# A GUIDE TO THE STUDY OF

# The United States of America

*Representative Books Reflecting the Development of*

*American Life and Thought*

Supplement

1956–1965

Prepared Under the Direction of Roy P. Basler

by Oliver H. Orr, Jr., and the Staff of the

Bibliography and Reference Correspondence Section

GENERAL REFERENCE AND BIBLIOGRAPHY DIVISION • REFERENCE DEPARTMEN

LIBRARY OF CONGRESS • Washington: 1976

Library of Congress Cataloging in Publication Data (Revised)

United States. Library of Congress. General Reference and Bibliography Division.

A guide to the study of the United States of America.

. . . . . . Supplement, 1956-1965.

Includes index.

Supt. of Docs. no.: LC 2.8:Un3/supp.

1. United States — Bibliography. I. Mugridge, Donald Henry. II. McCrum, Blanche Prichard, 1887–    . III. Orr, Oliver Hamilton.
Z1215.U53 Suppl. [E156]    016.973    60–60009
ISBN 0–8444–0164–1

FOR SALE BY THE SUPERINTENDENT OF DOCUMENTS, U.S. GOVERNMENT PRINTING OFFICE
WASHINGTON, D.C. 20402 - PRICE $12
STOCK NUMBER 030–010–00042–7

# Contents

# Introduction

When *A Guide to the Study of the United States of America* was published in 1960, the Library anticipated updating it with supplements or revisions. A supplement covering books published during the decade 1956-65 was decided upon, and a guideline limiting its contents to approximately half the number of entries contained in the 1960 *Guide* was adopted.

With only occasional exceptions, the *Supplement*'s designated time period, 1956-65, has been adhered to throughout. A few works appearing before 1956 are mentioned in annotations and headnotes because of their special relevance to the numbered entries, but they themselves are not regarded as entries in the formal sense. A few other pre-1956 publications are entered as parts of series or multivolume studies that began before 1956 and continued into the decade encompassed here. Also included in some instances are reprints or revisions, containing newly contributed annotations, bibliographies, textual alterations, or biographical or critical essays, of works first published before 1956. Although occasional projected works are referred to in the *Supplement*'s annotations, no books published after 1965 are mentioned, and no events occurring subsequent to that date are noted. Various chapters in the 1960 *Guide* describe books that appeared after its theoretical cutoff date of 1955; those books are excluded from the *Supplement*.

"Selected Readings in American Studies," an appendix to the 1960 *Guide,* has been omitted from the *Supplement,* inasmuch as scholarship in this field has begun to develop its own surveys and bibliographies.

The reader who seeks information about the origins of this bibliographic project, the manner in which books are selected for inclusion, and the nature of the bibliographic style and the annotations, should consult the general introduction in the 1960 *Guide* and the individual introductions to each of its chapters. The slight modifications in the 1960 *Guide*'s structure that were adopted in the *Supplement* are explained in the introductions to the chapters affected. The index follows the pattern of the one in the 1960 *Guide*.

The 1960 *Guide* lists a few publications that were not represented in the collections of the Library of Congress at the time the volume was compiled. All numbered entries in the *Supplement* are held by the Library, and the catalog card number and classification number or location are given for each.

No listing of names along with units of work accomplished can accurately reflect the contribution made by each of the many staff members of the General Reference and Bibliography Division who participated in the compilation of this *Supplement*. Some performed multiple piecemeal tasks (selecting books, writing portions of chapters, substituting new annotations for old); others concentrated on a few large undertakings, in many instances compiling entire chapters. Those given piecemeal tasks collectively compiled five chapters — VIII, General History; XV, Society; XVII, Science and Technology; XVIII, Medicine and Public Health; and XXVIII, Economic Life; they also contributed in one way or another to virtually every part of the *Supplement*. Foremost among them were Edward P. Cambio, Judith R. Farley, Betsy M. Fleet, Baiba Garoza, Stefan M. Harrow, John W. Kimball, Marvin W. Kranz, Sandra N. Pantages, Marie Schilling, Jerome L. Segal, Richard N. Sheldon, and Ruth E. Wennersten. Miss Garoza also prepared the index.

The basic content of each of the following chapters was determined by the person or persons indicated: I, Literature, Judith L. Richelieu and Donald H. Cresswell; II, Language, Dan O. Clemmer; III, Literary History and Criticism, Katherine M. Hanna; IV, Biography and Autobiography, Evalyn K. Shapiro; V, Periodicals and Journalism, Lucia J. Rather; VI, Geography, Suzy M. Slavin; VII, The American Indian, Lucia J. Rather; IX, Diplomatic History and Foreign Relations, Joyce Holland; X, Military History and the Armed Forces, Victor P. Margolin; XI, Intellectual History, William J. Studer; XII, Local History, Donald A. Baskerville; XIII, Travel and Travelers, Evalyn K. Shapiro; XIV, Population, Immigration, and Minorities, the late Donald H. Mugridge; XVI, Communications, William J. Studer; XIX, Entertainment, Lucia J. Rather; XX, Sports and Recreation, William J. Studer; XXI, Education, Natalie L. Miller; XXII, Philosophy and Psychology, Rande B. Langdon;

XXIII, Religion, Lucia J. Rather; XXIV, Folklore, Folk Music, Folk Art, Gail Shulman; XXV, Music, Alma S. Mather; XXVI, Art and Architecture, Lucia J. Rather; XXVII, Land and Agriculture, Suzy M. Slavin; XXIX, Constitution and Government, Henry J. Silverman; XXX, Law and Justice, Joyce Holland and John J. Beall; XXXI, Politics, Parties, Elections, Joyce Holland; and XXXII, Books and Libraries, Evelyn M. Timberlake.

Members of the Library staff outside the General Reference and Bibliography Division offered preliminary suggestions and criticized portions of the bibliography as the work progressed. Particularly helpful were personnel in the following offices: American-British Law Division, Law Library; Economics Division, Education and Public Welfare Division, and Senior Specialist Division, Congressional Research Service; and Geography and Map Division, Manuscript Division, Music Division, Prints and Photographs Division, and Science and Technology Division, Reference Department.

From outside the Library came the thoughtful assistance of Robert H. Walker, Professor of American Civilization, George Washington University, on Chapter I, Literature; Robert W. Burchfield, Editor, *Oxford English Dictionary Supplement,* Oxford, England, on Chapter II, Language; John Blake, Chief, History of Medicine Division, National Library of Medicine, on Chapter XVIII, Medicine and Public Health; Nelson R. Burr, author of bibliographical and historical works on religion in America and a retired LC staff member, on Chapter XXIII, Religion; and Benjamin A. Botkin, author and compiler of numerous books on folklore and a former LC staff member, on Chapter XXIV, Folklore, Folk Music, Folk Art.

The Specialist in American History in the General Reference and Bibliography Division functioned as the editor of the *Supplement.* Donald H. Mugridge, co-compiler of the 1960 *Guide,* held the position of specialist until his death in November 1964.

He was succeeded by James E. O'Neill, who resigned in August 1965. Oliver H. Orr, Jr., replaced O'Neill and, although he transferred to the Manuscript Division in 1969, served as editor until the *Supplement* was completed.

Helen D. Jones, Head of the Bibliography and Reference Correspondence Section, rendered invaluable help to the *Supplement* staff as general critic, as authority on bibliographical procedures and style, and — especially after the death of Mr. Mugridge — as repository of information about the compilation of the 1960 *Guide.* After Mrs. Jones' retirement in January 1969, her successor as Head of the Bibliography and Reference Correspondence Section, Ruth S. Freitag, was a constant source of encouragement, advice, and bibliographical expertise. The *Supplement's* index was prepared under the successive supervision of Mrs. Jones and Miss Freitag.

A second supplement, covering books published during the decade 1966-75, is now being compiled under the editorship of Marvin W. Kranz, the current Specialist in American History.

As Director of the Reference Department and, after October 1968, in my present capacity, I was able to devote to every chapter of the *Supplement,* at each stage of development, the same overall editorial attention that I gave to the 1960 *Guide.* I would be remiss, however, if I failed to acknowledge that chief credit for sustained accomplishment must go to Dr. Orr, and to the late Mr. Mugridge. The bridge between their respective terms was ably held by Dr. O'Neill. I would also be remiss if I failed to acknowledge that Robert H. Land, Chief of the General Reference and Bibliography Division, gave the best of supervision to the labors of all concerned, and I am sure he will join in a declaration that both the 1960 *Guide* and this *Supplement* are a monument to the special talent of Donald Mugridge, whose work enlightened both.

Roy P. Basler
*Chief, Manuscript Division*

# Literature (1607-1965)

OF THE 1960 *Guide's* 340 authors in Chapter I, 233 are represented here. Nineteen new authors who achieved prominence during the years 1956–65 have been added to Section F, which retains its original title except for an extension of the coverage dates from 1940–55 to 1940–65. The new authors, entered alphabetically among the others in Section F, are Edward Albee, John Barth, William Burroughs, John Cheever, James Dickey, Lawrence Ferlinghetti, Allen Ginsberg, Herbert Gold, Jack Kerouac, Bernard Malamud, James Michener, Vladimir Nabokov, Howard Nemerov, Flannery O'Connor, Philip Roth, Isaac Bashevis Singer, M. B. Tolson, John Updike, and Kurt Vonnegut. The criteria for their selection are those stated on page 1 in the 1960 *Guide*.

Headnotes for the new authors appear in the *Supplement* as they do for each author in the 1960 *Guide*. Some pre-1956 publications of the new authors are mentioned in their headnotes, but only their 1956–65 works are listed as formal entries. No headnotes are offered in the *Supplement* for the authors carried over from the 1960 *Guide;* instead, the entry numbers for their respective headnotes in the 1960 *Guide* are supplied.

Whereas the 1960 *Guide* usually omits biographical and critical works, referring the reader to inclusive publications such as the *Literary History of the United States* (no. 1214 in the *Supplement*) and *The Literature of the American People* (no. 2496 in the 1960 *Guide*), the *Supplement* seeks to be as representative of biographical and critical studies as of literary works. The chief reason for this change in policy is that the above-mentioned general histories are outdated for our purposes. The bibliography in the *Literary History of the United States* terminates with the year 1958 and *The Literature of the American People* has not been revised since its publication in 1951.

From the large number of reprints and revised editions of literary works, we have attempted to select those accompanied by such significant contributions as textual revisions, annotations, bibliographies, or essays about the author or the work. If the earlier edition appeared in the 1960 *Guide,* its entry number is supplied. From the biographical and critical studies, we have tried to choose those that develop fresh interpretations or provide syntheses of scholarship, or both.

Sections C and D, covering the periods often called the "American Renaissance" and the "Gilded Age," respectively, include large numbers of analytical works reflecting the influence of the New Criticism. More biographical and critical studies appear in these two sections than in the other four sections combined. Section F is distinctive for its understandable shortage of critical writings and its great body of new books by living authors.

The arrangement of entries under each author's name follows the pattern described on page 2 of the 1960 *Guide*.

# A. The Thirteen Colonies (1607-1763)

1. ANNE DUDLEY BRADSTREET, 1612?–1672

   No. 7 in 1960 *Guide.*

2. Piercy, Josephine K. Anne Bradstreet. New York, Twayne Publishers [1965] 144 p. (Twayne's United States authors series, 72)
   64–20722 PS712.P5
   Bibliographical notes: p. 121–128. Bibliography: p. 129–137.
   Mrs. Bradstreet's poetry and prose are examined as reflections of her spiritual and artistic development.

3. WILLIAM BYRD, 1674–1744

   No. 12 in 1960 *Guide.*

4. The London diary, 1717–1721, and other writings. Edited by Louis B. Wright and Marion Tinling. New York, Oxford University Press, 1958. 647 p. illus.        57–10389 F229.B9685
   Bibliographical footnotes.
   CONTENTS.—The life of William Byrd of Virginia, 1674–1744.—The secret diary of William Byrd of Westover from December 13, 1717, to May 19, 1721.—History of the dividing line.—A journey to the land of Eden.—A progress to the mines.
   The third section of Byrd's diary, the other two sections of which are no. 15 and 16 in the 1960 *Guide,* is published here for the first time, containing "all the passages that can be deciphered." Transcribed from a shorthand notebook in the library of the Virginia Historical Society, it portrays London under George I and describes life in Virginia during the development of its agrarian aristocracy. The last three works in the volume appear in an abridged text based on *The Westover Manuscripts* (1841), no. 13 in the 1960 *Guide.*

5. JOHN COTTON, 1584–1652

   No. 17 in 1960 *Guide.*

6. Emerson, Everett H. John Cotton. New York, Twayne Publishers [1965] 176 p. (Twayne's United States authors series, 80)
   65–13000 BX7260.C79E5
   Bibliographical notes: p. 159–162. Bibliography: p. 163–170.
   Cotton's treatises, sermons, pamphlets, and other writings are examined to indicate their literary and cultural significance within a historical context.

7. Ziff, Larzer. The career of John Cotton: Puritanism and the American experience. Princeton, N. J., Princeton University Press, 1962. 280 p.
   62–7415 BX7260.C79Z5
   "Bibliographical note": p. 261–271.
   A sociopolitical biography treating Cotton's career in England and America, his times, and his works.

8. JONATHAN EDWARDS, 1703–1758

   No. 21 in 1960 *Guide.*

9. The mind; a reconstructed text by Leon Howard. Berkeley, University of California Press, 1963. 151 p. (University of California publications. English studies, 28)    63–64061 B871.M5
   Appendix: The essays "Of Being" and "Of the Prejudices of Imagination": p. 137–148.
   Note on sources: p. 149.
   Using the holograph index to a lost manuscript, Howard has rearranged the earliest printed edition of Edwards' collection of notes entitled "The Mind." The reader is guided by an introduction, running commentary, and conclusion.

10. Works. Perry Miller, general editor. [New Haven, Yale University Press] 1957–59. 2 v.
    57–2336 BX7117.E3 1957
    CONTENTS.—v. 1. Freedom of the will.—v. 2. Religious affections.
    The 1754 edition of volume 1 and the 1746 edition of volume 2 are no. 26 and 25, respectively, in the 1960 *Guide.*

11. The select works of Jonathan Edwards; with an account of his life by Iain H. Murray. [London] Banner of Truth Trust [1958–61] 3 v.
    59–2646 BX7117.E3 1958
    Bibliography: v. 1, p. 60–62.
    CONTENTS.—v. 1. Memoir, by I. H. Murray. A narrative of surprising conversions. Sermons.—v. 2. Sermons.—v. 3. Treatise concerning the religious affections.
    The 1737 edition of *A Faithful Narrative of the Surprizing Work of God in the Conversion of Many Hundred Souls* . . . is no. 22 in the 1960 *Guide,* and the 1746 edition of *A Treatise Concerning Religious Affections* is no. 25.

12. Select works. v. 1. London, Banner of Truth
    Trust [1965] 244 p.
    66–4638 BX7117.E3 1965
*The Distinguishing Marks of a Work of the Spirit
of God* and *An Account of the Revival of Religion
in Northampton, 1740–1742* have been added to
this edition of volume 1, and Iain H. Murray's
"Memoir" has been omitted.

13. Aldridge, Alfred O. Jonathan Edwards. New
    York, Washington Square Press [1964] 181 p.
    (The Great American thinkers series, W881)
    65–935 BX7260.E3A59
Bibliography: p. 167–172.
A study of Edwards' philosophy in relation to the
intellectual currents of his time.

14. Elwood, Douglas J. The philosophical theol-
    ogy of Jonathan Edwards. New York, Colum-
bia University Press, 1960. 220 p.
    60–12503 BX7260.E3E5 1960
"Bibliography of Jonathan Edwards": p. [199]–
202. Bibliography: p. [203]–214.
Whereas other studies tend to concentrate on
either the religion or the philosophy of Edwards,
this one combines analyses of both.

15. COTTON MATHER, 1663–1728
    No. 40 in 1960 *Guide*.

16. The diary of Cotton Mather, D.D., F.R.S. for
    the year 1712. Edited, with an introduction
and notes, by William R. Manierre, II. Charlottesville, University Press of Virginia [1964] xxvii,
143 p. 64–13720 F67.M4214
This portion of Mather's diary had never before
been printed in its entirety, although extracts appeared in the *Panoplist and Missionary Magazine*
between 1816 and 1820.

17. Wendell, Barrett. Cotton Mather; the Puritan
    priest. New York, Harcourt, Brace & World
[1963] xxxi, 248 p. (A Harbinger book)
    63–12740 F67.M452 1963
Bibliography: p. [231]–233.
Alan Heimert's introduction reveals the continuing significance of this biography, first published in
1891.

18. SAMUEL SEWALL, 1652–1730
    No. 56 in 1960 *Guide*.

19. Winslow, Ola E. Samuel Sewall of Boston.
    New York, Macmillan [c1964] 235 p. illus.
    63–16140 F67.S547

Bibliographical notes: p. 209–220. Bibliography:
p. 221–224.
A narrative biography stressing material found in
Sewall's *Diary* (no. 57 in the 1960 *Guide*).

20. JOHN SMITH, 1579/80–1631
    No. 66 in 1960 *Guide*.

21. Barbour, Philip L. The three worlds of Cap-
    tain John Smith. Boston, Houghton Mifflin,
1964. xix, 553 p. illus. 64–10543 F229.S7145
    Bibliographical notes: p. [397]–490. Bibliog-
raphy: p. [493]–527.
Smith's career as adventurer, colonist, and promoter is examined in the light of hints and clues previously ignored.

22. Wharton, Henry. The life of John Smith,
    English soldier. Translated from the Latin
manuscript with an essay on Captain John Smith in
seventeenth-century literature by Laura Polanyi
Striker. Chapel Hill, Published for the Virginia
Historical Society by the University of North Caro-
lina Press [1957] 101 p. illus.
    57–13884 F229.S7W4
Bibliographical footnotes.
Written in 1685, Wharton's manuscript is pub-
lished here for the first time in English translation.
An essay on "Early American Interest in Wharton's
Manuscript," by Richard Beale Davis, is included.

23. EDWARD TAYLOR, 1642–1729
    No. 72 in 1960 *Guide*.

24. Christographia. Edited by Norman S. Grabo.
    New Haven, Yale University Press, 1962.
xlviii, 507 p. 62–10317 BX7117.T3
Bibliographical footnotes.
A series of 14 related sermons, delivered between
1701 and 1703, with correlative meditations in verse.
The editor's introduction provides both history and
interpretation.

25. Poems. Edited by Donald E. Stanford, with
    a foreword by Louis L. Martz. New Haven,
Yale University Press, 1960. lxii, 543 p.
    60–6432 PS850.T2A6 1960
Bibliographical references included in appendixes.
The complete text of the author's major work,
*Preparatory Meditations*, is printed here for the
first time.

26. Grabo, Norman S. Edward Taylor. New
    York, Twayne Publishers [1962, c1961] 192
p. (Twayne's United States authors series, 8)
    61–15668 BX7260.T28G7 1962

Bibliographical notes: p. 174–182. Bibliography: p. 183–187.

27. MICHAEL WIGGLESWORTH, 1631–1705

No. 79 in 1960 *Guide*.

28. Crowder, Richard. No featherbed to heaven, a biography of Michael Wigglesworth, 1631–1705. [East Lansing] Michigan State University Press [1962] 299 p.     61–16933  BX7260.W48C7
Bibliographical notes: p. 271–282. Bibliography: p. 283–293.

29. ROGER WILLIAMS, ca. 1603–1683

No. 84 in 1960 *Guide*.

30. Complete writings. New York, Russell & Russell, 1963. 7 v.
63–11034  BX6495.W55A2 1963
Volumes 1–6 are reprints of the Narragansett edition, no. 89 in the 1960 *Guide*. Volume 7 contains five tracts not printed in that edition, together with an introductory essay.
CONTENTS.—v. 7. Roger Williams: An essay in interpretation by Perry Miller. Christenings make not Christians. Experiments of spiritual life and health. The fourth paper presented by Major Butler. The hireling ministry none of Christs. The examiner—defended in a fair and sober answer.

31. Winslow, Ola E. Master Roger Williams, a biography. New York, Macmillan, 1957. 328 p.     57–10016  F82.W692
Bibliographical notes: p. 293–312. Bibliography: p. 313–316.
Miss Winslow seeks to avoid the myths, legends, and exaggerations surrounding her subject, for "His story is better as he lived it." Sources include Williams' letters and sermons, his *Works* (published in six volumes of the Narragansett Club *Publications*, no. 89 in the 1960 *Guide*), colony records, personal accounts of contemporaries, and pamphlet literature of the 1640's and 1650's.

32. JOHN WINTHROP, 1588–1649

No. 90 in 1960 *Guide*.

33. Morgan, Edmund S. The Puritan dilemma; the story of John Winthrop. Edited by Oscar Handlin. Boston, Little, Brown [1958] 224 p. (The Library of American biography)
58–6029  F67.W798
Bibliographical notes: p. [207]–215.
Interprets Winthrop's answer to the central Puritan problem involving man's responsibility to society. The author's principal sources are the 1853 edition of Winthrop's *Journal* (no. 91 in the 1960 *Guide*) and the *Winthrop Papers* (see biographical note, no. 90 in the 1960 *Guide*).

# B. The Revolution and the New Nation (1764–1819)

34. JOEL BARLOW, 1754–1812

No. 101 in 1960 *Guide*.

35. Woodress, James L. A Yankee's odyssey; the life of Joel Barlow. Philadelphia, Lippincott [1958] 347 p.     58–11128  PS705.W6
Bibliographical notes: p. 309–328.
A full-scale narrative biography. Primary sources include the major collection of Barlow manuscripts in the Harvard University Library. An appendix contains examples of Barlow's poetry.

36. HUGH HENRY BRACKENRIDGE, 1748–1816

No. 105 in 1960 *Guide*.

37. Modern chivalry, containing the adventures of Captain John Farrago and Teague O'Regan, his servant. Edited for the modern reader by Lewis Leary. New Haven, College & University Press [c1965] 335 p. (The Masterworks of literature series)     65–28257  PZ3.B7233Mo6
Reproduces the first four volumes of *Modern Chivalry*, published in 1792, 1793, and 1797. Subsequent additions and revisions have been omitted, although spelling and punctuation have been regularized and, when appropriate, modernized. See no. 106–108 in the 1960 *Guide*.

38. CHARLES BROCKDEN BROWN, 1771–1810

No. 109 in 1960 *Guide*.

39. Arthur Mervyn; or, Memoirs of the year 1793. Edited, with an introduction, by Warner Berthoff. New York, Holt, Rinehart & Winston [1962] 430 p. (Rinehart editions, 112)
62–9499  PZ3.B814Ar8
Bibliography: p. xxv–xxvii.
The text is based on that of the original edition,

published in two parts, 1799–1800 (no. 116 in the 1960 *Guide*). Minor changes have been made in the interest of typographic uniformity and orthographic consistency.

40. BENJAMIN FRANKLIN, 1706–1790

No. 122 in 1960 *Guide*.

41. The autobiography of Benjamin Franklin. Edited by Leonard W. Labaree [and others]. New Haven, Yale University Press, 1964. 351 p. illus.    64–12653    E302.6.F7A2 1964
Bibliography: p. 323–325.
Edited from the original manuscript in the Henry E. Huntington Library and Art Gallery. Aids to the reader include an introduction, footnotes, a Franklin chronology, Franklin's outline, and biographical notes concerning persons mentioned in the *Autobiography*. Descriptions of other editions may be found under no. 123–127 in the 1960 *Guide*.

42. Representative selections, with introduction, bibliography, and notes, by Chester E. Jorgenson and Frank Luther Mott. Rev. ed. New York, Hill & Wang [1962] clxxxix, 544 p. (American century series. American writers, ACW48)
            62–9491    PS745.A3M7 1962
Bibliography: p. cli-clxxxix.
A revised edition of no. 131 in the 1960 *Guide*. "*The Dissertation on Liberty and Necessity, Pleasure and Pain*, never before printed in an edition of Franklin's works or in a book of selections, is here printed from the London edition of 1725, retaining his peculiarities of italics, capitalization, and punctuation."

43. Amacher, Richard E. Benjamin Franklin. New York, Twayne Publishers [1962] 192 p. (Twayne's United States authors series, 12)
            61–18069    PS751.A5
Bibliographical notes: p. 159–178. Bibliography: p. 179–187.
A study of Franklin the writer, treating representative works in various literary genres, among them scientific papers, political journalism, and religious and philosophical tracts.

44. Granger, Bruce I. Benjamin Franklin; an American man of letters. Ithaca, N.Y., Cornell University Press [1964] 264 p.
            64–23360    PS751.G7
Bibliographical footnotes. "Bibliographical note": p. 253–255.
Assesses Franklin's achievement in the world of letters, focusing "on those writings that have belletristic qualities, not on scientific and official papers except as they are treated incidentally."

45. THOMAS JEFFERSON, 1743–1826

No. 149 in 1960 *Guide*.

46. Notes on the State of Virginia. Introduction to the Torchbook ed. by Thomas Perkins Abernethy. New York, Harper & Row [1964] 228 p. (Harper Torchbooks. The University library)    64–2956    F230.J5102 1964
Bibliographical footnotes.
A reprint of the edition published as part of volume 8 of *The Writings of Thomas Jefferson* (New York, H. W. Derby, 1861), edited by Henry A. Washington. Information regarding other editions is contained in the introduction and in no. 150–153 in the 1960 *Guide*.

47. THOMAS PAINE, 1737–1809

No. 154 in 1960 *Guide*.

48. Thomas Paine; representative selections, with introduction, bibliography, and notes, by Harry Hayden Clark. Rev. ed. New York, Hill & Wang [1961] clxiii, 436 p. (American century writers, ACW43)
            61–16873    JC177.A5 1961
Bibliography: p. cxxv-clxiii.
The bibliography has been updated in this reprinting of no. 158 in the 1960 *Guide*.

49. Gimbel, Richard. Thomas Paine, a bibliographical check list of Common sense, with an account of its publication. New Haven, Yale University Press, 1956. 124 p.    56–5942    Z8654.G5
Facsimiles of title pages from various editions of *Common Sense* illustrate the detailed introductory account. The checklist describes editions of the pamphlet and contains a list of materials relating to it.

50. SUSANNA HASWELL ROWSON, 1762–1824

No. 161 in 1960 *Guide*.

51. Charlotte Temple, a tale of truth. Edited for the modern reader by Clara M. and Rudolf Kirk. New York, Twayne Publishers [1964] 163 p. (Twayne's United States classics series)
            64–14446    PZ3.R799C35
Originally published by William Lane at his Minerva Press, London, in 1791, the first edition is reprinted here with an address entitled "To Ladies and Gentlemen, Patrons of Entertaining Literature" as preface. Two other editions are no. 162–163 in the 1960 *Guide*.

52. JOHN TRUMBULL, 1750–1831

No. 165 in 1960 *Guide*.

53. Satiric poems: The progress of dulness and M'Fingal. With illustrations from engravings by E. Tisdale. Edited, with a preface and notes, by Edwin T. Bowden. Austin, University of Texas Press [1962] 229 p. 61–15829 PS852.P7 1962
Presents "for the first time, an accurate reproduction of the first complete edition of each poem." *The Progress of Dulness* was first published in New Haven, Conn., in 1772–73. The text of *M'Fingal* is taken from the first complete version, published by Hudson and Goodwin, Hartford, Conn., in 1782. A revised edition of Trumbull's *Poetical Works* appeared in 1820 (no. 167 in the 1960 *Guide*).

54. MASON LOCKE WEEMS, 1759–1825
No. 171 in 1960 *Guide*.

55. The life of Washington. Edited by Marcus Cunliffe. Cambridge, Mass., Belknap Press of Harvard University Press, 1962. lxii, 226 p. illus. (The John Harvard library)
62–20253 E312.W3893
Bibliographical footnotes.
The text is based on that of the ninth edition, published in 1809 (other editions are no. 172-176 in the 1960 *Guide*). An extensive introduction honors Weems and his work, providing biographical and critical comment as well as a detailed publishing history of *The Life of Washington*.

56. JOHN WOOLMAN, 1720–1772
No. 178 in 1960 *Guide*.

57. Cady, Edwin H. John Woolman. New York, Washington Square Press [1965] 182 p. (The Great American thinkers series)
65–1754 BX7795.W7C3
Bibliography: p. 173–178.
A sympathetic evaluation of Woolman, illustrating his contributions to American culture in the 20th century as well as in his own time.

# C. Nationalism, Sectionalism, and Schism (1820-1870)

58. LOUISA MAY ALCOTT, 1832–1888
No. 188 in 1960 *Guide*.

59. Hospital sketches. Edited by Bessie Z. Jones. Cambridge, Belknap Press of Harvard University Press, 1960. xliv, 91 p. (The John Harvard library)
60–13289 E621.A34 1960
Reprinted from a copy of the first edition (1863) in the Houghton Library of Harvard University. The sketches are based on Miss Alcott's brief experiences as a volunteer nurse at a Georgetown, D.C., hospital during the Civil War.

60. Worthington, Marjorie M. Miss Alcott of Concord, a biography. Garden City, N.Y., Doubleday, 1958. 330 p. 58–11330 PS1018.W6
Bibliography: p. 323–326.

61. TIMOTHY SHAY ARTHUR, 1809–1885
No. 190 in 1960 *Guide*.

62. Ten nights in a bar-room, and what I saw there. Edited by Donald A. Koch. Cambridge, Belknap Press of Harvard University Press, 1964. lxxxiii, 240 p. (The John Harvard library)
64–25051 PZ3.A79Te10
The editor's introduction discusses Arthur's life and work in relation to the 19th-century temperance crusade. The text is a facsimile reprint of an 1854 edition bearing the combined imprint of L. P. Crown, Boston, and J. W. Bradley, Philadelphia. Another 1854 edition carries only the Bradley imprint (no. 191 in the 1960 *Guide*).

63. ROBERT MONTGOMERY BIRD, 1806–1854
No. 201 in 1960 *Guide*.

64. Dahl, Curtis. Robert Montgomery Bird. New York, Twayne Publishers [1963] 144 p. (Twayne's United States authors series, 31)
62–19475 PS1099.B5Z62
Bibliographical notes: p. 128–131. Bibliography: p. 132–140.
Sources include the collection of Bird manuscripts at the University of Pennsylvania as well as previously published biographical and critical material.

65. CHARLES FARRAR BROWNE ("ARTEMUS WARD"), 1834–1867
No. 209 in 1960 *Guide*.

66. Austin, James C. Artemus Ward. New York, Twayne Publishers [1964] 141 p. (Twayne's United States authors series, 51)
63–20610 PS1143.A9

Bibliographical notes: p. 122–131. Bibliography: p. 132–138.

An examination of Browne's career as a journalist, satiric lecturer, and letter-writer, demonstrating his contribution to the American comic tradition.

67. WILLIAM CULLEN BRYANT, 1794–1878

No. 216 in 1960 *Guide*.

68. McLean, Albert F. William Cullen Bryant. New York, Twayne Publishers [1964] 159 p. (Twayne's United States authors series, 59)
64–13955 PS1181.M3

Bibliographical notes: p. 139–148. Bibliography: p. 149–151.

The author contends "that William Cullen Bryant, as a poet, is far different from the gentlemanly man-of-letters handed down to us by his nineteenth-century admirers."

69. WILLIAM ELLERY CHANNING, 1780–1842

No. 230 in 1960 *Guide*.

70. Brown, Arthur W. Always young for liberty; a biography of William Ellery Channing. [Syracuse, N.Y.] Syracuse University Press [1956] 268 p.
56–9464 BX9869.C4B84

Reappraises Channing, focusing on his life and work "for a generation which knows him almost solely by association with other, more familiar names." Lacks footnotes but contains a critical essay on "Literature and Sources" (p. 245–261).

71. Rice, Madeleine H. Federal Street pastor; the life of William Ellery Channing. New York, Bookman Associates [1961] 360 p.
61–15676 BX9869.C4R5

Bibliographical notes: p. 303–332. Bibliography: p. 333–345.

The sources consulted by the author of this comprehensive study include manuscript collections, magazines, newspapers, published letters, diaries, and memoirs.

72. LYDIA MARIA FRANCIS CHILD, 1802–1880

No. 239 in 1960 *Guide*.

73. Baer, Helene G. The heart is like heaven; the life of Lydia Maria Child. Philadelphia, University of Pennsylvania Press [1964] 339 p. illus.
64–10895 E449.C5383

Bibliography: p. 317–333.

Emphasizes Mrs. Child's efforts for social reform and the abolition of slavery, examining her relationships with prominent figures within these movements.

74. Meltzer, Milton. Tongue of flame; the life of Lydia Maria Child. New York, Crowell [1965] 210 p.
65–14903 E449.C5393

Bibliography: p. [197]–204.

A narrative account based chiefly on Mrs. Child's books, articles, and correspondence. Unpublished letters and scrapbooks were also consulted.

75. JOHN ESTEN COOKE, 1830–1886

No. 245 in 1960 *Guide*.

76. Outlines from the outpost. Edited by Richard Harwell. Chicago, Lakeside Press, 1961. xxxiv, 413 p. (The Lakeside classics, 59)
62–6657 E470.2.C72

Bibliographical footnotes.

A collection of Civil War sketches and narratives, planned as a book that was described in the author's diary but never published. Many of the "Outlines" originally appeared in *The Southern Illustrated News;* others first appeared in *Wearing of the Gray* (1867), which also contained revised versions of sketches published earlier. One essay is printed here for the first time.

77. JAMES FENIMORE COOPER, 1789–1851

No. 252 in 1960 *Guide*.

78. The bravo. Edited for the modern reader by Donald A. Ringe. New York, Twayne Publishers [°1963] 382 p. (Twayne's United States classics series)
63–17405 PZ3.C786Br30

Bibliographical footnotes.

Cooper examines the relative values of democratic and autocratic governments in a romance of 18th-century Venice. Modern practice has been followed with regard to spelling and punctuation in a text based on that of the first American edition (Philadelphia, Carey & Lea, 1831. 2 v.).

79. The crater; or, Vulcan's Peak. Edited by Thomas Philbrick. Cambridge, Belknap Press of Harvard University Press, 1962. xxx, 471 p. (The John Harvard library)
62–11397 PZ3.C786Cr15

Bibliographical footnotes.

The establishment of a Utopian community in the Pacific provides the background for an explication of Cooper's views concerning socialism and democracy. The text is that of the first edition (New York, Burgess, Stringer, 1847. 2 v.). Minor typographical errors have been corrected and the spelling of foreign words regularized.

80. Letters and journals. Edited by James Franklin Beard. Cambridge, Belknap Press of Harvard University Press, 1960–64. 4 v. illus.
        60-5388  PS1431.A3  1960
CONTENTS.—v. 1. 1800–1830.—v. 2. 1830–1833.—v. 3. 1833–1839.—v. 4. 1840–1844.
Bibliographical footnotes.
Complete texts of all available letters and journals are included, as well as letters to editors and brief articles or notes written for newspapers and periodicals. Approximately two-thirds of the material has not been previously published. Entries are grouped in accordance with the periods of Cooper's life and are arranged chronologically.

81. Philbrick, Thomas. James Fenimore Cooper and the development of American sea fiction. Cambridge, Harvard University Press, 1961. 329 p. illus.    61–15276  PS1442.S4P45  1961
Considers the nautical novels of Cooper and his contemporaries up to 1851, when *Moby-Dick* was published; includes explanatory notes (p. [287]–326) and an extensive bibliography (p. [269]–286).

82. Ringe, Donald A. James Fenimore Cooper. New York, Twayne Publishers [1962] 175 p. (Twayne's United States authors series, 11)
        61–18068  PS1438.R5
Bibliographical notes: 157–164. Bibliography: p. 165–171.
The author concentrates on Cooper's later novels, stressing "the thematic interpretation of his tales and the means, sometimes highly successful, by which he gave his themes expression." Biographical and historical information is kept to a minimum.

83. RICHARD HENRY DANA, 1815–1882
No. 274 in 1960 *Guide.*

84. Two years before the mast; a personal narrative of life at sea. Edited from the original manuscript and from the first ed., with journals and letters of 1834–1836 and 1859–1860, and notes by John Haskell Kemble. With original illustrations by Robert A. Weinstein, and illustrated from contemporary paintings, prints, and charts. Los Angeles, Ward Ritchie Press, 1964. 2 v. illus. (part col.)    64–20444  G540.D2  1964
The 1840 edition is no. 275 in the 1960 *Guide.*

85. Shapiro, Samuel. Richard Henry Dana, Jr., 1815–1882. [East Lansing] Michigan State University Press, 1961. xi, 251 p.
        61–13704  E415.9.D15S5

Bibliographical notes: p. 199–240. Bibliography: p. 241–244.
Literature played a relatively minor role in Dana's life, as it does in this biography. Although his legal and political careers receive major emphasis, his literary achievement is spotlighted in the final chapter, "The History of a Book." The author's principal source is the collection of Dana papers divided between the Massachusetts Historical Society in Boston and the Longfellow House in Cambridge.

86. JOHN WILLIAM DE FOREST, 1826–1906
No. 277 in 1960 *Guide.*

87. Kate Beaumont. With an introduction by Joseph Jay Rubin. [State College, Pa., Bald Eagle Press, 1963] 424 p. (Monument edition, 3)
        63–7531  PZ3.D363Kat
This realistic portrayal of life in South Carolina before the Civil War first appeared in serial form in *The Atlantic Monthly,* January-December 1871; a book set from the corrected sheets was issued the following year. De Forest then added his own changes and revisions, and the text printed here is from this third and final version. The editor used a photostat of the novelist's corrected copy in the Yale University Library.

88. Honest John Vane. With an introduction by Joseph Jay Rubin. [State College, Pa., Bald Eagle Press, 1960] 232 p. (Monument edition, 1)
        60–5478  PZ3.D363Ho2
This indictment of political corruption in Washington during the Grant administration first appeared in five installments in *The Atlantic Monthly* in 1873. With the exception of minor mechanical changes, the present text is that of the only book edition, published by Richmond & Patten, New Haven, 1875.

89. Playing the mischief. With an introduction by Joseph Jay Rubin. [State College, Pa., Bald Eagle Press, 1961] 452 p. (Monument edition, 2)    61–10502  PZ3.D363Pl
This sequel to *Honest John Vane* began appearing serially in *Frank Leslie's Chimney Corner* in 1874. Harper & Brothers printed the book the following year, and De Forest revised it, as was his custom. The text printed here is based on Yale University's copy containing the author's corrections.

90. Light, James F. John William De Forest. New York, Twayne Publishers [1965] 192 p. (Twayne's United States authors series, 82)
        65–13002  PS1525.D5Z75

Bibliographical notes: p. 178–183. Bibliography: p. 184–188.

De Forest's major works are analyzed at length in a study which attempts "to reveal the relationship between the life and the work and by doing so to exhibit each a little more clearly." Primary sources include the De Forest materials in the Yale Collection of American Literature.

91. RALPH WALDO EMERSON, 1803–1882

No. 280 in 1960 *Guide*.

92. Selections from Ralph Waldo Emerson. Edited by Stephen E. Whicher. Boston, Houghton Mifflin [1957] 517 p. (Riverside editions, A13)
57–14108 PS1603.W45

Includes an introduction, a chronology, and full bibliographical notes (p. 469–510). The text is based on several previous publications, including the centenary edition of Emerson's *Complete Works* (no. 297 in the 1960 *Guide*) and Ralph L. Rusk's edition of the *Letters* (no. 296 in the 1960 *Guide*). Selections from the *Journals* (no. 294 in the 1960 *Guide*) have been corrected and amplified from manuscript sources.

93. Early lectures. Edited by Stephen E. Whicher and Robert E. Spiller. Cambridge, Harvard University Press, 1959–64. 2 v.
59–5160 PS1602.W5

Bibliographical footnotes. Bibliography: v. 1, p. 389–391; v. 2, p. 367–368.

CONTENTS.—v. 1. 1833–1836.—v. 2. 1836–1838.

This collection is newly edited from the Emerson papers in Harvard's Houghton Library. Publication of the lectures delivered through 1847 is contemplated for this edition.

94. Journals and miscellaneous notebooks. Edited by William H. Gilman [and others] Cambridge, Belknap Press of Harvard University Press, 1960–65. 5 v. illus. 60–11554 PS1631.A3 1960

Bibliographical footnotes.

Planned for completion in approximately 16 volumes, this edition is based on the Emerson papers in Harvard's Houghton Library. Regular journals, composition books, collections of quotations, and volumes on special topics will be included, the order of publication favoring personal and intellectual records. The first five volumes cover the years 1819–38 and include such items as a "Pocket Diary" and a "Catalogue of Books Read" in addition to the regular journals. The text "represents what Emerson wrote, in the way he wrote it, including cancellations, revision, and variants." An earlier edition, containing many alterations and deletions,

was edited by Emerson's son, Edward Waldo, and his nephew, Waldo Emerson Forbes, and was published during the years 1909–14 (no. 294 in the 1960 *Guide*).

95. The correspondence of Emerson and Carlyle. Edited by Joseph Slater. New York, Columbia University Press, 1964. 622 p. illus.
63–17539 PS1631.A35C3

Bibliography: p. [591]–601.

Treating the letters "as if they were sacred scripture," the editor presents unaltered texts based on manuscript copies, most of which are owned by the Ralph Waldo Emerson Memorial Association. A broad introduction (p. [3]–94) adds biographical and historical information.

96. Berry, Edmund G. Emerson's Plutarch. Cambridge, Harvard University Press, 1961. 337 p. 61–7389 PS1631.B4

Bibliographical notes: p. [293]–323. Bibliography: p. [289]–292.

Plutarch's works often provided anecdotes, expressions, and topics for Emerson's essays. Berry endeavors to "explore the exact extent of the influence of Plutarch on Emerson," maintaining that it extends to literary form as well as content.

97. Bishop, Jonathan. Emerson on the soul. Cambridge, Mass., Harvard University Press, 1964. 248 p. 64–25052 PS1642.R4B5

98. Nicoloff, Philip L. Emerson on race and history; an examination of English traits. New York, Columbia University Press, 1961. 315 p.
61–7361 PS1607.N5 1961

Bibliographical notes: p. [273]–295. Bibliography: p. [296]–300.

The author argues that "*English Traits* was not just an eccentric production contemporaneous with the great lecture series 'The Conduct of Life,' but an important complement to that series and a significant philosophical adventure in its own right."

99. TIMOTHY FLINT, 1780–1840

No. 307 in 1960 *Guide*.

100. Folsom, James K. Timothy Flint. New York, Twayne Publishers [1965] 191 p. (Twayne's United States authors series, 83)
65–13003 PS1679.F7Z67

Bibliographical notes: p. 171–179. Bibliography: p. 180–186.

Analyzes Flint's current reputation in relation to the excessive praise accorded his works during his lifetime.

101. (SARAH) MARGARET FULLER (MAR-
CHESA D'OSSOLI), 1810–1850
No. 313 in 1960 *Guide.*

102. Margaret Fuller: American Romantic; a selection from her writings and correspondence.
Edited by Perry Miller. Garden City, N.Y., Doubleday, 1963. 319 p. (Anchor books)
63–13082 PS2502.M5
Manuscripts in the Harvard University Library
and the Boston Public Library were used in the
preparation of this work. Holographs were followed whenever possible, with minimal editing. A
biographical essay and a bibliography are included.

103. Brown, Arthur W. Margaret Fuller. New
York, Twayne Publishers [1964] 159 p.
(Twayne's United States authors series, 48)
63–20612 PS2506.B77
Bibliographical notes: p. 135–147. Bibliography:
p. 148–153.
Attempts to soften the harsh judgments of Mar-
garet Fuller's contemporaries by basic reevaluation.

104. JAMES HALL, 1793–1868
No. 319 in 1960 *Guide.*

105. Randall, Randolph C. James Hall: spokesman of the new West. [Columbus] Ohio
State University Press [1964] 371 p.
63–18578 PS1779.H16Z86
Bibliographical notes: p. [281]–321. Bibliography: p. [323]–358.
Undertakes "to correct errors and misunderstandings in previous accounts, to present knowledge
from hundreds of manuscripts not used before in
studies of Hall, and to add nearly three hundred
items to the list of his known writings."

106. NATHANIEL HAWTHORNE, 1804–1864
No. 333 in 1960 *Guide.*

107. The scarlet letter; an annotated text, backgrounds and sources, essays in criticism.
Edited by Sculley Bradley, Richmond Croom Beatty
[and] E. Hudson Long. New York, Norton
[1962] 375 p. (Norton critical editions, N303)
62–9570 PZ3.H318Sc95
A critical edition containing the novel in a first-
edition text, as well as Hawthorne's preface to the
second edition, records of primary sources, and articles by noted scholars. Editions of 1850, 1947, and
1950 are no. 341–344 in the 1960 *Guide.*

108. The scarlet letter, a romance. Edited, with
an introduction by Larzer Ziff. Indianapolis,
Bobbs-Merrill [1963] 247 p. (The Library of
literature, 1) 62–21260 PZ3.H318Sc97
The centenary edition text (no. 110 below) is reprinted here, with a Hawthorne chronology, a bibliography, and the author's preface to the second
edition.

109. The house of the seven gables. With an introduction and newly edited text by Hyatt H.
Waggoner. Boston, Houghton Mifflin [1964]
xlvi, 281 p. (Riverside editions, A89)
64–55765 PZ3.H318Ho78
Bibliography: p. xlv–xlvi.
An entirely new critical text, produced by collat-
ing the manuscript with the first edition. Primary
authority is given the manuscript, located in the
Houghton Library at Harvard. Earlier editions are
no. 345–347 in the 1960 *Guide.*

110. The centenary edition of the works of
Nathaniel Hawthorne. [Editors: William
Charvat, and others. Columbus, Ohio State University Press, 1963–65, ©1962–65] 3 v.
63–750 PS1850.F63
Bibliographical footnotes.
CONTENTS.—v. 1. The scarlet letter.—v. 2. The
house of the seven gables.—v. 3. The Blithedale
romance. Fanshawe.
The centenary edition provides established texts
of the romances, tales, and shorter works in un-
modernized form. The texts have been constructed
through comparative critical use of early editions
and examination of extant manuscripts. Historical
and explanatory material is included in each volume, as well as a literary and textual introduction
to each work.

111. Bell, Millicent. Hawthorne's view of the
artist. [Albany] State University of New
York [1962] 214 p. 62–13566 PS1888.B4
Bibliographical footnotes.
The frequent appearance of the artist within
Hawthorne's fictional framework is examined with
reference to 19th-century Romanticism.

112. Fogle, Richard H. Hawthorne's fiction: the
light & the dark. [Rev. ed.] Norman, University of Oklahoma Press [1964] 240 p.
64–23334 PS1888.F6 1964
This revised edition of no. 361 in the 1960 *Guide*
is enlarged with two new essays. The bibliography
which appeared in the first edition has been dropped
in declared deference to Walter Blair's survey of
Hawthorne scholarship, supplemented by J. Chesley

Mathews, in a new edition of *Eight American Authors* (see no. 1253 in this *Supplement*).

113. Hoeltje, Hubert H. Inward sky; the mind and heart of Nathaniel Hawthorne. Durham, N.C., Duke University Press, 1962. 579 p. illus.   62–10052  PS1881.H6 1962
Bibliography: p. 563–571.
The entire range of Hawthorne's writing is examined, including letters, journals, and fiction, in an effort to correlate his inner thought patterns with the facts of his outward experience—"to disclose, as far as possible, the whole man."

114. Male, Roy R. Hawthorne's tragic vision. Austin, University of Texas Press [1957] 187 p.   57–7560  PS1888.M3
Bibliographical footnotes.
Although an essentially tragic view of life is expressed in Hawthorne's fiction, "the final mood of Hawthorne's tragedy is a tempered hopefulness." This study indicates the variety of technique and metaphor to be found in Hawthorne's work but stresses the unity and organic wholeness of its design.

115. Martin, Terence. Nathaniel Hawthorne. New York, Twayne Publishers [1965] 205 p. (Twayne's United States authors series, 75)   64–20725  PS1881.M28
Bibliographical notes: p. 181–184. Bibliography: p. 185–201.
Evaluates Hawthorne's literary achievement by exploring "the contours and issues of his career as a writer," his "method of imaginative creation," and "the pervasive thematic concerns" of his tales. The four major romances and six representative tales receive individual treatment.

116. Wagenknecht, Edward C. Nathaniel Hawthorne: man and writer. New York, Oxford University Press, 1961. 233 p.   61–6301  PS1881.W3
Bibliographical notes: p. 203–220. Bibliography: 221–223.
This account of Hawthorne's character and personality, based on his writings, letters, and journals, is described by the author as a psychograph, "neither a chronological biography nor a critical study."

117. Waggoner, Hyatt H. Hawthorne: a critical study. Rev. ed. Cambridge, Mass., Belknap Press of Harvard University Press, 1963. 278 p.   63–17215  PS1888.W3 1963
Bibliographical footnotes.
Extensive revisions, including the addition of one entirely new chapter, have been made in this new edition of no. 364 in the 1960 *Guide*.

118. OLIVER WENDELL HOLMES, 1809–1894
No. 368 in 1960 *Guide*.

119. The autocrat's miscellanies. Edited by Albert Mordell. New York, Twayne Publishers [1959] 356 p.   59–8382  PS1952.A8
A group of 30 previously uncollected articles on diverse topics, reflecting the kaleidoscopic aspects of Holmes' character and career. The editor's notes provide bibliographical and anecdotal information.

120. Small, Miriam R. Oliver Wendell Holmes. New York, Twayne Publishers [1963, °1962] 176 p. (Twayne's United States authors series, 29)   62–19473  PS1981.S5 1963
Bibliographical notes: p. 154–165. Bibliography: p. 166–172.
Holmes' public image as a writer is chronologically examined in relation to his professional career and private life. The author consulted published and unpublished materials, including the rich holdings of the Harvard University Library.

121. WASHINGTON IRVING, 1783–1859
No. 381 in 1960 *Guide*.

122. A history of New York. Edited for the modern reader by Edwin T. Bowden. New York, Twayne Publishers [°1964] 352 p. (Twayne's United States classics series)   64–19644  F122.1.I835 1964
Bibliography: p. 21–22.
Irving's first major revision of this work appeared in the second edition, published in New York and Philadelphia in 1812. As reprinted here, the second edition contains new material but preserves "the youthful drive and daring and nerve of the first." No. 382 in the 1960 *Guide* has information concerning the first edition (1809); a much later edition (1927) is described in no. 383. For the present text, spelling has been modernized and punctuation altered in the interest of clarity.

123. A tour on the prairies. Edited, with an introductory essay, by John Francis McDermott. Norman, University of Oklahoma Press [1956] xxxii, 214 p. (The Western Frontier library [7])   56–11232  F697.I743 1956
Bibliographical footnotes.
Irving's brief circuit of the Oklahoma prairies in 1832 provided the material for this frontier narrative. Based on the 1859 text, this edition includes

the author's original introduction to the American edition of 1835.

124.   Astoria; or, Anecdotes of an enterprise beyond the Rocky Mountains. [New ed.] Edited and with an introduction by Edgeley W. Todd. Norman, University of Oklahoma Press [1964] xlix, 556 p. illus. (The American exploration and travel series, 44)                    64–20765   F880.I75
Bibliographical footnotes. Bibliography: p. 524–534.

The text is that of the author's revised edition (1860–61), which has been collated with the first edition of 1836 (no. 391 in the 1960 *Guide*); differences between the two are indicated in the footnotes. The author's introduction and a lengthy prefatory essay by the editor are included.

125.   The adventures of Captain Bonneville, U.S.A., in the Rocky Mountains and the Far West, digested from his journal. Edited and with an introduction by Edgeley W. Todd. Norman, University of Oklahoma Press [1961] liv, 424 p. illus. (The American exploration and travel series, no. 34)
61–15144   F592.I73   1961
Bibliographical footnotes. Bibliography: p. 401–408.

Based on Captain Benjamin de Bonneville's records of his Northwest travels, 1832–35, this sequel to *Astoria* was first published in 1837. The text of the author's revised edition is reprinted here, retaining Irving's footnotes and appendix. The maps which appeared in the first edition are also reprinted.

126.   Hedges, William L. Washington Irving: an American study, 1802–1832. Baltimore, Johns Hopkins Press, 1965. 274 p. (The Goucher College series)   65–11663   PS2081.H35
Bibliographical footnotes.

Attempts to define Irving's major literary contributions in relation to the context and influence of his intellectual environment. Claiming that, after 1832, Irving "kept on writing but not developing as a writer," Hedges does not treat the final 27 years of his subject's life.

127.   Reichart, Walter A. Washington Irving and Germany. Ann Arbor, University of Michigan Press [1957] 212 p. (University of Michigan publications. Language and literature, v. 28)
57–7102   PS2081.R4
Bibliographical notes: p. 165–191.

In 1822–23, Irving toured Germany and Austria to collect materials for a "German Sketch Book," which became *Tales of a Traveller* (no. 390 in the 1960 *Guide*). The background of this tour and its

influence on his subsequent work are examined in depth. An appendix contains related material, including a catalog of the German books at Sunnyside, the Irving estate in Tarrytown, N. Y.

128.   Wagenknecht, Edward C. Washington Irving: moderation displayed. New York, Oxford University Press, 1962. 223 p.
62–9833   PS2081.W2
Bibliographical notes: p. 191–205. Bibliography: p. 207–212.

This literary portrait explores Irving's personality, which the author sees as "considerably more complicated than it is generally supposed to have been." Wagenknecht consulted manuscript material in the collections of several libraries, including the New York Public Library and the Sterling Library of Yale University.

129.   JOHN PENDLETON KENNEDY, 1795–1870

No. 405 in 1960 *Guide*.

130.   Swallow barn; or, A sojourn in the Old Dominion. With introduction and notes by William S. Osborne. Illustrations by Strother. New York, Hafner Pub. Co., 1962. lv, 506 p. (Hafner library of classics, no. 22)
62–11037   PZ3.K383S   15
Bibliography: p. [xliv]–xlv.

Follows the text of the revised second edition of 1851 and includes the preface to the first edition, a letter of dedication to William Wirt, and Wirt's reply. Published here for the first time are two fragments from Kennedy's *Swallow Barn* manuscript: "An Inn" and "Hoppergallop House." The first and second editions mentioned above are no. 406 and 407 respectively in the 1960 *Guide;* a 1929 reprint of the second edition is no. 408.

131.   Rob of the bowl; a legend of St. Inigoe's. Edited for the modern reader by William S. Osborne. New Haven, College & University Press [1965]   363 p. (The Masterworks of literature series)   65–25630   PZ3.K383R   5
Bibliographical footnotes.

The editor has supplied an introduction (p. 5–27) and has corrected printer's errors in this text of the revised second edition of 1854. Later editions are no. 412–413 in the 1960 *Guide*.

132.   Bohner, Charles H. John Pendleton Kennedy, gentleman from Baltimore. Baltimore, Johns Hopkins Press [1961] 266 p.
61–10735   E415.9.K35B6

Bibliography: p. 238–241. Bibliographical notes: p. [243]–258.

A comprehensive biography surveying Kennedy's literary, political, and business careers. The major source consulted is a collection of 130 volumes of John Pendleton Kennedy papers in the Peabody Institute, Baltimore.

133. CAROLINE MATILDA STANSBURY KIRKLAND, 1801–1864

No. 415 in 1960 *Guide.*

134. A new home — who'll follow? Glimpses of western life. Edited for the modern reader by William S. Osborne. New Haven, College & University Press [1965] 233 p. (Masterworks of literature series)  65–25629 PZ3.K635N 10
Bibliography: p. 25.

The first edition of this work is no. 416 in the 1960 *Guide,* followed by a 1953 edition as no. 417. The 1840 text of the second edition, incorporating revisions made by the author, is followed here. The editor's introduction appears on p. 5–24.

135. ABRAHAM LINCOLN, 1809–1865

No. 419 in 1960 *Guide.*

136. Warren, Louis A. Lincoln's Gettysburg declaration: "A new birth of freedom." Fort Wayne, Lincoln National Life Foundation, 1964. xix, 236 p. illus.  64–56025 E475.55.W39
Bibliography: p. [215]–222.

A detailed chronology of the events surrounding the writing, delivery, and reception of Lincoln's most famous address. An appendix contains the comparatively long oration delivered by Edward Everett, who preceded Lincoln on the platform at Gettysburg.

137. DAVID ROSS LOCKE ("PETROLEUM V. NASBY"), 1833–1888

No. 422 in 1960 *Guide.*

138. The struggles of Petroleum V. Nasby [pseud.] Original illustrations by Thomas Nast. Abridged ed. selected, edited, and with an introduction by Joseph Jones. Notes to the chapters by Gunther Barth. Boston, Beacon Press [1963] 246 p. (Beacon paperback)
63–8275 PN6161.L6373 1963
Bibliography: p. 246.

An abridged version of *The Struggles (Social, Financial and Political) of Petroleum V. Nasby,* no. 425 in the 1960 *Guide.* This abridgment contains one of the lectures, a selection of the illustra-

tions, and approximately one-third of the letters published in the original collection of 1872.

139. Austin, James C. Petroleum V. Nasby (David Ross Locke). New York, Twayne Publishers [1965] 159 p. (Twayne's United States authors series, 89)  65–18908 PS2248.L8Z59
Bibliographical notes: p. 141–147. Bibliography: p. 148–154.

Emphasizing analysis rather than biography, the author offers an overall view of Locke's works, illustrated by quotations from the collected and uncollected writings.

140. HENRY WADSWORTH LONGFELLOW, 1807–1882

No. 427 in 1960 *Guide.*

141. Kavanagh, a tale. Edited for the modern reader by Jean Downey. New Haven, College & University Press [1965] 125 p. (Masterworks of literature series)
65–25631 PZ3.L86K 15
Bibliography: p. 22.

An introduction has been added and minor technical corrections have been made in the text, which is based on that of the first edition (no. 430 in the 1960 *Guide*).

142. Arvin, Newton. Longfellow: his life and work. Boston, Little, Brown [1963] 338 p.
63–8312 PS2281.A6

143. Williams, Cecil B. Henry Wadsworth Longfellow. New York, Twayne Publishers (Twayne's United States authors series, 68) [°1964] 221 p. (Twayne's United States authors series, 68)  64–20718 PS2281.W47
Bibliographical notes: p. 201–207. Bibliography: p. 211–214.

Hoping to present "a truer picture of the real man and writer than any available hitherto," Williams explores the shifting nature of Longfellow's image and reputation. Both biography and criticism are offered, with emphasis on the interrelationship between Longfellow's literary and academic careers.

144. HERMAN MELVILLE, 1819–1891

No. 470 in 1960 *Guide.*

145. Moby-Dick; or, The whale. Edited, with an introduction and annotation, by Charles Feidelson, Jr. Indianapolis, Bobbs-Merrill [1964] xlv, 730 p. illus. (The Library of literature, 5)
64–16178 PZ3.M498Mo 73

Bibliography: p. xxv-xxvi.

The first American edition of *Moby-Dick* appeared in November 1851. With the exception of typographical changes, its text has been followed, supplemented by one short passage published in the first English edition of October 1851. The editor's notes define terms and expressions, explain allusions, explicate obscure or difficult passages, and suggest relationships among images and ideas. Editions of *Moby-Dick* and works of critical commentary are described in no. 481–483 in the 1960 *Guide*.

146. The confidence-man: his masquerade. Edited, with an introduction, by Hennig Cohen. New York, Holt, Rinehart & Winston [1964] xxxiii, 275 p. (Rinehart editions, 126)
64–12514 PZ3.M498Cp 5
Bibliography: p. xxxi-xxxiii.

The text follows that of the original American edition (no. 485 in the 1960 *Guide*), with typographical errors corrected and spelling and punctuation emended for the sake of consistency.

147. Battle-pieces; [poems]. Edited, with introduction and notes, by Hennig Cohen. New York, T. Yoseloff [1963] 302 p. illus.
62–14910 PS2384.B3 1963
Bibliography: p. [297]–299.

The first-edition text, published in 1866 under the title *Battle-Pieces and Aspects of the War* (no. 486 in the 1960 *Guide*), is reproduced and illustrated with contemporary Civil War drawings, principally from the Waud Collection in the Library of Congress.

148. Clarel, a poem and pilgrimage in the Holy Land. Edited by Walter E. Bezanson. New York, Hendricks House, 1960. cxvii, 652 p.
61–569 PS2384.C5 1960
CONTENTS.— Jerusalem.— The wilderness.— Mar Saba.— Bethlehem.

The text of the first American edition of 1876 is followed, with minor changes and with Melville's own revisions incorporated for the first time. The editor's long introduction is supplemented by maps, a chronology, a critical index of characters, and numerous explanatory and textual notes.

149. Billy Budd, sailor (an inside narrative). Reading text and genetic text, edited from the manuscript, with introduction and notes, by Harrison Hayford and Merton M. Sealts, Jr. [Chicago] University of Chicago Press [1962] 431 p.
62–17135 PZ3.M498Bl
Bibliography: p. 203–212.

Through interpretive analysis of the manuscript in Harvard's Houghton Library, the editors have prepared an annotated text for the general reader as well as a second text for the scholar. Notes to the reading text appear on p. 133–202, and the genetic text is accompanied by elaborate commentary and detailed description of the manuscript. The first edition of *Billy Budd* is no. 487 in the 1960 *Guide*.

150. The letters of Herman Melville. Edited by Merrell R. Davis and William H. Gilman. New Haven, Yale University Press, 1960. xxxi, 398 p. illus.
60–7822 PS2386.A57

This edition of 271 letters presents Melville's recoverable correspondence, whether in manuscript or printed form, including "letters to the editor," fragments, and first drafts. Fifty-five letters are published in full for the first time, and 42 are previously unpublished. Aids to the reader include an introduction, a checklist of unlocated letters, and extensive textual notes.

151. Selected poems. Edited by Hennig Cohen. Garden City, N. Y., Doubleday, 1964. xvi, 259 p. (Anchor books) 63–18037 PS2382.C6

In establishing this text, first editions were examined, as well as manuscripts in Harvard's Houghton Library. Selections were made on the basis of literary distinction. "Poems of lesser merit have been included, however, because they show Melville's artistic development, the range of his ideas, or important relationships to his prose."

152. Baird, James. Ishmael. Baltimore, Johns Hopkins Press, 1956. xxxviii, 445 p.
56–8064 PN56.P7B3
Bibliographical footnotes.

An exploratory study of "modern primitivism," emphasizing Melville's focal role as a symbolistic writer.

153. Berthoff, Warner. The example of Melville. Princeton, N. J., Princeton University Press, 1962. 218 p. 63–7065 PS2386.B4
Bibliographical footnotes.

Shunning the special concerns of literary criticism and scholarship, the author of this general study takes a direct look at Melville's exactness, explicitness, and urgency as defining elements of his artistic significance.

154. Bowen, Merlin. The long encounter; self and experience in the writings of Herman Melville. [Chicago] University of Chicago Press [1960] 282 p. 60–7232 PS2387.B6 1960
Considers Melville's works in the light of a per-

vading concern with the problem of self-discovery and self-realization, which influenced his choice of subject matter, his imagery, and the shape of his narratives.

155. Brodtkorb, Paul. Ishmael's white world; a phenomenological reading of Moby Dick. New Haven, Yale University Press, 1965. 170 p. (Yale publications in American studies, 9)
65–11176  PS2384.M62B7
Bibliography: p. 149–150. Bibliographical notes: p. [151]–166.
Within the critical framework of phenomenology, Ishmael's consciousness is analyzed as "the vessel that contains the book."

156. Finkelstein, Dorothee M. Melville's Orienda. New Haven, Yale University Press, 1961. 317 p. illus. (Yale publications in American studies, 5)  61–6312  PS2386.F5
Bibliographical footnotes. Bibliography: p. [283]–302.
Explores Melville's use of material and sources relating to the Near East, which in *Mardi* he called "old Orienda."

157. Fogle, Richard H. Melville's shorter tales. Norman, University of Oklahoma Press [1960] 150 p.  60–7741  PS2387.F6
Bibliographical footnotes.
A collection of critical essays offering general and individual analyses of the tales. Among those treated are "Bartleby," "The Encantadas," and "Benito Cereno."

158. Hetherington, Hugh W. Melville's reviewers, British and American, 1846–1891. Chapel Hill, University of North Carolina Press [1961] 304 p. illus.  61–12305  PS2387.H45
Bibliographical footnotes.
Examines numerous reviews which appeared during Melville's lifetime, demonstrating contemporary critical response to six major novels, including *Moby-Dick*.

159. Hillway, Tyrus. Herman Melville. New York, Twayne Publishers [1963] 176 p. (Twayne's United States authors series, 37)
63–10954  PS2386.H5
Bibliographical notes: p. 154–161. Bibliography: p. 162–170.
Without attempting to identify and answer the many questions surrounding Melville and his writing, Hillway presents a body of authentic information, a review of recent literature, and a summary of his critical judgment.

160. Sealts, Merton M. Melville as lecturer. Cambridge, Mass., Harvard University Press, 1957. 202 p. illus.  58–5542  PS2386.S4
Bibliographical footnotes.
Following his Mediterranean trip of 1856 and 1857, Melville traveled in the United States as a lecturer for three seasons. The lectures themselves were not printed after delivery, and the manuscripts have apparently been destroyed. Sealts analyzes this period of Melville's career and presents lecture texts reconstructed and annotated on the basis of contemporary newspaper reports.

161. Stern, Milton R. The fine hammered steel of Herman Melville. Urbana, University of Illinois Press, 1957. 297 p.  57–6959  PS2387.S7
Bibliographical footnotes. Bibliography: p. [251]–291.
Traces thematic and perceptual patterns developed throughout Melville's work, classifying his writings as "naturalistic" on the basis of interpretations of *Typee, Mardi, Pierre,* and *Billy Budd*. The comprehensive checklist of Melville studies includes dissertations.

162. JAMES KIRKE PAULDING, 1778–1860

No. 511 in 1960 *Guide*.

163. Letters. Edited by Ralph M. Aderman. Madison, University of Wisconsin Press, 1962. xxiv, 631 p. illus.
62–17397  PS2528.A45  1962
Includes all of the "available significant surviving correspondence," transcribed from manuscript sources when possible.

164. EDGAR ALLAN POE, 1809–1849

No. 520 in 1960 *Guide*.

165. Selected writings. Edited, with an introduction and notes, by Edward H. Davidson. Boston, Houghton Mifflin [1956] xxxii, 508 p. (Riverside editions, A11)  56–13895  PS2602.D3
Bibliography: p. xxix. Bibliographical notes: p. 487–506.
In addition to a selection of poems, essays, and criticism, this volume contains 16 tales and *The Narrative of Arthur Gordon Pym of Nantucket*. In most cases, the individual writings appear in texts bearing Poe's final revisions or approval, with exceptions indicated in the notes.

166. Poems. Edited, with an introduction, variant readings, and textual notes, by Floyd Stovall. Charlottesville, University Press of Virginia [1965] xxxvii, 361 p.  65–23455  PS2605.A1  1965a

The poems are chronologically arranged according to the date of first publication, insofar as that is known. Bibliographical notes and variant readings, constituting a history of the textual changes in the poems, appear on p. [147]–298. The complete text of Poe's poetic drama, *Politian — A Tragedy,* is included in an appendix.

167. Buranelli, Vincent. Edgar Allan Poe. New York, Twayne Publishers [1961] 157 p. (Twayne's United States authors series, 4)
61–9855 PS2631.B8
Bibliographical notes: p. 134–143. Bibliography: p. 144–151.

168. Davidson, Edward H. Poe, a critical study. Cambridge, Belknap Press of Harvard University Press, 1957. 296 p. 57–12965 PS2638.D3
Bibliographical notes: p. [263]–290.
Poe's mind and writings are examined within the philosophic context of 19th-century Romantic thought, with particular reference to the esthetic principles of Coleridge.

169. Moss, Sidney P. Poe's literary battles: the critic in the context of his literary milieu. Durham, N. C., Duke University Press, 1963. 266 p. 63–9010 PS2638.M6 1963
Bibliographical footnotes.
The author focuses on Poe's journalistic conflicts and their effect upon his characteristics and responses as a literary critic.

170. Parks, Edd W. Edgar Allan Poe as literary critic. Athens, University of Georgia Press [1964] 114 p. (Eugenia Dorothy Blount Lamar memorial lectures, 1964) 64–25841 PS2638.P3
Bibliographical notes: p. 97–108.
Maintaining that Poe's critical theories grew out of his work as a magazine editor and reviewer, the author discusses the development and nature of Poe's demand for a rhythmic harmony and unified design in literature.

171. Quinn, Patrick F. The French face of Edgar Poe. Carbondale, Southern Illinois University Press, 1957. 310 p. 56–10476 PS2638.Q5
Bibliographical notes: p. 279–293. Bibliography: p. 295–299.
This interpretation of the French response to Poe is mainly concerned with his importance as a writer of tales. Emphasis is placed upon the role played by Baudelaire and later French critics in revealing Poe to a European audience.

172. WILLIAM GILMORE SIMMS, 1806–1870
No. 546 in 1960 *Guide.*

173. The Yemassee; a romance of Carolina. Edited, with an introduction and notes, by C. Hugh Holman. Boston, Houghton Mifflin [1961] xxxi, 377 p. (Riverside editions, A65)
61–66407 PZ3.S592Y38
"Bibliographical note": p. [xxv]–xxvii.
Reprints the "new and revised" third edition of 1853, retaining the author's original punctuation with slight editorial changes indicated and explained. A Simms chronology and his poem "The Last of the Yemassees" are included. Other editions of *The Yemassee* are no. 548–549 in the 1960 *Guide.*

174. ———— Edited for the modern reader by Joseph V. Ridgely. New York, Twayne Publishers [1964] 415 p. (Twayne's United States classics series) 62–10274 PZ3.S592Yn 42
The text of the 1853 edition is again followed, with some alterations in spelling and punctuation. Simms' career is discussed in the editor's introductory essay.

175. Views and reviews in American literature, history and fiction: first series. Edited by C. Hugh Holman. Cambridge, Belknap Press of Harvard University Press, 1962. xliii, 292 p. (The John Harvard library) 62–17226 PS2850.V52
Bibliographical footnotes.
A reprint of the 1845 edition of 11 essays originally published in southern literary journals in the 1840's. The editor's notes identify individuals, places, and quotation sources whenever possible. A one-volume edition of the first and second series of this work is no. 551 in the 1960 *Guide.*

176. Woodcraft; or, Hawks about the dovecote; a story of the South at the close of the Revolution. Introduction by Richmond Croom Beatty. New York, Norton [1961] xvi, 518 p. (The Norton library, N507) 61–8921 PZ3.S592Wo 8
Bibliography: p. xv–xvi.
Reprinted from the revised edition of 1854, this work was first published in 1852 under the title *The Sword and the Distaff.*

177. Letters. Collected and edited by Mary C. Simms Oliphant, Alfred Taylor Odell [and] T. C. Duncan Eaves. Introduction by Donald Davidson. Biographical sketch by Alexander S. Salley. Columbia, University of South Carolina Press, 1952–56. 5 v. illus.
52–2352 PS2853.A4 1952
Bibliographical footnotes.
This edition of Simms' letters, no. 554 in the 1960 *Guide,* was completed with the publication in 1956 of volume 5, covering the period 1867-70.

178. Parks, Edd W. William Gilmore Simms as literary critic. Athens, University of Georgia Press, 1961. 152 p. (University of Georgia monographs, no. 7)     61–9795  PS2854.P3
Bibliographical notes: p. 114–144.
This monograph is the first of a three-volume study of antebellum southern critics; the final volume is *Edgar Allan Poe as Literary Critic* (no. 170 above). Parks examines Simms' criticism of fiction, poetry, and drama, concluding that "he was a good but not a great critic."

179. Ridgely, Joseph V. William Gilmore Simms. New York, Twayne Publishers [ᶜ1962] 144 p. (Twayne's United States authors series, 28)     62–16823  PS2853.R5
Bibliographical notes: p. 131–137. Bibliography: p. 138–141.
Treats Simms as a celebrator of the South who tried to create through fiction "the vision of an ideal Southern social structure." Biographical, historical, and source materials are reduced to a minimum.

180. HARRIET BEECHER STOWE, 1811–1896
No. 562 in 1960 *Guide*.

181. Uncle Tom's cabin; or, Life among the lowly. Edited by Kenneth S. Lynn. Cambridge, Mass., Belknap Press, 1962. xxviii, 460 p. (The John Harvard library)   62–9431  PZ3.S89Un 85
The text is that of the first American edition, published in Boston by J. P. Jewett, 1852 (no. 563 in the 1960 *Guide;* later editions are no. 564–567). The editor has contributed a lengthy introduction, a textual history, and a chronology of Mrs. Stowe's life.

182. The annotated Uncle Tom's cabin. Edited, with an introduction, by Philip Van Doren Stern. New York, P. S. Eriksson [1964] 591 p. illus.     64–15781  PZ3.S89An
Mrs. Stowe and her celebrated novel are discussed in the introduction, p. 7–37, and informative notes appear on p. 562–591. A selection of illustrations from the original edition is included.

183. Adams, John R. Harriet Beecher Stowe. New York, Twayne Publishers [ᶜ1963] 172 p. (Twayne's United States authors series, 42)     63–17370  PS2956.A6
Bibliographical notes: p. 143–158. Bibliography: p. 159–167.
"In a resolute effort to avoid myth-making," Adams focuses attention on Mrs. Stowe's writings (including more than 200 uncollected articles and stories).

184. Wagenknecht, Edward C. Harriet Beecher Stowe; the known and the unknown. New York, Oxford University Press, 1965. 267 p.
65–15615  PS2956.W3
Bibliographical notes: p. 221–251. Bibliography: p. 253–258.
This psychograph or character study of Mrs. Stowe regards her principally within the context of her familial relationships. The author has had access to a wide array of unpublished letters, many of which are contained in the collection of Stowe papers in the Women's Archives at Radcliffe College.

185. HENRY DAVID THOREAU, 1817–1862
No. 585 in 1960 *Guide*.

186. A week on the Concord and Merrimack Rivers. Edited, with introduction and notes, by Walter R. Harding. New York, Holt, Rinehart & Winston [1963] xxiii, 340 p. (Rinehart editions)
63–7886  F72.M7T5  1963
Bibliography: p. [xix]–xx.
The first edition of this work was published by James Munroe of Boston in 1849 (no. 587 in the 1960 *Guide;* a 1921 edition is no. 588). A "new and revised edition," published in 1868 by Ticknor & Fields, is followed here, with small revisions carefully noted.

187. The variorum Walden. Annotated and with an introduction by Walter R. Harding. New York, Twayne Publishers [1962] 320 p.
62–10273  PS3048.A1  1962a
Bibliographical notes: p. 267–319. Bibliography: p. 320.
The text is based on that of the first edition (Boston, Ticknor & Fields, 1854), no. 589 in the 1960 *Guide*. The editor's notes provide a collation of Thoreau scholarship and incorporate for the first time all the corrections made by Thoreau in his personal copy of *Walden*. Selected editions of this work are no. 590–593 in the 1960 *Guide*.

188. Walden and Civil disobedience. Edited, with an introduction and notes, by Sherman Paul. Boston, Houghton Mifflin [1960] xlvi, 266 p. (Riverside editions, A14)
60–16148  PS3048.A1  1960
Bibliography: p. [xlv]–xlvi.
The *Walden* text printed here follows the 1889 Riverside edition (Boston, Houghton Mifflin), which first included many of Thoreau's corrections and revisions. The reader is guided by an extended introduction, a Thoreau chronology, and a brief essay on the composition of *Walden*. Charles

Lane's article, "Life in the Woods," from *The Dial*, April 1844, has been appended.

189. Consciousness in Concord; the text of Thoreau's hitherto "lost journal," 1840–1841, together with notes and a commentary by Perry Miller. Boston, Houghton Mifflin, 1958. 243 p.
                58–7303 PS3053.A26
  Bibliographical notes: p. 221–240.
Based on a manuscript owned by the J. Pierpont Morgan Library, the text retains Thoreau's revisions and often eccentric punctuation, with textual variants indicated in the notes.

190. Correspondence. Edited by Walter R. Harding and Carl Bode. [New York] New York University Press, 1958. xxi, 665 p.
              58–11447 PS3053.A3 1958
The first inclusive edition of Thoreau's correspondence, chronologically arranged, contains "every available surviving letter written by and to Thoreau." The texts are based on original manuscripts whenever possible, with sources identified in the annotations.

191. Collected poems. Edited by Carl Bode. Enl. ed. Baltimore, Johns Hopkins Press, 1964. xxii, 413 p.
      64–12730 PS3041.B6 1964
This enlarged edition of no. 598 in the 1960 *Guide* incorporates the miscellaneous poems which have appeared since the original volume was published in 1943. Textual and explanatory notes appear on p. 281–377, with notes for the added poems on p. 400–404.

192. Christie, John A. Thoreau as world traveler. New York, Columbia University Press with the cooperation of the American Geographical Society, 1965. 358 p. illus. 65–24586 PS3056.C4
  Bibliographical notes: p. [275]–310.
Christie traces Thoreau's vicarious global adventures, exploring the influence and reflection of his "travel" through reading. The long bibliography of travel works read by Thoreau is partial evidence of the author's painstaking research.

193. Harding, Walter R. The days of Henry Thoreau. New York, Knopf, 1965. xvi, 472 p. 65–18766 PS3053.H3
  Bibliographical footnotes. Bibliography: p. 471–472.
A general and comprehensive biography, with "no thesis to present, no axe to grind." The text is augmented by a number of illustrations, including reproductions of photographs, daguerreotypes, and sketches.

194. Harding, Walter R. A Thoreau handbook. [New York] New York University Press, 1959. 229 p. 59–9918 PS3053.H32
This guide to Thoreau scholarship is divided into five sections, summarizing Thoreau's life, his works, the sources of his ideas, the ideas themselves, and the course of his fame. Each section presents an evaluation of previous work on the subject and includes an extended bibliography of related materials. A Thoreau chronology and a list of Thoreau bibliographies are included.

195. Meltzer, Milton, *and* Walter R. Harding, *eds*. A Thoreau profile. New York, Crowell [1962] 310 p. 62–16548 PS3053.M4
  Bibliographies: p. 294–297.
A pictorial biography featuring every known life portrait of Thoreau in addition to photographs, cartoons, news clippings, drawings, maps, and charts. The text is mainly derived from Thoreau's own writings, occasionally supplemented by the writings of his contemporaries.

196. Paul, Sherman. The shores of America: Thoreau's inward exploration. Urbana, University of Illinois Press, 1958. 433 p.
              58–6998 PS3053.P3
Bibliographical footnotes.
Through an examination of Thoreau's inner life, which was guided by the tenets of Transcendentalism, the author presents a work which "might be called a spiritual biography or a biography of vocation."

197. Shanley, James L. The making of Walden, with the text of the first version. [Chicago] University of Chicago Press [1957] 207 p.
              57–6990 PS3048.S5
Bibliographical footnotes.
Having established the proper manuscript order of Thoreau's first version of *Walden*, written in 1846–47, the author indicates how the work was rewritten and reshaped between 1848 and its publication in 1854. The text of the first version printed here is a transcript from the Huntington Library manuscript.

198. Stoller, Leo. After Walden; Thoreau's changing views on economic man. Stanford, Calif., Stanford University Press, 1957. 163 p.
             57–12516 PS3053.S8
Bibliographical footnotes. Bibliography: p. [157]–163.
Traces the evolution of Thoreau's economic philosophy and the development of his views concerning social legislation during the years following his stay at Walden Pond.

199. THOMAS BANGS THORPE, 1815–1878

No. 612 in 1960 *Guide*.

200. Rickels, Milton. Thomas Bangs Thorpe: humorist of the Old Southwest. Baton Rouge, Louisiana State University Press, 1962. 275 p. illus.      62–8018 PS3061.T6R5
Bibliographical footnotes. Bibliography: p. [257]–267.
A comprehensive biography of a versatile and lively observer of the mid-19th-century South.

201. HENRY TIMROD, 1828–1867

No. 614 in 1960 *Guide*.

202. Collected poems. A variorum ed. edited by Edd Winfield Parks and Aileen Wells Parks. Athens, University of Georgia Press [1965] 206 p.
65–25289 PS3070.A2 1965
The primary textual source is the memorial edition of Timrod's poems (no. 617 in the 1960 *Guide*), which in turn was based on the 1873 edition (no. 616 in the 1960 *Guide*). The notes appearing on p. 142–203 contain the publication record of each poem, explanatory comments, and variant readings.

203. Parks, Edd W. Henry Timrod. New York, Twayne Publishers [1964] 158 p. (Twayne's United States authors series, 53)
63–20607 PS3073.P3
Bibliographical notes: p. 117–145. Bibliography: p. 146–149.
A blend of biography and criticism, relating Timrod's life to the literary activities of Charleston in the 1850's.

204. WALT WHITMAN, 1819–1892

No. 619 in 1960 *Guide*.

205. Leaves of grass. 1st (1855) ed. Edited, with an introduction, by Malcolm Cowley. New York, Viking Press, 1959. xxxvii, 145 p.
59–13502 PS3201 1959
A reprint of the 1855 text (no. 620 in the 1960 *Guide*), with obvious typographical errors corrected. Facsimiles of the first-edition frontispiece and title page are included, as well as Whitman's prose introduction.

206. Leaves of grass. With an introduction by Roy Harvey Pearce. Facsim. ed. of the 1860 text. Ithaca, N.Y., Great Seal Books [1961] li, 467 p.
61–14850 PS3201 1860b
A cross-index of the 1860 and 1892 poems has been added to this facsimile reprint of the third edition (no. 622 in the 1960 *Guide*).

207. Leaves of grass. Edited by Harold W. Blodgett and Sculley Bradley. Comprehensive reader's ed. [New York] New York University Press, 1965. lviii, 768 p. illus. (The Collected writings of Walt Whitman)
65–1625 PS3201 1965
Bibliographical footnotes.
This edition contains the 1891–92 text (no. 626 in the 1960 *Guide*), with typographical errors corrected in the footnotes. In addition, the editors have included the annexes, prefaces, "A Backward Glance O'er Travel'd Roads," "Old Age Echoes," and uncollected and excluded poems and fragments. Various editions of *Leaves of Grass* are no. 620–630 in the 1960 *Guide*.

208. Memoranda during the war [&] Death of of Abraham Lincoln. Edited, with an introduction, by Roy P. Basler. Bloomington, Indiana University Press, 1962. 1 v. (various pagings)
62–8978 PS3216.A1 1962
*Memoranda During the War,* published in 1875–76, is reproduced in facsimile along with the text which Whitman used in delivering his lecture on Lincoln. Additional facsimiles of letters, manuscripts, and related material illustrate the volume. The introduction outlines the literary and historical background of each work.

209. Complete poetry and selected prose. Edited, with an introduction and glossary, by James E. Miller, Jr. Boston, Houghton Mifflin [1959] 516 p. (Riverside editions, A34)
59–2805 PS3200.F59
Contains all of the poetry written and published as *Leaves of Grass,* including the 29 poems which Whitman rejected from edition to edition. The text of the 1891–92 version is followed. *Democratic Vistas* and several of Whitman's prefaces are printed as prose selections.

210. The correspondence. Edited by Edwin Haviland Miller. [New York] New York University Press, 1961–64. 3 v. illus. (The Collected writings of Walt Whitman)
65–9834 PS3231.M48
Bibliographical footnotes.
CONTENTS.—v. 1. 1842–1867.—v. 2. 1868–1875.—v. 3. 1876–1885.
This edition includes all available letters, post cards, and notes, published in unabridged form and in chronological sequence, through 1885. The majority of the letters are based on original manuscripts, with editorial modifications made in the interest of readability. Additional materials include checklists of lost letters, manuscript sources, and letters written to Whitman.

211. The early poems and the fiction. Edited by Thomas L. Brasher. [New York] New York University Press, 1963. xxii, 352 p. (The Collected writings of Walt Whitman) 65–3935 PS3203.B7
Bibliographical footnotes.
Most of Whitman's early poems were published between 1838 and 1850 in New York or Long Island newspapers; his 24 tales appeared in periodicals between 1841 and 1848. The texts in this volume are based on Whitman's last printed versions, with variants indicated in the footnotes.

212. Prose works, 1892. Edited by Floyd Stovall. [New York] New York University Press, 1963–64. 2 v. illus. (The Collected writings of Walt Whitman) 65–3934 PS3202 1963
Bibliographical footnotes.
CONTENTS.—v. 1. Specimen days.—v. 2. Collect and other prose.
Except for the juvenile pieces, these two volumes contain all the material printed in Whitman's *Complete Prose Works* of 1892 (no. 638 in the 1960 *Guide*). The text of the 1892 edition is followed, with variant readings recorded in the notes and the appendix. A collection of prefaces, notes, and articles not in the earlier work has been added to this edition.

213. Allen, Gay W. Walt Whitman as man, poet, and legend. With a check list of Whitman publications, 1945–1960, by Evie Allison Allen. Carbondale, Southern Illinois University Press [1961] 260 p. 61–10924 PS3231.A698
Bibliographical notes: p. [247]–260.
Several of the essays in this collection are reprints or adaptations of previously published material. The comprehensive checklist records translations, theses, and uncollected writings, in addition to books and articles by and about Whitman. A number of notable letters concerning Whitman, the majority of which are in the Slocum Library of Ohio Wesleyan University, are printed in full for the first time.

214. Asselineau, Roger. The evolution of Walt Whitman. Cambridge, Belknap Press of Harvard University Press, 1960–62. 2 v. 60–13297 PS3231.A833
Bibliographical notes: v. 1, p. [273]–362; v. 2, p. [273]–379. Bibliography: v. 2, p. [261]–271.
CONTENTS.—v. 1. The creation of a personality. —[v. 2] The creation of a book.
The English translation of a work originally published in French in 1954. The first volume, translated by Richard P. Adams and the author, is essentially biographical; the second, translated by Burton L. Cooper and the author, is devoted to criticism of Whitman's work.

215. Dutton, Geoffrey. Whitman. New York, Grove Press [1961] 120 p. (Evergreen pilot books EP12) 61–17200 PS3231.D8 1961
Bibliographical footnotes. Bibliography: p. 118–120.
Divided into three sections, this concise study treats Whitman biographically in relation to his prose, analyzes his poetry, and discusses the reactions of individual critics.

216. Miller, James E. A critical guide to Leaves of grass. [Chicago] University of Chicago Press [1957] 268 p. 57–6982 PS3238.M5
Focusing on poetic structure, Miller's individual analyses of 10 Whitman poems and a panoramic view of *Leaves of Grass* "help dispel the common notion that Whitman was a formless, even a chaotic poet."

217. Miller, James E. Walt Whitman. New York, Twayne Publishers [1962] 188 p. (Twayne's United States authors series, 20) 62–13674 PS3231.M5
Bibliographical notes: p. 165–175. Bibliography: p. 176–181.
"Entrances" to Whitman's poetry are provided through discussions of its language, imagery, structure, wit, and wisdom.

218. JOHN GREENLEAF WHITTIER, 1807–1892

No. 662 in 1960 *Guide*.

219. Leary, Lewis G. John Greenleaf Whittier. New York, Twayne Publishers [1962, °1961] 189 p. (Twayne's United States authors series, 6) 61–15667 PS3288.L4 1962
Bibliographical notes: p. 172–179. Bibliography: p. 180–184.
This review of his major poetry seeks "to discover what Whittier, who spoke so clearly to his own time, has to say to ours."

220. Pickard, John B. John Greenleaf Whittier, an introduction and interpretation. New York, Barnes & Noble [1961] 145 p. illus. (American authors and critics series, AC4) 61–14752 PS3281.P48
Bibliography: p. 135–137.
Appraises Whittier's poetic achievement, correlating his literary, political, and humanitarian activities.

# D. The Gilded Age and After (1871-1914)

221. ANDY ADAMS, 1859–1935
No. 683 in 1960 *Guide*.

222. Why the Chisholm Trail forks, and other tales of the cattle country. Edited by Wilson M. Hudson. With illustrations by Malcolm Thurgood. Austin, University of Texas Press, 1956. 296 p.
56–11769  PZ3.A21Wh
Includes previously unpublished material.

223. Hudson, Wilson M. Andy Adams, his life and writings. Dallas, Southern Methodist University Press, 1964. xv, 274 p. illus.
64–16632  PS3501.D2152H8
Bibliographical notes: p. 227–258. Bibliography: p. 259–265.
Describes Adams' friendships with Walter Prescott Webb, J. Frank Dobie, Emerson Hough, and Eugene Manlove Rhodes and evaluates his place in western fiction.

224. HENRY ADAMS, 1838–1918
No. 688 in 1960 *Guide*.

225. A Henry Adams reader. Edited and with an introduction by Elizabeth Stevenson. Garden City, N.Y., Doubleday, 1958. xvi, 392 p. (Doubleday anchor books)    58–5929  AC8.A22
A selection from his letters, essays, biographies, histories, and poetry.

226. Hochfield, George. Henry Adams, an introduction and interpretation. New York, Barnes & Noble [1962] 150 p. illus. (American authors and critics series, AC5)
62–15370  E175.5.A1749
Bibliography: p. 145–147.

227. Levenson, Jacob C. The mind and art of Henry Adams. Boston, Houghton Mifflin, 1957. 430 p. illus.    57–6946  E175.5.A1765

228. Samuels, Ernest. Henry Adams; the major phase. Cambridge, Belknap Press of Harvard University Press, 1964. xv, 687 p.
64–21790  E175.5.A1776
"The writings of Henry Adams from 1892": p. [591]–594. Bibliographical notes: p. [595]–660. Bibliography: p. [661]–667.

Concludes Samuels' three-volume biography of Adams.

229. Samuels, Ernest. Henry Adams; the middle years. Cambridge, Belknap Press of Harvard University Press, 1958. 514 p.
58–12975  E175.5.A1777
"The writings of Henry Adams, 1878–1891": p. [423]–426. Bibliographical notes: p. [427]–488. Bibliography: p. [489]–497.
This sequel to Samuels' *The Young Henry Adams* (Cambridge, Harvard University Press, 1948. 378 p.) concentrates on Adams' life from 1877 to 1890.

230. GEORGE ADE, 1866–1944
No. 701 in 1960 *Guide*.

231. Artie, and Pink Marsh; two novels. Drawings by John T. McCutcheon. Introduction by James T. Farrell. Chicago, University of Chicago Press [1963] 224 p. (Chicago in fiction)
63–22584  PZ3.A228As

232. The America of George Ade, 1866–1944; fables, short stories, essays. Edited, with an introduction, by Jean Shepherd. New York, Putnam [1960] 284 p. illus.
60–8120  PS1006.A6A6  1960

233. Coyle, Lee. George Ade. New York, Twayne Publishers [1964] 159 p. (Twayne's United States authors series, 63)
64–20713  PS1006.A6Z6
Bibliographical notes: p. 141–149. Bibliography: p. 150–153.
Devotes considerable space to Ade's previously neglected career as a playwright.

234. JAMES LANE ALLEN, 1849–1925
No. 716 in 1960 *Guide*.

235. Bottorff, William K. James Lane Allen. New York, Twayne Publishers [1964] 176 p. (Twayne's United States authors series, 56)
63–20615  PS1036.B6
Bibliographical notes: p. 156–166. Bibliography: p. 167–172.

236. EDWARD BELLAMY, 1850–1898

No. 726 in 1960 *Guide.*

237. Bowman, Sylvia E., *and others.* Edward Bellamy abroad; an American prophet's influence. Preface by Maurice Le Breton. New York, Twayne Publishers [1962] xxv, 543 p. illus.
61–15672 HX806.B68
Bibliographical notes: p. 449–478. Bibliography: p. 479–528.

238. Bowman, Sylvia E. The year 2000: a critical biography of Edward Bellamy. New York, Bookman Associates [1958] 404 p. illus.
A 58–3939 HX84.B37B6
Bibliographical notes: p. 317–344. Bibliography: p. 345–393.

239. AMBROSE (GWINNETT) BIERCE, 1842–1914?

No. 732 in 1960 *Guide.*

240. Ambrose Bierce's Civil War. Edited and with an introduction by William McCann. Chicago, Gateway Editions; distributed by H. Regnery Co. [1956] 257 p. (A Gateway edition, 6015)
56–3957 E601.B594
CONTENTS. — War memoirs. — War stories.

241. The sardonic humor of Ambrose Bierce. Edited by George Barkin. New York, Dover Publications [1963] 232 p.
63–19487 PS1097.A6 1963
A new collection of verses and prose sketches selected from *The Collected Works of Ambrose Bierce* (New York, Neale Pub. Co., 1909–12. 12 v.).

242. Ghost and horror stories. Selected and introduced by E. F. Bleiler. New York, Dover Publications [1964] xxi, 199 p.
64–13459 PZ3.B479Gh
A new collection of short stories selected from *The Collected Works of Ambrose Bierce* (New York, Neale Pub. Co., 1909–12. 12 v.).

243. Woodruff, Stuart C. The short stories of Ambrose Bierce, a study in polarity. [Pittsburgh] University of Pittsburgh Press [1965, ᶜ1964] 193 p. (Critical essays in modern literature)
64–22147 PS1097.Z5W6
Bibliographical notes: p. 165–180. Bibliography: p. 181–191.
Analyzes representative works.

244. GEORGE WASHINGTON CABLE, 1844–1925

No. 745 in 1960 *Guide.*

245. Butcher, Charles P. George W. Cable. New York, Twayne Publishers [1962] 189 p. (Twayne's United States authors series, 24)
62–16819 PS1246.B78
Bibliographical notes: p. 168–177. Bibliography: p. 178–181.

246. WINSTON CHURCHILL, 1871–1947

No. 762 in 1960 *Guide.*

247. Titus, Warren I. Winston Churchill. New York, Twayne Publishers [ᶜ1963] 173 p. (Twayne's United States authors series, 43)
63–17371 PS1298.T5
Bibliographical notes: p. 151–162. Bibliography: p. 163–168.

248. SAMUEL LANGHORNE CLEMENS ("MARK TWAIN"), 1835–1910

No. 768 in 1960 *Guide.*

249. Adventures of Huckleberry Finn, an annotated text, backgrounds and sources, essays in criticism. Edited by Sculley Bradley, Richmond Croom Beatty [and] E. Hudson Long. New York, Norton [1962] 451 p. (Norton critical editions, N304)
62–9571 PZ3.C59A68
Bibliography: p. 449–451.
A photographic reproduction of the first American edition, no. 788 in the 1960 *Guide,* with annotated corrections of typographical errors. Other editions are no. 787 and 789–793.

250. The adventures of Colonel Sellers, being Mark Twain's share of The gilded age [1st ed., 1st issue], a novel which he wrote with Charles Dudley Warner. Now published separately for the first time and comprising, in effect, a new work. Edited and with an introduction and notes by Charles Neider. New York, Doubleday, 1965. 244 p.
65–11053 PZ3.C59Ac
*The Gilded Age* is no. 775-777 in the 1960 *Guide.*

251. The complete short stories of Mark Twain. Now collected for the first time. Edited, with an introduction, by Charles Neider. Garden City, N.Y., Hanover House, 1957. xxiv, 676 p.
57–5536 PZ3.C59Cm

252. The complete humorous sketches and tales of Mark Twain. Now collected for the first

time. Edited and with an introduction by Charles Neider. Drawings by Mark Twain. Garden City, N.Y., Hanover House [1961] 722 p.
61–6503 PS1303.N37

253. The complete essays of Mark Twain. Now collected for the first time. Edited and with an introduction by Charles Neider. Drawings by Mark Twain. Garden City, N.Y., Doubleday, 1963. xxv, 705 p. 63–7714 PS1302.N38

254. The complete novels of Mark Twain. Edited, with an introduction, by Charles Neider. Garden City, N.Y., Doubleday, 1964. 2 v.
64–19239 PZ3.C59Cg
The text of each novel is that of its first American edition. Minor changes have been made in the text where necessary, as in the case of obvious typographical errors.

255. Mark Twain of the Enterprise; newspaper articles & other documents, 1862–1864. Edited by Henry Nash Smith with the assistance of Frederick Anderson. Berkeley, University of California Press, 1957. 240 p. illus.
57–6543 PS1302.S5
Bibliographical notes: p. 209–224. Bibliography: p. 232–234.

256. Traveling with the innocents abroad; Mark Twain's original reports from Europe and the Holy Land. Edited by Daniel Morley Mc-Keithan. Norman, University of Oklahoma Press [1958] xviii, 324 p. 58–6858 PS1331.A3 1958
These journalistic sketches and letters, largely written for the San Francisco *Daily Alta California*, provided the raw material for *The Innocents Abroad*, no. 769–771 in the 1960 *Guide*.

257. Mark Twain-Howells letters; the correspondence of Samuel L. Clemens and William D. Howells, 1872–1910. Edited by Henry Nash Smith and William M. Gibson with the assistance of Frederick Anderson. Cambridge, Belknap Press of Harvard University Press, 1960. 2 v. (xxv, 948 p.) illus. 60–5397 PS1331.A3H6
Bibliographical references included in "Note on editorial practice" (v. 1, p. xxi–xxv). "Calendar of letters": v. 2, p. 883–903. "Index of works by Samuel L. Clemens and William D. Howells": v. 2, p. 943–948.

258. The travels of Mark Twain. Edited, with an introduction and notes, by Charles Neider. New York, Coward-McCann [1961] 448 p.
61–5434 PS1303.N4

Selected descriptions from American and foreign travels.

259. Life as I find it. Essays, sketches, tales, and other material, the majority of which is now published in book form for the first time. Edited, with an introduction and notes, by Charles Neider. Garden City, N.Y., Hanover House [1961] xvii, 411 p. 61–13327 PS1302.N4
Bibliography: p. [397]–399.

260. Letters from the earth. Edited by Bernard De Voto. With a preface by Henry Nash Smith. New York, Harper & Row [1962] 303 p.
62–14550 PS1331.A3 1962
"Bibliographical note": p. 303.
A selection of Twain's unfinished writings.

261. Blair, Walter. Mark Twain & Huck Finn. Berkeley, University of California Press, 1960. 436 p. illus. 59–15693 PS1305.B5
Bibliographical notes: p. 389–422. Bibliography: p. 423–427.
Depicts the creation of Twain's *Adventures of Huckleberry Finn*, no. 787–793 in the 1960 *Guide*, by discussing the author's life, his reading, his thinking, and his writing between 1874 and 1884.

262. Leary, Lewis G., *ed.* A casebook on Mark Twain's wound. New York, Crowell [1962] 351 p. (Crowell literary casebooks)
62–10282 PS1331.L42
Bibliographical footnotes. Bibliography: p. 337–346.
Van Wyck Brooks' *The Ordeal of Mark Twain* (1920) portrays Twain as a genius who was wounded and handicapped by his frontier environment. Bernard De Voto's *Mark Twain's America* (1932) argues that Twain profited from his Western heritage and utilized it in creating his literary art. Leary offers a selection from each of these books, together with comments by other critics upon the two conflicting views.

263. Long, Eugene Hudson. Mark Twain handbook. New York, Hendricks House [c1958] 454 p. 58–2265 PS1331.L6
Bibliographical footnotes. Bibliographies at ends of chapters.
Summarizes and evaluates Twain scholarship.

264. Meltzer, Milton. Mark Twain himself, a pictorial biography. New York, Crowell [1960] 303 p. 60–11545 PS1331.M38
"Picture sources": p. 295–297.
Among the pictures reproduced are daguerreo-

types, tintypes, stereographs, photographs, prints, drawings (including Twain's), paintings, broadsides, posters, cartoons, caricatures, illustrations from first editions, maps, news clippings, holographs, and even Twain's handprint.

265. Smith, Henry Nash. Mark Twain: the development of a writer. Cambridge, Belknap Press of Harvard University Press, 1962. 212 p.
62–19224 PS1331.S55 1962
Bibliographical references included in "Notes" (p. [189]–208).

266. STEPHEN CRANE, 1871–1900
No. 821 in 1960 *Guide*.

267. The red badge of courage, an annotated text, backgrounds and sources, essays in criticism. Edited by Sculley Bradley, Richmond Croom Beatty [and] E. Hudson Long. New York, Norton [1962] 344 p. (Norton critical editions, N305)
62–9572 PZ3.C852R 27
Bibliography: p. 342–344. Bibliographical footnotes.
Uses the text of the 1895 edition, no. 825 in the 1960 *Guide*. Other editions are no. 826–829.

268. Complete short stories & sketches. Edited, with an introduction, by Thomas A. Gullason. Garden City, N.Y., Doubleday, 1963. 790 p.
63–20507 PZ3.C852Co

269. Stephen Crane: letters. Edited by R. W. Stallman and Lillian Gilkes. With an introduction by R. W. Stallman. [New York] New York University Press, 1960. xxx, 366 p.
59–15192 PS1449.C85Z54
Bibliographical footnotes.
Reproduces 184 letters and autographs for the first time.

270. The war dispatches of Stephen Crane. Edited by R. W. Stallman and E. R. Hagemann. [New York] New York University Press, 1964. xv, 343 p. illus. 64–12559 PS1449.C85Z5
Bibliographical footnotes.
Narratives by Crane and his contemporaries from the Greco-Turkish War, the Spanish-American War, and the South African War.

271. Hoffman, Daniel G. The poetry of Stephen Crane. New York, Columbia University Press, 1957 [c1956] 304 p.
57–11017 PS1449.C85Z65
"Further uncollected poems of Stephen Crane": p. [281]–284. Bibliography: p. [285]–295.

272. EMILY DICKINSON, 1830–1886
No. 838 in 1960 *Guide*.

273. Complete poems. Edited by Thomas H. Johnson. Boston, Little, Brown [1960] 770 p. 60–11646 PS1541.A1 1960
The editor has selected one form of each poem from the variorum edition (no. 846 in the 1960 *Guide*) and has corrected some obvious textual errors.

274. Letters. Edited by Thomas H. Johnson. Associate editor: Theodora Ward. Cambridge, Belknap Press of Harvard University Press, 1958. 3 v. (xxvii, 999 p.) illus.
58–5594 PS1541.Z5A3 1958
This companion to *Poems* (no. 846 in the 1960 *Guide*) collects all of the letters known to have survived, including about 100 that are published for the first time.

275. Anderson, Charles R. Emily Dickinson's poetry: stairway of surprise. New York, Holt, Rinehart & Winston [1960] xviii, 334 p.
60–9546 PS1541.Z5A63
Analysis of selected poems.

276. Blake, Caesar R., *and* Carlton F. Wells, *eds.* The recognition of Emily Dickinson; selected criticism since 1890. Ann Arbor, University of Michigan Press [1964] xvi, 314 p.
64–10612 PS1541.Z5B55

277. Gelpi, Albert J. Emily Dickinson: the mind of the poet. Cambridge, Harvard University Press, 1965. 201 p. 65–13844 PS1541.Z5G4
Bibliography: p. 179–180. Bibliographical notes: p. 181–195.
Analysis of the ideas of Emily Dickinson in relation to American imaginative thought.

278. Leyda, Jay. The years and hours of Emily Dickinson. New Haven, Yale University Press, 1960. 2 v. illus. 60–11132 PS1541.Z5L4
"The sources": v. 2, p. 485–488. "Locations of manuscripts, illustrations, memorabilia": v. 2, p. 489–503.
A collection of chronologically arranged documents from manuscript and printed sources.

279. FINLEY PETER DUNNE ("MR. DOOLEY"), 1867–1936
No. 862 in 1960 *Guide*.

280. Mr. Dooley on ivrything and ivrybody. Selected and with an introduction by Robert

Hutchinson. New York, Dover Publications [1963] 244 p.                63–2652  PN6161.D8257

281. EDWARD EGGLESTON, 1837–1902

No. 867 in 1960 *Guide.*

282. Randel, William P. Edward Eggleston. New York, Twayne Publishers [ᶜ1963] 190 p. (Twayne's United States authors series, 45)
          63–17373  PS1583.R28
Bibliographical notes: p. 160–171. Bibliography: p. 172–187.

283. HAMLIN GARLAND, 1860–1940

No. 890 in 1960 *Guide.*

284. Crumbling idols; twelve essays on art dealing chiefly with literature, painting, and the drama. Edited by Jane Johnson. Cambridge, Belknap Press of Harvard University Press, 1960. xxxi, 150 p. (The John Harvard library)
          60–7994  PS1732.C7  1960
A new text (accompanied by explanatory and bibliographical footnotes and biographical glossary) recognizing variations in the periodical, lecture, and book versions. Earlier editions are no. 896–897 in the 1960 *Guide.*

285. Holloway, Jean. Hamlin Garland, a biography. Austin, University of Texas Press [1960] 346 p. illus.        59–8124  PS1733.H6
"Chronology of major Garland publications": p. [314]–332. Bibliography: p. 333–334.
Presents in chronological sequence the genesis and composition of Garland's various works and the critical reactions of his contemporaries.

286. LAFCADIO HEARN, 1850–1904

No. 945 in 1960 *Guide.*

287. Children of the levee. Edited by O. W. Frost. Introduction by John Ball. [Lexington] University of Kentucky Press [1957] 111 p. illus.        57–5834  F499.C5H39
Newspaper sketches of Negro life on the Ohio River from the *Cincinnati Enquirer* and *Cincinnati Commercial* during the period 1874–77.

288. Mordell, Albert. Discoveries: essays on Lafcadio Hearn. [Tokyo] Orient/West [1964] 240 p.        64–47174  PS1918.M6
Bibliographical footnotes.

289. Stevenson, Elizabeth. Lafcadio Hearn. New York, Macmillan, 1961. xvi, 362 p.
          61–10337  PS1918.S75
A biography.

290. Yu, Beongcheon. An ape of gods; the art and thought of Lafcadio Hearn. Detroit, Wayne State University Press, 1964. 346 p.
          64–10090  PS1918.Y8
Bibliographical notes: p. [295]–324. Bibliography: p. [325]–336.

291. ROBERT HERRICK, 1868–1938

No. 956 in 1960 *Guide.*

292. Nevius, Blake. Robert Herrick; the development of a novelist. Berkeley, University of California Press, 1962. xvi, 364 p.
          62–17569  PS1923.N4
Bibliographical notes: p. [345]–351. Bibliography: p. [352]–357.

293. EDGAR WATSON HOWE, 1853–1937

No. 959 in 1960 *Guide.*

294. The story of a country town. Edited by Claude M. Simpson. Cambridge, Belknap Press of Harvard University Press, 1961. xxxi, 347 p. (The John Harvard library)
          61–13736  PZ3.H8364S  12
Bibliography: p. xxxi.
The text is that of the 1884 edition published by J. R. Osgood & Company of Boston. The editor has corrected misprints, normalized contractions, and made slight changes in punctuation. Other editions are no. 960–963 in the 1960 *Guide.*

295. WILLIAM DEAN HOWELLS, 1837–1920

No. 964 in 1960 *Guide.*

296. Complete plays. [Edited, with an introduction, by] Walter J. Meserve. Under the general editorship of William M. Gibson and George Arms. [New York] New York University Press, 1960. xxxiii, 649 p.    59–15239  PS2026.A1  1960
Bibliography: p. 641–643.
"With the exception of the unpublished plays, which are printed here in what seems the most readable form, the texts of the plays in this volume are taken from the last American versions which Howells had an opportunity to revise."—Introduction.

297. Criticism and fiction, and other essays. Edited, with introductions and notes, by Clara Marburg Kirk and Rudolf Kirk. [New

York] New York University Press, 1959. xix,
413 p.                                59–6248 PN3451.H6
 Bibliographical notes: p. 385–395.
 Reprints the 1891 edition of *Criticism and Fiction*, no. 977 in the 1960 *Guide,* together with essays in criticism from numerous other sources.

298. Brooks, Van Wyck. Howells, his life and
      world. New York, Dutton, 1959. 296 p.
illus.                                59–10782 PS2033.B7
 Bibliographical footnotes.
 An impressionistic study.

299. Cady, Edwin H. The road to realism; the
      early years, 1837–1885, of William Dean
Howells. [Syracuse] Syracuse University Press
[1956] 283 p.                    56–11892 PS2033.C25
 "Bibliographical notes": p. 247–276.
 A study of Howells' emergence as an artist.

300. Cady, Edwin H. The realist at war; the ma-
      ture years, 1885–1920, of William Dean
Howells. [Syracuse] Syracuse University Press
[1958] 299 p.                    58–13106 PS2033.C23
 "Bibliographical notes": p. 273–292.
 Concentrates on Howells' achievements and significance.

301. Eble, Kenneth E., *ed.* Howells; a century of
      criticism. Dallas, Southern Methodist University Press [1962] 247 p.
                                      62–13275 PS2034.E2
 Bibliographical notes at the ends of articles.
 A collection of articles showing trends in the critical appraisal of Howells' work since 1860.

302. Kirk, Clara M. W. D. Howells and art in his
      time. New Brunswick, N. J., Rutgers University Press [1965] xvi, 336 p. illus.
                                      64–24736 PS2033.K49
 Bibliographical notes at the ends of chapters.
 Analysis of the interrelationship between Howells' views on social questions and his attitudes toward the various art theories of his day.

303. Kirk, Clara M. W. D. Howells, Traveler
      from Altruria, 1889–1894. New Brunswick,
N. J., Rutgers University Press [1962] 148 p.
illus.                                62–13762 PS2025.T72K5
 Bibliographical notes at the ends of chapters.
 A study of Howells' social and religious attitudes during the period of his association with the Church of the Carpenter in Boston.

304. HENRY JAMES, 1843–1916
      No. 986 in 1960 *Guide.*

305. Confidence, 1880. Now first edited from the
      manuscript. With notes, introduction, and
bibliography by Herbert Ruhm. With contemporary reviews, and excerpts from the notebooks.
New York, Grosset & Dunlap [1962] 238 p.
(The Universal library, UL146)
                                      62–52943 PZ3.J234Co 5
 The text of James' fifth novel is taken from one of the two complete surviving manuscripts of his novels.

306. The ambassadors: an authoritative text, the
      author on the novel, criticism. Edited by
S. P. Rosenbaum. New York, Norton [1963,
ᶜ1964] 486 p. (Norton critical editions)
                                      63–8035 PZ3.J234Amb 17
 "Bibliographies": p. 485–486.
 The text is taken from *Novels and Tales,* New York edition, no. 1004 in the 1960 *Guide.* Rosenbaum contributes textual notes and an essay, "Editions and Revisions." Other editions of *The Ambassadors* are no. 998–999 in the 1960 *Guide.*

307. The complete tales of Henry James. Edited,
      with an introduction, by Leon Edel. Philadelphia, Lippincott [1962–65, ᶜ1964] 12 v.
                                      62–11335 PZ3.J234Cl 2
 Reproduces the first texts to be published in book form.

308. The house of fiction, essays on the novel.
      Edited, with an introduction, by Leon Edel.
London, R. Hart-Davis, 1957. 286 p.
                                      58–1584 PN3499.J28
 Bibliographical footnotes. Bibliography: p. 281.

309. Literary reviews and essays, on American,
      English, and French literature. Edited by
Albert Mordell. New York, Twayne Publishers
[ᶜ1957] 409 p.                    58–249 PS2120.L5 1957
 Bibliographical notes: p. 354–402.
 Contains criticism by James never collected before.

310. Parisian sketches; letters to the New York
      tribune, 1875–1876. Edited, with an introduction, by Leon Edel and Ilse Dusoir Lind. [New
York] New York University Press, 1957. xxxvii,
262 p.                                57–7914 DC735.J3

311. Anderson, Quentin. The American Henry
      James. New Brunswick, N. J., Rutgers University Press, 1957. 369 p.
                                      57–6220 PS2124.A43 1957
 Bibliographical footnotes. Bibliography: p.
[355]–361.

An analysis of James' works as a reflection of his father's philosophy.

312. Cargill, Oscar. The novels of Henry James. New York, Macmillan, 1961. xviii, 505 p.
61–7434 PS2124.C25
Bibliographical notes at the ends of chapters.
Reviews "the best that has been said and written" about James' major fiction and contributes additional analysis.

313. Crews, Frederick C. The tragedy of manners; moral drama in the later novels of Henry James. New Haven, Yale University Press, 1957. 114 p. (Yale University. Undergraduate prize essays, v. 10) 57–10151 PS2124.C7

314. Edel, Leon. Henry James. Philadelphia, Lippincott [1953–62] 3 v. illus.
53–5421 PS2123.E33
Bibliographical notes at end of each chapter.
CONTENTS.—[1] The untried years, 1843–1870. —[2] The conquest of London, 1870–1881.—[3] The middle years, 1882–1895.
Volume 1 is no. 1020 in the 1960 *Guide*. The author has continued the story of James' life and times. Two additional volumes are in preparation.

315. Geismar, Maxwell D. Henry James and the Jacobites. Boston, Houghton Mifflin, 1963. 463 p. 63–10550 PS2123.G4
Bibliographical footnotes.
A vigorously adverse criticism of James and his admirers.

316. Holland, Laurence B. The expense of vision, essays on the craft of Henry James. Princeton, N. J., Princeton University Press, 1964. 414 p.
63–18644 PS2124.H64
Bibliographical footnotes.
Formal analysis of the interaction among James, his characters, and his audience.

317. Krook, Dorothea. The ordeal of consciousness in Henry James. Cambridge [Eng.] University Press, 1962. 422 p.
62–5617 PS2124.K7
Bibliographical footnotes.
A "collection of purely elucidatory studies of a selected number of James's works, connected by the theme of 'being and seeing'—the exploration and definition of consciousness in James's particular meaning of the term."

318. Lebowitz, Naomi. The imagination of loving; Henry James's legacy to the novel. De-troit, Wayne State University Press, 1965. 183 p.
65–14595 PS2128.L4
Bibliographical notes: p. 161–176. Bibliography: p. 177–180.

319. Stone, Edward. The battle and the books: some aspects of Henry James. Athens, Ohio University Press [1964] 234 p.
64–22886 PS2124.S79
Bibliographical notes: p. [221]–228.
Reviews the critical battles over James and examines selected works by him and his contemporaries.

320. Vaid, Krishna B. Technique in the tales of Henry James. Cambridge, Mass., Harvard University Press, 1964. 285 p.
64–22723 PS2124.V3 1964
Bibliographical notes: p. 267–281.

321. Wright, Walter F. The madness of art, a study of Henry James. Lincoln, University of Nebraska Press [1962] 269 p.
62–14665 PS2142.W7
Bibliographical footnotes. Bibliography: p. 255–266.
Presents a theory of the creative process in James' work and analyzes the ways in which ideas take form in the novels.

322. SARAH ORNE JEWETT, 1849–1909
No. 1023 in 1960 *Guide*.

323. Letters. Edited, with an introduction and notes, by Richard Cary. Waterville, Me., Colby College Press, 1956. 117 p. illus.
57–181 PS2133.A3 1956
"Books by Sarah Orne Jewett": p. [16] Bibliographical footnotes.
Ninety-four letters; more than half appear in print for the first time.

324. The world of Dunnett Landing, a Sarah Orne Jewett collection. Edited by David Bonnell Green. Lincoln, University of Nebraska Press [1962] 420 p. (A Bison book, BB147)
A62–8703 PZ3.J55Wo
The 1896 edition of *The Country of the Pointed Firs* (no. 1029 in the 1960 *Guide*) is reprinted, together with four additional sketches. The second part of the book contains critical essays about Miss Jewett by Martha H. Shackford, Mary Ellen Chase, Hyatt H. Waggoner, Warner Berthhoff, and David B. Green.

325. JACK (JOHN GRIFFITH) LONDON, 1876–1916

No. 1048 in 1960 *Guide*.

326. Stories of Hawaii. Edited by A. Grove Day. New York, Appleton-Century [1965] 282 p.
65–11682    PZ3.L846Sto

327. Letters from Jack London, containing an unpublished correspondence between London and Sinclair Lewis. Edited by King Hendricks and Irving Shepard. New York, Odyssey Press [1965] 502 p. illus.    65–22039    PS3523.O46Z53
Selections from London's voluminous correspondence.

328. O'Connor, Richard. Jack London, a biography. Boston, Little, Brown [1964] 430 p.
64–21486    PS3523.O46Z84
Bibliography: p. [411]–414. Bibliographical notes: p. [415]–419.

329. JOHN MUIR, 1838–1914

No. 1072 in 1960 *Guide*.

330. Smith, Herbert F. John Muir. New York, Twayne Publishers [1965] 158 p. (Twayne's United States authors series, 73)
64–20723    PS2447.M5Z85
Bibliographical notes: p. 148–151. Bibliography: p. 152–153.

331. (BENJAMIN) FRANK(LIN) NORRIS, 1870–1902

No. 1089 in 1960 *Guide*.

332. Letters. Edited by Franklin Walker. San Francisco, Book Club of California, 1956. 98 p.    56–3156    PS2473.A45    1956

333. Literary criticism. Edited by Donald Pizer. Austin, University of Texas Press [1964] xxiv, 247 p.    63–17618    PN99.U5N6
"Bibliographical note and Checklist of Norris' literary criticism": p. [233]–240.
A thematic survey, with interpretive introductions, covering the full range of Norris' critical writings.

334. French, Warren G. Frank Norris. New York, Twayne Publishers [1962] 160 p. (Twayne's United States authors series, 25)
62–16820    PS2473.F7
Bibliographical footnotes: p. 142–147. Bibliography: p. 148–154.

335. WILLIAM SYDNEY PORTER ("O. HENRY"), 1862–1910

No. 1111 in 1960 *Guide*.

336. Current-García, Eugene. O. Henry (William Sydney Porter). New York, Twayne Publishers [1965] 192 p. (Twayne's United States authors series, 77)    65–12997    PS2649.P5Z64
Bibliographical notes: p. 167–181. Bibliography: p. 182–187.
Analyzes representative stories and summarizes the growth and decline of O. Henry's reputation.

337. Langford, Gerald. Alias O. Henry; a biography of William Sydney Porter. New York, Macmillan, 1957. xix, 294 p.
57–8270    PS2649.P5Z7126
Bibliographical notes: p. 259–286.
Concentrates on O. Henry's life.

338. OWEN WISTER, 1860–1938

No. 1145 in 1960 *Guide*.

339. Owen Wister out west: his journals and letters. Edited by Fanny Kemble Wister. [Chicago] University of Chicago Press [1958] xix, 269 p. illus.    58–9609    PS3346.A3
"A Wister bibliography": p. 262–264.
A biographical introduction and the previously unpublished western memoirs provide a personal background to the writing of *The Virginian* (no. 1146–1148 in the 1960 *Guide*).

340. CONSTANCE FENIMORE WOOLSON, 1840–1894

No. 1149 in 1960 *Guide*.

341. Moore, Rayburn S. Constance Fenimore Woolson. New York, Twayne Publishers [1963] 173 p. (Twayne's United States authors series, 34)    62–19478    PS3363.M6
Bibliographical footnotes: p. 143–162. Bibliography: p. 163–165.

# E. The First World War
# and the Great Depression (1915-1939)

342. SAMUEL HOPKINS ADAMS, 1871–1958

No. 1155 in 1960 *Guide*.

343. Tenderloin. New York, Random House [ᶜ1959] 372 p.     59–5702 PZ3.A217Te
A novel set in New York City in the 1890's.

344. CONRAD POTTER AIKEN, 1889–

No. 1161 in 1960 *Guide*.

345. Mr. Arcularis, a play. Cambridge, Harvard University Press, 1957. 83 p.
     57–13535 PS3501.I5M5

346. Sheepfold Hill, fifteen poems. New York, Sagamore Press [1958] 62 p.
     58–9145 PS3501.I5S45

347. A reviewer's ABC; collected criticism of Conrad Aiken from 1916 to the present. Introduced by Rufus A. Blanshard. [New York] Meridian Books [1958] 414 p. (Greenwich editions)
     58–12328 PR99.A46
"Checklist of Conrad Aiken's critical writings": p. [395]–408.
Selections and excerpts representing the critical writing that Aiken wished to preserve.

348. Collected short stories. Preface by Mark Schorer. Cleveland, World Pub. Co. [1960] 566 p.     60–10537 PZ3.A2912Ck

349. The morning song of Lord Zero, poems old and new. New York, Oxford University Press, 1963. 130 p.     63–11915 PS3501.I5M6

350. Collected novels: Blue voyage, Great circle, King Coffin, A heart for the gods of Mexico [and] Conversation. Introduction by R. P. Blackmur. New York, Holt, Rinehart & Winston [1964] 575 p.     63–20431 PZ3.A2912Cf

351. Hoffman, Frederick J. Conrad Aiken. New York, Twayne Publishers [1962] 172 p. (Twayne's United States authors series, 17)
     62–13671 PS3501.I5Z68
Bibliographical notes: p. 156–163. Bibliography: p. 164–168.

352. Martin, Jay. Conrad Aiken: a life of his art. Princeton, N. J., Princeton University Press, 1962. 280 p.     62–11958 PS3501.I5Z75
Bibliographical notes: p. 251–258.

353. MAXWELL ANDERSON, 1888–1959

No. 1172 in 1960 *Guide*.

354. Bailey, Mabel D. Maxwell Anderson; the playwright as prophet. London, New York, Abelard-Schuman [1957] 200 p.
     57–6380 PS3501.N256Z57 1957
Bibliographical footnotes.
The first full-length evaluation of Anderson, structured with reference to his dramatic themes.

355. SHERWOOD ANDERSON, 1876–1941

No. 1178 in 1960 *Guide*.

356. Winesburg, Ohio. Introduction by Malcolm Cowley. [New ed.] New York, Viking Press, 1960. 247 p.     60–10867 PZ3.A55Win 7
The first new trade edition of this book of short stories since its original publication in 1919 (no. 1179 in the 1960 *Guide*).

357. Short stories. Edited and with an introduction by Maxwell Geismar. New York, Hill & Wang [1962] xxiii, 289 p. (American century series, AC52)     62–15213 PZ3.A55Sj
Bibliography: p. [291].
Stories first published in earlier collections such as *The Triumph of the Egg* (no. 1181 in the 1960 *Guide*).

358. Burbank, Rex J. Sherwood Anderson. New York, Twayne [1964] 159 p. (Twayne's United States authors series, 65)
     64–20715 PS3501.N4Z55
Bibliographical notes: p. 144–147. Bibliography: p. 148–152.

359. SAMUEL NATHANIEL BEHRMAN, 1893–

No. 1204 in 1960 *Guide*.

360. The cold wind and the warm, a play. Suggested by his New Yorker series and book, The Worcester account. New York, Random House [1959] 142 p. illus. (A Random House play)  59–9484  PS3503.E37C6

361. Lord Pengo; a comedy in three acts. Suggested by his New Yorker series, The days of Duveen. New York, Random House [1963] 132 p. illus.  63–14141  PS3503.E37L6

362. But for whom Charlie. New York, Random House [1964] 150 p.
64–17944  PS3503.E37B8
A play in three acts.

363. The suspended drawing room. New York, Stein & Day [1965] 253 p.
65–22989  PS3503.E37S8
Essays.

364. STEPHEN VINCENT BENÉT, 1898–1943
No. 1222 in 1960 *Guide*.

365. Selected poetry and prose; edited, with an introduction, by Basil Davenport. New York, Rinehart [1960] 336 p. (Rinehart editions, 100)
60–5174  PS3503.E5325A6  1960
Bibliography: p. xiv.

366. Selected letters. Edited by Charles A. Fenton. New Haven, Yale University Press, 1960. 436 p.  60–11231  PS3503.E5325Z54

367. Fenton, Charles A. Stephen Vincent Benét; the life and times of an American man of letters, 1898–1943. New Haven, Yale University Press, 1958. xv, 436 p. illus.
58–11252  PS3503.E5325Z62
Bibliographical notes: p. 375–409.

368. KAY BOYLE, 1903–
No. 1242 in 1960 *Guide*.

369. Generation without farewell. New York, Knopf, 1960 [ᶜ1959] 300 p.
59–11822  PZ3.B69796Gc
A novel about occupied Germany after World War II.

370. Collected poems. New York, Knopf, 1962. 105 p.  62–14759  PS3503.O9357A17  1962
Poems from the periods 1954–61 and 1926–43.

371. PEARL SYDENSTRICKER BUCK, 1892–
No. 1252 in 1960 *Guide*.

372. Imperial woman, a novel. New York, J. Day Co. [ᶜ1956] 376 p.
55–11370  PZ3.B8555Im

373. Letter from Peking, a novel. New York, J. Day Co. [1957] 252 p.
57–9389  PZ3.B8555Le

374. Command the morning, a novel. New York, J. Day Co. [1959] 317 p.
59–7169  PZ3.B8555Cr

375. Fourteen stories. New York, John Day Co. [1961] 250 p.  61–12716  PZ3.B8555Fo

376. A bridge for passing. New York, John Day Co. [1962] 256 p.
62–10937  PS3503.U198Z53  1962
The filming in Japan of her novel *The Big Wave* (1948) provides a basis for Miss Buck's comments on contemporary Japanese life.

377. The living reed, a novel. New York, John Day Co. [1963] 478 p.
63–10220  PZ3.B8555Li

378. Doyle, Paul A. Pearl S. Buck. New York, Twayne Publishers [1965] 175 p. (Twayne's United States authors series, 85)
65–18904  PS3503.U198Z64
Bibliographical notes: p. 157–168. Bibliography: p. 169–170.

379. JAMES BRANCH CABELL, 1897–1958
No. 1261 in 1960 *Guide*.

380. Between friends; letters of James Branch Cabell and others. Edited by Padraic Colum and Margaret Freeman Cabell. With an introduction by Carl Van Vechten. New York, Harcourt, Brace & World [1962] xvi, 304 p.
60–10935  PS3505.A153Z53
"Books by James Branch Cabell": p. 291–292.
Correspondence between Cabell and various literary figures, including Sinclair Lewis, F. Scott Fitzgerald, and Hugh Walpole.

381. Davis, Joe L. James Branch Cabell. New York, Twayne Publishers [1962] 174 p. (Twayne's United States authors series, 21)
62–16816  PS3505.A153Z62
Bibliographical notes: p. 152–161. Bibliography: p. 162–166.

382. ERSKINE CALDWELL, 1903–
No. 1270 in 1960 *Guide*.

383. Gulf coast stories. Boston, Little, Brown [1956] 248 p.    56–10634  PZ3.C12734Gu

384. Men and women; twenty-two stories selected and with an introduction by Carvel Collins. Boston, Little, Brown [1961] 313 p.
61–12810  PZ3.C12734Me

385. Around about America. Drawings by Virginia M. Caldwell. New York, Farrar, Straus [1964] 224 p.    64–16620  E169.C16
Observations and impressions recorded during a journey from St. Johnsbury, Vt., to Rheem Valley, Calif.

386. WILLA SIBERT CATHER, 1873–1947

No. 1276 in 1960 *Guide*.

387. Willa Cather in Europe; her own story of the first journey. With an introduction and incidental notes by George N. Kates. New York, Knopf, 1956. 178 p.    56–10906  PS3505.A87Z53
Essays written for newspaper publication during the author's 1902 European tour.

388. April twilights (1903); poems. Edited, with an introduction, by Bernice Slote. Lincoln, University of Nebraska Press [1962] xxxxviii, 72 p.    62–8899  PS3505.A87A8  1962
Bibliographical notes: p. 53-58. Bibliography: p. 59–72.
The origins of Willa Cather's first book are discussed in the introduction, which also examines her poems in relationship to her prose. The first-edition text, published in Boston by Richard G. Badger, is reprinted.

389. Willa Cather's collected short fiction, 1892–1912. Introduction by Mildred R. Bennett. Lincoln, University of Nebraska Press [1965] xli, 594 p.    65–10547  PZ3.C2858Wi
Bibliography: p. 593–594.
CONTENTS.—The Bohemian girl.—The troll garden.—On the Divide.—Appendix: Pseudonymous stories.
Forty-four early stories, only three of which were included by the author in the "Library Edition" of her work (no. 1277 in the 1960 *Guide*).

390. Bennett, Mildred R. The world of Willa Cather. New ed. with notes and index. Lincoln, University of Nebraska Press, 1961. 285 p. illus. (A Bison book, BB112)
61–7235  PS3505.A87Z58  1961
A revised edition of no. 1279 in the 1960 *Guide*.

391. Bloom, Edward A., *and* Lillian D. Bloom. Willa Cather's gift of sympathy. With a preface by Harry T. Moore. Carbondale, Southern Illinois University Press [1962] 260 p. (Crosscurrents: modern critiques)
62–7231  PS3505.A87Z583
The authors draw on the full Cather canon in examining her major themes: the frontier spirit, materialistic threats to that spirit, and the nature of the artist. *Death Comes for the Archbishop* receives special attention.

392. Randall, John H. The landscape and the looking glass; Willa Cather's search for value. Boston, Houghton Mifflin, 1960. 425 p. illus.
60–6225  PS3505.A87Z78
Bibliographical notes: p. 381–410. Bibliography: p. 413–415.
Applying techniques associated with the New Criticism, Randall analyzes theme, structure, tone, and imagery in Willa Cather's work in relation to the cultural influences of her time.

393. MARY ELLEN CHASE, 1887–

No. 1284 in 1960 *Guide*.

394. The edge of darkness. New York, Norton [1957] 235 p.    57–10637  PZ3.C3901Ed
A novel.

395. The lovely ambition, a novel. New York, Norton [1960] 288 p.
60–5843  PZ3.C3901Lo

396. A journey to Boston, a novel. New York, Norton [1965] 114 p.
64–23875  PZ3.C3901Jo

397. Westbrook, Perry D. Mary Ellen Chase. New York, Twayne Publishers [1965] 176 p. (Twayne's United States authors series, 86)
65–18905  PS3505.H48Z96
Bibliographical notes: p. 163–165. Bibliography: p. 166–171.

398. JAMES GOULD COZZENS, 1903–

No. 1298 in 1960 *Guide*.

399. By love possessed. New York, Harcourt, Brace [1957] 570 p.
57–10062  PZ3.C83983By
A novel.

400. Children and others. New York, Harcourt, Brace & World [1964] 343 p.

64–22665    PZ3.C83983Ch

Short stories.

401. Bracher, Frederick G. The novels of James Gould Cozzens. New York, Harcourt, Brace [1959]  306 p.  59–10245  PS3505.O99Z57

Bibliographical notes: p. 283–292. Bibliography: p. 293–297.

Evaluates Cozzens' achievement as a novelist with reference to his style, form, and point of view.

402. HART CRANE, 1899–1932

No. 1303 in 1960 *Guide*.

403. Quinn, Vincent G. Hart Crane. New York, Twayne Publishers [1963] 141 p. (Twayne's United States authors series, 35)

63–10952  PS3505.R272Z78

Bibliographical notes: p. 129–134. Bibliography: p. 135–138.

A survey of the themes of Crane's major poems, his attitudes toward poetry, and the opinions of his principal critics.

404. EDWARD ESTLIN CUMMINGS, 1894–1962

No. 1309 in 1960 *Guide*.

405. 95 poems. New York, Harcourt, Brace [1958]  95 p.

58–10909  PS3505.U334N5  1958

406. 73 poems. New York, Harcourt, Brace & World [1963]  1 v. (unpaged)

63–20271  PS3505.U334S4

407. A selection of poems. With an introduction by Horace Gregory. New York, Harcourt, Brace & World [1965] xiv, 194 p. (A Harvest book)  65–24992  PS3505.U334A17  1965

408. E. E. Cummings: a miscellany revised. Edited, with an introduction and notes, by George J. Firmage. Foreword by the author. New York, October House [1965] 335 p. illus.

64–13163  PS3505.U334A16  1965

A collection of short pieces originally published in a 1958 limited edition, reprinted with corrections and additions, including previously unpublished line drawings by the author.

409. Baum, Stanley V., *ed*. Ἐστί: e e c; E. E. Cummings and the critics. East Lansing,

Michigan State University Press [1962] 220 p.

61–13699  PS3505.U334Z56

Bibliography: p. 195–203.

A collection of essays by various writers, including Edmund Wilson, R. P. Blackmur, Karl Shapiro, and Randall Jarrell, designed to indicate the diversity of critical opinion concerning Cummings' work.

410. Friedman, Norman. E. E. Cummings; the growth of a writer. With a preface by Harry T. Moore. Carbondale, Southern Illinois University Press [1964] 193 p. (Crosscurrents: modern critiques)  64–11165  PS3505.U334Z66

Bibliography: p. [187]–188.

411. Norman, Charles. E. E. Cummings, the magic-maker. [Rev. ed.] New York, Duell, Sloan & Pearce [1964] 246 p.

64–12438  PS3505.U334Z8  1964

Bibliographical footnotes.

This revised and somewhat abridged version of Norman's 1958 biography conveys a profound affection for and knowledge of Cummings as writer and painter.

412. HAROLD LENOIR DAVIS, 1896–1960

No. 1314 in 1960 *Guide*.

413. The distant music. New York, Morrow, 1957.  311 p.  57–5424  PZ3.D29355Di

A novel.

414. Kettle of fire. New York, Morrow, 1959. 189 p.  59–11706  F881.2.D3

History, nature, and personal reminiscence are combined in a collection of essays on Oregon and the Northwest.

415. HILDA DOOLITTLE, 1886–1961

No. 1319 in 1960 *Guide*.

416. Selected poems. New York, Grove Press [1957] 128 p.

57–8646  PS3507.O726A17  1957

417. Bid me to live, a madrigal. New York, Grove Press [1960]  184 p.

60–6345  PZ4.D688Bi

418. Helen in Egypt. Introduction by Horace Gregory. New York, Grove Press [1961] 315 p.  61–12764  PS3507.O726H37

A poem.

419. Swann, Thomas B. The classical world of H. D. Lincoln, University of Nebraska Press, 1962. 217 p.          62–16782 PS3507.O726Z87
Bibliographical notes: p. 195–199. Bibliography: p. 201–206.
Investigates H. D.'s life and work in relation to her classical background, settings, and characters.

420. JOHN RODERIGO DOS PASSOS, 1896–
No. 1325 in 1960 *Guide.*

421. The great days. New York, Sagamore Press [1958] 312 p.          58–6966 PZ3.D74Gt
A novel.

422. Midcentury. Boston, Houghton, Mifflin, 1961. 496 p.          61–5359 PZ3.D74Mi
A novel.

423. Occasions and protests. [Chicago] H. Regnery Co., 1964. 323 p.
64–7914 PS3507.O743O25
Essays and observations on the American sociopolitical situation between 1936 and 1964.

424. Wrenn, John H. John Dos Passos. New York, Twayne Publishers [1962, ᶜ1961] 208 p. (Twayne's United States authors series, 9)
61–15669 PS3507.O743Z93 1962
Bibliographical notes: p. 188–197. Bibliography: p. 198–205.

425. THEODORE DREISER, 1871–1945
No. 1333 in 1960 *Guide.*

426. Sister Carrie. Edited, with an introduction, by Claude Simpson. Boston, Houghton Mifflin [1959] xxi, 418 p. (Riverside editions, A36)
59–1819 PZ3.D814S 31
A contents page has been added to the text of the first edition (no. 1334 in the 1960 *Guide*) and minor misprints have been corrected.

427. Letters of Theodore Dreiser: a selection. Edited, with preface and notes, by Robert H. Elias. Consulting editors: Sculley Bradley and Robert E. Spiller. Philadelphia, University of Pennsylvania Press [1959] 3 v. (1067 p.) illus.
58–8203 PS3507.R55Z54
Selects nearly 600 letters, written between 1897 and 1945, primarily from the Dreiser collection in the University of Pennsylvania Library. The letters chosen "should contribute to an understanding in particular of Dreiser as writer—that is, to Dreiser as man thinking."

428. Shapiro, Charles. Theodore Dreiser: our bitter patriot. With a preface by Harry T. Moore. Carbondale, Southern Illinois University Press [1962] xv, 137 p. (Crosscurrents: modern critiques)          62–16696 PS3507.R55Z83
Bibliographical notes: p. [124]–129.
Examines Dreiser's sprawling novels of hope and failure in the quest for the American dream.

429. Swanberg, W.A. Dreiser. New York, Scribner [1965] xvii, 614 p. illus.
65–13661 PS3507.R55Z84
Bibliographical notes: p. 535–581.
A comprehensive biography of "one of the most incredible of human beings, a man whose enormous gifts warred endlessly with grievous flaws."

430. RICHARD EBERHART, 1904–
No. 1350 in 1960 *Guide.*

431. Great praises. New York, Oxford University Press, 1957. 72 p.
57–2572 PS3509.B456G7
Poems.

432. Collected poems, 1930–1960, including 51 new poems. New York, Oxford University Press, 1960. 228 p.
60–14636 PS3509.B456A6 1960

433. Collected verse plays. Chapel Hill, University of North Carolina Press [1962] 167 p.
62–16088 PS3509.B456A19 1962

434. The quarry, new poems. New York, Oxford University Press, 1964. 114 p.
64–15009 PS3509.B456Q3

435. Selected poems, 1930–1965. [New York] New Directions [1965] 115 p. (A New Directions paperbook, NDP198)
65–17453 PS3509.B456A6 1965

436. THOMAS STEARNS ELIOT, 1888–1965
No. 1357 in 1960 *Guide.*

437. On poetry and poets. New York, Farrar, Straus & Cudahy, 1957. 308 p.
57–12154 PN511.E435
A collection of 16 essays written during the period 1926–56. Eliot's *Selected Essays* is no. 1358 in the 1960 *Guide.*

438. The elder statesman, a play. New York, Farrar, Straus & Cudahy [1959] 134 p.
59–6590 PS3509.L43E4

439. Collected plays. London, Faber & Faber [1962] 355 p.
   63–3627 PS3509.L43A19 1962
CONTENTS.— Murder in the cathedral.— The family reunion.— The cocktail party.— The confidential clerk.— The elder statesman.

440. Collected poems, 1909–1962. New York, Harcourt, Brace & World [1963] 221 p.
   63–21424 PS3509.L43A17 1963

441. Knowledge and experience in the philosophy of F. H. Bradley. New York, Farrar, Straus [1964] 216 p. 63–12865 B1618.B74E48 1964
Bibliographical notes: p. 170–176. Bibliography: p. 208–213.
Originally submitted to Harvard University in 1916 as a doctoral dissertation entitled *Experience and the Objects of Knowledge in the Philosophy of F. H. Bradley.* Eliot did not complete the requirements for a doctor's degree, although his dissertation was officially approved. Two 1916 essays on Leibniz are included in this volume.

442. To criticize the critic, and other writings. New York, Farrar, Straus & Giroux [1965] 188 p. 65–25139 PS3509.L43T6
CONTENTS.— To criticize the critic.— From Poe to Valéry.— American literature and the American language.— The aims of education.— What Dante means to me.— The literature of politics.— The classics and the man of letters — Ezra Pound: his metric and poetry.— Reflections on Vers libre.

443. Howarth, Herbert. Notes on some figures behind T. S. Eliot. Boston, Houghton Mifflin, 1964. 396 p. 62–8139 PS3509.L43Z684
Bibliographical notes: p. [343]–386.

444. Jones, Genesius. Approach to the purpose; a study of the poetry of T. S. Eliot. New York, Barnes & Noble [1965, c1964] 351 p.
   65–3788 PS3509.L43Z686 1965
Bibliography: p. 342–346.

445. Kenner, Hugh. The invisible poet: T. S. Eliot. New York, McDowell, Obolensky [1959] 346 p. 59–7118 PS3509.L43Z69
Contends that "opinion concerning the most influential man of letters of the twentieth century has not freed itself from a cloud of unknowing. He is the Invisible Poet in an age of systematized literary scrutiny, much of it directed at him."

446. Kenner, Hugh, *ed.* T. S. Eliot; a collection of critical essays. Englewood Cliffs, N. J., Prentice-Hall [1962] 210 p. (A Spectrum book: Twentieth century views, S–TC–2)
   62–9290 PS3509.L43Z6913

447. Smith, Carol H. T. S. Eliot's dramatic theory and practice, from Sweeney Agonistes to The elder statesman. Princeton, N. J., Princeton University Press, 1963. 251 p.
   63–7161 PS3509.L43Z867
Bibliography: p. 241–246.

448. Thompson, Eric. T. S. Eliot, the metaphysical perspective. With a preface by Harry T. Moore. Carbondale, Southern Illinois University Press [1963] 186 p. (Crosscurrents: modern critiques) 62–16697 PS3509.L43Z877
Bibliographical notes: p. [161]–180.
An exploration of Eliot's doctoral dissertation on F. H. Bradley (no. 441 above), tracing Bradley's influence on Eliot's poetry.

449. JAMES THOMAS FARRELL, 1904–
No. 1372 in 1960 *Guide.*

450. A dangerous woman, and other stories. New York, Vanguard Press [1957] 160 p.
   57–12256 PZ3.F2465Dan

451. The silence of history. Garden City, N. Y., Doubleday, 1963. 372 p.
   61–12518 PZ3.F2465Sj
A novel.

452. What time collects. Garden City, N. Y., Doubleday, 1964. 421 p.
   64–11695 PZ3.F2465Wf
A novel.

453. Selected essays. Edited by Luna Wolf. With an introduction by Don M. Wolfe. New York, McGraw-Hill [1964] xxiii, 199 p.
   64–16289 PS3511.A738A16 1964
Bibliographical footnotes.

454. The collected poems of James T. Farrell. New York, Fleet Pub. Corp. [1965] 82 p.
   65–16314 PS3511.A738A17 1965

455. WILLIAM FAULKNER, 1897–1962
No. 1379 in 1960 *Guide.*

456. As I lay dying. [New ed.] New York, Random House [1964, c1957] 250 p.
   64–12609 PZ3.F272As 3
Contains corrections based on a collation of the

first edition (no. 1384 in the 1960 *Guide*) with Faulkner's original manuscript and typescript.

457. The town. New York, Random House [1957] 371 p.      57–6656 PZ3.F272To
The second volume of the "Snopes" trilogy.

458. New Orleans sketches. Introduction by Carvel Collins. New Brunswick, N. J., Rutgers University Press, 1958. 223 p.
     57–12807 PZ3.F272Ne
Sixteen short pieces first published in 1925 in the New Orleans *Times-Picayune* and a group of sketches printed during the same year in a New Orleans literary magazine, *The Double Dealer*.

459. The mansion. New York, Random House [1959] 436 p.      59–10811 PZ3.F272Man
The third volume of the "Snopes" trilogy.

460. The reivers, a reminiscence. New York, Random House [1962] 305 p.
     62–10335 PZ3.F272Re
A novel.

461. William Faulkner: early prose and poetry. Compilation and introduction by Carvel Collins. Boston, Little, Brown [1962] 134 p.
     62–17953 PS3511.A86A6 1962
Bibliographical notes: p. 123–134.
Material published during the author's years at the University of Mississippi and shortly thereafter. Includes numerous drawings by Faulkner.

462. The hamlet. [3d ed.] New York, Random House [1964] 366 p.
     64–7972 PZ3.F272Ham 6
Earlier errors have been corrected through a collation of the author's typescript with the first edition of 1940 (no. 1391 in the 1960 *Guide*) and the second edition of 1956. *The Hamlet* is the first volume of Faulkner's "Snopes" trilogy.

463. The marble faun, and A green bough. New York, Random House [1965] 51, 67 p.
     65–27492 PS3511.A86M3 1965
Faulkner's two volumes of poetry reproduced from the original editions published in 1924 (*The Marble Faun*) and 1933 (*A Green Bough*).

464. Brooks, Cleanth. William Faulkner; the Yoknapatawpha country. New Haven, Yale University Press, 1963. xiv, 499 p.
     63–17023 PS3511.A86Z64
Bibliographical footnotes.

465. Hoffman, Frederick J., *and* Olga W. Vickery, *eds*. William Faulkner: three decades of criticism. [1960 ed. East Lansing] Michigan State University Press, 1960. 428 p.
     60–11481 PS3511.A86Z8 1960
Bibliography: p. 393–428.
A revised and updated edition of no. 1399 in the 1960 *Guide*.

466. Howe, Irving. William Faulkner: a critical study. 2d ed., rev. and expanded. New York, Vintage Books [1962] 299 p.
     62–2290 PS3511.A86Z84 1962
A new edition of no. 1400 in the 1960 *Guide*.

467. Runyan, Harry. A Faulkner glossary. New York, Citadel Press [1964] 310 p.
     64–15959 PS3511.A86Z965
An alphabetical guide to titles, characters, and places in Faulkner's writings. Seven appendixes offer critical and genealogical information as well as detailed bibliographies.

468. Tuck, Dorothy. Crowell's handbook of Faulkner. Lewis Leary, advisory editor. New York, Crowell [1964] xx, 259 p. (A Crowell reference book) 64–16536 PS3511.A86Z978
Bibliography: p. [247]–250.

469. Vickery, Olga W. The novels of William Faulkner; a critical interpretation. [Rev. ed. Baton Rouge] Louisiana State University Press [1964] 318 p. 64–23150 PS3511.A86Z98 1964

470. Waggoner, Hyatt H. William Faulkner: from Jefferson to the world. [Lexington] University of Kentucky Press [1959] 279 p.
     59–13268 PS3511.A86Z985
Bibliographical notes: p. [267]–274.
"The most significant meanings in Faulkner all start in Jefferson and radiate outward to meanings as various and as inexhaustible as myth."

471. EDNA FERBER, 1887–
No. 1403 in 1960 *Guide*.

472. Ice Palace. Garden City, N. Y., Doubleday, 1958. 411 p.      58–5936 PZ3.F38oIc
A novel.

473. A peculiar treasure. Garden City, N. Y., Doubleday, 1960. 383 p. illus.
     60–8865 PS3511.E46Z5 1960
Autobiography.

474. A kind of magic. Garden City, N. Y., Doubleday, 1963. 335 p.
63–18030  PS3511.E46Z52
Sequel to *A Peculiar Treasure.*

475. DOROTHEA FRANCES CANFIELD FISHER, 1879–1958
No. 1411 in 1960 *Guide.*

476. A harvest of stories, from a half century of writing. New York, Harcourt, Brace [1956] 352 p.  56–11298  PZ3.F53Har

477. VARDIS ALVERO FISHER, 1895–
No. 1420 in 1960 *Guide.*

478. Jesus came again, a parable. Denver, A. Swallow [1956]  359 p. (*His* The Testament of man [8])  56–13625  PZ3.F539Je

479. A goat for Azazel; a novel of Christian origins. Denver, A. Swallow [1956]  368 p. (*His* The Testament of man [9])
56–14254  PZ3.F539Gl

480. Pemmican; a novel of the Hudson's Bay Company. Garden City, N. Y., Doubleday, 1956. 319 p.  56–7740  PZ3.F539Pe

481. Peace like a river; a novel of Christian asceticism. Denver, A. Swallow [1957] 316 p. (*His* The Testament of man [10])
58–16346  PZ3.F539Pd

482. My holy satan; a novel of Christian twilight. Denver, A. Swallow [1958]  326 p. (*His* The Testament of man [11])
58–13022  PZ3.F539My

483. Tale of valor; a novel of the Lewis and Clark Expedition. Garden City, N. Y., Doubleday, 1958. 456 p.  58–7356  PZ3.F539Tal

484. Love and death; the complete stories of Vardis Fisher. Garden City, N. Y., Doubleday, 1959. 211 p.  59–10666  PZ3.F539Lo

485. Orphans in Gethsemane; a novel of the past in the present. Denver, A. Swallow [1960] 987 p. (*His* The Testament of man [12])
60–6113  PZ3.F539Or

486. Mountain man; a novel of male and female in the early American West. New York, Morrow, 1965. 372 p.  65–22970  PZ3.F539Mp

487. Flora, Joseph M. Vardis Fisher. New York, Twayne Publishers [1965] 158 p. (Twayne's United States authors series, 76)
65–12996  PS3511.I744Z63
Bibliographical notes: p. 145–148. Bibliography: p. 149–152.

488. FRANCIS SCOTT KEY FITZGERALD, 1896–1940
No. 1425 in 1960 *Guide.*

489. Afternoon of an author, a selection of uncollected stories and essays. With an introduction and notes by Arthur Mizener. Princeton, Princeton University Library, 1957. 226 p. illus.
58–3  PS3511.I9A6  1957

490. Six tales of the jazz age, and other stories. New York, Scribner [1960]  192 p.
60–6410  PZ3.F5754Si
Written between 1920 and 1924, these stories depict the era Fitzgerald named.

491. The Pat Hobby stories. With an introduction by Arnold Gingrich. New York, Scribner [1962]  159 p.  62–16655  PZ3.F5754Pat
These 17 previously uncollected stories provide a full-length portrait of one of Fitzgerald's tragicomic characters.

492. The Fitzgerald reader. Edited by Arthur Mizener. New York, Scribner [1963]  509 p.
62–9632  PS3511.I9A6  1963
Presents the entire text of *The Great Gatsby* (no. 1428 in the 1960 *Guide*) and portions of *Tender Is the Night* (included in *The Portable F. Scott Fitzgerald,* no. 1429 in the 1960 *Guide*) and *The Last Tycoon,* a novel left unfinished at Fitzgerald's death. A selection of stories, two novelettes, and four essays complete the anthology.

493. Letters. Edited by Andrew Turnbull. New York, Scribner [1963] xviii, 615 p. illus.
63–16755  PS3511.I9Z54
A selection.

494. Miller, James E. F. Scott Fitzgerald, his art and his technique. [New York] New York University Press, 1964. xiv, 173 p.
64–16900  PS3511.I9Z688
Bibliography: p. 163–165.

495. Mizener, Arthur. The far side of paradise, a biography of F. Scott Fitzgerald. Boston, Houghton Mifflin, 1965. xxviii, 416 p. illus. (Sentry edition, 46)  65–19307  PS3511.I9Z7  1965

Bibliographical notes: p. [353]–399. Bibliography: p. [400]–407.

A new edition of no. 1431 in the 1960 *Guide*, revised to include material made available since 1951, when the work was originally published.

496. Piper, Henry D. F. Scott Fitzgerald, a critical portrait. New York, Holt, Rinehart & Winston [1965] 334 p. 65–14435 PS3511.I9Z82
Bibliographical notes: p. 301–323.

Focuses on Fitzgerald's career as an author and sheds light on the position of the professional American writer during the twenties and thirties.

497. Trunbull, Andrew. Scott Fitzgerald. New York, Scribner [1962] 364 p. illus.
62–9315 PS3511.I9Z88

A full-scale biography.

498. WALDO DAVID FRANK, 1889–

No. 1445 in 1960 *Guide.*

499. Bittner, William R. The novels of Waldo Frank. Philadelphia, University of Pennsylvania Press [1958] 222 p.
58–6449 PS3511.R258Z57 1958
Includes bibliography.

500. ROBERT FROST, 1874–1963

No. 1451 in 1960 *Guide.*

501. In the clearing. New York, Holt, Rinehart & Winston [1962] 101 p.
62–11578 PS3511.R94I5
Poems.

502. The letters of Robert Frost to Louis Untermeyer. New York, Holt, Rinehart & Winston [1963] 388 p. 63–15383 PS3511.R94Z53

503. Selected letters. Edited by Lawrance Thompson. New York, Holt, Rinehart & Winston [1964] lxiv, 645 p. illus.
64–10767 PS3511.R94Z52 1964

504. Cook, Reginald L. The dimensions of Robert Frost. New York, Rinehart [1958] 241 p.
58–9351 PS3511.R94Z585
A personal interpretation of Frost's poetry by a close friend and director of the Bread Loaf School of English at Middlebury, Vt.

505. Cox, James M., *ed.* Robert Frost; a collection of critical essays. Englewood Cliffs, N. J., Prentice-Hall [1962] 205 p. (A Spectrum book:
Twentieth century views, S–TC–3)
62–9283 PS3511.R94Z588

506. Lynen, John F. The pastoral art of Robert Frost. New Haven, Yale Univeristy Press, 1960. 208 p. (Yale studies in English, v. 147)
60–7826 PS3511.R94Z77
Bibliography: p. 191–202.

507. Mertins, Marshall Louis. Robert Frost; life and talks-walking. Norman, University of Oklahoma Press [1965] 450 p. illus.
65–11238 PS3511.R94Z786
A portrait of Frost constructed from conversations which occurred over a period of 30 years.

508. Sergeant, Elizabeth S. Robert Frost; the trial by existence. New York, Holt, Rinehart & Winston [1960] xxvii, 451 p. illus.
60–8792 PS3511.R94Z92
A biography with frequent quotations from Frost's works.

509. ZONA GALE, 1874–1938

No. 1453 in 1960 *Guide.*

510. Simonson, Harold P. Zona Gale. New York, Twayne Publishers [1962] 157 p. (Twayne's United States authors series, 18)
62–13672 PS3513.A34Z85
Bibliographical footnotes: p. 141–146. Bibliography: p. 147–150.

511. ELLEN ANDERSON GHOLSON GLASGOW, 1874–1945

No. 1460 in 1960 *Guide.*

512. Collected stories. Edited by Richard K. Meeker. [Baton Rouge] Louisiana State University Press [1963] 254 p.
63–13240 PZ3.G464Co

513. McDowell, Frederick P. W. Ellen Glasgow and the ironic art of fiction. Madison, University of Wisconsin Press, 1960. 292 p.
60–9551 PS3513.L34Z68

514. CAROLINE GORDON, 1895–

No. 1464 in 1960 *Guide.*

515. The malefactors. New York, Harcourt, Brace [c1956] 312 p.
56–6653 PZ3.G6525Mal
A novel.

516. Old Red, and other stories. New York, Scribner [1963] 256 p.
63–17607  PZ3.G65250l

517. PAUL ELIOT GREEN, 1894–

No. 1473 in 1960 *Guide.*

518. The Confederacy; a symphonic outdoor drama based on the life of General Robert E. Lee. New York, S. French [1959]  123 p.
59–2086  PS3513.R452C65

519. The Stephen Foster story, a symphonic drama based on the life and music of the composer. New York, French [1960]  107 p.
60–1922  PS3513.R452S83

520. HORACE VICTOR GREGORY, 1898–

No. 1482 in 1960 *Guide.*

521. Collected poems. New York, Holt, Rinehart & Winston [1964]  226 p.
64–14359  PS3513.R558A6  1964

522. ALFRED BERTRAM GUTHRIE, 1901–

No. 1488 in 1960 *Guide.*

523. These thousand hills. Boston, Houghton Mifflin, 1956.  346 p.
56–13458  PZ3.G95876Th
A novel.

524. The blue hen's chick; a life in context. New York, McGraw-Hill [1965]  261 p.
64–66368  PS3513.U855Z5
Autobiography.

525. MOSS HART, 1904–1961

No. 1491 in 1960 *Guide.*

526. Act one, an autobiography. New York, Random House [1959] 444 p.
59–10813  PN2287.H27A3

527. ERNEST HEMINGWAY, 1899–1961

No. 1494 in 1960 *Guide.*

528. A moveable feast. New York, Scribner [1964]  211 p. illus.
64–15441  PS3515.E37Z525
Sketches of the author's life in Paris, 1921–26.

529. Baker, Carlos H., *ed.* Hemingway and his critics, an international anthology. Edited, with an introduction and a checklist of Hemingway criticism. New York, Hill & Wang [1961]  298 p. (American century series, AC36)
61–7565  PS3515.E37Z577
Includes bibliography.

530. Baker, Carlos H. Hemingway: the writer as artist. [3d ed.] Princeton, N. J., Princeton University Press, 1963. xx, 379 p.
63–25656  PS3515.E37Z58  1963
Bibliographical footnotes. "A working check-list of Hemingway's prose, poetry, and journalism, with notes": p. [349]–366.
A revised edition of no. 1502 in the 1960 *Guide.*

531. Hemingway, Leicester. My brother, Ernest Hemingway. Cleveland, World Pub. Co. [1962]  283 p. illus.  62–9043  PS3515.E37Z62

532. Weeks, Robert P., *ed.* Hemingway; a collection of critical essays. Englewood Cliffs, N. J., Prentice-Hall [1962]  180 p. (Twentieth century views. A Spectrum book, S–TC–8)
62–13652  PS3515.E37Z94
Bibliography: p. 179–180.

533. JOSEPH HERGESHEIMER, 1880–1954

No. 1506 in 1960 *Guide.*

534. Martin, Ronald E. The fiction of Joseph Hergesheimer. Philadelphia, University of Pennsylvania Press [1965]  288 p.
65–22570  PS3515.E628Z74
Bibliography: p. [271]–283.

535. ROBERT SILLIMAN HILLYER, 1895–1961

No. 1515 in 1960 *Guide.*

536. The relic & other poems. New York, Knopf, 1957.  93 p.  57–10308  PS3515.I69R4

537. Collected poems. New York, Knopf, 1961. 235 p.  61–8531  PS3515.I69A17  1961

538. LANGSTON HUGHES, 1902–

No. 1521 in 1960 *Guide.*

539. I wonder as I wander; an autobiographical journey. New York, Rinehart [1956]  405 p.
56–7254  PS3515.U274Z58

540. Simple stakes a claim. New York, Rinehart [1957]  191 p.  57–9628  PS3515.U274S54
Short stories.

541. The Langston Hughes reader. New York, G. Braziller, 1958. 501 p.
58–7871 PS3515.U274A6 1958

542. Selected poems. Drawings by E. McKnight Kauffer. New York, Knopf, 1959. 297 p.
58–10967 PS3515.U274A6 1959

543. Ask your mama: 12 moods for jazz. New York, Knopf, 1961. 92 p.
61–15039 PS3515.U274A8
A poem.

544. Five plays. Edited, with an introduction, by Webster Smalley. Bloomington, Indiana University Press [1963] 258 p.
63–7169 PS3515.U274A19 1963
CONTENTS.—Mulatto.—Soul gone home.—Little Ham.—Simply heavenly.—Tambourines to glory.

545. Simple's Uncle Sam. New York, Hill & Wang [1965] 180 p.
65–24717 PS3515.U274S6
Short stories.

546. FEDERICO SCHARMEL IRIS, 1889–
No. 1530 in 1960 Guide.

547. The seven hills of the dove. With a foreword by Padraic Colum. Boston, Bruce Humphries [1957] 72 p. illus. 56–6558 PS3517.R5S4
Poems.

548. A singing reed. [Chicago] R. F. Seymour [1963] 64 p. 64–444 PS3517.R5S5
Poems.

549. ROBINSON JEFFERS, 1887–1962
No. 1532 in 1960 Guide.

550. The beginning & the end, and other poems. New York, Random House [1963] 74 p.
63–9347 PS3519.E27B45

551. Squires, James Radcliffe. The loyalties of Robinson Jeffers. Ann Arbor, University of Michigan Press [1956] 202 p.
56–11031 PS3519.E27Z78
Bibliographical notes: p. 192–198. Bibliography: p. 199–202.

552. MacKINLAY KANTOR, 1904–
No. 1541 in 1960 Guide.

553. Spirit Lake. Cleveland, World Pub. Co. [1961] 957 p. 61–8164 PZ3.K142Sp
A novel.

554. OLIVER LA FARGE, 1901–1963
No. 1551 in 1960 Guide.

555. A pause in the desert; a collection of short stories. Boston, Houghton Mifflin, 1957. 235 p. 57–6381 PZ3.L129Pau

556. The door in the wall, stories. With a foreword by William Maxwell. Boston, Houghton Mifflin, 1965. 303 p.
64–24641 PZ3.L129Do

557. RING WILMER LARDNER, 1885–1933
No. 1554 in 1960 Guide.

558. Elder, Donald. Ring Lardner, a biography. Garden City, N. Y., Doubleday, 1956. 409 p. illus. 56–7656 PS3523.A7Z65

559. SINCLAIR LEWIS, 1885–1951
No. 1559 in 1960 Guide.

560. Schorer, Mark. Sinclair Lewis, an American life. New York, McGraw-Hill [1961] 867 p. illus. 61–12961 PS3523.E94Z78
Bibliography: p. 815–826.

561. Schorer, Mark, ed. Sinclair Lewis, a collection of critical essays. Englewood Cliffs, N. J., Prentice-Hall [1962] 174 p. (Twentieth century views. A Spectrum book, S-TC-6)
62–9311 PS3523.E94Z77

562. NICHOLAS VACHEL LINDSAY, 1879–1931
No. 1580 in 1960 Guide.

563. Ruggles, Eleanor. The west-going heart; a life of Vachel Lindsay. New York, Norton [1959] 448 p. 59–11337 PS3523.I58Z76
"Sources and acknowledgments": p. 437–441.

564. AMY LOWELL, 1874–1925
No. 1583 in 1960 Guide.

565. Gregory, Horace. Amy Lowell; portrait of the poet in her time. Edinburgh, New York, T. Nelson [1958] 213 p. illus.
58–11247 PS3523.O88Z67

566. ARCHIBALD MacLEISH, 1892–

No. 1585 in 1960 *Guide*.

567. J. B., a play in verse. Boston, Houghton Mifflin, 1958. 153 p.

58–1148 PS3525.A27J2 1958

568. Poetry and experience. Cambridge, Riverside Press, 1961 [ᶜ1960] 204 p.

60–12742 PN1031.M33

Criticism.

569. JOHN PHILLIPS MARQUAND, 1893–1960

No. 1589 in 1960 *Guide*.

570. Stopover: Tokyo. Boston, Little, Brown [ᶜ1957] 313 p. 57–5508 PZ3.B34466St

A novel.

571. Women and Thomas Harrow. Boston, Little, Brown [1958] 497 p.

58–10691 PZ3.M34466Wo

A novel.

572. Gross, John J. John P. Marquand. New York, Twayne Publishers [1963] 191 p. (Twayne's United States authors series, 33)

62–19477 PS3525.A6695Z68

Bibliographical notes: p. 176–180. Bibliography: p. 181–185.

573. HENRY LOUIS MENCKEN, 1880–1956

No. 1602 in 1960 *Guide*.

574. The bathtub hoax, and other blasts & bravos from the Chicago tribune. Edited, with an introduction and notes, by Robert McHugh. New York, Knopf, 1958. xvi, 286 p.

58–12629 PS3525.E43B3

575. Letters. Selected and annotated by Guy J. Forgue. With a personal note by Hamilton Owens. New York, Knopf, 1961. xxxviii, 506, xxii p. 61–12312 PS3525.E43A16 1961

576. The American scene, a reader. Selected and edited and with an introduction and commentary by Huntington Cairns. New York, Knopf, 1965. xxvii, 542 p.

65–11127 PS3525.E43A75 1965

Bibliography: p. 541–542.

577. HENRY MILLER, 1891–

No. 1611 in 1960 *Guide*.

578. Big Sur and the oranges of Hieronymus Bosch. [New York, New Directions, 1957] 404 p. illus. 57–5542 PS3525.I5454B5

Partly autobiographical nonfiction.

579. The Henry Miller reader. Edited by Lawrence Durrell. [New York] New Directions [1959] 397 p. 59–15022 PS3525.I5454A6 1959

Bibliography: p. 395–397.

580. Stand still like the hummingbird. [Norfolk, Conn.] New Directions [1962] 194 p.

62–10408 PS3525.I5454S75

Essays.

581. The rosy crucifixion. New York, Grove Press [ᶜ1965] 3 v.

65–23919 PZ3.M61468Ro

Autobiographical.

CONTENTS.—Book 1. Sexus.—Book 2. Plexus. —Book 3. Nexus.

582. Letters to Anaïs Nin. Edited and with an introduction by Gunther Stuhlmann. New York, Putnam [1965] xxvi, 356 p.

65–10859 PS3525.I5454Z57

Covers the period 1931–46.

583. MARGARET MITCHELL, 1900–1949

No. 1618 in 1960 *Guide*.

584. Farr, Finis. Margaret Mitchell of Atlanta, the author of Gone with the wind. New York, Morrow, 1965. 244 p.

65–22974 PS3525.I972Z67

585. MARIANNE MOORE, 1887–

No. 1620 in 1960 *Guide*.

586. A Marianne Moore reader. New York, Viking Press, 1961. 301 p.

61–17409 PS3525.O5616M3

587. Engel, Bernard F. Marianne Moore. New York, Twayne Publishers [1964] 176 p. (Twayne's United States authors series, 54)

63–20613 PS3525.O5616Z65

"Notes and references": p. 165–166. Bibliography: p. 167–169.

588. MERRILL MOORE, 1903–1957

No. 1623 in 1960 *Guide*.

589. The hill of Venus; poems of men and women reacting to, puzzled by, and suffering from

love, its fulfillments and its frustrations. New York, Twayne Publishers [1957] 71 p.
57–4764    PS3525.O563H5

590. Poems of American life. With an introduction by Louis Untermeyer. New York, Philosophical Library [1958] 275 p.
58–3315    PS3525.O563P63

591. OGDEN NASH, 1902–

No. 1629 in 1960 *Guide*.

592. You can't get there from here. Drawings by Maurice Sendak. Boston, Little, Brown [1957] 190 p.    57–7838    PS3527.A637Y6
Poems.

593. Everyone but thee and me. Illustrated by John Alcorn. Boston, Little, Brown [1962] 171 p.    62–16957    PS3527.A637E85
Poems.

594. Marriage lines; notes of a student husband. Illustrated by Isadore Seltzer. Boston, Little, Brown [1964] 108 p.
64–17471    PS3527.A637M35
Poems.

595. ROBERT GRUNTAL NATHAN, 1894–

No. 1635 in 1960 *Guide*.

596. The Mallot diaries. New York, Knopf, 1965. 174 p.    65–17384    PZ3.N195Mal
A novel.

597. EUGENE GLADSTONE O'NEILL, 1888–1953

No. 1647 in 1960 *Guide*.

598. Long day's journey into night. New Haven, Yale University Press, 1956 [ᶜ1955] 176 p.
56–5944    PS3529.N5L6
A play.

599. A touch of the poet. New Haven, Yale University Press, 1957. 182 p.
57–6342    PS3529.N5T6    1957
A play.

600. Cargill, Oscar, Nathan Bryllion Fagin, *and* William J. Fisher, *eds*. O'Neill and his plays; four decades of criticism. [New York] New York University Press, 1961. 528 p.
61–17631    PS3529.N5Z576
Bibliography: p. 487–517.

601. Falk, Doris V. Eugene O'Neill and the tragic tension; an interpretive study of the plays. New Brunswick, N. J., Rutgers University Press, 1958. 211 p.    58–10830    PS3529.N5Z64
A combination of psychological analysis and literary criticism.

602. Gassner, John, *ed*. O'Neill; a collection of critical essays. Englewood Cliffs, N. J., Prentice-Hall [1964] 180 p. (A Spectrum book. Twentieth century views, S–TC–39)
64–19679    PS3529.N5Z648
Bibliography: p. 177–180.

603. Gelb, Arthur, *and* Barbara Gelb. O'Neill. New York, Harper [1962] 970 p. illus.
61–13602    PS3529.N5Z653
A biography.

604. Raleigh, John H. The plays of Eugene O'Neill. With a preface by Harry T. Moore. Carbondale, Southern Illinois University Press [1965] xvi, 304 p. (Crosscurrents: modern critiques)    65–12387    PS3529.N5Z79
Bibliographical references included in "Notes" (p. [286]–297).

605. KATHERINE ANNE PORTER, 1894–

No. 1659 in 1960 *Guide*.

606. Ship of fools. Boston, Little, Brown [1962] 497 p.    62–9557    PZ3.P8215Sh
A novel.

607. Collected stories. New York, Harcourt, Brace & World [1965] 495 p.
65–14706    PZ3.P8315Co

608. Hendrick, George. Katherine Anne Porter. New York, Twayne Publishers [1965] 176 p. (Twayne's United States authors series, 90)
65–18909    PS3531.O752Z68
Bibliographical notes: p. 156–160. Bibliography: p. 161–171.

609. Nance, William L. Katherine Anne Porter & the art of rejection. Chapel Hill, University of North Carolina Press [1964] 258 p.
64–22525    PS3531.O752Z79    1964
Bibliography: p. [251]–253.

610. EZRA LOOMIS POUND, 1885–

No. 1664 in 1960 *Guide*.

611. Section: rock drill, 85–95 de los cantares. [New York, J. Laughlin, 1956] 107 p. (A New Directions book)
56–4113   PS3531.O82S4   1956
Half title: *Cantos 85–95 of Ezra Pound.*

612. Thrones; 96–109 de los cantares. [New York] New Directions [1959] 126 p.
59–13172   PS3531.O82T5
Half title: *Cantos 96–109 of Ezra Pound.*

613. Translations. With an introduction by Hugh Kenner. [Enl. ed. Norfolk, Conn.] New Directions [1963] 448 p. (A New Directions paperbook, 145)   64–1552   PN6020.P6   1963
An updated edition of no. 1667 in the 1960 *Guide.* Includes some original poems, with translations on opposite pages.

614. Davie, Donald. Ezra Pound: poet as sculptor. New York, Oxford University Press, 1964. 261 p.   64–24860   PS3531.O82Z58
Bibliographical footnotes.
A critical discussion of Pound's works.

615. Dekker, George. The cantos of Ezra Pound, a critical study. New York, Barnes & Noble [1963] xvi, 207 p.
63–23827   PS3531.O82C284   1963
First published in 1963 under title: *Sailing After Knowledge.*
Bibliographical footnotes.

616. Norman, Charles. Ezra Pound. New York, Macmillan, 1960. 493 p.
60–13141   PS3531.O82Z785
Notes: p. 469–477.
A critical biography.

617. Stock, Noel. Poet in exile: Ezra Pound. New York, Barnes & Noble [1964] 273 p.
64–4258   PS3531.O82Z84
Bibliography: p. 261–266.

618. JOHN CROWE RANSOM, 1888–
No. 1675 in 1960 *Guide.*

619. Selected poems. [2d] rev. and enl. ed. New York, Knopf, 1963. 110 p.
63–12791   PS3535.A635A6   1963
A revised edition of *Selected Poems* (1945), mentioned in no. 1679 in the 1960 *Guide.*

620. MARJORIE KINNAN RAWLINGS, 1896–1954
No. 1680 in 1960 *Guide.*

621. The Marjorie Rawlings reader. Selected and edited with an introduction by Julia Scribner Bingham. New York, Scribner [1956] 504 p.
56–10198   PS3535.A845A6   1956

622. EUGENE MANLOVE RHODES, 1869–1934
No. 1686 in 1960 *Guide.*

623. A Bar Cross man; the life & personal writings of Eugene Manlove Rhodes [by] W. H. Hutchinson. Norman, University of Oklahoma Press [1956] xix, 432 p. illus.
56–6001   PS3535.H68Z54
"Check list of Eugene Manlove Rhodes' writing": p. 392–407.

624. ELMER L. RICE, 1892–
No. 1688 in 1960 *Guide.*

625. Cue for passion, a play in five scenes. New York, Dramatists Play Service [1959] 121 p. illus.   59–4693   PS3535.I224C8

626. Minority report, an autobiography. New York, Simon & Schuster, 1963. 473 p.
63–15364   PS3535.I224Z5

627. Hogan, Robert G. The independence of Elmer Rice. With a preface by Harry T. Moore. Carbondale, Southern Illinois University Press [1965] 164 p. (Crosscurrents: modern critiques)   65–16535   PS3535.I224Z68
Bibliography: p. [155]–157.

628. CONRAD MICHAEL RICHTER, 1890–
No. 1691 in 1960 *Guide.*

629. The lady. New York, Knopf, 1957. 191 p.
57–5660   PZ3.R417Lad
A novel.

630. The waters of Kronos. New York, Knopf, 1960. 175 p.   60–7297   PZ3.R417Wat
A novel.

631. ELIZABETH MADOX ROBERTS, 1886–1941
No. 1697 in 1960 *Guide.*

632. McDowell, Frederick P. W. Elizabeth Madox Roberts. New York, Twayne Publishers [1963] 176 p. (Twayne's United States authors series, 38)   63–10955   PS3535.O172Z7

Bibliographical notes: p. 164–168. Bibliography: p. 169–172.

633. Rovit, Earl H. Herald to chaos; the novels of Elizabeth Madox Roberts. [Lexington] University of Kentucky Press [1960] 180 p.
60–13722   PS3535.O172Z8
Bibliography: p. [165]-169. Bibliographical notes: p. [171]- 178.

634. EDWIN ARLINGTON ROBINSON, 1869–1935
No. 1713 in 1960 *Guide.*

635. Selected early poems and letters. Edited by Charles T. Davis. New York, Holt, Rinehart & Winston [ᶜ1960] 238 p. (Rinehart editions, 107)   60–15097   PS3535.O25A6   1960

636. Selected poems. Edited by Morton Dauwen Zabel. With an introduction by James Dickey. New York, Macmillan [1965] xxviii, 257 p.   65–23550   PS3535.O25A6   1965
"Editor's note and bibliography": p. 247–254.

637. Smith, Chard P. Where the light falls; a portrait of Edwin Arlington Robinson. New York, Macmillan [1965] xx, 420 p. illus.
65–11479   PS3535.O25Z85
Bibliographical references included in "Notes" (p. 391–408).

638. ARCHIBALD HAMILTON RUTLEDGE, 1883–
No. 1724 in 1960 *Guide.*

639. Santee paradise. Indianapolis, Bobbs-Merrill Co. [1956] 232 p.
56–13274   F279.H25R82
Autobiographical.

640. Deep river, the complete poems. Columbia, S.C., R. L. Bryan Co. [1960] 635 p.
61–280   PS3535.U87A17   1960

641. CARL SANDBURG, 1878–
No. 1727 in 1960 *Guide.*

642. The Sandburg range. New York, Harcourt, Brace [1957] 459 p. illus.
57–12373   PS3537.A618A6   1957
Selections from the author's works.

643. Honey and salt. New York, Harcourt, Brace & World [1963] 111 p.
63–9836   PS3537.A618H63
Poems.

644. Crowder, Richard. Carl Sandburg. New York, Twayne Publishers [1964] 176 p. (Twayne's United States authors series, 47)
63–20606   PS3537.A618Z555
Bibliographical notes: p. 159–162. Bibliography: p. 163–168.

645. ROBERT EMMET SHERWOOD, 1896–1955
No. 1749 in 1960 *Guide.*

646. Brown, John Mason. The worlds of Robert E. Sherwood; mirror to his times, 1896–1939. New York, Harper & Row [1965] xviii, 409 p. illus.   65–20424   PS3537.H825Z63
"Works of Robert E. Sherwood": p. 387–390.

647. Shuman, Robert Baird. Robert E. Sherwood. New York, Twayne Publishers [1964] 160 p. (Twayne's United States authors series, 58)
64–13954   PS3537.H825Z87
Bibliographical notes: p. 147–150. Bibliography: p. 151–156.

648. UPTON BEALL SINCLAIR, 1878–
No. 1754 in 1960 *Guide.*

649. My lifetime in letters. Columbia, University of Missouri Press [1960] xxi, 412 p.
59–14141   PS3537.I85Z54

650. Autobiography. New York, Harcourt, Brace & World [1962] 342 p. illus.
62–19592   PS3537.I85Z517

651. LILLIAN EUGENIA SMITH, 1897–
No. 1759 in 1960 *Guide.*

652. One hour. New York, Harcourt, Brace [1959] 440 p.   57–5299   PZ3.S6536On
A novel.

653. GERTRUDE STEIN, 1874–1946
No. 1766 in 1960 *Guide.*

654. The Yale edition of the unpublished writings of Gertrude Stein. [Under the general editorship of Carl Van Vechten. New Haven, Yale University Press, 1951–58] 8 v.
51–6628   PS3537.T323A6
CONTENTS.—v. 1. Two: Gertrude Stein and her

brother, and other early portraits, 1908–12.—v. 2. Mrs. Reynolds, and five earlier novelettes.—v. 3. Bee time vine, and other pieces, 1913–1927.—v. 4. As fine as Melanctha, 1914–1930.—v. 5. Painted lace, and other pieces, 1914–1937.—v. 6. Stanzas in meditation, and other poems, 1929–1933.—v. 7. Alphabets and birthdays.—v. 8. A novel of thank you.

The first volume of this edition is no. 1772 in the 1960 *Guide*.

655. Brinnin, John M. The third rose; Gertrude Stein and her world. Boston, Little, Brown [1959] 427 p. illus. 59–13732 PS3537.T323Z57
"A selected bibliography of the works of Gertrude Stein": p. 411–413.

656. Reid, Benjamin L. Art by subtraction; a dissenting opinion of Gertrude Stein. Norman, University of Oklahoma Press [1958] 224 p. illus. 58–6852 PS3537.T323Z79
Bibliography: p. 209–216.

657. JOHN STEINBECK, 1902–

No. 1775 in 1960 *Guide*.

658. Travels with Charley; in search of America. New York, Viking Press [1962] 246 p.
62–12359 E169.S82
A travel account.

659. French, Warren G., *ed.* A companion to The grapes of wrath. New York, Viking Press [1963] 243 p. 63–17069 PS3537.T3234G85
Bibliography: p. 229–235.

660. Lisca, Peter. The wide world of John Steinbeck. New Brunswick, N. J., Rutgers University Press, 1958. 326 p.
57–10965 PC3537.T3234Z72
Includes bibliography.
A biographical and critical study which analyzes symbolism, style, and structure in Steinbeck's works.

661. WALLACE STEVENS, 1879–1955

No. 1782 in 1960 *Guide*.

662. Opus posthumous. Edited, with an introduction, by Samuel French Morse. New York, Knopf, 1957. 300 p.
57–7548 PS3537.T4753A6 1957
Poems, plays, and prose.

663. Brown, Ashley, *and* Robert S. Haller, *eds.* The achievement of Wallace Stevens. Phil-

adelphia, Lippincott [1962] 287 p.
62–10543 PS3537.T4753Z62
"For further reading: a bibliography of books and articles about Wallace Stevens and selected reviews of his work": p. 271–287.

664. Fuchs, Daniel. The comic spirit of Wallace Stevens. Durham, N. C., Duke University Press, 1963. 201 p. 63–9008 PS3537.T4753Z64
Bibliography: p. [193]–196.

665. Pearce, Roy Harvey, *and* Joseph Hillis Miller, *eds.* The act of the mind, essays on the poetry of Wallace Stevens. Baltimore, Johns Hopkins Press [1965] 287 p.
65–11666 PS3537.T4753Z75
Bibliographical footnotes.

666. Riddel, Joseph N. The clairvoyant eye; the poetry and poetics of Wallace Stevens. Baton Rouge, Louisiana State University Press, 1965. 308 p. 65–24679 PS3537.T4753Z76
"Index to Stevens titles": p. 299–303.
Bibliographical references included in "Notes" (p. 279–298).

667. RUTH SUCKOW, 1892–1960

No. 1796 in 1960 *Guide*.

668. The John Wood case, a novel. New York, Viking Press [1959] 314 p.
59–8615 PZ3.S942Jo

669. NEWTON BOOTH TARKINGTON, 1869–1946

No. 1802 in 1960 *Guide*.

670. On plays, playwrights, and playgoers; selections from the letters of Booth Tarkington to George C. Tyler and John Peter Toohey, 1918–1925. Edited by Alan S. Downer. Princeton, N. J., Princeton University Library, 1959. 100 p. illus. (Occasional publications sponsored by the Friends of the Princeton Library)
59–15575 PS2973.A38

671. ALLEN TATE, 1899–

No. 1809 in 1960 *Guide*.

672. Collected essays. Denver, A. Swallow [1959] 578 p. 59–15664 PN37.T27

673. Poems. New York, Scribner, 1960. 224 p.
62–3826 PS3539.A74P56

674. Meiners, R. K. The last alternatives; a study of the works of Allen Tate. Denver, A. Swallow [1963] 217 p.
63–14649 PS3539.A74Z7
Bibliography: p. 207–214.

675. SARA TEASDALE, 1884–1933
No. 1813 in 1960 *Guide.*

676. Carpenter, Margaret H. Sara Teasdale, a biography. New York, Schulte Pub. Co., 1960. 377 p. illus. 60–9646 PS3539.E15Z6

677. JAMES GROVER THURBER, 1894–1961
No. 1815 in 1960 *Guide.*

678. Alarms and diversions. New York, Harper [1957] 367 p. illus.
57–8181 PS3539.H94A7
Essays, parables, stories, and drawings, some of which appear here in book form for the first time.

679. The years with Ross. With drawings by the author. Boston, Little, Brown [1959] 310 p.
58–11443 PN4874.R65T5
A biography which describes the close personal and working relationships between the author and Harold Ross, founding editor of *The New Yorker.*

680. Lanterns & lances. New York, Harper [1961] 215 p. illus.
61–6444 PS3539.H94L3
Selected short pieces.

681. Morsberger, Robert E. James Thurber. New York, Twayne Publishers [1964] 224 p. (Twayne's United States authors series, 62)
64–13958 PS3539.H94Z77
Bibliographical notes: p. 200–206. Bibliography: p. 207–218.

682. MARK ALBERT VAN DOREN, 1894–
No. 1823 in 1960 *Guide.*

683. Autobiography. New York, Harcourt, Brace [1958] 371 p. illus.
58–10897 PS3543.A557Z52

684. The last days of Lincoln, a play in six scenes. New York, Hill & Wang, 1959. 152 p.
59–6708 PS3543.A557L27

685. The happy critic, and other essays. New York, Hill & Wang [1961] 177 p.
61–14476 PS3543.A557H3

686. Collected stories. New York, Hill & Wang [1962–65] 2 v. 62–15221 PZ3.V28686Co

687. Collected and new poems, 1924–1963. New York, Hill & Wang [1963] 615 p.
63–18480 PS3543.A557A17 1963

688. Narrative poems. New York, Hill & Wang [1964] 335 p. 64–24238 PS3543.A557N3
CONTENTS.—Jonathan Gentry.—A winter diary. —The eyes.—The Mayfield deer.—Mortal summer.—Anger in the room.

689. CARL VAN VECHTEN, 1880–1964
No. 1828 in 1960 *Guide.*

690. Lueders, Edward G. Carl Van Vechten, New York, Twayne Publishers [1965] 158 p. (Twayne's United States authors series, 74)
64–20724 PS3543.A653Z79
Bibliographical notes: p. 143–147. Bibliography: p. 148–152.

691. GLENWAY WESCOTT, 1901–
No. 1839 in 1960 *Guide.*

692. Rueckert, William H. Glenway Wescott. New York, Twayne Publishers [1965] 174 p. (Twayne's United States authors series, 87)
65–18906 PS3545.E827Z86
Bibliographical notes: p. 157–162. Bibliography: p. 165–171.

693. NATHANAEL WEST, 1902–1940
No. 1842 in 1960 *Guide.*

694. Complete works. New York, Farrar, Straus & Cudahy [1957] 421 p.
57–6259 PS3545.E8334 1957

695. Light, James F. Nathanael West; [an interpretative study. Evanston, Ill., Northwestern University Press, 1961] 220 p.
61–8746 PS3545.S8334Z75

696. EDITH NEWBOLD JONES WHARTON, 1862–1937
No. 1845 in 1960 *Guide.*

697. Best short stories. Edited, with an introduction by Wayne Andrews. New York, Scribner [1958] 292 p. 58–10825 PZ3.W555Be

698. Bell, Millicent. Edith Wharton & Henry James, the story of their friendship. New

York, G. Braziller [1965] 384 p.

65–10196 PS3545.H16Z59

Includes bibliographical references.

699. Howe, Irving, *ed*. Edith Wharton; a collection of critical essays. Englewood Cliffs, N. J., Prentice-Hall [1962] 181 p. (A Spectrum book. Twentieth century views, S–TC–20)

63–7990 PS3545.H16Z68

700. Lyde, Marilyn J. Edith Wharton: convention and morality in the work of a novelist. Norman, University of Oklahoma Press [1959] 194 p. illus. 59–7965 PS3545.H16Z74

701. JOHN HALL WHEELOCK, 1886–

No. 1857 in 1960 *Guide*.

702. The gardener, and other poems. New York, Scribner [1961] 94 p.

61–11582 PS3545.H33G3

703. ELWYN BROOKS WHITE, 1899–

No. 1859 in 1960 *Guide*.

704. The points of my compass; letters from the East, the West, the North, the South. New York, Harper & Row [1962] 240 p.

62–15724 PS3545.H5187P6

Contains articles originally published in *The New Yorker* and an essay which first appeared in *The Yale Review*.

705. THORNTON NIVEN WILDER, 1897–

No. 1864 in 1960 *Guide*.

706. Burbank, Rex J. Thornton Wilder. New York, Twayne Publishers [1961] 156 p. (Twayne's United States authors series, 5)

61–9854 PS3545.I345Z57

Bibliographical notes: p. 146–149. Bibliography: p. 150–153.

707. WILLIAM CARLOS WILLIAMS, 1883–1963

No. 1872 in 1960 *Guide*.

708. Paterson. [New York, New Directions, 1946–58] 5 v. 46–5910 PS3545.I544P3

The fifth volume completes this poem, the first four volumes of which are no. 1876 in the 1960 *Guide*.

709. Pictures from Brueghel, and other poems; including The desert music & Journey to love. [Norfolk, Conn., J. Laughlin, 1962] 184 p. (A New Directions paperbook, 118)

62–10410 PS3545.I544P45

710. The collected later poems. Rev. ed. [New York] New Directions [1963] 276 p.

62–19398 PS3545.I544A17 1963

711. Selected letters. Edited, with an introduction, by John C. Thirlwall. New York, McDowell, Obolensky [1957] 347 p.

57–12112 PS3545.I544Z53

712. THOMAS WOLFE, 1900–1938

No. 1887 in 1960 *Guide*.

713. Short novels. Edited, with an introduction and notes, by C. Hugh Holman. New York, Scribner [1961] xx, 323 p.

61–7212 PZ3.W8314Sh

CONTENTS.—A portrait of Bascom Hawke.—The web of earth.—No door.—"I have a thing to tell you."—The party at Jack's.

714. Kennedy, Richard S. The window of memory; the literary career of Thomas Wolfe, Chapel Hill, University of North Carolina Press [1962] 461 p. 62–16110 PS3545.O337Z737

Includes bibliography.

715. Nowell, Elizabeth. Thomas Wolfe, a biography. Garden City, N.Y., Doubleday, 1960. 456 p. illus. 60–8689 PS3545.O337Z74

716. MARYA ZATURENSKA, 1902–

No. 1905 in 1960 *Guide*.

717. Collected poems. New York, Viking Press [1965] 210 p.

65–23955 PS3549.A77A17 1965

# F. The Second World War and the Atomic Age (1940-1965)

718. JAMES AGEE, 1909–1955
No. 1907 in 1960 *Guide*.

719. A death in the family. New York, McDowell, Obolensky [1957] 339 p.
57–12114 PZ4.A265De
A novel.

720. Letters of James Agee to Father Flye. New York, G. Braziller, 1962. 235 p.
62–16270 PS3501.G35Z54 1962

721. EDWARD FRANKLIN ALBEE, 1928–

Albee's first one-act plays brought him immediate recognition as a spokesman for the symbolic and satiric theater of the absurd. His major themes, often veiled in obscure yet potent symbolism, are self-deception, hypocrisy, and alienation. Both *The Zoo Story* and *The Death of Bessie Smith* had their premieres in Berlin; *The Sandbox* was first produced in New York. Full length, three-act dramas by Albee, including adaptations of fictional works by other writers, have appeared regularly on the Broadway stage.

722. The zoo story; The death of Bessie Smith; The sandbox; three plays, introduced by the author. New York, Coward-McCann [1960] 158 p.
60–12478 PS3501.L178Z3

723. The American dream, a play. New York, Coward-McCann [1961] 93 p. [Coward-McCann contemporary drama, CM-6]
61–15067 PS3501.L178A7

724. Who's afraid of Virginia Woolf? A play. New York, Atheneum, 1962. 242 p.
62–17691 PS3501.L178W5

725. The play, The ballad of the sad café. Carson McCullers' novella adapted to the stage by Edward Albee. Boston, Houghton Mifflin, 1963. 150 p.
63–23325 PS3501.L178B3

726. Tiny Alice, a play. New York, Atheneum, 1965. 190 p.
65–15904 PS3501.L178T5

727. LOUIS AUCHINCLOSS, 1917–
No. 1909 in 1960 *Guide*.

728. The great world and Timothy Colt. Boston, Houghton Mifflin, 1956. 285 p.
56–9384 PZ3.A898Gr
A novel.

729. Venus in Sparta. Boston, Houghton Mifflin, 1958. 280 p.
58–9052 PZ3.A898Ve
A novel.

730. Pursuit of the prodigal. Boston, Houghton Mifflin, 1959. 292 p.
59–9633 PZ3.A898Pu
A novel.

731. The house of five talents. Boston, Houghton Mifflin, 1960. 369 p.
60–8761 PZ3.A898Ho
A novel.

732. Portrait in brownstone. Boston, Houghton Mifflin, 1962. 371 p.
62–8116 PZ3.A898Po
A novel.

733. Powers of attorney. Boston, Houghton Mifflin, 1963. 280 p.
63–9077 PZ3.A898Pq
Short stories.

734. The rector of Justin. Boston, Houghton Mifflin, 1964. 341 p.
64–14523 PZ3.A898Re
A novel.

735. JAMES BALDWIN, 1924–
No. 1914 in 1960 *Guide*.

736. Giovanni's room, a novel. New York, Dial Press, 1956. 248 p.
56–12125 PZ4.B18Gi

737. Another country. New York, Dial Press, 1962. 436 p.
61–7367 PZ4.B18An2
A novel.

738. Blues for Mister Charlie, a play. New York, Dial Press, 1964. 121 p.
64–15223 PS3552.A45B5

739. Going to meet the man. New York, Dial Press, 1965. 249 p.
65–15331 PS3552.A45G6
Short stories.

CONTENTS.—The rockpile.—The outing.—The man child.—Previous condition.—Sonny's blues.—This morning, this evening, so soon.—Come out the wilderness.—Going to meet the man.

740. SHIRLEY FRANCES BARKER, 1911–1965

No. 1916 in 1960 *Guide*.

741. Swear by Apollo. [New York] Random House [1958] 306 p. illus.
58–5282    PZ3.B2457Sw
A novel.

742. The last gentleman. New York, Random House [1960] 341 p.
60–6377    PZ3.B2457Las
A novel.

743. Strange wives. New York, Crown Publishers [1963] 377 p.
63–12062    PZ3.B2457St
A novel.

744. JOHN SIMMONS BARTH, 1930–

Barth's native Maryland, past or present, is often chosen as the setting for his fiction, which has been received with fascination, confusion, admiration, and occasional distaste. His curious plots, filled with digressions and sparked by Rabelaisian humor, are considered unique and undeniably the product of a masterful imagination. Barth's writing is concerned with matters of choice, value, and meaning in man's life, even when it takes the form of parody.

745. The floating opera. New York, Appleton-Century-Crofts [1956] 280 p.
56–10340    PZ4.B284Fl
A novel.

746. The end of the road. Garden City, N.Y., Doubleday, 1958. 230 p.
58–9381    PZ4.B284En
A novel.

747. The sot-weed factor. Garden City, N.Y., Doubleday, 1960. 806 p.
60–9467    PZ4.B284So
A novel.

748. SAUL BELLOW, 1915–

No. 1921 in 1960 *Guide*.

749. Seize the day, with three short stories and a one-act play. New York, Viking Press, 1956. 211 p.
56–10686    PS3503.E4488S4
*Seize the Day* is a brief novel previously published in *Partisan Review*.

750. Henderson, the rain king; a novel. New York, Viking Press, 1959. 341 p.
59–5649    PZ3.B41937He

751. Herzog. New York, Viking Press [1964] 341 p.
64–19794    PZ3.B41937Hh
A novel.

752. The last analysis, a play. New York, Viking Press [1965] 118 p.
65–16904    PS3503.E4488L3

753. JOHN BERRYMAN, 1914–

No. 1923 in 1960 *Guide*.

754. Homage to Mistress Bradstreet. With pictures by Ben Shahn. New York, Farrar, Straus & Cudahy [1956] 1 v. (unpaged)
56–6168    PS3503.E744H6
A poem.

755. 77 dream songs. New York, Farrar, Straus [1964] 84 p.    64–14107    PS3503.E744S4
Poems.

756. ELIZABETH BISHOP, 1911–

No. 1925 in 1960 *Guide*.

757. Questions of travel. New York, Farrar, Straus & Giroux [1965] 95 p.
65–22553    PS3503.I785Q4
Poems.

758. PAUL FREDERIC BOWLES, 1910–

No. 1927 in 1960 *Guide*.

759. A hundred camels in the courtyard. [San Francisco] City Lights Books [1962] 63 p.
62–51513    PZ3.B6826Hu
Short stories.

760. RAY BRADBURY, 1920–

No. 1932 in 1960 *Guide*.

761. Dandelion wine, a novel. Garden City, N.Y., Doubleday, 1957. 281 p.
57–7824    PZ3.B72453Dan

762. Something wicked this way comes, a novel. New York, Simon & Schuster, 1962. 317 p.
62–9604  PZ3.B72453So

763. The vintage Bradbury; Ray Bradbury's own selection of his best stories. With an introduction by Gilbert Highet. New York, Vintage Books [1965] 329 p.  65–18936  PZ3.B72453Vi

764. GWENDOLYN BROOKS, 1917–

No. 1937 in 1960 *Guide.*

765. The bean eaters. New York, Harper [1960] 71 p.  60–7521  PS3503.R7244B4
Poems.

766. Selected poems. New York, Harper & Row [1963]  127 p.
63–16503  PS3503.R7244A6  1963

767. WILLIAM SEWARD BURROUGHS, 1914–

Burroughs discarded the conventional style of his first novel, *Junkie* (1953), to adopt the radical surrealistic approach which has characterized his subsequent work. He achieved international prominence as a result of the controversy surrounding *The Naked Lunch,* a novel first published in Paris in 1959. This account of the protagonist's years as a drug addict has been condemned as the vilest pornography by some critics and acclaimed as the greatest innovation in recent literature by others. *The Soft Machine* (1961) and *Nova Express* (1964) continued Burrough's freestyle approach to the novel, while *The Yage Letters* (1963) established his affinity with the beat writers.

768. Naked lunch. New York, Grove Press [1962, ᶜ1959]  255 p.
60–11097  PZ4.B972Nak 2

769. The soft machine. Paris, Olympia Press [1961]  181 p. (The Traveller's companion series, no. 88)  64–5780  PZ4.B972So

770. The yage letters [by] William Burroughs & Allen Ginsberg. [San Francisco] City Lights Books [ᶜ1963] 68 p. illus.
63–12222  PS3552.U75Y3
CONTENTS.—In search of yage, 1953: William Burroughs to Allen Ginsberg.—Seven years later, 1960: Allen Ginsberg to William Burroughs. Burroughs' reply.—Epilogue, 1963.

771. Nova express. New York, Grove Press [1964]  187 p.  64–10597  PZ4.B972No
A novel.

772. TRUMAN CAPOTE, 1924–

No. 1944 in 1960 *Guide.*

773. Breakfast at Tiffany's, a short novel and three stories. New York, Random House [1958] 179 p.  58–10956  PZ3.C1724Br

774. JOHN CHEEVER, 1912–

A novelist and prolific writer of stories, Cheever observes contemporary urban and suburban life with facility and sophisticated style. He challenges the standards of a materialistic society in cynical, melancholy, and sometimes humorous tones. Early collections of his stories, which have appeared in *Esquire* and *The New Yorker,* include *The Way Some People Live* (1943) and *The Enormous Radio* (1953). Cheever won a National Book Award in 1958 for his first novel, *The Wapshot Chronicle.* The further adventures of this New England family were traced in *The Wapshot Scandal,* a sequel published in 1964.

775. The Wapshot chronicle. New York, Harper [1957] 307 p.  56–11100  PZ3.C3983Wap
A novel.

776. The housebreaker of Shady Hill, and other stories. New York, Harper [1958]  185 p.
58–11397  PZ3.C3983Ho

777. Some people, places, and things that will not appear in my next novel. New York, Harper [1961]  175 p.  61–7597  PZ3.C3983So
Short stories.

778. The brigadier and the golf widow. New York, Harper & Row [1964]  275 p.
64–20543  PZ3.C3983Br
Short stories.

779. The Wapshot scandal. New York, Harper & Row [ᶜ1964]  309 p.
63–20301  PZ3.C3983War
A novel.

780. JOHN CIARDI, 1916–

No. 1948 in 1960 *Guide.*

781. I marry you; a sheaf of love poems. New Brunswick, N.J., Rutgers University Press, 1958.  44 p.  58–9102  PS3505.I27I2

782. 39 poems. New Brunswick, N.J., Rutgers University Press, 1959.  86 p.
59–15628  PS3505.I27T5

783. In the stoneworks. New Brunswick, N.J., Rutgers University Press [1961] 83 p.
61–10256    PS3505.I27I5
Poems.

784. In fact. New Brunswick, N.J., Rutgers University Press [1962] 68 p.
62–18947    PS3505.I27I48
Poems.

785. Dialogue with an audience. Philadelphia, Lippincott [1963] 316 p.
63–15440    PN1064.C5
All but two of the articles collected here appeared in *The Saturday Review*.

786. Person to person. New Brunswick, N.J., Rutgers University Press [1964] 83 p.
64–18873    PS3505.I27P4
Poems.

787. AUGUST WILLIAM DERLETH, 1909–
No. 1959 in 1960 *Guide*.

788. The house on the mound. New York, Duell, Sloan & Pearce [1958] 335 p.
58–5563    PZ3.D445Hq
This novel is a sequel to *Bright Journey*, no. 1962 in the 1960 *Guide*.

789. The hills stand watch. New York, Duell, Sloan & Pearce [1960] 337 p.
60–5450    PZ3.D445Hi
A novel.

790. West of morning. Francestown, N.H., Golden Quill Press [1960] 64 p.
60–16459    PS3507.E69W4
Poems.

791. Walden West. Woodcuts by Grisha Dotzenko. New York, Duell, Sloan & Pearce [1961] 262 p.    61–14127    PS3507.E69W3
Vignettes of village life in Sac Prairie, Wis.

792. Wisconsin in their bones. New York, Duell, Sloan & Pearce [1961].
61-6918    PZ3.D445Wk
Short stories.

793. Countryman's journal. Illustrated by Grisha Dotzenko. New York, Duell, Sloan & Pearce [1963] 215 p.    63–16819    F589.S12D4
Descriptions of life in Sac Prairie, Wis.

794. The shadow in the glass. New York, Duell, Sloan & Pearce [1963] 471 p.
62–8520    PZ3.D445Sg
A novel.

795. Wisconsin country; a Sac Prairie journal. With decorations by Frank Utpatel. New York, Candlelight Press, 1965. 232 p. illus.
65–4011    F589.P83D4

796. JAMES LAFAYETTE DICKEY, 1923–
Dickey is a personal poet who looks into ordinary experience to re-create incidents from life. Free-verse images of his youth in the South, motor-cycle-riding, World War II, Korea, hunting, and other aspects of his past are used to create what he calls a "stripped kind of simplicity in verse in order to make effective statements." Dickey's first collection of poetry, "Into the Stone, and Other Poems," was published in *Poets of Today*, v. 7 (New York, Scribner, [1960]), p. 33–92, and he has since enjoyed an unusually successful career. The Wesleyan University Press has published several volumes of his poetry, the most acclaimed of which is *Buck-dancer's Choice* (1965). Dickey is also noted for his strong opinions as a critic.

797. Drowning with others, poems. Middletown, Conn., Wesleyan University Press [1962] 96 p.    62–10570    PS3507.I268D7

798. Helmets, poems. Middletown, Conn., Wesleyan University Press [1964] 93 p.
64–13610    PS3507.I268H4

799. The suspect in poetry. [Madison, Minn.] Sixties Press, 1964. 120 p.
62–21968    PS324.D5
Essays on recent poetry and poets.

800. Buckdancer's choice, poems. Middletown, Conn., Wesleyan University Press [1965] 79 p. (The Wesleyan poetry program)
65–21079    PS3507.I268B8

801. RALPH ELLISON, 1914–
No. 1966 in 1960 *Guide*.

802. Shadow and act. New York, Random House [1964] xxii, 317 p.
64–18928    PS153.N5E4    1964
Essays.

803. PAUL HAMILTON ENGLE, 1908–
No. 1968 in 1960 *Guide*.

804. For the Iowa dead. [Iowa City] State University of Iowa, 1956. [24] p.
56–27481    PS3509.N44F6
Poems.

805. Poems in praise. New York, Random House [1959] 97 p.    59–10822    PS3509.N44P6

806. A woman unashamed, and other poems. New York, Random House [1965] 109 p.
65–11277    PS3509.N44W53

807. HOWARD MELVIN FAST, 1914–
No. 1973 in 1960 *Guide.*

808. The story of Lola Gregg. New York, Blue Heron Press [1956] 219 p.
56–3199    PZ3.F265Ss
A novel.

809. Moses, Prince of Egypt. New York, Crown Publishers [1958] 303 p.
58–8324    PZ3.F265Mo
A novel.

810. The Winston affair. New York, Crown Publishers [1959] 221 p.
59–14020    PZ3.F265Wi
A novel.

811. April morning, a novel. New York, Crown Publishers [1961] 184 p.
61–10306    PZ3.F265Ap

812. Power, a novel. Garden City, N. Y., Doubleday, 1962. 378 p.    62–15943    PZ3.F265Po

813. The hill, an original screenplay. Garden City, N. Y., Doubleday, 1964. 123 p.
64–11381    PS3511.A784H5

814. LAWRENCE FERLINGHETTI, 1919–

After receiving a *doctorat de l'université* from the Sorbonne, Ferlinghetti returned to the United States, where he became a founder of the San Francisco City Lights Bookstore, reportedly the Nation's first all-paperback shop. He has been both an advocate and a practitioner of experimentation with literary forms and oral presentation of poetry. His first book of poems was *Pictures of the Gone World* (1955). An editor as well as a poet, he became the leading publisher of writers identified with the beat generation. *Howl of the Censor* (San Carlos, Calif., Nourse Pub. Co. [1961], 144 p.), a transcript of the trial in which he defended himself against charges of publishing obscene literature, indicates his concept of the poet's role in society.

815. A Coney Island of the mind, poems. [New York] New Directions [1958] 93 p. (New Directions paperbook no. 74)
58–7150    PS3511.E557C6
Includes new poems as well as selections from *Pictures of the Gone World.*

816. Her. [New York, New Directions, 1960] 156 p. (New Directions paperbook no. 88)
60–9221    PZ4.F357He
A novel.

817. Starting from San Francisco. [Norfolk, Conn.] New Directions [1961] 79 p. and phonodisc (2 s. 7 in. 33⅓ rpm. microgroove) in pocket.    61–14897    PS3511.E557S8
Poems.

818. Unfair arguments with existence, seven plays for a new theatre. [New York, New Directions Books, 1963] 118 p. (A New Directions paperbook ND 143)
63–21384    PS3511.E557U5 1963

819. Routines. [New York, Published for J. Laughlin by New Directions Pub. Corp., ᶜ1964] 52 p. (A New Directions paperbook NDP187)    64–23652    PS3511.E557R6
Experimental plays.

820. JEAN GARRIGUE, 1912–
No. 1981 in 1960 *Guide.*

821. A water walk by Villa d'Este. New York, St. Martin's Press [1959] 96 p.
59–15274    PS3513.A7217W3
Poems.

822. Country without maps. New York, Macmillan [1964] 82 p.
64–22600    PS3513.A7217C6
Poems.

823. ALLEN GINSBERG, 1926–

Ginsberg has been considered the leading poet of the beat generation. In a first prophetic volume entitled *Howl, and Other Poems* (1956), he used loosely structured lines, mystical obscurity, and a vocabulary sometimes selected for its shock value to discuss drug addiction, sex, jazz, alcohol, suicide, and materialism in American life. He has continued writing and publishing, especially in radical magazines, and has become widely known for his nonconformist views as well as for his poetry.

824. Howl, and other poems. San Francisco, City Lights Pocket Bookshop [1956] 44 p. (The Pocket poets series, No. 4)

56–8587 PS3513.I74H6

825. Kaddish, and other poems, 1958-1960. [San Francisco] City Lights Books [1961] 100 p. (The Pocket poets series, no. 14)

60–14775 PS3513.I74K3

826. Empty mirror, early poems. Introduction by William Carlos Williams. [New York] Totem Press [1961] 47 p.

61–14983 PS3513.I74E5

827. Reality sandwiches, 1953-60. [San Francisco] City Lights Books; [distributed by Paper Editions Corp., 1963] 98 p. (The Pocket poets series, no. 18) 63–12219 PS3513.I74R4

828. HERBERT GOLD, 1924–

Gold has gained widespread critical acclaim for his novels, short stories, and essays dealing with modern American life. In his first novel, *Birth of a Hero* (1951), Gold experimented with a stream-of-consciousness technique. His second novel, *The Prospect Before Us* (1954), exhibits his skill with colorful, colloquial language. In general, his writing has tended to emphasize theme and feeling over plot and structure.

829. The man who was not with it. Boston, Little, Brown [1956] 314 p.

56–5623 PZ4.G618Man

A novel.

830. The optimist, a novel. Boston, Little, Brown [1959] 395 p. 59–6475 PZ4.G618Op

831. Love & like. New York, Dial Press, 1960. 307 p. 60–8397 PZ4.G618Lo

Short stories.

CONTENTS.—The heart of the artichoke.—Susanna at the beach.—A celebration for Joe.—The burglars and the boy.—Encounter in Haiti.—Ti-Moune.—Paris and Cleveland are voyages.—Aristotle and the hired thugs.—The panic button.—Sello.—What's become of your creature?—Love and like.—A tale of two husbands.—Jim the man.—Postface: An aftermath about these stories.

832. Therefore be bold, a novel. New York, Dial Press, 1960. 256 p. 60–13431 PZ4.G618Th

833. The age of happy problems. New York, Dial Press, 1962. 238 p. 62–16333 E169.1.G58

Essays.

834. Salt, a novel. New York, Dial Press, 1963. 318 p. 63–10553 PZ4.G618Sal

835. WILLIAM GOYEN, 1915–

No. 1984 in 1960 *Guide*.

836. The faces of blood kindred, a novella and ten stories. [New York] Random House [1960] 167 p. 60–12124 PZ3.G7484Fac

837. The fair sister, a novel. Garden City, N. Y., Doubleday, 1963. 104 p.

63–17274 PZ3.G7484Fai

838. LILLIAN FLORENCE HELLMAN, 1905–

No. 1988 in 1960 *Guide*.

839. Toys in the attic, a new play. New York, Random House [1960] 116 p. illus.

60–12144 PS3515.E343T6

840. My mother, my father and me. Based on Burt Blechman's novel How much? New York, Random House [1963] 98 p. illus.

63–20244 PS3515.E343M9

A play.

841. JOHN RICHARD HERSEY, 1914–

No. 1992 in 1960 *Guide*.

842. A single pebble. New York, Knopf, 1956. 181 p. 56–7209 PZ3.H4385Si

A novel.

843. The war lover. New York, Knopf, 1959. 404 p. 59–13177 PZ3.H4385War

A novel.

844. The child buyer; a novel in the form of hearings before the Standing Committee on Education, Welfare, & Public Morality of a certain State Senate, investigating the conspiracy of Mr. Wissey Jones, with others, to purchase a male child. New York, Knopf, 1960. 257 p.

60–13850 PZ3.H4385Ch

845. Here to stay. New York, Knopf, 1963 [c1962] 335 p. 63–9123 G525.H43 1963

A selection of previously published articles.

846. White lotus. New York, Knopf, 1965. 683 p.      65–11104   PZ3.H4385Wh
A novel.

847. WILLIAM MOTTER INGE, 1913–

No. 1995 in 1960 *Guide.*

848. The dark at the top of the stairs, a new play. With an introduction by Tennessee Williams. New York, Random House [1958]  108 p.  illus.
58–8057   PS3517.N265D3

849. A loss of roses, a new play.  With a foreword by the author.  New York, Random House [1960]  127 p.  illus.  60–8376   PS3517.N265L6

850. Splendor in the grass, a screenplay.  New York, Bantam Books [1961]  121 p.  (A Bantam book, J2204)  61–65785   PS3517.N265S6

851. Summer brave, and eleven short plays.  New York, Random House [1962]  299 p.
62–12730   PS3517.N265P5   1962
The lead play in this volume is the rewritten version of the author's *Picnic,* no. 1997 in the 1960 *Guide.*

852. Natural affection.  New York, Random House [1963]  115 p.
63–16855   PS3517.N265N3
A play.

853. RANDALL JARRELL, 1914–1965

No. 1999 in 1960 *Guide.*

854. The woman at the Washington Zoo, poems & translations.  New York, Atheneum, 1960. 65 p.      60–11039   PS3519.A86W6

855. A sad heart at the supermarket, essays & fables.  New York, Atheneum, 1962.  211 p.
62–11681   PS3519.A86S3

856. Selected poems, including The woman at the Washington Zoo.  New York, Atheneum, 1964.  xxii, 205, vii–viii, 65 p.  (Atheneum paperbacks, 66)      64–54618   PS3519.A86A6   1964

857. The lost world.  New York, Macmillan [ᶜ1965]  69 p.  64–20736   PS3519.A86L63
Poems.

858. JAMES JONES, 1921–

No. 2003 in 1960 *Guide.*

859. The pistol.  New York, Scribner [1959, ᶜ1958]  158 p.      59–5785   PZ4.J77Pi
A novel.

860. The thin red line.  New York, Scribner [1962]  495 p.  illus.
62–12099   PZ4.J77Th
A novel.

861. JOHN ("JACK") KEROUAC, 1922–

Kerouac's fiction has taken the form of a series of autobiographical novels and reminiscences. His first work, *The Town & the City* (1950), is the story of a Massachusetts family during the period from 1910 through the years of World War II. Additional episodes from his youth form the basis for *Doctor Sax* (1959) and *Visions of Gerard* (1963).  American beat life is portrayed in his most famous work, *On the Road* (1957), an episodic novel about the aimless wanderings of an author. Later works about the beat generation, a term Kerouac is credited with coining, are *The Dharma Bums* (1958), *The Subterraneans* (1958), *Big Sur* (1962), and *Desolation Angels* (1965).

862. On the road.  New York, Viking Press, 1957. 310 p.      57–9425   PZ3.K4596On
A novel.

863. The Dharma bums.  New York, Viking Press, 1958.  244 p.
58–11734   PZ3.K4596Dh
A novel of the beat generation's search for a state of mind approximating the Buddhist concept of Dharma.

864. The subterraneans.  New York, Grove Press [1958]  111 p.  (Evergreen books, E–99)
58–6703   PZ3.K4596Su
A novel.

865. Mexico City blues.  New York, Grove Press [1959]  244 p.  59–12222  PS3521.E735M4
Poems of a "jazz poet."

866. Doctor Sax; Faust part three.  New York, Grove Press [1959]  245 p.
59–9806   PZ3.K4596Do
A novel.

867. Excerpts from Visions of Cody.  [New York, New Directions, 1959, ᶜ1960]  128 p.
60–4490   PZ3.K4596Ex
A character study of the renamed hero of *On the Road.*

868. Big Sur. New York, Farrar, Straus & Cudahy [1962] 241 p.
62–14957 PZ3.K4596Bi
A novel.

869. Visions of Gerard. New York, Farrar, Straus [1963] 151 p. illus.
63–16472 PZ3.K4596Vi 3
A novel.

870. Desolation angels, a novel. Introduction by Seymour Krim. New York, Coward-McCann [1965] xxviii, 366 p.
65–17524 PZ3.K4596De

871. ROBERT LOWELL, 1917–
No. 2007 in 1960 Guide.

872. Life studies. New York, Farrar, Straus, & Cudahy [1959] 90 p.
59–9174 PS3523.O89L5
Verse and prose.

873. Imitations. [New York, Noonday Press, 1962?] 149 p. (Noonday 233)
62–52845 PS3523.O89I4
Poems.

874. For the Union dead. New York, Farrar, Straus & Giroux [1964] 72 p.
64–21495 PS3523.O89F6
Poems.

875. The Old Glory. New York, Farrar, Straus & Giroux [1965] xix, 193 p. illus.
65–24026 PS3523.O89O4
"Theater trilogy . . . based on stories by Hawthorne and a novella by Melville."
CONTENTS.—Introduction, by Robert Brustein.—Director's note, by Jonathan Miller.—Endecott and the red cross.—My kinsman, Major Molineux.—Benito Cereno.

876. Mazzaro, Jerome. The poetic themes of Robert Lowell. Ann Arbor, University of Michigan Press [1965] 145 p.
65–20349 PS3523.O89Z77
Bibliography: p. 137–140.

877. ROBERT JAMES COLLAS LOWRY, 1919–
No. 2011 in 1960 Guide.

878. What's left of April. Garden City, N.Y., Doubleday, 1956. 247 p.
56–9399 PZ3.L9564Wh
A novel.

879. New York call girl. Garden City, N.Y., Doubleday, 1958. 237 p.
58–10029 PZ3.L9564Ne
Short stories.

880. MARY THERESE McCARTHY, 1912–
No. 2017 in 1960 Guide.

881. Memories of a Catholic girlhood. New York, Harcourt, Brace [1957] 245 p.
57–8842 PS3525.A1435Z55
Memoirs.

882. The group. New York, Harcourt, Brace & World [1963] 378 p.
63–15316 PZ3.M1272Gs
A novel.

883. Theatre chronicles, 1937–1962. New York, Farrar, Straus [1963] xxi, 248 p.
63–18449 PN2277.N5M22 1963
Most of the selections were originally published in Partisan Review and also in the author's Sights and Spectacles, 1937–1956 (1956).

884. CARSON SMITH McCULLERS, 1917–
No. 2023 in 1960 Guide.

885. The square root of wonderful, a play. Boston, Houghton Mifflin, 1958. 159 p.
58–6501 PS3525.A1772S63

886. Clock without hands. Boston, Houghton Mifflin, 1961. 241 p.
61–10351 PZ3.M13884Cl
A novel.

887. Evans, Oliver W. Carson McCullers; her life and work. London, P. Owen [1965] 220 p.
66–45393 PS3525.A1772Z6 1965
Bibliographical footnotes.

888. NORMAN MAILER, 1923–
No. 2025 in 1960 Guide.

889. Advertisements for myself. New York, Putnam [1959] 532 p.
59–11020 PS3525.A4152Z52
Short stories, articles, and essays, connected by an autobiographical narrative.

890. BERNARD MALAMUD, 1914–

In much of his fiction Malamud has drawn heavily upon his familiarity with Jewish culture, traditions, and folkways in America. The social implications of his work are by no means limited to a single ethnic group, however. His first novel, *The Natural,* was published in 1952. The critical response to this comic treatment of a baseball hero's attempt to achieve the American dream was mixed. He received the 1959 National Book Award for *The Magic Barrel* (1958), a volume of short stories, and has since won other prizes as well as popular acclaim for his novels and short stories.

891. The assistant, a novel. New York, Farrar, Straus & Cudahy [1957] 246 p.
57–7397　PZ4.M237As

892. The magic barrel. New York, Farrar, Straus & Cudahy [1958] 214 p.
58–6841　PZ4.M237Mag
Short stories.
CONTENTS.—The first seven years.—The mourners.—The girl of my dreams.—Angel Levine.—Behold the key.—Take pity.—The prison.—The lady of the lake.—A summer's reading.—The bill.—The last Mohican.—The loan.—The magic barrel.

893. A new life. New York, Farrar, Straus & Cudahy [1961] 367 p.
61–11416　PZ4.M237Ne
A novel.

894. Idiots first. New York, Farrar, Straus [1963] 212 p.　63–19562　PZ4.M237Id
Short stories and a scene from a play.
CONTENTS.—Idiots first.—Black is my favorite color.—Still life.—The death of me.—A choice of profession.—Life is better than death.—The Jewbird.—Naked nude.—The cost of living.—The maid's shoes.—Suppose a wedding (a scene of a play).—The German refugee.

895. WILLIAM KEEPERS MAXWELL, 1908–

No. 2029 in 1960 *Guide.*

896. The château. New York, Knopf, 1961. 401 p.　61–7125　PZ3.M4518Ch
A novel.

897. THOMAS MERTON, 1915–

No. 2034 in 1960 *Guide.*

898. The strange islands, poems. [New York, New Directions, 1957] 102 p.
57–8600　PS3525.E7174S8

899. Secular journal. New York, Farrar, Straus & Cudahy [1959] 270 p.
59–6588　BX4705.M542A28
A previously unpublished journal written by Merton before he became a Trappist monk.

900. Disputed questions. New York, Farrar, Straus & Cudahy [1960] 297 p.
60–12636　BX891.M45
Essays.

901. The behavior of Titans. [New York] New Directions [1961] 106 p.
60–10879　PS3525.E7174B4
Meditations.

902. New seeds of contemplation. [Norfolk, Conn.] New Directions [1962, ᶜ1961] 297 p.　61–17869　BX2350.2.M46
A revised edition of no. 2038 in the 1960 *Guide.*

903. A Thomas Merton reader. Edited by Thomas P. McDonnell. New York, Harcourt, Brace & World [1962] 553 p.
62–16737　PS3525.E7174A6　1962

904. Emblems of a season of fury. [Norfolk, Conn., J. Laughlin, 1963] 149 p. (A New Directions paperbook, no. 140)
63–18635　PS3525.E7174E4
Poems.

905. Seeds of destruction. New York, Farrar, Straus & Giroux [1965, ᶜ1964] xvi, 328 p.
64–19595　BT734.2.M4
CONTENTS.—Black revolution: Letters to a white liberal. The legend of Tucker Caliban.—The diaspora: The Christian in world crisis. The Christian in the diaspora. A tribute to Gandhi.—Letters in a time of crisis.

906. The way of Chuang-tzŭ. [New York] New Directions [1965] 159 p.
65–27556　BL1900.C483M4
Bibliography: p. 158.
Free renderings of selections from various translations of the works of Chuang-tzŭ.

907. JAMES ALBERT MICHENER, 1907–

Much of Michener's work has been based upon his studies of the islands in the Pacific. His first book of short stories, *Tales of the South Pacific* (1947), won the Pulitzer Prize for fiction in

1948. A series of novels followed. Michener described *Return to Paradise* (1951) as "half fiction, half hard reporting," *The Bridges at Toko-ri* (1953) as "an intense, bitterly controlled novel," and *Sayonara* (1954), as "a novella in an antique style." His epic work, *Hawaii* (1959), is a saga about the island complex and its inhabitants from geological beginnings to the present. In recent years, Michener has expanded his scope to include the Near and Middle East.

908. Hawaii. New York, Random House [1959] 937 p.                59–10815   PZ3.M583Haw

909. Caravans, a novel. New York, Random House [1963]  341 p.
63–16152   PZ3.M583Car 2
Set in Afghanistan.

910. The source, a novel. New York, Random House [1965]  909 p.
65–11255   PZ3.M583So
Set in Israel.

911. ARTHUR MILLER, 1915–

No. 2043 in 1960 *Guide.*

912. A view from the bridge, a play in two acts. With a new introduction. New York, Viking Press [1960]  86 p. (Compass books, C73)
60–4782   PS3525.I5156V5   1960
A revised and enlarged edition of the title play in no. 2049 in the 1960 *Guide.*

913. The misfits. New York, Viking Press [1961]  132 p.    61–6089   PZ3.M61224Mi
A "story conceived as a film." An earlier version appeared as a short story in *Esquire.*

914. After the fall, a play. [Rev. final stage version] New York, Viking Press [1964] 114 p.        66–1903   PS3525.I5156A66   1964a

915. Incident at Vichy, a play. New World, Viking Press [1965]  70 p.
65–12025   PS3525.I5156I5

916. Huftel, Sheila. Arthur Miller: the burning glass. New York, Citadel Press [1965] 256 p.        65–15492   PS3525.I5156Z7
A critical account of Miller's plays.

917. Welland, Dennis S. R. Arthur Miller. New York, Grove Press [1961]  124 p. (Ever-green pilot books, EP11)
61–12358   PS3525.I5156Z95   1961
Bibliography: p. 123–124.
A brief biography with criticism.

918. WRIGHT MORRIS, 1910–

No. 2052 in 1960 *Guide.*

919. The field of vision. New York, Harcourt, Brace [1956]  251 p.
56–8525   PZ3.M8346Fi
A novel.

920. Love among the cannibals. New York, Harcourt, Brace [1957]  253 p.
57–10060   PZ3.M8346Lo
A novel.

921. Ceremony in Lone Tree. New York, Atheneum, 1960.  304 p.
60–7775   PZ3.M8346Ce
A novel.

922. What a way to go. New York, Atheneum, 1962.  310 p.    62–17278   PZ3.M8346Wh
A novel.

923. One day. New York, Atheneum, 1965. 433 p.        65–12403   PZ3.M8346On
A novel.

924. Madden, David. Wright Morris. New York, Twayne Publishers [1965, °1964]  191 p. (Twayne's United States authors series, 71)
64–20721   PS3525.O7475Z7
Bibliographical notes: p. 172–176. Bibliography: p. 177–184.

925. VLADIMIR VLADIMIROVICH NABO-KOV, 1899–

Nabokov left Russia in 1919, acquired his higher education in England, resided at various times in Berlin and Paris, and came to the United States in 1940. His early works were written in Russian. His first novel in English, *The Real Life of Sebastian Knight* (1941), is the story of a Russian émigré in Paris. Nabokov taught in various universities while continuing to publish works such as *Bend Sinister* (1947), a novel; *Conclusive Evidence* (1951), an autobiography (entitled *Speak, Memory* in England); and *Poems 1929–1951* (1952). His novel *Lolita,* first published in Paris in 1955, became an overwhelming success. In all his works—novels, short stories, poems, translations, biography, and autobiography—Nabokov has displayed unusual skill in the creative use of language. His compositional acrostics represent a delightful challenge to many of his readers.

926. Pnin. Garden City, N.Y., Doubleday, 1957.
191 p.                    57–6299  PZ3.N121Pn
A novel.

927. Lolita. New York, Putnam [1958, ᶜ1955]
319 p.          58–10755  PZ3.N121Lo  2
A novel.

928. Nabokov's dozen, a collection of thirteen
stories. Garden City, N. Y., Doubleday, 1958.
214 p.              58–10032  PZ3.N121Nab
Includes those published in *Nine Stories* (New
York, New Directions, 1947. 126 p.).

929. Invitation to a beheading. Translated by
Dmitri Nabokov in collaboration with the
author. New York, Putnam [1959] 223 p.
                    59–11024  PZ3.N121In
A novel originally written in Russian in 1938,
translated by the author's son.

930. Poems. Drawings by Robin Jacques. Garden City, N. Y., Doubleday, 1959. 43 p.
                    59–10681  PS3527.A15P6

931. Pale fire, a novel. New York, Putnam
[1962] 315 p.          62–7351  PZ3.N121Pal

932. The gift, a novel. Translated from the Russian by Michael Scammell with the collaboration of the author. New York, Putnam [1963]
378 p.              63–9667  PZ3.N121Gi
The first Russian version appeared in *Sovre-
mennyia zapiski, annales contemporaines* (Paris),
in 1935–36.

933. The defense, a novel. Translated by Michael
Scammell in collaboration with the author.
New York [1964] 256 p.
                    64–13017  PZ3.N121Dc
Originally written in Russian in 1930.

934. HOWARD NEMEROV, 1920–

Nemerov is a versatile writer of novels, short
stories, plays, poetry, and criticism. His novels—
*The Melodramatists* (1949), *Federigo; or, The
Power of Love* (1954), and *The Homecoming
Game* (1957)—have satirized various aspects of life
in America. In his poems, on the other hand, he
treats such universal themes as life and death, the
mind and science, nature and man, and myth and
reality. Early volumes of his poetry include *The
Image and the Law* (1947), *Guide to the Ruins*
(1950), and *The Salt Garden* (1955).

935. The homecoming game, a novel. New York,
Simon & Schuster, 1957. 246 p.
                    57–5679  PS3527.E5H6

936. Mirrors & windows, poems. [Chicago]
University of Chicago Press, 1958. 101 p.
                    58–5683  PS3527.E5M5

937. A commodity of dreams & other stories. New
York, Simon & Schuster, 1959. 245 p.
                    59–6015  PZ3.N343Co

938. New & selected poems. [Chicago] University of Chicago Press, 1960. 115 p.
                    60–14236  PS3527.E5A17  1960

939. The next room of the dream, poems and two
plays. [Chicago] University of Chicago
Press [1962] 143 p.   62–22328  PS3527.E5N4

940. Poetry and fiction, essays. New Brunswick,
N. J., Rutgers University Press [ᶜ1963]
381 p.              63–16301  PN1136.N4
Critical lectures and book reviews.

941. JOHN FREDERICK NIMS, 1913–
No. 2060 in 1960 *Guide.*

942. Knowledge of the evening: poems, 1950–
1960. New Brunswick, N. J., Rutgers University Press [1960] 96 p.
                    60–11524  PS3527.I863K6

943. FLANNERY O'CONNOR, 1925–1964

Miss O'Connor's work is admired for its
acute sense of irony, insight, and comic nuance.
Her Southern gothic tales of the macabre and grotesque, although seldom pleasant, are greatly revealing of character and setting. An overtone of
religious conflict permeates her fiction. *Wise Blood,*
which first appeared in 1952, is described in the
author's preface to the second edition as "a comic
novel about a Christian *malgré lui,* and as such,
very serious, for all comic novels that are any good
must be about matters of life and death." Miss
O'Connor's 1955 collection of short stories, *A Good
Man Is Hard To Find,* was published in London
under the title *The Artificial Nigger* (1957).

944. The violent bear it away. New York, Farrar,
Straus & Cudahy [1960] 243 p.
                    60–6752  PZ4.O183Vi
A novel.

945. Wise blood. [2d ed.] New York, Farrar,
Straus & Cudahy [1962] 232 p.
                    62–5776  PZ4.O183Wi  5

946. Everything that rises must converge. New York, Farrar, Straus & Giroux [1965] xxxiv, 269 p.                65–13726 PZ4.O183Ev
A memoir by Robert Fitzgerald introduces this collection of short stories.

947. CLIFFORD ODETS, 1906–1963
No. 2063 in 1960 *Guide.*

948. Shuman, Robert Baird. Clifford Odets. New York, Twayne Publishers [c1962] 160 p. (Twayne's United States authors series, 30)
                62–19474 PS3529.D46Z87
Bibliographical notes: p. 149–151. Bibliography: p. 152–155.

949. JOHN HENRY O'HARA, 1905–
No. 2069 in 1960 *Guide.*

950. A family party. New York, Random House [1956] 64 p.    56–10932 PZ3.O3677Fam
A short story.

951. From the terrace, a novel. New York, Random House [1958] 897 p.
                58–12336 PZ3.O3677Fr

952. Ourselves to know, a novel. New York, Random House [1960] 408 p.
                60–5528 PZ3.O3677Ou

953. Sermons and soda-water. New York, Random House [1960] 3 v.
                60–16572 PZ3.O3677Sg
Three related novellas.
CONTENTS.—v. 1. The girl on the baggage truck. —v. 2. Imagine kissing Pete.—v. 3. We're friends again.

954. Assembly. New York, Random House [1961] 429 p.    61–12172 PZ3.O3677As
Short stories.

955. Five plays. New York, Random House [1961] xiv, 473 p.
                61–14888 PS3529.H29A19 1961
CONTENTS.—The farmers hotel.—The searching sun.—The champagne pool.—Veronique.—The way it was.

956. The Cape Cod lighter. New York, Random House [1962] 425 p.
                62–8455 PZ3.O3677Cap
Short stories.

957. Elizabeth Appleton, a novel. New York, Random House [1963] 310 p.
                63–14140 PZ3.O3677El

958. The hat on the bed. New York, Random House [1963] 405 p.
                63–20247 PZ3.O3677Hat
Stories.

959. The horse knows the way. New York, Random House [1964] 429 p.
                64–7751 PZ3.O3677Hr
Twenty-eight short stories.

960. KENNETH PATCHEN, 1911–
No. 2079 in 1960 *Guide.*

961. When we were here together. [New York] New Directions [1957] 112 p.
                57–13081 PS3531.A764W5
Poems.

962. Selected poems. Enl. ed. [New York] New Directions [1958, c1957] 145 p. illus. (The New classics series)
                58–590 PS3531.A764A6 1958
A revised and enlarged edition of no. 2083 in the 1960 *Guide.*

963. FREDERIC PROKOSCH, 1908–
No. 2087 in 1960 *Guide.*

964. A ballad of love. New York, Farrar, Straus & Cudahy [1960] 311 p.
                60–12517 PZ3.P9424Bal
A novel.

965. The seven sisters. New York, Farrar, Straus & Cudahy [1962] 405 p.
                62–18414 PZ3.P9424Sc
A novel.

966. The dark dancer. New York, Farrar, Straus [1964] 305 p.
                64–11268 PZ3.P9424Dar
A novel.

967. Squires, James Radcliffe. Frederic Prokosch. New York, Twayne Publishers [1964] 158 p. (Twayne's United States authors series, 61)
                64–13957 PS3531.R78Z87
Bibliographical notes: p. 148–150. Bibliography: p. 151–152.

968. KENNETH REXROTH, 1905–
No. 2098 in 1960 *Guide.*

969. In defense of the earth. [New York] New Directions [1956] 93 p.
56–13352  PS3535.T923I48
Poems.

970. Natural numbers; new and selected poems. [Norfolk, Conn.] New Directions, 1963. 119 p.      63–18636  PS3535.E923A17  1963

971. THEODORE ROETHKE, 1908–1963

No. 2103 in 1960 *Guide.*

972. Words for the wind, the collected verse. Garden City, N. Y., Doubleday, 1958. 212 p.
58–10039  PS3535.O39W6  1958

973. The far field. Garden City, N. Y., Doubleday, 1964. 95 p. 64–12105  PS3535.O39F3
Poems.

974. On the poet and his craft; selected prose. Edited with an introduction by Ralph J. Mills, Jr. Seattle, University of Washington Press, 1965. xvi, 154 p.      65–22387  PN1064.R6

975. Stein, Arnold S., *ed.* Theodore Roethke; essays on the poetry. Seattle, University of Washington Press [1965]  xx, 199 p.
65–23914  PS3535.O39Z87

976. PHILIP MILTON ROTH, 1933–

Roth received a National Book Award in 1960 for his first book, *Goodbye, Columbus.* Containing five short stories as well as the title novella, this collection conveys Roth's sharp sense of the pathos and humor in Jewish middle-class life in America. Roth has since become well known for his distinctive portrayals of this milieu.

977. Goodbye, Columbus, and five short stories. Boston, Houghton Mifflin, 1959. 298 p.
59–7579  PZ4.R8454Go

978. Letting go. New York, Random House [1962] 630 p.  62–8472  PZ4.R8454Le  2
A novel.

979. MURIEL RUKEYSER, 1913–

No. 2105 in 1960 *Guide.*

980. One life. New York, Simon & Schuster, 1957. 330 p.      57–5680  E748.W7R8
An imaginative work about Wendell Willkie, containing a blend of stories, poems, documents, and newspaper quotations.

981. Body of waking. New York, Harper [1958] 118 p.      57–11788  PS3535.U4B6
Poems.

982. Waterlily fire: poems, 1935–1962. New York, Macmillan, 1962. 200 p.
62–13595  PS3535.U4W33

983. JEROME DAVID SALINGER, 1919–

No. 2107 in 1960 *Guide.*

984. Franny and Zooey. Boston, Little, Brown [1961] 201 p.  61–14542  PZ4.S165Fr  3
Two stories previously published in *The New Yorker.*

985. Raise high the roof beam, carpenters, and Seymour—an introduction. Boston, Little, Brown [1963, ᶜ1959] 248 p.
63–8969  PZ4.S165Rai  5
Two stories previously published in *The New Yorker.*

986. French, Warren G.  J. D. Salinger. New York, Twayne Publishers [1963]  191 p. (Twayne's United States authors series, 40)
63–10957  PS3537.A426Z6
Bibliographical notes: p. 171–178. Bibliography: p. 179–186.

987. Grunwald, Henry A., *ed.* Salinger; a critical and personal portrait. New York, Harper [1962] 287 p.  62–11222  PS3537.A426Z62

988. Laser, Marvin, *and* Norman Fruman, *eds.* Studies in J. D. Salinger: reviews, essays, and critiques of The catcher in the rye, and other fiction. New York, Odyssey Press [1963]  272 p.
63–14023  PS3537.A426Z7
Includes bibliography.

989. WILLIAM SAROYAN, 1908–

No. 2110 in 1960 *Guide.*

990. The whole voyald, and other stories. Boston, Little, Brown [1956]  243 p. (An Atlantic Monthly Press book)  56–10653  PZ3.S246Wh

991. Mama, I love you. Boston, Little, Brown [1956]  245 p.  56–7051  PZ3.S246Mam
A novel.

992. Papa, you're crazy. Boston, Little, Brown [1957]  165 p.  57–7840  PZ3.S246Pap
A novel.

993. The cave dwellers, a play. New York, Putnam [1958] 187 p.
58–8902  PS3537.A826C3

994. Here comes, there goes, you know who. New York, Simon & Schuster, 1961. 273 p.
61–17926  PS3537.A826Z53
Autobiography.

995. After thirty years: the daring young man on the flying trapeze. New York, Harcourt, Brace & World [1964] 312 p.
64–7446  PZ3.S246Af
Saroyan's reminiscences of his life since the 1930's, together with a reprint of *The Daring Young Man on the Flying Trapeze and Other Stories.*

996. One day in the afternoon of the world. New York, Harcourt, Brace & World [1964] 245 p.
64–20194  PZ3.S246On
A novel.

997. MAY SARTON, 1912–
No. 2123 in 1960 *Guide.*

998. The birth of a grandfather. New York, Rinehart [1957] 277 p.
57–9630  PZ3.S249Bi
A novel.

999. In time like air, poems. New York, Rinehart [1958] 80 p.   58–5012  PS3537.A832I45

1000. I knew a phoenix; sketches for an autobiography. New York, Rinehart [1959] 222 p.
59–6569  PS3537.A832Z52

1001. Cloud, stone, sun, vine: poems, selected and new. New York, Norton [1961] 144 p.
61–13040  PS3537.A832C55

1002. The small room, a novel. New York, Norton [1961] 249 p.
61–11347  PZ3.S249Sm

1003. Mrs. Stevens hears the mermaids singing, a novel. New York, Norton [1965] 220 p.
65–18016  PZ3.S249Mi

1004. DELMORE SCHWARTZ, 1913–
No. 2133 in 1960 *Guide.*

1005. Summer knowledge: new and selected poems, 1938–1958. Garden City, N. Y., Doubleday, 1959. 240 p.
59–10689  PS3537.C79S8

1006. Successful love, and other stories. New York, Corinth Books, 1961. 242 p.
61–14981  PZ3.S405Su

1007. KARL JAY SHAPIRO, 1913–
No. 2139 in 1960 *Guide.*

1008. In defense of ignorance. New York, Random House [1960] 338 p.
60–5607  PS3537.H27I5
Essays in literary criticism.

1009. The bourgeois poet. New York, Random House [1964] 120 p.
64–10356  PS3537.H27B6
An autobiographical prose poem.

1010. IRWIN SHAW, 1913–
No. 2145 in 1960 *Guide.*

1011. Lucy Crown, a novel. New York, Random House [1956] 339 p.
55–8168  PZ3.S5357Lu

1012. Tip on a dead jockey, and other stories. New York, Random House [1957] 242 p.
57–5382  PZ3.S5357Ti

1013. Two weeks in another town. New York, Random House [1960] 372 p.
60–5560  PZ3.S5357Tw
A novel.

1014. Voices of a summer day. New York, Distributed by the Dial Press [1965] 223 p.
65–13414  PZ3.S5357Vo
A novel.

1015. ISAAC BASHEVIS SINGER, 1904–
Singer was educated at a rabbinical school in Warsaw, Poland. He came to the United States in 1935. His novels and short stories, written in Yiddish, convey a picture of the vanished world of Polish Jewry. His first work to be translated into English was *The Family Moskat* (1950), a conventional narrative about a family of Polish Jews during the period from the late 19th century until World War II. In 1955 he published a translation of *Satan in Goray,* a novel written in 1935. This work introduced his American audience to the elements of fantasy, irrationality, and the grotesque that pervade much of Singer's fiction.

1016. Gimpel the fool, and other stories. New York, Noonday Press [c1957] 205 p.
58–1234  PZ3.S61657Gi
Translated by Saul Bellow and others.

1017. The magician of Lublin. Translated from the Yiddish by Elaine Gottlieb and Joseph Singer. New York, Noonday Press [1960] 246 p.
60–10006 · PZ3.S61657Mag
A novel.

1018. The Spinoza of Market Street. New York, Farrar, Straus & Cudahy [1961] 214 p.
61–13676 PZ3.S61657Sp 3
Short stories, translated by Martha Glicklich and others.

1019. The slave, a novel. Translated from the Yiddish by the author and Cecil Hemley. New York, Farrar, Straus & Cudahy [1962] 311 p.
62–10501 PZ3.S61657Sl

1020. Short Friday, and other stories. New York, Farrar, Straus & Giroux [1964] 243 p.
64–23122 PZ3.S61657Sh
Translated by Joseph Singer and Roger Klein.

1021. HARRY ALLEN SMITH, 1907–
No. 2149 in 1960 *Guide*.

1022. The pig in the barber shop. Boston, Little, Brown [1958] 316 p.
58–11441 F1216.S57
A humorous account of a journey in Mexico.

1023. Let the crabgrass grow; H. Allen Smith's suburban almanac. Illustrated by Donald Madden. [New York] B. Geis Associates; distributed by Random House [1960] 256 p.
60–10125 PS3537.M4655L4
Anecdotes of suburban life.

1024. How to write without knowing nothing; a book largely concerned with the use and misuse of language at home and abroad. Boston, Little, Brown [1961] 179 p.
61–12813 PN6162.S65733
Essays.

1025. To hell in a handbasket. Garden City, N. Y., Doubleday, 1962. 341 p. illus.
62–7680 PN4874.S56A26
Autobiography.

1026. A short history of fingers, and other state papers. Illustrated by Leo Hershfield. Boston, Little, Brown [1963] 301 p.
63—17425 PS3537.M4655S5
A collection of articles.

1027. JEAN STAFFORD, 1915–
No. 2156 in 1960 *Guide*.

1028. Bad characters. New York, Farrar, Straus [1964] 276 p.   64–23037 PZ3.S7783Bad
Short stories.

1029. WALLACE EARLE STEGNER, 1909–
No. 2161 in 1960 *Guide*.

1030. The city of the living, and other stories. Boston, Houghton Mifflin, 1956. 206 p.
56–12088 PZ3.S818Ci

1031. A shooting star. New York, Viking Press, 1961. 433 p.   61–7037 PZ3.S818Sh
A novel.

1032. JESSE STUART, 1907–
No. 2166 in 1960 *Guide*.

1033. The year of my rebirth. Illustrated by Barry Martin. New York, McGraw-Hill [1956] 342 p.   56–12275 RC682.S8
A journal kept while recovering from a heart attack.

1034. Plowshare in heaven, stories. New York, McGraw-Hill [1958] 273 p. illus.
58–11194 PZ3.S9306Pl

1035. God's oddling; the story of Mick Stuart, my father. New York, McGraw-Hill [1960] 266 p.   60–15006 PS3537.T92516G6
Biographical stories.

1036. Hold April, new poems. Woodcuts by Walter Ferro. New York, McGraw-Hill [1962] 114 p.   61–18440 PS3537.T92516H6 1962

1037. Daughter of the legend. New York, McGraw-Hill [1965] 249 p.
65–25553 PZ3.S9306Dau
A novel.

1038. WILLIAM STYRON, 1925–
No. 2174 in 1960 *Guide*.

1039. Set this house on fire. New York, Random House [1960] 507 p.
60–5568 PZ4.S938Se
A novel.

1040. PETER HILLSMAN TAYLOR, 1917–
No. 2176 in 1960 *Guide*.

1041. Tennessee Day in St. Louis, a comedy. New York, Random House [1957] 177 p.
57–6463   PS3539.A9633T4
A play.

1042. Happy families are all alike, a collection of stories. New York, McDowell, Obolensky [1959] 305 p.   59–15376   PZ3.T21767Hap

1043. Miss Leonora when last seen, and fifteen other stories. New York, I. Obolensky [ᶜ1963] 398 p.   63–20872   PZ3.T21767Mi

1044. MELVIN BEAUNORUS TOLSON, 1900–

In an introduction to Tolson's *Harlem Gallery,* Karl Shapiro states: "A great poet has been living in our midst for decades and is almost totally unknown, even by the literati, even by poets." Tolson was born in Missouri, won a national poetry competition of the American Negro Exposition at Chicago in 1940, and published his first book of poems, *Rendezvous with America,* in 1944. He was named Poet Laureate of Liberia in 1947 and was commissioned to write the *Libretto for the Republic of Liberia* celebrating that country's centennial. *Poetry* magazine (Chicago) published a section of the poem in 1950; in a preface to the book (1953), Allen Tate expresses his appreciation of Tolson's talent, saying that "there is a great gift for language, a profound historical sense, and a first-rate intelligence at work in this poem from first to last." Tolson received *Poetry* magazine's Bess Hokin prize in 1951 for his poem "E. & O. E."

1045. Harlem gallery. With an introduction by Karl Shapiro. Book 1. The curator. New York, Twayne [1965] 173 p.
64–25063   PS3539.O334H3

1046. JOHN HOYER UPDIKE, 1932–

Since the first appearance of his stories, sketches, and verse in *The New Yorker,* Updike has been hailed as a master stylist and precocious technician. His fiction, which is often set in the small Pennsylvania town of his childhood, displays a special understanding of the sorrows of youth and old age. His novel *The Centaur* (1963) won the 1964 National Book Award.

1047. The carpentered hen, and other tame creatures, poems. New York, Harper [1958] 82 p.   58–6158   PS3541.P47C3

1048. The poorhouse fair. New York, Knopf, 1959 [ᶜ1958] 185 p.
59–5431   PZ4.U64Po
Updike's first novel.

1049. The same door, short stories. New York, Knopf, 1959. 241 p.
59–9776   PZ4.U64Sam

1050. Rabbit, run. New York, Knopf, 1960. 307 p.   60–12552   PZ4.U64Rab
A novel.

1051. Pigeon feathers, and other stories. New York, Knopf, 1962. 278 p.
61–17831   PZ4.U64Pi

1052. The centaur. New York, Knopf, 1963. 302 p.   63–7873   PZ4.U64Ce 2

1053. Telephone poles, and other poems. New York, Knopf, 1963. 83 p.
63–11047   PS3541.P47T4

1054. Of the farm. New York, Knopf, 1965. 173 p.   65–18763   PZ4.U64Of
A novel.

1055. Assorted prose. New York, Knopf, 1965. 326 p.   65–13460   PS3541.P47A16 1965
Collected nonfiction, including parodies, personal reports, and book reviews, most of which originally appeared in *The New Yorker.*

1056. GORE VIDAL, 1925–
No. 2180 in 1960 *Guide.*

1057. A thirsty evil, seven short stories. New York, Zero Press, 1956. 154 p.
56–11329   PZ3.V6668Th

1058. Visit to a small planet, and other television plays. Boston, Little, Brown [1956] 278 p.
57–5030   PS3543.I26V5
The title play of this volume was expanded for theatrical production and published as *Visit to a Small Planet; a Comedy Akin to a Vaudeville* (Boston, Little, Brown [1957] 158 p.).

1059. The best man; a play about politics. Boston, Little, Brown [1960] 168 p. illus.
60–13970   PS3543.I26B4

1060. Rocking the boat. Boston, Little, Brown [1962] 300 p.   62–13912   PS3543.I26R6
Essays.

1061. Julian, a novel. Boston, Little, Brown [1964] 503 p.
64–15048  PZ3.V6668Jw  2
Bibliography: p. 503.

1062. The city and the pillar revised, including an essay: Sex and the law, and An afterword. [Rev. ed.] New York, Dutton, 1965. 249 p.
65–18637  PZ3.V6668Ci  2
A revised edition of a novel mentioned in no. 2180 of the 1960 *Guide*.

1063. Messiah. [Rev. ed.] Boston, Little, Brown [1965] 243 p.
65–17660  PZ3.V6668Me  3
A revised edition of no. 2188 in the 1960 *Guide*.

1064. PETER ROBERT EDWIN VIERECK, 1916–

No. 2189 in 1960 *Guide*.

1065. The persimmon tree, new pastoral and lyrical poems. New York, Scribner [1956] 80 p.
56–10206  PS3543.I325P4

1066. The tree witch, a poem and play (first of all a poem). New York, Scribner [1961] 126 p.
61–7221  PS3543.I325T7  1961
A verse play.

1067. KURT VONNEGUT, 1922–

In his first novel, *Player Piano* (1952), Vonnegut established the science-fiction approach to location and situation which has characterized much of his subsequent work. His fusion of satire with serious morality has appealed to an increasingly wide circle of readers.

1068. The sirens of Titan. Boston, Houghton Mifflin, 1961 [c1959] 319 p.
61–6895  PZ4.V948Si  2
A novel.

1069. Cat's cradle. New York, Holt, Rinehart & Winston [1963] 233 p.
63–10930  PZ3.V948Cat
A novel.

1070. God bless you, Mr. Rosewater; or, Pearls before swine. New York, Holt, Rinehart & Winston [1965] 217 p. 65–16434  PZ4.V948Go
A novel.

1071. ROBERT PENN WARREN, 1905–

No. 2193 in 1960 *Guide*.

1072. Promises: poems 1954–1956. New York, Random House [1957] 84 p.
57–7894  PS3545.A748P7

1073. Selected essays. New York, Random House [1958] 305 p.  58–7674  PS121.W3

1074. The cave. New York, Random House [1959] 403 p.  59–5719  PZ3.W2549Cav
A novel.

1075. All the king's men, a play. New York, Random House [1960] 134 p.
60–8377  PS3545.A748A7  1960
Based on the 1946 novel of the same name, no. 2197 in the 1960 *Guide*.

1076. You, emperors, and others: poems, 1957–1960. New York, Random House [1960] 81 p.
60–12123  PS3545.A748Y6

1077. Wilderness; a tale of the Civil War. New York, Random House [1961] 310 p.
61–6248  PZ3.W2549Wi
A novel.

1078. Flood; a romance of our time. New York, Random House [1964] 440 p.
64–10357  PZ3.W2549Fl
A novel.

1079. Casper, Leonard. Robert Penn Warren: the dark and bloody ground. Seattle, University of Washington Press, 1960. 212 p.
60–14114  PS3545.A748Z65
A critical survey of Warren's novels and poems.

1080. Longley, John L., ed. Robert Penn Warren, a collection of critical essays. [New York] New York University Press, 1965. xix, 259 p.
65–13207  PS3545.A748Z77
Bibliography: p. 247–257.

1081. Strandberg, Victor H. A colder fire; the poetry of Robert Penn Warren. [Lexington] University of Kentucky Press [1965] 292 p.  65–27009  PS3545.A748Z87
Bibliographical references included in "Notes" (p. [283]–285).

1082. EUDORA WELTY, 1909–

No. 2202 in 1960 *Guide*.

1083. Appel, Alfred. A season of dreams; the fiction of Eudora Welty. Baton Rouge,

Louisiana State University, 1965. xvi, 274 p. (Southern literary studies)

65–20298 PS3545.E6Z56

Bibliography: p. 265–267.

1084. Vande Kieft, Ruth M. Eudora Welty. New York, Twayne Publishers [1962] 203 p. (Twayne's United States authors series, 15)

62–10272 PS3545.E6Z9

Bibliographical notes: p. 191–194. Bibliography: p. 195–199.

1085. JESSAMYN WEST, 1907–

No. 2210 in 1960 *Guide.*

1086. South of the Angels. New York, Harcourt, Brace [1960] 564 p.

60–6714 PZ3.W51903So

A novel.

1087. RICHARD PURDY WILBUR, 1921–

No. 2215 in 1960 *Guide.*

1088. Things of this world, poems. New York, Harcourt, Brace [1956] 50 p.

56–6655 PS3545.I32165T5

1089. Advice to a prophet, and other poems. New York, Harcourt, Brace & World [1961] 64 p. 61–15813 PS3545.I32165A7

1090. TENNESSEE WILLIAMS, 1914–

No. 2218 in 1960 *Guide.*

1091. Baby Doll: the script for the film, incorporating the two one-act plays which suggested it: 27 wagons full of cotton [and] The long stay cut short; or, The unsatisfactory supper. [New York] New Directions [1956] 208 p.

56–13347 PS3545.I5365B3 1956

1092. In the winter of cities, poems. [Norfolk, Conn.] New Directions [1956] 117 p.

56–13961 PS3545.I5365A17 1956

1093. Orpheus descending, with Battle of angels; two plays. [New York] New Directions [1958] 238 p. 57–13083 PS3545.I5365O7

1094. Suddenly last summer. [New York] New Directions [1958] 90 p.

58–9512 PS3545.I5365S83

A play.

1095. Sweet birth of youth. [New York] New Directions [1959] 114 p.

59–9492 PS3545.I5365S87

A play.

1096. Period of adjustment; high point over a cavern, a serious comedy. [New York] New Directions [1960] 120 p.

60–53248 PS3545.I5365P4

1097. The night of the iguana. [New York] New Directions, 1962 [ᶜ1961] 128 p.

62–10409 PS3545.I5365N5

A play.

1098. The eccentricities of a nightingale, and Summer and smoke; two plays. [New York, New Directions Pub. Corp., 1964?] 248 p. (A New Directions book)

64–23654 PS3545.I5365E2 1964

1099. The milk train doesn't stop here anymore. [Norfolk, Conn.] New Directions, 1964. 118 p. 63–13641 PS3545.I5365M5 1964

A play.

1100. Falk, Signi L. Tennessee Williams. New York, Twayne Publishers [1962, ᶜ1961] 224 p. (Twayne's United States authors series, 10)

61–15670 PS3545.I5365Z64 1962

Bibliographical notes: p. 191–205. Bibliography: p. 206–221.

1101. Jackson, Esther M. The broken world of Tennessee Williams. Madison, University of Wisconsin Press, 1965. xxiii, 179 p. illus.

64–8489 PS3545.I5365Z7

Works of Tennessee Williams: p. 161–163. Bibliography: p. 165–169.

An Aristotelian analysis which places Williams' major dramas in a perspective with the theater of the Western World.

1102. Tischler, Nancy M. P. Tennessee Williams: rebellious Puritan. New York, Citadel Press [1961] 319 p. 61–16975 PS3545.I5365Z85

A biography, with discussions of Williams' works and summaries of the plots of his major plays.

1103. HERMAN WOUK, 1915–

No. 2229 in 1960 *Guide.*

1104. Nature's way, a comedy in two acts. Garden City, N.Y., Doubleday, 1958. 134 p.

58–8463 PS3545.O98N3

1105. Youngblood Hawke, a novel. Garden City, N.Y., Doubleday, 1962. 783 p.

62–7698   PZ3.W923Yo

1106. Don't stop the carnival. Garden City, N.Y., Doubleday, 1965. 395 p.

64–22324.   PZ3.W923Do

A novel.

1107. RICHARD NATHANIEL WRIGHT, 1908–1960

No. 2232 in 1960 *Guide*.

1108. The long dream, a novel. Garden City, N.Y., Doubleday, 1958. 384 p.

58–12059   PZ3.W9352Lo

1109. Eight men. Cleveland, World Pub. Co. [1961] 250 p.

61–5636   PZ3.W9352Ei

Short stories.

1110. Lawd today. New York, Walker [1963] 189 p.   63–11769   PZ3.W9352Law

A novel.

# II

# Language

Perhaps the most significant trend in recent studies of American English has been the shift away from a normative grammatical approach toward an acceptance of wide variation within standard English. The validity of the traditional Latin-based English grammar is being questioned by those who favor an exposition of the language within the framework of American structural linguistics. The linguists have contended that grammar should be descriptive rather than prescriptive and have included in their analyses "substandard" constructions and "incorrect" words which are in common usage. In so doing, they have encountered opposition from those who consider that a grammar should represent a standard to be followed. The new trend is perhaps most clearly discernible in *Webster's Third New International Dictionary of the English Language* (no. 1114).

## A. Dictionaries

1111. Evans, Bergen, *and* Cornelia Evans. A dictionary of contemporary American usage. New York, Random House [1957] 567 p.
57–5379   PE2835.E84
"Designed for people who speak standard English but are uncertain about some details," this lucid dictionary of current English in the United States comments on grammar, idiomatic expressions, disputed usage, and common errors. The authors' approach is based on the findings of modern linguistic investigation, which reveal wide variations in standard English. Evans and his sister categorize usages with phrases such as "generally preferred," "acceptable in this country," and "nonstandard in the United States." Their preferences are influenced, however, by an admitted prejudice in favor of the forms used by the great writers of English rather than those found only in technical journals. Although *Current American Usage* (New York, Funk & Wagnalls [1962] 290 p.), edited by Margaret M.

Bryant, is narrower in scope and contains fewer entries than *A Dictionary of Contemporary American Usage,* it is based on a similar approach and has citations to sources of quotations and to scholarly studies.

1112. Nicholson, Margaret. A dictionary of American-English usage, based on Fowler's Modern English usage. New York, Oxford University Press, 1957. 671 p.   57–5560   PE2835.N5
Miss Nicholson's dictionary is intended as an adaptation of, not a replacement for, H. W. Fowler's monumental *A Dictionary of Modern English Usage,* first published in 1926. Many of the long articles have been shortened, and entries for words and expressions which occur rarely in American usage have been entirely omitted. New words and idioms that have come into the language since the initial publication of *Modern English Usage* have been added, as well as discussions of differences

66

between American and British spelling and pronunciation not recorded by Fowler.

1113. Thornton, Richard H. An American glossary; being an attempt to illustrate certain Americanisms upon historical principles. With an introduction by Margaret M. Bryant. New York, F. Ungar Pub. Co. [1962] 3 v.

61–13641  PE2835.T6  1962

The separately published parts of no. 2240 in the 1960 Guide are here united in a three-volume set.

1114. Webster's third new international dictionary of the English language, unabridged. A Merriam-Webster. Editor in chief: Philip Babcock Gove and the Merriam-Webster editorial staff. Springfield, Mass., G. & C. Merriam Co. [1961] 56a, 2662 p. illus.  61–65336  PE1625.W36  1961

Both denounced and praised by reviewers for its attitude toward pronunciation and usage, this dictionary marks a significant shift of direction in American lexicography. It assumes that change in language is continuous and normal and that "correctness" can be based only on usage, which itself is continuously changing. Consequently, the editors attempt to describe rather than prescribe current usage and pronunciation and to indicate acceptable variations. The definitions are based chiefly on examples collected since publication of the second edition (see the annotation for no. 2236 in the 1960 Guide) in 1934. In an attempt to provide "precise, sharp defining," the editors have developed a new dictionary style of "completely analytical one-phrase definitions." Various labels—"slang," "substandard," "nonstandard," "dialect"—are used, but the label "colloquial," which appeared in the second edition, has been dropped. Many of the reviews which greeted the arrival of the third edition are collected in *Dictionaries and That Dictionary; a Casebook on the Aims of Lexicographers and the Targets of Reviewers* (Chicago, Scott, Foresman [1962] 273 p.), edited by James H. Sledd and Wilma R. Ebbitt. The most recent edition of *Funk & Wagnalls New Standard Dictionary of the English Language* (New York, Funk & Wagnalls, 1963. 2816 p.) incorporates slight changes that distinguish it from the 1952 edition noted in the discussion of no. 2236 in the 1960 Guide.

## B. Grammars and General Studies

1115. Francis, Winthrop N. The structure of American English. With a chapter on American English dialects by Raven I. McDavid, Jr. New York, Ronald Press Co. [1958] 614 p. illus.

58–5647  PE2811.F67

Bibliography: p. 598–602.

A textbook for a graduate or undergraduate introductory course in the structure of English, particularly American English. Although Francis presents some original material, his stated purpose is to synthesize the work of many other structural linguists in order to bring it together in one volume. An introductory chapter entitled "Language, Languages, and Linguistic Science" is followed by others on phonetics, phonemics, morphemics, grammar, graphics, and the use of linguistics by teachers of English. McDavid contributes a chapter summarizing the work on a projected linguistic atlas of the United States and Canada, to be composed of several regional atlases (see the annotation for no. 1123 in this *Supplement*). Henry A. Gleason's *Linguistics and English Grammar* (New York, Holt, Rinehart & Winston [1965] 519 p.) is designed to interpret linguistics to teachers of English.

1116. Marckwardt, Albert H. American English. New York, Oxford University Press, 1958. 194 p. illus.  58–5374  PE2808.M3

A popular historical account of the development of English in the United States. The first English-speaking colonists tended to preserve words, meanings, and pronunciations long after they had dropped out of use in England. American English moved even further away from British English as it was supplemented by words borrowed from the American Indians, the early explorers, and immigrant groups. In addition, Marckwardt suggests, the vigor, the disregard for convention, and the ingenuity of the frontiersmen were among the factors contributing to the creation of many compound formations ("carpetbagger," "land office") and "mouth-filling" terms ("rambunctious," "catawampus"). The author also discusses the American tendency to glorify the commonplace ("saloon," "opera house"), to extend indiscriminately the use of honorifics ("doctor," "professor," and "honorable"), and to find euphemisms for delicate topics ("comfort station," "unmentionables," and "mortician").

1117. Mencken, Henry L. The American language; an inquiry into the development of English in the United States. The 4th ed. and the two supplements, abridged, with annotations and new materials, by Raven I. McDavid, Jr., with the assistance of David W. Maurer. New York, Knopf, 1963. xxv, 777, cxxiv p. 63–13628 PE2808.M43
Bibliographical footnotes.

A one-volume abridgement, condensation, and updating of Mencken's three volumes (no. 2248 in the 1960 *Guide*). Most of the editorial commentary and new material is enclosed in brackets. *Aspects of American English* (New York, Harcourt, Brace & World [1963] 272 p. Harbrace sourcebooks), compiled by Elizabeth M. Kerr and Ralph M. Aderman, is a collection of essays on the historical, regional, literary, colloquial, and social aspects of American English by authorities in these fields.

1118. Myers, Louis M. Guide to American English. 3d ed. Englewood Cliffs, N.J., Prentice-Hall, 1962. 446 p.
63–9823 PE1111.M954 1962
A thoroughly updated edition of no. 2249 in the 1960 *Guide*. The major revisions were made in the second edition, published in 1959.

1119. Roberts, Paul. Understanding English. New York, Harper [1958] xvii, 508 p. illus. 58–5110 PE1111.R736
Offered as a college text for freshman composition, this book also serves as an introduction to the analysis of American English. Roberts' point of view is that of linguistic science, and his writing is informal and frequently humorous. Among the various topics discussed are phonetics, the idiosyncrasies of English spelling, the approach of traditional grammarians, sentence patterns, punctuation, speech communities, disputed usage, slang, and etymology.

## C. Dialects, Regionalisms, and Foreign Languages in America

1120. American Dialect Society. Publication. no. 1+ Apr. 1944+ University, Ala. [etc.] Published for the Society by the University of Alabama Press [etc.] 2 no. a year (irregular)
72–1707 PE1702.A5
A continuation of no. 2254 in the 1960 *Guide*. Two of the longest publications appearing in the 1956-65 period are Dwight L. Bolinger's *Interrogative Structures of American English: The Direct Question* (1957 [i.e. 1958] 184 p. no. 28) and Einar I. Haugen's *Bilingualism in the Americas: A Bibliography and Research Guide* (1956. 159 p. no. 26). Among the topics covered in the other 18 publications issued during the period are expressions from Herman Melville and words and expressions designated in *Webster's Third New International Dictionary of the English Language* as nonstandard, substandard, or chiefly substandard.

1121. Atwood, Elmer Bagby. The regional vocabulary of Texas. Austin, University of Texas Press [1962] 273 p. illus.
62–9784 PE3101.T4A85
Bibliographical footnotes.

A study of the vocabulary of rural Texans of middle age and older. The data were collected by several of Atwood's advanced graduate students, who employed a questionnaire of items taken from the worksheets of the linguistic atlas of the United States and Canada (see the annotation for no. 1123 in this *Supplement*) as well as items designed to elicit vocabulary used mainly in the Southwest. Responses to the questionnaire are recorded in a chapter entitled "Topical Survey of the Vocabulary." On the basis of a comparison of vocabulary usage in Texas with that in eastern areas, it is concluded that the "regional vocabulary of Texas is basically Southern, with some admixture of Midland words and a considerably smaller proportion of Northern ones." Vocabulary occurrences are shown in a "Word Atlas," consisting of more than 120 pages of maps of Texas and surrounding States.

1122. Eliason, Norman E. Tarheel talk; an historical study of the English language in North Carolina to 1860. Chapel Hill, University of North Carolina Press [1956] 324 p. maps.
56–58593 PE3101.N76E4
Written for both the linguist and the general reader, this book is based on a study of manuscript materials—legal papers, commercial accounts, plantation records, church records, letters, children's writings, student writings, diaries, and journals. Usage since 1860, Eliason asserts, can best be derived from living informants. The chapter entitled "Language Attitudes and Differences" reveals a concern, among the writers represented in the manuscripts, for good English, particularly correct spell-

ing, but also shows that very few of them comment on the differences in pronunciation and vocabulary which they have encountered. The central chapter on vocabulary includes discussions of Americanisms, names, forbidden words, euphemisms, titles, and obsolete, slang, and local terms. A 50-page section on usage of some five hundred words is appended.

1123. Kurath, Hans, *and* Raven I. McDavid. The pronunciation of English in the Atlantic States; based upon the collections of the linguistic atlas of the Eastern United States. Ann Arbor, University of Michigan Press [1961] 182 p. (Studies in American English, 3)

        60–5671    PE2802.M53 v.3

This study of speech in the Eastern United States focuses on the pronunciation of both cultured and uncultured speakers from Maine to South Carolina. Materials are drawn from the collections of the linguistic atlas of the Eastern States, part of the planned linguistic atlas of the United States and Canada. This latter atlas project was begun in 1930 and has resulted thus far in one publication, *Linguistic Atlas of New England* (no. 2268 in the 1960 *Guide*), edited by Kurath. In *The Pronunciation of English in the Atlantic States,* symbols representing sounds are based on the International Phonetic Alphabet. *Dialects, U.S.A.* (Champaign, Ill., National Council of Teachers of English [1963] 62 p.), by Jean Malmstrom and Annabel Ashley, is a brief survey intended primarily for students in secondary schools but useful as well for the general reader.

## D. Miscellaneous

1124. Bronstein, Arthur J. The pronunciation of American English; an introduction to phonetics. New York, Appleton-Century-Crofts [1960] 320 p. illus.     60–6750   PE1137.B77

Bibliographies at the ends of chapters.

Part 1 deals with the International Phonetic Alphabet, the sound system, phonemes, dialects, and standard and disputed usage. Consonants, vowels, and complex consonant and vowel clusters are discussed in part 2. Part 3 covers the nature and types of sound change, pronunciation and influences affecting pronunciation; pitch levels, stress, and pause; and the melodies of American English. A brief historical survey of the development of the English language is appended. A comparison of the chief regional types of cultivated American pronunciation with standard British English can be found in Hans Kurath's brief survey of American English phonetics, *A Phonology and Prosody of Modern English* (Ann Arbor, University of Michigan Press [1964] 158 p.). Claude M. Wise's *Applied Phonetics* (Englewood Cliffs, N.J., Prentice-Hall, 1957. 546 p.) is a wide-ranging survey of the most important characteristics of general, southern, and eastern American speech; standard southern British speech; British regional dialects; American provincial dialects; and dialects of English spoken by foreigners or related to foreign languages.

1125. Evans, Bergen. Comfortable words. Illustrated by Tomi Ungerer. New York, Random House [1962] 379 p.

        62–10775   PE1460.E9

The author provides provocative comments on usage, pronunciation, etymology, idioms, and often-confused words in American English. He insists throughout on reason and naturalness in the use of language and eschews both artificiality and slavish obedience to norms. The entries are arranged alphabetically by the keywords in the phrases.

1126. Wentworth, Harold, *and* Stuart B. Flexner. Dictionary of American slang. New York, Crowell [1960] xviii, 669 p.

        60–6237   PE3729.U5W4

A scholarly treatment of American slang, "the body of words and expressions frequently used by or intelligible to a rather large portion of the general American public, but not accepted as good, formal usage by the majority." The authors consider all slang used in the United States to be "American," regardless of its origin. Many quotations are provided, with dates, to indicate usage for various meanings. The source of each quotation is cited, and, when the citation is abbreviated, fuller information is given in an extensive bibliography. Various wordlists are appended.

# III

# Literary History and Criticism

ALTHOUGH American literature of the 20th century is the major concern of recent literary scholarship, every period, many themes, and a wide variety of categories of writing receive attention in the books chosen for this chapter.

Among the broad categories of literature, fiction is the subject of the largest number of books. The novel of violence, the college novel, the social novel, the grotesque novel, the Negro novel, the realistic novel, and the short story—each of these is the topic of individual studies. Other specialized works deal with such themes as homicide in American fiction, the quest for paradise in American literature, human isolation and the American novel, psychoanalysis and American fiction, love and death in the American novel, and technology and the pastoral ideal in American literature. Poetry is examined in fewer works than fiction but in a similar manner. General appraisals are complemented by scrutinies of rhetoric and poetry, the influence of music on poetry, social themes in poetry, and the continuity of poetry. Recent drama is analyzed for, among other attributes, its political themes. Criticism and literary history are themselves the objects of critical review.

Regional studies concentrate on, for example, the early novel of the Southwest, the western farm novel, antebellum northern views of the South, and writers of the modern South. Cross-cultural ties with other nations are traced in studies of the Japanese tradition in British and American literature, the influence of German culture on American literature, the Mexican in American literature, American writers and artists in Italy, and Soviet attitudes toward American writing.

## A. Anthologies and Series

1127. Allen, Donald M., *ed.* The new American poetry, 1945–1960. New York, Grove Press [1960] 454 p.    60–6342 PS614.A59

The 44 poets represented in this collection make up "our avant-garde, the true continuers of the modern movement in American poetry." Their unity, according to Allen, lies in their "total rejection of all those qualities typical of academic verse." The editor has divided the 44 poets into five groups: those identified with the magazines *Origin* and *Black Mountain Review;* those of the 1947–49 San Francisco renaissance, such as Lawrence Ferlinghetti and Brother Antoninus; the poets of the "beat generation," including Allen Ginsberg and Jack Kerouac; the New York poets; and, finally, those who fit into no particular group. Concluding sections feature autobiographical notes from each of the poets, individual bibliographies, and statements on poetics.

1128. American literary forms. William Van O'Connor, general editor. New York, Crowell [1959–60] 5 v.

Those specific attitudes, topics, and qualities revealed in outstanding authors and legitimately referred to as "American" are studied in this series. Each volume, edited by a distinguished literary personality, is both a critical introduction to the literary history of a particular genre and an anthology which illustrates creative directions from colonial days to the mid-20th century. The volumes are as follows: *American Short Novels* ([1960] 398 p. 60–6314 PZ1.B56Am), edited by Richard P. Blackmur; *American Drama* ([1960] 261 p. 60–6315 PS625.D6), edited by Alan S. Downer; *American Literary Essays* ([1960] 318 p. 60–6316 PS682.L4), edited by Lewis G. Leary; *American Poetry* ([1960] 265 p. 60–6317 PS586.S43), edited by Karl J. Shapiro; and *American Short Stories* ([c1959] 267 p. 60–6318 PZ1.W5Am), edited by Ray B. West.

1129.  Auden, Wystan Hugh, *ed.* The Criterion book of modern American verse. New York, Criterion Books [1956] 336 p.

56–11366 PS614.A8

An anthology of 82 poets of the 20th century, arranged chronologically according to date of birth, from Edwin Arlington Robinson to Anthony Hecht. Although many of the poets are well known, several are minor figures who, in Auden's opinion, have achieved a measure of success in one or two poems. The poems represent a personal choice by the compiler and are often among the poet's less widely known works. Comparing English poets with those of the United States, Auden asserts that "from Bryant on, there is scarcely one American poet whose work, if unsigned, could be mistaken for that of an Englishman." The book appeared in England under the title *The Faber Book of Modern American Verse* (London, Faber & Faber [1956] 336 p.).

1130.  Best American plays. [1st] + ser.; 1939+ New York, Crown Publishers.

51–12830 PS634.B4

Title varies: 1st ser., *Twenty Best Plays of the Modern American Theatre.*—2d ser., *Best Plays of the Modern American Theatre.*

Editor: 1st–4th ser., John Gassner.

— — —  Supplementary volume, 1918–1958. Edited, with introduction, by John Gassner. New York, Crown Publishers [1961] xvi, 687 p.

PS634.B412

The first three series of *Best American Plays* are no. 2333–2335 in the 1960 *Guide.*

CONTENTS of the fourth series.—Introduction: and still it moves, by John Gassner.—I am a camera, by John Van Druten.—Cat on a hot tin roof, by Tennessee Williams.—The rose tattoo, by Tennes-

see Williams.—A moon for the misbegotten, by Eugene O'Neill.—A hatful of rain, by Michael V. Gazzo.—Picnic, by William Inge.—Bus stop, by William Inge.—Tea and sympathy, by Robert Anderson.—A view from the bridge, by Arthur Miller.—The crucible, by Arthur Miller.—Inherit the wind, by Jerome Lawrence and Robert E. Lee. —The Caine mutiny court-martial, by Herman Wouk.—The fourposter, by Jan de Hartog.—The seven year itch, by George Axelrod.—The Matchmaker, by Thornton Wilder.—No time for sergeants, by Ira Levin and Mac Hyman.—The solid gold Cadillac, by George S. Kaufman and Howard Teichmann.—A selective bibliography.—A supplementary list of plays.

CONTENTS of the supplementary volume.—Introduction, by John Gassner.—Clarence, by Booth Tarkington.—Rain, by John Colton.—The adding machine, by Elmer Rice.—Green grow the lilacs, by Lynn Riggs.—The house of Connelly, by Paul Green.—Children of darkness, by Edwin Justus Mayer.—Biography, by S. N. Behrman.—On borrowed time, by Paul Osborn.—Morning's at seven, by Paul Osborn.—Ethan Frome, by Owen Davis and Donald Davis.—Men in white, by Sidney Kingsley.—Yellow jack, by Sidney Howard.— Awake and sing!, by Clifford Odets.—Here come the clowns, by Philip Barry.—Harvey, by Mary Chase.—The teahouse of the August moon, by John Patrick.—The diary of Anne Frank, by Frances Goodrich and Albert Hackett.

1131.  Blair, Walter, Theodore Hornberger, *and* Randall Stewart, *eds.* The United States in literature. Introduction to modern poetry by Paul Engle. Composition guide by Don Otto. Novel discussion guides by Kenneth Sickal. Chicago, Scott, Foresman [1963] 820 p.

63–773 PS507.B527 1963

A revised edition of no. 2323 in the 1960 *Guide.*

1132.  Bradley, Edward Sculley, Richmond C. Beatty, *and* Eugene Hudson Long, *eds.* The American tradition in literature. Rev. New York, Norton [1961] 2 v.

61–8916 PS507.B74 1961

CONTENTS.—v. 1. Bradford to Lincoln.—v. 2. Whitman to the present.

A new edition of no. 2324 in the 1960 *Guide,* revised to include two full-length novels—*The Scarlet Letter* and *The Adventures of Huckleberry Finn*—and additional selections from the writings of Melville, James, Emerson, Whitman, Howells, Jonathan Edwards, and others. Robert Lowell, Richard Eberhart, Muriel Rukeyser, Richard Wilbur, and Marianne Moore are among those included in a new section on mid-20th-century poets.

1133. Brooks, Cleanth, *and* Robert Penn Warren, eds. Understanding fiction. 2d ed. New York, Appleton-Century-Crofts [1959] 688 p.

59–12844 PN3335.B7 1959

A revised edition of the influential teaching anthology mentioned in the annotation for no. 2378 in the 1960 *Guide.* The same publisher issued a shortened version in 1960 under the title, *The Scope of Fiction* (336 p.).

1134. Cerf, Bennett A., *ed.* Six American plays for today. Selected and with biographical notes by Bennett Cerf. New York, Modern Library [1961] 599 p. (The Modern library of the world's best books [38]) 61–11189 PS634.C418

CONTENTS.—Camino Real, by Tennessee Williams.—The dark at the top of the stairs, by William Inge.—Sunrise at Campobello, by Dore Schary.—A raisin in the sun, by Lorraine Hansberry.—The tenth man, by Paddy Chayefsky.—Toys in the attic, by Lillian Hellman.

Paul Kozelka has edited *15 American One-Act Plays* (New York, Washington Square Press [1961] 308 p. The ANTA series of distinguished plays), which includes "Thursday Evening," by Christopher Morley, "The Devil and Daniel Webster," by Stephen Vincent Benét, "Red Carnations," by Glenn Hughes, and "Trifles," by Susan Glaspell. Two anthologies of period plays from the Laurel Drama Series are *Famous American Plays of the 1930s* ([New York, Dell Pub. Co., ᶜ1959] 480 p.), edited by Harold Clurman, and *Famous American Plays of the 1940s* ([New York, Dell Pub. Co., 1960] 447 p.), edited by Henry Hewes.

1135. Edel, Leon, *and others, eds.* Masters of American literature. Boston, Houghton Mifflin [1959] 2 v. 59–1824 PS507.E3

According to the editors, the student of literature profits more through "close familiarity with a few writers than through superficial acquaintance with many." Further, "he will profit more from regarding the works he reads to be studied and enjoyed on their own terms than he will from viewing them as illustrations of the course of literary or cultural history." This anthology offers substantial selections from the works of writers from Jonathan Edwards to Faulkner and Frost.

1136. Elliott, George P., *ed.* Fifteen modern American poets. New York, Rinehart [1956] 315 p. (Rinehart editions, 79)

56–7952 PS614.E55

"This book aims," the editor noted in his 1956 preface, "to represent the middle generation of American poets," all of whom "have been known for several years." The oldest of the 15 poets is Richard Eberhart and the youngest Richard Wilbur. Short biobibliographical notes on poets and poems are appended. Selections from the works of 82 poets are presented in *The Modern Poets, an American-British Anthology* (New York, McGraw-Hill [1963] 427 p.), edited by John M. Brinnin and Bill Read, with 80 photographic portraits by Rollie McKenna.

1137. Engle, Paul, *ed.* Midland; twenty-five years of fiction and poetry selected from the writing workshops of the State University of Iowa. New York, Random House [1961] 600 p.

60–12132 PS536.E55

The university workshop in creative writing, a comparatively recent phenomenon, has caused considerable controversy among people interested in literature. The editor's introduction to this collection praises a pioneering institution in this field, but the anthology itself is the more convincing argument. Flannery O'Connor, Jean Stafford, Wallace Stegner, William Dickey, Jean Garrigue, Anthony Hecht, Donald Justice, W. D. Snodgrass, Leonard Unger, and Tennessee Williams are among the writers who have been associated with the program at the State University of Iowa during the last 25 years. Engle and Joseph Langland are the editors of *Poet's Choice* (New York, Dial Press, 1962. 303 p.), the result of an invitation to each of a hundred poets to select a favorite or crucial poem from his works and to comment about his selection.

1138. Fiedler, Leslie A., *ed.* The art of the essay. Edited with introductions, notes and exercise questions. New York, Crowell [1958] 640 p.

58–7917 PS682.F5

In this anthology, the editor aspires to restore the essay to its rightful place among literary forms. A noted practitioner of the art himself, Fiedler prefaces the general sections of his book with remarks on the history of the essay in Western culture. Letters, book reviews, extracts from lengthy prose works, and articles are arranged chronologically from Montaigne through such 20th-century American masters as Lionel Trilling, Constance Rourke, and Jacques Barzun. Each of the 60 essays is preceded by a short introduction to the author and his work.

1139. Foerster, Norman, *ed.* American poetry and prose. 4th ed., complete. Boston, Houghton Mifflin [1957] 1664 p.

57–13836 PS507.F6 1957

A revised edition of no. 2331 in the 1960 *Guide,* including additional works of substance by major authors, fewer selections from minor authors, and fuller notes accompanying individual selections.

Foerster and Robert P. Falk are coeditors of an abridged and revised edition, *American Poetry and Prose* (Boston, Houghton Mifflin [1960] 1223 p.).

1140. Foerster, Norman, *and* Robert P. Falk, *eds.*
Eight American writers, an anthology of American literature. New York, Norton [ᶜ1963] xvi, 1610 p.      62–20920 PS535.F6
  Bibliography: p. 1589–1605.
Selections from the works of eight authors whom the editors regard as constituting the classic core of American writing. The eight are Poe, Emerson, Thoreau, Hawthorne, Melville, Whitman, Mark Twain, and Henry James. Famous poems, stories, notebooks, letters, and chapters are reprinted here, along with substantial scholarly introductions to each author. A wider but still basic selection of standard figures is presented in *Classic American Writers* (Boston, Little, Brown [1962] 620 p.), edited by Harrison Hayford. The writers listed above are supplemented by Edward Taylor, Jonathan Edwards, Irving, Bryant, Longfellow, Whittier, Holmes, James Russell Lowell, Emily Dickinson, and Howells.

1141. Gordon, Caroline, *and* Allen Tate, *eds.* The house of fiction; an anthology of the short story, with commentary. 2d ed. New York, Scribner [1960] 469 p.      60–6360 PZ1.G653Ho
  Includes bibliography.
The formalist technique of textual analysis is demonstrated in this anthology of 23 stories. Each story is accompanied by a commentary on the fictional techniques at work in the selection, and a 20-page appendix explains the approaches used in the foregoing text. American short stories include "Young Goodman Brown," by Nathaniel Hawthorne; "The Fall of the House of Usher," by Edgar Allan Poe; "The Beast in the Jungle," by Henry James; "The Open Boat," by Stephen Crane; "Haircut," by Ring Lardner; "Old Mortality," by Katherine Anne Porter; "Spotted Horses," by William Faulkner; "Lions, Harts, Leaping Does," by J. F. Powers; "The Headless Hawk," by Truman Capote; "A Good Man Is Hard To Find," by Flannery O'Connor; "The Killers," by Ernest Hemingway; "Where a Man Dwells," by Herbert Gold; and "The Proud Suitor," by James Buechler. Another short-story anthology is *A New Southern Harvest* (New York, Bantam Books [1957] 294 p. A Bantam book, F1556), edited by Robert Penn Warren and Albert Erskine and featuring famous stories by recent southern writers.

1142. Hall, Donald, *ed.* Contemporary American poetry. Baltimore, Penguin Books [1963, ᶜ1962] 201 p. (Penguin poets)
            63–1971 PS614.H23 1963
Robert Lowell and Richard Wilbur are viewed as marking "the real beginning of postwar American poetry because they are the culmination of past poetries." In addition to the two mainstreams of modern poetry identified with William Carlos Williams and T. S. Eliot, Hall perceives the emergence of "a new kind of imagination" distinguished by a subjective attitude directed toward the external world. The postwar poets represented in this collection include John Ashbery, Reed Whittemore, Howard Nemerov, Robert Creeley, W. D. Snodgrass, Robert Lowell, and James Wright. With Robert Pack and Louis A. M. Simpson, Hall coedited *New Poets of England and America* (New York, Meridian Books, 1957. 351 p. Meridian books, M50). In *New Poets of England and America: Second Selection* (Cleveland, Meridian Books [1962] 384 p. Meridian books, M135), Hall edited the English poets and Pack the American. Sixteen poets under the age of 40 are represented in *American Poems; a Contemporary Collection* (Carbondale, Southern Illinois University Press [1964] 200 p. Crosscurrents; modern critiques), edited by Jascha F. Kessler.

1143. Jones, LeRoi, *ed.* The moderns; an anthology of new writing in America. New York, Corinth Books, 1963. xvi, 351 p.
            63–11408 PS536.J6
  Bibliographical references included in "Acknowledgments" (p. [vii-viii]).
The contemporary American poet who gathered these selections states that he has had more in mind a "prose medium" and quality of excitement than a record of a generation. The writers in this volume, says Jones, "exist out of a continuing tradition of populist modernism that has characterized the best of twentieth-century American writing." Rather than categorize the writers, Jones emphasizes the general and common qualities of the selections, which together make up "a body of work that seeks its identification and delineation as a departure from the main body of popular American fiction." Among the "moderns" included are William Eastlake, Edward Dorn, John Rechy, Michael Rumaker, Paul Metcalf, Robert Creeley, Diane Di Prima, Hubert Selby, and William Burroughs. Some of the same writers are represented in *Writers in Revolt, an Anthology* ([New York] Berkley Pub. Corp. [1965, ᶜ1963] 384 p. A Berkley medallion book), edited by Richard Seaver, Terry Southern, and Alexander Trocchi.

1144. Malin, Irving, *and* Irwin Stark, *eds.* Breakthrough: a treasury of contemporary

American-Jewish literature. New York, McGraw-Hill [1964] 376 p.    63–13261 PS508.J4M3

Ranges from Howard Nemerov and Allen Ginsberg to Philip Rahv, Alfred Kazin, and Philip Roth. An introductory essay on Jewish literature in the United States offers an abbreviated version of the ideas discussed in Malin's *Jews and Americans* (Carbondale, Southern Illinois University Press [1965] 193 p. Crosscurrents: modern critiques).

1145. Hill, Herbert, *ed.* Soon, one morning; new writing by American Negroes, 1940–1962. Selected and edited, with an introduction and biographical notes, by Herbert Hill. New York, Knopf, 1963. 617 p.    62–15567 PS508.N3H5

Essays, fiction, and poetry. Among the writers included are Ralph Ellison, James Baldwin, Langston Hughes, Richard Wright, Ann Petry, Gwendolyn Brooks, LeRoi Jones, and J. Saunders Redding. Arna Bontemps has edited an anthology, *American Negro Poetry* (New York, Hill & Wang [1963] 197 p.), showing the accomplishments of numerous Negro poets, including James Weldon Johnson, Paul Laurence Dunbar, Claude McKay, Jean Toomer, Countee Cullen, Margaret Walker, and Richard Wright.

1146. Miller, Perry, *ed.* Major writers of America. New York, Harcourt, Brace & World [1962] 2 v.    62–12181 PS507.M48

To "vindicate the study of American literature," this anthology includes those writers who have made their mark on world literature. Twenty-three noted literary specialists have individually edited chapters on 28 men of letters from William Bradford to William Faulkner. There are lengthy introductions for each author, generous selections from his shorter works, and suggestions for further reading. Among the editors and their subjects are Samuel Eliot Morison on William Bradford; Marius Bewley on Cooper and Bryant; R. W. B. Lewis on Whitman; Richard Wilbur on Poe; Richard Chase on Melville; Northrop Frye on Emily Dickinson; Eric Bentley on Eugene O'Neill; R. P. Blackmur on T. S. Eliot; and Irving Howe on Faulkner. Miller has also edited materials for *The Golden Age of American Literature* (New York, G. Braziller, 1959. 514 p.). He contends that a "golden age" in American literature was an actuality for the two decades prior to the Civil War and supports his contention with selections from Poe, Emerson, Thoreau, Hawthorne, Melville, and Whitman.

1147. Miller, Perry, *and* Thomas H. Johnson, *eds.* The Puritans. Rev. ed. New York, Harper & Row [1963] 2 v. (Harper torchbooks. The

Academy library)    63–1710 PS531.M5 1963

A revised edition of no. 2345 in the 1960 *Guide,* with bibliographies updated by George McCandlish.

1148. Olson, Elder, *ed.* American lyric poems, from colonial times to the present. New York, Appleton-Century-Crofts [1964] 166 p. (Goldentree books)    64–17762 PS593.L8O53

Observations on the qualities and history of American lyric poetry precede a collection of lyrics by 79 American poets. Olson traces the development of this poetic form from Edward Taylor and Anne Bradstreet to present-day lyricists.

1149. Partisan review. The Partisan review anthology. Edited by William Phillips and Philip Rahv. New York, Holt, Rinehart & Winston [1962] 490 p.    62–12136 AC5.P35

The first anthology of writings in the *Partisan Review* to draw selections from its entire history, beginning in 1937. Included are stories by Delmore Schwartz, Saul Bellow, Bernard Malamud, James Purdy, and others; among the American poets represented are Karl Shapiro, William Carlos Williams, Robert Penn Warren, Robert Lowell, and Elizabeth Bishop. Essays and reviews on literature and society are by Lionel Trilling, Irving Howe, T. S. Eliot, James Baldwin, Alfred Kazin, Daniel Aaron, and Leslie Fiedler. Anthologies of writings in other periodicals listed in the 1960 *Guide* have also been published recently: *Jubilee; One Hundred Years of the Atlantic* (Boston, Little, Brown [1957] 746 p.), selected and edited by Edward Weeks and Emily Flint; *Gentlemen, Scholars, and Scoundrels; a Treasury of the Best of Harper's Magazine From 1850 to the Present* (New York, Harper [1959] 696 p.), edited by Horace Knowles; *Opinions and Perspectives From The New York Times Book Review* (Boston, Houghton Mifflin, 1964. 441 p.), edited by Ernest Francis Brown; *The Saturday Review Gallery* (New York, Simon & Schuster, 1959. 481 p.), compiled by Jerome Beatty, Jr., and the editors of the *Saturday Review.* "Little magazine" anthologies include *Anthology* (New York, Vintage Books [1961] 461 p. A Vintage book, V–197), compiled by Frederick Morgan from *The Hudson Review; The Chicago Review Anthology* ([Chicago] University of Chicago Press [1959] 251 p.), edited by David Ray; and *A Country in the Mind; an Anthology of Stories and Poems From The Western Review* (Sausalito, Calif., Contact Editions [1962] 290 p. Contact editions, 2), edited by Ray B. West.

1150. Solomon, Eric, *ed.* The faded banners; a treasury of nineteenth-century Civil War

fiction. New York, T. Yoseloff [1960] 336 p.
60–6839 PZ1.S688Fad

1151. Steinmetz, Lee, *ed.* The poetry of the American Civil War. [East Lansing] Michigan State University Press [1960] 264 p.
59–15220 E647.S85

The change from a romantic idealization of battle to the grudging acceptance or hostile rejection of the realities of war is captured in Solomon's anthology of Civil War fiction. Literary merit was the first criterion for the selections included; there is no unity of viewpoint or sectional preference, and most of the works focus on the combat itself and the psychological impact of civil war upon ordinary Americans. Lee Steinmetz, in his anthology, has chosen 30 representative poems from among more than 200 poems written by Americans during the 1860's. He gives preference to the less familiar poets and emphasizes subject matter and theme more than esthetic quality. Each of five sections contains a general introduction to the subject matter of the poems and the historical background of the poetry, and each poem is, in addition, also related to the whole body of Civil War poetry.

1152. Twayne's United States authors series. Sylvia E. Bowman, editor. New York, Twayne Publishers, 1961+

A series of more than a hundred biographical and critical volumes, each approximately 175–200 pages in length, which discuss the accomplishments, reputation, and themes of a wide variety of American authors. Most of the books in the series have been written by professors at American colleges and universities and include selected bibliographical references and biographical chronologies. Each text is shaped according to the individual author being studied. For a little-known author, the Twayne authors series volume is often the only general biographical and critical treatment available. In the case of writers about whom many works have been published, the Twayne volume frequently serves to synthesize known facts and previously expressed interpretations. Many volumes in the Twayne series, each volume of which is separately cataloged, are listed under the individual authors in Chapter 1, "Literature," in this *Supplement.*

1153. University of Minnesota pamphlets on American writers. William Van O'Connor,

Allen Tate, and Robert Penn Warren, editors. Minneapolis, University of Minnesota Press, 1959+

A growing series of brief, inexpensive paperbacks which treat major and minor American authors and literary forms. Although most of the volumes are devoted to individual authors, some cover general topics, for example, Glauco Cambon's *Recent American Poetry* ([1962] 48 p. no. 16. 62–62784 PS324.C27), Alan S. Downer's *Recent American Drama* ([1961] 46 p. no. 7. 61–62514 PS351.D63), Jack B. Ludwig's *Recent American Novelists* ([1962] 47 p. no. 22. 62–63700 PS379.L82), and *The American Short Story* ([1961] 47 p. no. 14. 61–63843 PS374.S5R6 1961), by Danforth R. Ross.

1154. Untermeyer, Louis, *ed.* The Britannica library of great American writing. Edited, with historical notes and a running commentary. Chicago, Britannica Press; and distributed in association with J. B. Lippincott, Philadelphia [1960] 2 v. (xvii, 1764 p.) 60–14545 PS507.U5

Excerpts from the narratives, short stories, poems, and essays of American men of letters. Untermeyer has also edited *Modern American Poetry* [*and*] *Modern British Poetry,* a combined new and enlarged edition (New York, Harcourt, Brace & World [1962] 701, 541 p.).

1155. Weber, Brom, *ed.* An anthology of American humor. New York, Crowell [1962] 584 p. 62–10284 PN6162.W4
Includes bibliography.

1156. Carlisle, Henry C., *ed.* American satire in prose and verse. New York, Random House [1962] 464 p. 62–12727 PN6231.S2C3

American literary humor from the colonial period to the late 1950's is represented in Weber's compilation. Benjamin Franklin, Mark Twain, James Thurber, and George Washington Harris are among the widely recognized humorists included. Special attention is devoted to the humor of the masters of classic literature, including Hawthorne, Melville, Poe, James, Eliot, and Hart Crane. The writers represented in Carlisle's collection were chosen primarily for their skill in unmasking American folly and revealing the incongruities in American character and institutions. Selections range from the pre-Civil-War period to the present and are arranged according to objects of satirical criticism.

# B. History and Criticism

1157. Aaron, Daniel. Writers on the left; episodes in American literary communism. New York, Harcourt, Brace & World [1961] xvi, 460 p. (Communism in American life)

61–13349 PS228.C6A2

Bibliographical references included in "Notes" (p. 401-448).

In his "social chronicle" of American literary radicalism between 1912 and the early 1940's, Aaron traces the infatuation and ultimate disenchantment of a selected group of American writers with left-wing movements and ideologies. The earliest rebels, rooted in the tradition of Emerson and Whitman, rejected intellectual socialism and looked hopefully to the anarchism and syndicalism of the day for salvation. World War I and the Bolshevik Revolution ended this phase and opened a 20-year period of dalliance with communism, shattered only by the Russo-German pact of 1939. Although Aaron sees few writers or critics unaffected by communism between the wars, he regards his story as but "one more turn" in the longer cycle of literary revolt—like the others, beginning in hope and ending in disillusion.

1158. Allen, Walter E. Tradition and dream; the English and American novel from the twenties to our time. London, Phoenix House [1964] xxii, 346 p. 64–4173 PR881.A42 1964

The "dream" in Allen's title belongs to America; the "tradition," to England. The English writer of the 20th century has been constantly reminded, says the author, of his personal limitations and of his indebtedness to a mature literary and cultural heritage, while the American writer seems to have been impressed instead by his independence, his loneliness, his cultural isolation. Notable American exceptions have been regionalists like Ellen Glasgow and William Faulkner and, more recently, fiction writers examining America's Jewish and Negro communities, such as Saul Bellow and Ralph Ellison.

1159. Alvarez, Alfred. Stewards of excellence; studies in modern English and American poets. New York, Scribner [1958] 191 p.

58–12492 PR603.A4 1958

The London edition (Chatto & Windus) has the title *The Shaping Spirit*.

A young British critic, in comparing eight outstanding figures in modern American and British poetry, stresses the differences between the two traditions and the effect of cultural dissimilarities on poetic tradition. Yeats, Auden, Empson, and Lawrence are the English poets compared with Eliot, Pound, Hart Crane, and Stevens.

1160. Bewley, Marius. The eccentric design; form in the classic American novel. New York, Columbia University Press, 1959. 327 p.

59–13769 PS371.B4

Bibliographical references included in "Notes" (p. 314-324).

Having made a number of controversial statements in an earlier work, *The Complex Fate* (1952), the author devotes this study to detailing "the eccentric design" of the fate shared by major American writers. Abstraction and intelligence are the main characteristics of this tradition, and no room is left for "the so-called realists and naturalists" whose symbols are "exterior frosting." John Adams, Hamilton, and Jefferson are interpreted as being the first great figures who sought to resolve the conflicts inherent in American society.

1161. Bigelow, Gordon E. Rhetoric and American poetry of the early national period. Gainesville, University of Florida Press, 1960. 77 p. (University of Florida monographs. Humanities, no. 4) 60–63133 PS314.B5

Includes bibliography.

A literary history of American poetry and rhetoric from 1775 to 1815, concentrating on the major poets of the period. The author cites the rhetorical devices in the poetry of Freneau and other literary figures to support his charge that the young Nation encouraged politics and philosophies incompatible with "the emotional and imaginative insight which are necessary to poetic expression." A major part of the discussion concerns the relationship of poetry to rhetoric, the history of rhetoric, and the attitudes of the populace to these two disciplines.

1162. Blanck, Jacob N. Bibliography of American literature. New Haven, Yale University Press, 1955–63. 4 v. 54–5283 Z1225.B55

A monumental undertaking in American bibliography, supervised by the Bibliographical Society of America. Four volumes of the projected eight-volume series, to encompass American authors who, "in their own time at least, were known and read," had appeared by 1965. Some 35,000 items will ultimately be included. The entries are limited to writings by the selected authors, who are arranged alphabetically. The coverage of the first four volumes extends from Henry Adams through Joseph H. Ingraham. Blanck's preface in volume 1 describes the plan of the bibliography.

1163. Bode, Carl. The half-world of American culture; a miscellany. Preface by C. P. Snow. Carbondale, Southern Illinois University Press [1965] xii, 259 p.     64–20257 PS121.B596
In this volume of essays, the author writes chiefly about popular literature, analyzing such subjects as 19th-century pornography and the 20th-century "parish" of Lloyd C. Douglas. While serving as cultural attaché to the American embassay in London, Bode organized two series of lectures in which noted American scholar-critics discussed prominent figures and topics in American literature. The lectures were edited for publication by Bode and appeared as *The Young Rebel in American Literature* (New York, Praeger [1960, ᶜ1959] 170 p. Books that matter) and *The Great Experiment in American Literature* (New York, Praeger [1961] 151 p. Books that matter). Bode is also the author of *The American Lyceum* (New York, Oxford University Press, 1956. 275 p.).

1164. Bone, Robert A. The Negro novel in America. New Haven, Yale University Press, 1958. 268 p. (Yale publications in American studies, 3)     58–11249 PS153.N5B6
     Bibliography: p. 233–250.
The author believes that there is a distinctly "Negro" novel existing within and yet apart from the broader traditions of American fiction and deriving its distinctiveness from the uniqueness of the Negro experience in America. His book discusses Negro novelists from 1890 to 1952 and divides the subject into four distinct periods: 1890–1920, when the rising middle class dominated Negro literature; 1920–30, the days of the "Negro Renaissance" and the formation of a Negro intelligentsia; 1930–40, a period dominated by the weight of the depression, the flirtation with communism, the little magazines, and the Federal writers' projects; and 1940–52, when the Richard Wright school, raceless novels, and portrayals of Negro life and culture all occurred simultaneously and resulted in a flowering of the Negro novel. An appendix ranks the novelists from each of the four periods; a bibliography of 103 full-length Negro novels is included for specialists. *The American Negro Writer and His Roots* (New York, American Society of African Culture, 1960. 70 p.) comprises selected papers from the first Conference of Negro Writers, held in New York in March 1959, and features addresses by leading Negro writers.

1165. Bowden, Edwin T. The dungeon of the heart; human isolation and the American novel. New York, Macmillan, 1961. 175 p.
               61–8262 PS374.I8B6
Twelve American works of fiction which "form together an extended essay" on human isolation within American life are discussed, and the cultural conditions on which they are based are reviewed. They are *The Deerslayer; The Scarlet Letter; Huckleberry Finn; Moby Dick; My Antonia; The Portrait of a Lady; The Rise of Silas Lapham; Winesburg, Ohio; The Grapes of Wrath; Look Homeward, Angel; Light in August;* and *The Catcher in the Rye.*

1166. Brooks, Cleanth. The hidden God; studies in Hemingway, Faulkner, Yeats, Eliot, and Warren. New Haven, Yale University Press, 1963. 136 p.     63–9308 PS228.C5B7
Lectures originally delivered in 1955 to the Conference in Theology for College Faculty at Trinity College, Hartford, Conn. Although they were designed for a Christian audience, the emphasis is not upon Christian writers in any orthodox sense but upon the religious vision implicit within some literature which has been criticized as amoral or immoral. Brooks illustrates the kinship of these writers with the Christian theologian Paul Tillich and with the French existentialists: the theme common to all is a protest against the dehumanization of man and against the denial of free will.

1167. Brooks, Van Wyck. Days of the phoenix; the nineteen-twenties I remember. New York, Dutton, 1957. 193 p.
               57–5335 PS3503.R7297D3

1168. Brooks, Van Wyck. From the shadow of the mountain; my post-meridian years. New York, Dutton, 1961. 202 p.
               61–11417 PS3503.R7297Z5
The first volume of Brooks' autobiography, *Scenes and Portraits: Memories of Childhood and Youth* (one of the titles listed in the annotation for no. 2380 in the 1960 *Guide*), began the life story of this pioneer in the study of a national literature. *Days of the Phoenix* continues the story through the 1920's and is particularly notable for the account of the days he spent in a mental institution. The final volume of the trilogy, *From the Shadow of the Mountain,* begins in 1931 with his emergence from the institution and continues to his 75th year. Essays, aphorisms, sketches, and reminiscences, most

of them previously out of print, were published in *From a Writer's Notebook* (New York, Dutton, 1958. 182 p.).

1169. Brooks, Van Wyck. The dream of Arcadia; American writers and artists in Italy, 1760–1915. New York, Dutton, 1958. 272 p.

58–9597   DG457.A6B7

As a repository of Old World culture, Italy stimulated the minds and imaginations of generations of American artists and intellectuals who found there the "just taste" still wanting in the youthful United States. Through a discussion of mid-18th-century visits by painters and the later travels of Irving, Cooper, Longfellow, Hawthorne, James, Howells, and others, Brooks re-creates the scenes and atmosphere as they registered upon the impressionable minds of eager Americans who drew upon their Italian experiences in their writing. Nathalia Wright treats more directly the appearance of these influences in the fiction of American writers in her study *American Novelists in Italy* (Philadelphia, University of Pennsylvania Press [1965] 288 p.).

1170. Broussard, Louis. American drama; contemporary allegory from Eugene O'Neill to Tennessee Williams. Norman, University of Oklahoma Press [1962] 145 p.   62–16479   PS351.B7

Includes bibliography.

A study of 20th-century American reenactments of the "Everyman" theme by 10 "expressionistic" dramatists. Although focusing upon a limited number of plays, the author also touches on other plays which embody similar allegorical themes and on other art forms concerned with the same problems and conclusions. Following an introductory chapter on "The Motivating Force of Expressionism," the study examines playwrights Eugene O'Neill, Elmer Rice, John Howard Lawson, Philip Barry, T. S. Eliot, Thornton Wilder, Robert Sherwood, Tennessee Williams, Arthur Miller, and Archibald MacLeish.

1171. Brown, Deming B. Soviet attitudes toward American writing. Princeton, N.J., Princeton University Press, 1962. 338 p.

62–11954   PS159.R8B7

Includes bibliography.

A broad and authoritative investigation by a professor of Slavic literature and languages who also holds a degree in American literature. Brown made two trips to the USSR while gathering information on Soviet criticism of American literature. The book has several uses. It offers a description of the publication and reception of American books in the USSR, discussing censorship, the popularity of different American authors, and Soviet critical evalua-

tion of books from the 1920's to 1960; it presents ideological, esthetic, and political aspects of Soviet criticism, summarizes its strengths and weaknesses, and considers the effectiveness of critical propaganda in dictating esthetic choice to the reading public of the Soviet Union; and, finally, it evaluates the effectiveness of American writers in communicating a cultural understanding of the United States within a country where avowed opposition to American culture and values has been a virtue.

1172. Cambon, Glauco. The inclusive flame; studies in American poetry. Bloomington, Indiana University Press [1963] 248 p.

63–16612   PS305.C313

Bibliographical references included in "Notes" (p. [229]–245).

This work was originally published in 1956 as an introduction to American poetry for an Italian audience. The author translated his volume into English and has offered it to American readers as a scholarly contribution expressing the personal viewpoints of a native Italian who became a professor of comparative literature at Cambridge. Cambon takes his title from the effort of American poets to capture the totality of American experience through poetry. Nine American poets from Poe to Robert Lowell are studied in this search for "Americanness."

1173. Chase, Richard V. The American novel and its tradition. Garden City, N.Y., Doubleday, 1957. 266 p. (Doubleday anchor books, A116)   57–11412   PS371.C5

Includes bibliography.

A study in the comparative traditions of fiction in England and the United States. Although the American tradition inevitably sprang from its British parent, it is seen as coming under the influence of the romantic French and Russian writers during the 1880's and 1890's. The author's purpose is to assess "the significance of the fact that since the earliest days the American novel, in its most original and characteristic form, has worked out its destiny and defined itself by incorporating an element of romance." The result is a "freer, more daring, more brilliant fiction that contrasts with the solid moral inclusiveness and massive equability of the English novel." The romanticism of Brockden Brown, Cooper, Hawthorne, Melville, James, Mark Twain, Fitzgerald, Frank Norris, and Faulkner is studied in 10 essays. Two appendixes enlarge upon the text.

1174. Contemporary authors; the international bio-bibliographical guide to current authors and

their works. v. 1+ Detroit, Gale Research, 1962+
62–52046 Z1224.C6

A compendium of information on major and minor living authors in fields other than science and technology. Arranged alphabetically by author, the sketches are based on responses to questionnaires. Both personal and professional information is included, as well as lists of published writings and works in progress. Fourteen volumes had been published by the end of 1965. Indexes are cumulative, and information on authors is updated when new works appear.

1175. Cowley, Malcolm, *ed*. After the genteel tradition; American writers, 1910–1930. With a preface by Harry T. Moore. Carbondale, Southern Illinois University Press [1964] 210 p. (Crosscurrents; modern critiques)
64–11608 PS221.C645 1964

This revised edition of no. 2406 in the 1960 *Guide* includes a new foreword, an expanded "literary calendar" for the years 1911–30, and a new chapter on Robinson, written by the editor.

1176. Cunliffe, Marcus. The literature of the United States. [Rev. ed.] Baltimore, Penguin Books [1961] 384 p. (Pelican books, A289)
62–788 PS92.C8 1961

A critical-historical account of American literature from colonial times through the 1950's, written by an English scholar sympathetic to literary traditions in both Britain and the United States. Noting that his British readers often find the notion of a distinctly American literature difficult to accept, he makes a point of stressing the peculiarly American qualities of our national letters. In addition to discussing the traditional genres, the author shows enthusiasm for the history of American criticism, especially in its efforts to claim certain characteristics as peculiarly American.

1177. Davis, David B. Homicide in American fiction, 1798–1860; a study in social values. Ithaca, N.Y., Cornell University Press [1957] xviii, 346 p. 57–4688 PS374.H6D3
Bibliography: p. 315–340.

A study of American attitudes toward homicide as evidenced in both popular and classical novels of the 19th century. The author states in his preface that "this is a historical analysis of certain ideas associated with homicide, including beliefs concerning the origin and development of human evil, the extent of freedom and responsibility, the nature of mental and emotional abnormality, the influence of American social forces on violence, and the morality of capital punishment."

1178. Deutsch, Babette. Poetry in our time; a critical survey of poetry in the English-speaking world, 1900 to 1960. 2d ed., rev. and enl. Garden City, N.Y., Doubleday, 1963. 457 p. (Anchor books) 63–8763 PR601.D43 1963

Babette Deutsch was one of the first critics and historians of modern poetry and has been publishing and updating her studies for the last three decades. The best known of these is her *Poetry in Our Time*, no. 2414 in the 1960 *Guide*, which first appeared in 1952. The new edition is a revision and enlargement of the entire volume, written with the conviction that nothing can deal with the realities of the 20th century as meaningfully as the poetry of this century. Also revised and enlarged is her *Poetry Handbook* (New York, Funk & Wagnalls [1962] 181 p.), a "dictionary of the terms used in discussing verse techniques and some of the larger aspects of poetry, together with examples of poetic practice."

1179. Dickinson, A. T. American historical fiction. New York, Scarecrow Press, 1958. 314 p. 58–7803 PS374.H5D5
Bibliography: p. 225-230.

An annotated bibliography of 1,909 American novels, including classic works, popular narratives, regional tales, diaries, and chronicles. Annotations are objective rather than critical. Robert A. Lively's *Fiction Fights the Civil War* (Chapel Hill, University of North Carolina Press [1957] 230 p.) is a study of over five hundred novels about the war.

1180. Downer, Alan S., *ed*. American drama and its critics; a collection of critical essays. Chicago, University of Chicago Press [1965] xxi, 258 p. (Gemini books. Patterns of literary criticism)
65–24424 PS351.D59

Selections ranging from James A. Herne's end-of-the-century commentary to the more recent views of Eric Bentley, Tom Driver, and Robert Brustein are included in an anthology intended to indicate "the variety of critical experiences that accompanied the development of the modern American theater." A similar collection written from the viewpoint of the playwright is *American Playwrights on Drama* (New York, Hill & Wang [1965] 174 p. A Dramabook), edited by Horst Frenz and featuring 22 statements by 14 dramatists, including O'Neill, Maxwell Anderson, Thornton Wilder, Tennessee Williams, William Inge, Archibald MacLeish, Lorraine Hansberry, and Edward Albee.

1181. Dusenbury, Winifred L. The theme of loneliness in modern American drama. Gainesville, University of Florida Press, 1960. 231 p.
60–10228 PS338.L6D8 1960

Twenty-six major American plays since 1920 are discussed as they exemplify the theme of loneliness in American life. The criteria for the selection of plays required that they "meet the test of a truthful portrayal of American life" and "through their aesthetic heightening of the truth, have significance for modern audiences." The plays are categorized according to the cause of loneliness: personal failure, homelessness, an unhappy family life, the failure of a love affair, socioeconomic forces, a conflict between the material and the spiritual, the isolation of a hero, and unhappiness in the South. Arthur Miller, Eugene O'Neill, Carson McCullers, John Steinbeck, Tennessee Williams, William Saroyan, and William Inge are among the 20 playwrights represented.

1182. Eisinger, Chester E. Fiction of the forties. Chicago, University of Chicago Press [1963] 392 p. 63–20904 PS379.E4
Bibliographical references included in "Notes" (p. 368-383).
The writers of a troubled decade and their search for meaning in a rapidly changing world are discussed. The author believes that fiction mirrored the innermost fears and urges of the American people during the Second World War and the years immediately following. Naturalism, liberalism, conservatism, the "gothic spirit," and existentialism all found their best expression in the personal interpretations which juxtaposed self and society in a desperate struggle to discover both. The writers examined most closely include John Dos Passos, Nelson Algren, Eudora Welty, Truman Capote, James Gould Cozzens, and William Faulkner. An appendix gives a chronological listing of some 150 fiction titles published from 1939 to 1953.

1183. Falk, Robert P. The Victorian mode in American fiction, 1865–1885. [East Lansing] Michigan State University Press, 1965 [ᶜ1964] 188 p. 64–21643 PS377.F3
Bibliographical references included in "Notes" (p. 167–182).
Victorian realism is interpreted as coloring a distinct literary period, existing within its own life cycle, and moving from a hesitant Victorian romanticism to a mature "vision of reality." Falk places the novel at the center of his account. Henry James, William Dean Howells, John W. De Forest, and Mark Twain, the major practitioners of the craft at this time, are discussed in relation to the movement toward literary realism. Warner Berthoff's *The Ferment of Realism; American Literature, 1884–1919* (New York, Free Press [1965] 330 p.), attempts to trace the effects of realism in literary, so-

cial, intellectual, and historical works of a later period. *The Realistic Movement in American Writing* (New York, Odyssey Press [1965] 678 p. The Odyssey surveys of American writing), compiled by Bruce R. McElderry, is an anthology of fiction published during the period 1865–1900.

1184. Fiedler, Leslie A. Love and death in the American novel. New York, Criterion Books [1960] 603 p. 59–12195 PS374.L6F5
Fiedler draws upon the depth psychology of Freud and Jung to explain what he regards as a basic feature of American letters. Reflecting American society, the novel retreated into a fanciful world of nature and boyhood adventure, avoiding a conscious confrontation of sex and savagery. Submerged into the subconscious, these primeval forces have found symbolic expression in the repeated occurrence of thinly veiled homosexuality and demonic violence in American fiction. Mark Twain's Huck and Jim, along with Ishmael and Queequeg in *Moby Dick,* are thus seen as manifestations of repressed libido, while Cooper's tales become an outlet for the savagery lying beneath the surface of American life. Fiedler has also written numerous individual essays on literature, some of which have been collected in *No! In Thunder* (Boston, Beacon Press [1960] 336 p.). His *Waiting for the End* (New York, Stein & Day [1964] 256 p.) contains reflections on the present and future of American letters.

1185. Floan, Howard R. The South in northern eyes, 1831–1861. Austin, University of Texas Press [1958] 198 p.
57–8824 F213.F55 1958
Bibliographical footnotes.
The psychological conditioning for the "irrepressible" Civil War is studied through an examination of the views of major northern literary figures in the years prior to the conflict. The general pattern discerned is one of opposition to the South on the part of New England writers, balanced to some extent by sympathy among certain New Yorkers. To support his conclusions, the author cites the New England literary and general magazines as well as various regional writers, including Longfellow, Holmes, Hawthorne, Emerson, Thoreau, Lowell, Whittier, Garrison, and Wendell Phillips. Melville, Bryant, and Whitman express the partially sympathetic viewpoint of the New York area toward the South.

1186. Fraiberg, Louis B. Psychoanalysis & American literary criticism. Detroit, Wayne State University Press, 1960. 263 p.
59–11980 PS78.F7
The author discusses the use of Freudian theories

of psychoanalysis and art by various prominent American critics, including Van Wyck Brooks, Joseph Wood Krutch, Ludwig Lewisohn, Edmund Wilson, Kenneth Burke, and Lionel Trilling. Trilling is interpreted as adhering most faithfully to psychoanalytic findings.

1187. Frohock, Wilbur M. The novel of violence in America. [2d ed., rev. and enl.] Dallas, Southern Methodist University Press [1958, c1957] 238 p.      57–14767 PS379.F7 1958

A substantial revision of no. 2427 in the 1960 *Guide,* featuring a new preface and a "radical alteration" in the treatment of Faulkner and Hemingway. Three new chapters have been included: "Mr. Warren's Albatross," criticizing Robert Penn Warren's fiction for evasion of the actual; "James Agee — The Question of Wasted Talent," on the loss of potential novelists to film and magazine writing; and "The Menace of the Paperback," in which the relation of paperback "gimmick" fiction to the future of the novel is discussed.

1188. Frohock, Wilbur M. Strangers to this ground; cultural diversity in contemporary American writing. Dallas, Southern Methodist University Press [1961] 180 p.
     61–17183 PS221.F7

That national fiction affirms national diversity is the thesis established in this study of seven writers. The author believes that leaving home and beginning life in a new region and a different cultural environment constitute the decisive experience most Americans face — the "Great American Topos." Numerous novelists are cited as dealing with this problem, but Frohock concentrates on Fitzgerald, Pound, Emily Dickinson, Edna St. Vincent Millay, James Gould Cozzens, Lionel Trilling, and Jack Kerouac. The concluding essay considers the challenge to literary critics within the universities to relate literature, broadly conceived, to the cultural variety existing in American life.

1189. Fuller, Edmund. Man in modern fiction; some minority opinions on contemporary American writing. New York, Random House [1958] 171 p.      58–7664 PS379.F8

Writing from the viewpoint of the Judeo-Christian moral tradition, Fuller challenges the tendencies to depict deviates as representative of modern man and to view man as a godless, depraved creature whose life lacks both meaning and nobility. Writers singled out to illustrate the "destructive and anti-social" nature of much modern fiction and criticism include James Jones, Jack Kerouac, John Steinbeck, Norman Mailer, Tennessee Williams, and Nelson Algren. In *Books With Men Behind Them* (New York, Random House [1962] 240 p.), Fuller offers his candidates for "a renewed literature in the great tradition" of man as a rational, free, responsible, and purposeful creature of God: C. S. Lewis, C. P. Snow, Alan Paton, Thornton Wilder, Gladys Schmitt, J. R. R. Tolkien, and Charles Williams.

1190. Fussell, Edwin S. Frontier: American literature and the American West. Princeton, N. J., Princeton University Press, 1965. xv, 450 p.
     64–12181 PS169.W4F8

Bibliographical footnotes.

The author contends that the frontier was "the ideal *mimesis* for the mid-nineteenth century American literary problem, an almost perfect instrument for blending the most realistic native materials with the most far-reaching social criticism, moral commentary, or philosophical speculation." Accordingly, in penetrating the meaning of early American literature, "the word West, with all its derivatives and variants, is the all but inevitable key." Fussell begins by tracing possible origins for the various metaphors of the West and illustrating how the frontier metaphor developed and declined in the writings of major American authors. He alludes to the many uses of western names and places in the writings of Cooper, Hawthorne, Poe, Thoreau, Melville, and Whitman and finds the frontier metaphor a central factor in each. Wilson O. Clough, in *The Necessary Earth; Nature and Solitude in American Literature* (Austin, University of Texas Press [1964] 234 p.), offers conjectures on the frontier as a favorite source of native myth and on the extent to which this metaphor is influential in the 20th century.

1191. Gaston, Edwin W. The early novel of the Southwest. [Albuquerque] University of New Mexico Press [1961] xiii, 318 p.
     60–11693 PS277.G3

"Related studies": p. 288–291. Bibliography: p. 292–302.

A critical history of representative southwestern fiction written in the period 1819–1918 by authors who either lived in or had firsthand knowledge of the Southwest. A study of 40 novels leads to the conclusion that the general development of the early regional novel follows the romantic tradition of the mainstream of American fiction, evolving from the naive to the complex and mature. A general survey of the novels is followed by studies of plot types, techniques, character portrayal, impressions of geography, and intellectual or philosophical concepts. Appendixes contain synopses of the novels and biographical data on the authors.

1192. Gohdes, Clarence L. F. Bibliographical guide to the study of the literature of the U.S.A. 2d ed., rev. and enl. Durham, N.C., Duke University Press [1963] 125 p.
63–18575 Z1225.G6 1963
The author's 35 selective lists cover the methodology and technique of literary studies and American literary history and criticism as well as the authoritative works in such areas of Americana as biography, art, religion, and comparative literature. Brief annotations cover the scope and significance of the more than 700 books listed. A useful complement is James L. Woodress' *Dissertations in American Literature, 1891–1955, With Supplement, 1956–1961* (Durham, N.C., Duke University Press, 1962. 138 p.).

1193. Gossett, Louise Y. Violence in recent southern fiction. Durham, N.C., Duke University Press, 1965. xi, 207 p. 65–13656 PS261.G6
That violence is the dominating element in southern fiction since 1930 is the contention advanced in this study of the work of 11 writers, from the pre-1940 writings of William Faulkner, Erskine Caldwell, and Thomas Wolfe to the post-1940 work of William Styron, Flannery O'Connor, and Eudora Welty. Noting that recent southern fiction has been discussed in studies of the grotesque by William Van O'Connor and Irving Malin, Miss Gossett emphasizes the violence that often accompanies the incongruities and distortions. She sees violence as "part of the total response of creative artists to jarring changes in man's view of himself" and as an expression of the complicated history of the South.

1194. Haraszti, Zoltán. The enigma of the Bay Psalm Book. [Chicago] University of Chicago Press [1956] 143 p. facsims., port.
56–5128 BS1440.B415H3
Bibliographical references included in "Notes" (p. 119–139).
As only 11 copies of the original *Bay Psalm Book* of 1640 survive—and only five of these are complete—the University of Chicago issued *The Bay Psalm Book, a Facsimile Reprint of the First Edition of 1640* ([295] p.) in 1956. In this companion volume, Haraszti has examined the famous book as a literary object and has uncovered important facts and rectified misconceptions. He notes that, contrary to the usual assumption, John Cotton rather than Richard Mather wrote the preface. Haraszti also challenges earlier speculations concerning the authorship of the Puritan translation and discusses the historical background of the translation, the text of the book, and problems for the scholar in uncovering further clues to the authorship of individual passages.

1195. Hassan, Ihab H. Radical innocence; studies in the contemporary American novel. Princeton, N.J., Princeton University Press, 1961. 362 p. 61–7416 PS379.H32
Fiction after Hemingway and Faulkner is viewed as having created a new fictional hero, possessed by "radical innocence." As an existentialist who tries responsibly to reconcile himself to destructive encounters with experience, this victimized, innocent hero struggles to overcome defeat as he is initiated into the contradictions of his culture. After developing his metaphor for modern literature, Hassan considers nine novelists: William Styron, Harvey Swados, Norman Mailer, Frederick Buechner, Bernard Malamud, Ralph Ellison, Herbert Gold, John Cheever, and J. P. Donleavy. The last section discusses the synthesis between art and meaningful reality in the fiction of Carson McCullers, Truman Capote, J. D. Salinger, and Saul Bellow.

1196. Hicks, Granville, *ed*. The living novel, a symposium. New York, Macmillan, 1957. 230 p. 57–12221 PS379.H5
As a reply to those who regard the American novel as dead or dying, 10 contemporary novelists have written essays on their occupation. Although the tone varies from anger to detached and critical introspection, an intense devotion to craft is emphasized. The contributors are Saul Bellow, Flannery O'Connor, Herbert Gold, Ralph Ellison, Mark Harris, Paul Boles, John Brooks, Wright Morris, Harvey Swados, and Jessamyn West. Hicks concludes the volume with an afterword on "The Enemies of the Novel."

1197. Hoffman, Daniel G. Form and fable in American fiction. New York, Oxford University Press, 1961. 368 p. 61–8371 PS377.H6
Ten romances and tales are analyzed to show how folklore and mythology expressed the themes of 19th-century prose and affected the form and content of American fiction. Irving, Hawthorne, Melville, and Mark Twain, in their attempts to define the underlying themes of national life, are said to have turned inevitably toward the common archetypal patterns of journey, quest, and initiation. The meaning of the term "romance" is amplified and explored as Hoffman stresses the significant impact of magic, ritual, myth, and folklore upon our writers.

1198. Hoffman, Frederick J. Freudianism and the literary mind. 2d ed. Baton Rouge,

Louisiana State University Press, 1957. 350 p.
57–11542   PN49.H6 1957
Bibliography: p. 331–341.

A complete revision of a 1945 publication mentioned in the annotation for no. 2440 in the 1960 *Guide*. Although the substance of the original volume remains, Hoffman advises in his preface that he has amplified, cut, updated, and refined the language. In addition, he has included a detailed study of Fitzgerald's *Tender Is the Night* and an appendix reprinting an essay entitled "Psychology and Literature," first published in the *Kenyon Review* in 1957.

1199.  Hoffman, Frederick J., *ed*. Marginal manners; the variants of bohemia. Evanston, Ill., Row, Peterson [1962]  182 p.
62–4798  PS536.H6

A collection of essays, stories, and poems defining and describing the history of the socially dissident, the nonconformist, and the economic failure. Among these "marginal men" are beatniks, bohemians, expatriates, hipsters, bums, hoboes, and outsiders—types the author has distinguished from one another and related to the social history of different periods. Excerpts and essays are used to show that each group is identifiable on the basis of its language, values, and experiences.

1200.  Hoffman, Frederick J., *ed*. Perspectives on modern literature. Evanston, Ill., Row, Peterson [1962]  242 p.
62–4217  PR473.H6

A selection of readings arranged under such topics as "Culture and the Intellectual," "The Dignity and Responsibility of Art," "The 1930's—The Survival Values of Tradition," "The Leftist Imperative," and "The Revolt against Ideology." Among the authors represented are H. L. Mencken, Ezra Pound, Hart Crane, William Faulkner, and Norman Mailer.

1201.  Howard, Leon. Literature and the American tradition. Garden City, N.Y., Doubleday, 1960.  354 p.
60–5933  PS88.H65

A survey of American literature from the time of the Puritan and transcendental influences to the present, written to answer the question, "Does the literary history of America reveal the existence of an attitude of mind consistent and durable enough to be called an aspect of the national character?" Stressing the traditional periods and movements, Howard concludes that the key to the best in American literature lies in the attitude of Faulkner and Hemingway—their belief in "the creative power of the human spirit to endure and prevail and to exist in the meanest and queerest of individuals."

1202.  Hubbell, Jay B. South and Southwest; literary essays and reminiscences. Durham, N.C., Duke University Press, 1965.  369 p.
65–26839  PS121.H83
"Publications of Jay B. Hubbell": p. 365–369.

Sixteen essays, including reminiscences based upon the author's experiences as a teacher, editor, and author, as well as historical and literary studies supplementing the materials presented in his earlier publications. Among the essays are recollections of his years as editor of *Southwest Review*, 1924–27, as visiting professor in American literature at the University of Vienna, 1949–50, and as one of the founders of *American Literature*, for which he served as chairman of the board of editors from 1928 to 1954. In his *Southern Life in Fiction* (Athens, University of Georgia Press [1960]  99 p. Eugenia Dorothy Blount Lamar memorial lectures, 1959), Hubbell comments upon images of the South in literature and history, protesting that the South has often been misrepresented in fiction.

1203.  Hungerford, Edward B., *ed*. Poets in progress; critical prefaces to ten contemporary Americans. [Evanston, Ill.] Northwestern University Press, 1962.  213 p. 62–10612  PS324.H8
Bibliography: p. [209]–213.

Ten American poets who have won critical acclaim since World War II are discussed by current or former English professors at Northwestern University. Each of the contributors writes about a personal favorite, and several have previously written longer critical works on their subjects. The poets considered are Theodore Roethke, Robert Lowell, Stanley Kunitz, Richard Wilbur, Richard Eberhart, W. D. Snodgrass, Howard Nemerov, J. V. Cunningham, Randall Jarrell, and W. S. Merwin.

1204.  Hyman, Stanley E. The promised end; essays and reviews, 1942–1962. Cleveland, World Pub. Co. [°1963]  380 p.
63–18586  PN511.H9

These miscellaneous essays, dating from 1942 to 1962, treat a wide variety of themes and contexts but reflect Hyman's steady interest in American folk traditions, mythology, and contemporary writing and culture. The author has corrected errors of fact in the essays as they were initially published and has occasionally noted his disagreement with his own original opinions. Some of the writers who figure prominently in the essays are John Steinbeck, John Peale Bishop, Herman Melville, David Daiches, Isaac Babel, Richard Wright, and Ralph Ellison; general topics include "American Negro Literature and Folk Tradition," "Some Trends in the Novel," "Stances Toward Mass Culture," and "The Child Ballad in America."

1205. Jones, Howard Mumford. History and the contemporary; essays in nineteenth-century literature. Madison, University of Wisconsin Press, 1964. 176 p.          64–14505 PS201.J58
Includes bibliographical references.

Nine essays emphasizing the lasting qualities in the works of some 19th-century men of letters whom the author believes contemporary literary historians are apt to neglect. Jones holds that the intellectual giants of the 19th century assumed a responsibility for culture and the perpetuation of a literary tradition, whereas 20th-century writers have not. Cooper and Thoreau are interpreted as philosophic moralists, the former interested in cultural dilemmas and the latter sensitive to human nature. Holmes is evaluated as a free-ranging intellectual concerned with the great philosophical problems of history, while Poe is reread as offering an exercise in the psychology of a standard 19th-century hero. Whittier reconsidered is found to have given the best American expression of faith in the goodness of God and to have achieved lasting beauty in his poetry.

1206. Jones, Howard Mumford. The theory of American literature. Reissued, with a new concluding chapter and rev. bibliography. Ithaca, N.Y., Cornell University Press [1965] 225 p.
          66–272 PS31.J6 1965
Bibliography: p. 207–215.

An updated edition of no. 2446 in the 1960 *Guide*. The third edition of *Guide to American Literature and Its Backgrounds Since 1890* (Cambridge, Harvard University Press, 1964. 240 p.), compiled by Jones and Richard M. Ludwig, is a revised and enlarged edition of no. 2447 in the 1960 *Guide*.

1207. Kaul, A. N. The American vision; actual and ideal society in nineteenth-century fiction. New Haven, Yale University Press, 1963. 340 p. (Yale publications in American studies, 7)
          63–9309 PS374.S7K3 1963
Bibliography: p. 325–334.

A study of the social themes in the fiction of Melville, Hawthorne, Cooper, and Mark Twain. The author examines the dialectic between the real society which formed the background for each writer and the idealized society which each envisioned. A concluding note discusses "Social Reality and the Form of American Fiction."

1208. Kazin, Alfred. Contemporaries. [Essays] Boston, Little, Brown [1962] 513 p.
          62–10528 PS3521.A995C6

A catholic collection of literary essays, many previously published and well known, edited and arranged to indicate the intellectual heritage of modern American literature. Initial chapters discuss the relevance of the American past and the 19th-century classic writers. Saul Bellow, Robert Lowell, Norman Mailer, Karl Shapiro, Nelson Algren, James Agee, J. F. Powers, J. D. Salinger, Truman Capote, James Baldwin, Kenneth Rexroth, and Bernard Malamud are among the 20th-century writers included. Other chapters comment on "The European Current," "Freud and His Consequences," "The Puzzle of Modern Society," and "The Critic's Task."

1209. Klein, Marcus. After alienation; American novels in mid-century. Cleveland, World Pub. Co. [1964] 307 p.          63–19731 PS379.K5
Bibliography: p. 305–307.

1210. Baumbach, Jonathan. The landscape of nightmare: studies in the contemporary American novel. [New York] New York University Press, 1965. 173 p.          65–11761 PS379.B35
Bibliography: p. 171–173.

These two studies of the American novel in the post-World-War-II period share the conviction that the possibility of total annihilation, in combination with the alternative of dehumanized existence, has created a climate of terror which is reflected in recent fiction. Klein discusses five writers—Saul Bellow, Ralph Ellison, James Baldwin, Bernard Malamud, and Wright Morris—who have had to create a "literature of accommodation." Baumbach views the imaginative vision of nine modern novels in "a world which accommodates evil." The novels selected are *All the King's Men, The Victim, The Catcher in the Rye, Invisible Man, Wise Blood, The Assistant, Lie Down in Darkness, The Pawnbroker,* and *Ceremony in Lone Tree.* Sidney W. Finkelstein, in *Existentialism and Alienation in American Literature* (New York, International Publishers [1965] 314 p.), traces the philosophical development of existentialism in Europe through its manifestations in American literature.

1211. Kostelanetz, Richard, *ed.* On contemporary literature; an anthology of critical essays on the major movements and writers of contemporary literature. [New York, Avon Books, 1964] 638 p.
          64–55294 PN771.K6
Includes bibliographies.

A collection of more than 50 general essays on the major writers and movements in American, Canadian, and European literature since World War II. The initial 16 essays cover developments in the leading literary forms in seven countries; the rest of the book contains essays on individual writers, mostly American. Among the contributors are Ihab Hassan, Alfred Kazin, Norman Podhoretz, Leslie Fiedler, Randall Jarrell, Walter Allen, R. W. B. Lewis, William Barrett, Irving Howe, Eric Bentley, and Stanley Edgar Hyman. Individual authors discussed include Vladimir Nabokov, James Purdy, Theodore Roethke, William Styron, Robert Penn Warren, James Baldwin, Edward Albee, and Joseph Heller. Other anthologies of recent criticism on modern writing are *The Creative Present* (Garden City, N.Y., Doubleday, 1963. 265 p.), edited by Nona Balakian and Charles Simmons, and *Contemporary American Novelists* (Carbondale, Southern Illinois University Press [1964] 232 p. Crosscurrents: modern critiques), edited by Harry T. Moore.

1212. Lenhart, Charmenz S. Musical influence on American poetry. Athens, University of Georgia Press [1956]   337 p.

    56–7980   PS310.M8L4

Bibliography: p. 314–326.

Walt Whitman, Sidney Lanier, and Edgar Allan Poe are the central figures in this study of the poetic and musical arts in America during the 17th, 18th, and 19th centuries. To support his thesis that the "kinds of poetry written in a century often have depended upon the kinds of music heard in that century," the author identifies poems containing direct references to music, imitations of such musical forms as the symphony, and attempts to create the impression of music in poetry. The first chapter is devoted to a brief history of American music during three centuries; the following three chapters consider lyrical poetry and musical forms. The final chapters of the book discuss Whitman, Lanier, and Poe in detail.

1213. Levin, Harry. The power of blackness: Hawthorne, Poe, Melville. New York, Knopf, 1958. 263 p.   58–5826   PS1888.L4

Bibliography: p. 249–255.

The author demonstrates the preoccupation of three eminent writers with evil and examines the symbols they used. His *Contexts of Criticism* (Cambridge, Harvard University Press, 1957. 294 p. Harvard studies in comparative literature, 22) consists of academic essays on a wide variety of literary topics, including "Observations on the Style of Ernest Hemingway," "Don Quixote and Moby Dick," and "Criticism in Crisis."

1214. Literary history of the United States. Editors: Robert E. Spiller [and others] 3d ed.,

rev. New York, Macmillan, 1963. 2 v.

    63–17511   PS88.L522

Bibliography: v. 1, p. 1446–1481.

CONTENTS.— [1] History.— [2] Bibliography.

In the third edition of this now standard work, no. 2460–2461 in the 1960 *Guide,* the story of American letters is continued through the early 1960's. The second volume comprises the comprehensive bibliography published with the first edition in 1948 and the bibliographical supplement published in 1959, with a common index. Fifty-seven American scholars contributed the 83 chapters. In the revised "postscript" chapter for the third edition, Willard Thorp and Robert E. Spiller evaluate writers whose careers ended between the World Wars, and Ihab Hassan estimates the achievements of those who emerged after 1945 (including recent novelists, dramatists, poets, and literary critics) and the forces that have dominated literature in the postwar world.

1215. Litz, A. Walton, *ed.* Modern American fiction; essays in criticism. New York, Oxford University Press, 1963. 365 p. (A Galaxy book, GB100)   63–11919   PS379.L5

Critics representing a multiplicity of approaches to literature comment on the modern novel from Stephen Crane to Robert Penn Warren. Eleven essays are devoted to Fitzgerald, Hemingway, and Faulkner; others deal with Dreiser, Lewis, Dos Passos, Wolfe, Steinbeck, Sherwood Anderson, and Gertrude Stein. Theories of fiction which originated in the 19th-century with James, Howells, and Garland are balanced by the more recent speculations of Malcolm Cowley, Ihab Hassan, and Wright Morris. Maxwell D. Geismar's *American Moderns, From Rebellion to Conformity* (New York, Hill & Wang [1958] 265 p.) is a collection of critical essays from various periods. In *The Modern Novel in America* (Chicago, Gateway Editions; distributed by H. Regnery Co. [1956] 227 p. A Gateway edition, 6035), an earlier edition of which is no. 2360 in the 1960 *Guide,* Frederick J. Hoffman demonstrates the effects of artistic philosophy and technique upon the novel.

1216. Ludwig, Richard M., *ed.* Aspects of American poetry; essays presented to Howard Mumford Jones. [Columbus] Ohio State University Press [1963, ᶜ1962]   335 p.

    62–16217   PS305.L8

Includes bibliography.

After 43 years of leadership as a teacher, scholar, and humanist, Howard Mumford Jones retired in 1962 as Abbott Lawrence Lowell Professor of the Humanities at Harvard University. For the occasion, friends and former students supplied this festschrift of 12 essays on American poetry, along with a bibliography of Jones' writings. Contributors and essays are as follows: "The Meter-Making Argument," by Edwin Fussell; "Some Varieties of Inspiration," by G. Ferris Cronkhite; "Poe: Journalism and the Theory of Poetry," by William Charvat; "The Problem of Structure in Some Poems by Whitman," by Marvin Felheim; "Ezra Pound's London Years," by Richard M. Ludwig; "Robert Frost and Man's 'Royal Role,'" by Claude M. Simpson; "Sherwood Anderson's *Mid-American Chants*," by Walter B. Rideout; "*The Bridge* and Hart Crane's 'Span of Consciousness,'" by Albert Van Nostrand; "Wallace Stevens' Ice-Cream," by Richard Ellmann; "The Situation of Our Time: Auden in His American Phase," by Frederick P. W. McDowell; "Mr. Tate: Whose Wreath Should Be a Moral," by Radcliffe Squires; and "Deliberate Exiles: The Social Sources of Agrarian Poetics," by Wallace W. Douglas.

1217. Lyons, John O. The college novel in America. With a preface by Harry T. Moore. Carbondale, Southern Illinois University Press [1962] 208 p. (Crosscurrents: modern critiques)
62–17619 PS374.U52L9
Includes bibliography.

In this first full-length treatment of the college novel as a special literary genre, the author considers over 200 academic novels whose main characters are either students or professors. The orientation of the study is toward literary history rather than qualitative selection, although a critical approach is taken in the discussions of trends and types.

1218. Malin, Irving, *ed.* Psychoanalysis and American fiction. New York, Dutton, 1965. 316 p. (A Dutton paperback, D162)
65–2415 PS371.M26
Includes bibliographical references.

Fifteen essays in which the insights of psychoanalysis are applied to American writings. Cooper, James, Willa Cather, Erskine Caldwell, Faulkner, Mark Twain, Poe, Melville, and Frank Norris are among the writers considered; the critics include Simon Lesser, Patrick Quinn, Richard Chase, Leslie Fiedler, Edmund Wilson, Maxwell Geismar, and Leon Edel. In his *New American Gothic* (Carbondale, Southern Illinois University Press [1962] 175 p. Crosscurrents: modern critiques), Malin treats the private visions of six contemporary authors: Carson McCullers, Flannery O'Connor, John Hawkes, J. D. Salinger, Truman Capote, and James Purdy.

1219. Marx, Leo. The machine in the garden; technology and the pastoral ideal in America. New York, Oxford University Press, 1964. 392 p.
64–24864 E169.1.M35
Bibliographical references included in "Notes" (p. 367–384).

The author seeks "to describe and evaluate the uses of the pastoral ideal in the interpretation of American experience." After discussing the pastoral ideal in general, he examines its relationship to technology as depicted in the writings of Robert Beverley, Jefferson, Cooper, Thoreau, Melville, Mark Twain, Fitzgerald, Faulkner, and others.

1220. Maxwell, Desmond E. S. American fiction: the intellectual background. London, Routledge & K. Paul [1963] 306 p.
64–1077 PS371.M3 1963a
Bibliographical footnotes.

The idea that the American novel is a characteristic expression of romantic individualism, emerging from a shallow social order incapable of sustaining realistic fiction, is challenged in this account of the American social and literary scene from pre-Revolutionary days to the present. American politics, customs, laws, and social patterns are viewed as part of an intellectual dialectic, interacting with the classical European imagination to form a native American tradition more urban and civilized than the romantic, revolutionary tradition of American fiction. Edward Taylor, Philip Freneau, Edgar Allan Poe, James Fenimore Cooper, Herman Melville, Nathaniel Hawthorne, Mark Twain, Ernest Hemingway, John Dos Passos, F. Scott Fitzgerald, William Faulkner, and James Gould Cozzens are among the writers whose receptivity to European thought is examined.

1221. Meyer, Roy W. The middle western farm novel in the twentieth century. Lincoln, University of Nebraska Press [1965] 265 p.
64–17221 PS374.F3M4 1965
"An annotated bibliography of middle western farm fiction, 1891–1962": p. 200–242.
Bibliography: p. 243–252.

A study of 140 novels dealing with rural life in the Middle West and published from 1891 to 1962. The author considers that "farm" fiction is significant primarily as a social commentary rather than as part of the mainstream of artistic fiction. He notes that "the use of rural life as the substance of serious fiction was delayed until about the time when the United States changed from a predominantly rural to a predominantly urban country." Beginning with the initial efforts of Joseph Kirkland and Hamlin Garland, the farm novel as a genre grew slowly until after World War I, when suddenly it burgeoned.

1222. Millgate, Michael. American social fiction: James to Cozzens. New York, Barnes & Noble [1964] 217 p.     64–5659 PS379.M48
Bibliographical footnotes.
The author evaluates the quality of the social novel in America from 1877 to 1957 and defends its right to acclaim. Among the writers whose works he examines are Henry James, F. Scott Fitzgerald, William Dean Howells, Frank Norris, Edith Wharton, Theodore Dreiser, Sherwood Anderson, Sinclair Lewis, John Dos Passos, and James Gould Cozzens.

1223. Miner, Earl R. The Japanese tradition in British and American literature. Princeton, Princeton University Press, 1958. 312 p.
57–11934 PR129.J3M5
Includes bibliography.
An extended analysis of Japan's influence on American literature. The author notes that American impressionism, imagism, realism, and symbolism are all indebted to Japan for important features. The movements in the second decade of the 20th century toward a "new poetry" are carefully explored for the influence of the Japanese *haiku*. According to Miner, "Before Japanese poetry became known to the West, few poets would have felt they dared to write such a short poem about a moth and the moon unless they could discover a suitable moral to draw from the description." He is careful to differentiate between the roles of Pound, Amy Lowell, and John Gould Fletcher in the imagist movement and to delineate the place of Lafcadio Hearn in transmitting poetic influences. Frost, Williams, MacLeish, Aiken, Wilder, and Stevens are other figures judged to have made use of Japanese traditions.

1224. Mizener, Arthur. The sense of life in the modern novel. Boston, Houghton Mifflin, 1964 [*1963] 291 p.     62–11483 PS371.M59
The responsibilities of novelists and critics in creating and assessing the realistic novel are discussed in this study of English and American writers since the mid-19th century. Hemingway, Faulkner, Dos Passos, and Cozzens are emphasized. The problem for the writer is to reconcile his often eccentric sense of personal life with the social reality in which fiction must be rooted; the critic's problem is to compare the life represented in the novel to the actual patterns and deviations of society rather than to an abstract theory of "reality."

1225. More, Paul E. Shelburne essays on American literature. Selected and edited by Daniel Aaron. New York, Harcourt, Brace & World [*1963] 280 p.     63–19640 PS121.M6
CONTENTS.—Paul Elmer More: biographical and bibliographical note.—Paul Elmer More: introduction.—The spirit and poetry of early New England.—Jonathan Edwards.—Benjamin Franklin.—Philip Freneau.—The origins of Hawthorne and Poe.—A note on Poe's method.—The solitude of Nathaniel Hawthorne.—Hawthorne: looking before and after.—The centenary of Longfellow.—Whittier the poet.—Emerson.—The influence of Emerson.—A hermit's notes on Thoreau.—Thoreau's Journal.—Walt Whitman.—Charles Eliot Norton.—Henry Adams.
From the 11 volumes of *Shelburne Essays* (1904–21) and *The New Shelburne Essays* (1928), Daniel Aaron has selected and introduced this collection of More's writings on American letters. The essays exemplify More's neohumanist approach and the coherent critical philosophy by which he judged literature.

1226. Morris, Wright. The territory ahead. [New York] Harcourt, Brace [1958] 231 p.
58–10892 PS88.M6
The sense of the past as it dominated and transformed literature is the basis of this study of Thoreau, Whitman, Melville, Mark Twain, James, Wolfe, Hemingway, Fitzgerald, and Faulkner. Morris contends that a long line of major American novelists evaded their immediate present and sought refuge in a nostalgic past, which each translated through the genius of his craft. Only Henry James is considered to have approached the present with intellectual alertness and to have used raw materials and technique to fuse past and present effectively.

1227. O'Connor, William Van. The grotesque: an American genre, and other essays. With a preface by Harry T. Moore. Carbondale, Southern Illinois University Press [1962] 231 p. (Crosscurrents: modern critiques) 62–15004 PS121.O2
In 18 essays the author attempts to reveal the ethical philosophy concealed behind the apparent grotesqueness and nihilism of many American novels. There are discussions of Frost, Stevens, Emily Dickinson, Mark Twain, Hemingway, Hawthorne, Faulkner, Eliot, and Caroline Gordon, in addition to general essays on traditions in fiction, the relationship of the writer to his environment, and modern criticism. The concluding essay is an imaginative dialogue entitled "The Hawthorne Museum."

1228. Ostroff, Anthony, *ed*. The contemporary poet as artist and critic; eight symposia. Boston, Little, Brown [1964] 236 p.

64–18766 PS324.O83

CONTENTS.—On Richard Wilbur's "Love calls us to the things of this world."—On Theodore Roethke's "In a dark time."—On Stanley Kunitz's "Father and son."—On Robert Lowell's "Skunk hour."—On John Crowe Ransom's "Master's in the garden again."—On Richard Eberhart's "Am I my neighbor's keeper?"—On W. H. Auden's "A change of air."—On Karl Shapiro's "The bourgeois poet."—Notes and bibliography (p. 217-236).

A series of symposia, each consisting of an important contemporary poem, three critiques of the poem by fellow poets, and the poet's response to his critics' interpretations. Poets who act as critics, in addition to the poets above, are Muriel Rukeyser, W. D. Snodgrass, Léonie Adams, Louise Bogan, William Dickey, John Berryman, and Babette Deutsch. More general comments by another group of American poets may be found in *The Sullen Art* (New York, Corinth Books, 1963. 95 p.), by David Ossman.

1229. The Paris review. Writers at work, the Paris review interviews. Edited and with an introduction, by Malcolm Cowley. New York, Viking Press, 1958. 309 p. illus.

58–6046 PN453.P3 1963

In the spring of 1953, a group of young Americans in Paris launched the first issue of *The Paris Review,* an international literary quarterly containing fiction, poetry, literary documents, portfolios, and articles. Among the most popular contributions was a series of interviews with famous writers. This collection includes interviews with James Thurber, William Faulkner, Robert Penn Warren, and Truman Capote. *Writers at Work, the Paris Review Interviews, Second Series* (New York, Viking Press [1963] 368 p.) offers interviews with Robert Frost, T. S. Eliot, Katherine Anne Porter, Ernest Hemingway, and Robert Lowell, among others.

1230. Parkinson, Thomas F., *ed*. A casebook on the beat. New York, Crowell [1961] 326 p. (Crowell literary casebooks)

60–9938 PS536.P25

Includes bibliography.

Selections from the writings of nine spokesmen of the beat generation are combined with criticism and commentary. Among the authors are Allen Ginsberg, Jack Kerouac, William Burroughs, Lawrence Ferlinghetti, and Gregory Corso. The commentators include Kenneth Rexroth, Norman Podhoretz, Henry Miller, Herbert Gold, John Ciardi, and Thomas Parkinson.

1231. Pearce, Roy Harvey. The continuity of American poetry. Princeton, N.J., Princeton University Press, 1961. xv, 442 p.

61–7424 PS303.P4

Bibliographical footnotes.

In this effort to "comprehend as a continuing series" the texts of major poems in America, the author synthesizes esthetic criticism and cultural history and ends by forecasting a break in continuity after three centuries of poetry in the Puritan tradition. The "Adamic" and "mythic" perspectives of American poetic genius have been constant, he argues, but Wallace Stevens and T. S. Eliot have taken these traditions to their farthest limit. In reaching his conclusions, the author follows poetic development from Edward Taylor and the Puritans to Emerson and Whitman. From this point, all American poetry becomes "in essence, if not in substance, a series of arguments with Whitman."

1232. Pochmann, Henry A. German culture in America; philosophical and literary influences, 1600–1900. With the assistance of Arthur R. Schultz and others. Madison, University of Wisconsin Press, 1957. xv, 865 p.

55–6791 E169.1.P596

Bibliographical references included in "Notes" (p. 495–799).

A professor of American literature at the University of Wisconsin assesses the role of German intellectual and cultural movements in the shaping of American civilization. The book's scope is broad, and Pochmann attempts to balance the German contributions with those of native American or British origin. Two books which study the German reaction to American writing are Harvey W. Hewett-Thayer's *American Literature as Viewed in Germany, 1818–1861* (Chapel Hill, University of North Carolina Press [1958] 83 p. University of North Carolina studies in comparative literature, no. 22) and *The American Novel in Germany* (Hamburg, Cram, De Gruyter, 1960. 116 p. Britannica et Americana, Bd. 7), by Anne M. Springer, who examines the critical reception of 20th-century novelists between the two world wars.

1233. Podhoretz, Norman. Doings and undoings; the fifties and after in American writing. New York, Farrar, Straus [1964] 371 p.

64–12385 PS221.P6

In keeping with his belief that "literature is not an end in itself" but "a mode of public discourse that either illuminates or fails to illuminate the common ground on which we live," the editor of *Commentary,* in this collection of occasional essays written over a period of some 10 years, strikes a middle ground between the critic-scholars and the journalists. In the opening section, Podhoretz contrasts the early and current reputations and accomplishments of six American men of letters. The other two sections encompass literary, political, and social affairs. Among the many writers evaluated are Edmund Wilson, James Baldwin, John Updike, Norman Mailer, Joseph Heller, and Philip Roth.

1234. Rabkin, Gerald. Drama and commitment; politics in the American theatre of the thirties. Bloomington, Indiana University Press, 1964. 322 p.                     64–63003 PS338.P6R3
    Bibliography: p. 297–300.

1235. Himelstein, Morgan Y. Drama was a weapon: the left-wing theatre in New York, 1929–1941. With a foreword by John Gassner. New Brunswick, N.J., Rutgers University Press [1963] 300 p.           62–21161 PN2277.N5H5
    Includes bibliography.
    Two scholarly analyses of American drama from 1929 to 1941, stressing the political and social themes prominent in that period. Rabkin's book is of wider scope and purpose, treating all the manifestations of political activity, whereas Himelstein concentrates upon "leftist" (notably Communist) influence. A study of the years 1890–1959 is Caspar H. Nannes' *Politics in the American Drama* (Washington, Catholic University of America Press, 1960. 256 p.).

1236. Rahv, Philip, *ed.* Literature in America; an anthology of literary criticism. New York, Meridian Books, 1957. 452 p. Meridian giant original, MG11)           57–10840 PS121.R2
    Includes bibliography.
    A collection of 40 essays describing how literary figures have utilized native materials and reacted to the American heritage, illustrating the close relationship of talent to native bias. According to Rahv, the use of indigenous materials does not mean "allegiance simple, uniform, and thoughtless" but rather an emotional and intellectual involvement which often results in acute criticism. The historical scheme of the book permits the reader to witness changes in emphasis and problems of the American writer; for instance, whereas early writers often complained about the absence of cultural institutions, the later writers discovered that the proliferation of institutions outdistanced the progress made by the arts, creating unforeseeable problems.

1237. The Reader's encyclopedia of American literature, by Max J. Herzberg and the staff of the Thomas Y. Crowell Co. New York, Crowell [1962] 1280 p.           62–16546 PS21.R4
    A comprehensive index to authors, titles, personages, literary and historical movements, and other matters useful in the study of American literature. Both the United States and Canada, from colonial times to 1962, are covered in articles by scholars; many of the longer and more detailed essays are signed by the contributors, among whom are George Arms, Cleanth Brooks, Lewis Leary, Oscar Cargill, Max Lerner, Robert Stallman, and Ernest Leisy. Other useful reference works for American literature published or appearing in a new edition during the 1956–65 period include *American Authors and Books, 1640 to the Present Day* (New York, Crown Publishers [1962] 834 p.), by William J. Burke and Will D. Howe, no. 2391 in the 1960 *Guide,* now augmented and revised by Irving R. Weiss; *The Oxford Companion to American Literature,* 4th ed. (New York, Oxford University Press, 1965. 991 p.), by James D. Hart; *The Reader's Encyclopedia,* 2d ed. (New York, Crowell [1965] 1118 p.), edited by William R. Benet; and *A Library of Literary Criticism: Modern American Literature,* 3d ed. (New York, F. Ungar [1964] 620 p.), edited by Dorothy Nyren.

1238. Robinson, Cecil. With the ears of strangers; the Mexican in American literature. Drawings by H. Beaumont Williams. Tucson, University of Arizona Press, 1963. 338 p.
                        63–11971 PS173.M4R6
    Bibliography: p. 325–330.
    The result of the collision of the American mind with the alien temperament of Mexico has been recorded in a history of hostility softening to interested inquiry. Although many early journals, diaries, and novels discounted Mexicans as unclean, backward, and sensual, by the end of the 19th century writers were nostalgically recalling the beauty of the old mission culture and the Mexican traditions which had colored the Hispanic Southwest. Robinson illustrates, through a wide selection of novels and nonfictional accounts, the dawning realization that in this people sprung from Indian and Spanish progenitors lay a valuable literary source for continental myth and tradition. Whitman, Prescott, William Carlos Williams, Willa Cather, John Steinbeck, and Archibald MacLeish have been among the writers who showed interest in America's Mexican heritage; in addition, a score of enthusiasts have recorded in regional literature their hope for the fusion of Mexican and U.S. cultures.

1239. Rosenthal, Macha L. The modern poets; a critical introduction. New York, Oxford University Press, 1960. 228 p.

60–13204 PR601.R6

Includes bibliography.

Poetry and the modern "crisis of personality," which created a need for new idioms and voices, are related in this study of 20th-century poetry. Following an opening chapter on the poet and the reader and a comparison of past and present poetic sensibilities, Rosenthal devotes three chapters to the roles of Yeats, Pound, and Eliot as germinal figures in modern verse. He then analyzes the "rival idioms of the great generation" of poets, concentrating on Robinson, Frost, Williams, Stevens, Moore, Cummings, Sandburg, and Jeffers. Contemporary poets, ranging from Robert Lowell and Theodore Roethke to Allen Ginsberg and Charles Olson, are discussed in the final chapters.

1240. Rubin, Louis D. The faraway country; writers of the modern South. Seattle, University of Washington Press, 1963. xiv, 256 p.

63–19632 PS261.R63

Bibliographical references included in "Notes" (p. 241–247).

"The faraway country" is the country of the imagination whose special population consists of displaced Southerners who transcend and transform the actual Southern society through writing fiction. Three generations of novelists and poets, from George Washington Cable to William Styron, are interpreted as products of a specific time and place; changes in outlook from one generation of writers to the next are seen as indicative of changing Southern experiences. Other studies of Southern writers are contained in Rinaldo C. Simonini's anthology, *Southern Writers: Appraisals in Our Time* (Charlottesville, University Press of Virginia [1964] 191 p.), and John M. Bradbury's *Renaissance in the South; a Critical History of the Literature, 1920–1960* (Chapel Hill, University of North Carolina Press [1963] 222 p.).

1241. Rubin, Louis D., *and* John R. Moore, *eds.* The idea of an American novel. New York, Crowell [1961] 394 p. 61–6174 PS371.R8

Includes bibliography.

An unusual collection of "literary documents that bear on our intense and long-standing self-consciousness about the American novel." This history stretches back to early days of the Republic and first becomes visible as a conscious "call for a national literature" articulated by such prominent figures as Cooper, Emerson, Hawthorne, Melville, Whitman, and Poe. The dialogue increases in complexity and scope after the initial challenge has been met: writers in subsequent sections give their views on "The Scope of the 'Great American Novel'"; "The American Novel and 'Reality'"; "The American Character"; "Ideals for the American Novel"; and "American Art and American Experience." A long final section contains statements about 17 novelists from Cooper to William Styron and Robert Penn Warren. Throughout the text, commentaries from the works of distinguished authors or publications are presented.

1242. Sanford, Charles L. The quest for paradise; Europe and the American moral imagination. Urbana, University of Illinois Press, 1961. 282 p. 61–6539 E169.1.S245

Bibliographical footnotes.

An interdisciplinary study of the origins and developing traits of the American moral imagination, based on a historical theme of mental regression to an imaginative former state of paradise. The first five chapters describe a "journey pattern of modern history" involving an imaginative transfer of paradise from heaven to earth; the last eight essays expand the theory and describe its repercussions in American literature, society, and foreign and domestic affairs. Industrialism, science, the "American cult of newness," and ideals of nature are among the topics related to moral philosophy and in turn to literature. The reform movement is studied through the writings of Thoreau, Hawthorne, Whitman, Bellamy, Lincoln Steffens, Mark Twain, and John Steinbeck. Henry James' theme, presented in his international novels, is explained to be "the meaning of the fall from paradise as the condition of a greater humanity."

1243. Schneider, Robert W. Five novelists of the progressive era. New York, Columbia University Press, 1965. 290 p. 65–12110 PS379.S36

Bibliographical references included in "Notes" (p. [259]–281).

An attempt to reconstruct the intellectual history of the years 1890–1917. The author studies five representative novelists and demonstrates that the pull of traditional thought and Victorian attitudes was as strong an influence as the new scientific thought, which many literary historians have claimed resulted in a drastic intellectual revolution. Stephen Crane, Frank Norris, and Theodore Dreiser consciously accepted the new thought but unconsciously clung to many conventional attitudes. The early novels of William Dean Howells and the bestselling novels of Winston Churchill are regarded as more accurate mirrors of popular thought, which was not, according to the author, as progressive as is often claimed.

1244. Sensabaugh, George F. Milton in early America. Princeton, N.J., Princeton University Press, 1964. 320 p. 63–9997 PR3588.S45
Bibliographical footnotes.

The influence of the English poet John Milton upon the intellectual, spiritual, and moral life of early America is systematically explored. The author concludes that "for a while in American history Milton moved through the whole cultural community, impressing not only poets but also editors and free-lancers, statesmen and lawyers, schoolmasters and doctors and clerics." He is considered by Sensabaugh to be a greater influence than other writers and philosophers because he affected American speech, attitudes, institutions, and ideals, aiding the colonies and the early Republic in the search for national identity and standards of behavior. The study proceeds chronologically from the first 25 years of the Republic, when Milton's influence was greatest, concluding with his diminution of stature during the Romantic movement that swept the country in the middle years of the 19th century.

1245. Shapiro, Karl J., ed. Prose keys to modern poetry. Evanston, Ill., Row, Peterson [1962] 260 p. 62–4795 PN1136.S46

An anthology of critical essays, prefaces, and other prose selections designed to assist the reader in understanding modern poetry. The selections are divided into the classical and romantic traditions. The former includes pieces by Poe, Eliot, and Pound; the latter begins with Whitman and ends with D. H. Lawrence. A chronology of significant events in poetry between 1817 and 1960 is appended.

1246. Spencer, Benjamin T. The quest for nationality; an American literary campaign. [Syracuse, N.Y.] Syracuse University Press, 1957. xv, 389 p. 57–12017 PS88.S58
Bibliography: p. 341–372.

As a history of "the national literary will," Spencer's study charts the explicit and conscious attempts, from 1607 to 1892, to forge a national literature distinctly separate from British or European literature. The American writer's growing awareness of native themes and materials is emphasized, and the author notes that "scarcely a native author of any importance before 1900 failed to engage in the inquiry and to declare himself publicly on its issues." Although the maturing of the sense of nationality led to a shift in emphasis, there remained a dedication to commemorate a common heritage and to establish a "voice of a nation which for the first time in history had manifestly embraced a belief in both God and Reason."

1247. Spender, Stephen, and Donald Hall, eds. The concise encyclopedia of English and American poets and poetry. New York, Hawthorn Books [1963] 415 p. illus. 63–8015 PR19.S6
Bibliography: p. 367–392.

Articles on specific poets and poetic terms are interspersed with lengthier essays pursuing general topics in a compendium useful to both scholar and student. The editors have endeavored to represent complementary or opposing viewpoints where they exist. Portraits of many important poets are included in the text. Among the contributors are Marius Bewley, Glauco Cambon, Northrop Frye, Hugh Kenner, John Crowe Ransom, and Richard Wilbur.

1248. Spiller, Robert E. The third dimension; studies in literary history. New York, Macmillan, 1965. 245 p. 65–13122 PS121.S6 1965

The author considers that, in the interpretation of literature, the first dimension lies in understanding the text, the second in discovering the cultural and social patterns of the society, and the third in the perspective of history, particularly literary history. The 16 essays included here were written between 1929 and 1963, when Spiller was editing the *Literary History of the United States,* and express his views on the problems of writing American literary history. The essays are reprinted as they were originally conceived and are presented as historical documents of a major movement in American literary scholarship. Lewis G. Leary has edited a collection of papers on various aspects of literary studies during the past 30 years entitled *Contemporary Literary Scholarship: A Critical Review* (New York, Appleton-Century-Crofts [1958] 474 p.), sponsored by the Committee on Literary Scholarship and the Teaching of English of the National Council of Teachers of English.

1249. Stallman, Robert W. The houses that James built, and other literary studies. [East Lansing] Michigan State University Press, 1961. xii, 254 p. 60–53548 PS379.S7
Includes bibliographical references.

As a critic, Stallman has assimilated the methods of Henry James, T. S. Eliot, and the New Critics. He concentrates on the text of an individual work and then looks for linked analogies and ideas — such as confused identity — which can relate novels seemingly unrelated. His aim is to "illuminate the given work's hidden world, the substructure of multiple inter-relationships." He concentrates on the major novels of seven writers — Fitzgerald, Hemingway, Faulkner, Crane, James, Hardy, and Conrad — in addition to the New Critics and the "Marxist" critics, notably Philip Rahv. Essays are published for the first time on *Maggie, Tender Is the Night, The Snows of Kilimanjaro,* and *As I Lay Dying.* Many of the other studies have been expanded or substantially revised for this collection.

1250. Stepanchev, Stephen. American poetry since 1945; a critical survey. New York, Harper & Row [1965] 216 p.   65–20440 PS324.S68
   Bibliography: p. 211–213.
   A general survey of recent trends in poetry, with brief introductions to the main characteristics of the work of 21 poets. Stepanchev discerns five distinct movements in poetry since World War II, starting with a period of involvement in the horrors of war and moving in the late fifties and early sixties into the projective verse of Charles Olson and his contemporaries and the autobiographical rehearsals of the "confessional school." Among the poets discussed are Robert Lowell, Randall Jarrell, Elizabeth Bishop, Denise Levertov, James Wright, John Ashbery, James Dickey, Alan Dugan, LeRoi Jones, Louis Simpson, William Stafford, and May Swenson.

1251. Stewart, John L. The burden of time: the Fugitives and Agrarians; the Nashville groups of the 1920's and 1930's, and the writing of John Crowe Ransom, Allen Tate, and Robert Penn Warren. Princeton, N.J., Princeton University Press, 1965. xi, 551 p.   65–12994 PS255.N3S7
   Bibliographical footnotes.
   A historical and biographical study of the important Nashville writers in the twenties and thirties, with an analysis of the work of outstanding individuals in the group. Louise S. Cowan, in her literary history *The Fugitive Group* (Baton Rouge, Louisiana State University Press [1959] 277 p.), carefully distinguishes between the Fugitives and the Agrarians and confines her study to the 16 poets who, "having no particular program, met frequently from 1915 to 1928 for the purpose of reading and discussing their own work." *The Fugitives, a Critical Account* (Chapel Hill, University of North Carolina Press [1958] 300 p.), by John M. Bradbury, uses textual analysis to evaluate the poetry, fiction, and criticism of the group on the basis of published critical consensus rather than personal opinion, devoting most attention to Ransom, Tate, Warren, Davidson, and Cleanth Brooks.

1252. Stewart, Randall. American literature & Christian doctrine. Baton Rouge, Louisiana State University Press [1958] 154 p.
                        58–7936 PS166.S8
   As a latter-day exponent of a moral measure for literature, the author challenges the view of man implicit in the American doctrines of rationalism,

exaggerated individualism, and naturalism. He criticizes the works of Jefferson, Emerson, and Whitman, along with the modern naturalist literary school, as forsaking the responsibility to relate art to ethics and religion. Contrasted to the philosophy of these Americans, he finds Christian principles in the works of Hawthorne, Melville, James, Cather, Eliot, Faulkner, and Warren. Different conclusions are reached from a similar perspective by a group of Catholic scholars who evaluate 19th-century American writers in *American Classics Reconsidered* (New York, Scribner [1958] 307 p.), edited by Harold C. Gardiner. The ethics of critical theory from still another viewpoint — that of the neohumanist — are considered in *The Moral Measure of Literature* (Denver, A. Swallow [1961] 137 p.), by Keith F. McKean.

1253. Stovall, Floyd, *ed.* Eight American authors, a review of research and criticism, by Jay B. Hubbell [and others]. Bibliographical supplement by J. Chesley Mathews. New York, Norton [1963] 466 p. (The Norton library [N178])
                   70–8568 PS201.S8 1963
   Intended for advanced students and scholars, this collection of bibliographical essays describes the scholarly and critical writings on eight classic American authors. Poe is discussed by Jay Hubbell, Emerson by Floyd Stovall, Hawthorne by Walter Blair, Thoreau by Lewis Leary, Melville by Stanley Williams, Whitman by Willard Thorp, Mark Twain by Harry Hayden Clark, and James by Robert Spiller. J. Chesley Mathews' supplement is a selective checklist of works published between 1955 and 1962.

1254. Sutton, Walter E. Modern American criticism. Englewood Cliffs, N.J., Prentice-Hall, 1963. 293 p. (The Princeton studies, humanistic scholarship in America)
                        63–8462 PN99.U5S8
   A survey of the tendencies in 20th-century American criticism, combining a historical approach and a plea for the integration of formalist concerns with historical fact, cultural experience, and language studies. Movements surveyed include those of the New Humanists, the Marxist critics, the New Critics, the neo-Aristotelians, and the psychological and myth critics. *Learners and Discerners; a Newer Criticism* (Charlottesville, University Press of Virginia [1964] 177 p.), edited by Robert E. Scholes, contains five papers originally presented as Peters Rushton seminar lectures at the University of Virginia. Stephen G. Nichols has edited a collection of René Wellek's essays on literary theory, criticism, and history; entitled *Concepts of Criticism* (New

Haven, Yale University Press, 1963. 403 p.), the volume contains 13 essays on various methods of literary study, several of which relate specifically to American literature.

1255. Thorp, Willard. American writing in the twentieth century. Cambridge, Harvard University Press, 1960. 353 p. (The Library of Congress series in American civilization)
59–14739 PS221.T48
Includes bibliography.
A survey of the standard themes and periods of recent literary history. Emphasis is placed on detailed studies of 10 major writers associated with various periods and trends: Edith Wharton, Frost, Robinson, O'Neill, Willa Cather, Dos Passos, Hemingway, Stevens, Faulkner, and Eliot. Lively accounts of the "critical wars" and the Southern renaissance — two areas on which the author is an authority — are included, along with a discussion of naturalism in American fiction.

1256. The Times literary supplement. American writing today: its independence and vigor. Edited by Allan Angoff. [New York] New York University Press, 1957. 433 p.
56–10779 PS221.T5 1957
From a special issue published on Sept. 17, 1954, *The Times Literary Supplement,* London's distinguished literary weekly, selected 69 essays designed to present "as accurate a picture as we could paint of the state of writing in America today." General essays on all aspects of the literary scene are balanced with reprints of reviews on American books that made literary history, including *Spoon River Anthology, The Great Gatsby, An American Tragedy, A Farewell to Arms, Look Homeward, Angel, Soldier's Pay, Dodsworth,* and *Manhattan Transfer.* Most of the selections are unsigned, following the tradition of anonymity long established for regular issues. *The American Imagination* (New York, Atheneum, 1960. 209 p.) and *The Critical Moment: Literary Criticism in the 1960s* (New York, McGraw-Hill [1964] 164 p. McGraw-Hill paperbacks) are other anthologies selected from *The Times Literary Supplement.*

1257. Walcutt, Charles C. American literary naturalism; a divided stream. Minneapolis, University of Minnesota Press [c1956] 332 p.
56–12465 PS379.W28
A study of naturalism as a literary genre, reconciling the romantic and scientific attitudes which apparently collide in critical descriptions of the genre. The tension that results from asserting the compatibility of science and intuition has produced an area

of friction in naturalistic literature, a fact which leads Walcutt to trace the genre to its parent philosophy, American transcendentalism. Both philosophies run in a "divided stream," one branch approaching life scientifically, the other intuitively. Zola, Hemingway, Dos Passos, Steinbeck, and Faulkner are among the authors studied.

1258. Walker, Robert H. The poet and the gilded age; social themes in late 19th century American verse. Philadelphia, University of Pennsylvania Press [1963] xviii, 387 p.
62–11268 PS310.S7W3 1963
The author contends that the poets of the last quarter of the 19th century display a social awareness, an opinion contrary to that held by most literary historians. He supports his conclusion by analyzing, both verbally and statistically, the content of verse written by secondary poets. The subject matter of the poetry, rather than its esthetic value or internal form, is the primary criterion in this analysis. A more traditional literary review, one based on biographical treatment and poetic tradition, is Carlin T. Kindilien's *American Poetry in the Eighteen Nineties* (Providence, Brown University Press, 1956. 223 p. Brown University studies, v. 20).

1259. Warren, Austin. New England saints. Ann Arbor, University of Michigan Press [1956] 192 p.
56–9721 F3.W3
Includes bibliography.
A collection of portraits of saintly New England writers — "men I recognize and celebrate as those to whom reality was the spiritual life, whose spiritual integrity was their calling and vocation." The author, himself a native New Englander, writes this hagiography with a deep affection for the spiritual heritage of the region, finding a continuity in New England philosophy and attitudes through four centuries. The subjects treated include the 17th-century Puritan poets, the 18th-century parsons, Bronson Alcott and Emerson, the French Catholic Fénelon, the elder Henry James, the mariner Methodist preacher Edward Taylor, the agnostic Charles Eliot Norton, the neohumanist Irving Babbitt, and the poet John Brooks Wheelwright.

1260. Weales, Gerald C. American drama since World War II. New York, Harcourt, Brace & World [1962] 246 p. 62–14467 PS351.W4
Virtually every recent playwright with a claim to importance is dealt with in this critical survey of American drama, 1945–60. The author, an academic critic, analyzes the literary substance of drama and touches only incidentally upon the political or

cultural scene, box-office economics, or play-production. Dramatists are grouped, when possible, according to genre, and chapters discuss the various groups: poets and novelists who write for the theater; "video boys" who write serious drama; playwrights of the 1920's and 1930's who kept writing after World War II; dramatists who specialize in the adaptation of fiction to the stage; and playwrights who write for a particular audience. Arthur Miller and Tennessee Williams receive special attention. Another critical history of modern American drama, one which is more personal and evaluative in tone, is Allan Lewis' *American Plays and Playwrights of the Contemporary Theatre* (New York, Crown Publishers [1965] 272 p.).

1261. Witham, W. Tasker. The adolescent in the American novel, 1920–1960. New York, Ungar [1964] 345 p.      63–8849 PS374.Y6W5
Bibliography: p. 285–300. "Chronological list of American novels dealing with problems of adolescents": p. 301–332.
Some 500 American novels with plots built around adolescent problems form the basis for this study. After summarizing the genteel attitudes which dominated adolescent fiction during the first two decades of the century, the author traces the gradual acceptance of a new realism in the 1920's. Topical chapters offer brief discussions of novels whose theme or plot concerns sexual awakening, rebellion against parents and society, delinquency, educational and vocational adjustments, the influence of environment, and some "special problems," including mental and physical handicaps, alcohol, drugs, and the effects of war. The survey demonstrates that most novels with juvenile protagonists are first novels and largely autobiographical and that more than 90 percent of the best of such books center on boys.

1262. Wright, Austin M. The American short story in the twenties. [Chicago] University of Chicago Press [1961] 425 p.
61–14535 PS379.W7
Includes bibliography.
The author compares short-story writers from 1890 to 1919 with those of the 1920's and concludes that the experimental genius of the latter group created the short story's most brilliant period. Over 200 stories are analyzed on the basis of subject matter, form, and technique; 13 appendixes explain the criteria used in selection and evaluation. The writers of the 1920's whose work is considered here include Fitzgerald, Faulkner, Hemingway, Anderson, and Katherine Anne Porter. The earlier period is represented by James, Dreiser, Stephen Crane, Ambrose Bierce, and others. *The American Short Story* (Boston, Houghton Mifflin, 1964. 213 p.), by William H. Peden, analyzes the general themes and techniques of some 100 writers from 1940 to 1963.

1263. Yates, Norris W. The American humorist: conscience of the twentieth century. Ames, Iowa State University Press [1964] 410 p.
63–22161 PS438.Y3
Bibliographical references included in "Notes" (p. 363–391).
This study of 20th-century humor is primarily concerned with the social values and attitudes of 15 major humorists. Allowing these writers to speak for themselves, Yates offers a picture of an essentially middle-class America of cracker-barrel philosophers, "solid" citizens, and "little men" tyrannized by the natural facts of matrimony and sex and the unnatural facts of technology and science. Humorists treated include George Ade, Mr. Dooley, Will Rogers, H. L. Mencken, Ring Lardner, Don Marquis, Clarence Day, Robert Benchley, Dorothy Parker, James Thurber, E. B. White, and S. J. Perelman.

1264. Zabel, Morton D., *ed*. Literary opinion in America; essays illustrating the status, methods, and problems of criticism in the United States in the twentieth century. 3d ed., rev. New York, Harper & Row [1962] 2 v. (Harper torchbooks, TB3013–3014. The University library)
62–52885 PN771.Z2 1962
A revised edition of no. 2550 in the 1960 *Guide*. The second edition was distinguished by six bibliographical lists on recent American criticism up to 1951; to these have been added a list covering the period 1951–62. The only other changes are the inclusion of an essay on Fitzgerald by Arthur Mizener and the substitution of a critique by Irving Howe on Sherwood Anderson for another essay on that same writer which appeared in the second edition.

# C. Periodicals

1265. Book week. Sept. 15, 1963+ [New York, World Journal Tribune]

66–6410  Z1007.B71685

Distributed with the Sunday editions of the *New York Herald Tribune, The Washington Post,* and the *San Francisco Examiner.*

A weekly intended to provide "a national literary magazine that has the space and the distribution to talk about books and those who write and publish them with the high standards they deserve."

1266. Critique; studies in modern fiction. v. 1+ winter 1956+ [Minneapolis]

64–32236  PN3503.C7

Vol. 4, no. 2–3 published by the Bolingbroke Society; v. 5+ distributed by B. De Boer, Nutley, N.J.

Designed "to notice the best in contemporary fiction and to throw light on that recent fiction which has not received its rightful share of attention from perceptive critics." Published three times a year, *Critique* features book reviews and articles on both specific and general topics. Special issues have been devoted to individual writers, among them Flannery O'Connor, J. F. Powers, Wright Morris, and Saul Bellow.

1267. The New York review of books. v. 1+ [Feb. 25, 1963?]+ [Milford, Conn., A. W. Ellsworth]  68–6716  AP2.N655

Running title, Jan. 14, 1964+: *The New York Review.*

During the 1963 newspaper strike in New York City, a group of well-known critics and scholars wrote reviews for the first issue of the sort of literary journal which the editors and contributors felt was needed in America. In the first issue, Robert B. Silvers and Barbara Epstein, editors, note the intention to allocate neither time nor space to "books which are trivial in their intentions or venal in their effects, except occasionally to reduce a temporarily inflated reputation or to call attention to a fraud." A biweekly, *The New York Review* encourages contributors to treat the book review as a literary genre in its own right, using all the passion, precision, and intelligence they can muster.

1268. Poetry northwest. v. 1+ June 1959+ [Seattle, University of Washington]

65–32672  AP2.P746

Vol. 4, no. 3/4+ distributed by B. De Boer, Nutley, N.J.

A quarterly hospitable to "the young and inexperienced, the neglected mature, the rough major talents and the fragile minor ones." Translations, drawings, and notes on contributors and poetry meetings are included.

1269. Twentieth century literature; a scholarly and critical journal. v. 1+ Apr. 1955+ [Denver, Swallow Press]  56–1944  PN2.T8

Published quarterly, with the purpose of gleaning from all sources "the most significant of scholarly and critical writing dealing with literature of the first half of our century" and featuring an annotated bibliography of articles appearing in a wide range of periodicals.

1270. Wisconsin studies in contemporary literature. v. 1+ winter 1960+ [Madison, Wis.] University of Wisconsin.

64–6922  PN2.W55

Published three times a year and primarily devoted to a consideration of the new literature which has emerged since World War II on both sides of the Atlantic.

# IV

# Biography and Autobiography

Nos. 1271–1303

THIS chapter includes biographical works which do not fit precisely into other chapters but are considered useful for the study of American history and culture. It also encompasses the genre of biography and autobiography on the basis of its value as Americana, as history, and as literature. The works found appropriate to this chapter were disproportionately fewer in number than in the 1960 *Guide* because the *Supplement* covers only a 10-year period and because, in that period, fewer professional biographers were writing scholarly works. Since the chapter is thus limited in scope, the index should be used to ascertain whether a specific biography or autobiography has been included elsewhere in the *Supplement*.

1271. DEAN GOODERHAM ACHESON, 1893–

Dean Acheson, lawyer and public official, was Secretary of State from 1949 to 1953 and a major proponent of the containment policy implemented partially by the Marshall Plan and NATO. He is the author of *A Citizen Looks at Congress* (1957), *Power and Diplomacy* (1958), and *Sketches From Life of Men I Have Known* (1961).

1272. Morning and noon. Boston, Houghton Mifflin, 1965. 288 p. illus.

65–19308 E748.A15A3

Bibliographical references included in "Notes" (p. [231]–278).

Reminiscences which are "autobiographical but not an autobiography," concerning the author's early life and career to 1940. Acheson's strong sense of integrity and commitment is apparent in his recollections of an eventful life among the politically famous. He gives an account of his boyhood in Middletown, Conn., and his arrival in Washington in 1919 as Justice Louis D. Brandeis' law clerk. From 1921 to 1933 he practiced law with the firm of Covington, Burling, & Rublee, after which he received a succession of Federal appointments, including that of Under Secretary of the Treasury.

1273. ALFRED OWEN ALDRIDGE, 1915–

A professor of English and comparative literature in various universities in the United States and abroad, he is the author of *Franklin and His French Contemporaries* (1957) and *Jonathan Edwards* (1964).

1274. Man of reason, the life of Thomas Paine. Philadelphia, Lippincott [1959] 348 p. illus. 59–7777 JC178.V2A8

This new study contains information from a large number of recently discovered letters and essays by Paine, as well as from French, English, and American documents that were largely unknown to his previous biographers.

1275. IRVING HENRY BARTLETT, 1923–

Head of the history department at the Carnegie Institute of Technology; author of *From Slave to Citizen* (1953).

1276. Wendell Phillips, Brahmin radical. Boston, Beacon Press [1961] 438 p.

61–10570 E449.P5594

Bibliographical references included in "Notes": p. 402–432.

Radical abolitionist, intellectual, and eloquent crusader, Wendell Phillips (1811–1884) held strong Calvinist beliefs. Although born a Boston Brahmin and graduated a Harvard lawyer, he repudiated his aristocratic background to agitate for social and moral reform. His wife introduced him to the abolition movement, his religious convictions committed him to support it, and his masterful oratory soon made him a leader in the cause. He also used his rhetorical gifts to work for the immediate enfranchisement of the Negro, for women's rights, for the common laborer, and for currency reform. From Bartlett's biography emerges the multifaceted personality of a radical who unrelentingly criticized the institutions of American democracy out of a firm belief in the worth of the American way of life.

1277. FRANCIS BEVERLEY BIDDLE, 1886–

Francis Biddle, lawyer, author, and public official, was Attorney General under President Franklin D. Roosevelt from 1941 to 1945 and a member of the International Military Tribunal at Nuremberg from 1945 to 1946. He was active in the defense of civil liberties and chairman of several national organizations.

1278. A casual past. Garden City, N.Y., Doubleday, 1961. 408 p. illus.

61–9480   KF373.B5A3

1279. In brief authority. Garden City, N.Y., Doubleday, 1962. 494 p. illus.

62–16744   KF373.B5A32

Two volumes of reminiscences, published a year apart. In *A Casual Past,* Biddle brings to life some of the odd, lovable, and often eccentric individuals who peopled his background and youth. Here are the Randolphs of Virginia and the Biddles from the North, two families who represent the main lines in his American heritage and of whom he is proud. He writes of his years at Groton and Harvard and of his appointment as private secretary to Justice Holmes upon graduation. The volume ends with a review of his 20 years of law practice. *In Brief Authority* outlines Biddle's public work in association with Franklin D. Roosevelt, whom he first saw as a schoolboy at Groton. His characterization of President Roosevelt and other New Dealers includes numerous witty insights. Biddle also reports on the Nuremberg trial of German war criminals, at which he was the only American member of the International Military Tribunal.

1280. CATHERINE DRINKER BOWEN, 1897–

No. 2606 in 1960 *Guide.*

1281. Adventures of a biographer. Boston, Little, Brown [1959] 235 p.

59–11888   PS3503.O814Z52

Recollections from a career spanning 40 years of continuous and successful publication. Mrs. Bowen discusses the people she has encountered on her research travels, the places she has visited, and the problems of biographical research.

1282. WILLIAM ORVILLE DOUGLAS, 1898–

No. 2664 in 1960 *Guide.*

1283. My wilderness: the Pacific West. Illustrations by Francis Lee Jaques. Garden City, N.Y., Doubleday, 1960. 206 p.

60–13519   QH104.5.W4D6

1284. My wilderness: east to Katahdin. Illustrations by Francis Lee Jaques. Garden City, N.Y., Doubleday, 1961. 290 p.

61–12207   QH104.D68

These volumes reflect Justice Douglas' intimate knowledge and love of the wilderness. *East to Katahdin* concerns some of his favorite places in the Southwest, South, and East, including Baboquivari in Arizona, the Everglades, the Smoky Mountains, and Mt. Katahdin. *The Pacific West* covers the Brooks Range in Alaska, the Olympic Mountains, and the High Sierras, as well as other natural areas that have a special appeal for him.

1285. MARTIN B. DUBERMAN, 1930–

Professor of American history at Princeton. His *Charles Francis Adams* won the Bancroft Prize in 1962, and his *In White America, a Documentary Play* (1964) won the Vernon Rice Award for 1963–64.

1286. Charles Francis Adams, 1807–1886. Boston, Houghton Mifflin, 1961 [c1960] 525 p. illus.

61–5366   E467.1.A2D8

Bibliography: p. 401–421.

A biography concentrating chiefly on Adams' career as Massachusetts State representative and senator, U.S. Congressman, Minister to Great Britain during the Civil War, and leader of the Liberal Republican Party in 1872. A straightforward and exacting work, aided by the availablity of the Adams papers, this is the first biography of Adams published since *Charles Francis Adams* (1900), by Charles Francis Adams, Jr. (see no. 2581 in the 1960 *Guide*).

1287. RAYMOND BLAINE FOSDICK, 1883–

Brother of the spiritual leader Harry Emerson Fosdick, Raymond B. Fosdick was born in Buffalo, N.Y., into an unusually religious and joyous household. In his autobiography he presents a portrait of family life in a rural town before the turn of the century, together with accounts of his years at college, his career as a lawyer and public servant, and his friendship with Woodrow Wilson. He also describes his role in the League of Nations and his presidency of the Rockefeller Foundation. There are glimpses, sometimes brief and at other times lingering, of prominent people such as Edward H. House, Newton D. Baker, and Franklin D. Roosevelt.

1288. Chronicle of a generation, an autobiography. New York, Harper [1958] 306 p.
58–11047   E748.F69A3

1289. JOHN ARTHUR GARRATY, 1920–

John A. Garraty teaches history at Columbia University and is the author of several biographies. He has also edited *The Unforgettable Americans* (1960).

1290. Right-hand man; the life of George W. Perkins. New York, Harper [1960]   433 p. illus.   60–10404   HC102.5.P4G3

George Perkins (1862-1920) was one of the most successful and controversial Americans of the early 20th century. Self-made, without a high school education, he displayed so much ability and energy that at his death it was facetiously said he had lived 400 years in his span of 58. He revolutionized the insurance business, guided the International Harvester Corporation, and became J. P. Morgan's right-hand man. He helped organize the Progressive Party with Theodore Roosevelt, using the same methods he had applied to effect business reforms but with less success. He was engaged in voluntary organizational work in World War I.

1291. DICK GREGORY, 1932–

Dick Gregory, the entertainer and civil rights leader, whose full name is Richard Claxton Gregory, was born in St. Louis. His autobiography, entitled *Nigger* (he insists upon the use of the word to break the taboo), is representative of the struggle of American Negroes to escape from crippling poverty, although he makes the distinction that he was "not poor, just broke." One of six children reared by a mother who had been deserted by her husband, Gregory tells of the abuses and deprivations he endured. At school he was successful in athletics and distinguished himself in track. Later he chose entertainment as a career and became a successful comedian. He then began to devote an increasing amount of his time and money to the cause of civil rights. His book is a testament to his mother, who inspired him but did not live to see his many achievements.

1292. Nigger; an autobiography, by Dick Gregory with Robert Lipsyte. New York, Dutton, 1964.  224 p. illus.   64–11067  PN2287.G68A3

1293. STERLING HAYDEN, 1916–

Sterling Hayden is a seafaring actor who at 22, in his first command, took a schooner successfully around the world. His autobiography is an extremely personal account of a man in search of reason and self. It is a defiant, questioning, occasionally stumbling, and honest work that derives much of its intensity from Hayden's ties to the sea. The story begins in 1959 when, in violation of a court order, Hayden takes his children on a long sea voyage. His previous life emerges in a series of sometimes confusing flashbacks.

1294. Wanderer. New York, Knopf, 1963.  434 p.   63–20142  PN2287.H34A3

1295. ELEANOR ROOSEVELT ROOSEVELT, 1884–1962

Eleanor Roosevelt's autobiography includes abridged selections from three volumes of memoirs — *This Is My Story* (1937), *This I Remember* (1949), and *On My Own* (1958) — and several additional chapters that bring her account up to date. She writes of her childhood, the early years of growing up, and her marriage to her cousin, Franklin Delano Roosevelt. She gives a picture of her ever-broadening activites, from wife and mother to political helpmate and First Lady. As a widow, Mrs. Roosevelt became the chairman of the Human Rights Commission of the United Nations and a delegate to its General Assembly. This is a portrait of a shy young girl developing into a famous woman who, in accepting the numerous opportunities that life afforded her, contributed immeasurably to the cause of world peace and to the improvement of race relations.

1296. Autobiography. New York, Harper [1961] 454 p. illus.   61–12222  E807.1.R35

1297. ISHBEL ROSS, 1897–

Mrs. Ross, a former editor of the *New York Herald-Tribune,* is a professional biographer and author whose works include *Proud Kate, Portrait of an Ambitious Woman* (1953), *Angel of the Battlefield; the Life of Clara Barton* (1956), and *The General's Wife; the Life of Mrs. Ulysses S. Grant* (1959).

1298. Grace Coolidge and her era; the story of a President's wife. New York, Dodd, Mead, 1962.  370 p. illus.   62–8017  E792.1.C6R6
Bibliography: p. 353–355.

Grace Goodhue Coolidge (1879–1957) emerges as the perfect complement to her famous but reticent husband Calvin Coolidge. She was poised, unaffected, natural, and at ease in difficult situations. Mrs. Ross' detailed study takes up Mrs. Coolidge's lifelong interest in the deaf. The book also contributes to our understanding of the personality of the 30th President of the United States.

1299. LOUISE HALL THARP, 1898–

Author of several biographies, including *Until Victory: Horace Mann and Mary Peabody* (1953), mentioned in the annotation for no. 5125 in the 1960 *Guide.*

1300. Adventurous alliance; the story of the Agassiz family of Boston. Boston, Little, Brown [1959] 354 p. illus. 59–11886 QH31.A2T5
Includes bibliography.
A biography of the Agassiz family in 19th-century New England. The Swiss-born scientist, Louis Agassiz (1807–1873), whose studies ranged from fish to glaciers and who revolutionized the teaching of natural history at Harvard, came to the United States in 1846. He married Elizabeth Cabot Cary in 1850, after the death of his first wife. It was a successful union of two creative intellects. Included in their circle were such friends as Longfellow, William James, and Emerson. Mrs. Tharp follows the Agassiz' productive lives closely and includes information on their children and nearest relatives. The details of the founding of Radcliffe College by Elizabeth Agassiz, who became its first president, are presented.

1301. NORBERT WIENER, 1894–1964

Norbert Wiener was born in Columbus, Mo., and is best known for his theory of cybernetics, which he explained in *Cybernetics; or, Control and Communication in the Animal and the Machine* (1948). He won the National Book Award in 1965 for *God and Golem, Inc.* (1964).

1302. I am a mathematician; the later life of a prodigy, an autobiographical account of the mature years and career of Norbert Wiener and a continuation of the account of his childhood in Ex-prodigy. Garden City, N.Y., Doubleday, 1956. 380 p. 56–5598 QA29.W497A35
This is a companion volume to *Ex-Prodigy* (1953) but can be read independently. Wiener begins with what he terms his "mature years," when he arrived at the Massachusetts Institute of Technology in 1919 at the age of 24. He remained there until his death in 1964. He concentrates on his career as scientist and mathematician and avoids the personal details of his life, which he preferred to keep private.

THURMAN WILKINS

1303. Clarence King, a biography. New York, Macmillan, 1958. 441 p. illus.
58–6965 QE22.K5W5
Bibliography: p. 357–378.
A biography of the "debonair adventurer," Clarence King (1842–1901), founder of the U.S. Geological Survey, explorer, mountaineer, mining expert, and good friend of William Dean Howells and Henry Adams. Some of his scientific achievements are described in his well-known *Mountaineering in the Sierra Nevada* (1872), no. 4210 in the 1960 *Guide.* Wilkins attempts to piece together the story of King's entire life from letters, papers, diaries, fieldbooks, reminiscences, memoirs, court records, and contemporary newspapers and periodicals.

# V

# Periodicals and Journalism

I TS RIGHT to free expression guarded by the Constitution, the press in the United States has traditionally served as a trustee of moral values. Another of its major functions is perhaps dual in nature: to explain the world we live in and to prepare us for change in that world. According to authors entered in Sections A and F, the press no longer adequately fulfills these roles; rather, journalism has become big business. Newspaper monopolies, some observers fear, by their very nature threaten diversity and freedom of opinion and lower the quality of the content of their papers; yet spiraling production costs and labor demands appear to encourage monopolies. Section I raises another problem, that of the delicate relationship between government and the press. Two of the authors stress the tendency of governmental bodies and agencies on all levels to become increasingly secretive about their activities and to withhold information from reporters.

Less thorny aspects of journalism are covered in Section D, comprising biographies of newspapermen who have made significant contributions to the field, and Sections G and H, devoted to histories of magazines which have, except for the political journals, been largely concerned with entertainment, culture, and noncontroversial information.

## A. Newspapers: General

1304. Emery, Edwin. The press and America, an interpretative history of journalism. 2d ed. Englewood Cliffs, N.J., Prentice-Hall, 1962. 801 p. illus. (Prentice-Hall journalism series)

62–15294 PN4855.E6 1962

An updated edition of no. 2845 in the 1960 *Guide.*

1305. Lindstrom, Carl E. The fading American newspaper. Garden City, N.Y., Doubleday, 1960. 283 p. 60–13541 PN4867.L55

A critical survey of the newspaper industry in

America today, based on the ideas that the journalistic function has migrated to other communications media and that "the major problem for the newspaper journalist is to keep his readers from migrating too." The author, formerly managing editor of *The Hartford Times* and currently a professor of journalism at the University of Michigan, trenchantly attacks those aspects of newspaper practice which he considers to be anachronistic, wasteful, or shortsighted. He particularly condemns the futile effort to publish the latest news in the shortest time, a race already lost to the radio and television industry; the failure to follow up yesterday's news story, thus abandoning a rich field to other journalistic media; the lack of competent reviewers in the fields of literature and the arts; and the disappearance of controversy as a result of the growth of newspaper chains and monopolies.

1306. Mott, Frank Luther. American journalism, a history, 1690–1960. 3d ed. New York, Macmillan [1962] 901 p. illus.

62–7157 PN4855.M63 1962

An updated edition of no. 2847 in the 1960 *Guide.*

1307. Tebbel, John W. The compact history of the American newspaper. New York, Hawthorn Books [1963] 286 p.

63–16771 PN4855.T4

"Suggested reading": p. 269–274.

A popular treatment by a former newspaperman and editor who is now chairman of the Department of Journalism at New York University. The author views the history of the American newspaper as "a record of the Establishment's effort to control the news and of private individuals to disclose it without restriction." From the colonial period to the 1830's, the American newspaper was essentially a propaganda device; the establishment of James Gordon Bennett's *New York Herald* in 1835 began what the author calls "the era of personal journalism." During the colorful period from 1865 to 1900, the newspaper enjoyed its heyday, far surpassing in influence and popularity other printed media. Out of the "gaudy struggle" between Pulitzer and Hearst emerged the concept of the newspaper as a business institution, and a new era began. The author sees three formidable problems which are causing a crisis in the press today; these are monopoly control (destroying the diversity of viewpoint which is the real strength of democracy), the automation of the industry (making monopoly control a business necessity), and a loss of purpose (the proper function of the newspaper being to explain the world to the people who live in it by significant news, rather than to multiply advertisements and entertainment features).

1308. Weisberger, Bernard A. The American newspaperman. Chicago, University of Chicago Press [1961] 226 p. illus. (The Chicago history of American civilization)

61–8647 PN4855.W4

Since the appearance in 1690 of the first and only issue of *Publick Occurrences Both Forreign and Domestick,* the American newspaper has evolved from a printer's sideline into a multimillion-dollar business. Accompanying this process has been a transformation of the functions of the individuals engaged in daily journalism. Weisberger examines the social, political, and technological factors which produced the age of the printer, the age of the partisan editor, the age of the publisher and personalized journalism, and the age of the reporter and columnist. In the concluding chapter he considers the public relations boom as a threat to the integrity and independence of the newspaperman. A section of "Suggested Reading" (p. 207–216) provides a brief annotated survey of selected literature in the field.

## B. Newspapers: Periods, Regions, and Topics

1309. Becker, Stephen D. Comic art in America; a social history of the funnies, the political cartoons, magazine humor, sporting cartoons, and animated cartoons. With an introduction by Rube Goldberg. New York, Simon & Schuster, 1959. xi, 387 p. illus. 59–13140 NC1420.B4

Political cartoons became a regular feature of newspapers in the latter part of the 19th century, and sports cartoons and comic strips followed shortly thereafter. The author presents a chronological history of the comic strip, from *The Yellow Kid* to *Pogo* and *Peanuts,* and also reviews other forms of comic art. Although emphasis is placed on social history, Becker shows a considerable knowledge of the artistic and technical problems involved as well. More critical discussions, as well as an extensive bibliography, can be found in *The Funnies, an American Idiom* ([New York] Free Press of Glencoe [1963] 304 p.), an anthology edited by David Manning White and Robert H. Abel, which includes both original and reprinted essays.

1310. Crozier, Emmet. American reporters on the Western Front, 1914–1918. New York, Oxford University Press, 1959. 299 p.

59–10968 D632.C72

Military censorship of the news probably reached an all-time high during World War I. During the first half of the war, the British and French armies allowed little or no press coverage, and news was derived from the official communiqué, from rumor, or occasionally from the unauthorized exploits of enterprising newsmen. The Allied armies eventually allowed a few accredited reporters to cover the war but kept tight control on their dispatches. The author, a retired newspaperman, relates the activities of such American correspondents as Herbert Corey, Floyd Gibbons, Westbrook Pegler, John T. McCutcheon, and Heywood Broun. Crozier employed a similar approach in *Yankee Reporters, 1861–65* (New York, Oxford University Press, 1956. 441 p.), accompanying it with nine unusual Civil War maps which show the disposition and movements not of troops but of reporters.

1311. Forsyth, David P. The business press in America. [v. 1] 1750–1865. Philadelphia, Chilton Books [ᶜ1964] xx, 394 p. illus.
64–10959 PN4784.C7F6
Bibliography: v. 1, p. 363–370.
This study, the first in a projected set, traces business publications from their origins as broadside price-currents just before the Revolution down to the period preceding their greatest growth. The record shows increasing diversification as commercial, railroad, and banking journals make their appearance, and Forsyth discusses each type of paper against a background of American economic history. A chronological list is given of papers published from 1750 to 1865, with their inclusive dates of publication, and it is noted that their survival rates have been higher than those of general or literary magazines.

1312. Hohenberg, John. Foreign correspondence; the great reporters and their times. New York, Columbia University Press, 1964. xix, 502 p.
64–22762 PN4784.F6H6
Bibliography: p. [475]–480.
The author, a professor at Columbia University's Graduate School of Journalism, explores "the effect of the foreign correspondent on his times and the influence he has exerted on the jagged course of international relations." The study is organized into a series of short narratives which together portray the origin and evolution of news-gathering abroad. Although the study is worldwide in scope, emphasis is placed on the United States, which with England has been a leader in developing an independent foreign correspondence. Considerable attention is devoted to the growth of the Associated Press, the United Press, and the foreign reporting sponsored by *The New York Times*, the *New York Herald*,

*The World* (New York), and *The Chicago Daily News*.

1313. Hohenberg, John, *ed.* The Pulitzer prize story; news stories, editorials, cartoons, and pictures from the Pulitzer prize collection at Columbia University. New York, Columbia University Press, 1959. 375 p. illus. 59–7702 PS647.N4H6
The Pulitzer Prize was established by Joseph Pulitzer in 1903 for the "encouragement of public service, public morals, American literature and the advancement of education." Since the bestowal of the prizes was contingent upon the opening of the Columbia University School of Journalism, no awards were conferred until 1917, six years after Pulitzer's death. Awards are made in letters, music (since 1943), and in eight fields of journalism. Compiled by the executive secretary of the Pulitzer Prize Advisory Board, this anthology contains 64 news stories and editorials which won journalism prizes. Notes providing the background of the article and biographical information on the journalists precede each piece. The material is arranged under 11 general subject headings and is accompanied by some of the prize-winning cartoons and photographs. An appendix contains a brief history of the prize and a complete list of the awards made in all fields since 1917. The complete series of Pulitzer Prize cartoons, with commentary, is reproduced in *The Lines Are Drawn; American Life Since the First World War as Reflected in the Pulitzer Prize Cartoons* (Philadelphia, Lippincott [1958] 224 p.), by Gerald W. Johnson.

1314. Knight, Oliver. Following the Indian wars; the story of the newspaper correspondents among the Indian campaigners. Norman, University of Oklahoma Press [1960] 348 p.
60–8751 E83.866.K58
Bibliography: p. 331–338.
A history of the newspapermen who reported the military campaigns against the Indians in the West from the close of the Civil War to the Battle of Wounded Knee, S. Dak. in 1890. Most of these campaigns were conducted by small units far from their base of supply, and the correspondents perforce became members of the expeditions. A professor of journalism and former newspaperman, Knight has concentrated on the 20 identifiable correspondents, accredited between 1867 and 1881, of whom Henry M. Stanley is the best known. The treatment is chronological by campaign and includes information on the reporters' backgrounds. The battles themselves are described and the accuracy of the reporting is evaluated.

# C. Individual Newspapers

1315.  Canham, Erwin D.  Commitment to freedom; the story of *The Christian Science Monitor*.  Boston, Houghton Mifflin, 1958.  454 p. illus.                          58–9055  PN4899.B65C53

*The Christian Science Monitor* is considered to rank among the most influential papers published in the United States today.  It was established in Boston in 1908 by mandate of Mary Baker Eddy, the founder of Christian Science, who intended it to be a regular newspaper with the "spiritual mission" of supplying accurate information and interpretation of current events to Christian Scientists and others. A policy of "meaningful journalism" has been maintained by the paper.  Crime, disaster, and scandal are reported only when a "necessary social purpose" is involved.  This history of the *Monitor,* written by the man who has served as editor since 1945, is uncritical of policies and performance but supplies much inside information revealing how and why the *Monitor,* "which is to professionals a kind of daily astonishment," has grown and developed the reputation it holds today.

1316.  Conrad, William C., Kathleen F. Wilson, *and* Dale Wilson.  *The Milwaukee Journal:* the first eighty years.  With a foreword by Arthur Ochs Sulzberger.  Madison, University of Wisconsin Press, 1964.  xv, 232 p.  illus.
64–19175  PN4899.M37J67

*The Milwaukee Journal* was founded in 1882 and, under the capable editorship of Lucius W. Nieman, soon rose to a position of leadership in Wisconsin.  Through most of its existence the *Journal* has been a fiercely independent paper, often to the point of supporting candidates from opposing parties in the same election.  Before and during World War I, the paper attacked the propaganda published by the German-language newspapers of the area and solidly backed the Nation's efforts to prosecute the war.  For this crusade in a predominantly German area, it won the Pulitzer Prize for public service in 1919.  In the thirties, the paper supported the New Deal; in the fifties it opposed Senator McCarthy in his own State.  Today the *Journal* is frequently ranked among the first five papers in the Nation on the basis of typographic excellence as well as widespread news coverage and independence in viewpoint.  Appropriately, the history of this employee-owned paper is written by three former staff members in the simple but positive style characteristic of the paper itself.

1317.  Hart, Jim Allee.  A history of the *St. Louis Globe-Democrat*.  Columbia, University of Missouri Press [1961]  298 p. illus.
61–12425  PN4899.S27G55  1961
Bibliography: p. 281–290.

The *St. Louis Globe-Democrat* had its origins in the *Daily Missouri Democrat,* founded in 1852. After its merger with the *St. Louis Globe* in 1875, the paper achieved great influence under the editorship of Joseph B. McCullagh.  "Little Mack," who considered the essence of running a newspaper to be "the art of guessing where hell is likely to break loose next," spent more for telegraphed and cabled news than any of his editorial contemporaries and, when there was no local news, set about creating it by means which have subsequently been imitated by the American press as a whole.  After McCullagh's suicide in 1896 and a brief fling with yellow journalism, the paper settled down into conservative, pedestrian ways and by 1950 was overshadowed by the more imaginative and hard-driving *St. Louis Post-Dispatch*.  In 1955 the *Globe-Democrat* was sold to the Newhouse chain and, despite a crippling strike in 1959, seemed to be emerging as a crusading newspaper.

1318.  Perkin, Robert L.  The first hundred years; an informal history of Denver and *The Rocky Mountain News*.  With a foreword by Gene Fowler.  Garden City, N.Y., Doubleday, 1959. 624 p. illus.                          59–9786  PN4899.D45R6

*The Rocky Mountain News* was established in 1859, during the Pike's Peak gold rush.  The paper changed hands many times, with corresponding alterations in political and journalistic philosophy. The *News* was purchased by the Scripps-Howard Newspapers in 1926, and Roy Howard immediately engaged in a newspaper war — referred to as the "battle of the century" — with Fred Bonfils and the profitmaking vehicle of his yellow journalism, *The Denver Post*.  The exhausted publishers finally signed a truce in 1928.  Today the *News* is a thriving local tabloid with a lively journalistic style. The growth of another western newspaper is described in John Middagh's *Frontier Newspaper: The El Paso Times* (El Paso, Texas Western Press, 1958. 333 p.).

# D. Newspapermen

1319. Baillie, Hugh. High tension; the recollections of Hugh Baillie. New York, Harper [1959] 300 p. illus. 59–6299 PN4874.B24A3

The United Press (now United Press International) was founded in 1907 by E. W. Scripps to compete with the Associated Press, which provided news service only to its member newspapers. The UP sold news on a contract basis to any newspaper that wished to subscribe. The UP was forced to scramble for news, and Hugh Baillie, its president from 1935 to 1955, lacking the well-established pipelines of the more sedate AP, maintained a vigorous, aggressive agency. Baillie was a writing executive who, whenever possible, covered the news himself, and this book is an account of his journalistic experiences, emphasizing his interviews with many famous personalities.

1320. [Cockerill] King, Homer W. Pulitzer's prize editor; a biography of John A. Cockerill, 1845–1896. Durham, N.C., Duke University Press, 1965. xx, 336 p. illus.
64–7798 PN4874.C6Z7
Bibliography: p. [324]-329.

The New York *World* was not exclusively the product of Joseph Pulitzer's inspiration and effort. When Pulitzer installed John A. Cockerill as managing editor of the *St. Louis Post-Dispatch,* the "Colonel" had had a distinguished record of editorial work on *The Cincinnati Enquirer, The Washington Post,* which he founded with Stilson Hutchins, and the *Baltimore Gazette.* Cockerill and Pulitzer were in accord in their crusading zeal to publish a fearless, factual, provocative newspaper. Pulitzer purchased *The World* in 1883 and made Cockerill managing editor. The latter's willingness to experiment throughout his career won him the appellation, "father of the new journalism." A pioneer in the use of pictures and editorial cartoon caricatures and in starting a Sunday newspaper for all the family, he discovered and developed Bill Nye, Nellie Bly, and Lafcadio Hearn.

1321. Cooper, Kent. Kent Cooper and the Associated Press, an autobiography. New York, Random House [1959] 334 p. illus.
59–6640 PN4874.C685A3

Kent Cooper (1880-1965) joined the Associated Press in 1910 and was its general manager and executive director from 1925 to 1951. Under his leadership the AP was transformed from a cautious, conservative news agency for the United States into a dynamic organization serving papers all over the world. In this account Cooper covers the many tributes which he received from prominent members of the press over the years and also singles out many AP staff members for special mention. Photographs are included of many well-known editors, publishers, and reporters. Cooper's views on government intervention in the communications field are set forth in his book *The Right to Know; an Exposition of the Evils of News Suppression and Propaganda* (New York, Farrar, Straus & Cudahy [1956] 335 p.).

1322. Daniels, Jonathan. They will be heard; America's crusading newspaper editors. New York, McGraw-Hill [1965] 336 p.
64–66019 PN4855.D3
Bibliography: p. 325–330.

The continuing fight by zealous editors for a free press is the underlying theme of this work. The author dramatizes the persistent struggle to exercise —in the words used by Andrew Hamilton in the famous libel case against John Peter Zenger—"the liberty both of exposing and opposing arbitrary Power by speaking and writing Truth." The discussion begins with Benjamin Harris' newspaper, *Publick Occurrences Both Forreign and Domestick,* which appeared on September 25, 1690, with the announced purpose of exposing false rumors. Among the later editors who receive attention are Edmund Ruffin, Horace Greeley, Joseph Pulitzer, and William Allen White. The concluding anecdote concerns the efforts of Carl McGee, against vigorous resistance from Secretary of the Interior Albert B. Fall, to expose the corruption in the Teapot Dome oil leases in 1922.

1323. [Daniels] Morrison, Joseph L. Josephus Daniels says . . . An editor's political odyssey from Bryan to Wilson and F. D. R., 1894–1913. Chapel Hill, University of North Carolina Press [1962] 339 p. 62–53249 PN4874.D33M6
Bibliography: p. [320]–332.

Josephus Daniels (1862–1948), publisher of *The News and Observer* (Raleigh, N.C.) for more than 50 years, was a spokesman for the "New South" and the Democratic Party. Through his brand of personal journalism, the paper gained the largest circulation in the State and, although later surpassed by the *Charlotte Observer*, has remained the most influential political voice in eastern North Carolina. Daniels was a loyal and liberal Democrat who fought against the railroad interests and child labor and championed State-supported education and nationwide prohibition. He worked for economic and educational progress for the Negro while continuing to support white supremacy. Morrison has confined his attention to Daniels' early career as an editor, from the time he took control of *The News and Observer* to his appointment as Wilson's Secretary of the Navy. Emphasis is placed on his political activities and the controversies in which he and the newspaper became involved.

1324. [Davis] Burlingame, Roger. Don't let them scare you; the life and times of Elmer Davis. Philadelphia, Lippincott [1961] 352 p.
    61–8669 PN4874.D36B8

Elmer Davis (1890–1958) was a newspaperman, freelance writer, novelist, public official, and radio commentator. Born in a small Indiana town, he never lost his midwestern twang or his ability to express complicated ideas and events in language which was simple, uncommonly clear, and forceful. After 10 years with *The New York Times,* he turned to freelance writing for *Collier's, Harper's,* and other prominent journals. As World War II approached, Davis returned to reporting, this time as a news analyst for CBS. During the war, he served as head of the Office of War Information and became engaged in well-publicized disagreements with Robert Sherwood and a group of OWI writers, including Henry F. Pringle and Arthur M. Schlesinger, Jr. As a radio commentator for ABC in the early 1950's, he was highly critical of the tactics of the late Senator Joseph McCarthy. The author expresses considerable admiration for Davis' broadcasting. The professional experiences of another newspaperman and radio commentator are related in Raymond Swing's *"Good Evening!" A Professional Memoir* (New York, Harcourt, Brace & World [1964] 311 p.).

1325. [Hearst] Swanberg, W.A. Citizen Hearst; a biography of William Randolph Hearst. New York, Scribner [1961] 555 p. illus.
    61–7220 PN4874.H4S83

Controversy characterized most of William Randolph Hearst's life (1863–1951), and this book, the latest and largest of the many Hearst biographies, has itself been a storm center. In 1962, it was unanimously nominated by the Pulitzer Advisory Board for the biography award, but in an unprecedented action the trustees of Columbia University vetoed the nomination and declined to give any prize for biography. Swanberg's account is generally acknowledged to be an uncommonly thorough analysis of this contradictory personality. Although unable to gain access to the greater part of the Hearst correspondence, Swanberg nevertheless amassed a vast amount of information through research in newspapers, secondary sources, and hundreds of personal interviews.

1326. [Lippmann] Childs, Marquis W., *and* James B. Reston, *eds.* Walter Lippmann and his times. New York, Harcourt, Brace [1959] 246 p. 59–10255 PN4874.L45C5
    Bibliographical footnotes.

A volume of 12 essays honoring Walter Lippmann (b. 1889) in his 70th year. Lippmann has been writing and commenting on the political scene since 1914, when he joined Herbert Croly on *The New Republic*. After World War I he became editor of the New York *World* and, after that paper's demise, he undertook a syndicated column for the *New York Herald Tribune*. Two-thirds of these essays deal with Lippmann's life, ideas, and influence, and the remainder with aspects of foreign policy or the democratic press suggested by his work. Marquis Childs and James Reston provide an introduction to Lippmann the political analyst and a picture of Lippmann the man. Allan Nevins writes of Lippmann's years at *The World*, Frank Moraes discusses the columnist's influence in Asia, and Arthur M. Schlesinger, Jr., treats him as a case study in the relationship of the intellectual to practical politics. Whereas Lippmann operates from an Olympian viewpoint, Joseph and Stewart Alsop practice personal and often emotional involvement with international events. A description of their mode of operation is provided in the first five chapters of their work, *The Reporter's Trade* (New York, Reynal [1958] 377 p.); the remainder of the volume is made up of representative selections from their published columns, 1946–57.

1327. Newton, Virgil M. Crusade for democracy. Ames, Iowa State University Press [1961] 316 p. 61–10549 PN4899.T35T75

An account of the newspaper campaigns fought by *The Tampa Tribune* and its editor, Virgil M. (Red) Newton, Jr. Newton joined the *Tribune* in 1930 and became its managing editor in 1943. Under his leadership, the paper inaugurated a series of crusades that helped turn out the corrupt government which had dominated Tampa for 17 years, exposed the existence of a flourishing gambling underworld, and aroused public opinion on substandard schools. With Tampa on the road to reform, Newton turned to State government and trenchantly attacked abuses in the prison system, campaigned for reapportionment of the legislature, and exposed graft and corruption among high officials. In 1953 Newton became chairman of the Freedom of Information Committee of Sigma Delta Chi and thereupon turned his indefatigable energy to an investigation of secrecy in the Federal Government, in particular that surrounding the expenditure of public funds. A man of strong opinion, Newton displays an almost total confidence in the righteousness of the causes he has espoused.

1328. [Pegler] Pilat, Oliver R. Pegler, angry man of the press. Boston, Beacon Press [1963] 288 p. illus.    63–11391 PN4874.P43P5

In an age when newspapers strive to present the news impartially, personal journalism has survived in the writings of the syndicated columnists who are allowed wide scope in giving their own interpretation of the significance of current events. As a sportswriter and nationally known columnist, Westbrook Pegler took advantage of this freedom to write a column notorious for its unrestrained attacks on well-known contemporaries. Pegler made his reputation in the 1930's as an uncompromising opponent of fascism. During this period, he won a Pulitzer Prize for articles on abuses in organized labor. His political beliefs subsequently shifted to the right, and in the 1950's he was a supporter of Senator Joseph McCarthy. His columns became increasingly intemperate, and in 1962 he terminated his contract with King Features as a result of their censorship of his column. Later he wrote a monthly column for *American Opinion,* owned and edited by Robert Welch of the John Birch Society. This biography by an editor of the *New York Post* attempts to provide a rounded and objective picture of the controversial journalist. Pilat describes many of Pegler's more famous attacks and his libel suits in some detail and tries to show how far the columnist's accusations were justified and wherein they were distorted. The result is a portrayal of a sensitive, emotional, and vindictive man who sees himself as "the reporter who tells the truth and walks alone."

1329. Seltzer, Louis B. The years were good. Introduction by Bruce Catton. Cleveland, World Pub. Co. [1956]  317 p.

56–10431  PN4874.S427A3

The *Cleveland Press,* established in 1878 by E. W. Scripps, was the first newspaper in what was to become the Scripps-Howard chain. Since 1928 the *Press* has been edited by Louis B. Seltzer (b. 1897), and under his leadership it has maintained its position as a hard-hitting, crusading newspaper. Seltzer left school at 13 to become an office boy for *The Cleveland Leader.* He was city editor of the *Cleveland Press* at 19 and had become its editor before he was 31. Through the years, he and the paper have become identified with the development, growth, and improvement of the city. In crisp journalistic style, this autobiography describes Seltzer's personal philosophy of journalism, as well as many of the paper's crusades and campaigns.

1330. [Swope] Kahn, Ely J. The world of Swope. New York, Simon & Schuster [1965]  510 p.  illus.

65–11976  CT275.S9874K3

Bibliography: p. 476–482.

An anecdotal, authorized biography by a long-time staff writer for *The New Yorker.* The son of German-Jewish parents, Herbert Bayard Swope (1882–1958) was a flamboyant figure of many facets. He began his newspaper career at the age of 17 on the *St. Louis Post-Dispatch;* he served the New York *World* from 1909 to 1925 with ingenuity and distinction. He disclaimed having any rules for success but offered a sure formula for failure: "Try to please everyone." He was most successful in making money and in seeming to know everyone of consequence. Woodrow Wilson, Alfred E. Smith, Franklin D. Roosevelt, and Bernard Baruch sought and accepted his advice. High-salaried consultant of large corporations, member of civic committees, founder and director of Freedom House, New York Racing Commissioner, consultant to the Secretary of War during World War II, he was referred to as a "creator of statesmen" and "editor emeritus of public opinion."

# E. Foreign-Language Periodicals

1331. Arndt, Karl J. R., *and* May E. Olson. German-American newspapers and periodicals, 1732-1955; history and bibliography. 2d rev. ed. New York, Johnson Reprint Corp. [1965] 810 p. facsims.    66–2897 Z6953.5.G3A7 1965

Added t.p.: *Deutsch-amerikanische Zeitungen und Zeitschriften, 1732–1955.*

German-language newspapers and periodicals

have probably been the greatest in number and influence among America's foreign-language press. They flourished at the turn of the century but suffered a disastrous blow during World War I, when public sentiment caused many to cease publication. In some cases back issues were even destroyed, and with them a great deal of source material on local history was lost. To fill this gap, the authors have sought to compile a complete bibliography of German-language papers published in the United States and to locate files of these publications whenever possible. In some cases complete holdings could only be found in European libraries. About 5,000 titles are included, arranged by State and city. Each entry includes dates of publication, changes of title, names of editors and publishers, and often a brief commentary. The section for each State begins with a short introductory summary giving statistics of the German element. The main body of the work is followed by a title index, an extensive bibliography, and an appendix listing 111 additional serials, mostly prisoner-of-war camp papers.

1332. Hunter, Edward. In many voices; our fabulous foreign-language press. Norman Park, Ga., Norman College [1960] 190 p.

60–3673 PN4884.H8

The foreign-language press is not the influential voice in America today that it was 50 years ago before curbs were placed on immigration, but it is still a factor in American political life and a reminder of the diverse national origins of American citizens. In 1960, there were 65 daily foreign-langue newspapers and more than 200 weeklies in 33 languages. Since second- and third-generation Americans have tended to lose interest in their ancestral lands and languages, many of the surviving papers have accepted sponsorship by nationality societies or religious groups or have shifted to publication in English. A small number are under Communist control. Individual publications are discussed briefly in this survey, which is the first attempt at a general view since *The Immigrant Press and Its Control* (1922), by Robert E. Park, no. 2897 in the 1960 *Guide*.

# F. The Practice of Journalism

1333. Arnold, Edmund C. Functional newspaper design. New York, Harper [1956] 340 p. illus. 56–6442 Z253.A7

Attractive packaging is one of the most important factors in promoting sales of any commodity, and newspapers are no exception. The author, who is editor of *The Linotype News,* states that today's papers "must make reading as easy as possible and make it appear even easier" in order to meet the stiff competition from the electronic media. The "tools" in the hands of the newspaper designer are typography and layout. Both have been modernized and improved in the 20th century, the most notable changes being a larger and simpler typeface, tabloid size ("five columns by approximately 15 inches"), and style. Topics discussed include typeface in headlines and in the body of the text, pictures, layouts in general and on the specialized pages, and recent technological changes. Although this volume is intended as a manual for professional newsmen, its clear style, explanation of technical terms, and numerous illustrations make it accessible to the nonprofessional reader.

1334. Brucker, Herbert. Journalist, eyewitness to history. New York, Macmillan [1962]

211 p. (Career book series)

62–14794 PN4775.B735

A description of the journalistic profession today. The author is editor of *The Hartford Courant* and a former professor of journalism at Columbia University. The discussion covers all types of journalism, including radio and television, photojournalism, public relations, and in particular, newspaper work. Much of the book is devoted to practical advice on educational preparation, job availability, and advancement. Opportunities for women entering the field are noted, and the requirements, rewards, and sacrifices of day-to-day reporting are outlined. Brucker also analyzes the rights involved in the freedom of the press and discusses the decline in the number of newspapers, the rise in costs, the competition from other journalistic media, and the control of the press by businessmen rather than editors.

1335. Byerly, Kenneth R. Community journalism. Philadelphia, Chilton Co., Book Division [1961] 435 p. 61–7188 PN4784.C73B9

The term "country weekly" has become passé, the cracker-barrel philosopher-editor has disappeared, and the number of smalltown newspapers has decreased by more than 40 percent in the last 50 years, but community journalism nonetheless remains a thriving aspect of the newspaper profession. The total size and circulation of the surviving papers have increased, and new papers are being started in the rapidly growing suburban areas. This is a practical textbook on how to run a community newspaper, written by a newspaperman with many years' experience as owner and editor of weekly and daily papers in the South and West. Byerly considers that the two major functions of a community paper are to provide local news and to serve as "an influence, voice, and builder" in stimulating thought and action on projects and issues. Such papers "must be written with more intimacy and more concern about the reader's reception" than city dailies; they constitute the "last stronghold of personal journalism in America." The book's final section is devoted to the newspaper as a business, with emphasis on public relations and sound accounting methods.

1336. Casey, Ralph D., *ed.* The press in perspective. Baton Rouge, Louisiana State University Press [1963] 217 p. 63–16657 PN4857.C27
Bibliographical references included in "Notes" (p. 207–213).

A collection of annual lectures financed by the Newspaper Guild of the Twin Cities and delivered at the University of Minnesota School of Journalism from 1947 to 1962. The lecturers included James Reston, Elmer Davis, Pierre Salinger, James Hagerty, John Fischer, Gerald W. Johnson, Eric Sevareid, Herbert Block, Joseph Alsop, Reinhold Niebuhr, and Henry S. Commager. In general, the series attempts to define the place of the press "within a social context." Recurrent themes are that the press should devote more emphasis to the background and interpretation of the news and should improve its own performance "as a trustee of the public interest."

1337. Elfenbein, Julien. Business journalism. 2d rev. ed. New York, Harper [1960] 352 p. 60–5712 PN4784.C7E4 1960
An updated edition of no. 2902 in the 1960 *Guide.*

1338. Hohenberg, John. The professional journalist; a guide to modern reporting practice. New York, Holt [1960] 423 p. 60–7795 PN4775.H44
A basic textbook on the problems and techniques of reporting the news for newspapers and wire services, including sections on the techniques of newswriting, newsgathering, and specialized reporting. Emphasis is placed on reporting as a public service, but the ethical aspects of determining how news is to be gathered and what news is to be printed are discussed realistically in the light of present practices. Hohenberg's approach is practical and detailed; there are several chapters on "newspaper style," showing the difference between the English found in the newspapers and everyday written and spoken English. Hillier Krieghbaum's *Facts in Perspective* (Englewood Cliffs, N.J., Prentice-Hall, 1956. 518 p. Prentice-Hall journalism series) is a practical guide to editorial writing and news interpretation. Roland E. Wolseley's *Critical Writing for the Journalist* (Philadelphia, Chilton Co., Book Division [1959] 207 p.) presents a discriminating view of literary and artistic criticism as practiced in news media today.

1339. MacDougall, Curtis D. Newsroom problems and policies. [Rev. and enl. ed.] New York, Dover Publications [1963] viii, 493 p. 63–17910 PN4731.M27 1963
An updated edition of no. 2905 in the 1960 *Guide.* MacDougall has also published a slightly modified version of the updated text under the title *The Press and Its Problems* (Dubuque, Iowa, W. C. Brown Co. [1964] 532 p. Journalism series).

1340. Nieman reports. Reporting the news; selections from Nieman reports. Edited, with an introduction, by Louis M. Lyons. Cambridge, Belknap Press of Harvard University Press, 1965. 443 p. 65–19825 PN4853.N5
Louis M. Lyons, who for 25 years was curator of the Nieman Fellowships for newspapermen at Harvard University, selected and edited *Reporting the News* from the quarterly publication of the Nieman Fellows. The fellowships provide experienced newspapermen with a year at Harvard to pursue studies of their choice and to attend discussions on journalism with their colleagues. *Nieman Reports* has based its philosophy on the concept of "the responsibility of the press." The articles reprinted here are objective, realistic, and often penetrating.

1341. Rucker, Frank W., *and* Herbert Lee Williams. Newspaper organization and management. 2d ed. Ames, Iowa State University Press [1965] xv, 544 p. illus. 65–10573 PN4775.R8 1965
Bibliography: p. 529–534.
An updated edition of no. 2909 in the 1960 *Guide.*

1342. Woods, Allan. Modern newspaper production. New York, Harper & Row [1963]

238 p. illus.        63–12054  PN4734.W6

A clear and sometimes witty explanation of the technical side of newspaper publishing. The author, a former production manager of *Newsday,* considers such subjects as printers' unions, the flow of work through the composing room and press-room, high-speed machines, problems of newsprint supply, and the photoengraving processes. The final chapter concerns the crisis caused by spiraling costs. Woods describes the search for new and cheaper production methods as exemplified by the Teletypesetter and offset printing. He concludes that since most of these new cost-cutting devices can only be used effectively for smaller issues, the result may be a rise in the number of small local papers after many of the large papers have priced themselves out of the field. This volume is intended to familiarize journalism students with the technical side of the newspaper business. It is written in language which can be understood by the nonspecialist, and all technical terms are italicized the first time they appear and explained in an extensive glossary at the end (p. 193–223).

## G. Magazines: General

1343.  Davenport, Walter, *and* James C. Derieux. Ladies, gentlemen, and editors. Garden City, N.Y., Doubleday, 1960.  386 p.

60–11379  PN4871.D3

Includes bibliography.

Biographical essays on some of the more interesting editors and publishers of the 19th and early 20th centuries. The authors, former editors of *Collier's,* have chosen strong personalities, without regard for the relative merits of their magazines. No living editors and no appraisals of existing magazines in their present form are included. Having ruled out all reasonable possibilities of legal reprisal, the authors have produced a collection of uninhibited accounts of such people as William d'Alton Mann of *Town Topics,* William Cowper Brann of *The Iconoclast,* William Marion Reedy of *The Mirror,* and Richard Kyle Fox of *The Police Gazette,* as well as such well-known editors as Edward William Bok, Sarah Josepha Hale, William Lloyd Garrison, and George Horace Lorimer. Scholarship has been blended with a racy conversational style, replete with colloquial expressions and incomplete sentences. An account of Reedy and the influence of his St. Louis magazine on American literature during the period 1890–1920 can be found in *The Man in the Mirror* (Cambridge, Harvard University Press, 1963.  351 p.), by Max Putzel. Brann's controversial life and violent death are described against the background of Waco, Tex., in the 1890's in Charles Carver's *Brann and The Iconoclast* (Austin, University of Texas Press [1957]  196 p.).

1344.  Ferguson, Rowena. Editing the small magazine. New York, Columbia University Press, 1958.  271 p.        57–10746  PN4775.F4

Small magazines or specialized journals with limited circulation constitute 95 percent of the magazines published in this country. Generally issued by or for organized agencies, these publications reflect the needs and interests of the parent body and its members. Because of their small size and limited budgets, they are often edited by staff members with little editorial experience or training. This book is designed as a how-to-do-it manual for such editors. The first half is a detailed breakdown of the technical aspects of editorial work; the second section is concerned with the executive functions of the editor. There is a brief bibliographic essay (p. 259–264) on books useful to beginning and experienced editors alike. A discussion is included of the "little magazine," a specific type of literary magazine appealing to a small, sophisticated audience. Reed Whittemore's *Little Magazines* (Minneapolis, University of Minnesota Press [1963] 47 p. University of Minnesota pamphlets on American writers, no. 32) is a critical and witty essay on the aims, influence, and future of this class of publication, with which the author has been actively concerned during most of his life.

1345.  Peterson, Theodore B. Magazines in the twentieth century. [2d ed.] Urbana, University of Illinois Press, 1964.  484 p. illus.

64–18668  PN4877.P4  1964

An updated edition of no. 2918 in the 1960 *Guide.* Roland E. Wolseley's *Understanding Magazines* (Ames, Iowa State University Press, 1965.  451 p.) is a revision, with a different theme and a new plan of organization, of *The Magazine World* (1951), which is described in the annotation for no. 2919 in the 1960 *Guide.*

# H. Individual Magazines

1346. Lyon, Peter. Success story; the life and times of S. S. McClure. New York, Scribner [1963] 433 p. illus.

63–16757    PN4874.M35L9

"Author's note and bibliography": p. 413–422.

Samuel S. McClure (1857–1949), an Irish immigrant of brilliant mind but erratic personality, organized one of the first successful syndicates for the sale of popular fiction to city newspapers when he was only 28. In 1893 he founded *McClure's Magazine,* which was priced at 15 cents a copy and contained high-quality fiction and well-written articles on topics of current interest. By 1900 *McClure's* had the second highest circulation among general magazines and had revolutionized the periodical world. The January 1903 issue, with articles by Ida Tarbell, Ray Stannard Baker, and Lincoln Steffens, marked the beginning of the muckraking era and the pinnacle of McClure's success. By 1912, however, McClure had been ousted from the editorship and the magazine had begun the slow decline which ended with its demise in 1929. Lyon maintains that McClure was "the greatest magazine editor this country had yet produced" and that *McClure's* from 1895 to 1910 was "probably the best general magazine ever to be published anywhere." McClure's *My Autobiography* (New York, Ungar [1963] 266 p. American classics) is a reprint, with an introduction by Louis Filler, of the original 1914 work ghostwritten by Willa Cather.

1347. Skipper, Ottis C. J. D. B. De Bow, magazinist of the Old South. Athens, University of Georgia Press [1958] 269 p. illus.

58–9172    PN4874.D395S53

Bibliography: p. 248–258.

James Dunwoody Brownson De Bow (1820–1867) founded and edited *De Bow's Review,* for some years the most influential and widely circulated magazine of the ante bellum South. The *Review,* founded in 1846 in New Orleans, was primarily a commercial and statistical magazine, although from time to time it included articles on literature and history. De Bow was a zealous advocate of slavery and, by the middle 1850's, was proposing secession as the only method of preserving Southern unity. A year after the outbreak of the Civil War, the *Review* suspended publication because of a lack of funds. De Bow revived it in 1866 but died the following year; the *Review* was continued irregularly by other publishers until 1880. Its chief importance today lies in its value as "interpreter of the antebellum South." Skipper, a professional historian, concludes that the *Review* was a reflection of the thinking of the times rather than an influence upon them.

1348. Turner, Susan J. A history of *The Freeman,* literary landmark of the early twenties. New York, Columbia University Press, 1963. 204 p.

63–19075    PN4900.F7T85

Bibliography: p. [187]–197.

Few periodicals that have lasted for so short a time as *The Freeman* (New York) of 1920–24 have lingered so persistently in memory. In 1917 Francis Neilson, an English single-taxer who had broken with the Liberal Party, married Mrs. Helen Swift Morris of the wealthy Chicago meatpacking family. Two years later, since the *Nation* could not be purchased, she established *The Freeman* to serve as his vehicle. Neilson allowed most of the work of editing and writing to pass into the hands of an American single-taxer, Albert Jay Nock, but became quite resentful at the outcome. The political viewpoint of *The Freeman* approached philosophical anarchism: the state was to wither away as the development of ideas left it high and dry. This view was uncongenial to the American left of the day, however, and the subscribers never exceeded 10,000. The magazine's brilliant literary department, headed by Van Wyck Brooks, Harold Stearns, and Lewis Mumford and aided by a corps of reviewers that looks impressive 40 years later, won general admiration but did not make up for the failure to attract a political following. When the Neilsons withdrew support at the end of the fourth year, *The Freeman* ceased publication.

# I. The Press and Society

1349. Cater, Douglass. The fourth branch of government. Boston, Houghton Mifflin, 1959. 194 p.                   59–7616 PN4738.C3

A study of the interaction between the national government and the Washington press corps. The author, a former special assistant to the Secretary of the Army and Washington correspondent for *The Reporter,* maintains that the influence of the press is such that it constitutes a fourth branch of government. With the proliferation of agencies since 1933, the reporter has become "the indispensable broker and middleman among the subgovernments." Cater contends that the new generation of politicians uses the press to build national reputations which are sometimes unrelated to legislative accomplishment; officials, on the other hand, jealously guard new programs against the glare of public exposure until policy has become so set that public opinion can no longer affect it. Since the press is thus forced to obtain information in unsystematic fashion, news is often incomplete and its treatment unbalanced. The press itself exercises great power by deciding what constitutes important news and what will be relegated to the inside pages or omitted entirely. Cater offers few panaceas, but his postscript describing reporting in Moscow makes it clear that conditions could be worse.

1350. Pollard, James E. The Presidents and the press, Truman to Johnson. Washington, Public Affairs Press [1964] 125 p.
                   64–8753 JK518.P6

"References": p. 121–125.

This supplement to no. 2930 in the 1960 *Guide* treats the press relations of recent U.S. Presidents. The author traces the initiation and development of the White House news conference, which originated in President Wilson's administration and has been continued with varying success to the present time. Franklin D. Roosevelt, who extended the news conference with his "fireside chats" by radio, was "unsurpassed in the uses to which he put the device or in his skill in managing it." His methods were continued and expanded by Harry S. Truman. Pollard states that Dwight D. Eisenhower appeared to endure the news conferences rather than to enjoy them, but was the first to extend them to television. John F. Kennedy was convivial, quick in response, and ready with word or fact in reply to a question. Lyndon B. Johnson proved informal and im-

promptu; news conferences were likely to be held in unusual places and under unaccustomed conditions—at the "L.B.J." ranch, for example, or in a rapid walking tour of the White House grounds. Another book on the same subject, *Presidential Leadership of Public Opinion* (Bloomington, Indiana University Press, 1965. 370 p.), by Elmer E. Cornwell, traces relations between President and press from Theodore Roosevelt through John F. Kennedy.

1351. Wiggins, James R. Freedom or secrecy? New York, Oxford University Press, 1956. 242 p.                   56–11115 JC599.U5W53

A discussion of the increasing secrecy in government—national, State and local, legislative, judicial, and executive alike—which the author believes is threatening freedom of the press. Wiggins, who is executive editor of *The Washington Post,* finds that after three centuries of progress in making information available to the people events now appear to be moving in the opposite direction. He complains that committees of Congress hold their executive sessions behind doors closed to press and public; all Federal and many State courts exclude cameras from the courtroom; records of the expenditure of millions of dollars of Federal funds are held confidential and privileged; and the military establishments keep spreading the cover of security over matters to which it has small if any relevance. The several elements of freedom of information and the press are reviewed, and the history of these rights is traced from their beginnings in English law to their present status in America, with illustrations from pertinent legal cases. The last chapter is concerned with various criticisms of newspaper practice today. After an analysis of each charge, Wiggins concludes that "the professed fears that information furnished by government will be distorted by the press or misunderstood by the people are fears that spring from a lack of faith in democratic institutions and beliefs."

1352. Zenger, John Peter, *defendant.* A brief narrative of the case and trial of John Peter Zenger, printer of the *New York Weekly Journal.* By James Alexander. Edited by Stanley Nider Katz. Cambridge, Mass., Belknap Press of Harvard University, 1963. 238 p. (The John Harvard library)                   63–19133 KF223.Z4K38 1963

Bibliographical notes: 205–232.

The trial and acquittal of John Peter Zenger (1697?–1746), printer of the *New York Weekly Journal,* for criminal libel in 1736 has traditionally been considered a foundation stone in the establishment of freedom of the press in this country. Recent investigation has brought about a more cautious evaluation. Katz reviews the proceedings in their contemporary context, notes that the decision was considered at the time to be "a politically motivated legal anomaly," and concludes that "the reformation of the law of libel and the associated unshackling of the press came about, when they did, as if Peter Zenger had never existed." The importance of the case lies in allowing us "to see in dramatic detail the nature of the forces developing in the early eighteenth century which would end, two generations later, in the transformation of both politics and the law." Katz points out that the *Brief Narrative,* ostensibly by Zenger, was probably written by James Alexander, the actual editor of the *Journal. The Trial of Peter Zenger* ([New York] New York University Press, 1957. 152 p.), edited by Vincent Buranelli, presents the text in abridged form, prefaced by a lengthy introduction in which the editor describes the trial and takes the traditional view in attributing far-reaching consequences to Zenger's acquittal.

# VI

# Geography

BASIC to an understanding of American civilization is the study of the natural setting in which it arose and on which it must depend for sustenance. This chapter contains works which describe the physical features of the Anglo-American continent and others which examine the reciprocal relationship between continent and human culture. Although entry no. 1355 in Section A treats geography as a discipline—listing variations in American methodology from environmentalism to economic geography—the other selections in the section deal with specific aspects of the Nation's environment, such as the diversity of landforms or the cultural use of the land.

Climate and weather are perennial topics; the entries in Section C each study an extreme manifestation: aridity, hurricanes, and hailstorms, respectively. The books on plants and animals in Section D are supplemented by others in Sections G and H of Chapter XXVII, Land and Agriculture, in which works devoted to the conservation of wildlife have been placed. As in the 1960 *Guide,* the brevity of Section E indicates that few geographers have approached the specialty of historical geography per se. There are, however, accounts of historic explorations in the polar regions in Section F.

## A. General and Physical Geography

1353. American heritage. The American heritage book of natural wonders, by the editors of American heritage, the magazine of history. Editor in charge: Alvin M. Josephy. [New York] American Heritage Pub. Co.; book trade distribution by Simon & Schuster [1963] 384 p.

             63–17026   E169.A496

1354. Farb, Peter. Face of North America; the natural history of a continent. Illustrations by Jerome Connolly. New York, Harper & Row [1963] 316 p.     62–14598   QH104.F3

Readings: p. 299–305.

The editors of *American Heritage* present the spectacular in the American landscape. Each of eight writers—Peter Matthiessen, William O. Douglas, Jan de Hartog, Bruce Catton, Paul Engle, Wallace Stegner, George R. Stewart, and Harold Gilliam—characterizes, with his own particular emphasis and personal enthusiasm, a broad region of the United States by the dimensions of landscape, the diversity of place names, and local color. The illustrations are a notable contribution of this volume and combine historic American prints and paintings, maps and drawings by the early naturalists, and photographs of wildlife, landscapes, and natural resource development. *Face of North America* complements the wondrous and remarkable in the American landscape with an introductory study of the diversity of landforms that label and link the regions of this continent. Concentration on the geological development and ecological cooperation involved in the cycle of land formation emphasizes impermanence and change, the constant "rise and fall of the land." Each section considers a broad landform, which is further defined in the subsections. Numerous drawings and photographs clarify the process of development visually. An appendix lists the "Outstanding Natural Areas of North America, by State and Province."

1355. Platt, Robert S., *ed.* Field study in American geography; the development of theory and method exemplified by selections. Chicago, 1959. 405 p. (University of Chicago. Dept. of Geography. Research paper no. 61)

60–205 H31.C514 no. 61

This volume was compiled on the assumption that successive methods of field work during the last 150 years of American geography, although varying in content from environmentalism to economics, have been progressive and cumulative in the development of geographic knowledge. Chosen as representative mileposts in geographic research where there is direct contact between researcher and subject, these selections are drawn from diverse sources. The work as a whole is designed for specialists and categorizes the materials with such terms as "exploratory traverse," "explanatory physical," and "analytical economic." At the same time, the excerpts themselves are often appropriate for the layman, representing, as they do, such readable authors as Lewis and Clark and Ellen C. Semple. An introduction places each study and its author in historical perspective. William Warntz' *Geography Now and Then; Some Notes on the History of Academic Geography in the United States* (New York, American Geographical Society, 1964. 162 p. American Geographical Society research series, no. 25) is a survey of the characteristics and

role of geography as a discipline in this country since its colonial beginnings.

1356. Thornbury, William D. Regional geomorphology of the United States. New York, Wiley [1965] 609 p. illus. 65–12698 QE77.T5 Chapter references.

A reference and textbook incorporating new research data to update Nevin M. Fenneman's *Physiography of Western United States* (1931) and *Physiography of Eastern United States* (1938), no. 2935 and 2936, respectively, in the 1960 *Guide.* This study combines the origin of landforms with the regional distribution and geomorphic histories of landscapes. Limited in length, the treatment is necessarily selective and economical in comparison with its predecessors but follows the same general classification. *Geomorphology Before Davis* ([London] Methuen; [New York] Wiley [1964] 678 p.), the first volume of *The History of the Study of Landforms,* by Richard J. Chorley, Anthony J. Dunn, and Robert P. Beckinsale, is an account of the evolution of European and American ideas "relating to the development of the physical landscape," enriched by many excerpts from original sources.

1357. White, Charles Langdon, Edwin J. Foscue, *and* Tom L. McKnight. Regional geography of Anglo-America. 3d ed. Englewood Cliffs, N. J., Prentice-Hall [1964] xvii, 524 p. illus.

64–10071 E169.W54 1964

References at the ends of chapters.

An updated edition of no. 2940 in the 1960 *Guide.* Two other textbooks are Earl B. Shaw's *Anglo-America, a Regional Geography* (New York, Wiley [1959] 480 p.), a brief and selective survey, emphasizing economic geography, and James Wreford Watson's *North America, Its Countries and Regions* ([London] Longmans [1963] 854 p. Geographies for advanced study), which stresses historical settlement and cultural use of the land.

## B. Geology and Soil

1358. Clark, Thomas H., *and* Colin W. Stearn. The geological evolution of North America; a regional approach to historical geology. New York, Ronald Press Co. [1960] 434 p.

60–6154 QE71.C55

1359. King, Philip B. The evolution of North America. Princeton, N.J., Princeton University Press, 1959. 189 p. illus. 59–5598 QE71.K54

Reference material: p. vii–ix.

These two volumes treat the progressive growth of North America by region. The first, a textbook for students familiar with physical geology, presents the three major structural units of the continent: the bordering geosynclines, the stable interior, and the Canadian Shield. Maps and diagrams are uncluttered and well integrated. The evolution of life is discussed in a final section, and appendixes summarize the biological classifications. *The Evolution of North America,* by a geologist with the U.S. Geological Survey, was compiled from a lecture series for a college course. It does not aim to be comprehensive but gives detailed consideration to selected regions which illustrate principles of the continent's development. The book retains the informality of its original oral delivery.

1360. Eardley, Armand J. Structural geology of North America. 2d ed. New York, Harper & Row [c1962] xv, 743 p. illus. (Harper's geoscience series)   62–17482 QE71.E17 1962
    Bibliography: p. 709–738.
    A revised edition of no. 2942 in the 1960 *Guide.*

1361. Wright, Herbert E., *and* David G. Frey, *eds.*
    The Quaternary of the United States: a review volume for the VII Congress of the International Association for Quaternary Research. Princeton, N.J., Princeton University Press, 1965.   922 p. illus.   65–14304 QE696.W93
    Bibliographical footnotes.
    A scholarly and technical interdisciplinary report on the era of geologic time covering the last ice age to the present. This period, which includes the evolution of modern man, is "unique among the geologic periods for the relative perfection of its stratigraphic record." On a basis of uniformitarianism, the unusual stratigraphy permits a broad selection of American scholars in representative fields of scientific learning to collaborate in detailing and analyzing development. The four major sections are devoted to geology, biogeology, archeology, and miscellany; subsections defined principally by region contain detailed chronological description, summaries, extensive references, and brief notes on the authors' credentials.

## C. Climate and Weather

1362. American Association for the Advancement of Science. *Committee on Desert and Arid Zones Research.* Aridity and man; the challenge of the arid lands in the United States. Carle Hodge, editor; Peter C. Duisberg, associate editor. Washington, American Association for the Advancement of Science, 1963. xx, 584 p. illus. ([American Association for the Advancement of Science] Publication no. 74)   63–22003 GB614.A5
    Bibliography: p. 555-560.
    One-third of the 48 contiguous States of the United States are deficient in moisture. This volume, composed of case histories and chapters on the relationship of aridity to weather, terrain, vegetation, soils and minerals, and historical settlement and development, portrays the sum of U.S. experience in arid lands. Conceived as a working tool for a UNESCO symposium on arid zones research, this interdisciplinary study, scholarly but readable, useful to researchers as well as to administrative and governmental leaders, emphasizes arid zones where development has failed. In a more general introduction, *The North American Deserts* (Stanford, Calif., Stanford University Press, 1957. 308 p.), by Edmund C. Jaeger, combines regional descriptions of the five North American deserts with a field guide of common desert flora and fauna.

1363. Dunn, Gordon E., *and* Banner I. Miller. Atlantic hurricanes. [Rev. ed. Baton Rouge] Louisiana State University Press [1964] xx, 377 p. illus.   64–21598 QC945.D8 1964
    Bibliography: p. 299–301, 363–368.
    Through meteorological work at the National Hurricane Center in Florida, the authors acquired experience and familiarity with "the most destructive of all weather phenomena." Serving both as an explanation for the layman and an analytical description for the student, this treatment of the tropical storm supplies information on current scholarship, as well as on climatology, physical processes, tracking, forecasting, hazard intensity, and historical storms of the 20th century. A thoroughly documented specialized study is David M. Ludlum's *Early American Hurricanes, 1492–1870* (Boston, American Meteorological Society [c1963] 198 p. The History of American weather, no. 1).

1364. Flora, Snowden D. Hailstorms of the United States. Norman, University of Oklahoma Press [1956] 201 p. illus.
    56–11231 QC929.H1F4
    Because "hail is even more destructive than tornadoes," the author has supplemented an earlier volume, *Tornadoes of the United States* (1954), no. 2948 in the 1960 *Guide,* with a comprehensive general introduction emphasizing the why, when, and where of hailstorms. Employing devices of content and format similar to those used in his previous work, the author here tabulates damage and risk according to States, notes the phenomenal, records the past effectiveness of forecasting, and advises on the practicalities of insurance.

# D. Plants and Animals

1365. Bent, Arthur C. Life histories of North American blackbirds, orioles, tanagers, and allies. Order: Passeriformes; families: Proceidae, Icteridae, and Thraupidae. Washington, Smithsonian Institution, 1958. 549 p. (U.S. National Museum. Bulletin 211) 58–60425 Q11.U6 no. 211
Bibliography: p. 510–531.
This is the 17th and final title of Bent's unique series of life histories of North American birds. Issued by the Smithsonian Institution in a total of 20 volumes over a period of almost 40 years, the studies together have been described as the "most comprehensive, most complete, and most-used single source of information" on the birds of North America. In this volume, as in the others, the author interweaves easy narrative with terse facts and blends his own findings with those of other observers. The text is both readable and useful and is accompanied by a section of black and white photographic illustrations. Dover Publications has reprinted, in paperback, the entire set as it was originally issued, complete with pictures. Henry H. Collins, Jr., has edited a two-volume abridgement to which he has given the title *Life Histories of North American Birds* (New York, Harper [1960]).

1366. National Geographic Society, *Washington, D.C. Book Service*. Natural science library. Washington, National Geographic Society, 1960–65. 6 v.
Entries no. 1367 through 1370 below describe four of the six volumes thus far published in this series. The two volumes omitted are devoted to domesticated nature (one is on dogs, the other on gardens) rather than to life still relatively wild and free. As the titles indicate, three of the four volumes listed concern birds and fishes; the book on animals is restricted to mammals. All of these volumes combine informative text with drawings, paintings, and photographs that are esthetic as well as instructive. Two other National Geographic Society publications resembling the Natural Science Library in subject and presentation are *Stalking Birds With Color Camera* [2d rev. ed.] ([1963] 351 p.), by Arthur A. Allen and others, and *The Book of Fishes* ([1961] 339 p.), edited by John O. La Gorce.

1367. Wetmore, Alexander, *and others*. Song and garden birds of North America. Foreword by Melville Bell Grosvenor. [1964] 400 p. 64–23367 QL681.W46
"Acknowledgments and reference guide": p. 398–[399].
"Bird songs of garden, woodland and meadow, by Arthur A. Allen and Peter Paul Kellogg" (12 p. and phonodiscs: 12 s. 7 in. 33⅓ rpm.) in pocket.

1368. Wetmore, Alexander, *and others*. Water, prey, and game birds of North America. Foreword by Melville Bell Grosvenor. [1965] 464 p. 65–24605 QL681.W48
Bibliographical references included in "Acknowledgments" (p. 463).
"Bird sounds of marsh, upland, and shore, by Peter Paul Kellogg" (12 p. and phonodiscs: 12 s. 7 in. 33⅓ rpm.) in pocket.

1369. National Geographic Society, *Washington, D.C. Book Service*. Wild animals of North America. Foreword by Melville Bell Grosvenor. [1960] 400 p. 60–15019 QL715.N3

1370. National Geographic Society, *Washington, D.C.* Wondrous world of fishes. [Editor-in-chief, Melville Bell Grosvenor. Washington, 1965] 366 p. 65–11482 QL625.N33

1371. Shelford, Victor E. The ecology of North America. Urbana, University of Illinois Press, 1963. xxii, 610 p. illus. 63–7255 QH102.S5
Bibliography: p. 495–531.
An extension of a previous work sponsored by Nature Conservancy (formerly Committee on the Preservation of Natural Conditions, Ecological Society of America) and edited by Shelford: *Naturalist's Guide to the Americas* (1926), no. 2956 in the 1960 *Guide*. In the new study, Shelford presents a comprehensive picture of plant and animal communities in 16th-century North America. He describes the continent's forest regions in terms of their component biomes — ecological formations of living organisms in their physical environments. Biomes are identified on the basis of their characteristic flora. This is a technical reference work, founded on research data from a vast array of sources. A useful tool for conjunctive study is Au-

gust W. Küchler's *Potential Natural Vegetation of the Conterminous United States* (New York, American Geographical Society, 1964. col. map 95 x 149 cm. Special publication no. 36) with its *Manual To Accompany the Map* (36, 116 p.), which discusses plant-life regions of the United States in a visual format with interpretive photographs and descriptive data. *The Natural Geography of Plants* (New York, Columbia University Press, 1964. 420 p.), by Henry A. Gleason and Arthur Cronquist, is an introductory discussion of the distribution and classification of plants in the United States.

## E. Historical Geography and Atlases

1372. Lunny, Robert M. Early maps of North America. Newark, New Jersey Historical Society, 1961. 48 p.  62–13718 GA401.L8
"Check list of an exhibition: Early maps of North America, December 12, 1961–January 20, 1962 at the New Jersey Historical Society": p. 47–48.

1373. Rand, McNally and Company. Pioneer atlas of the American West; containing facsimile reproductions of maps and indexes from the 1876 first edition of Rand, McNally & Company's Business atlas of the great Mississippi Valley and Pacific slope; together with contemporary railroad maps and travel literature. Historical text by Dale L. Morgan. Chicago [1956] 51 p.
Map 57–5 G1380.R35 1956
Two map publishers have celebrated company anniversaries with the publication of these volumes of maps commemorating historical epochs of settlement. In the first, C. S. Hammond and Company, in cooperation with the New Jersey Historical Society, has reproduced maps from a variety of private and institutional sources. Lunny's accompanying text, although it contains many historical bibliographical references, is primarily a brief, descriptive, cartographic history with diverse notes on each plate. The maps themselves are revealing examples of how the early French, Dutch, English, and Spanish explorers interpreted the New World. Rand, McNally and Company, which early specialized in railroad mapping, has reproduced an 1876 gazetteer, the "first atlas which frankly embraced the West." A sketch of the early history of the firm, a historical outline of mapping in the transcontinental West, detailed maps of 16 Western States with individual essays on settlement and mapping, and decorative maps, posters, and timetables—all of these emphasize the role of the railroad in the human geography, development, and expansion of the West.

1374. Rand, McNally and Company. Commercial atlas and marketing guide. 96th ed. Chicago, 1965. 508, 65A p.  Map 6–9 G1019.R22
Revised annually, this large volume is probably the most widely known and used cartographic reference that emphasizes economically oriented geographical information on the United States. Its maps, tables, and indexes pertaining to the 50 states and the territories are supplemented with world maps and maps of foreign countries.

1375. Stewart, George R. Names on the land; a historical account of place-naming in the United States. Rev. and enl. ed. Boston, Houghton Mifflin, 1958, 511 p. illus.
57–10780 E155.S8 1958
Notes and references: p. 442–482.
An updated edition of no. 2976 in the 1960 *Guide*. Two additional reference volumes further delineate the influences of historical antecedents and contemporary commerciality on the geography of the United States. In *The American Counties*, rev. ed. (New York, Scarecrow Press, 1962. 540 p.), Joseph N. Kane supplies information on each of the Nation's 3,072 counties. Kane is also coauthor with Gerard L. Alexander of *Nicknames of Cities and States of the U.S.* (New York, Scarecrow Press, 1965. 341 p.).

# F. Polar Exploration

1376. Caswell, John E.  Arctic frontiers; United States explorations in the Far North.  Norman, University of Oklahoma Press [1956]  232 p.
56–11235  G630.A5C3
Bibliography: p. 216–225.

1377. Mitterling, Philip I.  America in the Antarctic to 1840.  Urbana, University of Illinois Press, 1959.  201 p.  illus.  59–10555  G870.M67
Essay on sources: p. 169–186.

Two historical surveys of 19th-century polar exploration, each well documented and concise.  The first describes northern polar expeditions between 1850 and 1909, the period when, as Vilhjalmur Stefansson has written, "explorers tended to become pioneers of science if not martyrs of science."  After brief introductory mention of earlier European polar thrusts, this volume emphasizes the historical continuity, including the chain of friendships, in expeditions from Edwin Jesse De Haven to Robert E. Peary and the cumulatively increasing data base of scientific knowledge that resulted.  Photographs, drawings, and maps of persons and places increase the historical perspective of Caswell's text.  The bulk of Mitterling's material covers early 19th-century discovery of the South Atlantic islands and the coastal rim of a new continent.  A synthesis of many private papers, this chronological narrative stresses the motivations of the explorers, who varied widely in purpose, ranging from those who sought profits in the fur-seal trade to those who pursued information and understanding on scientific and governmental missions.  In an extensive bibliography, the author evaluates the sources of his facts.

1378. Siple, Paul.  90° South; the story of the American South Pole conquest.  New York, Putnam [1959]  384 p.
59–11029  G850  1957.S5
Paul Siple made his first trip to Antarctica as the Boy Scout chosen to accompany the Richard E. Byrd Expedition of 1928–30.  This reminiscence, an intimate and descriptive review of American Antarctic exploration in the 20th century, first surveys the author's five expeditions with Byrd and then comprehensively details the 18 months Siple spent at the South Pole as the scientific leader of 17 men undertaking investigations for the U.S. contribution to the International Geophysical Year.  An informal narrative, *90° South* reveals the problems of physical existence in the "deepfreeze" as well as the emotional and intellectual reactions it provokes.  Photographs intensify the description of a stark and frigid life.  A general historical account of the search for the South Pole, by a *New York Times* correspondent who took part in three expeditions, is Walter Sullivan's *Quest for a Continent* (New York, McGraw-Hill [ᶜ1957]  372 p.).

# VII

# The American Indian

UNTIL the 20th century, the general attitude toward the American Indian was characterized by the self-contradictory term "noble savage." On the one hand, the Indian was romanticized through such writings as Longfellow's "Song of Hiawatha." On the other hand, public policy, framed on the basis of conquest and premised on the belief that the Indian was either a barbarian or a child, became a source of national embarrassment. Neither attitude encouraged the objective study of the Indian's ancient cultural heritage.

Despite increasing governmental efforts, the American Indian has continued to fare very poorly. He has been deprived of the opportunity to live in the manner of his inherited culture and at the same time has been denied privileges in the white community. Historians, social scientists, and professional writers interested in the Indian have, however, been more enlightened than the general public. Underlying most of the following selections, which range from scientific analyses to artistic descriptions of various Indian groups, is the assumption that American Indians from Alaska to the southern tip of South America possess cultural and tribal identities which are, in many cases, very rich.

Among the selections are archeological and anthropological studies; histories, both of tribes and of Indian affairs as a continuing aspect of American history; critiques of governmental policy toward the Indians; and studies of various aspects of Indian culture and life.

## A. General Works

1379. The Civilization of the American Indian series. Norman, University of Oklahoma Press, 1932–65. 79 v.

This long, continuing series "has as its purpose the reconstruction of American Indian civilization by presenting aboriginal, historical, and contemporary Indian life." The volumes, some of which are unnumbered, range from informal autobiographical accounts to scholarly monographs. Several of them are entered by subject in the 1960 *Guide*. Others appear elsewhere in this *Supplement*. Representa-

tive new volumes reflecting the scope of the series are listed below as no. 1380 through 1382.

1380. Hassrick, Royal B. The Sioux; life and customs of a warrior society. In collaboration with Dorothy Maxwell and Cile M. Bach. [1964] 337 p. illus. (no. 72)    64–11331   E99.D1H3
Bibliography: p. 314–319.

1381. Newcomb, Franc J. Hosteen Klah, Navaho medicine man and sand painter. [1964]

xxxiii, 227 p. illus. (no. 73)

64–20759 E99.N3N37

Bibliography: p. 221.

1382. Young, Mary E. Redskins, ruffleshirts, and rednecks; Indian allotments in Alabama and Mississippi, 1830–1860. [1961] 217 p. illus. (no. 61)

61–15150 E98.L3Y6

1383. Driver, Harold E. Indians of North America. [Chicago] University of Chicago Press [1961] 667 p. illus. 61–5604 E58.D68

Bibliography: p. 613–633.

In the history of North American Indian groups, the high points of cultural development vary considerably, ranging from the 16th century for the Indians in Mexico to the 19th century for those of Canada and parts of the United States. Driver discusses the primary aspects of these cultural peaks for tribes from Central America to Alaska. Topical chapters on such subjects as subsistence patterns, education, religion, and language are subdivided into geographic areas of culture; this arrangement facilitates a comparative survey. Thirty-seven maps showing the geographic relationships of various cultural patterns are included. *The Native Americans: Prehistory and Ethnology of the North American Indians* (New York, Harper & Row [1965] 539 p.), by Robert F. Spencer and seven other anthropologists, covers essentially the same subject but offers less comparative analysis of the cultural groups. In 1964, Driver edited a short anthology, *The Americas on the Eve of Discovery* (Englewood Cliffs, N.J., Prentice-Hall [1964] 179 p. The Global history series, S–93), portraying Indian life at the time the New World was penetrated by Europeans.

1384. La Farge, Oliver. A pictorial history of the American Indian. New York, Crown Publishers [1956] 272 p. 56–11375 E77.L245

A comprehensive collection of pictures of the North American Indian, with accompanying explanatory text. It reproduces drawings by John White, paintings by George Catlin and Frederic Remington, stylized illustrations by contemporary Indian artists, 19th-century pictures of reluctant Indian subjects, and colorful publicity photographs of contemporary reservation Indians. Other illustrations show a wide range of artifacts and primitive art. The author, a trained anthropologist who lived and worked with the Indians, divides his subject by geographical area and concludes with a general account of the problems facing the Indians today.

1385. Mead, Margaret, *and* Ruth L. Bunzel, *eds.* The golden age of American anthropology. New York, G. Braziller, 1960. 630 p. illus.

60–11668 E77.M48

"Suggestions for further reading": p. 629–630.

The editors of this anthology have selected the years 1880 to 1920 as the "golden age" for anthropological studies of the United States. A period in which the first attempts at systematic and scientific study were made, it was also a time when anthropologists could base their investigations on firsthand accounts from Indians who had experienced patterns of living that have now disappeared. The selections actually cover a much greater timespan than this 40-year interval. They begin with reports of the early Spanish explorers, continue through accounts of American missionaries, traders, and artists, and conclude with anthropological studies of the early part of the 20th century. In general, the articles are written in nontechnical language, and short introductory paragraphs place the authors of the selections in historical context. Particular attention is paid to Franz Boas, who dominated American anthropology for more than 40 years.

# B. Archeology and Prehistory

1386. Gladwin, Harold S. A history of the ancient Southwest. Portland, Me., Bond Wheelwright Co., 1957. 383 p. 57–6941 E78.S7G42

Bibliography: p. 363–372.

The story of the inhabitants of Colorado, Utah, New Mexico, Arizona, and parts of Mexico, emphasizing the period from 200 to 1450. Based primarily on 30 years of research performed by an eminent amateur archeologist and his associates, the study is chronologically arranged and is accompanied by numerous drawings, photographs, and maps. A number of Gladwin's theories are at variance with the orthodox ideas of professional scholars, but he is careful to point out these controversial areas.

1387. Hibben, Frank C. Digging up America. New York, Hill & Wang [1960] 239 p. illus. 60–10518 E58.H49

"A suggested list of further readings in American archaeology": p. 227-228.

Systematic study of prehistoric man in America did not really begin until the last of the frontiers vanished. Since that time, extensive investigations have been inaugurated under the auspices of Government agencies and educational institutions. Delicate techniques of excavation and increasingly accurate methods of determining age have been developed. In a popular style, Hibben describes the theories formulated and then discarded, the monumental discoveries, and the uncharted areas yet to be explored. He discusses the problems of when and from where the first men came, the origins of agriculture, the mystery of the mounds, the pueblos of the Southwest, the recent discoveries of ancient Eskimo cultures, and the highly developed Incan, Mayan, and Aztec civilizations.

1388. Quimby, George I. Indian life in the Upper Great Lakes, 11,000 B.C. to A.D. 1800. [Chicago] University of Chicago Press [1960] 182 p.          60-11799  E78.G7Q5
   Bibliography: p. 166-176.

When the glaciers disappeared from the region around Lakes Superior, Michigan, and Huron and the land became habitable, Indians settled there. The first half of Quimby's book describes the prehistoric period of those settlements and examines the evidence relating to them. In the second half, he devotes his attention to the 17th- and 18th-century cultures of the Miami, Sauk, Fox, Winnebago, Menominee, Chippewa, Huron, Ottawa, and Potawatomi tribes. The book is directed toward the general reader or beginning student and includes a large number of maps and illustrations and a glossary.

1389. Vaillant, George C. Aztecs of Mexico: origin, rise, and fall of the Aztec Nation. Rev. by Suzannah B. Vaillant. Garden City, N.Y., Doubleday, 1962. 312 p. illus.
           62-10466  F1219.V13  1962
   Bibliography: p. [257]-297.
   An updated edition of no. 2997 in the 1960 *Guide*.

1390. Wauchope, Robert. Lost tribes & sunken continents; myth and method in the study of American Indians. [Chicago] University of Chicago Press [1962] 155 p. illus.
          62-18112  E61.W33
   Bibliography: p. [139]-145.

The origins of the American Indians have not only been fiercely disputed by scholars but have also been the basis for unchecked theorizing by amateur anthropologists and archeologists. Some of the amateurs' theories hold that the earliest inhabitants of the New World migrated from ancient Egypt or from the lost continents of Atlantis or Mu. Others identify the Indians as the Lost Tribes of Israel, or as descendants of sailors from the fleets of Alexander the Great. Wauchope summarizes the basic arguments supporting these notions, refutes them, and describes their sometimes eccentric proponents in informal fashion. In *No Stone Unturned, an Almanac of North American Prehistory* (New York, Random House [1959] 370 p.), Louis A. Brennan accepts the orthodox premise that the first inhabitants arrived by way of Siberia and the Bering Strait but argues for an earlier arrival than is generally advanced by professional scholars.

1391. Wedel, Waldo R. Prehistoric man on the Great Plains. Norman, University of Oklahoma Press [1961] xviii, 355 p. illus.
          61-9002  E78.W5W4
   Bibliography: p. 312-340.

Until as recently as 35 years ago, little was known about the prehistoric occupants of the Great Plains; there was, indeed, some doubt as to their existence. In the last three decades, however, a wealth of evidence relating to ancient cultures in that region has been uncovered. The work-relief agencies of the 1930's conducted systematic investigations, and Federal dam-building projects have prompted intensive studies in areas slated to be inundated. A summary of the information revealed by these activities, Wedel's volume is designed to serve both scholar and general reader. An introductory chapter describes the tools used by the archeologist; later chapters deal with the prehistory of the various subareas within the Great Plains.

## C. Tribes and Tribal Groups

1392. Ewers, John C. The Blackfeet; raiders on the Northwestern Plains. Norman, University of Oklahoma Press [1958] xviii, 348 p. illus.

(The Civilization of the American Indian series, 49)         58-7778  E99.S54E78
   Bibliography: p. 329-336.

Blackfeet is a group name for the Piegan, Kainah, and Siksika tribes who occupied the northern portions of the Midwest. This historical and ethnological account depicts the progress of these tribes from stone-age men who traveled on foot to mobile buffalo hunters on horseback. It also narrates their subsequent decline as the white settlers moved into their lands and the buffalo vanished. Ewers has combined recollections of elderly Indians on reservations with Government reports, newspaper accounts, and scholarly articles to provide a balanced, nontechnical survey.

1393. Hughes, Charles C. An Eskimo village in the modern world. With the collaboration of Jane M. Hughes. Ithaca, N.Y., Cornell University Press [1960] xiv, 419 p. illus. (Cornell studies in anthropology) 60–2605 E99.E7H95
Bibliography: p. 399–410.
In 1940 Alexander H. Leighton and Dorothea C. Leighton made an anthropological survey of Eskimo life in Gambell, a small and isolated village on St. Lawrence Island off the coast of Alaska. In 1955 Hughes studied the sociological changes which had occurred during the intervening 15 years, a period in which the U.S. Government established air and military bases in the vicinity and the people of the island came into close contact with the Alaskan mainland. This volume contains the results of that study. The author begins with a short history of the village and then discusses population growth, economic factors, and cultural change and breakdown. A glossary of Eskimo terms is appended. A similar study of Barrow, Alaska, can be found in *The North Alaskan Eskimo; a Study in Ecology and Society* (Washington, U.S. Govt. Print. Off., 1959. 490 p. [U.S.] Bureau of American Ethnology. Bulletin 171), by Robert F. Spencer.

1394. Josephy, Alvin M. The patriot chiefs; a chronicle of American Indian leadership. New York, Viking Press, 1961. 364 p. illus. 61–17039 E89.J78
Bibliography: p. 349–356.
The story of nine chiefs—Hiawatha, King Philip, Popé, Pontiac, Tecumseh, Osceola, Black Hawk, Crazy Horse, and Chief Joseph—who tried to help their people retain their liberty and cultural integrity. Of special interest is Josephy's chapter on Hiawatha, an Iroquois chief who inspired his people to form a confederation based on democratic principles a hundred years before the first white explorers appeared. The author, an editor of *American Heritage,* has taken his information from secondary sources, most of which are listed in an extensive bibliography. Maps at the beginning of each chapter indicate location of the principal tribes and the more significant battles. Full-length biographies of many of these chiefs have already been published. One of the more recent is Merrill D. Beal's *"I Will Fight No More Forever"; Chief Joseph and the Nez Perce War* (Seattle, University of Washington Press, 1963. 366 p.).

1395. Newcomb, William W. The Indians of Texas, from prehistoric to modern times. With drawings by Hal M. Story. Austin, University of Texas Press [1961] 404 p. 60–14312 E78.T4N4
Bibliography: p. 365–377.
This anthropological study of the 10 Indian tribes known to have occupied the area now called Texas was written to help substantiate the thesis that all races have basically the same capabilities. Tribal differences, Newcomb asserts, were caused by varying cultural environments which evolved slowly and perpetuated themselves. He describes the early savages: Coahuiltecans and Karankawas; the horseback-riding warriors: Lipan Apaches, Tonkawas, Comanches, and Kiowas; and the primitive farmers: Jumanos, Wichitas, Caddo Confederacies, and Atakapans. One chapter is devoted to each tribe, with descriptions of appearance, material culture, social organization, and religious beliefs. The last chapter is a historical account of the defeat and extermination of the tribes as the whites moved into the area. Newcomb's study is a synthesis of material taken from such primary sources as the journals of explorers, soldiers, missionaries, and captives and from secondary materials which included scholarly ethnological articles and monographs.

# D. Religion, Art, and Folklore

1396. Dockstader, Frederick J. Indian art in America; the arts and crafts of the North American Indian. Greenwich, Conn., New York Graphic Society [1961] 224 p. 60–8921 H98.A7D57
Bibliography: p. 222–224.

Indian artifacts and decorations presented in 250 photographs, some of which are in color. The author, director of the Museum of the American Indian, Heye Foundation, has limited the survey to North America, but he tries to show examples from every important region and of all major artistic techniques. The plates are divided into two sections, prehistoric and historic, which are subdivided roughly by geographic area. Each illustration is accompanied by a brief description indicating where and approximately when the article was made and its size, significance, and present location (usually the Museum of the American Indian). Especially striking are the colorful carved masks and statues made by the tribes of the northern Pacific coast and the stylized watercolors painted by contemporary artists. These watercolors are reproduced and discussed more extensively in Clara L. Tanner's *Southwest Indian Painting* (Tucson, University of Arizona Press [1957] 157 p.).

1397. Miles, Charles. Indian and Eskimo artifacts of North America. Chicago, H. Regnery Co., 1963. 224 p.    62–19386 E77.M62
    Bibliography: p. 238–239.
Drawing heavily on his personal collection, Miles has compiled an illustrated catalog of North American Indian artifacts. He includes items of native design, such as tools, clothing, personal decorations, musical instruments, toys, and pipes, but omits artifacts inspired by the white man's culture — modern Southwestern pottery, for example. The objects are arranged by function into chapters, each of which is preceded by an informative introduction. No attempt is made to identify each item by date

and origin because the evidence needed for reliable identification is usually unavailable.

1398. Schoolcraft, Henry Rowe. Indian legends from Algic researches (The myth of Hiawatha, Oneóta, the red race in America) and historical and statistical information respecting the Indian tribes of the United States; edited by Mentor L. Williams. [East Lansing] Michigan State University Press, 1956. xxii, 322 p.
    55–11688 E98.F6S32
    Bibliography: p. 320–322.
Schoolcraft (1793–1864) was an explorer, geologist, Indian agent, and pioneer ethnologist (see biographical sketch, entry no. 2892 in the 1960 *Guide*). In 1823 he married a halfblood Chippewa. From his numerous Indian acquaintances and relatives by marriage he collected legends and folklore of the Algonquian tribes in the Northeast. Longfellow drew upon Schoolcraft's writings for his tales of Hiawatha, as did several authors of children's books. Today it is recognized that Schoolcraft's informants were sometimes confused in their renditions of the tales and also that his transcriptions were not always completely faithful. His collection, however, remains one of the most authentic available. Williams has selected for this volume the principal legends from Schoolcraft's major works. He provides a short critical history of Schoolcraft's life and writings and supplies new footnotes to the tales. A collection of California Indian legends rewritten with skill can be found in *The Inland Whale* (Bloomington, Indiana University Press [1959] 205 p.), by Theodora Kroeber.

# E. The White Advance

1399. Andrist, Ralph K. The long death; the last days of the Plains Indian. Maps by Rafael D. Palacios. New York, Macmillan [1964] 371 p.
    64–12545 E78.W5A593
    Bibliography: p. 355–357.
An account of the Indian wars on the Great Plains from the establishment of the boundary of a "permanent" Indian country in 1840 to the massacre at Wounded Knee Creek in 1890. This is a bloody tale of broken promises and betrayals by the whites and savage atrocities by the Indians who fought to save their lands and way of life. Andrist is sympathetic toward the Indians, and he marshals his facts in support of his ideas. He describes the Sioux wars

in Minnesota in 1862, Chivington's massacre of the Cheyennes at Sand Creek in 1864, the annihilation of Captain Fetterman and his men at Fort Philip Kearny in 1866, the Modoc War, Custer and the Battle of Little Bighorn, and the last stand of the Nez Percés under the leadership of Chief Joseph. Numerous maps enhance the value of this study. Another well-mapped history is *The Military Conquest of the Southern Plains* (Norman, University of Oklahoma Press [1963] 269 p.), by William H. Leckie, which is amply footnoted and includes an extensive bibliography. *The Modocs and Their War* (Norman, University of Oklahoma Press [1959] 346 p. The Civilization of the American

Indian series, 52), by Keith A. Murray, is a detailed account of the Indian war in which Gen. Edward R. S. Canby was killed by Indians while he was negotiating with them.

1400. Flexner, James T. Mohawk baronet: Sir William Johnson of New York. New York, Harper [1959] 400 p. illus.

59–10581 E195.J659

Bibliography: p. 362–368.

Johnson (1715–1774) was an Irish emigrant who came to the New World in the late 1730's to manage his uncle's estate on the Mohawk River. He quickly gained the friendship of the Indians in New York and for most of his life played a dual role as both adopted Mohawk and Iroquois chief and British superintendent of Indian affairs. He was responsible in large part for keeping the Iroquois on the English side in the French and Indian wars and received an English baronetcy in recognition of his services. He opened the Mohawk Valley for colonization and at his death was one of the largest landowners in the Colonies. Johnson tried to create a situation in which the Iroquois tribes could have stabilized holdings, but he failed to foresee the wave of white settlers who, soon after his death, would clamor for more and more land. Based on extensive research, this biography provides a vivid picture of one of the most influential figures in the long history of relations between the Indian and the white man.

1401. Hagan, William T. American Indians. [Chicago] University of Chicago Press [1961] 190 p. illus. (The Chicago history of American civilization)

61–1555 E93.H2

"Suggested reading": p. 175–183.

The author provides a brief but lucid introduction to the complex history of the American Indian. He graphically portrays the Indian tribes fighting to save a way of life, the whites continually pressing for more land, and the Government repeatedly failing to establish permanent protective boundaries. The last chapter is devoted to recent public policy. *The Indian and the White Man* (Garden City, N.Y., Anchor Books, 1964. 480 p. Documents in American civilization series), edited by Wilcomb E. Washburn, is a collection of annotated primary sources useful for supplementary reading.

1402. Leach, Douglas E. Flintlock and tomahawk; New England in King Philip's War. New York, Macmillan, 1958. 304 p. illus.

58–5467 E83.67.L4

Bibliography: p. 271–290.

1403. Vaughan, Alden T. New England frontier; Puritans and Indians, 1620–1675. Boston, Little, Brown [1965] 430 p. illus.

65–20736 F7.V3

Bibliography: p. [401]–420.

In June 1675, after years of comparative peace, a number of the Algonquian tribes submerged their historic feuds and combined in an uneasy confederation led by King Philip, a Wampanoag chief, in an effort to drive out the English settlers. Many of the frontier towns were destroyed and more than a thousand settlers killed, but by August 1676 King Philip was dead and the uprising crushed. Leach's study, based on extensive research in primary sources, supplies a well-rounded picture of the desperate struggle. Vaughan focuses on the relationships between Puritan and Indian in the years from the settlement at Plymouth up to this destructive war. He concludes that, contrary to the widely held view of white oppression, the Puritans were more enlightened than most of their contemporaries and "followed a remarkably humane, considerate, and just policy in their dealings with the Indians."

1404. Pearce, Roy Harvey. The savages of America; a study of the Indian and the idea of civilization. Rev. ed. Baltimore, Johns Hopkins Press, 1965. xv, 260 p. illus.

65–2719 E93.P4 1965

Bibliographical footnotes.

An updated edition of no. 3031 in the 1960 *Guide*.

1405. Prucha, Francis P. American Indian policy in the formative years: the Indian trade and intercourse acts, 1790–1834. Cambridge, Harvard University Press, 1962. 303 p.

62–9428 E93.P965

"Bibliographical note": p. [279]–292.

The early Indian policy of the U.S. Government consisted of a body of law designed to promote a gradual and peaceful westward advance of the white settlers and at the same time to reserve to the Indians specified liberties and land areas. Prucha has studied the emergence, implementation, and modification of that policy. He reveals the way in which it developed in response to the pressures of Indians and whites and the manner in which it was either executed successfully by the Government or frustrated by the land-hungry frontiersmen. Other studies of the attempts to regulate the Indian affairs at various times include Allen W. Trelease's *Indian Affairs in Colonial New York: The Seventeenth Century* (Ithaca, N.Y., Cornell University Press [1960] 379 p.) and *The Movement for Indian Assimilation, 1860–1890* (Philadelphia, University of Pennsylvania Press [1963] 244 p.), by Henry E. Fritz.

1406. Spicer, Edward H. Cycles of conquest; the impact of Spain, Mexico, and the United States on the Indians of the Southwest, 1533–1960. Drawings by Hazel Fontana. Tucson, University of Arizona Press [1962] 609 p.

61–14500    E78.S7S6

"Bibliographic notes to chapters": p. 587–599.

As the Governments of Spain, Mexico, and the United States successively obtained political control of the Southwest, they attempted, with varying degrees of success, to impose their cultural patterns on the Indians. Basing his conclusions on the works of historians and anthropologists who have studied individual tribes in detail, Spicer analyzes the effects of interethnic contact and shows how the impact of European civilization on Indian culture resulted in changes unexpected by both Indians and whites. He traces the instances of contact and conquest as they occurred, examines the policies of the conquering groups, and describes the political, linguistic, social, and economic developments that followed. *The Indian Traders* (Norman, University of Oklahoma Press [1962] 393 p.), by Frank McNitt, describes the American traders in the Southwest, who provided much of the firsthand contact between the Indians and the whites.

## F. The Twentieth Century

1407. Fey, Harold E., *and* D'Arcy McNickle. Indians and other Americans; two ways of life meet. New York, Harper [1959] 220 p. illus.

58–10368    E93.F37

The National Government did not, according to authors Fey and McNickle, adopt a policy designed to meet the needs of the Indians in a constructive and realistic fashion until the Meriam survey of 1926–28 (the report of the survey is no. 3038 in the 1960 *Guide*) and the Indian Reorganization Act of 1934. The new approach called for promoting tribal organization, assisting in economic development, improving educational facilities, and reviving Indian cultures. This program did not endure long, however. Its opponents strongly favored decreasing public responsibility for the Indians' welfare. In the 1950's the Government began to reduce its support and to plan for the eventual division of all Indian lands into individual allotments. The authors condemn this trend as premature and urge continued aids and controls until the Indians, economically and socially, reach a stage of development at which they can contend equally in the white communities that will assimilate them.

1408. Kroeber, Theodora. Ishi in two worlds; a biography of the last wild Indian in North America. Berkeley, University of California Press, 1961. 255 p. illus.    61–7530    E90.I8K7

Bibliography: p. [245]–255.

Ishi, the last surviving member of the Yahi tribe, was found trapped by barking dogs in a corral on a farm near Oroville, Calif., in August 1911. Unable to speak or understand English and with no direct knowledge of the whites, Ishi was a man of the Stone Age. Two young anthropologists, T. T. Waterman and Alfred L. Kroeber, brought him to the Museum of Anthropology in San Francisco. Ishi adjusted with unexpected ease to 20th-century life. The museum paid him a small salary and permitted him to live in its own quarters. He described his primitive early existence to anthropologists and ethnologists and patiently entertained thousands of museum visitors by building fires and chipping arrowheads. By the time of his death in 1916, he had made many close friends among the staff members of the museum and the people of the city, in which he had learned to travel alone. Mrs. Kroeber tells with warmth and insight the poignant story of Ishi and the demise of the Yahi tribe.

1409. Lange, Charles H. Cochití: a New Mexico pueblo, past and present. Austin, University of Texas Press [1960, ᶜ1959] xxiv, 618 p. illus.    58–10852    E99.C84L3

Bibliography: p. [575]–585.

A study in depth of contemporary life and customs in a single New Mexican pueblo. The author spent several summers in Cochití and has here combined his observations with information gleaned from the reports of anthropologists who studied the pueblo between 1880 and 1950. Lange describes the village's current economic situation, ceremonial life, and social structure and relates them to the past, showing the impact of European civilization. He also compares the cultural characteristics of Cochití with those of neighboring pueblos in the Rio Grande Valley. Extensive appendixes include statistics, rosters of members of religious societies, pictures of costumes used in religious ceremonies, and choreography and music for ritualistic dances. An analysis of European influence on six western Indian groups may be found in *Perspectives in American Indian Culture Change* ([Chicago] University of Chicago Press [1961] 549 p.), edited by Edward H. Spicer for the Interuniversity Summer Research Seminar held at the University of New Mexico in 1956.

1410. Wilson, Edmund. Apologies to the Iroquois. With a study of The Mohawks in high steel by Joseph Mitchell. New York, Farrar, Straus & Cudahy [1960] 310 p. illus.

59–9177    E99.I7W56

Well known for his versatility as an author, Wilson became interested in the Iroquois in 1957, when their attempts to reclaim their historic tribal lands received newspaper publicity. In ensuing years he visited reservations in New York and Canada and talked with many Indian leaders. This small volume contains a collection of articles which he wrote as a result of his investigations and which originally appeared in *The New Yorker*. Wilson summarizes the history of the Iroquois Confederation, discusses the life of the tribes today, describes some of their ceremonies, and analyzes the growth of the Iroquois nationalist movement. His detailed accounts of recent Indian struggles to prevent the preemption of their lands for public works projects are of special interest. Mitchell's brief contribution is an essay on the unexpected fondness and talent Indians in the New York area have shown for working on the high steel frameworks of bridges and buildings.

# VIII

# General History

THE INTERPRETIVE essay which introduces this chapter in the 1960 *Guide* places in perspective the concept of "general history" as it evolved and as it has been applied in this country since its origin. The chapter's entries survey the whole range of historical development in that "portion of the earth's surface which is now the United States" and, in the process, take account of the changing attitudes of mind by which successive generations of historians conceived their task of recording that development.

The concept that the historian's approach to his subject and his selection and use of materials undergo a continuing process of review and revision is one which the *Supplement* also follows with an eye to recognizing the shifting currents of historical scholarship. This chapter is partly a review of the history of history. Section A contains works devoted to historiography, and the remaining selections show the increased velocity with which the change in viewpoint is taking place, corresponding to the rapidly rising volume of historical writing. The selections also contain the implications, with which few historians today would quarrel, that historical perspective in any given period is aligned to and conditioned by the social, political, economic, and cultural milieu in which it operates and that the presuppositions which guide historians in any age tend to develop in a process of reaction to the mode and temper of their predecessors.

In the developmental process, for example, that began with the birth of "scientific history" before the turn of the century, there eventually emerged, from the eclecticism of its university environment, a corrective—"New"—history, intended to widen the scope of the discipline's purview, to relate it to the present, and to link it with the social sciences. The new historians, writing through the 1920's and 1930's, viewed their subject with an abiding sense of change and progress and a growing awareness of the social and economic conflicts that characterized and motivated their own times. In some, this experience hardened into an economic determinism. Others reacted with a heightened interest in the role of contending ideas, ideals, and values as dynamic factors in the growth and progress of the Nation. With the rise of intellectual history and biography, the historian's task moved far beyond its traditional preoccupation with military and political events, brought into play a still wider spectrum of the social sciences, and extended the burgeoning accumulation of historical source material.

Since the early 1950's, it has been evident that another modification is under way. In some quarters the seeming internal contradictions in postwar affairs have diminished the status of the liberal faith in the idea of progress. The pendulatory swing has favored a search for stability, continuity, and tradition in American life, a search that is reflected in the way historians contemplate the past. In this view, sectional divisiveness and class and ethnic cleavages are seen to have been more apparent than real, and scholars search for national unity and for the nature and efficacy of something called the national character.

Just as the complexity of historical thought and introspection has increased, so the phenomenal growth of historical source materials imposes an awesome burden on the modern writer, as the books in this chapter reveal. His conscious or unconscious involvement with the social sciences, new techniques of quantitative analysis, and the output of data processing requires a painful duty in merely "keeping up." The "new self-consciousness" referred to in the 1960 *Guide* now concerns itself with the historian's ability to use this pyramiding body of research and fact and with the quality and purpose of the history he is producing. Journal articles and convention papers testify to the profession's desire to sustain standards of literary artistry and readability. The fragmentation and specialization of historical inquiry have created conditions that are not conducive to the production of what was formerly defined as "general history." The grand design is today seldom attempted by an individual; rather, it is normally the aim of ventures in cooperative authorship and of works in series under pivotal editorship.

Yet the fact remains that the 10-year period under review has perhaps produced an unprecedented array of skillfully researched, engagingly written, and handsomely presented historical works. They provide for the bibliographer a new challenge in selection and organization. The divisions of labor in American historical writing are becoming less distinct and more difficult to define. The point where intellectual history merges into historiography or with the philosophy of history is that point at which we attempt to place selections accurately either in this chapter or in Chapter XI, Intellectual History, or Chapter XXII, Philosophy and Psychology. Biography poses a special dilemma. The vastly increased popularity of this genre has resulted in many scholarly and well-written — even prize-winning — biographies of relatively minor figures often within the context of regional or local history. The stature of the subject, rather than the excellence of his biographer, must often guide us here, and a great many worthy studies must be omitted. Many biographical works are placed in chapters on other topics or in Chapter IV, Biography and Autobiography. In the section on historiography we have attempted to choose the broader surveys and representative biographies of historians that will make the problems and purposes of the craft intelligible to those outside. The reader may find that some of the books he expects to encounter in this chapter are in Chapter XII, Local History. History is being writ small, but in microcosm; nearly all, be it noted, is posed within the larger framework of national relevance.

## A. Historiography

1411. America, history and life. v. 1+ July 1964+ [Santa Barbara, Calif.] Published by Clio Press for American Bibliographical Center.

64–25630    Z1236.A48

Four numbers a year, one of which is the annual index.

Editor: Eric H. Boehm.

A bibliographic review and abstracting service, which surveys about 500 U.S. and Canadian periodicals for articles within the entire range of American and Canadian history and on current American and Canadian life. Abstracts are grouped by topic.

1412. Beers, Henry P. The French & British in the Old Northwest; a bibliographical guide to archive and manuscript sources. Detroit, Wayne State University Press, 1964. 297 p.

64–13305    F478.2.B4

The area covered by this guide includes Michigan, Ohio, Indiana, Illinois, Wisconsin, Minnesota, and the Dakotas, with some reference to the western portions of Pennsylvania and New York. It presents "an historical account of the acquisition, preservation, and publication by American and Canadian institutions of the original records created by French and British officials in the Old Northwest (the region south of the Great Lakes) chiefly during the eighteenth century, and of officials and governing bodies of Canada relating to that region." Historical notes and introductions also provide descriptions of the government of the region, the land-grant system, and ecclesiastical organizations. The nature, extent, and location of all important archival and manuscript materials are recorded, and the existence of copies or transcripts is noted. The concluding chapter is a 61-page list of bibliographical sources.

1413. Borning, Bernard C. The political and social thought of Charles A. Beard. Seattle, University of Washington Press, 1962. xxv, 315 p.

62–12129 E175.5.B382

Bibliography: p. 257–295.

The author, a political scientist at the University of Idaho, systematically explores the development of Beard's ideas from 1898 to 1948. His purpose is to describe Beard's impact on the political opinion of his time and, by a careful study of his writings and the response of his contemporaries, to relate the significance of his ideas to the prevailing intellectual environment. The analytical techniques of the social sciences are applied to both Beard and Frederick Jackson Turner in Lee Benson's *Turner and Beard; American Historical Writing Reconsidered* (Glencoe, Ill., Free Press [1960] 241 p.). Benson reviews their economic writings against a background of European influences, in particular that of the Italian economist, Achille Loria. He finds that the two historians' economic theories tend to converge and takes to task not their ideas but rather the mistaken conclusions of thir critics. In *The Pragmatic Revolt in American History: Carl Becker and Charles Beard* (New Haven, Yale University Press, 1958. 182 p. Yale historical publications. The Wallace Norstein essays, no. 3), Cushing Strout poses Beard against yet another historian. Two temperamentally dissimilar iconoclasts are brought together for their common attacks on the scientifically oriented historical positivism of their times and are carefully examined, in alternating chapters, for the internal merits or practical inadequacies of the pragmatic relativism which each espoused.

1414. Cartwright, William H., *and* Richard L. Watson, *eds.* Interpreting and teaching American history. Washington, National Council for Social Studies, a Dept. of the National Education Association [1961] xvi, 430 p. (National Council for the Social Studies. Yearbook, 31st, 1961)

31–6192 H62.A1N3 v. 31, 1961

Directed toward improving the teaching of American history at all levels, this book is designed to update the Council's 17th yearbook, *The Study and Teaching of American History* (1946), no. 3059 in the 1960 *Guide*. The greater part of the

book consists of a series of bibliographical essays on all major aspects of American history. Arranged in chronological order and intended to balance, in each period, interpretation with bibliographical references, the essays seek to introduce the student to a wide variety of interpretations by relating these to the works and to the scholars responsible. Three contributions to this section originally appeared in virtually the same form, in the similarly oriented pamphlet series published by the Service Center for Teachers of History of the American Historical Association.

1415. Curti, Merle E. The making of an American community; a case study of democracy in a frontier county. With the assistance of Robert Daniel [and others]. Stanford, Calif., Stanford University Press, 1959. 483 p. maps, diagrs.

59–5051 HN79.W62T73

"Bibliographical notes": p. 467–469.

Frederick Jackson Turner (1861–1932) advanced the theory that the frontier experience fostered the development of a democratic way of life in America. Curti examines Turner's thesis by applying it to a specific case, the settling of Trempealeau County in western Wisconsin. He is of the opinion that Turner perhaps underestimated the tremendous obstacles to the acquisition of frontier land, over-emphasized the frontier as a promoter of democracy, and neglected the role of other factors such as industrialism. Curti believes that Turner probably saw more democracy in the relations among frontier people than was really there but concludes that, if Trempealeau County was a typical frontier area, then this investigation bears out Turner's thesis. He notes in particular the fostering of such "democratic traits" as self-reliance, social equality, and tolerance of personal differences. In honor of the centennial of Turner's birth, the Wisconsin State Historical Society published *Wisconsin Witness to Frederick Jackson Turner; a Collection of Essays on the Historian and the Thesis* (Madison, 1961. 204 p.), compiled by O. Lawrence Burnette, Jr. *Frederick Jackson Turner's Legacy; Unpublished Writings in American History* (San Marino, Calif., Huntington Library, 1965. 217 p. Huntington Library publications), edited by Wilbur R. Jacobs, is a selection of speeches, essays, lectures, and memorandums.

1416. Doughty, Howard. Francis Parkman. New York, Macmillan, 1962. 414 p.

61–12191 E175.5.P212

Bibliographical note: p. 402–403.

A deeply sensitive examination of Parkman's life and work, composed with an architecture and style very much like Parkman's own. It is primarily with Parkman as a man of letters that the author is concerned, and his critical appreciation of the historian's literary gifts is displayed in a minute textual analysis of his works. Parkman's heritage, early life, studies, wilderness excursions, and physical frailty are described in their manifold relations to the development of his narrative artistry. More than 400 Parkman letters are annotated and published in *Letters of Francis Parkman* (Norman, University of Oklahoma Press [1960] 2 v.), edited by Wilbur R. Jacobs. Two works more conventional in their biographical approach to eminent historians are Abraham S. Eisenstadt's *Charles McLean Andrews, a Study in American Historical Writing* (New York, Columbia University Press, 1956. 273 p. Columbia studies in the social sciences, no. 588) and Jacob E. Cooke's *Frederic Bancroft, Historian* (Norman, University of Oklahoma Press [1957] 282 p.), which contains three of Bancroft's previously unpublished essays on the colonization of American Negroes from 1801 to 1865. Milton Berman's *John Fiske; the Evolution of a Popularizer* (Cambridge, Harvard University Press, 1961. 297 p. Harvard historical monographs, 48) portrays a less original but lucid and immensely popular historian.

1417. Posner, Ernst. American State archives. Chicago, University of Chicago Press [1964] xiv, 397 p.        64–23425  CD3024.P6
"Basic bibliography of writings on public archives administration in the United States": p. 377–386.
The published results of a study of State archival programs sponsored by the Society of American Archivists under a grant from the Council on Library Resources, Inc. On the basis of written questionnaires and survey visits to each State, Posner presents a State-by-State analysis of the background development, organization, and legal status of the archival and records programs of all 50 States and Puerto Rico. The individual State evaluations are preceded by a chapter on "The Genesis and Evolution of American State Archives" and followed by a chapter entitled "A Summary of Findings" and another on "Standards for State Archival Agencies." *In Support of Clio; Essays in Memory of Herbert A. Kellar* (Madison, State Historical Society of Wisconsin, 1958. 214 p.), edited by William B. Hesseltine and Donald R. McNeil, offers a more selective evaluation of prevailing aids to historical study in a collection of essays by prominent scholars on such topics as the Historical Records Survey, manuscript collecting, public archives, mechanical aids in historical research, foundations and the study of history, and historical organizations as aids to history.

1418. Saveth, Edward N., *ed*. American history and the social sciences. [New York] Free Press of Glencoe [1964] 599 p.
64–20308  E175.S36
Bibliographical references included in "Notes" (p. 537–591).
A selection of essays arranged to illustrate and evaluate the implications of the current confluence of history and the social sciences in American scholarship. To systematize the essays' mutual scrutiny of method and approach, the editor has divided this large and close-packed volume into five parts. The first defines the problem—the "difference between the professional climates of history and the social science disciplines"—in terms of what is involved in the social science approach and its relationship to adjacent areas of traditional historiography. The second part presents views by representatives of the disciplines, and the third deals with a wide range of social science concepts, defined for their relevance to historical inquiry and illustrating their application to the data of American history. Part 4 concentrates on "quantitative concepts and machine processes applied to historical research." The final part allows selected historians the right of reply in defining from their own experience the "limits of the social science approach." Among the contributors to the volume are Walt W. Rostow, Margaret Mead, Richard Hofstadter, Oscar and Mary Handlin, Henry Steele Commager, Merle Curti, John Higham, Cushing Strout, and Arthur M. Schlesinger, Jr.

1419. Sheehan, Donald H., *and* Harold C. Syrett, *eds*. Essays in American historiography; papers presented in honor of Allan Nevins. New York, Columbia University Press, 1960. 320 p.
60–8187  E175.S48
CONTENTS.—Allan Nevins: an appreciation, by John A. Krout.—Scientific history in America: eclipse of an idea, by Edward N. Saveth.—Thoughts on the Confederacy, by Robert C. Black, III.—Radical Reconstruction, by Donald Sheehan.—The New South, by Jacob E. Cooke.—American historians and national politics from the Civil War to the First World War, by James A. Rawley.—Reflections on urban history and urban reform, 1865–1915, by Mark D. Hirsch.—The idea of the robber barons in American history, by Hal Bridges.—Some aspects of European migration to the United States, by Carlton C. Qualey.—The evolution controversy, by Joseph A. Boromé.—Pragmatism in America, by Sidney Ratner.—Populism: its significance in American history, by Everett Walters.—Imperialism and racism, by James P. Shenton.—The muckrakers: in flower and in failure, by Louis Filler.—

A cycle of revisionism between two wars, by Harry W. Baehr.—An interpretation of Franklin D. Roosevelt, by Bernard Bellush.

1420.  Social Science Research Council. *Committee on Historical Analysis.* Generalization in the writing of history; a report. Edited by Louis Gottschalk. [Chicago] University of Chicago Press [1963] 255 p.                63–13064  D13.S595

This third report of the Social Science Research Council on the nature of history is a set of essays dealing with the problem of generalization by the historian in several different contexts and from several varying points of view. The first report, *Theory and Practice in Historical Study* (1946), is no. 3065 in the 1960 *Guide.* The second is *The Social Sciences in Historical Study* (1954).

CONTENTS.— Reflections upon the problem of generalization, by Chester G. Starr.—Generalizations in ancient history, by M. I. Finley.—On the uses of generalization in the study of Chinese history, by Arthur F. Wright.—Comments on the paper of Arthur F. Wright, by Derk Bodde.—Generalizations about revolution: a case study, by Robert R. Palmer.—Generalizations about national character: an analytical essay, by Walter P. Metzger.—The historian's use of social role, by Thomas C. Cochran. —Categories of historiographical generalization, by Louis Gottschalk.—The genealogy of historical generalizations, by Roy F. Nichols.—Notes on the problem of historical generalization, by William O. Aydelotte.—Explicit data and implicit assumptions in historical study, by David M. Potter.—Summary, by Louis Gottschalk.— Bibliography of writings on historiography and the philosophy of history, by Martin Klein.

1421.  Van Tassel, David D. Recording America's past; an interpretation of the development of historical studies in America, 1607–1884. [Chicago] University of Chicago Press [1960] 222 p.
60–14404  E175.V3  1960
Bibliography: p. 191–212.

1422.  Higham, John, Leonard Krieger, *and* Felix Gilbert. History. Englewood Cliffs, N.J., Prentice-Hall [1965] xiv, 402 p. (The Princeton studies: humanistic scholarship in America)
64–23563  D13.H43
Bibliographical footnotes.
Viewed by the author himself as a mere chapter in what a full history of the "whole range of American historical studies" could be, *Recording America's Past* explores such developments as the colonial origins and formative role of the local historian; the early genesis of historical societies on the frontier; the impetus for the writing of community, territorial, and State history; and, finally, the rise of national history. Most striking is the author's recognition of the services of the amateur historian in broadening the scope of historical inquiry beyond the conventional limits of European precedents and in shaping and recording the growth and historical sense of the Nation. Whereas Van Tassel concludes with the triumph of national history, Higham begins with the accession of the professional historian. Their narratives overlap with the founding of the American Historical Association in 1884 and the subsequent institutionalization of historical study in the universities. From this point, Higham and his colleagues seek to interpret the progress and present status of the professional historians in America in terms of their theories, general conceptions, and motivation. Particular merits of their work are its broad erudition and the large body of information that is packed into a volume of reasonable size.

1423.  Whitehill, Walter Muir. Independent historical societies, an enquiry into their research and publication functions and their financial future. [Boston] Boston Athenaeum; distributed by Harvard University Press, 1962. xviii, 593 p.
63–1190  E172.W5
Bibliographical footnotes.
Under the auspices of the Council on Library Resources, Inc., the author visited "three quarters of the fifty states" to probe a considerably wider range of subjects than is indicated by the title. The principal independent historical societies are described and their historical background and evolution are outlined. Other allied organizations are presented more briefly, with emphasis on their present activities. The final chapters, often marked by a frank irreverence and wit, concern such topics as State-supported societies, historical associations, manuscript collections and Presidental libraries, genealogists, museums, and State archives. *Keepers of the Past* (Chapel Hill, University of North Carolina Press [1965] 241 p.), edited by Clifford L. Lord, offers a series of biographical essays devoted to key figures in various fields of historical preservation who pioneered and "made notable things happen" in developing historical societies, public archives, museums, special collections, and historic sites.

1424.  Wilkins, Burleigh T. Carl Becker; a biographical study in American intellectual history. Cambridge, M.I.T. Press, 1961. 246 p.
61–7870  D15.B33W5
Described by the author "mainly as an exercise in

historical understanding," this biography is, in addition, a sensitive, perceptive, and at times critical study of the intellectual development of this philosopher-historian and of the changing dimensions of his mind in relation to the emerging pattern of his life. "By relating his 'thoughts' to his 'environment,'" Wilkins has "tried to see Becker 'whole' while at the same time discriminating between the major and minor aspects of his work." The elements of the environment are found by the author in Becker's family, its religion and politics; in the conditioning influence of a prolonged college and university milieu; and in the remarkable circle of eminent friends with whom he corresponded all his life. The alchemy of these forces, the impact of the times in which he lived, the shifting tides of political and historical philosophy, the disturbing effect of two world wars, and the elements in his own character are carefully examined. Charlotte W. Smith's *Carl Becker: On History & the Climate of Opinion* (Ithaca, N.Y., Cornell University Press, 1956. 225 p.) centers on American historiography and Becker's historical relativism.

1425. Wish, Harvey. The American historian; a social-intellectual history of the writing of the American past. New York, Oxford University Press, 1960. 366 p. 60–13202 E175.W5
    Bibliographic notes: p. 351–360.
    In a general survey devoted to examining the social and intellectual assumptions underlying various stages of American historical writing, the author studies representative historians from William Bradford to Allan Nevins. The traditional biographical approach is subordinated to an exploration of the subjective factors which emerge from a study of their writings and of the critical secondary literature their writings have evoked. A closer look at the environmental influences of the 19th century on historical scholarship is provided in each of three widely dissimilar but equally incisive works. In *History as Romantic Art: Bancroft, Prescott, Motley, and Parkman* (Stanford, Calif., Stanford University Press, 1959. 260 p. Stanford studies in language and literature, 20), David Levin examines the relationship between four historians' assumptions and their literary techniques. Wendell Holmes Stephenson's *Southern History in the Making; Pioneer Historians of the South* ([Baton Rouge] Louisiana State University Press, 1964. 294 p.), a companion volume to his *The South Lives in History* (mentioned in the annotation for no. 3057 in the 1960 *Guide*), contains detailed studies of nine historians of the South. In *The German Historical School in American Scholarship; a Study in the Transfer of Culture* (Ithaca, Cornell University Press [1965] 262 p.), Jurgen Herbst examines the rise and decline of the German historical school of social science in the United States between 1876 and 1914.

# B. General Works

1426. Adams, James Truslow, *ed.* Dictionary of American history. James Truslow Adams, editor in chief; R. V. Coleman, managing editor. 2d ed. rev. New York, Scribner, 1942–61. 6 v.
    44–1876 E174.A43 1942
    On title page of v. 6: Supplement 1; issued without edition statement.
    *Supplement 1* adds new, revised, and updated material to the five-volume set entered as no. 3071 in the 1960 *Guide*. Also revised and updated is the *Index Volume* (New York, Scribner [1963] 266 p.). The *Concise Dictionary of American History* (New York, Scribner [1962] 1156 p.) is a condensed version of the *Dictionary of American History*, including *Supplement 1*. Michael R. Martin and Leonard Gelber have written *The New Dictionary of American History* (New York, Philosophical Library [1965] 714 p.), revised by Arthur W. Littlefield, which includes brief biographical studies.

1427. The Adams papers. L. H. Butterfield, editor in chief. Cambridge, Belknap Press of Harvard University Press, 1961–65. 11 v.
    When publication is completed, the Adams papers will consist of 80 to 100 volumes. As of 1965, the volumes were divided into three principal series: the Adams Diaries, the Adams Family Correspondence, and General Correspondence and Other Papers. The following volumes had then been published in the Adams Diaries: John Adams' *Diary and Autobiography* (1961. 4 v. 60–5387 E322.A3), edited by Butterfield, and the first two of an estimated 18 volumes of Charles Francis Adam's *Diary* (1964. 64–20588 E467.1.A2A15), edited by Aïda D. Donald and David H. Donald. The first two volumes of the *Adams Family Correspondence* (1963. 63–14964 E322.1.A27), also edited by Butterfield, had appeared. The initial volumes in the third series are the *Legal Papers of*

*John Adams* (1965. 3 v. 65–13855 Law), edited by L. Kinvin Wroth and Hiller B. Zobel.

1428. Berger, Josef, *and* Dorothy Berger, *eds.* Diary of America; the intimate story of our nation, told by 100 diarists—public figures and plain citizens, natives and visitors—over the five centuries from Columbus, the Pilgrims, and George Washington to Thomas Edison, Will Rogers, and our own time. New York, Simon & Schuster, 1957. 621 p.                                    57–10976  E173.B38
"Sources and acknowledgments": p. 618–621.
An assemblage of diary selections spanning American history from Columbus to General Joseph W. ("Vinegar Joe") Stilwell. The diarists include persons from all walks of life, whose recorded experiences range from family matters and love affairs to travel, entertainment, and politics. *The American Spirit; United States History as Seen by Contemporaries* (Boston, Heath [1963] 964 p.), edited by Thomas A. Bailey, is another collection of writings, including selections from "letters, diaries, autobiographies, editorials, propaganda leaflets, public debates, and interviews."

1429. Billington, Ray Allen. Westward expansion; a history of the American frontier by Ray Allen Billington, with the collaboration of James Blaine Hedges. 2d ed. New York, Macmillan [1960]  xv, 893 p. illus.
                             60–5482  E179.5.B63  1960
"Bibliographical note": p. 759–854.
An updated edition of no. 3074 in the 1960 *Guide,* incorporating new viewpoints on the frontier. In *A Concise Study Guide to the American Frontier* (Lincoln, University of Nebraska Press, 1964. 269 p.), Nelson Klose discusses the leading theories of the frontier, explains different types of frontiers, and analyzes problems of the frontier in general. The early history of the West is recounted by Francis S. Philbrick in *The Rise of the West, 1754–1830* (New York, Harper & Row [1965]  398 p. New American Nation series).

1430. Boorstin, Daniel J.  The Americans: the colonial experience. New York, Random House [1958]  434 p.       58–9884  E188.B72
"Bibliographical notes": p. 375–421.

1431. Boorstin, Daniel J.  The Americans: the national experience. New York, Random House [1965]  517 p.       65–17440  E301.B6
"Bibliographical notes": p. 433–495.
In these two volumes, Boorstin attempts to show how the experience of settling the United States created a unique American character. Together they review and interpret American history up to the Civil War. The author emphasizes nonpolitical history, tracing the development of such activities as law, medicine, agriculture, science, warfare, and business.

1432. Carruth, Gorton.  The encyclopedia of American facts and dates. Edited by Gorton Carruth and associates. 3d ed. New York, Crowell [1962]  758 p.  (A Crowell reference book)
                             62–14453  E174.C3  1962
An updated edition of no. 3076 in the 1960 *Guide.*

1433. Commager, Henry Steele, *ed.* Documents of American history. 7th ed. New York, Appleton-Century-Crofts [1963]  632,'739 p.
                             63–9300  E173.C66  1963
A revised and updated edition of no. 3079 in the 1960 *Guide.*
*A Documentary History of the United States* ([New York]  New American Library [1965] 336 p.  A Mentor Book, MT605), edited by Richard D. Heffner, is a revised and expanded edition of a work mentioned in the annotation for no. 3079 in the 1960 *Guide.*

1434. Dictionary of American biography, published under the auspices of the American Council of Learned Societies. New York, Scribner, 1943–58. 22 v.       44–41895  E176.D562
Volume 22, *Supplement Two,* an addition to no. 3080 in the 1960 *Guide,* contains biographies of 585 persons who died between 1936 and 1940. The *Concise Dictionary of American Biography* (New York, Scribner [1964]  1273 p.) is a short version of the *Dictionary of American Biography,* including both supplements, and provides an entry, varying in length from "minimal" to "extended," for each biographical sketch in the larger work.

1435. Eisenstadt, Abraham S., *ed.* American history: recent interpretations. New York, Crowell [1962]  2 v.       62–10281  E178.6.E44
Designed to meet the need for supplementary readings in college courses, these two volumes contain articles by reputable historians covering various aspects and periods of the American past. The articles, most of which were published in scholarly journals after 1945, have been selected to represent new viewpoints in the interpretation of American history. *The American Past; Conflicting Interpretations of the Great Issues,* 2d ed. (New York, Macmillan [1965]  2 v.), edited by Sidney A. Fine and Gerald S. Brown, is another collection of readings, including both journal articles and selections from books.

1436. Kull, Irving S., *and* Nell M. Kull. An encyclopedia of American history. Newly enl. and updated by Stanley H. Friedelbaum. New York, Popular Library [1965] 637 p. (Eagle books, Z25)      65–1251  E174.5.K8 1965

An enlarged and updated edition of no. 3077 in the 1960 *Guide*. The previous edition was entitled *A Short Chronology of American History, 1492–1950*.

1437. Morison, Samuel Eliot, *and* Henry Steele Commager. The growth of the American Republic. [5th ed., rev. and enl.] New York, Oxford University Press [1962] 2 v. illus.
61–13567  E178.M85 1962

Includes bibliographies.

A revised and enlarged edition of no. 3103 in the 1960 *Guide*. Other notable two-volume college texts include *A History of the American People,* 2d ed., rev. (New York, Knopf, 1960–61), by Harry J. Carman, Harold C. Syrett, and Bernard W. Wishy; *The Federal Union; a History of the United States to 1877,* 4th ed. (Boston, Houghton Mifflin [1964] 729 p.), by John D. Hicks, George E. Mowry, and Robert E. Burke, and *The American Nation; a History of the United States From 1865 to the Present,* 4th ed. (Boston, Houghton Mifflin, 1965. 832 p.), a revised edition of no. 3436 in the 1960 *Guide,* by the same authors; *Empire for Liberty: The Genesis and Growth of the United States of America* (New York, Appleton-Century-Crofts [1960]), by Dumas Malone and Basil Rauch; and *A History of the United States,* 2d ed., rev. (New York, Knopf, 1964), by Thomas Harry Williams, Richard N. Current, and Frank Freidel.

1438. Morison, Samuel Eliot. The Oxford history of the American people. New York, Oxford University Press, 1965. xxvii, 1150 p. illus.
65–12468  E178.M855

A history of the United States for the general reader. Morison does not slight politics but puts equitable emphasis on social and economic development. He also includes a brief account of Canadian history. Two other broad histories for the general reader are *A New History of the United States* (New York, G. Braziller, 1958. 474 p.), by William Miller, who provides a balanced narrative, and *The Americans; a New History of the People of the United States* (Boston, Little, Brown [1963] 434 p.), by Oscar Handlin, who features the role of the immigrant in American life.

1439. Morris, Richard B., *ed.* Encyclopedia of American history. Updated and rev. New York, Harper & Row [1965] xiv, 843 p. illus.
65–22859  E174.5.M847 1965

An updated edition of no. 3072 in the 1960 *Guide*.

1440. Parkes, Henry Bamford. The United States of America, a history. 2d ed., rev. New York, Knopf, 1959. 783 p. illus.
59–6118  E178.P25 1959

Bibliography: p. 779–783.

An updated edition of no. 3104 in the 1960 *Guide*. Among other one-volume college texts are *The American Pageant; a History of the Republic* (Boston, Heath [1956] 1007 p.), by Thomas A. Bailey; *The Stream of American History,* 3d ed. (New York, American Book Co. [1965] 832 p.), by Leland D. Baldwin and Robert L. Kelley; *The United States; a History of a Democracy,* 2d ed. (New York, McGraw-Hill, 1960. 713 p. McGraw-Hill series in American history), edited by Wesley M. Gewehr and others; and *A History of American Life and Thought; Revision of A Short History of American Life* (New York, McGraw-Hill, 1963. 622 p. McGraw-Hill series in American history), by Nelson M. Blake.

1441. Problems in American civilization; readings selected by the Department of American Studies, Amherst College. Boston, Heath, 1949– [65] 45 v.

Sixteen new volumes, as well as four revised editions, have been added to this series (no. 3107 in the 1960 *Guide*). Among the added volumes are *The Causes of the American Revolution,* rev. ed. ([1962] 131 p. 62–3817 E210.W3 1962), edited by John C. Wahlke; *The Debate Over Thermonuclear Strategy* ([1965] 114 p. 65–6618 UA23.W362), edited by Arthur I. Waskow; and *Desegregation and the Supreme Court* ([1958] 116 p. 58–2326 Law), edited by Benjamin M. Ziegler.

1442. Riegel, Robert E., *and* Robert G. Athearn. America moves west. 4th ed. New York. Holt, Rinehart & Winston [1964] xiv, 651 p. illus.
64–19649  F591.R53 1964

Includes bibliographies.

An updated edition of no. 3137 in the 1960 *Guide*.

1443. Schlesinger, Arthur M. Paths to the present. With a foreword by Arthur M. Schlesinger, Jr., Rev. and enl. Boston, Houghton Hifflin, 1964. viii, 293 p. (Sentry edition, 36)
64–2185  E178.S33 1964

"For further reading": p. [265]–289.

An updated edition of no. 3140 in the 1960 *Guide*.

1444. U.S. *Bureau of the Census.* The statistical history of the United States from colonial times to the present. Stamford, Conn., Fairfield Publishers; distributed by Horizon Press, New York [1965] xxiv, 789 p. illus.

65–21873   HA202.A385   1965

"Up-dated edition, containing two reference works prepared by 125 distinguished scholars under the direction of the U.S. Bureau of the Census with the cooperation of the Social Science Research Council: Historical statistics of the United States, colonial times to 1957, published 1960, and Continuation to 1962 and revisions, published in 1965."

The objective of this work is to combine in a single volume historical statistics from a multiplic-ity of sources. Text annotations refer to sources of more detailed information. Broad in scope, the book is divided into 24 chapters, among which are "Population," "Labor," "Construction and Housing," "Agriculture," and "Colonial Statistics."

1445. Wish, Harvey. Society and thought in America. v. 2. Society and thought in modern America; a social and intellectual history of the American people from 1865. 2d ed. New York, D. McKay Co. [1962]   644 p.   illus.

61–18349   E169.1.W652, v. 2

Bibliography: p. 607–629.

An updated edition of v. 2 of no. 3150 in the 1960 *Guide.*

# C. The New World

1446. Bolton, Herbert E. Bolton and the Spanish borderlands. Edited and with an introduction by John Francis Bannon. Norman, University of Oklahoma Press [1964]   xi, 346 p.

64–11336   E123.B69

"A Bolton bibliography": p. 333–341.

A collection of essays, many of them previously unpublished or relatively inaccessible, by Herbert E. Bolton (1870–1953), one of the pioneer historians of the Spanish influence in the Southwest and Florida. Bannon has included essays written between 1911 and 1939, each of which covers one specific aspect of the Spanish settlement of the North American frontier. Among the topics chosen are the initial exploration, the strategic importance of the Borderlands, and the mission as a frontier institution. The introductory essay defines Bolton's place in American historiography. Maurice G. Holmes' *From New Spain by Sea to the Californias, 1519–1668* (Glendale, Calif., A. H. Clark Co., 1963. 307 p. Spain in the West, 9), a study of the Spanish politics behind the exploration of California, is based on much research in Spain.

1447. Morison, Samuel Eliot, *ed. and tr.* Journals and other documents on the life and voyages of Christopher Columbus. Illustrated by Lima de Freitas. New York, Printed for the members of the Limited Editions Club, 1963, xv, 417 p.

64–1683   E111.M865

Bibliography included in "Abbreviations used in introductions to documents and in footnotes" (p. xvi).

This edition of Columbian documents is an outgrowth of several years of research. While work-ing on his biography of Columbus, *Admiral of the Ocean Sea,* no. 3164 in the 1960 *Guide,* Morison discovered that most of the translations of the documents were untrustworthy. In his own translations he chose to sacrifice modern literary style to literal accuracy. For inclusion in this work he selected those documents which seemed "the most informing, interesting, and significant" in his own work on the life of Columbus. Many of these have not appeared in other collections. The arrangement is chronological, with emphasis on the establishment of Columbus' identity and on the four voyages. Benjamin Keen has translated, with annotations, Fernando Colón's *Historie del S. D. Fernando Colombo* (1571) under the title of *The Life of the Admiral Christopher Columbus by His Son, Ferdinand* (New Brunswick, N.J., Rutgers University Press [1959]   316 p.).

1448. Williamson, James A. The age of Drake. 4th ed. London, A. & C. Black [1960] viii, 399 p.   maps.   (The Pioneer histories)

63–4459   DA355.W484   1960

Imprint covered by label: New York, Barnes & Noble.

A revised edition of no. 3173 in the 1960 *Guide.* Williamson has updated parts of the section on the events of 1588 and 1589 and has made many minor corrections.

1449. Williamson, James A. The Cabot voyages and Bristol discovery under Henry VII. With the cartography of the voyages by R. A. Skelton. Cambridge [Eng.] Published for the Hakluyt

Society at the University Press, 1962. xvi, 332 p. illus. (Hakluyt Society. Works, 2d ser., no. 120)
63–195  G161.H2  2d ser. no. 120
"Documents": p. [173]–291.
Bibliography: p. xv-xvi.

Although in this volume Williamson uses much material from his earlier work, *The Voyages of the Cabots and the English Discovery of North America under Henry VII and Henry VIII* (no. 3174 in the 1960 *Guide*), 30 years of scholarly research on the voyages prompted him to make substantial changes in the text. The present volume is limited primarily to a discussion of the voyages of various Bristol merchants and of John Cabot and his son Sebastian between 1480 and 1509. The author expands his discussion of the background of the Cabot voyages, with emphasis on the significance of Bristol as a stimulus for exploration. He includes documents which were unavailable when he did his earlier work and adds an essay, "The Cartography of the Voyages," which Raleigh A. Skelton wrote expressly for this volume.

1450.  Wright, Louis B.  The Elizabethans' America; a collection of early reports by Englishmen on the New World. Cambridge, Harvard University Press, 1965. 295 p. (The Stratford-upon-Avon library)  65–8877  E141.W7
Bibliographical references included in "Notes" (p. 282–295).

A collection of early British descriptions of North America as recorded by explorers, traders, privateers, and settlers. Most of the accounts selected were written during the last quarter of the 16th century and the first quarter of the 17th century. Because one of Wright's principal criteria in making selections was the propaganda value of the reports in promoting colonization and development of the New World, the documents indicate the early image of America in Britain, both accurate and inaccurate. In the introduction, the editor discusses the importance of such propaganda in helping to create in the British Isles an attitude favorable to the colonization of North America.

# D.  The Thirteen Colonies

1451.  Akers, Charles W.  Called unto liberty; a life of Jonathan Mayhew, 1720–1766. Cambridge, Harvard University Press, 1964. xii, 285 p. illus.  64–21783  BX9869.M45A7
"Bibliography of Jonathan Mayhew, with short titles used in the Notes": p. [238]–241. Bibliographical references included in "Notes" (p. [243]–272).

As the minister of the West Church in Boston from 1747 to 1766, Jonathan Mayhew excited controversy in both England and New England by preaching a rational brand of theology and the political doctrine of inalienable rights. By 1765, when he delivered a sermon against the Stamp Act, he was recognized as one of the leaders of colonial dissent. Akers' biography of Mayhew is primarily intellectual; he explores his religious and political views against the background of controversies both within New England and between New England and the mother country. John A. Schultz' *William Shirley: King's Governor of Massachusetts* (Chapel Hill, Published for the Institute of Early American History and Culture at Williamsburg, Va., by the University of North Carolina Press [1961]  292 p.) is a biography of a Massachusetts Governor (1741-56) whose administration "brought an era of relative good feeling" to the colony.

1452.  Barck, Oscar T., *and* Hugh T. Lefler. Colonial America. New York, Macmillan [1958]  767 p. illus.  58–5913  E188.B26
Bibliography: p. 731–747.

This textbook, which covers the period from the first colonization to the ratification of the Constitution, is organized primarily as a chonological narrative with occasional chapters devoted to topical problems. Other textbooks are *A History of Colonial America,* 3d ed. (New York, Harper [1961] 745 p. Harper's historical series), by Oliver P. Chitwood; *The Roots of American Civilization,* 2d ed. (New York, Appleton-Century-Crofts [1963] 748 p.), by Curtis P. Nettels; and *A History of Colonial America,* rev. ed. (New York, Holt, Rinehart & Winston [1964]  701 p.), written by Max Savelle and revised by Robert Middlekauff.

1453.  Bronner, Edwin B.  William Penn's holy experiment; the founding of Pennsylvania, 1681–1701. New York, Temple University Publications; distributed by Columbia University Press, 1962. 306 p. illus.  62–14819  F152.B84
Includes bibliography.

A chronological study of Pennsylvania politics between 1681, when Charles II granted the original charter to William Penn, and 1701, when the General Assembly of Pennsylvania adopted the Charter of Privileges. In probing the reasons behind the failure of Pennsylvania to become the Quaker utopia envisaged by Penn and its success in establishing itself within 20 years as a viable political and economic entity, Bronner examines three sets of factors: religious, economic, and political dissensions; relations between William Penn and the colonials; and the position of Pennsylvania within the colonial system as subject to British-French balance-of-power politics. In *War Comes to Quaker Pennsylvania, 1682–1756* (New York, Published for Temple University Publications by Columbia University Press, 1957. 245 p.), Robert L. D. Davidson focuses on the external pressures from the Indians and the French which corroded Quaker pacifism and resulted in Pennsylvania's entry into war in 1756. Joseph E. Illick's *William Penn, the Politician: His Relations with the English Government* (Ithaca, N.Y., Cornell University Press [1965] 267 p.) ascribes much of Penn's success in establishing a proprietary colony to his political acumen in dealing with the English Government.

1454. Brown, Richard M. The South Carolina Regulators. Cambridge, Belknap Press of Harvard University Press, 1963. xi, 230 p. illus. (A publication of the Center for the Study of the History of Liberty in America, Harvard University)

           63–7589  F272.B75

Bibliography: p. 161–177.

The Regulator movement consisted of a well-organized vigilante group formed in 1767 to put down outlawry in the back country of South Carolina. It assumed virtually full control over back-country affairs during the next two years and was squelched in 1769 by the Moderators, a movement organized for the specific purpose of ending Regulator domination. Although the Regulators often employed terroristic methods, they were instrumental in bringing law and order into the back country, which was both socially chaotic and out-of-touch with the colonial government in Charleston.

1455. Dunn, Richard S. Puritans and Yankees; the Winthrop dynasty of New England, 1630–1717. Princeton, N.J., Princeton University Press, 1962. xi, 379 p. illus.

           62–7400  F67.W7957

"Bibliographical note": p. 359–361. Bibliographical footnotes.

One of the central themes in the history of early New England is the discrepancy between the religious ideals of its founders and the secular institutions which they developed. Dunn's study of four members of the first three generations of Win-

throps, who were "indisputably the first family of New England," shows how this dynasty reflected the secularization of life there. The careers of John Winthrop (1588–1649), John Winthrop, Jr. (1606–1676), and two of the latter's sons, Fitz J. Winthrop (1638–1707) and Wait S. Winthrop (1642–1717), were integrally bound up with a dual development: the transition of New England from domination by a Puritan ethos to domination by a secular ethos and the gradual acceptance of a dependent status within the British Empire. In *Winthrop's Boston; Portrait of a Puritan Town, 1630–1649* (Chapel Hill, Published for the Institute of Early American History and Culture at Williamsburg, Va., by the University of North Carolina Press [1965] 324 p.), Darrett B. Rutman considers the same problem through an examination of the developing institutions of Boston.

1456. Franklin, Benjamin. Papers. Leonard W. Labaree, editor. Whitfield J. Bell, Jr., associate editor. Helen C. Boatfield and Helene H. Fineman, assistant editors. New Haven, Yale University Press, 1959–65. 8 v. illus.

           59–12697  E302.F82  1959

"Sponsored by the American Philosophical Society and Yale University."

Bibliographical footnotes.

CONTENTS.—v. 1. Jan. 6, 1706, through Dec. 31, 1734.—v. 2. Jan. 1, 1735, through Dec. 31, 1744.—v. 3. Jan. 1, 1745, through June 30, 1750.—v. 4. July 1, 1750, through June 30, 1753.—v. 5. July 1, 1753, through Mar. 31, 1755.—v. 6. Apr. 1, 1755, through Sept. 30, 1756.—v. 7. Oct. 1, 1756, through Mar. 31, 1758.—v. 8. Apr. 1, 1758, through Dec. 31, 1759.

Projected as a 40-volume work, this comprehensive edition is planned to contain the full text of every document, signed or unsigned, known to have been written by Franklin or by Franklin with others. Volume 1 includes an introduction and a genealogy; each volume is indexed and contains a chronology. In *Benjamin Franklin, Philosopher & Man* (Philadelphia, Lippincott [1965] 438 p.), Alfred O. Aldridge attempts to "synthesize all that is known about Franklin's life and character." In *Benjamin Franklin and Pennsylvania Politics* (Stanford, Calif., Stanford University Press, 1964. 239 p.), a study of Pennsylvania local politics from 1750 to 1776, William S. Hanna concludes that Franklin, as well as other Pennsylvania public leaders, acted on practical expedients as often as on idealistic objectives.

1457. Gipson, Lawrence H. The British Empire before the American Revolution. Caldwell,

Id., Caxton Printers, 1936–65. 12 v. illus.
36–20870  DA500.G5
Vols. 4–12 have imprint: New York, A. A. Knopf.
Bibliographical footnotes.
Volumes 10–12 are a continuation of no. 3188 in the 1960 *Guide*.
CONTENTS.—v. 10. The triumphant Empire: Thunder-clouds gather in the west, 1763–1766.—v. 11. The triumphant Empire: The rumbling of the coming storm, 1766–1770.—v. 12. The triumphant Empire: Britain sails into the storm, 1770–1779.
In these three volumes, Gipson continues his analysis of American colonial development as it was affected both by internal circumstances and by the relative position of the Colonies within the British Empire. Revised editions of v. 1–3 have been published by A. A. Knopf, 1958–60.

1458. Green, Jack P. The quest for power; the lower houses of assembly in the Southern Royal Colonies, 1689–1776. Chapel Hill, Published for the Institute of Early American History and Culture at Williamsburg, Va., by the University of North Carolina Press [1963] xi, 528 p.
63–21077  JK2508.G7
"Bibliographical essay": p. [496]–504.
An institutional analysis of the development of the lower houses of Virginia, the two Carolinas, and Georgia from 1689 to 1783. Greene bases his study on an anlaysis of the basic issues of power between Great Britain and each colony: control over finances, the civil list, legislative proceedings, and executive affairs. Although the colonial burgesses were apparently not primarily motivated by abstract principles of government, their pragmatic assumption of power prepared them to become the backbone of responsible government after the break from Great Britain.

1459. Hall, Michael G. Edward Randolph and the American Colonies, 1676–1703. Chapel Hill, Published for the Institute of Early American History and Culture by the University of North Carolina Press [1960] 241 p.
60–16352  E191.H29
"Bibliographical essay": p. 224–230. Bibliographical footnotes.
Edward Randolph served the Crown as a British agent to the Colonies from 1676 to 1703. As a representative of the King, he antagonized the Colonies by trying to enforce unpopular trade laws and by trying to bring the Colonies directly under the political control of the King. On the basis of an examination of the numerous Crown-colony legal cases which Randolph either instigated or in which

he was implicated, Hall argues that Randolph was one of the chief architects of a uniform pattern of commercial and legal administration. *The Glorious Revolution in America; Documents on the Colonial Crisis of 1689* (Chapel Hill, Published for the Institute of Early American History and Culture at Williamsburg, Va., by the University of North Carolina Press [1964] 216 p. Documentary problems in early American history), edited by Michael G. Hall, Lawrence H. Leder, and Michael G. Kammen, includes British and colonial documents, both public and private, which demonstrate the effects of the Glorious Revolution on internal colonial administration and on Crown-colony relations.

1460. Labaree, Benjamin W. The Boston Tea Party. New York, Oxford University Press, 1964. 347 p.                64–18337  E215.7.L3
Bibliography: p. 317–330.
The author portrays the Boston Tea Party as the catalyst which brought on the Revolution. It was a violent incident that broke the relatively calm relations between Britain and America and gave the Thirteen Colonies a common cause. The dumping of the tea in Boston harbor resulted from the American conviction that the East India Company's sale of tea—temptingly cheap in price but subject to a duty—was part of a British conspiracy to achieve colonial acceptance of Parliament's right to tax. Britain's reaction to the Tea Party was extreme, and she punished Massachusetts with the tyrannical Coercive Acts, which the colonists viewed, according to the author, as raising the question of whether they had any rights at all. The hardships inflicted on Boston by these measures aroused sympathy throughout the Colonies and inspired a fear that freedom throughout America was threatened. Eighteen months after the Boston Tea Party, the colonists united in war against Britain.

1461. Leder, Lawrence H. Robert Livingston, 1654–1728, and the politics of colonial New York. Chapel Hill, Published for the Institute of Early American History and Culture at Williamsburg, Va., by the University of North Carolina Press [1961] xii, 306 p. illus.
61–62687  F122.L43
"Bibliographical note": p. 293–297. Bibliographical footnotes.
Robert Livingston, the son of a Scotch Calvinist who had emigrated to Holland to avoid religious persecution, came to Albany in 1674 at the age of 20. He began his political career as a town clerk and secretary of the board of commissioners for Indian affairs in Albany and rose, through marriage, land acquisition, commercial activity, and political

acumen, to become one of the leading merchants and public servants of New York. When he died, he left a political dynasty which remained influential until the mid-19th century. Leder explores Livingston's career against the background of the complex social, economic, and political activities of the New York aristocracy and its relationship to the British colonial government.

1462. Merrens, Harry R. Colonial North Carolina in the eighteenth century; a study in historical geography. Chapel Hill, University of North Carolina Press [1964] 293 p.

64–13555 F257.M4

Bibliography: p. [266]–288.

In this study of the human ecology of North Carolina from 1750 to 1775, Merrens discusses the changing economic patterns resulting from the interplay of geographic, demographic, and production factors. He emphasizes the following features of development: the land, immigration and population distribution, commerce and the production of naval stores, agriculture, and the function of the town as a commercial center for rural areas. The work presents a picture of North Carolina as a colony in which there were many diverse patterns of economic development. In *The Lower Cape Fear in Colonial Days* (Chapel Hill, University of North Carolina Press [1965] 334 p.), Enoch Lawrence Lee analyzes the economic and political development of an important commercial area of North Carolina from the first settlement in 1665 until the end of the Revolution.

1463. Morton, Richard L. Colonial Virginia. Chapel Hill, Published for the Virginia Historical Society by the University of North Carolina Press, 1960. 2 v. (xiv, 883 p.) illus.

60–51846 F229.M75

Bibliography: p. 401–408, 833–844.

CONTENTS.—v. 1. The Tidewater period, 1607–1710.—v. 2. Westward expansion and prelude to Revolution, 1710–1763.

A comprehensive chronological narrative with emphasis on political events. In examining the evolution of Virginia from a series of scattered and uncertain British settlements to a politically and economically mature colony which produced a large number of revolutionary leaders, Morton emphasizes the significance of Virginia's contributions to the formation of the United States. In *Give Me Liberty; the Struggle for Self-Government in Virginia* (Philadelphia, American Philosophical Society, 1958. 275 p. Memoirs of the American Philosophical Society, v. 46), an interpretive essay, Thomas J. Wertenbaker traces the evolution of self-

government and the mounting struggle of the Virginians for their rights as Englishmen. *William Fitzhugh and his Chesapeake World, 1676–1701; the Fitzhugh Letters and Other Documents* (Chapel Hill, Published for the Virginia Historical Society by the University of North Carolina Press, 1963. 399 p. Virginia Historical Society [Richmond] Documents, v. 3), edited by Richard B. Davis, provides much firsthand information about the life of a lawyer, planter, and public servant who emigrated from England to Virginia in the early 1670's.

1464. Peckham, Howard H. The colonial wars, 1689–1762. Chicago, University of Chicago Press [1964] 239 p. illus. (The Chicago history of American civilization) 64–12606 E195.P4

Bibliography: p. 226–231.

In this survey of the major military and diplomatic events of the four colonial wars, Peckham distinguishes between those aspects of the wars which were determined by European power conflicts and those aspects which were endemic to colonial relationships with the Indians and the French colonials in Canada. He emphasizes two closely related peculiarities of colonial warfare: the development of a nonmilitaristic attitude and the adaptation of methods of war to the American environment. As a result of British colonial military organization, the Colonies built up a foundation for intercolonial cooperation and a bias against the British yoke. In *The French and Indian Wars; the Story of Battles and Forts in the Wilderness* (Garden City, N.Y., Doubleday, 1962. 318 p. Mainstream of America series), Edward P. Hamilton emphasizes the conditions of war in the frontier regions. Harrison Bird's *Battle for a Continent* (New York, Oxford University Press, 1965. 376 p.) is a detailed narrative of military events on the Canadian frontier during the Seven Years' War, 1756–63.

1465. Powell, Sumner C. Puritan village; the formation of a New England town. Middletown, Conn., Wesleyan University Press [1963] xx, 215 p. illus. 63–8862 F74.S94P74

Bibliographical references included in "Notes" (p. [149]–161). Bibliography: p. [197]–211.

An analysis of the development of Sudbury, Mass., from 1638, when the land grant for the town was made, until 1655–57, when a large number of the younger generation seceded to form a new town which was in many ways a replica of Sudbury. Powell began his research with a fairly complete set of town records from Sudbury and was able to trace the English backgrounds of 13 of the 16 original selectmen and of 79 percent of the first land grantees. On the basis of a comparison of the diverse experiences of the settlers in England with their activities in Sudbury, especially with respect to the three basic institutions of land system, town meeting, and town church, Powell concludes that, although the New England town in some respects resembled the English village, the settlers succeeded in creating a new kind of political community. Charles S. Grant's *Democracy in the Connecticut Frontier Town of Kent* (New York, Columbia University Press, 1961. 227 p. Columbia studies in the social sciences, no. 601) is a study of economic opportunity and democracy in Kent from its initial settlement in 1739 to the end of the 18th century.

1466. Reese, Trevor R. Colonial Georgia; a study in British imperial policy in the eighteenth century. Athens, University of Georgia Press [1963] 172 p. 63–17349 F289.R4
Includes bibliography.

An examination of British colonial policy as it was worked out by the administrators in Georgia between 1732, when the initial charter was granted, and 1765, roughly when Georgia began to enter her revolutionary phase. The author focuses on three strands of British policy: commercial, strategic, and social. Because British policy often operated against the interest of the Georgia settlers, the colonial administration was in part responsible for establishing conditions conducive to revolutionary agitation. Other works on the history of the colonial government of Georgia are *The Journal of the Earl of Egmont; Abstract of the Trustees Proceedings for Establishing the Colony of Georgia, 1732–1738* (Athens, University of Georgia Press [1962] 414 p. Wormsloe Foundation. Publications, no. 5), edited by Robert G. McPherson; *The Journal of William Stephens* (Athens, University of Georgia Press [1958–59] 2 v. Wormsloe Foundation. Publications, no. 2–3.), edited by Ellis Merton Coulter; and *The Royal Governors of Georgia, 1754–1775* (Chapel Hill, Published for the Institute of Early American History and Culture at Williamsburg by the University of North Carolina Press [1959] 198 p.), by William W. Abbot.

1467. TePaske, John J. The governorship of Spanish Florida, 1700–1763. Durham, N.C., Duke University Press, 1964. xiii, 248 p. 64–18659 F314.T3
Bibliography: p. [234]–238.
An institutional analysis of the administration of Spanish Florida from 1700, when control of Spain shifted from the Habsburg to the Bourbon dynasty, to 1763, when Florida became a British possession. The author treats his subject as a case study of insti-

tutional devolopment on the frontier. By examining such problems as finance, Indian policies, the church, and balance-of-power politics, he shows how the colonial administration functioned primarily as a strategic outpost of the Spanish Government in the New World. Because internal colonial policies were subordinate to Spanish military considerations, Spain failed to develop a viable economic and political unit in Florida.

1468. Ver Steeg, Clarence L. The formative years, 1607–1763. New York, Hill & Wang [1964] 342 p. illus. (The Making of America) 64–14682 E188.V49
"Bibliographical essay": p. 307–336.
A survey of colonial development from the founding of the Colonies until the end of the fourth French and Indian War and the beginning of the series of incidents which precipitated the War for Independence. The author traces the evolution of transplanted British and European social, economic, political, and religious attitudes and institutions into their peculiarly American forms. Although the geographic and chronological scope of the survey is broad, the developments which characterized individual colonies are taken into consideration. Changing patterns in the relationships between the Colonies and Great Britain within the context of the European balance-of-power system are also analyzed.

1469. Wainwright, Nicholas B. George Croghan, wilderness diplomat. Chapel Hill, Published for the Institute of Early American History and Culture at Williamsburg by the University of North Carolina Press [1959] 334 p. 59–2353 F483.C76W3
"Bibliographical essay": p. [311]–316. Bibliographical footnotes.
George Croghan came from Ireland to Pennsylvania in 1741 to escape a potato famine. Within a few years he established himself as a prominent Indian trader and mediator between Pennsylvania and the Indian tribes in the Ohio Valley. He was one of the major architects of Pennsylvania's Indian policy, which consisted of attempts to draw the Indians away from French influence through treaties and gifts. Sir William Johnson's deputy superintendent of Indian affairs from 1756 to 1772, he served as the principal negotiator between the British Empire and the Indians of the Northwest. He later became involved in the organization of a number of Western land companies. Wainwright's biography, based on Croghan's personal papers, places his colorful career in the perspective of colonial frontier development and British-French rivalry.

# E. The American Revolution

1470. Bailyn, Bernard, *ed.* Pamphlets of the American Revolution, 1750–1776, edited by Bernard Bailyn, with the assistance of Jane N. Garrett. v. 1. 1750–1765. Cambridge, Belknap Press of Harvard University Press, 1965. 771 p. illus. (The John Harvard library)   64–21784  E203.B3

Much of the important characteristic writing of the American Revolution appeared, originally or ultimately, in pamphlet form. The pamphlets were initially concerned with political problems related to the conflict with Britain but eventually dealt with broader issues. Although the pamphleteers looked to past theorists for sources and traditions to buttress their contention that British measures amounted to an active conspiracy of power against liberty, they not only created what is most original in American political thought but also helped develop the American radicalism of the Revolution, a radicalism which was unique in that it sought not to change or overthrow but to establish in principle the way of life that was an existing reality. This is the first volume of a planned four-volume set. It covers the period 1750–65 and contains a 200-page general introduction by Bailyn as well as reprints of 14 pamphlets, from Jonathan Mayhew's *A Discourse Concerning Unlimited Submission* (1750) to John Dickinson's *The Late Regulations* (1765), each with a critical essay by the editor. A useful companion work is Thomas R. Adam's *American Independence: The Growth of an Idea; a Bibliographical Study of the American Political Pamphlets Printed Between 1764 and 1776 Dealing With the Dispute Between Great Britain and Her Colonies* (Providence, Brown University Press, 1965. 200 p. Brown University bicentennial publications: studies in the fields of general scholarship).

1471. Cary, John H. Joseph Warren: physician, politician, patriot. Urbana, University of Illinois Press, 1961. 260 p.

61–62763  E263.M4W234

Bibliography: p. 227–243.

Although Warren (1741–1775) has been known chiefly as the man who sent Paul Revere on his midnight ride to Lexington, he played a major role as a propagandist in Massachusetts during the critical years that culminated in the outbreak of the Revolutionary War. He was an important figure in the incidents following the seizure of John Hancock's sloop *Liberty* in 1768, as well as in the events leading to the Boston Tea Party in 1773. He also wrote the influential Suffolk Resolves in 1774 and was president of the Provincial Congress of Massachusetts in 1775. Appointed a major general, he went to Bunker Hill to observe and was killed while heroically assisting in the fruitless effort to hold the redoubt on Breed's Hill.

1472. Commager, Henry Steele, *and* Richard B. Morris, *eds*. The spirit of 'seventy-six; the story of the American Revolution as told by participants. Indianapolis, Bobbs-Merrill [1958]   2 v. (1348 p.)  illus.        58–12330  E203.C69

Bibliography: v. 2, p. 1297–1319.

A collection of contemporary writings dating from 1773 to 1783 and drawn from orations, essays, songs, ballads, journals, diaries, private correspondence, and British and American official papers. Campaigns and battles receive the most generous treatment, but material is included on the coming of the war and on political and other nonmilitary aspects of the war years. Source collections bearing on limited phases of the Revolution are *The Road to Independence; a Documentary History of the Causes of the American Revolution: 1763–1776* (New York, Putman [1963]  314 p.), by John Braeman, and *The American Revolution Through British Eyes* (Evanston, Ill., Row, Peterson [1962]  180 p.), edited by Martin Kallich and Andrew MacLeish, which helps to show "how England really felt about America."

1473. Donoughue, Bernard. British politics and the American Revolution; the path to war, 1773–75. London, Macmillan; New York, St. Martin's Press, 1964 [i.e. 1965]  323 p. (England in the age of the American Revolution)

64–21438  E210.D6  1965

Bibliography: p.295–309.

From the Boston Tea Party to the outbreak of the Revolution, the Ministry of Lord North received the support of both King and Commons. Confident that effective opinion was behind them, the Ministers met the challenge of the Boston Tea Party with a policy based on the belief that the total subordination of America was necessary for the maintenance of the Empire. The Americans, however, refused to be coerced and resorted instead to an organized resistance that led to war. In *The Chatham Administration, 1766–1768* (London, Macmillan; New

York, St. Martin's Press, 1956. 400 p. England in the age of the American Revolution), John Brooke tells of the earlier failure of William Pitt, Earl of Chatham, to maintain the initial acceptance of his Ministry by both King and Commons. This failure led to the hardening of political parties into the forms they assumed during the Revolution. In *The End of North's Ministry, 1780–1782* (London, Macmillan; New York, St. Martin's Press, 1958. 428 p. England in the age of the American Revolution), Ian R. Christie discusses the undermining and collapse of the North Ministry following news of the British defeat at Yorktown.

1474. Ferguson, Elmer James. The power of the purse; a history of American public finance, 1776–1790. Chapel Hill, Published for the Institute of Early American History and Culture at Williamsburg, Va., by the University of North Carolina Press [1961] 358 p.            61–325 HJ247.F4
"Bibliographical essay": p. [344]–347. Bibliographical footnotes.
The traditionally unfavorable view of Revolutionary finance has been based on the writings of the 19th-century scholars who were "sound money" men involved in currency controversies. From his 20th-century viewpoint, Ferguson accepts fiat money and regulated economies as the norm and portrays Revolutionary finance as "reasonable if not inevitable." The Federal income for the first five years of the war came primarily from paper money. This policy was based upon the similar and generally successful financial system employed during colonial times. The problems of public finance were also of major importance during the postwar years as they influenced the new Nation's political and constitutional development. The question of whether the States or Congress should pay the domestic and foreign debt, mostly acquired during the latter years of the war, was intimately involved in the movement to strengthen the Federal Government, a development which led to the adoption of the Constitution and the rise of political parties.

1475. Knollenberg, Bernhard. George Washington: the Virginia period, 1732–1775. Durham, N.C., Duke University Press, 1964. 238 p.
64–24989 E312.2.K56
Bibliography: p. [197]–210.
This biographical treatment of Washington's early life is based solely on contemporary evidence. Knollenberg examines Washington's own writings critically and finds much in his early career which is not wholly praiseworthy. In order to clarify Washington's diverse activities, a topical rather than a chronological approach is taken.

1476. Knollenberg, Bernhard. Origin of the American Revolution: 1759–1766. New York, Macmillan, 1960. 486 p.         59–10990 E210.K65
Bibliography: p. 397–452.
The author argues that "while the British Stamp Act of 1765 greatly contributed to and touched off the colonial uprising of 1765–1766, the colonists had been brought to the brink of rebellion by a number of other provocative British measures from 1759 to 1764, most of which persisted after the Stamp Act was repealed in 1766 and contributed to the mounting colonial discontent culminating in the American Revolution of 1775–1783." The first of these acts was the Privy Council's order (1759) that any bill passed by the Virginia legislature repealing or amending an existing act must contain a clause suspending its operation until approved by the Privy Council in England. This order was soon followed by the application of the same requirement to Massachusetts and South Carolina and by other measures, such as general writs of assistance. In 1764, new colonial revenue legislation came under the jurisdiction of the British vice-admiralty courts in America. In *The Vice-Admiralty Courts and the American Revolution* (Chapel Hill, Published for the Institute of Early American History and Culture, Williamsburg, Va., by the University of North Carolina Press, 1960. 242 p.), Carl Ubbelohde tells of the colonists' opposition to these courts, which he considers "a minor, but persistent, cause of the American Revolution."

1477. Main, Jackson Turner. The social structure of revolutionary America. Princeton, N.J., Princeton University Press, 1965. 330 p.
65–17146 HN57.M265
Bibliographical footnotes.
This statistical study of the American social structure from 1763 to 1788 reveals an economic class system which was based upon inequalities in property and income and reflected a concentration of wealth and great disparity between rich and poor. Yet because of material abundance and the absence of legal impediments for whites, the system was remarkably mobile. Also dependent upon economic inequalities was the social hierarchy. It was characterized by a consciousness of class distinctions and a prestige order but was relatively democratic in that it set up no barriers that property could not surmount. Main concludes that the Revolution at least temporarily reversed a long-term trend toward social and economic inequality and more marked class distinctions.

1478. Morison, Samuel Eliot. John Paul Jones, a sailor's biography. With charts and diagrs.

by Erwin Raisz and with photos. Boston, Little, Brown [1959] xxii, 453 p. 59–5285 E207.J7M6
Bibliography: p. [431]–443.

"Commodore" Jones (1747–1792), whose official naval rank was captain, has been the subject of much romance and controversy but has received relatively little scholarly attention. Morison, a retired admiral as well as a historian, wrote this Pulitzer-Prize-winning biography of Jones in order to tell "what a sailor has to say about him." The author presents the Commodore's career in the Continental Navy and describes in detail the famous battle between the *Bonhomme Richard* and the *Serapis* in 1779. The book also offers a full picture of Jones' personal life, including his several romances, and clears away longstanding myths, especially those created by a few previous biographers whose works Morison considers to be largely fictional.

1479. Nelson, William H. The American Tory. Oxford, Clarendon Press, 1961. 194 p.
62-8 E277.N48

The author discusses the Tory's quarrel with his fellow Americans and the totality of his defeat. During the years of argument before 1775, the Tory leaders were unable to gain sufficient support in the Colonies to secure power. With the outbreak of hostilities they became Loyalists because they continued to hold social or political opinions that could be realized in America only with British assistance. The war brought disenchantment and defeat to the Loyalists. The British neither gave them sufficient support nor put down the rebellion, and as a result these Americans suffered silencing and expulsion. The role of the Loyalists in British military policy is described in Paul H. Smith's *Loyalists and Redcoats* (Chapel Hill, Published for the Institute of Early American History and Culture at Williamsburg, Va., by the University of North Carolina Press [1964] 199 p.). *The King's Friends* (Providence, Brown University Press, 1965. 411 p.), by Wallace Brown, is a study of the Loyalists through an investigation of the extant records of the claims commission set up by the British to indemnify these Americans for losses caused by the Revolution. A Tory's hostile view of the Revolution is presented in Peter Oliver's *Origin & Progress of the American Rebellion* (San Marino, Calif., Huntington Library, 1961. 173 p. Huntington Library publications), edited by Douglass Adair and John A. Schutz from a previously unpublished manuscript by a prosperous colonial Massachusetts judge.

1480. Quarles, Benjamin. The Negro in the American Revolution. Chapel Hill, Published for the Institute of Early American History and Culture, Williamsburg, Va., by the University North Carolina Press [1961] xiii, 231 p.
61–66795 E269.N3Q3
Bibliography: p. [201]–223.

Supporting whichever side locally invoked the image of liberty, Negroes in the Revolution fought with both British and American forces and benefited from an era which Quarles believes "marked out an irreversible path toward freedom." The Americans were slow to make more than limited use of the Negro because of an unwillingness to deprive a master of his apprenticed servant or chattel slave and from a fear of arming people who, for the most part, were not free. Although free Negroes fought in the North from the beginning, it took a shortage of white manpower plus British appeals to the blacks to force Congress and the Northern States to recruit slaves and grant them freedom as the reward for faithful service. The South resisted for a time, but all the plantation States except South Carolina and Georgia eventually used free Negroes as soldiers or sailors, and Maryland provided for the enlistment of slaves. The British employed runaway slaves and free Negroes primarily as military laborers, evacuating them along with the regular troops at the end of the war.

1481. Schlesinger, Arthur M. Prelude to independence; the newspaper war on Britain, 1764–1776. New York, Knopf, 1958 [ᶜ1957] 318, xvi p. 57–12068 PN4861.S3
"Bibliographical note": p. 316–318. Bibliographical footnotes.

Schlesinger's purpose is to "assess the role of the newspaper in undermining loyalty to the mother country and creating a demand for separation." Many factors from the Sugar Act onward helped provoke the Revolution, but the movement would have failed had not the patriot editors vehemently championed the American cause at every crisis and personally participated in subversive activities. Through the use of propaganda, these editors kept the people in constant opposition to Britain while preparing them for armed rebellion. In addition to fostering the movement toward independence, Schlesinger concludes, the Revolutionary newspapers promoted a freedom of utterance that has proved to be a boon to American journalism and the democratic process.

1482. Shy, John W. Toward Lexington; the role of the British Army in the coming of the American Revolution. Princeton, N.J., Princeton University Press, 1965. 463 p. maps.
65–17160 E210.S5
Bibliographical footnotes.

In responce to the demands of defense, imperial regulation, and especially Indian affairs, the British maintained a large army on the American frontier during the years of peace that followed the Seven Years' War. The author notes that this reasonable military policy antagonized the colonists and helped bring on a constitutional crisis when Parliament decided to tax the Colonies for part of the soldiers' upkeep. In 1768 most of the troops were moved to the East, where their presence in peacetime convinced Americans that the British wanted an army not 'o defend but to control the Colonies. By this tim' the colonial challenge to Parliament's sovereignty was a major problem. Although the British we:e united in their refusal to negotiate on the issue of parliamentary authority, they were divided on the question of the army's role in the Colonies and were unable to decide between the alternatives of removing the army in adherence to Whig concepts of militarism or using it against the colonists. The events of 1775 made the decision for them.

1483. Sosin, Jack M. Agents and merchants; British colonial policy and the origins of the American Revolution, 1763–1775. Lincoln, University of Nebraska Press, 1965. xvi, 267 p. illus.
65–13913    E210.S73

Bibliography: p. 235–250.

On the eve of the Revolution, Britain's policy on colonial America was influenced by the efforts of two groups: agents retained by various Colonies to represent their interests in London and English merchants who traded with the Colonies. Because they believed that the prosperity of Britain depended upon the well-being of the American Colonies, the merchants worked with the colonial agents to modify measures considered obnoxious in America. This lobby was especially successful during the years following the French and Indian War. It could count among its important accomplishments the repeal of both the Stamp Act and the Townshend duties. Yet the combination of agents and merchants was ultimately unsuccessful. According to the author, it failed primarily because the American challenge to British authority expanded from a simple question of taxation, on which compromise was possible, to one of Parliament's sovereignty, which was not negotiable from Britain's point of view. In *Whitehall and the Wilderness; the Middle West in British Colonial Policy, 1760–1775* (Lincoln, University of Nebraska Press, 1961. 307 p.), Sosin again expounds British administration and policy.

# F. Federal America (1783-1815)

1484. Bernhard, Winfred E. A. Fisher Ames, Federalist and statesman, 1758–1808. Chapel Hill, Published for the Institute of Early American History and Culture at Williamsburg, Va., by the University of North Carolina Press [1965] xiii, 372 p. illus.    65–23142  E302.6.A5B4
"A note on the sources": p. 355–360.

The appearance of a number of political biographies of early second-rank Federalist leaders has increased understanding of the formation of America's first political party and of its attempts to establish a balance between local and national interests. One of the most notable of such leaders was Fisher Ames, Harvard graduate and lawyer, who entered politics in 1788 as a member of the Massachusetts convention called to consider ratification of the Constitution. A year later, Ames was elected to the U.S. House of Representatives, where he maintained a position of leadership by virtue of his legislative and oratorical skills until his retirement in 1797. Although Ames never wholly accepted the party system, he served as a major spokesman for Hamilton's

fiscal and economic policies and supported the predominantly Federalist view that a centralized government should foster native commerce and industry. Biographies of other Federalist leaders who had careers in Congress from Connecticut, Massachusetts, and South Carolina, respectively, are as follows: Chester M. Destler's *Joshua Coit, American Federalist: 1758–1798* (Middletown, Conn., Wesleyan University Press [1962] 191 p.), Richard E. Welch's *Theodore Sedgwick, Federalist; a Political Portrait* (Middletown, Conn., Wesleyan University Press [1965] 276 p.), and George C. Rogers' *Evolution of a Federalist: William Loughton Smith of Charleston (1758–1812)* (Columbia, University of South Carolina Press, 1962. 439 p.).

1485. Brant, Irving. James Madison. Indianapolis, Bobbs-Merrill [1941–61] 6 v. illus.
41–19279  E342.B7
Includes bibliographies.
CONTENTS—[1] The Virginia revolutionist. —[2] The nationalist, 1780–1787.—[3] Father of

the Constitution, 1787–1800.—[4] Secretary of State, 1800–1809.—[5] The President, 1809–1812. —[6] Commander in Chief, 1812–1836.

The first five volumes of this six-volume biography are no. 3282 in the 1960 *Guide*. The final volume carries Madison's career from 1812, the fourth year of his first term as President, to his death in 1836. More a narrative of the critical events of Madison's Presidency than a full-scale biographical treatment, this volume heavily emphasizes the military and political strategies and issues of the War of 1812. Brant's overall assessment of Madison's administration is that it strengthened and consolidated the Union without weakening the instruments of self-government. The first four volumes of Madison's *Papers* ([Chicago] University of Chicago Press [1962–65]), edited by William T. Hutchinson and William M. E. Rachal, cover the years from his birth in 1751 to July 1782, when he represented Virginia in the Continental Congress.

1486. Brown, Roger H. The Republic in peril: 1812. New York, Columbia University Press, 1964. 238 p.      64–12498 E357.B88
Bibliographical references included in "Notes": p. [197]–231.

On the basis of his analysis of the papers of Republican Congressmen, Brown presents the thesis that by 1812 war was the only alternative to commercial submission to Great Britain. Beginning with Jefferson, the Republican administration based its policy on the premise that the proof of republicanism as a viable form of government depended on the maintenance of self-regulated commercial enterprise. War was the logical consequence of Great Britain's unwillingness to negotiate commercial peace despite repeated American pressures on the British Government and British commerce. The options, as the Republican leadership understood them, were either to submit to British domination, thus destroying the Republican Party and admitting the failure of the republican experiment, or to declare war.

1487. Dangerfield, George. Chancellor Robert R. Livingston of New York, 1746–1813. New York, Harcourt, Brace [1960] 532 p.
60–10924 E302.6.L72D3
"A bibliographical note": p. 441–450.
Robert Livingston's political career began in 1775 when he became a member of the New York provincial convention and of the Second Continental Congress. In 1777 he was chosen to be the first chancellor of the State of New York, a position he held until 1801. He was influential in domestic politics at the local, State, and national levels and held a number of important diplomatic posts, including that of Minister to France from 1801 until 1805, when he retired from politics. Dangerfield deals with his subject almost as the New York analog of Thomas Jefferson. His picture of Livingston as an aristocratic Republican who based his political attitudes on the agrarian ideal and on the belief in property rights supports his thesis that during the Federalist period the New York aristocracy became both more republican and less democratic in resistance to the democratic attempt to purge American society of aristocratic elements.

1488. Fischer, David H. The revolution of American conservatism; the Federalist party in the era of Jeffersonian democracy. New York, Harper & Row [1965] xx, 455 p.      65–14680 E331.F5
Bibliographical footnotes.

The author analyzes Federalist organization between 1800 and 1816 in order to shed further light on the democratization of politics during Jefferson's administration. His data, much of which is drawn from a study of relatively younger Federalist leaders, supports his contention that political organization killed the Federalist movement. Fischer suggests that, whereas the Federalists began as an interest group based on elitist concepts of political leadership, the necessity of building up a power base against the Jeffersonians forced the adoption of Jeffersonian techniques of party organization. In the process of borrowing methods of mass political appeal such as the use of conventions, electioneering, and widespread publicity, the Federalists were forced to compromise their elitist ideals. During the Jeffersonian period, they were unable to find an organizing issue strong enough to replace elitism.

1489. Hamilton, Alexander. Papers. Harold C. Syrett, editor; Jacob E. Cooke, associate editor. New York, Columbia University Press, 1961–65. 9 v. illus.      61–15593 E302.H247
CONTENTS.—v. 1. 1768–1778.—v. 2. 1779–1781. —v. 3. 1782–1786.—v. 4. Jan. 1787–May 1788.— v. 5. June 1788–Nov. 1789.—v. 6. Dec. 1789– Aug. 1790.—v. 7. Sept. 1790–Jan. 1791.—v. 8. Feb. 1791–July 1791.—v. 9. Aug. 1791–Dec. 1791.
These volumes contain letters and documents by Hamilton, letters to him, and some additional documents that directly concern him. Many routine items are simply calendared. In *Number 7: Alexander Hamilton's Secret Attempts to Control American Foreign Policy* (Princeton, N.J., Princeton University Press, 1964. 166 p.), Julian P. Boyd uses documents from his edition of the Jefferson *Papers* (no. 1491 below) to indict Hamilton on the grounds

that he deliberately tried to subvert George Washington's policy toward England.

1490. Jackson, Donald D., *ed*. Letters of the Lewis and Clark Expedition, with related documents, 1783–1854. Urbana, University of Illinois Press [1962] xxi, 728 p. illus.

62–7119 F592.7.J14

Bibliography: p. 681–694.

Includes letters written by members of the Lewis and Clark expedition and by others who were directly interested in it. Most of the letters were written between 1801 and 1816 and cover the details of the expedition, its purposes and findings, and foreign reaction to it. More than half the 428 items were previously unpublished. Richard H. Dillon's biography, *Meriwether Lewis* (New York, Coward-McCann, 1965. 364 p.), focuses on the role of Lewis as the commander of the expedition and uses the journals and other contemporary literature to describe the conditions of exploration.

1491. Jefferson, Thomas, *Pres. U.S.* Papers. Julian P. Boyd, editor; Lyman H. Butterfield and [others], associate editors. Princeton, Princeton University Press, 1950–65. 17 v. illus.

58–7486 E302.J463

Volumes 1–13 of this multivolume edition and the first volume of the *Index* are no. 3292 in the 1960 *Guide*.

CONTENTS.—v. 14. 8 Oct. 1788 to 26 Mar. 1789. —v. 15. 27 Mar. 1789 to 30 Nov. 1789.—v. 16. 30 Nov. 1789 to 4 July 1790.—v. 17. 6 July 1790 to 3 Nov. 1790.

A second volume of the *Index* (Princeton, Princeton University Press, 1958. 207 p.), compiled by Elizabeth J. Sherwood, covers v. 7–12 of the *Papers*.

1492. Malone, Dumas. Jefferson and his time. Boston, Little, Brown, 1948–62. 3 v. illus.

48–5972 E332.M25

Includes bibliographies.

CONTENTS.—v. 1. Jefferson the Virginian.—v. 2. Jefferson and the rights of man.—v. 3. Jefferson and the ordeal of liberty.

The first two volumes of this multivolume biography are no. 3295 in the 1960 *Guide*. Volume 3 covers the period from 1792 to 1801, during which Jefferson served for three years as George Washington's Secretary of State and for four years as Vice President under John Adams. Jefferson is viewed as a democratic child of the Enlightenment, a philosopher-turned-statesman who was guided by the determination that "men should be set free and kept free in order to move forward in the light of ever-expanding knowledge." He was branded as a rank opportunist by some critics and as an impractical idealist by others; Malone answers both charges. Although Jefferson was a founder and leader of the Republican Party, Malone considers that he was a reluctant partisan who used the party only in the service of unity and democracy. Alexander Balinky's *Albert Gallatin: Fiscal Theories and Policies* (New Brunswick, N.J., Rutgers University Press, 1958. 275 p.) concludes that Gallatin, as Jefferson's Secretary of the Treasury, "subordinated fiscal considerations and principles to the political and economic (though nonfiscal) objectives of his party."

1493. Miller, John C. The Federalist era, 1789–1801. New York, Harper [1960] 304 p. (The New American nation series)

60–15321 E310.M5

Bibliography: p. 279–298.

This chronological survey of the chief political and diplomatic events during the Presidencies of George Washington and John Adams focuses on the issues and personalities from which the first American party system originated. Two themes dominate the study: the search for national unity and the demand for individual liberty. In tracing the development of these themes, Miller follows with special care the activities of Alexander Hamilton and to a lesser extent those of Thomas Jefferson. In *The Nation Takes Shape, 1789–1837* ([Chicago] University of Chicago Press [1959] 222 p. The Chicago history of American civilization), a descriptive and interpretive essay, Marcus Cunliffe briefly surveys the critical years between the adoption of the Constitution and the end of Andrew Jackson's Presidency.

1494. Mitchell, Broadus. Alexander Hamilton. New York, Macmillan, 1957–62. 2 v. illus.

57–5506 E302.6.H2M6

Bibliography: p. 775–792.

CONTENTS.—[1] Youth to maturity, 1755–1788. —[2] The national adventure, 1788–1804.

Volume 1 of this biography is no. 3291 in the 1960 *Guide*. Most of the second volume is a detailed analysis of Hamilton's economic theories and an examination of his fiscal policies. Hamilton was motivated by a sense of national honor translated into the moral imperative of respecting and discharging national monetary obligations. As Secretary of the Treasury, he established public credit and introduced order into finance, with the result that when he left the Treasury in 1795, the Nation was solvent. In *Alexander Hamilton: Portrait in Paradox* (New York, Harper [1959] 659 p.), the result of more than a decade of research, John C. Miller presents a broader analysis, showing Hamilton's behavior in relation to the intricate political and diplomatic events of Washington's Presidency.

1495. Monroe, James, *Pres. U.S.* Autobiography. Edited, and with an introduction, by Stuart Gerry Brown, with the assistance of Donald G. Baker. [Syracuse] Syracuse University Press [1959] xi, 236 p. illus.    59–13117 E372.A3

Brown considers James Monroe (1758–1831) to be the first important professional politician in the United States. Monroe began his autobiography in 1827 but died before completing it. The manuscript, a fragmentary rough draft, covers Monroe's career until 1807, by which time he had seen military service in the Revolution and had been a U.S. Senator, Governor of Virginia, and Minister to France and Great Britain. Nearly half of the autobiography is devoted to his first mission to France, 1794–96.

1496. Smith, Page. John Adams. Garden City, N.Y., Doubleday, 1962. 2 v. (xx, 1170 p.) illus.    63–7188 E322.S64

Includes bibliographical references.

CONTENTS.— v. 1.  1735–1784.— v. 2.  1784–1826.

The author is the first biographer of John Adams to have access to the complete papers of the Adams family, which provided the basis for his painstaking reconstruction of Adams' life, both private and public. He has chosen a narrative style and, through a copious use of direct quotations, allows Adams to tell much of the story. Since it was the author's intention to depict John Adams as a three-dimensional figure and his world as he himself perceived and experienced it, the subject matter is arranged chronologically rather than topically. The result is a constant juxtaposition of slight personal incidents and events of major historical significance. Lester J. Cappon has edited *The Adams-Jefferson Letters; the Complete Correspondence Between Thomas Jefferson and Abigail and John Adams* (Chapel Hill, Published for the Institute of Early American History and Culture at Williamsburg, Va., by the University of North Carolina Press [1959] 2 v.).

## G. The "Middle Period" (1815-60)

1497. Benson, Lee. The concept of Jacksonian democracy; New York as a test case. Princeton, N.J., Princeton University Press, 1961. 351 p.    61–6286 F123.B49

Bibliographical footnotes.

A study of the relevance of Jacksonian democracy to New York State politics, 1816 through 1844, coupled with an investigation of group voting patterns that crystallized in the 1844 presidential election. Benson argues that the traditional portrayal of the Jackson Party as a democratic movement opposed by aristocratic, antiegalitarian Whigs is historically inaccurate. Because the Jacksonian Democrats adhered to the doctrines of States rights and negative government, the Whigs came "closer than the Democrats to satisfying the requirements of historians in search of nineteenth-century precursors to twentieth-century New Dealers." The author also finds that New York voters in 1844 were influenced by ethnocultural and religious factors rather than by campaign issues. *Jacksonian Democracy in Mississippi* (Chapel Hill, University of North Carolina Press, 1960. 192 p. The James Sprunt studies in history and political science, v. 42), by Edwin A. Miles, and *The Jacksonian Heritage; Pennsylvania Politics, 1833–1848* (Harrisburg, Pennsylvania Historical and Museum Commission, 1958.

256 p.), by Charles M. Snyder, treat the diverse characteristics of Jacksonian politics in these individual States.

1498. Capers, Gerald M. John C. Calhoun, opportunist; a reappraisal. Gainesville, University of Florida Press, 1960. 275 p.    60–15788 E340.C15C25

"Bibliographical Note": p. 267–269.

The author interprets Calhoun (1782–1850) as a politician motivated by presidential aspirations. Calhoun, South Carolina legislator, Congressman, Secretary of War in Monroe's Cabinet, and Vice President under John Quincy Adams and Andrew Jackson, is portrayed as clearly revealing this motive in his career. First announcing his candidacy in 1821, he actively sought the nomination in later presidential campaigns. Calhoun emerges here as a self-seeking politician, a nationalist turned sectionalist, advocating nullification and States' rights as his principles of government. The first two volumes of the projected multivolume set of Calhoun's *Papers* (Columbia, Published by the University of South Carolina Press for the South Caroliniana Society, 1959–63), edited by the late Robert L. Meriwether and William Edwin Hemphill, contain chronologically arranged letters, speeches, comments, and reports of Calhoun from 1801 through July 1818.

1499. Clarke, Dwight L. Stephen Watts Kearny, soldier of the West. Norman, University of Oklahoma Press [1961] xv, 448 p. illus.

61–15148 E403.1.K2C5

"Notes on sources": p. 401–426.

The 36-year Army career of Stephen Watts Kearny (1794–1848) began with his enlistment at the outbreak of the War of 1812 and lasted through the Mexican War. Kearny served mainly in the West and founded many frontier posts. In 1846 he commanded the Army of the West and led the expedition to invade and seize New Mexico. His successful campaign resulted in annexation, and Kearny became the first Governor of the territory. Clarke believes that Kearny has become a neglected figure in history because he brought court-martial charges against Lt. John C. Frémont, the popular son-in-law of Senator Thomas Hart Benton, and because he was too taciturn to defend himself adequately at the time and did not leave records that could be used by historians for that purpose.

1500. Clay, Henry. Papers. James F. Hopkins, editor; Mary W. M. Hargreaves, associate editor. [Lexington] University of Kentucky Press [ᶜ1959–63] 3 v. illus. 59–13605 E337.8.C597

CONTENTS.—v. 1. The rising statesman, 1797–1814.—v. 2. The rising statesman, 1815–1820.—v. 3. Presidential candidate, 1821–1824.

These three volumes are part of a projected 10-volume edition. Included are the texts of letters written by Clay and of selected letters received by him, as well as speeches, financial papers, and other documents relating to his career. The first volume treats Clay's career through the signing of the Treaty of Ghent, the second covers the period when he emerged as an influential politician, and the third reveals him in his first unsuccessful presidential campaign and as Speaker of the House of Representatives.

1501. Dangerfield, George. The awakening of American nationalism, 1815–1828. New York, Harper & Row [ᶜ1965] 331 p. illus. (The New American Nation series) 64–25112 E338.D3

"Bibliographical essay": p. 303–321. Bibliographical footnotes.

The author characterizes the period between the signing of the Treaty of Ghent in December 1814 and the election of Jackson as President in 1828 as a conflict between economic nationalism and democratic nationalism. Andrew Jackson emerges triumphant over Henry Clay, John Quincy Adams,

and their adherents. In his synthesis Dangerfield treats presidential elections, the Presidents and their Cabinets, the Monroe Doctrine, and the politics of the Missouri Compromise, as well as the panic of 1819, Clay's American system, and the Tariff of Abominations.

1502. Goetzmann, William H. Army exploration in the American West, 1803–1863. New Haven, Yale University Press, 1959. xx, 509 p. illus. (Yale publications in American studies, 4)

59–12694 F591.G6

"Bibliographical essay": p. 461–480. Bibliographical footnotes.

The author is primarily interested in the record of the Corps of Topographical Engineers from its creation by Congress in 1838 until it merged into the Corps of Engineers in 1863. The Topographical Engineers led the way in observing, surveying, and mapping trails, rivers, and mountain passes in the trans-Mississippi West. They also supervised the construction of roads, built dams, laid out coastal fortifications, and collected, cataloged, and inventoried scientific information.

1503. Hamilton, Holman. Prologue to conflict; the crisis and Compromise of 1850. [Lexington] University of Kentucky Press [1964] 236 p. 64–13999 E423.H2

"Bibliographical essay": p. [209]–216. Bibliographical footnotes.

A comprehensive analysis of the personalities and politics connected with the adoption of the Compromise of 1850. Researches in the *Congressional Globe,* manuscript collections, and newspapers reveal the complex legislative maneuvers involved in securing passage of the compromise as five separate acts. The author highlights the roles played by President Fillmore and Stephen A. Douglas. He also emphasizes the influence of banker William W. Corcoran, whose lobbying for Federal assumption of the Texas debt strengthened support for the compromise. Tables showing rollcall votes in the House and Senate on the compromise measures are appended.

1504. Kirwan, Albert D. John J. Crittenden; the struggle for the Union. [Lexington] University of Kentucky Press [1962] 514 p. illus. 62–19380 E340.C9K5

"Critical essay on authorities": p. 481–491.

In his 50-year career in Kentucky and national politics as a State legislator, Governor, Congressman, Senator, and three-time Cabinet member, John J. Crittenden (1787–1863) witnessed the major political events of the ante bellum period. A member of the Whig Party, he learned the art of politics from his fellow Kentuckian Henry Clay. Clay's prominence and influence obscured Crittenden until the mid-1840's, when he emerged as a capable party leader. Well-versed in the tactics of compromise, Crittenden sought a settlement of the slavery controversy to prevent the dissolution of the Union. His proposals for settling the issue through constitutional amendments failed, but he was instrumental in keeping Kentucky in the Union.

1505. Klein, Philip S. President James Buchanan, a biography. University Park, Pennsylvania State University Press [1962] xviii, 506 p. illus.

62–12623  E437.K53

Bibliography: p. 473–490.

With the demise of the Federalist Party, James Buchanan (1791–1868) became a conservative Democrat. Buchanan served as a Congressman and Senator, as Minister to Russia and Great Britain, as Secretary of State in Polk's Cabinet, and as 15th President of the United States. In 1854 Buchanan helped draw up the Ostend Manifesto calling for the acquisition of Cuba as slave territory. Hostile opposition, however, forced President Pierce to repudiate the proposal, and Buchanan was discredited. As President, Buchanan's efforts at compromise between North and South merely alienated extremists of both sides. Buchanan lacked the initiative needed, Klein believes, to handle the secession crisis.

1506. Merk, Frederick. Manifest destiny and mission in American history; a reinterpretation. With the collaboration of Lois Bannister Merk. New York, Knopf, 1963. 265 p.

63–8204  E179.5.M4

Includes bibliography.

The author explores in depth the configuration of the ideas, prevalent in America during the years 1840 through 1890, that resulted in the general national spirit of manifest destiny. Proponents of manifest destiny, Merk points out, were primarily concerned with the extension of the continental limits of the United States. Later, when this idea was transformed into a defense of Caribbean and international expansion, involving the assimilation of non-Anglo-Saxon people, the doctrine lost its intense emotional vogue and its political importance.

1507. Nichols, Roy F. Franklin Pierce, Young Hickory of the Granite Hills. [2d ed., completely rev.] Philadelphia, University of Pennsylvania Press [1958] xvii, 625 p. illus.

58–7750  E432.N63 1958

Bibliography: p. 577–593.

An updated edition of no. 3347 in the 1960 *Guide*.

1508. Rayback, Robert J. Millard Fillmore; biography of a President. Buffalo, Published for the Buffalo Historical Society by H. Stewart, 1959. xiv, 470 p. illus. (Publications of the Buffalo Historical Society, v. 40)  59–14009  F129.B8B88, v. 40

Bibliography: p. [447]–457.

Upon the death of Zachary Taylor after 16 months in office, Millard Fillmore (1800–1874) became the 13th President of the United States. As a Whig politician from Buffalo, N.Y., Fillmore shared the limelight with Thurlow Weed and William H. Seward and served in the State Assembly and in Congress. Rayback notes that, in his desire to preserve the Union and to enforce the Compromise of 1850, particularly the Fugitive Slave Law, Fillmore alienated both the North and the South. He failed to gain antislavery Whig support and thus lost the presidential nomination in 1852 to General Winfield Scott. Fillmore ran in 1856, however, as the candidate of the American (Know-Nothing) Party. After the Civil War, he retired from politics and worked for Buffalo's economic, educational, and cultural betterment.

1509. Seager, Robert. And Tyler too; a biography of John & Julia Gardiner Tyler. New York, McGraw-Hill [1963] xvii, 681 p.

63–14259  E397.S4

Bibliography: p. 647–654.

At the death of his first wife after 29 years of marriage, John Tyler (1790–1862) took as his bride Julia Gardiner, 30 years his junior. Their life in the White House and at their Virginia plantation, "Sherwood Forest," together with their seven children, is the subject of this informal biography. Correspondence of the proud and ambitious Gardiner family reveals both the private and public sides of the Tyler-Gardiner alliance. Against the backdrop of "the political and sectional history of the United States from 1810 to 1890," John Tyler and Julia Gardiner are revealed as distinctly warm and sympathetic individuals. Claude H. Hall's *Abel Parker Upshur, Conservative Virginian, 1790–1844* (Madison, State Historical Society of Wisconsin, 1963 [i.e. 1964] 271 p.) examines the career of the man who served Tyler first as Secretary of the Navy and then as Secretary of State.

1510. Spencer, Ivor D. The victor and the spoils; a life of William L. Marcy. Providence, Brown University Press, 1959. 438 p. illus.

59–6898  E415.9.M18S6

Includes bibliography.

William L. Marcy (1786–1857), prominent politician from New York State, began his long service in government as a founder of the "Albany Regency," the political machine opposing De Witt Clinton. As a loyal Jacksonian Democrat in the U.S. Senate, Marcy uttered his statement that "to the victor belong the spoils" while defending the confirmation of Martin Van Buren as Minister to England. Three times Governor of New York, Marcy ably met the financial and banking problems of the era. He served as Secretary of War in Polk's Cabinet and demonstrated administrative acumen during the Mexican War. His statesmanship in negotiating the Gadsden Purchase, improving trade relations, and dealing with England in Central America capped his career.

1511. Van Deusen, Glyndon G. The Jacksonian era, 1828–1848. New York, Harper [1959] 291 p. illus. (The New American Nation series) 58–13810 E338.V2
"Bibliographical essay": p. 267–283. Bibliographical footnotes.

A survey of American politics from the election of Andrew Jackson through that of Zachary Taylor. Van Deusen's main emphasis is on national events, issues, and personalities. In his analysis the author frequently compares and contrasts Whig and Jacksonian political methods and practices. He points out that, although the Jacksonian Party understood the needs and aspirations of the common man, it lacked an adequate economic program. The Whigs, on the other hand, had a clear and comprehensive program for the economic development of the country, but they did not have the means at their disposal to win the support of the people. *Jacksonian Democracy and the Working Class, a Study of the New York Workingmen's Movement, 1829–1837* (Stanford, Stanford University Press, 1960. 286 p. Stanford studies in history, economics, and political science, 19), by Walter E. Hugins, examines the labor movement and its leaders and their relationship to the Jacksonian Party and program.

# H. Slavery, the Civil War, and Reconstruction (to 1877)

1512. Brodie, Fawn M. Thaddeus Stevens: scourge of the South. New York, Norton [1959] 448 p. illus. 59–9236 E415.9.S84B7
Bibliography: p. 401–433.
A member of the U.S. House of Representatives during 1849–53 and 1859–68, Thaddeus Stevens is acknowledged as the father of the 14th amendment and the leading architect of Republican Reconstruction policy. Mrs. Brodie applies two analytical methods in her study of Stevens' tempestuous career. In the first quarter of the book, she explores the circumstances of Stevens' childhood and early career in order to determine the psychological factors behind his uncompromising idealism and extreme radicalism. She devotes the remainder of the volume to a discussion of the political, social, and economic temper of the times, with emphasis on those conditions which made it possible for Stevens to play a dominant role.

1513. Cain, Marvin R. Lincoln's Attorney General: Edward Bates of Missouri. Columbia, University of Missouri Press [1965] 361 p. illus. 65–13690 E415.9.B2C3
Bibliography: p. 334–352.
Although Edward Bates' diary of the war years has long been an important source of information on the Lincoln administration, Cain is the first historian to write a full-scale biography of this conservative

political leader from Missouri. Cain's study of Bates (1793–1869), whom historians have regarded as relatively colorless and unimportant, focuses on the transitional rather than the turbulent elements of the Civil War decade. According to the author, Bates represented a generation "caught between the agrarian idealism of Jeffersonian society and the material promise of young America and facing formidable problems engendered by slavery, sectionalism, and the industrial awakening." Although he was not one of the more influential members of Lincoln's Cabinet, he did effect some legal and administrative restraints on radical military activity.

1514. Carter, Hodding. The angry scar; the story of Reconstruction. Garden City, N.Y., Doubleday, 1959. 425 p. (Mainstream of America series) 58–9377 E668.C3
Bibliography: p. [411]–414.
The author, a Southern journalist, takes as his point of departure the current conflicts between North and South. His study is "essentially an interpretive synthesis of a considerable body of writing on the Reconstruction period," with emphasis on the effects of post-Civil-War Republican policy on future generations rather than on explanations for the failure of Reconstruction to achieve its objectives. Carter believes that, instead of uniting the American

people, Reconstruction rigidified Southern white culture and hardened Southern opposition to change far into the 20th century.

1515. Donald, David H. Charles Sumner and the coming of the Civil War. New York, Knopf, 1960. 392 p. illus. 60–9144 E415.9.S9D6
Bibliographical footnotes.

A biography of the Boston lawyer who was one of the leading proponents of abolition in the U.S. Senate. From 1845, when his antislavery idealism brought him actively into Massachusetts politics over the issue of the annexation of Texas, until his death, Charles Sumner (1811–1874) gained a reputation as a doctrinaire moral crusader and radical extremist. Donald approaches his subject primarily as a problem of understanding the complex personality of a man who was successful in both the intellectual circles and the political arenas of mid-19th-century America. The analysis of Sumner's intellectual and emotional development is based partly on a study of his speeches and writings and the reactions of his contemporaries. The volume ends with the year 1861; a companion volume covering Sumner's later career is projected.

1516. Douglas, Stephen A. Letters. Edited by Robert W. Johannsen. Urbana, University of Illinois Press, 1961. xxxi, 558 p. illus.
61–62768 E415.9.D73A4

A complete collection of the known correspondence of Stephen A. Douglas (1813–1861), an Illinois Democrat whose politics were based on his belief in manifest destiny and popular sovereignty. The letters cover his active political years (1833–61) during which he held many State and national offices, including those of Representative and Senator in the U.S. Congress, and was an unsuccessful candidate for the Presidency in 1860. This volume is intended in part to serve as a corrective balance to Douglas' historical image as a rigid supporter of States rights, a reputation which he gained in part through his debates with Lincoln in 1858.

1517. Duberman, Martin B., ed. The antislavery vanguard; new essays on the abolitionists. Princeton, N.J., Princeton University Press, 1965. 508 p. 65–10824 E449.D84
Bibliographical footnotes.

A collection of 17 essays which reexamine and redefine abolitionism. The essays represent a revisionist swing away from the long-prevalent interpretation of the abolitionists as cranks and fanatics. The editor notes that, although "most of the contributors to this volume may be said to be sympathetic to the abolitionists, they have not seen their function as one

of vindication or special pleading"; the "large majority have dealt in neutral terms of analysis." The essays cover a wide range of approaches, including moral, social, political, and psychological. In *The Bold Brahmins; New England's War Against Slavery, 1831–1863* (New York, Dutton, 1961. 318 p.), Lawrence Lader presents a study of that part of the antislavery movement which originated and centered in Boston.

1518. Duff, John J. A. Lincoln: prairie lawyer. New York, Rinehart [1960] 433 p. illus.
60–5228 E457.2.D8
Bibliography: p. 403–413.

A study of Lincoln's legal career from 1837, when he was sworn in before the Illinois bar and commenced practice in Springfield, the State capital, until his election as President in 1860. The author considers Lincoln's legal career against the background of the legal profession in the Middle West during the period when that region was passing from frontier status to political and social maturity. Primary emphasis is given to Lincoln's use of his legal practice as preparation for his political career and his years in the Presidency. Duff draws much of his evidence from an examination of the cases, many of which were politically relevant, that Lincoln argued before Illinois and Federal courts, as well as from a scrutiny of Lincoln's law partners, John T. Stuart, Stephen T. Logan, and William H. Herndon.

1519. Franklin, John Hope. Reconstruction: after the Civil War. [Chicago] University of Chicago Press [1961] 258 p. illus. (The Chicago history of American civilization)
61–15931 E668.F7
"Suggested reading": p. 232–242.

A survey of Reconstruction policy and its political, economic, and social effects during the post-Civil-War decade. The author treats the emergence of the New South, with its cities, factories, and racial problems, in the context of the larger national problems posed by industrialization. Much of the volume centers on the decline of old socioeconomic groups, the emergence of new groups, and the shifting political interactions between groups. Franklin concludes that the failure of Reconstruction was due as much to Northern acquiescence in Southern prejudices as to Southern attitudes.

1520. Gara, Larry. The liberty line; the legend of the underground railroad. Lexington, University of Kentucky Press [1961] 201 p.
61–6552 E450.G22
Bibliographical footnotes.

The author dissects the legend of the underground railroad and poses its elements against the reality of escape from slavery. In his attempt to separate fact from fancy, Gara examines abolitionist memoirs and contemporary newspapers, both Northern and Southern. Finding little reason for acceptance of the romantic notion of the underground as a well-organized conspiracy in which the white abolitionist played the hero, he assigns primary importance to the legend as propaganda. Even though the underground railroad was less instrumental in facilitating escape than is commonly supposed, the propagation of the myth of its utility was an important ingredient of abolitionist agitation.

1521. Genovese, Eugene D. The political economy of slavery; studies in the economy & society of the slave South. New York, Pantheon Books [1965] xiv, 304 p.          65–14583 E442.G45
"Bibliographical note": p. 289–292. Bibliographical footnotes at the ends of chapters.

The slaveholding system was at the basis of a civilization which was not only different from but also antagonistic to the more industrially oriented Northern States and European nations. The South was thus increasingly put in a defensive posture, but the relative inefficiency of its agrarian economic system undermined the viability of its institutions. In *Slavery; a Problem in American Institutional and Intellectual Life* ([Chicago] University of Chicago Press [1959] 247 p.), Stanley M. Elkins uses psychological analogies and comparative institutional analyses to discuss the effects of slavery on the Negro in America.

522. McKitrick, Eric L. Andrew Johnson and Reconstruction. [Chicago] University of Chicago Press [1960] 533 p.
60–5467 E668.M156
"Selected bibliography, with notes": p. 511–521.

This analysis of Federal Reconstruction policy from 1865 to 1869 traces the development of the conflict between Andrew Johnson and Congress within the context of partisan politics. McKitrick argues that the President, by virtue of his uncompromising nonpartisanship, bore major responsibility for the inability of the Federal Government to achieve a moderate solution for the problems of the South. By promulgating Reconstruction policies which were unacceptable to his own party, Johnson failed to conciliate the South and at the same time alienated the North. *Politics, Principle, and Prejudice, 1865–1866; Dilemma of Reconstruction America* ([New York] Free Press of Glencoe [1963] 294 p.), by LaWanda C. F. Cox and John H. Cox, examines the development of power blocs within the Democratic and Republican Parties during the first year of Johnson's Presidency.

1523. McPherson, James M. The struggle for equality; abolitionists and the Negro in the Civil War and Reconstruction. Princeton, N.J., Princeton University Press, 1964. 474 p. illus.
63–23411 E449.M176
"Bibliographical essay": p. 433–450.

A study of the abolitionist movement in the North from 1860 to the ratification of the 15th amendment in 1870. McPherson contends that the abolitionists, in their struggle for racial equality, served as the conscience of the radical Republicans. He traces the activities of a number of groups and individuals, many of them either Garrisonian or derivative from the Garrison movement, which stood for immediate, unconditional, and universal abolition of slavery in 1860. *The Negro's Civil War; How American Negroes Felt and Acted During the War for the Union* (New York, Pantheon Books [1965] 358 p.), also by McPherson, is a collection of documents arranged in narrative form, with connecting interpretive and factual information.

1524. Merrill, Walter M. Against wind and tide, a biography of Wm. Lloyd Garrison. Cambridge, Harvard University Press, 1963. xvi, 391 p. illus.
63–10871 E449.G2557
Bibliographical references included in "Introduction" (p. xiii–xvi) and in "Notes" (p. 335–377).

A biography inspired by the author's discovery and acquisition of an extensive group of manuscripts relating to Garrison. Basing his story on these papers and the publicly available collections, Merrill undertakes to "re-evaluate the character and personality of Garrison the man, and to afford a solid basis for appraisal of his position in the American antislavery movement." He places Garrison in the context of his family and his closest associates, "a side of Garrison neglected by other biographers," and describes "the fiery radical, the orator, the politician, the writer of florid editorials as well as the man of family, the kindhearted father and friend, the vain and humorous punster, and the writer of bad verse." He replies to his subject's recent critics, concluding that "As editor and personality, Garrison remains the chief symbol of the abolition crusade."

1525. Nevins, Allan. The War for the Union. New York, Scribner [1959–60] 2 v. illus. (*His* The Ordeal of the Union, v. 5–6)
59–3690 E468.N43
Includes bibliographical references.
CONTENTS.—v. 1. The improvised war, 1861–1862.—v. 2. War becomes revolution, 1862–1863.

A continuation of The Ordeal of the Union, the first four volumes of which are no. 3398–3399 in the 1960 Guide. The primary theme of these two volumes, which cover slightly more than the first two years of the conflict, is the impact of the war on national character. The author contends that the Civil War forged a new unity in a nation of individualists and that the military exigencies of popular warfare demanded new forms of administrative, industrial, transportation, political, and social organization. Tragic Years, 1860–1865; a Documentary History of the American Civil War (New York, Simon & Schuster, 1960. 2 v.), by Paul M. Angle and Earl Schenck Miers, uses contemporary accounts to reveal the social revolution which occurred during the Civil War.

1526. Nichols, Roy F. The stakes of power, 1845–
      1877. New York, Hill & Wang [1961] 246
p. illus. (The Making of America)
                           61–7560  E415.7.N5
"Bibliographical note": p. 231–240.
A survey organized around the theme of the struggle between North and South for the control of the political and economic power of the Federal Government. The author notes that, as America expanded and as Americans made more demands on the Federal Government, the stakes of power grew higher and politics became a serious struggle between those who wanted power and those who were afraid of losing it. The Civil War and the bitterness of Reconstruction, according to Nichols, were logical consequences of the "either/or" character of national politics during the 1840's and 1850's and the inability to compromise on the issues of ideology and lifestyle.

1527. Quarles, Benjamin. Lincoln and the Negro.
      New York, Oxford University Press, 1962.
275 p. illus.          62–9829  E457.2.Q3
  Bibliography: p. 251–264.
Lincoln brought to the Presidency in 1860 "a grasp of the political and constitutional aspects of slavery unsurpassed by any public person of his day." Negroes have almost universally regarded him as the hero-liberator of their race, the author indicates, and the act of emancipation is one of the foundation stones of the Lincoln legend. Lincoln's attitude toward the Negro and toward slavery was not as consistent as the legend would suggest, however. Quarles' study of the development of Lincoln's attitudes toward the Negro issue over his lifetime reveals a man of "complex and many-sided character" and of political astuteness.

1528. Randall, James G., and David H. Donald.
      The Civil War and Reconstruction. 2d ed.
Boston, Heath [1961]  820 p. illus.
                        61–10357  E468.R26  1961
  Bibliography: p. 703–788.
An updated, revised edition of no. 3408 in the 1960 Guide. Donald, a student of Randall's, has made most of the major changes in the Reconstruction section, shifting the emphasis from sectional to national problems and issues. The Tragic Conflict; the Civil War and Reconstruction (New York, G. Braziller, 1962. 528 p. The American epochs series), edited by William B. Hesseltine, is a collection of contemporary accounts documenting a variety of attitudes toward the war. Two works dealing primarily with structural and political weaknesses in the Confederacy are Why the North Won the Civil War ([Baton Rouge] Louisiana State University Press [1960] 128 p.), a collection of essays edited by Donald, and War Within a War; the Confederacy Against Itself (Philadelphia, Chilton Books [1965] 177 p.), by Carleton Beals.

1529. Sewell, Richard H. John P. Hale and the
      politics of abolition. Cambridge, Harvard
University Press, 1965. 290 p.
                        65–13849  E415.9.H15S4  1965
  Includes bibliographies.
Many recent studies of individual abolitionists have contributed to an understanding of the complexity and variety of motivations, attitudes, and activities which have been grouped together under the generic term "abolition movement." One such work is Sewell's biography of John P. Hale (1806–1873), New Hampshire lawyer, politician, and diplomat, who gained a national reputation as an anti-slavery spokesman. Other studies of prominent abolitionists are Hinton Rowan Helper, Abolitionist-Racist (University, University of Alabama Press [1965] 256 p. Southern historical publications, no. 7), by Hugh C. Bailey, and Elijah P. Lovejoy, Abolitionist Editor (Urbana, University of Illinois Press, 1961. 190 p.), by Merton L. Dillon.

1530. Sharkey, Robert P. Money, class, and party;
      an economic study of Civil War and Reconstruction. Baltimore, Johns Hopkins Press, 1959.
346 p. (The Johns Hopkins University studies in historical and political science, ser. 77, no. 2)
                        59–15423  H31.J6  ser. 77, no. 2
  Bibliography: p. 312–333.
An analysis of the financial views of various economic and political groups from 1865 to 1870. The author accepts Charles A. Beard's general interpretation that the major historical significance of the Civil War and Reconstruction lies in the profound social revolution which they brought about. Sharkey concludes, however, that close examination

of the activities of manufacturers, farmers, laborers, bankers, and various subgroups within the Republican and Democratic Parties with respect to the greenback, tariff, and banking issues does not bear out Beard's thesis that the crux of the revolution was the political overthrow of the Southern planter aristocracy by a Northern and Eastern capitalist-Republican group. The theory of monolithic class revolution, Sharkey believes, does not adequately represent the diversity and complexity of the economic and political groupings of post-Civil-War society.

1531. Stampp, Kenneth M. The era of Reconstruction, 1865–1877. New York, Knopf, 1965. 228, [1] p.          64–13447 E668.S79
"Bibliographical note": p. 217–[229].
A synthesis of revisionist scholarship on the Reconstruction period. The author's purpose is to dispel the lingering notion that the post-Civil-War South was the scene of almost unbridled licentiousness and brutality perpetrated by a group of irresponsible Republican politicians who dictated Reconstruction policy. The weaknesses and failures of Reconstruction leaders are exposed, but their lofty intentions and genuine accomplishments, particularly the adoption of the 14th and 15th amendments, are credited with enduring significance. The provisional governments established in the South by Johnson are blamed for introducing the patterns of segregation and discrimination.

1532. Stern, Philip Van Doren. When the guns roared; world aspects of the American Civil War. Garden City, N.Y., Doubleday, 1965. 385 p. illus.          65–12826 E469.S9
Bibliographical references included in "Notes" (p. [353]–372).
A study of the international impact of the Civil War and of the effect of foreign attitudes on the outcome of the war. On the basis of an analysis of official and unofficial diplomacy and of popular reactions, the author concludes that the balance of international opinion remained on the side of the North. The Confederacy's defeat was in part due to her failure to gain England, and hence other nations, as an ally to her cause. Abroad, the Civil War appeared primarily as a conflict between good and evil, freedom and slavery, and the Confederacy could not overcome this disadvantage.

1533. Thomas, Benjamin P., *and* Harold M. Hyman. Stanton; the life and times of Lincoln's Secretary of War. New York, Knopf, 1962. 642 p. illus.          61–17829 E467.1.S8T45
Bibliographical footnotes.
A biography of the Ohio lawyer (1814–1869) who moved into the Federal Government as Buchanan's Attorney General in 1860 and served as Secretary of War under Lincoln and Johnson from 1862 to 1868. The authors devote most of their study to Stanton's activities in the Lincoln and Johnson Cabinets. As Civil War administrator of the Army, he was one of the key figures in the reorganization of the Government to meet the demands of military supply. As a radical reconstructionist in the Johnson Cabinet, he was one of the leaders of the movement to impeach the President.

1534. Wade, Richard C. Slavery in the cities; the South, 1820–1860. New York, Oxford University Press, 1964. 340 p.
          64–22366 E443.W3
Bibliographical references included in "Notes" (p. [287]–323).
The author traces the decline of the institution of slavery from 1820 to 1860. On the basis of his examination of various aspects of urban slavery, Wade concludes that it began to deteriorate in most Southern cities between 1835 and 1845. Although slavery remained as viable economically as it had been between 1820 and 1840, when the slave population had grown proportionately with the white population, it became increasingly difficult to discipline slaves during their off-work hours. As a result, cities began to devise schemes for decreasing black populations and for exercising rigid controls on Negroes who remained in the city.

1535. Warren, Robert Penn. The legacy of the Civil War; meditations on the centennial. New York, Random House [1961] 109 p.
          61–7261 E649.W27
An impressionistic and discursive essay by the poet and novelist. Warren identifies the Civil War as *the* formative American experience. His essay, which has both poetic and metaphysical overtones, represents an excursion into the national psyche. The legacy of the Civil War cannot be cost-accounted; there is no way of balancing the industrialization of the North against the backwardness of the South. The historical significance of the Civil War continues through the mid-20th century because it serves as the American restatement of the classic conflict, as yet unresolved, between will and inevitability, and because "we see how the individual men, despite failings, blindness, and vice, may affirm for us the possibility of the dignity of life."

1536. Welles, Gideon. Selected essays. Compiled by Albert Mordell. New York, Twayne Publishers [1959–60] 2 v. 60–11329 E458.W4
CONTENTS.—[1] Civil War and Reconstruction. —[2] Lincoln's administration.

A collection of essays by the man who served as Secretary of the Navy under Lincoln and Johnson. Gideon Welles (1802–1878) came to the Cabinet with a background in journalism and politics. These essays, which originally appeared as articles in the *Galaxy* and the *Atlantic Monthly* during 1870–78, were intended in part to correct contemporary misconceptions about Lincoln's administration and in part to vindicate the author's Cabinet activities. They serve as a source of information on the methods by which Lincoln arrived at some of the crucial decisions of the Civil War.

# I. Grant to McKinley (1869-1901)

1537. Diamond, Sigmund, *ed.* The Nation transformed; the creation of an industrial society. New York, G. Braziller, 1963. xiv, 528 p.

63–17876 HN57.D53

Bibliography: p. 524–528.

A selection of writings on the Gilded Age, stressing its economic, social, and intellectual developments. The accelerated growth of industry altered the existing environment and created numerous problems in American society. At the turn of the century, the American people realized that organized programs were needed to cope with the changing economy and the glaring inequalities that it had produced. *The Nationalizing of American Life, 1877–1900* (New York, Free Press [1965] 338 p. Sources in American history, 6), edited by Ray Ginger, is another series of excerpts pertaining to the political, economic, social, and cultural problems of the age. *The Gilded Age, a Reappraisel* ([Syracuse, N.Y.] Syracuse University Press, 1963. 286 p.), edited by Howard Wayne Morgan, consists of essays by 10 historians on American life during this period. John S. Blay's *After the Civil War; a Pictorial Profile of America from 1865 to 1900* (New York, Crowell [1960] 312 p.), reflects the transformation of the United States during this 35-year span.

1538. Faulkner, Harold U. Politics, reform, and expansion, 1890–1900. New York, Harper [1959] 312 p. illus. (The New American Nation series)

56–6022 E661.F3

Bibliography: p. 281–304.

A descriptive history, concentrating on the political, economic, social, and expansionist activities of the United States. Faulkner notes that the shift from a predominantly rural and agricultural environment to an urban and industrial society caused profound changes in the economic and social structure of the Nation. During this decade reform movements were initiated to cope with the problems of a modern industrial state, and the country moved from a position of relative isolation to one of involvement in world politics. The victory over Spain and the imperialism which resulted from it, according to Faulkner, signaled the dawn of a new age. The 1890's were a watershed separating "not only two centuries but two eras in American history."

1539. Glad, Paul W. McKinley, Bryan, and the people. Philadelphia, Lippincott [1964] 222 p. (Critical periods of history)

64–11853 E710.G55

"Bibliographical essay": p. 211–218.

During the campaign of 1896 both William Jennings Bryan, the Democratic and Populist nominee, and William McKinley, the Republican candidate, emerged as spokesmen for a particular economic order and the social values connected with it. McKinley was a representative of business and industry and subscribed to the concept of the "self-made man." William Jennings Bryan represented an agrarian ideal that stressed the role of the independent yeoman farmer in the tradition of Jefferson. The author considers that the election of 1896 signified the triumph of industrialism over agrarianism. Henceforth farmers would no longer play their previously powerful role in American politics.

1540. Hayes, Rutherford B., *Pres. U.S.* Hayes: the diary of a President, 1875–1881, covering the disputed election, the end of Reconstruction, and the beginning of civil service. Edited by T. Harry Williams. New York, D. McKay Co. [1964] 329 p.

64–10784 E682.H48

The diary of Rutherford Birchard Hayes (1822–1893) covers his nomination for the Presidency, the 1876 campaign, the controversial election and its outcome, and his record as Chief Executive. Not a day-to-day journal, it is significant for Hayes' comments on the end of Reconstruction, the Republican Party, reform in the Gilded Age, the role of the President, and his relations with Congress. There is much detail on Hayes' views on the money and currency question, civil service, and the struggle with Congress over the rider bills. The diary also depicts the social activities of President Hayes and his wife. This edition, based on a typed copy of the original manuscript, includes an introduction, a chronology of Hayes' administration, and biographical notes on his contemporaries. In *Hayes of the Twenty-third; the Civil War Volunteer Officer* (New York, Knopf, 1965. 324 p.), T. Harry Williams studies Hayes' four-year service in the Twenty-third Ohio Volunteer Infantry.

1541. Hays, Samuel P. The response to industrialism, 1885–1914. [Chicago] University of Chicago Press [1957] 210 p. (The Chicago history of American civilization)

57–6981 HC105.H35

The period discussed in this work was marked by vast changes in the American economic system. Technological innovation and industrial expansion greatly altered traditional functions of work and employment. The author states that industrialism provided for every American an opportunity to enjoy a higher standard of living, but it also demanded drastic changes in his life. "It forced upon every one a new atmosphere, a new setting, to which he had to adjust in his thought, play, worship, and work." During these years new political parties, such as the Populists, Progressives, and Socialists, sought in their programs to reform a society increasingly regimented and dehumanized by industrialism. Ray Ginger's *Age of Excess; the United States From 1877 to 1914* (New York, Macmillan [1965] 386 p.) aims at synthesizing the economic, social, cultural, and political issues of the Gilded Age.

1542. Merrill, Horace S. Bourbon leader: Grover Cleveland and the Democratic Party. Edited by Oscar Handlin. Boston, Little, Brown [1957] 224 p. (The Library of American biography)

57–12002 E697.M4

"A Note on the sources": p. [209]–210.

A critical biography reappraising Grover Cleveland (1837–1908). The first Democratic President after the Civil War, Cleveland took office in 1885 but lost to Benjamin Harrison in 1888. He regained the Presidency in the election of 1892. During his early years in New York State politics, Cleveland had acquired a reputation for efficiency and honesty as an elected official. In 1884 he was the choice of the Bourbon Democrats, the most influential men in the party, to receive the presidential nomination. The Bourbon Democrats, "the conservative spokesmen of business," backed Cleveland during both of his administrations. By following Bourbon strategy, Cleveland ran two successful presidential campaigns

on the platform of ending corruption and waste in governmental operations. *The Cabinet Diary of William L. Wilson, 1896–1897* (Chapel Hill, University of North Carolina Press [1957] 276 p.), edited by Festus P. Summers, is a private account of the last 14 months of Cleveland's second administration from the viewpoint of his Postmaster General. In *"I Am a Democrat"; the Political Career of David Bennett Hill* ([Syracuse, N.Y.] Syracuse University Press, 1961. 315 p.), Herbert J. Bass concentrates on Hill's career as Governor of New York State, 1885–91, and his subsequent influence in the Democratic Party as U.S. Senator, 1892–97.

1543. Morgan, Howard Wayne. William McKinley and his America. [Syracuse, N.Y.] Syracuse University Press, 1963. 595 p. illus.

63–19723 E711.6.M7

Bibliographical references included in "Notes to chapters."

This biography presents William McKinley (1843–1901) as a transitional figure in the history of the American Presidency. He had neither the conservative views of Cleveland, his predecessor, nor the modern ones of Theodore Roosevelt, who followed him. The author places special emphasis on McKinley's 30-year career in national politics and illustrates his role as an internationalist in the formulation of American foreign policy. He also shows that, contrary to current historical interpretations, McKinley sympathized with labor and outlived his rigid conservatism on the tariff question. The 25th President, Morgan maintains, was of much stronger moral and political vision than is usually recognized. McKinley Republicanism helped restore confidence and prosperity to a depression-stricken generation. In *the Days of McKinley* (New York, Harper [1959] 686 p.), by Margaret Leech, is a detailed review of McKinley's first administration.

1544. Nye, Russel B. Midwestern progressive politics; a historical study of its origins and development, 1870–1958. [East Lansing] Michigan State University Press [1959] 398 p.

58–9111 F354.N8 1959

An updated edition of no. 3446 in the 1960 *Guide.* In *The Populist Response to Industrial America, Midwestern Populist Thought* (Cambridge, Harvard University Press, 1962. 166 p.), Norman Pollack considers Populism as "a progressive social force" and the Populist Party as a group seeking to alleviate the economic and social inequalities created by industrialism. *Ignatius Donnelly; the Portrait of a Politician* ([Chicago] University of Chicago

Press [1962] 427 p.), by Martin Ridge, is a full-length treatment of the Minnesota reformer and Congressman.

1545. Sage, Leland L. William Boyd Allison; a study in practical politics. Iowa City, State Historical Society of Iowa, 1956. 401 p. illus.

56–63186 E664.A43S3

"Bibliography: manuscript collections": p. 333–334. Bibliographical references included in "Footnotes" (p. 335–383).

William Boyd Allison (1829–1908) represented the State of Iowa in the U.S. Congress for 43 years. His political career began in 1863 with his election as a Republican to the House of Representatives, where he served for eight years. He was elected Senator in 1872 and continued in that office for six terms. Allison maintained a high standing in the Republican Party and was a serious contender for the presidential nomination in 1888. He was offered Cabinet positions during the administrations of Garfield, Harrison, and McKinley but chose to retain the chairmanship of the Appropriations Committee instead. The Iowa Senator is perhaps best remembered for the bill bearing his name, the Bland-Allison Act of 1878, which provided for the coinage of silver dollars. *Shelby M. Cullom, Prairie State Republican* (Urbana, University of Illinois Press, 1962. 328 p. Illinois studies in the social sciences, v. 51), by James W. Neilson, is a biography of the U.S. Senator from Illinois who was instrumental in establishing the Interstate Commerce Commission.

1546. Sievers, Harry J. Benjamin Harrison. Introduction by Hilton U. Brown. Chicago, H. Regnery Co., 1952–[59] 2 v. illus.

67–27226 E702.S54

Vol. 2 has imprint: New York, University Publishers.

Bibliography at end of each volume.

CONTENTS.— 1. Hoosier warrior, 1833–1865.— 2. Hoosier statesman; from the Civil War to the White House, 1865–1888.

The first two volumes of this projected three-volume study of Benjamin Harrison (1833–1901) chronicle his rise from local political leadership in Indiana to his election as the 23d President in 1888. Volume 1 covers Harrison's early life through his Civil War service as a Union officer. After the war Harrison returned to his law practice in Indianapolis and reentered State politics. He was defeated in the gubernatorial election of 1876 but was elected U.S. Senator five years later. Harrison was nominated as the Republican presidential candidate in 1888 to run against Grover Cleveland. Although Cleveland received a plurality of the popular vote, Harrison was elected with a majority of the electoral votes. A second edition, revised, of the first volume of this biography, *Hoosier Warrior; Through the Civil War Years, 1833–1865* (New York, University Publishers [ᶜ1960] 374 p.) contains a new preface and an enlarged index.

## J. Theodore Roosevelt to Wilson (1901-21)

1547. Barck, Oscar T., *and* Nelson M. Blake. Since 1900; a history of the United States in our times. 4th ed. New York, Macmillan [1965] 963 p. illus.      65–14074 E741.B34 1965

An updated edition of no. 3452 in the 1960 *Guide*.

1548. Coletta, Paolo E. William Jennings Bryan. v. 1. Political evangelist, 1860–1908. Lincoln, University of Nebraska Press, 1964. 486 p.

64–11352 E664.B87C55

Bibliography: p. 446–477.

The first volume of this projected multivolume biography deals with the political career of William Jennings Bryan (1860–1925) and his effects on the domestic and foreign policies of the Nation. Three times defeated as the Democratic candidate for President, Bryan exemplified agrarian America in an era of rapid industrial growth. The author's study of published and unpublished material provides new insights into Bryan's personality and political style. Viewing political and economic questions in moral terms, Bryan maintained a provincial outlook. He urged, however, that the Federal Government play a greater role in the solution of national problems, particularly in matters of currency reform. In *The Trumpet Soundeth; William Jennings Bryan and His Democracy, 1896–1912* ([Lincoln] University of Nebraska Press, 1960. 242 p.), Paul W. Glad studies Bryan during the most important period of his leadership. *Defender of the Faith: William Jennings Bryan; the Last Decade, 1915–1925* (New York, Oxford University Press, 1965. 386 p.), by Lawrence W. Levine, traces Bryan's career after his resignation as Secretary of State in 1915.

1549. Daniels, Josephus. The Cabinet diaries of Josephus Daniels, 1913–1921. Edited by E. David Cronon. Lincoln, University of Nebraska Press [1963] 648 p. illus.

62–7874 E766.D29 1963

Josephus Daniels (1862–1948), Secretary of the Navy in both of President Wilson's administrations, took office on March 5, 1913, and kept a diary for the duration of his service. Diary entries for the years 1914 and 1916, however, are missing. Daniels' diaries record and comment upon Cabinet deliberations, fellow Cabinet members, and other prominent officials, including Franklin D. Roosevelt, his Assistant Secretary of the Navy. Notations are fullest for Wilson's second administration, emphasizing the debates on preparedness; wartime problems; and postwar domestic and foreign issues.

1550. Grantham, Dewey W. Hoke Smith and the politics of the New South. Baton Rouge, Louisiana State University Press, 1958. 396 p. illus. (Southern biography series)

58–9209 E748.S663G7

"Critical essay on authorities": p. 372–377. Bibliographical footnotes.

As lawyer, newspaper publisher, and politician, Hoke Smith (1855–1931) served and represented his adopted State of Georgia. Professional and financial success as a damage-suit lawyer turned Smith toward politics. The vigorous support of his newspaper, *The Atlanta Journal,* for Grover Cleveland brought Smith the Cabinet position of Secretary of the Interior in 1893. His belief in sound money, however, meant exile from the Democratic Party's national leadership for the decade after 1896. Smith was inaugurated Governor of Georgia in 1907; he failed to win the nomination in 1908 but won again in 1910. He resigned from the governorship in November 1911 in order to take a seat in the U.S. Senate, where he served until 1921. Grantham concludes that, from the days of the Bourbon Democrats through the Progressive Era, Hoke Smith's career in Georgia and Washington politics was constructive but marked with "far greater promise than fulfillment."

1551. Link, Arthur S. Wilson. Princeton, Princeton University Press, 1947–65. 5 v. illus.

47–3554 E767.L65

Includes bibliographies.

CONTENTS.—[1] The road to the White House.—[2] The new freedom.—[3] The struggle for neutrality, 1914–1915.—[4] Confusions and crises, 1915–1916.—[5] Campaigns for progressivism and peace, 1916–1917.

Volumes 1 and 2 of this multivolume biography are no. 3472 in the 1960 *Guide.* Volumes 3–5 examine Wilson's transformation from a national leader interested primarily in domestic reform to an international leader in a world on the brink of war. In *Woodrow Wilson and the Politics of Morality* (Boston, Little, Brown [1956] 215 p. The Library of American biography), John M. Blum stresses the role of Wilson's Calvinist principles in shaping his views of domestic and international affairs. In *An Affair of Honor; Woodrow Wilson and the Occupation of Veracruz* ([Lexington] Published for the Mississippi Valley Historical Association [by] University of Kentucky Press [1962] 184 p.), Robert E. Quirk details Wilson's decision in 1914 to send American troups to Veracruz and the consequences of this aggressive act against Mexico.

1552. Lorant, Stefan. The life and times of Theodore Roosevelt. Garden City, N.Y., Doubleday [1959] 640 p. illus. 58–10732 E757.L85

Bibliography: p. 635.

A pictorial history of Theodore Roosevelt (1858–1919) and his era. Reproductions of photographs, cartoons, letters, and diary entries, coupled with textual information, depict Roosevelt in his youth, his early political campaigns, his Presidency, and his triumphs and defeats after 1909. This graphic presentation shows the diversity of Roosevelt's interests, re-creating his love for politics, world travel, nature, and family.

1553. Maxwell, Robert S. La Follette and the rise of the Progressives in Wisconsin. [Madison] State Historical Society of Wisconsin [1956] 271 p. illus. 56–58533 E664.L16M

Bibliography: p. 245–255.

A concise history of "the development, the course, and the results of the Progressive Movement in Wisconsin during its initial phase, the years from 1900 to 1915." Robert M. La Follette (1855–1925), first as Governor and then as U.S. Senator, dominated Wisconsin progressivism and inaugurated comprehensive political, economic, and social reform measures. His political program, known as the Wisconsin Idea, served as a model of enlightened Midwestern progressivism. Hoyt L. Warner's *Progressivism in Ohio, 1897–1917* ([Columbus] Ohio State University Press for the Ohio Historical Society [1964] 556 p.) provides a specialized study of the Progressive Movement in Ohio.

1554. Mowry, George E. The era of Theodore Roosevelt, 1900–1912. New York, Harper [1958] 330 p. illus. (The New American Nation series) 58–8835 E756.M

Bibliography: p. 297–316.

This survey includes an analysis of the origins and nature of progressivism and a reevaluation of the role of Theodore Roosevelt during this period. The author describes the Progressive Movement as "a compound of many curious elements" and Theodore Roosevelt as its foremost national spokesman. Roosevelt emerges as a constructive, capable President, responsive to the changes in the political, economic, and social structure of the Nation. In *Governor Theodore Roosevelt; the Albany Apprenticeship, 1898–1900* (Cambridge, Harvard University Press. 1965. 335 p.), G. Wallace Chessman appraises Roosevelt's governorship and the many reforms he inaugurated in New York State.

1555. Peterson, Horace C., *and* Gilbert C. Fite. Opponents of war, 1917–1918. Madison, University of Wisconsin Press, 1957. xiii, 399 p. illus.                              57–5239  E780.P4
    Bibliography: p. 351–371.

This study, completed by Fite after Peterson's death, describes "what individuals or groups opposed the war, why they acted as they did, and what happened to them." Antiwar sentiment bred by the Socialists, the Industrial Workers of the World, conscientious objectors, pacifists, and religious groups was met with repression and reprisals in the United States. Minority groups and aliens as well as the clergy, teachers, and the press were subject to violations of civil rights and intimidation. The intolerance directed against those who professed antiwar beliefs demonstrates how fundamental liberties were ignored during this time of crisis.

1556. Preston, William. Aliens and dissenters: Federal suppression of radicals, 1903–1933. Cambridge, Harvard University Press, 1963. 352 p.                              63–10873  E743.5.P7
    "Bibliographical note": p. [279]–286. Bibliographical references included in "Notes": p. [287]–345.

Since the late 19th century, according to Preston, aliens and radicals living in the United States have suffered violations of their personal and political liberties. He notes that nativism, born of economic depression, social conflict, and international uncertainties, manifested itself in antidemocratic actions by local and Federal authorities. The "red scare" of 1919–20, culminating in the "Palmer raids" in those years under the direction of Attorney General A. Mitchell Palmer, was merely one episode in the history of intolerance and retaliation against radicals. Stanley Coben's *A. Mitchell Palmer: Politician* (New York, Columbia University Press, 1963. 351 p.) treats Palmer as a political opportunist who led the Department of Justice to take repressive action against radicals in the hope of winning the presidential nomination of 1920.

1557. Wish, Harvey. Contemporary America, the national scene since 1900. 3d ed. New York, Harper [1961]  776 p.  illus.
                              61–6391  E741.W78  1961
    Bibliography: p. 747–762.
    An updated edition of no. 3474 in the 1960 *Guide*.

# K. Since 1920

1558. Baruch, Bernard M. Baruch. New York, Holt [1957–60]  2 v. illus.
                              57–11982  E748.B32A3
    Vol. 2 published by Holt, Rinehart & Winston.
    CONTENTS.—[1] My own story.—[2] The public years.

In these two volumes of autobiography, Bernard Baruch (1870–1965) traces the course of his development as a financier, philanthropist, and influential adviser to Presidents Wilson, Roosevelt, and Truman. In the first volume he recounts his early years in South Carolina, his college days in New York, and his subsequent career as a Wall Street financier. Volume 2 is devoted to his years in public service, which began when he was asked by President Wilson to take charge of mobilizing America's industrial resources during World War I. Also included in this volume is an account of the author's service on the United Nations Atomic Energy Commission after World War II, in the course of which he proposed a plan for the international control of atomic energy. A biography of Baruch based on extensive research is Margaret L. Coit's *Mr. Baruch* (Boston, Houghton Mifflin, 1957. 784 p.).

1559. Blum, John M. From the Morgenthau diaries. Boston, Houghton Mifflin, 1959–65. 2 v. illus.                              59–8853  HJ257.B6
    CONTENTS.—[1] Years of crisis, 1928–1938.—[2] Years of urgency, 1938–1941.

The first two volumes of a three-volume biography of Henry Morgenthau (1891–1967), who served as

Franklin Roosevelt's Secretary of the Treasury from 1934 to 1945. Blum's biography is based primarily on Morgenthau's diaries, which provide a detailed account of his career. Volume 1 covers the period during which Morgenthau worked in the New York State government, headed the Farm Credit Administration, and served as Secretary of the Treasury. Volume 2 discusses Morgenthau's years as Secretary of the Treasury. In *Minister of Relief; Harry Hopkins and the Depression* ([Syracuse, N.Y.] Syracuse University Press, 1963. 286 p.), Searle F. Charles discusses Hopkins' administration of three major Federal relief agencies during the New Deal years. *Rexford Tugwell and the New Deal* (New Brunswick, N.J., Rutgers University Press [1964] 535 p.), by Bernard Sternsher, contains a general discussion of Tugwell's thought as well as an account of his role during Roosevelt's first administration.

1560. Eisenhower, Dwight D., *Pres. U.S.* The White House years. Garden City, N.Y., Doubleday, 1963–65. 2 v. illus.

63–18447   E835.E47

CONTENTS.— [1] Mandate for change, 1953–1956.— [2] Waging peace, 1956–1961.

Dwight D. Eisenhower's personal memoirs of his Presidency. Volume 1, which includes an account of the 1952 presidential campaign, covers the first term, and volume 2, which begins with the 1956 campaign, covers the second. Written in an informal style, the memoirs provide insight into Eisenhower's responses to the many significant events with which he was confronted as President. Among these were the increase and decline of Senator Joseph McCarthy's influence, the formation of the Southeast Asian Treaty Organization (SEATO), the launching of Sputnik, and the sending of Federal troops into Little Rock. The former President also describes his personal life during these years.

1561. Hicks, John D. Republican ascendancy, 1921–1933. New York, Harper [1960] 318 p. illus. (The New American Nation series)

60–7528   E784.H5

Bibliography: p. 281–301.

1562. Leuchtenburg, William E. The perils of prosperity, 1914–32. [Chicago] University of Chicago Press [1958] 313 p. (The Chicago history of American civilization)

58–5680   HC106.3.L3957

Bibliography: p. 277–297.

Hicks sees the years 1921–33 as an interlude characterized by a lack of strong political leadership in domestic and foreign affairs. A business mentality dominated, and the United States experienced th[e] most severe economic crisis in its history. Emphasi[s] is placed on the economic and political history o[f] the period, but Hicks also gives due attention to problems of foreign policy. In *The Perils of Prosperity, 1914–32,* Leuchtenburg describes the transition from Wilson's New Freedom to the policies o[f] the succeeding Republican years. He then show[s] how various trends came to a head at the end of th[e] 1920's and resulted in the stock market crash, which "was taken as a judgement pronounced on th[e] whole era."

1563. Leuchtenburg, William E. Franklin D[.] Roosevelt and the New Deal, 1932–1940[.] New York, Harper & Row [1963] 393 p. illus[.] (The New American Nation series)

63–12053   E806.L47[?]

Bibliography: p. 349–363.

The author provides an overview of the Ne[w] Deal years, beginning with Franklin Roosevelt'[s] campaign for the Presidency in 1932 and endin[g] with his reelection to a third term in 1940. He de[-] votes considerable attention to the political and socia[l] events of the period and offers insight into suc[h] phenomena as party politics, social conditions, an[d] prominent personalities. Roosevelt's administrativ[e] programs and his appointees such as Hopkins, Lili[-] enthal, and Tugwell are also discussed. In additio[n] to the domestic scene, Leuchtenburg deals wit[h] events abroad and shows how American foreig[n] policy developed during these years in response t[o] the threat of involvement in another world war.

1564. Lilienthal, David E. The journals of Davi[d] E. Lilienthal. Introduction by Henry Steel[e] Commager. New York, Harper & Row [1964] 2 v. illus.   64–18056   E748.L7A3[?]

CONTENTS.— v. 1. The TVA years, 1939–194[5] — v. 2. The atomic energy years, 1945–1950.

Among his various achievements, David Lilien[-] thal (b. 1899) led in the development of the Ten[-] nessee Valley Authority, became the first Chairma[n] of the Atomic Energy Commission, and, later, be[-] gan to put the TVA idea to work in the develop[-] ing regions of the world. Volume 1 of his *Journal[s]* contains an account of the early development o[f] TVA and includes selected journal entries from pre[-] ceding years. Volume 2 deals primarily with Lilien[-] thal's years as AEC chairman. In *Men and Deci[-] sions* (Garden City, N.Y., Doubleday, 1962. 46[8] p.), Lewis L. Strauss surveys his life in business an[d] public service, emphasizing his association with th[e] AEC and his tenure as Chairman during the Eisen[-] hower administration.

1565. Link, Arthur S. American epoch, a history of the United States since the 1890's. With the collaboration of William B. Catton. 2d ed., rev. and rewritten. New York, Knopf, 1963. xxiv, 917, xiii p. illus. 63–12398 E741.L55 1963

Bibliography: p. [885]–917.

A revised and enlarged edition of no. 3489 in the 1960 *Guide*. The authors adopt a broad perspective and include economics, politics, diplomatic relations, and the arts. The entire text has been rewritten, and new information and interpretations have been incorporated. *The Shaping of Twentieth-Century America; Interpretive Articles* (Boston, Little, Brown [1965] 682 p.), edited by Richard M. Abrams and Lawrence W. Levine, is a collection of journal articles which deal with various aspects of American history from the late 19th century to the mid-1960's. John Braeman, Robert H. Bremner, and Everett Walters have edited *Change and Continuity in Twentieth-Century America* ([Columbus] Ohio State University Press [1965, c1964] 287 p. Modern America, no. 1), a selection of scholarly essays related to the theme of tradition and innovation. *The Urban Nation, 1920–1960* (New York, Hill & Wang [1965] 278 p. The Making of America), by George E. Mowry, offers an introduction to the period between the wars, with emphasis on the interrelation between urban development and politics.

1566. Morison, Elting E. Turmoil and tradition; a study of the life and times of Henry L. Stimson. Boston, Houghton Mifflin, 1960. 686 p. illus. 60–10132 E748.S883M6

Bibliography: p. 657–662.

As a lawyer and statesman, Henry L. Stimson (1867–1950) was active in public life for more than 50 years. He served as Governor General of the Philippines and in the Cabinets of three Presidents. Under Hoover he was Secretary of State, and under Taft and Franklin D. Roosevelt he was Secretary of War. Stimson was President Roosevelt's chief adviser on atomic energy policy during World War II and later served President Truman in the same capacity. Morison's detailed biography covers Stimson's entire life. Although the emphasis is on Stimson's career and the events in which he was involved, the author also describes his family background and school years.

1567. Schlesinger, Arthur M., Jr. The age of Roosevelt. Boston, Houghton Mifflin, 1957– 60. 3 v. 56–10293 E806.S34
Includes bibliographies.

CONTENTS.—[1] The crisis of the old order, 1919–1933.— 2. The coming of the New Deal.— 3. The politics of upheaval.

Volume 1 of this projected multivolume work is no. 3500 in the 1960 *Guide*. In the second and third volumes, Schlesinger concentrates on Roosevelt's domestic policy during his first term. Volume 2 is devoted mainly to domestic events which occurred during 1933 and 1934, although the narrative is continued into the following years when necessary. In volume 3, the author recounts the Roosevelt administration's history through the 1936 election. Foreign policy during the first term will be treated in a later volume. Thomas H. Greer's *What Roosevelt Thought; the Social and Political Ideas of Franklin D. Roosevelt* ([East Lansing] Michigan State University Press, 1958. 244 p.) is an examination of Roosevelt's views on a variety of subjects, including human rights, the Constitution, and the role of the President. In *Roosevelt and Howe* (New York, Knopf, 1962. 479 p.), Alfred B. Rollins tells the story of Roosevelt's relationship with Louis Howe, his secretary and assistant for more than 20 years.

1568. Sorensen, Theodore C. Kennedy. New York, Harper & Row [1965] 783 p. 65–14660 E841.S6

1568a. Schlesinger, Arthur M., Jr. A thousand days; John F. Kennedy in the White House. Boston, Houghton Mifflin, 1965. xiv, 1087 p. 65–20218 E841.S3

As former Kennedy staff members, the authors of these two books about President Kennedy (1917–1963) were personally involved in many of the events which they discuss. Both volumes are based on a combination of firsthand knowledge and extensive research. Sorensen concentrates on Kennedy's years in the White House, but also provides ample coverage of the late President's Senate career and the 1960 presidential campaign. His account of the Kennedy Presidency is, in general, most vivid when he deals with domestic affairs. In Schlesinger's history of the Kennedy administration, which deals in less detail with the events leading up to Kennedy's election, the emphasis is on foreign policy.

1569. U.S. *President*. Public papers of the Presidents of the United States, containing the public messages, speeches, and statements of the President. [Washington, U.S. Govt. Print. Off., 1958]–65. 20 v. 58–61050 J80.A283
Published by the Office of the Federal Register of the National Archives and Records Service.

A continuing series, based on White House releases and transcripts of news conferences. The material ranges from informal statements to nation-wide broadcasts. Official documents such as proclamations and Executive orders are not included, however, since they are published elsewhere. As of 1965, published volumes contained the papers of Harry S. Truman, 1945–51 (7 v.); Dwight D. Eisenhower, 1953–61 (8 v.); John F. Kennedy, 1961–63 (3 v.); and Lyndon B. Johnson, 1963–64 (2 v.).

1570. Warren, Harris G. Herbert Hoover and the great depression. New York, Oxford University Press, 1959. 372 p.

59–5663 E801.W28

Bibliographical references included in "Notes" (p. 305–352).

The author has attempted a balanced appraisal of the Hoover Presidency and seeks to avoid the extreme praise or deprecation which has dominated much of the literature on Hoover's career. A political and economic history of the Hoover administration, the book covers not only events in which Hoover played a dominant role but also matters in which his influence was minor. Warren concludes that Hoover's conduct in public office, both as Secretary of Commerce and as President of the United States, indicates that he was "the greatest Republican of his generation." Albert U. Romasco's *The Poverty of Abundance; Hoover, the Nation, the Depression* (New York, Oxford University Press, 1965. 282 p.) also deals with the years of Hoover's Presidency and emphasizes the ways in which the depression caused the Nation's leaders to change existing institutions in order to solve the economic crisis.

# IX

# Diplomatic History and Foreign Relations

THE DUAL title and organization of this chapter are consistent with the general approach established for the 1960 *Guide*. The books classified as Diplomatic History (Section A) are primarily but not exclusively retrospective and deal with political relations between the United States and other nations from the beginning of the American Revolution to the present. Publications on the growing American involvement in Africa and the Middle East have been placed under Subsection Aix, the title for which has been changed from Asia to Asia, Africa, and the Middle East. The entries in Section B, Foreign Relations, deal almost entirely with the process of formulating and executing foreign policy within the framework of the U.S. political system.

## A. Diplomatic History

### Ai. GENERAL WORKS

1571. The American foreign policy library. Cambridge, Harvard University Press, 1947–64. 19 v.

A continuation of no. 3501 in the 1960 *Guide*. Five of the original 15 volumes, no. 3502–3516 in the 1960 *Guide*, have been revised, and four new volumes have been added to the series. These nine works are listed as no. 1572–1580 below.

1572. Brown, William Norman. The United States and India and Pakistan. Rev. and enl. ed. 1963. 444 p.

                63–13807   DS480.84.B73  1963

    Bibliography: p. [403]–418.

A revised edition of no. 3503 in the 1960 *Guide*.

1573. Cline, Howard F. The United States and Mexico. Rev. ed., enl. New York, Atheneum, 1963. 484 p. (Atheneum paperbacks, 40)
63–24587 F1226.C6 1963
"Suggested reading": p. [444]–453. "A bibliographical supplement, 1953–1962": p. [454]–471.
A revised edition of no. 3504 in the 1960 *Guide*.

1574. Fairbank, John King. The United States and China. New ed., completely rev. and enl. 1958. 365 p.    58–11552 DS735.F3 1958
"Suggested reading": p. [321]–344.
A revised edition of no. 3506 in the 1960 *Guide*.

1575. Gallagher, Charles F. The United States and North Africa: Morocco, Algeria, and Tunisia. 1963. 275 p.    63–20766 DT194.G15
Bibliography: p. [257]–263.

1576. Grattan, Clinton Hartley. The United States and the Southwest Pacific. 1961. 273 p.
61–5583 DU30.G7

1577. Hughes, Henry Stuart. The United States and Italy. Rev. ed. 1965. 297 p.
65–13845 DG577.H8 1965
"Suggested reading": p. [276]–286.
A revised editon of no. 3507 in the 1960 *Guide*.

1578. Polk, William R. The United States and the Arab world. 1965. xiv, 320 p.
65–16688 DS63.2.U5P6
"Suggested reading": p. [297]–311.

1579. Reischauer, Edwin O. The United States and Japan. 3d ed. 1965. xxv, 396 p.
64–8057 E183.8.J3R4 1965
Bibliography: p. [382]–384.
A revised edition of no. 3510 in the 1960 *Guide*.

1580. Safran, Nadav. The United States and Israel. 1963. 341 p. 63–17212 E183.8.I7S2
Bibliography: p. [319]–332.

1581. Bailey, Thomas A. A diplomatic history of the American people. 7th ed. New York, Appleton-Century-Crofts [1964] 973 p.
64–10909 E183.7.B29 1964
Bibliography: p. 912–947.
A revised edition of no. 3517 in the 1960 *Guide*.

1582. Bartlett, Ruhl J., *ed.* The record of American diplomacy; documents and readings in the history of American foreign relations. 4th ed. enl. New York, Knopf, 1964. xxiv, 892, xxii p.
64–23887 E183.7.B35 196
Bibliography: p. 891–892.
A revised edition of no. 3518 in the 1960 *Guide*.

1583. Bemis, Samuel Flagg. American foreign policy and the blessings of liberty, and other essays. New Haven, Yale University Press, 1962. 423 p.    62–16561 E183.7.B4
A selection of works written since 1918 by th noted diplomatic historian. The title essay poses th question whether the diplomatic history of th United States can "strengthen our judgment i facing problems today which include nothing les than the survival of our nation." This the autho answers in the affirmative. Today's problems, ac cording to Bemis, must be understood in the contex of their origin and development. Specifically Americans need to relate current policy to historica tradition and to the fundamental human values o "life, liberty, and the pursuit of happiness." A might be expected from the author of two such im portant studies as *Jay's Treaty,* 2d ed. (1962. 520 p.) and *Pinckney's Treaty,* rev. ed. (1960. 372 p.) both published in New Haven by the Yale Univer sity Press, most of the other essays relate to Amer ican diplomacy in the early days of the United States A chronologically arranged bibliography of Bemis writings from 1913 to 1962 is included (p. 417– 423).

1584. Bemis, Samuel Flagg, *ed.* The American Secretaries of State and their diplomacy. v 11–14. Robert H. Ferrell, editor. New York Cooper Square Publishers, 1963–65. 4 v.
62–20139 E183.7.B46
Includes bibliographies.
For a description of the first 10 volumes, see no 3519 in the 1960 *Guide*. Volumes 11–14 cover th administrations of Frank B. Kellogg (1925–29) Henry L. Stimson (1929–33), Cordell Hull (1933– 44), Edward R. Stettinius, Jr. (1944–45), and Jame F. Byrnes (1945–47).

1585. Bemis, Samuel Flagg. A diplomatic history of the United States. 5th ed. New York Holt, Rinehart & Winston [1965] 1062 p. illus.
65–11841 E183.7.B4682 196
Bibliographical footnotes.
A revised edition of no. 3520 in the 1960 *Guide*.

1586. De Conde, Alexander. A history of American foreign policy. New York, Scribne [1963] 914 p.    63–7615 E183.7.D4
"Supplementary readings": p. 863–896.

A survey of American diplomatic history from colonial times to the Kennedy administration, emphasizing the influence of political, social, and economic developments on foreign policy. A third of the book is devoted to the U.S. role in the cold war and to contemporary American policy toward the Far East, Latin America, the Middle East, Europe, and Africa. Useful features of this book are its extensive appendixes and a bibliography arranged by chapter. A brief introduction to the whole scope of American diplomatic history is Ruhl J. Bartlett's concise and lucid *Policy and Power* (New York, Hill & Wang [1963] 303 p.).

1587. Graebner, Norman A., *ed*. Ideas and diplomacy; readings in the intellectual tradition of American foreign policy. New York, Oxford University Press, 1964. 892 p.

64–15011 E173.G78

Bibliographical footnotes.

These documents on American diplomacy were chosen for the importance of the concepts and ideas they express rather than for their relevance to specific historical problems. Although the general student may be unfamiliar with some of the readings, as a group they serve to portray the intellectual conflict over diplomacy that has confronted the United States since the 18th century. Graebner considers that two functional concepts have determined the American diplomatic response: the analytical approach to diplomacy, corresponding roughly to the realism of the 18th- and 19th-century diplomatic tradition, and the ideological approach, exemplified in the idealism that has characterized the 20th century. A short introduction precedes each of the 12 divisions of the book and indicates the major theme of the readings.

1588. Leopold, Richard W. The growth of American foreign policy, a history. New York, Knopf, 1962. xxii, 848, xxix p.

62–13894 E183.7.L47

"Bibliographical essay": p. [819]–848.

A survey designed for the general reader and college student. The principles and practices of the first century of U.S. foreign policy are briefly described. Detailed coverage begins with the inauguration of Benjamin Harrison in 1889, and the book concludes with seven chapters on the diplomacy of the Eisenhower administration. Featured throughout are character portrayals of the Presidents, their Secretaries of State, and congressional leaders involved in the making of foreign policy.

1589. Perkins, Dexter. The American approach to foreign policy. Rev. ed. Cambridge, Harvard University Press, 1962. 247 p.

62–11400 E183.7.P46 1962

Bibliography: p. 233–237.

A revised edition of no. 3523 in the 1960 *Guide*.

1590. Smith, Daniel M., *ed*. Major problems in American diplomatic history: documents and readings. Boston, Heath [1964] 677 p. maps.

63–22521 E183.7.S56

Includes bibliographies.

Smith divides the history of American foreign policy into two successive phases: the country's expansion until 1889 and its subsequent emergence as a great world power. The documents are organized around 20 diplomatic problems, each of which is discussed in an interpretive essay. Among the problems presented are those concerning the Jefferson-Hamilton rivalry, the Monroe Doctrine, the Mexican War, the rejection of the Versailles Treaty, and the agreements reached at the Yalta Conference. The final chapter considers "currents in American foreign policy since 1952" and ends with selections from President Kennedy's statements relating to the confrontation with the Soviet Union over offensive missiles in Cuba and his replies to De Gaulle's challenges to American leadership in Europe.

## Aii. PERIOD STUDIES

1591. Davids, Jules. America and the world of our time; United States diplomacy in the twentieth century. New York, Random House [1960] 597 p. 60–5563 E744.D25

Bibliography: p. 563–599.

A general introduction that seeks to place 20th-century American foreign policy in the context of world affairs. Two main themes of the book are the growth of American power and influence in the world and the reluctant shift from isolationism to internationalism. Emphasis is placed on "the circumstances which contributed to America's involvement in power politics; the great changes that were brought about by World War II; and the diplomatic background of the Cold War." The neutrality legislation of the 1930's—the zenith in American isolationism in the 20th century—is examined by Robert A. Divine in *The Illusion of Neutrality* ([Chicago] University of Chicago Press [1962] 370 p.). Two other general studies of American diplomacy since World War I are Jean B. Duroselle's *From Wilson to Roosevelt* (Cambridge, Harvard University Press, 1963. 499 p.), translated by Nancy L. Roelker, and Dexter Perkins' *Foreign Policy and the American Spirit, Essays* (Ithaca, N.Y., Cornell University Press [1957] 254 p.), edited by Glyndon G. Van Deusen and Richard C. Wade.

1592. Feis, Herbert. Between war and peace; the Potsdam Conference. Princeton, N.J., Princeton University Press, 1960. 367 p. maps.

60–12230   D734.B4  1945ad

Bibliography: p. 355–357.

1593. Feis, Herbert. Churchill, Roosevelt, Stalin; the war they waged and the peace they sought. Princeton, N.J., Princeton University Press, 1957. 692 p. maps.          57–5470  D748.F4

Bibliographical footnotes.

Two studies in sequence that examine the wartime relations between Great Britain, the United States, and the Soviet Union. Using a chronological approach in the first volume, the author threads his way through the complex diplomatic crises taking place between 1940 and the German surrender in May 1945. He presents a balanced and penetrating account of such Allied wartime decisions as the doctrine of unconditional surrender, the Normandy invasion, and allowing Berlin to fall to the Russians. The Yalta Agreement and the corrosion within the coalition thereafter are analyzed carefully and dispassionately. The second volume begins by describing the events surrounding Germany's surrender to the Allies. Feis then traces the flow of dissension which subsequently exposed the long-developing fractures within the alliance. With the groundwork thus laid, the proceedings at Potsdam are reviewed, as unfavorable circumstances pitted two relatively inexperienced Western negotiators, Truman and Attlee, against the shrewd and intransigent Stalin. In an often arresting narrative, the author describes the hammering out of the vital questions of Germany's future, while the grand alliance collapsed and the cold war began. Briefer and more concise than Feis' studies are two volumes in the America in Crisis series: *The Reluctant Belligerent; American Entry Into World War II* (New York, Wiley [1965] 172 p.), by Robert A. Divine, and Gaddis Smith's *American Diplomacy During the Second World War, 1941–1945* (New York, Wiley [1965] 194 p.). Important source materials for these works were the proceedings compiled by the U.S. Department of State: *The Conferences at Malta and Yalta, 1945* (Washington, U.S. Govt. Print. Off., 1955. 1032 p. Foreign relations of the United States: diplomatic papers) and *The Conference of Berlin; the Potsdam Conference, 1945* (Washington, U.S. Govt. Print. Off., 1960. 2 v. Foreign relations of the United States: diplomatic papers), issued as Department of State Publications 6199 and 7015, respectively.

1594. Ferrell, Robert H. American diplomacy in the great depression; Hoover-Stimson foreign policy, 1929–1933. New Haven, Yale University Press, 1957. 319 p. (Yale historical publications. Studies, 17)          57–11913  E801.F4

"Bibliographical essays": p. 283–308.

The second volume of a projected three-volume history of American diplomacy from 1927 to 1937. The initial work, *Peace in Their Time; the Origins of the Kellogg-Briand Pact* (New Haven, Yale University Press, 1952. 293 p. Yale historical publications. Miscellany, 55), is a study of the period 1927–29 and the efforts to establish a basis for lasting peace through treaty pledges. In this middle volume, U.S. foreign policy under President Hoover and Henry L. Stimson, his Secretary of State, is examined. Drawing much of his material from the diaries of William Castle, the Under Secretary of State, Ferrell depicts the effect of the great depression on the maintenance of world order as catastrophic and declares that never was an economic disaster so evident in the shaping of American diplomacy. Although the crisis explains much of the country's policy, the author finds American diplomatic principles of the 1920's, based on isolationism and "moral" leadership, inadequate to meet the increasingly intricate international problems confronting the Hoover-Stimson administration. Lewis Ethan Ellis notes similar inadequacies in the period preceding the Hoover Presidency in his book *Frank B. Kellogg and American Foreign Relations, 1925–1929* (New Brunswick, N.J., Rutgers University Press [1961] 303 p.). Robert H. Ferrell's *American Diplomacy, a History* (New York, Norton [1959] 576 p.) is a general introduction to these and other periods of U.S. foreign policy.

1595. LaFeber, Walter. The new empire; an interpretation of American expansion, 1860–1898. Ithaca, N.Y., Published for the American Historical Association [by] Cornell University Press [1963] 444 p.          63–20868  E661.7.L2

Bibliography: p. 418–426.

This study of the major period of U.S. overseas expansion emphasizes the economic forces motivating commercial and territorial aggrandizement. Although many accounts interpret American expansionist activity as accidental and spur-of-the-moment, LaFeber views it as a natural culmination within a maturing nation of the impetus created by the industrial revolution. Characterizing Secretary of State Seward as one of the great statesmen of the era, the author also emphasizes the impact of the ideas of such men as Frederick Jackson Turner and Alfred Thayer Mahan on the attitudes of the time. Foster Rhea Dulles has written a general study of the period: *Prelude to World Power; American Diplomatic History, 1860–1900* (New York, Macmillan

[1965] 238 p. History of American foreign policy series). A concise account of the Spanish-American War period is Howard Wayne Morgan's *American Road to Empire* (New York, Wiley [1965] 124 p. America in crisis), which, in support of LaFeber, interprets the expansionism of 1898 as the culmination of a generation's tendencies in world affairs.

1596. Link, Arthur S. Wilson the diplomatist; a look at his major foreign policies. Baltimore, Johns Hopkins Press, 1957. 165 p. (The Albert Shaw lectures on diplomatic history, 1956)

57–12120 E767.L66

The author, a noted Wilson scholar, attempts to answer major questions concerning the President's diplomatic role in World War I. Link states that until 1917 Wilson was better able to accept the Allied maritime blockade than German submarine warfare because the former threatened American neutrality less than the latter. The Peace Conference is seen as a clear clash of Wilsonian idealism and Allied ambitions, and the author absolves Wilson of blame for those aspects of the Versailles Treaty that failed to fulfill his idealistic aspirations. The book concludes with a discussion of the "Great Debate" over the acceptance of the League of Nations by the American people and the Senate. Because of his intransigence over compromise on the Covenant, Wilson is seen as a "prophet" rather than a statesman. *The Inquiry; American Preparations for Peace, 1917–1919* (New Haven, Yale University Press, 1963. 387 p.), by Lawrence E. Gelfand, receives its title from the name of a little-known Government agency, created by the President in 1917 to plan and gather information for the forthcoming peace.

1597. May, Ernest R. Imperial democracy; the emergence of America as a great power. New York, Harcourt, Brace & World [1961] 318 p.

61–13354 E661.M34

Bibliography: p. 273–299.

Until the late 1880's, according to the author, the United States was dealt with as a second-rate power, but by the early 20th century Europe was beginning to look upon American strength with increased respect and concern. Although concentrating primarily on the events of the Spanish-American War, the author amply illustrates a wide range of causes contributing to the emergence of the United States as a great power. Showing the American people themselves as a driving force in this development, the book becomes a social and economic history as well as one of foreign relations. Of considerable interest are the varying views of European govern-

ments and statesmen toward American imperialism and growth during the period. Equally interesting is America's ambivalence, which is demonstrated during this time of intense nationalism by the country's desire to find ways for bringing about peaceful settlement of international conflicts. America's efforts to maintain world peace are examined by Calvin D. Davis in *The United States and the First Hague Peace Conference* (Ithaca, N.Y., Published for the American Historical Association [by] Cornell University Press [1962] 236 p.). In *The Awkward Years; American Foreign Relations Under Garfield and Arthur* (Columbia, University of Missouri Press [c1962] 381 p.), David M. Pletcher shows that the foreign policies of the 1880's, although inadequately shaped, "foreshadowed attitudes and expedients of later imperialist years."

1598. May, Ernest R. The World War and American isolation, 1914–1917. Cambridge, Harvard University Press, 1959. 482 p. (Harvard historical studies, v. 71)

58–12971 D619.M383

"Bibliographical essay": p. [439]–466.

Dealing with the familiar story of President Wilson's dilemma as he reluctantly committed his Nation to war, this book emphasizes both the domestic politics of the United States and the diplomacy of the Allies and the Central Powers. Primary in the discussion are submarine warfare, the blockading of sea transport, and the interaction of Britain's policies toward her French and Russian allies with her policies toward the United States. Crucial in the making of America's decision to join the Allies was the triumph in Germany of the proponents of unlimited submarine warfare while British leaders maintained restraint in executing maritime policies that adversely affected the United States.

1599. Morris, Richard B. The peacemakers; the great powers and American independence. New York, Harper & Row [1965] xviii, 572 p. illus.

65–20435 E249.M68

Bibliographical references included in "Notes" (p. 467–552).

An extensive account of the complicated diplomacy surrounding negotiations for the Treaty of Paris which resolved the American Revolutionary War. With scholarly care and precision, Morris traces the intricate steps by which the American peace commissioners attacked their central problem, that of cutting the bonds of the French alliance in order to arrive at a settlement with Great Britain. By the terms of the peace, the author contends, the United States emerged as an undisputed sovereign nation, accomplishing possibly "the greatest victory in the annals of American diplomacy." In describing the endeavor, he explores the motivations and objectives of the major European powers, as well as their maneuvers and intrigues. A major part of the story is revealed through portraits of the principal diplomatic personalities: American commissioners John Jay, John Adams, Henry Laurens, and Benjamin Franklin; England's Richard Oswald and the Earl of Shelburne; the French Foreign Minister, the Comte de Vergennes; and Spain's Ambassador to France, the Conde de Aranda. Short sketches of innumerable opposition leaders, spies, intriguers, and self-appointed advisers complete the gallery. Further insight and flavor are added to the account by occasional glimpses into the "backstairs diplomacy" which characterized relations among European nations in this period.

1600. Varg, Paul A. Foreign policies of the founding fathers. [East Lansing] Michigan State University Press, 1963 [i.e. 1964, ᶜ1963] 316 p.
63–19117 E310.7.V3
In a topical narrative tracing the development of American foreign policy from 1773 to 1812, the author attempts to demonstrate the close relationship between domestic and foreign issues in the conduct of the Nation's diplomacy. Varg considers that foreign affairs played a major role in undermining the Government under the Articles of Confederation and later, under the Constitution, became a focal point of debate that resulted in the rise of political parties. During the Jefferson administration, the viewpoint on relations abroad shifted, the author maintains, from the preeminence of Hamiltonian realism toward an increasing idealism. In his book To the Farewell Address (Princeton, N.J., Princeton University Press, 1961. 173 p.), Felix Gilbert approaches the early development of American foreign policy from the vantage point of intellectual history, focusing on the interrelationship between the European heritage of the Enlightenment and the American colonial experience.

### Aiii. PERSONAL RECORDS

1601. Murphy, Robert D. Diplomat among warriors. Garden City, N.Y., Doubleday, 1964. 470 p. 64–11305 E744.M87
In this firsthand account the author reviews some of the most important historical events of the 20th century. A diplomat in the Department of State for more than 40 years, Murphy went in 1921 to Munich, where he met Hitler and other members of the Nazi leadership and observed their early careers. Serving in Paris during the period 1930–40, he witnessed the fall of France and was then assigned as Chargé d'Affaires to the Vichy Government.

President Roosevelt made Murphy his personal representative in Africa, where he conducted exploratory missions and made preparations for the entry of French West Africa into the war. The author was present during the important Casablanca Conference in 1942, helped negotiate the Italian surrender in 1943, and served as political adviser to the Supreme Headquarters of the Allied Expeditionary Force in Europe (SHAEF) in planning and carrying out the occupation of Germany. During the Eisenhower administration, this experienced diplomat, serving as Deputy Under Secretary and then Under Secretary of State for Political Affairs, took part in policy decisions relating to events such as the Korean armistice, the Suez crisis, and the U-2 incident. Because of his role as a participant, Murphy is able to present many facts never before publicly revealed.

### Aiv. THE BRITISH EMPIRE

1602. Allen, Harry C. Conflict and concord; the Anglo-American relationship since 1783. New York, St. Martins Press [1960, ᶜ1959] 247 p. illus. 59–15565 E183.8.G7A47 1960
A revised and enlarged edition of part 1 of Great Britain and the United States; a History of Anglo-American Relations, 1783–1952, no. 3551 in the 1960 Guide.

1603. Campbell, Charles S. Anglo-American understanding, 1898–1903. Baltimore, Johns Hopkins Press [1957] 385 p.
57–9518 E183.8.G7C28
"Bibliographical note": p. 369–374. Bibliographical footnotes.
Great Britain and the United States, realizing that a comprehensive understanding was in the interest of both, resolved a striking number of outstanding differences during the relatively brief period encompassed by this study. Under the leadership of Secretary of State John Hay and British Ambassador Pauncefote, settlement was reached on the boundary dispute in southeastern Alaska and on hunting rights in the Bering Sea, and the basis was laid for a final agreement on fishing rights off Newfoundland's outer banks. In addition, the two nations mutually consented in 1899 to partition Samoa, and in 1901 Britain signed the Hay-Pauncefote Treaty renouncing all joint rights with the United States to an Isthmian Canal. Although disagreements were to arise later, Campbell notes that the Anglo-American understanding achieved in this period created a firm and enduring basis for the relations of the two nations in the 20th century.

1604. Gelber, Lionel M. America in Britain's place; the leadership of the West and Anglo-American unity. New York, Praeger [1961] 356 p. (Books that matter)     61–11059 E744.G45

A Canadian's analysis of Anglo-American unity, written in the light of the shift in Western leadership from Britain to the United States since World War II. Constructively critical toward both countries, this work attempts to set American policies in contemporary perspective. The author notes the deep-rooted capacity of the two countries for working together and sees in their unity the basic element in the Western alliance. While allowing for divergence in attitudes and interpretation between London and Washington, Gelber demonstrates, through his discussion of the Hungarian and Suez crises in 1956, the dangers inherent in any wide misunderstanding. Another book dealing with much the same theme is Herbert G. Nicholas' *Britain and the U.S.A.* (Baltimore, Johns Hopkins Press, 1963. 191 p. The Albert Shaw lectures on diplomatic history, 1961). In *The Debatable Alliance* (London, New York, Oxford University Press, 1964. 130 p. Chatham House essays, 3), Coral Bell, an Australian, considers the Anglo-American relationship as an element in the central international balance of power.

1605. Perkins, Bradford. Prologue to war; England and the United States, 1805–1812. Berkeley, University of California Press, 1961. 457 p.     61–14018 E357.P66

"Notes on the sources": p. 439–446. Bibliographical footnotes.

1606. Perkins, Bradford. Castlereagh and Adams; England and the United States, 1812–1823. Berkeley, University of California Press, 1964. 364 p.     64–19696 E358.P4

Includes bibliographical references.

Two of three volumes that the author has devoted to the study of Anglo-American relations in the critical 30 years after 1795. The initial volume, *The First Rapprochement* (Philadelphia, University of Pennsylvania Press, 1955. 257 p.), dealt with the 10-year period of generally happy relations between the two countries following ratification of Jay's Treaty. The second and third volumes are organized around the central theme of America's search for "national respectability and true independence from Europe." Although accepting the common interpretation that the War of 1812 finally erupted after repeated British violations of American sovereignty on the high seas, Perkins contends that too little attention has been given to the influences of national pride, sensitivity, and frustration. His argument is bolstered by evidence from many heretofore unexploited British sources, especially newspapers. As America groped for identity after the end of the war, England demonstrated an increasing willingness to accept the former colony as a truly independent and sovereign nation. Perkins maintains that both countries, wary of ambitious, autocratic Europe, recognized the mutual benefits to be gained from reconciliation. Through the capable and bold diplomacy of Castlereagh and Adams, a new relationship of cooperation was built.

1607. Winks, Robin W. Canada and the United States: the Civil War years. Baltimore, Johns Hopkins Press [1960] xviii, 430 p.     60–14699 E469.W5

"A note on sources": p. 382–397. Bibliographical footnotes.

Writing on a virtually ignored aspect of Civil War diplomacy, the author intersperses scenes of Confederate intriguers sipping mint juleps in Montreal with general analyses of Canadian and American attitudes and their effects on the delicate problems of Anglo-American relations. Of special impact was a southern guerrilla raid on St. Albans, Maine, launched from across the Canadian border. The book also deals with various aspects of British colonial administration and with the consolidation of Canada as a nation. John S. Dickey has edited for the American Assembly a concise background study on historical and contemporary American-Canadian relations, *The United States and Canada* (Englewood Cliffs, N.J., Prentice-Hall [1964] 184 p. A Spectrum book, S–AA–12). A narrower period is investigated by Robert C. Brown in *Canada's National Policy, 1883–1900* (Princeton, N.J., Princeton University Press, 1964. 436 p.), which places heavy emphasis on Canadian domestic politics but treats diplomacy as well.

## Av. RUSSIA

1608. Kennan, George F. Soviet-American relations, 1917–1920. Princeton, N.J., Princeton University Press, 1956–58. 2 v. illus.     56–8382 E183.8.R9K4

Includes bibliographies.

CONTENTS.—v. 1. Russia leaves the war.—v. 2. The decision to intervene.

An intricate appraisal of Soviet-American diplomatic relations in a critical period. The initial volume deals with events between the November Revolution of 1917 and Russia's final departure from the war in March 1918, following the Brest-Litovsk peace agreement with Germany. Kennan states that, failing to understand the true motivations, needs, and intent of the Bolsheviks, the United States and the Western Allies maneuvered to keep the Russians in the war as the Russians in turn sought an expedient peace which would permit them to consolidate their position within. Volume 2 deals with the first consolidation of the Communist forces, British intervention, Japanese activities in Siberia, the saga of the Czech Legion, and finally the decision of the United States to send troops into Russia. This decision, asserts Kennan, was made principally in deference to the pressures of the Western Allies against the better judgment of President Wilson. Although ostensibly directed against possible German encroachment, the intervention assumed an anti-Bolshevik character and laid the foundations of relations between the West and Russia for the next 25 years and beyond. Kennan's *Russia and the West Under Lenin and Stalin* (Boston, Little, Brown [1961] 411 p.) is a comprehensive history of these relations. In *The Ignorant Armies* (New York, Harper [1960] 232 p.), Ernest M. Halliday describes the experience of U.S. troops in Russia during 1918 and argues that the commitment was both unwitting and unfortunate, since Allied intent to intervene in Russian internal affairs must have been evident to Wilson, if not to other American leaders.

## Avi. OTHER EUROPEAN NATIONS

1609. Beloff, Max. The United States and the unity of Europe. Washington, Brookings Institution [1963] 124 p.
63–15630 D1065.U5B4
Includes bibliography.

In this concise study the author describes the main currents of U.S. official policy and public opinion concerning the movement toward an integrated European community since World War II. The central force of this concerted effort on the part of France, Germany, Italy, and the Benelux nations was derived from three initial arrangements: the European Coal and Steel Community, the European Economic Community, and the European Atomic Energy Community. According to Beloff, American opinion toward European union moved through fluctuating phases until 1962, when a position of clear commitment to continental integration was assumed.

1610. Blumenthal, Henry. A reappraisal of Franco-American relations, 1830–1871. Chapel Hill, University of North Carolina Press [1959] xiv, 255 p.
59–65128 E183.8.F8B55
Bibliography: p. [212]–242.

"The myth of the uninterrupted historic friendship between France and the United States has been perpetuated in spite of the overwhelming evidence against it." Using this idea as his main theme, the author explores the diplomatic history of Franco-American relations from the July Revolution in France through the American Civil War and the Maximilian affair, ending with the neutral stance of the United States during the Franco-Prussian War. A growing rivalry, chiefly commercial in nature but heightened by secondary ideological and religious suspicions, impelled the two countries to the brink of war on several occasions. Influential in this increasingly negative relationship was the competitiveness of the other European powers: Britain, Russia, and the emerging German nation.

1611. De Conde, Alexander. Entangling alliance; politics & diplomacy under George Washington. Durham, N.C., Duke University Press, 1958. xiv, 536 p.
58–8500 E311.D4
Bibliographical footnotes.

An extensive monograph centering on the American alliance with France during President Washington's administration. Through a synthesis of the themes of foreign policy and domestic politics, the author shows how the early bonds of friendship between the two countries were weakened and destroyed, bringing the nations close to war. At the same time, this heavily documented study details the partisan response of French supporters in America to the Hamilton-inspired, British-oriented policy, a conflict which helped to lay the foundations for the formation of political parties. The roles of Jefferson, Madison, and Monroe are analyzed with particular care.

1612. Kertesz, Stephen D., ed. The fate of East Central Europe: hopes and failures of American foreign policy. Notre Dame, Ind., University of Notre Dame Press, 1956. 436 p. (International studies of the Committee on International Relations, University of Notre Dame)
56–9731 D376.U6K4
Bibliographical footnotes.

Although Americans have long maintained a sympathetic concern for the fate of Central Europe, this region has been historically regarded as remote from the national interest. As a result, Kertesz maintains, "the United States has seldom had a comprehensive foreign policy for East Central Europe." The authors whose works are included in this volume examine the breadth and scope of American policy in the area through the years, the post-1945 political history of the individual countries, the economic problems between the Soviet and non-Soviet worlds, and economic trends in the "captive countries." Attention is also given to earlier postwar relations between the Soviet bloc and non-Soviet areas. Contemporary U.S. efforts in the region are examined by John C. Campbell in *American Policy Toward Communist Eastern Europe: The Choices Ahead* (Minneapolis, University of Minnesota Press [1965] 136 p.). In the 1963–64 Elihu Root lectures, *On Dealing With the Communist World* (New York, Published for the Council on Foreign Relations by Harper & Row [1964] 57 p.), George F. Kennan discusses pertinent considerations of an American-Soviet coexistence policy in central Europe.

## Avii. LATIN AMERICA: GENERAL

1613. Munro. Dana G. Intervention and dollar diplomacy in the Caribbean, 1900–1921. Princeton, N.J., Princeton University Press, 1964. 553 p.                              63–18647  F1418.M92
Bibliographical footnotes.
"The problems that confronted the United States in the Caribbean in the first two decades were much like the problems that confront us there today." Within the framework of the disorder and economic backwardness which existed in these unstable Latin nations, the author traces the evolution of the United States intervention policy in the early 20th century. Maintaining that the motivations were more political than economic, he examines pertinent aspects of the Roosevelt Corollary: the military occupation of Nicaragua, Haiti, and the Dominican Republic; Wilson's doctrine of nonrecognition of revolutionary governments; and the use of dollar persuasion. Access to Department of State records and Presidential papers of the time greatly facilitated this study of the effects of U.S. policy on diplomatic relations in the Western Hemisphere.

## Aviii. LATIN AMERICA: INDIVIDUAL

1614. Carey, James C. Peru and the United States, 1900–1962. [Notre Dame, Ind.] University of Notre Dame Press, 1964. 243 p. (International studies of the Committee on International Relations, University of Notre Dame)
                              64–23666  E183.8.P4C3
Includes bibliographical references.
Relations with Peru are examined as representing a middle ground in the development of U.S. policy toward Latin American countries. Rather than offering a recital of treaty negotiations, the author reviews the history of both public and private activities, between which, he notes, there has been no distinct line. According to Carey, the incidents during

Vice President Richard M. Nixon's 1958 visit to Peru, at which time he was subjected to demonstrations of hostility against the United States, represented a turning point in the course of relations between the two countries. The Peruvian unrest, in Carey's view, was generated by the longstanding need for internal reform and by heavy U.S. investment control in the economy. It is noted that, a year before the Nixon visit, the newspaper *El Mundo* called upon the U.S. Government to talk less lyrically and act more forcefully with respect to an economic program to help eliminate misery in Peru so that the chances of communist growth would be lessened.

1615. Clendenen, Clarence C. The United States and Pancho Villa; a study in unconventional diplomacy. Ithaca, N.Y., Published for the American Historical Association [by] Cornell University Press [1961] 352 p. illus.
                              61–18097  F1234.C64  1961
Bibliography: p. 323–339.
Choosing not to emphasize the more colorful and romantic aspects of Villa's life, the author regards the Mexican revolutionary leader as one whose activities and policies affected events far beyond the borders of his own country. The Mexican revolution and its leaders are treated primarily for their impact on the formulation and conduct of U.S. external policy. The elements of President Wilson's policy of "watchful waiting" toward Mexico, coinciding with his efforts to keep the United States neutral during the early years of World War I, are traced in the tangled and uncertain diplomatic relations south of the border. From contemporary interviews, news correspondents, and diplomatic and consular archives, the author has drawn the materials which he uses to examine the sources of Villa's influence and to interpret the motives and designs behind his varied relationships with U.S. envoys. The American response to such issues as expropriation, intervention, and recognition is placed within the context of the larger Wilsonian foreign policy. The author strongly suggests — while admitting that the evidence is circumstantial — that because of the disturbed relations between the United States and Mexico, Germany was in some measure encouraged to embark upon its policy of unrestricted submarine warfare.

1616. Peterson. Harold F. Argentina and the United States, 1810–1960. [Albany] State University of New York; [University Publishers, New York, sole distributors] 1964. xxii, 627 p. illus.                    62–21414  E183.8.A7P46
Bibliography: p. 553–582.

According to the author, the dominant characteristic of a century and a half of relationships between Argentina and the United States has been more often rivalry and estrangement than friendship and cooperation. He describes the development of these discordant relations in detail, stressing conflicts over economic competition, the infiltration of ideological totalitarianism into Argentina, and the recent failure of American diplomacy to construct a system of inter-American solidarity.

1617. Pike, Fredrick B. Chile and the United States, 1880–1962; the emergence of Chile's social crisis and the challenge to United States diplomacy. [Notre Dame, Ind.] University of Notre Dame Press, 1963. 466 p. (International studies of the Committee on International Relations, University of Notre Dame) 63–9097 E183.8.C4P5
Bibliographical footnotes.
Citing Chile as unique in Latin America for its history of political stability, this interpretive account begins at 1880 because, according to the author, diplomatic relations between Chile and the United States were relatively unimportant before that date. Through 1933, the discussion is devoted to conferences, minor incidents, and treaty exchanges. From 1933 to the 1960's, the study of Chilean internal development is emphasized, and great importance is attributed to the role of Chilean social ferment as an influence on relations with the United States.

## Aix. ASIA, AFRICA, AND THE MIDDLE EAST

1618. American Assembly. The United States and Africa. Edited by Walter Goldschmidt. Rev. ed. New York, Praeger [1963] xvi, 298 p. illus. 63–20154 DT38.A65 1963
Originally prepared as background reading for participants in the American Assembly, 1958.
Problems of the new African nations and U.S. policy toward them are discussed in this collection of essays. Noting the great diversity among the peoples and states of Africa and the pressures working upon them, the authors stress that a uniform policy toward the continent as a whole would be an unrealistic approach. An appendix provides a summary of operations of U.S. Government agencies, including the Department of State, the Agency for International Development, the U.S. Information Agency, and the Peace Corps, in Africa. The problems and U.S. alternatives in southern Africa are examined by Waldemar A. Nielsen in *African Battleline* (New York, Published for the Council on Foreign Relations by Harper & Row [1965] 155 p.

Policy book series of the Council on Foreign Relations).

1619. Darling, Frank C. Thailand and the United States. Washington, Public Affairs Press [1965] 243 p. 65–16717 E183.8.T4D3
Bibliography: p. 229–239.
An assessment of the influence of American foreign policy on the evolution of Thailand's political system since 1945. The author discusses the history of 20th-century constitutional government in the Southeast Asian nation, with emphasis on the struggle between civilian liberalism and military rule. Darling considers that U.S. policies have often had the effect of weakening civilian governments but concludes that much has been done to enhance Thailand's national security. The administration of foreign aid and the role of the Southeast Asia Treaty Organization (SEATO) are outlined and suggestions for future U.S. policies are offered.

1620. DeNovo, John A. American interests and policies in the Middle East, 1900–1939. Minneapolis, University of Minnesota Press [1963] 447 p. maps. 63–21129 DS63.2.U5D4
Bibliography: p. 397–410.

1621. Campbell, John C. Defense of the Middle East; problems of American policy. Rev. [i.e. 2d] ed. New York, Published for the Council on Foreign Relations by Harper, 1960. 400 p. illus. 60–9110 DS63.2.U5D3 1960
The Middle East was not an area of primary diplomatic involvement for the United States until the end of World War II. DeNovo contends, however, that important cultural and economic ties developed over four decades before the war and so conditioned the American approach as to complicate adjustments to a more serious commitment in the region after 1945. While the area was dominated by Ottoman rulers and by the European power struggle, official American activities were restricted to fostering and protecting the cultural and commercial interests of her citizens. After a brief venture into Middle Eastern politics following World War I, the United States acknowledged the area to be a British sphere of influence. A major exception was the strong American support given to an "open door" principle on oil exploitation. Campbell discusses U.S. diplomacy in the area since the end of World War II. With British and French power dramatically reduced, the United States assumed a larger role in time to encounter the emotions of rising nationalism and Arab hostility engendered by the Palestine issue. Campbell asserts that, as a newly emerging diplomatic leader in the Middle East, the United States fumbled for a policy which would

help maintain Western presence in this unstable area. He seeks a basis for successful American initiative, exploring questions of military policy, economic assistance, and conflict with the Soviet Union. *The United States and the Middle East* (Englewood Cliffs, N. J., Prentice-Hall [1964] 182 p. A Spectrum book), an American Assembly publication prepared under the editorial supervision of Georgiana G. Stevens, is of value for general background.

1622. Dulles, Foster Rhea. Yankees and samurai; America's role in the emergence of modern Japan: 1791–1900. New York, Harper & Row [1965] 275 p. illus.   65–20427   E183.8.J3D84
"Bibliographical notes": p. 255–268.

The year 1791 marked the first recorded contact between "the Red Hairs from a Land called America" and feudal Japan. It was not until 1853, however, that Commodore Matthew Perry anchored in Yedo (Tokyo) Bay and successfully opened the door to commercial and political intercourse between the two countries. The author relies on personal diaries and accounts of seamen, visitors, and diplomats, as well as official records and logs of the period, to relate the unusual and highly significant courtship that ultimately "helped shape the entire course of subsequent Far Eastern history." Emphasis is placed on cultural contact, and care is taken to separate legend from fact. A general history which brings the subject up to the time of the U.S. occupation following World War II is William L. Neumann's *America Encounters Japan; From Perry to MacArthur* (Baltimore, Johns Hopkins Press, 1963. 353 p. The Goucher College series).

1623. Evans, Laurence. United States policy and the partition of Turkey, 1914–1924. Baltimore, Johns Hopkins Press [1965] 437 p. (Johns Hopkins University. Studies in historical and political science, ser. 82, no. 2)
65–11660   E183.8.T8E9
Bibliography: p. 418–420.

Based on extensive investigation of official documents, memoirs, and personal papers of participants, this study is presented from the viewpoint of the President and the Secretary of State as the primary formulators of foreign policy. Evans traces the development of the U.S. position on the Middle East from complete noninvolvement during World War I to intense concern during the Peace Conference and back to noninvolvement following the Senate's rejection of the Versailles Treaty. He discusses in detail the relationships of the United States with the main protagonists: the major powers of Europe, the Turks, and the Arabs. President Wilson had a deep concern for the mandate solu-

tion in the Middle East and, according to Evans, performed exceptionally well on the matter at Paris. Nevertheless, the ultimate settlement was the product of European rather than Middle Eastern political factors. After 1920, the U.S. Department of State's interest was directed more toward an "open door" for commercial exploitation and the protection of rights for American citizens than toward the welfare of the former Turkish possessions.

1624. Fifield, Russell H. Southeast Asia in United States policy. New York, Published for the Council on Foreign Relations by Praeger [1963] 488 p.   63–20144   DS518.8.F48
"Bibliographical note": p. 441–472.

In this study of American policy in Southeast Asia since World War II, Fifield argues that the immediate problem is to mobilize effective opposition to the indirect aggression being waged against the nations there. At the same time, Communist China must be convinced that it cannot accomplish its major objective of ultimate supremacy in this area through the threat or use of force. Much of the book covers the background of a wide range of issues influencing U.S. policy, such as problems of economic growth and political stability in Southeast Asia, as well as the role of the Southeast Asia Treaty Organization (SEATO). Of particular note is the discussion projecting the future influence that Indian and Japanese political and economic growth might exert in counteracting aggression in the area. The role of the Soviet Union and Communist China in this region is summarized by Oliver Edmund Clubb in *The United States and the Sino-Soviet Bloc in Southeast Asia* (Washington, Brookings Institution [1962] 173 p.), where numerous alternative U.S. policies are suggested and briefly appraised. A detailed study of the policies of the Southeast Asian countries may be found in Russell H. Fifield's *The Diplomacy of Southeast Asia: 1945–1958* (New York, Harper [1958] 584 p.).

1625. Rappaport, Armin. Henry L. Stimson and Japan, 1931–33. Chicago, University of Chicago Press [1963] 238 p.
63–18847   E183.8.J3R3
"A note on the sources": p. 233–234. Bibliographical footnotes.

1626. Borg, Dorothy. The United States and the Far Eastern crisis of 1933–1938; from the Manchurian incident through the initial stage of the undeclared Sino-Japanese war. Cambridge, Harvard University Press, 1964. 674 p. (Harvard East Asian series, 14)
64–13421   DS784.B65   1964
Bibliography: p. [547]–561.

In summarizing a significant episode in the diplomatic origins of World War II, Rappaport attempts to explain why the United States and Great Britain did nothing to stop Japan in Manchuria between 1931 and 1933. He views the U.S. doctrine of nonrecognition as essentially "the pistol which, unhappily, was not loaded," concluding that the fault lay not with Stimson but with public opinion both in America and abroad. Neither here nor in Europe were people willing to become responsibly involved in the affairs of the Far East. Dorothy Borg examines the crucial years of American-Japanese relations between 1933 and 1938. Rejecting the frequently expressed allegation that Roosevelt's intransigence was a major cause of the breakdown of peaceful relations, she underscores the President's tendency to look for a means of reaching an understanding with Japan. At the same time, she demonstrates Roosevelt's clear concern over the threat of Japanese imperialism to international order and reveals his tendency toward the creation of a stiffer policy, which became increasingly manifest after the outbreak of the Sino-Japanese War in 1937.

1627. Taylor, George E. The Philippines and the United States: problems of partnership. New York, Published for the Council on Foreign Relations by Praeger [1964] 325 p.
64–12080 DS672.8.T3 1964
Bibliographical footnotes.

A history of U.S. relations with the Philippines as a U.S. colony and as an independent nation. Although several aspects of the experiment with colonialism were commendable, Taylor asserts that the American Government made no serious or effective effort to build a sound economic base for political democracy in the islands during its half century of rule. Thus, until Communist aggressions and con-

quests in Asia altered the American outlook and approach, the colonial policy was generally unsatisfactory and contributed to the serious economic and political crises which followed achievement of Philippine independence in 1946. The search for Philippine national identity, with its concomitant tensions between newly introduced democratic political institutions and traditional value systems, is viewed as the single most important problem affecting the two countries.

1628. Tsou, Tang. America's failure in China, 1941–50. [Chicago] University of Chicago Press [1963] 614 p. 63–13072 DS777.53.T866

According to the author, an unwillingness to use military power and an adherence to idealistic objectives formed the basis of U.S. policy in China. In turn, this dual policy was responsible for the misjudgments and faulty assumptions regarding the Nationalist Government, the Soviet Union, and the Chinese Communists and denied to America any chance for lasting success in China. The author was born and raised in China and received his Ph.D. degree in political science from the University of Chicago, where he later taught. The conception that American interests in China were not worth a war on the mainland, Tsou believes, had its roots in the tradition of the "open door." He emphasizes policy decisions which put limited military objectives above broad political goals, names Chiang as the single person most responsible for those decisions, and traces America's failures at each major stage. In an effort to promote a general understanding of contemporary problems and policies in the area, the American Assembly has issued *The United States and the Far East*, 2d ed. (Englewood Cliffs, N.J., Prentice-Hall [1962] 188 p. A Spectrum book, S–AA–6), edited by Willard L. Thorp.

# B. Foreign Relations

## Bi. ADMINISTRATION

1629. Dulles, Allen Welsh. The craft of intelligence. New York, Harper & Row [1963] 277 p. illus. 63–16507 UB270.D8
Bibliography: p. 265–267.

The author, a former director of the Central Intelligence Agency, traces the evolution of intelligence work from the Israelites in Canaan to the present. After justifying the creation and continuing work of the CIA, Dulles describes the collection

of information, counterintelligence methods, and administrative aspects. He also draws a composite picture of the American agent and devotes a chapter to defectors, whom he prefers to call volunteers, and the information they provide. Reflecting the American concern over communism, Dulles discusses the Soviet espionage network, the intelligence services of the European satellites and Red China, the utilization of intelligence by policymakers in the Departments of State and Defense, and the role of intelligence in the cold war era. By explaining the place of the CIA in the Government hierarchy and the controls and limitations on its activities, he attempts to refute charges that our intelligence system can become a threat to our freedoms.

1630. Dyer, Murray. The weapon on the wall; rethinking psychological warfare. Baltimore, Johns Hopkins Press [1959] 269 p.

59–14234 E744.D93

The author outlines the role and nature of psychological warfare, now used by many nations as a major instrument of foreign policy, and discusses its major premises and operating principles. The American people, he believes, have a distorted conception of this type of propaganda and thus are reluctant to accept it as an appropriate instrument of foreign relations. Striving to create a realistic perspective, Dyer traces the origins of psychological warfare, the difficulties presented by its use, and the requirements for developing it as an effective and responsible weapon. In *Strategic Psychological Operations and American Foreign Policy* ([Chicago] University of Chicago Press [1960] 243 p.), a study illustrated with case histories, Robert T. Holt and Robert W. Van de Velde also express the opinion that Americans have never fully understood the nature of psychological warfare.

1631. Graebner, Norman A., *ed.* An uncertain tradition; American Secretaries of State in the twentieth century. New York, McGraw-Hill, 1961. 341 p. (McGraw-Hill series in American history) 61–8654 E744.G7

Bibliography: p. 309–327.

A symposium of essays on the careers of 14 Secretaries of State, from John Hay to John Foster Dulles. The first essay, "The Year of Transition," sets the tone for the collection, depicting 1898 as a crucial turning point. In that year, the United States shifted from a relatively unblurred diplomatic tradition of 19th-century realism to a less easily characterized viewpoint. The new attitude was shaped on the one hand by the complexities of world politics and on the other by the American sense of moral obligation for the whole world. The essays vary according to the importance of each Secretary and the length of his term in office. Among the Secretaries included, in addition to Hay and Dulles, are Elihu Root, Robert Lansing, George Marshall, and Dean Acheson. A bibliographical note for each man is appended. A brief historical introduction to the office of Secretary of State is Alexander De Conde's *The American Secretary of State: An Interpretation* (New York, Praeger [1962] 182 p. Books that matter).

1632. Ilchman, Warren F. Professional diplomacy in the United States, 1779–1939; a study in administrative history. [Chicago] University of Chicago Press [1961] 254 p.

61–11991 JX1705.I4

"Bibliographical essays": p. 244–248. Bibliographical footnotes.

Part of a larger study by Ilchman on the growth of professional U.S. diplomacy, this volume traces the evolution of a career service for conducting foreign affairs. The diplomatic service is shown to have been characterized until the 1880's by the refusal of the Government either to consider overseas missions as permanent or to regard the members of a mission as part of a career diplomatic corps. As early as the 1860's, however, the demands of Civil War diplomacy and the later campaign for administrative reform in government caused a noticeable change. Ultimately, the emergence of the United States as a world power at the turn of the 19th century stimulated a professionalization of the service, which largely culminated in reorganization under the Rogers Act in 1924. Since then, democratization and specialization have been the characteristic trends. The contemporary organization and functions of the Department of State are examined by Robert E. Elder in *The Policy Machine* ([Syracuse, N.Y.] Syracuse University Press, 1960. 238 p.).

1633. Ransom, Harry H. Central intelligence and national security. Cambridge, Harvard University Press, 1958. xiv, 287 p.

58–12972 JK468.I6R3

Bibliography: p. 233–256.

Noting that "one simply can not apply to this subject the usual rigorous standards of data gathering and documentation," Ransom seeks to clarify the essential nature of a widely misunderstood field. In so doing, he describes the growth and function of intelligence as an aspect of U.S. national policy and investigates the complex organizational structure, which, in addition to the Central Intelligence Agency, includes a separate intelligence branch for each of the armed services and the Department of State and requires shared responsibilities with the National Security Agency, the Federal Bureau of Investigation, and the Atomic Energy Commission. Besides the problems of coordination that invariably arise, the author analyzes the delicate question of surveillance by Congress. Paul W. Blackstock concentrates on the theory and practice of covert political operations abroad in *The Strategy of Subversion* (Chicago, Quadrangle Books, 1964. 351 p.).

1634. Scott, Andrew M., *and* Raymond H. Dawson, *eds.* Readings in the making of American foreign policy. New York, Macmillan [1965] 551 p.     65–13587  E183.7.S39

Includes bibliographical references.

This volume brings together analytic essays on the formulation and execution of American foreign policy. The authors—some represented by other entries in this chapter—examine the problems of public opinion, pressure groups, and consensus within our system. The role of Congress is treated, as are the organization, functions, and responsibilities within the executive branch. The impact of military, intellectual, scientific, and research communities on policy is also investigated.

1635. Thompson, Kenneth W. American diplomacy and emergent patterns. [New York] New York University Press, 1962. 273 p. (James Stokes lectureship on politics, New York University, Stokes Foundation)

62–14654  JX1705.T47

Includes bibliography.

Maintaining that the patterns of American diplomacy are not fixed but evolving, Thompson attempts to determine what part of the Nation's past experience is relevant to the present. Topics discussed include the philosophy of diplomacy and politics, American professionalism, the flexible role of the Executive as outlined by the Constitution, and the evolution of diplomatic practice throughout the Nation's history. The last chapter is devoted to diplomacy in a changing world.

1636. Warren, Sidney. The President as world leader. Philadelphia, Lippincott [1964] 480 p.     64–22183  E744.W295

Bibliographical references included in "Chapter notes" (p. 439–457). Bibliography: p. 458–470.

The expansion of Presidential powers over the years has resulted primarily "from the impact of the great Presidents who gave the office new dimensions, invigorated it and provided a legacy that even weaker men could not dissipate." In the 20th century the expansion has occurred notably in the conduct of foreign affairs, according to the author. Beginning with the administration of Theodore Roosevelt, Warren examines the effect each President has had on this aspect of Executive power, particularly through his responses to specific international emergencies. He points out that, in the current era of almost perpetual crisis, a distinction can no longer be made between a wartime and a peacetime head of state.

## Bii. DEMOCRATIC CONTROL

1637. Carroll, Holbert N. The House of Representatives and foreign affairs. Pittsburgh, University of Pittsburgh [1958] 365 p.

58–10705  JK1319.C3

Bibliography: p. 351–357.

The Constitution assigns to the House of Representatives a much smaller role in foreign relations than is granted to the Senate. The author maintains, however, that the House, beginning in World War II, has assumed increased responsibilities. Much of this new power, he points out, has evolved out of the monetary needs created by complex international policies requiring legislative action. The purpose of this book is to analyze the nature of this expanding role and its influence on the formulation of U.S. foreign policy. A short history of the House precedes a thorough discussion of the organization and operation of its internal power structure. Particular importance is attached to the relationship between the Appropriations and the Foreign Affairs Committees. Two short chapters are devoted to the external relations of the House of Representatives with the Senate and the President.

1638. Cohen, Bernard C. The press and foreign policy. Princeton, N.J., Princeton University Press, 1963. 288 p.     63–12668  PN4745.C6

Bibliographical footnotes.

A systematic investigation of foreign affairs reporting in Washington, D.C., based on extensive interviews with reporters and foreign policy officials. The author emphasizes a basic conflict between the two groups. On the one hand, policymakers stress the need to conduct delicate negotiations in private; on the other, the press maintains the right of the people to be informed of the decisions being considered before they become irrevocable. The resulting climate of suspicion gives rise to reporting which is "spasmodic, piecemeal, impressionistic, and oversimplified, sometimes inaccurate and garbled." Although limited in scope, the book is a pioneer study in an increasingly important field.

1639. Crabb, Cecil V. Bipartisan foreign policy: myth or reality? Evanston, Ill., Row, Peterson [1957] 279 p.     57–11349  E744.C8

Bibliography: p. 264–270.

An examination of the intricate role played by party politics in the formulation of American foreign policy. Although agreeing that important programs would have failed at the outset without bipartisan support, the author contends that the advantages of such an approach may at times be outweighed by more serious disadvantages. Using case studies of major postwar programs developed on a bipartisan basis, Crabb discusses difficulties which are sometimes created by conducting foreign affairs in this manner. In *Senatorial Politics & Foreign Policy* ([Lexington] University of Kentucky Press [c1962] 214 p.), Malcolm E. Jewell seeks to illustrate the transformation that can occur in the voting records of both parties when the representative majority shifts from one party to the other.

1640. Robinson, James A. Congress and foreign policy-making; a study in legislative influence and initiative. Homewood, Ill., Dorsey Press, 1962. 262 p. (The Dorsey series in political science)　　　　62–11289　JK1081.R6
　Bibliography: p. 235–253.

The author states that at present the influence of Congress upon foreign policy is "primarily (and increasingly) one of legitimating and amending policies initiated by the executive." To a significant degree, according to Robinson, this situation is attributable to "the changing character of the information or intelligence needs in modern policy-making." This trend, he maintains, is not inevitable or irreversible, and as one means of offsetting it he suggests a more centralized leadership in the House and Senate. Reviewing congressional involvement in major foreign policy decisions since the 1930's, he discusses the concept and use of congressional influence, legislative-executive liaison on foreign policy, and the communications network between Congress and the Department of State.

1641. Thomson, Charles A., *and* Walter H. C. Laves. Cultural relations and U.S. foreign policy. Bloomington, Indiana University Press [1963] 227 p.　　　　63–7167　E744.5.T5 1963
　Bibliographical footnotes.

Evolving largely from an initial effort in 1938 to counteract Nazi-Fascist penetration in Latin America, cultural exchange is a rapidly growing facet of U.S. foreign relations. This book examines both the evolution of the Government's programs and the role that cultural activities play in American diplomacy. The authors discuss the often heated debates surrounding the programs, which by their nature tend to generate apprehensions and misunderstandings. The final chapter suggests guidelines to increase future effectiveness. Philip H. Coombs briefly surveys the same subject in *The Fourth Dimension of Foreign Policy; Educational and Cultural Affairs* (New York, Published for the Council on Foreign Relations by Harper & Row [1964] 158 p. Policy books).

## Biii. POLICIES

1642. Bloomfield, Lincoln P. The United Nations and U.S. foreign policy; a new look at the national interest. Boston, Little, Brown [1960] 276 p.　　　　60–15453　JX1977.2.U5B62

A study initiated for the purpose of reevaluating the United Nations from the standpoint of U.S. national interests. Among these interests are the broad categories of political and military security, stability and welfare, and world order. The author finds that there are important political advantages to be gained by supporting programs of the world organization which are consistent with overall American policies. The national interest is also central to the theme of Richard N. Gardner's *In Pursuit of World Order; U.S. Foreign Policy and International Organization* (New York, Praeger [1964] 263 p.). Gardner sees in the United Nations a unique opportunity for debate, negotiation, and action. In *United Nations and U.S. Foreign Economic Policy* (Homewood, Ill., R. D. Irwin, 1962. 235 p. Irwin series in economics), Benjamin H. Higgins discusses multilateral versus bilateral economic aid for underdeveloped countries and urges the channeling of more American aid through the agencies of the United Nations.

1643. Kissinger, Henry A. Nuclear weapons and foreign policy. New York, Published for the Council on Foreign Relations by Harper, 1957. 455 p. illus.　　　　57–7801　UA23.K49

"Mastery of the challenges of the nuclear age will depend on our ability to combine physical and psychological factors, to develop weapon systems which do not paralyze our will, and to devise strategies which permit us to shift the risks of counteraction to the other side." The author contends that, with the nature of warfare vastly changed by the technology of nuclear weapons, the basic challenge to the United States is to formulate a sound strategic doctrine. Topics discussed include the dilemma of American security, all-out war and limited war, the contemporary challenge to diplomacy, the obsolescence of some traditional military concepts, the complexities of disarmament and international inspection, and Sino-Soviet strategic thought.

1644. Osgood, Robert E. NATO, the entangling alliance. [Chicago] University of Chicago Press [1962] 416 p.　　　　62–8348　UA646.3.O8
　Bibliographical footnotes.

A history of the North Atlantic Treaty Organization from its inception in 1949, this study examines one phase of contemporary U.S. foreign policy as transformed by the changing conditions of the postwar era. Osgood notes that new political, economic, and military developments have either invalidated or introduced complexities into the original assumptions upon which the NATO alliance was built. Among these changes are the economic resurgence of Europe, the active reassertion of separate European purposes, and the growth of Soviet power. With these in mind, the author attempts to define the role of military power in a nuclear age and to assess the alliance within the overall political and military purposes of the West. Recognizing the continued need for allied cooperation, Osgood asks for an enlarged contribution from Europe on behalf of its own defense. A study which presents both American and European views on the major issues confronting the Atlantic community is *NATO in Quest of Cohesion* (New York, Published for the Hoover Institution on War, Revolution, and Peace by Praeger [1965] 476 p. Hoover Institution publications), edited by Karl H. Cerny and Henry W. Briefs. The problems surrounding effective uses of military power in the nuclear age are examined by Osgood in *Limited War; the Challenge to American Strategy* ([Chicago] University of Chicago Press [1957] 315 p.).

1645. Spanier, John W. American foreign policy since World War II. Rev. ed. New York, Praeger [1962] 275 p.
      62–13739 E744.S8 1962
 Bibliography: p. 259–267.
This critical analysis of U.S. policy in the cold war is based on the thesis that an intense distaste for power politics has hindered an adequate response by American policymakers to the ideological, social, and strategic challenges of our age. According to the author, this underlying national belief that power is an immoral, antidemocratic instrument has produced an inadequate answer to the Soviet threat of expansionism. Supporting this thesis, Spanier examines decisions and actions relevant to such policy issues as the Truman Doctrine, the North Atlantic Treaty Organization, the Korean War, the Middle East, Cuba, and Berlin. As a solution, the author advocates a foreign policy which recognizes the mutual relationship between power and diplomacy and a new attempt to understand the social changes underlying the "revolution of rising expectations" throughout the developing areas. In a collection of essays entitled *The Impasse of American Foreign Policy* ([Chicago] University of Chicago Press [1962] 312 p.), the second volume of *Politics in the Twentieth Century,* Hans J. Morgenthau criticizes U.S. policy for remaining static since the Korean War and failing to meet the new circum-

stances of the Soviet challenges in various areas of the world. In *The United States in the World Arena* (New York, Harper [1960] 568 p. Massachusetts Institute of Technology. Center for International Studies. American project series) Walt W. Rostow seeks to evaluate the manner in which the Nation's overall evolution has affected its military and foreign policy performance over the last 25 years.

## Biv. ECONOMIC POLICY

1646. Feis, Herbert. Foreign aid and foreign policy. New York, St. Martin's Press [1964] 246 p.     64–18364 HC60.F35
 Bibliographical footnotes.
The author discusses the need for comprehensive planning in American foreign-aid programs, emphasizing the fact that achievement of economic growth in the developing areas requires fundamental social changes as well as capital investment. Feis provides a general review of the evolution of foreign aid and notes a growing affiliation between U.S. aid and diplomacy, showing the complexities involved in pursuing political aims while maintaining feasible and balanced economic programs. In *The New Statecraft; Foreign Aid in American Foreign Policy* ([Chicago] University of Chicago Press [1960] 246 p.), George Liska counsels the use of foreign aid in such a way that optimum control will rest with the aid-giving country. Edward S. Mason, in *Foreign Aid and Foreign Policy* (New York, Published for the Council on Foreign Relations by Harper & Row [1964] 118 p. The Elihu Root lectures, 1962-63), outlines basic aid principles and gives a concise description and interpretation of the Alliance for Progress program in action.

1647. Ranis, Gustav, *ed.* The United States and the developing economies. New York, Norton [1964] xx, 174 p. (Problems of the modern economy)     63–21712 HC60.R2
 Bibliography: p. 173–174.
A series of essays which investigate the rationale, significance, and effectiveness of foreign-aid programs. Following a general descriptive introduction, "The Poor Nations," by Barbara Ward, the book is divided into three major parts: "The Developing Economies: A New Commitment," "Aid Instruments and Allocation Criteria," and "The Economics of Foreign Assistance." In addition to the contributions of such authorities as Milton Friedman, Robert Asher, and Thomas Schelling, a selection is included from the 1963 Clay Committee Report examining American assistance programs. In *Witness for AID* (Boston, Houghton Mifflin,

1964. 273 p.), Frank M. Coffin, former Deputy Administrator of the Agency for International Development, notes the continuing confusion over the purpose of foreign aid in U.S. policy and stresses the vital need for a working consensus to back the program.

# X

# Military History and the Armed Forces

Bотн the quality and variety of the books chosen for this chapter reflect the growing interest in military affairs evident since the end of World War II. From university study centers, the historical units of the armed services, and the commercial presses, come books which define and clarify the American military establishment: what it has been, what it is, and what it may become.

Of the three gaps in the literature that were noted in the 1960 *Guide,* two remain unfilled in spite of the current upsurge in scholarship. There is still no adequate general history of the Army or comprehensive operational history of World War I. But the military history of the Revolutionary War, comparatively neglected before, has recently begun to receive attention.

The arrangement of the sections follows the order of the 1960 *Guide,* with two exceptions: a section on the Air Force (D) has been added; and in what is now Section E, Wars of the United States, a new subdivision covers the Korean war. Because of a dearth of appropriate material in the period covered by this *Supplement,* no subsection is devoted to the Vietnam conflict. As in the 1960 *Guide,* this chapter includes more works on the Civil War than on any other, indicating the continuing fascination with this era in the Nation's history.

## A. General Works

1648. Hammond, Paul Y. Organizing for de-
     defense; the American military establishment
in the twentieth century. Princeton, N.J., Princeton University Press, 1961. 403 p.
                     61–7398   UB23.H3
Bibliographical footnotes.

This study of defense administration relates the organization and functioning of the armed services departments to their public and political environment. Major emphasis is placed on the roles of Congress and the President in influencing the structure of military administration. The author covers organizational changes and developments from about 1900 to 1960. Particular attention is devoted to departmental operations during World Wars I and II, when important principles of administration were tested, and to the unification of the services in the Department of Defense in 1947. A briefer work on defense organization is *The Management of Defense; Organization and Control of the U.S. Armed Services* (Baltimore, Johns Hopkins Press [1964] 228 p.), by John C. Ries.

1649. Huntington, Samuel P. The soldier and the state; the theory and politics of civil-military relations. Cambridge, Belknap Press of Harvard University Press, 1957. xiii, 534 p.

57–6349    UA23.H95

Bibliographical references included in "Notes" (p. 469–517).

The author looks at civil-military relations as a system which involves a complex equilibrium between the authority of military and nonmilitary groups in a society. The premise of the book is that a general theory of the nature and purpose of military institutions can be used to analyze the civil-military relations of any society and to determine the degree to which those relations affect military security. The first part of the book contains a theoretical and historical discussion of military institutions and the state in the Western World. In the second and third parts the author applies his theories to a historical analysis of civil-military relations in the United States. His focus is on the officer corps, whose relation to the state, he believes, reflects the general relations between the military and the rest of society. In *The Civilian and the Military* (New York, Oxford University Press, 1956. 340 p.), Arthur A. Ekirch examines the traditional American tendency to oppose a conscript army and a large military establishment.

1650. Janowitz, Morris. The professional soldier, a social and political portrait. Glencoe, Ill., Free Press [1960] 464 p.    60–7090  UB147.J3

Includes bibliography.

One of the few sociologists to study the American military environment, Janowitz examines the military profession as it has evolved during the first half of this century. Using sociological concepts, he studies the officer corps as a professional group and analyzes the social origins of the officers as well as their career motivations, political beliefs, and style of life. There is a new emphasis, he states, on the military professionals' capacity for critical judgment. Furthermore, developments in technology have created the need for an increasing number of technical specialists in the military. Overall, the differences between military and nonmilitary organizations have been greatly reduced.

1651. Kaufmann, William W. The McNamara strategy. New York, Harper & Row [1964] 339 p.    64–12672  UA23.K37

Bibliographical references included in "Notes" (p. 320–334).

Under President Kennedy, Robert McNamara, as Secretary of Defense, accomplished significant changes in defense administration and policy. His strategic concept of "multiple options" emphasized preparation for both nuclear and nonnuclear war. Through the application of a "planning-programming-budgeting system" within the Defense Department, he increased the degree of control which the Secretary could maintain over the formulation and execution of defense policy and initiated a large-scale program of cost reduction. Kaufmann reviews Secretary McNamara's tenure throughout the Kennedy administration, quoting at length from the Secretary's speeches as well as from those of other officials. Arnold A. Rogow's *James Forrestal, a Study of Personality, Politics, and Policy* (New York, Macmillian [°1963] 397 p.) is a "psychological portrait" of the Secretary of the Navy who became the first Secretary of Defense.

1652. Millis, Walter. Arms and men; a study in American military history. New York, Putnam [1956] 382 p.    56–10240  E181.M699

Bibliography: p. 367–371.

A commentary on the history of American military policy. The author concludes that military force can no longer be "brought rationally to bear upon the decision of any of the political, economic, emotional or philosophical issues by which men still remain divided." *American Military Policy, Its Development Since 1775*, 2d ed. (Harrisburg, Pa., Military Service Division, Stackpole Co. [1961] 548 p.), by C. Joseph Bernardo and Eugene H. Bacon, is a slightly revised edition of no. 3643 in the 1960 *Guide*. Two other pertinent works are *American Defense Policy in Perspective, From Colonial Times to the Present* (New York, Wiley [1965] 377 p.), a collection of readings edited by Raymond G. O'Connor, and *The Minute Man in Peace and War; a History of the National Guard* (Harrisburg, Pa., Stackpole Co. [1964] 585 p.), by Jim D. Hill.

1653. Millis, Walter. Arms and the state; civil-military elements in national policy, by Walter Millis, with Harvey C. Mansfield and Harold Stein. New York, Twentieth Century Fund, 1958. 436 p.    58–11837  E744.M56

Bibliography: p. 415–420.

This volume is part of a Twentieth Century Fund study of civil-military relations in the United States. The period from 1930 to the end of World War II is discussed by Mansfield and Stein. The postwar period is treated by Millis, who describes defense reorganization, the development of the cold war, and the war in Korea. *American Civil-Military Decisions; a Book of Case Studies* ([University, Ala.] Published in cooperation with the Inter-University Case Program by University of Alabama Press, 1963. 705 p.), edited by Harold Stein, is another volume in The Twentieth Century Fund's project. It offers discussions of separate incidents exemplifying civilian and military participation in the process of decisionmaking. In *The Common Defense; Strategic Programs in National Politics* (New York, Columbia University Press, 1961. 500 p.), Samuel P. Huntington analyzes changes in American military policy between 1945 and 1960.

1654. U.S. *Military Academy, West Point. Dept. of Military Art and Engineering.* The West Point atlas of American wars. Chief editor: Vincent J. Esposito. With an introductory letter by Dwight D. Eisenhower. New York, Praeger [1959] 2 v. col. maps. (Books that matter)

59–7452   G1201.S1U5   1959

Includes bibliographies.

CONTENTS.—v. 1. 1689–1900.—v. 2. 1900–1953. Designed initially for use by cadets at the U.S. Military Academy, this atlas provides detailed maps of battles and campaigns of all wars, up to and including the Korean war, in which the United States has taken part. Although American actions are featured, each war is treated as a whole, and engagements in which the United States did not participate, as well as those undertaken with allies, are traced. Because air and naval operations do not lend themselves to the type of portrayal used in this work, the maps, with few exceptions, depict the operations of land forces.

## B. The Army

1655. Dupuy, Richard Ernest. The compact history of the United States Army. Illustrated by Gil Walker. New and rev. ed. New York, Hawthorn Books [1961] 318 p. illus.

61–7827   E181.D78   1961

Bibliography: p. 297–300.

Colonel Dupuy brings to his work many years of experience in the Army and writes with enthusiasm about his subject. The book covers, in a popular fashion, the various wars and campaigns in which the United States has been engaged. *Uncommon Valor; the Exciting Story of the Army* (Chicago, Rand McNally [1964] 512 p.), edited by James M. Merrill, contains a selection of first-hand accounts of army life from 1775 to 1962, culled from such sources as personal letters, diaries, official correspondence, and unit histories. *A Guide to the Military Posts of the United States, 1789–1895* (Madison, State Historical Society of Wisconsin, 1964. 178 p.), by Francis P. Prucha, consists mainly of regional maps with post locations and a catalog of the posts established during this period.

1656. Ginzberg, Eli, *and others.* The ineffective soldier; lessons for management and the nation. New York, Columbia University Press, 1959. 3 v. illus.   59–7701   UB323.G5   1959

Includes bibliographies.

CONTENTS.—1. The lost divisions.—2. Breakdown and recovery.—3. Patterns of performance.

Prepared by the staff of the Conservation of Human Resources Project at Columbia University. A major objective was to discover why, during World War II, about 2.5 million men were rejected from the Army or, having been accepted, were then prematurely separated because of mental or emotional disorders. Another significant objective was to examine the postwar adjustment of these men and to seek to determine why some men recovered early, others after a delay, and some not at all. The study was based primarily on medical and personnel records, and the volumes include both statistical data and case material.

1657. Progue, Forrest C. George C. Marshall. [v. 1] Education of a general, 1880-1939. With the editorial assistance of Gordon Harrison. Foreword by Omar N. Bradley. New York, Viking Press [1963] xvii, 421 p. illus.

63–18373   E745.M37P6

The first volume of a projected three-volume biography of George C. Marshall (1880–1959), who was chairman of the Allied Chiefs of Staff during World War II and who served as Secretary of State and Secretary of Defense under President Truman. It covers the first 60 years of Marshall's life, during which time he carried out various military assignments in the Philippines, France, China, and the United States. It ends with his appointment as U.S. Army Chief of Staff in 1939. *Soldier: The Memoirs of Matthew B. Ridgway* (New York, Harper [1956] 371 p.), by General Ridgway as told to Harold H. Martin, is an autobiographical account of 38 years of military service, ending with the general's retirement as U.S. Army Chief of Staff in 1955.

1658. Risch, Erna. Quartermaster support of the Army; a history of the corps, 1775–1939. Washington, Quartermaster Historian's Office, Office of the Quartermaster General, 1962. xvii, 796 p. illus.     62–60012    UC34.R5
  Bibliography: p. [749]–766.
Prepared as part of the Quartermaster Corps' historical program, this substantial volume traces the growth and evolution of the Corps from 1775, the date of its establishment, to 1939. Miss Risch shows how an organization that was to a large extent civilian in character developed into a militarized corps with permanent headquarters in Washington. The author also emphasizes the Quartermaster Corps' support operations during five major wars, from the Revolution through World War I. Another contribution to Army administrative history is *The Story of the U.S. Army Signal Corps* (New York, F. Watts [1965] 305 p. The Watts

landpower library), edited by Max L. Marshall. A popular account of the artillery is Fairfax D. Downey's *Sound of the Guns; the Story of American Artillery From the Ancient and Honorable Company to the Atom Cannon and Guided Missile* (New York, D. McKay Co. [1956] 337 p.).

1659. Weigley, Russell F. Towards an American army; military thought from Washington to Marshall. New York, Columbia University Press, 1962. 297 p.     62–15388    UA25.W4
  Bibliography: p. [277]–285.
A history of ideas concerning the formation of an American army. The author discusses and contrasts the concepts of a number of men, mostly in military life, from the time of the American Revolution to the mid-20th century. The debate has centered primarily on whether the United States should maintain a professional army or rely on a well-trained citizen militia, and Weigley shows that this problem has not yet been fully resolved. Stephen E. Ambrose's *Upton and the Army* (Baton Rouge, Louisiana State University Press, 1964. 190 p.) is a study of Emory Upton (1839–1881), a career officer whose writings had a profound influence on the development of a modern army in the United States. The early years of the War Department are described in *The Department of War, 1781–1795* ([Pittsburgh] University of Pittsburgh Press [1962] 287 p.), by Harry M. Ward.

## C. The Navy

1660. Albion, Robert G., *and* Robert H. Connery. Forrestal and the Navy. With the collaboration of Jennie Barnes Pope. New York, Columbia University Press, 1962. 359 p. illus.
    62–9974    E748.F68A6
  Bibliography: p. [335]–342.
An account of the career of James Forrestal (1892–1949) as Secretary of the Navy from 1944 to 1947. Combining biographical material with naval administrative history, the authors present a case study of a civilian executive in charge of a military service. They discuss the Navy Department and Navy organization during this period and also analyze the problems of interservice coordination and unified theater commands in World War II. Forrestal's views on postwar military preparedness, as well as his role in the movement for a unification of the armed forces, are examined. When the new position of Secretary of Defense was created in 1947, he was chosen to fill it.

1661. Braisted, William R. The United States Navy in the Pacific, 1897–1909. Austin, University of Texas Press [1958] 282 p. fold. map (in pocket)     57–12530    E182.B73
  Bibliography: p. 247–262.
The author examines the relation between American naval and diplomatic policies in the Pacific from the beginning of the Spanish-American War through the end of Theodore Roosevelt's second administration. During this expansionist period, the United States, pursuing its economic and strategic interests in the Far East, formulated basic foreign policies which were to make increasing demands on the Navy in the years to come. In *Prelude to Pearl Harbor; the United States Navy and the Far East, 1921–1931* (Columbia, University of Missouri Press [1963] 212 p.), Gerald E. Wheeler describes the manner in which the Navy was readied for action during the 1920's and the development of its Far Eastern policies during that period. Robert E. John-

son's *Thence Round Cape Horn; the Story of United States Naval Forces on Pacific Station, 1818–1923* (Annapolis, United States Naval Institute [1963] 276 p.) chronicles the increasing importance of the eastern Pacific Ocean to the Navy and discusses the policies responsible for the Navy's presence there.

1662. Heinl, Robert D. Soldiers of the sea; the United States Marine Corps, 1775–1962. Foreword by B. H. Liddell Hart. Annapolis, United States Naval Institute [1962] 692 p. illus.
61–18078 VE23.H4
Bibliography: p. 649–659.
Combining sea, land, and air action, the Marine Corps represents the prototype of an integrated fighting force. Colonel Heinl traces the evolution of the Corps from its origin in 1775 to 1962. The Marines have served in every major war in American history and in numerous minor encounters and skirmishes. The author amply covers their activities, especially in World War II. Taking a broad approach to military history, he deals with "planning, policy, command, administration, traditions and personalities," as well as with battle accounts. A more condensed general history of the Marines, written by Philip N. Pierce and Frank O. Hough, is *The Compact History of the United States Marine Corps,* new and rev. ed. (New York, Hawthorn Books [1964] 334 p.).

1663. Pratt, Fletcher. The compact history of the United States Navy. Revised by Hartley E. Howe. Illustrated by Louis Priscilla. New and rev. ed. New York, Hawthorn Books [1962] 350 p.
62–9039 E182.P84 1962
A popular history of the Navy's formation and growth. In addition to describing battles and engagements, the book tells the story of the American sailor—"who he has been and who he is today; where he came from at first and where he comes from today; what he has done to the Navy; and what the Navy has done to him." In the *Picture History of the U.S. Navy, From Old Navy to New, 1776–1897* (New York, Scribner, 1956. 1 v., unpaged), by Theodore Roscoe and Fred Freeman, more than 1,000 prints, photographs, maps, and

other visual materials are reproduced. Marshall Smelser, in *The Congress Founds the Navy, 1787–1798* ([Notre Dame, Ind.] University of Notre Dame Press, 1959. 229 p.), focuses on the political origins of the Navy and shows that partisan politics was the major influence on naval decisions in the Federalist period. *The Navy League of the United States* (Detroit, Wayne State University Press, 1962. 271 p.), by Armin Rappaport, is the history of an organization founded in 1902 and dedicated to the promotion of a "big navy."

1664. U.S. *Naval History Division.* Dictionary of American naval fighting ships. Washington, 1959–63. 2 v. illus.
60–60198 VA61.A53
The first two volumes in a multivolume series intended to present historical and statistical data on more than 10,000 ships which have formed part of the Continental and U.S. Navies since 1775. The information, arranged alphabetically by name of ship, includes such data (whenever available) as the name of the builder, identity of sponsor, launching date, tonnage or displacement, length, speed, class, armament, and operational history. The second volume carries the list of ships through the letter "F" and contains appendixes on aircraft carriers and on vessels of the Confederate Navy.

1665. The Watts histories of the United States Navy. New York, Watts [1965] 4 v.
Four volumes planned as part of a coordinated history of the Navy. In *A Chronology of the U.S. Navy, 1775–1965* (471 p. 65–21636 E182.C73), David M. Cooney provides brief descriptions of significant events in the history of both the Navy and the Marine Corps. Daniel J. Carrison, in *The Navy From Wood to Steel, 1860–1890* (186 p. 65–11939 E591.C3), concentrates on the role of the Navy in the Civil War. Brayton Harris, in *The Age of the Battleship, 1890–1922* (212 p. 65–21634 E182.H25), follows the Navy through an expansionist period, which ended with the convening in Washington of the International Conference on the Limitation of Naval Armaments. *The United States Nuclear Navy* (199 p. 65–21635 VM317.G5), by Herbert J. Gimpel, features the development of naval technology since World War II.

# D. The Air Force

1666. Goldberg, Alfred, *ed.* A history of the United States Air Force, 1907–1957. Princeton, N.J., Van Nostrand [1957] 277 p. illus.
57–14552 UG633.G6

"Select bibliography": p. 259–263.
Members of the USAF Historical Division prepared this profusely illustrated volume to mark the 50th anniversary of military aviation in the United

States, and the 10th anniversary of the establishment of the Department of the Air Force. Because of space limitations and the fact that other Air Force publications have covered or are planned to cover the period through World War II in detail, the book emphasizes the period after 1947. *The Compact History of the United States Air Force* (New York, Hawthorn Books [1963] 339 p.), by Carroll V. Glines, is a general narrative. *The United States Army Air Arm, April 1861 to April 1917* ([Montgomery, Ala.] USAF Historical Division, Research Studies Institute, Air University, 1958. 260 p. USAF historical studies, no. 98), by Juliette A. Hennessy, is the first of three monographs which will take the history to 1939.

1667. Wagner, Ray. American combat planes. Garden City, N.Y., Hanover House, 1960

[i.e. 1961] 447 p. illus.

60–14913    TL685.3.W17

This history of military aircraft covers all combat planes built in the United States or purchased abroad for the American Army, the Air Force, and Navy. The book contains photographs of the planes as well as information about their dimensions, weight, and performance. Two works on specific types of planes are *United States Army and Air Force Fighters, 1916–1961* (Letchworth, Herts, Harleyford Publications, 1961. 256 p.), compiled by Kimbrough S. Brown and others, and *Flying Fortress; the Illustrated Biography of the B-17s and the Men Who Flew Them* (Garden City, N.Y., Doubleday, 1965. 362 p.), by Edward Jablonski. In *A History of the U.S. Air Force Ballistic Missiles* (New York, Praeger [1965] 264 p.), Ernest G. Schwiebert describes the development of the Air Force ballistic missile program between 1954 and 1964.

## E. Wars of the United States

### Ei. WARS: THE REVOLUTION

1668. Billias, George A., *ed.* George Washington's generals. New York, W. Morrow, 1964. xvii, 327 p. illus.        64–12038    E206.B5

Bibliographies at the ends of chapters.

A collection of essays reexamining the careers of the most important Continental Army commanders, including Washington himself, in the light of recent scholarship. The other generals discussed are Charles Lee, Philip Schuyler, Horatio Gates, Nathanael Greene, John Sullivan, Benedict Arnold, Benjamin Lincoln, the Marquis de Lafayette, Henry Knox, Anthony Wayne, and Daniel Morgan, all of whom were selected on the basis of the significance of their contributions to the war effort and the fact that they served with Washington in some capacity. Three of the book's contributing historians have also published full-length biographies of their subjects: *Henry Knox* (New York, Rinehart [1958] 404 p.), by North Callahan; *Daniel Morgan* (Chapel Hill, Published for the Institute of Early American History and Culture at Williamsburg, Va., by the University of North Carolina Press [1961] 239 p.), by Don Higginbotham; and *A General of the Revolution, John Sullivan of New Hampshire* (New York, Columbia University Press, 1961. 317 p.), by Charles P. Whittemore.

1669. Mackesy, Piers. The war for America, 1775–1783. Cambridge, Harvard University

Press, 1964. xx, 565 p. illus.

64–2777    E208.M14

Bibliography: p. [528]–535.

With sympathy for the difficulties faced by the Ministers, Mackesy examines the making and execution of England's strategy in the American Revolution and judges the War Ministry according to circumstance rather than results. Problems related to space, time, and weather were often complicated by uncertainty, miscalculation, and poor communications across the Atlantic, and an adequate number of ships were not detached to America because of the fear that England and her Mediterranean garrisons might be attacked. There were leadership problems also. A Ministry divided between aggressiveness and timidity did not have wide popular support, and except for Cornwallis the generals were characterized by their lack of the boldness needed for victory. William B. Willcox' *Portrait of a General: Sir Henry Clinton in the War of Independence* (New York, Knopf; [distributed by Random House] 1964. 534 p.), is a biography of the English commander in chief (1778–81) whose personal shortcomings contributed to the British defeat.

1670. Peckham, Howard H. The War for Independence, a military history. [Chicago] University of Chicago Press [1958] 226 p. (The Chicago history of American civilization)

58–5685    E230.P36

Includes bibliography.

Following a brief survey of the causes for conflict between Britain and the Colonies, Peckham summarizes the military aspects of the Revolution from Lexington and Concord in 1775 to the evacuation of British troops eight years later. He contends that the American victory was primarily due to high troop morale, new tactics, and dedication and perseverance of a few leaders, and the role of George Washington, whose character "prevented the Revolution from either failing or from ending in tyranny and excess." In *This Glorious Cause* (Princeton, N.J., Princeton University Press, 1958. 254 p.), Herbert T. Wade and Robert A. Lively relate the day-to-day experiences of two Massachusetts company officers in the Continental Army from 1775 to 1779. Hugh F. Rankin, in *The American Revolution* (New York, Putnam [1964] 382 p.), presents materials from correspondence, journals, and diaries that relate to the land war. Primary sources for the first year of the war at sea are found in the U.S. Naval History Division's *Naval Documents of the American Revolution*, v. 1 (Washington [For sale by the Supt. of Docs., U.S. Govt. Print. Off.] 1964. 1451 p.), edited by William Bell Clark.

1671. Thayer, Theodore G. Nathanael Greene; strategist of the American Revolution. New York, Twayne Publishers, 1960. 500 p. illus.

60–8546 E207.G9T48

Bibliography: p. 477–486.

From a provincial middle-class Quaker home in Potowomut, R.I., Nathanael Greene (1742–1786) rose to become a major general in the Continental Army. The author portrays Greene as the mastermind of Washington's campaigns in the North and the executor of such brilliant Southern victories as those at Guilford Court House, N.C., and in South Carolina, where Cornwallis was shut within the narrow limits of Charleston and the immediate neighborhood. Greene was an ardent nationalist whose personal ambitions did not impair his loyalty to his country's cause or to his commander and whose insight into America's political, economic, and constitutional problems inspired him to advocate the kind of strong central government embodied in the Constitution after his death. M. F. Treacy's *Prelude to Yorktown; the Southern Campaign of Nathanael Greene, 1780–1781* (Chapel Hill, University of North Carolina Press [1963] 261 p.) pictures Greene as an excellent planner but one who demonstrated a lack of self-assurance and personal force.

## Eii. WARS: 1798–1848

1672. Forester, Cecil S. The age of the fighting sail; the story of the naval War of 1812. Garden City, N.Y., Doubleday, 1956. 284 p. (Mainstream of America series)

56—7741 E360.F69

A narrative of the naval War of 1812 by the author of the Horatio Hornblower stories and other novels of the sea. Forester discusses American unpreparedness for war and the lassitude with which the Executive administration and the Congress built an effective fleet. Despite these handicaps, the new Nation won memorable victories before an exasperated England began to even the score. The book has no table of contents or chapter titles, but an index provides access to specific names and incidents. The war on the Great Lakes and in Canada is the focus for *The Incredible War of 1812; a Military History* ([Toronto] University of Toronto Press [1965] 265 p.), written from a Canadian viewpoint by J. Mackay Hitsman. *The War of 1812* (Chicago, University of Chicago Press [1965] 298 p. The Chicago history of American civilization), by Harry L. Coles, is an introduction to the war with an emphasis on military aspects.

1673. Singletary, Otis A. The Mexican War. [Chicago] University of Chicago Press [1960] 181 p. illus. (The Chicago history of American civilization) 60–7248 E404.S5

"Suggested reading": p. 166–168.

A very brief introduction to the first offensive war launched by the United States. Singletary concentrates on the military aspects of the war but includes brief summaries of the causes of the conflict and of the diplomacy preceding and following it. The author devotes a chapter each to Zachary Taylor's victories in northern Mexico, to the occupation of New Mexico and California, and to Winfield Scott's capture of Mexico City. The dissension between President Polk, a Democrat, and his two ambitious Whig generals, Scott and Taylor, is described, with none of them emerging untarnished. Further discord is the topic of the chapter entitled "The Hidden War." Here the author describes the jealousy and rivalry between Scott and Taylor, the hostility between the well-trained regular soldiers and the undisciplined volunteers, and the friction generated by joint operations of the Army and the Navy.

## Eiii. WARS: THE CIVIL WAR

1674. Barrett, John G. Sherman's march through the Carolinas. Chapel Hill, University of

North Carolina Press, 1956. 325 p.

56–14242 E477.7.B3

Bibliography: p. [282]–309.

Although less well known than the march to the sea, Gen. William Tecumseh Sherman's march from Savannah to Raleigh—much of it over dangerous terrain—was an outstanding military accomplishment. The Army traveled through swamps, often in rainy weather, building bridges and corduroy roads as it progressed northward. Sherman conducted a campaign of "total war," and the destruction of the Carolinas was executed with a high degree of efficiency. Much of this scholarly study is based on diaries and correspondence of eyewitnesses. A narrative of Sherman's famous marches is *Those 163 Days; a Southern Account of Sherman's March from Atlanta to Raleigh* (New York, Coward-McCann [1961] 317 p.), by John M. Gibson. *From the Cannon's Mouth: the Civil War Letters of General Alpheus S. Williams* (Detroit, Wayne State University Press, 1959. 405 p.), edited by Milo M. Quaife, is a record of the general who commanded the 20th Corps in Sherman's Army.

1675. Catton, Bruce. The centennial history of the Civil War. E. B. Long, director of research. Garden City, N.Y., Doubleday, 1961–65. 3 v. col. illus. 61–12502 E468.C29

Includes bibliographies.

CONTENTS.—v. 1. The coming fury.—v. 2. Terrible swift sword.—v. 3. Never call retreat.

A general history of the Civil War. The first volume opens with the Democratic presidential convention of 1860 and ends after the first Battle of Bull Run. Volume 2 continues the narrative through Antietam and its aftermath in the fall of 1862. The final volume concludes with the surrender at Appomattox and Lincoln's assassination. *The American Heritage Picture History of the Civil War* (New York, American Heritage Pub. Co.; book trade distribution by Doubleday [1960] 630 p.), edited by Richard M. Ketchum and with text by Bruce Catton, reproduces drawings, paintings, maps, and photographs. Also by Catton are *This Hallowed Ground: the Story of the Union Side of the Civil War* (Garden City, N.Y., Doubleday, 1956. 437 p. Mainstream of America series) and *Grant Moves South* (Boston, Little, Brown [1960] 564 p.), a continuation of Lloyd Lewis' *Captain Sam Grant,* mentioned in the annotation for no. 3696 in the 1960 *Guide.*

1676. Cornish, Dudley T. The sable arm; Negro troops in the Union Army, 1861–1865. New York, Longmans, Green, 1956. 337 p.

56–6219 E540.N3C77

Bibliography: p. 316–332.

A history of the use of Negro troops in the Union Army. Attempts to allow Negroes to serve, even as volunteers, failed at first. As the war progressed, however, the Negro was accepted as a fighting soldier and "was permitted to do more for the freedom of his race than drive a supply wagon, cook for white soldiers, or labor on fortifications." Consequently, problems in administrative policy and army practice arose. Cornish examines how the Negro was recruited, trained, armed, employed, and compensated for his service in the Union Army and assesses his contribution to the war's outcome.

1677. Foote, Shelby. The Civil War, a narrative. New York, Random House [1958–63] 2 v. maps. 58–9882 E468-F7

CONTENTS.—1. Fort Sumter to Perryville.—2. Fredericksburg to Meridian.

The first volume traces events from the firing on Fort Sumter to the battle at Perryville, Ky., in October 1862, and the second proceeds from the Fredericksburg campaign through Grant's appointment to command of all the Federal Armies. A third and concluding volume is projected. Another general survey is *The Compact History of the Civil War* (New York, Hawthorn Books [1960] 445 p.), by Richard Ernest Dupuy and Trevor N. Dupuy. *The Civil War Dictionary* (New York, D. McKay Co. [1959] 974 p.), by Mark M. Boatner, is an alphabetically arranged reference work on all aspects of the war.

1678. Jones, Archer. Confederate strategy from Shiloh to Vicksburg. Baton Rouge, Louisiana State University Press [1961] xxi, 258 p.

61–7085 E470.8.J6 1961

Bibliography: p. 241–249. Bibliographical footnotes.

The author analyzes the efforts of Jefferson Davis, his Secretaries of War George W. Randolph and James A. Seddon, and his commanders in the field to devise a plan for Confederate operations, particularly in the West. Southern strategy, based primarily on territorial defense, called for the creation of departments, each charged with defending a specific area. Jones concludes that Davis was not "a narrow and ignorant despot" but a leader who formulated strategy in harmony with the States' rights philosophy and the limited logistical means at the Confederacy's disposal. *Lee's Maverick General, Daniel Harvey Hill* (New York, McGraw-Hill [1961] 323 p.), by Leonard Hal Bridges, and *General William J. Hardee: Old Reliable* (Baton Rouge, Louisiana State University Press [1965] 329 p. Southern biography series), by Nathaniel C. Hughes, concentrate on the Civil War careers of their respective subjects.

1679. Jones, Virgil C. The Civil War at sea. Foreword by E. M. Eller. New York, Holt, Rinehart, Winston [1960–62] 3 v.

60–14457 E591.J6

Includes bibliographies.

CONTENTS.—v. 1. The blockaders, January 1861–March 1862.—v. 2. The river war, March 1862–July 1863.—v. 3. The final effort, July 1863–November 1865.

This trilogy describes the naval operations of the Union and Confederate forces, emphasizing battles, blockade and coastal activities, tactics, and technological developments. Volume 1 is focused on the blockade against the South and the *Monitor-Merrimack* engagement. In the second volume Jones considers the effects of superior Northern sea power as it was used to tighten the blockade, patrol the coast, control the inland waterways, and combine operations with the Army. Volume 3 carries the narrative through the end of the war at sea, when the Confederate cruiser *Shenandoah* landed in Liverpool months after the South's surrender. *Infernal Machines; the Story of Confederate Submarine and Mine Warfare* ([Baton Rouge] Louisiana State University Press [1965] 230 p.), by Milton F. Perry, details the technological advances effected by the Confederacy in naval warfare. *Mr. Lincoln's Admirals* (New York, Funk & Wagnalls, 1956. 335 p.), by Clarence E. N. Macartney, and *Mr. Lincoln's Navy* (New York, Longmans, Green, 1957. 328 p.), by Richard S. West, concentrate on Northern naval operations.

1680. Lamers, William M. The edge of glory; a biography of General William S. Rosecrans, U.S.A. New York, Harcourt, Brace [1961] 499 p. illus. 61–7688 E467.1R7L3

Bibliography: p. 453–471.

The author devotes most of his biography on "Old Rosy" to a study of the general and his battles. Rosecrans was an able, although tactless, commander. His notable victories at Murfreesboro (December 31, 1862–January 3, 1863) and in the Tullahoma campaign (1863) demonstrated his competence on the battlefield. His Army of the Cumberland suffered severely at Chickamauga, and he was subsequently removed from command. The author goes into detail on the circumstances of Rosecrans' dismissal, which he views as partly stemming from the personal animosity of Grant and Secretary of War Edwin M. Stanton toward Rosecrans. A biography of the general who assumed command of Rosecrans' Army is *Education in Violence: The Life of George H. Thomas and the History of the Army of the Cumberland* (Detroit, Wayne State University Press, 1961. 530 p.), by Francis F. McKinney.

1681. Lee, Robert E. The wartime papers of R. E. Lee. Clifford Dowdey, editor; Louis H. Manarin, associate editor. With connective narratives by Clifford Dowdey and maps by Samuel H. Bryant. Virginia Civil War Commission. Boston, Little, Brown [1961] xiv, 994 p. illus. (Virginia Civil War centennial, 1961–1965)

61–5737 E470.L49

Bibliographical references included in "Notes" (p. [943]–968).

A collection of 1,006 letters, dispatches, orders, and reports. The papers are arranged chronologically, beginning with Lee's resignation from the U.S. Army on April 20, 1861, and ending with his letter to Jefferson Davis on April 20, 1865, calling for the "suspension of hostilities and the restoration of peace." Also included are letters to his wife and family. Three recent books on Lee are Burke Davis' *Gray Fox: Robert E. Lee and the Civil War* (New York, Rinehart [1956] 466 p.) and Clifford Dowdey's two studies, *Lee* (Boston, Little, Brown [1965] 781 p.) and *Lee's Last Campaign; the Story of Lee and His Men Against Grant—1864* (Boston, Little, Brown [1960] 415 p.).

1682. Warner, Ezra J. Generals in blue; lives of the Union commanders. [Baton Rouge] Louisiana State University Press [1964] xxiv, 679, [1] p. illus. 64–21593 E467.W29

Bibliography: p. 673–[680].

Biographical sketches and portraits of the 583 men appointed to the rank of general officer in the Union Army. Appended are the names of the generals grouped together by State or country of birth, a roster of brevetted generals, and an alphabetical list of campaigns and battles. Warren W. Hassler's *Commanders of the Army of the Potomac* (Baton Rouge, Louisiana State University Press [1962] 281 p.) examines the careers of the seven Union generals from McDowell to Grant who led the Army of the Potomac. Hassler has also written a biography of the most controversial commander of the Army of the Potomac: *General George B. McClellan, Shield of the Union* (Baton Rouge, Louisiana State University Press [1957] 350 p.). *Quartermaster General of the Union Army; a Biography of M. C. Meigs* (New York, Columbia University Press, 1959. 396 p.), by Russell F. Weigley, is an account of the supply services of the Union Army and the man who presided over the sprawling system.

1683. Warner, Ezra J. Generals in gray; lives of the Confederate commanders. [Baton Rouge] Louisiana State University Press [1959] xxvii, 420 p. illus.          58–7551 E467.W3
Bibliography: p. 401–420.
Biographical sketches and portraits of the 425 men commissioned to the rank of general officer in the Confederate Army. Appended are a roster of officers assigned to duty in the Trans-Mississippi area but not officially appointed by Jefferson Davis and a list of campaigns and battles. Full-length biographies of Confederate generals are *Stonewall Jackson* (New York, W. Morrow, 1959. 2 v.), by Lenoir Chambers; *A Different Valor, the Story of General Joseph E. Johnston, C.S.A.* (New York, Bobbs-Merrill [1956] 470 p.), by Gilbert E. Govan and James W. Livingood; and *General Leonidas Polk, C.S.A.: The Fighting Bishop* ([Baton Rouge] Louisiana State University Press [1962] 408 p. Southern biography series), by Joseph H. Parks.

1684. Williams, Kenneth P. Lincoln finds a general; a military study of the Civil War. With maps by Clark Ray. New York, Macmillan, 1949–59. 5 v.          49–11530 E470.W765
Includes bibliographies.
The first three volumes of this multivolume study are no. 3706 in the 1960 *Guide*. Volume 4 covers the campaigns from Iuka to Vicksburg. The author died during the preparation of the final volume; he had concluded the ninth chapter, which carries the account to Chickamauga. His notes indicate that he had planned two additional chapters, which would have continued the story to March 1864, when Grant was made commander in chief of the Union armies. Stephen E. Ambrose's *Halleck: Lincoln's Chief of Staff* (Baton Rouge, Louisiana State University Press [1962] 226 p.) portrays Gen. Henry W. Halleck as an able administrator and organizer but a poor field commander. Freeman Cleaves' *Meade of Gettysburg* (Norman, University of Oklahoma Press [1960] 384 p.) defends Gen. George G. Meade against criticism for having failed to pursue Lee after the battle of Gettysburg.

## Eiv. WARS: THE SPANISH-AMERICAN WAR

1685. Freidel, Frank B. The splendid little war. Boston, Little, Brown [1958] 314 p. illus.          58–10069 E715.F7
Bibliography: p. 313–314.
A pictorial history of the Spanish-American War, the conflict which John Hay, Ambassador to England at the time, called "a splendid little war." Freidel asserts that, although it may have been "splen-did" for those at home reading newspaper accounts of the battles, it was as grim and bloody as any war in history. Furthermore, it was "little" only because of the ineptitude of the Spaniards and the good luck of the Americans. Some 300 reproductions of photographs, sketches, and paintings show the toll of war on men and the land as well as the more commonplace aspects of military life. Among the photographers and artists represented are James Burton, Dwight L. Elmendorf, Frederic Remington, and Howard Chandler Christy. Whenever possible, the author has used the words of participants and war correspondents to tell the story.

## Ev. WARS: WORLD WAR I

1686. Mason, Herbert M. The Lafayette Escadrille. New York, Random House [1964] 340 p. illus.          64–20035 D603.M34
Bibliography: p. 326–329.
The Lafayette Escadrille was a fighter squadron created by American fliers who served as volunteers in the French Air Corps in the early years of World War I while the United States remained neutral. The author describes the flamboyant spirit of these men and narrates their daring escapades against the Germans. The book portrays military aviation in its infancy and illustrates the technical problems faced by the first fighter pilots. Mason includes many anecdotes about the Escadrille's members, their operations, and their exploits aloft and on the ground. Appended are a list of confirmed victories, the Lafayette Flying Corps Roster, and aids to understanding the language of aerial warfare. *Memoirs of World War I: "From Start to Finish of Our Greatest War"* (New York, Random House [1960] 312 p.) is the wartime diary of Brig. Gen. William ("Billy") Mitchell.

1687. Stallings, Laurence. The Doughboys; the story of the AEF, 1917–1918. Maps by Harry Scott. New York, Harper & Row [1963] 404 p.          62–14547 D570.S75
"A reader's guide": p. 383–390.
An account of the American Expeditionary Force in Europe from the average soldier's viewpoint. The author, a veteran of World War I, details the adventures of the AEF, its difficulties and achievements, its battlescarred heroes and grim casualties. The accounts of Cantigny, Chateau-Thierry, Saint-Mihiel, and Meuse-Argonne illustrate the problems of command, the strategy of operations, and the experiences of the men at the front. *Over There; the Story of America's First Great Overseas Crusade* (Boston, Little, Brown [1964] 385 p.), by Frank

B. Freidel, is a pictorial history of the AEF. In *At Belleau Wood* (New York, Putnam [1965] 375 p.), Robert B. Asprey details the tactics of this American offensive of June 1918.

1688. Trask, David F. The United States in the Supreme War Council; American war aims and inter-Allied strategy, 1917–1918. Middletown, Conn., Wesleyan University Press [1961] 244 p.
61–14237   D544.T7

The Supreme War Council, organized in 1917, coordinated the political and military strategies of England, France, Italy, and the United States. As military representative on the Council, Gen. Tasker H. Bliss devoted great energy to assist in arranging an inter-Allied military strategy against the Central Powers. Bliss refused to approve Allied proposals when they warranted military commitments that would jeopardize President Wilson's plan for peace. The author charts the Wilson administration's course in supporting the Allies and at the same time striving to avoid diplomatic entanglements.

## Evi.  WARS: WORLD WAR II

1689. Buchanan, Albert R. The United States and World War II. New York, Harper & Row [1964]  2 v. (xvii, 635 p.)  illus. (New American Nation series)   63–20287   D769.B8
Bibliography: p. 595–612. Bibliographical footnotes.

The author covers the battles and campaigns in all theaters, matters of policy and strategy, and war mobilization at home. Another overall history of the war is Kenneth S. Davis' *Experience of War: the United States in World War II* (Garden City, N.Y., Doubleday, 1965. Mainstream of America series). In *Pearl Harbor; Warning and Decision* (Stanford, Calif., Stanford University Press, 1962. 426 p.), Roberta Wohlstetter analyzes the United States' lack of preparedness for the Pearl Harbor attack.

1690. Morison, Samuel Eliot. History of United States naval operations in World War II. Boston, Little, Brown, 1947–62.  15 v.  illus.
47–1571   D773.M6
Bibliographical footnotes.

Five additional volumes conclude this 15-volume work; the first 10 volumes are no. 3721 in the 1960 *Guide*. Morison has also written *The Two-Ocean War, a Short History of the United States Navy in the Second World War* (Boston, Little, Brown [1963] 611 p.), which is not a condensation of his larger study but rather a narrative of the Navy's

most important battles and campaigns. Other aspects of U.S. sea operations during the war are covered in Felix Riesenberg's *Sea War; the Story of the U.S. Merchant Marine in World War II* (New York, Rinehart [1956]  320 p.) and *The U.S. Coast Guard in World War II* (Annapolis, United States Naval Institute [1957]  347 p.), by Malcolm F. Willoughby.

1691. Ryan, Cornelius. The longest day: June 6, 1944. New York, Simon & Schuster, 1959. 350 p. illus.   59–9499   D756.5.N6R9
Bibliography: p. 336–339.

This account of the Normandy invasion centers on the events of a single day. Ryan describes the landings of the Allied airborne armies and the assault on the five invasion beaches along the Normandy coast. Another book on the Normandy invasion is Samuel L. A. Marshall's *Night Drop; the American Airborne Invasion of Normandy* (Boston, Little, Brown [1962]  425 p.). In *The Duel for France, 1944* (Boston, Houghton Mifflin, 1963. 432 p.), Martin Blumenson covers the fighting in France from July to September 1944. John Toland's *Battle, the Story of the Bulge* (New York, Random House [1959]  400 p.) describes one of the major battles of the war.

1692. U.S. *Air Force. USAF Historical Division.* The Army Air Forces in World War II. Prepared under the editorship of Wesley Frank Craven [and] James Lea Cate. [Chicago] University of Chicago Press [1948–58]  7 v.  illus.
48–3657   D790.A47

The first six volumes of this history are no. 3727 in the 1960 *Guide*. Volume 7, *Services Around the World*, describes nontactical units such as the Air Transport Command, the Aviation Engineers, and the AAF Weather Service. Also included are chapters on medical services and women in the AAF.

1693. U.S. *Dept. of the Army. Office of Military History.* United States Army in World War II. Washington, 1947–65.  62 v.  illus., maps.
47–46404   D769.A533

A continuation of no. 3726 in the 1960 *Guide*. More than 85 volumes were planned for this series, and 62 have been published thus far. New subseries added since the publication of the 1960 *Guide* include *The Western Hemisphere* and *The Mediterranean Theater of Operations*. The *Master Index: Reader's Guide II* (1960. 145 p.) contains brief summaries of all volumes in the series as well as some projected volumes. *American Strategy in World War II: A Reconsideration* (Baltimore, Johns Hopkins Press, 1963. 145 p.), by Kent R. Greenfield, chief historian of the Department of the Army from 1946 to 1958, deals with such subjects as Anglo-American strategy, Roosevelt as commander in chief, and strategy and air power. Greenfield is also the editor of *Command Decisions* (Washington, 1960. 565 p.), a collection of articles issued by the U.S. Department of the Army, Office of the Chief of Military History, analyzing various strategic decisions made by the Allied and Axis powers during the war.

1694. U.S. *Marine Corps.* History of U.S. Marine Corps operations in World War II. [Washington] Historical Branch, G-3 Division, Headquarters, U.S. Marine Corps [1958–63] 2 v. illus.                58–60002  D769.369.U53

The first two volumes in a projected five-volume series. Volume 1 outlines the development of the Marine Corps' amphibious mission and describes the defense of Wake Island, the campaign in the Philippines, the fight for Midway, and the battle for Guadalcanal. The focus in the second volume is on the drive to occupy Rabaul. Also described are the occupation of the New Georgia Islands, operations in the northern Solomons, and the New Britain campaign. Robert Leckie's *Strong Men Armed: The United States Marines Against Japan* (New York, Random House [1962] 563 p.) is a popular history of Marine Corps operations in the Pacific during World War II.

Evii. WARS: THE KOREAN WAR

1695. Appleman, Roy E. South to the Naktong, north to the Yalu; June–November 1950. Washington, Office of the Chief of Military History, Department of the Army, 1961. xxiv, 813 p. illus. (United States Army in the Korean War, 1)
                60–60043  DS918.U5246 vol. 1
Bibliographical footnotes.

The first volume in the U.S. Army's official history, *United States Army in the Korean War*. The activities of other branches of the military service in Korea are described in *The United States Air Force in Korea, 1950–1953* (New York, Duell, Sloan & Pearce [1961] 774 p.), by Robert F. Futrell; James A. Field's *History of United States Naval Operations: Korea* (Washington [U.S. Govt. Print. Off.] 1962. 499 p.); and the first four volumes of a pro-

posed five-volume Marine Corps publication, *U.S. Marine Operations in Korea, 1950–1953* (Washington, Historical Branch, G-3, Headquarters, U.S. Marine Corps, 1954 [i.e. 1955]–62).

1696. Leckie, Robert. Conflict; the history of the Korean War, 1950–53. New York, Putnam [1962] 448 p. illus.        62–10975  DS918.L36
    Bibliography: p. 431–434.

An account of the Korean War for the general reader. The author traces the course of the war and provides detailed descriptions of the battles and operations as well as a discussion of the strategy involved. A more scholarly history of the war is *Korea: The Limited War* (New York, St. Martin's Press, 1964. 511 p.), by David Rees, a British historian. Rees discusses the development of American policy toward Korea, amply covers the military operations, and deals with the British response to the war. In *Pork Chop Hill; the American Fighting Man in Action, Korea, Spring, 1953* (New York, Morrow, 1956. 315 p.), Samuel L. A. Marshall analyzes in detail an encounter in which the Americans won an important victory.

1697. Spanier, John W. The Truman-MacArthur controversy and the Korean War. Cambridge, Mass., Belknap Press, 1959. 311 p. illus.
                59–12976  DS919.S62
    Bibliographical references included in "Notes" (p. 281–297). Bibliography: p. 298–306.

A major issue during the early part of the Korean War was the policy disagreement between President Truman and General MacArthur which subsequently led to MacArthur's dismissal from all of his commands. Spanier traces the origins of the policy differences between the two men and shows how and why these differences developed to the point at which Truman had no alternative but to relieve MacArthur of his duties. The author, in addition, uses the controversy to analyze the problem of civil-military relations during a limited war. A briefer interpretation of the disagreement between Truman and MacArthur is Trumbull Higgins' *Korea and the Fall of MacArthur; a Précis in Limited War* (New York, Oxford University Press, 1960. 229 p.).

# XI

# Intellectual History

Aᴛᴛᴇᴍᴘᴛꜱ to impose accurate limits upon the scope of intellectual history frequently end in frustration. Only a thin line of demarcation separates this chapter from those concerned with literature, society, politics, philosophy, and history, all of which may be regarded as supplementary. The books described here portray the development and transition of the American intellectual and cultural scene from its beginnings, when a knowledge of the classics was a prerequisite for being regarded as an intellectual and when the colonists looked to Europe as the source of civilization and culture. In general, the influence of European thinkers on the American mind was overwhelming in the early years, but after the American Revolution the flow of ideas moved in both directions.

Diverse and independent trends developed as this country went its own way and manifested an increasing inclination to divorce itself from the traditionalism of European countries. The authors represented in this chapter display a wide range of opinion concerning the people and ideas that have most profoundly influenced American thought. Many writers have selected Jefferson as a major figure in this field, but in his time he was often denounced as an atheist and a divisive influence in his political concepts. Writing of the decades between 1800 and 1860, Perry Miller (no. 1705) draws attention to the importance of the drive toward moral uplift as a primary force in maintaining "the grand unity of national strength." The Bohemian revolt against narrow middle-class respectability and convention during the first quarter of the 20th century was succeeded in the 1950's by the beat generation's more sweeping rejection of contemporary American life and values. Richard Hofstadter (no. 1699) traces a tradition of hostility to intellectualism throughout American history.

## A. General Works

1698. Curti, Merle E. The growth of American thought. 3d ed. New York, Harper & Row [1964] xx, 939 p. illus.

        64–12796   E169.1.C87   1964

  Bibliography: p. 797–900.

  An updated edition of no. 3729 in the 1960 *Guide.*

1699. Hofstadter, Richard. Anti-intellectualism in American life. New York, Knopf, 1963. 434, xiii p.                63–14086   E169.1.H74

  Bibliographical footnotes.

  Hostility to intellectualism in America, Hofstadter maintains, is older than the Nation; it reached a cyclical peak in the 1950's in an attack led by

Senator Joseph R. McCarthy. The launching of Sputnik by the Soviets shocked the American public into a reappraisal of the school system and a protest against the slackness of American education. The author defines and explains his concept of intellectualism and traces some of the social movements in our history in which "intellect has been dissevered from its co-ordinate place among the human virtues and assigned the position of a special kind of vice." He believes the United States possesses the only educational system whose vital segments have fallen into the hands of people who proclaim their hostility to intellect and identify with children who show the least intellectual promise.

1700. Lerner, Max. America as a civilization; life and thought in the United States today. New York, Simon & Schuster, 1957. 1036 p.
57–10979 E169.1.L532
Bibliography: p. 955–998.
A monumental study and interpretation, the purpose of which is to grasp "the pattern and inner meaning of contemporary American civilization and its relationship to the world today." It is not intended as a history or mere description of life in America; neither is it "a celebration of 'the American way' or a lament about it." In an effort to arrive at a composite picture, Lerner has carried through an encyclopedic investigation of society and its institutions in the United States, ranging from religion and cultural patterns to economics and political power. Particularly interesting chapters dissect "Class and Status in America," the "Life Cycle of the American," "Character and Society," and "The Arts and Popular Culture." His detailed inquiries have led him to conclude that conformism, fanaticism, and rigidity have not dried up the native sources of creativity. He sees "still in the American potential the plastic strength that has shaped a great civilization." Gerald N. Grob and Robert N. Beck have compiled and edited the writings of theologians, philosophers, political theorists, statesmen, and historians under the title *American Ideas; Source Readings in the Intellectual History of the United States* ([New York] Free Press of Glencoe [1963] 2 v.).

1701. Whittemore, Robert C. Makers of the American mind. New York, Morrow, 1964. 497 p.
64–12525 B851.W48
Bibliographical references at the ends of chapters.

This book is neither a history of philosophy nor an interpretation of American civilization. Rather it is a careful effort "to present in compact form, and as much as possible in their own words, the essentials of the philosophy of those thinkers and doers whose influence upon our culture is, or has been, such as justify calling them the makers of the American Mind." The author, a professor of philosophy at Tulane University, traces the shapers of our national consciousness from John Cotton to Alfred North Whitehead. Along with the familiar names of Franklin, Jefferson, Emerson, Thoreau, Santayana, and John Dewey are those of such less widely known men as Solomon Stoddard, Theodore J. Frelinghuysen, Charles Chauncey, Cadwallader Colden, and Abner Kneeland. The author concludes that no thinker comparable to any of the men whose thought he reviews here is "on the scene" today and laments what he believes to be a current hostility to intellectual excellence.

# B. Periods

1702. American Studies Association. American perspectives; the national self-image in the twentieth century. Edited by Robert E. Spiller and Eric Larrabee; associate editors: Ralph Henry Gabriel, Henry Nash Smith [and] Edward N. Waters. Cambridge, Harvard University Press, 1961. 216 p. (Library of Congress series in American civilization)
61–8841 E169.1.A49
This volume was planned to synthesize the diverse aspects of American culture treated in the rest of the Library of Congress series and to answer the question, "What do we think of ourselves?" It includes essays by specialists in history, literature, philosophy, politics, economics, sociology, art, music, popular arts, and the mass media. The authors express diverse and independent viewpoints in attempting to impart "a general impression of the emotional and intellectual trends which America experienced while living through the vast ideological and technological changes of this half century."

1703. Gummere, Richard M. The American colonial mind and the classical tradition; essays in comparative culture. Cambridge, Harvard University Press, 1963. 228 p.  63–20767 E162.G88
Bibliography and notes: p. [201]–223.

A scholarly account of the impact of Greek and Roman ideas on the lives and thought of the American colonists. The author makes it clear that the foundations of this country were laid by men who possessed sound scholarship; the majority were college-educated or were well grounded in the classics, from which they derived wisdom and idealism. The religious motive was very strong, and the rights of the individual under the English law were assumed. The Bible, the English common law, and the classics were basic for the education of the colonists, who applied them to illustrate their own ideas and to deal with their own problems.

1704. May, Henry F. The end of American innocence; a study of the first years of our own time, 1912–1917. New York, Knopf, 1959. 412 p.
59–11236 E169.1.M496

An examination of American thought as expressed in various areas of the social sciences and humanities from politics to philosophy. The author seeks to demonstrate that the cultural upheaval and intellectual revolt commonly associated with the 1920's and attributed to the disillusioning experiences of World War I were already present beneath the surface of an illusive Victorian calm during the five years before the United States entered the conflict. The "standard American culture" or consensus made up of idealism, moralism, progressivism, and optimism was even then crumbling in a ferment generated by the ideas of Darwin, Marx, Nietzsche, Freud, Shaw, Veblen, John Dewey, Dreiser, Lincoln Steffens, and many others. The voices of dissent filled such journals as *The Smart Set, Little Review, The New Republic, The Masses,* and *Glebe.* The final chapter considers the war and its aftermath, which accelerated the disintegration of the old consensus.

1705. Miller, Perry. The life of the mind in America, from the Revolution to the Civil War. New York, Harcourt, Brace & World [1965] 338 p.
65–19065 E169.1.M6273

The author planned an extensive work divided into nine books. He wrote book 1, on religious revivalism and morality, and book 2, on the law, but had finished only the first chapter of book 3, on science, at the time of his death. The completed portions are published here along with a working script for the projected chapters of book 3 and a list of the six unwritten books. Miller explores the search for a character and a national identity worthy of the opportunities in the new and unexploited land to which the European colonists came. "To elevate the moral condition of our race," he concludes, was the objective carried out with missionary zeal in early 19th-century America. It dominated every facet of American life and was the prime force in maintaining the "grand unity of national strength."

1706. Sanford, Charles L., *ed.* Quest for America, 1810–1824. Garden City, N.Y., Anchor Books, 1964. xxxvii, 474 p. illus. (Documents in American civilization series) 64–11311 E165.S25
"Suggested readings": (p. [471]–474).

This novel sourcebook presents the cultural history of the period through 108 "documents," 41 of which consist of one or more illustrations with a page or so of explanatory or interpretative text. Through them and a 23-page introduction, the editor seeks to depict his book's 15 years as peculiarly a period of transition, with 1815 as a turning point at which America's homogenous and stable agrarian society began to break up. Hugh S. Legaré's Fourth of July oration delivered at Charleston, S.C., in 1823, is chosen to express the view that America, by restoring the republican simplicity of the classical era, had divorced herself from "the antiquated and corrupt systems of the old world." Word and image are drawn upon to illustrate expressions of national feeling in war and peace, in art (especially John Trumbull's "The Declaration of Independence," the large version of which was completed in 1818), science, political economy, foreign relations, education, and literature. The search for a characteristic American style is exemplified in the designs of steam engines and steamboats, bridges, and plows.

# C. Topics

1707. Bode, Carl. The anatomy of American popular culture, 1840–1861. Berkeley, University of California Press, 1959. 292 p. illus.
59–8759 E169.1.B657

A synthetic treatment of American culture during a period when such factors as the mass production of printed matter, the advent of general literacy, and a rising prosperity were molding that culture into its modern shape. The author's aim is to depict the popular arts, identify and display the most prominent varieties of the printed word, and suggest how the American character revealed itself through its cultural preferences. He finds four sets of qualities manifested in the American character in this era: a somewhat chauvinistic patriotism counterbalanced by a reluctant belief in Europe's cultural superiority; an aggressiveness, combined with optimism and restlessness, which emphasized the importance of material success; a religiosity evidenced by reverence for the Bible, a revival of Puritanism, and a humanitarian zeal for reform; and a sentimental preoccupation with love, both romantic and filial.

1708. Churchill, Allen. The improper bohemians; a re-creation of Greenwich Village in its heyday. New York, Dutton, 1959. 349 p. illus.

58–9604  F128.68.G8C45
Bibliography: p. 339–343.

Drawing on the personal reminiscences of survivors of the period, magazine articles, and some 50 retrospective books, the author has put together an anecdotal account of Greenwich Village life from 1912 to 1930. This was the golden era when such revolutionary magazines as *The Masses, The Seven Arts,* and *The Quill* were born and flourished and when Mrs. Mabel Dodge (later Mrs. Luhan of Taos) played hostess to the Village intelligentsia, whose names read like a who's who in American art and letters for these years. The final chapter describes the Village's rapid loss of artistic eminence after 1930.

1709. Cleveland, Harlan, Gerard J. Mangone, *and* John C. Adams. The overseas Americans. New York, McGraw-Hill [1960]  316 p. (The Carnegie series in American education)

60–10598  E169.1.C56

A survey by three members of the Maxwell Graduate School of Citizenship and Public Affairs of Syracuse University, undertaken to assess the problems of overseas living confronting the more than a million and a half American businessmen, missionaries, Armed Forces personnel, government employees, teachers, and students employed abroad. After analyzing data collected from interviews with 244 Americans of various professions residing in six foreign countries, the authors suggest five elements pertinent to successful living abroad: technical skill, belief in one's mission, cultural empathy, a sense of politics, and organizing ability. The latter portion of the book is devoted to an examination of deficiencies and needed improvements in existing educational programs for prospective overseas Americans. The lack of competence in foreign languages is emphasized as a particularly serious and widespread handicap; it is also desirable that Americans planning to be abroad should know their own country well.

1710. Hofstadter, Richard. Social Darwinism in American thought. Rev. ed. New York, G. Braziller, 1959 [°1955]  248 p.

59–9543  HM22.U5H6  1959
Bibliography: p. [205]–216.

An updated edition of no. 3755 in the 1960 *Guide.*

1711. Kiger, Joseph C. American learned societies. Washington, Public Affairs Press [1963]  291 p.           63–16497  AS25.K5
Bibliography: p. 246–261.

This study of the 60 foremost learned societies and of four councils and five institutes (national associations of related learned societies) in the United States "is an attempt to set forth and interpret the historical development of these organizations, provide a compendium on them [origins, purpose, history, organization, activities, publications, membership, etc.], and to shed light on their operations and relationships to each other and to other domestic and international organizations concerned with scientific and cultural advancement." The author takes into account the changing roles of philanthropic foundations, government, industry, and universities as the societies' sources of financial support, and he notes that a gradual broadening of scope has led to widespread participation by the societies in relevant international conferences and congresses since World War II. In the final chapter, four major future trends are predicted: an ever-increasing involvement with international affairs; a growing awareness that national needs must be served; agreement on the necessity of greater financial support from the Federal Government and from industry for humanistic and social science societies and councils; and an increase in the number and scope of organizations established for the purpose of bridging outmoded barriers between disciplines.

1712. Lipton, Lawrence. The holy barbarians. New York, Messner [1959]  318 p. illus.

59–7135  E169.1.L547

The author, who conducts a poetry and jazz workshop in Venice, Calif., and who has associated intimately with this particular "community of disaffiliates," has produced a sympathetic analysis of beat life. By means of vivid dialogs and case histories, Lipton reveals many aspects of the beat generation's bizarre life and the beats' attitudes toward love, sex, morals, art, music, literature, government, and drugs. He discusses some reasons for their rebellion against a society which they regard as dominated by materialism and militarism and compares the present-day beats with the bohemians of former eras. He concludes that "this is not just another alienation. It is a deep-going change, a revolution under the ribs."

1713. Parry, Albert. Garrets and pretenders; a history of bohemianism in America. Rev. ed. New York, Dover Publications [°1960] 422 p. illus. 61–549 PS138.P3 1960
Bibliography: p. 397–406.

A revised edition of no. 3757 in the 1960 *Guide,* including a new introduction, addenda which serve to correct or elaborate the original text, and two additional chapters: "Greenwich Village Revisited:

1948," by the author, and "Enter Beatniks: the Bohème of 1960," by Harry T. Moore.

1714. Wolfe, Don M. The image of man in America. Dallas, Southern Methodist University Press [1957] 482 p.
57–14766 E169.1.W68
Bibliography: p. 441–462.

Discusses a variety of American answers to the question of whether the environmental or the genetic factor is dominant in shaping human nature. The author does not attempt to prove or disprove these theories but instead analyzes the views of such writers as Jefferson, Emerson, Lincoln, Mark Twain, William James, John Dewey, and Theodore Dreiser and examines the social climates and personal backgrounds that gave rise to their beliefs.

## D. Localities

1715. Davis, Richard Beale. Intellectual life of Jefferson's Virginia, 1790–1830. Chapel Hill, University of North Carolina Press [1964] 507 p. 64–13548 F230.D3
"Bibliography and notes": p. [439]–482.

The author explores the reasons why the period between 1790 and 1830 in what he calls Jefferson's Virginia "held a political and intellectual primacy which was acknowledged and often envied by her sister states and indeed by much of the European world." Born to privileges, the Virginia planter was required by his code of conduct to have the ability to dance, to fence, to know Latin and Greek, to be well grounded in the classics, and to be conversant in the theories of law and government. Reared under the concept of *noblesse oblige,* he occupied a social position that exacted the acceptance of civic responsibilities. He was interested in good architecture, fine furniture, religion, educating his children, and collecting books. He was especially interested in good government. With his fellow

*ferson Image in the American Mind* (New York, Oxford University Press, 1960. 548 p.), by Merrill D. Peterson, is a scholarly treatment of a century of interpretation, misinterpretation, and reinterpreta-Virginians he was prompted to fulfill the destiny for which the forefathers had sacrificed. *The Jef*tion of Jefferson's ideas and of how they have affected his image and American intellectual development from the time of his death through the 1930's.

1716. Eaton, Clement. The freedom-of-thought struggle in the Old South. New York, Harper & Row [1964] xiii, 418 p. illus. (Harper torchbooks. The Academy library, TB 1150)
65–321 F209.E15 1964
Bibliographical footnotes.

A new edition of no. 3766 in the 1960 *Guide,* with a modified title, a new preface, and three chapters added on censorship of the mails, freedom of conscience in politics, and American nationalists in the prewar South.

## E. International Influences: General

1717. Boorstin, Daniel J. America and the image of Europe: reflections on American thought. New York, Meridian Books [1960] 192 p. (Meridian books, M89) 60–6769 E169.1.B75

Eight essays treating the misconceptions which Americans harbor about their relationship to European culture, their history, and their national character. Boorstin is concerned with showing what is unique and distinct about the United States. He contends that Americans should stop judging their culture by decreasingly relevant European standards and should instead view themselves in the perspective of the non-European civilizations of Asia and Africa, in order to present a clearer image of their country to themselves and to the world.

1718. Jones, Howard Mumford. O strange new world; American culture: the formative years. New York, Viking Press [1964] xiv, 464 p. illus. 64–15062 E169.1.J644 1964
"Reference notes": p. 397–449.
Awarded the 1965 Pulitzer Prize in the general nonfiction category, this book is the first of a projected two-volume study of the effect of the Old World civilizations on the New. Beginning with Christopher Columbus' first report from the *Nina* in 1493 and continuing to the 1840's, the author traces European influences on the development of American culture. "The Old World projected into the New a rich, complex, and contradictory set of habits, forces, practices, values, and presuppositions; and the New World accepted, modified, or rejected these or fused them with inventions of its own." Jones marshals large bodies of detailed information in illustration of a wide range of provocative ideas. Reviewing the economic, political, religious, literary, artistic, and sociological aspects of the classical Greek and Roman civilizations, he relates them to the Spanish, English, Dutch, Portuguese, German, and French cultures which contributed to the American mind.

1719. Joseph, Franz M., *ed.* As others see us; the United States through foreign eyes. With contributions by Raymond Aron [and others]

Princeton, N.J., Princeton University Press, 1959. 360 p. 59–13872 E169.1.J67
These essays by visitors from 20 nations on five continents resulted from a project of the American European Foundation and were written more or less simultaneously in 1957. Each author seeks to convey his impressions of the United States and to relate them to the image of this country which is generally held by his countrymen. The depth and perceptive qualities of the analyses are uneven and there is a remarkable sameness in much of the commentary, but valuable questions are posed, insights into our national character are offered, and the impact of modern America on these writers and their countries is illustrated.

1720. Skard, Sigmund. The American myth and the European mind; American studies in Europe, 1776–1960. Philadelphia, University of Pennsylvania Press [1961] 112 p. (Studies in American civilization) 61–15199 E175.8.S64
Four lectures which summarize and comment upon the author's two-volume *American Studies in Europe: Their History and Present Organization* (Philadelphia, University of Pennsylvania Press, 1958), cited on page 1081 in the 1960 *Guide.* He divides his subject into four periods, ending with 1865, 1918, 1945, and 1960, respectively, and in each describing the major developments in writing about America and the teaching of American subjects in the several European nations and concluding each chapter with thumbnail sketches of representative figures such as Johan Kortüm, M. Y. Ostrogorsky, and Charles Cestre. He stresses the degree to which radical or conservative sentiment has determined the fortunes of the subject and shows how American studies have been a symbolic issue in the efforts of European minds to transcend traditionalism and understand the modern world and their place in it.

# F. International Influences: By Country

1721. Chisolm, Lawrence W. Fenollosa: the Far East and American culture. New Haven, Yale University Press, 1963. 297 p. (Yale publications in American studies, 8)
63–17024 N8375.F375C5
Bibliography: p. [255]–277.
The author has written the first full-length biography of Ernest Francisco Fenollosa (1853–1908), philosopher, historian, and reforming prophet, who "searched the cultures of East and West for the

outlines of an emerging world civilization." After interpreting Japanese art to the Japanese while resident professor of Western philosophy, Fenollosa returned to the United States to interpret Far Eastern civilization to Westerners and to work vigorously toward the fusion of East and West. Considered the world's leading authority on the history of Japanese art, he is remembered by art historians for his pioneer Far Eastern studies; in literary circles for his influence, as a translator of Chinese poetry and Japanese drama, on Ezra Pound and William Butler Yeats; and by museum curators for his role in developing the Freer collections now in the Smithsonian Institution. He taught Confucius' theory of the fundamental relation of art to character and to the state: "to keep the soul free through art."

1722. Thistlethwaite, Frank. The Anglo-American connection in the early nineteenth century. Philadelphia, University of Pennsylvania Press [1959] 222 p. (Dept. of American Civilization, Graduate School of Arts and Sciences, University of Pennsylvania. Studies in American civilization)          57–11957   E183.8.G7T4

Based on lectures delivered at the University of Pennsylvania while the author was visiting professor of American civilization, this volume explores the economic, political, social, educational, and humanitarian interrelationships between Britain and the United States which bound the two countries into a closely tied "Atlantic community" between the Peace of Ghent and the American Civil War. This interchange of goods, ideas, and people flourished despite the conspicuous animosities on the political level. The author notes, however, that the connection was limited in America to the Northern States and in Britain to the elements seeking to overturn the establishment and that it disappeared as a result of the vast displacement of forces brought about by the Civil War.

# XII

# Local History: Regions, States, and Cities

THE EFFLORESCENCE of local and regional history is one of the most striking developments in the field of historical writing during the period under review. As the production of large-scale general studies has declined, regional history in particular has attracted the interests of writers and provided them with a forum for a variety of special interests. (The movement away from comprehensive national histories has been remarked in the introduction to Chapter VIII, where it is noted that the mounting array and diversity of source materials increasingly recommends the smaller unit of history and the selective view.)

As this generation proceeds to explore and reinterpret the elements of American growth and civilization, it is carefully choosing its ground. The unexplored areas of local development and the more familiar territory of sectional controversy both provide manageable targets for the revisionists and may be examined in isolation or as a pattern for wider application. Similarly, academic historians are finding an inexhaustible mine of neglected problems and forgotten data as subjects for scholarly research. Further, the resources of regional history offer a convenient testing site for the resolution of a problem that is affecting the historian with increasing urgency: the need to evaluate the contribution of the social sciences to historical inquiry. The reactions of professional historians range from defensive skepticism to wholehearted acceptance of the demographic probes, statistical methods, and behavioral studies that appear in carefully selected and controlled areas of investigation.

Whether these activities are pursued for their own sake or are the logical—perhaps inevitable—extension of the historian's craft, they add to the total experience and understanding, and, in the process, local and regional history become at once the source and the consumer of an expanding accumulation of historical knowledge. Somewhat paradoxically, at a time of increasing specialization in historical scholarship, the scope of local and especially regional studies is being extended. Old geographical boundaries become less confining and political boundaries less meaningful as common cultural, economic, ethnic, historical, and social factors are assembled to plot an area distinct in itself. Just as the county has all but lost its significance for some types of study, so the history of States has assumed additional dimensions. Seldom does an author's preface in a modern State history fail to indicate that he has attempted to relate the internal affairs of his subject with the larger issues of national development.

The many adjacent areas between the pursuits of local and national history indicate a greater mutual contribution than is perhaps immediately apparent. The integrity of this exchange depends ultimately on the vision, skill, and purposes of the individual historian. And, in this regard, the selections that follow here offer considerable promise. More and more, the field is being populated with prominent and established historians, social scientists, journalists, and other writers, who are proving that history can be both popular and accurate and that, in the confluence of many disciplines and in concert with the literary and pictorial arts, opportunities for variety in selection, approach, and presentation are virtually endless.

This aspect of a rapidly expanding branch of history inevitably caused difficulties in the compilation of the present chapter. With traditional divisions of labor falling into disregard and new guidelines scarcely envisaged by the profession itself, the categorization of books becomes almost arbitrary. Titles immediately betray the calculated violations of disciplinary lines. Period studies often achieve significance by virtue of their regional importance. The problem of determining whether a closely focused study is to be classified as local, general, intellectual, economic, or social history, or as one of a number of other categories, can often be decided only on the basis of the author's declared intent. Works on local history may therefore be found elsewhere in this *Supplement,* in topical chapters more appropriate to their special emphases.

Overseas Possessions, Section U in the 1960 *Guide,* has been changed to Section V in the *Supplement* in order to make room for a new Section U, covering Alaska and Hawaii.

# A. General Works, Including Series

1723.  American guide series. [Compiled and written by the Federal Writers' Project and the Writers' Program] 1936–43. 155 v.

Entry no. 3786 in the 1960 *Guide* describes the compilation of this series; the volumes are listed as no. 3787–3941, with new editions and reprints substituted for original publications. Two substantially revised editions which have appeared since 1955 are entered below as no. 1724 and 1725.

1724.  Oklahoma; a guide to the Sooner State, compiled by Kent Ruth and the staff of the University of Oklahoma Press, with articles by leading authorities and photographic sections arranged by J. Eldon Peek. [Rev. ed.] Norman, University of Oklahoma Press [1957] xxxv, 532 p. illus.

57–7333   F694.R8

Bibliography: p. 504–511.
A revised edition of no. 3908 in the 1960 *Guide.*

1725.  New Mexico; a guide to the colorful State. Compiled by workers of the Writers' Program of the Work Projects Administration in the State of New Mexico. New and completely revised edition by Joseph Miller; edited by Henry G. Alsberg. New York, Hastings House, 1962. xxxii, 472 p. illus.        62–53065   F794.3.W7 1962

Bibliography: p. 436–440.
A revised edition of no. 3924 in the 1960 *Guide.*

1726.  The Rivers of America; as planned and started by Constance Lindsay Skinner [various editors] New York, Holt, Rinehart & Winston, 1937–[65] 56 v.

For a description of this series, a listing of 51 volumes, and an identification of editors, see no. 3969–4025 in the 1960 *Guide*. Carl Carmer, who edited the last seven volumes entered in the *Guide*, has continued as the series editor. The volumes issued before 1962 bear the imprint of Rinehart as publisher; thereafter the name is Holt, Rinehart & Winston. Volumes appearing since 1955 include *The Genesee* ([1963]   338 p.   63–12079   F127.-

G2C5), by Henry W. Clune; *The St. Croix: Midwest Border River* ([1965]   309 p.   65–14452   F612.S2D78), by James Taylor Dunn; *The Merrimack* ([1958]   306 p.   58–10701   F72.M6H6), by Raymond P. Holden; *The Minnesota: Forgotten River* ([1962]   306 p.   62–8340   F612.M4J6), by Evan Jones; and *The Cape Fear* ([1965]   340 p.   65–22461   F262.C2R6), by Malcolm H. Ross.

## B.  New England: General

1727.  Dodge, Ernest S.   New England and the South Seas.   Cambridge, Mass., Harvard University Press, 1965.   xv, 216 p.   illus.
65–19823   DU28.3.D6
   Bibliography: p. 199–204.
   The director of the Peabody Museum of Salem employs the resources of his institution's distinguished collection and that of the Essex Institute to sketch the history of Yankee trade in the Pacific during the 19th century. Based on a series of lectures delivered in 1962 at the Lowell Institute, Boston, the book is devoted primarily to the opening of the South Seas trade by the merchants and seamen of Massachusetts and Connecticut and to the dissemination of Yankee products and civilization throughout the South Pacific islands. Emphasizing "the common facets of New England and South Sea history, and the economic, cultural, religious, and political effect of the one region upon the other —but especially of Yankee influence in the Pacific," the author traces the continuing impact of missionary zeal, the political influence of commercial agents, and the mutual legacy of native and New England artifacts. Selections drawn primarily from the same Massachusetts collections have been edited by Norman R. Bennett and George E. Brooks in *New England Merchants in Africa; a History Through Documents, 1802 to 1865* ([Brookline, Mass.] Bos-

ton University Press, 1965.   576 p.   Boston University.   African research studies, no. 7).

1728.  Holbrook, Stewart H.   The Old Post Road; the story of the Boston Post Road.   New York, McGraw-Hill [1962]   273 p.   illus.   (American trails series)   62–9989   F5.H6
   Bibliography: p. 261–263.
   An affectionate and nostalgic "account of selected places, people, things, and events which seem to have been of some special significance in the life of the first post road in the present United States." Beginning with the first post rider who was dispatched from New York on January 22, 1673, and reached Boston on February 5, the historical and geographical milestones of early New England coach travel are traced through four States. In reality, three post roads branched off at New Haven to proceed independently to Boston. The original, or Old Boston Post Road, went by way of Hartford, Springfield, and Worcester; the Lower Road led through New London, Bristol, and Attleboro; and the Middle Road forked at Hartford past Coventry, Pomfret, and Uxbridge. On the basis of his own travels and local inquiry, the author takes the reader over each, stage by stage, in the manner of a historical and biographical Baedeker.

## C.  New England: Local

### NEW HAMPSHIRE AND VERMONT

1729.  Hill, Ralph Nading.   Yankee kingdom: Vermont and New Hampshire.   Illustrations by George Daly.   New York, Harper [1960]   338 p.

(A Regions of America book)   60–7529   F49.H555
   Bibliography: p. 311–324.
   The author takes exception to Arnold Toynbee's dismissal of this northeast corner of the United States as beyond the line of optimum response and

as populated with "certain woodmen, watermen, and hunters." Hill sets out to establish that the region not only has bred some rather singular qualities in its inhabitants, but has also supplied a high percentage of remarkable figures whose influence has been felt far beyond its borders. There follows a series of pointed biographical sketches of such men as Daniel Webster, Horace Greeley, Stephen A. Douglas, Franklin Pierce, and Thaddeus Stevens within the context of the historical, geographical, and social milieu from which they emerged. A particular merit of the work is in the author's unusual selection of his material. Something, for example, of the laconic quality of the legendary Yankee is evident in his portrayal of the religious independence of the region through incisive accounts of the Shaker society and the career of Mary Baker Eddy.

## MASSACHUSETTS

1730. Howe, Henry F. Massachusetts: there she is—behold her. Illustrations and maps by John O'Hara Cosgrave II. New York, Harper [1960] 290 p. (A Regions of America book)
60–13447  F64.H75
Bibliography: p. 269–277.

With pride and a measure of nostalgia, a physician-historian offers a social and economic account of the State. Written for the general reader, the story is told through a selection of "typical incidents and general discussion of characteristic problems in each period." Massachusetts' participation in the Nation's affairs is presented largely through notes on the lives of its great leaders; the democratic virtues of its local government are considered in relation to the tradition of the town meeting. Howe's perspective is extensive, and he is at ease in dealing with the 17th and 18th centuries. He deplores the impact of urbanization and suburbanization on the Yankee smalltown culture. A studied corrective to the Boston-dominated histories of the State, his wider view embraces the local self-education and self-government and the economic arrangements of the peripheral areas: the south coast, western Massachusetts, and the Connecticut valley.

1731. Kirker, Harold, and James Kirker. Bulfinch's Boston, 1787–1817. New York, Oxford University Press, 1964. 305 p. illus.
64–24862  F73.44.K5
"Bibliographical notes": p. 275–298.

When Charles Bulfinch sailed for his grand European tour in 1785, not a single important building had been constructed in Boston for the previous 25 years. Thirty years later, according to the authors, it was "the most perfect architectural city in the nation." This is the story of the architectural transformation of Boston in the Federal period and of one man's involvement in its local affairs for three decades. A product of the aristocratic Province House set—Palladian in taste and Royalist in sentiment—Bulfinch brought the neoclassical revival from the London of Robert Adam and the Whig aristocrats. The loss of his own fortune was the origin of his participation and leadership—as chairman of the Board of Selectmen and as chief of police—in the politics, society, planning, and education, as well as in the artistic development, of Boston. The measure of his achievement is in his ability to translate the new architectural form, along with his own vision and taste, into a style appropriate for the meager circumstance and reluctant atmosphere of the small colonial town then dominated by the commercial Essex Junto.

1732. Whitehill, Walter Muir. Boston, a topographical history. Cambridge, Belknap Press of Harvard University Press, 1959. xxix, 244 p. illus.
59–12978  F73.3.W57
Bibliographical references included in "Notes" (p. [207]–233).

A series of eight lectures delivered in 1958 by the director and librarian of the Boston Athenaeum. The author traces the physical evolution and architectural growth of Boston from its founding in 1630 to the present. The illustrations—maps, drawings, prints, and photographs — were chosen primarily to explain this process of change. The designs of Charles Bulfinch receive special attention. The author has also written Boston: Portrait of a City (Barre, Mass., Barre Publishers, 1964. 112 p.), illustrated with Katharine Knowles' photographs of the city's present-day appearance in all seasons.

## RHODE ISLAND

1733. Coleman, Peter J. The transformation of Rhode Island, 1790–1860. Providence, Brown University Press, 1963. xiv, 314 p. illus.
63–14420  F83.C6
Bibliographical footnotes.

On the basis of a thorough demographic analysis, Coleman identifies the central factor in Rhode Island's history as the "extraordinary disparity from one town to another." Anchoring his interpretations in the locally diverse reaction to changing conditions, he traces the State's transformation from a maritime to an industrial society. In the colonial period, he notes, a severely limited area, a peculiar pattern of population development, and a restricted agricultural potential forced the people to wrest a livelihood from the sea. Early in the 19th century a manufacturing economy began to emerge. The entrepreneurial class, despite its reputation for sharpish, even piratical, business practices, is credited with having responded creatively to the challenge of declining sea trade. By 1860, Rhode Island was the most highly industrialized State in the Union. Numerous tables and maps fortify the author's statistical approach and deliberately narrow treatment.

1734. Lippincott, Bertram. Indians, privateers, and high society; a Rhode Island sampler. Philadelphia, Lippincott [1961] 301 p. illus.

61–8683 F79.L5

Bibliography: p. 289–294.

"Little Rhode Island packs more bizarre and incredible history per square foot than any other state in the Union." Lippincott's historical sketches "attempt to give highlights and sidelights on the career of this hectic little state, from the earliest times to the present." He has assembled a collection of episodes that serve to reinforce his view of Rhode Island's singular development. His style is informal and his selections are governed by an ironic humor and a sense of the dramatic.

## CONNECTICUT

1735. Van Dusen, Albert E. Connecticut. New York, Random House [1961] 470 p.

61–6263 F94.V3

Bibliographical references included in "Notes" (p. 421–461).

A general history written by the State historian at the request of the State Library Committee. Surveying a period of 325 years, it begins with the persecution of the Puritans in England and the emigration of Thomas Hooker and his followers to the New World and concludes with the economic and industrial expansion occurring after World War II. The arrangement is chronological, and the treatment balances political, economic, and social aspects. The author traces the strong spirit of self-reliance and independence that characterized the founding of the theocratic colonies along the Connecticut River and that is manifest in the political behavior of the modern State. A generous selection of contemporary illustrations accompanies the text.

## MAINE

1736. Rich, Louise Dickinson. The coast of Maine, an informal history. Rev. ed. New York, Crowell [1962] 340 p. illus.

62–12804 F19.R5 1962

1736a. Morison, Samuel Eliot. The story of Mount Desert Island, Maine. Boston, Little, Brown [1960] 81 p. illus.

60–9352 F27.M9M6

Originally published in 1956, Mrs. Rich's revised and enlarged volume is a modern guidebook as well as a light, anecdotal, historical narrative. Her material on the coastal towns, islands, and resorts of Maine has been selected with an eye for the eccentric and the picturesque and is presented with a frank, warm, personal attachment. She begins with the earliest prehistoric formation of the region and thereafter becomes chiefly concerned with latter-day rusticators and the beauty and charm of coastal living accumulated and preserved to the present time. Similar in approach; Morison's *The Story of Mount Desert Island, Maine* is a short, informal history and personal reminiscence of life —mostly summer life— on the rocky island at the mouth of the Penobscot River. As the author indicates, his small book is a labor of love. The island's varied inhabitants are described with a wit and amiability usually reserved for friends and neighbors.

1737. Rich, Louise Dickinson. State o' Maine. Illustrations by Aldren A. Watson. New York, Harper & Row [1964] xvi, 302 p. (Regions of America) 64–12679 F19.R52

Bibliography: p. 291–292.

A history of Maine as a way of life emerging from the remote and unique environment. Maine was a province for a considerably longer period of time than it has been a State, and fully half the book is devoted to this prolonged formative period. For many facets of Maine life, the characteristics of this period have continued into statehood. The author probes the thin layer of modernity to expose the rough-hewn qualities that persist today. There are few commercial statistics, and scant attention is given to urban development, closely fought elections, or machine politics. Instead, the broad currents of historical development—or lack of it—are traced against the larger movements of the world outside. In an uneven topical arrangement, which in each case goes back to beginnings, the effects of geography, climate, occupation, and hoary tradition upon the singular deportment of the inhabitants are described and illustrated.

# D. The Middle Atlantic States

## NEW YORK

1738. Carmer, Carl L., *ed.* The tavern lamps are burning; literary journeys through six regions and four centuries of New York State. New York, D. McKay Co. [1964] xix, 567 p. illus.
64–13201 PS548.N7C3

A personal literary anthology that is unusual in its scope and design and in the experience and authority of its editor. Carmer has devoted the greater part of his own study and writings to American regional history and to the history of New York State in particular. That "Upstate" New York possesses a unique quality has long been contended by many of its residents. Partly in an effort to prove this point, Carmer here presents a collection of imaginative writings—fiction, nonfiction, and verse—culled from his own wide reading on the subject. The selections are grouped according to six geographical areas and arranged chronologically within each group. The use of the term "literary journeys" in the volume's subtitle is amply justified; included are pieces by Washington Irving, James Fenimore Cooper, William Cullen Bryant, Edna St. Vincent Millay, Francis Parkman, Herman Melville, Nathaniel Hawthorne, Theodore Dreiser, and Mark Twain, among many others.

1739. Ellis, David M., *and others.* A short history of New York State. Ithaca, N.Y. Published in co-operation with the New York State Historical Association by Cornell University Press [1957] 705 p.
57–4153 F119.E46

A well-balanced and closely knit summary of State history since 1609, prepared over a 10-year period by four New York scholars. Coauthors with Ellis are James A. Frost, Harold C. Syrett, and Harry J. Carman. Book 1, divided into three time periods, tells the story of New York to 1865. Book 2, covering the years since the Civil War, is organized into three topical divisions, political, economic, and cultural, among which the division on economic growth is the longest. The volume has an extensive critical bibliographical essay (p. 655–690).

1740. Gordon, John, *and* L. Rust Hills, *eds.* New York, New York; the city as seen by masters of art and literature. New York, Shorecrest [1965] 403 p.
65–23717 PS509.N5G6

More than 100 paintings, watercolors, and drawings of New York City scenes have been selected by John Gordon, curator of the Whitney Museum of American Art; many are presented in color. Although they are chosen for their intrinsic worth, their chronological arrangement indicates an evolution not only of form but of artistic perception and temperament. The progression from an early wood engraving to abstract painting includes the romantic, the impressionist, and the surrealist. In his selection of short stories by a group of well-known American writers, L. Rust Hills, fiction editor for the *Saturday Evening Post,* illustrates a number of common themes evoked by life in the big city. Behind the variety of mood and approach he finds a recurring emphasis, for example, on the discrepancies that emerge between dream and reality and between the hope of freedom and opportunity and the actuality of loneliness and indifference.

1741. McKelvey, Blake. Rochester: an emerging metropolis, 1925–1961. Rochester, N.Y., Christopher Press, 1961. 404 p. illus. (Rochester Public Library. Kate Gleason Fund publications. Publication 4)
61–18763 F129.R7M228

Few cities in the United States have been studied as carefully by a reliable scholar as has Rochester. This volume concludes McKelvey's four-volume account. The first three are no. 4050–4052 in the 1960 *Guide.* In his preface the author warns readers not to be misled by the title: he has not attempted, as one might expect, a synthetic study of the nature and evolution of a metropolis. His purpose, he insists, is to present a "biographical review of the experiences of a particular community in the throes of such a transformation." The dividing line is a thin one, however, and he deliberately steps across it in the fifth and concluding part of the book, where he discusses Rochester's attainment of metropolitan economy, government, and culture.

## NEW JERSEY

1742. The New Jersey historical series. Edited by Richard M. Huber [and] Wheaton J. Lane. Princeton, N. J., Van Nostrand, 1964–65. 31 v.

This series was conceived by a committee of Jerseymen—Julian P. Boyd, Wesley Frank Craven, John T. Cunningham, David S. Davies, and Richard P. McCormick—and published under the auspices of the New Jersey Tercentenary Commission. Twenty-six numbered volumes and five supplements had appeared by the end of 1965. Issued at a rapid rate, the series contains both chronological surveys and topical studies. Two major themes are common to almost all of the volumes: the elements of unity in the historical development of an otherwise heterogeneous population and the special identity of New Jersey as separate from New York and Pennsylvania. Seven of the more general historical works are no. 1743 through 1749 below.

1743. (Vol. 1) McCormick, Richard P. New Jersey from Colony to State, 1609–1789. 1964. xv, 191 p. illus.      64–17954  F137.M2
"Bibliographical note": p. 176–178.
A general survey of State history from Hudson's voyage of discovery through the ratification of the Federal Constitution.

1744. (Vol. 2) Miers, Earl Schenck, ed. New Jersey and the Civil War: an album of contemporary accounts. 1964. 135 p. illus.
64–2652  E521.M5
Collected from letters, diaries, newspapers, and other sources, this work begins with Lincoln's visit to New Jersey as President-elect in February 1861 and concludes with a New Jersey officer's description of the tragedy at Ford's Theater.

1745. (Vol. 3) Craven, Wesley Frank. New Jersey and the English colonization of North America. 1964. 114 p. illus.
64–2612  F137.C896
"Bibliographical note": p. 103–108.
The founding of East and West New Jersey is discussed in relation to the history of the middle Colonies and England's developing interest in North America.

1746. (Vol. 9) Pomfret, John E. The New Jersey proprietors and their lands, 1664–1776. 1964. xviii, 135 p. illus.      64–7009  F137.P72
"Bibliographical note": p. 124–128.
Relates the essentially feudal character of the proprietary land system to the persistent and continuing struggle by the colonists to preserve their local assemblies, courts, and rights of protest and petition.

1747. (Vol. 10) Leiby, Adrian C. The early Dutch and Swedish settlers of New Jersey. 1964. xiv, 139 p. illus.      64–22336  F145.D9L4
"Bibliographical note": p. 122–129.
The Dutch and Swedish did not settle in New Jersey until after the advent of British rule and came from other Colonies in America rather than from overseas. The origins of their communities are discussed, therefore, within the context of the history of New Netherland and New Sweden.

1748. (Vol. 11) Bill, Alfred Hoyt. New Jersey and the Revolutionary War. 1964. 117 p. illus.      64–23965  E263.N5B5
Bibliography: p. 106–109.
An appraisal of the contribution of this bitterly and almost equally divided State (the "cockpit of the Revolution") amid the pressures and conflicting loyalties of its neighbors.

1749. (Vol. 21) Burr, Nelson R. A narrative and descriptive bibliography of New Jersey. 1964. xxii, 266 p. illus.      65–862  Z1313.B8
This bibliography is drawn from the Library of Congress catalogs, periodical indexes, abstracts of dissertations, *Writings on American History,* and the bibliographies in general histories. The author sets these references in a running commentary, which might stand alone as a brief history of the State.

1750. Pomfret, John E. The Province of West New Jersey, 1609–1702; a history of the origins of an American colony. Princeton, N. J., Princeton University Press, 1956. xii, 298 p. (The Princeton history of New Jersey series)
55–6700  F137.P74
Bibliographical footnotes.

1751. Pomfret, John E. The Province of East New Jersey, 1609–1702, the rebellious proprietary. Princeton, N. J., Princeton University Press, 1962. x, 407 p. (The Princeton history of New Jersey series)      62–7045  F137.P73
Bibliographical footnotes.
Devoting a separate volume to each of the two settlements that were united by the Crown in 1702, Pomfret emphasizes their individual historical identities. The West Jersey proprietary, a Quaker colony, developed with deliberation and in relative tranquility. It remained essentially a rural society, based upon the family unit, with a simple system of land tenure. Individual farms were widely dispersed and government was diffused. The West Jerseymen had more in common with their Quaker neighbors in Pennsylvania than with their partners to the east. By sharp contrast, East Jersey was composed of a heterogeneous population compactly settled in townships where local government, influenced by Puritan and Calvinist religious views, was centered. The two areas suffered in common a period of slow growth, imposed largely by the uncertainties and contradictions within the proprietary system. The union resulting from the surrender of proprietary charters in 1702 was far from complete. West Jersey was largely a part of the hinterland of

Philadelphia, and East Jersey was dominated by the port of New York.

## PENNSYLVANIA

1752. Burt, Nathaniel. The perennial Philadelphians; the anatomy of an American aristocracy. Boston, Little, Brown [1963] xiv, 625 p. illus. 63–14956 F158.3.B97

Bibliography: p. 604–608.

This book "does not pretend to be a full-length study or portrait," the author insists. "This particular portrait is of the head only—of Philadelphia's upper class; a head of such importance in the city that the portrait turns out to be a rather elaborate one. It can be justified on the assumption that Philadelphia, even more than most places, is characterized and dominated by its head—that is, its upper class, the 'Old Philadelphians'; what they are, how they got that way. But it is not a thesis; it is not meant to prove or demonstrate, merely to present, to introduce." The author, a novelist and poet, portrays this social oligarchy in all its charm and parochialism and with its "tinge of decadence."

1753. Lorant, Stefan, ed. Pittsburgh; the story of an American city. Garden City, N. Y., Doubleday [1964] 520 p.

64–23508 F159.P6L68

Bibliography: p. 507–512.

CONTENTS.—Forts in the wilderness, by Henry Steele Commager.—Gateway to the West, by Stefan Lorant.—The city grows, by Oscar Handlin.—The Civil War and its aftermath, by J. Cutler Andrews.—The hearth of the Nation, by Sylvester K. Stevens.—Problems of labor, by Henry David.—The entrepreneurs, by John Morton Blum.—The muckraking era, by Gerald W. Johnson.—Between two wars, by Stefan Lorant.—Rebirth, by David L. Lawrence (as told to John P. Robin and Stefan Lorant).

The editor devoted 10 years to collecting the more than a thousand illustrations—reproducing maps, sketches, contemporary prints and photographs, and original art work—and has brought together a group of contributors whose combined chapters form a unified history of the city. A 50-page chronology of events, compiled by Mel Seidenberg, Lois Mulkearn, and James W. Hess, concludes the volume.

1754. O'Meara, Walter. Guns at the forks. Englewood Cliffs, N. J., Prentice-Hall [1965] 275 p. illus. (The American forts series)

65–12921 F159.P6O4

Bibliography: p. 259–263.

On the site of today's "Golden Triangle" in Pittsburgh, Fort Duquesne and then Fort Pitt guarded three river routes of frontier travel: the Allegheny, connecting with Lake Erie by way of a chain of French forts; the Monongahela, leading toward the Potomac Valley; and the Ohio, opening to the Mississippi and the wide frontier beyond. O'Meara's book is an account of the part these forts played in the French and British colonial rivalry during the French and Indian War (Seven Years' War). The story begins in 1753 with young Major George Washington's mission demanding a peaceful departure of all French from the Ohio. Most of the narrative thereafter concerns the immediate consequences of that ultimatum within a limited area. The shifting fortunes of small armies reach a climax with the victory of British troops under Col. Henry Bouquet at the Battle of Bushy Run in 1760. An epilogue briefly traces the history of Fort Pitt from the end of the war to the present.

1755. Stevens, Sylvester K. Pennsylvania, birthplace of a nation. New York, Random House [1964] 399 p. illus. 64–18930 F149.S77

"What to read about Pennsylvania": p. 379–390.

The executive director of the Pennsylvania Historical and Museum Commission, a former State historian, wrote this volume to meet his State's need for a "good and sound history." Earlier historical surveys of Pennsylvania, including his own lengthy work, *Pennsylvania, the Keystone State* (New York, American Historical Co. [1956] 2 v.), were viewed by the author as inadequate. In the new study, Stevens places major emphasis upon the Pennsylvania story since 1865; three chapters center on the history of the State since 1900. The discussion covers the "growth and even the temporary decline of the economy of Pennsylvania," as well as social and cultural affairs. The text is extensively illustrated, and the appendix contains a detailed chronology, a historical sketch of Pennsylvania counties, a list of State executives, and a bibliographical essay. Stevens also served as coeditor, with Donald H. Kent, of the Historical and Museum Commission's *Bibliography of Pennsylvania History*, 2d ed. (Harrisburg, 1957. 826 p.), compiled by Norman B. Wilkinson. Also written for the general reader by another member of the commission, Paul A. W. Wallace's *Pennsylvania: Seed of a Nation* (New York, Harper & Row [1962] 322 p. A Regions of America book) is a history of the State from its geological beginnings to the present.

# DISTRICT OF COLUMBIA

1756. Aikman, Lonnelle. We, the people; the story of the United States Capitol, its past and its promise. [3d ed.] Washington, United States Capitol Historical Society, 1965. 143 p.

65–20721 F204.C2A45 1965

1756a. The White House; an historic guide. Washington, White House Historical Association, 1962. 129 p. 62–18058 F204.W5W6

*We, the People,* which has an introduction by Allan Nevins, is the story of the building and site where Congress meets. Through the generous use of illustrations and the words of eminent lawmakers, the Capitol is presented as a continuing inspiration and a "symbol in stone of the success of our republic." *The White House* is the first official guidebook to the Executive Mansion. Mrs. John N. Pearce, curator of the White House, wrote the text and selected the illustrations. Mrs. Jacqueline Kennedy states in the foreword that the guidebook was originally planned for children, but "as research went on and so many little-known facts were gleaned from forgotten papers, it was decided to make it a book that could be of profit to adults and scholars also." Both these volumes were published in cooperation with the National Geographic Society, which lent the photographic and production skills of its staff and—for no. 1756—the services of Mrs. Aikman of the Senior Editorial Staff as author.

1757. Carpenter, Frank G. Carp's Washington. Arranged and edited by Frances Carpenter. Introduction by Cleveland Amory. New York, McGraw-Hill [1960] 314 p. 60–9844 F196.C3

A collection of early articles by Frank G. Carpenter, a Washington correspondent for the *Cleveland Leader* who wrote a widely copied column of gossip and social commentary on the Washington scene. Preserved in scrapbooks by his wife, the articles are here arranged and edited by his daughter and published in book form for the first time. Beginning in 1882 and continuing into "Ben Harrison's era," Carpenter's reporting covered the trivia as well as the potentially momentous news of Capitol Hill, the White House, and both high and low society. "Whether considering President Cleveland's love-life, the low-cut evening gowns of Washington hostesses, the Congressmen's spittoons, or women 'enameling' themselves, Carp does so with a contemporary, present-tense style that brilliantly brings his era to life," Amory asserts in his introduction.

1758. Green, Constance McLaughlin. Washington. Princeton, N. J., Princeton University Press, 1962–63. 2 v. 62–7402 F194.G7

Bibliography: v. 1, p. 405–427; v. 2, p. 513–529.

CONTENTS — v. 1. Village and Capital, 1800–1878. — v. 2. Capital City, 1879–1950.

Mrs. Green was awarded the Pulitzer Prize for the first volume of this history of the Nation's Capital. The overall purpose of the study is to develop "a better understanding of the nature of urban growth in the United States and its place in American history." The author examines the evolution of race relations and problems posed by the city's delicate position between North and South; the "psychological impermanence" of its inhabitants that continues to impede the organization of civic energies and is aggravated by the absence of the vote and of local participation in city government; and above all, the problem of municipal management in a city unable to tax its largest landowner. Because of the nature of the source material available for the period before 1878, Mrs. Green notes, the first volume is "more narrative than analytical." The second volume benefits from 20th-century community and urban studies and, in drawing upon interviews with contemporaries, becomes progressively more incisive.

1759. Smith, Arthur Robert, *and* Arnold Eric Sevareid. Washington: magnificent capital. Photography by Fred J. Maroon. Garden City, N. Y., Doubleday, 1965. 248 p.

65–24912 F200.S63

A volume of brief, pithy essays by two Washington correspondents on the sights, institutions, life, culture, and government of the Nation's Capital. Topics discussed include the legislators and the halls of Congress, the President and his mansion, the diplomats on "Embassy Row" and their social haunts, the military and its citadel, members of the press, Supreme Court Justices, and both high and low society. Full-page photographs—many of them in color—illustrate the chapters.

# E. The South: General

1760. Clark, Thomas D. The emerging South. New York, Oxford University Press, 1961. 317 p.                    61–8368  F209.C58
"Selected bibliography": p. 287–303.

The author, a Mississippian by birth, reviews the changes in Southern life since the 1920's. Aside from the sources listed in his bibliography, he writes effectively from his own experience. Observations from the 19th century travel accounts of Frederick Law Olmsted are followed by Clark's analyses of such subjects as public health, education, population and the urban movement, the growth of the tourist trade, racial integration, agricultural depression, and the rise of industry. Although the rapid expansion of modern industry is conveyed as the most pervasive economic development since the depression, agriculture receives a larger share of attention. Political history is omitted. "The South in Cultural Change" was contributed by Clark as one of eight papers presented to the 1962 conference at Duke University on "The Impact of Political and Legal Change in the Postwar South." These papers were edited by Allan P. Sindler and published under the title *Change in the Contemporary South* (Durham, N. C., Duke University Press, 1963. 247 p.).

1761. Eaton, Clement. The growth of Southern civilization, 1790–1860. New York, Harper [1961] xvii, 357 p. illus. (The New American Nation series)                    61–12219  F213.E18
Bibliography: p. 325–344.

A study of the structure of Southern society as "a federalism of cultures—the Creole civilization, the lowland and the upland cultures, the mores of the black belts and of the pinelands of the Southwest, and city life." In an introductory chapter, Eaton reviews the ubiquity of the ideal of the English country gentleman and sets the stage for the rise of the cotton kingdom. Despite his affection for the Old South, the author reveals its paradoxes, its restrictions on thought, its determination to retain slavery, its pursuit of profits, its self-centeredness, and its self-esteem. Political history after the Jackson era and intellectual history in general are left for other authors in the New American Nation Series. A useful supplement to this volume is Eaton's book *The Mind of the Old South* ([Baton Rouge] Louisiana State University Press [1964] 271 p.), which is based on the Fleming Lectures in Southern History which he delivered at Louisiana State University in 1961.

1762. Ezell, John S. The South since 1865. New York, Macmillan [1963] 511 p. illus.
                    63–13126  F215.E94
Bibliography: p. 479–492.

Underlying the task of reintegrating the defeated South into the Union after 1865 were "the twin problems of the South's attitude toward its new citizens—the freed Negro slaves who composed one-third of the population—and its feelings for the nation it had tried to destroy. What the minimum changes were which the North would accept, as well as what concessions the South would make voluntarily, were the core of Southern history after 1865 and are the theme of this book." The author asserts that, although the legacies of the past were still regional characteristics of the South, "the evidence was clear that the South was moving back into the 'mainstream' of American life." He traces developments in the realms of urbanization, race, religion, education, and politics that have "brought the South in line with the prevailing national culture to a greater degree than ever before in its history."

1763. Hesseltine, William B., *and* David L. Smiley. The South in American history. 2d ed. Englewood Cliffs, N. J., Prentice-Hall, 1960. 630 p. illus.          60–6880  F209.H48  1960

A revised edition of no. 4071 in the 1960 *Guide.* The "Selected bibliography" appearing at the end of each chapter in the first edition has been deleted.

1764. A history of the South. Edited by Wendell Holmes Stephenson and E. Merton Coulter. Baton Rouge, Louisiana State University Press, 1947–61. 8 v.

Entry no. 4072 in the 1960 *Guide* describes this series. The first six volumes issued are no. 4073–4078. The two volumes that appeared after 1955 are listed below as no. 1765 and 1766.

1765. (Vol. 3) Alden, John R. The South in the Revolution, 1763–1789. 1957. xv, 442 p. illus.                    57–12096  F213.A4
"Critical essay on authorities": p. 401–426.

The author, James B. Duke Professor of History at Duke University, stresses four principal themes: "the role of the Southerners (not yet generally called by that name) in the struggle for independence; the rise of sectional controversy between North and South, which is as old as the nation; the internal reformation below the Mason-Dixon line that proceeded from the contest with Britain; and the part taken by the South in the making of the Federal union formed at the end of the Revolutionary time."

1766. (Vol. 4) Abernethy, Thomas P. The South in the new nation, 1789–1819. 1961. xvi, 529 p. illus.          61–15488  F213.A2
"Critical essay on authorities": p. 476–499.
The frontier, the international power politics that played upon it, the pattern and process of settlement, and the side-by-side growth of a democracy and a landed gentry receive the emphasis in this volume. Sectionalism is a secondary theme, and for social and economic development the reader is referred to the succeeding volume in the series (entry no. 4074 in the 1960 Guide).

1767. Kane, Harnett T., ed. The romantic South. New York, Coward-McCann [1961] 385 p. (American vista series)          61–5424  F209.K33
Author of more than 20 books on the South, Kane has here compiled an attractively produced literary album of this "most regional of American regions." In discussing the South's literary heritage, he attempts to represent "all or most schools of thought and writing" and "to strike a balance between classic material and the less familiar." The volume as a whole is chronological, but the selections are divided into six categories, some of which overlap or parallel each other in time, and the writers are entered by subject. For example, part 1, entitled "Finders and Founders," covers the period from the explorations of the 16th century through the age of Jefferson; the writers range in time from Giovanni da Verrazzano to Marshall Fishwick. Parts 2–6 deal respectively with "flush times" in the Southeast, 1815–1860; plantation life in the deep South and the Southwest; the rise of Texas; Civil War and Reconstruction; and the recent South. Part 6 reflects the high literary productivity of Southerners in the 20th century.

1768. Sellers, Charles G., ed. The Southerner as American. Chapel Hill, University of North Carolina Press [1960] 216 p. 60–4104 F209.S44
Bibliographical notes: p. 203–216.
CONTENTS.—"As for our history . . . ," by John Hope Franklin.—Americans below the Potomac, by Thomas P. Govan.—The travail of slavery, by Charles Grier Sellers, Jr.—The Southerner as a fighting man, by David Donald.—Reconstruction: index to Americanism, by Grady McWhiney.—The central theme revisited, by George B. Tindall.—The Negro as Southerner and American, by L. D. Reddick.—An American politics for the South, by Dewey W. Grantham, Jr.—The Southerner as American writer, by C. Hugh Holman.

Nine writers who "share a common approach to Southern history" reexamine the region's traditions and institutions and attempt to determine the extent to which they are compatible with the "American way of life." The rationale for this cooperative effort is briefly as follows: the South is facing a period of severe crisis; the manner in which it responds to this crisis depends to a large degree upon its image of itself; in the past historians have contributed to a distorted image by a preoccupation with the differentness of the South; historians must now help the South to form a new image, one in which the region's bonds with the Nation are highlighted.

1769. Simkins, Francis Butler. A history of the South. 3d ed. New York, Knopf, 1963. xiii, 675, xxiv p.          63–16714  F209.S5 1963
Bibliography: p. 635–675.

1770. Simkins, Francis Butler. The everlasting South. [Baton Rouge] Louisiana State University Press [1963] xv, 103 p.
                                    63–20407  F209.S488
A History of the South is a revised edition of no. 4082 in the 1960 Guide. In The Everlasting South, a volume of five brief essays, Simkins renders explicit and succinct his conservative statement of the South's position that is the pervading theme of his textbook and appeals for the continued realization of the South's identity as a region with a distinct culture and behavior of its own. "Indeed," he asserts, "it can be argued that the region, despite many changes, is as much different from the rest of the United States today as it was in 1860."

1771. Southern Historical Association. The pursuit of Southern history; presidential addresses of the Southern Historical Association, 1935–1963. Edited by George Brown Tindall. Baton Rouge, Louisiana State University Press, 1964. xxi, 541 p.          64–21595  F209.S74
Bibliographical references included in "Notes" (p. 495–534).
Although all of the addresses are devoted to the history of the South, they were not planned to be related in content. Tindall's introduction places them in perspective and reveals that most of them fall into three basic categories: historiography, sectionalism, and life in the Southern States. The

origins of southern historiography are discussed by E. Merton Coulter, Philip M. Hamer, Joseph G. de Roulhac Hamilton, and Wendell H. Stephenson. Sectionalism is most explicit in Frank L. Owsley's discourse on the Northeast's "egocentric sectionalism" as the fundamental cause of the Civil War. Charles S. Sydnor, Fletcher M. Green, James W. Patton, and Walter B. Posey provide glimpses into the life of the Old South. Thomas D. Clark, Rembert W. Patrick, Clement Eaton, and James W. Silver discuss society in the New South. Silver's "Mississippi: The Closed Society," which received wide newspaper coverage and appeared in expanded form as a book with the same title (no. 1795 in this *Supplement*), is a primary source in itself. As a group, Tindall notes in his introductory essay, these presidential addresses touch upon points in a wide spectrum and suggest areas for further exploration. Although they devote little attention to subjects such as Reconstruction, economic development, intellectual history, and the race problem from the Negro's point of view, they "constitute a remarkably broad and distinguished cross-section of southern historical scholarship over a period of three decades."

1772. Woodward, Comer Vann. The burden of southern history. Baton Rouge, Louisiana State University Press [1960] 205 p.

60–13169 F209.W6

Eight essays reflecting the author's search for identifying elements in the Southern character. All but one, "A Southern Critique for the Gilded Age," have previously appeared in periodicals. Woodward seeks to isolate and understand qualities in the Southern mind which have made the inhabitants of the South distinctive or have combined to produce a "regional essence." These elements he finds in the Southern past. He examines selected historical incidents in which the "collective experience" of the Southern people differs essentially from that of the rest of America. By a series of contrasts he concludes that the differentness is derived in large part from the Southern experience with poverty, defeat, and the tragic evil of slavery. In a Nation where "success and victory are still national habits of mind," he sees the effects of the South's frustration and failure. Against the legend of American innocence and moral complacency—untainted by the Old World evils of feudalism and monarchism—is posed the South's "un-American adventure in feudal fantasy" and its experience with the realities of human tragedy and bondage.

# F. The South Atlantic States: Local

## VIRGINIA

1773. Bodine, A. Aubrey. The face of Virginia. Baltimore, Bodine [1963] 176 p. (chiefly illus.)

63–19830 F227.B6

A collection of photographs taken over a period of some 30 years by a photographer. In an introduction, Virginius Dabney states that the book portrays "Virginia, both old and new, with a balance, range, artistry and charm which in my opinion has never been equalled in any portfolio of views on the Old Dominion." Credit is also given to J. Albert Caldwell and Son and to what the author describes as their "amazing process" of Unitone lithography. Bodine's views do equal justice to the natural beauty of the Virginia landscape, the State's wealth of historic and educational buildings, the impingement of recent military installations, and the wide variety of economic enterprise. The present volume is the latest in a series that also includes *The Face of Maryland* (Baltimore, Bodine; distributed by Viking Press, New York [1961] 144 p.).

1774. Fishwick, Marshall W. Virginia: a new look at the Old Dominion. New York, Harper [1959] 305 p. illus. (A Regions of America book)

58–6148 F226.F49

"Bibliographical note": p. 282–283.

An analysis of the nature and persistence of the "Virginia tradition" and its effect upon the social and political views of successive generations of Virginians. The author pursued this theme earlier in a brief work, *The Virginia Tradition* (Washington, Public Affairs Press [1956] 111 p.). His later and longer account shows Virginians caught up in a self-perpetuating mythology: "What Virginians think they are has a lot to do with what they have become." Legend becomes historical fact when viewed as a pervasive influence in the development of regional culture. Probing life in the Allegheny cabin or the tidewater plantation, among the poor whites or the "First Families of Virginia," the author balances early glories and modern frustrations. To the familiar predicament of Virginia's position in the Union—the pull between North and South—

are added the disturbing implications of the internal tensions generated by the east-west divisions of the State. A final chapter offers a comparative review of historical writing in Virginia.

1775. Wertenbaker, Thomas J. Norfolk: historic Southern port. 2d ed., edited by Marvin W. Schlegel. Durham, N.C., Duke University Press [1962] 417 p. illus.

        62–10054   F234.N8W4  1962

A revised edition of no. 4088 in the 1960 *Guide.* Wertenbaker's death interrupted the work of revision; Schlegel edited the manuscript and wrote parts of two chapters on the post-World-War-II period.

## WEST VIRGINIA

1776. Ambler, Charles H., *and* Festus P. Summers. West Virginia, the Mountain State. 2d ed. Englewood Cliffs, N.J., Prentice-Hall, 1958. 584 p. illus.    57–12033  F241.A523  1958

"Bibliographical note": p. 562–564.

A revised edition of no. 4089 in the 1960 *Guide.* Beginning chapters are recast, those covering the period since 1870 have been entirely rewritten, and additions bring the story up to the present. Special studies of the State's history are *The Smokeless Coal Fields of West Virginia; a Brief History* (Morgantown, West Virginia University Library, 1963. 106 p.), by W. P. Tams, and Roy B. Clarkson's abundantly illustrated *Tumult on the Mountains; Lumbering in West Virginia, 1770–1920* (Parsons, W.Va., McClain Print. Co., 1964. 410 p.).

## NORTH CAROLINA

1777. Lefler, Hugh T., *and* Albert Ray Newsome. North Carolina, the history of a Southern State. Rev. ed. Chapel Hill, University of North Carolina Press [1963] 756 p.

        63–3932   F254.L39  1963

Bibliography: p. [681]–713.

A revised edition of no. 4090 in the 1960 *Guide.* Lefler has reorganized and rewritten that portion of the book dealing with the period after 1896. He has also edited a fourth edition of his *North Carolina History Told by Contemporaries* (Chapel Hill, University of North Carolina Press [1965] 580 p.). A helpful array of facts and figures about the State, past and present, is *North Carolina; an Economic and Social Profile* (Chapel Hill, University of North Carolina Press [1958] 380 p.), by Samuel Huntington Hobbs.

## SOUTH CAROLINA

1778. Guess, William Francis. South Carolina: annals of pride and protest. Illustrations and maps by John O'Hara Cosgrave, II. New York, Harper [1960] 337 p. illus. (A Regions of America book)    58–12450  F269.G85

Bibliography: p. 325–329.

As in many of the volumes in the Regions of America series, this history of South Carolina is introduced by a personal prologue establishing the author's relationship and approach to his subject and setting the style of the work. Directed toward the general reader, the book is a broad episodic review of the South Carolinian ethos from colonial times to the present, rich in biography, literary allusion, and regional pride and idiom. Selections he makes from contemporary diaries and letters provide insight into "the marvelously informing drama of acute and archetypal minds at grips with crucial experience." Guess leans heavily on Ulrich B. Phillips' assertion that white supremacy was the "central theme" in Southern history. The effect of the Negro's presence within the fabric of South Carolina's social, political, and economic affairs is a constant ingredient in his discussion of the State's development.

## GEORGIA

1779. Averitt, Jack N. Georgia's coastal plain. New York, Lewis Historical Pub. Co. [<sup>c</sup>1964] 3 v.    65–2086  F286.A9

A formidable two-volume history (accompanied by a third volume of biographical sketches) of the original coastal counties of southeastern Georgia. The author includes an account of the region's contribution to the development of the State and its influence on the role played by the State in national affairs. Georgia's colonial history is almost entirely confined to these southeastern counties. Conspicuous early traits were a pattern of political unity and conservatism and a tendency toward a predominant interest in economic affairs, accompanied by a cultural and artistic cosmopolitanism surrounding the port of Savannah. The first volume is largely a narrative of events from Oglethorpe's first settlement to the eve of the Civil War. Volume 2 begins with a discussion of Georgia in the Civil War and the Reconstruction period and then follows a primarily topical arrangement, tracing in turn the southeastern region's agricultural, political, financial, industrial, and cultural development to the present time. In all, attention is devoted to a range of individuals and details which tend to be neglected in general histories. A final chapter describes briefly each of the 40 modern counties in the area today.

1780. Coulter, Ellis Merton. Georgia, a short history. Rev. and enl. ed. Chapel Hill, University of North Carolina Press [1960] 537 p.
60–16233 F286.C78 1960
An updated edition of no. 4094 in the 1960 *Guide*.

## FLORIDA

1781. Covington, James W. The story of southwestern Florida. New York, Lewis Historical Pub. Co., 1957. 2 v. illus.
58–880 F311.C67
Vol. 2 has subtitle: *Family and Personal History*. Includes bibliographical references.

A general account of the development of southwestern Florida from the earliest times to the present, based largely on secondary sources and local newspaper files. Nearly half the work deals with the 20th century. Arranged topically, it describes the area's rapid expansion following each of the two world wars. The progress of activities that make up a large part of Florida's regional image — real estate promotion, the tourist trade, citrus and fishing industries, baseball's winter quarters — is fully explored, as are such standard ingredients of regional history as flora, fauna, scenery, transportation, communication, religion, and education.

# G. The Old Southwest: General

1782. Arnow, Harriette L. S. Seedtime on the Cumberland. New York, Macmillan, 1960. xviii, 449 p.
60–7414 F442.2.A7
Bibliographical footnotes.

1783. Arnow, Harriette L. S. Flowering of the Cumberland. New York, Macmillan [1963] xviii, 441 p.
63–15672 F442.2.A69
Bibliographical footnotes.

The author, a novelist, has produced two nonfiction volumes on pioneer life in the valley of the Cumberland from 1780 to 1803. Together they represent the culmination of a lifetime of collection and assimilation. Her facts come from a wide range of local records, memoirs, and other written sources and from her own cultural inheritance in her native Kentucky. "This work," she writes in the acknowledgments in the first volume, "is not a history, nor is it concerned with the lives of famous men and women, nor does it pretend to be an exhaustive study of the pioneer. I have tried to re-create a few of the more important aspects of pioneer life as it was lived on the Cumberland by ordinary men and women." The same statements apply equally well to the second volume. Different themes, more than different time periods, distinguish the two volumes. *Seedtime* emphasizes the settler's ability to conquer a new environment, whereas *Flowering* is concerned chiefly with his success in transplanting Old World culture. Within this dual arrangement the organization is essentially esthetic; the end result is considerably more than a historical scrapbook. Both themes are developed with an intimate familiarity and an easy narrative style.

1784. Daniels, Jonathan. The devil's backbone; the story of the Natchez Trace. With map and headpieces by the Dillons. New York, McGraw-Hill [1962] 278 p. illus. (The American trails series)
61–18131 F341.D24
"Sources and acknowledgments": p. 259–267.

The Natchez Trace was used mostly in one direction — from the Mississippi River at the future site of Natchez northward through the lands of the Choctaws and the Chickasaws, and across Tennessee to the Cumberland River at Nashville. It was the road back for traders and boatmen who freighted their products downstream by barge, keelboat, and raft along the Cumberland, Ohio, and Mississippi Rivers from Kentucky, Indiana, and Pennsylvania. The author populates this ancient pathway, which followed roughly an old Indian trail, with a wide spectrum of figures and tells the early histories of such various personalities as Abraham Lincoln, General James Wilkinson, Aaron Burr, Meriwether Lewis, and, in particular, Andrew Jackson, who rode on his wedding journey down the Trace with Rachel Donelson and later marched down it to the Battle of New Orleans.

1785. Havighurst, Walter. Voices on the river; the story of the Mississippi waterways. New York, Macmillan [1964] 310 p. illus.
64–11761 HE630.M6H35
Bibliography: p. 287–297.
"A survey of three centuries of transportation on the Mississippi system, from Indian canoes to the barge fleets that now dwarf the vanished steamboat traffic." The author traces the course of river craft

by the cry of the steersman on raft or keelboat, the pitch of a steamboat whistle, or the varied sounds of a ship's bell signaling the passage of time and the rivalries of commerce. More a collection of storied lore than a history of transport, the book makes its subject—"the everlasting river"—the setting for travelers' tales, the pageant of explorer, fur trader, and peddler, and the romance of steamboat travel.

# H. The Old Southwest: Local

## LOUISIANA

1786. Davis, Edwin Adams. Louisiana, a narrative history. 2d ed. Baton Rouge, Claitor's Book Store, 1965. 394 p.

65–3751 F369.D24 1965

Bibliography: p. 385–394.

First published in 1961, this sizable history—of greater dimensions than the usual textbook—is used as a general reading and study guide on the college level. With some justice, the author repeatedly characterizes the story of Louisiana history as a "fabulous saga." The political, legal, and social aspects of Louisiana's French and Spanish origins reflect an experience not shared by other States. During the "War for Southern Independence" and the military occupation that followed, Louisiana suffered more and longer than most of her neighbors. This era is presented with an undisguised regret and mordancy. Another of the State's unique adventures is related in a clear and balanced account of the rise of Huey Long. A closeup view of New Orleans and its flamboyant growth after the Louisiana Purchase is found in Albert E. Fossier's *New Orleans; the Glamour Period, 1800–1840* (New Orleans, Pelican Pub. Co. [ᶜ1957] 520 p.).

## ARKANSAS

1787. White, Lonnie J. Politics on the Southwestern Frontier: Arkansas Territory, 1819–1836. Memphis, Memphis State University Press, 1964. 219 p. illus.

64–55971 F411.W49

Bibliography: p. [206]–212.

A minutely documented, factual account, largely from local newspaper sources, of the rise of factionalism in territorial politics during a period when alignments were often based upon personalities rather than issues and political differences were sometimes settled at the dueling grounds. The author's principal objective is to examine the political foundations which were established for the future State of Arkansas during the 17 years of territorial status. The successive elections during this period are examined in detail as the training ground for future political leaders under statehood.

## TENNESSEE

1788. Folmsbee, Stanley J., Robert E. Corlew, *and* Enoch L. Mitchell. History of Tennessee. New York, Lewis Historical Pub. Co., 1960. 4 v. illus., maps.

61–2736 F436.F64

Vols. 3–4 have subtitle: *Family and Personal History.*

Bibliography: v. 2, p. 395–430.

Two weighty volumes of history, supplemented by two volumes of biographical sketches. The three authors share about equally the task of relating the story of the State's progress from the earliest times to the present day. Folmsbee introduces the work with a topographical chapter that is especially useful in view of the later stormy territorial and statehood boundary problems. He also discusses the entry of the State into the Union and recounts its role in the War of 1812. Corlew covers the 19th century, with particular reference to the Jacksonian era and the deep divisions caused by the Civil War and Reconstruction. Tennessee's development in the 20th century is recounted by Mitchell, who examines the course of politics, education, religion, and conservation and describes society and culture at midcentury.

1789. Govan, Gilbert E., *and* James W. Livingood. The Chattanooga country, 1540–1962; from tomahawks to TVA. [Rev. ed.] Chapel Hill, University of North Carolina Press [1963] 526 p.

63–4206 F444.C4G6 1963

Bibliography: p. 495–512.

A revised edition of no. 4104 in the 1960 *Guide.*

## KENTUCKY

1790. Clark, Thomas D. A history of Kentucky. [Rev. ed.] Lexington, Ky., John Bradford Press, 1960. 516 p. 61–1846 F451.C63 1960

Bibliography: p. 461–493.

A revised edition of no. 4106 in the 1960 *Guide.*

1791. Moore, Arthur K. The frontier mind; a cultural analysis of the Kentucky frontiersman.

[Lexington] University of Kentucky Press [1957] 264 p.                    57–11379 F454.M65
   Includes bibliographies.
   The author approaches the Kentucky frontiersman through his reflection in literature and the tall tale; his study is more a report of what nonfrontiersmen thought about this "buckskin hero" or "playful savage" than a penetration of his mind and culture. Moore reverses the well-known thesis of Frederick Jackson Turner, stating that frontier democracy had its origins not in the forest but in the European heritage. What emerged from the forest was the "alligator-horse" (yet another sobriquet for the frontiersman, after a familiar myth), "invested with all the rights and privileges of republican citizenship and ill prepared to exercise them." Regarding the myths of the earthly paradise and the noble savage as operative factors in the occupation and development of Kentucky, the author has produced a lively polemic against primitivism, charging that it underlies the inadequacies of midwestern culture, both in the age of settlement and considerably later.

## MISSOURI

1792. Kirschten, Ernest. Catfish and crystal. Bicentenary edition of the St. Louis story. Garden City, N.Y., Doubleday [1965] 508 p.
                    65–22575 F474.S2K5 1965
   A history of the "Gateway City" by an editorial writer for the *St. Louis Post-Dispatch*. First published in 1960, this book in its bicentenary edition begins with French control and ends with a postscript chapter which, among other new items, announces another world series for the Cardinals. A fast-moving parade of anecdotes, historical asides, and personality sketches make up the St. Louis "story." Reports on machine politics, backroom deals, social scandal, tenderloin, baseball, and breweries are culled from the files, as well as tales of explorers, traders, missionaries, settlers, civic leaders, churches, and art societies as the constituent elements in the growth and progress of a great crossroads city.

1793. McReynolds, Edwin C. Missouri; a history of the Crossroads State. Norman, University of Oklahoma Press [1962] xiv, 483 p. illus.
                    62–18052 F466.M2
   Bibliography: p. 459–466.
   Beginning with the early Spanish explorers and the national rivalries and first settlements in the Mississippi Valley, McReynolds presents a compressed factual narrative of the acquisition of the Missouri Territory in the Louisiana Purchase of 1803 and its subsequent rise to statehood in 1821. From this point forward, emphasis is upon Missouri's place in the history of the United States. The Missouri regional strategy in the opening of the Far West, the central role of the State in western railroad development, and the national attention drawn to the Missouri Compromise are covered. With a secessionist Governor and a unionist population, the State mirrored the national agony on the eve of the Civil War. The State's agricultural development and the granger, populist, isolationist, and reform movements are described within the context of the policies and fortunes—and the long successive tenures—of the Democratic and Republican Parties. Prominent Missourians are discussed in the context of their appearance on the national scene and in the tangle of national party politics. Particular reference is made to figures such as Thomas Hart Benton, David Barton, and the younger Francis P. Blair, as well as to the Pendergast politics of the 1930's, and the rise of Harry S. Truman.

1794. Meyer, Duane G. The heritage of Missouri, a history. Saint Louis, State Pub. Co., 1963. 843 p. illus.                    63–1213 F466.M578
   Bibliographies at the ends of chapters.
   "The scope of the book is broad; the social, economic, and political development of Missouri is reviewed from the era of the mastodon to the age of the missile." Written as a comprehensive text, this work is enhanced by its abundant illustrations and clear chronological organization. The author defines and evaluates the State's historical legacy in terms of its geographical position as the pioneer center of river, rail, and air transportation; the varied national and racial elements of its population that precluded the growth of a clear-cut regional image; and its dual economy—commercial and agricultural—characterized by financial conservatism and the lack of dramatic economic development. The region along the Missouri River has historically been a center of activity, and the State's wealth, political power, and cultural life are concentrated along the axis between Kansas City and St. Louis. The mid-State area's predominant role during the formative period receives closer scrutiny in Andrew Theodore Brown's *Kansas City to 1870* (Columbia, Mo., University of Missouri Press [1964, ᶜ1963] 235 p.), the first volume of his *Frontier Community*.

## MISSISSIPPI

1795. Silver, James W. Mississippi: the closed society. New York, Harcourt, Brace &

World [1964] xxii, 250 p.    64–19939  F345.S5
Bibliographical footnotes.

An expansion of the author's 1963 presidential address before the Southern Historical Association. It examines historically certain political and racial parallels between the slavery era in Mississippi and the subsequent regime of white supremacy in that State. The immediate occasion for the address and this volume was Silver's experience as an eyewitness to the mob violence which attended the court-ordered admission of James Howard Meredith, a Negro, to the University of Mississippi on September 30, 1962. The author has set down a strong indictment of Mississippi society, laws, and govern-ment officials in relation to the past, to other States, to the Federal Government, and to the laws of the land. He asserts that in its racial arrangements since the Civil War Mississippi has continuously perpetuated a system of exclusion, in defense of which its highest officials invoke an elaborate structure of historical myth, political and social pressure, and legal oppression. "Today the closed society of Mississippi imposes on all its people acceptance of and obedience to an official orthodoxy almost identical with the one developed in the middle of the 19th century. In fact the philosophical basis for slavery has become the catechism of white supremacy."

# I. The Old Northwest: General

1796. Hatcher, Harlan H., and Erich A. Walter.
    A pictorial history of the Great Lakes, by Harlan Hatcher and Erich A. Walter, assisted by Orin W. Kaye, Jr. New York, Crown Publishers [ᶜ1963]  344 p.          63–12068  F551.H37
    Bibliography: p. 338.
Hatcher, the author of *The Great Lakes* (1944) and *The Western Reserve* (1949), no. 4114 and 4118, respectively, in the 1960 *Guide,* has joined with Walter and Kaye in arranging a collection of illustrations, including reproductions of photographs, museum prints, and maps, in a striking companion to his earlier works. The full range and development of lake shipping is portrayed in detail—even to an unusual poster of the standard stack colors of the Great Lakes fleets. Early and modern scenes appear together, and views of locks, canals, lighthouses, bridges, cities, and industrial centers sustain the theme of a vigorous maritime and commercial expansion. A compact narrative carries the coverage to the opening of the St. Lawrence Seaway in 1959.

1797. Havighurst, Walter. The Heartland: Ohio,
    Indiana, Illinois. Illustrations by Grattan Condon. New York, Harper & Row [1962]  400 p. (A Regions of America book)
                   62–14531  F479.H28
    Bibliography: p. 379–388.
Readers who have followed Havighurst's excursions into the history of the Old Northwest will find many familiar landmarks here: the early Indian treaties; Fallen Timbers; the land rush that followed the Black Hawk War; Little Turtle, Chief of the Miami Nation; Chicago, "the upstart village"; the coming of the railroad; and the death of smalltown America. For the author, political boundaries disappear. These three States share a common idiom, attitude, and history, and Havighurst's view of the land, its meteoric development and growth, its enormous productive capacity in agriculture and industry, is panoramic. The "Heartland" is the "center of America's population and the source of important currents of its political, economic, and cultural life." The rapidity of change in the area is seen in the fact that Ohio, Indiana, and Illinois, formed in the early 1800's, had by 1840 reached the end of their frontier period. Numerous anecdotes from the history and legend of the region are included.

1798. Havighurst, Walter. Wilderness for sale;
    the story of the first western land rush. New York, Hastings House [1956]  372 p. illus. (American procession series)  56–8123  F479.H33
    Bibliography: p. 359–361.
The author's purpose is "to picture the first huge western frontier in America, and the process of its acquisition from the Indians, its survey, sale, settlement, and the beginnings of its culture and economy." The mingled pattern of farmer, squatter, speculator, and promoter of big land schemes is described from the first strong surge of migration in 1800 until, 40 years later, one of Ohio's citizens was elected President of the United States. In episodic style the author relates the story of prairie life, the birth of cities, the growth of river transport, and the politics of public land administration. He peoples his account with such characters as Tecumseh, Johnny Appleseed, Robert Owen, the eccentric Harman Blennerhassett, and William Henry Har-

rison. In Congress, Harrison drafted the land act of 1800 that opened the floodgates of the great migration, and his election as President in 1840 signalized its fulfillment. Havighurst has also edited *Land of the Long Horizons* (New York, Coward-McCann [°1960] 437 p. American vista series: The Midwest), a volume of readings on the history of the Midwest, illustrated with reproductions of paintings, drawings, engravings, and photographs.

1799. Murray, John J., *ed.* The heritage of the Middle West. Norman, University of Oklahoma Press [1958] xiv, 303 p. illus.
      58–11607   F351.M86
   Bibliographical footnotes.

1800. McAvoy, Thomas T., *ed.* The Midwest: myth or reality? A symposium. [Notre Dame, Ind.] University of Notre Dame Press [1961] 96 p.          61–10848   F355.M2
   Includes bibliographies.
   In these two anthologies midwestern scholars attempt to define the region's geographic boundaries, its heritage from the past and early development, its modern industrial and agricultural growth, and the character of its inhabitants as seen in their politics, religion, education, art, and literature. Although its geographical limits are inexact, the Midwest's existence is emphatically asserted and its claim to a separate regional identity is upheld. McAvoy's small volume is the result of a symposium in

which the contributors of the papers respond to a number of almost standard criticisms concerning such topics as midwestern isolationism, farm-bloc politics, and economic and financial relationships with the East. The 12 contributors to *The Heritage of the Middle West* make individual assessments according to topic and the historical perspective of each. Together these essays sketch the evolution of an essentially conservative segment of the Nation's population, in whom, these authors testify, the demands for radical change and adjustment have fashioned a unique and unmistakable manner and style.

1801. Van Every, Dale. Forth to the wilderness; the first American frontier, 1754–1774. New York, Morrow, 1961. 369 p. illus.
      61–11223   E195.V3
   Includes bibliography.
   The first of four volumes in a series which follows the frontier across America from the Appalachian Mountains to the west coast (1754–1845). In this volume, Van Every focuses on the conquest of the Appalachian Mountains and the conflicts between the Europeans in the East and the Indians in the West. Other volumes in the series are *A Company of Heroes; the American Frontier, 1775–1783* (1962. 328 p.); *Ark of Empire; the American Frontier, 1784–1803* (1963. 383 p.); and *The Final Challenge; the American Frontier, 1804–1845* (1964. 378 p.).

## J. The Old Northwest: Local

### OHIO

1802. Butler, Margaret Manor. A pictorial history of the Western Reserve, 1796 to 1860. Cleveland, Early Settlers Association of the Western Reserve, 1963. xi, 155 p. (Early Settlers Association of the Western Reserve. Publication no. 1–63)
      63–19645   F486.W58 no. 117
   Western Reserve Historical Society. Publication no. 117.
   Bibliography: p. 152–[153].
   As official historian of the Early Settlers Association of the Western Reserve, the author collected the sketches, woodcuts, paintings, and photographs included here to portray pioneer life in this northeastern corner of Ohio. A historical account covering the period between the first surveying party led by

Moses Cleveland in 1796 and the Civil War accompanies the illustrations of early terrain, pioneer homes and furnishings, art, education, religion, and recreation. Kenneth V. Lottich's *New England Transplanted, a Study of the Development of Educational and Other Cultural Agencies in the Connecticut Western Reserve in Their National and Philosophical Setting* (Dallas, Royal Pub. Co., 1964. 314 p.) explores the impact of the importation of New England school and religious systems to northeastern Ohio upon the public educational leadership of both the Connecticut Reserve and, ultimately, the State of Ohio.

1803. Smith, William E., *and* Ophia D. Smith. History of southwestern Ohio, the Miami

Valleys. New York, Lewis Historical Pub. Co. [1964] 3 v. illus.         65–5412  F497.M64S5
A lengthy history of the 14 counties in the watershed of the Great and Little Miami Rivers. Volumes 1 and 2 are arranged into topical chapters in chronological order, and the third volume is devoted to personal and family history. The area's earliest inhabitants, its flora and fauna, the emergence of the frontier, towns, transport, industry, and learning are covered in detail. The progress of modern institutions is pursued into the 20th century and developments in banking, public education, religion, fine arts, medicine, agriculture, politics, and municipal government are depicted.

## INDIANA

1804. Thornbrough, Emma Lou. Indiana in the Civil War era, 1850–1880. Indianapolis, Indiana Historical Bureau, 1965. xii, 758 p. illus. (The History of Indiana, v. 3)
                    66–63323  F526.H55 vol. 3
"Bibliographical essay": p. 715–736.
CONTENTS.—Attitudes and issues at midcentury. —Political realignments in the fifties.—Secession and Civil War.—Military contribution.—Disunion at home.—Politics and legislation of the Reconstruction Era.—Depression and politics, 1873–1879.— The transportation revolution. — Agriculture. — Foundations of industrialization: mining, manufacturing, banking, labor.—Education.—Population growth and social change.—Religion.—Intellectual, cultural, and social life.
Published in observance of the sesquicentennial of Indiana's statehood in 1966, this is one volume in a projected five-volume history of the State.

## ILLINOIS

1805. Pease, Theodore C. The story of Illinois. 3d ed., revised by Marguerita Jenison Pease. Chicago, University of Chicago Press [1965] xvi, 331 p. illus.        65–17299  F541.P36 1965
Bibliography: p. 301–314.
A revised edition of no. 4133 in the 1960 *Guide*.

## MICHIGAN

1806. Bald, Frederick C. Michigan in four centuries. Line drawings by William Thomas Woodward. Rev. and enl. ed. New York, Harper [1961] 528 p.        61–17179  F566.B2 1961
Includes bibliography.
A revised and enlarged edition of no. 4137 in the 1960 *Guide*.

1807. Dunbar, Willis Frederick. Michigan: a history of the Wolverine State. Watercolors and drawings by Reynold Weidenaar. Grand Rapids, W. B. Eerdmans Pub. Co. [1965] 800 p.
                    64–8579  F566.D84
Bibliography: p. 757–774.
A comprehensive history of the State, designed to provide readers with "information and understanding that will help them to contribute effectively to the building of Michigan's future." Emphasis is placed on the rich heritage of the State's many national and racial stocks and on the sustained efficacy of the economic motive since the early days of settlement. Dunbar's work is divided by centuries into four parts, each of which is prefaced with a brief summary and evaluation of the period. The discussion of the late 19th and 20th centuries covers such topics as social, educational, and cultural development; political hegemony (78 years of Republican domination that ended with the great depression); and the coming of the automobile, which at once transformed Michigan from an extracting into a processing economy, from an agricultural into an industrial State.

## MINNESOTA

1808. Blegen, Theodore C. Minnesota; a history of the State. [Minneapolis] University of Minnesota Press [1963] 688 p. illus.
                    63–13124  F606.B668
Bibliography: p. 601–624.
Blegen, the author of several scholarly monographs on Minnesota history, here offers the State's story from its geological prehistory to the present day for "the general public—citizens of Minnesota and people elsewhere who may be interested." He has produced a compactly written sourcebook of factual information, with helpful maps and illustrations. The book was sponsored by the Minnesota Historical Society, of which the author is a former superintendent. Blegen has also contributed an introduction to a centennial album of essays and illustrations: *Minnesota Heritage; a Panoramic Narrative of the Historical Development of the North Star State* (Minneapolis, T. S. Denison [ᶜ1960] 430 p.), edited by Lawrence M. Brings. William Van O'Connor has edited *A History of the Arts in Minnesota* (Minneapolis, University of Minnesota Press [1958] 63, 40, 62 p.), a small centennial volume on music, theater, books, authors, art, and architecture.

1809. Minnesota history. Selections from Minnesota history; a fiftieth anniversary anthology. Edited by Rhoda R. Gilman and June Drenning

Holmquist. St. Paul, Minnesota Historical Society, 1965. 369 p. illus. (Publications of the Minnesota Historical Society) 65–25992 F606.M6637
Bibliographical references included in "Footnotes" (p. 324–352).

On the occasion of this magazine's golden anniversary, 26 articles from more than 500 published over the years were selected for this anthology. They were chosen according to four criteria: "the importance of the subject, the breadth and depth with which it was treated, the continuing interest of the piece as a whole, and the readability of its presentation. Several representative articles were also selected, since the committee felt that the anthology should reflect the general contents and character of the magazine." In addition, certain topics which have received emphasis in the magazine were included: the fur trade, pioneer social life, immigration, and third-party political movements in the State. The articles are arranged chronologically by subject rather than by date of publication.

## K. The Far West

1810. Bartlett, Richard A. Great surveys of the American West. Norman, University of Oklahoma Press [1962] xxiii, 408 p. illus. (The American exploration and travel series [38])
62–16475 F594.B28
Bibliography: p. 377–390.
After the Civil War, four geographical and geological surveys were conducted over large areas of the West from 1867 until 1879, when the U.S. Geological Survey was founded. Two were under the administration of the War Department: the United States Geological Exploration of the Fortieth Parallel, headed by Clarence King, and the United States Geographical Surveys West of the One Hundredth Meridian, led by Lt. George Montague Wheeler. Two others, under the Department of the Interior, were the United States Geological and Geographical Survey of the Territories, directed by Ferdinand Hayden, and the United States Geographical and Geological Survey of the Rocky Mountain Region, led by John Wesley Powell. In an attempt to bring all four surveys under comparative examination, the author presents each expedition in turn, spotlighting the achievements of the more important scientists, journalists, painters, and photographers and recording the most notable accomplishments of their extensive and varied explorations. In the process, he renders a very large subject intelligible to the general reader and opens a fertile field of scholarship.

1811. Conference on the History of Western America. 1st, Santa Fe, N.M., 1961. Probing the American West; papers. Edited by K. Ross Toole [and others] With an introduction by Ray A. Billington. Santa Fe, Museum of New Mexico Press [1962] 216 p. 62–53525 F591.C75 1961
Bibliographical references included in "Notes" (p. 193–205).

1812. Conference on the History of Western America. 2d, Denver, 1962. The American West, an appraisal; papers. Edited by Robert G. Ferris. Editorial advisers: Le Roy R. Hafen, Allen D. Breck [and] Robert M. Utley. Introduction by Ray A. Billington. Preface by James Taylor Forrest. Santa Fe, Museum of New Mexico Press [c1963] 287 p. 63–22144 F591.C75 1962
Bibliographical references included in "Notes" (p. 226–251).
The papers presented in these two volumes reflect new tendencies in western historical research and writing signalized by the Santa Fe Conference on the History of Western America and the subsequent formation of the Western History Association, which publishes a quarterly journal entitled *The American West*. Ray A. Billington, in an introduction to the first volume and in one of the papers in the second, heralds a new surge of activity in western studies which he sees as the latest pendular swing in the pattern of alternating enthusiasm and neglect that has followed Frederick Jackson Turner's provocative essay "The Significance of the Frontier in American History." The renewed energy is also viewed as the spontaneous result of the rapid changes which have occurred in western life during the last decade. The association and these papers represent a movement away from the provincial antiquarian, the purveyor of western glamor, and the highly distilled Turnerian theorist toward more resourceful scholars who, through functional and interpretive works, attempt to bring the frontier past into a more meaningful relationship to the present and to the Nation as a whole.

1813. Hart, Herbert M. Old forts of the Northwest. Illustrated by Paul J. Hartle. Seattle, Superior Pub. Co. [1963] 192 p. (*His* Forts of

the old West)        63–15215   UA26.N6H3
  Bibliography: p. 186–188.

1814.  Hart, Herbert M.  Old forts of the South-
       west.  Drawings by Paul J. Hartle.  Seattle,
Superior Pub. Co. [1964]  192 p.  (*His* Forts of the
old West)        64–21316   UA26.S6H3

1815.  Hart, Herbert M.  Old forts of the Far
       West.  Drawings by Paul J. Hartle.  Seattle,
Superior Pub. Co. [1965]  192 p. (*His* Forts of the
old West)        65–23448   UA26.W4H3
  Bibliography: p. 186–189.
Nearly all the Army posts described in these
works on the forts of the Old West have been
visited by the author, who provides directions to the
present-day sites and a brief account of the historical
significance of each.  The objective of his travels
and of the supporting research has been to rediscover and underline the Army's role as guardian of
the westward movement between 1850 and 1890.
Robert W. Frazer's *Forts of the West; Military
Forts and Presidios, and Posts Commonly Called
Forts, West of the Mississippi River to 1898* (Norman, University of Oklahoma Press [1965]  246 p.)
supplies the date of establishment, purpose, and location of each post; the name, rank, and military unit
of the person establishing it; and its present status.
Kent Ruth's *Great Day in the West: Forts, Posts,
and Rendezvous Beyond the Mississippi* (Norman,
University of Oklahoma Press [1963]  308 p.)
depicts 147 important sites along the western trails
as they were at the moment of their greatest contribution to western development.  Each description is accompanied by a contemporary illustration
and a modern photograph.

1816.  Hine, Robert V., *and* Edwin R. Bingham,
       *eds*.  The frontier experience; readings in
the Trans-Mississippi West.  Belmont, Calif., Wadsworth Pub. Co. [1963]  xiv, 418 p.  illus.
                 63–18663   F591.H67
  Includes bibliographical references.
Two professors of American history have col-
laborated to edit an anthology of excerpts from the
journals, reports, local archives, literature, and histories of the 19th-century western frontier.  They
take as their theme Frederick Jackson Turner's
assertion that from the conditions of frontier life
came intellectual traits of profound importance.
Their selections are intended to illustrate the interaction—or contradiction—of two such traits and
their opposites: "the individualistic and the innova-
tive threads of frontier experience, versus the cooperative and traditional threads" in the formation of
the American character.  In their chapter introduc-

tions and explanatory paragraphs the editors seek to
place each selection in its appropriate context.  The
self-reliance and independence of the explorers and
the mountain men, for example, provide an insight
into the force of individual resourcefulness and the
unfettered spontaneous response to the wilderness
challenge.

1817.  Lavender, David S.  The fist in the wilder-
       ness.  Garden City, N.Y., Doubleday, 1964.
xiv, 490 p.  illus.     64–16203   HD9944.U48A47
  Bibliography: p. 424–480.
A contribution to the history of the American fur
trade and an understanding of the Astorian achievement.  The system of barter with the Indians of the
Upper Missouri and Great Lakes region for musk-
rat, raccoon, and deer hides—and, later, buffalo
robes—was the "true foundation of the huge mercantile empires that influenced the destiny of nations."  The author's central figure is Ramsey
Crooks, John Jacob Astor's lieutenant and "fist" in
the wilderness, whose enterprise, perception, and
energy captured the French and British trade for
the American Fur Company.  Crooks was one of
that small group of wilderness entrepreneurs who
wielded an influence in world capitals out of proportion to their numbers by their knowledge of
the frontier outposts and their control over the Indians.  Ruthless, resourceful, and fiercely competitive, Crooks led a continuing struggle for the operation of free enterprise against governmental
restrictions.  When the settlers came, and with them
the money trade, he helped to guide "the entire
transition of the fur trade from an instrument of
history to a plain business."

1818.  Lavender, David S.  Westward vision; the
       story of the Oregon Trail.  With illustra-
tions by Marian Ebert.  New York, McGraw-Hill
[1963]  424 p.  (American trails series)
                 63–16467   F880.L39
  Bibliography: p. 401–412.

1819.  Stewart, George R.  The California trail, an
       epic with many heroes.  New York, McGraw-
Hill [1962]  339 p.  illus.  (American trails series)
                 62–18977   F591.S83
  Bibliographical notes: p. 329–332.
Much of Lavender's work is concerned with the
earliest searches for a westward passage to the Pacific: the French voyageurs of the 18th century, the
British penetration in the early 19th century, and
the American exploration that began with the Lewis
and Clark expedition.  From this point the author
traces in detail, using excerpts from diaries, journals, and contemporary accounts, the farflung net-

work of trails opened by the exploring, fur-trading, or missionary ventures that often led far wide of the eventual route to the Columbia. Only in the final quarter of this volume does the reader glimpse the Oregon Trail itself and the beginnings of family migrations in the 1840's. Stewart, for many years a latter-day explorer of the California Trail, continues the theme begun by Lavender. The California—or Oregon—Trail forked at the Snake River and was variously named according to one's destination. Following closely the diaries and journals of this "folk movement" from 1841 to 1850, the author presents a vivid and detailed account of the light wagons, the oxen and mules which drew them, the supplies carried, life on the trail, the peculiarities of each stage of the journey, and the cumulative experience gained by successive wagon trains.

1820. Monaghan, James, ed. The book of the American West. Jay Monaghan, editor in chief. Clarence P. Hornung, art director. Authors: Ramon F. Adams [and others] New York, Messner [°1963] 608 p. illus. 63–17415 F591.M76
Bibliography: p. 593–595.
Ten writers on western Americana cover the history of half a continent in this elaborately illustrated volume. Subjects treated include the early explorers and mountain men, transportation, mining, Indians and soldiers, law and justice, cowboys, guns, wildlife, folklore, and song. A final section entitled "A Gallery of Western Art" was written by Clarence P. Hornung. The other contributors are Dale Morgan, Oscar Osburn Winther, Oscar Lewis, Don Russell, Wayne Gard, Ramon F. Adams, Robert Easton, Natt N. Dodge, and Benjamin A. Botkin.

1821. Moody, Ralph. The old trails west. New York, T. Y. Crowell Co. [1963] xiv, 318 p. illus. 63–15093 F591.M8
Bibliography: p. 303–306.
The author pursues a lifelong fascination with the early western trails, particularly in their beginnings and in the circumstances that determined their course and destination. On the theory that few trails wander aimlessly in the primordial forest, he inquires how and why they were first worn into the topography of the wilderness. Prehistoric origins are traced to animal tracks leading to grazing lands, salt licks, and water. These were later followed as routes to rivers and through the mountain barriers by Indians, explorers, trappers, miners, missionaries, settlers, and armies. From the stories of the oldtimers, his own travels, and his reading in mainly secondary sources, the author has reconstructed "from origin to obliteration" the progress

and proliferation of the main overland routes to the Pacific.

1822. Morgan, Dale L., ed. Overland in 1846; diaries and letters of the California-Oregon Trail. Georgetown, Calif., Talisman Press, 1963. 2 v. (825 p.) illus. 62–11493 F592.M7
Bibliographical references included in "Notes" (v. 1, p. 369–457; v. 2, p. 743–799).
Bernard De Voto's The Year of Decision, 1846 (no. 3331 in the 1960 Guide) is taken as the point of departure for this collection of sources, although Morgan is concerned with only one aspect of the total pattern of contemporary events that is the great merit of the earlier work. Morgan has focused on the migration along the Oregon Trail, which reached its high point in 1846, and has collected its contemporary records. The emigrants were intent, for various reasons that emerge from their letters and diaries, on getting to California and Oregon. "How they got there, and what happened along the way, as they themselves saw fit to record the facts, is the business of this book."

1823. Morgan, Dale L., ed. The West of William H. Ashley; the international struggle for the fur trade of the Missouri, the Rocky Mountains, and the Columbia, with explorations beyond the Continental Divide, recorded in the diaries and letters of William H. Ashley and his contemporaries, 1822–1838. Denver, Old West Pub. Co., 1964. liv, 341 p. illus. 63–21637 F592.M72
This very large and expensive volume fulfills Morgan's pledge, made during his work on Jedediah Smith and the Opening of the West (1953), to publish the Ashley papers. The general reader will probably be most attracted to the biographical sketch of Ashley in the beginning section, which covers his early life and his interest in mining, politics, and surveying, and to the section entitled "Fur Trade Exploration Before the Ashley Era." Ashley's fur trade activities are traced in the documents, composed of letters, newspaper accounts, business records, trading documents, and diaries. Morgan's major concern is with Ashley as a dominant figure in western history whose enterprise and energy helped establish the fur trade permanently in the Rockies and who introduced its distinctive American features.

1824. Smith, Alson J. Men against the mountains; Jedediah Smith and the South West Expedition of 1826–1829. New York, John Day Co. [1965] 320 p. illus. 64–14206 F592.S655
Bibliographical references included in "Notes" (p. [270]–292).

Much of the color and rambunctious energy of the early journeys into the West is related here. The greater aim of this book, however, is to trace the adventure and achievement in the western explorations of Jedediah Smith. With David Jackson and William Sublette, Smith purchased the fur business of Gen. William Ashley. After the rendezvous of 1826 at Cache Valley in what is now northern Utah, Smith traveled south with a company of 17 seasoned companions to explore first to the south and west of the Great Salt Lake, then north to Vancouver. Although the expedition was profitless to the firm of Smith, Jackson, and Sublette and to the fur trade, it was a landmark in western exploration. During the years under review Smith piled up an impressive list of firsts. He was the first American to reach California overland, to cross the Sierra Nevadas, to travel all the way across the Great Basin, to journey up the central valley of California, and to enter Oregon from the south. In the north he discovered and mapped the routes later used by settlers in California and Oregon.

1825. Tilden, Freeman. Following the frontier with F. Jay Haynes, pioneer photographer of the old West. New York, Knopf, 1964. 406 p. illus.      64–12327   TR140.H39T5

From the resources and collections of the Haynes Museum at Boseman, Mont., Freeman Tilden has sorted several hundred photographs that are reproduced in this album-*cum*-biography of the remarkable F. Jay Haynes. During a career that flourished through the last quarter of the 19th century, the itinerate photographer traveled by horseback, stagecoach, and riverboat to mining camps and Indian villages and with surveying parties to nearly every section of the frontier West. As official photographer for the Northern Pacific Railroad, he used a specially outfitted studio car that dramatically extended his range and diversity beyond that of other pioneer photographers. Ralph W. Andrews' *Photographers of the Frontier West; Their Lives and Works, 1875 to 1915* (Seattle, Superior Pub. Co. [1965] 182 p.) describes and illustrates the artistry of 12 other pioneer photographers from a wide variety of frontier locales in the United States and Canada. *Photographer of the Southwest, Adam Clark Vroman, 1856–1916* ([Los Angeles] Ward Ritchie Press, 1961. 127 p.), edited by Ruth I. Mahood, contains introductory materials on Vroman, a short piece by him, and reproductions of more than 90 of his photographs.

## L. The Great Plains: General

1826. Drago, Harry S. Great American cattle trails; the story of the old cow paths of the East and the longhorn highways of the plains. New York, Dodd, Mead [1965] 274 p. illus.
     65–12347   E179.5.D8
Bibliography: p. 261–262.

The author has made a generous contribution to the field of western fiction under several different pen names. Here, as historian, he is a revisionist, debunking and correcting old accounts, sifting fact from a large body of legend. He enlivens the retelling of familiar tales by critical commentary on the texts of other writers and in a carefully molded popular style. In this book he explores the history of the early New England cowpaths and the Oregon and Northern Trails to the end of the open range in the great "die-up" of 1886. The roads and trails and the towns at trail's end (Abilene, Wichita, Caldwell, Dodge City) are peopled with famous outlaws, marshals, dancehall girls, and cowboys. Jack W. Schaefer's *Heroes Without Glory; Some Goodmen of the Old West* (Boston, Houghton Mifflin, 1965.

323 p.) is about 10 representative "goodmen" who outclassed the "badmen" in skill, courage, endur- *Old West in Fact* (New York, I. Obelensky [1962] 446 p.), edited by Irwin R. Blacker, is an anthology of firsthand accounts which the editor selected as being readable, enjoyable, and significant in the history of the region.

1827. Lass, William E. A history of steamboating on the Upper Missouri River. Lincoln, University of Nebraska Press [1962] 215 p. illus.
     62–14663   HE630.M63L3
Bibliography: p. 201–210.

"This study traces the development of commercial navigation on the Upper Missouri from 1819, when the first steam vessel entered the waters of the Missouri, until 1936, when the last commercial navigation company on the Upper Missouri went out of existence." Based on steamboat company reports, tonnage and wage records, business ledgers, and government sources, the work is chiefly concerned with the financial and managerial problems of the river entrepreneur. Of particular value to the local historian, however, is the ensuing analysis of river-town economics. It traces not only the impact of the railroads but also the effects of government ex- ance, and gallantry "right across the board." *The* penditures, through avenues such as army contracts and Indian annuities, on the region's prosperity.

1828. Miller, Nyle H., *and* Joseph W. Snell. Why the West was wild; a contemporary look at the antics of some highly publicized Kansas cow-town personalities. Topeka, Kansas State Historical Society, 1963. 685 p. illus.   63–63480   F680.M5
   Bibliographical footnotes.
   By their persistent adherence to contemporary sources — State, county, and city archives, police dockets, and especially newspapers — the authors at-tempt to put back into perspective the stories of seven Kansas cowtowns which have been "knocked askew" somewhere between the doing and the tell-ing. For the period from 1867 to 1885, the careers of 57 lawmen and "certain other persons who were either astraddle or outside the law" are followed through the records without benefit of reminiscences or secondhand coloring matter. Various figures popularized by television, such as Wyatt Berry Stapp Earp, James Butler Hickok, John Henry Holliday, and William B. Masterson, emerge more or less in-tact and suffer little for having been made credible. There are exceptions, however, as the following in-dex entry shows: "Dillon, Matt: no police officer by

this name ever served in early Dodge City. Sorry." *The Album of Gunfighters* ([San Antonio? 1965] 236 p.), by John Marvin Hunter and Noah H. Rose, offers a selection from the Rose Collection of "Old Time Photographs" of frontier characters and scenes, with a brief narrative describing the role each played in the history of the West. A number of subjects are photographed "laid-out" in last re-pose complete with bullet holes, nooses, coffins, and other terminal devices. End papers are decorated with a variety of venomous insects and reptiles.

1829. Sandoz, Mari. Love song to the Plains. Illustrations and map by Bryan Forsyth. New York, Harper [1961]  303 p. (A Regions of America book)   61–6441   F591.S32
   Bibliography: p. 277–287.
   The author writes of the Great Plains with a sweeping lyric style she has developed through many books and articles describing the land of her childhood and the way its people lived and died. She attests to early maneuvering for "special rela-tionships, special rhythm patterns" to describe this region and the movement of the world past her own threshold. The history of Nebraska extends geo-graphically outward into Wyoming, Kansas, and the Dakotas and chronologically from the Spanish explorers to the intrusions of modern science. Miss Sandoz' account is not a historian's history but an impressionistic filling-in of invisible outlines with lore, tales, and half-legends.

## M. The Great Plains: Local

### NORTH DAKOTA AND SOUTH DAKOTA

1830. Lamar, Howard Roberts. Dakota Territory, 1861–1889; a study of frontier politics. New Haven, Yale University Press, 1956. 304 p. illus. (Yale historical publications. Miscellany 64)
   56–10098   F655.L25
   "Bibliographical note": p. 285–291.
   The author finds that Federal and local govern-ment was a highly important factor in making set-tlement possible in the Dakota Territory. Partly because of this experience, Dakotan miners and farmers tended to seek political approaches to eco-nomic problems. Patterns developed in such move-ments as the Farmers Alliance, the Populist Party, and the Non-Partisan League, which were neither radical nor conservative but the product of the new environment. Lamar sees these patterns as still be-ing adhered to in North Dakota today. *Dakota*

*Panorama* ([Sioux Falls?] 1961. 468 p.), edited by John Leonard Jennewein and Jane Boorman and published by the Dakota Territory Centennial Com-mission of South Dakota, is a collection of essays illustrated by photographs and maps.

1831. Schell, Herbert S. History of South Dakota. Line drawings by Jack Brodie. Lincoln, University of Nebraska Press, 1961. 424 p.
   61–7234   F651.S29
   "Supplementary reading": p. 393–404.
   The centennial of the Organic Act of 1861, which created the Dakota Territory, emphasized the need and the possibility for a full-scale history of the area. "The pick-and-shovel work in the vast body of available documents and primary sources seems to have progressed sufficiently in most areas to war-rant a synthesis on a wide basis." The first eight chapters of Schell's book constitute such a synthesis

of the prehistoric sources and early explorations of the upper Missouri River. From this point his emphasis is largely upon the growth of political institutions during the Territorial period and the political history of South Dakota after statehood. Political growth is discussed within the context of the area's unique economic problems, derived from special aspects of pioneering in the Great Plains; the rise of large-scale agriculture and its dependence upon such external forces as railroad expansion, eastern capital, and Federal land and Indian policies; and the anomalous adoption of measures for State regulation and State-owned enterprises by an essentially agrarian and conservative population. The author candidly includes a survey of the State's industrial activities "with the idea of providing a backdrop for the current campaign to attract industry to South Dakota." He concludes with four chapters of "reappraisal" of the State's Indian affairs, its farm and ranch economy, manufacturing and mining, and the social and cultural aspects of South Dakota life.

## KANSAS

1832. Zornow, William F. Kansas; a history of the Jayhawk State. Norman, University of Oklahoma Press [1957] 417 p. 57–7334 F681.Z6
Bibliography: p. 379–400.

1833. Kansas, the first century. New York, Lewis Historical Pub. Co. [ᶜ1956] 4 v.
57–1389 F681.K193
Vols. 1–2 edited by John D. Bright. Vols. 3–4 have subtitle: *Family and Personal History*.
Two histories of Kansas published in anticipation of the State's centennial in 1961. An underlying theme in each is that the story of Kansas' past, as a worthy subject for scholarly investigation, should consist of much more than the seven years of turmoil preceding the Civil War which has thus far preoccupied historians. Both works therefore reach back to the area's early history—to Coronado and the quest for Quivira, to the Indians and the French frontier—and continue their coverage up to the present day. Zornow's history is intended as "a general survey which traces some of the pertinent developments in the political, economic, social, and intellectual life of Kansas." The two volumes edited by Bright contain chapter essays by 27 contributors and follow, in greater detail, the same topical arrangement in chronological sequence. *Kansas, a Pictorial History* (Topeka, Kansas Centennial Commission, 1961. 320 p.), by Nyle H. Miller, Edgar Langsdorf, and Robert W. Richmond, is the "first attempt to tell the story of Kansas largely through pictures, with text to supplement the illustrations."

## OKLAHOMA

1834. Litton, Gaston L. History of Oklahoma at the golden anniversary of statehood. New York, Lewis Historical Pub. Co., 1957. 4 v. illus.
57–3664 F694.L58
Vols. 3–4 have subtitle: *Family and Personal History*. Includes bibliographies.
The first comprehensive multivolume history of the State to be written since 1929. Litton, the former archivist of the University of Oklahoma, has prepared a survey of imposing dimensions. The first volume is a chronological account of the region's history from the earliest times to the election of 1946. Volume 2, arranged topically, covers the development of agriculture, business, transportation, mineral resources, education, and social and religious life.

1835. Morris, John W., *and* Edwin C. McReynolds. Historical atlas of Oklahoma. Norman, University of Oklahoma Press [1965] xxvi, 70 p.
Map 65–1 G1366.S1M6 1965
Bibliography: p. ix-xv.
The authors' purpose is to present specific aspects of the State's history by means of a series of maps. Each full-page map is accompanied by a brief historical or geographical statement to explain its importance. The first maps place the State in its national setting and show its outstanding physical characteristics, such as landforms, rainfall, rivers, and lakes. Another series depicts the chronological development of the history of the State: Indian lands, exploration routes, forts, battles, cattle trails, and territory, State, and county boundaries. A final series shows the locations of incorporated communities as they were in 1960.

# N. The Rocky Mountain Region: General

1836. Athearn, Robert G. High country empire; the high plains and Rockies. New York, McGraw-Hill [1960] 358 p. 60–8822 F598.A8
Bibliographical essay: p. 335–352.

America's last frontier—an area which now includes the States of Montana, Wyoming, Colorado, North and South Dakota, Nebraska, and Kansas—is viewed as a whole "in an effort to understand its relationship to the larger story of American growth and to bring out any dominant highlights that characterize its history." The most persistent theme is that of exploitation carried on by remote control from the more settled parts of America, by successive armies of mountain men, miners, cattlemen, land speculators, timber barons, and oil wildcatters in their role of "git-and-git-out" extractors. Settlement by farmers ultimately led to a new economy with cash crops made possible by the railroads. Then came a realization of a gigantic cul-de-sac and the recognition of permanent agricultural ailments. Climate, the demands of eastern creditors, and the arbitrary exactions of the railroads combined to produce mass anger—the "agrarian revolt." The 20th century has seen the development of a full-blown stubborn tradition of political protest against the fluctuations of a national economy and the apparent vagaries of Federal farm policies. In all, this book is a strong indictment of an attitude of irresponsibility that has led to abuse of the high country.

1837. Cline, Gloria G. Exploring the Great Basin. Norman, University of Oklahoma Press [1963] 254 p. (The American exploration and travel series [39]) 63–8988 F592.C635
Bibliography: p. 217–240.

The earliest explorations of this last part of the country to yield up its secrets are traced through the archives of the Hudson's Bay Company, the Canadian Archives, and the journals of explorers and fur traders. The Great Basin, which encompasses parts of Utah, Wyoming, Idaho, Oregon, and Southern California and nearly all of Nevada, lies across the path of a long parade of travelers who had little or no knowledge of the nature of the terrain they sought to cross. It lured fur traders, treasure seekers in search of legendary kingdoms, and explorers who looked for a river system linking America with the Pacific and the Orient. In the 1840's the Great Basin became a corridor to California and Oregon, through which groups of emigrants passed with no understanding of its geographical character. In 1844, John C. Frémont applied to the area the name of "Great Basin," an appropriate title for a vast, unique area of interior drainage without an outlet to the sea. Mrs. Cline's record of the adventurers in the basin begins with the 18th-century Spanish explorers and continues through the mid-19th century.

1838. Sprague, Marshall. The great gates; the story of the Rocky Mountain passes. Boston, Little, Brown [1964] 468 p. illus., maps.
64–13189 F721.S76
Bibliography: p. [356]–364.

Two thousand miles of Rocky Mountain passes, from the San Juans in northern New Mexico to Canada's Jasper National Park, are traced with historical perspective. "The story opens with the sixteenth-century Spaniards, and runs through the pass adventures of British and American explorers and trappers until the whole chain stood revealed around 1830." From this point, the narrative continues with the development of the passes by army engineers, empire builders, gold seekers, scientists, railroaders, and motorists. Sprague bases his study on maps, photographs, archives, contemporary accounts, railroad histories, and other documents, as well as his own wide travels by jeep and aircraft. Geographically, the routes are often located by reference to modern highway numbers. Historically, the process of their discovery and exploration is related to the continuing development of the areas on either side of the Continental Divide. A list of some 800 passes is included, with historical and current travel information on each.

# O. The Rocky Mountain Region: Local

## MONTANA

1839. Burlingame, Merrill G., *and* Kenneth Ross Toole. A history of Montana. New York, Lewis Historical Pub. Co. [1957] 3 v.
57–37892 F731.B95
Vol. 3 has title: *A History of Montana, Family and Personal History.*

1840. Toole, Kenneth Ross. Montana: an uncommon land. Norman, University of Oklahoma Press [1959] 278 p. 59–7489 F731.T65
"Selected bibliography": p. 259–269.
The authors of *A History of Montana* have assembled an extensive compendium of fact. In apportioning their material they have tried to avoid the imbalance that characterizes some State histories; familiar and popular facets of the past — such as, in Montana's case, the early gold camps, the vigilante movement, and political party feuds — have been compressed to give more attention to 20th-century economic, industrial, and social developments hitherto neglected. The story of the open range gives way to a fuller treatment of the livestock industry, the air age is favored over that of the railroads, and modern progress in health and welfare, commerce, industry, and literature is more completely examined than is customary. In the process the authors have provided both a basis and a stimulus for additional historical studies. In *Montana: An Uncommon Land,* Toole interprets the brief, traumatic history of the State "in a series of roughly chronological essays which point up the themes that course through the years." At the same time he conveys an impression of the immoderate variety of the land, its people, and its history.

1841. Hamilton, James M. From wilderness to statehood; a history of Montana, 1805–1900. Foreword by A. L. Strand; edited by Merrill G. Burlingame. Pen sketches by Betty G. Ryan. Portland, Or., Binfords & Mort [1957] 620 p.
57–9233 F731.H28
Includes bibliographies.
Written by Hamilton several years before his death in 1940, this work was planned as a two-volume study of Montana's entire history. The unfinished manuscript was finally published, the editor explains, because of the realization that, almost 20 years after the author's death, materials were not yet available from which to write a history of the State with anything like the detail and clarity which characterize this volume. "Detail and interpretation are included here that are not available in any other published history."

## WYOMING

1842. Larson, Taft A. History of Wyoming. Line drawings by Jack Brodie. Lincoln, University of Nebraska Press, 1965. 619 p.
65–15277 F761.L3
"Sources": p. 583–599.
A detailed and clearly presented treatment of Territorial and State history. The author indicates that this is the first critical history of Wyoming for adult readers. The periods of explorers, fur traders, and the California, Oregon, and Mormon trails are briefly summarized. Emphasis is placed primarily on political and economic events, although social and cultural developments are adequately described. The interrelations of these forces are highlighted in the discussion of the impact of the railroads on the organization of the Territory and the effect of woman suffrage in the movement toward statehood.

## COLORADO

1843. Ubbelohde, Carl. A Colorado history. Boulder, Colo., Pruett Press [ᶜ1965] 339 p.
65–27239 F776.U195
Bibliographical footnotes.
A general history of Colorado, emphasizing the political and economic development of the State. The narrative runs from the days of the prehistoric Indians through the present. An analysis is included of social, religious, and educational trends in the State.

## UTAH

1844. Crampton, Charles Gregory. Standing up country: the canyon lands of Utah and Arizona. New York, Knopf, 1964. xv, 191 p.
64–20165 F788.C79
Bibliography: p. 181–191.
In this "biography of a region" Crampton portrays a sculptured land of 100 square miles in the heart of the Colorado plateau. His geographical

and historical review of the canyon lands and rivers emerged from a series of historical field studies which were part of a cooperative venture in archeology, ecology, and geology sponsored by the National Park Service and carried out by the University of Utah and the Museum of Northern Arizona. The studies were prompted by the desire to examine the historical remains and physical characteristics that would be jeoparidzed or destroyed by Lake Powell, the reservoir that would result from the building of Glen Canyon Dam on the Colorado River. The text combines a sensitive description of the physical wonders of the area with a history of the successive explorers, inhabitants, and cultures: Indian, Spanish, American, fur traders, miners, Mormons, and scientists. The volume includes 15 full-page color plates and more than a hundred scenes and portraits in black and white.

1845. Stegner, Wallace E. The gathering of Zion; the story of the Mormon Trail. New York, McGraw-Hill [1964] 331 p. illus. (American trails series) 64–19216 F593.S85
Bibliography: p. 315–319.
"This narrative begins at Nauvoo [Illinois] in the last months of 1845; its primary subjects are the Mormon migration from the bank of the Mississippi to the bank of City Creek in Salt Lake Valley, and the Gathering of Zion that took place over essentially the same route during the next twenty-two years." The author emphasizes the supreme importance today of the trail as an integral part of the Mormon faith, sustained by an enormous literature of diaries, journals, archives, reminiscences, and genealogical records and exalted to a central symbol in Mormon art and practice. In their literal belief in the promised land and the Kingdom of God on earth, the pioneer Mormons imposed a religious dynamic on the prevailing westward movement of the time; and because they were part of that movement they thrived. Although their wandering in the wilderness coincided more often than not with the California and Oregon Trails, the exodus of the Mormon hosts is described in terms of their religious and social organization. "They were the most systematic, organized, disciplined, and successful pioneers in our history."

## NEVADA

1846. Hulse, James W. The Nevada adventure, a history. Illustrations by Don Kerr. Reno, University of Nevada Press, 1965. 311 p.
64–8467 F841.H8
Bibliography: p. [301]–306.
Although State law requires the teaching of Nevada history in the schools and universities, there has previously been no single adequate book upon which courses could be based. The author, a professor of history at the University of Nevada, has sought to supply a longstanding "need for a short non-technical history of Nevada." Explicitly intended as a textbook, it is nonetheless rewarding to adult readers. Early history is covered chronologically in the initial chapters; recent times are discussed in topical chapters on mining, transportation and tourism, the impact of Federal Government projects, political problems, and the atomic age in Nevada.

# P. The Far Southwest: General

1847. Carter, Hodding. Doomed road of empire; the Spanish trail of conquest, by Hodding Carter, with Betty W. Carter. Illustrations by Don Almquist. New York, McGraw-Hill [°1963] 408 p. (The American trails series)
63–20189 F389.C25
Bibliography: p. 375–394.
The story of "El Camino Real para los Texas," the route that stretched through New Spain — eventually from Mexico to Natchitoches on the Red River at the northeastern edge of Texas. The author notes that the road was called by various names during the 150 years of religious conflict and national rivalries that surrounded it. Carter devotes only minimal attention to the road itself, emphasizing instead a sequence of narrative episodes from the history of colonial, borderland, and revolutionary Texas through the Treaty of Guadalupe Hidalgo in 1848.

1848. Hollon, William Eugene. The Southwest: old and new. New York, Knopf, 1961. xiv, 486, xviii p. illus. 61–9232 F786.H6
"Bibliographical notes": p. 465–[487].
The somewhat nebulous boundaries of the "Southwest" are here taken to include the States of Texas, Oklahoma, New Mexico, and Arizona — an

area which constitutes no particular social, political, or cultural entity but is distinguished by its variety, contrasts, and extremes in both its physical aspects and the behavior of its inhabitants. Hollon's account traces the history of the region as a whole through the successive explorations and occupations (Spanish, French, and Anglo-American), the impact of the war with Mexico, and the Civil War. The generally chronological arrangement of the book is relieved by descriptive chapters depicting life in the Texas Republic, Indian affairs, climate and topography, the ranching industry, transportation, manufacturing, politics, and urbanization. The author's synthesis frequently includes the more flamboyant episodes and personalities—particularly in the last half of the book, which deals with the States severally and their economic and political development since statehood.

## Q. The Far Southwest: Local

### TEXAS

1849. Bainbridge, John. The super-Americans; a picture of life in the United States, as brought into focus, bigger than life, in the land of the millionaires—Texas. Garden City, N.Y., Doubleday, 1961. 395 p.     61–16775 F391.2.B3

There is deliberately little or no form or organization to this impressionistic portrait of top-drawer Texans. Its chapters are not titled, but two themes persist through all of them: millionaires and money. Millionaires come in various kinds and sizes; there are more of them in Texan than in other States, and they have an attitude toward money which is difficult to define but which can be described at length. If this segment of the State of Texas is somewhat overdrawn, it is an indulgence justified by the subject. "Free-wheeling," "hi-jinks," and "wheeler-dealer" are terms repeatedly applied to the people, the "deals," and the tax deductions; irony is the device most frequently employed in describing the tastes, politics, eccentricities, or way of life of this wide-open society. Much of the material for this work originated as a series of articles in *The New Yorker*.

1850. Richardson, Rupert N. Texas, the Lone Star State. 2d ed. Englewood Cliffs, N.J., Prentice-Hall, 1958. 460 p. illus.

58–9834 F386.R52 1958

"Selected bibliography" at the end of each chapter.

A revised edition of no. 4194 in the 1960 *Guide*. In the rewriting, "a chapter has been added on the course of public affairs during the last fifteen years, and the various topics have been brought up to date. A simpler, more direct view of the period since 1876 has resulted in its condensation into fewer chapters, providing space for new maps, charts, and illustrations."

1851. Siegel, Stanley. A political history of the Texas Republic, 1836–1845. Austin, University of Texas Press, 1956. xiv, 281 p.

56–7478 F390.S55

Bibliography: p. 259–268.

Politics in the Texas Republic were essentially personal in character. There were no political parties comparable to those in the United States, and alignments on the basis of political principles did not emerge after independence. Siegel traces the clash of personalities over the staggering array of problems that beset the young Nation in such areas as finance, military defense, and foreign affairs. Based on the letters, journals, manuscript sources, and public documents of the period, his study of the administrations of David Burnet, Mirabeau Lamar, Anson Jones, and, above all, Sam Houston is particularly concerned with their policies toward finance, relations with Mexico, and the diplomatic maneuvers for annexation. In a prelude to the history of the Republic, *The Last Years of Spanish Texas, 1778–1821* (The Hague, Mouton, 1964. 156 p. Studies in American history, 4), Odie B. Faulk offers a study of Spanish colonial administration and reveals successes as well as failures while explaining the alienation of the settlers from the Government.

1852. Wallace, Ernest, *ed*. Documents of Texas history. With the assistance of David M. Vigness. [Austin, Tex.] Steck Co. [1963] 293 p.

63–24468 F386.W32

Brings together the traditional literature that has been the basis for narrative history. The materials included are those that "most graphically illustrate the Texas past as it unfolded" and that provide "examples of what seems most worthy of preservation in the Texas heritage." They consist of outstanding contemporary narratives, speeches, treaties, State documents, proclamations, and court decisions.

1853. Wisehart, Marion K. Sam Houston, American giant. Washington, R. B. Luce [1962] 712 p.                    62–20000   F390.H868
   Bibliography: p. 681–692.

The University of Texas in 1943 completed publication of eight volumes of *The Writings of Sam Houston.* In the light of that contemporary testament, the author reevaluates "the outstanding traits of character that made him the man he was and the following major phases of his career: (1) his decision to go to Texas; (2) his relations as Commander in Chief with the General Council, the legislative body of the first provincial government; (3) his plans for defending Texas without sacrificing the Alamo Garrison; (4) his strategy during the forty-day campaign which culminated in the victory at San Jacinto; (5) his anti-war policy as President of the Texas Republic; (6) his annexation policy; (7) his thirteen years of service in the United States Senate and his attempts to check the drift toward war and to heal the breach between North and South; and (8) his anti-secession policy as Governor of Texas." Sue Flanagan's pictorial biography, *Sam Houston's Texas* (Austin, University of Texas Press [1964] 213 p.), adds a graphic dimension. Traveling more than 7,000 miles in eastern Texas, she visited and photographed "every place where evidence indicated he had ever been."

## NEW MEXICO

1854. Beck, Warren A. New Mexico; a history of four centuries. Norman, University of Oklahoma Press [1962] 363 p.   62–16470   F796.B4
   Bibliography: p. 337–352.

"Intended for readers who want a brief yet reasonably comprehensive treatment of the development of the state," this is a popular but substantial account. Early history is reviewed, with particular attention to Territorial affairs and the Spanish rule and heritage. About a third of the book is devoted to a description of economic, political, urban, and cultural advancement since statehood.

## ARIZONA

1855. Cross, Jack L., Elizabeth H. Shaw, *and* Kathleen Scheifele, *eds.* Arizona: its people and resources. Tucson, University of Arizona Press, 1960. 385 p.        60–15913   F811.C79
   Published by the University of Arizona as part of
   Bibliography: p. 378–385.
its 75th anniversary celebration, this unusual compendium is based on 64 separate topical essays assembled by a group of specialists, most of whom are members of the university faculty. Their contributions are correlated under five subject headings for the State: its people and their past, lands and resources, government and social services, the economy, and cultural institutions. By this treatment both fact and method become visible, and the various techniques and viewpoints of natural scientists, political scientists, economists, sociologists, historians, and students of other disciplines are applied.

1856. Peplow, Edward H. History of Arizona. New York, Lewis Historical Pub. Co. [1958] 3 v. illus.           58–42516   F811.P4
   Vol. 3: *Family and Personal History.*
   Bibliography: v. 2, p. 549–565.

The author points out that Arizona was, at the time of his writing, the youngest State in the Union, yet it contains what is believed to be the oldest continuously inhabited community on the continent. Climate and topography have made it an ideal workshop for archeologists and anthropologists. It is, he asserts, the only State to have its history, from wilderness to modern times, chronicled in the newspapers, and a large number of those who contributed to the State's growth and progress are still alive to tell the story. From this wealth of source material he has produced a sober and systematic history of the 48th State. The first volume opens with a discussion of the mute relics of geological times and continues chronologically through the Indian wars and the settlement of the territory. Volume 2 is essentially a history of the period of statehood, recounted in topical discussions of economic, political, and cultural developments. A much more specialized and detailed look at the genesis of the Arizona Territory composed on the occasion of its centennial, is B. Sacks' *Be It Enacted: The Creation of the Territory of Arizona* (Phoenix, Arizona Historical Foundation, 1964. 200 p.) The work is an expansion of a two-part article originally published in *Arizona and the West.*

# R. California

1857. Caughey, John W., *and* LaRee Caughey, *eds.* California heritage; an anthology of history and literature. Los Angeles, Ward Ritchie Press, 1962. 536 p. illus.   62–20999 PS571.C2C35
"Other books to read": p. 527–532.
Selections by 137 writers are brought together as an expression of the variety of moods, lands, and people that make up the California story. The editors consider "some of it sober history, much of it lyrical and analytical description, some of it indubitably creative writing." The first and last selections are by Robinson Jeffers; in between, the contributors are as varied as Ambrose Bierce and Aimee Semple McPherson, Jack London and Lawrence Ferlinghetti. The collection is divided according to subject matter, beginning with the Indians and continuing to the present. A brief introduction accompanies each section and a biographical headnote is included for each writer.

1858. Cleland, Robert Glass. From wilderness to empire; a history of California. A combined and revised edition of From wilderness to empire, 1542–1900, & California in our time, 1900–1940. Edited and brought down to date by Glenn S. Dumke. New York, Knopf, 1959. 445 p. illus.
59–8037 F861.C598
Bibliography: p. 435–445.
A combined and revised edition of no. 4203 and 4204 in the 1960 *Guide.*

1859. Lewis, Oscar, *ed.* This was San Francisco, being first-hand accounts of the evolution of one of America's favorite cities. New York, D. McKay Co. [1962] 291 p. illus.
61–18348 F869.S3L613
Bibliography: p. 285–288.
Contemporary views and attitudes have been sorted out and embedded in a narrative that covers the San Francisco scene from the discovery of the Bay in 1776 to the "catastrophic visitation" of April 18, 1906. Not a traditional anthology, the book aims "to emphasize those phases that have long set San Francisco apart from other cities." Lewis offers little-known selections representing the testimony of observers or participants in the events described. His witnesses are a disparate company of travelers and residents, including Ambrose Bierce, Anthony Trollope, Richard H. Dana, Rudyard Kipling, and a host of others, whose comments are culled from the books, pamphlets, newspapers, and magazines of the time. Another contemporary collection, *San Franicsco as It Is; Gleanings From the Picayune* (Georgetown, Calif., Talisman Press, 1964. 285 p.), edited by Kenneth M. Johnson, offers excerpts of articles and news commentary in the first afternoon newspaper in San Francisco from its third issue, August 5, 1850, until its eclipse on April 17, 1852.

1860. Pourade, Richard F. The history of San Diego. Commissioned by James S. Copley. [San Diego] Union-Tribune Pub. Co. [1960–65] 5 v.   F869.S22H5
A venture in local history that has been expanded to impressive scholarly and artistic proportions. Suggested and commissioned by the publisher of the *San Diego Union* and *Evening Tribune,* the five volumes that have appeared contain a wealth of source material. For the text and illustrations the author has drawn from contemporary journals, diaries, correspondence, and art collections located here and abroad. Some original paintings were commissioned for the work. The result is a set of large, lavishly illustrated volumes, containing text and reproductions of paintings, drawings, and photographs. Volume 1, *The Explorers* ([1960] 203 p.  60–53624), deals with the discovery and settlement of California from Juan Rodríguez to Juan Bautista de Anza. Volume 2, *Time of the Bells* ([1961]  262 p.  61–14059), covers the mission period, the years of the Franciscan domination of California from 1769 to 1835. Volume 3, *The Silver Dons* ([°1963]  286 p.  63–7055), encompasses the years 1830–65, beginning with the secularization of the missions and ending with the close of the Civil War. Volume 4, *The Glory Years* ([1964]  276 p.  64–17561), explores the "boom and bust" period between 1865 and 1900. Volume 5, *Gold in the Sun* ([1965]  282 p.  65–23410), examines the period from the turn of the century to the roaring twenties.

1861. Riesenberg, Felix. The Golden Road; the story of California's Spanish mission trail. New York, McGraw-Hill [1962]  315 p. illus. (The American trails series) 62–17374 F861.R54
Bibliography: p. 290–302.

The California Camino Real, the coastal route from Mexico to San Diego, San Francisco, and eventually to the Oregon border, was once composed of connecting trails between the missions. It grew into a commercial route for a rich cattle country and carried the march of conquest in 1846. The author uses the highway as a starting point from which to present episodes in the development of southern California, including the gold-rush days, the stagecoach era, and, in 1869, the coming of the "octopus"—the Southern Pacific Railway that opened the floodgates of immigration. Riesenberg notes that the 20th century began with only a few of the Nation's 10,000 horseless carriages in California. Within 20 years, however, the State had one million automobiles and from this point travelers are legion: tourists, Okies, tramps, and bootleggers. In 1925 the Camino Real became U.S. Highway 101.

1862. Rolle, Andrew F. California; a history. New York, Crowell [1963] 649 p. illus.
63–8480 F861.R78
"Selected readings" follow each chapter.

California is noted for the diversity of its geography, climate, history, and people. This basic textbook succeeds in drawing together various characteristics into an ordered and intelligible whole. The use of short sections with meaningful headings relieves the necessity for involved transitions and supplies a valuable outline. The relative independence of California's historical development from that of the rest of the United States is noted. The author recounts the State's history from its origins to the present, seeking to interpret every phase of the story without recourse to burdensome or extraneous detail. His work is based in part on *A Short History of California* (1929), by Rockwell D. Hunt and Nellie Van de Grift Sánchez.

## S. The Pacific Northwest: General

1863. Johansen, Dorothy O., *and* Charles M. Gates. Empire of the Columbia; a history of the Pacific Northwest. New York, Harper [1957] xv, 685 p. illus. 56–11074 F852.J67
Bibliographical footnotes.

A collaborative study of the region that includes the present States of Oregon, Washington, and Idaho and, for early history, a large area to the north as well. Dorothy Johansen covers the years up to the period of Territorial government and Oregon statehood in the 1880's. Gates continues with a study of the transitional period in politics, transportation, industry, and urban affairs and a topical appraisal of these together with 20th-century progress in reclamation, conservation, forestry, fishing, and cultural affairs. Described as an "essay in regional analysis," the work also relates local problems to the national and international scene. The search for Quivira or a northwest passage and the rivalries of the fur trade, for example, are viewed as part of the contemporary expansion of Western Europe. The period of explosive growth and change between 1880 and 1910 was a part and product of a pattern of enterprise and industrial growth in the country as a whole.

1864. Lavender, David S. Land of giants; the drive to the Pacific Northwest, 1750–1950. Garden City, N.Y., Doubleday, 1958. 468 p. illus. (Mainstream of America series) 58–12049 F851.L4
Bibliography: p. 447–457.

A study of the explorers, "sea peddlers," fur traders, miners, lumbermen, and settlers who migrated to the Pacific Northwest. Lavender traces their motives, quarrels, and conquests and includes a wealth of detail and anecdote. Particular attention is devoted to the exploits and rivalries of the mountain men and to trade, gold, and lumber bonanzas. The final chapters cover 20th-century developments in forestry, reclamation, and conservation.

1865. Pomeroy, Earl S. The Pacific slope; a history of California, Oregon, Washington, Idaho, Utah, and Nevada. New York, Knopf, 1965. 403, xvi p. illus. 65–11128 F851.P57
"Notes on further reading": p. 399–[404].

Eschewing the conventional beginnings with "explorers who came when almost no one else was there," Pomeroy places more emphasis on "Western society that men now living can remember." He attempts "to focus on men and events that explain the West as a developing community, emphasizing traits and institutions," and justifies the scope of his work by clearly demonstrating that State boundaries have ignored the natural, climatic, economic, and institutional affinities within the area. Beginning in the 1830's and 1840's, Pomeroy in his interpretive approach selects formative factors upon which he imposes his own synthesis of what was and is important. "When one approaches Western history from the point of view of the development of communities, traits, and institutions, farms, cities, political parties, and social ideas loom larger than trouble with the Indians, who were never the barrier to settlement west of tthe Rockies that they were to the east."

## T. The Pacific Northwest: Local

### WASHINGTON

1866. Avery, Mary W. Washington: a history of the Evergreen State. Seattle, University of Washington Press [1965] 362 p.
65–4963  F891.A82

Bibliography: p. 331–340.

A revision of the history section of the author's *History and Government of the State of Washington* (Seattle, University of Washington Press, 1961. 583 p.), which was prepared as a combined textbook for history and government courses in the State. Intended for the general public, the present work provides a background to more specialized study. The narrative surveys early explorations, the fur trade, Indian wars, and political development. Topical discussions are included of geology, Indian culture, industrial progress, and cultural growth, with the exception of literature and art.

1867. Stewart, Edgar I. Washington: Northwest frontier. New York, Lewis Historical Pub. Co. [1957] 4 v. illus.
58–320  F891.S87

Includes bibliographical references.

This general history traces the development of the State from the 16th-century exploration of the Northwest to the present. Although the author focuses on local history, he emphasizes events and developments which were significant within the context of national history. The first two volumes are historical, the last two biographical.

### IDAHO

1868. Beal, Merrill D., *and* Merle W. Wells. History of Idaho. New York, Lewis Historical Pub. Co. [1959] 3 v.
59–4740  F746.B335

Vol. 3 has title: *History of Idaho; Personal and Family History.*

"Bibliographical essay": v. 1, p. [xi]–xiv. Includes bibliographical references.

Traces the development of the State from the Lewis and Clark Expedition (1805–6) to the present. The authors emphasize the effect of major national events and social forces on the history of Idaho.

## U. Alaska and Hawaii

### ALASKA

1869. Sherwood, Morgan B. Exploration of Alaska, 1865–1900. New Haven, Yale University Press, 1965. xiv, 207 p. illus. (Yale Western Americana series, 7)
65–11187  F908.S6

Bibliographical footnotes.

The progress of exploration is a logical and substantive theme for Alaskan history during the period covered. Commercial affairs were limited geographically, and the sparse civilized population precluded an emphasis on political activity. At the time of the American purchase in 1867, Alaska was a vast terra incognita. By 1900, as a result of Ameri-can exploration, problems in gross geography had largely been solved. The author's purpose is to trace the course of exploration by variously sponsored expeditions and to determine to what extent it resembled the exploration phase of the stateside westward expansion of a half century earlier. He concludes that the institutional patterns were similar with respect to commercial motive, the quest for scientific knowledge, and governmental responsibility. In view of the social attitudes in the United States at the time and Alaska's infinitesimal population, the exploration activities in these years and especially the role played by the Federal Government can be considered extensive.

## HAWAII

1870. Day, Arthur Grove, *and* Carl Stroven, *eds.*
A Hawaiian reader. With an introduction by James A. Michener. New York, Appleton-Century-Crofts [1959] 363 p.

59–14048 DU620.3.D3

An anthology containing 37 selections from the work of 30 authors who have written about Hawaii. The excerpts are arranged chronologically according to the date of the incidents, beginning with the discovery of the islands by Captain James Cook. A brief introduction precedes each selection. Included are five pieces on ancient Hawaiian folklore and literature. *Ruling Chiefs of Hawaii* (Honolulu, Kamehameha Schools Press [1961] 440 p.), by Samuel M. Kamakau, presents the "historical and ethnographic record of Hawaii."

1871. Kuykendall, Ralph S., *and* Arthur Grove Day. Hawaii: a history, from Polynesian kingdom to American State. Rev. ed. Englewood Cliffs, N.J., Prentice-Hall [1961] 331 p. illus.

61–8894 DU625.K778 1961

This revised edition of no. 4220 in the 1960 *Guide* brings the history of Hawaii up to date by documenting the final steps toward statehood, achieved in 1959. In *The Hawaiian Revolution, 1893–94* (Selinsgrove, Pa., Susquehanna University Press, 1959. 372 p.) and its sequel, *The Hawaiian Republic, 1894–98* (Selinsgrove, Pa., Susquehanna University Press, 1961. 398 p.), William A. Russ recounts the events which led to the annexation of Hawaii to the United States.

# V. Overseas Possessions

1872. Coulter, John W. The Pacific dependencies of the United States. New York, Macmillan, 1957. 388 p. illus. 57–9543 F970.C6
Includes bibliographies.

A comparative study of land utilization, land tenure, and population in the Pacific Islands under American trusteeship, based on 13 years of research and travel among the Pacific Islanders. Particular attention is devoted to differences in island geography and agricultural methods. Among the islands discussed are Hawaii, Samoa, Guam, the Marianas, and the Marshalls. The author concludes that, in every South Sea area invaded by the West, native cultures have slowly disintegrated and some of the best and much of the worst of alien ways have been adopted.

## AMERICAN SAMOA

1873. Gray, John A. C. Amerika Samoa; a history of American Samoa and its United States Naval Administration. Annapolis, United States Naval Institute [1960] 295 p. illus.

60–12080 DU819.A1G7

In 1899 Samoa was partitioned under American and German rule. The first part of Gray's book presents an anthropological and historical survey of the islands prior to 1900; the second part is a description of "Amerika Samoa" or "Eastern Samoa" and its progress under U.S. rule. The territory was governed by the United States Naval Administration until 1951, when the responsibility was transferred to the Department of the Interior.

## PUERTO RICO

1874. Lewis, Gordon K. Puerto Rico; freedom and power in the Caribbean. New York [Monthly Review Press] 1963. 626 p.

63–20065 F1958.L4

Bibliographical references included in "Notes" (p. 575–613).

Contending that the literature on Puerto Rico, an independent Commonwealth in association with the United States, depicts it as a "tropical terminus of the American way of life rather than as a threshold to the wider Caribbean and Middle American worlds," Lewis seeks to correct the distortion. Part 1 deals with "The Past," from the voyage of Columbus in the 15th century to the emergence of the Popular Democratic Party in the 1940's. The author characterizes the island as a continuing neocolonial society and the United States consequently as a continuing neocolonial power. The topics covered in part 2, "The Present," offer evidence for such portrayals and also provide further material for "an extensive examination of the general experience of Puerto Rican life and thought." The last purpose of this scholarly study—to use the island as a prototype of the mass of new problems caused by the mutual confrontation of the developed and underdeveloped societies in the modern world—underlies the entire volume and is given final expression in part 3, which concerns the future for Puerto Rico and world society.

# XIII

# Travel and Travelers

A. *General Works*                                          1875–1877

B. *19 Selected Travelers, 1754–1898*
    (chronologically arranged by the date of their travels)    1878–1915

No ENTRIES appropriate to the 1960 *Guide's* Section B, Anthologies, were located for the decade covered by this *Supplement,* and the designation "B" has therefore been assigned to the list of selected travelers, which was Section C in the original volume. The list of travelers below is limited to 19, as compared to 50 in the initial *Guide.* Four of the 19 (no. 1880, 1882, 1888, and 1894) are in the 1960 *Guide,* and the entry numbers for their headnotes there are provided in the *Supplement.* Of the 15 newly listed travelers at least six (no. 1878, 1896, 1900, 1904, 1906, and 1914) are authors of works previously unpublished, or published only in part. At least three others (no. 1884, 1890, and 1898) are the authors of works not heretofore available in full in English. Although most of the travels are from the period before 1865—as in the case of those reported in the 1960 *Guide*—one of them took place in 1898, four years after the terminal date of the final account listed in the earlier volume. In addition to the observations of visitors from France, Switzerland, England, Sweden, Poland, Germany, and Spain, the new Section B also records accounts by three native Americans.

## A. General Works

1875. Clark, Thomas D., *ed.* Travels in the Old South, a bibliography. Norman, University of Oklahoma Press [1956–59] 3 v. illus. (The American exploration and travel series, no. 19)
    56–8016  Z1251.S7C4

CONTENTS.—v. 1. The formative years, 1527–1783; from the Spanish explorations through the American Revolution.—v. 2. The expanding South, 1750–1825: the Ohio Valley and the cotton frontier.—v. 3. The ante-bellum South, 1825–1860: cotton, slavery, and conflict.

1876. Clark, Thomas D., *ed.* Travels in the new South, a bibliography. Norman, University of Oklahoma Press [1962] 2 v. illus. (The American exploration and travel series, v. 36)
    62–10772  Z1251.S7C38

In v. 2, this work is incorrectly listed as v. 37 in the series.

CONTENTS.—v. 1. The postwar South, 1865–1900.—v. 2. The twentieth-century South, 1900—1955.

A two-part series of more than 2,000 annotated entries arranged alphabetically within each chronological period, beginning with the early Spanish travelers in the 16th century and the English settlement in 1606. The years 1860–65 are omitted in deference to Ellis Merton Coulter's *Travels in the Confederate States, a Bibliography* (1948), no. 3365 in the 1960 *Guide.* The series attempts to appraise and evaluate the valid aspects of the travel accounts, including geographies, atlases, surveys, and statistical reports. There is also peripheral literature of a regional nature, but the bibliographies do not touch on magazines, newspapers, or fugitive miscellaneous publications. Seeking "to follow the established rules of bibliography which make for clarified usability," the compilers have devoted considerable space to the annotations and to supplemental notes.

1877. Hubach, Robert R. Early Midwestern travel narratives; an annotated bibliography, 1634–1850. Detroit, Wayne State University Press, 1961. 149 p.                60–15110   Z1251.W5H8

The Midwest is defined as "that section of America as far east as the western border of Pennsylvania and including all territory north of the Ohio River and north of the present states of Arkansas and Oklahoma to the Canadian border." Hubach's bibliography includes both published and unpublished materials, generously annotated and arranged in chronological order. Exceptions to the chronological arrangement are treated in separate units. Further notes for each chapter appear at the end of the book.

# B. 19 Selected Travelers, 1754 - 1898
*(chronologically arranged by the date of their travels)*

1878.  1754–1813.  JOHN GOTTLIEB ERNESTUS HECKEWELDER (1743–1823)

"A man on the move," Heckewelder, an American Moravian missionary, came to this country from England at the age of 12 and lived and traveled among the Indians for nearly 60 years. He journeyed extensively through the eastern woods and crossed the Allegheny mountains 30 times, making numerous trips through Pennsylvania, Ohio, and Indiana. "As a reporter of Indian life during his time and in his vicinity he has no superior," the editor of his journals maintains. Heckewelder also assisted in various advisory and administrative capacities in dealing with the Indians. Twelve edited manuscript journals of his travels provide the major source for the narratives presented here, which are told in an unobtrusive and simple manner. His final years were spent in the preparation of historical and linguistic records of Pennsylvania tribes.

1879.  Thirty thousand miles with John Heckewelder, edited by Paul A. W. Wallace. [Pittsburgh] University of Pittsburgh Press [1958] xvii, 474 p. illus.          58–6422   E163.H4

Heckwelder's travel journals, gathered from various repositories, and selections from his published reminiscences woven into a connected story.

1880.  1773–1778.    WILLIAM    BARTRAM (1739–1823)

No. 4247 in 1960 *Guide*.

1881.  Travels. Edited with commentary and an annotated index by Francis Harper. Naturalist's ed. New Haven, Yale University Press, 1958. lxi, 727 p. illus.          57–11916   F213.B2893
Bibliography: p. 668–694.

A revised edition of no. 4248–4250 in the 1900 *Guide*. The editor provides an introduction with an account of Bartram's life and travels; a long commentary principally on his geographical routes; and an inclusive annotated index, identifying, among other things, the plants, animals, minerals, persons, and Indian tribes that Bartram notes or describes.

1882.  1780–1782.  FRANÇOIS JEAN, MARQUIS DE CHASTELLUX (1734–1788)

No. 4251 in 1960 *Guide*.

1883.  Travels in North America in the years 1780, 1781, and 1782.

A revised translation with introduction and notes by Howard C. Rice, Jr. Chapel Hill, Published for the Institute of Early American History and Culture at Williamsburg, Va., by the University of North Carolina Press [1963] 2 v. (xxiv, 688 p.) illus.          63–18103   E163.C59   1963
"Note on bibliographic and cartographic sources": v. 2, p. 556–561.

A drastically revised version of George Grieve's 18th-century translation, no. 4253 in the 1960 *Guide*, through which Chastellux' book has been known to English-speaking readers. Passages have been clarified, archaisms modernized, and efforts made to convey the exact meaning and general spirit of the original. The journals have been divided into chapters, and notes have been supplied at the back of the book.

1884.  1783–1784.  FRANCISCO DE MIRANDA (1750–1816)

Miranda was born in Caracas, the son of a prosperous linen merchant and planter. A cultured, enigmatic military hero, he deserted the Spanish army in 1783 by slipping aboard an American whaler bound for the United States from Cuba. As a fugitive he spent his life trying to liberate the Spanish colonies. Eventually he died in prison in Cadiz. His diary displays a strong sense of history and records his tour through the Carolinas, Pennsylvania, Delaware, New Jersey, New York, Connecticut, Rhode Island, Massachusetts, and New Hampshire and most of the major communities on the eastern coast. His intellectual interests and his accounts of numerous influential acquaintances have produced a description of life in America which fills an important gap in our firsthand knowledge of the period.

1885. The new democracy in America; travels of Francisco de Miranda in the United States, 1783–84. Translated by Judson P. Wood. Edited by John S. Ezell. Norman, University of Oklahoma Press [1963] xxxii, 217 p. illus. (The American exploration and travel series, 40)

63–9959    E164.M673

Bibliographical references included in "Editor's preface."

The first complete translation into English of that portion of Miranda's diary which deals with his travels in the United States.

1886. 1785–1798. MICHEL GUILLAUME ST. JEAN DE CRÈVECOEUR (1735–1813)

Michel Guillaume St. Jean de Crèvecoeur became famous after the publication of his *Letters From an American Farmer* (1782), no. 4500–4501 in the 1960 *Guide*. Often compared to Thoreau because of his love of nature and his agrarian philosophy, Crèvecoeur demonstrates the resemblance in his *Journey Into Northern Pennsylvania and the State of New York*. He uses the literary device of a "found" or "shipwrecked" manuscript, alleging that he is merely the translator. The element of travel is secondary. It is in the pastoral descriptions, romantic legends, adventure sagas, and the telling of Indian lore that the author excels.

1887. Journey into northern Pennsylvania and the State of New York. Translated by Clarissa Spencer Bostelmann. Ann Arbor, University of Michigan Press [1964] xviii, 619 p.

63–14014    F153.C923    1964

1888. 1788. JACQUES PIERRE BRISSOT DE WARVILLE (1754–1793)

No. 4258 in 1960 *Guide*.

1889. New travels in the United States of America, 1788. Translated by Mara Soceanu Vamos

and Durand Echeverria. Edited by Durand Echeverria. Cambridge, Mass., Belknap Press of Harvard University Press, 1964. xxviii, 477 p. illus. (The John Harvard library)

64–19579    E164.B89285

Bibliographical footnotes.

A new translation and a complete rendering of the French text, no. 4259 in the 1960 *Guide*. No. 4260 in the 1960 *Guide* is a translation of the first two of the three volumes in the original French edition.

1890. 1797–1807. JULIAN URSYN NIEMCEWICZ (1758–1841)

Niemcewicz was a Polish patriot, a statesman, and a prolific author. He was born in Lithuania and elected to the Polish parliament in 1788. Later he became Kosciuszko's aide-de-camp during the insurrection of 1794 and was captured and imprisoned. Upon his release he left for the United States with Kosciuszko in 1797. After living briefly in Philadelphia, he settled in Elizabeth, N.J., where he married a prominent widow. Family obligations recalled him to Poland in 1802, and he remained there for two years. From 1804 to 1807 he lived again in America, keeping journals that describe his domestic and private life and local people and scenes. Impressionistic in nature, the journals reflect the early and relatively unexplored history of American-Polish cultural relations.

1891. Under their vine and fig tree; travels through America in 1797–1799, 1805, with some further account of life in New Jersey. Translated and edited, with an introduction and notes, by Metchie J. E. Budka. Elizabeth, N.J., Grassmann Pub. Co. [1965] lvii, 398 p. illus. (Collections of the New Jersey Historical Society at Newark, v. 14)

65–15378    F131.N62    vol. 14

A translation of the author's manuscript notebooks, originally written in French or Polish and first published in Polish under the title *Podróze po Ameryce, 1797–1807* (1959).

1892. 1817–1818. WILLIAM COBBETT (1763–1835)

In 1817 William Cobbett, one of the most unruly figures in English literature and politics, fled to the United States to avoid possible arrest for his violently expressed demands for measures in behalf of the poor. Renting a farm on Long Island, N.Y., he read, experimented with crops, and wrote *A Year's Residence in the United States of America*. The diary shows his journalistic skill as he describes the customs, manners, and agricultural techniques of the Americans and remarks upon natural phenomena. His comments are frequently bare and fragmented, but he notes conditions with precision. He prefers "to deal a little in particular instances" rather than in general descriptions, and his details give veracity to the journal. Cobbett includes Thomas Hulme's "Journal of a Tour in the Western Countries of America" (p. 253–283), copied from Hulme's manuscript, which covers his visit to the West as far as Illinois during the period September 30, 1818, to August 7, 1819.

1893. A year's residence in the United States of America: treating of the face of the country, the climate, the soil, the products, the mode of cultivating the land, the prices of land, of labour, of food, of raiment; of the expenses of housekeeping, and of the usual manner of living; of the manners and customs of the people; and of the institutions of the country, civil, political, and religious. Carbondale, Southern Illinois University Press [1965, c1964] 338 p. illus. (Centaur classics) 64–14796 E165.C668

1894. 1833–1835. MICHEL CHEVALIER (1806–1879)

No. 4312 in 1960 *Guide.*

1895. Society, manners, and politics in the United States; letters on North America. Edited and with an introduction by John William Ward. Translated after the T. G. Bradford ed. Garden City, N.Y., Doubleday, 1961. 419 p. (Anchor books, A259) 61–9754 E165.C54 1961
Translation of *Lettres sur l'Amérique du Nord.*

A new edition of no. 4314 in the 1960 *Guide,* containing approximately 5,000 corrections of Bradford's translation and supplying materials that he omitted. According to the editor, it is the "first complete edition of Chevalier's *Lettres* in English." The footnotes from the original translation have been omitted, since they are now deemed unnecessary.

1896. 1836–1837. THOMAS CATHER.

Thomas Cather, a lawyer and member of the Royal Irish Academy from County Londonderry, was best known for his study of the Gaelic origins of local place names. At the age of 23 he traveled to America, accompanied by his friend Henry Tyler. He covered some 12,000 miles in all, with visits to New York, Philadelphia, Detroit, Baltimore, and Charleston. After a side trip to Cuba he took a Mississippi steamer to Kentucky and from there traveled by horseback, stagecoach,

and wagon deep into the frontier, entering observations and minute details in his journals. He was intolerant of American coarseness and passion for money but admired the strength of the new Nation. He foresaw the Civil War a quarter of a century before its occurrence.

1897. Voyage to America; the journals of Thomas Cather, edited with an introduction by Thomas Yoseloff. Illustrated with contemporary drawings by Harry Tyler. New York, T. Yoseloff [1961] 176 p. illus. 60–6841 E165.C35
The text of the first three months of the journal was published in London in 1955 under the title *Journal of a Voyage to America in 1836.*

1898. 1841–1858. GUSTAF ELIAS MARIUS UNONIUS (1810–1902)

Gustaf Unonius was a Finn who moved to Sweden with his family when his homeland came under Russian domination. He studied law at Uppsala University and became a clerk for the provincial government at Uppsala. At 31 he emigrated to America and took orders in the Protestant Episcopal Church. Seventeen years later, disappointed in the United States and in his hopes for a utopian colony, he returned to Sweden and published two volumes of his *Memoirs.* In the first volume he describes his arrival in New York and his journey by steamer and canalboat to Wisconsin, with stops along the way at Albany, Buffalo, Detroit, and Milwaukee. Unonius' privation as a pioneer farmer and minister of the gospel is faithfully detailed. Much material of a secondary nature about American life in the 1850's has been deleted by the editor, but nothing of autobiographical interest has been omitted. Throughout the work, Unonius seeks to uphold the viewpoint of the Episcopal Church and shows bias in his judgments of other denominations. The second volume introduces further lengthy descriptions of his experiences as an immigrant in Wisconsin and Illinois a century ago.

1899. A pioneer in Northwest America, 1841–1858; the memoirs of Gustaf Unonius. Translated from the Swedish by Jonas Oscar Backlund; edited by Nils William Olsson. With an introduction by George M. Stephenson. Minneapolis, Published for the Swedish Pioneer Historical Society by the University of Minnesota Press [1950–60] 2 v. illus. 50–11209 E166.U593
Bibliographical references included in "Notes" (p. 327–342).
The first English translation of *Minnen från en sjuttonårig vistelse i nordvestra Amerika* (1862. 2 v.).

1900. 1842–1844. WILLIAM BOLLAERT (1807–1876)

At 13 William Bollaert of Hampshire, England, entered the Royal Institution as a laboratory assistant; he published some of his original discoveries when he was only 16. He later worked as an assayer and chemist in Peru and as an agent of diplomatic intrigue for the Carlists in Spain, where he spent six years. In 1841 he made arrangements to explore Texas, with the idea of possibly settling there. He had followed the eastern coast to the most heavily populated areas, to the low country, and to the prairies when agitation for the annexation of Texas to the United States changed his plans; he returned to London in 1844. His sympathetic and appealing account of life in the frontier republic is full of scientific data, portrayals of social life, and random observations and is here accompanied by voluminous footnotes supplied by the editors.

1901. William Bollaert's Texas, edited by W. Eugene Hollon and Ruth Lapham Butler. Norman, University of Oklahoma Press [1956] xxiii, 423 p. illus. (The American exploration and travel series, 21)  56–11228  F390.B68
  Bibliography: p. 390–396.
Edited from manuscripts in the Newberry Library.

1902. 1853–1858. DAVID HUNTER STROTHER ("PORTE CRAYON") (1816–1888)

Strother was born into an illustrious Virginia family which included such literary figures as John Pendleton Kennedy, John Esten Cooke, and Philip Pendleton Cooke. An invalid in childhood, he developed an early interest in the arts. When his health subsequently improved he turned to exploration and employed his talents at sketching to record his journeys. His work eventually came to the attention of *Harper's Monthly,* and he became one of its highest paid contributors as writer and illustrator. His portrayals of leisurely, rural America, the Appalachian mountaineer, and the Negro were intended to combine instruction with amusement. Strother's entire career as artist, writer, soldier, and diplomat is treated in Cecil D. Eby's *"Porte Crayon": The Life of David Hunter Strother* (Chapel Hill, University of North Carolina Press [1960] 258 p.).

1903. The Old South illustrated. Profusely illustrated by the author. Edited with an introduction by Cecil D. Eby, Jr. Chapel Hill, University of North Carolina [ᵉ1959] xxi, 296 p.
  60–687  F213.S87

"Taken from . . . [the author's] articles scattered in *Harper's Monthly* between 1853 and 1858."
  "Bibliographical appendix": p. [293]–296.
Selections from Strother's articles in *Harper's Monthly,* 1853–58.

1904. 1859–1862. ISRAEL JOSEPH BENJAMIN (1818–1864)

Benjamin was born to a traditionally orthodox Jewish family in the Turkish province of Moldavia. He failed as a lumber-trader at 25 and decided to become a *maggid,* a type of moralistic, itinerant preacher. He spent his life traveling, preaching, and writing of his travels. This is a record of one of his journeys and is one of the few accounts of American life before 1870 by a Jewish writer. Interested primarily in moralizing, Benjamin makes no attempt at either scholarship or accuracy and presents an entertaining and informative, if somewhat prejudiced, description of the United States. Although he remained in New York for more than a year, he treats only California at length. The ferment over slavery prevented his traveling in the South. Oscar Handlin's introduction to the edition entered below provides a historical setting for this translation of Benjamin's hitherto unpublished journal.

1905. Three years in America, 1859–1862; translated from the German by Charles Reznikoff, with an introduction by Oscar Handlin. Philadelphia, Jewish Publication Society of America, 1956. 2 v. (The Jacob R. Schiff library of Jewish contributions to American democracy)
  56–7957  F594.B462

1906. 1859–1861. BARON SALOMON DE ROTHSCHILD (1835–1864)

Grandson to the founder of the powerful banking dynasty, Salomon de Rothschild came to America from France in 1859, ostensibly on family business. He stayed for 18 months, at the height of the debate on slavery, and visited New York, Jamestown, Saratoga, Newport, Baltimore, and New Orleans. He wrote well but in a contemptuous vein about the provincialism of Americans. He was arrogant and self-confident and more impressed with the failings of the United States than with its accomplishments. Strongly attracted to the South, he attempted unsuccessfully to influence his country on behalf of the Confederacy. He died at the age of 29, three years after his return to Paris.

1907. A casual view of America; the home letters of Salomon de Rothschild, 1859–1861.

Translated and edited by Sigmund Diamond. Stanford, Calif., Stanford University Press, 1961. 136 p.

61–14650 E166.R823

Translated from a manuscript volume in the Bibliothèque Nationale.

1908. 1861. CAMILLE FERRI-PISANI

Camille Ferri-Pisani was born in Coudray, near Paris, the son of a Corsican. He had a brilliant career as a professional soldier, and at the time of his visit to America in 1861 he was an aide-de-camp to Joseph Bonaparte, Prince Napoléon. The responsibility of keeping a record of the trip, which was regarded as a private visit, fell to Ferri-Pisani. The tour was of two months' duration and included a meeting with President Lincoln, excursions through the Northern and Western States, visits to New York, Philadelphia, Cleveland, Detroit, Boston, Washington, Pittsburgh, and other cities. Ferri-Pisani emphasizes the meetings with Civil War leaders and the military and political circumstances in which his group found itself.

1909. Prince Napoleon in America, 1861. Letters from his aide-de-camp. Translated with a preface by George J. Joyaux. Foreword by Bruce Catton. Illustrated by Gil Walker. Bloomington, Indiana University Press, 1959. 317 p. illus.

59–9248 E167.F383

Translation of Lettres sur les États-Unis d' Amérique (1862).

Bibliographical references included in "Notes" (p. [309]–317).

1910. 1865–1866. JOHN RICHARD DENNETT (1838–1874)

Brought to Massachusetts from New Brunswick as a child, John Richard Dennett attended Harvard, became editor of the Harvard Magazine, and was chosen class poet in his senior year. In 1865, when The Nation was conceived, he was invited to join the staff as a special correspondent covering the South. He traveled widely in Virginia, the Carolinas, Georgia, Mississippi, Alabama, and Louisiana, reporting what he saw and heard in a series of weekly letters which captured the idiom and speech of the day through the use of dialects. His observations were penetrating and objective, based on interviews in isolated rural areas as well as in urban centers. This volume brings the Dennett letters together in book form for the first time.

1911. The South as it is: 1865–1866. Edited and with an introduction by Henry M. Christman. New York, Viking Press [1965] 370 p.

65–19271 F216.D4 1965

1912. 1876–1878. HENRYK SIENKIEWICZ (1846–1916)

Sienkiewicz, born in Russian Poland to a family of impoverished gentry, is best known as the author of Quo Vadis? (1895) and recipient of the Nobel Prize for literature (1905). At 30 he joined a Polish group in a plan to establish a small utopian colony in California. Sent ahead with one companion to choose a location, Sienkiewicz financed his journey by writing articles for Polish newspapers. He arrived in New York in 1876 and, after a brief stay there, set out for California via Chicago over the recently completed transcontinental railroad. His reports, most of which were originally published as a series in Gazeta polska (Warsaw), contain accounts of the democratization of America and of encounters with American customs, sensitive descriptions of the land and the people, and a comparison between America and Europe. The colony was founded but quickly collapsed, and Sienkiewicz was back in Poland by 1878.

1913. Portrait of America, letters. Edited & translated by Charles Morley. New York, Columbia University Press, 1959. 300 p. illus.

59–7371 E168.S5763

Translation of v. 41–42 of Listy z podrózy do Ameryki (1947–55).

1914. 1898. BEATRICE POTTER WEBB (1858–1943)

Beatrice Potter was born in an upper-class Victorian home in Gloucester. Ill as a child, she received her education informally at home. She married Sidney Webb of the Fabian Society, and for 50 years they were leaders of major social and economic reform movements in England. This journal is the result of a trip the Webbs took to the United States in 1898. Mrs. Webb emphasizes her investigations of local governments in the cities of New York, Boston, Cincinnati, Denver, Salt Lake City, and San Francisco. Interviews with two future Presidents, Theodore Roosevelt and Woodrow Wilson, are included. Mrs. Webb's descriptions and impressions of the country and of the many prominent people she sought out are perceptive but somewhat provincial and condescending in tone.

1915. American diary, 1898. Edited by David A. Shannon. Madison, University of Wisconsin Press, 1963. 181 p. illus. 63–8436 E168.W4

The first publication of a manuscript in the British Library of Political and Economic Science, London School of Economics.

# XIV

# Population, Immigration, and Minorities

Sᴇᴄᴛɪᴏɴ A, Population, reflects the increasing concern with population growth in the United States as a whole and in the metropolitan centers in particular. The movement to the cities magnifies the difficulty of providing adequate housing, water supply, waste disposal, education, medical care, transportation, police protection, and other services. What the population explosion is doing to destroy man's natural environment is discussed in Sections G and H of Chapter XVII, Land and Agriculture. Section A of the present chapter includes studies which deal statistically with the characteristics of the population as such, its geographical distribution, age grouping, marital status, and relationship to economic trends.

Since the publication of the 1960 *Guide,* a number of social scientists, historians, and journalists have studied the situations of minority groups in the large urban areas. This chapter lists both current and historical analyses of the Negroes, Jews, Irish, Italians, and Puerto Ricans in New York, the Chinese in San Francisco, the Italians in Boston, and the Negroes in Chicago. The chapter also includes books on other minority groups, such as the Finns, Poles, Scotch-Irish, Norwegians, and Greeks. These works are mostly historical, as are the volumes on immigration. The increasing emphasis on books by and about Negroes is reflected in the large number of selections for Section E. A few of these might well have been placed in the chapters covering history, labor, or housing, but they seemed most appropriate for this chapter. Books on civil liberties and civil rights can be found in Chapters XXIX and XXX, and works on the Negro churches are in Chapter XXIII. Other works on the Negro in American society can be found through the index.

## A. Population

1916. Freedman, Ronald, Pascal K. Whelpton, *and* Arthur A. Campbell. Family planning, sterility and population growth. New York, McGraw-Hill, 1959. 515 p. illus. (McGraw-Hill series in sociology)          58–14348   HQ766.5.U5F7

Precise information concerning the extent and success in American society of "family planning"— use of the several means, variously approved and variously reliable, of avoiding pregnancy—has been notoriously lacking. This book reports upon a considerable attempt to supply such information, conducted by the Scripps Foundation for Research in Population Problems of Miami University and the Survey Research Center of the University of Michigan and largely financed by the Rockefeller Foundation. It is based upon interviews with 2,713 white married women between the ages of 18 and 39, living with their husbands or separated temporarily by the latter's military service. The "sample" was widely spread geographically and included diverse income levels and modes of living. The results show that "subfecundity" and actual sterility are very common and productive of much individual unhappiness, but that they make no great difference—at most a reduction of 10 or 15 percent—in the total number of births. They show that family limitation is generally approved and practiced and that there is a notable national consensus on family size—childlessness and a single child are both thought undesirable, whereas from two to four children are generally wanted and obtained. The authors report remarkably little variation between income levels, which may indicate that the sample was deficient in slumdwellers and "problem" families. The present family ideals, however, are sufficient to point toward rapid population growth and a probable total U.S. population of 312 million by A.D. 2000, with the present sex ratio but a larger proportion of children under 18. *Family Growth in Metropolitan America* (Princeton, N.J., Princeton University Press, 1961. 433 p.), by Charles F. Westoff and others, investigates the social and psychological factors thought to relate to differences in fertility among American couples living in the largest population centers of the Nation.

1917. Hauser, Philip M. Population perspectives. New Brunswick, N.J., Rutgers University Press [1961, °1960] 183 p. illus.

61–7090  HB3505.H3

Includes bibliography.

In these Brown and Haley lectures delivered at the University of Puget Sound, Hauser discusses the facts and consequences of three "explosions"—that in world population, as background, and those in U.S. total and metropolitan population, as main themes. People who derive encouragement from the economic stimulation provided by accelerated population growth, he argues, are shortsighted, missing short-run disadvantages and long-run dangers alike. Growth at the present rates means greatly reduced nonrenewable natural resources per head, an increased proportion of dependent persons young and old, increased pressure on virtually all public services, a decline in the already inadequate facilities for the aged, the spread of the lowered

quality of elementary education to the higher grades, and the demand upon an inelastic economy for millions of additional jobs. The explosive spread of metropolitan areas has brought about a decline of civic responsibility, housing shortages affecting many groups, commuter congestion, and the impossibility of enforcing codes for building maintenance. Hauser also claims that the Negro's higher rate of reproduction and his lack of preparation for urban living create a special set of problems. The primary element in all these explosions, the author insists, is "death control," the sharp reduction in mortality rates brought about by modern public health and medical practices; the only way to stabilize the population is through birth control and deliberate family limitation. Lincoln H. Day and Alice Taylor Day, in *Too Many Americans* (Boston, Houghton Mifflin, 1964. 298 p.), enumerate their arguments for seeking early attainment of population stability in the United States and discuss how this goal might best be achieved.

1918. Kuznets, Simon S., *and* Dorothy S. Thomas, eds. Population redistribution and economic growth: United States, 1870–1950. Prepared under the direction of Simon Kuznets and Dorothy Swaine Thomas. Philadelphia, American Philosophical Society, 1957–64. 3 v. illus. (Memoirs of the American Philosophical Society, v. 45, 51, 61)

57–10071  HB1965.K8

Bibliographical references.

CONTENTS.—1. Methodological considerations and reference tables, by Everett S. Lee and others.—2. Analyses of economic change, by Simon Kuznets, Ann R. Miller, and Richard A. Easterlin.—3. Demographic analyses and interrelations, by Hope T. Eldridge and Dorothy S. Thomas.

This study emphasizes "the many and close links between economic growth and population redistribution; the interdependence of the various distributions and redistributions of population and of economic opportunities; and the importance of migration as the principal mechanism by which job-seeking elements in the population are adjusted numerically and by characteristics to changing temporal-spatial distributions of opportunities." The discussions are accompanied by numerous tables listing data on population growth, population movement, wages, incomes, and economic activity.

1919. Maclachlan, John M., *and* Joe S. Floyd. This changing South. Gainesville, University of Florida Press, 1956. 154 p.

56–12858  HB3511.M35

As a result of interregional migration, the population of the South has been growing more slowly than that of the United States as a whole (an increase of 12.7 as against 14.5 percent between 1940 and 1950), despite its higher rate of natural increase. The white population in the South increased by 16.5 percent between 1940 and 1950, while the black population rose only 1.5 percent in the area as a whole and decreased in six of the 13 Southern States. The majority of the South's counties—those predominately rural—lost population, but the remainder showed rapid rates of increase, and the cities of the South grew more rapidly than those of "non-southern America." Income in the South, especially in the States worst off in 1940, likewise rose more rapidly than in other regions. A precipitous decline in the agricultural labor force was offset by a rapid rise in the white female labor force. All these figures point to basic and irreversible changes in the traditional patterns of Southern society.

1920. Sheldon, Henry D. The older population of the United States. With introductory and summary chapters by Clark Tibbitts. For the Social Science Research Council in cooperation with the U.S. Dept. of Commerce, Bureau of the Census. New York, Wiley [1958] 223 p. (Census monograph series)          58–6086  HB1545.S5

Eleven special monographs were published with the census of 1920, but depression and war prevented such studies of the censuses of 1930 and 1940. The Social Science Research Council and the Russell Sage Foundation cooperated with the Bureau of the Census in ensuring the appearance of this Census Monograph Series interpreting the 1950 figures. Four of the volumes were noted in the 1960 *Guide* (no. 4395), and another is no. 1921 below. During the first half of the 20th century, while the population of the United States nearly doubled, the segment aged 65 or over nearly quadrupled, rising from 3.1 million to 12.3 million. Within this older population, the number of males for each 100 females declined during the period from 102.1 to 89.6. Sheldon examines the statistical characteristics of this group with respect to geographic distribution, employment and occupation, living arrangements, and income. In 1950, 42 percent of the men over 64 remained in the labor force, as compared to 68 percent in 1890. The author states that earlier retirement does not necessarily mean sufficient income, adequate housing, proper medical care, or opportunities for utilizing leisure. Statistics on housing indicate, for example, that among households headed by persons over 64 in 1950, one-third lived in substandard housing, as against one-fourth for the middle-aged group. The other volumes in this series are *American Families* (240 p.), by Paul C. Glick, and *Farm Housing* (194 p.), by Glenn H. Beyer and J. Hugh Rose, both published in New York by Wiley in 1957.

1921. Taeuber, Conrad, *and* Irene B. Taeuber. The changing population of the United States. For the Social Science Research Council in cooperation with the U.S. Dept. of Commerce, Bureau of the Census. New York, Wiley [1958] 357 p. (Census monograph series)

57–13451  HB3505.T3

"Sources for national demographic statistics": p. 327–334. Bibliographical footnotes.

This most general volume of the Census Monograph Series (see no. 1920 above) is concerned with the trends of greatest significance in all the fields covered by the census of 1950. In some instances the First Census of 1790 is the point of departure, but developments are more often limited to the present century. It is noted, for example, that the overall density of the population had risen by 1950 to 50.7 persons per square mile. A quarter of the population was contained in 28 of the Nation's 3,103 counties, as against 39 counties in 1910. Significant changes in internal migration occurred in the 20th century, and marriage became a more general condition. The authors conclude with some very cautious projections, the point of doubt being whether the recent unusually high fertility rates will be maintained. Another commentary on the census of 1950 is provided by Donald J. Bogue in *The Population of the United States* (Glencoe, Ill., Free Press [c1959] xix, 873 p.). Intended primarily for reference use, it has an even greater proportion of tables, graphs, and maps than the Taeubers' volume and seeks to interpret the changes of the 1950's as revealed in the *Current Population Reports* of the Bureau of the Census and elsewhere. Bogue treats a number of topics which the Taeubers omit, including industrial composition, unemployment, confinement to institutions, religious affiliation, housing, and the populations of Alaska and Hawaii.

# B. Immigration: General

1922. Ander, Oscar Fritiof, *ed*. In the trek of the immigrants, essays presented to Carl Wittke. Rock Island, Ill., Augustana College Library, 1964. xvi, 325 p. (Augustana Library publications, no. 31)　　　　　64–19873　E184.A1A66
　Bibliographical references included in "Notes" (p. 266–299).
　　　CONTENTS.—Preface, by Clarence W. Sorensen. —Introduction, by O. Fritiof Ander.—Carl Wittke, historian, by Harvey Wish.—Four historians of immigration, by O. Fritiof Ander.—Immigration, emigration, migration, by Carlton C. Qualey.—Bibliography of works by Carl Wittke, by Clarence H. Cramer.—A forgotten theory of immigration, by Edward P. Hutchinson.—Agrarian myths of English immigrants, by Charlotte Erickson.—A brief history of immigrant groups in Ohio, by Francis P. Weisenburger.—The German in American fiction, by John T. Flanagan.—English migration to the American West, 1865–1900, by Oscar Osborn Winther.—Saga in steel and concrete, by Kenneth O. Bjork.—Finnish immigrant farmers in New York, 1910–1960, by A. William Hoglund.—The immigrant and the American national idea, by Walter O. Forster.—British backtrailers: working-class immigrants return, by Wilbur S. Shepperson.—Exodus U.S.A., by Theodore Saloutos.—The Negro in the old Northwest, by James H. Rodabaugh.—The American Negro: an old immigrant on a new frontier, by J. Iverne Dowie.

1923. Handlin, Oscar. Boston's immigrants [1790–1880]; a study in acculturation. Rev. and enl. ed. Cambridge, Mass., Belknap Press of Harvard University Press, 1959. 382 p. illus.
　　　　　59–7653　F73.9.A1H3　1959

A revised edition of no. 4410 in the 1960 *Guide*.

1924. Jones, Maldwyn A. American immigration. [Chicago] University of Chicago Press [1960] 359 p. (The Chicago history of American civilization)　　　60–8301　JV6450.J6
　Bibliography: p. 325–341.
　The author, a Welsh scholar, regards immigration as "the most persistent and the most pervasive influence" in America's development and notes that "as a social process it has shown little variation" from 1607 to the present. He finds a pervasive Americanism at work throughout the separate activities of ethnic groups and points out that the facts of immigration have forced Americans to broaden their concept of equality and have given a new meaning to the national motto "E pluribus unum": "the unity that has developed from the mingling of peoples diverse in origin but sharing a common devotion to liberty, democracy, and tolerance." Oscar Handlin has compiled a selection of important readings, mostly from original sources, in his *Immigration as a Factor in American History* (Englewood Cliffs, N.J., Prentice-Hall, 1959. 206 p.). In *A Nation of Immigrants,* rev. and enl. ed. (New York, Harper & Row [1964] 111 p.), John F. Kennedy reviews U.S. immigration history, stresses multinational contributions to American cultural and economic life, and offers recommendations for improvements in present Government policy.

1925. Wittke, Carl F. We who built America; the saga of the immigrant. [Rev. ed. Cleveland] Press of Western Reserve University [1964]. xviii, 550 p.　　　64–20939　JV6455.W55　1964
　Includes bibliographical references.
　An updated edition of no. 4417 in the 1960 *Guide*.

# C. Immigration: Policy

1926. Bennett, Marion T. American immigration policies, a history. Washington, Public Affairs Press [1963] 362 p.　　63–10815　JV6465.B4
　Bibliography: p. 347–356.
　This careful study by a Commissioner of the U.S. Court of Claims deals chiefly with the McCarran-

Walter Act of 1952, which codified the scattered legislation on immigration for the first time and confirmed and entrenched the restrictions inaugurated by the quota system in 1924. Bennett summarizes the history of immigration down to 1950 and the legislation which it provoked, noting that the first

Federal law to restrict immigration was passed in 1875, when certain classes of orientals were excluded. He also discusses the Senate report of 1950 on the study (authorized in 1947 and extended to March 1950) which constituted "the first broadscale investigation of our immigration system by Congress since the one in the years 1907–1911," which was less comprehensive. Chapters 12 and 13 present 26 detailed criticisms of the act, most of which were voiced by Presidents Truman and Eisenhower, with answers drawn from statements by the cosponsors of the act and by Richard Arens, the staff director of the Senate Subcommittee To Investigate Immigration and Naturalization. The several relaxations of the law in President Eisenhower's administration are reviewed. The quota plan is judged to have failed in its original intention, that of preserving the dominant national origins of the American people, because of various alternative principles admitted in the act itself and in subsequent legislation—such as family unity, asylum to refugees, and Western Hemisphere solidarity through unrestricted migration. The author discusses problems of the future and points out that, between the restrictionists and the antirestrictionists, there is a large middle ground, favoring "sufficient restrictions to bar those who have nothing worthy to contribute to our society," yet welcoming those who seek freedom and support American institutions.

1927. Common Council for American Unity. The alien and the immigration law; a study of 1446 cases arising under the immigration and naturalization laws of the United States. A study under the direction of Edith Lowenstein. New York, Oceana Publications, 1958 [ᶜ1957] 388 p.

57–12992 KF4800.C6 1958

Shortly after publishing this study, the Common

Council for American Unity merged with another organization to become the American Council for Nationalities Service; one of its functions remains the provision of legal aid to immigrants and would-be immigrants. The study describes the difficulties encountered, the assistance received, and the conclusions reached in connection with applications since the Immigration and Nationality Act, usually referred to as the McCarran-Walter Act, went into effect in 1952. The cases are arranged under the headings of Immigration, Status, Deportation, Naturalization, and Nationality; some cases are discussed under more than one heading. Read Lewis, the Executive Director of the Common Council, notes that the immigration act of September 11, 1957, alleviated some hardships but fails to "cover all the situations in which administrative discretion to ease hardship is needed." This closeup view of the actual working of the immigration code can be supplemented by *A Research Study Concerning Illegal Entrants and Illegal Aliens in the United States* (Carbondale, Ill., Southern Illinois University, 1958. 199 p.), by James C. Messersmith, who treats the problems encountered by the Immigration and Naturalization Service in guarding the country's borders. The author discusses factors that lead aliens to attempt illegal entry and describes the enforcement activities of the four regional offices of the Service.

1928. Higham, John. Strangers in the land; patterns of American nativism, 1860–1925. Corrected and with a new preface. New York, Atheneum, 1963. 431 p. (Atheneum paperbacks, 32)

63–3476 E184.A1H5 1963

Includes bibliography.

A corrected edition of no. 4422 in the 1960 *Guide.*

# D. Minorities

1929. Glazer, Nathan, *and* Daniel P. Moynihan. Beyond the melting pot; the Negroes, Puerto Ricans, Jews, Italians, and Irish of New York City. Cambridge, Mass. M.I.T. Press, 1963. 360 p. (Publications of the Joint Center for Urban Studies of the Massachusetts Institute of Technology and Harvard University)

63–18005 F128.9.A1G55

Bibliographical references included in "Notes" (p. 325–347).

The authors examine the continuance of strong ethnic consciousness among the large immigrant groups of New York City and attempt to explain

why these groups have not been assimilated by the "melting pot." Four major events or social processes of the past generation are distinguished which have prevented the assimilation of Jews, Catholics, Negroes, and Puerto Ricans, respectively. Oscar Handlin concentrates on two of these groups in *The Newcomers: Negroes and Puerto Ricans in a Changing Metropolis* (Cambridge, Harvard University Press, 1959. 171 p. New York metropolitan region study). *The Urban Villagers: Group and Class in the Life of Italian-Americans* ([New York] Free Press of Glencoe [1962] 367 p.), by Herbert J.

Gans, is a report on life in a Boston slum about to undergo clearance. The author concludes that the behavior patterns and values of working-class subcultures ought to be understood and taken into account by urban planners.

1930. Gossett, Thomas F. Race; the history of an idea in America. Dallas, Southern Methodist University Press, 1963. 512 p.

63–21187 E184.A1G6

Bibliographical references included in "Notes" (p. 461–501).

The evolution of ideas on race is traced, with emphasis given to their impact on currents of thought in the United States. The author discusses race relations at the times that specific racial doctrines were being propagated, summarizes early race theories, and explores the ideas that were prevalent in the Colonies and through the 18th, 19th, and 20th centuries. Gossett notes that significant changes took place in intellectual attitudes during the 1920's, when racists first encountered from the sciences a serious check to their theories of innate racial inferiority. Although many still believe that character, intelligence, and human worth are often matters of race, this attitude is rapidly losing support and the academic disciplines in general have abandoned it. Idus A. Newby's *Jim Crow's Defense; Anti-Negro Thought in America, 1900–1930* (Baton Rouge, Louisiana State University Press, 1965. 230 p.) details one era in the development of anti-Negro racism.

1931. Handlin, Oscar. The American people in the twentieth century. Boston, Beacon Press [1963] 248 p. 63–2687 E169.1.H265 1963

Bibliographical notes: p. [237]–239.

An updated edition of no. 4429 in the 1960 *Guide*.

1932. Javits, Jacob K. Discrimination—U.S.A. New York, Harcourt, Brace [1960] 310 p.

60–10926 E184.A1J3

Bibliographical references included in "Notes" (p. 287–300).

Senator Javits (b. 1904) vividly recalls the poverty and restrictions of his boyhood in New York's Lower East Side, noting the general advance which has been made since 1900, when the United States was a "white, Protestant, Anglo-Saxon country" and an effective majority was concerned to keep it so. After tracing the struggle for effective civil rights legislation in Congress, he surveys the fields in which discrimination bears most severely on Negroes and other minorities and notes recent steps to curb its effects. Discrimination has been worst in employment, but since 1941 the Federal Govern-

ment has repudiated it, 16 States have passed enforceable laws against it, and 45 cities have adopted ordinances to the same end. Politics, housing, the schools, public accommodation and transportation, and the administration of justice are other fields where discrimination is still powerful but where many recent checks have been imposed upon it. The complete elimination of many types of discrimination in Washington, D.C., during the preceding decade is presented as "a clear pilot-plant operation." The passage of the Civil Rights Act of 1960 is treated as the climax of an extended effort.

1933. Marden, Charles F., *and* Gladys E. Meyer. Minorities in American society. 2d ed. New York, American Book Co. [1962] 497 p. (American sociology series)

62–4432 E184.A1M3 1962

"Suggested reading" at the end of each chapter.

A revised edition of no. 4432 in the 1960 *Guide*, with a new coauthor. Recent developments in relations between the various minorities and the dominant group are discussed, particularly Negro-white relations in the South since the desegregation decision of 1954. New theoretical insights and research findings are included, especially in an added chapter on "Sociological Theory and Dominant-Minority Relations." In *American Minorities; a Textbook of Readings in Intergroup Relations* (New York, Knopf, 1957. 518 p.), edited by Milton L. Barron, are assembled 50 pieces, chiefly articles from periodicals or symposia but with a few extracts from textbooks and monographs. Editorial comments and notes on the contributors enhance the book's usefulness. Negro-white, Roman Catholic-Protestant, and Jewish-gentile relations are given separate chapters. The last 14 selections, arranged under the headings "Minority Group Reactions and Adjustment" and "Toward Intergroup Harmony and Equality," are oriented toward the philosophy of "social inclusivism."

1934. Vander Zanden, James W. American minority relations; the sociology of race and ethnic groups. New York, Ronald Press [1963] 470 p. 63–13576 E184.A1V3

Bibliography: p. 515–538.

A textbook on race and minority relations in the United States. The first part establishes a groundwork of concepts and discusses the facts and myths of racial knowledge. Parts 2 and 3 consider the sources of prejudice and discrimination and their extension into society in the form of intergroup conflict, segregation, and stratification. Part 4 concerns itself with the attitudes of the disadvantaged minorities. Particular attention is devoted to the reactions of acceptance, aggression, avoidance, and assimilation directed by these groups toward society. The final chapters discuss the inevitability of social change and the dangers inherent in a society that seeks to remain static. A résumé of the five-volume report submitted by the U.S. Commission on Civil Rights in 1961 is presented by Wallace Mendelson in *Discrimination* (Englewood Cliffs, N.J., Prentice-Hall [1962] 175 p. A Spectrum book, S–45).

# E. Negroes

1935. Bardolph, Richard. The Negro vanguard. New York, Rinehart [1959] 388 p.
59–6571  E185.96.B28
"Essay on authorities": p. 343–369.

1936. Lomax, Louis E. The Negro revolt. New York, Harper [1962] 271 p.
62–7911  E185.61.L668

Bardolph's book "takes as its theme several hundred Negro Americans, from the days of the American Revolution to the present, who may fairly be counted among the makers and shakers of American social history." His study begins with Crispus Attucks, the first victim of the Boston Massacre in 1770, and concludes with Althea Gibson, who swept the major women's tennis events at home and abroad in 1957–58. Under the auspices of the Guggenheim Foundation, Bardolph interviewed 131 well-known Negro Americans, seeking to objectively evaluate their achievements and to relate their careers to social and racial circumstances. He frequently asserts or implies that achievement might have been greater if obstructions because of their race had been fewer. Lomax discusses the "do-it-yourself" movement among Negroes, primarily in the South but with widespread effects throughout the country. He assigns its beginning a precise date, December 1, 1955, when Mrs. Rosa Parks refused to yield her seat on an Alabama bus to a white man. He states that, as the folkways of segregation were worked out and became rigid between 1880 and 1920, the Negro world became "an enclave of terror" and the Negro masses "were trapped in their separate hell." The author describes the successive phases of the sit-ins and the freedom rides and indicates that activist organizations such as the Congress of Racial Equality are cutting into the older, relatively conservative leadership of the National Association for the Advancement of Colored People. The Negro crime rate is discounted as being the product of social conditions imposed upon the Negro community.

1937. Brown, Claude. Manchild in the promised land. New York, Macmillan [1965] 415 p.
65–16938  E185.97.B86A3

The autobiography of a Harlemite (b. 1937) who decided at age 16 to give up street life and return to school. The author offers his life history as representative of that generation of Northern urban Negroes whose parents migrated from the South during the post-depression years. Because he was a leader in the streets, Brown can provide keen personal insight into ghetto society and the institutions which shape it. *The Autobiography of Malcolm X* (New York, Grove Press [1965] 455 p.), written by Malcolm Little (1925–1965) with the assistance of Alex Haley, describes the experiences of a leader in the Black Muslim movement.

1938. Cable, George Washington. The Negro question; a selection of writings on civil rights in the South. Edited by Arlin Turner. Garden City, N.Y., Doubleday, 1958. 286 p. (Doubleday anchor books)
58–7796  E185.61.C19  1958a

1939. Rudwick, Elliott M. W. E. B. Du Bois; a study in minority group leadership. Philadelphia, University of Pennsyvania Press [1960] 382 p.          60–6754  E185.97.D73R8
Bibliography: p. 350–368.

Cable (1844–1925) had fought for the Confederacy and after the war became an admired writer of Southern local-color fiction. His sense of justice led him into controversy on behalf of Negro children in the New Orleans public schools as early as 1875, and in 1884 he entered upon an intensive campaign on behalf of the Negro's civil and political rights. He demonstrated in a series of addresses and essays that the full concession of such rights was not merely just but essential to the welfare of the white South. In consequence, he was assailed and ostracized as the southern antislavery men had been half a century earlier, and for the last 40 years of his life he resided in Massachusetts. William Edward Burghardt Du Bois (1868–1963) began his career with moderate views, but the intransigence of the white superiority bloc soon turned him into an advocate of protest and resistance. He initiated the Niagara Movement in 1905 and became the editor of *The Crisis,* the journal of the National Association for the Advancement of Colored People. After the death of Booker T. Washington in 1915, he was long the most conspicuous figure among Negro Americans, but he remained an individualist and a theorist rather than an organizer. A difference on policy in the Depression led him to resign from the NAACP in 1934. Rudwick's study defines both Du Bois' doctrines and his limitations.

1940. Davis, Allison, Burleigh B. Gardner, *and* Mary R. Gardner. Deep South; a social anthropological study of caste and class. With a new foreword by James W. Silver and a retrospect by the authors. Abridged ed. Chicago, University of Chicago Press [1965] xix, 364 p. (Phoenix books, P204)        65–27759   HN79.A2D3   1965
    Bibliographical footnotes.
    An updated edition of no. 4438 in the 1960 *Guide.*

1941. Drake, St. Clair, *and* Horace R. Cayton. Black metropolis; a study of Negro life in a Northern city. Introduction by Richard Wright. Introduction to Torchbook edition by Everett C. Hughes. [Rev. and enl. ed.] New York, Harper & Row [1962] 2 v. (Harper torchbooks, TB1086–1087. The Academy library)
            62–52869   F548.9.N3D68   1962
    Includes bibliography.
    An updated edition of no. 4439 in the 1960 *Guide.*

1942. Essien-Udom, Essien U. Black nationalism; a search for an identity in America. [Chicago] University of Chicago Press [1962] 367 p. illus.        62–12632   E185.61.E75
    Bibliography: p. 351–360.
    An investigation of one aspect of the efforts by American Negroes "to resolve the fundamental problem of identity." Black nationalism, the author asserts, provides a meaningful context for moral, cultural, and material advancement within the limitations set by American society. The study focuses on the Nation of Islam movement headed by Elijah Muhammad. The author outlines the tradition of Negro nationalism and its effects on Negro thought and social action and explains the reasons for which Negroes join and remain in the movement. Other chapters deal with its ideology, organization, programs, and limitations. A final section sets forth conclusions and identifies significant trends for the future. Charles Eric Lincoln brings together much concrete information about the same "intensely

dedicated, tightly disciplined block" in *The Black Muslims in America* (Boston, Beacon Press [1961] 276 p.). In *The New World of Negro Americans* (New York, John Day Co. [1963] 366 p.), Harold R. Isaacs probes the effects of rising African nationalism on Negro thought in the United States.

1943. Frazier, Edward Franklin. Black bourgeoisie. With a new preface by the author. New York, Collier Books [1962] 222 p. illus. (Collier books, AS347)
            A 62–8728   E185.61.F833   1962
    A "sociological analysis of the behavior, the attitudes, and values" of the Negro middle class. The first part treats economic and social status and political, educational, and cultural backgrounds. Part 2 discusses the "world of make-believe" that the "bourgeois" Negro has created to cope with his feelings of inferiority in white America and his alienation from the Negro masses. In *Transformation of the Negro American* (New York, Harper & Row [1965] 207 p.), Leonard Broom and Norval D. Glenn offer a sociological review of information about the Negro in the United States and his evolving position in society through the years. *A Pictorial History of the Negro in America,* new rev. ed. (New York, Crown Publishers [1963] 337 p.), by Langston Hughes and Milton Meltzer, is a revised edition of a work mentioned in the annotation for no. 4440 in the 1960 *Guide.*

1944. Hughes, Langston. Fight for freedom; the story of the NAACP. New York, Norton [1962] 224 p. illus.   62–14352   E185.5.N276H8
    Bibliography: p. 207–208.
    A history of the National Association for the Advancement of Colored People. Established in 1909, the NAACP waged a slow, often discouraging battle to improve the condition of the Negro American. The author devotes particular attention to the legal victories achieved over the last 50 years, including the high point of the 1954 Supreme Court decision which ruled segregation in the public schools unlawful. Major campaigns conducted by the NAACP have included efforts to ensure enforcement of laws against lynching, end discrimination in the armed services, and gain equal access to the franchise and better housing. Hughes presents sketches of prominent NAACP leaders and supporters, such as W. E. B. Du Bois and presidents Moorfield Storey, Joel and Arthur Spingarn, and Roy Wilkins. In *The National Association for the Advancement of Colored People: A Case Study in Pressure Groups* (New York, Exposition Press [1958] 252 p. An Exposition-university book), Warren D. St. James investigates the problems,

effectiveness, and achievements of the organization. In *SNCC; the New Abolitionists,* 2d ed. (Boston, Beacon Press [1965] 286 p.), Howard Zinn chronicles the activities of the Student Nonviolent Coordinating Committee in the South between 1960 and 1964.

1945. Lewis, Anthony. Portrait of a decade; the second American revolution [by] Anthony Lewis and the New York Times. New York, Random House [1964] 322 p. illus.

      64–14832   E185.61.L52   1964

A description of the "civil rights revolution," beginning with the 1954 school segregation cases and ending with the passage of the Civil Rights Act in 1964. Into his account Lewis weaves articles or portions of articles written by various authors for *The New York Times.* Included are reportorial descriptions of the Montgomery, Ala., bus boycott, James Meredith's entry into the University of Mississippi, the integration of schools in Little Rock, Ark., and the acceleration of voter registration. Martin Luther King's *Why We Can't Wait* (New York, Harper & Row [1964] 178 p.) explains the motivations, purposes, and aspirations of the Negro movement. A portrait of a moderate Southern community (Chapel Hill, N.C.) experiencing an effort at integration is drawn by John Ehle in *The Free Men* (New York, Harper & Row [1965] 340 p.). William M. McCord recounts a significant phase of the civil rights movement during 1964 in *Mississippi: The Long Hot Summer* (New York, Norton [1965] 222 p.).

1946. Litwack, Leon F. North of slavery; the Negro in the free States, 1790–1860. [Chicago] University of Chicago Press [1961] 318 p.

      61–10869   E185.9.L5

Bibliographical essay: p. 280–303.

"Discrimination against the Negro and a firmly held belief in the superiority of the white race were not restricted to one section but were shared by an overwhelming majority of white Americans in both the North and the South." Public opinion, laws, and extralegal measures restricted the Negro in the antebellum North. Federal Government policy, particularly in the Dred Scott decision, further reduced the Negro's status. Nonetheless, the Northern Negro was free and could work toward the improvement of his position. He could organize and petition, accumulate property, publish newspapers, and engage in business. In *The Negro in the Making of America* (New York, Collier Books [1964] 288 p. A Collier books original), Benjamin Quarles discusses the black man's role as

pioneer, soldier, freedman, and aspirant for civil rights.

1947. Logan, Rayford W. The betrayal of the Negro, from Rutherford B. Hayes to Woodrow Wilson. New enl. ed. New York, Collier Books [1965] 447 p.

      65–23835   E185.61.L64   1965

Bibliographical references included in "Notes" (p. 397–430).

A revised edition of *The Negro in American Life and Thought: The Nadir, 1877–1901* (1954), no. 4445 in the 1960 *Guide.*

1948. Meier, August. Negro thought in America, 1880–1915; racial ideologies in the age of Booker T. Washington. Ann Arbor, University of Michigan Press [1963] 336 p.

      63–14008   E185.6.M5

"Bibliographical note": p. 280–282. Bibliographical references included in "Notes" (p. 283–316).

An analysis of the prevailing racial ideologies as expressed by articulate Negroes from the post-Reconstruction era through the outbreak of World War I. Emphasis is on the role of Booker T. Washington and his philosophy of self-help and racial solidarity in influencing Negro thought in the United States. For two decades Washington was accepted by whites and Negroes as the spokesman of Negro opinion. Criticism of Washington's leadership, however, crystallized under W. E. B. Du Bois and led to the formation of the National Association for the Advancement of Colored People. Another study of Negro thought in America is *The Mind of the Negro; an Intellectual History of Afro-Americans* (Baton Rouge, La., Ortlieb Press [1961] 562 p.), by Earl E. Thorpe.

1949. Myrdal, Gunnar. An American dilemma; the Negro problem and modern democracy. With the assistance of Richard Sterner and Arnold Rose. 20th anniversary ed. New York, Harper & Row [1962] 1483 p. illus.

      62–19706   E185.6.M95   1962

Bibliography: p. 1144–1180.

This revised edition of no. 4446 in the 1960 *Guide* adds a brief preface by the author and a longer "Postscript Twenty Years Later: Social Change and the Negro Problem" by Arnold N. Rose, Myrdal's former assistant. Myrdal calls attention to the accuracy of his prediction "that an area of more than half a century in which there had been no fundamental change [in interracial relations] was approaching its close" and praises the late Frederick P. Keppel, then president of the Carnegie Corporation, for his courage in giving the inquiry a completely free hand and in persevering with publication during the most anxious months of the war. Rose summarizes Negro progress in several fields and identifies the forces operative in each. "The changes in American race relations from 1940 to 1962 appear to be the most rapid and dramatic in world history without violent revolution," he maintains, predicting that in another 30 years racial prejudice in America will have dwindled to "the minor order of Catholic-Protestant prejudice." In *A Profile of the Negro American* (Princeton, N.J., Van Nostrand [1964] 250 p.), Thomas F. Pettigrew concludes that many Negro traits often attributed to race have actually resulted from environmental influences, such as poverty and discrimination.

1950. Negro heritage library. Yonkers, N.Y., Educational Heritage [1964–65] 4 v.
A series on the Negro's contribution to society. The volumes pertaining to the Negro in the United States are *Negro Heritage Reader for Young People* ([c1965] 320 p. 66–2716 PE1121.C3) and *The Winding Road to Freedom; a Documentary Survey of Negro Experiences in America* ([1965] 384 p. 65–5735 E185.C14), both edited by Alfred E. Cain; the first volume, covering the period 1619–1900, of *Profiles of Negro Womanhood* ([1964] 352 p. 64–25013 E185.96.D25, v. 1), by Sylvia G. L. Dannett; and *A Martin Luther King Treasury* ([1964] 352 p. 65–391 E185.61.K535).

1951. Northrup, Herbert R., *and* Richard L. Rowan, *eds.* The Negro and employment opportunity; problems and practices. Ann Arbor, Bureau of Industrial Relations, Graduate School of Business Administration, University of Michigan [1965] 411 p. illus. 65–63900 E185.8.N649
This collection of 28 papers is divided into sections on the overall job problems of Negroes, equal opportunity legislation, representative companies, unions, community activities, Negro employment in the urban market, and Negro entrepreneurial activities. *Employing the Negro in American Industry; a Study of Management Practices* (New York, Industrial Relations Counselors, 1959. 171 p. Industrial relations monographs, no. 17), by Paul H. Norgren and others, is a pioneer study based on the experience of 44 company and plant managements that employ Negroes as well as whites. In *The Negro and Organized Labor* (New York, Wiley [1965] 327 p.), F. Ray Marshall analyzes the factors responsible for the evolution of union racial practices. In *The Urban Negro in the South* (New York, Vantage Press [1962] 272 p.), Wilmoth A. Carter examines a typical Negro residential and business district in a Southern city (Raleigh, N.C.) and concludes that the progress of desegregation is likely to close out Negro small businesses altogether.

1952. Silberman, Charles E. Crisis in black and white. New York, Random House [1964] 370 p. 64–14843 E185.61.S57
Bibliographical footnotes.
Silberman's primary purpose is to define what can and cannot be accomplished by integration. Observations are included on circumstances which influence the Negro's family, employment opportunities, and quality of education. The author further describes the impact of these circumstances on individual and group motivation, direction, and stability. From his material, Silberman evolves two main arguments: that to achieve meaningful improvement in their situation, Negroes must acquire some realistic economic and political power, and that any successful welfare program must be executed *by* Negroes as well as for them. Of added interest is a chapter on the work and achievement of Chicago's controversial neighborhood organizer, Saul Alinsky. In *The New Equality* (New York, Viking Press [1964] 243 p.), Nat Hentoff stresses the close relationship between poverty and the race problem and urges underprivileged people, white as well as black, to unite in an effort to improve their economic status.

1953. Taeuber, Karl E., *and* Alma F. Taeuber. Negroes in cities; residential segregation and neighborhood change. Chicago, Aldine Pub. Co. [1965] xvii, 284 p. illus. (Population Research and Training Center monographs) 65–12459 E185.89.H6T3
Bibliography: p. 267–277.
A statistical examination of urban segregation in the United States. Using both quantitative and empirical methods, the authors reveal that significant variations exist in residential patterns from city to city as well as from region to region. Important changes are shown to have occurred throughout the country since 1950, and evidence exposes as fallacious numerous beliefs regarding comparative white and Negro residential behavior. The most important change in the character of Negro influx into cities is that in-migrants are former residents of another city, with the rural sharecropper no longer constituting a significant proportion. In *The Negro Population of Chicago; a Study of Residential Succession* ([Chicago] University of Chicago Press [1957] 367 p. Monograph series of the Chicago Community Inventory of the University of Chicago), Otis D. Duncan and Beverly Duncan trace

Negro population distribution and growth from 1910 to 1950 in a Northern terminal of the Negro migration route from the South.

1954. Welsch, Erwin K. The Negro in the United States; a research guide. Bloomington, Indiana University Press, 1965. 142 p.
        65–23085  Z1361.N39W4  1965
Bibliography: p. 108–138.
The author has compiled a descriptive bibliography of books, periodicals, and essays pertinent to the study of the Negro in America. The book is divided into four parts: "Science, Philosophy, and Race," "Historical and Sociological Background," "The Major Issues Today," and "The Negro and the Arts." The appendixes include a discussion of additional bibliographies and a list of periodicals, both of which are useful for Negro studies. Organizations that issue information or try to shape public opinion concerning the Negro are also listed.

# F. Jews

1955. Levinger, Lee J. A history of the Jews in the United States. [20th rev. ed.] New York, Union of American Hebrew Congregations [1961] 616 p. illus. (Commission on Jewish Education of the Union of American Hebrew Congregations and [the] Central Conference of American Rabbis. Union graded series)
        63–39  E184.J5L664  1961
Includes bibliography.
An updated edition of no. 4461 in the 1960 *Guide.*

1956. Rischin, Moses. The promised city; New York's Jews, 1870-1914. Cambridge, Harvard University Press, 1962. 342 p. illus.
        62–11402  F128.9.J5R5
"Bibliographical note": p. [275]–282.

1957. Gordon, Albert I. Jews in suburbia. Boston, Beacon Press [1959] 264 p.
        59–12322  E184.J5G67
The Jewish community in New York City dates back to the mid-17th century but remained small during its first two centuries. Rischin's volume covers the period during which more than one-third of the Jewish inhabitants of Russia and Rumania left their homes and, for the most part, came to New York's Lower East Side and took over tenements from the Irish, the Germans, and other earlier occupants. By 1915 they numbered nearly 1,400,000, more than New York's total population in 1870. Although he describes the economic bases and the abominable living conditions of this "immigrant Jewish cosmopolis," he is primarily concerned with its intense intellectual life. Rischin describes the friction between German and Russian Jews, the spread of a Yiddish press and culture, the rise of secular social idealism, the origin and progress of labor unionism, the entry into municipal politics, and the achievement of power and position by the garment unions. The outbreak of war in Europe in 1914 not only brought the great migration to an end but provoked a new hostility to foreigners in the society at large, a situation which complicated the problems of the Jewish community. American Jewry did not remain in the Lower East Side and other primary areas of urban concentration, however, but moved in hundreds of thousands to suburban areas, especially after 1946. Gordon, who drew on his experience as a rabbi in Minneapolis to write *Jews in Transition* (1949), no 4456 in the 1960 *Guide,* later transferred to Temple Emmanuel in Newton, Mass. In gathering evidence for *Jews in Suburbia* he polled fellow rabbis as well as lay leaders in 89 suburban communities, mostly in Massachusetts, New York, New Jersey, Maryland, and California. He found that these Jews had attained a high degree of integration with their communities and liked their situation — as one respondent put it: "Here, at least, we feel like people." Since Jewish secular organizations imperfectly adapted themselves to this exodus, the synagogue, usually a conservative one, became the real center of suburban Jewish life and took on secular functions without any serious loss in religious ones. On these points Gordon is confirmed by a study of "North City" (presumably Minneapolis): *Children of the Gilded Ghetto; Conflict Resolutions of Three Generations of American Jews* (New Haven, Yale University Press, 1961. 228 p.), by Judith R. Kramer and Seymour Leventman.

1958. Sklare, Marshall, *ed.* The Jews; social patterns of an American group. Glencoe, Ill., Free Press [1958] 669 p.    57–9318  E184.J5S55
CONTENTS.—The historical setting.—Demographic aspects and the factor of social mobility.—The Jewish community: institutions, social patterns,

status structure, and levels of integration.—The Jewish religion: aspects of continuity and change.— Psychological aspects: group belongingness and Jewish identification.—Some cultural aspects and value orientations.

1959. Sherman, Charles Bezalel. The Jew within American society; a study in ethnic individuality. Detroit, Wayne State University Press, 1961. 260 p.                   60–16839   E184.J5S46
   Bibliography: p. 245–249.
Sklare has assembled 33 articles, more than half of which were specially prepared for this collection. The articles range from the particularity of "The

Jewish Organizational Elite of Atlanta, Georgia," by Solomon Sutker, to the generality of "Sources of Jewish Internationalism and Liberalism," by Lawrence H. Fuchs. Sherman's shorter and more unitary volume is based not only on published sources but also on the author's regular visits to Jewish communities and his attendance at the conventions and conferences of major Jewish organizations. He considers the recent strengthening of the Jewish Americans' "ethnic individuality" as evidence that they will continue as a distinct ethnic minority "on the level of spiritual uniqueness, religious separateness, ethnic consolidation and communal solidarity, but not in a political sense."

# G. Orientals

1960. Barth, Gunther P. Bitter strength; a history of the Chinese in the United States, 1850– 1870. Cambridge, Harvard University Press, 1964. 305 p. (A publication of the Center for the Study of the History of Liberty in America, Harvard University)                   64–21785   E184.C5B23
"Sources": p. [223]–231. Bibliographical references included in "Notes" (p. [235]–285).
An analysis of the development of race prejudice against the Chinese, based on a study of the first two decades of Chinese experience in America. From an examination of the backgrounds of the sojourners, the circumstances of their arrival, and their subsequent life in the mines, Barth concludes that the Chinese, by their activities and attitudes, contributed to the development of anti-oriental feelings among the white people in California. Many of the first Chinese came without the intention of becoming American; they came to earn money and return home. They were further isolated by the "credit ticket system" which indebted them to their own countrymen and extended the Chinese social structure to the United States. Acceptance of the Chinese as Americans began to come only when they took on the attitude of permanent settlers.

1961. Daniels, Roger. The politics of prejudice, the anti-Japanese movement in California, and the struggle for Japanese exclusion. Berkeley, University of California Press, 1962. 165 p. (University of California publications in history, v. 71)
                   62–63248   E173.C15 vol. 71
   Bibliography: p. 153–160.
The author traces California's struggle for more than a quarter of a century to achieve Japanese ex-

clusion. The effort successfully culminated with the passage of the Immigration Act of 1924 by the U.S. Congress. The study emphasizes the policies and actions of the "excluders" rather than the "excluded." Antipathy toward the Japanese immigrant was to some extent a continuation of longtime agitation against the Chinese. Labor interests, strong in California, viewed the orientals as potential strikebreakers and a threat to wage levels and working conditions. Unlike the Chinese, the Issei, first-generation Japanese settlers, rapidly began to challenge whites in numerous business and professional enterprises. "Nonrational fears," stemming from racial and cultural differences, were compounded by the growing unpopularity of Japan and its increasing militancy.

1962. Lee, Rose Hum. The Chinese in the United States of America. [Hong Kong] Hong Kong University Press, 1960. 465 p.
                   60–3959   E184.C5L53
   Bibliography: p. [441]–446.
"The present writer is the only American of Chinese ancestry to head a university department of Sociology [Roosevelt University, Chicago], and her text-book [The City, 1955] is widely used." Based primarily upon the author's earlier detailed studies of the Chinese in the San Francisco area, this work is designed to develop an "understanding of how the process of acculturation, assimilation and integration operates when persons with distinguishable physical characteristics, bearing a different culture, come into contact with people of European origin." Professor Lee shows that the Chinese-American communities have recently undergone

great changes: they have risen above the lower economic strata to occupy a median position; the old "sojourners" can no longer return to China when their working career is over; and there are more women, more families, and more American-born children than ever before. The author sympathetically presents the social tensions within these communities and describes the elements making for social and personal disorganization, of which chronically inadequate housing is among the most important. Although Shien-woo Kung's *Chinese in American Life: Some Aspects of Their History, Status, Problems, and Contributions* (Seattle, University of Washington Press, 1962. 352 p.) does not rival Professor Lee's book in depth or subtlety of sociological analysis, it contains a fuller account of recent immigration regulations and their effects and some straightforward descriptions of Chinese communities and their problems which usefully supplement the larger work.

# H. North Americans

1963. Berry, Brewton. Almost white. New York, Macmillan [1963] 212 p. illus.
63–8997 E184.A1B43
Bibliography: p.191–203.
A study of mestizos in the Eastern States. Settled in largely self-contained communities, these "triracial isolates" share an obscurity of heritage. For the most part, the people live as outcasts suspended between races, rejected by whites, marginally accepted by Indians, and unwilling to identify with Negroes. On the basis of evidence gathered from extensive fieldwork, the author describes the mestizos' culture and mores, the obstacles they face as a minority people, and the attitudes toward them among whites and Negroes.

1964. Padilla, Elena. Up from Puerto Rico. New York, Columbia University Press, 1958. 317 p. illus.
58–7171 F128.9.P8P3

1965. Rand, Christopher. The Puerto Ricans. New York, Oxford University Press, 1958. 178 p.
58–10733 F128.9.P8R3
Miss Padilla spent 3½ years among the Puerto Ricans of Manhattan's Lower East Side (which she calls "Eastville") doing fieldwork for the Anthropology Department of Columbia University. Her results are humanely presented in chapters on group feeling, relations with neighbors of other ethnic backgrounds, the family and the household, childhood and its dangers, "cliques and the social grapevine" (including a considerable treatment of drug addiction), adjustments to non-Hispano New York, and problems of health and morale. Rand undertook his inspection of the Puerto Ricans of East Harlem for *The New Yorker,* and his chapters first appeared, in somewhat different form, in its issues. In the course of trying to understand this people, he made an extended visit to Puerto Rico itself, which Puerto Ricans leave "because there are too many of them there." Although considerably less systematic than Miss Padilla, Rand has a talent for penetrating the minds and the essential situation of the migrants "among the cold people." He evidences respect for a group which maintains its traditions and its dignity in the worst slums of the United States; he illustrates, however, the peculiar problems arising from this first airborne mass migration, whose members show less desire to learn English, to assimilate, or to rise in the economic scale than their predecessors. Dan Wakefield's *Island in the City; the World of Spanish Harlem* (Boston, Houghton Mifflin, 1959. 278 p.) has much of interest in its extended and literal descriptions, but its reportage is considerably more diffuse than Rand's. Clarence O. Senior in *The Puerto Ricans: Strangers—Then Nieghbors* (Chicago, Published in cooperation with the Anti-Defamation League of B'nai B'rith by Quadrangle Books [1965] 128 p.) reviews the major aspects of life among the group and discusses the progress achieved thus far in assimilating the Caribbean immigrants into the mainland society.

# I. Scandinavians

1966. Björk, Kenneth. West of the Great Divide; Norwegian migration to the Pacific Coast, 1847–1893. Northfield, Minn., Norwegian-American Historical Association, 1958. 671 p. illus., maps. (Publications of the Norwegian-American Historical Association)

58–4511 E184.S2B48

The author surveys early Norwegian settlements in the Rocky Mountain and Pacific Coast States, British Columbia, Alaska, and Hawaii, down to the panic of 1893. The earliest Scandinavian pioneers were, in fact, a Dane and a Swede who took part in the original Mormon trek to the Great Salt Lake in 1847; others joined in the California Gold Rush soon thereafter. San Francisco became a haven for Norwegian seamen, many of whom married local girls, but the other settlements were occupied by men and families who had stayed some time in the Middle West before moving overland. An entire chapter is devoted to Snowshoe Thompson (born Jon Thoreson Rue), a remarkable figure who during the later 1850's carried the mail over the Sierras on skis. In an autobiography, *Moorings Old and New* (Madison, State Historical Society of Wisconsin, 1963. 276 p.), Paul Knaplund offers detailed recollections of his life in Norway and as an immigrant settler in the United States.

# J. Other Stocks

1967. Conway, Alan, *ed.* The Welsh in America; letters from the immigrants. Minneapolis, University of Minnesota Press [1961] 341 p.

61–7724 E184.W4C6

Bibliography: p. 330–332.

This collection of 97 letters or parts of letters written between 1817 and 1895 by Welsh immigrants in America, usually to their friends at home. The letters, most of which are translated from the Welsh language, are taken from manuscripts and from the files of 32 Welsh newspapers and non-conformist periodicals published in Wales or, in a few cases, in the United States. Conway employs a flexible topical arrangement: an initial section on the crossing; four on agricultural settlers in areas from the Middle Atlantic States to the Pacific Northwest; three sections on Welsh migrants in coal mining, in iron and steel milling, and in the frontier mining rushes; and concluding ones on the Civil War and the Welsh Mormons. The Welsh, being skilled and dependable, were at first great favorites with American mineowners, but fell from grace when it was found that they would stand on their rights and lead their fellow miners in strikes. The Welsh-Americans, with their evangelical roots, were natural abolitionists, Unionists, and Lincoln men. Conway also notes the frustration of those who sought to perpetuate the Welsh language and nationality in America. In *The Character of Early* *Welsh Emigration to the United States* (Cardiff, University of Wales Press, 1957. 40 p.), Arthur H. Dodd describes a persistent trickle of individuals and groups during the two centuries preceding 1840, an equal persistence of religious motivation, and a tendency for migrating Welshmen to choose the middle Colonies rather than New England or the South and to move farther west as the opportunity presented itself.

1968. Govorchin, Gerald G. Americans from Yugoslavia. Gainesville, University of Florida Press, 1961. 352 p. 61–11312 E184.Y7G6

Includes bibliographical references.

The study of immigration from present-day Yugoslavia has a weaker statistical basis than that of other ethnic groups, official American statistics did not distinguish between the various national groups within the Austro-Hungarian monarchy until the U.S. Immigration Commission was established in 1907, and Bulgarians were counted with Serbians until the end of World War I. Since the initial imposition of the quota system in 1921, Southern Slav immigration has been reduced to a trickle. The mass of the Yugoslavs entered the United States between 1880 and 1914: no estimated total appears here, but the census of 1930 found the number of living immigrants just short of 470,000, and the author puts the present Yugoslav stock of the first three generations at a round million. Peasants at home, in America the South Slavs largely turned to mining and heavy industry. Thus they have concentrated most heavily in the industrial belt of the East North Central States and to a lesser degree in the Middle Atlantic and the West North Central States. Govorchin includes chapters on the Croatian Fraternal Union and other ethnic societies which combine mutual help with recreation; on the Yugoslav press, which began in San Francisco in 1884 and still numbers 26 newspapers; and on the general character of immigrant life, marked by a lessening of mutual distrust among Croat, Serb, and Slovene along with progressive Americanization. The final chapters are devoted, in traditional style, to Slavs of distinction, such as Nikola Tesla, Louis Adamic, and Frank J. Lausche and to Yugoslav contributions to America.

1969. Hoglund, Arthur W. Finnish immigrants in America, 1880–1920. Madison, University of Wisconsin Press, 1960. 213 p.

60–5662   E184.F5H58   1960
"Sources": p. 196–203.

The author has winnowed a surprisingly large body of Finnish-language newspapers, magazines, and annuals in order to study cultural change among the newcomers during the four major decades of Finnish immigration. As many as 300,000 Finns may have entered the United States during these years. The great majority were landless persons from rural areas, especially from the two southeastern Baltic provinces of Vaasa and Turku-Pori, but with a remarkably small percentage of illiteracy. The largest concentration of Finns in the United States was attracted by the new mining areas of Minnesota and the northwestern peninsula of Michigan. Here the early immigrants won themselves a formidable reputation for the depth of their drinking and the ferocity of the brawls to which it led, the author notes, but the Finnish community itself developed a strong temperance movement, and a variety of ethnic organizations urged decorous family life and economic prudence upon their compatriots. As their earnings permitted, many of the miners and workers in other industries purchased farms and returned to the land; the census of 1920 recorded nearly 15,000 Finnish-born operators of farms. By this time, immigration from the old country was only a trickle, and the numerous ethnic organizations were faced with the problem of defections among the American-born generations.

1970. Leyburn, James G. The Scotch-Irish: a social history. Chapel Hill, University of North Carolina Press [1962] xix, 377 p.

62–16063   E184.S4L5
Bibliography: p. [354]–372.

The author, whose *Frontier Folkways* was published in 1935, here seeks to bring continuity and precision into the story of the migrations of the Scotch-Irish. He sets out to establish the social character of the Lowland Scots about 1600, before the plantation of Ulster began, and notes that they were already a dour and resistant people who lacked the peasant mentality. During their century or more in Ulster before the American immigration began (1717), they passed from the feudal order of Scotland to one in which freedom of labor and movement were habitual, and distinctions based upon property and leadership gave rise to a new, homemade gentry. The migration to the United States, which went on sporadically until the American Revolution, was in large part determined by the English Parliament's legislation discriminating against their economic enterprise and their Presbyterianism. The final third of the book gives a very clear outline of the course and character of their settlements in the Thirteen Colonies and conducts a sharply critical inquiry into what is here called the "mythology" of the Scotch-Irish. Chiefly, however, it proves to have been an exaggeration of their homogeneity and uniformity. Leyburn states that the Scotch-Irish settlers who got beyond the reach of organized Presbyterianism soon became lax or semibarbarous in their ways and that, once the Regulator movement in the Carolinas had been suppressed, its Scotch-Irish participants gave small support to the patriot cause. Yet the greater part of the Scotch-Irish formed an intercolonial patriot bloc, with a national rather than a provincial patriotism.

1971. Saloutos, Theodore. The Greeks in the United States. Cambridge, Harvard University Press, 1964. xiv, 445 p.

64–13428   E184.G7S29
Bibliography: p. [389]–400.

A chronological study of Greek immigration and settlement in America based on research conducted in both the United States and Greece. Greek immigration, chiefly a product of the late 19th and early 20th centuries, was motivated by political, economic, cultural, and spiritual conditions in the mother country. The immigrants, while developing quick attachments to the United States, brought with them a strong Greek nationalism, which emphasized the idea of preserving a Hellenic identity. The steady process of Americanization, however, particularly in the second generation, gradually worked to integrate the Greeks into the American community.

In *They Remember America; the Story of the Repatriated Greek-Americans* (Berkeley, University of California Press, 1956. 153 p.), Saloutos studies the years 1908–24, when 168,847 of the 366,454 Greek immigrants voluntarily returned to their native land.

1972. Schrier, Arnold. Ireland and the American emigration, 1850–1900. Minneapolis, University of Minnesota Press [1958] 210 p.

        58–10303   JV7711.Z79U57

"Notes and bibliography": p. 171–205.

During the six decades between 1841 and 1901, the population of Ireland declined from 8,196,000 to 4,456,000, and the provinces of Munster and Connaught lost well over half their inhabitants. More than four million Irish left their homeland, and 85 percent of them made their way to the United States. Here they constituted nearly 43 percent of the foreign-born in 1850, and 10 years later one American in 20 was an Irish immigrant. Schrier has examined the effects of this exodus upon Ireland itself, where it aroused a chorus of protest in press and pulpit. Nothing was done to check it, however, or to remedy the fundamental maladjustments that had brought it about. The author attributes to emigration the consolidation of many small landholdings and a major changeover from tillage to pasture in the Irish economy. He describes the "American wake," an imitative but no less bibulous rite to mark the loss of a near relative to the New World, and notes the steady return of $250 million in remittances during the half century—unfortunately in sums so small that, although they could ameliorate hardship, they rarely enabled the recipients at home to put their affairs on a more prosperous basis. George W. Potter's *To the Golden Door; the Story of the Irish in Ireland and America* (Boston, Little, Brown [1960] 631 p.), unfinished when its author died in 1959, was published without references of any kind, a serious lack in a work which so frequently quotes from primary sources. A substantial section on Irish society at the beginning of the emigration is followed by a shorter one, "How They Got Across the Ocean," and, much the longest (p. 161–631), "What Befell Them in America." In all three the subject is developed by brief and vivid episodes; the author would presumably have bound them more tightly together and provided summary views had he been able to complete the work. As it stands, however, it is an uncommonly sympathetic presentation of the human experience involved in the Irish colonization of America and the nativist reaction which it provoked. In *The American Irish* (New York, Macmillan [1963] 458 p.), William V. Shannon gives special attention to elected officials and political bosses.

1973. Shepperson, Wilbur S. Emigration and disenchantment; portraits of Englishmen repatriated from the United States. Norman, University of Oklahoma Press [1965] 211 p.

        65–11248   E184.B7S48

Bibliography: p. 197–204. Bibliographical footnotes.

Early in the first crucial decades of settlement, the return of immigrants to their homelands provoked concern in the American Colonies. In this study, Shepperson examines the magnitude and significance of the return movement of British settlers through 1865. In an age of rising urbanization and industrialization, many Britons came to America in pursuit of the economic and social betterment which had eluded them at home. To their dismay and disillusionment, they often encountered many of the same conditions from which they had fled, as well as new and unexpected ones. The collapse of their often exaggerated and romanticized expectations motivated them to return to more familiar environments.

1974. Wytrwal, Joseph A. America's Polish heritage; a social history of the Poles in America. Detroit, Endurance Press, 1961. 350 p.

        60–15742   E184.P7W9

Bibliography: p. 295–309.

Poland emerged as a nation in the 10th century, disappeared after the Third Partition of 1795, and regained independence only by the Treaty of Versailles in 1919. The census of 1790 counted 468 Poles in the United States; the recurrent uprisings and suppressions of the 19th century had brought some 50,000 Poles here by 1870. After that year a larger emigration, economic rather than political in its drive, began. Within half a century the Polish-American community had reached an estimated 3,000,000. After a general treatment of each of these movements, Wytrwal concentrates on the ethnic organizations of the later period, in particular the Polish Roman Catholic Union, established in 1873, and the Polish National Alliance, established in 1880, whose combined membership reaches 600,000. The special interest of the Union was to maintain the autonomy of Polish-American Catholics against the Irish-dominated American Catholic hierarchy. The Alliance was organized to promote the independence of the Polish homeland. The organizations have not always worked in harmony. An episode of the earlier period is reconstructed by Jerzy Jan Lerski in *A Polish Chapter in Jacksonian America; the United States and the Polish Exiles of*

*1831* (Madison, University of Wisconsin Press, 1958. 242 p. Poland's millennium series of the Kości-uszko Foundation). In documented detail it tells the story of the American-Polish Committee in Paris, which included James Fenimore Cooper, Samuel Gridley Howe, and Samuel F. B. Morse, as well as Lafayette, among its members; the reception of some 425 Polish exiles in America; and the formation of the first Polish-American organizations in the United States.

1975. Yearley, Clifton K. Britons in American labor; a history of the influence of the United Kingdom immigrants on American labor, 1820–1914. Baltimore, Johns Hopkins Press, 1957. 332 p. (The Johns Hopkins University studies in historical and political science, ser. 75, no. 1)

          57–12122 H31.J6, ser. 75, no. 1
  Bibliography: p. 318–322.

The author amplifies the more general record presented in Rowland T. Berthoff's *British Immigrants in Industrial America,* no. 4488 in the 1960 *Guide.* Yearley describes the numerous ties between British and American labor during the second half of the 19th century and emphasizes the role of British organizers in the American movement. Represented as sinister incendiaries by upper-class opinion in the United States, they were actually "in an overwhelming number of cases moderate and constructive men." He pays particular attention to the career of Thomas Phillips, a Lancashire shoemaker who came to Philadelphia in 1852 at the age of 19, spread the cooperative ideas of G. J. Holyoake, and in 1862 founded the Union Co-operative Association there. In the 20th century British influence in the American labor movement waned rapidly.

# XV

# Society

FOR THE most part, the writers selected for this chapter—whether they are academic sociologists, social philosophers, city planners, or social workers—seem to agree that the dominant characteristics of American society must be analyzed within the context of urbanization, industrialization, and technology.

A high proportion of the works in this chapter are problem centered and issue oriented. During the decade covered by the *Supplement,* the social sciences in the United States appear to have passed from a period of relative stability and complacency to one of dynamism and dissatisfaction. The academic sociologists and social activists tend to be reformist in outlook, and this trend is reflected in the subjects which they choose to examine.

Topics that recur frequently among the works entered here include the following: mass society and alienation; egalitarianism versus status-orientation; the crisis of the city and the function of planning; and the question of the ability of Americans to plan society while maintaining a spirit of democracy, diversity, and individuality.

## A. Some General Views

1976. American heritage. The American heritage cookbook and illustrated history of American eating & drinking. With chapters by Cleveland Amory [and others]. Historical foods consultant: Helen Duprey Bullock. Recipes editor: Helen McCully; associate: Eleanor Noderer. [New York] American Heritage Pub. Co.; Distribution by Simon & Schuster [1964] 629 p. 64–21278 TX705.A65

Brillat-Savarin noted in the 19th century that the "destiny of nations depends on how they nourish themselves." A like view is held by the editors of this two-part volume on the history of our Nation's food and drink. Each part is distinct in purpose, abundantly detailed, and separately indexed. The first, an "Illustrated History of American Eating and Drinking," contains historical essays and vignettes which are richly visualized with reproductions of photographs, paintings, engravings, and sketches. The second is entirely devoted to traditional menus and dishes, some of them originating from the Thirteen Colonies and adapted for today's use. Background notes accompany recipes that are of particular historical interest.

1977. Boorstin, Daniel J. The image; or, What happened to the American dream. New York, Atheneum, 1962 [°1961] 315 p.

62–7936   E169.1.B752

"Suggestions for Further Reading (and Writing)": p. 263–294.

In the United States, creating images in one form or another is a commonplace, according to the author, and contemporary American culture, with its significantly complex changes, tends to substitute the acquisition of an image for the pursuit of an ideal. This book is about the art and practice of self-deception and the dangers involved in hiding reality from oneself. Boorstin notes that specious statements or quasi-truths immerse the individual in a sense of comfort and well-being. He places no blame, however, but rather traces our faults to our strengths—literacy, progress, and wealth—and urges each of us to discover his own illusions, to moderate his expectations, and to decide for himself where he wants to go.

1978. Chase, Stuart. American credos. New York, Harper [1962] 216 p.

62–9887   E169.1.C4525

"Appendix of Sources": p. 203–212.

To find out what representative Americans believe about many important issues of the day, the author has compiled related testimony from polltakers. Foreign policy, education, science, civil liberties, and personal problems are some of the subjects for which results from the various pollings are compared. "What do the people want? How deeply do they want it, and how long will they continue to want it?" In trying to arrive at some answers, Chase has organized an abundance of material. He endeavors to show that in these polls the personal problems of Americans, which he refers to as "privatism," seem to outrank all others, except in time of actual war. Concerning work, the attitude appears paradoxical. The majority say they like their jobs, but in-depth interviews reveal negative responses. The author finds that automation does not bring satisfaction, that professional workers are gaining status, and that disarmament and the prevention of nuclear war are very much desired.

1979. Gardner, John W. Excellence: Can we be equal and excellent too? New York, Harper [1961] 171 p.   61–6194   HM146.G29

Bibliographical references included in "Notes" (p. 163–167).

"This book is concerned with the difficult, puzzling, delicate and important business of toning up a whole society, of bringing a whole people to that fine edge of morale and conviction and zest that makes for greatness." The author, who was president of the Carnegie Corporation of New York and the Carnegie Foundation for the Advancement of Teaching when this book appeared, examines two conflicting maxims basic in American democratic thought: "All men are created equal" and "May the best man win." After exploring the problems inherent in this paradox of equality and competitive performance, he points out the danger of extreme emphasis on either. Warning Americans that "the idea for which this nation stands will not survive if the highest goal free men can set themselves is an amiable mediocrity," Gardner calls for a striving toward the highest standards of performance in every phase of life and in every occupation.

1980. Morison, Elting E., ed. The American style, essays in value and performance; a report on the Dedham conference of May 23–27, 1957. New York, Harper [1958] 426 p. (Massachusetts Institute of Technology. Center for International Studies. American project series)

58–11042   E169.1.M8

Includes bibliographical references.

How men cope with problems in the ordinary course of their lives is considered to reflect a national style. Analysis of these problem-solving activities can be used as a basis for identification of primary national characteristics. The classic American style developed in the early 19th century, as the surge to the West began and the Founding Fathers passed from the scene. This volume is a record of a conference on contemporary America sponsored by the Center for International Studies at the Massachusetts Institute of Technology. The explicit purpose of the meeting was to examine societies and institutions of all persuasions in the United States and to present background papers as a framework for debate. Some of the topics covered are the clash between good and evil in man as a social animal, between theory and fact, and between order and innovation in human organization.

1981. Reissman, Leonard. Class in American society. Glencoe, Ill., Free Press [1960, °1959] 436 p.   59–6825   HN57.R45

Bibliographical references included in "Notes" (p. 405–429).

A systematic treatment of "class" as social reality and part of the fabric of society, with a description of the logic and methodology used in the analysis. Popular acceptance of class was prevented for decades by professed values of equality and equal accessibility of opportunity. The idea of "status," a less materialistic and more ambiguous concept, has been readily accepted. Reissman analyzes social stratification and the economic processes that set the basic molds of class distinctions. He believes that the democratic affirmation of social equality and the desire of most Americans "to be like everyone else" account in large measure for the overwhelming size of the middle class in the United States.

1982. Schlesinger, Arthur M., *and* Morton White, *eds.*
Paths of American thought. Boston, Houghton Mifflin, 1963. 614 p.        63–14184  B851.S37
"Notes and further reading": p. 541–592.
Essays selected to present various aspects of the evolution of American intellectual and social life. Dividing the Nation's history into colonial, Federal, national, and international phases, the editors isolate a pattern of ideas running parallel to this division. They note that the major ideas of each age possess internal coherence but that the degree to which national thought corresponds to the realities of social life in any given era varies from period to period. The pattern of the past is reversed in the present: today, the intellectual contends with American life as it is, yet there is no unifying philosophy which embodies America's convictions on basic problems. Whatever the present and future, in the 350 years of its germination the national mind succeeded for the most part in adjusting society to changing economic and moral circumstances.

1983. Smith, Bradford. Why we behave like Americans. Philadelphia, Lippincott [1957] 322 p.        57–11954  E169.1.S596
Bibliography: p. 309–313.
There is no visible single pattern of American character. Successive waves of immigration to the United States have complicated our diverse racial and cultural origins and make for puzzling contradictions in American behavior. This survey of community and family life, education, recreation, culture, politics, economics, science, and historical backgrounds attempts to assay the basic characteristics of present-day America and its people. Smith portrays Americans as insisting upon conformity in fundamentals but as being manipulative and free in day-to-day techniques in order to achieve success. He notes that a high value is placed upon success, particularly that which is measurable. Whether it is material reward or recognition of accomplishment, Americans never cease to struggle for it. Erving Goffman's *Behavior in Public Places* ([New York] Free Press of Glencoe [1963] 248 p.) is a psychological study of interaction between persons confronting each other primarily on social occasions.

# B. Social History: Periods

1984. Lord, Walter. The good years: from 1900 to the First World War. New York, Harper [1960] 369 p. illus.        59–10585  E756.L68
Bibliography: p. 348–354.
The author chose this title to reflect the fact that, in the first years of the 20th century, "whatever the trouble, people were sure they could fix it." His highly selective account of American society during that period covers such topics as reform movements, politics, achievements, military exploits, and disasters. The 1900's brought confidence in a glorious new age, a confidence which survived many crises but was finally shattered by the onset of the First World War. The author's parade of events includes American involvement in the Boxer Rebellion, the assassination of President McKinley, the San Francisco fire, Commodore Peary's discovery of the North Pole, the 1912 nomination of Woodrow Wilson, and the movement to abolish child labor.

1985. Wilson, Edmund. The American earthquake; a documentary of the twenties and thirties. Garden City, N.Y., Doubleday, 1958. 576 p. (Doubleday anchor books)        58–5584  E169.W658
A companion volume to Wilson's *The Shores of Light*, no. 2541 in the 1960 *Guide*, this is a compilation of almost 100 short "nonliterary" articles written between 1923 and 1934 for various journals. The "earthquake" of the title refers to the Great Depression. The author's views are clearly liberal and anticapitalist. In one of the longest articles, he presents a grim picture of life in automotive plants in Detroit. In another he describes the tumultuous

events surrounding the trial of the Scottsboro boys. Other articles, political and nonpolitical, focus on vaudeville, the movies, the theater, Sacco and Van-zetti, Communist demonstrations, striking coal miners in West Viriginia, and the coming of the New Deal.

## C. Social History: Topics

1986. Amory, Cleveland. Who killed society? New York, Harper [1960] 599 p. illus.
60–15314   E161.A4
Bibliography: p. 553–555.
A highly detailed, anecdotal look at the Nation's fashionable, powerful, and wealthy, from 1607 to the present. In answer to those who bemoan the death of "Society" and blame its demise on such causes as the *nouveaux riches*, Franklin D. Roosevelt, the servant problem, and taxes, Amory asserts that there was no murder. If, he reasons, "people have complained about Society not being what it used to be for some 350 years, the stark, inescapable conclusion seems to be that Society, as such, never was." Although the focus is on the Northeast, the author also discusses society in the Midwest, the Southwest, the Far West, and the Old South. Chapters on American aristocracy, club life, celebrities, and Jewish society are included. A 45-page index, mostly of names, is appended.

1987. Baltzell, Edward Digby. The Protestant establishment: aristocracy & caste in America. New York, Random House [1964] xviii, 429 p. illus.   64–14840   HN57.B26
Bibliographical references included in "Notes" (p. 388–403).
Convinced that the United States has need of an aristocratic class to create and perpetuate a set of traditional and authoritative standards, Baltzell argues that such a class must be representative of the society as a whole if it wants to stay in power. He finds that since the early years of the 20th century the great majority of the members of the Anglo-Saxon Protestant establishment have been unwilling to share their privileges by absorbing talented members of minority ethnic groups. Ethnic minorities have been excluded from the select social organizations, from the best educational institutions, and from the higher levels of management, according to the author. Consequently, this portion of the establishment has declined in power. Baltzell focuses on anti-Semitism to illustrate the "nature of the conflict between the social forces of caste and aristocracy" because he finds the prejudice against Negroes too complex for his purposes.

1988. Burlingame, Roger. The American conscience. New York, Knopf, 1957. 420 p.
56–5782   E169.1.B938
Bibliography: p. 407–420.
The author's premise is that American moral attitudes differed from those of our European ancestors because of a set of special determinants which include isolation, the movement of the frontier, and the natural wealth encountered in the march across the continent. These combined with various secondary determinants to produce the "peculiar American compulsion to assign moral values to every historical event, economic theory, or social trend." The author begins with the rise and fall of theocracy in New England and follows with discussions of the Enlightenment in the United States, the "Great Awakening," "manifest destiny," abolition, the struggle for land, and frontier morality. The last chapter, "Our Most Wanton Orgy," focuses on the shrill nativism, corruption, and contempt for law of the 1920's.

1989. Flexner, Eleanor. Century of struggle; the woman's rights movement in the United States. Cambridge, Belknap Press of Harvard University Press, 1959. 384 p. illus.
59–9273   HQ1410.F6
"Bibliographical Summary": p. 335–338.
"Notes": p. [339]–373.
This history covers the women's rights movement from its beginnings in the early 19th century to 1920 and the ratification of the 19th amendment giving women the right to vote. Almost half the book deals with woman suffrage, but the author also discusses the role of women in the abolition movement, labor unions, and various other reform activities. Such participation provided women with the knowledge of the basic organizational skills necessary in attempts to gain equal status with men. Miss Flexner concludes by saying that suffrage did not bring the millenium for which millions of women hoped. Despite gains in status relative to men, women's pay is still unequal, and only a handful have climbed to the highest positions in government, business, education, and the professions. In *The Better Half; the Emancipation of the American Woman* (New York, Harper & Row [1965]  401 p.), Andrew Sinclair

covers much the same ground but includes two chapters on the changes—and lack of them—brought about by woman suffrage.

1990. Habenstein, Robert W., *and* William M. Lamers. The history of American funeral directing. Rev. ed. Milwaukee, Bulfin Printers, 1962. 638 p. illus. 62–16553 GT3150.H3 1962
Bibliographical notes.

A revised edition of no. 4527 in the 1960 *Guide*. In *The American Way of Death* (New York, Simon & Schuster, 1963. 333 p.), Jessica Mitford aims at the "vast majority of ethical undertakers" for whom "to be 'ethical' merely means to adhere to a prevailing code of morality, in this case one devised over the years by the undertakers themselves for their own purposes." An appendix contains a directory of memorial societies, instructions for organizing such a society, and information about the donation of bodies for the use of medical science.

1991. Holbrook, Stewart H. Dreamers of the American dream. Garden City, N.Y., Doubleday, 1957. 369 p. (Mainstream of America series) 57–11424 HN57.H55
Bibliography: p. 350–353.

A sympathetic introductory picture of the "daft, earnest, honest, and all but incredible lot of men and women"—some of them little known—who dared be "shakers of trees" when society was ripe, or almost ripe, for change. The efforts of Dorothea Dix, Thomas Hopkins Gallaudet, and Samuel Gridley Howe to secure humane and enlightened treatment for the insane, the mute, and the blind are movingly presented. Other subjects include controversies over land rights and the land reform movement; prohibition and its attack on the "viper in the glass"; the struggle for women's rights; the fight of laboring men to gain acceptance for their unions; and John Humphrey Noyes' colony of perfectionists at Oneida, N.Y.

1992. Lynes, Russell. The domesticated Americans. New York, Harper & Row [1963] 308 p. illus. 62–14538 E161.L9
"Sources and acknowledgments": p. 293–295.

"Partly a discussion of manners, partly an opinionated critique of domestic architecture, and partly an exercise in social history," Lynes' book focuses on American houses inside and out and on the inability of Americans to establish a permanent domestic architecture. Population mobility removed the need for structural permanence; most families stay in one house only until they can afford to move into a better one. As the increasing scarcity of servants dictated the building of smaller houses, luxury became associated with conveniences rather than with space. And despite their pragmatic spirit, Americans often sacrificed comfort and realism for romantic and sentimental illusions in the form of little Louvres, replicas of Greek temples, and small versions of Elizabethan country houses.

1993. Sinclair, Andrew. Prohibition, the era of excess. With a preface by Richard Hofstadter. Boston, Little, Brown [1962] 480 p. illus. 62–8071 HV5089.S56
Bibliographical references included in "Notes" (p. 421–461).

A dispassionate history of the victory and subsequent failure of the movement to prohibit the manufacture and sale of alcoholic beverages. Sinclair's thesis is that prohibition was advocated with an excess of zeal and was resisted in the same manner. Supported most strongly by women, some feminists, progressives, churches, and rural Americans, the movement had all the fervor of a Protestant revival. If the drys had been willing to compromise and accept a less stringent law—one legalizing beer and wine, for instance—there probably would have been less resistance. The wets were also guilty of excessive zeal and helped to promote their own temporary downfall by an unwillingness to control the liquor traffic and close the worst saloons. *The Life and Times of the Late Demon Rum* (New York, Putnam [1965] 381 p.), by Joseph C. Furnas, is an account of the temperance movement from the 18th century to about 1920. Another, more specialized, book is *The Social History of Bourbon, an Unhurried Account of Our Star-Spangled American Drink* (New York, Dodd, Mead [1963] 280 p.), an entertaining look at "the distinctive spirit of the United States," by Gerald Carson.

1994. Webber, Everett. Escape to Utopia; the communal movement in America. New York, Hastings House Publishers [1959] 444 p. illus. (American procession series) 58–12525 HX653.W4
Bibliography: p. 421–435.

A somewhat ironic and unsympathetic view of attempts to establish and maintain utopian communities in the United States. The author suggests that most of the leaders and their followers were attempting to escape from the unpleasantness they found in society. The leaders generally failed to establish successful communities because of their blindness to the need for organization, to economic realities, and to the actual nature of man. "They were not men of vision, but of visions." Few of the followers who came to live in communes did so because of philosophical or religious convictions. According to Webber, the movement appealed mostly to the "spiritually and socially inept," to those who wanted to be cared for and told what to do, and to the idle.

# D. Social Thought

1995. Allen, Philip J., *ed*. Pitirim A. Sorokin in review. Durham, N.C., Duke University Press, 1963. xxii, 527 p. illus. (The American sociological forum)    63–7634   HM22.U6S6
Bibliographical footnotes.

Sorokin was among the first to apply statistical methods to the analysis of historical processes. He was also a pioneer contributor to the study of rural life and became the first chairman of Harvard's department of sociology. This volume, divided into three parts, presents a broad view of Sorokin's comprehensive studies of human society. The first part contains his own account of the factors which influenced the development of his thought. The second and major part comprises a group of critical essays by outstanding sociologists, psychologists, and historians who discuss aspects of Sorokin's work from the perspectives of their various disciplines. The third part consists of Sorokin's lengthy reply to the critiques of his colleagues and is followed by a chronological bibliography of his publications (p. [497]–506). A supplementary book is Sorokin's autobiography, *A Long Journey* (New Haven, Conn., College & University Press [1963] 327 p.).

1996. Black, Max, *ed*. The social theories of Talcott Parsons; a critical examination. Englewood Cliffs, N.J., Prentice-Hall, 1961. 363 p. illus.
61–8220   HM15.B55
Bibliographical footnotes.

A foremost theorist among contemporary American sociologists is Talcott Parsons, founder and first chairman of the department of social relations at Harvard University. In his prolific writings, he has developed a synoptic "general theory of action" to explain the functioning of the individual within the social system, based on his wide knowledge of biology, psychology, economics, political science, and anthropology. Parsons' theories were discussed by 10 faculty members at Cornell University in a series of public seminars; their papers, in revised form, make up the present volume. The authors—psychologists, sociologists, economists, and a philosopher—subject Parsons' work to close analysis and are divided in their estimation of its value as a systematic theory of society. Also included in the volume is Parsons' response to his colleagues' review of his writings.

1997. Lipset, Seymour M., *and* Leo Lowenthal, *eds*. Culture and social character; the work of David Riesman reviewed. [New York, Free Press of Glencoe, 1961] xiv, 466 p. (Continuities in social research)    61–9169   BF755.A5R525
Bibliographical footnotes.

This work was undertaken to assess the value of David Riesman's study *The Lonely Crowd,* no. 4555 in the 1960 *Guide,* 10 years after its initial publication. In order to achieve a balanced appraisal of the book and its significance, the editors solicited papers from persons with varied backgrounds. Also included is a critical reevaluation of the book by its author in collaboration with Nathan Glazer. The papers are grouped into several sections, among which are "Cultures and Societies," "Politics," and "Personality and Education." Some of the writers, in lieu of discussing the book's contents, provide reports of original research related to its major themes.

1998. Loomis, Charles P., *and* Zona K. Loomis. Modern social theories; selected American writers. 2d ed. Princeton, N.J., Van Nostrand [1965] xxiv, 800 p. illus. (Van Nostrand series in sociology)    65–1947   HM24.L8   1965
Bibliography: p. 741–779.

The theories of eight leading sociologists are systematically presented. Although divergent in their delineations of the elements which constitute a social system, the theorists share a search for the interrelationships among social phenomena. The sociologists whose work is examined are Howard Becker, Kingsley Davis, George C. Homans, Robert K. Merton, Talcott Parsons, Pitirim A. Sorokin, Robin M. Williams, and Alvin Gouldner. The authors outline each sociologist's main concerns and discuss his theories in detail. Each discussion is based on a conceptual model of social processes developed by Charles P. Loomis in an earlier book, *Social Systems: Essays on Their Persistence and Change* (Princeton, N.J., Van Nostrand [1960] 349 p. The Van Nostrand series in sociology). The extensive footnotes, as well as the charts, diagrams, and chronological bibliographies, render this book especially relevant to the needs of the student of sociology.

1999. Mills, Charles Wright. The sociological imagination. New York, Oxford University Press, 1959. 234 p.    59–7506   H61.M5
Bibliographical footnotes.

In this study C. Wright Mills (1916–1962) seeks to determine the relevance of social science to present-day society. He defines the "sociological imagination" as the capacity to shift perspectives in order to build up a total view of the social world and considers that it can help men to make issues explicit and thus identify choices for action. Mills holds that American sociology has lost the push for reform with which it began, because of the bias of many sociologists toward scattered and unrelated studies or abstract general theories. He stresses the importance of studying social problems within a historical context, emphasizes the close relation of sociology to other disciplines and proposes a unified social science. A collection of Mills' essays, *Power, Politics, and People* (New York, Oxford University Press, 1963. 657 p.), has been edited and introduced by Irving L. Horowitz.

# E. General Sociology; Social Psychology

2000.  Goodman, Walter.  All honorable men; corruption and compromise in American life. Boston, Little, Brown [1963]  342 p.
63–13978  HN58.G6
Bibliography: p. [330]–334.
In an exploration of recent public scandals in business, government, and the mass media, the author discusses incidents such as price-fixing, the Sherman Adams and Bernard Goldfine case, and TV quiz-show rigging. Strikingly evident is the public's condonement, which the author feels originates deep within our society. According to Goodman, superficial allegiance to ethical convention thinly veils the common acceptance of perverted values stemming from the "amoral cash nexus of our age." Although honesty prevails on an individual basis, the author maintains that its absence is often tolerated in group activity, where responsibility is diffused. Another portrayal of the alleged ethical collapse is *The Pseudo-Ethic: A Speculation on American Politics and Morals* (New York, Simon & Schuster, 1963. 127 p.), by Margaret Halsey. In *The Power Elite* (New York, Oxford University Press, 1956. 423 p.), C. Wright Mills concludes: "The higher immorality is a systematic feature of the American elite." Vance O. Packard alerts the reader to the widespread invasion of privacy by business, government, and other interests in *The Naked Society* (New York, D. McKay Co. [1964] 369 p.).

2001.  Hodges, Harold M.  Social stratification; class in America. Cambridge, Mass., Schenkman Pub. Co. [1964]  307 p.
64–13290  HN57.H538
Bibliography: p. 281–300.
A broad, humanistic treatment, intended for the layman, in which the author claims to have shunned "a fact-grubbing, questionnaire-type sociology." Hodges' basic contentions are the universality of social stratification in complex societies and the far-reaching effects of stratification on every facet of life. The discussion covers the theorists, novelists, and empiricists of social class. Hodges concludes that, in spite of the creed of classlessness, American society is stratified, but the country nonetheless comes closer to the ideal of an open society than many other nations. Another account of social class is found in *The Status Seekers; an Exploration of Class Behavior in America and the Hidden Barriers That Affect You, Your Community, Your Future* (New York, D. McKay Co. [1959] 376 p.), by Vance O. Packard.

2002.  Keniston, Kenneth.  The uncommitted; alienated youth in American society. New York, Harcourt, Brace & World [1965]  500 p. illus.
65–19062  HM136.K45
Bibliography: p. [499]–500.
This analysis of the complex roots of alienation is based on a study of 12 "extremely alienated" Harvard undergraduates. Alienation is broadly defined as "a response by selectively predisposed individuals to problems and dilemmas confronting our entire society." After analyzing the psychological origins of the problem, the author examines basic characteristics of American society which foster traits that appear in their extreme in the alienated. Chronic social change, empiricism, fragmentation, and the "deification" of technological values are considered to engender rootlessness, a lack of individual identity, and the subordination of emotion. The significant implication of alienation, according to Keniston, is seen in the heavy human toll exacted by our technological society.

2003.  Miller, Delbert C., *and* William H. Form. Industrial sociology: the sociology of work organizations. 2d ed. New York, Harper & Row [1964]  xxii, 873 p.
64–10221  HD6961.M55  1964
Bibliographies at the ends of chapters.
An updated edition of no. 4552 in the 1960 *Guide*.

The same authors explore business, labor, and community relations in *Industry, Labor, and Community* (New York, Harper [1960] 739 p. Harper's social science series). *Social Mobility in Industrial Society* (Berkeley, University of California Press, 1959. 309 p.), by Seymour M. Lipset and Reinhard Bendix, is a scholarly treatment of mobility, based on the Labor Mobility Survey conducted in 1949 in Oakland, Calif., and on other American and foreign surveys. The results of the studies tend to disprove the commonly held beliefs that social mobility is less extensive in Europe than in the United States, that social mobility declines as industrial societies mature, and that penetration into the business elite becomes more difficult with increasing industrialization.

2004. Olson, Philip, *ed.* America as a mass society; changing community and identity. [New York] Free Press of Glencoe [1963] 576 p.

63–13541 HN58.04

Bibliographical notes.

The impact upon the individual of the changing American social structure is the central theme of this substantial anthology of representative and illustrative essays. The emerging concept of "mass society" indicates concern over a basic, historically rooted issue in our culture: freedom of the individual versus institutional control. Some view mass society as a stultifying influence that contributes to loss of individuality and absorption of community by the all-engulfing, centrally controlled mass structure. Others regard it as a liberating influence which destroys the stifling effects of a traditional and hierarchial social order. The predominant outlook favors the former interpretation.

2005. Whyte, William H. The organization man. New York, Simon & Schuster, 1956. 429 p. illus. 56–9926 BF697.W47

The author postulates the birth of a "Social Ethic" in response to the modern American's attempt to legitimize morally his seemingly inevitable subjection to the pressures of industrial society characterized by a growing collectivism. An "organization man"—a doctor in a corporate clinic, a scientist in a government laboratory, or a corporation executive—holds the belief that the group is superior to the individual and that "belongingness" is his basic need. Pledging unquestioning loyalty to the organization, which he regards as benevolent, he accepts its dictates in all spheres of his life. The author views the increasing collectivism as a result of an overemphasis on egalitarianism and community spirit. To restore the balance, he advocates a return to the primacy of the individual. "The fault is not in organization, in short; it is in our worship of it." In *The Pyramid Climbers* (New York, McGraw-Hill [1962] 339 p.), Vance O. Packard elaborates on the corporation executive.

2006. Williams, Robin M. American society: a sociological interpretation. 2d ed., rev. New York, Knopf, 1960. 575 p.

60–6472 HN57.W55 1960

Bibliographies at the ends of chapters.

An updated edition of no. 4558 in the 1960 *Guide*. A statistical perspective of American society is presented in *This U.S.A.: An Unexpected Family Portrait of 194,067,296 Americans Drawn From the Census* (Garden City, N.Y., Doubleday, 1965. 520 p.), by Ben J. Wattenberg in collaboration with Richard M. Scammon.

## F. The Family

2007. Bossard, James H. S., *and* Eleanor S. Boll. The sociology of child development. 3d ed. New York, Harper [1960] 706 p. illus. (Harper's social science series)

60–7016 HQ781.B67 1960

Includes bibliography.

A revised edition of no. 4559 in the 1960 *Guide,* containing new material as well as structural changes. *The Family, Society, and the Individual* (Boston, Houghton Mifflin [1961] 690 p.), by William M. Kephart, is a readable textbook on the family as a social institution. The author believes that problems of the family frequently represent some antipathy centering on the "needs of the individual and the requirements of the social order." These forces must balance in order to effect maximum social integration. A U.S. Department of Labor publication, *The Negro Family; the Case for National Action* ([Washington, For sale by the Supt. of Docs., U.S. Govt. Print. Off.] 1965. 78 p.), often referred to as the Moynihan report, traces the structural breakdown of the Negro family and recommends national action.

2008. Coleman, James S. The adolescent society; the social life of the teenager and its impact on education, by James S. Coleman with the assistance of John W. C. Johnstone and Kurt Jonassohn.

[New York] Free Press of Glencoe [1961] xvi, 368 p. illus.        61–14725   HQ796.C64
Bibliographical footnotes.

Ten Illinois high schools were selected for this study on the basis of their differences rather than their "representativeness." Students, parents, and teachers contributed replies to written inquiries and informal interviews. Coleman provides a creative and thoughtful analysis of the importance and consequence of student status achieved through behavior, dress, scholastic and social success, use of leisure time, leadership, habits, and sports. *Adolescents and the Schools* (New York, Basic Books [1965] 121 p.), by the same author, contains additional material.

2009.  Goode, William J.  After divorce. Glencoe, Ill., Free Press [°1956]  xv, 381 p.
55–10992   HQ814.G6
Bibliographical footnotes.

This exploratory report on the "process of adjustment after divorce" surveys many problems but offers no solutions. "Sociologically, the most important justification for the study of divorce is not that we thereby deal with unhappiness, but that we thereby locate and analyze *points of strain,* personal and social." Four-fifths of the divorced mothers surveyed were convinced of the necessity of separating from their former husbands and confident that they had improved their situation.

2010.  Goodman, Paul.  Growing up absurd; problems of youth in the organized system. New York, Random House [1960]  296 p.
60–12137   HQ796.G645

In this study of the present waste of human resources, Goodman probes the connection between the organized system of American life and the disaffected youth of today. Believing that organized society wants not men but movable parts for the machine, he attempts to show how difficult it is "for an average child to grow up to be a man." Youth is confronted with three alternatives—to accept the role of the organization man, to try to remain in society but independent of it, or to drop out completely. After discussing the job opportunities concomitant with these choices, the author examines the earlier and character-molding factors which impede growth. He cites, for example, the stupidity, the lack of patriotism and faith, and the sexual confusion of the "average adjusted boy." If the youths who are trapped by the system can recognize its evil, he asks, why cannot the adults who perpetrated it effect a change? In *The Vanishing Adolescent* (Boston, Beacon Press [1959] 144 p.), Edgar Z. Friedenberg also deplores the increasing emphasis in schools on "adjustment" and points

to resulting difficulties which young people have in developing self-respect and maturity.

2011.  Lifton, Robert J., *ed.*  The woman in America. Boston, Houghton Mifflin, 1965.  293 p. illus. (The Daedalus library [3])
65–15157   HQ1420.L5
Bibliographies at the ends of chapters.

Pithy opinions on the changing status of women by such authorities as Erik H. Erikson, Edna G. Rostow, David Riesman, and Diana Trilling. Based on a series of dialogues held at the American Academy of Arts and Sciences, the papers discuss such topics as the enduring aspects of the extent to which woman's psychological life is determined by her anatomy and biology, the opportunities American society offers to its women, and the special problems of women. In *The Feminine Mystique* (New York, Norton [1963] 410 p.), Betty Friedan examines American woman since World War II, emphasizing her dissatisfactions.

2012.  Mudd, Emily H., *and* Aron M. Krich, *eds.*  Man and wife; a source book of family attitudes, sexual behavior and marriage counseling. New York, W. W. Norton [1957]  291 p.
57–11241   HQ734.M88
Bibliography: p. 277–279.

2013.  Mudd, Emily H., Howard E. Mitchell, *and* Sara B. Taubin.  Success in family living. New York, Association Press [1965]  254 p. illus.
65–11096   HQ10.M8
Bibliographical footnotes.

These two collaborative efforts explore wider areas than Emily Mudd's earlier book, *The Practice of Marriage Counseling* (no. 4570 in the 1960 *Guide*). In *Man and Wife,* a series of lectures on family attitudes and sexual behavior, marital problems and marital counseling are discussed by psychologists, psychiatrists, religious leaders, and lawyers. The lecturers depict the customs and values of families with different religious faiths and discuss practical assistance. *Success in Family Living* correlates various findings of a program known as the "All-American Family Search," sponsored by the National Institute of Mental Health. In 1957 and again in 1960, an entire family was selected from each State and the District of Columbia to attend a conference. Led by the Grolier Society, Inc., teams of research interviewers were in residence with the families for the express purpose of discovering methods for further improvement of the family unit. Although the families' occupations, educational levels, and financial situations differed, a common denominator of a democratic way of life seemed to emerge.

2014. Schur, Edwin M., *ed*. The family and the sexual revolution; selected readings. Bloomington, Indiana University Press, 1964. xv, 427 p.
64–18819   HQ535.S34

Bibliography: p. 423–427.

Compiled almost a generation after the "Kinsey Reports" (no. 4565 and 4566 in the 1960 *Guide*), this collection of articles by recognized authorities upholds its precursors' view that uninhibited discussion of sexual behavior in our time is desirable. Part 1, "Changing Sex Standards," constituting half the volume, deals with American attitudes on the relaxation of morals and speculates on why the direction is so liberal. One of the predominant answers given is the lifting of restrictions on magazines, books, and films. The subjects of premarital sexual experience, fidelity, and extramarital relations are discussed. Part 2, "The Woman Problem," and part 3, "Birth Control," discuss the social and biological expectations of women. Part 3 also includes a history of the turbulence that has surrounded the subject of family planning and a summary of its present legal status.

## G. Communities: General

2015. Conkin, Paul K. Tomorrow a new world: the New Deal community program. Ithaca, N.Y., Published for the American Historical Association [by] Cornell University Press [1959] 350 p. illus.
59–65124   HD1761.C66

"Bibliographical notes": p. 338–340. Bibliographical footnotes.

Frequently in the history of the United States there have been efforts to establish new communities in rural settings. These projects have been inspired partly by a conviction that urbanization is inimical to man's nature and partly as a solution to unemployment and poverty in the cities. The author reviews the establishment of 100 such communities during the period 1933–38 as part of the New Deal program. Their planning and development involved a clash between the conflicting ideological strains in New Deal thinking—collectivism and Jeffersonian individualism. The author examines the ideological background of the communities' creation, traces the development of each type of program from its inception to its abandonment, and concludes with studies of specific communities illustrative of each type of program.

2016. Stein, Maurice R. The eclipse of community; an interpretation of American studies. Princeton, N.J., Princeton University Press, 1960. 354 p.
60–5757   HT123.S78

Bibliography: p. 339–342.

The author attempts to present a general view of community life in America by reviewing the findings of studies of specific communities against the background of American society as a whole. Stein identifies an "eclipse of community," related to the increased interdependence and decreased local autonomy of modern life and characterized by a discarding of traditional values when they interfere with the pursuit of commodities or careers, destruction of community and even family ties, and a general feeling of loneliness and existential "shipwreck." *Community Structure and Analysis* (New York, Crowell [1959] 454 p.), edited by Marvin B. Sussman, includes selections from the works of various specialists in the social sciences.

2017. Warren, Roland L. The community in America. Chicago, Rand McNally [1963] 347 p. (Rand McNally sociology series)
63–8327   HT123.W25

Bibliographical footnotes.

This introduction to the study of the community explores the common traits of urban and rural social units. Warren considers that the traditional concept of the community as a group living in a specific geographic area and having certain common institutions and values no longer applies in the United States. Geographic areas overlap and intermingle and the sharing of community values and customs has declined. Various manifestations of the great change in social units are discussed, among them the "increasing orientation of local community units toward extracommunity systems of which they are a part, with a corresponding decline in community cohesion and autonomy." *The Community; an Introduction to a Social System* (New York, Ronald Press Co. [1958] 431 p.), by Irwin T. Sanders, is a useful textbook. Louis Wirth's selected papers, *Community Life and Social Policy* ([Chicago] University of Chicago Press [1956] 431 p.), edited by Elizabeth W. Marwick and Albert J. Reiss, deal with such aspects of community life as the ghetto, rural-urban differences, and life in the city.

# H. Communities: Rural

2018. Taylor, Miller Lee, *and* Arthur R. Jones. Rural life and urbanized society. New York, Oxford University Press, 1964. xiv, 493 p. illus. 64–11239 HN58.T3

Includes bibliographical references.

The authors contend that there are no longer any entirely rural communities in the United States. The country has developed a predominantly urban society as a result of the expansion of nationwide transportation and communications systems, scientific agricultural techniques, and the tremendous mobility of people. The diversity of the more rural 19th century has given way to the mass values of modern industrial America.

2019. Vidich, Arthur J., *and* Joseph Bensman. Small town in mass society; class, power, and religion in a rural community. Princeton, Princeton University Press, 1958. xvi, 329 p. 57–14576 HT431.V5

A study of a rural community in upstate New York, pseudonymously called "Springdale." The relationships between such a community and modern industrial society are investigated on the basis of an analysis of Springdale's economic and social history, self-image, political character, and religious affairs. Springdalers were bound to be ambivalent toward mass society, realizing their inferior cultural and economic opportunities but celebrating their ability to live a rural life and yet visit the city for its advantages. In *People of Coal Town* (New York, Columbia University Press, 1958. 310 p.),

Herman R. Lantz studies a community in economic decline, describing a depressed and cynical people with a dim future.

2020. Wheeler, Thomas C., *ed.* A vanishing America; the life and times of the small town. Twelve regional towns by Hodding Carter [and others]. Introduction by Wallace Stegner. New York, Holt, Rinehart & Winston [1964] 191 p. illus. 64–21932 E161.W487

Wallace Stegner describes this volume as "an unabashed invitation to nostalgia." Twelve eminent regional writers, many of whose larger works appear elsewhere in this *Supplement,* record the biographies of 12 American towns viewed as prototypes. The essays vary in approach but share a romantic harking back to village mores, quiet, and natural beauty and a common rejection of encroaching bigness, noise, ugliness, and pollution in the modern metropolis. The authors and their subjects are as follows: W. Storrs Lee—Middlebury, Vt.; Conrad Richter—Pine Grove, Pa.; Thomas D. Clark—Harrodsburg, Ky.; Hodding Carter—Holly Springs, Miss.; William E. Wilson—New Harmony, Ind.; James Gray—Marine on St. Croix, Minn.; John Edward Weems—Nacogdoches, Tex.; Winfield Townley Scott — Chimayo, N. M.; David Lavender—Telluride, Colo.; A. B. Guthrie, Jr. —Choteau, Mont.; Oscar Lewis—Red Bluff, Calif.; and William O. Douglas—Forks, Wash. Biographical sketches of the authors appear at the end of the book.

# I. Communities: Urban

2021. Bollens, John C., *and* Henry J. Schmandt. The metropolis: its people, politics, and economic life. New York, Harper & Row [1965] xvi, 643 p. illus. 65–19489 JS422.B6

"A commentary on bibliography": p. [599]–608.

An introduction to the study of metropolitan areas, with emphasis on social characteristics and trends, economic developments, government and politics, and the roles of citizens. The authors also discuss problems associated with metropolitan growth and functioning and the various attempts to solve them. It is suggested that the role of

government is to provide an appropriate system within which other community institutions may work to improve the quality of urban life. In *Governing the Metropolis* (New York, Wiley [1962] 153 p.), Scott A. Greer summarizes many studies of metropolitan areas as a basis for his analysis of big city government.

2022. Cole, Donald B. Immigrant city: Lawrence, Massachusetts, 1845–1921. Chapel Hill, University of North Carolina Press [1963] 248 p. illus. 63–3915 F74.L4C6

Bibliography: p. [232]–237. Bibliographical footnotes.

The author believes that the 1912 textile strike of the International Workers of the World in Lawrence created an image of the city as un-American, anarchistic, and impoverished and of immigrants in general as poverty-stricken, insecure radicals. Cole challenges these stereotypes, proposing that the foreign workers were not as hopelessly poor, ultra-liberal, or insecure as was thought and that the city was not as extreme as the activity during the strike indicated. The book is a careful study of Lawrence from its beginning as a city of immigrants to its emergence as a city of Americans.

2023. Dobriner, William M. Class in suburbia. Englewood Cliffs, N.J., Prentice-Hall [1963] 166 p. illus. (A Spectrum book)
63–7772 HT351.D48
Bibliographical footnotes.

The author's thesis is that all suburbs are not alike but vary according to the class of people living in them. He asserts that the typical image of suburbia as a place where city dwellers are transformed from working class to middle class and from Democrats to Republicans, where they "rediscover religion, the PTA, and the bridge club," and where life in general seems to become "one frenetic garden party" is erroneous. Dobriner cites various studies which reveal that the move from the city to the suburb has very little effect on behavior and notes that these stereotypes are distinctively middle class and are not typical of working-class suburbs. *The Suburban Community* (New York, Putnam [1958] 416 p.), edited by Dobriner, is a textbook focusing on the creation, outer forms, and internal processes of the suburb.

2024. Duhl, Leonard J., *ed.* The urban condition; people and policy in the metropolis. Edited by Leonard J. Duhl, with the assistance of John Powell. New York, Basic Books [1963] 410 p.
63–12844 HT123.D76
Bibliographies at the ends of chapters.

Thirty-two writers from various fields attempt to provide insights into the kind of planning needed to achieve mental health for our urban society. A general conclusion is that simplistic, cause-and-effect approaches to urban problems are inadequate and that the complexity of relationships within an urban industrial society must be taken into consideration. The papers are arranged into sections dealing with new ways of thinking about urban problems; urban renewal and the attendant dislocations and relocations; slums, public housing, poverty, and mental illness; philosophies of social planning and social action; and the ecology of the social environment. The editors of *Fortune* discuss the problems of the cities and draw attention to the process of urban sprawl in *The Exploding Metropolis* (Garden City, N.Y., Doubleday, 1958. 193 p.)

2025. Gottmann, Jean. Megalopolis; the urbanized northeastern seaboard of the United States. New York, Twentieth Century Fund, 1961. 810 p. illus. 61–17298 HT123.5.A12G6
Bibliographical footnotes.

A systematic analysis of the development and present state of "Megalopolis," the string of metropolitan regions stretching from Boston to Washington, D.C. In addition to its high population density, Megalopolis is noteworthy for its prime role in the Nation's political and economic activities and as one of the largest industrial belts in the world. The area includes pockets of wilderness and agricultural areas that are achieving a new kind of integration with the cities. Gottmann contends that slums and urban crowding are growing pains and that, as a whole, people in Megalopolis are healthier, richer, more successful, and better off than comparable groups elsewhere in the world. As "the cradle of a new order in the organization of inhabited space," Megalopolis presents a major challenge to modern civilization. The central findings of the study are discussed in nontechnical language and presented in graphic form in the Twentieth Century Fund report, *The Challenge of Megalopolis* ([New York?] Macmillan, 1964. 126 p.), by Wolf Von Eckhardt.

2026. McKelvey, Blake. The urbanization of America, 1860–1915. New Brunswick, N.J., Rutgers University Press [1963] 370 p. illus.
62–21248 HT123.M23
Bibliography: p. [333]–357.

The author examines the character and causes of city growth during the late 19th and early 20th centuries and its relationship to other developments during that period. McKelvey, who has also written an authoritative history of Rochester, N.Y., regards the city as a constantly changing and developing entity in human society. After identifying the "economic and demographic forces that tended to multiply and scatter urban centers across the land," he traces the internal civic and political evolution of the cities and examines social and cultural developments as they became embodied in urban customs and institutions. The discussion closes at a turning point in urban history, when many cities were becoming complex metropolitan centers with new and perplexing needs. Additional historical accounts of American cities are *The Urban Frontier; the Rise of Western Cities, 1790–*

*1830* (Cambridge, Harvard University Press, 1959. 362 p. Harvard historical monographs, 41), by Richard C. Wade, and *The Rise of Urban America* (New York, Harper & Row [1965] 208 p.), by Constance McLaughlin Green. The latter book is a brief survey of urban life from the 1600's to the 1960's.

2027. Vernon, Raymond. Metropolis 1985; an interpretation of the findings of the New York metropolitan region study. Cambridge, Mass., Harvard University Press, 1960. 252 p. illus. (New York metropolitan region study 9)
60–15243 HC108.N7V4
Bibliographical references included in "Notes" (p. [241]–244).

The New York Metropolitan Region Study, directed by Raymond Vernon, is a comprehensive analysis of the region's major economic and demographic features, with projections to 1965, 1975, and 1985. The nine-volume study covers 22 counties in three States. In one volume of the study, *Anatomy of a Metropolis* (Cambridge, Harvard University Press, 1959. 345 p.), Edgar M. Hoover and Raymond Vernon discuss the changing distribution of people and jobs within the New York metropolitan area. *Metropolis 1985,* an interpretive summary of the other eight volumes, emphasizes economic development in projecting the region's growth for a 25-year period. Additional volumes in the series are entered by subject elsewhere in this *Supplement.*

## J. City Planning; Housing

2028. Abrahamson, Julia. A neighborhood finds itself. New York, Harper [1959] 370 p.
59–7061 HN80.C5A6
"Source Material": p. 358–360.
An eloquent story of people of all races and creeds working together to save their 100-year-old, declining community. As cochairman of the Social Order Committee of a Quaker group in Chicago, the author helped organize the Hyde Park-Kenwood Community conference, which became one of the most ambitious urban renewal undertakings in the United States. The Federal Housing and Home Finance Agency approved its plans in 1958 and allocated $25,835,000 for assistance. Active group participation, with block leaders and interracial involvement at the grassroots level, are held to be chiefly responsible for the success of the project. In *Slums and Social Insecurity* (Washington, U.S. Govt. Print. Off. [1963] 168 p. U.S. Social Security Administration. Division of Research and Statistics. Research report no. 1), Alvin L. Schorr evaluates housing policies in relation to the elimination of poverty.

2029. Abrams, Charles. The city is the frontier. New York, Harper & Row [1965] 394 p.
64–25145 HT123.A6
Bibliographical footnotes.
The author, who has been associated with the housing program in the United States since its inception in 1933, explores the financial, political, and legal entanglements of the program and concludes that material improvements without regard to human relationships are inadequate. Urban re-

newal "calls for something more than tearing down a few slums, putting up another string of public projects, or another row of apartment houses." It requires that the central city with all its problems be "acknowledged as one of the vital options in American life."

2030. Futterman, Robert A. The future of our cities. Introduction by Victor Gruen. Graphics and cartography by Stephen Kraft. Garden City, N.Y., Doubleday, 1961. 360 p. illus.
61–8884 NA9108.F8
The author, a successful builder and developer, likens the city to a living organism that changes even while it is being examined. Analyzing the American city as a fundamentally democratic and humanistic entity, Futterman notes that although a dominant industry can promote a city's growth it may simultaneously control it, and the single economic base is thus to be avoided. He considers that some cities flourish because of their "eternally valuable location" while others decline when their resources are drained. The latter half of the volume is devoted to capsule histories of 19 large cities in the United States.

2031. Gallion, Arthur B., *and* Simon Eisner. The urban pattern; city planning and design. Chapter title sketches by Anthony Stoner. 2d ed. Princeton, N.J., Van Nostrand [1963] 435 p.
63–24088 NA9031.G3 1963
Bibliography: p. 401–423.
A revised edition of no. 4606 in the 1960 *Guide,* with additional material and new photographs. In *The Making of Urban America; a History of City*

*Planning in the United States* (Princeton, N.J., Princeton University Press, 1965. 574 p.), John W. Reps documents the important influences that have molded America's cities in the last 400 years. "To provide a general survey and basic history of this neglected aspect of the nation's growth," he traces the European heritage and major design forms from the beginning of American colonization to the start of modern urban planning. More than 300 reproductions of original plans and historic maps are included, as well as quotations from diarists in the late 17th century.

2032. Jacobs, Jane. The death and life of great American cities. [New York] Random House [1961] 458 p. 61–6262 NA9108.J3

A critique of past and current city planning in the United States. Citing errors that she attributes to careless planning theories, the author concentrates on the inner areas of the cities and the numerous related problems of ethnic and community groups. For her, "The pseudoscience of city planning and its companion, the art of city design, have not yet broken with the special comfort of wishes, familiar superstitions, over-simplification, and symbols, and have not yet embarked upon the adventure of probing the real world." In *The Heart of Our Cities; the Urban Crisis: Diagnosis and Cure* (New York, Simon & Schuster, 1964. 368 p.), Victor Gruen urges wide participation in city planning.

2033. McEntire, Davis. Residence and race; final and comprehensive report to the Commission on Race and Housing. Berkeley, University of California Press, 1960. xxii, 409 p. illus. (Publications of the Commission on Race and Housing) 60–13020 HD7293.M22

Bibliography: p. [381]–400.

"One of the basic liberties of citizens in a free society is the freedom to move and to choose a place of residence," says the author in his introduction, and he proceeds to consider the political, social, and economic forces which influence residential patterns in the United States. Drawn largely from related studies by social scientists and experts on minority housing, this report also contains considerable data from governmental sources. McEntire

finds that most private housing developments, except those intended primarily for minority occupancy, still exclude minority groups entirely. Thus, although building and financing methods have altered, traditional racial policies have remained much as before. Asserting that his findings are "not limited to the specific problems of housing and race relations" but are basic to research in human behavior, the author concludes with constructive principles for action. In *Urban Renewal Politics; Slum Clearance in Newark* (New York, Columbia University Press, 1963. 219 p. Metropolitan politics series, no. 1), Harold Kaplan seeks to determine what kind of local political structure is conducive to rapid, planned change.

2034. Meyerson, Martin, Barbara Terrett, *and* William L. C. Wheaton. Housing, people, and cities. New York, McGraw-Hill, 1962. xiv, 386 p. illus. (ACTION series in housing and community development) 61–16532 HD7293.M4

Bibliography: p. 355–365.

The final volume of a series sponsored by ACTION (The American Council To Improve Our Neighborhoods) to investigate obstructions to the improvement of housing and urban environment. Under the headings, "The Setting," "The Consumer," "The Producer," "The Investor," "The Federal Government," and "The Community," the authors measure demographic trends in family life in the United States and the present housing needs of the consumer. Factors determining the buying, selling, financing, and construction of dwellings are discussed in detail. Though disagreement over appropriate involvement of the Government in future planning remains a central issue, the authors suggest that private enterprise and public effort should complement one another in their attempts to develop desirable community rehabilitation. Three relevant studies on housing are *Housing Markets and Public Policy* (Philadelphia, University of Pennsylvania Press [1963] 346 p. City planning series), by William G. Grigsby; *Property Values and Race* (Berkeley, University of California Press, 1960. 256 p.), by Luigi Laurenti; and *The Urban Complex; Human Values in Urban Life* (Garden City, N.Y., Doubleday, 1964. 297 p.), by Robert C. Weaver.

## K. Social Problems; Social Work

2035. Andrews, Frank Emerson. Philanthropic foundations. New York, Russell Sage Foundation, 1956. 459 p. illus. 56–5824 HV97.A3A67

Bibliography: p. 355–387.

As defined by the author, a philanthropic foundation is "a nongovernmental, nonprofit organization having a principal fund of its own, managed by its own trustees or directors, and established to maintain or aid social, educational, charitable, religious, or other activities serving the common welfare." Essentially a 20th-century institution, the foundation in the United States grants private funds for public use and participates in a broad range of social and economic activity. Andrews discusses the operation, types, establishment, and finances of foundations, as well as their trustees, personnel, and administration. Criteria for grants and current trends in this sphere of philanthropy are also outlined. John E. Lankford's *Congress and the Foundations in the Twentieth Century* (River Falls, Wisconsin State University, 1964. 142 p.) is a specialized study that centers on congressional investigations of the functions of foundations.

2036. Bremner, Robert H. American philanthropy. [Chicago] University of Chicago Press [1960] 230 p. (The Chicago history of American civilization) 60–7246 HV91.B67
Bibliography: p. 198–212.
Philanthropic activities in the United States are surveyed from the colonial period to the present, and the principal individuals, institutions, and movements are noted. Stating that economic developments such as industrialism and the accumulation of great wealth influenced the nature of philanthropic ideas and activity in a beneficial way, Bremner illustrates the role philanthropy has played in the areas of humanitarian reform, charity, social service, education, research, religion, and war relief. In addition, he discusses the overall contribution of philanthropy to the improvement of humanity. Merle E. Curti's *American Philanthropy Abroad: A History* (New Brunswick, N.J., Rutgers University Press [1963] 651 p.) is a comprehensive account of the motivations, programs, and accomplishments of American philanthropic efforts in foreign countries.

2037. Bruno, Frank J. Trends in social work, 1874–1956; a history based on the Proceedings of the National Conference of Social Work. With chapters by Louis Towley. [2d ed.] New York, Columbia University Press, 1957. xviii, 462 p. 57–9699 HV91.B75 1957
Bibliographical footnotes.
An updated edition of no. 4618 in the 1960 *Guide*. Two complementary books are *The Heritage of American Social Work; Readings in Its Philosophical and Institutional Development* (New York, Columbia University Press, 1961. 452 p.), edited by Ralph E. Pumphrey and Muriel W. Pumphrey, and Nathan E. Cohen's *Social Work in the American*

*Tradition* (New York, Dryden Press [1958] 404 p.), an analysis and evaluation of the purposes and goals of social work.

2038. Cohen, Nathan E., *ed*. Social work and social problems. New York, National Association of Social Workers [1964] xiv, 391 p. 64–20628 HV15.C58
Bibliographical footnotes.
A study of the contribution of social work to the solution of social problems. The topics covered include poverty, marital incompatibility, child neglect, deterioration of the inner city, unmarried mothers, broken families, and racial discrimination. A model for problem analysis is presented which focuses attention on the relationship between actual and ideal objectives in social work. Within this frame of reference, a basis for action is defined. Emphasis is placed on the need for preventive techniques through which problems are anticipated and kept from developing.

2039. Cuber, John F., William F. Kenkel, *and* Robert A. Harper. Problems of American society; values in conflict. 4th ed. New York, Holt, Rinehart & Winston [1964] 422 p. 64–12925 HN57.C8 1964
Suggested readings at the ends of chapters.
A revised edition of no. 4619 in the 1960 *Guide*. Problems of industrial and urban society in the United States are discussed in *Social Problems: Dissensus and Deviation in an Industrial Society* (New York, Oxford University Press, 1964. 594 p.), by Russell R. Dynes and others, and *Social Problems in Our Time; a Sociological Analysis* (Englewood Cliffs, N.J., Prentice-Hall, 1960. 600 p. Prentice-Hall sociology series), by Samuel K. Weinberg.

2040. Cutlip, Scott M. Fund raising in the United States; its role in America's philanthropy. Foreword by Merle Curti. New Brunswick, N.J., Rutgers University Press [1965] xiv, 553 p. 64–8261 HV41.C87
Bibliography: p. 541–546.
Focusing on 20th-century developments, the author examines the operations, techniques, and individuals involved in fundraising campaigns. The small-scale philanthropic activities before 1900 are discussed briefly. The book concentrates on the evolution of fundraising into a unique business operation directed by professional fundraisers and public relations experts. Early YMCA campaigns, Red Cross drives during World War I, community chest activities, relief funding in the Depression, national health campaigns, World War II appeals,

and contemporary fundraising methods are covered in detail. Cutlip notes that America philanthropy, now a billion-dollar enterprise, has adapted the business methods of the modern corporation to the task of charitable activities.

2041. Fink, Arthur E., Everett E. Wilson, *and* Merrill B. Conover. The field of social work. 4th ed. New York, Holt, Rinehart & Winston [1963] 560 p. 63–11337 HV40.F5 1963

Includes bibliography.

An updated edition of no. 4621 in the 1960 *Guide.* In *The Professional Altruist; the Emergence of Social Work as a Career, 1880–1930* (Cambridge, Harvard University Press, 1965. 291 p. A Publication of the Center for the Study of the History of Liberty in America, Harvard University), Roy Lubove traces the development of social work from a voluntary and personal service to an efficient and bureaucratic profession.

## L. Dependency; Social Security

2042. Allan, W. Scott. Rehabilitation: a community challenge. New York, Wiley [1958] 347 p. illus. 58–7894 HV3011.A65
Bibliography: p. 226–240.
Rehabilitation of the physically handicapped encompasses a broad range of services, programs, personnel, and facilities. The need to rehabilitate the greatest number of disabled persons requires coordinated action among therapists, physicians, government, and health agencies, according to Allan. To be effective, "rehabilitation must be broad in scope, practical in purpose and integrated in practice." Emphasis is placed upon the importance of community-level planning. *Hearing and Deafness,* rev. ed. (New York, Holt, Rinehart & Winston [1960] 573 p.), edited by Hallowell Davis and Sol Richard Silverman, is a comprehensive treatment of the field of audiology and the problems of deafness. In *Hope Deferred; Public Welfare and the Blind* (Berkeley, University of California Press, 1959. 272 p.), Jacobus Ten Broek and Floyd W. Matson examine major legislation to aid the blind.

2043. De Grazia, Alfred, *and* Ted Gurr. American welfare. [New York] New York University Press, 1961. xv, 470 p. illus.
60–14432 HV91.D45
Bibliography: p. 451–454.
A general overview of the American welfare system. The roles of religious groups, fraternal and service organizations, business, labor unions, and statewide and nationwide services are explained, as well as the functions of local, State, and National Governments and their relation to welfare practices. A chapter on American welfare programs abroad is included. In *The Wasted Americans; Cost of Our Welfare Dilemma* (New York, Harper & Row [°1964] 227 p.), Edgar May describes the frustrating conditions facing welfare caseworkers and recipients alike and the problems created and perpetuated by the system. A text combining the disciplines of sociology and social work is *Industrial Society and Social Welfare; the Impact of Industrialization on the Supply and Organization of Social Welfare Services in the United States* (New York, Russell Sage Foundation, 1958. 401 p.), by Harold L. Wilensky and Charles N. Lebeaux.

2044. Harrington, Michael. The other America; poverty in the United States. New York, Macmillian, 1962. 191 p. 62–8555 HV91.H3
The author notes that national abundance often conceals the extent and nature of poverty in the United States. In contrast to the standards and goals of an affluent society, the unskilled, the rural poor, the migratory farm laborer, the aged, and minority groups subsist in a subculture of impoverishment. Harrington outlines the general sociological and cultural status of the millions of poor Americans, who lack adequate food, shelter, education, and medical care, and stresses the need for a comprehensive program by the Federal Government to alleviate the problems of the poor. *From the Depths; the Discovery of Poverty in the United States* (New York, New York University Press [1956] 364 p.), by Robert H. Bremner, traces the changing awareness of poverty as a social problem from the mid-19th century to the 1920's. *Poverty in America; a Book of Readings* (Ann Arbor, University of Michigan Press [1965] 532 p.), edited by Louis A. Ferman, Joyce L. Kornbluh, and Alan Haber, is a selection of articles describing and analyzing the poverty problem. *Poverty in America* (San Francisco, Chandler Pub. Co. [1965] 465 p. Chandler publications in political science) is the proceedings of the Conference on Poverty in America, held at the University of California at Berkeley in 1965. These papers, edited by Margaret S.

Gordon, discuss the effectiveness of current and proposed programs and policies.

2045. Myers, Robert J. Social insurance and allied Government programs. Homewood, Ill., R. D. Irwin, 1965. 258 p. (The Irwin series in risk and insurance) 64–24696 HD7125.M9
Bibliography: p. 247–254.

The book charts the growth of social insurance and security programs since the Depression of the 1930's and their effect on the social, economic, and political history of the United States. Greater emphasis is placed on the development of social insurance than on public assistance programs. Basic principles and provisions for administration, coverage, benefits, and financing are explained. In addition, the author includes a summary of social security programs of various foreign countries. An extensive analysis of social security problems and policy questions is presented by Eveline M. R. Burns in *Social Security and Public Policy* (New York, McGraw-Hill, 1956. 291 p. Economics handbook series). Edwin E. Witte's *Social Security Perspectives* (Madison, University of Wisconsin Press, 1962. 419 p.), edited by Robert J. Lampman, traces the evolution of Witte's thinking on social security issues.

2046. Vedder, Clyde B., *comp.* Gerontology; a book of readings. Springfield, Ill., C. C. Thomas [1963] 430 p. 62–21330 HQ1061.V4
Bibliography: p. 417–422.

A collection of reprinted articles on the sociology of aging, with particular reference to demographic, economic, medical, and sociocultural aspects. The growing importance of gerontology in the social sciences is noted and recommendations are made for training and curricula in this field. Comprehensive treatments of the subject are presented in the *Handbook of Aging and the Individual; Psychological and Biological Aspects* ([Chicago] University of Chicago Press [1960] 939 p.), edited by James E. Birren, and *Handbook of Social Gerontology; Societal Aspects of Aging* ([Chicago] University of Chicago Press [1960] 770 p.), edited by Clark Tibbits.

# M. Delinquency and Correction

2047. Barnes, Harry E., *and* Negley K. Teeters. New horizons in criminology. 3d ed. Englewood Cliffs, N.J., Prentice-Hall, 1959. 654 p. illus. (Prentice-Hall sociology series)
59–5873 HV6025.B3 1959
Bibliographical footnotes.

An updated edition of no. 4639 in the 1960 *Guide.* A brief study of crime and its sociological complexities is Gresham M. Sykes' *Crime and Society* (New York, Random House [1956] 125 p. Random House studies in sociology, 14). *Organized Crime in America; a Book of Readings* (Ann Arbor, University of Michigan Press [1962] 421 p.), edited by Gus Tyler, is a general treatment of the subject. *Readings in Criminology and Penology* (New York, Columbia University Press, 1964. 698 p.), edited by David Dressler, includes representative selections by writers in disciplines other than sociology.

2048. Chein, Isidor, *and others.* The road to H: narcotics, delinquency, and social policy. New York, Basic Books [1964] 482 p. illus.
63–17342 HV5822.H4C47
Bibliographical footnotes.

A study of juvenile drug users in New York City, based on research conducted from 1949 through 1954. The authors describe the social environment and psychology of the addicts and conclude that changes must be made in public policy dealing with them. Although drugs users were found to be "clearly related to the delinquent subculture," their use of drugs did not lead to an overall increase in the number of crimes but rather to a reduction in crimes of physical violence and an increase in crimes for money. At the time of this survey, most drug users lived in high delinquency areas, were from poor and disrupted families, and were members of ethnic minority groups. Drugs provided a means of escape from misery. The authors recommend that drugs be legalized and their prescription by physicians permitted.

2049. Cloward, Richard A., *and* Lloyd E. Ohlin. Delinquency and opportunity; a theory of delinquent gangs. Glencoe, Ill., Free Press [1960] 220 p. 60–10892 HV9069.C52
Bibliographical footnotes.

From a study of juvenile gangs in large cities, the authors have developed an environmental theory of criminology based on the principle of opportunity. They argue that youths become delinquent because of a lack of opportunities to succeed in normal society and that the form of delinquency is likewise determined by environmental opportunities. A young delinquent gravitates to a particular type of delinquent subculture or gang, and the norms of conduct and patterns of delinquency of the gang determine his subsequent adult behavior. This theory is further explored in Irving Spergel's *Racketville, Slumtown, Haulburg; an Exploratory Study of Delinquent Subcultures* (Chicago, University of Chicago Press [1964] 211 p.).

2050. Dressler, David. Practice and theory of probation and parole. New York, Columbia University Press, 1959. 252 p.

59–11177   HV9278.D72

Bibliographical footnotes.

This textbook is more systematic than the author's earlier *Probation and Parole* (no. 4643 in the 1960 *Guide*) and includes an account of the origins of probation and parole and a discussion of current practice. The author concludes that the lack of scientific studies in this area has made it difficult to evaluate the effectiveness of probation and parole in the treatment of criminals and that a more scientific attitude must be taken toward crime and its treatment.

2051. Glueck, Sheldon, *and* Eleanor T. Glueck. Physique and delinquency. New York, Harper [1956] xviii, 339 p. illus.

56–6432   HV9069.G54

Bibliographical footnotes.

One of a series of monographs in which the authors explore various causes of delinquency. In this study, based on research with 500 delinquents and an equal number of nondelinquents, evidence is presented that body type is a factor in delinquency. The relationship between physique and other characteristics such as personality and intelligence is also discussed. In *Family Environment and Delinquency* (Boston, Houghton Mifflin [1962] 328 p.), the Gluecks analyze the effects of sociocultural influences on the basis of evidence from the same study. Both works are elaborations on findings originally described in the authors' *Unraveling Juvenile Delinquency* (no. 4650 in the 1960 *Guide*).

2052. Shulman, Harry M. Juvenile delinquency in American society. New York, Harper [1961] 802 p. illus. (Harper's social science series)   61–8555   HV9104.S47

Bibliographies at the ends of chapters.

A comprehensive textbook. The author views juvenile delinquency as a product of urban life and considers that adults contribute to the problem by forfeiting to the police and the courts many of their parental and civic responsibilities. Topics covered include personality, intelligence, the family, peer groups, the legal machinery for dealing with delinquency, methods of group treatment, social control, and the causes of delinquency. Comparisons between American and European delinquency are also presented. Current theories of juvenile delinquency are challenged in David Matza's *Delinquency and Drift* (New York, Wiley [1964] 199 p.). An extensive selection of readings on the subject is included in *The Problem of Delinquency* (Boston, Houghton Mifflin [1959] 1183 p.), edited by Sheldon Glueck.

2053. Smith, Bruce. Police systems in the United States. Rev. by Bruce Smith, Jr. 2d rev. ed. New York, Harper [1960] 338 p. illus.

60–11498 HV8138.S58 1960

Bibliographical footnotes.

An updated edition of no. 4655 in the 1960 *Guide*. In *Racial Factors and Urban Law Enforcement* (Philadelphia, University of Pennsylvania Press [1957] 209 p.), William M. Kephart analyzes integration in the Philadelphia Police Department and interrelationships between white and Negro policemen and offenders. *The FBI Story; a Report to the People* (New York, Random House [1956] 368 p.), by Don Whitehead, is a history of the Federal Bureau of Investigation.

2054. Sykes, Gresham M. The society of captives; a study of a maximum security prison. Princeton, N.J., Princeton University Press, 1958. 144 p.   58–10054 HV9475.N52T7

Bibliographical footnotes.

The prison is presented as a small-scale totalitarian system which can provide answers to social questions larger than those usually posed by penology. The major elements in this social system are two: the adjustments made by the inmates to their various deprivations, and the constant tension and friction existing between the inmates and the prison staff. The author concludes that the public should be realistic about prisons and prison reform. By "expecting less and demanding less we may achieve more," he advises, "for a chronically disillusioned public is apt to drift into indifference." Don C. Gibbons' *Changing the Lawbreaker; the Treatment of Delinquents and Criminals* (Englewood Cliffs, N.J., Prentice–Hall [1965] 306 p.) is a brief theoretical examination of the causes and cures of criminal behavior. *Penology: A Realistic Approach* (Springfield, Ill., C. C. Thomas [1964] 345 p.) is a book of readings compiled and edited by Clyde B. Vedder and Barbara A. Kay.

2055. Wilson, Orlando W. Police administration. 2d ed. New York, McGraw-Hill [1963] 528 p. illus. (McGraw-Hill series in political science)                63–9827 HV7935.W48 1963

A revised edition of no. 4660 in the 1960 *Guide.*

2056. Wolfgang, Marvin E. Patterns in criminal homicide. Philadelphia, University of Pensylvania [1958] xiv, 413 p. illus.

56–11803 HV6534.P5W6

Bibliography: p. 341–360.

An analysis of 588 cases of criminal homicide, based on the records of the Philadelphia Police Department during the period 1948-52. The author briefly explains the distinctions of homicidal crimes according to Pennsylvania statutes. Specific data on the perpetrators as well as the victims of homicide are analyzed according to race, sex, age, weapons, and motives. Interpersonal relationships between victim and offender play a significant part in explaining the reasons for the crime. The author also provides a detailed account of what happens to the offender after the homicide. Included in the text are statistical tabulations and research material relevant to each phase of the study.

# XVI

# Communications

CHANGES occur swiftly in the communications field, and their effects go deep into the structure of American life. This chapter presents books dealing with current changes as well as historical studies in such subject areas as the postal system, the express companies, and the telegraph, telephone, and cable services. In addition, there are works on air and transatlantic mail and Radio Free Europe.

The majority of books on communications concern some aspect of television: advertising, the reaction to the real or supposed threat of governmental restraints, the effect of TV on children, the use of closed circuit TV in the classroom, and the wide and growing variety of programs on noncommercial broadcasting with educational, industrial, scientific, and military applications. The ever-widening influence of TV has added to the impulse toward the development of an essentially new discipline, the study of mass communications in general; a new section on this subject, Section F, has been added.

## A. The Post Office; Express Companies

2057. Baratz, Morton S. The economics of the postal service. Washington, Public Affairs Press [1962] 104 p.        62–21124   HE6371.B3

As of 1961, the U.S. Post Office comprised some 35,000 stations staffed by 580,000 employees. A total of 65 billion pieces of mail were handled per year. Annual expenditures were $4 billion, but revenues were only slightly over $3 billion. This study seeks to evaluate the economic performance of this vast public enterprise. The author outlines the historical evolution of fiscal policies against a background of constantly increasing demand for postal service and sets forth the rate structure of the four classes of mail, the concepts underlying rate differentials, and the relation of costs to income within each class. Baratz concludes that postal service must be priced to provide "an impersonal and effective rationing mechanism," that the amount of subsidy which the Post Office should receive cannot be objectively determined and may be left to the congressional majority, and that, although no overall rating system is applicable, some of the existing rate differentials are discriminatory and inequitable.

2058. Doherty, William C. Mailman, U.S.A. New York, D. McKay Co. [1960]   308 p.
60–14594   HD6515.P7D6

The longtime president of the National Association of Letter Carriers critically reviews Post Office Department policies, most of which, he asserts, have consistently denied the mailman a living wage, adequate fringe benefits, and decent working conditions, as well as having unnecessarily curtailed mail service. Doherty outlines the history of the association from its founding in 1889 and traces its campaigns for pay raises, shorter working hours, job security, and insurance benefits. The development of postal administration is discussed, and portraits are presented of the men who have held the position of Postmaster General and other high offices in the Department. The final chapter makes general recommendations for reforms and improvements throughout the postal system. In *The Silent Investigators* (New York, Dutton, 1959. 319 p.), John N. Makris describes a series of cases illustrating the two primary functions of the postal inspector: "(1) Service investigations to insure the best possible service to the American public, and (2) criminal investigations leading to the apprehension of those who violate postal laws."

2059. Fuller, Wayne E. RFD, the changing face of rural America. Bloomington, Indiana University Press [1964] xii, 361 p. illus.
64–19374    HE6455.F8
"A note on sources": p. 315–316. Bibliographical references included in "Notes" (p. 317–350).
A history of how Rural Free Delivery promoted and reflected a transition from the old to the new in rural America. The RFD system, created despite the opposition of merchants, postmasters in small towns, and budget balancers in Washington, led to an extension of the circulation of daily newspapers, a phenomenal growth of mail-order houses, and the construction of improved roads. The early rural mailman not only delivered mail but also carried news from farm to farm and ran errands for his patrons. Written in a light vein but based on sound

research, the book gives an authentic picture of the effects of RFD on U.S. society.

2060. Summerfield, Arthur E. U.S. mail: The story of the United States postal service, by Arthur E. Summerfield as told to Charles Hurd. New York, Holt, Rinehart & Winston [1960] 256 p. illus.    60–10747   HE6371.S8
The Postmaster General in the Eisenhower administration surveys the development of a postal system in this country from the beginning of intercolonial mail service in 1672. Topics covered include philatelic history, the pony express, the inception of airmail service, automated post offices, facsimile letter-transmission, the work of postal inspectors, and the problems of mail-order pornography and mail fraud. The business and fiscal operations of the Post Office Department are reviewed and suggestions for reforms and modernization are presented. In *The Story of Pitney-Bowes* (New York, Harper [1961] 262 p.), William Cahn chronicles the origin and growth of the Pitney-Bowes Company of Stamford, Conn., best known for its development and dissemination of the postage meter. Early developments in reciprocal postal service between Great Britain and North America are recorded in *The Transatlantic Mail* ([Southampton] A. Coles: New York, J. De Graff [1956] 191 p.), in which author Frank Staff traces its progress from the 17th-century practice of depositing mail at the coffee houses or taverns frequented by seamen, through the early 18th-century introduction of packet boats chartered by the British government to carry mail, and as far as the mid-19th-century advent of steamships, which rapidly replaced the slower and less regular sailing packets.

## B. Telegraph, Cable, Telephone

2061. Clarke, Arthur C. Voice across the sea. New York, Harper [1958] 208 p.
58–8868   TK5605.C55
A general historical account of the original transatlantic cable and of the laying of the first submarine telephone cable between Europe and the United States in 1955–56.

2062. Costain, Thomas B. The chord of steel; the story of the invention of the telephone. Garden City, N.Y., Doubleday, 1960. 238 p.
60–10085   TK6143.B4C6

A biographical study covering six years in the life of Alexander Graham Bell, beginning with his family's move from London to Brantford, Ontario, in 1870. The author outlines the series of experiments leading up to the inventions of the multiple telegraph and telephone but places primary emphasis on Bell's personality. The reader is afforded glimpses of the inventor's boyhood in England, his early and continuing interest in the science of speech, his devotion to teaching the deaf to speak, his family life, and the great verve with which he pursued his inventions.

2063. Harder, Warren J. Daniel Drawbaugh; the Edison of the Cumberland Valley. Philadelphia, University of Pennsylvania Press [1960] 227 p. 59–9201 TK6018.D8H3 1960

A portrayal of the life and work of a prolific inventor from Pennsylvania who narrowly missed fame by delaying his application for a patent. Drawbaugh patented a telephone apparatus in 1880 and sold his rights to several men who formed the People's Telephone Company in New York City. The Bell Telephone Company promptly filed suit for violation of its patent rights. Much of the book is devoted to the ensuing eight years of litigation, which concluded with a Supreme Court decision dismissing Drawbaugh's claim of an original invention. Several court decisions are quoted in full.

## C. Radio, Television: Broadcasting

2064. Blum, Daniel C. Pictorial history of television. Philadelphia, Chilton Co., Book Division [1959] 288 p. 59–9640 PN1992.5.B55

Hundreds of photographs cover the major television programs from 1939, when NBC presented Gertrude Lawrence in scenes from the Broadway play *Susan and God,* through 1959. The arrangement is chronological within 22 subject categories. A brief text gives information on the shows and their principal performers. *A Pictorial History of Radio* (New York, Citadel Press [1960] 176 p.), by Irving Settel includes photographs illustrating radio's technological development, as well as scenes from a variety of programs and portraits of the stars who made them famous. The narrative text incorporates excerpts from actual scripts. A year-by-year chronicle of network programing is given in *A Thirty-Year History of Programs Carried on National Radio Networks in the United States, 1926–1956* ([Columbus, Ohio State University] 1958. 228 p.), by Harrison B. Summers. Annual tables list all broadcasts of 10 minutes or longer. Information is included on the sponsor, number of winter seasons on the air, carrying network, day and hour of broadcast or weekly frequency, length and popularity rating.

2065. Chester, Giraud, Garnet R. Garrison, *and* Edgar E. Willis. Television and radio. 3d ed. New York, Appleton-Century-Crofts [1963] 659 p. 63–11954 TK6550.C43 1963
Bibliography: p. 631–642.
An updated edition of no. 4686 in the 1960 *Guide.*

2066. The Eighth art; twenty-three views of television today. Contributors: Eugene Burdick [and others] Introd. by Robert Lewis Shayon. New York, Holt, Rinehart & Winston [1962] 269 p. 62–18758 PN1992.5.E43

In these essays, television's purveyors and audiences are the targets of an almost unbroken stream of adverse comment by critics within the television industry and without. The articles were originally commissioned by the CBS Television Network for inclusion in a projected quarterly magazine. Television is discussed as a medium for the other seven arts, for news, and for politics. Marya Mannes contends that the quality of television has suffered because intellectuals have failed to support its best efforts. Leo Rosten, on the other hand, argues that the mass media are meant for the masses, not for the intellectuals. Other contributors include Walter Cronkite, Moses Hadas, Tyrone Guthrie, George Balanchine, Gilbert Seldes, Ashley Montagu, Richard H. Rovere, and Charles A. Siepmann.

2067. Head, Sydney W. Broadcasting in America; a survey of television and radio. Boston, Houghton Mifflin [1956] 502 p.
56–13974 HE8698.H4

The director of broadcasting and film services at the University of Miami argues that our private-enterprise, competitive, advertising-supported, and syndicated broadcasting system is basically sound and stable. Proceeding on this assumption, he aims in this encyclopedic analysis of the industry "to provide a basis for appraising American broadcasting by standards relevant to service as it exists here and now." The author believes that the medium has been judged by irrelevant criteria developed for other modes of mass communication. Criticisms and suggestions for improvement are here formulated within the framework of discussions concerning such aspects as technological and organizational growth, interrelationships of the various mass media, pros and cons of government regulation, the uses, kinds, and influence of advertising, financial organization, social forces operating on the medium, and the effects of the broadcasting process on society. An overview of the field designed for both radio and television station employees is *The Modern Broadcaster: The Station Book* (New York, Harper [1961] 351 p.), by Sherman P. Lawton, who concentrates on describing overall station organization and the techniques employed in various jobs at the station level.

2068. Holt, Robert T. Radio Free Europe. Minneapolis, University of Minnesota Press [1958] xii, 249 p.          58–7621 DR1.R253
Bibliographical references included in "Notes" (p. 232–242).

Established in 1949 as a division of the Free Europe Committee, Radio Free Europe was intended to break the monopoly of the airwaves held by the Communist governments of central and eastern Europe. By 1957 it was operating 29 transmitters and broadcasting nearly 3,000 hours per week to Poland, Czechoslovakia, Hungary, Romania, and Bulgaria. The author discusses RFE's organizational structure, program content, transmission problems, and large-scale propaganda campaigns from 1953 to 1957 and evaluates its position as an "officially nonofficial" instrument of American foreign policy. Investigations of its effectiveness by the Audience Analysis Section "demonstrate the dominant position that RFE holds among the 'big three' western broadcasters" (the other two being the British Broadcasting Corporation and the Voice of America).

2069. Lessing, Lawrence P. Man of high fidelity: Edwin Howard Armstrong, a biography. Philadelphia, Lippincott [1956] 320 p.
56–11677     TK6545.A7L4
The author, who considers Armstrong (1890–1954) to be the "single most important inventor of modern radio," traces his life from his childhood in New York City through his years as professor of electrical engineering at Columbia University. Armstrong's experiments, which resulted in such basic innovations as the regenerative amplifier (1912) and frequency modulation (1933) are described, together with the ensuing bitter and expensive litigations concerning his patents. Particular attention is devoted to Lee De Forest's claim to prior invention of the regenerative process and RCA's disregard for Armstrong's patent rights in the use of FM. Lessing depicts his subject as a stubborn and courageous individualist who, in general, was treated unjustly by corporations, the Patent Office, the Federal courts, and the Federal Communications Commission.

2070. Mehling, Harold. The great time-killer. Cleveland, World Pub. Co. [1962] 352 p.
62–9044     PN1992.3.U5M4
An indictment of commercial television and the practices engaged in by the "networks, by sponsors and their Madison Avenue advertising agencies, and by the hired hands in the Hollywood laugh-laugh mills." Topics discussed include the quiz scandals, sponsors' taboos, advertising agency influence, the excesses of commercials, the rating systems, the blacklisting of TV writers, Federal regulation, and pay-TV. Although his study recognizes some of television's successes and its ability to carry good programs to a vast audience when it chooses, Mehling concentrates on the abuses which he considers have made TV a "vast wasteland." A more temperate appraisal of the world of television is Stan Opotowsky's *TV, the Big Picture,* new, rev. ed. (New York, Collier Books [1962] 285 p. Collier books, AS327X). Supplementing published sources with information gathered in interviews with professionals of all classes, the author explores many of the same areas as Mehling but without pronouncing judgment.

2071. Minow, Newton N. Equal time; the private broadcaster and the public interest. New York, Atheneum, 1964. xvi, 316 p.
64–22102     PN1992.3.U5M5
A collection of speeches made by the author when he was Chairman of the Federal Communications Commission during the Kennedy administration. Emphasizing the responsibility of public service but recognizing that television programs are dependent in a large measure on public approval, Minow states that "nothing in the history of man approaches the potential of television for information and misinformation, for enlightenment and obfuscation, for sheer reach and sheer impact." He points out the failures and successes of the system of mass communication in the United States and notes its importance in the cultivation of cultural values. Harry J. Skornia's *Television and Society: An Inquest and Agenda for Improvement* (New York, McGraw-Hill [1965] 268 p.) analyzes the weaknesses of American television and offers some proposals and recommendations for change.

2072. Roe, Yale. The television dilemma; search for a solution. New York, Hastings House [1962] 184 p. (Communication arts books)
62–19678     HE8698.R6
The author, a network sales executive, considers television to be a commercial enterprise which is justified in making profits from mass-audience shows but which also has a moral responsibility to provide public-service programs that will "better inform, better educate, better strengthen the American people with the knowledge, the perspective, the culture, and the values vital for a society's perseverance." Suggested means for achieving this balance include a self-enforced code of goals and responsibilities, a central foundation to solicit paid sponsorship for educational TV, tax exemptions for business invest-

ments in public-service programs, a daily or weekly period set aside during prime viewing time for simultaneous broadcasts in the public interest on all networks, and a Federal Communications Commission that tempers its regulation with stimulation.

2073. Seehafer, Eugene F., *and* Jack W. Laemmar. Successful television and radio advertising. New York, McGraw-Hill, 1959. 648 p. (McGraw-Hill series in marketing and advertising)
59–9994   HF6146.R3S42

The tremendous growth in the scope and influence of television as an advertising medium between 1951 and 1958 and the consequent losses to radio prompted the authors to update their *Successful Radio and Television Advertising* (no. 4696 in the 1960 *Guide*). The present study analyzes a wide range of advertising forms, methods, techniques, and principles, defines the new roles of television and radio, and seeks to show how both media can be employed by national and local advertisers. After describing the structure of the broadcasting system and typical programs in the United States, the authors concentrate on research to predict or measure the effectiveness of advertising, advertising campaigns, and station management. Arthur Bellaire's *TV Advertising; a Handbook of Modern Practice* (New York, Harper [1959]   292 p.) is compact and practical.

2074. Stanford University. *Institute for Communication Research.* Educational television, the next ten years; a report and summary of major studies on the problems and potential of educational television, conducted under the auspices of the U.S. Office of Education. Stanford, 1962. xi, 375 p. illus.
62–13346   LB1044.7.S8

Includes bibliographies.

Educational television met with much greater success than had been anticipated, and 56 stations were operating in the United States by 1962. In 1960 the U.S. Office of Education commissioned several studies designed to ascertain the plans of educational systems and communities for the use of educational television and to analyze potential problems in such areas as the exchange of teaching materials, finance, program quality, personnel, and engineering. The research was conducted by the National Association of Educational Broadcasters,

the University of Nebraska, and the Institute for Communication Research at Stanford, and the results are reported in this volume, which was edited by Wilbur Schramm. John Walker Powell's *Channels of Learning; the Story of Educational Television* (Washington, Public Affairs Press [1962]   178 p.) recounts the benefactions of the Ford Foundation's Fund for Adult Education, which funneled more than $12 million into educational TV between 1951 and 1961.

2075. Stasheff, Edward, *and* Rudolf Bretz.   The television program: its direction and production.   [3d ed]   New York, Hill & Wang [1962]   335 p.            62–10860   PN1992.5.S8   1962

Full-length treatments of television writing have appeared since the second edition of this work was published (no. 4697 in the 1960 *Guide*), and the authors have therefore eliminated their chapters on writing in order to include "more material, and more advanced material on production theory and practice" in this much revised edition. *Television in the Public Interest* (New York, Hastings House [1961]   192 p. Communication arts books), by A. William Bluem, John F. Cox, and Gene McPherson, provides basic information on the planning, preparation, and performance of public service programs. The production of educational motion-picture films is discussed in Lewis H. Herman's *Educational Films: Writing, Directing, and Producing for Classroom, Television, and Industry* (New York, Crown Publications [1965] 338 p.). In *Television Production; the Creative Techniques and Language of TV Today* (New York, Hastings House [1957]   231 p. Communication arts books), Harry W. McMahan defines more than 2,000 words and phrases used in the television industry.

2076. Zworykin, Vladimir K., E. G. Ramberg, *and* L. E. Flory.   Television in science and industry.   New York, Wiley [1958]   300 p.  illus.
58–6089   TK6680.Z9

A nontechnical introduction to the current and potential uses of closed-circuit television. The authors outline the historical development of closed-circuit TV, describe the apparatus used, and discuss application in such fields as business and industry, banking, transportation, the biological and physical sciences, prison supervision, and marine salvage.

# D. Radio, Television: The Audience

2077. Bogart, Leo.  The age of television; a study of viewing habits and the impact of television on American life.  2d ed., rev. and enl.  New

York, F. Ungar Pub. Co. [1958]   367 p.
58–6788   HE8698.B6   1958
An updated edition of no. 4699 in the 1960 *Guide*.

2078. Schramm, Wilbur L., Jack Lyle, *and* Edwin
      B. Parker. Television in the lives of our
children. With a psychiatrist's comment on the
effects of television, by Lawrence Z. Freedman.
Stanford, Calif., Stanford University Press, 1961.
324 p.                          61–6533  HQ784.T4S35
   "Annotated bibliography": p. 297–317.
   A study based on a three-year research project
involving 6,000 children, 2,000 parents, and 300
educators from 10 communities in the United States
and Canada representing every major television
environment, "including the condition of *no television.*" Among the topics considered were the
changes TV has made in the child's world, the
amount and kind of TV viewed at different ages,
and the chief elements in a child's makeup that
determine what uses he makes of television. The
results suggest that "for most children, under *most*
conditions, *most* television is probably neither particularly harmful nor particularly beneficial"; they use
it primarily to satisfy a need for fantasy which was
previously fulfilled by radio, comic books, movies,
and escape magazines. The authors indicate that
some of the consequences for which TV is blamed
might properly be assigned to careless parents and
conclude with some pointed questions addressed to
broadcasters, teachers, parents, and researchers. Descriptions of 425 programs designed for at-home
viewing by children four to 12 years old form
the substance of *For the Young Viewer; Television
Programming for Children, at the Local Level*
(New York, McGraw-Hill [1962] 181 p.), edited
by Ralph Garry, Frederick B. Rainsberry, and
Charles Winick. Criteria employed in selecting the
programs were "feasibility for a broadcaster" and
"desirability for children," and the descriptions are
based on replies to questionnaires addressed to all
TV stations in the United States.

2079. Steiner, Gary A. The people look at televi-
      sion; a study of audience attitudes. New
York, Knopf, 1963. xvii, 422 p.
                          63–9124  PN1992.5.S83
   At the beginning of 1961 approximately 90 percent of American homes had TV sets, and these
sets were being viewed for an average of five to six
hours each day. To determine the viewer's reaction
to, feelings about, and uses of television, the author
obtained responses from 2,500 adults to a list of
more than 100 questions concerning their viewing
habits. In addition, 300 persons who had kept
detailed diaries of their complete viewing for a
week were interviewed. The results of the surveys
are evaluated and a detailed breakdown of the data
obtained is presented.

# E. Government Regulation

2080. Emery, Walter B. Broadcasting and gov-
      ernment: responsibilities and regulations.
[East Lansing] Michigan State University Press
[1961] xxiv, 482 p.      60–16416  KF2805.E4
   Bibliography: p. 469–473. Includes bibliographical references.
   The Federal Communications Commission and
its control of broadcasting are discussed by a former
member of the FCC legal staff. The development
of a regulatory system for broadcasting is outlined
and the policies and rules which govern various
communications systems in the United States are
reviewed. Current problems of regulation are analyzed and suggestions for clarifying legislation are
made. Extensive supplemental material is appended, including relevant parts of the Communications
Act of 1934 and a documented chronology of the
FCC from 1934 to 1960. *Network Broadcasting*
(Washington, U.S. Govt. Print. Off., 1958. 737 p.
85th Congress, 2d session. House report no. 1297),
a report of the House Committee on Interstate and
Foreign Commerce, incorporates the findings and
recommendations of a study initiated by the FCC
in 1955. The study's purpose was to determine
whether current network structure and practices
foster or impede competition among broadcasting
systems and whether the advent of television and
the resultant changes in the radio industry call for
revision of the chain-broadcasting rules adopted in
1943. In *Broadcast Regulation and Joint Ownership of Media* ([New York] New York University
Press, 1960. 219 p.), Harvey J. Levin traces the
patterns and trends of multimedia ownership and
compares its effects with those of intermedia competition. Levin concludes that the FCC's policy of
giving preference to applicants for a broadcasting
license without holdings in nonbroadcasting media
over those with such holdings, other qualifications
being equal, should be strengthened. The competition induced by this "diversification policy" can,
according to the author, improve the fairness, balance, diversity of coverage, thoroughness, and accuracy of the media output.

2081. Radio and television. [Durham, N.C.] School of Law, Duke University, 1957–58. 2 v. (Law and contemporary problems, v. 22, no. 4-v. 23, no. 1) 58–1782 HE8693.U6R3

The merits and defects of radio and television are analyzed in relation to the structure of the communications industry and its regulation by the Federal Government. Part 1 of this symposium seeks to present a cross section of opinion regarding the need for greater or lesser control and the desirability of change in the present structure, organization, and practices of the industry. The articles in part 2 cover a broader range of issues, including the role of the advertising lawyer in radio and television, labor relations, and authors' and performers' rights. *Freedom and Responsibility in Broadcasting* ([Evanston, Ill.] Northwestern University Press, 1961. 252 p.), edited by John E. Coons, contains tthe proceedings of a conference sponsored by the Northwestern University School of Law in August 1961 "to consider the state of the broadcasting industry and the divergent proposals for its repair."

# F. Mass Communications

2082. Emery, Edwin, Phillip H. Ault, *and* Warren K. Agee. Introduction to mass communications. 2d ed. New York, Dodd, Mead, 1965. 434 p. 65–15617 P90.E4 1965

Bibliography: p. 399–422.

A journalist and two professors of journalism review such media as newspapers, magazines, radio and television, books, and motion pictures, with particular reference to their origins and functions; political, economic, and social importance; and technological growth. Detailed descriptions are included of the organization and operation of each media industry and of such related agencies as news syndicates and advertising and public relations firms. Career opportunities and qualifications are outlined and the state of education for work in mass communications is surveyed. *The Mass Communicators; Public Relations, Public Opinion, and Mass Media* (New York, Harper [1959] 470 p.), by Charles S. Steinberg, defines public relations and its component parts of publicity, promotion, and advertising and describes the principles and techniques employed in using each of the media to inform and create desired climates of public opinion on behalf of social, cultural, educational, and business organizations. *Organizations, Publications, and Directories in the Mass Media of Communications,* 2d ed. (Iowa City, Iowa [1962] 40 p.), compiled by Wilbur Peterson, provides an extensive listing and description of organizations and reference materials, including registers of State press and broadcasting associations.

2083. Klapper, Joseph T. The effects of mass communication. Glencoe, Ill., Free Press [1960] 302 p. (Foundations of communications research, v. 3) 60–14402 P91.K4

Bibliography: p. 258–274.

A survey of the findings of some 270 "published reports of disciplined social research" and "the considered conjectures" of informed persons on the social and psychological effects of mass communications. The author concludes that the mass media are not direct causes of the various social ills for which they are blamed but rather exert only a contributory influence on behavior among such forces as audience predisposition, group membership and norms, and personality. Similar conclusions are reached by Theodore B. Peterson, Jay W. Jensen, and William L. Rivers in *The Mass Media and Modern Society* (New York, Holt, Rinehart & Winston [1965] 259 p.).

2084. Schramm, Wilbur L., *ed.* Mass communications; a book of readings. [2d ed.] Urbana, University of Illinois Press, 1960. 695 p. 60–8343 P90.S37 1960

"Suggestions for further reading": p. 669–678.

An introductory survey covering such diverse topics as the history, growth, structure, economics, functions, government control, ownership, content, audiences, effects, and responsibilities of the mass media. The authors include Llewellyn White, Harold D. Lasswell, Daniel Katz, Elihu Katz, Margaret Mead, Frank Luther Mott, Paul F. Lazarsfeld, Walter Lippmann, Bernard Berelson, Gilbert Seldes, Neil H. Borden, and Leo Bogart. Richard E. Chapin's *Mass Communications; a Statistical Analysis* (East Lansing, Michigan State University Press [1957] 148 p.) brings together the available statistical data for each medium from Government publications, trade journals, and accessible research studies.

2085. Schramm, Wilbur L. Responsibility in mass communication. New York, Harper [1957] xxiii, 391 p. (Series on ethics and economic life) 57–10951 P90.S383

Bibliography: p. 370–374. Bibliographical references included in "Notes" (p. 375–384).

The author argues that increased centralization of the ownership and control of mass communication industries and the resulting reduction in the number of independent outlets for voicing differences of opinion impose new obligations on the communicators for accurate, fair, truthful, and balanced presentations. More than 100 case histories are discussed in an attempt to define the boundary between responsibility and irresponsibility. The author concludes that responsibility for media content is shared by the media themselves, the public, and government. The general public must be alert to media performance and vocal in expressing its needs and judgments, and, to avoid an undesirable increase in government regulations, the media must become patently responsible.

2086. Tamiment Institute. Culture for the millions? Mass media in modern society. Edited by Norman Jacobs; with an introduction by Paul Lazarsfeld. Princeton, N.J., Van Nostrand [1961] xxv, 200 p.          61–8537 P91.T3

Fifteen papers presented at a seminar sponsored jointly by the Tamiment Institute and *Daedalus,* the journal of the American Academy of Arts and Sciences, in 1959. Diverse opinions are expressed concerning the origins, nature, and functions of mass society and its culture, the role which mass media have played in shaping the standards, values, and tastes of this society, and the relationship of art and the artist to the social and cultural order. A final section records the panel discussion which followed the formal symposium. The authors are Paul F. Lazarsfeld, Edward Shils, Leo Lowenthal, Hannah Arendt, Ernest van den Haag, Oscar Handlin, Leo Rosten, Frank Stanton, James J. Sweeney, Randall Jarrell, Arthur Berger, James Baldwin, Stanley E. Hyman, H. Stuart Hughes, and Arthur M. Schlesinger, Jr.

# XVII

# Science and Technology

SECTION A indicates that the scientific community, frequently accused of self-containment in recent decades, is concerning itself with the society within which and for which it is presumably working. Section B reflects continuing need for histories of individual sciences. As Section C demonstrates, biographical studies of scientists tend to be more appealing to authors than general historical analyses. Invention is seldom now a matter of the work of one lone scientist, and the books on the subject must rely largely on earlier periods for their subject matter. Some of the major issues which arise and are reflected throughout the selections in this chapter are the following: What kinds of scientific research should be performed? Who should determine national priorities? What is the proper role between government and science? To what uses should research be put? Should the scientist assume responsibility for the results of his research? Are science and democracy compatible?

## A. General Works

2087. American men of science; a biographical directory. 10th ed. Edited by Jaques Cattell. Tempe, Ariz., Jaques Cattell Press, 1960–62. 5 v.      6–7326   Q141.A47

An updated edition of no. 4712 in the 1960 *Guide.* Entries for the physical and biological sciences are combined under one alphabet in the first four volumes. The fifth volume covers the social and behavioral sciences. Approximately 120,000 biographies are featured, representing an increase of about one-third over the ninth edition.

2088. Bates, Ralph S. Scientific societies in the United States. 3d ed. Cambridge, Mass., M.I.T. Press [1965] 326 p.      65–8325   Q11.A1B3 1965
Bibliography: p. [245]–293.

This revised edition of no. 4713 in the 1960 *Guide* includes new chapters on the atomic age and the space age, an updated and enlarged bibliography, and a chronology of science in the United States. *Industrial Research Laboratories of the United States,* 12th ed. (Washington, Bowker Associates, 1965. 746 p.), edited by William W. Buchanan, and *Scientific and Technical Societies of the United States and Canada,* 7th ed. (Washington, National Academy of Sciences—National Research Council, 1961. 413, 54 p. National Research Council. Publication 900) are revisions of no. 4720 and 4728, respectively, in the 1960 *Guide.*

2089. Brady, Robert A. Organization, automation, and society; the scientific revolution in industry. Berkeley, University of California Press,

1961. xiv, 481 p. (Publications of the Institute of Business and Economic Research, University of California) 61–7535 HD31.B723

Bibliographical references included in "Notes" (p. [425]–466).

An analysis of methodologies for applying advances in science and engineering to the productive resources of the economy. In *Who Needs People?* (Washington, R. B. Luce [1963] 114 p.), Robert E. Cubbedge discusses the possibility that the machine will one day transcend man.

2090. Bulletin of the Atomic Scientists. The atomic age; scientists in national and world affairs. Articles from the Bulletin of the Atomic Scientists, 1945–1962. Edited and with introductions by Morton Grodzins and Eugene Rabinowitch. New York, Basic Books, 1963. xviii, 616 p.
63–21583 D842.B78

A collection of 65 articles reflecting the scientist's involvement in politics since World War II. The *Bulletin* was founded in 1945 in an effort to awaken the public to the problems created by atomic power. The material in the present work is grouped into four sections: "Failure," dealing with the unsuccessful efforts to achieve international control over nuclear weapons after the war; "Peril," reflecting the consequent dangers and the efforts toward arms control and disarmament; "Fear," describing the effects of the problem at the national level; and "Hope," giving examples of international cooperation in science and technology and presenting some bases for improving society through peaceful applications of nuclear power.

2091. Columbia University. *Seminar on Technology and Social Change.* Technology and social change. Edited for the Columbia University Seminar on Technology and Social Change, by Eli Ginzberg. New York, Columbia University Press, 1964. 158 p. illus. 64–17158 HC106.5.C6244

Six representatives from science, industry, and education inquire into the nature and causes of technological change and the problems of social adaptation that it precipitates. *The impact of Science on Technology* (New York, Columbia University Press, 1965. 221 p.), edited by Aaron W. Warner, Dean Morse, and Alfred S. Eichner, is a record of the Columbia University Seminar on Technology and Social Change during its second year of existence.

2092. Elbers, Gerald W., *and* Paul Duncan, *eds.* The scientific revolution: challenge and promise. Published in cooperation with the President's Committee on Scientists and Engineers.

Washington, Public Affairs Press [1959] 280 p.
59–6977 Q127.U6E4

Papers presented at a conference at Yale University in 1958 with the purpose of clarifying the basic issues of the scientific challenge presented by the launching of the first Soviet sputniks. Among the topics discussed are the necessity of an adequate science program, the role of science in society, the effects of public indifference, and the urgency of raising educational standards.

2093. Fortune. Great American scientists; America's rise to the forefront of world science, by the editors of Fortune. Englewood Cliffs, N.J., Prentice-Hall [1961] 144 p.
61–6215 Q127.U6F6

First published in *Fortune* in 1960, these articles trace recent developments in physics, chemistry, astronomy, and biology by describing the major achievements of 40 living scientists. Scientific concepts and discoveries are discussed in terms readily understandable to the general reader. *The Scientific Life* (New York, Coward-McCann [1962] 308 p.), by Theodore Berland, presents the major accomplishments of nine prominent American scientists, with emphasis on the personal characteristics and philosophies of the men and their habits of work. In *This High Man: The Life of Robert H. Goddard* (New York, Farrar, Straus [1963] 430 p.), Milton Lehman discusses the career of a pioneer in astronautics.

2094. Gilman, William. Science U.S.A. New York, Viking Press [1965] 499 p.
65–23995 Q127.U6G47

A discussion of the economic, social, and political aspects of science and technology in the United States. Part 1, "State of the Establishment," is concerned with the power wielded by leaders in various fields of science and the financing of scientific research. Part 2, "State of the Art," covers significant research projects in specific fields. The author attempts to maintain an objective approach throughout his analysis of the problems confronting scientists but also argues that the scientific profession must be conscious of the fact that it has definite responsibilities to the society as a whole.

2095. Jaffe, Bernard. Men of science in America: The story of American science told through the lives and achievements of twenty outstanding men from earliest colonial times to the present day. Rev. ed. New York, Simon & Schuster, 1958. 715 p. illus. 58–59443 Q127.U6J27 1958

"Sources and reference material": p. 654–670.

This revised edition of no. 4721 in the 1960 *Guide*

includes a new chapter on Enrico Fermi and an updated discussion of the future of science in America.

2096. National Advanced-Technology Management Conference, *Seattle, 1962.* Science, technology, and management; proceedings. Edited by Fremont E. Kast and James E. Rosenzweig. New York, McGraw-Hill [1963] 368 p. illus.
63–11852 TA168.N3 1962
Bibliography: p. 350–358.

The record of a conference at which some 900 representatives of various fields of science and technology discussed the development and practical application of modern systems management. The participants included Edward Teller, Warren G. Magnuson, and Wernher von Braun.

2097. Reingold, Nathan, *ed.* Science in nineteenth-century America, a documentary history. New York, Hill & Wang [1964] 339 p. illus. (American century series) 64–24830 Q127.U6R4

Documents and commentary on the careers of several key figures in American science, together with a discussion of the growth of formal scientific institutions and other facets of scientific activity during the century in which present American attitudes toward science were largely molded. The author notes that Americans lagged considerably behind their European counterparts during the 19th century and that the early tendency to emphasize applied research at the expense of basic research is a persisting weakness of American science today. Dirk Jan Struik's *Yankee Science in the Making* (New York, Collier Books [1962] 544 p. Collier books, BS50) is an updated edition of no. 4730 in the 1960 *Guide.*

2098. Resources for the Future. Science and resources: prospects and implications of tech-

nological advance; essays by George W. Beadle [and others] Edited by Henry Jarrett. Baltimore, Johns Hopkins Press [1959] 250 p. illus.
59–14232 Q171.R43

Papers presented at the Resources for the Future Forum held in Washington, D.C. in 1959. Emphasis is placed on the close link between technology and natural resources and on the impetus given to resource technology by modern science. Six areas in which new developments are of great significance to resources and their utilization are discussed: genetics, weather modification, minerals exploration, chemical technology, nuclear energy, and space exploration. Current research in each area is reviewed by a leading natural scientist, and authorities in such other fields as business, economics, and agriculture analyze the impact of science on resources from their particular perspectives.

2099. Technology and social change [by] Francis R. Allen [and others] New York, Appleton-Century-Crofts [1957] 529 p. illus. (Appleton-Century-Crofts sociology series)
57–5944 HM221.T4
Bibliographies at end of each chapter.

PARTIAL CONTENTS.— The meaning of technology, by William F. Ogburn.— Obstacles to innovation, by Meyer F. Nimkoff.— The automobile, by Francis R. Allen.— Radio and television, by Delbert C. Miller.— Atomic energy, by Hornell Hart.— Influence of technology on industry, by Delbert C. Miller.— Technology and the family, by Meyer F. Nimkoff. —Influence of technology on war, by Francis R. Allen.— Technology and the practice of medicine, by Francis R. Allen.— The hypothesis of cultural lag: a present-day view, by Hornell Hart.— Predicting future trends, by Hornell Hart.— Human adjustment and the atom, by Hornell Hart.

A college textbook.

# B. Particular Sciences

2100. Botanical Society of America. Fifty years of botany; golden jubilee volume of the Botanical Society of America, edited by William Campbell Steere. New York, McGraw-Hill, 1958. 638 p. illus. 57–14685 QK81.B697
Bibliographies at end of each chapter.

Specialists from various branches of botanical science discuss major developments in the field from the early years of the 20th century through the 1950's.

2101. Caidin, Martin. The moon: new world for men. Indianapolis, Bobbs-Merrill [1963] 406 p. illus. 63–14583 TL799.M6C295

A discussion of Project Apollo and the advantages of space exploration in general. The author notes the benefits accruing to American industry and labor from the program, the potential discoveries, and, in particular, the military advantages associated with the control of space. Edwin Diamond, in *The Rise and Fall of the Space Age* (Garden City, N.Y.,

Doubleday, 1964. 158 p.), laments the nationalistic, uncooperative character of the space race.

2102. Clark, Paul F. Pioneer microbiologists of America. Madison, University of Wisconsin Press, 1961. 369 p. illus. 60–11441 QR21.C55
Bibliographical references included in "Notes" (p. 333–355).
A historical study of American microbiology from the late 17th century, when Cotton Mather became interested in inoculation against smallpox, up to World War I. Emphasis is placed on medical science, and both cause (micro-organisms) and effect (disease) are discussed. The dependence of early American microbiology on European research is noted. Clark includes various narrative episodes, among them a vivid description of the yellow-fever epidemic that claimed the lives of a tenth of the population of Philadelphia in 1793.

2103. Cohen, I. Bernard. Franklin and Newton; an inquiry into speculative Newtonian experimental science and Franklin's work in electricity as an example thereof. Philadelphia, American Philosophical Society, 1956. xxvi, 657 p. illus. (Memoirs of the American Philosophical Society, v. 43) 56–13224 QC7.C65
Bibliography: p. 603–650.
A study designed "to illuminate the nature of scientific thought by considering the interaction between the creative scientist and his scientific environment." The author relates the personalities of Franklin and Newton to their scientific thought and reputations, describes aspects of Newton's scientific accomplishments, analyzes the most important Newtonian works that were studied by experimental scientists in the 18th century, traces the formation of Franklin's concepts in electrical science against the background of Newtonian science, and discusses the reception, application, and eventual influence of those concepts.

2104. Groves, Leslie R. Now it can be told; the story of the Manhattan project. New York,

Harper [1962] xv, 464 p. illus.
61–10208 QC773.A1G7
The story of the development of the atomic bomb, as told by the general who was in command of the Manhattan Project. In addition to describing the work at Los Alamos. Groves discusses the elaborate intelligence operation conducted to determine exactly how far the Germans had progressed in their nuclear program, the selection and training of the air units that dropped the bombs at Hiroshima and Nagasaki, and the creation of the Atomic Energy Commission to place peacetime atomic research under civilian control. Robert Jungk's *Brighter Than a Thousand Suns; a Personal History of the Atomic Scientists* (New York, Harcourt, Brace [1958] 369 p.), translated by James Cleugh, deals with the same subject but places greater emphasis on the lives of the scientists involved.

2105. Strauss, Anselm L., *and* Lee Rainwater. The professional scientist; a study of American chemists, by Anselm L. Strauss and Lee Rainwater, with Marc J. Swartz and Barbara G. Berger and with a contribution by W. Lloyd Warner. Foreword by Albert L. Elder. Chicago, Aldine Pub. Co. [1962] 282 p. illus. (Social research studies in contemporary life) 62–13512 QD39.5.S8
Bibliographical footnotes.
A study of the attitudes of chemists and others toward the profession, the role of the American Chemical Society, and related matters, based on a survey of members of the society conducted by Social Research, Inc. This introspective professional analysis covers such matters as the various types of specialties within the field of chemistry, the potential careers available to college chemistry majors, and the views of laymen concerning chemists. *The Rise of the American Chemistry Profession, 1850–1900* (Gainesville, University of Florida Press, 1964. 76 p. University of Florida monographs. Social sciences, no. 23), by Edward H. Beardsley, traces the development of American chemistry from a state of almost complete dependence on Europe to one of near self-sufficiency.

## C. Individual Scientists

2106. [Agassiz] Lurie, Edward. Louis Agassiz: a life in science. [Chicago] University of Chicago Press [1960] xiv, 449 p. illus.
59–11623 QH31.A2L8
Bibliographical references included in "Notes" (p. 391–419). "Essay on sources": p. 421–430.

An interpretation, based on the examination of extensive manuscript materials, of the personal life and scientific endeavors of Louis Agassiz (1807–1873), who "taught men to appreciate specialized knowledge and impressed society with the need to support science and advance the professional status of its practitioners." Agassiz' effectiveness in attracting public support and money for his projects, especially for the Museum of Comparative Zoology at Harvard, was without precedent. His refusal to accept Darwin's theory of evolution, however, although popular with laymen, alienated much of the scientific community. *Correspondence Between Spencer Fullerton Baird and Louis Agassiz — Two Pioneer American Naturalists* (Washington, Smithsonian Institution, 1963. 237 p. Smithsonian Institution. Publication 4515), collected and edited by Elmer C. Herber, contains the 297 known letters between these two 19th-century scientists.

2107. [Audubon] Ford, Alice E. John James Audubon. Norman, University of Oklahoma Press [1964] xiv, 488 p. illus.
64–20757   QL31.A9F6
Bibliography: p. 451–469.

Careful research into previously inaccessible private collections of documents, records, and letters forms the basis of this factual biography of John James Audubon (1785–1851), an immigrant of French descent. Audubon's attempts at business were numerous and unsuccessful, as he devoted himself increasingly to being a painter and naturalist. In 1826 he went to England to exhibit and publish his drawings of birds. *The Birds of America,* with engravings by Robert Havell, was published in elephant folio size between 1827 and 1838. William Macgillivray's collaboration on *Ornithological Biography* (1831–39. 5 v.) provided a scientific treatise to accompany the engravings. *Louis Agassiz Fuertes: His Life Briefly Told and His Correspondence* (New York, Oxford University Press, 1956. 317 p.), edited by Mary F. Boynton, is devoted to the 20th-century painter of birds whose works are regarded by many as second only to Audubon's in quality.

2108. [Gray] Dupree, A. Hunter. Asa Gray, 1810–1888. Cambridge, Belknap Press of Harvard University Press, 1959. x, 505 p. illus.
59–12967   QK31.G8D8
"Note on the sources": p. [423]–425. Bibliographical references included in "Notes" (p. [427]–476).

A biography detailing the scientific contributions of Asa Gray to the descriptive botany of North America, to plant classification, and to the field of plant geography. Gray was appointed Fisher Professor of Natural History at Harvard in 1842 and founded the department of botany at that institution. His articles and textbooks popularized the study of botany and provided a history of botanical development, and his *Manual of the Botany of the Northern United States* (1848) remains a standard reference for identifying native plant life. Gray's analysis of the similarity between Japanese and North American flora reinforced the theory of evolution, and his debates on Darwinism with his colleague Louis Agassiz captured nationwide attention. Dupree has also edited a new edition of Gray's *Darwiniana: Essays and Reviews Pertaining to Darwinism* (Cambridge, Belknap Press of Harvard University Press, 1963. 327 p. The John Harvard library). *John Clayton, Pioneer of American Botany* (Chapel Hill, University of North Carolina [1963] 236 p.), by Edmund Berkeley and Dorothy S. Berkeley, is an account of the life and contributions of this 18th-century botanist.

2109. [Maury] Williams, Frances L. Matthew Fontaine Maury, scientist of the sea. New Brunswick, Rutgers University Press [1963] xx, 720 p. illus.
63–10564   GC30.M4W5
Bibliography: p. 659–692. "Bibliography of the published works of Matthew Fontaine Maury": p. 693–710.

A detailed account of the life of Matthew Fontaine Maury (1806–1873), the first superintendent of the U.S. Naval Observatory and Hydrographical Office. Under Maury's direction the Navy conducted scientific studies of the currents, tides, depths, salinity, and temperatures of the sea. His publications of wind and current charts provided data for safer and shorter sailing routes, and *The Physical Geography of the Sea,* which he published in 1855, is considered to be the first textbook of modern oceanography. At the outbreak of the Civil War Maury resigned his commission to work on Confederate naval defenses, and he later served as a Southern agent in England. Ultimately he became known as a crusader for international scientific cooperation.

2110. [Rittenhouse] Hindle, Brooke. David Rittenhouse. Princeton, N.J., Princeton University Press, 1964. 394 p. illus.
63–23407   QB36.R4H5
"Bibliographical note": p. 367–375.

A chronological study of the life of David Rittenhouse (1732–1796), who was not only a scientist but also a craftsman, patriot, and politician. Rittenhouse worked as a clockmaker and instrument-maker, constructed orreries for the College of Philadelphia and the College of New Jersey, and established a reputation as an astronomer on the basis of his precise observation of the transit of Venus in 1769. A member of the American Philosophical Society, he was highly respected within the scientific and intellectual communities of the 18th century. *Knight of the White Eagle, Sir Benjamin Thompson, Count Rumford of Woburn, Mass.* (New York, T. Y. Crowell Co. [1965, °1964] 301 p.), by W. J. Sparrow, is an account of the multi-faceted career of a man who was scientist, inventor, Revolutionary War turncoat, financial wizard, philanthropist-reformer, and Bavarian general.

2111. [Van Hise] Vance, Maurice M. Charles Richard Van Hise; scientist progressive. Madison State Historical Society of Wisconsin, 1960. 246 p.          60–63390  LD6125  1903.V3
    Bibliography: p. 223–237.
    Van Hise (1857–1918) pursued a long and distinguished career at the University of Wisconsin. His activities spanned the fields of geology, conservation, and education. Having participated in the U.S. Geological Survey at Lake Superior while still a graduate student at Wisconsin, he subsequently received the first academic doctoral degree awarded by the university and accepted a professorship in the geology department. He was an authority on pre-Cambrian rock formations and published *A Treatise on Metamorphism* (1904), a work noted for its comprehensiveness and its quantative approach to the study of geological problems. He also attended the White House Conservation Conference in 1908, served on the National Conservation Commission, and wrote *The Conservation of Natural Resources in the United States* (1901). As president of the University of Wisconsin, Van Hise was a vigorous supporter of Gov. Robert La Follette's progressive program that soon became known as the "Wisconsin idea."

2112. [Wiley] Anderson, Oscar E. The health of a nation; Harvey W. Wiley and the fight for pure food. [Chicago] Published for the University of Cincinnati by the University of Chicago Press [1958] 332 p. illus.          58–11945  TX518.W5A5
    Bibliographical references included in "Notes" (p. 283–321).

During his 29 years as chief chemist of the U.S. Department of Agriculture, Wiley (1844–1930) played a vital role in the long fight for Federal food and drug legislation which culminated in the passage of the Pure Food and Drug Act of 1906. Before accepting a position in Washington, Wiley was professor of chemistry at Purdue University, where he established a reputation as a sugar chemist through his work on sorghum. Under his leadership the Department of Agriculture instituted new techniques for the analysis of foods and their adulterants. He published a study entitled *Foods and Their Adulteration* in 1907 and continued to campaign for enforcement of the Pure Food and Drug Act after his retirement from Government service in 1912.

2113. [Wilson] Cantwell, Robert. Alexander Wilson: naturalist and pioneer, a biography. With decorations by Robert Ball. Philadelphia, Lippincott [1961] 318 p. illus.
          61–12246  QL31.W7C3
    "Sources": p. 306–310.
    Originally a weaver by trade, Wilson (1766–1813) became one of America's great ornithologists. After emigrating from Scotland he taught school in Pennsylvania, where he met the naturalist William Bartram. Bartram encourged Wilson's interest in studying and drawing birds, and as his skill increased Wilson wrote to a friend that he was beginning his work of drawing "all the finest birds of America." While working as assistant editor of Abraham Rees' *Cyclopaedia* he devoted much of his time to his ornithological research, a project that culminated in the publication of *The American Ornithology* (1808–14. 9 v.). *Mark Catesby: The Colonial Audubon* (Urbana, University of Illinois Press, 1961. 137 p.) by George F. Frick and Raymond P. Stearns, is a scholarly account of the 18th-century pioneer American naturalist.

## D. Science and Government

2114. Dupree, A. Hunter. Science in the Federal Government, a history of policies and activities to 1940. Cambridge, Mass., Belknap Press of Harvard University Press, 1957. 460 p. illus.
          57–5484  Q127.U6D78
Includes bibliographical references.
A history of the first century and a half of Ameri-

can science and the science policies of the Federal Government. The author notes that Government promotion of applied science began as early as 1789. The Lewis and Clark expedition is cited as an example of Government-sponsored scientific exploratation. The scope of applied science was considerably broadened during the Civil War, and after 1865 a scientific establishment arose within the Government. In *Science and State Government* (Chapel Hill [Published for the Institute for Research in Social Science by] the University of North Carolina Press [1959] 161 p.), Frederic N. Cleaveland presents studies of the science policies of six representative States. *Science and the Nation; Policy and Politics* (Englewood Cliffs, N.J., Prentice-Hall [1962] 181 p. A Spectrum book, S–25), by Joseph Stefan Dupré and Sanford A. Lakoff, stresses recent developments in Government sponsorship of science.

2115. Kaplan, Norman, *ed.* Science and society. Chicago, Rand McNally [1965] 615 p. (Rand McNally sociology series)

65–26582    Q125.K3

Bibliography: p. 581–595.

A collection of essays by journalists, scientists, economists, sociologists, and historians on the interrelations of science and society. A recurrent theme of the contributors is that science as an activity is not separate from society as a whole. The average citizen exerts an influence upon scientific research, directly or indirectly, and likewise benefits from the results of much research. Kaplan has selected these essays with a view to placing science in a historical context. He emphasizes the fact that an understanding of scientific subject matter alone is insufficient in defining the role of science in society.

2116. Kidd, Charles V. American universities and Federal research. Foreword by Paul E. Klopsteg. Cambridge, Mass., Belknap Press, 1959. 272 p. illus.    59–12974    Q127.U6K5

Bibliographical references included in "Notes" (p. 251–267).

The author's central thesis is that "large-scale federal financing of research has set in motion irreversible forces that are affecting the nature of universities, altering their capacity to teach, changing their financial status, modifying the character of parts of the federal administrative structure, establishing new political relations, and changing the way research itself is organized." He predicts that large amounts of Federal money will probably continue to be made available for research in universities and considers that this situation should be accepted without being "immobilized by staring fixedly into the eye of the danger of federal control." The extent and purposes of recent Federal support for scientific research are outlined in *The National Science Foundation: A General Review of Its First 15 Years* (Washington, U.S. Govt. Print. Off., 1965. 286 p.), a report prepared by the Legislative Reference Service of the Library of Congress.

2117. Price, Don K. The scientific estate. Cambridge, Mass., Belknap Press of Harvard University Press, 1965. 323 p.

65–22047    Q127.U6P73

Bibliographical references included in "Notes" (p. 279–305).

The dean of the Graduate School of Public Administration at Harvard discusses the role of the scientist - turned - administrator, notes that abridgments of liberties have occurred when science is supported by the Government, and advocates the separation of politics from science.

2118. Wiesner, Jerome B. Where science and politics meet. New York, McGraw-Hill [1965] 302 p.    65–16157    Q127.U6W5

A collection of speeches and papers by the science adviser to Presidents Kennedy and Johnson. Topics covered include the organization of scientific research, educational needs, and arms-limitation measures. Science policy is also discussed in *Scientists and National Policy-Making* (New York, Columbia University Press, 1964. 307 p.), edited by Robert Gilpin and Christopher Wright, and *The Politics of American Science, 1939 to the Present* (Chicago, Rand McNally [1965] 287 p. Rand McNally history series), edited by James L. Penick and others.

# E. Invention

2119. De Camp, Lyon Sprague. The heroic age of American invention. Garden City, N.Y., Doubleday, 1961. 290 p. illus.

61–7646    T212.D4

"Notes": p. [264]–271. Bibliography: p. [272]–276.

Invention flourishes, according to the author, under conditions which combine the requisite materials and technical skills, a society that is receptive to a given innovation, and a patent law that offers the inventor sufficient protection. De Camp considers that such conditions prevailed in the United States between 1836, when the Patent Office was reorganized, and 1917, before the profession of inventing became highly organized and subject to corporate control. The lives and work of such men as Samuel F. B. Morse, Ottmar Mergenthaler, and Alexander Graham Bell are discussed against this background, and the role their inventions played in the development of modern patent law is reviewed.

2120. Universities-National Bureau Committee for Economic Research. The rate and direction of inventive activity: economic and social factors; a conference of the Universities-National Bureau Committee for Economic Research and the Committee on Economic Growth of the Social Science Research Council. Princeton, Princeton University Press, 1962. 635 p. illus. (National Bureau of Economic Research. Special conference series, 13)

62–7044 HD69.175U5

Bibliographical footnotes.

PARTIAL CONTENTS.—Inventive activity: problems of definition and measurement.—The economics of research and development.—Major product and process innovations, 1920 to 1950.—Intellect and motive in scientific inventors: implications for supply.—The link between science and invention: the case of the transistor.—Inventive activity: Government controls and the legal environment.

# F. Engineering

2121. Ackerman, Edward A. *and* George O. G. Löf. Technology in American water development, by Edward A. Ackerman and George O. G. Löf, with the assistance of Conrad Seipp. Baltimore, Published for Resources for the Future by Johns Hopkins Press [1959]

59–10066 TD345.A25

Bibliographical footnotes. "General references": p. 667–672.

PARTIAL CONTENTS.— The geographical nature of water occurrence.— The general nature of water use in the United States.— Techniques and technical events affecting water development and its administration: introduction. — Technical improvements promoting the scale economies: six cases.— Technical activities in progress and related to water use: introduction.—Expanding the physical range of recovery: future use of sea water and saline inland waters. — The organization of operational management.

2122. Calhoun, Daniel H. The American civil engineer: origins and conflict. Cambridge, Technology Press, Massachusetts Institute of Technology; distributed by Harvard University Press, 1960. xiv, 295 p. illus. 59–15742 TA23.C3

"Bibliographical note": p. [219]–237.

The history of American civil engineering is traced to the early decades of the 19th century, when the majority of engineers were employed in the construction and maintenance of canals and railroads. The author notes that, although most of the corporate and governmental sponsors of these projects recognized the value of engineering knowledge, the engineer had to adjust to the organization before he could get his job done. The development of the profession is outlined and various crises are described, including the panic of 1837, which left many engineers unemployed, and investigations of bankrupt internal improvement projects by various State legislatures which led to attacks on the profession itself. The role of Army engineers in railroad construction, surveying, and river and harbor improvement is discussed. In *The Story of Engineering* (Garden City, N.Y., Doubleday, 1960. 528 p. Anchor books, A214), James K. Finch traces engineering in Western civilization from the building of the pyramids to the 20th century.

2123. Condit, Carl W. American building art: the nineteenth century. New York, Oxford University Press, 1960. xvii, 371 p. illus.

59–11752 TA23.C56

"Notes": p 275–[344]. Bibliography: p. 345–351.

2124. Condit, Carl W. American building art: the twentieth century. New York, Oxford University Press, 1961. xviii, 427 p. illus.

61–8369 TA23.C57

"Notes": p. 307–391. Bibliography: p. 393–405.

A history of building techniques and the development of a structural basis for modern construction. The first volume covers wood framing, wooden bridge trusses, iron bridge trusses, suspension bridges, iron arch bridges, railway trainsheds, and concrete construction, and the second deals with steel frames, metropolitan railway terminals, steel truss and girder bridges, suspension bridges, concrete building construction, concrete bridges, concrete dams and waterway control, and the metropolitan parkway. The author notes that most of the essential practices of contemporary building were devised before 1900.

# XVIII

# Medicine and Public Health

THE LITERATURE on medicine in the United States reflects not only phenomenal gains in medical knowledge and skills but also growing concern over the shortage of doctors and nurses, the increasing cost of medical services, the safety and effectiveness of prescription drugs, and the desirability of governmental participation in medical insurance.

Various aspects of the history of medicine are brought out in the works listed in Section A. Histories of such influential institutions as the Rockefeller Foundation and the American Medical Association are included. Section B presents biographies of notable men and women in medicine, and Section C covers mental health in the United States and care for the mentally ill. Occupational health, dentistry, and pathology are the subjects of studies in Section D. The remaining sections include works that shed light on the controversies in such areas as the adequacy of medical care, problems of medical education, programs for public health, and increases in the costs that must be borne by the patient.

## A. Medicine in General

2125. Burrow, James G. AMA: voice of American medicine. [Baltimore] Johns Hopkins Press, 1963. 430 p.          63–15347  R15.B9
"Bibliographical essay": p. 414–416. Bibliographical footnotes.

This extensively documented history traces the professional, social, and political activities of the American Medical Association from its modest beginnings in 1848 to its position of significant national power in the mid-20th century. The AMA's continuing opposition to "socialized medicine," in particular to compulsory health insurance plans, is traced, as are the various programs which the association has undertaken to improve the quality of medical care, support stringent Federal food and drug laws, and provide alternatives to compulsory health insurance. In *The Troubled Calling; Crisis in the Medical Establishment* (New York, Macmillan [1965] 398 p.), Selig Greenberg criticizes private enterprise on the ground that "the doctor's need to get paid inevitably conflicts at times with the patient's need to get well."

2126. Corner, George W. A history of the Rockefeller Institute, 1901–1953; origins and growth. New York, Rockefeller Institute Press, 1964 [1965] 635 p. illus.

64–24275  R862.R64C6

"Major documentary sources": p. [597]–598. Bibliographical references included in "Notes on the text" (p. [547]–573).

A detailed history of the institute established by John D. Rockefeller in New York City in 1901 to encourage research in the medical sciences. The institute was organized to sponsor basic research in areas of medicine where the achievement of practical results was uncertain and is independent of existing hospitals or universities. In its first year of existence, the institute achieved fame by financing a study that related widespread infant sickness and mortality to a high bacterial content in milk sold in open cans to tenement dwellers in New York City. The institute has since expanded its activities, assembled a large and distinguished staff, and achieved a preeminent position in the United States and the world.

2127. Lasagna, Louis. The doctors' dilemmas. New York, Harper [1962] 306 p.
                                    62–7906  R114.L34
"Suggested reading": p. 292–295.

A popular survey of problems encountered in the practice of medicine today. The author discusses such diverse topics as superstitions, quackery, medical education, medical organizations, the drug industry, congressional investigations, medical jurisprudence, and the mass media's view of medicine. Various controversial issues are discussed in *The Crisis in American Medicine* (New York, Harper [1961] 149 p.), edited by Marion K. Sanders, a collection of 11 short articles, and *Challenges to Contemporary Medicine* (New York, Columbia University Press, 1956. 120 p. Bampton lectures in America, no. 6), by Alan Gregg.

2128. Roueché, Berton. The incurable wound, and further narratives of medical detection. Boston, Little, Brown [1958, °1957] 177 p.
                                    58–5653  RC66.R63
Six true accounts, all of which appeared originally in *The New Yorker*. The subjects include the discovery of rabies in North American bats, amnesia, accidental poisonings by overexposure to chemicals used in a drycleaning plant and through a child's mistaking aspirin for candy, the reference service provided by the Poison Control Center in New York City, and an unusual reaction to cortisone. The author has collected 11 additional accounts in *A Man Named Hoffman, and Other Narratives of Medical Detection* (Boston, Little, Brown [1965] 276 p.).

2129. Shryock, Richard H. Medicine and society in America, 1660–1860. [New York] New York University Press, 1960. 182 p. (Anson G. Phelps lectureship on early American history)
                                    60–6417  R148.S45
Bibliographical footnotes.

Four lectures portraying medicine in its social setting from the early colonial period to the Civil War. The author notes that in the Colonies the doctor served as physician, surgeon, and pharmacist, in contrast to the division of labor practiced in England and Scotland. The founding of hospitals and medical schools and the beginning of medical licensing and publication are traced, and the fact that relatively little attention was given to medical research in the Colonies is noted. Public health and epidemiology are discussed, and a general review is presented of the period from 1820 to 1860, when quackery was rampant and plans for improving medical education ended in frustration. *History of American Medicine, a Symposium* (New York, MD Publications [°1959] 181 p. MD international symposia, no. 5), edited by Félix Martí Ibáñez, is a collection of 14 essays, originally published in the *International Record of Medicine*, on various aspects of medicine in the United States.

2130. Shryock, Richard H. National Tuberculosis Association, 1904–1954; a study of the voluntary health movement in the United States. New York, National Tuberculosis Association, 1957. 342 p. illus. (National Tuberculosis Association. Historical series, no. 8)  43–1648  RC306.N386 no. 8
Bibliography: p. [313]–317.

A history of the National Tuberculosis Association's campaigns for the prevention and cure of tuberculosis. The association brought together physicians, laymen, and welfare workers to fight the disease as a social as well as a medical problem. The Christmas Seal program and other activities designed to arouse public concern over tuberculosis are reviewed. The work of several other voluntary health societies is discussed in *The Gentle Legions* (Garden City, N.Y., Doubleday, 1961. 335 p.), by Richard Carter.

2131. Young, James H. The toadstool millionaires; a social history of patent medicines in America before Federal regulation. Princeton, N.J., Princeton University Press, 1961. 282 p. illus.
                                    61–7428  RM671.A1Y6
"A Note on the Sources": p. 263–269.

An account of the escapades of the most successful promoters of patent medicines in the United States up to 1906, when the Pure Food and Drug Act was passed by Congress. Although a great number of these promoters were outright charlatans, some sincerely believed that their potions were beneficial to mankind. The author notes that huge fortunes were amassed through the sale of products that seldom had any therapeutic value and were often extremely harmful. *The Golden Age of Quackery* (New York, Macmillan, 1959. 302 p.), by Stewart H. Holbrook, is a more popular treatment of the same subject.

## B. Physicians and Surgeons

2132. Blochman, Lawrence G. Doctor Squibb; the life and times of a rugged idealist. New York, Simon & Schuster, 1958. 371 p. illus.
58–11805   R154.S73B55

A biography based on Edward Robinson Squibb's private journals, which cover more than half a century. Squibb, who is regarded by Blochman as "the grandfather of the Pure Food and Drug Act," was unable to secure nationwide regulation of drugs in his lifetime but did write a pure food and drug act which became law in the States of New York and New Jersey around 1880. A year before the *Journal* of the American Medical Association was founded, Squibb established a periodical entitled *An Ephemeris* which described and evaluated new medicines, apparatus, and techniques. A pioneer in anesthesia, he invented a method for the manufacture of pure ether of uniform potency, studied effective dosage, and perfected the techniques of administration through the use of a mask instead of an inhaler.

2133. Bluemel, Elinor. Florence Sabin; Colorado woman of the century. Boulder, University of Colorado Press [1959]   238 p.   illus.
59–1235   R154.S115B55

Bibliography: p. 223–232.

Anatomist Florence Rena Sabin (1871–1953) is renowned for her cellular studies at the Rockefeller Institute for Medical Research in New York and for her struggle to improve the health laws of Colorado. She was a professor at the Johns Hopkins University School of Medicine, where she taught the freshman course in anatomy from 1902 to 1925, and was the first woman to be elected to life membership in the National Academy of Sciences. In *Doctor Kate, Angel on Snowshoes* (New York, Rinehart [1956]   339 p.) Adele Comandini relates the life story of Kate Pelham Newcomb, an outstanding and warmhearted general practitioner in the north woods of Wisconsin.

2134. Cohn, Isidore, *and* Hermann B. Deutsch. Rudolph Matas; a biography of one of the great pioneers in surgery. Garden City, N.Y., Doubleday, 1960. 431 p. illus.
60–9471   R154.M29875C6

A review of the personal and professional life of the man who is regarded as the father of modern vascular surgery, presented in the context of a century of surgical progress in the United States. Considerable attention is also given to Lafcadio Hearn, who was one of the surgeon's closest friends. An appendix lists the degrees, honorary awards, foreign decorations, and official positions held by Matas. Paul B. Magnuson's autobiography, *Ring the Night Bell* (Boston, Little, Brown [1960] 376 p.), edited by Finley Peter Dunne, stresses the author's interest in curative surgery and rehabilitation for bone and joint disorders.

2135. Davis, Audrey W. Dr. Kelly of Hopkins: surgeon, scientist, Christian. Baltimore, Johns Hopkins Press [1959]   242 p.   illus.
59–14235   R154.K27D3

A portrait of Howard Atwood Kelly, one of the four surgeons who inaugurated the Johns Hopkins Hospital and helped establish the School of Medicine at the Johns Hopkins University. Kelly's *Operative Gynecology* (1898) became the definitive text in the field and also introduced the type of vivid illustration that was to revolutionize medical publishing. Among Kelly's numerous contributions to gynecology, urology, and general surgery were his introduction of the open-air method of cystoscopy, his invention of the perineal and ovariotomy cushions, and his development of successful procedures for operation through the abdomen. Kelly's writings, numbering some 575 items in all, cover a variety of medical fields. Samuel J. Crowe's *Halsted of Johns Hopkins: The Man and His Men* (Springfield, Ill., C. C. Thomas [1957]   247 p.), is an intimate view of William Stewart Halsted and the Halsted era in surgery. Edward H. Richardson, a surgical specialist in gynecology and urology associated with the Johns Hopkins University School of Medicine for 52 years, relates his experiences and observations in *A Doctor Remembers* (New York, Vantage Press [1959]   252 p.).

2136. Dunlop, Richard. Doctors of the American frontier. Garden City, N.Y., Doubleday, 1965. 228 p. illus.   65–13979   R152.D85

Bibliography: p. [210]–221.

The frontier doctor's cures were sometimes blunt and crude, sometimes ingenious. The author reviews the practice of medicine on the frontier and notes that great medical achievements were sometimes made under primitive conditions. Ephraim McDowell, for example, braved a lynch mob in Kentucky to perform the first ovariectomy in medical history, and at a Great Lakes military outpost William Beaumont studied human digestion through a shotgun wound in a patient's stomach. The lives of three pioneers of medicine in the United States are portrayed in *Daniel Drake, 1785–1852, Pioneer Physician of the Midwest* (Philadelphia, University of Pennsylvania Press [1961] 425 p.), by Emmet F. Horine; *David Hosack, Citizen of New York* (Philadelphia, American Philosophical Society, 1964. 246 p. Memoirs of the American Philosophical Society, v. 62), by Christine C. Robbins; and *John Morgan, Continental Doctor* (Philadelphia, University of Pennsylvania Press [1965] 301 p.), by Whitfield J. Bell.

2137. King, George S. Doctor on a bicycle. New York, Rinehart [1958] 275 p.

    58–11521 R154.K32A3

The autobiography of a general practitioner. King notes the incredible progress made in medicine and surgery during his 59 years of medical service in New York but voices strong opposition to the present trend toward specialization. He believes that in general practice the physician is oriented toward an overall, complete diagnosis, but that the specialist is frequently "like the mariner who, looking through his glass at the horizon, sees only the field upon which he focuses, while the rest of the sky escapes him." Two other autobiographies which relate typical medical experiences of general practitioners are *One Hundred Dollars & a Horse; the Reminiscences of a Country Doctor* (New York, Morrow, 1965 [c1963] 272 p.), by James Gordon Bryson, and *The Last Stitch* (Philadelphia, Lippincott [1956] 250 p.), by William L. Crosthwait and Ernest G. Fischer.

2138. Rackemann, Francis M. The inquisitive physician: the life and times of George Richards Minot, A. B., M. D., D. SC. Cambridge, Harvard University Press, 1956. 288 p.

    56–6521 R154.M645R3

"References": p. 277–282.

The author, a specialist in allergy at the Massachusetts General Hospital and Minot's cousin and intimate friend, recounts the physician's distinguished career. Minot's life was saved as a result of the discovery of insulin, and he in turn saved countless other lives through his discovery, with William P. Murphy and George H. Whipple, of the liver treatment for pernicious anemia, an achievement that earned them the 1934 Nobel Prize in Physiology and Medicine. In *George Hoyt Whipple and His Friends; the Life-Story of a Nobel Prize Pathologist* (Philadelphia, Lippincott [1963] 335 p.), George W. Corner emphasizes Whipple's research on the liver, blood, iron, and proteins.

2139. Rowntree, Leonard G. Amid masters of twentieth century medicine; a panorama of persons and pictures. With an introduction by George F. Lull. Springfield, Ill., C. C. Thomas [1958] 684 p. illus.

    58–8432 R154.R77A3 1958

"Sources of bibliographical notes": p. xii-xvi.

As teacher, research worker, clinician, and medical administrator, the author was closely associated with outstanding leaders of the medical profession during one of the most important periods in its history. His autobiography provides intimate portraits of these men and their work. Rowntree studied at the Johns Hopkins Medical School and subsequently served as chief of medicine of the Mayo Foundation and medical director of Selective Service during World War II. He was a cofounder of the School of Medicine of the University of Miami. Walter C. Alvarez, internist, authority on gastroenterology, and writer of a syndicated health column, tells the story of his life and the remarkable developments he witnessed in medicine in *Incurable Physician, an Autobiography* (Englewood Cliffs, N.J., Prentice-Hall [1963] 274 p.).

# C. Psychiatry

2140. Dain, Norman. Concepts of insanity in the United States, 1789–1865. New Brunswick, N.J., Rutgers University Press [1964] xv, 304 p.

    63–16302 RC443.D3

"Notes": p. [211]–261. "Selected bibliography": p. [263]–291.

Beginning in 1789, when Benjamin Rush petitioned for humanitarian reforms in the treatment of the mentally ill at the Pennsylvania Hospital, the author traces the development of an increasingly sympathetic, therapeutic approach to mental illness. Psychiatry became a recognized specialty in medicine, but by the 1850's an emphasis on heredity as a cause of insanity had resulted in a gradual shift from optimism to pessimism concerning curability. Institutional neglect of the insane again became widespread, and only after World War II was there a significant renewal of concern for victims of mental illness. The mental health movement and its leaders are discussed in *Mental Health in the United States; a Fifty-Year History* (Cambridge, Published for the Commonwealth Fund by Harvard University Press, 1961. 146 p.), by Nina A. Ridenour, and *Pioneers in Mental Health* (New York, Dodd, Mead, 1961. 242 p.), by Robin McKown.

2141. Gorman, Mike. Every other bed. Cleveland, World [1956] 318 p.
56–5310   RC443.G6
"Acknowledgements": p. 311–314.
Noting that one-half of the hospital beds in the United States are in mental hospitals, the author reviews "the parlous state of psychiatric research and training" and contends that treatment of the mentally ill "still smacks of superstition, negativism, niggardliness, and unimaginativeness." *The Patient and the Mental Hospital; Contributions of Research in the Science of Social Behavior* (Glencoe, Ill., Free Press [1957] 658 p.), edited by Milton Greenblatt, Daniel J. Levinson, and Richard H. Williams, is a collection of papers and discussions from the Conference on Socio-Environmental Aspects of Patient Treatment in Mental Hospitals. In *The Community Mental Health Center: An Analysis of Existing Models* (Washington, 1964. 219 p.), the Joint Information Service of the American Psychiatric Association and the National Association for Mental

Health presents 11 models of successful community mental health programs.

2142. Rolo, Charles J., *ed.* Psychiatry in American life. Boston, Little, Brown [1963] 246 p.                63–13977   RC458.R65
"Readings in psychiatry": p. [241]–243.
Essays on diverse aspects of psychiatry. The theory and practice of psychiatry are reviewed and the relationship of psychiatry to society and culture is analyzed. *Americans View Their Mental Health* (New York, Basic Books [1960] 444 p. Joint Commission on Mental Illness and Health. Monograph series, no. 4), by Gerald Gurin, Joseph Veroff, and Sheila Feld, is based on a nationwide series of personal interviews.

2143. Winslow, Walker. The Menninger story. Garden City, N.Y., Doubleday, 1956. 350 p. illus.                56–6531   R154.M57W5
Bibliography: p. [338]–339.
Two generations of the Menninger family are portrayed. Charles Frederick Menninger began his medical practice in Topeka, Kans., in 1889. His sons Karl and William also became doctors and Karl chose to specialize in psychiatry. The three Menningers and their associates developed a number of important medical institutions in Topeka, including a psychiatric clinic, a sanitarium, and a school for mentally ill children. The Menninger Foundation for Psychiatric Education and Research was established in 1941 and the Menninger School of Psychiatry in 1945. Together, these institutions have had a worldwide influence on the teaching and practice of psychiatry. Karl A. Menninger's writings are compiled in *A Psychiatrist's World, Selected Papers* (New York, Viking Press, 1959. 2 v.), edited by Bernard H. Hall.

# D. Other Specialties

2144. Long, Esmond R. A history of American pathology. Springfield, Ill., C. C. Thomas [1962] 460 p. illus.                62–10161   RB15.L6
Bibliographical references included in "Notes": p. 393–427.
A survey of the evolution of the discipline concerned with the fundamental nature of disease. The growth of pathology in the United States and Canada is traced from the 16th century to the post-World War II era, with emphasis on the contribu-

tions of various outstanding researchers and teachers in the field.

2145. McCluggage, Robert W. A history of the American Dental Association; a century of health service. Chicago, American Dental Association, 1959. 520 p. illus. 59–14780   RK1.A543M3
Bibliography: p. 442–507.
A comprehensive review of the activities of the American Dental Association since its founding in

1859. The work also serves as a general history of the evolution of the dental profession, covering such additional aspects as the development of local societies and journals, progress in dental education, and the formation of national organizations.

2146. Selleck, Henry B. Occupational health in America. In collaboration with Alfred H. Whittaker. Detroit, Wayne State University Press, 1962. 523 p. illus.        61–16777  RC963.S42
    Bibliographical references included in "Notes": p. 469–486.
    The author traces the history of the Industrial

Medical Association and provides a comprehensive account of the development in the United States of the medical specialty that "deals with the restoration and conservation of health in relation to work, the working environment, and maximum efficiency." The activities of physicians in this specialty are reviewed in *The Physician in Industry* (New York, Blakiston Division, McGraw-Hill [1961] 290 p.), by William P. Shepard. In *Mental Health in Industry* (New York, Blakiston Division, McGraw-Hill, 1958. 262 p.), Alan A. McLean and Graham C. Taylor examine the role of psychiatry in industrial medicine.

# E. Hospitals and Nursing

2147. Chesney, Alan M. The Johns Hopkins Hospital and the Johns Hopkins University School of Medicine; a chronicle. Baltimore, Johns Hopkins Press, 1943–63. 3 v. illus.
        SG44—2  R747.J62C5
    Bibliographical footnotes.
    CONTENTS.—I. Early years, 1867–1893.—II. 1893–1905.—III. 1905–1914.
    The first volume of Chesney's history is no. 4845 in the 1960 *Guide*. The second volume covers the 12-year period from the opening of the School of Medicine to the resignation of Dr. William Osler as professor of medicine in the Johns Hopkins University and as physician in chief to the Johns Hopkins Hospital. The third volume continues the narrative to the hospital's 25th anniversary.

2148. Faxon, Nathaniel W. The Massachusetts General Hospital, 1935–1955. Cambridge, Mass., Harvard University Press, 1959. 490 p. illus.
        59–12968  RA982.B7M515
    Bibliographical references included in "Notes": p. 467–472.
    A continuation of the historical survey begun by Frederic A. Washburn in *The Massachusetts General Hospital; Its Development, 1900–1935* (no. 4853 in the 1960 *Guide*). Faxon reviews the activities of the hospital under his own directorship and, for the period 1949–55, under that of his successor Dean A. Clark. Accomplishments during the period covered include the addition of eight new departments, construction of five major new buildings, establishment of a blood bank in 1942, reorganization of the Nursing School, and extensive expansion of research facilities. Particularly noteworthy are the hospital's successful handling of the Coconut Grove disaster in 1942 and the polio epi-

demic of 1955. In *New England Hospitals, 1790–1833* (Ann Arbor, University of Michigan Press [1957] 282 p.), Leonard K. Eaton defines the tradition of New England hospitals as one of "creative conservatism." He notes that New Englanders were first to accept the principle of State responsibility for care of the indigent insane.

2149. Georgopoulos, Basil S., *and* Floyd C. Mann. The community general hospital. New York, Macmillan [1962] 693 p.
        62–13440  RA963.G4
    Bibliographical references at the end of each chapter.
    An examination of the structure and functions of the short-stay community general hospital, based on a study of 12 Michigan hospitals made by the Institute for Social Research at the University of Michigan. Among the topics discussed are leadership and supervision, intraorganizational strain, communication, and organizational effectiveness. *The Community and Its Hospitals; a Comparative Analysis* ([Syracuse, N.Y.] Syracuse University Press, 1963. 234 p.), by Ivan Belknap and John G. Steinle, stresses the importance of relating the hospital's functions to the leadership and welfare services of the community. Esther L. Brown's *Newer Dimensions of Patient Care* (New York, Russell Sage Foundation, 1965. 159, 194, 163 p.) focuses on selected psychosocial and cultural aspects of patient care.

2150. Hughes, Everett C., Helen M. Hughes, *and* Irwin Deutscher. Twenty thousand nurses tell their story; a report on studies of nursing functions sponsored by the American Nurses' Association. With a foreword by Agnes Ohlson.

Philadelphia, Lippincott [1958] 280 p. illus.
58–11876   RT82.H78
Bibliography: p. 278–280.

The findings of a five-year study of nursing functions are reported and prognoses concerning the future of nursing are presented. The authors note that the best-educated nurses are being employed at desks and filing cabinets and in administrative positions while "it is left to practical nurses and aides to supply the human warmth and comfort that so many laymen think of when they think of ladies in white caps and uniforms." *The Story of Nursing,* new ed. (Boston, Little, Brown [1965] 244 p.), by Bertha S. Dodge, touches upon the highlights of the heritage of American nursing. Edna Yost's *American Women of Nursing* (Philadelphia, Lippincott [1965] 197 p.) is a revised edition of no. 4854 in the 1960 *Guide.*

2151.  Klarman, Herbert E.  Hospital care in New York City; the roles of voluntary and municipal hospitals. New York, Columbia University Press, 1963. 573 p.   62–19901   RA982.N5A88

Bibliographical notes: p. [529]–556.

A statistical analysis of hospital service in New York City and the various influences shaping it. The author's intent was "to assess in each hospital system the adequacy of available resources to perform its share of the total task. The respective roles of the voluntary and municipal hospital systems were to be ascertained by comparing the characteristics of patients served as well as trends in the volume of services rendered. Appraisal of resources was to include the availability of money and of real resources, such as key personnel and physical plant, and also their organization and coordination." In *Hospital City* (New York, Crown [1957] 282 p.), John Starr relates the history of New York's Bellevue Hospital, "the most famous hospital in the world, a breeder of great men and women, of great ideas and greater legends." Milton L. Zisowitz' *One Patient at a Time; a Medical Center at Work* (New York, Random House [1961] 287 p.) describes the day-to-day activities of the New York Hospital-Cornell Medical Center in training doctors and nurses and in caring for the sick.

# F. Medical Education

2152.  Becker, Howard S., *and others.* Boys in white; student culture in medical school. [Chicago] University of Chicago Press [1961] 456 p. illus.   61–16622   R737.B4

The results of a study conducted at the University of Kansas Medical School to determine the nonacademic effects of medical school on future doctors. The curriculum is dealt with only as it influences the attitudes of students toward their studies and their future profession. The authors note that during the four years of medical school the students adopt a series of perspectives which they use in orienting themselves to their work and in defining their long-range goals. Among the students' concerns are determining the relevant material for study and dealing with the faculty members who examine and grade them. The distinction between the problems of the medical student and those of the professional physician is stressed. *The Student-Physician; Introductory Studies in the Sociology of Medical Education* (Cambridge, Published for the Commonwealth Fund by Harvard University Press, 1957. 360 p.), edited by Robert K. Merton, George G. Reader, and Patricia L. Kendall, is a set of reports on studies conducted by the Bureau of Applied Social Research of Columbia University.

2153.  Corner, George W.  Two centuries of medicine; a history of the School of Medicine, University of Pennsylvania. Philadelphia, Lippincott [1965] 363 p. illus.
65–11358   R747.P42   1965
"Notes and references": p. 324–346.

The growth of the University of Pennsylvania School of Medicine is traced from 1765, the year of its founding, to 1965. In addition to detailing many events in the school's history, the author describes the contributions of the numerous individuals who shaped its development. In *A History of Colonial Medical Education: In the Province of New York, With Its Subsequent Development, 1767–1830* (Springfield, Ill., C. C. Thomas [1962] 286 p.), Byron P. Stookey relates the early history of the King's College Medical School, which later became the Columbia University College of Physicians and Surgeons. The influence of German, Austrian, and Swiss universities on American medical education is recounted by Thomas N. Bonner in *American Doctors and German Universities; a Chapter in International Intellectual Relations, 1870–1914* (Lincoln, University of Nebraska Press [1963] 210 p.).

2154. Evans, Lester J. The crisis in medical education. Ann Arbor, University of Michigan Press [1964] 101 p. illus. ([Ann Arbor science library]) 64–17436 R740.E78
Bibliographical references included in "Notes" (p. [99]–101).

The author states that bureaucracy and specialization have prevented medical schools from including the latest concepts of health care in their curricula and urges the universities, as institutions with objectives broader than mere professional training, to take the lead in shaping medical education. The necessity of team effort in curing illness and the importance of combining all patient care and clinical activities into an integrated whole are stressed. Evans proposes that medical education include the humanities and social sciences as well as the traditional medical disciplines. *Preparation for Medical Education, a Restudy* (New York, Blakiston Division, McGraw-Hill [1961] 404 p.) is the report of a survey prepared for the Association of American Medical Colleges to determine progress in medical education since the publication of *Preparation for Education in the Liberal Arts College,* which was mentioned in the annotation for no. 4861 in the 1960 *Guide.*

# G. Public Health

2155. Dunning, James M. Principles of dental public health. Cambridge, Harvard University Press, 1962. 543 p. illus.
62–7096 RK52.D8
"References": p. 507–530.

A textbook intended for the student and the general practitioner of dentistry. The author includes an introduction to the field of public health as a whole, in addition to detailed material on the development of dental public health programs.

2156. Freeman, Ruth B., *and* Edward M. Holmes. Administration of public health services. Philadelphia, Saunders, 1960. 507 p.
60–7455 RA393.F7
Includes bibliography.

The authors note that since the turn of the century, when the major public health concerns were basic sanitation and control of communicable diseases, this field has become a complex integral function of government with expenditures reaching billions of dollars annually. Services have been expanded to include the prevention and cure of major chronic diseases, mental health problems, drug addiction and alcoholism, control of environmental pollution, medical care, and rehabilitation. Broad support is also being given to basic and applied research. Greater managerial and administrative skills are consequently being demanded of public health officers, and the authors attempt to provide guidance in the application of basic principles of management to the problems encountered in the administration of public health services. *Administration of Community Health Services* (Chicago, International City Managers' Association, 1961. 560 p. The International City Managers' Association. Municipal management series), edited by Eugene A. Confrey, is a comprehensive training and reference manual for administrators at the city and county level and for public health workers.

2157. Johns Hopkins University Conference on Drugs in Our Society, *1963.* Drugs in our society, based on a conference sponsored by the Johns Hopkins University. Edited by Paul Talalay, assisted by Jane H. Murnaghan. Contributors: Owsei Temkin [and others] Baltimore, Johns Hopkins Press [1964] 311 p.
64–16306 RS99.J6 1963c
Bibliographical footnotes at the end of each chapter.

The 21 papers presented at this conference by experts in various fields form the main body of this work. Among the chief issues discussed are drug safety and effectiveness, the role of government, the support of research to develop new drugs, the education of physicians and the public in the intelligent use of drugs, the cost of medicine, and the legal and ethical considerations of drug use. *The Impact of the Food and Drug Administration on Our Society* (New York, MD Publications, 1956. 144 p.), edited by Henry Welch and Félix Martí Ibáñez, documents the many contributions the FDA has made. In *The Therapeutic Nightmare* (Boston, Houghton Mifflin, 1965. 590 p.), Morton Mintz states that the testing of drugs is frequently inadequate or fraudulent and pleads for a stronger Food and Drug Administration. In *The Real Voice* (New York, Macmillan [1964] 245 p.) Richard Harris reports on the investigation of the drug industry by Senator Estes Kefauver's Subcommittee on Antitrust and Monopoly, the public support which aided his cause, and the regulatory legislation which resulted.

2158. Knutson, Andie L. The individual, society, and health behavior. New York, Russell Sage Foundation, 1965. 533 p. illus.

65–21057 RA418.K55

Bibliographical footnotes at the end of each chapter.

An analysis of the health behavior of the individual, based on the concepts of social psychology. Emphasis is placed on the role of communication in motivating people to acquire attitudes beneficial to society's general welfare as well as their own.

2159. Lerner, Monroe, and Odin W. Anderson. Health progress in the United States, 1900–1960; a report of Health Information Foundation. Chicago, University of Chicago Press [1963] xv, 354 p. illus.                 63–18854 RA445.L45

Bibliographical footnotes.

An analysis of the causes, extent, and consequences of improved public health. The authors note that although the mortality rate has dropped sharply since 1900, chiefly because of the control of communicable diseases, the morbidity rate has tended to rise with increasing longevity. Accurate assessment of current health levels requires that both rates be taken into consideration. Lerner and Anderson find degenerative diseases and accidents to be the major recent causes of death, partly owing to the growth of urbanization and industrialization. They also conclude that, in spite of improved health conditions, chronic and acute illnesses are widespread. Stating that "good health is now considered by many as a 'right' flowing naturally out of the fact of common human association," the authors observe that people are disturbed by relatively minor manifestations of ill health and aspire to a degree of physiological well-being that is perhaps impossible of attainment.

2160. Lewis, Howard R. With every breath you take; the poisons of air pollution, how they are injuring our health, and what we must do about them. New York, Crown [1965] xvii, 322 p. illus.                 64–23821 RA576.L5

Bibliographical references included in "Notes" (p. 287–313).

A public health consultant views air pollution not simply as a nuisance but as a significant and increasingly menacing health problem. More than 43 million people in over 300 cities are reported to be living under a major air pollution hazard. Lewis advocates programs involving community action groups, stepped-up research, increased Federal participation, and stringent regulations. The hazards of another source of pollution are explored in *Radiation, Genes, and Man* (New York, Holt [1959] 205 p.), by Bruce Wallace and Theodo-sius G. Dobzhansky. The Committee on Environmental Health Problems of the U.S. Public Health Service, in its *Report to the Surgeon General* ([Washington] U.S. Dept. of Health, Education, and Welfare, Public Health Service, 1962. 288 p. U.S. Public Health Service. Publication no. 908), reviews various environmental health problems and proposes long-range objectives.

2161. Means, Richard K. A history of health education in the United States. Philadelphia, Lea & Febiger, 1962. 412 p. illus. (Health education, physical education, and recreation series)

62–17823 RA440.3.U5M4

Bibliographical notes and suggested readings at the end of each chapter.

Health education is presented as a distinct discipline and a significant professional field. Beginning with its origins in the late 18th century, the author traces its uneven but persistent growth, highlighting the work of pioneers in the field, the role of health organizations, child health conferences, the development of a literature, and the impact of research. Personal interviews with key figures in the development of health education, as well as published sources, are the basis for the study.

2162. Osborn, Barbara M. Introduction to community health. Boston, Allyn & Bacon, 1964. xiv, 327 p. illus.                 64–12894 RA427.O8

Bibliographies at the end of nearly every chapter.

An introductory college text covering such topics as the history of public health programs, health facilities, the functions of public and private organizations, current American and world health problems, the role of the behavioral sciences in community health, and the education of the public in good health practices. The author defines community health as "the organized effort of all agencies working toward the promotion of the physical, emotional, and social health of people" and notes that underlying this effort are a concept of health as a primary asset of the individual and consequently of society as a whole and an assumption that the highest levels of health can best be achieved through community programs. A panoramic view of the expanding public health field is presented in *Health and the Community; Readings in the Philosophy and Sciences of Public Health* (New York, Free Press [1965] 877 p.), edited by Alfred H. Katz and Jean S. Felton.

2163. Rosenberg, Charles E. The cholera years; the United States in 1832, 1849, and 1866. [Chicago] University of Chicago Press [1962] 257 p.                 62–18121 RC131.A3R6

"Annotated bibliography": p. 235–252.

Compared to malaria and tuberculosis, cholera claimed few victims in the 19th century, but it was nonetheless "novel and terrifying, a crisis demanding response in every area of American life and thought." Between 1832 and 1866, both piety and abstract rationalism were replaced by a more critical temper in medicine, and sanitary reform instead of morality was recommended to ensure good health in growing cities. The cholera epidemics were highly instrumental in overcoming government indifference in the field of public health. Social, political, and economic aspects of public health are treated in John B. Blake's *Public Health in the Town of Boston, 1630–1822* (Cambridge, Harvard University Press, 1959. 278 p. Harvard historical studies, v. 72). *Charles V. Chapin and the Public Health Movement* (Cambridge, Harvard University Press, 1962. 310 p.), by James H. Cassedy, traces the contributions of a pioneer in sanitation.

2164. U.S. *President's Commission on Heart Disease, Cancer and Stroke.* A national program to conquer heart disease, cancer and stroke; report to the President. [Washington] 1964–65. 2 v. illus. 65–60405 RC682.U49
Bibliography: v. 1, p. 102–113.
The conclusions reached by a Commission appointed to recommend steps for prevention and treatment of the three diseases responsible for more than 70 percent of the deaths in the United States today. In volume 1, the summary report, the problems and available resources are examined, and 35 specific recommendations are made. A national network of diagnostic and medical care, added support for medical education and research, and a buttressing of State and local programs of control are considered prime objectives. Volume 2 contains the full reports of the eight subcommittees of the Commission, as well as additional scientific and technical documentation.

# H. Medical Economics

2165. Carter, Richard. The doctor business. Garden City, N.Y., Doubleday, 1958. 283 p.
59–5577 R728.C32
A criticism of the economics of medical service. The author claims that the fee system is often arbitrary and unfair, that organized medicine opposes reforms because it fears public control, and that the public has tended to acquiesce, without protest, to its desires. Fee-paying relations between patient and physician are uneconomical according to Carter, who suggests improved insurance plans as one remedy. Describing the individual physician as generally responsible and dedicated, he places primary blame on the professional organization with "its largely voiceless rank and file."

2166. Follmann, Joseph F. Medical care and health insurance; a study in social progress. Homewood, Ill., R. D. Irwin, 1963. 503 p. (The Irwin series in risk and insurance)
63–10321 HG9396.F6
Bibliographical footnotes.
A discussion of methods for financing medical assistance in the United States and in other countries. Emphasis is placed on recent developments in private health insurance, including coverage of the aged, farm residents, the temporarily unemployed, the mentally ill, and those needing dental care. *Blue Cross and Private Health Insurance Coverage of Older Americans* (Washington, U.S. Govt. Print.

Off., 1964. 153 p.), a report by the Subcommittee on Health of the Elderly to the Senate Special Committee on Aging, concludes that private health insurance is unable to provide adequate hospital coverage for most older Americans.

2167. Somers, Herman M., and Anne R. Somers. Doctors, patients, and health insurance; the organization and financing of medical care. Washington, Brookings Institution [1961] xix, 576 p. illus. 61–13235 RA410.S6
Bibliographical footnotes.
According to the authors, personal medical care not only has failed to keep pace with advances in medical science and technology, but is also being transformed "from an individual profession into a highly organized and institutionalized industry." Historical perspectives and current data are provided on the structure, distribution, and financing of health services, with emphasis on private health insurance. *The Economics of American Medicine* (New York, Macmillan [1964] 508 p.), by Seymour E. Harris, considers the complex financial aspects of medicine and health in the United States.

2168. Weisbrod, Burton A. Economics of public health; measuring the economic impact of diseases. Philadelphia, University of Pennsylvania Press [1961] 127 p. illus.
61–5545 RA410.W4 1961

Bibliography: p. [121]–124.

The techniques of economics are applied to an analysis of the costs and benefits of public health in an attempt to provide meaningful and scientifically defensible standards for use in evaluating benefits accruing from various public health programs. Such standards involve the measurement of the economic losses to society from a disease, and the data obtained can be used in "making a priority listing of health projects according to anticipated economic benefits." After developing his standards, Weisbrod applies them in a quantitative evaluation of programs to eliminate cancer, tuberculosis, and poliomyelitis. The use of this type of procedure, the author hopes, would provide legislators, public health administrators, and hospital planners with a basis for resource-allocation decisions.

# XIX

# Entertainment

THE OVERLAPPING subject matter of books within the area defined as "Entertainment" and the relationship between this area and others in this *Supplement* are discussed in the prefatory notes to Chapter XIX, Entertainment, and Chapter XX, Sports and Recreation, in the 1960 *Guide.* Relative to the 1960 *Guide,* this chapter of the *Supplement* contains proportionately fewer works on the American stage and more on motion pictures. The number of bibliographies of notable personalities in both fields is conspicuously smaller here. The *Supplement,* like the 1960 *Guide,* has a subsection on radio and television, but in both bibliographies the major works on the subject are more suitable for inclusion in Chapter XVI, Communications, than the chapter on entertainment. An analysis of the personalities and the script materials of 16 comedians who achieved eminence on television is the only entry in the radio and television portion of this chapter. The section devoted to general works, consisting of entries on comedians, tent Chautauqua, stars of stage, screen, and television, and the relationship between the performing arts and their critics, is almost equal in size to the comparable section in the 1960 *Guide.*

# A. General Works

2169. Cahn, William. The laugh makers; a pictorial history of American comedians. New York, Putnam [1957] 192 p.

57–14516 PN2285.C2

Although jokes have changed, basic joke situations in the United States have persisted since Thomas Wignell, the first major American comedian, entertained George Washington. This brief popular account traces the history of comedy from 1787 to 1957. Almost all the important comedians in the history of show business, including radio, motion pictures, and television, are mentioned. The emphasis is on the 20th century, and among the personalities receiving the most attention are George M. Cohan, Will Rogers, W. C. Fields, Charlie Chaplin, Ed Wynn, Groucho Marx, and Jimmie Durante.

2170. Harrison, Harry P. Culture under canvas; the story of tent Chautauqua, by Harry P. Harrison as told to Karl Detzer. New York, Hastings House [°1958] 287 p.

57–12799 LC6301.C5H3

As the 19-year-old school principal in Wiota, Iowa, the author was called upon to manage the town's winter lyceum course. Four years later, in 1901, he was attending Cornell College when Keith Vawter, of Vawter's Standard Lecture Bureau, visited the campus in search of summertime agents. Harrison went to work for him, and in that same year Vawter bought a third interest in the well-established Redpath Lyceum Bureau. Closing his own agency, Vawter assumed the position of western manager for Redpath. Harrison became a permanent employee, rising eventually to the position of treasurer and general manager. Here he surveys the whole traveling lyceum and Chautauqua movement, blending historical settings with anecdotes about himself and famous performers. In *The Chautauqua Movement; an Episode in the Continuing American Revolution* ([New York] State University of New York, 1961. 108 p.), Joseph E. Gould discusses "the beginnings of the most significant venture in popular education in the United States."

2171. Ross, Lillian, *and* Helen Ross. The player; a profile of an art. With photographs by Lillian Ross. New York, Simon & Schuster, 1962. 459 p.

62–16986 PN2285.R6

Biographical sketches of 55 stars of stage, screen, and television. Most of the players were born in the United States; all are well known for their performances in this country. The information was elicited through informal interviews, conducted between 1958 and 1962. Twenty-one of the sketches originally appeared in *The New Yorker.* Each piece traces the subject's life and career up to the time of the interview and is accompanied by a photograph. The interviewees include Melvyn Douglas, Hume Cronyn, Henry Fonda, Sidney Poitier, Katherine Cornell, Andy Griffith, Paul Newman, Rod Steiger, Dana Andrews, Kim Hunter, Fredric March, Angela Lansbury, and Robert Preston.

2172. Seldes, Gilbert V. The public arts. New York, Simon & Schuster, 1956. 303 p.

56–7488 PN1992.5.S38

In *The Seven Lively Arts* (1924), Seldes praised the gaiety and vigor of popular entertainments in the United States; in *The Great Audience* (1950), no. 4895 in the 1960 *Guide,* he warned that the very same entertainments could be used as mass media to keep Americans complacent and immature. *The Public Arts* is based on the author's new theory, in which the lively arts and the mass media are viewed as two aspects of a single phenomenon. He stresses the desirability of an audience enticed by the entertainer, instructed by the reporter-critic, and unified and shared by both. The problems involved in achieving this ideal are analyzed in detail by the author. In *The Performing Arts; Problems and Prospects* (New York, McGraw-Hill [1965] 258 p.), a Rockefeller Brothers Fund report on the future of the theater, the dance, and music, the problems of development and support on national, State, and local levels are examined.

# B. The American Stage

## Bi. HISTORY

2173. Gassner, John. Theatre at the crossroads; plays and playwrights of the mid-century American stage. New York, Holt, Rinehart & Winston [1960] 327 p. 60–9272 PN1851.G3
Bibliographical note: p. 313–314.

An assessment of the New York theater in the 1950's. The first section consists of general essays on tragedy, social drama, the state of the theater, and such influential playwrights as Eugene O'Neill, Tennessee Williams, and Jean Giraudoux. The second section is a selective "chronicle" of the theater, on Broadway and off, for this 10-year period. The author discusses both American and European plays, examining them as literature and noting the degree of effectiveness with which they were presented on the stage.

2174. Hewitt, Barnard. Theatre U.S.A., 1668 to 1957. New York, McGraw-Hill, 1959. 528 p. 58–11982 PN2221.H4
Bibliography: p. 506–513.

Through extensive use of firsthand accounts, the author conveys the contemporary atmosphere of the American theater at various periods and relates players and plays to their era. The documentation provided for the period through 1800 consists of playbills, newspaper advertisements, letters, and journals; critical reviews constitute the primary source of information for the years after 1800. A connecting commentary gives background information, notes innovations and trends, and provides current perspectives for earlier enthusiasms. A concluding section, "The Selections and Their Authors," identifies each quotation and supplies a short biographical note for each writer.

2175. Oppenheimer, George, ed. The passionate playgoer; a personal scrapbook. New York, Viking Press, 1958. 623 p. 58–12377 PN2266.O6

This collection of affectionate sketches is intended to convey that part of the theater's essence that eludes systematically researched surveys. The author presents selections that have made the greatest impression on him in his 40 years of involvement with the stage. Here, among others, are essays by Dorothy Parker on audiences, Robert Sherwood on the Lunts, John Dos Passos on Isadora Duncan, Tallulah Bankhead on touring shows, and Elia

Kazan on *A Streetcar Named Desire*. The se[c]tions are arranged loosely under general topics, an index provides access to individual items. [?]*American Drama Since 1918* [Rev. ed.] (N[ew] York, G. Braziller, 1957. 344 p.), an updated [edi]tion of a work mentioned in the annotation for 4900 in the 1960 *Guide,* contains essays by Jos[eph] Wood Krutch.

2176. Rankin, Hugh F. The theater in colon[ial] America. Chapel Hill, University of No[rth] Carolina Press [1965] 239 p.
65–16333 PN2237.[?]
Bibliographical references included in "Not[es]" (p. 203–223).

The colonial theater had obvious limitations. [It] was derivative in nature; it produced practically [no] playwrights; and its stylized acting ignored [the] more natural innovations introduced to the Engl[ish] stage by David Garrick. But it did bring a liv[ely] and vigorous entertainment from the Old World [to] the New and demonstrated that a tiny colon[ial] capital, such as Williamsburg or Annapolis, co[uld] sustain one of the important ornaments of civili[zed] life, a repertory theater." The first local comp[any] was formed in 1752 by William and Lewis Halla[m.] Disbanded in 1758 after a tour of the West Ind[ies,] it was reorganized in that same year by Da[vid] Douglass. In 1775, after the Continental Congr[ess] adopted a resolution designed to discourage, amo[ng] assorted frivolities, "exhibition of shews, plays, a[nd] other expensive diversions," Douglass took the co[m]pany to Jamaica to await the restoration of "tr[an]quility." Rankin's account of these early beginni[ngs] of the theater in the United States is based [on] extensive research in the fragmentary records t[hat] have been preserved.

2177. Taubman, Hyman Howard. The maki[ng] of the American theatre. New York, Cow[ard] McCann [1965] 385 p. 65–20410 PN2221.T[?]

Although this broad survey covers the theater [in] the United States from the earliest colonial touri[ng] companies to the present, its main emphasis is [on] the 20th century. The author, a former dra[ma] critic for the *New York Times,* examines not o[nly] the Broadway stage but also the experimental thea[ter] off Broadway and the revival of local repert[ory] theater across the country. *A Pictorial History [of] the American Theatre; 100 Years: 1860–1960* (P[?]

adelphia, Chilton Co., Book Division [1960] 384 p.), by Daniel C. Blum, has small pictures arranged together on individual pages and a brief text containing information on the plays. *The American Theatre as Seen by Hirschfeld* (New York, G. Braziller, 1961. unpaged) is a collection of Albert Hirschfeld's humorous drawings that appeared in the Sunday drama section of the *New York Times.*

## Bii. CRITICISM

2178. Brustein, Robert S. Seasons of discontent; dramatic opinions, 1959–1965. New York, Simon & Schuster [1965] 322 p.
        65–22268  PN2266.B73

The author, a professor of English at Columbia University, had had little direct experience with the American stage when he became drama critic for *The New Republic* in 1959, and what he saw came as a shock. He was "appalled at the absence of distinguished drama" and astonished that theater standards were "being arbitrated (often in less than two hours of hurried scribbling) by newspaper reporters, many of whom had prepared for dramatic criticism through stints in such departments as music, foreign affairs, dining and dancing, and sports." His writing took the form of "destructive criticism" offered for constructive purposes. In the essays presented here, most of which originally appeared in *The New Republic,* Brustein discusses the theater on and off Broadway, plays from abroad, activities of companies, and a variety of other subjects. Among the Broadway plays reviewed are *The Dark at the Top of the Stairs,* by William Inge, *The Night of the Iguana,* by Tennessee Williams, and *Who's Afraid of Virginia Woolf?,* by Edward Albee.

2179. Kerr, Walter. The theater in spite of itself. New York, Simon & Schuster, 1963. 319 p.
        63–11143  PN2277.N5K4  1963

First-night reviews and other articles on the theater by the drama critic for the *New York Herald Tribune.* The author can be devastating in the presence of a poor production, but his general outlook on the contemporary theater is kindly. This collection reflects his appreciative but penetrating analytical approach. Some of Kerr's earlier reviews appear in his *Pieces at Eight* (New York, Simon & Schuster, 1957. 244 p.).

2180. Rice, Elmer L. The living theatre. New York, Harper [1959] 306 p.
        59–6317  PN2037.R5

A study of the theater as a social institution.

Drawing on more than 40 years' experience as playwright, stage director, and producer, the author describes conditions in the theater internationally and discusses the problems peculiar to the American stage. Among the many topics considered are the narrow line between commercialism and art, the theater as a business dependent upon such factors as labor unions and real estate values, and the roles played by critic, actor, director, designer, and audience in producing successful plays. Chapters are included on the Federal Theatre Project of the 1930's and on the cooperative theater groups— Neighborhood Playhouse, Theatre Guild, Group Theatre, and Playwrights' Company. Rice also describes in some detail the troubles that beset the production of his Pulitzer Prize-winning play *Street Scene.*

## Biii. PARTICULAR STAGE GROUPS, THEATERS, MOVEMENTS, ETC.

2181. Blau, Herbert. The impossible theater, a manifesto. New York, Macmillan [1964] 309 p. illus.      64–24008  PN2266.B56

A small but vocal segment of the theater of the 1950's and 1960's was engaged in the search for a new drama concerned with the meanings of human existence. In the vanguard of this search was the San Francisco Actor's Workshop, founded by the author and Jules Irving. In this "manifesto" Blau combines a brief history of the workshop with extensive discourses on theory, relating the theater to the existentialist, crisis-ridden world and this world to the theater.

2182. Crowley, Alice L. The Neighborhood Playhouse; leaves from a theatre scrapbook. New York, Theatre Arts Books [1959] 266 p.
        59–13239  PN2277.N6N42

A reminiscence by a founder of the Neighborhood Playhouse (1912-27), which had its origins in the festivals of the Henry Street Settlement on New York's lower East Side. Under the generous financial support of Irene and Alice Lewisohn, it produced unusual artistic plays from all over the world. Especially notable were the productions of the Hindu comedy *The Little Clay Cart* and the Russian-Jewish drama *The Dybbuk.* The playhouse also staged modern drama, housed dance festivals, and annually produced a satiric revue, "The Grand Street Follies."

2183. Hodge, Francis. Yankee theatre; the image of America on the stage, 1825–1850. Austin, University of Texas Press [1964] 320 p.
        64–19417  PN2248.H6

Bibliography: p. [273]–296.

A study of native American comedy as a reflection of New England character. The author examines closely the careers of four American comedians— James H. Hackett, George H. Hill, Dan Marble, and Joshua Silsbee—who, as the famous "Stage Yankees," performed throughout the United States and in London. Hodge views their eccentric dialect humor as an "honest exploitation of the materials of American life for an audience in search of its own identification." Other monographs on the history of the 19th-century theater are Reese D. James' *Cradle of Culture, 1800–1810, the Philadelphia Stage* (Philadelphia, University of Pennsylvania Press [1957] 156 p.), Margaret G. Watson's *Silver Theatre, Amusements of the Mining Frontier in Early Nevada, 1850 to 1864* (Glendale, Calif., A. H. Clark Co., 1964. 387 p.), Joseph Gallegly's *Footlights on the Border; the Galveston and Houston Stage Before 1900* ('s-Gravenhage, Mouton, 1962. 262 p.), and Alice H. Ernst's *Trouping in the Oregon Country; a History of Frontier Theatre* (Portland, Oregon Historical Society [1961] 197 p.).

2184. Lifson, David S. The Yiddish theatre in America. New York, T. Yoseloff [1965] 659 p. illus.  64–17112  PN3035.L46 1965
Bibliography: p. 626–647.

Tracing the history of the Yiddish-language dramatic theater from its origins in the 19th century to its decline after 1940, the author reveals its dependence on Central European writers, actors, directors, producers, and audiences and demonstrates its complexities, its development of such talented performers as Paul Muni, and its applications of the theory of German expressionism and the methods of the Stanislavsky school.

### Biv. BIOGRAPHY: ACTORS AND ACTRESSES

2185. Alpert, Hollis. The Barrymores. New York, Dial Press, 1964. xviii, 397 p. illus.
64–20278  PN2285.A45
Bibliography: p. xvii-xviii.

A collective biography of the fascinating family that predominated in the American theater for over 50 years, by the film critic for the *Saturday Review*. After briefly discussing the lives of Mrs. John Drew, John Drew, Jr., Georgie Drew, and her husband, Maurice Barrymore, the author concentrates on the three Barrymore children, Lionel, Ethel, and John. Lionel was thought by many critics to be the most

important character actor of his period; Ethel was often referred to as the "first lady of the theater"; and John's portrayals of Richard III and Hamlet were considered to be among the finest ever rendered. Elliott Nugent's *Events Leading Up to the Comedy* (New York, Trident Press, 1965. 204 p.) is the wry, dryly humorous autobiography of an actor who became a playwright and wrote, with James Thurber, *The Male Animal* (1940).

2186. Moody, Richard. Edwin Forrest, first star of the American stage. New York, Knopf, 1960. 415 p. illus.  60–6648  PN2287.F6M57
Notes on sources: p. 408–[416]

Forrest (1806-1872) became a star with his portrayal of Othello in New York at the age of 20. Subsequently, because of his powerful portrayals of Lear, Coriolanus, and Spartacus, his reputation spread across the country and to Europe. His later life was embittered by the lengthy and scandalous divorce proceedings that he and his wife brought against each other and by a running feud with British actor William C. Macready, which is closely examined by Moody in *The Astor Place Riot* (Bloomington, Indiana University Press, 1958. 243 p.).

2187. Overmyer, Grace. America's first Hamlet. Washington Square [New York] New York University Press, 1957. 439 p. illus.
56–12391  PN2287.P25O8
Bibliographical references included in "Notes" (p. 389–414).
Bibliography: p. 423–431.

A biography of John Howard Payne (1791–1852) that reveals extensive use of manuscript materials. Remembered chiefly as the author of the words to "Home, Sweet Home," Payne probably considered these verses less important than many of his other achievements. He was successful as translator, playwright, and actor; he collected information about the Cherokee Indians and defended their interests; and he served as United States consul in Tunisia. Appearing as Hamlet in Boston in 1809, he became the first native American to enact the role. Miss Overmyer's biography is based to a large extent on manuscript materials.

2188. Robbins, Phyllis. Maude Adams; an intimate portrait. New York, Putnam [1956] 308 p. illus.  56–6625  PN2287.A4R6

The great popularity of James M. Barrie's sentimental comedies in the first two decades of the 20th century was due in large part to the charm and ability of Maude Adams (1872–1953), who acted a wide range of parts in the stage productions of Barrie's works, from Lady Babbie in *The Little Minister* to the title role in *Peter Pan*. Miss Adams' most enduring fame still rests on her portrayal of the latter character. The author draws heavily upon her long friendship with her subject but never allows sentimentality or affection to cloud the biography. Appended to the text are a genealogy of the actress and a chronological list of her performances.

2189. Zolotow, Maurice. Stagestruck; the romance of Alfred Lunt and Lynn Fontanne. New York, Harcourt, Brace & World [1965] 278 p.

65–11995  PN2287.L8Z6

When Lunt, talented young star of Booth Tarkington's *Clarence,* married British-born actress Fontanne in 1922, a partnership formed that was to illuminate the American stage for the next 25 years. During the twenties and thirties, the Lunts were mainstays of the Theatre Guild and provided it with deft performances of sophisticated comedies, including *Arms and the Man,* by George Bernard Shaw, and *The Guardsman,* by Ferenc Molnar. They also proved their capabilities in such dramas as *There Shall Be No Night,* by Robert E. Sherwood, and *The Visit,* by Friedrich Durrenmatt. Zolotow, drama critic and personal friend of the Lunts, presents an intimate, informal account, illustrated with photographs of the pair in their most notable roles. A large collection of pictures is offered in *The Lunts; an Illustrated Study of Their Work, With a List of Their Appearances on Stage and Screen* (New York, Macmillan, 1958 [°1957] 134 p. Theatre world monograph no. 10), by George Freedley.

## Bv.  BIOGRAPHY: DIRECTORS, PRODUCERS, ETC.

2190. Felheim, Marvin. The theater of Augustin Daly; an account of the late nineteenth century American stage. Cambridge, Harvard University Press, 1956. 329 p. illus.

56–7214  PN2287.D254F4

Daly (1838–1899) was one of the foremost American theater managers of the late 19th century. Under his autocratic direction, his companies, whose performers included Fanny Davenport, Ada Rehan, John Drew, and Otis Skinner, achieved a high degree of precision and style. He favored his own melodramatic dramas, free adaptations of French and German plays, and bowdlerizations of Shakespeare. The author reviews the little that is known of Daly's private life, then offers a detailed study of his productions. The book is indexed, but for footnotes and bibliography the reader is referred to Felheim's doctoral thesis in English at Harvard University, "The Career of Augustin Daly" (1948).

2191. Gilroy, Frank D. About those roses; or, How not to do a play and succeed, and the text of The subject was roses. New York, Random House [1965] 210 p.

65–17873  PS3513.I6437S87

The author states that this book is for "those who like fairy tales." Reviewers of the book called it the story of a "miracle." In the form of excerpts from Gilroy's journal, it describes how his three-character play *The Subject Was Roses* was brought to Broadway in a low-budget production starring little-known actors, with a producer, a director, a scenic artist, and a general manager, none of whom had ever had a Broadway show. Opening at the end of the season in May 1964, the play received rave reviews, was supported financially by a devoted few until it caught the attention of the public, and in May 1965 won the Pulitzer Prize for drama. Gilroy, who fought successfully to maintain the integrity of his play in the face of commercial expediency, tells the story with verve and humor. In *The Seesaw Log; a Chronicle of the Stage Production, With the Text, of Two for the Seesaw* (New York, Knopf, 1959. 273 p.), William Gibson recalls the trials of bringing another successful play to the New York stage. Less fortunate than Gilroy in his negotiations with producers and actors, Gibson was forced to make changes in conflict with his conception of his play.

2192. Helburn, Theresa. A wayward quest; the autobiography of Theresa Helburn. Boston, Little, Brown [1960] 344 p. illus.

60–9333  PN2287.H415A3

Theresa Helburn (1887–1959) was probably involved in the production of more Broadway plays than any other woman in theater history. Shortly after the founding of the Theatre Guild in 1919, she became its executive director and, with Lawrence Langner, was the driving force behind it for many years. She elected to star Alfred Lunt and Lynn Fontanne in their first joint roles in *The Guardsman* (1924), by Ferenc Molnar. She also inspired and backed *Oklahoma!* (1943), by Richard Rodgers and Oscar Hammerstein, against the advice of most of the New York theatrical world. Her autobiography, completed after her death by Elinore Denniston, serves as a history of the Broadway theater for a period of more than 20 years.

2193. Stevens, David H., *ed*. Ten talents in the American theatre. Norman, University of Oklahoma Press [1957] 299 p.

57–5960 PN2285.S725

A collection of essays on the theater by Robert E. Gard, Paul Baker, Alan Schneider, Margo Jones, Frederic McConnell, Barclay Leathem, Gilmor Brown, Leslie Cheek, Jr., George C. Izenour, and Paul Green. As a director, producer, playwright, designer, or technician, each author has been closely identified with the American theater for more than 20 years. Several of them have been involved with Broadway, but in general their interests have lain in the development of grassroots theater where each one has pioneered in a special field of endeavor.

# C. Motion Pictures

## Ci. HISTORY

2194. Griffith, Richard, *and* Arthur Mayer. The movies; the sixty-year story of the world of Hollywood and its effect on America, from pre-nickelodeon days to the present. New York, Simon & Schuster, 1957. 422 p. illus.

57–10977 PN1993.5.U6G78

Bibliography: 6th prelim. page.

Griffith, the curator of the Museum of Modern Art Film Library, and Mayer, a veteran of the film industry, have combined an authoritative text with a collection of photographs taken primarily from the Film Library's extensive holdings. More than half of the book is devoted to the silent era; movies of the last three decades receive sketchy treatment. Paul Michael's compilation *The Academy Awards: A Pictorial History* (Indianapolis, Bobbs-Merrill [1964] 341 p.) includes a list of the winners in each category from 1928, the year of the first awards, to 1963. *The Western, From Silents to Cinerama* (New York, Orion Press [ᶜ1962] 362 p.), by George N. Fenin and William K. Everson, is a historical, critical, and pictorial survey.

2195. Hendricks, Gordon. The Edison motion picture myth. Berkeley, University of California Press, 1961. 216 p. illus.

61–7532 TR848.H4

Bibliographical footnotes.

History and tradition have generally credited the invention of the motion picture process to Thomas A. Edison. After extensive examination of the records of Edison's East Orange laboratory, Hendricks concluded that William Kennedy Laurie Dickson, one of Edison's assistants, actually invented the first motion picture apparatus, the Kinetoscope, with little help or encouragement from Edison. A day-by-day account of Dickson's work from 1889 up to May 1891, when the Kinetoscope made its public debut, is presented here. Dickson's later contributions to other motion picture processes such as the Mutoscope and the Biograph are described in the same author's *Beginnings of the Biograph; the Story of the Invention of the Mutoscope and the Biograph and Their Supplying Camera* (New York, Beginnings of the American Film, 1964. 78 p.).

2196. Knight, Arthur. The liveliest art; a panoramic history of the movies. New York, Macmillan, 1957. 383 p.

57–12222 PN1993.5.A1K6

The film industry was born almost simultaneously in the major countries of Europe and in the United States. From the beginning, filmmakers borrowed new techniques and copied successful themes with little regard for national boundaries. This survey by a noted lecturer and critic for the *Saturday Review* traces the growth and influence of foreign as well as American films. Knight is primarily concerned with the development of the film as an art form. He discusses the major directors and shows how they creatively utilized such technological innovations as sound, color, and wide screens. The technical aspects of filmmaking are emphasized in *Behind the Screen; the History and Techniques of the Motion Picture* (New York [Delacorte Press, 1965] 528 p.), by Kenneth Macgowan.

2197. Wagenknecht, Edward. The movies in the age of innocence. Norman, University of Oklahoma Press [1962] 280 p. illus.

62–16473 PN1993.5.A1W2

Bibliographical footnotes.

A nostalgic history of the silent films by a noted literary historian who asserts that he has not written a definitive work. His main objective is "to record what the first motion pictures looked like to the generation for which they were created." Discussing primarily those stars, directors, and pictures that appeal to him personally, he devotes almost half of his book to D. W. Griffith, Mary Pickford, and Lillian Gish. Joe Franklin's *Classics of the Silent*

*Screen; a Pictorial Treasury* (New York, Citadel Press [1960, ʿ1959] 255 p.) surveys 50 films and 75 stars. A previously neglected topic in the history of the motion picture in the United States is the subject of Kalton C. Lahue's *Continued Next Week; a History of the Moving Picture Serial* (Norman, University of Oklahoma Press [1964?] 293 p.).

## Cii. SPECIAL ASPECTS AND ANALYSES

2198. Agee, James. Agee on film. Drawings by Tomi Ungerer. [New York] McDowell, Obolensky [1958–60] 2 v.

58–12581    PN1993.5.A1A35

In addition to his novel, *A Death in the Family* (1959), for which he won a Pulitzer Prize, Agee (1909–1955) was well known for his film criticism and his screenplays. The first volume of this anthology includes all his film columns appearing in *The Nation* from 1942 to 1948 and selections from his reviews for *Time* between 1941 and 1948. Although Agee could be bitingly critical, he preferred to look for qualities to admire. His reviews reveal warmth and understanding in his attempts to comprehend the aims and limitations of each motion picture. The second volume contains his film scripts for *Noa Noa, The African Queen, The Night of the Hunter, The Bride Comes to Yellow Sky,* and *The Blue Hotel.*

2199. Bluestone, George. Novels into film. Baltimore, Johns Hopkins Press, 1957. 237 p. illus.                57–8449    PN1997.85.B5

Bibliography: p. 221–228.

An analysis of the essential differences between novels and films, as art forms and as vehicles for entertainment. The author points out that the novel is a linguistic medium. Furthermore, its audience is often a relatively small, well-educated class, and its length is highly flexible. The film, on the other hand, is primarily visual, must reach a wide audience to be commercially successful, and is constrained by limitations in viewing time. The author closely examines six films based on novels — *The Informer, Wuthering Heights, Pride and Prejudice, The Grapes of Wrath, The Ox-Bow Incident,* and *Madame Bovary* — and shows what happened to the original stories in their conversion to motion pictures. His conclusion, sustained by these examples, is that "the filmist becomes not a translator for an established author, but a new author in his own right."

2200. Crowther, Bosley. The lion's share; the story of an entertainment empire. New York, Dutton, 1957. 320 p.

57–5325    PN1993.5.U6C7

Metro-Goldwyn-Mayer resulted from the merger of several small struggling companies in 1924, with Louis B. Mayer as vice president and general manager in charge of film production. Through the thirties and forties, the studio prospered with polished productions and the largest group of stars in Hollywood, including Greta Garbo, Jean Harlow, Lon Chaney, Norma Shearer, Clark Gable, Spencer Tracy, Mickey Rooney, and Judy Garland. It was not until the advent of television that this "entertainment empire" began to decline, primarily because of its inability to adjust to new conditions. Crowther, a motion-picture critic for the *New York Times,* tells the colorful story of the rise of the studio. He describes the early struggles to develop talking pictures, the remarkable career of Mayer's brilliant assistant Irving Thalberg, and the filming of such notable pictures as the first *Ben Hur* and *Gone With the Wind.* Much of the same material can be found in the author's *Hollywood Rajah; the Life and Times of Louis B. Mayer* (New York, Holt [1960] 339 p.), which carries the account up to the time of Mayer's death in October 1957.

2201. Hall, Ben M. The best remaining seats; the story of the golden age of the movie palace. New York, C. N. Potter [1961] 266 p. illus.

61–11763    NA6845.H3

With the emergence of the full-length motion picture as entertainment for all social classes, enterprising showmen began to build palatial theaters in large cities. Epitomized by the Roxy ("The Cathedral of the Motion Picture"), which Samuel Lionel Rothafel opened in New York in 1927, these lavishly decorated theaters featured — along with the main film — chorus lines, ballets, full orchestras, Wurlitzer organs, and platoons of drilled ushers. In addition to the Roxy, among the more spectacular buildings were the Rivoli and the Rialto in New York, the Paradise and the Avalon in Chicago, and the Fox in San Francisco. Hall's account is actually an obituary, for with the decline in movie audiences, most of the palaces have been torn down. Numerous photographs of theaters and facsimiles of playbills, programs, and advertisements accompany the text.

2202. Schumach, Murray. The face on the cutting room floor; the story of movie and television censorship. New York, Morrow, 1964. 305 p. illus.                64–17880    PN1994.A2S3

Ever since the movies became a favorite American entertainment, they have been subjected to censorship by religious organizations, minority groups, government bodies, and cautious film producers. The author describes the scandals of the twenties that provoked the first public demand for censorship, the establishment of the Motion Picture Production Code and its implementation, the Congressional probes of the film industry and the unacknowledged blacklist that resulted, instances in which protesting groups were able to have "offensive" segments of film deleted, and instances in which ingenious filmmakers circumvented existing prohibitions. One chapter is devoted to television censorship, which has often tended to discourage programs on controversial subjects. Schumach concludes that the Motion Picture Production Code has shown remarkable flexibility in adjusting to the changing mores of society; he strongly advocates, however, a voluntary system of classification for both movies and television. An appendix describes censorship practices in foreign countries and includes the text of the Production Code.

### Ciii.  BIOGRAPHY: ACTORS AND ACTRESSES

2203.  Noble, Peter.  The fabulous Orson Welles. London, Hutchinson [1956]  276 p.

    57–580   PN2287.W456N6   1956

 Welles became famous in 1938 when his Mercury Theatre radio broadcast of *The War of the Worlds* panicked many half-attentive listeners into believing the United States had been invaded by Martians. Later his film productions of *Citizen Kane,* in which he starred, and *The Magnificent Ambersons,* which he directed but in which he did not appear, exhibited original techniques in narration, wide-angle photography, dramatic lighting, functional music, and overlapping dialogue. His subsequent work as a writer, actor, director, and producer has taken place more often in Europe than in the United States. Although critics tend to agree that he has never attained the creative fulfillment promised by youthful achievements, his total contribution has had a lasting impression on American cinematic art and entertainment. This biography conveys the energetic personality of the man, his brilliance, his foibles, and his diversity of interests.

### Civ.  BIOGRAPHY: DIRECTORS, PRODUCERS, ETC.

2204.  De Mille, Cecil B.  Autobiography.  Edited by Donald Hayne.  Englewood Cliffs, N.J., Prentice-Hall [1959]  465 p.  illus.

    59–15367   PN1998.A3D37

 The motion picture career of director-producer Cecil B. De Mille covered more than 40 years, from *The Squaw Man* (1914), one of the earliest features to be made in Hollywood, to the highly popular film *The Ten Commandments* (1956). He is primarily remembered as the producer of super-spectacles replete with thousands of extras and laced generously with sexual symbols. One of the reasons for his phenomenal success was his uncanny ability to sense what the general public would demand in new films. Hayne, a longtime member of De Mille's staff, selected and arranged materials for this autobiography from notes and preliminary drafts prepared by De Mille before his death. The narrative recalls the highlights of De Mille's career and the many prominent motion picture figures with whom he worked. Phil A. Koury's *Yes, Mr. De Mille* (New York, Putnam [1959] 319 p.), with its portrait of the temperamental, sometimes irascible, director, provides a balance to De Mille's recollections.

## D. Other Forms of Entertainment

### Di.  RADIO AND TELEVISION

2205.  Allen, Steve.  The funny men.  New York, Simon & Schuster, 1956.  279 p.

    56–7492   PN1992.4.A2A7

 The author, a "funny man" fascinated by the art of his profession, informally and sympathetically analyzes the personalities and script materials of 16 successful television comedians. They are "not *necessarily* the funniest or the most important" performers, Allen asserts; they were selected because he happened to have a "certain number of things to say" about them. They are Fred Allen, Jack Benny, Milton Berle, Red Buttons, Sid Caesar, Eddie Cantor, Wally Cox, Jackie Gleason, George Gobel, Arthur Godfrey, Bob Hope, Sam Levenson, Jerry Lewis, Groucho Marx, Phil Silvers, and Red Skelton. John Henry Faulk's *Fear on Trial* (New York, Simon & Schuster, 1964.  398 p.) is the account of an ordeal experienced by a humorist who, upon being blacklisted for alleged Communist activities, lost his position as a radio performer with the Columbia Broadcasting System and who eventually, with Louis Nizer as his attorney, won a suit for damages.

## Dii. THE DANCE IN AMERICA

2206. Maynard, Olga. The American ballet. Philadelphia, Macrae Smith Co. [ᶜ1959] 353 p.
59-13260  GV1787.M36
Bibliographical footnotes: p. 337–342.

From the time of Augusta Maywood, who made her debut in 1837, the United States produced individual dancers of excellence; with the eventual establishment of companies, a distinctive American ballet emerged. The author describes the development and operation of the New York City Ballet, the Ballets Russes de Monte Carlo (which was founded in Europe but moved to America in 1938), the American Ballet Theatre, and a number of smaller companies. She views love as the predominant theme in American ballet and supports her opinion with discussions of *Billy the Kid, Rodeo, Fancy Free, Fall River Legend,* and *The Cage.* Lew Christensen, Eugene Loring, Agnes De Mille, and Jerome Robbins serve as representative choreographers; the School of American Ballet in New York and the American School of Dance in Hollywood illustrate, respectively, "Classic" training and "Freestyle" training. George Balanchine, head of the School of American Ballet and choreographer for the New York City Ballet, is the subject of Bernard Taper's *Balanchine* (New York, Harper & Row [ᶜ1963] 342 p.). In *And Promenade Home* (Boston, Little, Brown [1958] 301 p.), Agnes De Mille continues the autobiographical account begun in *Dance to the Piper* (1952), no. 4970 in the 1960 *Guide.*

2207. Terry, Walter. The dance in America. New York, Harper [1956] 248 p. illus.
56-8767  GV1623.T4

The author, veteran dance critic of the *New York Herald Tribune,* briefly sketches the history of the dance from its uses by the American Indian to its place in ballet, musical theater, motion pictures, and television today. He emphasizes modern dance and the influence of such artists as Isadora Duncan, Ruth St. Denis, Ted Shawn, Martha Graham, and Doris Humphrey. Jack Mitchell's *American Dance Portfolio* (New York, Dodd, Mead [1964] 128. p.) consists of black-and-white photographs from the files of a highly acclaimed dance photographer.

2208. Terry, Walter. Isadora Duncan; her life, her art, her legacy. New York, Dodd, Mead [1964, ᶜ1963] xiv, 174 p. illus.
64-10954  GV1785.D8T4
Bibliography: p. 169.

From humble beginnings in California to her accidental death in Nice, Isadora Duncan lived a tempestuous and rebellious life. She brought to the world of dance a new freedom and a zest for experiment. The author evaluates her career, her philosophy, and her enduring influence on the modern dance. A more detailed biography is Allan R. Macdougall's *Isadora; a Revolutionary in Art and Love* (Edinburgh, New York, T. Nelson [1960] 296 p.). Informal autobiographies by two recent dance performers are Ted Shawn's *One Thousand and One Night Stands* (Garden City, N.Y., Doubleday, 1960. 228 p.) and Fred Astaire's *Steps in Time* (New York, Harper [1959] 338 p.).

## Diii. VAUDEVILLE AND BURLESQUE

2209. McLean, Albert F. American vaudeville as ritual. [Lexington, Ky.] University of Kentucky Press [1965] xvii, 250 p.
65–11830  PN1968.U5M3
Bibliographical references included in "Notes" (p. 223–238).

The author examines audiences, performers, and performances in an attempt to "make sense and some sort of order out of the tinsel and glitter known as vaudeville" and concludes that it was a "ritualistic enactment charged with symbols of the social beliefs and attitudes of the American industrial civilization." "Its place in American life was neither that of a crude monument to national vitality and gaiety, nor was it simply a kind of relaxation. Instead it served as a means of assimilation and crystallization of very important and historically significant value judgments upon life in an expanding industrial democracy. Vaudeville, in short, was one way by which the American people, passing through a neoprimitive stage, sought perspectives upon their common experience." *A Pictorial History of Vaudeville* (New York, Citadel Press [1961] 224 p.), by Bernard Sobel, is a nostalgic panorama of the personalities who toured the circuits. Fred Allen's autobiographical *Much Ado About Me* (Boston, Little, Brown [1956] 380 p.) covers his years in vaudeville and theater to 1928.

2210. Sobel, Bernard. A pictorial history of burlesque. New York, Putnam [1956] 194 p.
56–10246  PN1947.S6

"When it reached its peak in the early years of this century, burlesque was a composite entertainment that took its components from the minstrel show, variety, extravaganza, comedy 'bits,' and extra added attractions such as boxing bouts and the hootchykootchy." Sobel's story begins with "Lydia Thompson and her British Blondes," who came to New York in 1869, and essentially ends with the inability of Morton and Herbert K. Minsky to renew their license to operate a theater in New York in

1939. One of the causes of the decline of burlesque was the appearance of revues, which the author characterizes as "lacquered burlesque." A famous revue is described, with many illustrations, by Marjorie Farnsworth in *The Ziegfeld Follies* (New York, Putnam [1956] 194 p.). In *Gypsy, a Memoir* (New York, Harper [1957] 337 p.), Gypsy Rose Lee, one of burlesque's most popular stars, recalls her rise to fame. *The Night They Raided Minsky's* ([New York] Simon & Schuster, 1960. 351 p.), by Rowland Barber, combines research and a free imagination to recapture the flamboyance of burlesque in the mid-twenties.

### Div. SHOWBOATS, CIRCUSES, ETC.

2211. Chindahl, George L. A history of the circus in America. Caldwell, Idaho, Caxton Printers, 1959. 279 p. illus. 58–5336 GV1803.C47

Bibliography: p. 272–279.

The spectacular bigness of the combination show became the distinctive characteristic of the circus in the United States. Beginning with the display of wild animals in the early 18th century, the author traces the evolution of the circus and points out factors determining its form and quality. The book has no index, but the table of contents is extensive, and an appendix lists American circuses and their dates. Robert W. G. Vail's *Random Notes on the History of the Early American Circus* (Barre, Mass., Barre Gazette, 1956. 92 p.), drawn largely from the rich circus research materials in the library of the American Antiquarian Society, is devoted to the development of the circus in the 18th and early 19th centuries. John and Alice Durant's *Pictorial History of the American Circus* (New York, A. S. Barnes [1957] 328 p.) re-creates the story of the circus through reproductions of photographs and circus advertisements and artwork. *The One-Horse Show* (Jamestown, N.Y. [1962] 434 p.), by John C. Kunzog, is the biography of Dan Rice, one of America's first well-known clowns and a circus operator for four decades beginning in the 1840's.

2212. North, Henry Ringling, *and* Alden Hatch. The circus kings; our Ringling family story. Garden City, N.Y., Doubleday, 1960. 383 p. illus. 60–8877 GV1821.R5N6

An intimate history of the Ringlings and the Norths and their devotion to the circus world. The Ringling Brothers show began in 1871 in Baraboo, Wis., with a five-cent admission price and a domestic goat as the star performer; it became, at its zenith, the traveling "Big Top" of Ringling Brothers-Barnum & Bailey Combined Shows, the "Greatest Show on Earth." Today it is an indoor spectacle displayed for a season of 11 months. The key figures in the story are John Ringling, the most famous of five brothers, and his nephew, John Ringling North, who became the president of the company in 1937 and adapted it successfully to modern conditions. The tents were abandoned, for example, because the increasingly congested cities had no fields large enough to accommodate the circus, its performers, and its equipment. Coauthor Henry Ringling North, a brother of John Ringling North, retired as vice president in 1958. *A Ticket to the Circus* (Seattle, Superior Pub. Co. [1959] 184 p.), by Charles P. Fox, is a pictorial history of the "incredible Ringlings." *The Fabulous Showman* (New York, Knopf, 1959. 317 p.), by Irving Wallace, is a biography of the American impresario and showman, the master of humbuggery, Phineas T. Barnum.

2213. Russell, Don. The lives and legends of Buffalo Bill. Norman, University of Oklahoma Press [1960] 514 p.

60–13470 F594.C6867

Bibliography: p. 482–503.

William F. Cody was an all-round champion of the westward expansion movement, "that great rodeo of the plains and the mountains in the last half of the 19th century." He was scout, Indian fighter, cowboy, hunter, horseman, wagon driver, dime-novel hero, and showman. In a carefully documented biography of "a great liar in the Mark Twain style," the author stresses the drama of Cody's career and the melodrama of his legend. Buffalo Bill's Wild West Show—his "historical and educational exhibition"—was an original and distinctly American type of entertainment. Although public interest in such shows declined rapidly after Cody's death in 1917, their influence lives on in the television and motion-picture images of cowboy and Indian.

# XX

# Sports and Recreation

THE SECTION devoted to general works on sports and recreation is proportionately equal in size to the same section in the 1960 *Guide* and includes a study of sport as a social phenomenon, a pictorial sports history, the reminiscences of an eminent sportswriter, a selection of sports writings from a popular magazine, and an introduction to outdoor sports. Also in this section are a general history of recreation and an analysis of increasing leisure as a social problem.

The section on community and scholastic activities has the same number of entries as the parallel section in the 1960 *Guide* and thus is proportionately larger. Community recreation, general recreation, college athletics, and athletics at Harvard University are the respective subjects of the four entries. The number of entries on particular sports and recreations is also proportionately greater than the number in the 1960 *Guide*. The major increases are in the respective subsections on baseball, boating, and miscellaneous sports, the last of which includes entries on three sports—basketball, bicycling, and rowing—not represented by separate publications in the 1960 *Guide*.

The section on general field sports is proportionately smaller than in the 1960 *Guide* and is devoted entirely to hunting and fishing.

## A. General

2214. Boyle, Robert H. Sport: mirror of American life. Boston, Little, Brown [1963] 293 p. 63–17429 GV583.B6
"Bibliographical note": p. [277]–286.

An analysis of the social and psychological roots of sport in the United States and its impact on daily living. The author relates sport to such disparate topics as social status, race relations, business life, automobile design, clothing style, language, and ethical values and examines such subjects as the Negro in baseball, the hot-rod cult, the country club, and the latest of the annual (since 1875)

Harvard-Yale football contests. The final chapter is devoted to a study of Gilbert Patten's fictional character Frank Merriwell, the "unreal ideal" sportsman who, from 1896 to 1914, "performed unmatchable feats of derring-do in *Tip Top Weekly,* the most widely read nickel novel" of the time.

2215.  Dulles, Foster Rhea. A history of recreation;
America learns to play. 2d ed. New York, Appleton-Century-Crofts [1965] xvii, 446 p.
65–25489 E161.D852 1965
Bibliographical references included in "Notes" (p. 401–434).
An updated edition of *America Learns To Play; a History of Popular Recreation,* no. 4985 in the 1960 *Guide.*

2216.  Durant, John, *and* Otto Bettmann. Pictorial
history of American sports, from colonial times to the present. Rev. ed. [New York] Barnes [1965] 312 p. illus.
64–21453 GV583.D85 1965
An updated edition of no. 4986 in the 1960 *Guide.*

2217.  Larrabee, Eric, *and* Rolf Meyersohn, *eds.*
Mass leisure. Glencoe, Ill., Free Press [1958] 429 p. 58–9397 GV53.L3
"A comprehensive bibliography on leisure, 1900–1958 . . . by Rolf Meyersohn, with the assistance of Marilyn Marc": p. 389–419.
Wealth was formerly the basis of a leisure class, but modern mechanization has provided leisure in varying degrees to all classes. This volume is concerned with leisure as a social phenomenon and as a problem. Such contributors as Bertrand Russell, Margaret Mead, and Aldous Huxley, among others, review the possibilities for using leisure fruitfully. People interested in the opportunities for self-cultivation in music, literature, and the arts have no problem, but others, lacking preparation to meet increasing leisure, may be faced with a great emptiness. The authors discuss desirable methods of filling this emptiness, offer statistics on the present usage of leisure, and note the fusion of work and leisure in the modern industrial society. Margaret E. Mulac's *Hobbies; the Creative Use of Leisure* (New York, Harper [1959] 271 p.) surveys briefly the hobbies falling into four categories—making, collecting, doing, and learning—and provides lists of readings.

2218.  The Saturday Evening Post. Sport U.S.A.;
the best from *The Saturday Evening Post.* Edited by Harry T. Paxton. New York, Nelson [1961] 463 p. illus. 61–12630 GV576.S3
A selection of 61 articles, stories, and autobio-

graphical sketches published between 1901 and 1961 and touching upon virtually every sport. Other compilations are *Sports: The American Scene; Memorable Moments From the Pages of Sports Illustrated* (New York, McGraw-Hill [1963] 283 p.), edited by Robert M. Smith; *The World of Sport, the Best From Sport Magazine* (New York, Holt, Rinehart & Winston [1962] 358 p.), edited by Al Silverman; *Sportswriters' Choice; Their Best Stories, as Selected by the Authors* (New York, A. S. Barnes [1958] 332 p.), edited by Richard P. Goldman; *The Grantland Rice Award Prize Sports Stories* (Garden City, N.Y., Doubleday, 1962. 345 p.), edited by Robert M. Smith; *Best of the Best Sports Stories* (New York, Dutton, 1964. 480 p.), edited by Irving T. Marsh and Edward Ehre; and *The Best of Red Smith* (New York, J. L. Pratt [1963] 184 p. The American sports library), by Walter W. Smith.

2219.  Sports Illustrated (*New York*). Book of the
outdoors. Text by John O'Reilly. New York, Golden Press [1959] 322 p. (A Ridge Press book) 59–14665 SK601.S78
As the Nation's population shifts toward the engulfing megalopolis, Americans show an increasing inclination to spend their leisure time in the outdoors. This book, containing many illustrations in color, is designed to provide a perspective of the broad range of recreational environments from coastal waters to inland lakes, streams, forests, plains, mountains, and deserts. Outdoor pastimes as diverse in appeal as water-skiing and bird-watching are depicted. *The Spectacle of Sport, From Sports Illustrated* (Englewood Cliffs, N.J., Prentice-Hall, 1957. 317 p.), compiled and edited by Norton Wood, aims at capturing the kaleidoscopic view of the wide variety of sport. Among the authors represented are William Saroyan (baseball), William Faulkner (horse-racing), and A. J. Liebling (boxing).

2220.  Tunis, John R. The American way in
sport. New York, Duell, Sloan & Pearce [1958] 180 p. 58–12268 GV583.T8
Drawing on the experiences of a lifetime spent as a player and reporter of various sports, the author critically examines the growth and maturity of sport in a society that has pursued it with an intensity and devotion equaled in no other. Once played in an almost casual manner, such games as baseball, football, basketball, and even golf and tennis have become, at the most expert levels, big-business, mass-spectator exhibitions. The author categorically denounces "spectatoritis" and the profit motive as having corrupted games and distorted the original notions of their purpose in society. He is not

against competitive athletics; he is against extreme commercialism in sport and against its deplorable overemphasis in the educational system. He suggests the possible separation of so-called amateur athletics from education by the establishment of training schools to turn out champion athletes for entertainment purposes. Students interested primarily in obtaining an education would attend schools that stressed learning but permitted sports for exercise and relaxation.

## B. Community and Scholastic Activities

2221. Butler, George D. Introduction to community recreation, prepared for the National Recreation Association. 3d ed. New York, McGraw-Hill, 1959. 577 p.

59–8531 GV171.B85 1959

An updated edition of no. 4997 in the 1960 *Guide*.

2222. Carlson, Reynold E., Theodore R. Deppe, *and* Janet R. MacLean. Recreation in American life. Belmont, Calif., Wadsworth Pub. Co. [1963] 530 p. 63–8481 GV53.C3

A textbook on recreation, "its philosophy, historical background, leadership, organization, and program." The authors discuss the responsibility of families, schools, voluntary youth organizations, churches, industrial corporations, and local, State, and Federal governments to cooperate in developing recreation opportunities and facilities. The need for professional leadership is asserted, standards for recreation professionals are suggested, pros and cons of program planning are outlined, and 11 categories of possible recreational activities (from sports and outdoor recreation to drama and music) are explored. The many facets of recreation in an era of rapid change furnish the themes of *Spotlight on Recreation U.S.A.: Recreation in a Mobile America* ([New York, National Recreation Association, 1962] 135 p.), which consists of papers presented at the 43d National Recreation Congress in Detroit, 1961, and *Recreation in the Age of Automation* (Philadelphia, American Academy of Political and Social Science, 1957. 208 p. *Its* Annals, v. 313), a volume of essays. Detailed information on the Nation's present and potential recreational facilities is in the U.S. Outdoor Recreation Resources Review Commission's 27 study reports (Washington, U.S. Govt. Print. Off., 1962. 29 v.) and its final assessment, *Outdoor Recreation for America, a Report to the President and to the Congress* (Washington, 1962. 245 p.).

2223. Christenson, Ade. The verdict of the scoreboard; a study of the values and practices underlying college athletics today. New York, American Press [°1958] 190 p.

58–13844 GV706.C47

A rhetorical plea by a 35-year veteran of college athletics coaching and administration to change the concept of college sports from one of professional entertainment back to one of wholesome amateur competition. In the author's opinion, the scoreboard has become master, and overwhelming pressures to win have made victory an end to be attained by practically any means; the coach is "told to win, asked to recruit—but not to get caught." Christenson firmly believes that intercollegiate sports have a role well worth preserving, but he laments the "establishment of scholarships, grants, free rides [secret subsidies to student athletes] and gift convertibles, as living testimony to what is considered important in American education."

2224. Movius, Geoffrey H., *ed*. The second H book of Harvard athletics, 1923–1963. Cambridge, Harvard Varsity Club, 1964. xvii, 941 p.

64–17169 GV691.H3M6

A continuation of the narrative begun in a much earlier work, *The H Book of Harvard Athletics, 1852-1922* (1923), edited by John A. Blanchard. The new volume includes articles on football, soccer, basketball, boxing (dropped by Harvard as an intercollegiate sport after 1937), fencing, hockey, skiing, squash, swimming, wrestling, baseball, crew, lightweight crew, golf, lacrosse, rugby, sailing, tennis, and track and cross country. Photographs, team statistics, and a list of players awarded the major letter "H" supplement the text. James E. Pollard's *Ohio State Athletics, 1879-1959* ([Columbus, 1959] 306 p.) is a detailed history of a program that is representative, in a general way, of intercollegiate and intramural sports programs in many large universities throughout the country.

# C. Particular Sports and Recreations

## Ci. AUTO-RACING AND MOTORING

2225. Bentley, John. Great American automobiles; a dramatic account of their achievements in competition. Englewood Cliffs, N.J., Prentice-Hall [1957] 374 p. illus.

57–8467 GV1029.B4

Confining his scope to the first three decades of the 20th century, the author offers an abundance of semitechnical details on the various models of motorcars, shows the speed records set on Florida's Daytona Beach, and describes the numerous races of the period, including such classic events as the Vanderbilt Cup, the Glidden Tours, the 1908 New York to Paris marathon, and the first Indianapolis 500. He also traces the work of the designers who developed the American competition automobile, among them Alexander Winton, James W. Packard, and Harry C. Stutz. Road racing is the subject of *The Checkered Flag* (New York, Scribner [1961] 178 p.), by Peter Helck, whose drawings complement his narrative of the exploits of men and machines from the first race between Chicago and Evanston in 1895 through America's participation in the European Bennett Race (1900–1905) into the annual classics: the Vanderbilt Cup (1904–16) and the American Grand Prize (1908–16). The story of a group of enthusiasts who kept road racing alive during the thirties and paved the way for modern sports car racing is told in John C. Rueter's *American Road Racing; the Automobile Racing Club of America in the 1930's* (New York, Barnes [1963] 139 p.).

2226. Bloemker, Al. 500 miles to go; the story of the Indianapolis Speedway. New York, Coward-McCann [1961] 287 p. illus.

61–6839 GV1029.B55

The author, publicity director of the Speedway, describes in detail its inception, ownership, and management, the individual races and drivers, the cars and their builders, and the mechanical evolution of the automobiles. He reveals that in the 44 contests staged between 1911 and 1960, the average winning speed gradually increased from 74.59 miles an hour to 138.78 and the duration of the race lessened from nearly seven hours to little more than 3.5. Additional accounts of the annual Memorial Day spectacle and its home are provided by Brock Yates in *The Indianapolis 500; the Story of the Motor Speedway*, rev. "Golden Anniversary" ed. (New York, Harper [1961] 182 p.), and *Famous Indianapolis Cars and Drivers* (New York, Harper [1960] 219 p.). Photographs by Bob Verlin and a brief accompanying text by Angelo Angelopolous have been combined in *The Race* (Indianapolis, Bobbs-Merrill [1958] unpaged) to re-create the setting, mood, and experiences of the modern 500-mile race.

2227. Nolan, William F. Barney Oldfield; the life and times of America's legendary speed king. New York, Putnam [1961] 251 p. illus.

61–12739 GV1032.O4N6

During the late 1890's Oldfield was a successful bicycle racer, but in 1902 victory in his first motorcar race marked the beginning of a flamboyant career that spread his name across the country and helped popularize the automobile before it reached the masses. In 1903 he became the first to drive a gas-powered car a mile a minute, and in the next 15 years he placed his name beside almost every record on the books and in the winning column of almost every race. In this popular biography the author covers Oldfield's professional racing career and describes his turbulent nature, his weakness for alcohol, his three marriages, his relationships with industrialists and film actors of his time, and his several business ventures. In May 1946 Oldfield was honored at Detroit's Golden Jubilee as one of the Nation's automotive pioneers; four months later he died of a cerebral hemorrhage. The racing careers of three of America's top drivers since World War II are the respective subjects of the same author's *Phil Hill: Yankee Champion; First American to Win the Driving Championship of the World* (New York, Putnam [1963, ᶜ1962] 256 p.); *Challenger, Mickey Thompson's Own Story of His Life of Speed* (Englewood Cliffs, N.J., Prentice-Hall [1964] 237 p.), by Mickey Thompson with the assistance of Griffith Borgeson; and *Adventure on Wheels; the Autobiography of a Road Racing Champion* (New York, Putnam [1959] 284 p.), by John Fitch with the assistance of William F. Nolan.

## Cii. BASEBALL

2228. Allen, Lee. The American League story. Rev. ed. New York, Hill & Wang [1965] 258 p. illus. 65–17425 GV875.A15A45 1965

2229. Allen, Lee. The National League story; the official history. Rev. ed. New York, Hill & Wang [1965] 293 p. illus.

65–17426 GV875.A3A7 1965

The author writes of the players, managers, owners, presidents, and commissioners whose abilities and personalities have contributed to the development and color of baseball's National League and American League, founded in 1876 and 1901 respectively. He also treats famous games, plays, and teams, as well as the intermittent periods of glory, tragedy, and scandal that have been the lot of both leagues. The longstanding rivalry between two well-known National League teams is the theme of another book by the same author, *The Giants and the Dodgers, the Fabulous Story of Baseball's Fiercest Feud* (New York, Putnam [1964] 255 p.). The annual postseason contest between the pennant winners of each league is one of the Nation's foremost sports spectacles; its origin and history are explored by John Durant in *Highlights of the World Series* (New York, Hastings House [1963] 187 p.) and by Frederick G. Lieb in *The Story of the World Series* (New York, Putnam [1965] 438 p.). The notorious scandal that erupted when eight members of the Chicago White Sox club conspired to throw a series to the Cincinnati Reds is the subject of Eliot Asinof's *Eight Men Out; the Black Sox and the 1919 World Series* (New York, Holt, Rinehart & Winston [1963] 302 p.).

2230. Cobb, Tyrus R. My life in baseball; the true record, by Ty Cobb, with Al Stump. Garden City, N.Y., Doubleday, 1961. 283 p. illus.

61–12504 GV865.C6A3

The author, regarded by many as the greatest baseball player of all time, set more than 90 records in a lengthy career (1905–28) with the Detroit Tigers and the Philadelphia Athletics. His book was written in part to dispel the legend that he had been "a spike-slashing demon of the diamond with a wide streak of cruelty in his nature." He recounts many of his own experiences, reminisces about other great players, and offers outspoken opinions of today's game, which he regards as inferior to that of his own time. Two other autobiographical accounts by record-setting performers are *My War With Baseball* (New York, Coward-McCann [1962] 253 p.), by Rogers Hornsby and Bill Surface, and *Stan Musial: "The Man's" Own Story* (Garden City, N.Y., Doubleday, 1964. 328 p.), by Stanley F. Musial as told to Robert M. Broeg. Hornsby, one of the greatest batters in National League history, mingles reminiscences and anecdotes with acid comments on the national sport and the way it is played. Musial, a National League star of more recent times,

is considerably less critical of the sport that made him famous and of his fellow players than are Cobb and Hornsby. His book is a straightforward narrative of his career from obscure beginnings in a Pennsylvania steel town to national renown.

2231. Graham, Frank. The New York Yankees, an informal history. New and rev. ed. New York, Putnam [1958] 352 p.

58–9514 GV875.N4G7 1958

The Yankees were not remarkably successful during their first two decades, but between 1921 and 1959 they captured 24 pennants and 18 world championships—a record unapproached by any other club in baseball. Graham chronicles the founding and fortunes of the club and sketches the personalities of its chief officials and players. In *The Yankee Story* (New York, Dutton, 1960. 224 p.), Thomas Meany concentrates on the people who played dominant roles in the team's history. *Casey at the Bat* (New York, Random House [1962] 254 p.), by Casey Stengel, is an account of the author's 50 years in baseball, emphasizing his 12 years (1949–60) as Yankee manager, during which the team won 10 pennants and seven world championships.

2232. Gregory, Paul M. The baseball player: an economic study. Washington, Public Affairs Press [1956] 213 p. 56–6598 GV880.G7

"Baseball as a part of our American culture is intimately related to capitalism and democracy," and in this study by a professor of economics at the University of Alabama, emphasis is placed on the "analysis and interpretation of baseball as a game, a business, and an occupation." The author examines the worth of a player in terms of such standards as performance and gate appeal, discusses the financial rewards of playing, examines the industry's legal structure with particular reference to players' contracts and baseball law, traces the stormy development of player-management relations from the early unions to the present representative system, describes the players' job opportunities after retirement, and delineates theories and principles of baseball economics. *The Long Season* (New York, Harper [1960] 273 p.) is an informal journal of the experiences of Jim Brosnan, a pitcher who started the 1959 season with the St. Louis Cardinals and finished with the Cincinnati Reds.

2233. Meany, Thomas. There've been some changes in the world of sports. New York, Nelson [1962] 313 p. 61–12631 GV191.M37

The author believes that baseball, as well as most other sports, is played better today than it was in 1923, when he began covering the Brooklyn Dodgers. He reminisces about the many sports events and personalities he observed in 40 years of sports writing and he discusses the modifications in the style of play of individual games and the drastic changes in the general environment of the world of sport, brought about by such innovations as radio, arc lights (permitting night play), air travel, and television. Many sports are touched on in these memoirs, but baseball was and is the author's forte. Thirty-two of his magazine articles (1939–57) are reprinted in *Mostly Baseball* (New York, Barnes [1958] 441 p.); 25 of them deal with baseball topics and the rest are scattered among hockey, golf, football, horse-racing, boxing, and basketball. Four baseball anthologies of varying aim and scope are *The Fireside Book of Baseball* (New York, Simon & Schuster, 1956. 394 p.) and *The Second Fireside Book of Baseball* (New York, Simon & Schuster, 1958. 395 p.), two collections of nonfiction, fiction, and poetry that span the game's entire history, selected and edited by Charles Einstein; *The Best of Baseball; the Game's Immortal Men and Moments as Selected From Baseball Magazine* (New York, Putnam [1956] 248 p.), 38 articles (1908–56) selected by Sidney Offit from the first magazine devoted exclusively to the sport; and *Baseball's Unforgettable Games* (New York, Ronald Press [1960] 362 p.), by Joe Reichler and Ben Olan, who describe 100 games judged by them to be the best since 1870.

2234. Robinson, John R. Baseball has done it, by Jackie Robinson. Edited by Charles Dexter. Philadelphia, Lippincott [1964] 216 p.

64–14467 GV865.R6A2

When Branch Rickey recruited Jackie Robinson for the Brooklyn Dodgers in 1947, he introduced the first Negro to major league baseball and began the assault on the sport's rigid color line. Since then Negroes have played for every major league club and in every minor league. Robinson tells how he turned the other cheek in the face of countless humiliations during his first two years and presents accounts by other outstanding Negro ballplayers, including Carl Erskine, Ernie Banks, Roy Campanella, Hank Aaron, Elston Howard, and Monte Irvin, of experience with race prejudice. In *Negro Firsts in Sports* (Chicago, Johnson Pub. Co. [1963] 301 p.), by Andrew S. N. ("Doc") Young records noteworthy accomplishments of Negro athletes, examines racial handicaps they faced, and surveys the changed position of Negroes in today's sports world, where they "approach closer to the democratic ideal than in any other facet of American life."

2235. Seymour, Harold. Baseball: the early years. New York, Oxford University Press, 1960. 373 p. 60–5799 GV863.S37

The author traces baseball from its origins in the English game of rounders through its evolution from a boyish pastime to an amateur sport for young gentlemen, then to a well-organized business monopoly run by professional promoters, staffed with highly skilled players, and performed for the entertainment of paying spectators. Although Seymour gives attention to outstanding players, teams, and records, his emphasis is on the economic and social aspects of baseball and how it both reflected and contributed to the shaping of American life. He also scotches the myth of the importance of Abner Doubleday and Cooperstown, N.Y., in the origin of the game. This volume carries the chronicle to 1903, and an intended sequel will examine the 20th century. Three general histories that follow the conventional pattern of episodic treatment with concentration on the exploits of teams and players are *The History of Baseball: Its Great Players, Teams and Managers* (Englewood Cliffs, N.J., Prentice-Hall [1959] 412 p.), by Allison Danzig and Joe Reichler; *The Story of Baseball in Words and Pictures* (New York, Hastings House [1959] 298 p.), by John Durant; and Robert M. Smith's *Baseball in America* (New York, Holt, Rinehart & Winston [1961] 278 p.). *The American Diamond; a Documentary of the Game of Baseball* (New York, Simon & Schuster, 1965. 204 p.), by Branch Rickey, begins with Alexander Cartwright, who is identified as the founder of the game, continues to the present, and contains an "All-Time Team" of 30 players.

## Ciii. BOATING

2236. Brooks, Jerome E. The $30,000,000 cup; the stormy history of the defense of the America's Cup. New York, Simon & Schuster, 1958. 275 p. illus. 58–10359 GV829.B87

2237. Stone, Herbert L., *and* William H. Taylor. The America's Cup races. Princeton, N.J., Van Nostrand [1958] 254 p. illus.

58–9435 GV829.S7 1958

In the summer of 1851 the invading schooner *America* badly defeated the 17 entries of the Royal Yacht Squadron in a race around the Isle of Wight, capturing the trophy (known then as the Hundred Guinea Cup) that for more than a century now has been the symbol of top-level international yachting competition. In 1957 the owners of the *America* turned the cup over to the New York Yacht Club in trust, "to be held as a permanent challenge cup, open to competition by any organized yacht club of any foreign country." Between 1870 and 1937 the cup was defended successfully against 16 challengers from Britain or Canada. Both of these chronicles describe the dramatic circumstances, events, and sidelights of the original competition and the subsequent races, with special attention to the people concerned. The closest contest occurred in 1934 when the *Rainbow* crossed the finish line only five seconds ahead of the English *Endeavour*. *Sailing for America's Cup* (New York, Harper & Row [1964] 216 p.), by Everett B. Morris, and *The Pictorial History of the America's Cup Races* (New York, Viking Press [1964] 194 p. A Studio book), by Robert W. Carrick, are primarily photographic records covering the races through 1962 and 1964, respectively.

2238. McKeown, William T., *ed.* Boating in America. New York, Ziff-Davis Pub. Co. [1960] 303 p.                 60–8224  E41.M2

Postwar improvements in equipment (making boating safer and more comfortable), the development of many new lakes, reservoirs, and waterways, the greater mobility of the population (putting water facilities within reach of almost everyone), and a steadily growing personal income have all combined to make pleasure-boating "America's fastest growing sport." These 44 short articles selected from *Popular Boating* magazine describe boating areas and facilities along both coastlines and across the entire expanse of the country. Each description is accompanied by a photograph, often an aerial view.

2239. Rosenfeld, Morris. The story of American yachting, told in pictures, with photographs by Morris Rosenfeld and text by William H. Taylor and Stanley Rosenfeld. New York, Appleton-Century-Crofts [1958] 276 p.
                 57–12332  GV815.R6

A work intended to provide both the new and the veteran sailor with a panorama of American yachting from its beginnings in the 1840's. All but 12 of some 200 black-and-white photographs were made by the author. The reproductions of old prints and paintings were drawn mainly from the collections of the New York Historical Society and the Marine Association of Mystic, Conn. The illustrations were chosen to reflect the moods of the sailors and of the sea, as well as to add visual substance and continuity to the story. The text summarizes the developments in American yacht design and building, records the history of the America's Cup and ocean racing, and describes the contemporary yachting scene in the United States. More of Rosenfeld's photographs of various classes of yachts in all kinds of settings are collected in his *Sail Ho! Great Yachting Pictures* (1947) and *Under Full Sail* (Englewood Cliffs, N.J., Prentice-Hall [1957] 212 p.).

2240. Wallace, William N. The Macmillan book of boating. New York, Macmillan [1964] 249 p.                 64–19473  GV815.W25
Bibliography: p. 249.

A survey of American boating from the first pleasure craft, *Cleopatra's Barge* (1816), to Henry Ford II's *Santa Maria,* built in 1963 at a cost of $7,000,000. "It is essentially a story of the evolution of naval architecture, which means the interplay between men capable of designing fine boats and men capable of paying for them." From the beginning, when a few yachts were built for the very wealthy, boat design and construction have expanded through the production of many classes of sail, steam, outboard motor, and power vessels. Interspersed among the discussions of designers, owners, skippers, and yachts are numerous illustrations, some of which are in color.

### Civ. BOXING

2241. Farr, Finis. Black champion; the life and times of Jack Johnson. New York, Scribner [1964] 245 p.                 64–13631  GV1132.J73F3

2242. Dempsey, Jack. Dempsey, by the man himself, as told to Bob Considine and Bill Slocum. New York, Simon & Schuster, 1960. 249 p.
                 60–6719  GV1132.D4A28

2243. Fleischer, Nathaniel S. The Louis legend; the amazing story of the Brown Bomber's rise to the heavyweight championship of the world and his retirement from boxing. [n.p., °1956] 181 p.                 57–3410  GV1132.L6F5

When Jack Johnson (1878-1946) defeated Tommy Burns in 1908, he became the first Negro to wear the heavyweight crown, and in some minds his victory transformed the title into a defiant symbol of racial supremacy. Jim Jeffries was coaxed from retirement to champion the white man's primacy, but was defeated by "the greatest heavyweight of all time," as Nat Fleischer has called Johnson. In Farr's biography, Johnson's pugilistic career and his notorious personal life are examined. Jack Dempsey, born in Manassa, Colo., in 1895 and originally named William Harrison Dempsey, was a peripatetic jack-of-all-trades before becoming an established prize-fighter. On July 4, 1919, the "Manassa Mauler" knocked out Jess Willard in three rounds and thus became the heavyweight champion. In his candid autobiography, Dempsey reflects not only on his 16 years in the ring but also on such personal topics as the abject poverty of his youth and his three marriages. *The Louis Legend* is a biography of Joseph Louis Barrow, who under the name of

Joe Louis revitalized a sport sapped by lackluster combatants and the Great Depression. He successfully defended his crown against all contenders from 1937, when he won the championship from Jim Braddock, until 1949 when he announced his retirement. Prompted by the need for money to pay back taxes, Louis attempted a ring "comeback" and a wrestling career in the early 1950's but was unsuccessful at both.

2244. Fleischer, Nathaniel S. 50 years at ringside. New York, Fleet Pub. Corp. [1958] 296 p.
58–8780 GV1125.F55

The founder and longtime editor of *The Ring* magazine discusses the fighting qualities and eccentricities of the top pugilists and gives glimpses of the noncombatants closely associated with the sport's promotion, management, matchmaking, and supervision. He selects the 10 alltime best fighters in each weight division and concludes that in recent years "fighting talent has gone into an amazing decline." *A Pictorial History of Boxing* (New York, Citadel Press [1959] 316 p.), by Fleischer and Sam Andre, includes pictures from the two authors' respective collections and from the files of *The Ring*.

2245. Fleischer, Nathaniel S. The heavyweight championship; an informal history of heavyweight boxing from 1719 to the present day. Rev. ed. New York, Putnam [1961] 318 p.
61–5821 GV1121.F6 1961

This updated edition of no. 5026 in the 1960 *Guide* continues the story through the second Floyd Patterson-Ingemar Johansson title bout (1960), when Patterson became the first ex-champion to win back the heavyweight crown. In *The Heavyweight Champions* (New York, Hastings House [1960] 150 p.), John Durant discusses each titleholder, describes the growth and changes of the sport, and reviews the matches in some detail from England's first recognized champion, James Figg (1719), to Johansson.

2246. Liebling, Abbott J. The sweet science. New York, Viking Press, 1956. 306 p.
56–9224 GV1125.L5

A collection of the author's pieces in *The New Yorker* on the "Sweet Science of Bruising," from the Louis-Savold fight on June 1951 to Archie Moore's unsuccessful bid to wrest the heavyweight crown from Rocky Marciano in September 1955. In between are accounts of other notable ring battles, the exploits of such minor heroes as Sandy Saddler, and the work of trainer-seconds, whom the author believes to be the prime movers of the efficient and artistic pugilist. An observer of prizefighting since 1918 and a onetime amateur boxer, Liebling spices his chronicles with retrospective comparisons of fighters and offbeat conversations with sparring partners, promoters, trainers, and cab drivers. His writing is also included in *The Fireside Book of Boxing* (New York, Simon & Schuster, 1961. 408 p.), edited by Wilfred C. Heinz, a potpourri of fact, fiction, and poetry, which follows the course of boxing history since Homer's *Iliad* but concentrates on the American ring.

2247. Samuels, Charles. The magnificent rube; the life and gaudy times of Tex Rickard. New York, McGraw-Hill [1957] 301 p.
57–8627 GV165.R5S3

George Lewis Rickard (1875-1929), better known as Tex, was responsible for two milestones in boxing history: in 1921 he promoted the match between Jack Dempsey and Georges Carpentier that drew the first million-dollar gate; and in 1925 he built the new Madison Square Garden. Beginning in poverty in Texas, he rose from cowboy, town marshal, gold prospector, gambler, and saloon-owner in the Klondike and Nevada gold rushes to become boxing's colorful millionaire promoter during the 1920's.

## Cv. FOOTBALL

2248. Gottehrer, Barry. The Giants of New York; the history of professional football's most fabulous dynasty. New York, Putnam [1963] 319 p. illus.
63–16182 GV956.N4G65

The author traces the development and fortunes of the Giants from the 1925 inaugural season through the 1962 playoff against the Green Bay Packers, which marked the club's 13th participation in a final championship game. In a style frequently anecdotal, Gottehrer supplies details of memorable games and recalls such great coaches as Steve Owen and Jim Lee Howell and such outstanding players as Benny Friedman, Ken Strong, Mel Hein, Charlie Conerly, and Frank Gifford. An 11-page section of alltime records is appended. *Y. A. Title: I Pass! My Story as Told to Don Smith* (New York, F. Watts [1964] 290 p.) is the autobiography of a former Giant quarterback, Yelberton A. Tittle.

2249. Johnson, Chuck. The Green Bay Packers; pro football's pioneer team. [2d ed.] New York, Nelson [1963, ᶜ1961] 171, 31 p.
63–19351 GV956.G7J6 1963

"Supplement" (31 p.) inserted at end.

The author has chronicled the vacillating fortunes of the professional club that Earl L. (Curly) Lambeau founded in 1919 and coached until 1950. Under the revitalizing leadership of Vince Lombardi, fourth in a succession of coaches after Lambeau, the Packers captured the National Football League championship in both 1961 and 1962. *Run to Daylight!* (Englewood Cliffs, N.J., Prentice-Hall [1963] 299 p.), by Vince Lombardi with W. C. Heinz, recounts, hour by hour, a seven-day period in which the Packers prepared for and played a game during the 1962 season. More than 100 photographs by Robert Riger portray the week's happenings.

2250. Maule, Hamilton. The game, by Tex Maule; the official picture history of the National Football League. Rev. ed. including the Giant-Bear championship game in color. New York, Random House [1964] 249 p.

    64–22444 GV956.N38M35 1964

After briefly summarizing the origins and development of professional football and the National Football League (founded in 1920), the author provides a team-by-team history of the NFL's 14 members. More than 200 photographs (28 colored) complement the text. *The Pros* (New York, Simon & Schuster, 1960. 191 p.), by Robert Riger with commentary by Maule, is primarily pictorial. Riger utilizes his own drawings to depict professional football's growth from 1920 to 1950, then uses his photographs to create a panoramic view of the sport as played during the decade 1950-60.

2251. Smith, Robert M. Pro football; the history of the game and the great players. Garden City, N.Y., Doubleday, 1963. 230 p. illus.

    62–15915 GV938.S6

2252. Claassen, Harold. The history of professional football. Englewood Cliffs, N.J., Prentice-Hall [1963] 526 p. illus.

    63–18119 GV938.C52

Smith surveys the professional game from its beginnings in the 1890's as an offshoot of intercollegiate football. Drawing on recorded facts and personal recollections, he explains the adaptation of American football from English rugby and traces the evolution of rules which changed the style of play from an irregular free-for-all requiring mostly brute strength to the game of today with its emphasis on precision and specialization. He describes outstanding teams and the great players who made them successful. The period covered by Claassen is essentially the same as Smith's, but he offers a more methodical, straightforward chronicle with extensive statistical material. The history of each team now in the National Football League is

sketched, and each championship game from 1933 to 1962 is described in detail. What it is like to play one year of professional football—from the off-season through training camp and exhibition engagements to the 14-game grind of the regular season—is depicted by Lee Grosscup in *Fourth and One* (New York, Harper & Row [1963] 310 p.). In *Pro Football's Hall of Fame* (Chicago, Quadrangle Books, 1963. 248 p.), Arthur Daley reviews the gridiron careers of the 17 men who were the first selections for the National Professional Football Hall of Fame.

2253. Wallace, Francis. Knute Rockne. Garden City, N.Y., Doubleday, 1960. 286 p. illus.

    60–13749 GV939.R6W3

In his 13 years as head football coach at Notre Dame (1918-30), Knute Rockne not only achieved a record of five seasons without a defeat but also played an essential role in creating the climate in which college football grew into a national institution. The author, a sportswriter and reporter who was also Rockne's lifetime friend and associate, has written a biography which attempts to capture the spirit of his subject's inspiring personality and dynamic energy. Rockne was born in Voss, Norway, in 1888, spent his childhood in Chicago, and worked briefly as a postal clerk in that city. He attended college at Notre Dame and starred on the gridiron. After serving as chemistry instructor and assistant football coach, he was appointed head coach. On March 31, 1931, an airplane crash ended his brilliant career, and the spontaneous outpouring of grief from millions of Americans testified to the esteem and affection with which he was regarded. *A Treasury of Notre Dame Football* (New York, Funk & Wagnalls [1962] 340 p.), edited by Gene Schoor, incorporates 66 pieces ranging from historical essays and biographical sketches to discussions of notable seasons and teams and descriptions of memorable games and feats.

2254. Weyand, Alexander M. Football immortals. Foreword by Earl "Red" Blaik. New York, Macmillan [1962] 290 p. illus.

    62–19433 GV939.A1W4

Biographical sketches of 55 stars of college and professional fame. Fred Russell and George Leonard describe the annual college bowl engagements in *Big Bowl Football; the Great Postseason Classics* (New York, Ronald Press [1963] 416 p.). Short items of fact, fiction, and humor make up *The Fireside Book of Football* (New York, Simon & Schuster, 1964. 347 p.), edited by Jack Newcombe. The stories of two great coaches are told by Robert B. Considine in *The Unreconstructed Amateur; a*

*Pictorial Biography of Amos Alonzo Stagg* (San Francisco, Amos Alonzo Stagg Foundation, 1962. 154 p.), edited by Ralph Cahn, and *You Have To Pay the Price* (New York, Holt, Rinehart & Winston [1960] 430 p.), an autobiography by Earl H. Blaik with Tim Cohane.

## Cvi. GOLF AND TENNIS

2255. Cummings, Parke. American tennis; the story of a game and its people. Boston, Little, Brown [1957] 182 p. 57–11347 GV993.C8

A profusely illustrated history of the game since its importation into the United States from Bermuda in 1847. Emphasis is placed on outstanding players from the first national champions of the 1880's, Dick Sears and Ellen Hansell, to the major present-day figures in national and international competition. The author provides a background of the changing social, political, economic, and scientific environment in which tennis has developed. A separate chapter describes the evolution of rackets, courts, and costumes. Championship and match records of the United States Lawn Tennis Association are appended. The restless life and career of a tennis star is reconstructed in *Man With a Racket; the Autobiography of Pancho Gonzales* (New York, Barnes [1959] 254 p.), as told to Cy Rice by Gonzales. Born to Mexican-American parents in Los Angeles in 1928, Gonzales became obsessed with tennis at an early age and won the United States singles championship when he was only 20.

2256. Jones, Robert T. Golf is my game. Garden City, N.Y., Doubleday, 1960. 255 p. illus. 60–13386 GV965.J63

2257. Snead, Samuel. The education of a golfer, by Sam Snead with Al Stump. New York, Simon & Schuster, 1962. 248 p. illus. 62–9601 GV964.S6A3

Along with suggestions on improving one's game and one's mental approach to golf, Bobby Jones offers autobiographical reflections on the development of his own skills from the age of six. He records in detail the year (1930) of his "Grand Slam": a winning sweep of the British Amateur, British Open, U.S. Open, and U.S. Amateur tourneys. He also expresses his thoughts on golf-course design, discusses his participation in the design and construction of the Augusta National Golf Course, where the Masters tournament is held each spring, and describes (with diagrams) the best ways of playing each hole. A year-by-year chronicle (1934–60 with the exception of the war years 1943–45) of the Augusta Masters tournament is provided by Tom Flaherty in *The Masters; the Story of Golf's Greatest Tournament* (New York, Holt, Rinehart & Winston [1961] 150 p.). In *The Education of a Golfer,* "Slammin' Sammy" Snead (b. 1912 in Ashwood, Va.), who won special fame because of his long tee shots, reveals how determined practice coupled with a natural bent for the game enabled him to rise from errand boy and handyman on the courses of Virginia and West Virginia summer resorts to become one of the ablest professional golfers in the United States. He won his first tournament in 1936; among his other victories were three Masters Championships (1949, 1952, and 1954).

2258. Price, Charles. The world of golf; a panorama of six centuries of the game's history. Foreword by Bobby Jones. New York, Random House [1962] 307 p. 62–16287 GV963.P7

A copiously illustrated history, in which the author reviews the beginnings of the game in Scotland and narrates the highlights of golf in the United States from the founding of the first permanent club, St. Andrews Golf Club of Yonkers, N.Y., in 1888. Price concentrates on interpretive descriptions of the champions, their style of play, and the tournaments which brought them fame. He has also edited *The American Golfer* (New York, Random House [1964] 241 p.), an anthology from *The American Golfer Magazine,* 1920-35. A pictorial tour of 63 of the best courses across the length and breadth of the Nation is assembled in *Golfing America* (Garden City, N.Y., Doubleday [1958] 128 p.), edited by Edward A. Hamilton and Charles Preston, with text (mostly captions) by Al Laney, diagrams of courses, and numerous illustrations in color.

## Cvii. HORSE-RACING

2259. Robertson, William H. P. The history of thoroughbred racing in America. Englewood Cliffs, N.J., Prentice-Hall [1964] xi, 621 p. 64–17364 SF335.U5R6

In 1610, seven horses were sent to Virginia by the London Company, and 20 mares, "beautiful and full of courage," arrived in 1620. From this beginning, racing has developed into a highly organized, thoroughly controlled, and jealously guarded industry of coast-to-coast proportions. This book is lavishly illustrated with paintings and photographs. Extensive charts show the leading money-winners by seasons; leading jockeys, trainers, owners, breeders, and sires; yearlings sold, average prices, and revenues to States; time records; and champions by seasons, classified as to category.

2260. Woods, David F., *ed.* The fireside book of horse racing. New York, Simon & Schuster, 1963. 341 p. illus.          63–15369 SF301.W6

Although not entirely confined to racing in the United States, this collection of turf fact and fiction edited by a former racetrack publicist is an addition to the sparse literature on one of America's foremost spectator sports. Included in its more than 50 selections are profiles of great American horses, descriptions of famous races, sketches of various aspects of the racing milieu by such well-known sports writers as Joe H. Palmer, Grantland Rice, Red Smith, and Frank Graham, and short stories with a racetrack setting by Donn Byrne, J. P. Marquand, Damon Runyon, and Sherwood Anderson.

## Cviii. MISCELLANEOUS

2261. Alama, Malcolm R. Mark of the oarsmen; a narrative history of rowing at Syracuse University. Syracuse, N.Y., Syracuse Alumni Rowing Association, 1963. 370 p. illus.
          63–24968 GV807.S9A6

Bibliography: p. 343–344.

A chronicle of more than 60 years of rowing history, detailing triumphs and defeats and recording the deeds of the oarsmen, coxwains, coaches, riggers, trainers, alumni, and university officials who directed the fortunes of the Syracuse crews. The work focuses on rowing at Syracuse and the work of James A. Ten Eyck, coach from 1903 until his death in 1938, but includes information on the sport at other colleges and universities and on the Intercollegiate Rowing Association.

2262. Bowen, Ezra. The book of American skiing. Design and layout by Martin Nathan. Philadelphia, Lippincott [1963] 229 p.
          63–21412 GV854.4.B6

The ski editor of *Sports Illustrated* has assembled this pictorial volume, which, with accompanying text, "is intended as a panoramic view of the sport, with details on personalities, places, techniques, history." A recreation which is rapidly becoming the most popular participant winter sport in the United States, skiing was brought to this country long before it reached Central Europe, having been introduced in the mid–19th century by Scandinavian miners searching for gold in the California mountains.

2263. Gallico, Paul. The golden people. Garden City, N.Y., Doubleday, 1965. 315 p. illus.
          65–19889 GV697.A1G3

The author has done what he vowed he never would do when he "read and listened to the old-timers going on about the greats of their era." He has reminisced about the sports stars of his own time. Selecting the outstanding athletes in many fields, he has expanded articles he wrote from 1923 through 1936 for the *Chicago Tribune* and the New York *Daily News* and has added touches of nostalgia and sentimentality. Having known and socialized with Babe Ruth, Gertrude Ederle, Jack Dempsey, Gene Tunney, William T. Tilden, Knute Rockne, Helen Wills, Tex Rickard, Ty Cobb, Johnny Weissmuller, Babe Didrikson, Red Grange, and Bobby Jones, he discusses their lives and characters as well as their great athletic prowess. In an article entitled "Saint Bambino" in the appendix, he brings Babe Ruth back to advise youth on the value and rewards of playing baseball.

2264. Kieran, John, *and* Arthur Daley. The story of the Olympic games, 776 B.C. to 1964. [Rev. ed.] Philadelphia, Lippincott [1965] 448 p. illus.          65–3495 GV23.K5 1965

With symbolic rituals intended to recall the religious aspect of the original Greek contests, the first of the modern games was inaugurated in 1896, fittingly in Athens. There was no "official team" from the United States, but the 13 American athletes carried off first honors in nine of the 12 events in track and field. This work provides, in chronological order, a record of events, participants, and settings from 1896, when 285 athletes from 12 nations vied for honors, through 1964, when more than 5,000 from 94 nations competed in Tokyo. Track and field sports are emphasized, and, since American participants have repeatedly dominated these contests, most of the book is devoted to accomplishments of athletes from the United States. In *An Illustrated History of the Olympics* (New York, Knopf [1963] 319 p.), Richard Schaap offers a similar, albeit less detailed, chronicle containing some 400 photographs. A brief survey concentrating on the outstanding athletes (mostly American) and events is provided by John Durant's *Highlights of the Olympics, From Ancient Times to the Present* (New York, Hastings House [1961] 160 p.).

2265. Palmer, Arthur J. Riding high; the story of the bicycle. New York, Dutton [1956] 191 p.          56–8322 GV1041.P3

The original bicycle was invented in 1816 by Baron Karl von Drais in Karlsruhe, Germany, and was called the Draisine; it had no pedals and was propelled by a walking-scooting motion. In 1866 the so-called velocipede was introduced into the United States by a French inventor, Pierre Lallement. Its brief popularity led to a rapid series of improvements during the 1870's and 1880's, eventuating in a chain-driven, rubber-tired bicycle essentially the same as present-day models. During the Gay Nineties the enthusiasm for bicycles spread rapidly. The author devotes chapters to multicycles (for more than one rider), early motorcycles, "oddities and offshoots" of the bicycle, and racing. The numerous photographs and drawings include illustrations showing a decemtuple, a bicycle built for 10, now in the Ford Museum, and an eight-man tricycle that weighed 1½ tons, with two of its wheels 11 feet in diameter.

2266. Weyand, Alexander M. The cavalcade of basketball. New York, Macmillan, 1960. 271 p. illus.                60–11609  GV885.W47

Basketball was originated by Dr. James Naismith in 1891 at the Young Men's Christian Association Training School in Springfield, Mass.; a soccer ball was tossed at goals consisting of peach baskets. Extensive changes in equipment and in the original 13 rules (one of which allowed from three to 40 players per side) have taken place since then. The author traces the game's development from its Y.M.C.A. club beginnings to its present position as one of the Nation's most popular spectator sports. Although the book was designed primarily as a season-by-season history of college basketball, recalling hundreds of its outstanding organizers, coaches, and players, its concluding chapters are devoted to the national tournaments of the Amateur Athletic Union since 1897, to women's basketball, which spread from Canada to the United States, to international developments (the first major competition

occurring at the Berlin Olympics in 1936), and to "the pro game," which has grown rapidly since World War II.

2267. Wilson, Charles M. The magnificent scufflers; revealing the great day when America wrestled the world. Illustrations by Jon Corbino. Brattleboro, Vt., Stephen Greene Press, 1959. 105 p.
59–13812  GV1195.W5

Wrestling was introduced into colonial America by Irish immigrants, but it was not until the mid-19th century that it really took root in the upstate communities of Vermont—the cradle of American scufflers—which produced three stalwart champions: Henry Dufur (born Dunn), John McMahon, and Ed Decker. During the Civil War, the U.S. Army adopted "collar and elbow" as a favorite recreation. In the 1870's and 1880's, matches with gate receipts of $1,000 and up were held in cities from New England to the Midwest and Pacific coast, and in the 1890's wrestling continued to spread, making its way into the athletic programs of most secondary schools, colleges, and universities. Although its popularity was surpassed by other sports during the early 20th century, it remained well patronized until the Great Depression. The sport revived briefly during World War II, but by the late 1940's true scufflers were being replaced by television performers whose wrestling bouts were palpable charlatanism. In this study, the author discusses eminent wrestlers, traces the evolution of wrestling styles and rules, and describes vicissitudes encountered by the sport.

# D. General Field Sports

2268. Field and Stream. The sportsman's world; for every hunter and fisherman, a richly illustrated guide to sport in seventeen areas of the United States and abroad. By the editors of *Field and Stream*. New York, Holt [1959] 272 p.
59–13595  SK33.F386

A collection of articles originally published in *Field and Stream* (1956–59). More than half the articles (p. 104–232) pertain to the United States; the rest deal largely with Canadian and Caribbean areas readily accessible to Americans. Each article elaborates on the fish and game resources of an area; describes the natural setting; advises on the most favorable seasons, the best means of transportation, and the most desirable equipment; and ana-

lyzes the average costs of fishing and hunting trips. The volume is abundantly illustrated with color photographs. In *The World of "Wood, Field and Stream," an Outdoorsman's Collection From the Columns of the New York Times* (New York, Holt, Rinehart & Winston [1962] 177 p.), the late outdoor editor John W. Randolph injects wit, satire, and irony into 91 tales of his own adventures as hunter and fisherman.

2269. Migdalski, Edward C. Angler's guide to the fresh water sport fishes of North America. New York, Ronald Press [1962] 431 p. illus.
62–9760  SH462.M5

An encyclopedic work on the physical appearance, behavior, habitat, distribution, migration, and reproduction of freshwater game fish. The text is accompanied by photographs, and identification charts (annotated outline drawings) of each species appear at the back of the volume. Introductory chapters note that the great increase in freshwater fishing has occurred mainly because of the remarkable increase during the last 20 years of manmade bodies of water and because of improved conservation techniques. The author notes the dangers of water pollution and urges sportsmen to support remedial legislation. Migdalski has also written *Angler's Guide to the Salt Water Game Fishes, Atlantic and Pacific* (New York, Ronald Press [1958] 506 p.). *America's Favorite Fishing; a Complete Guide to Angling for Panfish* (New York, Outdoor Life [1964] 285 p.), by F. Philip Rice, is a handbook on small game fish.

2270.  Outdoor Life. The story of American hunting and firearms, by the editors of *Outdoor Life,* with paintings by Ralph Crosby Smith, drawings by Nicholas Eggenhofer and Ray Pioch. New York, McGraw-Hill [1959] 172 p.

59–14109  SK41.O9

A history of hunting practices and firearms development from the 17th century's cumbersome muzzle-loading muskets, used to take game in the New England forests to the variety of modern high-velocity hunting rifles and the strictly regulated sport of today. The early colonists used guns imported from or designed in Europe. The first truly American firearm was the Kentucky rifle with a reduced bore and a lengthened barrel, which for more than a century furnished the frontiersman with both a hunting and a military weapon. In the early 1800's the breech-loader and a rudimentary percussion system replaced the awkward process of muzzle-loading and the undependable flint lock. By the beginning of the Civil War, firearms were basically similar to those in use today. This work depicts the hunting opportunities that opened up as the Nation expanded westward and describes the wholesale slaughter of many species of game in the late 19th century. Some kinds of birds and animals were saved from extinction by the conservation laws of the early decades of the 20th century, but others succumbed to hunting and the loss of favorable habitat.

2271.  Ulrich, Heinz. America's best bay, surf, and shoreline fishing. New York, Barnes [1960] 240 p. illus.     60–9867  SH463.U4

2272.  Ulrich, Heinz. America's best lake, stream, and river fishing. New York, Barnes [1962] 367 p. illus.     62–10179  SH463.U42

2273.  Ulrich, Heinz. America's best deep-sea fishing. New York, Barnes [1963] 316 p. illus.     63–18263  SH457.U4  1963

Three volumes which form a comprehensive guide to saltwater and freshwater angling throughout the United States and its coastal waters. For each region or State discussesd, Ulrich indicates the choicest areas and kinds of fish available, seasons for the best catches, facilities for the visiting angler, and sources to write to for more detailed information. He discusses each species with regard to edibility, identifying features, size ranges, behavior patterns, baits that attract it, and tackle that can land it. A final section in each book offers general advice to both the amateur and the veteran angler on fishing methods and gear. A pictorial cross section of varieties of fishing in our inland and shoreline waters is provided in *Fishing America* (Garden City, N.Y., Doubleday [1958] 128 p.), edited by Edward A. Hamilton and Charles Preston. *The Treasury of Angling* (New York, Golden Press [1963] 251 p.), by Lawrence R. Koller, is an illustrated miscellany that presents the evolution of sport fishing in America from the late 18th century, describes the changing paraphernalia used in the art of angling, discusses various species of fish, and gives advice on how best to catch them.

2274.  Walsh, Roy E. Gunning the Chesapeake; duck and goose shooting on the Eastern Shore. Cambridge, Md., Tidewater Publishers, 1960. 117 p.     60–15800  SK327.W3

The Chesapeake Bay and the Eastern Shore of Maryland and Virginia remain among the most fertile hunting grounds in the country. The author describes the life habits of the great variety of waterfowl to be found in this maze of rivers, inlets, ponds, marshes, creeks, sloughs, and streams. He offers both the novice and seasoned gunner advice on the best hunting methods and devotes individual chapters to the carved wooden decoy and the Chesapeake Bay retriever, "a true specialist" who shares his master's zeal for the hunt. Numerous photographs and drawings of the region supplement the text, and a final section provides plates and information designed to aid in identifying the various species. In *The Hunting Dogs of America* (Garden City, N.Y., Doubleday, 1964. 311 p.), Jeff Griffen discusses the history, characteristics, and training of the 44 breeds of hunting dogs used in the United States.

# XXI

# Education

SINCE the compilation of the 1960 *Guide,* books on education have continued to be published in large numbers. Although the authors of the new works have in general shared the preoccupations of the writers represented in the 1960 *Guide,* the entries in Section F, Methods and Techniques, and Section G, Contemporary Problems and Controversies, in the *Supplement* reflect an intensified effort to find ways to improve the educational process. In Section F are the report of the chairman of the Woods Hole Conference of 1959, an introduction to teaching with audiovisual aids, an analysis of the nature of reading from the point of view of linguistics, a study of the guidance function in the schools, a volume of readings on team teaching, and a textbook on measuring scholastic achievement.

Section G in the *Supplement* is proportionately more than twice as large as in the 1960 *Guide.* Readers interested in contemporary educational problems will find entries devoted to familiar topics. Among them are religion and the public schools, Negro education, Communists and the schools, public responsibility and the schools, the training of teachers, the need to upgrade standards of achievement, the Federal Government's involvement in education, reading instruction, and education and democracy.

## A. General Works

### Ai. HISTORICAL AND DESCRIPTIVE

2275. Alexander, Carter, *and* Arvid J. Burke. How to locate educational information and data; an aid to quick utilization of the literature of education. 4th ed., rev. New York, Bureau of Publications, Teachers College, Columbia University, 1958. 419 p.    58–10058  Z711.A37 1958

A revised edition of no. 5098 in the 1960 *Guide*.

2276. Encyclopedia of educational research; a project of the American Educational Research Association. Edited by Chester W. Harris, with the assistance of Marie R. Liba. 3d ed. New York, Macmillan, 1960. xxix, 1564 p.

60–275  LB15.E48  1960

Includes bibliographies.

A revised edition of no. 5111 in the 1960 *Guide*.

2277. Good, Harry G. A history of American education. 2d ed. New York, Macmillan [1962] 610 p. illus.

62–8150  LA209.G58  1962

Bibliography at the end of each chapter.

Education in the United States is constantly changing. The most massive of all the great changes is the prodigious increase in the amount of education offered and undertaken in the last 100 years. Although modifications have come about as a result of external pressure or inner growth, education itself has been alternately viewed as a means for personal development and as an instrument of national policy. The author cautions that the two goals are not mutually exclusive and that the recent shift to the latter may go too far. In another textbook, *An Educational History of the American People* (New York, McGraw-Hill, 1957. 444 p. McGraw-Hill series in education), Adolph E. Meyer interweaves the American educational past with its cultural context. In *Education in the Forming of American Society; Needs and Opportunities for Study* (Chapel Hill, Published for the Institute of Early American History and Culture at Williamsburg, Va., by the University of North Carolina Press [1960] 147 p. Needs and opportunities for study series), historian Bernard Bailyn maintains that the history of American education has suffered from narrow, slanted approaches by educational specialists and crusaders for professionalism. He views education broadly, defining it as the entire process by which a culture transmits itself across the generations and offering fresh insights into that process in the colonial period.

2278. Gross, Richard E., ed. Heritage of American education. Boston, Allyn & Bacon, 1962. 544 p.

62–13069  LA205.G75

Bibliography at the end of each chapter.

CONTENTS.— 1. Heritage of American education; an introduction, by Richard E. Gross.—2. Our debt to the ancients of the Western World, by Richard E. Gross and Arthur H. Moehlman.—3. Judaic roots of modern education, by Eugene B. Borowitz. —4. The Catholic heritage, by Bernard J. Kohlbrenner.—5. Islamic contributions to American education, by Ray H. Muessig and Dwight W. Allen.—6. The Protestant heritage in American education, by Joseph S. Roucek.—7. The European impact upon American educational history, by Joseph S. Roucek and Richard E. Gross.—8. Key ideas from great foreign educational thinkers, by William E. Drake.—9. What do we owe to our American neighbors? by Joseph Katz and Patricia Grinager.—10. Contributions from minorities, elites, and special educational organizations, by Robert M. Frumkin and Joseph S. Roucek.—11. What is indigenous in American education? by Kenneth V. Lottich.—12. America and education in the world, by Richard E. Gross and Joseph S. Roucek.

Beginning in the 1930's, interest in courses on the history of education declined. This volume, with an innovational approach, stresses the need for a revival.

2279. Kursh, Harry. The United States Office of Education: a century of service. Philadelphia, Chilton Books [°1965] xvi, 192 p.

65–11513  LB2807.K8

Bibliography: p. 139–142.

The year 1967 marks the centennial of the U.S. Office of Education. The author's purpose is to tell how and why the Office of Education was created, what it does today, and how it does it. He reviews the history of the Office, summarizes its basic functions, and describes the duties of the Commissioner, his immediate staff, and the three bureaus under which the operating divisions of the Office have been organized. He also discusses the agency's role in the process of accreditation, its methods of distributing educational information, the type of professional personnel it employs, and some of the major problems and issues with which it is concerned. Four appendixes serve as guides to further reading.

2280. Lee, Gordon C. An introduction to education in modern America. Rev. ed. New York, Holt [1957] 624 p.

57–5705  LA209.2.L43  1957

Bibliography at the end of each chapter.

A revised edition of no. 5109 in the 1960 *Guide*. *Public Education in America; a New Interpretation of Purpose and Practice* (New York, Harper [1958] 212 p.), edited by George Z. F. Bereday and Luigi Volpicelli, is the product of a symposium undertaken with the intention of explaining American education to foreign audiences. The 15 contributing educators explore basic educational issues in the United States today. *American Education Today* (New York, McGraw-Hill [1963] 292 p.), edited by Paul Woodring and John Scanlon, is a collection of 30 essays taken from the "Education in America" section of *Saturday Review*.

2281. Welter, Rush. Popular education and democratic thought in America. New York, Columbia University Press, 1962. 473 p.

62–19909   LA212.W4

Bibliography: p. [389]–435.

An analysis of the dynamic interrelationships between two of the most characteristic American political commitments, popular rule and public education. The author traces the historical development of the American belief in education in terms of representative schools of political and social theory and points out that the idea of education has played an influential role in determining the content of our political thought. In the 20th century a significant change has occurred. The people continue to have great faith in formal education, but their confidence in informal, democratic, political education has weakened. In Welter's view, the change threatens the theory of democracy. He concludes, nevertheless, that faith in education has been and remains America's most characteristic political belief.

2282. Wesley, Edgar B. NEA: the first hundred years; the building of the teaching profession. New York, Harper [1957] 419 p.

56–11918   L13.N49W4

Bibliographical footnotes.

The National Education Association of the United States has played a major role in American life as a builder of the teaching profession, a proponent of educational ideas, and a disseminator of educational information. "An account of the rise and progress of the NEA in its broadest sense would be the history of American education; in its narrowest sense it would be the internal story of the growth of a great organization." The author has chosen the middle way between these two extremes by selecting the *Proceedings* of the association from 1857 to 1956 as his main source. His account is, therefore, the history of some aspects of American education in which the NEA was actively involved as a contributor. A historian and sociologist, Wesley was chosen by the NEA to write its history for the occasion of its centennial celebration.

### Aii. PHILOSOPHICAL AND THEORETICAL

2283. Brameld, Theodore B. H. Toward a reconstructed philosophy of education. [New York] Dryden Press [1956] 417 p. (Dryden Press professional books in education)

56–13909   LB875.B724

Bibliography: p. 399–406.

The philosophy of reconstructionism in education as conceived and developed here is essentially an extension and a reformulation of the philosophy of progressivism. It seeks to correct the latter's weaknesses and strengthen its achievements. Many contributions made by the philosophies of perennialism and essentialism are also incorporated into the reconstructionist pattern, however. After discussing the background and underlying philosophical beliefs of reconstructionism, the author elaborates on its theory of education. In *Cultural Foundations of Education: An Interdisciplinary Exploration* (New York, Harper [1957] 330 p.), the same author examines and interprets aspects of culture theory that have implications for philosophy and for the practice of education. In *The Ideal and the Community; a Philosophy of Education* (New York, Harper [1958] 302 p.), Isaac B. Berkson proposes a philosophy of reconstructionism more conservative than Brameld's. Although Berkson's point of departure is experimentalism, he is inclined toward the idealism that is characteristic of traditional philosophy.

2284. Johnston, Herbert. A philosophy of education. New York, McGraw-Hill [1963] 362 p. (McGraw-Hill Catholic series in education)

62–18857   LB885.J58

Bibliographical footnotes.

A neo-Thomist exposition that proceeds from considerations of the nature of man and of those powers that make him "educable." Although the book, written by a professor of philosophy at the University of Notre Dame, is intentionally doctrinal rather than historical in character, it does include cogent analyses of other philosophies. Questions and cases intended to stimulate philosophical discussion are appended to each chapter. In *Public Schools and Moral Education; the Influence of Horace Mann, William Torrey Harris, and John Dewey* (New York, Columbia University Press, 1958. 315 p.), Neil G. McCluskey, a Jesuit priest, discusses the problem that religious pluralism poses for the public schools in their quest for a philosophy of values.

2285. Morris, Van Cleve. Philosophy and the American school; an introduction to the philosophy of education. Boston, Houghton Mifflin [1961] 492 p. 61–16124   LB885.M67

Writing from the positions of experimentalism in philosophy and progressivism in educational theory, the author employs what he designates as the "philosophy-to-policy-to-practice" approach to the philosophical questions of ontology, epistemology, and axiology. He explains how each question is dealt with by exponents of idealism, realism, neo-Thomism, experimentalism, and existentialism and relates their views to educational theory. He also synthesizes the various concepts into a policy for managing American education and depicts the classroom operation of philosophical theory and stated policy.

2286. Phenix, Philip H. Philosophy of education. New York, Holt [1958] 623 p.
58–6308 LB885.P5
Bibliography: p. 591–612.

A professor of educational philosophy at Teachers College, Columbia University, analyzes a wide range of topics in the light of variant philosophical positions. In order to prevent the reader from being influenced except by the persuasiveness of the ideas and arguments themselves, the author presents each position without reference to the authorities who have advocated it. In *Education and the Common Good; a Moral Philosophy of the Curriculum* (New York, Harper [1961] 271 p.), the same author proposes that the content of school instruction be based on a consideration of the major problems facing contemporary civilization. He maintains that the cardinal goal of instruction in all fields should be "the development of loyalty to what is excellent, instead of success in satisfying desires."

2287. Riesman, David. Constraint and variety in American education. [Lincoln] University of Nebraska Press [1956] 160 p. ([Nebraska. University] The university lectures in the humanities, 1)
56–13482 LA210.R5

"To place American higher and secondary school education in its cultural context" is the plan for the author's three sociological essays, based on lectures delivered at the University of Nebraska. In "The Academic Profession," he points out the ways in which universities imitate one another, follow national models, and tend toward "institutional homogenization." In "The Intellectual Veto Groups," he focuses on the interdisciplinary problems and conflicts within the social sciences. "Secondary Education and 'Counter-Cyclical' Policy" is a discussion of the vulnerability of high schools to local pressures; here Riesman presents "a theory of education as desirably 'counter-cyclical,' that is, a theory that education should oppose momentary booms and busts in our cultural economy." The view of education from the position of sociology is depicted in greater detail by Robert J. Havighurst and Bernice L. Neugarten in *Society and Education,* 2d ed. (Boston, Allyn & Bacon, 1962. 585 p.). The perspective from two other social sciences is revealed

in *Educational Anthropology: An Introduction* (New York, Wiley [1965] 171 p.), by George F. Kneller, and *Educational Psychology; Psychological Foundations of Education,* 2d ed. (Boston, Allyn & Bacon, 1964. 589 p.), by James M. Sawrey and Charles W. Telford.

2288. Ulich, Robert. Philosophy of education. New York, American Book Co. [1961] 286 p. 61–2970 LB875.U63
Bibliography at the end of each chapter.

A Harvard University professor of education writes from a philosophical point of view which might be defined as a combination of idealism, existentialism, and humanism. Examining the role that education plays within the ever-expanding continuum of civilization, he points out the dependence of man's progress upon his success in keeping the apparently contrasting aspects of life, or the polarities of civilization, in constructive harmony and balance. As the ideal basis for instruction, he proposes the concept of "cosmic reverence" expressed in Goethe's *Wilhelm Meisters Wanderjahre,* which to Ulich means "not only a person's respect and love for other persons or for a cherished idea or institution, but a sense of the belongingness of all created things to a common ground of life, religiously expressed by such terms as God, the Father, the Creator, or naturalistically expressed—though mostly with a religious overtone—by such terms as *nature, the creation, the universe, the cosmos.*" *Education and the Idea of Mankind* (New York, Harcourt, Brace & World [1964] 279 p.), edited by Ulich and published under the auspices of the Council for the Study of Mankind, views education as a means for helping mankind realize its fundamental unity and brotherhood while it maintains a diversity in ideas and beliefs.

2289. Wegener, Frank C. The organic philosophy of education. Dubuque, Iowa, W. C. Brown [1957] xx, 472 p.
A58–5794 LB885.W4
Bibliographical footnotes at the end of each chapter.

An attempt to achieve a synthesis in the philosophy of education. The author believes that the arguments about educational philosophies in terms of such dichotomies as realism versus idealism, naturalism versus supernaturalism, and modernism versus classicism are now anachronistic. Far from being eclectic, the organic philosophy, with its bipolar theory of education, holds that the nature of man and the world is such that the divergent views of conservatism and progressivism are not mutually exclusive but can and must operate side by side. This orientation is in the tradition extending from

Plato and Aristotle to Alfred North Whitehead, all of whose writings influenced the author's thought. After establishing his philosophical foundations, Wegener applies his propositions to the crucial problems of educational philosophy. Whitehead's technical terminology, which can be troublesome to the general reader, is defined in a special appended glossary.

# B. Primary and Secondary Schools

## Bi. GENERAL AND HISTORICAL WORKS

2290. Carpenter, Charles H. History of American schoolbooks. Philadelphia, University of Pennsylvania Press [1963] 322 p. illus.
62–10747  LT23.C3  1963
Bibliography: p. 279–300.
An analysis of the evolution of textbooks in the United States and "along with this, as a requisite accompaniment, a picture of the pioneer-day school system — this latter only insofar as it had to do with schoolbook production and early usage." Because of the large number of books involved, the author, whose personal collection alone totals about 3,000, limits his study to outstanding works. These include such elementary texts as the New England primer, such readers as those in the McGuffey series, and specialized subject-area works from grammars to geographies. In Ruth M. Elson's *Guardians of Tradition; American Schoolbooks of the Nineteenth Century* (Lincoln, University of Nebraska Press [1964] 424 p.), more than a thousand popular texts used in the first eight grades are examined with respect to their ideological teachings on such subjects as God, nature, race, and religion. In *Old Textbooks* ([Pittsburgh] University of Pittsburgh Press [1961] 364 p.), John A. Nietz surveys and analyzes some 8,000 works used by the schools before 1900.

2291. Cremin, Lawrence A. The transformation of the school; progressivism in American education, 1876–1957. New York, Knopf, 1961. 387 p.            61–11000  LA209.C7
Bibliographical note: p. 355–387.
"The story of the progressive education movement: of its genesis in the decades immediately following the Civil War; of its widespread appeal among the intellectuals at the turn of the century; of its gathering political momentum during the decade before World War I; of its conquest of the organized teaching profession; of its pervasive impact on American schools and colleges, public and private; of its fragmentation during the 1920's and 1930's; and of its ultimate collapse after World War II; is the substance of this volume." In the author's view, progressive education was a parallel to political progressivism; it was the educational phase of the widespread humanitarian and political effort to fulfill the "promise of American life."

2292. Edwards, Newton, *and* Herman G. Richey. The school in the American social order. 2d ed. Boston, Houghton Mifflin [1963] 694 p. illus.            63–4262  LA205.E3  1963
Bibliography at the end of each chapter.
A revised edition of no. 5140 in the 1960 *Guide*.

2293. Gross, Neal C. Who runs our schools? New York, Wiley [1958] 195 p.
58–12523  LB2806.G74
In Massachusetts, 105 superintendents and 508 board members were interviewed by investigators who asked such questions as "What are the major obstacles you face in your efforts to do a good job in your community?" The answers are here summarized and examined, and the reader's thoughts are directed to proposed answers to the question, "What can be done?" In *Education and the Cult of Efficiency* ([Chicago] University of Chicago Press [1962] 273 p.), Raymond E. Callahan traces the origin and development of the adoption of business values and practices in educational administration. He protests that school administrators have begun to consider themselves business managers rather than scholars and educational philosophers and urges Americans to concentrate more on excellence than on efficiency and economy in education.

2294. Kandel, Isaac L. American education in the twentieth century. Cambridge, Harvard University Press, 1957. 247 p. (The Library of Congress series in American civilization)
57–11658  LA209.2.K26
Bibliographical notes: p. 231–238.
"The fifty years of this century have witnessed a radical transformation of a theory of education [i.e., progressivism] that has achieved notoriety both because of the vociferous claims put forward in its behalf and because the roseate picture was painted against a backdrop of an 'evil' educational tradi-

tion." In this study of public elementary and secondary education, the author acknowledges that the public schools in the United States have improved. He maintains, however, that the improvement resulted mainly from the contributions of psychology and child study rather than from progressive or "modern" theories. Kandel takes the traditional or "essentialist" viewpoint espoused by William C. Bagley, whose biography he presents in *William Chandler Bagley, Stalwart Educator* (New York, Bureau of Publications, Teachers College, Columbia University, 1961. 131 p.). Kandel also shares with Bagley the conviction that teachers must have thorough scholarly training as well as high pedagogical skills.

2295. Mort, Paul R., Walter C. Reusser, *and* John W. Polley. Public school finance: its background, structure, and operation. 3d ed. New York, McGraw-Hill, 1960. 512 p. (McGraw-Hill series in education)
59–11940  LB2825.M598  1960
Bibliography at the end of each chapter.
A revised edition of no. 5144 in the 1960 *Guide*. Arvid J. Burke's *Financing Public Schools in the United States,* rev. ed. (New York, Harper [1957] 679 p. Exploration series in education) is an updated edition of a work mentioned in the annotation for *Public School Finance* in the 1960 *Guide*.

2296. Thayer, Vivian T. The role of the school in American society. New York, Dodd, Mead, 1960. 530 p.           60–6781  LC191.T48
Bibliography at the end of each chapter.
The author considers selected assumptions and formative ideas about education, analyzes transformations in the social and economic status of youth that have affected the curriculum, examines the relationship between educational theories and curriculum, methods of teaching, and administrative structure, and discusses issues currently facing the schools. He enlarges upon one of his topics in a subsequent work, *Formative Ideas in American Education, From the Colonial Period to the Present* (New York, Dodd, Mead, 1965. 394 p.).

## Bii. PRESCHOOL AND PRIMARY GRADES

2297. Caswell, Hollis L., *and* Arthur Wellesley Foshay. Education in the elementary school. 3d ed. New York, American Book Co. [1957] 430 p. illus. (American education series)
57–753  LB1555.C35  1957
Bibliography at the end of each chapter. Bibliography: p. 420–421.

A revised edition of no. 5147 in the 1960 *Guide*. *Nursery-Kindergarten Education* (New York, McGraw-Hill, 1958. 365 p.), edited by Jerome E. Leavitt, is a collection of essays written by 11 educators to help students, teachers, and parents become oriented to the methods, curriculum, philosophy, and basic principles of nursery school and kindergarten. Nancy M. Rambusch's *Learning How to Learn; an American Approach to Montessori* (Baltimore, Helicon [1963, °1962] 183 p.) is focused on the educational methods developed for preschool children by Maria Montessori and on the use of these methods in the United States. Gilbert E. Donahue's 481-item bibliography of writings by and about Montessori is appended.

2298. Otto, Henry J., *and* David C. Sanders. Elementary school organization and administration. 4th ed. New York, Appleton-Century-Crofts [1964] 409 p.    64–11518  LB2805.O76  1964
Bibliographical footnotes.
A revised edition of no. 5151 in the 1960 *Guide*.

## Biii. SECONDARY SCHOOLS

2299. Conant, James B. The American high school today: a first report to interested citizens. New York, McGraw-Hill [1959] 140 p. (Carnegie series in American education, 1)
59–8527  LB1607.C647
From 1957 to 1959, the author and his staff of four assistants, on a grant from the Carnegie Corporation of America, conducted an investigation of "comprehensive" high schools in 26 States. A comprehensive high school is one which accommodates all the high-school-age youths of a community and is typical of American secondary education in the United States. Having no equivalent in any European country, "it has come into being because of our economic history and our devotion to the ideals of equality of opportunity and equality of status." The main objectives of such a school, Conant maintains, are to provide a general education for all, a variety of nonacademic elective programs, and special arrangements for academically talented students. Convinced that small schools cannot attain these objectives, he urges that they be abolished wherever possible. He also presents a list of 21 additional recommendations concerning the major existing weaknesses of public secondary education. The same author's later volume, *The Child, the Parent, and the State* (Cambridge, Harvard University Press, 1959. 211 p.), is based on addresses that largely grew out of the same study. His *Recommendations for Education in the Junior High School Years; a Memorandum to School*

*Boards* (Princeton, N.J., Educational Testing Service [1960] 46 p.) derives from a second investigation conducted during the 1959–60 school year.

2300. Downey, Lawrence W. The secondary phase of education. New York, Blaisdell Pub. Co. [1965] xvi, 226 p. (A Blaisdell book in the social and behavioral sciences) 64–24820 LB1607.D67
Annotated bibliography at the end of each chapter.
The author maintains that secondary education has been characterized by a lack of order and system. Scholarly studies in the field have not been adequately related, and no guiding comprehensive concept of the total process of education has been developed. Downey's purpose is to facilitate fruitful research by advancing a conceptual system for the study of secondary education. In *The American Secondary School Curriculum* (New York, Macmillan [1965] 453 p.), Leonard H. Clark, Raymond L. Klein, and John B. Burks describe the background theory and present substance of the junior and senior high school curriculum. Harl R. Douglass has revised his two textbooks: *Modern Administration of Secondary Schools; Organization and Administration of Junior and Senior High Schools,* 2d ed. (Boston, Ginn [1963] 636 p.), the first edition of which is no. 5154 in the 1960 *Guide,* and *Secondary Education in the United States,* 2d ed. (New York, Ronald Press [1964] 475 p.), the original edition of which is entitled *Secondary Education for Life Adjustment of American Youth* (1952) and is mentioned in the annotation for no. 5224 in the 1960 *Guide.*

2301. Krug, Edward A. The shaping of the American high school. New York, Harper & Row [1964] 486 p. (Exploration series in education) 64–12801 LA222.K7
Bibliographical note: p. 449–466.
In the author's view, the high school assumed its modern shape and characteristics during the period between 1880 and 1920. Caught in a vast complex of reform, the high school was subjected to extensive criticism. The *Report of the Committee on Secondary School Studies* (1893) "aroused the educational world to discussion and controversy." Prepared by a committee of the National Education Association, it is generally referred to as the "Report of the Committee of Ten." An extensive account of this document is contained in Theodore R. Sizer's *Secondary Schools at the Turn of the Century* (New Haven, Yale University Press, 1946. 304 p.). "For fifteen years after its publication," Sizer says of the report, "it served as gospel for the curriculum writers of the burgeoning high schools; in our own time it serves as the explicit rallying point for those who feel that our secondary schools have forgotten their central role in training the intellect."

2302. Middlekauff, Robert. Ancients and axioms: secondary education in eighteenth-century New England. New Haven, Yale University Press, 1963. 218 p. (Yale historical publications. Miscellany 77) 63–7941 LA222.M53
Bibliographical note: p. 196–203.
An analysis of the English educational tradition in its New England setting. From 1700 to 1783 the Puritan, or liberal, tradition persisted in such educational patterns as the development of private education and the adherence to a classical curriculum. From 1784 to 1800 the tradition was weakened by the decline of the grammar schools and the emergence of the academy with its addition of higher mathematics and vocational subjects to the curriculum. The author points out that the distinctive achievements of the Puritan system are difficult to discern, but he indicates its influence on the lives of boys and on cultural developments in New England. He concludes that although the liberal tradition did not by itself produce a new frame of mind, "it did reinforce tendencies already present — a concern for this world, religious apathy, and especially the rational strain within Puritanism."

# C. Colleges and Universities

## Ci. GENERAL AND HISTORICAL WORKS

2303. American Council on Education. American universities and colleges. Edited by Allan M. Cartter. 9th ed. Washington [1964] xv, 1339 p. 28–5598 LA226.A65

A revised edition of no. 5161 in the 1960 *Guide.* Parts 1 and 2 and appendixes 1, 4, and 6 have been separately published under the title *Higher Education in the United States* (Washington [1965] 197 p.).

2304. Berelson, Bernard. Graduate education in the United States. New York, McGraw-Hill, 1960. 346 p. (The Carnegie series in American education) 60–12759 LB2371.B4
Bibliography: p. 265–270.

Graduate education began in the United States in 1876 with the opening of Johns Hopkins University. The author reviews the history of that institution's program as background for an anlysis of major current trends and problems. In his conclusions and recommendations he takes the position that graduate education is basically sound but can be improved by a few adaptive changes. In *Graduate Education; a Critique and a Program* (New York, Harper [1961] 213 p.), Oliver C. Carmichael characterizes the graduate school as the most inefficient and, in some ways, the most ineffective division of the modern university and suggests a specific, thoroughgoing program of reform and reorganization. *Graduate Education Today* (Washington, American Council on Education [1965] 246 p.), edited by Everett Walters, consists of the views of 13 graduate school deans.

2305. Brick, Michael. Forum and focus for the junior college movement: the American Association of Junior Colleges. New York, Bureau of Publications, Teachers College, Columbia University, 1964 [°1963] 222 p. (Teachers College studies in education) 64–14816 LB2301.A24B7
Bibliography: p. 209–222.

As a voluntary, national organization, the American Association of Junior Colleges provides leadership, direction, and cohesion for the Nation's two-year colleges. The author traces the history of the association from its inception in 1920 through its annual meeting in 1962 and examines the junior college movement as a whole. In *The Junior College: Progress and Prospect* (New York, McGraw-Hill, 1960. 367 p. The Carnegie series in American education), Leland L. Medsker, past president of the association, describes the effectiveness with which the junior college performs its major functions. *The Open Door College: A Case Study* (New York, McGraw-Hill, 1960. 207 p. The Carnegie series in American education), by Burton R. Clark, is a study of San Jose Junior College, California, which is an administrative part of the local school district and has a strong tendency toward secondary school orientation. *The Two-Year College; a Social Synthesis* (Englewood Cliffs, N.J., Prentice-Hall [1965] 298 p. Prentice-Hall series in education), by Clyde E. Blocker, Robert H. Plummer, and Richard C. Richardson, is focused upon the relationship between the two-year college as an institution and the society it was created to serve.

2306. Brubacher, John S., *and* Willis Rudy. Higher education in transition; an American history, 1636–1956. New York, Harper [1958] 494 p. 58–7978 LA226.B75
Bibliographical footnotes: p. 391–479.

A summing up of the development of higher education from its beginnings in the small colonial church-related colleges to the variety of forms it takes today. The discussion includes the New England hilltop college, the school of technology, the complex municipal college or university, the community or junior college, and the large secular State university. Each of these diverse forms represents a significant stage in the growth of American civilization. All possess the distinguishing imprint of democracy. Endorsing Jacksonian egalitarianism, the authors conclude that "American higher education, far from reinforcing caste, has helped to foster social mobility; instead of ratifying the recruitment of an elite by ascription, it has thrown its influence in the direction of the selection of a leadership by achievement."

2307. Goodman, Paul. The community of scholars. New York, Random House [1962] 175 p. 62–17163 LB2321.G63

"A little treatise in anarchist theory" is the definition given by the author to this critique of colleges and universities in the United States. He believes in free association and federation rather than from-the-top management and administration and advocates a revival of the ancient but neglected notion of the community of scholars. He proposes that groups of faculty members secede from established institutions and create conditions under which they can teach and learn without external obstruction and regulation by administrators. An attempt to develop a community of scholars within the framework of the established university system is described in a collection of 11 essays, *A Community of Scholars; the University Seminars at Columbia* (New York, Praeger [1965] 177 p.), edited by Frank Tannenbaum, the founder and director of the seminar movement at Columbia University, where for 20 years informal groups of scholars and intellectuals from many departments and institutions have met monthly for dialog on broad subjects.

2308. Harris, Seymour E. Higher education: resources and finance. New York, McGraw-Hill, 1962. xxxviii, 713 p. illus. 61–18311 LB2342.H34
Bibliographical footnotes.

An economist attacks the problems of getting more resources into higher education and utilizing them more effectively. He reviews present trends.

projects a 1970 budget for all colleges and universities combined, and discusses such topics as tuition, scholarships and loans, Federal and State aid, the declining significance of endowment–fund income, mistakes in management, costs and economies, and the economic status of the faculty. *Philanthropy in the Shaping of American Higher Education* (New Brunswick, N.J., Rutgers University Press [1965] 340 p.), by Merle E. Curti and Roderick Nash, is devoted to the broad question, "What difference did the giving of billions of dollars to American colleges and universities make?" The land-grant movement from its beginnings to the present is the subject of Edward D. Eddy's *Colleges for Our Land and Time; the Land-Grant Idea in American Education* (New York, Harper [1957] 328 p.).

2309. Hofstadter, Richard, *and* Wilson Smith, *eds.* American higher education, a documentary history. [Chicago] University of Chicago Press [1961] 2 v. 61–15935 LA226.H53 1961
Bibliographical footnotes.

A highly readable anthology covering three centuries of educational history. The selections range from John Eliot's earnest appeal for a college in the Massachusetts Bay Colony in 1633 to the 1947 report of the President's Commission on Higher Education and Robert M. Hutchins' critical commentary on it. Many of the documents have long been out of print and inaccessible except in the largest libraries. Together they reveal "the diffusion of the educational system throughout the country; the problems created by sectarian affiliations; the character and functions of presidents and trustees; the evolution of curricular controversies and educational ideals; the institutional position and role of the professor and the conditions of professorial life; the development of academic freedom." Each part of the anthology is prefaced by an introductory essay identifying the documents and placing them in context.

2310. Kerr, Clark. The uses of the university. Cambridge, Mass., Harvard University Press, 1963. 140 p. (The Godkin lectures at Harvard University, 1963) 63–20770 LB2325.K43
Bibliographical footnotes: p. 127–135.

In his eight-year presidency, the author led the University of California through a period of tremendous growth and change. In this volume, based on three lectures that he delivered at Harvard University in 1963, he describes recent developments in higher education. He maintains that the university is being reshaped by the widespread recognition that new knowledge is the most important factor in economic and social growth. In *The Academic*

*President: Educator or Caretaker?* (New York, McGraw-Hill, 1962. 294 p. The Carnegie series in American education), Harold W. Dodds, president of Princeton University from 1933 to 1957, stresses that a college president's prime function should be to furnish educational leadership rather than to devote himself to such activities as fundraising and public relations. In *Academic Procession; Reflections of a College President* (New York, Columbia University Press, 1959. 222 p.), Henry M. Wriston, president emeritus of Brown University, asserts that scholarly achievement is the principal qualification for the head of an institution of higher learning.

2311. McGrath, Earl J. The predominantly Negro colleges and universities in transition. [New York] Published for the Institute of Higher Education by the Bureau of Publications, Teachers College, Columbia University [1965] xv, 204 p. (Publications of the Institute of Higher Education) 65–19733 LC2801.M28
Bibliography: p. 194–204.

A former U. S. Commissioner of Education presents an overview of the characteristics, needs, and prospects of 123 predominantly Negro institutions that provide the main educational opportunity for Negro youth. He emphasizes the necessity for massive support from private foundations, government, and other benefactors. *The Negro Woman's College Education* (New York, Teachers College, Columbia University, 1956. 163 p. TC studies in education), by Jeanne L. Noble, is a brief discussion of current conditions.

2312. Newcomer, Mabel. A century of higher education for American women. New York, Harper [1959] 266 p. 59–13797 LC1756.N4
Bibliographical note: p. 257–259. Bibliography at the end of each chapter.

An interpretive history of higher education for women from its beginnings at Oberlin College in 1837. Written as a tribute to Vassar College on the occasion of its centennial celebration, the book emphasizes, because of the important roles they have played, some of the older institutions, including — in addition to Vassar — Bryn Mawr, Radcliffe, Mount Holyoke, and Wellesley.

2313. Power, Edward J. A history of Catholic higher education in the United States. Milwaukee, Bruce Pub. Co. [1958] 383 p. 58–9981 LC487.P65
Bibliography: p. 359–373.

The author centers his attention on the origins and development of Catholic colleges for men. The first four-year Catholic college for women was not established until 1896, and it, like others that followed, was essentially patterned after the existing men's colleges. In addition, the men's institutions, although they are less numerous than their counterparts for women, enroll four times as many students. Appendixes provide brief historical sketches of 267 men's colleges, in order by date of founding, and lists of men's and women's colleges, arranged by States.

2314. Rudolph, Frederick. The American college and university, a history. New York, Knopf, 1962. 516 p. (Knopf publications in education) 62–12991 LA226.R72

Bibliography: p. [497]–516.

"For some time now the general reader and the professional historian have had greater access to the history of almost any skirmish of the Civil War than they have had to the history of education in the United States. This book is intended in some way to redress the balance, as far as the American experience with higher education is concerned." The author draws on 300 years of educational development to provide informed answers to the questions of how, why, and with what results colleges and universities have developed as they have. He discusses the role and status of faculties and administration, conflicts over the curriculum, and extracurricular activities. A bibliography is supplemented by a commentary on the historiography of higher education and by suggestions concerning needs and opportunities for further study in this field.

2315. Sanford, Nevitt, ed. The American college; a psychological and social interpretation of the higher learning. Prepared for the Society for the Psychological Study of Social Issues. New York, Wiley [1962] xvi, 1084 p.
61–17362 LA228.S3

Includes bibliographies.

The editor states that the major purpose of this volume is to help put the resources of the newer social sciences into the service of liberal education. The 30 contributors are social scientists who are convinced that colleges are failing to achieve their stated purposes and who advocate searching for remedies through studies of the processes of college education. Here they undertake to indicate what has been done and what needs to be done in the field of undergraduate education. The college is analyzed as a complex, diverse whole, constantly influenced and changed by the society and culture in which it exists.

2316. Schmidt, George P. The liberal arts college; a chapter in American cultural history. New Brunswick, N.J., Rutgers University Press, 1957. 310 p. 57–8640 LA226.S36

Bibliography: p. 297–299.

The liberal arts college was the original institution of higher learning in the United States. Its history is traced here, from the colonial period to the present, by a Rutgers University historian. He views the liberal arts college as an institution that has changed from one dominating the educational scene to one struggling to maintain its identity and existence. The author concludes that its future is dependent on the continued vitality of the principle of academic freedom. The nonconformist must be allowed to express himself. "What was said by them of old time contains the wisdom of the ages, which the liberal college must preserve and transmit to posterity. But whenever a prophet of new ideals arises to speak with the authority that rests on fullness of knowledge and conscientious conviction, it is the duty of the liberal college to give him a hearing."

2317. Veysey, Laurence R. The emergence of the American university. Chicago, University of Chicago Press [1965] xiv, 505 p.
65–24427 LA226.V47

Bibliography: p. 448–460.

From the Civil War until about 1890, the main issue concerning the university in the United States was the problem of defining its basic purpose and function. In the nineties, the dispute centered on the kind and degree of control to be exerted by the administration. Accordingly, this study, covering the period from 1865 to 1910, is divided into two parts. "The first considers in turn each of the principal academic philosophies which vied for dominance of higher learning in the United States during the decades after 1865. Interspersed among the accounts of these philosophies are brief analyses of some of the individual leaders who were more or less associated with each of them. The second part of the study, largely devoted to developments after 1890, describes the academic structure which came into being, the younger men who took command of it, and its effect on a variety of professional temperaments. Here again brief discussions of particular leading figures have been used to illustrate the general themes."

2318. Wilson, Logan, ed. Emerging patterns in American higher education. Washington, American Council on Education [1965] 292 p.
65–19783 LB2325.W49

Includes bibliographies.

Thirty-six essays, most of which were prepared for the annual meeting of the American Council on Education in San Francisco, October 1–2, 1964. They are focused on the problems arising from the growth of new patterns of organization and administration within colleges and universities. *Higher Education: Some Newer Developments* (New York, McGraw-Hill [1965] 342 p.), edited by Samuel Baskin, is devoted to recent experimentation. In *The Citadel of Learning* (New Haven, Yale University Press, 1956. 79 p.), James B. Conant reflects on the two main functions of a university, teaching and research, and their interrelationship. William C. De Vane, in *Higher Education in Twentieth-Century America* (Cambridge, Harvard University Press, 1965. 211 p. Library of Congress series in American civilization), identifies and describes movements and trends.

## Cii. INDIVIDUAL INSTITUTIONS

2319. Durkin, Joseph T. Georgetown University: the middle years, 1840–1900. Washington, Georgetown University Press, 1963. 333 p. illus.
63–22294 LD1961.G52D8
"Bibliographical essay": p. 319–322.
Georgetown University was the first institution of Catholic higher education in the United States. Father Durkin continues the narrative begun by Father John M. Daley, S.J., in *Georgetown University: Origin and Early Years* (Washington, Georgetown University Press, 1957. 324 p.), which recounts the events surrounding the founding of the college in 1789 and the subsequent 50 years of growth. Among the major figures in Father Durkin's study are Father James Ryder, during whose presidency the medical school was opened in 1851; Father Bernard Maguire, who in his last commencement address in 1870 announced the opening of the law school; and Father Patrick F. Healy, who played a dominant role in the decision to make the institution a university.

2320. Foster, Margery S. "Out of smalle beginnings . . ." an economic history of Harvard College in the Puritan period (1636 to 1712). Cambridge, Belknap Press of Harvard University Press, 1962. 243 p. illus. 62–13266 LD2152.F63
Bibliography: p. [209]–216.
"The object of this study is to describe the economic situation of Harvard College in the Puritan Period, and to show how general economic factors of the period influenced the College, as well as how factors other than economic affected Harvard's economics." The author also differentiates between current practices that have colonial origins and those that are new. *Social Sciences at Harvard, 1860–1920; From Inculcation to the Open Mind* (Cambridge, Harvard University Press, 1965. 320 p.), edited by Pearl H. Buck, consists of essays by five graduate students who view the introduction of the scientific method of inquiry, by which college teaching changed from the revelation of a fixed body of truth to the search for truth, as the principal impulse that transformed Harvard from the classical college of 1850 to the great university of 1900.

2321. Meigs, Cornelia L. What makes a college? A history of Bryn Mawr. New York, Macmillan, 1956. 277 p. illus.
56–7323 LD7063.M4
The history of a small, prestigious, liberal arts college for women, located near Philadelphia, Pa. The author concludes that the institution's success has been due to the mutual harmony of its presidents, trustees, alumnae, faculty, and students, in short, all who have shared in its growth. The source of the harmony has been "an unspoken loyalty, an unshakable belief in the power of human learning, in the power of men's minds as a force as great as any that exists in a universe of infinite forces." Margaret F. Thorp's *Neilson of Smith* (New York, Oxford University Press, 1956. 363 p.) is the biography of William A. Neilson, teacher and scholar who, from 1917 to 1939, was president of Smith College, another outstanding liberal arts college for women, located in Northampton, Mass.

2322. Michigan University. The University of Michigan, an encyclopedic survey. Wilfred B. Shaw, editor. Ann Arbor, University of Michigan Press, 1942–58. 4 v. (2066 p.) illus.
61–63636 LD3278.A242
Vols. 3–4 edited by Walter A. Donnelly and others. Includes bibliographies.
This survey, entered as no. 5201 in the 1960 *Guide,* was completed with the publication of volume 4 in 1958. It has also been issued in eight volumes. The recent history of a large Southern State university is traced by Louis R. Wilson in *The University of North Carolina, 1900–1930; the Making of a Modern University* (Chapel Hill, University of North Carolina Press [1957] 633 p.) and *The University of North Carolina Under Consolidation, 1931–1963: History and Appraisal* (Chapel Hill, University of North Carolina, Consolidated Office, 1964. 483 p.). Intimately connected with the university's growth since 1901 as librarian, teacher, and founder of the institution's library school, extension service, and press, Wilson draws fruitfully upon personal experience in developing his narrative.

2323. Rudolph, Frederick. Mark Hopkins and the log; Williams College, 1836–1872. New Haven, Yale University Press, 1956. 267 p. illus. (Yale historical publications. Miscellany 63)

56–5946  LD6072.7  1836.R8

Bibliography: p. [239]–256.

Williams College, a small liberal arts institution for men in northwestern Massachusetts, "has become in the folklore of American education a symbol of what Americans have often meant by a college education." A legend has grown up around the figure of Mark Hopkins, who served as president from 1836 to 1872. Many students of higher education consider James A. Garfield's well-known aphorism, "The ideal college is Mark Hopkins on one end of a log and a student on the other," to be the most satisfactory definition of what an American college ought to be. The author attempts to recover Hopkins, his college, and its students from mythology and to determine the extent to which they and their contemporaries on other college campuses influence education today.

## D. Education of Special Groups

2324. Baker, Harry J. Introduction to exceptional children. 3d ed. New York, Macmillan [1959] 523 p. illus.

59–5106  LC3965.B32  1959

Bibliography at the end of each chapter.

A revised edition of no. 5207 in the 1960 *Guide*. *Special Education for the Exceptional* (Boston, P. Sargent [1955–56] 3 v.), edited by Merle E. Frampton and Elena D. Gall, which is mentioned in the annotation for no. 5207 in the 1960 *Guide*, is now complete with the publication of volume 3. Samuel A. Kirk's *Educating Exceptional Children* (Boston, Houghton Mifflin [1962] 415 p.) is a textbook that applies the concept of discrepancies in growth to the study of exceptional children and has chapters on the intellectually gifted, the mentally retarded, the auditorily handicapped, the visually handicapped, the speech defective, the orthopedically handicapped, and the emotionally disturbed. Elmer W. Weber's *Mentally Retarded Children and Their Education* (Springfield, Ill., C. C. Thomas [1963] 338 p.) is a study of one large category of exceptional children.

2325. Gold, Milton J. Education of the intellectually gifted. Columbus, Ohio, C. E. Merrill Books [1965] 472 p. (Merrill's international education series)  65–21168  LC3993.G54

Bibliography: p. 446–465.

"The real issue in education of the gifted, as in the education of children with moderate and low intellectual ability, is individualization in content, materials, and method." One of the problems engendered by the typically comprehensive public school is the difficulty in providing for a wide range of individual abilities within a single classroom. The author believes that gifted children have been neglected, and he stresses the need for developing programs in which the individual is the chief concern. Additional works on the same subject include *Educating Gifted Children*, rev. and enl. ed. ([Chicago] University of Chicago Press [1961] 362 p.), by Robert F. DeHaan and Robert J. Havighurst; *The Gifted Student* (New York, Oxford University Press, 1964. 296 p.), by William K. Durr; and the National Society for the Study of Education publication *Education for the Gifted* (Chicago, NSSE; distributed by the University of Chicago Press, 1958. 420 p. Yearbook of the National Society for the Study of Education [new ser.] 57th, pt. 2), edited by Nelson B. Henry.

2326. Handbook of adult education in the United States. [4th ed.] Malcom S. Knowles, editor. Chicago, Adult Education Association of the U.S.A., 1960. 624 p.  60–7359  LC5251.H3

Bibliographies and bibliographical footnotes at the ends of chapters.

A revised edition of no. 5209 in the 1960 *Guide*. In *The Adult Education Movement in the United States* (New York, Holt, Rinehart & Winston [1962] 335 p.), Malcolm S. Knowles traces the movement's history, showing how other social forces influenced and were influenced by it. He examines the contributions of such organizations as the American Association for Adult Education, the Department of Adult Education of the National Education Association, and the Adult Education Association and anticipates future trends and problems. *Volunteers for Learning; a Study of Educational Pursuits of American Adults* (Chicago, Aldine Pub. Co. [1965] 624 p. National Opinion Research Center. Monographs in social research, 4) is the final report, coauthored by John W. C. Johnstone and Ramon J. Rivera, on the National Opinion Research Center's investigation into the nature of adult education in the United States.

2327. Riessman, Frank. The culturally deprived child. New York, Harper [1962] 140 p.
62–9915 LC4069.S6R5

Bibliography: p. 131–133.

One of the major problems facing education today is the lack of preparation for coping with the needs of children who are "culturally deprived" or "disadvantaged." The author aims to provide teachers, social workers, psychologists, and psychiatrists with a picture of the deprived individual, enabling them to work with him in a fruitful, nonpatronizing manner. Riessman emphasizes what he regards as previously ignored, positive aspects of the under-privileged child's cultural heritage. In *Slums and Suburbs; a Commentary on Schools in Metropolitan Areas* (New York, McGraw-Hill [1961] 147 p.), James B. Conant contrasts high schools in the slums of large cities with those in the wealthy suburbs and explores the problems facing both. *Teaching the Culturally Disadvantaged Pupil* (Springfield, Ill., C. C. Thomas [1965] 335 p.), compiled and edited by John M. Beck and Richard W. Saxe, contains suggestions concerning methods and materials for use in improving the education of culturally disadvantaged children in elementary schools.

# E. Teachers and Teaching

2328. Caplow, Theodore, *and* Reece J. McGee. The academic marketplace. With a foreword by Jacques Barzun. New York, Basic Books [1958] 262 p.
58–13156 LB1778.C3

The academic labor market is a peculiar and sometimes disillusioning operation. Faculty members are selected on the basis of repute rather than performance. "Men are hired, to put it baldly, on the basis of how good they will look to others." When an academic man's reputation has crystallized, the possibilities of changing it are slight. "A man may, for example, publish what would be, in other circumstances, a brilliant contribution to his field, but if he is too old, or too young, or located in the minor league, it will not be recognized as brilliant and will not bring him the professional advancement which he could claim if he were of the proper age and located at the proper university." Such are some of the conclusions arrived at by sociologists Caplow and McGee on the basis of interviews with administrative officers and 418 professors at 10 major universities. Numerous suggestions for reform are offered. In *Professor; Problems and Rewards in College Teaching* (New York, Macmillan, 1961. 189 p. Macmillan career book), Fred B. Millett discusses the training, activities, and responsibilities of the college teacher in 20th-century America.

2329. Conant, James B. The education of American teachers. New York, McGraw-Hill [1963] 275 p. (Carnegie series in American education)
63–20444 LB1715.C617 1963

Bibliographical footnotes.

The author, with the collaboration of nine eminent educators, made a two-year investigation of the education of teachers for elementary and secondary schools. During the first year, he and his traveling staff visited 77 "teacher-preparing" institutions in 22 States. All types and categories of institutions were represented. In the second year of the study, Conant focused attention on the State regulations that place limitations on the local school board's freedom to employ teachers. He concentrated almost exclusively on the 16 most populous States, representing each geographical section of the United States. Foremost among the author's recommendations is the shifting of responsibility for certification from State departments of education to the 1,150 institutions which educate teachers, a move designed to eliminate the former's "bankrupt" policies and to invigorate the latter.

2330. Flexner, Abraham. Abraham Flexner; an autobiography. Introduction by Allan Nevins. New York, Simon & Schuster, 1960. xvi, 302 p.
60–8007 LB875.F583A3 1960

"A revision, brought up to date, of the author's I remember, published in 1940."

The author's two major achievements were the revolution he effected in American medical education and the establishment of the Institute of Advanced Study at Princeton. This revision of his autobiography was completed before his death in 1959 at the age of 92. It is not only the story of a modest and humane scholar, told with color and humor, but also a history of the educational developments made possible by philanthropy guided by perceptive minds. In *The Gentle Puritan; a Life of Ezra Stiles, 1727–1795* (Published for the Institute of Early American History and Culture, Williamsburg, Va. New Haven, Yale University Press, 1962. 490 p.), Edmund S. Morgan examines the papers of a man of extraordinary learning who served as president of Yale from 1778 to 1795, and whose journals and notebooks furnish access to the intellectual life of 18th-century New England.

2331. Gage, Nathaniel L., *ed.* Handbook of research on teaching; a project of the American Educational Research Association. Chicago, Rand McNally [1963] 1218 p. illus.

63–7142 LB1028.G3

"Whatever else it may be, teaching is an intriguing, important, and complex process. Because it is intriguing, it attracts scientific attention. Because it is important, it merits careful research. Because it is complex, research on teaching needs many-sided preparation. It is toward this preparation that the *Handbook of Research on Teaching* is aimed." The contributors collectively attempt to summarize, analyze, and integrate the vast body of research on teaching. Although this long volume is intended primarily for the graduate or advanced undergraduate student preparing to do research on teaching, it can be useful to school administrators, teachers, and citizens interested in education.

2332. Lieberman, Myron. The future of public education. [Chicago] University of Chicago Press [1960] 294 p.

59–15108 LA216.L5

Bibliographical footnotes.

A discussion of the structure and organization of the teaching profession. The author maintains that public education in the United States is much less effective than it can and ought to be. In his opinion, the most important cause of this ineffectiveness is an anachronistic and dysfunctional power structure, toward which he directs the attention of teachers. "The basic educational reforms needed in the United States will have to be initiated and carried out by the teachers themselves. It follows from this that the study of teachers' organizations— their programs, leadership, political sophistication, strategy, and tactics—must be accorded high priority by those who wish to bring about fundamental improvements." In an earlier work entitled *Education as a Profession* (Englewood Cliffs, N.J., Prentice-Hall, 1956. 540 p.), the same author sets forth the criteria of a profession and describes and analyzes the status of education with respect to them.

## F. Methods and Techniques

2333. Brown, James W., Richard B. Lewis, *and* Fred F. Harcleroad. A-V instruction: materials and methods. 2d ed. New York, McGraw-Hill [1964] 592 p. illus. (McGraw-Hill series in education) 63–22154 LB1043.B75 1964

Bibliographies at the ends of chapters.

Examples of instructional media drawn from many subject fields and from various school levels, kindergarten to college. Emphasis is placed upon the interrelatedness of these materials and their multiple uses. The authors deal with readymade products, such as textbooks, films, television and radio programs, globes and maps, and programmed materials, and a large group of "created" materials and techniques. Practical guidance in the operation of audiovisual equipment commonly found in schools today is appended to the text. Specialized works on two important types of audiovisual media are, respectively, *Teaching Machines and Programmed Learning; a Source Book* ([Washington] Dept. of Audio-Visual Instruction, National Education Association [1960–65] 2 v.), edited by Arthur A. Lumsdaine and Robert Glaser, and *TV and Our School Crisis* (New York, Dodd, Mead, 1958. 198 p.), by Charles A. Siepmann. *Administering Educational Media* (New York, McGraw-Hill [1965]

357 p.), by James W. Brown and Kenneth D. Norberg, is focused on the control and organization of audiovisual materials in grade schools, high schools, colleges, universities, and State departments of education.

2334. Bruner, Jerome S. The process of education. Cambridge, Harvard University Press, 1960. 97 p. 60–15235 LB885.B78

The chairman's report of the Woods Hole Conference of 1959, at which some 35 scholars, scientists, and educators discussed possible means of improving the public schools. Among the major topics are the role of intuition in thought, the stimulation of the desire to learn, the proposition that "the foundations of any subject may be taught to anybody at any age in some form," and the need to teach the fundamental ideas of a subject rather than mere facts and techniques.

2335. Fries, Charles C. Linguistics and reading. New York, Holt, Rinehart & Winston [1963] 265 p. illus. 63–14410 LB1050.F7

Bibliographical notes: p. 216–255.

"This book presents the first attempt to bring together a nontechnical descriptive survey of modern linguistic knowledge, an analysis of the nature of the reading process in the light of that knowledge, and a somewhat detailed linguistic examination of the kinds of materials to which the reader must develop high-speed recognition responses." Romalda B. Spalding and Walter T. Spalding explain the Unified Phonics Method for teaching speech, writing, spelling, and reading in *The Writing Road to Reading; a Modern Method of Phonics for Teaching Children to Read*, rev. ed. (New York, Whiteside & Morrow, 1962. 248 p.). In *American Reading Instruction* (Newark, Del., International Reading Association [1965] 449 p.), by Nila B. Smith, and *Reading in the Elementary School* (Boston, Allyn & Bacon, 1964. 356 p.), by George D. Spache, various current methods of teaching reading are reviewed. *The Teaching of Reading*, rev. ed. (New York, Holt, Rinehart & Winston [1964] 422 p.), by John J. De Boer and Martha Dallmann, is a textbook designed to illustrate the problems of reading instruction in the elementary school.

2336. Hutson, Percival W. The guidance function in education. New York, Appleton-Century-Crofts [1958] 680 p. illus.
58–11064  LB1027.5.H86
Bibliographies at the ends of chapters.

The author, who selected references on guidance for inclusion in *The School Review* (no. 5249 in the 1960 *Guide*) for 24 years, here draws upon a large body of literature to present "the accumulated understandings of the guidance function and of the features which implement it." His gleanings from the writings of other authors are integrated with his own appraisals and interpretations. In *Management and Improvement of Guidance* (New York, Appleton-Century-Crofts [1965] 508 p.), George E. Hill stresses the practical aspects of guidance in elementary and secondary schools. In *Using Tests in Counseling* (New York, Appleton-Century-Crofts [1961] 434 p. The Century psychology series), Leo Goldman aims to help guidance workers gain competence in employing tests as tools in the counseling process. Merle M. Ohlsen's *Guidance Services in the Modern School* (New York, Harcourt, Brace & World [1964] 515 p.) is a textbook for teachers, administrators, and counselors, presenting the basic guidance services and the relationships among them.

2337. Shaplin, Judson T., *and* Henry F. Olds, *eds.* Team teaching. With chapters by Judson T. Shaplin [and others] New York, Harper & Row [ᶜ1964] xv, 430 p. (Exploration series in educa-tion)  64–10224  LB1027.S466
Bibliography: p. 379–421.

*"Team teaching is a type of instructional organization, involving teaching personnel and the students assigned to them, in which two or more teachers are given responsibility, working together, for all or a significant part of the instruction of the same group of students."* This new pattern of organization has emerged in American education since 1954 and is becoming a major educational movement. It is estimated that some 1,500 teachers and 45,000 students are now involved in team teaching projects. In many team-taught classes, the grading of student achievement is eliminated. The theoretical basis and practical operation of nongraded schools is clarified by John I. Goodlad and Robert H. Anderson in *The Nongraded Elementary School*, rev. ed. (New York, Harcourt, Brace & World [1963] 248 p.) and by Bartley F. Brown in *The Nongraded High School* (Englewood Cliffs, N.J., Prentice-Hall [1963] 223 p.). *Innovation in Education* (New York, Bureau of Publications, Teachers College, Columbia University, 1964. 689 p.), edited by Matthew B. Miles, is a collection of essays on various other new educational trends.

2338. Stanley, Julian C. Measurement in today's schools. 4th ed. Englewood Cliffs, N.J., Prentice-Hall [1964] xviii, 414 p. illus.
64–20454  LB1131.S74  1964
First to third editions by C. C. Ross.
Bibliographies at the ends of chapters.

The fourth edition of a work mentioned in the annotation for no. 5229 in the 1960 *Guide*. This basic textbook deals with fundamental principles of measurement and with the construction and use of measuring instruments. *The Fifth Mental Measurements Yearbook* (Highland Park, N.J., Gryphon Press, 1959. 1292 p.), edited by Oscar K. Buros, supplements the editor's previous yearbooks, which are also mentioned in the annotation for no. 5229 in the 1960 *Guide*. It covers the years from 1952 through 1958 and contains a test list, test reviews, references on the construction, use, and limitations of specific tests, a book list, and excerpts from book reviews. *Measurement and Evaluation in the Modern School* (New York, D. McKay Co. [1962] 622 p.), by Joseph Raymond Gerberich, Harry A. Greene, and Albert N. Jorgensen, has a particularly strong section on measuring and evaluating in school subjects. Frederick B. Davis' *Educational Measurements and Their Interpretation* (Belmont, Calif., Wadsworth Pub. Co. [1964] 422 p.) includes in the appendixes definitions of statistical terms.

# G. Contemporary Problems and Controversies

2339. Boles, Donald E.  The Bible, religion, and the public schools.  [3d ed.]  Ames, Iowa State University Press, 1965.  408 p.

65–16369  LC111.B55  1965

Bibliographical references included in "Notes" (p. 345–370).

Bibliography: p. 375–379.

"Two fundamental propositions basic to our public school system are: public funds shall not be granted to sectarian schools, and sectarian instruction shall not be given in public schools."  The author examines the second principle, presenting the arguments on both side of the controversy concerning Bible readings and related programs in the public schools.  He discusses European and colonial backgrounds, State constitutions, statutes, and court decisions, and the United States Supreme Court decisions of 1962 and 1963 banning State-sponsored prayer and State-sponsored Bible readings in the public schools as violations of the first and 14th amendments of the Federal Constitution.  In *Freedom of Choice in Education,* rev. ed.  (Glen Rock, N.J., Paulist Press [1963] 224 p. Deus Books), Father Virgil C. Blum, a Catholic, advocates public financial support for private schools.

2340. Clift, Virgil A., Archibald W. Anderson, *and* H. Gordon Hullfish, *eds.*  Negro education in America; its adequacy, problems, and needs.  New York, Harper [1962] xxiii, 315 p.  (Yearbook of the John Dewey Society, 16th)

62–9485  L101.U6J6  16th, 1962

Bibliographical footnotes.

An appraisal of education as an instrument for helping Negroes become freely and fully functioning first-class citizens.  Historical, anthropological, sociological, and psychological data are provided as background, and the Supreme Court's decision in *Brown* v. *Board of Education* (1954), which declared segregation by race in the public schools unconstitutional, is discussed.  The aftermath of the Court's decision is the subject of Benjamin Muse's *Ten Years of Prelude: The Story of Integration Since the Supreme Court's 1954 Decision* (New York, Viking Press [1964] 308 p.), in which are examined the desegregation of public schools in the South and the beginnings of the broad movement against all forms of race discrimination in the United States.

2341. Iversen, Robert W.  The Communists & the schools.  New York, Harcourt, Brace [1959] 423 p.  (Communism in American life)

59–11769  LA209.I9

Bibliographical notes: p. 375–410.

Although the educational system in the United States was not initially an object of Communist attention, there is a record of Communist activity relating to the schools from the 1920's on.  The author is concerned with the nature, magnitude, and impact of this activity.  Focusing on the 1930's, when Communism was at its height in this country, he discloses that the Communists contributed little or nothing to the philosophy of education, to educational methods, or to curriculum and textbooks.  In the area of personnel relations, evidence of influence is "inchoate and inconclusive."  The Communists achieved their most significant success in student extracurricular activities; there was also some activity in front organizations on the faculty level.  Communist leadership was briefly influential in the New York local of the American Federation of Teachers.  Iversen concludes that "perhaps the most important single consequence of American Communist activity in the field of education has been the massive retaliation it provoked."

2342. Keats, John C.  Schools without scholars.  Boston, Houghton Mifflin, 1958.  202 p.

57–10790  LA209.2.K4

In considering the multiple question of "why we should teach what to whom," the author contrasts traditional and progressive methods and materials.  In his opinion, the function of the public school is to serve its community, and the responsibility of the public is to see that it does.  Therefore, the public rather than professional educators should decide the content of instruction.  Keats describes what one community did to improve the quality of its schools.  He shares with Paul Goodman the belief that Americans have been oversold on the idea of higher education.  Both men contend that too many, not too few, high school graduates go to college.  In *The Sheepskin Psychosis* (Philadelphia, Lippincott [1965] 190 p.), Keats supports the improvement of high schools as being preferable to the establishment of additional colleges.  In *Compulsory Mis-education* (New York, Horizon Press [1964] 189 p.), Goodman opposes lengthy formal schooling as a "mass superstition" that is inept and psychologicaly, politically, and professionally damaging. Among the alternatives to college proposed by the two writers are guided travel abroad, practical apprentice training, work camps, little theaters, local newspapers, farm schools, community service, and Army enlistment.

2343. Koerner, James D. The miseducation of American teachers. With an introduction by Sterling M. McMurrin. Boston, Houghton Mifflin, 1963. 360 p.          63–9082 LB1715.K6

Based on a two-year study of 63 accredited institutions with programs in teacher education, the author's findings indicate an urgent need for reform. "Education as an academic discipline has poor credentials." Koerner states that the intellectual quality of the education faculty is often inferior and that education students do not compare favorably to other students in academic ability. Required courses in education are excessive in quantity—in the case of undergraduate elementary education students, about 40 percent of the total course load—and are "often puerile, repetitious, dull, and ambiguous." At the graduate level, admission standards are low, work in a liberal arts field is seldom included, and "dissertations, when they are done at all, are frequently triumphs of trivia." Koerner is executive secretary of the Council for Basic Education, a lay-oriented group devoted to the maintenance of quality in American education. He has edited a collection of 18 essays sponsored by the Council and entitled *The Case for Basic Education; a Program of Aims for Public Schools* (Boston, Little, Brown [1959] 256 p.). Additional arguments for basic education are presented by John F. Latimer in *What's Happened to Our High Schools?* (Washington, Public Affairs Press [1958] 196 p.) and by Philip Marson in *A Teacher Speaks* (New York, D. McKay Co. [1960] 230 p.).

2344. Rickover, Hyman G. Education and freedom. New York, Dutton, 1959. 256 p.
59–5810 LA209.2.R53

A collection of speeches, modified for book publication, by the naval officer who was the chief figure in the experimental work that led to the adoption of nuclear propulsion by the U.S. Navy. Rickover maintains that massive upgrading of the scholastic standards of the Nation's schools is necessary to guarantee the future prosperity and freedom of the Republic. Highly critical of "life-adjustment" concepts of education, he stresses that youth must have vigorous mental training to ensure flexible and versatile minds for life in a constantly changing world. In *American Education, a National Failure; the Problem of Our Schools and*

*What We Can Learn From England* (New York, Dutton, 1963. 502 p.) and *Swiss Schools and Ours; Why Theirs Are Better* ([Boston] Little, Brown [1962] 219 p.), Rickover describes educational practices abroad that merit emulation in the United States.

2345. Rudy, Solomon Willis. Schools in an age of mass culture; an exploration of selected themes in the history of twentieth-century American education. Englewood Cliffs, N.J., Prentice-Hall [1965] 374 p. (Prentice-Hall education series)
65–11037 LA209.2.R79
Bibliographical footnotes.

The author, a professor of history, includes among his topics the child study movement, child-centered schools, the concept of "adjustment" as an educational goal, parent-teacher associations, philanthropic foundations, school segregation, and the separation of church and state. In The Rockefeller Brothers Fund report *The Pursuit of Excellence; Education and the Future of America* (Garden City, N.Y., Doubleday, 1958. 48 p. *Its* Special studies report, 5), the point is stressed that in a democracy there is no inherent clash between equality of opportunity and the pursuit of excellence; education can be provided for the masses and for the gifted. Mortimer J. Adler and Milton Mayer set forth the controversial issues in American education in *The Revolution in Education* ([Chicago] University of Chicago Press [1958] 224 p.). *Crucial Issues in Education,* 3d ed. (New York, Holt, Rinehart & Winston [1964] 374 p.), edited by Henry Ehlers and Gordon C. Lee, is a revision of a work mentioned in the annotation for no. 5236 in the 1960 *Guide.*

2346. *U.S. Congress. House. Committee on Education and Labor.* The Federal Government and education: [a report on a study of education programs in which the Federal Government is involved] Presented by Mrs. Green of Oregon. Washington, U.S. Govt. Print. Off., 1963. xv, 178 p. (88th Cong., 1st sess. House document no. 159)
63–65276 LB2825.A452 1963a
Bibliography: p. 166.

This report, prepared under the supervision of Representative Edith Green, reviews the Federal Government's involvement in improving facilities, equipment, and curricula, in supporting research in colleges and universities, in extending grants to students, and in financing other programs at home and abroad. *Federal Assistance for Educational Purposes* (Washington, U.S. Govt. Print. Off., 1963. 166 p. 87th Cong., 2d sess.), by Helen A. Miller and Andrew J. Shea, and *Federal Educational Policies, Programs and Proposals* (Washington, U.S.

Govt. Print. Off., 1960. 3 pts. 86th Cong., 2d sess.), by Charles A. Quattlebaum, are surveys prepared for the House Committee on Education and Labor by staff members of the Legislative Reference Service of the Library of Congress. Homer D. Babbidge and Robert M. Rosenzweig sketch the background and development of relations between the Federal Government and the American higher education community in *The Federal Interest in Higher Education* (New York, McGraw-Hill, 1962. 214 p.).

2347. Walcutt, Charles C., *ed*. Tomorrow's illiterates: the state of reading instruction today. With an introduction by Jacques Barzun. Boston, Little, Brown [1961] xvii, 168 p.

61–12822 LB1050.W3

Bibliographical references included in "Notes" (p. 165–168).

A group of specialists place responsibility for the widespread illiteracy among graduates of our public schools on such "progressive" reading methods as "look-and-say" or "whole word," which, together with the vocabulary control of basal readers and the application of such concepts as "reading readiness," dominated educationist thought for four decades. In a concluding essay, editor Walcutt, professor of English at Queens College, describes various phonics methods which are now being used with success. *Reading Without Dick and Jane* (Chicago, Regnery,

1965. 186 p.), by Arther S. Trace, *The Right to Learn* (Chicago, Regnery, 1959. 228 p.), by Glenn McCracken, and *Reading: Chaos and Cure* (New York, McGraw-Hill [1958] 285 p.), by Sibyl Terman and Charles C. Walcutt, also advocate the use of phonics in reading instruction.

2348. Woodring, Paul. A fourth of a nation. New York, McGraw-Hill [1957] 255 p.

57–10232 LA209.2.W63

Bibliographical references included in "Notes" (p. 245–248).

The classic thesis that education is the development of the mind is juxtaposed to the pragmatic antithesis that education is the nurturing of the whole child. The author's synthesis is that the proper aim of education is to prepare the individual to make wise decisions. "The educated man is one who can choose between good and bad, between truth and falsehood, between the beautiful and the ugly, between the worthwhile and the trivial." In *Voices in the Classroom; Public Schools and Public Attitudes* (Boston, Beacon Press [1965] 292 p.), Peter Schrag examines a variety of schools and communities. In *The Schools* (New York, Harper [1961] 446 p.), Martin Mayer offers for the benefit of parents a description of what he has observed happening in classrooms from kindergarten through high school.

## H. Periodicals and Yearbooks

2349. The Educational record. v. 1+ Jan. 1920+ [Washington, The American Council on Education] E21–40 L11.E46

Quarterly.

The articles focus on higher education in the United States.

2350. The Harvard educational review. v. 1+ Feb. 1931+ Cambridge, Mass., Graduate School of Education, Harvard University.

34–7870 L11.H3

Quarterly.

Articles and book reviews by teachers, scholars, and research workers in education.

2351. History of education quarterly. v. 1+ Mar. 1961+ [Pittsburgh, University of Pittsburgh] 63–24253 L11.H67

Official organ of the History of Education Society. Although the scope is worldwide, a great number of the articles and book reviews are concerned with education in the United States.

2352. The Phi delta kappan, a journal for the promotion of research, service, and leadership in education. v. 1+ Nov. 1915+ [Homewood, Ill., Phi Delta Kappa] 46–35485 LJ121.P4

Published 10 times a year.

Journal of Phi Delta Kappa, professional fraternity for men in education; "solicits and publishes articles designed to advance thinking in the fields of educational research, service, and leadership." A "Books for Leaders" column is also included.

2353. Teachers College record. v. 1+ Jan. 1900+ New York City [Bureau of Publications]

Teachers College, Columbia University.

6–14087 L11.T4

Issued eight months a year, October through May. Edited (1965) by Maxine Greene. Primarily a forum for teachers covering a broad range of topics, it is a "journal of contemporary thought in the humanities and behavioral sciences as they illuminate the process of education." Book reviews.

# XXII

# Philosophy and Psychology

THE GENERAL works on philosophy range from broad histories and studies of specific philosophical movements to introductory anthologies of the writings of eminent philosophers and collections reflecting recent philosophical thinking.  Nine of the 18 representative philosophers chosen for Section B in the 1960 *Guide* are included in this *Supplement*.  The other nine were omitted because of the absence of books by or about them that are appropriate for this chapter.  One additional philosopher, Arthur O. Lovejoy, was selected for inclusion in the *Supplement*.  As in the 1960 *Guide,* the writings of some of the philosophers are entered in other chapters, especially Chapter I, Literature.  Except in the case of Lovejoy, for whom a biographical headnote is provided, the entry for each philosopher's name refers to the headnote in the 1960 *Guide*. A revised edition of a history of American psychology entered in the 1960 *Guide* is the only entry in Section C of this chapter.  Works on psychiatry appear in Chapter XVIII, Medicine and Public Health.

## A.  Philosophy: General Works

2354.  Anderson, Paul R. Platonism in the Midwest.  Philadelphia, Temple University Publications; distributed by Columbia University Press, 1963.  216 p.                63–11694  B944.P5A5
One purpose of this monograph is to reinforce the conclusion that "no one section of the country, no one hereditary strain, and no one center of population has given a definitive character to our national life."  Anderson argues that New England, commonly considered the intellectual center of 19th-century America, was no oasis in the wilderness; on the contrary, he finds that the social environment of the Mississippi Valley between 1860 and 1890 precipitated intellectual activity that surpassed the East in its youth, courage, and self-confidence and, in fact, influenced the culture of New England.  In St. Louis was a well-known Hegelian group, which the author discusses only generally, and in Jacksonville, Ill., was a Platonist group, which is the main object of this study.

Anderson describes the organizations, including the Plato Club led by Hiram K. Jones, that made Jacksonville the center of midwestern Platonism.  Another group devoted to Plato flourished in western Missouri under Thomas M. Johnson, the "Sage of the Osage."  After 1888 the movement lost its impetus.  The author's conclusion is that the people sought something germane to the American mind and consequently rejected the readymade principles of the ancient Greeks.

2355.  Black, Max, *ed.* Philosophy in America, essays [by] William P. Alston [and others] Ithaca, N.Y., Cornell University Press [1965] 307 p.  (Muirhead library of philosophy)
                          65–15046  B934.B56 1965
Bibliographical footnotes.
The editor has assembled a group of papers representing the work of a number of young philosophers teaching at American universities.  Their contribu-

tions represent "work in progress," and Black states that one main purpose of this collection is to encourage others to make further progress toward solving the problems dealt with by the authors. Some, although not all, of the papers employ technical terminology and are most relevant for students of philosophy. Among the topics included are "Aesthetic Problems of Modern Philosophy," "Explanations in Psychology," "Quantum Physics and the Philosophy of Whitehead," and "Reasons and Reasoning."

2356. Christy, Arthur. The Orient in American transcendentalism; a study of Emerson, Thoreau, and Alcott. New York, Octagon Books, 1963 [ᶜ1960] xix, 382 p. (Columbia University studies in English and comparative literature)
63–20888    B905.C5  1963

Originally published in 1932, this book is a study of the beginnings of American interest in oriental thought and its flowering in New England transcendentalism. The author concentrates upon Ralph Waldo Emerson, Henry David Thoreau, and Amos Bronson Alcott as representative of transcendentalism as a whole. His account shows how these three men borrowed from the literature of India, China, and Persia and from classical and European thought, blending all together in an eclectic synthesis thoroughly characteristic of transcendentalism. The bulk of the work is devoted to Emerson and discusses the influence of the Orient on his philosophical ideas; Thoreau and Alcott are studied through an examination of their application of orientalism to their conduct of life. The volume includes an annotated bibliography (p. 273–323) of the oriental reading of these three transcendentalists.

2357. Frankel, Charles, ed. The golden age of American philosophy. New York, G. Braziller, 1960.  534 p.         60–5612  B934.F7

2358. Konvitz, Milton R., and Gail Kennedy, eds. The American pragmatists; selected writings. New York, Meridian Books [1960]  413 p. (Meridian books, M105)         60–12329  B832.K6

2359. Peterfreund, Sheldon P. An introduction to American philosophy. New York, Odyssey Press [1959]  291 p.         59–2030  B934.P4

Frankel's compendium presents a "profile" of American philosophy from the Civil War to the Great Depression by means of extracts from the major works of Chauncey Wright, Charles Peirce, William James, Josiah Royce, George Santayana, Ralph Barton Perry, Clarence Irving Lewis, and Morris Raphael Cohen. The "golden age" of American philosophy is defined as the time when American philosophers took their places as full partners with the great philosophers of other lands. Another anthology for the beginner seeking a first acquaintance with American philosophy is the compilation by Konvitz and Kennedy, which includes selections from the writings of Emerson, Justice Oliver Wendell Holmes, and Sidney Hook. Peterfreund's volume is designed as an introduction to the major systematic philosophers and includes selections from the works of Peirce, William James, Royce, Santayana, and Dewey, arranged in an order intended to display the logical progression of their central ideas.

2360. Margolis, Joseph Z., ed. Philosophy looks at the arts; contemporary readings in aesthetics. New York, Scribner [1962]  235 p.
62–16652  BH21.M3

CONTENTS.—Introduction.—What makes a situation aesthetic, by J. O. Urmson.—The concept of expression in art, by Vincent Tomas.—The role of theory in aesthetics, by Morris Weitz.—Aesthetic concepts, by Frank Sibley.—The intentional fallacy, by William K. Wimsatt, Jr., and Monroe C. Beardsley.—The logic of interpretation, by Joseph Margolis.—On the reasons that can be given for the interpretation of a poem, by Charles L. Stevenson.—Critical communication, by Arnold Isenberg. —Reasons in art criticism, by Paul Ziff.—The language of fiction, by Margaret MacDonald.—Implied truths in literature, by John Hospers.—Metaphor, by Max Black.

Esthetics as a separate discipline of American philosophy was for years relatively neglected, but the founding of the American Society of Aesthetics and the *Journal of Aesthetics and Art Criticism* (1942) signaled a change. The esthetician has become interested in an analytical approach to the philosophy of art and has focused his attention on art and art forms. In this anthology Margolis brings together samples of the writing of estheticians of the analytic stamp, along with a wide range of problems. An introduction by the editor and a bibliography accompany each selection.

2361. Muelder, Walter G., Laurence Sears, and Anne V. Schlabach, eds. The development of American philosophy; a book of readings. 2d ed. [Boston] Houghton Mifflin [1960]  643 p.
60–16272  B851.M8  1960

A revised edition of no. 5259 in the 1960 *Guide*, to which has been added a section on recent developments in American philosophy in relation to 20th-century science, with extracts from the writings of such men as Alfred North Whitehead and George

H. Mead. The section on naturalism and realism has been expanded by the addition of extracts from the writings of Arthur O. Lovejoy, Ralph Barton Perry, and Evander Bradley McGilvary, and other sections have been enlarged to include selected writings of newly ascendant philosophers. The selected bibliographies have also been brought up to date.

2362. Reck, Andrew J. Recent American philosophy; studies of ten representative thinkers. New York, Pantheon Books [1964] xxiii, 343 p.
64–13268 B893.R4 1964

The author maintains that the history of thought is a "cooperative social process to which by means of concurrence and dissent, countless obscure or forgotten thinkers contribute" and that philosophic thought can never gain perspective as long as it focuses exclusively on a few such major figures as Peirce, James, Royce, Santayana, Dewey, and Whitehead. He chooses for analysis 10 less intensively studied philosophers who reached the peak of their intellectual activity between the two World Wars: Ralph Barton Perry, William Ernest Hocking, George H. Mead, John Elof Boodin, Wilbur Marshall Urban, DeWitt H. Parker, Roy Wood Sellars, Arthur O. Lovejoy, Elijah Jordan, and Edgar S. Brightman.

2363. Schneider, Herbert W. A history of American philosophy. 2d ed. New York, Columbia University Press, 1963. 590 p.
63–14114 B851.S4 1963

A revised edition of no. 5261 in the 1960 *Guide* with an additional section on the development of the 20th-century school of philosophic realism, entitled "Emergence of Naturalistic Realisms."

2364. Smith, John E. The spirit of American philosophy. New York, Oxford University Press, 1963. 219 p.
63–12553 B851.S48

An interpretation chiefly of the writings of Charles Peirce, William James, Josiah Royce, John Dewey, and Alfred North Whitehead. In the author's view an understanding of the main contribution of each man "requires that more attention be paid to basic doctrines and their reflection of American convictions than to the internal development of a philosophical system." He omits George Santayana as unrepresentative of the main drift of American thinking and finds significant common convictions held by the five philosophers he has chosen. The spirit of American philosophy from the Civil War to the 1930's is interpreted as a modern version of ancient humanism. Although American philosophers were interested in nature and science, their true focus was on the use of knowledge and the value of things for human purposes.

2365. Smith, Wilson. Professors & public ethics; studies of Northern moral philosophers before the Civil War. Ithaca, N.Y., Published for the American Historical Association [by] Cornell University Press [1956] 244 p.
57–13532 BJ352.S56

Bibliography: p. 217–237.

An assessment of the relationship between American rationalistic moral philosophy, an inheritance from the Enlightenment, and secular life in the 19th century, as evidenced in pre-Civil War public affairs. In the first of three essays, the author identifies 48 academic moral philosophers (listed in the appendix, p. 211–216), of whom at least 33 participated in public affairs outside their own church and college. He indicates their religious affiliations (the majority were clergymen) and describes their large indebtedness to the English moral theologian William Paley. In the second essay he analyzes the thought and public careers of John D. Gros of Columbia, Francis Lieber of South Carolina College, Charles B. Haddock of Dartmouth, and Francis Wayland, president of Brown. The last essay is devoted entirely to James Walker of Harvard, who, in untypical neutralism, would not commit himself on partisan secular issues.

2366. Van Wesep, Hendrikus B. Seven sages; the story of American philosophy: Franklin, Emerson, James, Dewey, Santayana, Peirce [and] Whitehead. New York, Longmans, Green, 1960. 450 p.
60–15278 B851.V3 1960

This book sums up American philosophy as a forward-looking, indigenous "excelsiorism." The author's subjects all agreed in being realists, pluralists, evolutionists, freedom lovers, and anti-absolutionists; all stood for broadening the discipline of philosophy to include elements once considered too everyday or too practical; and all were secularly minded and concerned for a better life in the New World.

# B. Representative Philosophers

2367. MORRIS RAPHAEL COHEN, 1880–1947

No. 5267 in 1960 *Guide*.

2368. Rosenfield, Leonora D. C. Portrait of a philosopher: Morris R. Cohen in life and letters. New York, Harcourt, Brace & World [1962] 461 p. 61–19591 B945.C54R6

Mrs. Rosenfield, author of books on French literature and the history of ideas, has based this biography largely on her father's diaries and his correspondence with his wife, the former Mary Ryshpan, and with friends, students, and many eminent men of his day, including Cardozo, Frankfurter, Learned Hand, Einstein, Bertrand Russell, and John Dewey. The account is enriched by the author's personal reminiscences. She describes Cohen's social environment, the intellectual and emotional aspects of his life and work, his wide range of interests, his effectiveness as a teacher, and his role as an innovator in the realm of ideas, as well as life in New York's lower East Side, Harvard at the turn of the century, and the atmosphere of the City College of New York in the twenties and thirties.

2369. JOHN DEWEY, 1859–1952

No. 5271 in 1960 *Guide*.

2370. Philosophy, psychology and social practice; essays. Selected, edited and with a foreword by Joseph Ratner. New York, Putnam [1963] 315 p. 63–16188 B945.D41R22 1963

CONTENTS.—Knowledge and the relativity of feeling.—Kant and philosophic method.—The new psychology.—Soul and body.—The psychological standpoint.—Psychology as a philosophic method.—"Illusory Psychology."—Knowledge as idealization.—On some current conceptions of the term "self."—How do concepts arise from percepts?—The superstition of necessity.—The ego as cause.—The psychology of infant language.—The theory of emotion.—The reflex arc concept in psychology.—The psychology of effort.—Interpretation of the savage mind.—Psychology and social practice.

Only two of these essays, "The Reflex Arc Concept in Psychology" and "Interpretation of the Savage Mind," are found in the collection *Philosophy and Civilization* (1931), no. 5281 in the 1960 *Guide*. In the early years of his career, Dewey was an adherent of a form of Hegelian idealism. The first nine essays, originally published during the period 1883–90, are products of this discipleship. The remainder reveal the emergence of an original, creative thinker working on the foundations of his own philosophic system. *John Dewey and Arthur F. Bentley: A Philosophical Correspondence, 1932–1951* (New Brunswick, N.J., Rutgers University Press [1964] 737 p.), selected and edited by Sidney Ratner and Jules Altman, contains approximately 2,000 communications, "the most extensive correspondence of any two contemporary philosophers published in America or Europe." Most of the letters were exchanged during the years 1943–49, when Dewey and Bentley were collaborating on *Knowing and the Known,* no. 5286 in the 1960 *Guide.*

2371. Blewett, John, *ed.* John Dewey: his thought and influence. New York, Fordham University Press [1960] 242 p. (The Orestes Brownson series on contemporary thought and affairs, no. 2) 60–10737 B945.D44B55

CONTENTS.—Introduction, by John Blewett.—The genesis of Dewey's naturalism, by James Collins.—Democracy as religion: unity in human relations, by John Blewett.—Dewey's theory of knowledge, by Beatrice H. Zedler.—John Dewey and progressive education, by Sister Joseph Mary Raby.—Dewey and the problem of technology, by John W. Donohue.—Dewey's ambivalent attitude toward history, by Thomas P. Neill.—Process and experience, by Robert C. Pollock.—Dewey's influence in China, by Thomas Berry.

Fordham University held a symposium in honor of the centennial of Dewey's birth and assembled this sympathetic but critical volume of essays upon aspects of his philosophy and its influence. John S. Brubacher's foreword says, "When his philosophical critics and adversaries join in the celebration we can take it as a great compliment to the length of his shadow." In *John Dewey and Self-Realization* (Englewood Cliffs, N.J., Prentice-Hall [1963, ᶜ1962] 152 p.), Robert J. Roth develops Dewey's ideas without completely endorsing them.

2372. Geiger, George R. John Dewey in perspective. New York, Oxford University Press, 1958. 248 p. 58–9463 B945.D44G4

The author maintains that Dewey was the philosophic spokesman of democratic social liberalism and progressivism in education and that his views have had a profound impact on psychological and social thought as well as pedagogy. His general extension of the logical method of modern experimental science to moral and social problems has gained him a large audience. At the same time, his thought has been rejected by those who discount the authority of science, who do not agree with social liberalism, or who attribute the shortcomings of the public schools to educational progressivism. Geiger suggests that too often a limited focus of discussion is to blame for misconceptions of Dewey's ideas, which he seeks to place in a wide context.

2373. Hendel, Charles W., *ed.* John Dewey and the experimental spirit in philosophy; four lectures delivered at Yale University commemorating the 100th anniversary of the birth of John Dewey. New York, Liberal Arts Press [1959] 119 p.　　　59–15785　B945.D44H38

Lectures by members of the Yale philosophy department presenting enduring ideas in Dewey's writing rather than a comprehensive statement or reappraisal of his work. In a brief biographical sketch, Hendel places the philosopher in his time and environment and looks for precursors of his empiricism in such philosophical traditions as Hegelian idealism. The underlying theme of the other lectures is Dewey's empirical spirit. Nathaniel M. Lawrence develops the social basis of Dewey's educational theories; Richard J. Bernstein relates his naturalism to his epistemology, process of valuation, and concept of freedom; and John E. Smith summarizes, in "John Dewey: Philosopher of Experience," the pragmatist's views on evolution, experience, and metaphysics.

2374. WILLIAM ERNEST HOCKING, 1873–

No. 5310 in 1960 *Guide.*

2375. Types of philosophy, by William Ernest Hocking, with the collaboration of Richard Boyle O'Reilly Hocking. 3d ed. New York, Scribner [1959] 340 p.　BD21.H6 1959 59–8019

Includes bibliography.

A revised edition of Hocking's widely used textbook, mentioned in no. 5310 in the 1960 *Guide.*

2376. ARTHUR ONCKEN LOVEJOY, 1873–1962

An astute critic of American philosophy, Lovejoy is recognized as a leader of the critical realists and as a pioneer in the modern study of the history of ideas, which grew to maturity under his influence and with its own journal (*The Journal of the History of Ideas*). Lovejoy described his philosophy as a "temporalistic realism." The "realism" grew out of his reactions to idealism, evolutionism, and prag-

matism. In his presidential address to the Western Division of the American Philosophical Association, he explicitly rejected idealism and pronounced the "obsolescence of the eternal." From this position he developed an epistemological dualism that became the essence of his critical realism. His "temporalism" consists of an "emergent evolutionism," a theory that changes occur and new entities come into existence. Lovejoy's philosophy has been overshadowed by the influence of his studies in the history of ideas, in which he probed behind past systems and movements to discover primary and recurrent units of thought. One of his most significant contributions to intellectual history is *The Great Chain of Being, a Study of the History of an Idea* (1936); two other major works are *Essays in the History of Ideas* (1948) and *Reflections on Human Nature* (1961).

2377. The reason, the understanding, and time. Baltimore, Johns Hopkins Press [1961] 210 p.　　　61–8177　B945.L583R4

A series of essays which originated as lectures delivered at Princeton in 1939. Lovejoy critically analyzes Henri Bergson's creative evolutionism, the German Romantics as precursors of his philosophy, and his claim to originality. Explicit throughout is a contrast of Lovejoy's own temporalism with that of the French philosopher.

2378. The revolt against dualism: an inquiry concerning the existence of ideas. 2d ed. La Salle, Ill., Open Court Pub. Co., 1960. 405 p. (The Paul Carus lectures, ser. 2)
　　　　　　60–53406　B812.L6　1960

Lovejoy here examines the main strands of the revolt in the first quarter of the 20th century against 17th-century epistemological dualism. Included are discussions of the roles of the "new realism," objective relativism, Whiteheadian epistemology, and Bertrand Russell's attempt to unify mind and matter. The author concludes with a statement of his own dualistic theory of knowledge, which stands at the center of his "critical realism."

2379. The thirteen pragmatisms, and other essays. Baltimore, Johns Hopkins Press [1963] 290 p.　　　63–11890　B832.L6

A compilation of essays largely concerned with the vagueness of present-day pragmatism.

2380. CHARLES SANDERS PEIRCE, 1839–1914

No. 5345 in 1960 *Guide.*

2381. Moore, Edward C., *and* Richard S. Robin, *eds.* Studies in the philosophy of Charles

Sanders Peirce. Second series. Amherst, University of Massachusetts Press, 1964. 525 p.

65–3174   B945.P44M5

A sequel to no. 5353 in the 1960 *Guide*. Although concerned with Peirce's philosophical system as a whole, this volume emphasizes his role as "scientist." The essays indicate an increase in foreign interest in Peirce. Among the contributors are Arthur N. Prior of the University of Manchester, Nynfa Bosco of the University of Turin, and Thomas A. Goudge and David Savan of the University of Toronto.

2382. Murphey, Murray G. The development of Peirce's philosophy. Cambridge, Mass., Harvard University Press, 1961. 432 p.

61–13739   B945.P44M8

Making extensive use of Peirce's manuscripts, the author seeks to prove that his subject at all times aimed to be a systematic philosopher. Despite an inchoate appearance, the structure of Peirce's thought is derived from an "architectonic" theory of philosophy, which is in turn based on formal logic. Murphey discovers four major phases in Peirce's philosophical development. The first extended from his earliest papers of 1857 until 1865 or 1866, a period during which he was strongly influenced by Kantian logic. "The second began with the discovery of the irreducibility of the three syllogistic figures in 1866, and extended until 1869 or 1870. The third was inaugurated by the discovery of the logic of relations and continued until 1884." The last stemmed from the discovery of quantification and set theory and continued until Peirce's death in 1914. Murphey's book follows a chronological scheme except for a section which is concerned solely with Peirce's mathematics. In a more specialized study, *Charles Peirce and Scholastic Realism* (Seattle, University of Washington Press, 1963. 177 p.), John F. Boler examines Peirce's relation to the medieval realist John Duns Scotus, whom Peirce acknowledged as a precursor but whose ideas he did not hesitate to transform. *Values in a Universe of Chance* (Garden City, N.Y., Doubleday, 1958. 466 p. Doubleday anchor books, A126), edited by Philip P. Wiener, is made up of a number of Peirce's less technical papers and letters, some of which are not included in his *Collected Papers* (no. 5346 in the 1960 *Guide*).

2383. JOSIAH ROYCE, 1855–1916

No. 5354 in 1960 *Guide*.

2384. Buranelli, Vincent. Josiah Royce. New York, Twayne Publishers [1964] 174 p.

(Twayne's United States authors series, 49)

63–20608   B945.R64B8

Bibliography: p. 160–166.

"This volume is an attempt to present Josiah Royce as he has not been presented before—to describe him through his multifarious aspects from novelist and literary critic to logician and metaphysician." It is a nontechnical introduction, omitting detail in favor of a panoramic view of Royce's thought. The author approaches the philosopher's metaphysics largely through his literary and historical achievements but devotes a chapter to his logical methods and another to his system of absolute idealism. Buranelli also estimates Royce's relevance for Americans, selecting as the Nation's foremost philosophers "Peirce, Royce, and Edwards in that order."

2385. Costello, Harry T. Josiah Royce's seminar, 1913–1914: as recorded in the notebooks of Harry T. Costello. Edited by Grover Smith. With an essay on the philosophy of Royce by Richard Hocking. New Brunswick, N.J., Rutgers University Press [1963] 209 p. 62–18949 BD241.C65

Recording secretary Costello and (excluding dropouts) nine other students, among them T. S. Eliot, were enrolled in Royce's Tuesday evening seminar on scientific methods at Harvard during the academic year reported here. The philosopher welcomed to his seminar, in addition to the regular students, professional colleagues from other disciplines. Lawrence J. Henderson, biological chemist, Elmer E. Southard, head of the Psychopathic Hospital in Boston, and Frederick A. Woods, lecturer at the Massachusetts Institute of Technology, were among the regular visitors. Royce was convinced that the "community of scholars" was the best laboratory for gaining new insight into scientific questions. Possessing an argumentative but amicable personality, he provoked lively discussions. Costello summarizes the papers presented at the seminar and notes remarks made in the discussion, principally those offered by Royce. Costello's published writings are listed in an appendix (p. 196–203).

2386. GEORGE SANTAYANA, 1863–1952

No. 5365 in 1960 *Guide*.

2387. Cory, Daniel. Santayana: the later years; a portrait with letters. New York, G. Braziller [1963] 330 p. 63–19573 B945.S24C65

The author, Santayana's friend and secretary, has written a memoir of the philosopher's life from 1927 until his death in 1952. He has woven his reminiscences around the diary he kept during his early association with Santayana, the more than 300 letters he received from him, and innumerable conversations with him. He makes observations on the philosopher's work and associates, his daily routines of life, and his personal habits and portrays him as an "affable old-fashioned gentleman." He also shows Santayana's productivity in old age, his diligence in creating *Realms of Being* (no. 5371 in the 1960 *Guide*), and his satisfaction at the enthusiastic reception given his bestselling novel, *The Last Puritan* (no. 1736 in the 1960 *Guide*). In *Santayana: Saint of the Imagination* ([Toronto] University of Toronto Press, 1961. 240 p.), Mossie M. W. Kirkwood interprets the philosopher's life and provides concise summaries of his philosophy, following the transition of his thought from the supernaturalism of his youth to the naturalism of his maturity.

2388. Munson, Thomas N. The essential wisdom of George Santayana. New York, Columbia University Press, 1962. 224 p.
62–10453    B945.S24M85
Bibliography: p. 229–232.
The author's purpose is to "clarify Santayana's philosophy, appreciate his methods, and make a judgment regarding his contribution to philosophical knowledge." An appendix (p. 138–150) includes Munson's correspondence with Santayana and an associate's interview with him. A special aspect of Santayana's philosophy is analyzed in Irving Singer's *Santayana's Aesthetics* (Cambridge, Harvard University Press, 1957. 235 p.).

2389. PAUL WEISS, 1901–
No. 5378 in 1960 *Guide*.

2390. History: written and lived. Carbondale, Southern Illinois University Press [1962] 245 p.    62–15006    D16.8.W39
This study proceeds from a "conviction that philosophy ought to be carried out on two levels. It should have a speculative dimension, where the whole of being and knowledge is in principle dealt with systematically by a distinctive method and in a distinctive style. There should also be an empirically oriented set of studies revealing the experienceable significance of realities." Weiss' philosophy of history belongs to the second field of investigation, which he recognizes as a comparatively new and distinct subject area, and he attempts to define its limits and method of study. He inquires into the historian's objectives and presuppositions and maintains that history cannot be studied through established categories and methods but requires a fresh empirical approach.

2391. Our public life. Bloomington, Indiana University Press [1959] 256 p.
59–9852    HM51.W4
A statement of Weiss' social and political philosophy, in which he has "tried to present a systematic speculative account of the nature and need for such important groups as society, state, culture, and civilization." He examines man's role within social divisions, depicts the kind of classes which should constitute the ideal society, and considers such topics as "native rights," sovereignty, natural law, and "man's persistent drive to achieve a satisfying and enriching public existence." Sections of this book were delivered as the Mahlon Powell lectures at Indiana University in 1958.

2392. The world of art. Carbondale, Southern Illinois University Press [1961] 193 p.
61–5168    N66.W34

2393. Nine basic arts. Carbondale, Southern Illinois University Press [1961] 238 p.
61–7164    N66.W32

2394. Religion and art. Milwaukee, Marquette University Press, 1963. 97 p. (The Aquinas lecture, 1963)    63–13170    N72.W4
Taken together, these works express Weiss' philosophy of esthetics. In *The World of Art* he isolates general principles, discusses problems inherent in art, and examines its relationship to other fields, such as science. *Nine Basic Arts* is an analysis of the distinguishing features of selected major arts (including both "musicry" and music), with the objective of stating the common properties of all fine art. Art is seen as distinct from other endeavors in that it "demands a fresh and unmistakable act of creativity, terminating in the production of self-sufficient excellence." In *Religion and Art,* Weiss asserts that religious and artistic strivings alike provide "an answer to man's basic need to be perfected."

2395. ALFRED NORTH WHITEHEAD, 1861–1947
No. 5383 in 1960 *Guide*.

2396. American essays in social philosophy. Edited with an introduction by A. H. Johnson. New York, Harper [1959] 206 p.
59–9943    H33.W5
CONTENTS.— The problem of reconstruction.— The study of the past.— Memories.— England and the Narrow Seas.— An appeal to sanity.— The importance of friendly relations between England and the United States.— The education of an English-

man.—Harvard: the future.—Historical changes.
—Universities and their function.

A collection of periodical articles, the majority of
which appeared originally in *The Atlantic Monthly,*
between 1926 and 1942.

2397. Christian, William A. An interpretation of
Whitehead's metaphysics. New Haven, Yale
University Press, 1959. 419 p.
59–6794   B1674.W354C5

2398. Leclerc, Ivor. Whitehead's metaphysics: an
introductory exposition. London, Allen &
Unwin; New York, Macmillan [1958] 233 p.
58–4842   B1674.W354L4

Whitehead's search for a cosmology equal in pro-
fundity to the Newtonian synthesis resulted in a shift
of interest in his later works, particularly *Process
and Reality,* from science to a new set of problems
with esthetic, ethical, and social implications. The
authors of these two monographs seek to clarify
some of his solutions to metaphysical problems.
Christian, guided by his own concern with how
"God transcends the world," is especially interested
in the theological implications of Whitehead's metaphysics. Leclerc contributes a detailed exposition of
the categorical structure of Whitehead's system,
postponing evaluation to a projected second volume
of the study. In *A Whiteheadian Aesthetic* (New
Haven, Yale University Press, 1961. 219 p.),
Donald W. Sherburne examines the relationship between Whitehead's metaphysics and his philosophy
of art.

2399. Johnson, Allison H. Whitehead's philosophy
of civilization. New York, Dover Publications, 1962. 211 p.
62–51278   CB19.W49J6 1962

A brief introduction, originally published in 1958,
to Whitehead's views of society, history, education,
and religion.

2400. Leclerc, Ivor, *ed.* The relevance of Whitehead; philosophical essays in commemoration
of the centenary of the birth of Alfred North Whitehead. London, Allen & Unwin; New York, Macmillan [1961] 383 p. (The Muirhead library of
philosophy)   61–3432   B1674.W354L38 1961

Contents.—Whitehead and contemporary philosophy, by Charles Hartshorne.—Some uses of
reason, by William A. Christian. Sketch of a philosophy, by Frederic B. Fitch.—Metaphysics and
the modality of existential judgments, by Charles
Hartshorne.—Whitehead on the uses of language,
by Allison H. Johnson.—Time, value, and the self,
by Nathaniel Lawrence.—Form and actuality, by

Ivor Leclerc.—The approach to metaphysics, by Victor Lowe.—Metaphysics as *Scientia Universalis* and
as *Ontologia Generalis,* by Gottfried Martin.—The
relevance of "On Mathematical Concepts of the Material World" to Whitehead's philosophy, by W.
Mays.—Aesthetic perception, by Eva Schaper.—In
defence of the humanism of science: Kant and
Whitehead, by Hermann Wein.—History and objective immortality, by Paul Weiss.—Whitehead's
empiricism, by William P. D. Wightman.—Deity,
monarchy, and metaphysics: Whitehead's critique
of the theological tradition, by Daniel D. Williams.

Essays which exemplify the continuing influence
and significance of Whitehead's thought.

2401. Lowe, Victor. Understanding Whitehead.
Baltimore, Johns Hopkins Press, 1962. 398 p.
62–15312   B1674.W354L6

A nontechnical introduction that assumes no prior
knowledge of Whitehead's thought. The author
surveys the entire scope of the philosopher's system
(metaphysics, philosophy of science, and philosophy
of religion) and traces his philosophical development from mathematics to the philosophy of science
and, ultimately, to a metaphysical system and a
philosophy of civilization. Lowe finds Whitehead
"immediately productive and constructively original
in each new field" and concludes that his cosmology
represents "a culmination of Western tradition."
Another book designed for the nonspecialist is
*Whitehead's Philosophical Development* (Berkeley,
University of California Press, 1956. 370 p.), by
Nathaniel M. Lawrence, who aims at providing
a foundation from which *Process and Reality* can
profitably be studied. A recent collection edited
by George L. Kline, *Alfred North Whitehead, Essays
on his Philosophy* (Englewood Cliffs, N.J., Prentice-
Hall [1963] 214 p. A Spectrum book), includes
18 papers.

2402. CHAUNCEY WRIGHT, 1830-1875

No. 5386 in 1960 *Guide.*

2403. Madden, Edward H. Chauncey Wright and
the foundations of pragmatism. Seattle,
University of Washington Press, 1963. 203 p.
63–9939   B945.W74M3

An introduction to Wright's moral philosophy,
epistemology, metaphysics, philosophy of science,
and psychology, with discussions of his agnosticism,
utilitarianism, and view of "self-consciousness" and
extensive references to his essays and letters.
Wright's empirical theory of knowledge led him to
the conclusion that sufficient evidence is not yet
available either to prove or to disprove the existence

of God. Madden is also the author of another introductory work, *Chauncey Wright* (New York, Washington Square press [1964] 170 p. The Great American thinkers series.), as well as the editor of an anthology of Wright's works, *Philosophical Writings; Representative Selections* (New York, Liberal Arts Press [1958] 145 p. The American heritage series, no. 23).

# C. Psychology

2404. Roback, Abraham A. History of American psychology. New, rev. ed. New York, Collier Books [1964] 575 p.

64–16138   BF108.U5R6

Bibliography: p. 539–546.

A revised edition of no. 5392 in the 1960 *Guide*. The author has added chapters entitled "E. W. Scripture—Experimental Avant-Gardist," "Lightner Widmer, Pioneer in Clinical Psychology," "E. L. Thorndike, the Connectionist," "Hull and his Behavior System," "Lashley—Iconoclast in Neuro-psychology," "Boring and his Zeitgeist," and "Operant Conditioning" as well as others on psychobiology, the test movement, and the phenomenal expansion of psychology in the United States. In *The Influence of Freud on American Psychology* (New York, International Universities Press, 1964. 243 p. Psychological issues, v. 4, no. 1. Monograph 13), David Shakow and David Rapaport measure the impact of psychoanalysis on the evolution of psychology in this country.

# XXIII

# Religion

SECTION A, General Works, which contains more entries than the parallel section in the 1960 *Guide,* perhaps reflects an increased demand for basic books with a scope sufficiently broad to reveal the identities of the various religious groups in the United States, past and present, their origins, and their geographical distribution. Among the entries are three guides to the modern denominations, three general histories of religion, two histories of Protestantism, two studies of the current nature of Protestantism, a historical atlas of religion, and a documentary history of Christianity.

Section C, Church and State, also containing more entries than its counterpart in the 1960 *Guide,* suggests the nature of recent interest in the applications of the provisions regarding religion in the first amendment to the Constitution. The entries include a documentary history of religious liberty, a condensed and updated version of a three-volume study of the same subject, two analyses of religion and the political process, an examination of Protestant concepts of church and state, a Jesuit theologian's view of Catholicism and democracy, a Methodist minister's appraisal of the relationship between communism and the churches, an argument for complete separation of religion and the public schools, and a defense of neutrality as the proper role for the state.

## A. General Works

2405. Gaustad, Edwin Scott. Historical atlas of religion in America. New York, Harper & Row [1962] 179 p. illus.
     Map 62-51 G1201.E4G3 1962
An account of the growth of the larger religious groups, accompanied by maps showing the location of their principal adherents and graphs indicating their comparative size. The author comments on the lack of reliable statistics (each church counts its membership in its own way) and, wherever possible, provides both the number of churches and the number of members as indications of size. The first three sections treat the subject chronologically; the last section concerns special groups (Indians, Jews, and Negroes) and special areas (Alaska and Hawaii).

2406. Hudson, Winthrop S. American Protestantism. [Chicago] University of Chicago Press [1961] 198 p. (The Chicago history of American civilization) 61–15936 BR515.H78
     "Suggested reading": p. 187–191.

2407. Littell, Franklin H. From state church to pluralism; a Protestant interpretation of religion in American history. Garden City, N.Y., Anchor Books, 1962. 174 p. (Anchor books, A294)
61–9530 BR515.L55

Two historical analyses of the growth and decline of Protestant influence in America. Both authors consider Protestantism today to be a culture religion equating itself with Americanism; the major denominations have liberalized their membership standards and softened their theological differences. *American Protestantism* completes the studies of the principal religions of the United States in the University of Chicago's series on American civilization. Earlier volumes, no. 5448 and 5458 in the 1960 *Guide,* respectively, contain analyses of the growth of Catholicism and Judaism. Hudson emphasizes ideas and movements and minimizes dates and details. Littell attacks in his history the notion that the United States was once a " 'Christian nation' (i.e., Protestant controlled)" as a myth and a stumbling block in Protestantism's effort to assess its current position and potential in today's religiously plural society.

2408. Hudson, Winthrop S. Religion in America. New York, Scribner [1965] 447 p.
65–28188 BR515.H79

Bibliographical footnotes.

A study of religion from colonial times to the present. The author does not trace individual denominations; rather, he concentrates on major religious forces working in the society in specific periods and correlates the emergence of new religious groups with their environments and backgrounds. Discussions of the Holiness movement, Fundamentalism, Eastern Orthodoxy, Judaism, and, to a more limited degree, Roman Catholicism are deferred to the periods when those groups began to loom large on the American scene. The post-Civil War years receive as much attention as the longer time interval preceding the war.

2409. McLoughlin, William G. Modern revivalism: Charles Grandison Finney to Billy Graham. New York, Ronald Press [1959] 551 p.
58–12959 BV3773.M3

"Notes on the sources": p. 531–535.

A history of revivalism from the early 19th century to the present. The author sees revivalism as a social, rather than a religious, phenomenon, arising from the need to adjust Protestantism to cultural changes. Charles G. Finney "made revivalism a profession," and Dwight L. Moody gave it the aspects of a well-organized business, employing planning, extensive advertising, and sound financing.

McLoughlin devotes most of his attention to Finney, Moody, Billy Sunday, and Billy Graham and notes in passing numerous minor evangelists. Revivalism between 1840 and 1865 is explored in Timothy L. Smith's *Revivalism and Social Reform in Mid-Nineteenth-Century America* (New York, Abingdon Press [1957] 253 p.). A biography of Dwight L. Moody is Richard K. Curtis' *They Call Him Mister Moody* (Garden City, N.Y., Doubleday, 1962. 378 p.).

2410. Mayer, Frederick E. The religious bodies of America. 4th ed., rev. by Arthur Carl Piepkorn. Saint Louis, Concordia Pub. House, 1961. 598 p. 61–15535 BR516.5.M3 1961

An updated edition of no. 5397 in the 1960 *Guide.*

2411. Mead, Frank S. Handbook of denominations in the United States. New 4th ed. New York, Abingdon Press [1965] 271 p.
65–21980 BR516.5.M38 1965

Bibliography: p. 246–256.

An updated edition of no. 5398 in the 1960 *Guide.*

2412. Olmstead, Clifton E. History of religion in the United States. Englewood Cliffs, N.J., Prentice-Hall, 1960. 628 p.
60–10355 BR515.O4

Essentially a theological history, this work nevertheless places religion against a background of political, social, and economic developments. In an annotated bibliography (p. 595–611), the author suggests additional reading and evaluates some of the more specialized studies. In 1961, he published a brief survey, *Religion in America, Past and Present* (Englewood Cliffs, N.J., Prentice-Hall. 172 p. A Spectrum book, S–20).

2413. Osborn, Ronald E. The spirit of American Christianity. New York, Harper [1958] 241 p. 57–9881 BR516.O74

"Bibliographical note": p. 225–234.

2414. Marty, Martin E. The new shape of American religion. New York, Harper [1959] 180 p. 59–10336 BR526.M35

Each of these volumes examines the current nature of Protestantism. Osborn, professor of church history at Christian Theological Seminary, writes primarily for a European audience and concerns himself largely with such aspects of religion as the separation of church and state, denominationalism, and the general indifference to theology and liturgy. In his role of interpreter for interested foreigners, the author tries to provide a factual but sympathetic picture. Marty has a sharply contrasting objective; he strives to arouse lethargic religious leaders at home. *The New Shape of American Religion* is an indictment of contemporary Protestantism, which, the author contends, has been eroded by the social environment, leaving only a "religion-in-general" differing little from the secular "religion of democracy." He urges Protestants to accept religious pluralism and revitalize their religious outlook. Other aspects of contemporary Protestantism are analyzed in Sidney E. Mead's collection of essays, *The Lively Experiment: The Shaping of Christianity in America* (New York, Harper & Row [1963] 220 p.).

2415. Smith, Hilrie Shelton, Robert T. Handy, *and* Lefferts A. Loetscher. American Christianity; an historical interpretation with representative documents. New York, Scribner [1960–63] 2 v. illus.                    60–8117  BR514.S55
   CONTENTS.— v. 1.  1607–1820.— v. 2.  1820–1960.
   A collection of documents on Protestant and Catholic history. The range of selection is wide, including excerpts from Dale's Laws, Jefferson's views on Christian orthodoxy, the report of John Carroll on American Catholicism in 1785, the Plan of Union of the Presbyterian and Congregational Churches, essays by Reinhold Niebuhr, Paul Tillich, and John Courtney Murray, and Martin Luther King's views on the ethics of nonviolence. The compilers have divided their material chronologically and topically. Each chapter has a general introduction and a concluding essay on bibliography, and each document is prefaced by biographical and historical information.

2416. Smith, James Ward, *and* Albert Leland Jamison, *eds.* Religion in American life. Princeton, N.J., Princeton University Press, 1961. 3 v. in 4. illus. (Princeton studies in American civilization, no. 5)                    61–5383  BR515.S6
   Volume 4 by Nelson R. Burr in collaboration with the editors.
   CONTENTS.— 1.  The shaping of American religion.— 2.  Religious perspective in American culture.— 4.  A critical bibliography of religion in America.  2 v.
   These volumes grew out of the experience of the Special Program in American Civilization at Princeton University in offering seminars during the academic years 1948–49, 1953–54, and 1957–58. The program was devoted to the study of "the religious dimensions of American culture, and the cultural dimensions of American religion," and the essays in the first two volumes cover a wide range of topics. The author of the volumes devoted to bibliography has woven the titles of books, articles, and unpublished theses, along with critical and historical notes, into a continuous narrative text. A projected volume 3, by Jacob Viner, is to be on the subject of the European background of religious thought and the economic society.

2417. Williams, John P.  What Americans believe and how they worship. Rev. ed. New York, Harper & Row [1962] 530 p.
                    62–7308  BR516.5.W5  1962
   An updated edition of no. 5404 in the 1960 *Guide*.

# B. Period Histories

2418. Bailey, Kenneth K.  Southern white Protestantism in the twentieth century. New York, Harper & Row [1964] 180 p.
                    64–19493  BR535.B3
   "A bibliographical essay": p. 169–172.
   A survey of the positions taken by the three major Southern Protestant groups (Baptist, Methodist, and Presbyterian) on such basic issues as fundamentalism, evolution, prohibition, social reform, and race relations. The author describes the antievolution campaigns, the continuing vigilance against the encroachment of liberal theology, and the stand taken by the churches against Al Smith in the 1928 presidential election because of his Roman Catholicism and his opposition to prohibition. Bailey notes that denominational leaders have been ahead of their congregations in favoring equal rights for the races.

He concludes that although religion remains a dominant factor in the South today, the churches have lost some of the influence they held at the beginning of the century.

2419. Cavert, Samuel McCrea.  On the road to Christian unity; an appraisal of the ecumenical movement. New York, Harper [1961] 192 p.
                    61–12823  BX8.2.C3
   "Selected bibliography": p. 177–187.
   A former general secretary of the National Council of Churches surveys the world ecumenical movement as it has been influenced by, and as it has influenced, the religious scene in the United States. An account of the growth of cooperation through State and local interdenominational effort is offered by Ross W. Sanderson in *Church Cooperation in*

the United States; the Nation-Wide Backgrounds and Ecumenical Significance of State and Local Councils of Churches in Their Historical Perspective ([New York] Association of Council Secretaries, 1960. 272 p.). The Challenge to Reunion (New York, McGraw-Hill [1963] 292 p.), compiled and edited by Robert M. Brown and David H. Scott, is a collection of essays dealing with the historical, theological, and social aspects of the proposed merger of the major Presbyterian, Episcopalian, Methodist, and United Church bodies in the United States.

2420. Gaustad, Edwin Scott. The Great Awakening in New England. New York, Harper [1957] 173 p. illus.    57–9888  BR520.G2

A history of the wave of revivals that swept the British colonies in the first half of the 18th century as they affected New England. Led by Jonathan Edwards, George Whitefield, and Gilbert Tennent, the movement reached its peak between 1740 and 1742 and then quickly declined. The controversies it generated caused a progressive hardening of church doctrines, promoted the growth of separatism, and led to the destruction of the parish system. In Revivalism and Separatism in New England, 1740–1800 (New Haven, Yale University Press, 1962. 370 p. Yale publications in religion, 2), C. C. Goen surveys the churches which arose as a result of the Great Awakening and traces the subsequent conversion of most of them to Baptist principles.

2421. Miyakawa, Tetsuo Scott. Protestants and pioneers; individualism and conformity on the American frontier. Chicago, University of Chicago Press [1964] 306 p.
64–22247  BR545.M5

Bibliography: p. 275–293.

A sociological study, extensively documented, of western pioneer life, especially among the Methodists and the Baptists, the largest and perhaps most characteristic denominations. The Presbyterians and the Quakers are included as extremes in belief and polity. In the author's view, the pioneers were members of disciplined religious groups and as such helped to create a society in which people were willing to cooperate to achieve objectives unattainable by individuals.

## C. Church and State

2422. Blau, Joseph L., ed. Cornerstones of religious freedom in America. Rev. and enl. ed. New York, Harper & Row [1964] 344, 9 p. (Harper torchbooks. The Cloister library)
64–6727  BR516.B55  1964

"List of sources": p. 338–341.

An updated edition of no. 5418 in the 1960 Guide.

2423. Murray, John Courtney. We hold these truths; Catholic reflections on the American proposition. New York, Sheed & Ward [1960] 336 p.    60–12876  BR516.M84

"The question is sometimes raised," says the author, "whether Catholicism is compatible with American democracy." A Jesuit theologian at Woodstock College, he offers here an affirmative answer. In this collection of essays and occasional papers published over a 10-year period, he discusses the basic propositions of American political theory and their relevance to Catholic ideas on education, censorship, government support for religion, and natural law. A more recent statement of the Catholic position is Religion, the Courts, and Public Policy (New York, McGraw-Hill [1963] 261 p.), in which Robert F. Drinan confines his attention to those problems which have become legal and constitutional issues.

2424. Roy, Ralph L. Communism and the churches. New York, Harcourt, Brace [1960] 495 p. (Communism in American life)
60–10941  BR517.R64

An investigation of the relationship between communism and religion in the United States from the founding of the American Communist Party in 1919 through the 1950's. The author, a Methodist minister, discusses the reactions of the churches to policies of the Soviet Government, the attitude of the Communist Party of America toward religion, and alleged Communist infiltration of the churches. He concludes that the party never undertook a full-scale campaign to subvert the churches, that the number of party members among the clergy was between 50 and 200 over a 30-year period, that the efforts of the party to enlist religious leaders were made mainly through front organizations, and that there is virtually no Communist influence in the churches today.

2425. Sanders, Thomas G. Protestant concepts of church and state; historical backgrounds and approaches for the future. New York, Holt, Rinehart & Winston [1964] 339 p. (Studies of church and state) 64–11275 BV630.2.S3
Bibliographical notes: p. 301–329.

2426. Blanshard, Paul. Religion and the schools; the great controversy. Boston, Beacon Press [1963] 265 p. 63–18730 LC111.B53
Bibliography: p. [247]–249. Bibliographical notes: p. [250]–260.

2427. Bennett, John C. Christians and the state. New York, Scribner [1958] 302 p.
58–11638 BV630.2.B4
Historically, Protestants have advocated positions on church and state ranging from total union to complete separation. Sanders analyzes many of these positions and isolates five distinct Protestant attitudes. Beginning with the European origins of each, he traces its development and current popularity in America. An articulate and controversial exponent of complete separation has been Paul Blanshard. His early books, no. 5444 in the 1960 *Guide* and another title mentioned in the annotation for no. 5444–5445, deal with what he regards as Catholic threats to American freedom and have been vigorously denounced and rebutted by Catholic defenders. A subsequent work, *God and Man in Washington* (Boston, Beacon Press [°1960] 251 p.), reveals his overall view of religion and its relationship to the American political system. Blanshard's *Religion and the Schools* is primarily concerned with the U.S. Supreme Court's decisions on the New York Board of Regents' prayer in 1962 and on Bible reading and the Lord's Prayer in 1963. Taking a more moderate stand in the church-state debate, John C. Bennett, dean of the Union Theological Seminary, sees complete separation as undesirable and advocates a neutral rather than a secular state. His book surveys the nature and functions of the state in the light of Christian understanding against a background of the institutions and problems of the United States.

2428. Stedman, Murray S. Religion and politics in America. New York, Harcourt, Brace & World [1964] 168 p. 64–19366 BR516.S8
Bibliography: p. 159–161.

2429. Geyer, Alan F. Piety and politics: American Protestantism in the world arena. Richmond, John Knox Press [1963] 173 p. illus.
63–15198 BR115.P7G44
Bibliography: p. [168]–169. Bibliographical notes: p. [157]–167.
Analyses of the interrelationships between religion and political processes. Stedman is chiefly concerned with domestic politics and the role of churches in political decisionmaking. Many churches that are too different to act together attempt individually to influence government in the promotion of their respective interests; in turn, government and economic groups try to use the churches to provide the moral justifications for secular purposes. The author concludes that religious groups can best promote the public interest through their "judgmental role" in assessing "the moral aspects of great political issues." In Geyer's opinion, a nation's moral and religious outlook plays an important part in the development of its foreign policy, primarily by setting restraints on the choices available to policymakers. He argues that "the Puritan ethos has given Americans their most distinctive vision of their role in international affairs" and finds examples in the moralistic approach to foreign relations of Woodrow Wilson and John Foster Dulles. He concludes that unreasoning religious influence has often promoted irresponsible or vindictive diplomacy and urges religious leaders to recognize their importance as "decision influencers" and to acquire the necessary knowledge of politics and economics to exercise their function well.

2430. Stokes, Anson Phelps, *and* Leo Pfeffer. Church and state in the United States. Rev. one-volume ed. New York, Harper & Row [1964] 660 p. 64–14382 BR516.S85 1964
Bibliography: p. 623–631.
A condensed and updated edition of no. 5420 in the 1960 *Guide,* with an added chapter on the decisions of the U.S. Supreme Court in the area of church-state relationships. The texts of the major court decisions, including majority and minority opinions, have been compiled by Joseph Tussman in *The Supreme Court on Church & State* (New York, Oxford University Press, 1962. 305 p.), and are analyzed by Philip B. Kurland in *Religion and the Law of Church and State and the Supreme Court* (Chicago, Aldine Pub. Co. [1962] 127 p.).

# D. Religious Thought; Theology

2431. Carter, Paul A. The decline and revival of the social gospel; social and political liberalism in American Protestant churches, 1920–1940. Ithaca, N.Y., Cornell University Press [1956, °1954] 265 p.                A56–5089  HN39.U6C35
Bibliography: p. 251–260.

2432. Meyer, Donald B. The Protestant search for political realism, 1919–1941. Berkeley, University of California Press, 1960. 482 p.
60–9648  HN39.U6M45
Bibliography: p. 463–474.
These studies analyze neo-orthodox theology and its relationship to the social gospel movement which flourished at the turn of the century. Carter sees in the growth of ecumenicalism and the views of Reinhold Niebuhr the rise of a new social gospel, highly theological in structure and realistic in outlook. He describes the distinctive beliefs of the theologians of the old social gospel movement and of the neo-orthodoxy, with primary attention to their social and political influence. Meyer examines the theologians' views in much greater detail and concludes that Niebuhr's ideas did not revive the social gospel; rather, they destroyed it. Under his influence the "Protestant social concern ended as a criticism of religion."

2433. Cauthen, Kenneth. The impact of American religious liberalism. New York, Harper & Row [1962] 290 p.   62–14573  BR1615.C35
A systematic investigation of the dominant theological movement in American Protestantism during the first 30 years of this century. The author characterizes religious liberalism as an attempt to "relate the enduring Christian message to a constantly changing cultural situation." He distinguishes between "evangelical liberalism," which sought a theology to continue the Christian tradition without conflicting with the modern view of the world, and "modernistic liberalism," which attempted to use the methodologies of 20th-century science and philosophy to preserve and reinterpret what was valuable in Christian tradition. With the 1930's came the rise of the school of neo-orthodox thought and the decline of the liberal movement, a change attributed by Cauthen to the increasing recognition that "liberalism was in large part a cultural faith expressed in Christian terminology and not a genuine reinterpretation of the Christian revelation."

2434. Gasper, Louis. The fundamentalist movement. The Hague, Mouton [1963] 181 p.
63–24282  BT82.2.G3
Fundamentalism reached its zenith in the 1920's with the Scopes trial and the formation of the World Christian Fundamentals Association; then the association collapsed and bad publicity from the trial seemed to signify the demise of the movement. This study of fundamentalism since 1930 shows, however, that by midcentury the movement had again achieved national prominence. The author describes its division in the early 1940's into two national groups: the conservative and militant American Council of Christian Churches, dominated by Carl McIntire; and the more conciliatory and moderate National Association of Evangelicals, led by Harold John Ockenga. Gasper also discusses the aggressive attacks on religious and political liberalism by the American Council, the attempts of "neo-evangelical" scholars to relate their conceptions of the Bible to the scientific method, the growth of Bible Institutes, and the resurgence of revivalism under the leadership of Billy Graham.

2435. James, William. The varieties of religious experience; a study in human nature. Enl. ed., with appendices and introduction by Joseph Ratner. New Hyde Park, N.Y., University Books [1963] xlii, 626 p. (Gifford lectures on natural religion, 1901–02)   63–14505  BR110.J3  1963
An updated edition of no. 5431 in the 1960 *Guide*.

2436. Morgan, Edmund S. Visible saints; the history of a Puritan idea. [New York] New York University Press, 1963. 159 p.
63–9999  BX9322.M6
In this study the author argues that the New England Puritans developed the notion of the church as an exclusive body of those who had been demonstrably "saved" through the conversion experience. Although this idea had only a short life in the 17th century, it was revived almost 90 years later by Jonathan Edwards and remains influential today.

# E. Religious Bodies

2437. [Baptist] Torbet, Robert G. A history of the Baptists. With a foreword by Kenneth Scott Latourette. Rev. Valley Forge, Judson Press [1963] 553 p. 63–8225 BX6231.T6 1963
An updated edition of no. 5443 in the 1960 *Guide*.

2438. [Catholic] Cross, Robert D. The emergence of liberal Catholicism in America. Cambridge, Mass., Harvard University Press, 1958. 328 p. 58–5593 BX1407.A5C7
Bibliography: p. [295]–312.

In the last half of the 19th century, Catholicism in the United States was torn by controversy between conservatives, who thought the church should assume a defensive position against a Protestant world, and liberals, who optimistically sought "a friendly interaction between their religion and American life." Cross, a non-Catholic, presents a study of the liberal group. Against a background of the activities of James Cardinal Gibbons, John Ireland (Archbishop of St. Paul), and Isaac Hecker, the founder of the Paulists, he describes the liberal ideas on cooperation with Protestants, church and state relationships, labor unions, socialism, and education. He maintains that although the controversy was disruptive, "in the long run the spirited debate probably facilitated the orderly adaptation of the church to a swiftly changing American society." One of the concluding events of the struggle was the condemnation of "Americanism" by the Pope in 1899. This episode is examined by Thomas T. McAvoy in *The Great Crisis in American Catholic History, 1895–1900* (Chicago, Regnery, 1957. 402 p.). The reaction of the Catholic Church to the problems of urbanization and industrialization is discussed in Aaron I. Abell's *American Catholicism and Social Action: A Search for Social Justice, 1865–1950* (Garden City, N.Y., Hanover House, 1960. 306 p.).

2439. Ellis, John Tracy. Documents of American Catholic history. [2d ed.] Milwaukee, Bruce Pub. Co. [1962] xxii, 667 p. 62–12432 BX1405.E4 1962
An updated edition of no. 5449 in the 1960 *Guide*. Michael V. Gannon has used original documents to write *The Cross in the Sand; the Early Catholic Church in Florida, 1513–1870* (Gainesville, University of Florida Press, 1965. 210 p.), a history of the oldest establishment of the Christian faith in the United States.

2440. Scharper, Philip, *ed*. American Catholics: a Protestant-Jewish view [by] Stringfellow Barr [and others] With an afterword by Gustave Weigel. New York, Sheed & Ward [1959] 235 p. 59–12093 BX1406.S36

2441. Brown, Robert McAfee, and Gustave Weigel. An American dialogue; a Protestant looks at Catholicism and a Catholic looks at Protestantism. With a foreword by Will Herberg. Garden City, N.Y., Doubleday, 1960. 216 p. 60–13750 BX4818.3.B7

In 1959, Sheed & Ward commissioned Stringfellow Barr, Martin E. Marty, Robert McAfee Brown, Arthur A. Cohen, Arthur Gilbert, and Allyn P. Robinson, representing Protestant and Jewish faiths, to write essays on aspects of Roman Catholicism which most concern other religious groups. The essays in *American Catholics: A Protestant-Jewish View* are characterized by candor and directness, combined with an attempt to understand the Catholic point of view. Catholic reluctance to participate in exchanges of views with non-Catholic groups and the prevailing apprehension of the Catholic Church's attitude on religious freedom are the two dominant themes. In an appended essay, Gustave Weigel, a Jesuit professor at Woodstock College, calls on Catholics to use these "calm evaluations" as an aid in promoting interfaith understanding. Weigel and Robert McAfee Brown, professor of religion at Union Theological Seminary, advance this program of mutual evaluation in *An American Dialogue*. Brown discusses contemporary American Catholicism, the issues dividing Protestants and Catholics, and the attitude of the Catholic Church toward the ecumenical movement. Weigel presents a Catholic picture of Protestantism, its principles, fears, and inconsistencies. The authors see little chance of union or of complete resolution of differences, but they urge tolerance and cooperation.

2442. [Episcopal] Manross, William W. A history of the American Episcopal Church. [3d ed., rev.] New York, Morehouse-Gorham, 1959. 420 p. 59–1356 BX5880.M35 1959

2443. Albright, Raymond W. A history of the Protestant Episcopal Church. New York, Macmillan [°1964] 406 p.

64–21168 BX5580.A4

Bibliography: p. 382–397.

More than half of the volume by Manross, which is a revised and updated edition of no. 5456 in the 1960 *Guide*, is devoted to the period before the American Revolution. Albright's highly detailed study devotes relatively more attention to recent history. In *Mitre and Sceptre; Transatlantic Faiths, Ideas, Personalities, and Politics, 1689–1775* (New York, Oxford University Press, 1962. 354 p.), Carl Bridenbaugh discusses the conflicts generated by the efforts to establish the Anglican Church in the American Colonies and examines religion as a fundamental cause of the American Revolution.

2444. [Jehovah's Witnesses] Whalen, William J. Armageddon around the corner; a report on Jehovah's Witnesses. New York, J. Day Co. [1962] 249 p. illus. 62–10958 BX8526.W47

Bibliography: p. 235–238.

A brief account, written in a popular style, by a Roman Catholic layman. The Jehovah's Witnesses, one of the "three major indigenous religious movements in this country," had their origins in the small study groups organized by Charles Taze Russell in the 1870's. Russell's belief in the imminence of the end of the world remains the dominant tenet of the sect today. Renouncing worldly concerns, Witnesses refuse to vote, salute the flag, or perform military service. These ideas, in combination with their militant evangelism, have often subjected them to mob violence and prosecution in the courts.

2445. [Judaism] Wouk, Herman. This is my God. Garden City, N.Y., Doubleday, 1959. 356 p. 59–11617 BM561.W65

A novelist's personal testament of the significance of the Jewish faith. Wouk describes the essence of Judaism, both for Jews who have fallen away from the old observances and for interested Gentiles. Although he treats Judaism in general, his point of view is American and Orthodox. He offers information on American Judaism as well as a plea for recognition of the values to be found in conscientious observance of the Mosaic law. Moshe Davis describes the rise of Conservative Judaism in opposition to the spread of the Reform movement in *The Emergence of Conservative Judaism: the Historical School in 19th Century America* (Philadelphia, Jewish Publication Society of America, 1963. 527 p. The Jacob R. Schiff library of Jewish contributions to American democracy, no. 15).

2446. [Lutheran] Wentz, Abdel R. A basic history of Lutheranism in America. Rev. ed. Philadelphia, Fortress Press [1964] 439 p. 64–12996 BX8041.W38 1964

Bibliography: p. 398–421.

An updated edition of no. 5461 in the 1960 *Guide*.

2447. [Methodist] Harmon, Nolan Bailey. The organization of the Methodist Church; historic development and present working structure. 2d rev. ed. Nashville, Methodist Pub. House [1962] 287 p. 62–12436 BX8388.H3 1962

An updated edition of a study mentioned in the annotation for no. 5463 in the 1960 *Guide*.

2448. The History of American Methodism. Editorial Board: Emory Stevens Bucke, general editor [and others] New York, Abingdon Press [1964] 3 v. illus. 64–10013 BX8235.H5

The first official history of American Methodism since its beginnings in 1784. Authorized by the General Conference of the Methodist Church in 1956, this multivolume work was written by 44 scholars and clergymen. From the arrival in America of the Wesleys and George Whitefield, the story follows the founding of the early societies, the activities of Francis Asbury as circuit rider and first bishop, the schisms in the first part of the 19th century, the growth of the various Methodist denominations after the Civil War, and the union in 1939 of the three major groups which now form the Methodist Church. Each volume of this history includes bibliographies, and the whole is extensively documented and indexed. Francis Asbury's *Journal and Letters* (London, Epworth Press; Nashville, Abingdon Press [1958] 3 v.), edited by Elmer T. Clark, J. Manning Potts, and Jacob S. Payton, is an eyewitness account of the early days of Methodism.

2449. [Mormon] O'Dea, Thomas F. The Mormons. [Chicago] University of Chicago Press [1957] 288 p. 57–6984 BX8611.O3

A study of the Mormon Church by a non-Mormon sociologist. After presenting a brief history, the author discusses theology, institutional development, and the characteristic Mormon way of life. A final chapter analyzes the position of the church in today's secular society. O'Dea lived in Utah for several years while collecting material for this study and openly displays his admiration for the Mormons and their accomplishments. Accounts written by some of the early travelers and curiosity seekers who visited the Mormon settlements have been collected and edited by William Mulder and

Arlington Russell Mortensen in *Among the Mormons; Historic Accounts by Contemporary Observers* (New York, Knopf, 1958. 482 p.).

2450. [Presbyterian] Thompson, Ernest Trice. Presbyterians in the South. v. 1. 1607–1861. Richmond, John Knox Press [ᶜ1963] 629 p.                    63–19121   BX8941.T5 v. 1
    Bibliography: p. [597]–608.
    A professor of church history at the Union Theological Seminary in Virginia traces the institutional and theological history of ante bellum Southern Presbyterianism. Beginning with the first scattered Presbyterians in Virginia, he follows the growth of the denomination through adversity and persecution in colonial times, post-Revolutionary eminence, and controversy and schism in the period before the Civil War. He also discusses such topics as slavery, missions, morals, and education. A more limited study is Robert Hastings Nichols' *Presbyterianism in New York State; a History of the Synod and Its Predecessors* (Philadelphia, Published for the Presbyterian Historical Society by the Westminster Press [1963] 288 p.), issued in the Presbyterian Historical Society's Studies in Presbyterian History series. Another volume in the same series is *The Presbyterian Ministry in American Culture; a Study in Changing Concepts, 1700–1900* (1962. 269 p.), by Elwyn Allen Smith, who surveys theological ideas and educational practices and shows how they influence the denomination's conception of its mission.

# F. Representative Leaders

2451. [Ballou] Cassara, Ernest. Hosea Ballou; the challenge to orthodoxy. Boston, Universalist Historical Society [1961] 226 p.
                    61–6545   BX9969.B3C3
    Bibliography: p. 177–190.
    Universalism was a product of the revolt of New England's lower classes against Calvinist orthodoxy. Its central idea of universal salvation first appeared in the American Colonies with the arrival of John Murray in New Jersey in 1770. Universalism spread slowly at first but gained impetus after the conversion, in 1789, of Hosea Ballou (1771–1852) from Baptist Calvinism. Ballou possessed little formal education, but his rough eloquence made him the leading Universalist minister. In *A Treatise on the Atonement*, mentioned in the annotation for no. 5473 in the 1960 *Guide*, he introduced the Unitarian ideas which were gradually accepted by the Universalist congregations. This biography analyzes his theology and supplies an extensive list of his publications.

2452. [Graham] High, Stanley. Billy Graham; the personal story of the man, his message, and his mission. New York, McGraw-Hill [1956] 274 p.        56–11952   BV3785.G69H5

2453. McLoughlin, William G. Billy Graham; revivalist in a secular age. New York, Ronald Press [1960] 269 p.
                    59–12122   BV3785.G69M3
    High, a senior editor of *The Reader's Digest,* was assigned to interview Graham in 1954, and his account is the result of the interest and admiration he developed at that time. Written in a popular style and at the height of the Graham crusades, this biography reflects the cooperation accorded the author by Graham's family and associates and includes excerpts from letters and personal anecdotes. McLoughlin's volume, published four years later, is a critical analysis. The author, associate professor of history at Brown University, describes the evangelist's career and examines his theological, social, and political ideas, his pulpit techniques, the mechanics of his campaigns, and the commercialism surrounding his activities. McLoughlin has attempted to present all sides in his investigation, although his views are unsympathetic to Graham's ideas and to revivalism in general.

2454. [Ingersoll] Larson, Orvin P. American infidel: Robert G. Ingersoll, a biography. New York, Citadel Press [1962] 316 p. illus.
                    62–10223   BL2790.I6L3
    Bibliography: p. 286–290.
    Ingersoll (1833–1899), one of the finest orators of the 19th century, was an apostle of antireligion. Inveighing against the Bible, organized religion, and the clergy, he spoke to packed houses all over the country on such topics as "Some Mistakes of Moses," "Myth and Miracle," and "About the Holy Bible." His ideas derived from a passionate belief in freedom of thought, and he was active in political affairs, supporting such causes as votes for women and the abolition of obscenity laws. The interest of his biographer, chairman of the department of speech at Brooklyn College, centers on Ingersoll the orator, but nevertheless a picture emerges of a man

who, while attacking religious beliefs and organizations, helped to promote an atmosphere conducive to critical research and thought. A general analysis of the influence of atheistic, agnostic, deistic, and theistic thought is made by Martin E. Marty in *The Infidel; Freethought and American Religion* (Cleveland, Meridian Books [1961] 224 p. Living age books, LA34).

2455. [Jones] Vining, Elizabeth Gray. Friend of life; the biography of Rufus M. Jones. Philadelphia, Lippincott [1958] 347 p. illus.
58–11131 BX7795.J55V5
"Books by Rufus M. Jones": p. 331–333.
Jones (1863–1948), sometimes called the modern spiritual leader of Quakerism, combined a life oriented toward intellectual pursuits with one of active service in organized Quaker philanthropy. He published more than 40 books on Quaker philosophy and history and served for many years as chairman of the American Friends Service Committee. Several accounts of his life and work have appeared since his death. *Friend of Life* is the most recent of these and one of the most detailed.

2456. [Wise] Heller, James G. Isaac M. Wise: his life, work, and thought. [New York] Union of American Hebrew Congregations [1965] xxi, 819 p. 64–24340 BM755.W5H5
Bibliography, including works of and about Rabbi Wise: p. 677–692.
Rabbi Heller has written not only a biography of a pivotal figure in Jewish history in the United States but also a full account of the Reform Judaism which Rabbi Wise (1819–1900) introduced into this country. Most of the book is a straightforward narrative of Wise's life and achievements, which included the founding of the Union of Hebrew Congregations, the Hebrew Union College, and the Central Conference of American Rabbis. A separate section of the volume sets forth a systematic outline of Wise's thinking on subjects that interested and concerned him. Whenever possible the author has allowed Wise to speak for himself through excerpts from his letters and speeches. Among the subjects discussed are religion in general, Judaism and Reform Judaism, colonization and Zionism, Christianity, and civil rights for Jews.

## G. Church and Society

2457. Berger, Peter L. The noise of solemn assemblies; Christian commitment and the religious establishment in America. Garden City, N.Y., Doubleday, 1961. 189 p.
61–14587 BR526.B45

2458. Winter, Gibson. The suburban captivity of the churches; an analysis of Protestant responsibility in the expanding metropolis. Garden City, N.Y., Doubleday, 1961. 216 p.
61–7667 BV637.7.W5

2459. Shippey, Frederick A. Protestantism in suburban life. New York, Abingdon Press [1964] 221 p. 64–20521 BV637.7.S46
Bibliography: p. 203–212.
In a manual prepared for the National Student Christian Federation, Berger sees the churches as a "religious establishment" existing in American society as a "segregated enclave, surrounded by actions that have little if any relationship to religious motives." Maintaining that they are no longer able to take the lead in forwarding the work of Christian mission, he discusses alternative ways, including new "organizational forms," in which this mission might be carried out apart from existing organiza-

tions. In *The Suburban Captivity of the Churches* Winter analyzes the role of the church in metropolitan areas and stresses the exodus of the Protestant churches from the socially disorganized inner city to the middle-class suburbs. He contends that although the minority and low-income groups in midcity have the greatest need of religion, a ministry here demands great outlay of money and personnel with little tangible return. The suburbs, on the other hand, are a fertile field for the growth of financially prosperous, homogenous congregations. Condemning this "exclusiveness," the author emphasizes the "inclusiveness" of the Christian mission and advocates the enlargement of the lay ministry and the reorganization of the parish to include both suburban and inner city areas. He develops these ideas further in *The New Creation as Metropolis* (New York, Macmillan [1963] 152 p.). The attempts of one group to deal with the problems of the inner city by living and working among the people are graphically depicted in Bruce Kenrick's *Come Out the Wilderness; the Story of East Harlem Protestant Parish* (New York, Harper [1962] 220 p.). The author of *Protestantism in Suburban Life* asserts that the suburbs are no longer the exclusive domain of the Protestant middle class.

Citing contemporary surveys, Shippey describes the influx of Roman Catholics, Jews, Negroes, blue-collar workers, and sect groups which have made suburbia "the greatest American spiritual frontier for all faiths." His book is a discussion of the problems arising in the fringe areas of the city and a defense of the activities of the organized churches. Catholic suburbia is described in *The Church and the Suburbs* (New York, Sheed & Ward [1959] 206 p.), by Andrew M. Greeley.

2460. Cox, Harvey G. The secular city; secularization and urbanization in theological perspective. New York, Macmillan [1965] 276 p.
65–16713 BR115.W6C65
Bibliography: p. 271–276. Includes bibliographical references.

A theological essay calling for a reassessment and redefinition of Christian thought and action in order to make Christianity responsive to the demands of urban secular society. The author, associate professor of church and society in the Divinity School of Harvard University, is viewed in some quarters as one of the Nation's most radical and respected young Christian thinkers. Although he chooses the broad historical context of Western civilization, his criticisms of modern Christianity derive from his analysis of the disjuncture between church and society in the United States. In its adherence to outworn doctrines, institutions, and ethical codes, he argues, modern Christianity has diverged from the spiritual values which were at the core of Christ's teachings. By recognizing that other institutions have taken over economic, social, political, and educational functions which were once its province, the church can free itself to continue the process of spiritual fermentation.

2461. Herberg, Will. Protestant, Catholic, Jew; an essay in American religious sociology. New ed., completely rev. Garden City, N.Y., Anchor Books, 1960. 309 p. (A Doubleday Anchor book, A195) 60–5931 BR526.H4 1960
Includes bibliography.

An updated edition of no. 5488 in the 1960 *Guide*.

2462. Lee, Robert. The social sources of church unity; an interpretation of unitive movements in American Protestantism. New York, Abingdon Press [1960] 238 p.
60–9199 BX8.2.L4
Bibliography: p. 225–231.

In *The Social Sources of Denominationalism* (1929), Helmut Richard Niebuhr, a pioneer in the sociology of religion, argues that religious differentiation in the United States is largely based on social class rather than on theology. Lee's book, as its title suggests, is a parallel study conducted 30 years later. Accepting Niebuhr's thesis, Lee contends that in the period since 1929, cultural unity, rather than diversity, has become increasingly apparent in society and is a basic factor in the current ecumenical movement. After demonstrating the diminution of social and cultural distinctions, he turns to the various aspects of ecumenicalism—the National Council of Churches, local church councils, denominational mergers and reunions, community churches, and comity. He also examines separatist movements, including the growth of the Holiness sects and the rapid expansion of the antiecumenical Southern Baptist Convention.

2463. Lenski, Gerhard E. The religious factor; a sociological study of religion's impact on politics, economics, and family life. Garden City, N.Y., Doubleday, 1961. 381 p.
61–9197 BL60.L44
Bibliographical footnotes.

The author presents and interprets the results of personal interviews with a cross section of people from metropolitan Detroit, conducted with the cooperation of the University of Michigan's Detroit Area Study. He shows a high correlation between religious affiliation and attitudes, practices, and relative success in daily life. Reports and conclusions of a similar survey conducted by the staff of the Chicago Theological Seminary in an anonymous rural midwestern county are included in *The Church and Faith in Mid-America* (Philadelphia, Westminster Press [1963] 174 p.), by Victor Obenhaus, and *Religion in American Culture; Unity and Diversity in a Midwestern County* ([New York] Free Press of Glencoe [1964] 254 p.), by Obenhaus and W. Widick Schroeder. Reports on a nationwide survey of religious belief are contained in John L. Thomas' *Religion and the American People* (Westminster, Md., Newman Press, 1963. 307 p.).

2464. Moberg, David O. The church as a social institution; the sociology of American religion. Englewood Cliffs, N.J., Prentice-Hall, 1962. 569 p. (Prentice-Hall sociology series)
62–10140 BV625.M6
Includes bibliography.

The influence of religion as a factor of sociological significance was for many years discounted by sociologists and political scientists. Around the turn of the century Emile Durkheim and Max Weber published studies that tried to identify the role played by religion in influencing social institutions and social change, but it was not until after World War II that American social scientists in general came to recognize the sociology of religion as a valid field of study in the United States. In this textbook, one of several appearing in recent years, the author argues that the church is an integral part of society and that clearer knowledge of its institutional characteristics is necessary to enable religious leaders to plan wisely for the future.

2465. Pfeffer, Leo. Creeds in competition: a creative force in American culture. [New York] Harper [1958] 176 p.

58–10373   BR516.5.P43

An analysis of the effects of religious pluralism on American culture. The author, professor of constitutional law at Yeshiva University, discusses the efforts of Protestants, Catholics, Jews, and secular humanists to promote their own ideas of society and behavior through "governmental action either in the enactment of laws or in the operation of governmental institutions." In his opinion the conflicts among the various religious groups generate "creative competition." He presents the views of each group on such subjects as education, censorship, morals, family life, and social reform.

## H. The Negro's Church

2466.   Weatherford, Willis D. American churches and the Negro; an historical study from early slave days to the present. Boston, Christopher Pub. House [1957] 310 p.

57–9842   BR563.N4W4

A study of the relationship of the primarily white religious denominations to the Negro in the United States, both before and after the abolition of slavery. The author avers that religious groups before the Civil War took the Negroes into their churches and considered their spiritual needs to be of primary concern but that after the war the Negroes became generally unwelcome. He notes that the churches are belatedly beginning to resume their original mission and calls for an end to segregation in church membership and activities. *In White Protestantism and the Negro* (New York, Oxford University Press, 1965. 236 p.), David M. Reimers pursues his topic from the beginning of the 19th century to the early 1960's and concludes that Protestantism's treatment of the Negro was "no better and no worse than that of American society as a whole." In *The Negro Church in America* (New York, Schocken Books [1964, °1963] 92 p. Studies in sociology), Edward Franklin Frazier contends that, following the Civil War, the Negro church became the most influential Negro institution, its other-worldly emphasis providing a refuge from the harsh realities of life.

# XXIV

# Folklore, Folk Music, Folk Art

THE ENTRIES in Section A, Legends and Tales: General, include a treasury of anecdotes and a dictionary of proverbs and proverbial phrases. Section B has entries for works on local lore in Maine, Texas, North Carolina, Illinois, and Nebraska and among such social groups as the folk associated with the oil industry and the Pennsylvania Dutch miners. Murder ballads, Negro folk music, and chanteys are among the subjects of entries in Section C, and in Section D are works on local ballads and songs from Virginia, Utah, Pennsylvania, the Catskills, New England, and the Southwest, as well as biographies of a folk composer of the Northeast woods and a folk hero of the Rio Grande borderland.

Because of the lack of suitable entries, no section on Games and Dances, which is Section E in the 1960 *Guide,* appears in the *Supplement.* The section on Folk Art and Crafts, Section F in the 1960 *Guide,* is Section E in the *Supplement.*

## A. Legends and Tales: General

2467. Beck, Horace P., *ed.* Folklore in action; essays for discussion in honor of MacEdward Leach. Philadelphia, American Folklore Society, 1962. 210 p. (Publications of the American Folklore Society. Bibliographical and special series, v. 14) 62–12687 GR15.B4
Includes bibliographical references.

For years professor of Middle English at the University of Pennsylvania, Leach became chairman of the institution's graduate department in folklore in 1962. A group of his former students and close friends, as well as past presidents of the American Folklore Society, have here contributed what they consider to be "their most worthwhile, definitive work in a particular field." The essays are of a general rather than a specific nature and cover a number of major areas of folklore in an attempt to represent Leach's multifarious interests. Several of the essays are reprinted or adapted from other publications. *Studies in Folklore, in Honor of Distinguished Service Professor Stith Thompson* (Bloomington, Indiana University Press, 1957. 270 p. Indiana University publications. Folklore series, no. 9), edited by Winthrop Edson Richmond, is a tribute to a scholar probably best known for his accomplishments in the area of comparative folklore. The contributors include students and colleagues associated with the major phases of his career both in the United States and abroad.

2468. Botkin, Benjamin A., *ed.* A Civil War treasury of tales, legends, and folklore; illustrated by Warren Chappell. New York, Random House [1960] 625 p. 60–5530 E655.B65
Bibliographical notes: p. 577–607.
"Before the Civil War became our writingest and

storytellingest war, it was our talkingest war." A favorite campfire pastime in both armies was swapping gossip and anecdotes. These sessions were rituals in which all could take part and which united each narrator with the group. "The soldier's stories were his folk literature, leveling individual differences, codifying his beliefs and attitudes, and giving him a sense of belonging." The main sources of this collection are reminiscences, personal narratives, and unit histories, with additions from letters, diaries, scrapbooks, newspapers, periodicals, pamphlets, and miscellaneous ephemera. The editor presents it as "the first attempt at a Civil War folk history and story history based on a wide variety of contemporary sources." The selections have been arranged in six parts, one devoted to each year, 1861–65, and a sixth to the "aftermath." These parts are in turn divided by content into sections, in each of which the materials are offered as nearly in chronological order as possible.

2469. Botkin, Benjamin A., *ed.* A treasury of American anecdotes; sly, salty, shaggy stories of heroes and hellions, beguilers and buffoons, spellbinders and scapegoats, gagsters and gossips, from the grassroots and sidewalks of America. New York, Random House [1957] 321 p.
57–10053 PN6261.B6

These anecdotes are "short, pointed, pithy, pungent illustrative or attributed stories" which belong to what the editor calls "floating literature—literature without known authorship or fixed form." The collection includes tall tales, jokes, and regional lore arranged geographically in 14 sections (with introductions) devoted to such types or motifs as "Whopper Wit," "Barnyard and Barroom," and "Wit's End." Botkin has gone to many kinds of sources, oral and printed, old and new, in his effort to make the book representative of the whole range of the raconteur's art and repertoire. "If this book proves anything about American storytelling," he observes, "it is that 'Old stories never die.'"

2470. Dorson, Richard M. American folklore. [Chicago] University of Chicago Press [1959] 328 p. (The Chicago history of American civilization) 59–12283 GR105.D65
"Bibliographical notes": p. 282–300.

2471. Dorson, Richard M. Buying the wind: regional folklore in the United States. Chicago, University of Chicago Press [1964] xvii, 573 p. 64–13010 GR105.D66
Bibliography: p. [536]–[544].

Dorson contends that "the only meaningful approach to the folk traditions of the United States must be made against the background of American history, with its unique circumstances and environment." No "other history—or folklore—grapples in the same measure with the factors of colonization, immigration, Negro slavery, the westward movement, or mass culture." The outline of *American Folklore* follows, accordingly, the broad sweep of the Nation's development. The author draws his material from authentic collections and studies, eschewing "fakelore," in which the raw data of folklore has been refined and falsified to make it more palatable and more marketable. Supplementary to this volume, and in particular to its chapter on "Regional Folk Cultures," is *Buying the Wind,* described as a "volume of texts." A "text" is defined as an "inviolable document" that "comes from the lips of a speaker or singer and is set down with word for word exactness by a collector." For each item the informant is named and the collector is cited. Seven regional groups are represented: Maine Down-Easters, Pennsylvania Dutchmen, Southern Mountaineers, Louisiana Cajuns, Illinois Egyptians, Southwest Mexicans, and Utah Mormons.

2472. Goldstein, Kenneth S. A guide for field workers in folklore. Preface by Hamish Henderson. Hatboro, Pa., Folklore Associates, 1964. xviii, 199 p. 64–24801 GR40.G6
Bibliography: p. 177–188.

If folklore studies are to achieve full academic status, Hamish Henderson observes in the preface to this book, the folklorists' reputation for "bizarre waywardness and indiscipline" must be liquidated. Goldstein's manual is designed precisely to meet that objective. Its explicit aim is to raise the discipline of folklore to the level of a science and to turn amateur practitioners into professionals. The author envisions a social science with close ties to the humanities. He shows how folklore can borrow from the ethnographic approach to field work and at the same time avoid its "extreme functionalist attitude." The reader does not need academic training in folklore in order to understand the instructions offered here. He is warned, however, that the reading will not necessarily convert him into a professional collector. If he lacks the required temperament, he will not become a successful fieldworker even by using the recommended methods and techniques.

2473. Taylor, Archer, *and* Bartlett J. Whiting, *comps.* A dictionary of American proverbs and proverbial phrases, 1820–1880. Cambridge, Belknap Press of Harvard University Press, 1958. xxii, 418 p. 58–10406 PN6426.T28
Bibliography: xii–xxii.

In the opinion of the compilers, "There is no

exaggeration in the statement that at no other time have so many American writers made proverbs so obvious an ingredient in their style." The authors whose writings are included in the dictionary were chosen "as representative of various regions and for their popularity." Two regional collections are *Proverbs and Proverbial Phrases of Illinois* (Car-bondale, Southern Illinois University Press [1965] 213 p.), edited by Frances M. Barbour, and *A Dictionary of Proverbs and Proverbial Phrases From Books Published by Indiana Authors Before 1890* (Bloomington, Indiana University Press, 1961. 168 p. Indiana University folklore series, no. 15), compiled by Jan H. Brunvand.

# B. Legends and Tales: Local

2474. Beck, Horace P. The folklore of Maine. Drawings by Arthur K. D. Healy. Philadelphia, Lippincott [1957] 284 p.
57–8948 GR110.M2B4
Bibliography: p. 273–276.
"This is not a scholarly book in the pedantic sense nor is it intended to be one. Neither is it a complete collection of Maine folklore. Rather, it is a selection of tales, beliefs, superstitions, songs, and customs of people of English-speaking stock in Maine. It is a book that attempts to give illustrations of most of the major aspects of folklore that are, or have been within the last twenty years, extant in the state." The materials are incorporated into a historical setting in order that the reader may see the folk record of history through the centuries. Most of the stories have been paraphrased to facilitate reading.

2475. Boatright, Mody C. Folklore of the oil industry. With illustrations by William D. Wittliff. Dallas, Southern Methodist University Press [°1963] 220 p.    63–21186 TN872.A5B6
Bibliographical references included in "Notes" (p. 205–213).
"The oil industry is a little more than a hundred years old—old enough to have generated a considerable body of tradition, young enough to exemplify the generation of tradition in a literate, industrial society." Some of the more prevalent forms of this tradition are examined here. Based largely on field-work in Texas, the study is buttressed by research in libraries and by additional fieldwork in Pennsylvania, West Virginia, Ohio, Kansas, and Oklahoma. The author divides his discussion into three parts: one on stories concerned with the search for oil, another on figures already stereotyped in the industry (including the "promoter" and the "shooter"), and a third devoted to miscellaneous tales and songs. Although the folk of the oil industry created their own mythical heroes, they also borrowed from other settings. Even Paul Bunyan found time in his busy life to drill for oil, building one rig so tall that it reached to heaven, where his crew lived until the well was finished.

2476. Boatright, Mody C., Wilson M. Hudson, *and* Allen Maxwell, *eds*. Singers and story-tellers. Dallas, Southern Methodist University Press [1961] 298 p. (Publications of the Texas Folklore Society, no. 30)
60–15894 GR1.T4 no. 30
A collection of 28 articles, some of which are collections of tales and most of which pertain to Texas. The contributors are as varied as the subjects about which they write. Articles by J. Frank Dobie, MacEdward Leach, and editor Boatright are intermixed with others by a senior English major at the University of Texas, a geography teacher at Louisiana State University, and a soil conservationist. Boatright has also joined with Robert B. Downs and John T. Flanagan as coauthor of *The Family Saga and Other Phases of American Folklore* (Urbana, University of Illinois Press, 1958. 65 p. Sixth annual Windsor lectures, 1958), a small volume consisting of one lecture by each man.

2477. Botkin, Benjamin A., *ed*. A treasury of New England folklore; stories, ballads, and traditions of Yankee folk. Rev. ed. New York, Crown Publishers [1965] xxii, 618 p. music.
64–17848 GR106.B6 1965
A revised edition of no. 5524 in the 1960 *Guide*, containing a new introduction and some additional material.

2478. Brewer, John Mason. Worser days and better times; the folklore of the North Carolina Negro. With preface & notes by Warren E. Roberts. Drawings by R. L. Toben. Chicago, Quadrangle Books [1965] 192 p.    65–18245 GR103.B72
Bibliography: p. 17–18.
A broad sampling of contemporary Negro folk-tales and other folklore from North Carolina. Collected while the author, a Negro folklorist, was teaching at Livingstone College, Salisbury, the tales,

talk, superstitions, song texts, and verses were chosen to illustrate characteristics which Brewer considers typical of the North Carolina Negro. Among the traits identified are an attitude of superiority toward Negroes in States to the south, especially South Carolina and Georgia; an absorbing desire to go to New York City to live; seriousness about religion and religious leaders; closely knit family and neighborhood relationships; a "slow and steady" and suspicious nature; and replacement of the "other worldly" thinking of slavery days with "reality thinking." Brewer makes less use of dialect than in his earlier work, *Dog Ghosts, and Other Texas Negro Folk Tales* (Austin, University of Texas Press [1958] 124 p.) and keeps "editorial interference" at a minimum "in order to preserve the peculiar folk flavor of the individual offerings."

2479. Campbell, Marie. Tales from the cloud walking country. Illustrated by Clare Leighton. Bloomington, Indiana University Press [1958] 270 p.      58–12212 GR110.K4C3
   Bibliography: p. 267–270.

Seventy-eight tales from the oral tradition of the eastern Kentucky mountains. Narrated by six "right main tale-tellers" who had a "fine sleight at tale-telling," the items consist largely of what the layman would call fairytales, even though few of them are about fairies. All of them came originally "from across the ocean waters" and were brought to Kentucky by "our foreparents way back in time." The author collected these materials, using a self-devised system of shorthand, while teaching school among the rural people in the 1920's and 1930's. *Up Cutshin and Down Greasy; Folkways of a Kentucky Family* ([Lexington] University of Kentucky Press [1959] 165 p.), by Leonard W. Roberts, is the history of Jim Couch and his relatives, with one chapter consisting of their typical stories and songs.

2480. Dorson, Richard M., *ed.* Negro tales from Pine Bluff, Arkansas, and Calvin, Michigan. Bloomington, Indiana University Press, 1958. xviii, 292 p. (Indiana University publications. Folklore series, no. 12)      58–63484 GR108.D6
   Bibliography: p. 289–292. Includes bibliographical references.

The editor has explored in two directions the "incomparably rich" narrative lore of the Southern Negro. Approximately half of the materials came from a single outstanding storyteller, James D. Suggs. Although Suggs had grown up in Mississippi, he lived in Michigan at the time his stories were recorded. The other half of the contributions were collected from a number of narrators on a field

trip to a Negro community in southeastern Arkansas. Dorson calls special attention to a small group of "protest tales" which correspond to the better known genre, "protest songs." These were solicited from a man of mixed heritage (Indian and Negro), who aroused some uneasiness in his own community because—in Dorson's words—"his stream of anecdotes sidestepped the conventional plots about Brother Rabbit and Old Marster, to center on the racial situation."

2481. Duke University, *Durham, N.C. Library.*
   *Frank C. Brown Collection of North Carolina Folklore.* The Frank C. Brown Collection of North Carolina Folklore; the folklore of North Carolina, collected by Dr. Frank C. Brown during the years 1912 to 1943, in collaboration with the North Carolina Folklore Society. General editor: Newman Ivey White; associate editors: Henry M. Belden [and others]. Wood engravings by Clare Leighton. Durham, N.C., Duke University Press [1952–64] 7 v. illus., music. (Duke University publications).
   Includes bibliographies.
   CONTENTS.—v. 1. Games and rhymes. Beliefs and customs. Riddles. Proverbs. Speech. Tales and legends.—v. 2. Folk ballads from North Carolina. —v. 3. Folk songs from North Carolina.—v. 4. The music of the ballads.—v. 5. The music of the folk songs.—v. 6–7. Popular beliefs and superstitions from North Carolina.
             52–10967 GR110.N8D8

With the publication of volumes 5–7, this collection, entered as no. 5536 in the 1960 *Guide,* is complete. Volumes 6 and 7, edited by Wayland D. Hand, are now the published model for the arrangement of American folk beliefs. Another major regional collection that follows the same arrangement is Ray B. Browne's *Popular Beliefs and Practices From Alabama* (Berkeley, University of California Press, 1958. 271 p. University of California publications. Folklore studies, 9).

2482. Hyatt, Harry M. Folk-lore from Adams County, Illinois. 2d and rev. ed. [n.p.] 1965. 920 p. (Memoirs of the Alma Egan Hyatt Foundation)      66–6468 GR110.I3H9 1965

The author interviewed his informants personally and sought to obtain stories based on real experiences rather than unsupported statements. Although the text of the first edition, *Folk-lore From Adams County, Illinois,* is enhanced by an extensive index, the second edition has no index at all. Hyatt points out that "one very special treasure of this book, probably the only one in existence," is a picture of a "Witch Wreath." Found in a child's cradle pillow, the wreath consisted of feathers set in skin resembling a chicken breast and allegedly nourishing the feathers so that they grew in size.

2483. Korson, George G. Black rock; mining folklore of the Pennsylvania Dutch. Baltimore, Johns Hopkins Press [1960] 453 p.

60–16892  GR900.K65

"Folk songs and ballads": p. 348–402. Bibliographical references included in "Source notes" (p. 403–436).

Contrary to popular belief, the Pennsylvania Dutch played a dominant role in the development of the anthracite coal industry in the second half of the 19th century. This survey of the miners living in western Schuylkill County, Pa., portrays an agricultural people adjusting to an industrial environment. The author was one of the first folklorists to recognize the richness of the industrial community's lore and tradition. After tracing the geographical settlement and economic history of the Pennsylvania Dutch in the region, he concentrates on daily activities as reflected through folk habits in speech, medicine, games, cooking, religion, tales, and a collection of songs and ballads. Here, as throughout his field research and writing, Korson emphasizes the intrinsic worth of the people among whom he works and the rewards of winning their confidence.

2484. Pound, Louise. Nebraska folklore. Lincoln, University of Nebraska Press, 1959. 243 p.

59–9868  GR110.N2P6

Scholar and athlete, the first woman president of the Modern Language Association of America and the first woman elected to the Nebraska Sports Hall of Fame, the author was a professor at the University of Nebraska for 50 years and a recognized authority in the field of folklore. Shortly before her death in 1958, she prepared for publication this collection of her writings on the folklore of her home State. Included are selections on cave lore, snake lore, and rain lore, as well as legends, hoaxes, and folk customs. Three scholarly papers read by the author at professional conferences are appended. *Kansas Folklore* (Lincoln, University of Nebraska Press, 1961. 251 p.), edited by Samuel J. Sackett and William E. Koch, comes from a quantity of lore, "identifiably Kansan," created within the State's borders and revealing the nature of its land and people.

2485. Randolph, Vance, *ed*. Sticks in the knapsack, and other Ozark folk tales. With notes by Ernest W. Baughman. Illustrated by Glen Rounds. New York, Columbia University Press,

1958. 171 p.    58–13670  GR110.M77R28  1958

Bibliography: p. 167–171.

2486. Randolph, Vance, *ed*. Hot springs and hell; and other folk jests and anecdotes from the Ozarks. Illustrated by William Cechak. Hatboro, Pa., Folklore Associates, 1965. xxviii, 297 p.

65–26776  GR110.M77R274

Bibliography: p. 281–297.

"The Ozark Mountain region is a strange land, and few outsiders know anything about it," Randolph asserts in the introduction to *Sticks in the Knapsack*. "The people who live in the Ozarks are not like country folk elsewhere, and city dwellers do not understand them." One of the differences is in the use of leisure time, which is apparently abundant for the backwoodsman. "When a city slicker takes a holiday, he goes somewhere and does something strenuous or debilitating. But the Ozarker just sits down, and talks with his neighbors. He likes to crack old jokes and tell old stories." These two books are composed of gleanings from 45 years of listening by the editor. At various times he collected with the use of a pen or pencil, a stenographer, or recording equipment. Whatever the method of collection, he attempts here to reproduce each story essentially as it was told to him. He leaves the idiom and the stylistic flaws and retains sexual or scatological terms. He often cuts out profanity, however, and he omits some stories that he regards as unprintable without a censorship that would ruin them.

2487. Wyld, Lionel D. Low bridge! Folklore and the Erie Canal. [Syracuse, N.Y.] Syracuse University Press, 1962. 212 p.

62–10627  F127.E5W9

Bibliographical notes: p. 182–206.

The Erie Canal, or "Clinton's ditch," is an inland waterway 360 miles long, connecting the Hudson River with Lake Erie. Since its construction early in the 19th century, it has contributed directly to the development of the region through which it passes and to the growth of Buffalo, Albany, and New York City. By 1900 railroad competition had caused a decline in the use of the canal, but it is still in service today as a part of the New York State Barge Canal System. This volume surveys the "cultural mosaic" that the Erie Canal helped to create. The social historian, the folklorist, and the general reader will each find chapters of interest. Wyld discusses the building of the canal, the way of life that was generated upon it as well as along it, and the vocabulary, the ballads, and the tales that it evoked. He also examines at length the role of the canal as a subject for stories, novels, stage plays, and motion pictures.

# C. Folksongs and Ballads: General

2488. Bronson, Bertrand H., *ed*. The traditional tunes of the Child ballads; with their texts, according to the extant records of Great Britain and America. Princeton, N.J., Princeton University Press, 1959–62. 2 v.   57–5468 ML3650.B82

In *The English and Scottish Popular Ballads* (mentioned in the annotation for no. 5550 in the 1960 *Guide*), Francis James Child included 350 ballads which he believed to represent, as he wrote in an unpublished introduction, "everything in the Engl[ish] language that by the most liberal interpretation could be called a popular ballad, and all the known versions of such." Bronson has elected to complement and supplement the Child ballads with the musical record where text and tune have both survived. His introduction is "designed to answer questions about the name and nature of the undertaking as a whole, to justify its purpose, account for its limitations, and describe its manner of proceeding." Each ballad is allotted a chapter detailing its history and listing variants with their sources. These are followed by tunes and full texts. The two volumes, containing 1,000 variants of 113 ballads, parallel the materials in the first two of Child's five volumes, and Bronson indicates his hopes for finding support that will enable him to continue the work.

2489. Burt, Olive W., *ed*. American murder ballads and their stories. New York, Oxford University Press, 1958. 272 p.
58–5382 ML3551.B93
Includes unaccompanied melodies.

The editor traces her interest in this subject to the sad ballads that she heard in childhood from her mother. Later, while a journalist, she became interested in true crime stories. Their frequent references to ballads gradually led her to study the folklore of murder. This collection is the product of 20 years of hunting, listening, and copying. "Here are only American songs, composed on the spot, indigenous to this country. They cover the entire period of our history and the whole area of the United States. They relate murders committed from all sorts of motives." They are "the voice of the people, speaking authoritatively upon one of the tragic but very real aspects of our civilization."

2490. Coffin, Tristram P. The British traditional ballad in North America. Rev. ed. Philadelphia, American Folklore Society, 1963. xvii, 186 p. (Publications of the American Folklore Society. Bibliographical series, v. 2)
63–22101/MN ML3553.C6 1963
Bibliography: p. 173–182.
A revised edition of no. 5550 in the 1960 *Guide*.

2491. Courlander, Harold. Negro folk music, U.S.A. New York, Columbia University Press, 1963. 324 p.   63–18019/MN ML3556.C7
Bibliography: p. [299]–301; Discography: p. [302]–308.

The author examines Negro folk music as a whole and searches for cultural continuity and for relationships with other kinds of traditions. In his opinion, Negro music is probably the largest body of genuine folk music still alive in this country and merits "an effort to see it in the round." The melodies and words of 43 songs are included in a special section at the end of the text. Courlander has also compiled *Negro Songs From Alabama*, rev. and enl. 2d ed. (New York, Oak Publications [1963] 111 p.). Examples of recent Negro folk music are included in *We Shall Overcome! Songs of the Southern Freedom Movement* ([New York] Oak Publications [1963] 112 p.), compiled by Guy and Candie Carawan.

2492. Harlow, Frederick P. Chanteying aboard American ships. Barre, Mass., Barre Gazette, 1962. 250 p.   62–9370 ML3551.H28
Includes unaccompanied melodies.

"A chantey (pronounced 'Shanty') is a song sung by sailors aboard ship while doing various kinds of manual work of a heavy nature," the author explains. It is a combination of chant and song. A "chanteyman" (or more commonly, "shantyman") leads off with a solo for one or two lines, and the crew members unite in a chorus. The author was a sailor on a square rigger in the 1870's, and he offers here the chanteys he joined in singing as he worked at chores on the ship. He warns that different versions of the words are common. No one was required to adhere to tradition, and impromptu rhyming was frequent. Some songs of the sea and of whaling supplement the chanteys. *Songs the Whalemen Sang* (Barre, Mass., Barre Publishers, 1964. 328 p.), edited by Gale Huntington, is a collection gathered largely from the journals and log books of the whalemen of southeastern Massachusetts, which was once the center of the whaling industry.

2493. Laws, George Malcolm. Native American balladry, a descriptive study and a bibliographical syllabus. Rev. ed. Philadelphia, American Folklore Society, 1964. xiv, 298 p. (Publications of the American Folklore Society. Bibliographical and special series, v. 1)

64–17007/MN ML3551.L3 1964

Bibliography: p. 281–288.

A revised edition of no. 5556 in the 1960 *Guide*. *A Pioneer Songster; Texts From the Stevens-Douglass Manuscript of Western New York, 1841–1856* (Ithaca, N.Y., Cornell University Press [1958] 203 p.), edited by Harold W. Thompson, contains British and American ballads sung in English in the United States.

2494. Lomax, Alan, *ed.* The folk songs of North America, in the English language. Melodies and guitar chords transcribed by Peggy Seeger, with one hundred piano arrangements by Matyas Seiber and Don Banks. Illustrated by Michael Leonard. Editorial assistant, Shirley Collins. Garden City, N.Y., Doubleday [1960] 623 p.

M 60–1043 M1629.L83F6 1960a

Bibliography: p. 597–600. Discography: p. 608–615.

"The intention of this volume is to put a choice selection of our folk songs into their historical and social setting so that they tell the story of the people who made and sang them—to compose, in a word, a folk history, or a history of the folk of America." The editor maintains that folksongs provide outlets for unconscious fantasies and for wishes and emotional conflicts too disturbing to be openly stated. They can be taken as signposts of persistent patterns of community emotion and can project light into dark corners of both past and present. An ideal folksong study could be a history of popular feeling, Lomax asserts, and in this volume he tries to suggest what such a history could reveal.

2495. Nettl, Bruno. An introduction to folk music in the United States. [Rev. ed. with index] Detroit, Wayne State University Press, 1962. 126 p. (Waynebook, no. 7)

62–16346/MN ML3551.N47 1962

Includes 32 unaccompanied melodies, some with words.

Bibliographical aids: p. 118–122.

Folklorist Richard M. Dorson suggested the idea for this book, which is intended to be different from the many other books in the field in that it offers an overall survey or summary of the subject in its entirety. It does not pretend to be definitive or comprehensive, or to present new material. Its purpose is merely to introduce the layman to the great variety of forms and cultures represented in the folk music of this country. Although many song types, instruments, and ethnic groups are omitted, a glimpse into each of the large categories of folk music is provided. The emphasis is on the music itself; words are a secondary consideration.

2496. Oliver, Paul. Blues fell this morning; the meaning of the blues. With a foreword by Richard Wright. New York, Horizon Press [1961, ᶜ1960] 355 p. 61–14275 ML3561.J304 1961

An examination of 350 lyrics derived mainly from the country and urban folk blues rather than from either the hollers (work songs improvised on the job) or the classic blues. In *Conversation With the Blues* (New York, Horizon Press [1965] 217 p.), the same author describes an extended tour of the United States during which he interviewed blues singers and musicians. *The Country Blues* (New York, Rinehart [1959] 288 p.), by Samuel B. Charters, is a study of early blues singers and their recordings and includes a discussion of the marketing and sales of blues records. Both urban and country blues with accompaniments for guitar and banjo make up the contents of *The Book of the Blues* (New York, Leeds Music Corp. [1963] 301 p.), edited by Kay Shirley and annotated by Frank Driggs.

2497. Silber, Irwin, *ed.* Songs of the Civil War. Piano and guitar arrangements by Jerry Silverman. New York, Columbia University Press, 1960. 385 p. M 60–1027 M1637.S5S6

Selections arranged by such subjects as songs of the Union and of the Confederacy, sentimental songs, songs of battles and campaigns, and songs the soldiers sang. Each song is documented, and its historical background is discussed briefly. Nearly all the numerous illustrations in the book are from wood engravings by artists of the Civil War period.

2498. Wilgus, D. K. Anglo-American folksong scholarship since 1898. New Brunswick, N.J., Rutgers University Press, 1959. xx, 466 p.

59–7517 ML3553.W48

"A selected discography of folk music performances on long-playing records": p. [365]–382. Bibliographical references included in "Notes" (p. [383]–407). Bibliography: p. [409]–427.

"This is a history of British and American scholarship devoted to ballads and folksongs in English." Although the scholars themselves are discussed, their personalities are subordinated to their work. The author maintains that although 20th-century scholarship has emphasized the ballad in the narrow sense, the entire field has been broadened by an interest in folksong study. The song and the singer, the performance and the function—all have become subjects of investigation. Two chapters of this history (approximately half of the volume) are devoted to the prolonged controversy over the question of whether or not the ballad is

more nearly the product of the entire society than of an individual. The other two chapters deal respectively with the collection and publication of folksongs and the methodology of folksong scholarship, past, present, and future. In an appendix the author discusses the origins of the Negro spiritual and concludes that it must be viewed as a hybrid, a folk music derived from African tradition combined with elements of the songs that the Negro heard in the United States.

## D. Folksongs and Ballads: Local

2499. Cazden, Norman, ed. The Abelard folk song book; more than 101 ballads to sing. Edited and arranged for piano and guitar. Illustrated by Abner Graboff. New York, Abelard Schuman, °1958. 2 pts. in 1 v. (127, 127 p.)

M 58–1011 M1629.C28A2

Bibliography: [pt. 1], p. 124–127; [pt. 2], p. 125–127.

The editor divides his offerings into "Songs for Every Day" and "Songs for Saturday Night." Those in the first group were collected in the Catskill Mountain region of New York State and treat a range of topics "as varied and comprehensive as human activity and human sympathy." A few of these songs are indigenous to the Catskills, but many are found in variant forms in other parts of the United States and have origins in the British Isles. A large number of them have rarely been published in their present form, however. Love with its attendant sorrows and joys is the theme of most of the "Songs for Saturday Night." There are "suggestive, uninhibited, often lusty passages in many of these songs, expressed through imagery that is at once bold and subtle." Complete accompaniments for piano or guitar are provided with all the songs, and notes on original sources are supplied at the end of each of the two groups.

2500. Davis, Arthur Kyle, ed. More traditional ballads of Virginia; collected with the cooperation of members of the Virginia Folklore Society. Chapel Hill, University of North Carolina Press [1960] 371 p. 60–51689 ML3551.D2M7

Includes melodies.

Bibliography: p. [361]–366.

Forty-six traditional or Child ballads selected from a large body of folksong collected by the Virginia Folklore Society and housed at the University of Virginia. Each of the ballads is prefaced by an essay re-

lating the variant texts and tunes to the total known tradition of the ballad. Sources are cited for each transcription. This scholarly study, including significant fresh material, is written to appeal to the amateur and general reader as well as the specialist. Two earlier volumes compiled by Davis establish editorial continuity and provide background. Traditional Ballads of Virginia (1929) is a selection of 51 Child ballads, 35 of which are represented in More Traditional Ballads of Virginia with additional texts and tunes. Folksongs of Virginia (1949) is a checklist of the almost 3,200 items in the University of Virginia collection, with a brief history of the collection and its classification system.

2501. Flanders, Helen Hartness, ed. Ancient ballads traditionally sung in New England, from the Helen Hartness Flanders ballad collection, Middlebury College, Middlebury, Vt. Correlated with the numbered Francis James Child collection. Critical analyses by Tristram P. Coffin. Music annotations by Bruno Nettl. Philadelphia, University of Pennsylvania Press [1960–65] 4 v.

M 59–1030 M1629.F58A5

These texts and tunes, some of which have appeared in earlier publications compiled by the editor, have been gathered in New England since 1930. Preceding each ballad is a note on its symbolism, its relationship to other ballads, and its sources. For some items there are many textual versions, several of which are very rare. Texts are printed and tunes are noted exactly as the singers rendered them. For each tune the structure, rhythm, contour, and scale are given. The musical annotations express the tunes' characteristics and facilitate comparative work.

2502. Hubbard, Lester A., ed. Ballads and songs from Utah. Music transcription by Kenly

W. Whitelock. Salt Lake City, University of Utah Press, 1961. xxi, 475 p.

M 61–1720 M1629.H86

Unaccompanied melodies.

Bibliography: p. 464–466.

The Mormon experience in Utah in the 19th century was distinctive. The practice of polygamy, although relatively limited in time and extent, inspired the creation of such gently humorous songs as "The Cohabs" and "In the Mormon Beds Out West," as well as many that were not — in the language of one source used for this compilation — "nice." Forty-six of the 250 pieces selected from the Hubbard collection for this volume are grouped together under the heading, "Utah and the Mormons." The remainder, imported from outside the State, are similar to songs collected elsewhere in the United States and are arranged in such familiar categories as "Love and Courtship," "Youth and Childhood," and "Domestic Relations."

2503. Ives, Edward D. Larry Gorman: the man who made the songs. Bloomington, Indiana University Press, 1964. xv, 225 p.

64–63000/MN ML410.G645 I 9

Bibliography: p. 213–217. Bibliographical footnotes.

A biography of a folk composer and poet of the northeastern woods. Gorman was a farmer, fisherman, woodsman, river driver, and millhand, "an angular cantankerous individual who lived his lonely life, dying as obscurely as he was born." But as a writer and singer of satirical songs, he made men laugh. His songs reflected the traditions and living patterns of his fellow immigrants: the farmers, fishermen, and woodsmen of Prince Edward Island, New Brunswick, and Maine. This is a study of his songs "in the context of his life," designed to "shed some light on the creation of folksongs in general and the relation of the individual songmaker to his tradition." The author describes Gorman's compositions and the people who inspired them and relates the whole of his work to Anglo-American traditions of satirical song. All his extant songs and poems are included, with sources for tunes, texts, and variants.

2504. Moore, Ethel, *and* Chauncey O. Moore, *comps*. Ballads and folk songs of the Southwest: more than 600 titles, melodies, and texts collected in Oklahoma. Norman, University of Oklahoma Press [1964] xv, 414 p.

64–11329/M M1629.M84B3

Bibliography: p. 393–396.

In the southwestern States, "a happy and tolerant blend of peoples from the North, South, East, and West" were assimilated into "an essentially Western tradition." With the mingling of dissimilar peoples occurred a cross-fertilization of folksongs. A different type of music, "at once varied and democratic," was created, and new life was infused into old songs. Words such as "lord" and "lady" were replaced by "young" and "fair." Local place names and personal names were substituted for traditional ones. The Moores built their collection, from which the pieces in this volume were selected, by a door-to-door search over a period of 25 years, largely in the city of Tulsa, where they lived.

2505. Paredes, Américo. "With his pistol in his hand," a border ballad and its hero. Austin, University of Texas Press [1958] 262 p.

58–10853 PQ7297.A1C63

Bibliography: p. 251–258.

The "corrido," or Mexican narrative folksong of epic theme, evolved from the Spanish "romance," influenced by the Scottish medieval border ballad. It depicted a story of resistance rather than of military victory. In 1901 Gregorio Cortez killed a sheriff under circumstances that a jury later agreed had been self-defense, but in the intervening period he was a fugitive who killed again in order to elude unsympathetic "gringo" justice. The first half of this book discusses the life of Cortez in fact and legend. It also offers a study of relations between English-speaking Texans and Texans of Spanish origin in the isolated communities along the lower border of the Rio Grande. The author then proceeds to a comprehensive treatment of the border ballad form in general and of "El Corrido de Gregorio Cortez" in detail. He traces the ballad's origins, imagery, structure, and versification and supplies textual variations in both Spanish and English.

2506. Yoder, Don. Pennsylvania spirituals. Lancaster, Pennsylvania Folklife Society, 1961. 528 p.

62–13444 ML3555.Y6

Bibliography: p. 483–498.

"Much of what we call Pennsylvania Dutch folk-culture is not a transplantation of Continental European practices onto Pennslyvania soil, but a new American production shaped by acculturation with the Scotch-Irish and English Quaker neighbors who lived beside the Dutchman in 18th and 19th Century America. That in brief is the theme of this book." The chief emphasis is on a neglected religious pattern, that of the "Bush-Meeting Dutch." "Bush-meeting" is an early Pennsylvania synonym for "camp-meeting." "Bush-Meeting Religion" refers to a family of revivalist sects that arose in the

State at the time of the Second Awakening. Influenced by early American Methodism, these new native sects began with the United Brethren, the Evangelicals, and the Church of God. Yoder offers 150 song texts, with brief editorial notes. In addition he presents five chapters on the Pennsylvania spiritual and the type of religion that produced it; two chapters on sources and bibliography for the specialist; and two more on the themes of the spirituals and their diffusion among other groups.

# E. Folk Art and Crafts

2507. Christensen, Erwin O. American crafts and folk arts. Washington, R. B. Luce [1964] 90 p. illus. (America today series, no. 4)
64–19601 NK805.C48
Bibliography: p. 88–90.

In this brief introductory guide, "crafts" and "folk arts" are deliberately used in a loose sense. Often both may be applied to a single object. Pennsylvania German pottery, for example, is both craft and folk art. The author states that although the only native "American art" is that of the Indian, today the expression ordinarily refers to the art developed by the European settlers and their descendants. The modern meaning is the one followed here. One chapter is on the art of the American Indian; the rest of the chapters concentrate on the white society. The chronological picture is sketched in chapters on crafts of the colonial period, primitive painters, and popular art in the 19th century. Topical themes include "The American Eagle," "European Folk Art Transplanted," and "The Handicraft Movement and Today's Leisure-Time Craftsmen."

2508. Espinosa, José E. Saints in the valleys; Christian sacred images in the history, life, and folk art of Spanish New Mexico. [Albuquerque] University of New Mexico Press, 1960. 122 p. illus.
60–5656 N7910.N6E8
Bibliography: p. 101–107.

In early New Mexico a sacred image was referred to by the generic name "santo." A santo could take any of several forms. It could be a figure carved in the round from pine or cottonwood, a modeled bas-relief, a flat painting on a pine panel, or a group of such objects used as an altar screen. The folk artists who created santos were "santeros," white men who adapted European and Mexican religious art to the new environment. The golden age of santo-making was approximately 1795 to 1860. After that time the art declined, fading out completely in the last decade of the 19th century. Espinosa traces the santo and its place in New Mexican life from the landing of Cortez on the coast of Mexico in 1519 to the present. Forty-six black-and-white illustrations of santos are included. *Popular Arts of Colonial New Mexico* (Santa Fe, Museum of International Folk Art, 1959. 51 p.), by Elizabeth B. W. Hall—writing under the pseudonym of E. Boyd—is a brief survey, illustrated partly in color.

2509. Stoudt, John J. Early Pennsylvania arts and crafts. New York, A. S. Barnes [1964] 364 p.
64–21360 NK835.P4S72

An interpretive study of the period from the end of the 17th century to the middle of the 19th, during which, in the author's opinion, Pennsylvania was the cultural center of the United States. The distinction between folk arts and fine arts was related to the cultural, spiritual, geographic, and economic differences between the Piedmont, home of the "plain" Pennsylvania Dutch, and the Tidewater, inhabited by Quakers who soon reflected European elegance. Pennsylvania folk art came from the hands of experienced craftsmen with a religious point of view. Faced by a new environment, they produced imaginative and sophisticated architectural structures, furniture, works of art, assorted handicrafts, and illuminated manuscripts, which Stoudt describes in turn. He views these creations as "keys which unlock the spirit of those who made them and of those who have used them." Large in format, the volume is lavishly illustrated.

2510. Whaling Museum Society, *Cold Spring Harbor, N.Y.* Scrimshaw; folk art of the whalers. Text by Walter K. Earle, curator. Illustrations by Jane Davenport (Mrs. Jas. A. de Tomasi), assistant curator. Cold Spring Harbor [1957] 36 p.
59–471 NK5903.W47

"Scrimshaw" is the name Yankee whalemen created for the items they made at sea, mostly with a jackknife. "Scrimshawing" provided diversion and entertainment in the long and monotonous hours when there was nothing to do. It was an art practiced only by sailors engaged in whaling. Similar products are made today by Eskimos and Aleutian

Indians, and others are machine-made in the United States and Europe; readily distinguishable from scrimshaw, the modern products are "beautiful and in good demand although lacking the inherent charm" of the whalemen's art. Because of the scarcity of literature on the subject, the Whaling Museum Society offers this very short review of the birth of scrimshaw and the nature of the art, illustrated with drawings of pieces in the museum at Cold Spring Harbor.

# XXV

# Music

THIS chapter's section on popular music is proportionately twice as large as its counterpart in the 1960 *Guide*. In contrast, the respective sections on orchestras and bands and on choirs are conspicuously smaller. These differences may reflect changing interests in the society. No shift in public interest in music, however, accounts for this chapter's proportionately small section on individual musicians. The section is open to works on any person in any area of music, but the publications appropriate for inclusion are limited to an autobiography of a jazz musician, a biography of an opera singer, and a biography of a composer-critic. Although semibiographical works are entered in other sections, the contents of this chapter clearly reveal that few eminent people in the field of music, for whatever reasons, attracted scholarly biographers in this period, and fewer still published full, candid, and perceptive autobiographies.

## A. General Histories and Reference Works

2511. Howard, John T. Our American music; a comprehensive history from 1620 to the present. 4th ed. New York, Crowell [1965] xxii, 944 p. illus.          65–18697/MN  ML200.H8  1965

"Bibliography, rev. and brought up to date (1964) by Karl Kroeger": p. 769–845.

A revised edition of no. 5607 in the 1960 *Guide*. The author has also written, in collaboration with George K. Bellows, *A Short History of Music in America* (New York, Crowell [1957] 470 p.).

2512. Lowens, Irving. Music and musicians in early America. New York, Norton [1964] 328 p. illus.          64–17518/MN  ML200.L7

"A check-list of writings about music in the periodicals of American transcendentalism (1835–50)": p. 311–321.

The chief music critic for the Washington *Evening Star* has selected from his previous writings 18 scholarly but easily read articles on the history of music in the United States, with emphasis on the period to 1850. Some of the original articles were revised and updated by the author for this compilation. Lowens discusses such musical events as the publication of John Tuft's *Introduction to the Singing of Psalm-Tunes* (1721), the first American music textbook; major musical figures, including Benjamin Carr, Joseph Hewitt, and Louis Moreau Gottschalk; and diverse philosophical topics, among which are "American Democracy and American Music (1830–1914)" and "Music and American Transcendentalism (1835–50)." Commentaries on music from 1861 to 1961 are collected in *One Hundred Years of Music in America* (New York, G. Schirmer; distributor to the book trade: Grosset & Dunlap [1961] 322 p.), edited by Paul H. Láng.

2513. Mattfeld, Julius. Variety music cavalcade 1620–1961. A chronology of vocal and instrumental music popular in the United States. Rev. ed. With an introduction by Abel Green. Englewood Cliffs, N.J., Prentice-Hall [1962] xxiii, 713 p.          62–16317   ML128.V7M4   1962

2514. Shapiro, Nat, *ed.* Popular music; an annotated index of American popular songs. New York, Adrian Press [1964–65] 2 v.
                  64—23761/MN   ML120.U5S5
CONTENTS—v. 1. 1950–59.—v. 2. 1940–49.
Two selective lists of popular music. Although *Variety Music Cavalcade* includes very few compositions for the years before 1800, it surveys virtually the full period of American history. Following the roster of each year's music, the concurrent political and cultural events of major importance are noted. *Popular Music* lists music titles chronologically by year of publication or copyright and for each piece shows its composer, lyricist, and publisher, as well as its origin, such as motion picture or musical comedy. Additional volumes for the years 1900–40 are planned. *Popular Music* contains more entries per year than does *Variety Music Cavalcade;* the latter retains the usefulness of a comprehensive one-volume work. A relatively brief reference to the identity of more than 3,000 bestselling songs is *Index to Top-Hit Tunes, 1900–1950* (Boston, B. Humphries [1962] 249 p.), compiled by John H. Chipman.

2515. Mellers, Wilfrid H. Music in a new found land; themes and developments in the history of American music. New York, Knopf, 1965 [ᶜ1964]  xv, 543 p.  music.
          64–17706/MN   ML200.M44   1965
    Bibliography: p. [450]–451. Discography: p. [452]–519.
"The nature of this book is accurately defined by its sub-title—themes and developments in American music." It is not an attempt at a comprehensive history. Written by an English scholar and published while he was a visiting professor at the University of Pittsburgh, it deals with comparatively few composers, each of whom was chosen by avowedly arbitrary criteria. Representative chapters include "Realism and transcendentalism; Charles Ives as American hero"; "Skyscraper and prairie: Aaron Copland and the American isolation"; and "Orgy and alienation: country blues, barrelhouse piano, and piano rag."

2516. Wolfe, Richard J. Secular music in America, 1801–1825; a bibliography. Introduction by Carleton Sprague Smith. New York, The New York Public Library, 1964. 3 v.
          64–25006/MN   ML120.U5W57
A list of more than 10,000 compositions in alphabetical order by composer or arranger. The description of each entry includes "all title-page information (or the caption title and imprint when a title-page is absent), together with printed or supplied date of publication, pagination, and size of the largest copy encountered." If the music is known to be extant, its present location in a library or private collection is indicated; otherwise a contemporary announcement of its publication is cited. Brief biographical sketches of many of the composers are provided. Volume 3 contains a general index as well as separate indexes of titles, first lines, publishers, engravers, printers, and publishers' plate and publication numbering systems. Wolfe's compilation supplements *A Bibliography of Early Secular American Music (18th Century),* by Oscar George Theodore Sonneck, revised and enlarged by William Treat Upton (no. 5610 in the 1960 *Guide*), and contains an appendix listing items not recorded in that work.

# B. Contemporary Surveys and Special Topics

2517. Browne, Charles A. The story of our national ballads. Rev. by Willard A. Heaps. New York, Crowell [1960]  314 p.
          60–15255   ML3551.B88   1960

A revised edition of no. 5616 in the 1960 *Guide*.

2518. Read, Oliver, *and* Walter L. Welch. From tin foil to stereo: evolution of the phonograph. Indianapolis, H. W. Sams [1959] xvi, 524 p. illus.        59–15832  TS2301.P3R4

Bibliography: p. 495–502.

"No industrial development has had a more romantic past than the phonograph. Ingenuity, loyalty, perseverance, and honesty have contended with piracy, jealousy, rapacity, and treachery in many-sided struggles for financial success." Thomas A. Edison's original tinfoil phonograph was patented in 1878. From this primitive beginning the authors trace the evolution of the instrument and the history of the industry that ultimately mass-produced it. The story is "replete with strong and unusual personalities, intrigues, bitter litigation, corporate manipulations, and struggles for survival."

2519. Schickel, Richard. The world of Carnegie Hall. New York, Messner [ᶜ1960] 438 p. illus.        60–13802  ML200.8.N52C34

When the cornerstone of Carnegie Hall (then known as Music Hall) was laid in 1890, Andrew Carnegie expressed the hope that the building would "intertwine itself with the history of our country." Schickel reveals the extent to which Carnegie's hope has been fulfilled. Blending anecdotes about debuts, premieres, and lectures with references to social, economic, and political trends, he places the "very small world of Carnegie Hall" in perspective against the "very large world" which has surrounded it. A few of the many personages in the field of music who appear in the book are Tchaikovsky, Paderewski, Isadora Duncan, Yehudi Menuhin, Walter Damrosch, Olin Downes, Fritz Kreisler, Arturo Toscanini, and Leonard Bernstein. Among the nonmusical performances described are Winston Churchill's defense of Britain's role in the Boer War, William Butler Yeats' plea for Irish independence, and Clarence Darrow's ridicule of evolution and prohibition.

2520. Wells, L. Jeanette. A history of the music festival at Chautauqua Institution from 1874 to 1957. Washington, Catholic University of Amer-

ica Press, 1958. 310 p. A 58-6036  ML38.C53W4

"Selected bibliography": p. 300–304.

The Chautauqua Institution, known today for its general educational program, was founded in 1874 as a summer institute for training Sunday school teachers. There was little music other than group singing that first year. The beginning of instruction in music in 1875 heralded the steady growth of a music program. The Chautauqua School of Music was organized in 1879. In 1906 a Music Week for concerts and competitions was designated, and in 1914 it was renamed Music Festival Week. Concerts increased in number and variety. In 1957 the Chautauqua music season ran for 54 days with more than 130 events, including operas, recitals, and symphonic, chamber, and choral music. The author discusses Chautauqua's music and reviews in chronological order the significant episodes in the history of the Nation's oldest continuous summer music festival.

2521. Woodworth, George W. The world of music. Cambridge, Mass., Belknap Press of Harvard University Press, 1964. 207 p.
64–13432/MN  ML200.5.W65

Includes bibliographical footnotes.

"Music in our day is a vast subject. It is not one subject, but many; not one field of activity, but dozens. Music is an art, a science, a literature, one of the humanities, and a field of learning. It is an area of education from kindergarten to graduate school, a craft, a business, an article of commerce. It is bought and sold. It is a powerful tool of the Madison Avenue advertiser, and it is an agent in propaganda. It permeates our life." The modern uses of music provoke the author into raising questions about its meaning to the people who make it and those who hear it. Does it stimulate activity of thought? Does it enlarge receptiveness to beauty? Does it nurture humane feeling? An outgrowth of lectures delivered at the Lowell Institute in Boston during the spring of 1961, the book is directed toward the amateur rather than the professional.

## C. Localities

2522. Keefer, Lubov B. Baltimore's music; the haven of the American composer. Baltimore, 1962. xvii, 343 p.
62–53630/MN  ML200.8.B19K4

Bibliography: p. 298–312.

One of Baltimore's characteristics, manifest particularly in the period before the Civil War, was its

receptivity to all kinds of music. The city was "able to strike a Golden Mean between the uplifting and the pleasurable, the sacred and the profane, the scholarly and the homely. There was a balance between vocal and instrumental idioms, between what expressed the common man and the individual. Opera and oratorio, ditty and string quartet, mature artist and prodigy—all peopled the scene without dominating it." Of the numerous alien influences, the strongest and longest lasting was German. What "could have developed into a strangle hold of German thought was aborted by the indefatigable activity of Asger Hamerik," head of the Peabody Institute. Hamerik encouraged many American composers and arranged for the performance of their works in Baltimore. Although the author discusses music in Baltimore from colonial times to the present, he concentrates on the 19th century, the period in which the city could most appropriately be described as a "haven" for native composers.

2523. Pichierri, Louis. Music in New Hampshire, 1623–1800. New York, Columbia University Press, 1960. 297 p. 60–13940 ML200.7.N4P5
    Bibliography: p. [271]–281.

New Hampshire was first settled in 1623. The earliest sources indicating the presence of musical instruments are dated 1633 and mention drums, recorders, and hautboys. Although the Colony apparently was never subjected to any Puritan restraints on its musical life, development was slow and documentary evidence is scarce. Delving into "unpublished wills, legal documents, letters, diaries, contemporary newspapers, periodicals, and tune books," the author collected his fragments of information. In order to fill gaps, perceive relationships, and gain perspectives, he turned to secondary sources. In this probing study of music in one American Colony, he strives primarily to present a large body of data hitherto unknown or disregarded by previous researchers, reserving critical examination of the music itself for a projected companion volume.

## D.  Religious Music

2524. Barbour, James M. The church music of William Billings. [East Lansing] Michigan State University Press [1960] xvi, 167 p. music.
    60–15105 ML410.B588B4
    Bibliography: p. 159–163.
    A tanner by trade, Billings (1756–1800), was the "most important composer of the pioneer period of American church music, the last third of the 18th century." His first collection of hymns and anthems, *The New England Psalm Singer,* was published in 1770. Five other collections followed. The author of this study offers analytical chapters

entitled "Texts," "Rhythm and Meter," "Melody," "Counterpoint and Harmony," "Modality and Tonality," and "Texture and Form." He supplies numerous examples from Billings' compositions and also, for comparative purposes, from the compositions of his American contemporaries and his English predecessors. Billings' critics have called him musically illiterate. Barbour refutes this charge and concludes that as a composer of church music, Billings was superior both to other Americans of the time and to the English composers whose works were performed in 18th-century America.

## E.  Popular Music

2525. Dachs, David. Anything goes; the world of popular music. Indianapolis, Bobbs-Merrill [1964] 328 p. illus.
    63–18993/MN ML200.5.D32
    The author views popular music today as a big, money-hungry business. Sales promotion and selling techniques play a larger part than ever before, and popularity is measured largely in terms of sales of recordings. Dach's book is primarily about the record business and how it functions. He deals with all aspects—recording, distribution, and promotion. Critical of both the music and the com-

merce, he bemoans the decline in esthetic standards, a development that he attributes to the influence of "hacks and puffed-up adolescents, teenage idols, and their shrewd, calculating personal managers and booking agencies."

2526. Ewen, David. Complete book of the American musical theater; a guide to more than 300 productions of the American musical theater from The black crook (1866) to the present, with plot, production history, stars, songs, composers, librettists, and lyricists. New York, Holt [1958] xxvii, 447 p. illus. 58–11220 ML1711.E9

A reference book on musical productions. The author's avowed purpose is twofold: "to satisfy curiosity in regard to productions of the past about which much still is said but little remembered, and to revive in theatergoers memories of enchanted evenings." For each of 47 composers a brief biography is provided, followed by information on his most significant musicals, with plot summaries, production histories, names of stars, principal songs and writers, and numbers of performances. The majority of the musicals were produced during the 20th century. Other composers' works dating from 1866 to 1958 are discussed in an appendix. Also useful for reference is *The World of Musical Comedy; the Story of the American Musical Stage As Told Through the Careers of Its Foremost Composers and Lyricists* (New York, Grosset & Dunlap [1962] 397 p.), by Stanley Green.

2527. Ewen, David, *ed.* Popular American composers from Revolutionary times to the present; a biographical and critical guide. New York, H. W. Wilson, 1962. 217 p. illus.

62–9024 ML390.E845

A biographical directory ranging chronologically from William Billings to André Previn and alphabetically from Richard Adler to Victor Young. The representation of deceased composers is comprehensive. In the case of those still living at the time of publication—approximately one-third of the 130 included—the editor was necessarily selective. He chose the ones, who in his opinion, were "of most interest to most people by virtue of their success, their productiveness, their contribution to our popular music." The majority of the sketches are accompanied by a photograph, as well as references to books or articles. A chronological list of composers and an index of songs and other compositions are included.

2528. Goldberg, Isaac. Tin Pan Alley; a chronicle of American popular music. Introduction by George Gershwin. With a supplement: From sweet and swing to rock 'n' roll, by Edward Jablonski. New York, Ungar [ᶜ1961] 371 p. illus.

60–53364 ML2811.G65 1961

An updated edition of no. 5635 in the 1960 *Guide.*

2529. Mates, Julian. The American musical stage before 1800. New Brunswick, N.J., Rutgers University Press [1962] 331 p. illus.

61–12409 ML1711.M4

Bibliography: p. 299–313.

Although *The Black Crook* (1866) has often been designated as the first American musical comedy, Mates traces the lineage of the musical stage back to *The Archers* (1796) and to many other entertainments that were musical and closely related to the theater. With *The Archers* as a focal point, he reveals the beginning of a tradition of musical drama in the 18th century. The Old American Company, which put on the first performance of *The Archers* at the John Street Theatre in New York was "one of the two best acting companies in the United States, and was composed of actors, singers, and dancers renowned in England and France as well as native-born Americans." The orchestra "was composed of the best musicians of the day and represented the culmination of efforts to build a good, professional theatre band in New York."

2530. Nathan, Hans. Dan Emmett and the rise of early Negro minstrelsy. Norman, University of Oklahoma Press [1962] xiv, 496 p. illus. 62–10769 ML410.E5N4

Includes unaccompanied melodies.

"Bibliography of the works of D. D. Emmett": p. 290–306; "Anthology" (principally melodies with piano acc.): p. [311]–491.

Many of the best-known songs, dances, and banjo tunes of the mid-19th century, including "Dixie," were composed by Daniel Decatur Emmett. The son of a blacksmith in rural Ohio, he learned the printer's trade but early abandoned it for a career as an entertainer. For the rest of his active life he made his living as a banjoist, fiddler, singer, and comedian. His compositions are important in the history of popular music and have intrinsic value for "their hard-bitten humor, their naive freshness, and their native flavor." He lived to be 88 years of age and during the final decade depended for support upon a weekly stipend of five dollars from the Actor's Fund of America. A simple, unassuming man, he was nonetheless proud of his most famous achievement; in signing his name he usually added "author of Dixie." Nathan intermingles biography with historical discussions and includes selections from Emmett's works as well as from songs and tunes of the time.

# F. Jazz

2531. Blesh, Rudi, *and* Harriet G. Janis. They all played ragtime; the true story of an American music. [1st rev. ed.] New York, Grove Press [1959] 345 p. illus.
         59–13575   ML3561.J3B49  1959
A revised edition of no. 5641 in the 1960 *Guide.*

2532. Feather, Leonard G. The encyclopedia of jazz. Completely rev., enl. and brought up to date. New York, Horizon Press, 1960. 527 p.
        55–10774   ML3561.J3F39  1960
A revised edition of no. 5642 in the 1960 *Guide,* containing new material as well as information from the author's two yearbooks: *The Encyclopedia Yearbook of Jazz* (New York, Horizon Press, 1956. 190 p.) and *The New Yearbook of Jazz* (New York, Horizon Press, 1958. 187 p.).

2533. Leonard, Neil. Jazz and the white Americans; the acceptance of a new art form. [Chicago] University of Chicago Press [1962] 215 p. illus.   62–19626  ML3561.J3L46
   Bibliography: p. 193–206.
In 1917, "phonograph records and a growing number of bands introduced collectively improvised jazz to the general public." Before long the new music became a controversial issue. Many critics called it distasteful and charged that it provoked immoral behavior. In two decades, however, the "mean of public opinion" had shifted from puzzlement and dislike to tolerance and acceptance. Jazz became respectable. It was taken into the "sanctums of the concert hall and the conservatory." Books were written about it. "A growing number of Americans took pride in what some of them believed to be their country's greatest contribution to the arts." Starting with the 19th-century background of the controversy, the author seeks to "illuminate the proper place of jazz both in American life and in the world of art."

2534. Newton, Francis. The jazz scene. New York, Monthly Review Press, 1960. 303 p. illus.   60–8435  ML3561.J3N47
   Bibliography: p. 296–298.
A British intellectual, critic for the *New Statesman,* offers a group of essays on an American creation. His main object is "to survey the world of jazz for the benefit of the intelligent layman, who knows nothing about it, and perhaps also for that of the expert who has hitherto overlooked some of its non-technical corners." He observes, however, that "it is impossible to look at jazz with any sort of curiosity without trying to find out, however crudely, how it fits into the general framework of twentieth-century civilization." He renders many judgments on the society that produced jazz, the business that both sustains and is sustained by it, the musicians from whom it emanates, the people who are its public, and its reciprocal effects on society.

# G Orchestras and Bands

2535. Goldman, Richard Franko. The wind band, its literature and technique. Boston, Allyn & Bacon, 1961 [ᶜ1962] xvi, 286 p. illus.
        62–8835   ML1300.G65
   Bibliography: p. [269]–278.
Today there are nearly 30,000 bands of all types in the United States. Until about 1925 bands were formed largely by military units, municipalities, or individual leaders. Since then, the sponsorship has shifted largely to schools and colleges. The author discusses the European origins of the modern band and the history of band music in the United States. An experienced conductor, he surveys the major problems that bands encounter and offers suggestions for coping with them. He also describes some contemporary bands, including the concert band founded by his father, Edwin Frarko Goldman.

# H. Opera

2536. Bloomfield, Arthur J. The San Francisco Opera, 1923–1961. New York, Appleton-Century-Crofts [1961] 250 p. illus.
61–16610 ML1711.8.S2B6
The San Francisco Opera has operated continuously since its founding by Gaetano Merola in 1923. Its record of achievement is long. It presented, for example, the American premieres of Richard Strauss' *Die Frau Ohne Schatten,* Maurice Ravel's *L'Enfant et les Sortileges,* and William Turner Walton's *Troilus and Cressida.* Renata Tebaldi and Richard Lewis made their American debuts there. Leontyne Price, Eileen Farrell, Mary Costa, and Elizabeth Schwartzkopf have sung there often. The San Francisco Opera now gives more performances each year than any other company in the United States outside New York. The author begins his story with the organization's background and founding. The significant events of each season, 1924–61, are treated chronologically, year by year. Appendixes list the company's complete repertoire and the entire casts for all the San Francisco performances.

2537. Davis, Ronald L. A history of opera in the American West. Englewood Cliffs, N.J., Prentice-Hall [1965] 178 p. illus.
65–12168/MN ML1711.D4
Bibliographical footnotes.
A review of the development of opera in the West that emphasizes Chicago, New Orleans, San Francisco, Dallas, Santa Fe, and Central City, Colo. The author includes a brief discussion of the San Antonio Opera Festival as representative of the activities of small companies. New Orleans was the site of the first opera performance in the United States (circa 1793) and the home of the first American opera company. A regular feature of the city's cultural life during the 19th century, opera declined in significance with the rise of jazz. In the other cities, opera appeared at a much later date. City by city, Davis discusses the resident companies that developed and the traveling organizations that visited. He concludes that the "American West, traditionally the most culturally barren section of the country, has blossomed into a region frought with lyric vitality."

2538. Eaton, Quaintance. The Boston Opera Company. New York, Appleton-Century [1965] xiv, 338 p. illus.
65–12607/MN ML1711.8.B7E2
The Boston Opera Company, the city's first resident grand opera company, came into being in 1909 and lasted five seasons. During that time it presented Boston with grand opera that was long remembered. Among the leading divas were Nellie Melba, Lillian Nordica, Emmy Destinn, and Mary Garden, whose love scene with Vanni Marcoux in the performance of *Tosca* was so passionate that the city mayor issued instructions for restraint. In May 1915 the company filed bankruptcy proceedings. A revival under new management collapsed early in its second year.

2539. Eaton, Quaintance. Opera caravan; adventures of the Metropolitan on tour, 1883–1956. New York, Farrar, Straus & Cudahy, 1957. xv, 400 p. illus. 57–7116 ML1711.8.N3M425
The Metropolitan Opera House opened in October 1883 with Henry Eugene Abbey as the company manager. The season was an artistic success but a financial failure, as Abbey hired high-salaried singers for his elaborate and costly productions. Hoping to recoup his losses, he took the company on tour. Its first appearance away from home was in the Boston Theatre, December 26, 1883. From 1883 through 1956, the Metropolitan went on tour annually, with five exceptions. The tour of 1906 ended after the company experienced the earthquake in San Francisco. In 1910 came a successful venture in Paris. This account, sponsored by the Metropolitan Opera Guild, touches on the high points of the company's travels and includes a chronological list of tour casts, 1883–1956. *The Golden Horseshoe* (New York, Viking Press [1965] 319 p. A Studio book), by Frank Merkling and others, is a pictorial history of the Metropolitan Opera House.

2540. Graf, Herbert. Producing opera for America. Zürich, New York, Atlantis Books [1961] 211 p. illus. 61–3898 ML1700.G75P7
"What is the place of opera in the cultural life of the American community today, and by what methods can opera in America achieve artistic and economic support?" In seeking answers to these questions the author—for many years the stage director for the Metropolitan Opera Company—first turns to Europe, where opera originated. There it

is solidly entrenched in historic tradition; governments recognize and subsidize it as a cultural obligation to the citizenry. In the United States, on the other hand, opera has a very insecure artistic and economic existence. It is not able to achieve either a consistent artistic policy or modern standards of production. However, Graf offers reasons for optimism. He describes new methods of sponsorship, a growing popularity of concert performances of operas, numerous projects for new theaters, and the emergence of opera workshops, television opera, and a wealth of operatic talent. "From these foundations," he predicts, "opera in the United States will rise and find its proper place in American cultural life."

# I. Choirs

2541. Johnson, Harold Earle. Hallelujah, amen! The story of the Handel and Haydn Society of Boston. Boston, B. Humphries [1965] 256 p. illus.                65–19351/MN ML200.8.B7H34
  Bibliographical references included in "Notes" (p. 244–248).
  The Handel and Haydn Society "rests secure in its status as America's oldest oratorio society." Incorporated in 1816, it comprised, with few exceptions, tradesmen and musical amateurs. Membership was then and has remained a male prerogative, although women are permitted to sing in the chorus. Discipline has been necessary to vitality and quality. At intervals, indifferent members have been suspended, and elderly members, suffering from "impaired voice and musical ear," have received tactful letters suggesting that they retire from the chorus. Until comparatively recently, the society retained choral works of the 18th and 19th centuries as the staples of its repertoire. Within the past few years, however, it has ventured to perform contemporary music. The author was invited by the society to write this "anecdotal history" for its 150th anniversary.

# J. Music Education

2542. Bukofzer, Manfred F. The place of musicology in American institutions of higher learning. New York, Liberal Arts Press [1957] 52 p.                57–4920 ML3797.B8
  Musicology, virtually unknown in the United States in the early 1920's, has developed in the intervening years into a recognized field of study. Its ultimate goal is "understanding." "Through understanding, music becomes a more intense aesthetic experience with wider and richer associations, greater sensual pleasure, and deepened spiritual satisfaction." To obtain this understanding, the musicologist gathers all types of musical knowledge. He tries to discover all the forms that music has taken and sees each one as a manifestation of the human mind. The author was a member of the Committee on Musicology of the American Council of Learned Societies and volunteered to write this brochure as part of a series designed by the committee to advance the cause of musicology. The place for teaching this relatively new discipline, he asserts, is the graduate school, where the entering student should have had a general education with courses in language and history, as well as a broad orientation in music and music history.

2543. Riker, Charles C. The Eastman School of Music, 1947–1962. Rochester, N.Y., University of Rochester, 1963. 119 p. illus.
              49–2415./MN MT4.R6E247 Suppl.
  A supplement to The Eastman School of Music; Its First Quarter Century, 1921–1946, no. 5671 in the 1960 Guide.

# K. Individual Musicians

2544. Béchet, Sidney. Treat it gentle. New York, Hill & Wang [1960] 245 p. illus.

       60–15935   ML419.B23A3  1960a

A jazz musician reminisces about his family, his childhood in New Orleans, and his musical career. Béchet (1897–1959) learned to play the clarinet as a child and at 22 was an established virtuoso who had performed in such cities as New Orleans, Chicago, and New York. He went on tour to Europe in 1919 and, over the next 30 years, alternated between engagements there and in the United States. For the last few years of his life he resided in France and rarely left the continent. Among the many musicians and singers who appear in his story are Joe Oliver, Louis Armstrong, Clarence Williams, Bessie Smith, and Duke Ellington. The major portion of his highly imaginative autobiography, including a romanticized account of the death of Béchet's grandfather, was elicited from the author by Joan Reid, who recorded his comments. She put the material into writing, and he approved it. A chronological catalog of every title known to have been recorded by Béchet is included.

2545. Glackens, Ira. Yankee diva; Lillian Nordica and the golden days of opera. With Lillian Nordica's Hints to singers. New York, Coleridge Press [1963] 366 p. illus.

       63–22042/MN  ML420.N733G6

Bibliography: p. 275–277. Discography: p. 292–300.

Lillian Norton (1857–1914) of Farmington, Maine, studied voice in the United States and went to Europe to begin her career. She returned with a reputation as an operatic soprano and the professional name of Nordica. After being acclaimed in Milan, St. Petersburg, and Paris, she made her American debut in 1883 at the New York Academy of Music. Later she joined the Metropolitan Opera Company and became especially noted for her Wagnerian roles. Among opera singers born and trained in the United States, Nordica was one of the earliest to achieve world fame. In this biography, the author traces the fortunes and misfortunes of the girl who went from the New England Conservatory of Music and Patrick C. Gilmore's band to successive triumphs in the world's leading opera houses.

2546. Hoover, Kathleen O., *and* John Cage. Virgil Thomson: his life and music. New York, T. Yoseloff [1959] 288 p. illus.

       58–12144  ML410.T452H6

Composer and critic, Thomson was born in 1896 in Kansas City, Mo., where he received his early musical training. Subsequently he studied at Harvard, in Paris (with Nadia Boulanger), and in New York. Having found the atmosphere of Paris congenial, he returned in 1925 and remained there for much of the next 15 years. Friendship with Gertrude Stein led to collaboration on *Four Saints in Three Acts,* an opera which received its premiere in Hartford, Conn., in 1934 with an all-Negro cast. When Thomson returned to the United States in 1940, he joined the staff of the *New York Herald Tribune,* and in the ensuing 14 years he distinguished himself as an adept, articulate, and controversial music critic. He continued composing and in 1949 received a Pulitzer Prize for his music for the documentary film *Louisiana Story.* At the end of the text of the biography is a list of Thomson's compositions through 1957.

# XXVI

# Art and Architecture

THE LARGE number of works appropriate for inclusion in Section A, The Arts, and Section B, Architecture: General, help to offset the scarcity of publications suitable for such specialized sections as those on sculpture, prints and photographs, and museums. Section H, Prints and Photographs, consists merely of two works, each of which reproduces photographs by a modern artist; the same section in the 1960 *Guide* emphasizes printmaking. Section J, Museums, is limited to a history of the preservation movement and a guide to art museums and galleries, in contrast to the same section in the 1960 *Guide*, which is devoted largely to works on individual museums. Although books on the architecture of single cities were excluded from the 1960 *Guide*, two such works have been included here in Section C, Architecture: Special. Art and History, Section K in the 1960 *Guide*, has been omitted from this *Supplement* because of the lack of books with a fitting blend of history and art or a clear focus on history as revealed through works of art.

## A. The Arts

2547. Brown, Milton W. The story of the Armory show. [n.p.] Joseph H. Hirshorn Foundation; distributed by New York Graphic Society [Greenwich, Conn., 1963] 320 p. illus.

63–13496    N5015.A8B7

Bibliography: p. 303–306.

Originally planned as an exhibition of American art, the Armory Show of 1913 was widened in scope to include the best of the contemporary European schools of painting. It thus became one of the most influential art events ever held in the United States. Crowds filling the New York Armory during the month of the exhibition were exposed to the new trends, and many American artists came away from the European sections with new vision. Using recently discovered records, the author wrote a detailed history of the show, its organization, and its results, to which he appends an amplified catalog listing all the identifiable works in the exhibition, together with their prices in 1913 and their location today. Much of this information was discovered by the Munson-Williams-Proctor Institute in the course of its research for a reconstruction of the Armory show, which exhibited as many of the original entries as could be assembled. The institute's catalog, *1913 Armory Show; 50th Anniversary Exhibition, 1963* ([Utica, 1963] 212 p.), includes colored as well as black-and-white reproductions.

2548. Dunlap, William. History of the rise and progress of the arts of design in the United States. Introduction by William P. Campbell. Newly edited by Alexander Wyckoff, incorporating the notes and additions compiled by Frank W. Bayley and Charles Goodspeed. [New ed., rev. and enl. New York] B. Blom [1965] 3 v.

       65–16236 N6505.D9 1965

Running title: History of the arts of design.
Bibliography: v. 3, p. 346–377B.
An updated edition of no. 5690 in the 1960 *Guide*.

2549. Larkin, Oliver W. Art and life in America. Rev. and enl. ed. New York, Holt, Rinehart & Winston [1960] xvii, 559 p. illus.

       60–6491 N6505.L37 1960

"Bibliographical notes": p. 491–525.
An updated edition of no. 5693 in the 1960 *Guide*.

2550. Mendelowitz, Daniel M. A history of American art. New York, Holt, Rinehart & Winston [1960] 662 p. 60–10762 N6505.M4
Includes bibliography.

A basic factual text for the beginning art student presupposing little knowledge of the visual arts. The author begins his survey with Indian artifacts and ornaments, then follows the development of art from the colonial period to the present. He treats painting, sculpture, architecture, and the decorative arts, including furniture, metalwork, ceramics, glass, and textiles. Nearly all the works discussed are illustrated by small black-and-white photographs. In 1955, as an aid in art education, the Carnegie Corporation of New York provided the financial support for compiling a collection of reproductions to represent American art in all phases; some 4,000 works were selected for color photography, and the resulting slides are reproduced and cataloged in *Arts of the United States; a Pictorial Survey* (New York, McGraw-Hill [1960] 452 p.), edited by William H. Pierson and Martha Davidson.

2551. New York. Museum of Modern Art. Americans 1963. Edited by Dorothy C. Miller, with statements by the artists and others. Garden City, N.Y., Distributed by Doubleday [1963] 112 p. illus. 63–17994 N6512.N416
"Catalog of the exhibition, May 20 through August 18, 1963": p. 106–112.
Since its founding in 1929, the Museum of Modern Art has periodically presented group exhibitions of American painting and sculpture, featuring small numbers of artists whose work is current and of more than passing interest. Earlier exhibition catalogs in this series include *Sixteen Americans* (1959. 96 p.) and *12 Americans* ([1956] 95 p.), both edited by Dorothy C. Miller. The chief value of the catalogs of the early shows lies in the wide range of art represented. The latest catalogs, however, provide a survey of some of the newer and more controversial art forms. *Americans 1963* features the work of 15 painters and sculptors, including the pop art of James Rosenquist and Claes Oldenburg, the op art of Richard Anuszkiewicz, the gray canvases of Ad Reinhardt, and the welded steel and plaster forms of Edward Higgins.

2552. New York Historical Society. Dictionary of artists in America, 1564–1860, by George C. Groce and David H. Wallace. New Haven, Yale University Press, 1957. xxvii, 759 p.

       57–6338 N6536.N4

A biographical dictionary arranged alphabetically. The full name and dates and places of birth and death of each artist are provided; the media in which he customarily worked and subjects he most frequently chose are identified; and the names of his outstanding pupils, the dates and places of major exhibitions of his creations, and, occasionally, the current locations of representative works are supplied. Each entry is documented, and an extensive "Key to Sources" (p. 713–759) is appended. Between 10,000 and 11,000 painters, draftsmen, sculptors, and printmakers are listed. Architects are included only if they also worked in one of the above artistic fields.

2553. Saarinen, Aline B. The proud possessors; the lives, times, and tastes of some adventurous American art collectors. New York, Random House [1958] 423 p. illus. 58–9890 N8383.S2
Includes bibliography.

Private art collectors in the United States have done much to influence the development of American art. Most of the great collectors gratified their personal tastes, but almost all were guided in their selections by professionals in the art world. When such a collector acquired a work of art, often its value was enhanced and the reputation of the artist was strengthened. The collectors functioned both as tastemakers and benefactors of the public, for most of the collections were eventually given to museums. Among the people whose lives and collections are discussed in this study are Mrs. Potter Palmer, Isabella Steward Gardner, John G. Johnson, the Stein family, John Quinn, Joseph H. Hirshhorn, Electra Havemeyer Webb, and Peggy Guggenheim, for each of whom "the collecting of art was a primary means of expression." The author describes their artistic quests, their eccentricities, and their contributions to the art world. In *Art Collecting in the United States of America; an Outline of a History* (London, New York, Nelson [1964] 210 p.), William G. Constable discusses deceased collectors whose collections have passed into public hands.

2554. Whitney Museum of American Art, *New York*. American art of our century [by] Lloyd Goodrich, director, [and] John I. H. Baur,

associate director. New York, Praeger [196 309 p.                         61–15642 N6512.W

A historical and critical analysis of America painting and sculpture in the 20th century, based the collections in the Whitney Museum. Goodri deals with the period 1900–1939; Baur covers 194 60. All the significant schools of art are represente and the text is accompanied by numerous black-an white reproductions, as well as 81 color plates. A pendixes include a catalog of the 1,371 pieces in t museum's collection and a list of the exhibitio staged by the museum and its predecessors fro 1941 to 1960.

# B. Architecture: General

2555. Burchard, John E., *and* Albert Bush-Brown. The architecture of America; a social and cultural history. Boston, Little, Brown [1961] 595 p. illus.                         61–5736 NA705.B8
Bibliography: p. [513]–517.
This is a panoramic survey of the influence of American geography, economic and social life, and literary and artistic trends on the development of distinctly American styles of architecture and engineering. Commissioned as part of the centennial celebration of the American Institute of Architects in 1957, this study by two faculty members of the Massachusetts Institute of Technology begins with an essay on the nature of architecture, then describes building and construction generally from 1600 to the present. More than half of the book deals with the last 85 years. Wayne Andrews' *Architecture in America; a Photographic History From the Colonial Period to the Present* (New York, Atheneum Publishers, 1960. 179 p.) is a brief pictorial survey.

2556. Fitch, James M. Architecture and the esthetics of plenty. New York, Columbia University Press, 1961. 304 p. illus.
61–8510 NA705.F53
The essays and lectures in this collection were written over many years and cover such diverse topics as the architectural ingenuity of Thomas Jefferson, the esthetic concepts of Horatio Greenough, the idealized architectural forms of Mies van der Rohe, and the Gruen plan for the reconstruction of downtown Fort Worth. A professor of history at the Columbia University School of Architecture, the author is primarily concerned with the difficulty of creating new architectural ideas and making them effective in the United States, where material and

technical resources are abundant but where the ci zen is an "ignorant consumer," the designer is "isolated, powerless specialist," and both are co fronted with "properties, potentialities, and limi tions of almost stupefying complexity."

2557. Gowans, Alan. Images of American livin four centuries of architecture and furnitu as cultural expression. Philadelphia, Lippinc [1964] 498 p. illus.         63–17676 NA705.C
A broad survey of American design from the fi settlement in Jamestown to the present. The a thor, chairman of the department of art and art h tory at the University of Delaware, maintains th although most American architecture and furnitu was, until recently, based on European design, Ame ican craftsmen modified the original patterns to co form to native use and taste. These America modifications provide tangible indications of the d velopment of American culture. This volume is n encyclopedic; Gowans is interested in broad tren and patterns. He describes the important architec the social and economic conditions which influenc building forms, and the succession of styles whi dominated artistic thinking.

2558. McCallum, Ian R. M. Architecture U.S. New York, Reinhold Pub. Corp. [195 216 p.                         59–16224 NA712.M
Bibliography: p. 213–216.
Largely because of the achievements of such m as Wright, Mies van der Rohe, and Gropius, t United States is in the forefront in the developme of contemporary architecture. The author, a Briti architectural critic, maintains that "for the you European architect an American Grand Tour is b

coming as important as the Italian was to the eighteenth-century English gentleman." Addressing himself primarily to architects outside the United States, McCallum begins with a short historical essay on the development of American architecture, then discusses 33 architects from Sullivan, Wright, Mies, Neutra, and Johnson to such lesser known figures as A. Quincy Jones, Edward L. Barnes, and Ulrich Franzen. Each architect is accorded a biographical sketch, accompanied by numerous photographs with explanatory notes. Other pictorial surveys of contemporary architecture include the American Institute of Architects' *Mid-Century Architecture in America* (Baltimore, Johns Hopkins Press [1961] 254 p.), edited by Wolf Von Eckardt and listing the institute's honor awards from 1949 to 1961, and *The Second Treasury of Contemporary Houses* ([New York] F. W. Dodge Corp., ᶜ1959. 216 p.), selected by the editors of *Architectural Record*.

2559. Makers of contemporary architecture. [New York, G. Braziller, 1962] 4 v.
The architects represented in this series are contemporary artistic or technical innovators whose work has been watched with great interest but whose place in the history of American architecture had not been fixed at the time of publication. Each volume consists of a critical essay followed by photographs, plans, and bibliographies. The volumes which pertain to American architects are as follows:

*Philip Johnson* (127 p. 62–16264 NA737.J6J3), by John M. Jacobus; *R. Buckminster Fuller* (127 p. 62–16263 NA737.F8M2), by John McHale; *Louis I. Kahn* (127 p. 62–16265 NA737.K32S38), by Vincent J. Scully; and *Eero Saarinen* (127 p. 62–16266 NA737.S28T4), by Allan Temko.

2560. The Masters of world architecture series. Edited by William Alex. New York, G. Braziller, 1960. 6 v.
Of the American architects in this series, only Sullivan and Wright were native born. The others were naturalized citizens who, except for Neutra, did considerable work in Europe before establishing themselves in the United States. All, however, have executed much of their finest work and have exercised their greatest influence in this country. Each volume consists of a critical essay, photographs, plans, and a bibliography. The volumes on Americans are as follows: *Louis Sullivan* (128 p. 60–13306 NA737.S9B8), by Albert Bush-Brown; *Ludwig Mies van der Rohe* (127 p. 60–6077 NA1088.M65D7), by Arthur Drexler; *Walter Gropius* (128 p. 60–13308 NA1088.G85F5), by James M. Fitch; *Richard Neutra* (128 p. 60–13309 NA737.N4M3 1960a), by Esther McCoy; *Frank Lloyd Wright* (125 p. 60–6075 NA737.W7S3), by Vincent J. Scully; and *Eric Mendelsohn* (128 p. 60–14514 NA1088.M57V6), by Wolf Von Eckardt.

# C. Architecture: Special

2561. Broderick, Robert C. Historic churches of the United States. Drawings by Virginia Broderick. New York, W. Funk [1958] 262 p.
58–7142 NA5205.B7
A study of notable church buildings currently in use, ranging from early Spanish missions to recent examples of contemporary architecture. The author provides a brief history of each church, describes the circumstances regarding its planning and construction, and notes unusual or especially beautiful features. Photographs of many of the churches enhance the text. Intended for the general reader, this survey contains little technical information. An intensive study of a subject of more limited scope is provided by Edmund W. Sinnott in *Meetinghouse & Church in Early New England* (New York, McGraw-Hill [1963] 243 p.); a "Check List of New England Meetinghouses and Churches Built by 1830 and Still Standing" is appended. *The Colonial Houses of Worship in America, Built in the English*

*Colonies Before the Republic, 1607–1789, and Still Standing* (New York, Hastings House [1964, ᶜ1963] 574 p.), by Harold W. Rose, has numerous photographs.

2562. Burnham, Alan, *ed.* New York landmarks; a study & index of architecturally notable structures in greater New York. Middletown, Conn., Published under the auspices of the Municipal Art Society of New York by the Wesleyan University Press [1963] 430 p.
63–17794 NA735.N5B8
Bibliography: p. 391–412.
A pictorial study based on the "Index of Architecturally Notable Structures in Greater New York" compiled by the Committee on Historical Architecture of the Municipal Art Society of New York. Full-page photographs of 148 buildings (none later than 1930) are presented, together with small maps and short descriptive annotations. *Chicago's Fa-*

*mous Buildings; a Photographic Guide to the City's Architectural Landmarks and Other Notable Buildings* ( [Chicago] University of Chicago Press [1965] 230 p.), edited by Arthur S. Siegel, contains photographs and plans of notable buildings selected by the Commission on Architectural Landmarks of Chicago, ranging from the oldest-known building (1836) still standing to the skyscrapers of the 1960's.

2563. Condit, Carl W. The Chicago school of architecture; a history of commercial and public building in the Chicago area, 1875–1925. Chicago, University of Chicago Press [1964] xviii, 238 p. 196 illus. 64–13287 NA735.C4C6 1964
Bibliography: p. 221-225.
A revised and greatly enlarged edition of the author's 1952 work, *The Rise of the Skyscraper*, no. 5705 in the 1960 *Guide*. Part of the new material concerns the development of the second generation of Chicago architects after World War I.

2564. Maass, John. The gingerbread age; a view of Victorian America. New York, Rinehart [1957] 212 p. 57–7370 NA710.M3
Includes bibliography.
A sympathetic treatment of the Victorian architecture which flourished between 1837 and 1876. Dividing buildings into three distinct styles, Gothic, Italianate, and Mansardic, the author maintains that beneath the ornate decoration lay a strength of design and construction almost unknown today. Drawings and photographs illustrate his thesis. A prefatory chapter on manners, furnishings, and dress reveals a close stylistic relationship between architecture and other arts of the period.

2565. McCoy, Esther. Five California architects. New York, Reinhold Pub. Corp. [1960] 200 p. illus. 60–10551 NA730.C2M3
Although California architects have worked in a variety of styles, nearly all have been noted for a natural and human approach, contrasting sharply with the more austere designs of Mies van der Rohe and Gropius. In this volume, the author discusses the work of Bernard Maybeck, Irving Gill, Charles and Henry Greene, and R. M. Schindler, all of whom have died in recent years. Characterizing the five as innovators who first conceived of many of the principles and methods which are standard today, she analyzes their most important structures and their influence on contemporary styles.

2566. Pratt, Dorothy, *and* Richard Pratt. The treasury of early American homes. New, rev. and enl. ed. New York, Hawthorn Books [1959] 144 p. col. illus. 59–12178 NA7205.P685

An updated edition of no. 5722 in the 1960 *Guide*. *The Second Treasury of Early American Homes* (New York, Hawthorn Books. 143 p.), by the same authors, was also reissued in a revised and enlarged form in 1959. Arnold Nicholson's *American Houses in History* (New York, Viking Press [1965] 260 p. A Studio book) reflects the rich and varied heritage of the builders: Spaniards, Englishmen, Dutchmen, Germans, and Swedes. Henry L. Williams and Ottalie K. Williams present a popular account in *A Guide to Old American Houses, 1700–1900* (New York, A. S. Barnes [1962] 168 p.).

2567. Williamsburg architectural studies. [Williamsburg, Va., Colonial Williamsburg, 1958–60] 2 v. illus. 58–3504 NA735.W5W47
CONTENTS.— v. 1. The public buildings of Williamsburg, colonial capital of Virginia; an architectural history, by Marcus Whiffen.— [v. 2] The eighteenth-century houses of Williamsburg; a study of architecture and building in the colonial capital of Virginia, by Marcus Whiffen.
Studies prepared by the architectural historian of Colonial Williamsburg and based on research conducted for the restoration project. In volume one the author concentrates on the construction of the public buildings, their relation to contemporary English architecture, and their influence on architectural design in Virginia. He briefly summarizes their history from the time of the removal of the capital to Richmond in 1780 to their reconstruction after 1928. Volume two is an examination of existing houses on the basis of external evidence and building practices known to have been prevalent in Virginia at the time. Building materials, methods, and design are discussed, and descriptions and pictures of 32 of the restored houses are offered.

2568. Wright, Frank Lloyd. Writings and buildings. Selected by Edgar Kaufmann and Ben Raeburn. [New York] Horizon Press [1960] 346 p. 60–8166 NA737.W7A48 1960a
Considered by many as this country's greatest modern architect, Wright (1869–1959) has been the subject of numerous biographical and critical surveys. This volume contains selections from his many published writings, including *An Autobiography* (1932), *A Testament* (1957), and various articles and speeches revealing the development of his ideas. Accompanying the text are photographs of such notable buildings as the Coonley House, the Imperial Hotel in Tokyo, the Price Tower, and the Guggenheim Museum, a geographical list of structures completed between 1893 and 1959 and still standing in 1960 (p. 333–346), and plans and sketches for many unexecuted projects. Wright's

*Drawings for a Living Architecture* (New York, Published for the Bear Run Foundation and the Edgar J. Kaufmann Charitable Foundation by Horizon Press, 1959. 255 p.) features many reproductions in color. *Frank Lloyd Wright:* [v. 1] *To 1910: The First Golden Age* (New York, Reinhold [1958] 227 p.), by Grant C. Manson, is the first volume of a projected three-volume biography.

## D. Interiors

2569. Boston. Museum of Fine Arts. American furniture in the Museum of Fine Arts, Boston [by] Richard H. Randall. Boston [1965] xvii, 276 p.          65–24149   NK2406.B65
A catalog of 17th- and 18th-century furniture given to the Boston Museum of Fine Arts by collectors and donors interested in preserving family heirlooms. Each black-and-white plate is accompanied by detailed descriptive and historical notes. Other volumes on various periods of American furniture from the 17th through the 19th centuries are *Masterpieces of American Furniture, 1620–1840* (New York, Architectural Book Pub. Co. [1965] 256 p.), by Lester Margon; *American Country Furniture, 1780–1875* (New York, Crown [1965] 248 p.), by Ralph M. Kovel and Terry Kovel; and *American Furniture of the Nineteenth Century* (New York, Viking Press [1965] 229 p. A Studio book), by Celia J. Otto.

2570. Comstock, Helen. American furniture: seventeenth, eighteenth, and nineteenth century styles. New York, Viking Press [1962] 336 p. (A Studio book)          62–18074   NK2406.C58
Bibliography: p. 319–324.
An introduction to American furniture design. The author presents the various styles in relation to their European backgrounds, pointing out local variations and adaptations. She treats the Jacobean, William and Mary, Queen Anne, Chippendale, classical, and early Victorian styles in turn, concluding with the 1870's, when mechanization and mass production became prevalent in the furniture industry. Each chapter includes an introductory essay, biographical sketches of the more important cabinetmakers, a chart indicating principal woods, techniques, and designs, and photographs. *The Cabinetmakers of America* (Garden City, N.Y., Doubleday, 1957. 252 p.), by Ethel H. Bjerkoe, is a biographical dictionary of furniture craftsmen in the 17th, 18th, and early 19th centuries.

2571. Iverson, Marion D. The American chair, 1630–1890. Illustrated by Ernest Donnelly. New York, Hastings House [c1957] 241 p. illus.          57–11664   NK2715.I85
Bibliography: p. 231–232.
The author describes the most important types of chairs, from the wainscot structures of the early Puritans to the ornate pieces of the later 19th century. Anecdotes about the owners of historic chairs serve to relate chair design to the cultural climate in which each style flourished. *The Ornamented Chair: Its Development in America, 1700–1890* (Rutland, Vt., C. E. Tuttle Co. [1960] 173 p.), edited by Zilla R. Lea, is a comprehensive pictorial history of decorated chairs, based on information and pictures collected by Esther Stevens Brazer before her death in 1945 and added to by seven members of the Historical Society of Early American Decoration.

## E. Sculpture

2572. New York. Metropolitan Museum of Art. American sculpture; a catalogue of the collection of the Metropolitan Museum of Art [by] Albert Ten Eyck Gardner. Greenwich, Conn., Distributed by New York Graphic Society [1965] 192 p. illus.          65–10579   NB205.N38
A catalog of the Metropolitan's American sculpture collection, which has grown to include 354 works by 176 artists since William B. Astor presented the museum with its first piece of American sculpture in 1872. The collection, treated in this volume chronologically by the artists' year of birth, is representative of sculptural trends during the 19th and 20th centuries. The author provides a biographical sketch of each sculptor, a description of each piece of sculpture, and lists of additional read-

ings. *The Literary Sculptors* (Durham, N.C., Duke University Press, 1965. 206 p.), by Margaret F. Thorp, is a study of some of the American sculptors who studied and worked in Rome between 1825 and 1875.

2573. Wright, Nathalia. Horatio Greenough, the first American sculptor. Philadelphia, University of Pennsylvania Press [1963] 382 p. illus.
62–11261   NB237.G8W7
Bibliographical references included in "Notes" (p. 307–358).

Greenough (1805–1852) was one of the first American sculptors to receive national recognition.

Today his reputation rests on writings as art critic and pamphleteer as well as on his works of art, most of which consists of portrait busts done in the classical style. One of his best-known portraits is the half-draped sculpture of George Washington, now in the Smithsonian Institution, which was commissioned through the influence of James Fenimore Cooper. Avant-garde and traditional sculptures of the 20th century are represented, respectively, in *William Zorach* (New York, Published for the Whitney Museum of American Art by Praeger, 1959. 116 p. Books that matter), by John I. H. Baur, and *Paul Manship* (New York, Macmillan, 1957. 198 p.), by Edwin Murtha.

# F. Painting

2574. 2574. Baur, John I. H., *ed.* New art in America: fifty painters of the 20th century. Greenwich, Conn., New York Graphic Society in cooperation with Praeger, New York [1957] 280 p.
57–9100   ND212.B38
Biographical sketches and reproductions of representative works of painters "who did the most" to shape American art in the 20th century. The coverage extends from Sloan, Benton, and Wyeth and their representational works to Pollock and De Kooning and their abstract creations. One large color plate and several small black-and-white reproductions are provided for each artist. *Morris Graves* (1956. 61 p.), *Hans Hofmann* (1957. 66 p.), and *Arthur G. Dove* (1958. 96 p.), written by Frederick S. Wight and published in Berkeley by the University of California Press, and *Arshile Gorky* ([°1962] 56 p.), *Mark Tobey* ([1962] 112 p.), and *Hans Hofmann* ([1963] 64 p.), written by William C. Seitz, published in New York by the Museum of Modern Art, and distributed in Garden City by Doubleday, are brief works issued on the occasions of large one-man exhibitions.

2575. Belknap, Waldron P. American colonial painting: materials for a history. Cambridge, Mass., Belknap Press of Harvard University Press, 1959. xxi, 377 p.   59–10313   ND1311.B39
Bibliography: p. 337–344.
At the time of his death in 1949, Belknap had spent five years examining the works of painters of the American Colonies and Bermuda in preparation for writing a history of colonial painting. This volume contains some of his materials, which are now in the collection of the Henry Francis du Pont Winterthur Museum. Edited by the museum's li-

brarian, Charles Coleman Sellers, the selections include two previously published articles—"The Identity of Robert Feke" and "Feke and Smibert: Note on Two Portraits"—as well as genealogical notes on the New York portrait painters and diverse materials on other painters and craftsmen and on such painting practices as the use of British mezzotints as models for figures and backgrounds in portraiture.

2576. Boston. Museum of Fine Arts. M. & M. Karolik collection of American water colors & drawings, 1800–1875. Boston, 1962. 2 v.
62–21319   N6510.B74
"Exhibition held . . . October 18, 1962-January 6, 1963."
Includes bibliographies.
From 1935 to 1962, Maxim and Martha Karolik worked closely with the Boston Museum of Fine Arts to assemble a collection of furniture, paintings, and drawings representative of 18th- and 19th-century America. *Eighteenth-Century American Arts* (1941), commemorating the achievements of American artists and craftsmen, 1720–1820, and *M. and M. Karolik Collection of American Paintings, 1815 to 1865* (no. 5745 in the 1960 *Guide*) are catalogs of materials in the collection. This third catalog lists about 1,500 of the 3,000 items in the collection and includes works by academic artists, foreign visitors, folk artists, and Civil War illustrators. A few prints and statues are also listed. Each item is described, biographical information about the artist is supplied wherever possible, and a general index and supplementary indexes are provided. Numerous black-and-white reproductions and 24 color plates illustrate the text. Bartlett H. Hayes' *American Drawings* (New York, Shorewood Pub-

lishers [1965] 141 p. Drawings of the masters) is a survey of American compositions, with biographical notes on the artists, most of whom are later than those in the Karolik collection.

2577. Flexner, James T. That wilder image; the painting of America's native school from Thomas Cole to Winslow Homer. Boston, Little, Brown [1962] 407 p. illus.

62–16956 ND210.F6

"Selected bibliographies": p. 375–394.

The author surveyed the early years of American painting in two previous works (no. 5750 and 5751 in the 1960 Guide). This volume is devoted to the years 1825–1910, when American painting was relatively uninfluenced by European ideas and methods. Flexner begins with the romantic landscapes of Thomas Cole and Asher B. Durand, includes such genre painting as that of William Sidney Mount and George Caleb Bingham as well as works of artists who concentrated on Indians and the Far West and those who belonged to the Hudson River School, and ends with the naturalistic creations of Winslow Homer. The text is accompanied by 111 reproductions in black and white.

2578. Garbisch, Edgar W. 101 masterpieces of American primitive painting, from the collection of Edgar William & Bernice Chrysler Garbisch. Foreword by James J. Rorimer. Preface by John Walker. Introduction by Albert Ten Eyck Gardner. New ed. [New York] American Federation of Arts; distributed by Doubleday [1962] 159 p. 64–6629 ND207.G3 1962

The Garbisch collection of more than 2,000 pictures is the most comprehensive collection of American primitive paintings in existence. This volume is a catalog of an exhibition which was shown in many of the major museums in the United States from 1961 to 1964. The pictures were painted in the 18th and 19th centuries and range from the crude efforts of unknown portrait painters to the relatively polished work of Ralph Earl. Each painting is reproduced in color, and biographical data is supplied for 29 of the artists whose work is represented.

2579. The Great American artists series. New York, G. Braziller, 1959. 6 v.

The volumes in this series are as follows: Albert P. Ryder (128 p. 59–12227. ND237.R8G6) and Winslow Homer (127 p. 59–12226. ND237.H7G58), by Lloyd Goodrich; Stuart Davis (128 p. 59–12223. ND237.D333G6), by E. C. Goossen; Willem de Kooning (128 p. 59–12224. ND237.D334H4), by Thomas B. Hess; Jackson Pollock (125 p. 59–12228. ND237.P73O4), by Frank O'Hara; and Thomas Eakins (127 p. 59–12225.

ND237.E15P6), by Fairfield Porter. Each volume contains a critical essay on the artist and his work, approximately 80 black-and-white or color plates, a chronology of the painter's life, and a selected bibliography.

2580. James, Henry. The painter's eye; notes and essays on the pictorial arts. Selected and edited with an introduction by John L. Sweeney. London, R. Hart-Davis, 1956. 274 p. illus.

57–1066 N7445.J23

Includes bibliographies.

From 1868 to 1882 and in 1897, James contributed essays on art to the Atlantic Monthly, Nation, New York Tribune, Galaxy, Harper's Weekly, and other serial publications. Thirty of these essays have been collected and published together for the first time. James was a painter during his early years and studied with John La Farge. As an art critic, he based his opinions of paintings on his "disposition to enjoy them." These critical pieces discuss painters and exhibitions on both side of the Atlantic. Included are comments on Whistler, Sargent, Homer, Duveneck, and other American painters; an account of the beginnings of the Metropolitan Museum of Art; and reviews of several American exhibitions. An appendix contains a list of James' essays on art which were omitted from this volume.

2581. New York. Metropolitan Museum of Art. American paintings; a catalogue of the collection of the Metropolitan Museum of Art. v. 1. Painters born by 1819. [By] Albert Ten Eyck Gardner [and] Stuart P. Feld. Greenwich, Conn., Distributed by New York Graphic Society [1965] 292 p. 65–16834 ND205.N364

Includes bibliographical references.

This first volume of a projected three-volume catalog includes approximately 250 black-and-white photographs of oil paintings by many masters and a number of little-known or unidentified artists. Wherever possible, each picture is accompanied by a brief biography of the artist and historical and technical information about the painting. Three Hundred Years of American Painting (New York, Time Inc., 1957. 318 p.), a popular history by Alexander Eliot, art editor of Time, includes more than 150 color reproductions and a guide to 100 permanent collections of American paintings.

2582. Nordness, Lee, ed. Arts: USA: now. Text by Allen S. Weller. New York, Viking Press [1963] 2 v. (475 p.) (A Studio book)

62–19607 ND212.N6

Convinced that American art critics and museums have paid undue attention to "abstract expressionism" in the United States, Nordness set out to redress the balance by compiling a book that would present a cross section of contemporary painting. He interested S. C. Johnson & Son, Inc., in sponsoring a traveling exhibition representative of the many styles in modern American art. The works obtained for the exhibition form the basis for this study, which for each of 102 living artists (as of April 1962) supplies a biographical sketch, photographs of the artist, small black-and-white reproductions of some of his more important paintings, and one large color reproduction.

2583. Richardson, Edgar P. Painting in America, from 1502 to the present. New York, Crowell [1965] 456 p. illus.

65–23777 ND205.R53 1965

Bibliography: p. 425–435.

An updated edition of no. 5756 in the 1960 *Guide*, an updated and abridged edition of which has been published under the title *A Short History of Painting in America; the Story of 450 Years* (New York, Crowell [1963] 348 p.).

## G. Painting: Individual Artists

2584. [Bingham] McDermott, John F. George Caleb Bingham, river portraitist. Norman, University of Oklahoma Press [1959] xxviii, 454 p.

59–13474 ND237.B59M3

Bibliography: p. 438–446.

Bingham (1811–1879) was one of the most important genre painters of the 19th century. In this extensively documented biography, the author, a historian, debunks a number of legends about the painter's early years. He describes the community and surrounding countryside in which Bingham grew up, offers a chronological narrative of his painting career, and concludes with a critical analysis of his work. The text is illustrated by 79 plates and 112 sketches. A checklist of more than 350 of Bingham's paintings is appended.

2585. [Catlin] McCracken, Harold. George Catlin and the old frontier. New York, Dial Press, 1959. 216 p.

59–9434 ND237.C35M3 1959

Bibliography: p. [212]–214.

Catlin (1796–1872) was the first artist of note to travel widely among the Indians with the idea of documenting their way of life. From 1830 to 1836, often alone except for his horse, he journeyed from the headwaters of the Mississippi to the far Southwest, producing colorful and detailed portraits of Indians, collecting artifacts, and keeping a written account of his experiences. Upon his return to the East in 1836, he organized an unsuccessful Indian Museum based on his collections. His paintings and artifacts were ultimately donated to the Smithsonian Institution. This biography is illustrated with many color and black-and-white reproductions of Catlin's paintings. *The Charles M. Russell Book; the Life and Work of the Cowboy Artist* (Garden City, N.Y., Doubleday, 1957. 236 p.), by the same author, and *Seth Eastman, Pictorial Historian of the*

*Indian* (Norman, University of Oklahoma Press [1961] 270 p.), by John F. McDermott, are biographies of other artists who painted people and scenes of the West.

2586. [Feininger] Hess, Hans. Lyonel Feininger. New York, Abrams [1961] xvi, 354 p.

61–9389 ND237.F33H43

Bibliography: p. 319–344.

Feininger (1871–1956) was born in New York City but spent more than half his life in Germany, where he first achieved prominence as a cartoonist before turning to painting at the age of 39. From 1919 to 1932, he was associated with Walter Gropius and the Bauhaus. He returned to the United States to live in 1937. Feininger's paintings and drawings are characterized by broken lines and repeated geometric shapes related to early Cubism, Paul Klee's fantasies, and Italian Futurist paintings. This study by the director of the Museum of York, England, is primarily an account of Feininger's artistic development and an evaluation of his work. Twenty-eight color and 72 black-and-white plates as well as numerous small illustrations accompany the text. An illustrated catalog of all of Feininger's known paintings, prepared by his wife Julia, and a chronological list of exhibitions are appended. A more detailed account of Feininger's career as a cartoonist appears in Ernst Scheyer's *Lyonel Feininger: Caricature & Fantasy* (Detroit, Wayne State University Press, 1964. 196 p.).

2587. [Glackens] Glackens, Ira. William Glackens and the Ashcan group; the emergence of realism in American art. New York, Crown Publishers [1957] 267 p.

57–8771 ND237.G5G55

In 1908, an exhibition at the Macbeth Galleries brought to public attention the works of a group of young American painters who diverged sharply from the sentimental, anecdotal, and highly finished style of the members of the National Academy. Five of the "Eight" who exhibited—Robert Henri, George Luks, Everett Shinn, John Sloan, and William Glackens (1870–1938)—were later known as the "Ashcan School" (for their insistence on painting the realities of everyday life); and the paintings of the other three—Arthur B. Davies, Ernest Lawson, and Maurice Prendergast—deviated from the prescribed forms in other ways. The friendship which joined this group is warmly described in Ira Glackens' account of his father and his father's associates. Numerous drawings and photographs of Glackens' family and friends, as well as some reproductions of his work, accompany the text.

2588. [Gorky] Schwabacher, Ethel. Arshile Gorky. With a preface by Lloyd Goodrich and an introduction by Meyer Schapiro. New York, Published for the Whitney Museum of American Art by Macmillan, 1957. 159 p.

57–12946 ND237.G613S36

Bibliography: p. 153–155.

Gorky (1905–1948) was an Armenian who came to America in 1920. Largely self-taught, he painted in a succession of styles, following such modern masters as Cézanne, Picasso, and Miró until, in the 1940's, he developed his own distinctive form of expression. After years of extreme poverty, he seemed on the verge of receiving wide recognition and financial security when he committed suicide in 1948. The author was Gorky's pupil and friend and based the biography on personal experience and on the letters and memories of the artist's associates and family. Eight illustrations in color and 70 in black and white are included. Harold Rosenberg's *Arshile Gorky: The Man, the Time, the Idea* (New York, Horizon Press [1962] 144 p.) is a blend of biography and criticism.

2589. [Homer] Gardner, Albert Ten Eyck. Winslow Homer, American artist: his world and his work. New York, C. N. Potter [ᶜ1961] 262 p.

61–11762 ND237.H7G3

Bibliography: p. [235].

An enlargement of the author's introductory essay in the catalog of the exhibition held by the National Gallery of Art and the Metropolitan Museum of Art in 1958 and 1959. Gardner, associate curator of American art at the Metropolitan Museum, relates Homer and his work to the main course of American cultural life and examines the artistic trends—both American and foreign—which affected his art. Special emphasis is placed on the influence of Japanese art on Homer's sense of composition and design.

The text is complemented by more than 200 illustrations in color as well as in black and white.

2590. [Prendergast] Rhys, Hedley H. Maurice Prendergast, 1859–1924. Cambridge, Harvard University Press, 1960. 156 p.

60–16756 ND237.P85R5

"Catalogue of the exhibition [October 26-December 4, 1960) prepared by Peter A. Wick": p. [65]–108.

Bibliography: p. 64.

Largely unappreciated during his lifetime, Prendergast was ultimately viewed by critics as this country's first important postimpressionist. He was one of the first American artists to emphasize artistic form over subject matter, and his colorful pictures of parties, promenades, and picnics serve as vehicles for exquisite patterns of shape and color. This small volume was prepared on the occasion of a memorial exhibition, shown in various part of the country in 1960 and 1961, and includes, in addition to a long essay on the artist's life and work, a catalog of the pictures exhibited. Most of these are reproduced in color or in black and white. *Sketches, 1899* ([Boston, Museum of Fine Arts, 1960] 96 p.) is a facsimile edition of one of Prendergast's sketchbooks.

2591. Shahn, Ben. Paintings. Text by James Thrall Soby. New York, G. Braziller, 1963. 144 p.

63–18187 ND237.S465S62

Bibliography: p. 139–144.

Shahn (b. 1898) was brought to the United States from Lithuania when he was eight years old. Employed in his youth as a lithographer's apprentice, he supported himself by this trade until he was 30. When he turned to painting, this training became evident in his attention to detail, sureness of line, and love of lettering. In the beginning Shahn saw his painting as a form of social protest, and his first significant work was a series of gouache paintings depicting the trial and execution of Sacco and Vanzetti. During the depression and the early forties, he was employed in painting murals, making photographs, and designing posters for various Government agencies. After World War II, he produced many paintings and drawings notable for their bitter reality and their compassion. This volume contains 98 plates, many of which are in color. Soby also wrote the text for *Ben Shahn: His Graphic Art* (New York, G. Braziller, 1957. 139 p.).

2592. [Stuart] Mount, Charles M. Gilbert Stuart, a biography. New York, Norton [1964] 384 p. illus.

63–15881 ND237.S8M65

"The works of Gilbert Stuart": p. [357]–379.

Bibliographical notes: p. [333]–356.

A detailed biography of one of the great portrait painters of the 18th and 19th centuries, whose subjects included the notables of England, Ireland, and the United States. The author, a portrait painter in his own right, supplies insight into Stuart's portraits through his knowledge of painting techniques. Much of his account is based on research in England and Ireland. Acknowledging the extent to which Stuart borrowed from earlier masters, Mount argues that the artist was a painter in the "Georgian mode" and, like Reynolds and Gainsborough, "systematically employed the best works of other artists as sources for the perfection in his own." A catalog of the painter's known works is appended.

2593. [West] Evans, Grose. Benjamin West and the taste of his times. Carbondale, Southern Illinois University Press, 1959. 144 p. 73 illus., col. plate.
      58–12322   ND237.W45E85
  Bibliography: p. 129–138.

West (1738–1820) was one of the most influential of the Anglo-American painters of the 18th and 19th centuries. Born in Pennsylvania, he traveled as a young man to Italy, where he perfected his painting techniques before settling in London for the rest of his life. There he became a friend of royalty and, through government subsidies, was able to devote his time to historical canvases in the heroic mode. Prominent in helping to found the Royal Academy, he became its second president. American painters often found a haven in his home, where they absorbed his precepts and techniques. Appraising West's art in the light of the artistic aims of the 18th century, the author asserts that the painter, while upholding the ideals of the classicists, absorbed many of the new theories which appeared in his time and in the end showed the way to neoclassical and romantic art.

2594. [Whistler] Sutton, Denys. Nocturne: the art of James McNeill Whistler. Philadelphia, Lippincott, 1964 [c1963] 153 p. illus. (part col.).
      64–22181   ND237.W6S84  1964
  Bibliographical footnotes.

In his lifetime, Whistler's reputation as a painter was enhanced by the public interest in his eccentric personality and barbed wit. After his death, however, the critics of art turned their attention to other radical innovators. This volume is a historical account of Whistler's career as a painter rather than a conventional biography. Details of his personal life are included only where necessary to explain his art. The author discusses the influences of Velasquez, Courbet, and the Japanese artists on Whistler's distinctive style—a kind of pictorial shorthand characterized by carefully chosen, restrained color and by masterful understatement. *The World of James McNeill Whistler* (New York, Nelson [1959] 255 p.), by Horace Gregory, is a critical appraisal of the man and his work.

## H. Prints and Photographs

2595. Steichen, Edward. A life in photography. Published in collaboration with the Museum of Modern Art. Garden City, N.Y., Doubleday, 1963. 1 v. (unpaged) 249 illus.
      63–11119   TR140.S68A25

An autobiography in which brief chapters of text are followed by reproduction of the author's best photographs, some in color. Steichen (b. 1879) became associated with Alfred Stieglitz in 1905 and for many years produced "art" photographs characterized by blurring of focus and alteration of texture. From the beginning, however, he displayed a genius for portraits and an ability to get important people to sit for his camera. In his mid-sixties he photographed the carrier war in the Pacific; on his return he became director of the Department of Photography at the Museum of Modern Art, where he organized his memorable exhibition "The Family of Man." The museum has also published *Steichen the Photographer* (Garden City, N.Y., Distributed by Doubleday [1961] 80 p.), containing reproductions of 48 of his photographs, mostly portraits, and short essays by Carl Sandburg, Alexander Liberman, and René d'Harnoncourt.

2596. Thoreau, Henry David. In wildness is the preservation of the world. Selections & photographs by Eliot Porter. Introduction by Joseph Wood Krutch. San Francisco, Sierra Club [1962] 167 p.    62–20527   TR660.T5

A photographic essay which captures the spirit of Thoreau's "world of American Nature," as Krutch calls it. Porter's full-color photographs and Thoreau's word pictures evoke the moods of New England's shifting seasons by focusing on the details of nature. *Not Man Apart; Lines From Robinson Jeffers* (San Francisco, Sierra Club [1965] 159 p. Sierra Club exhibit format series, 10) depicts the

Big Sur country in California through the poetry of Jeffers and the photographs of Ansel Adams and other west-coast photographers.

# I. Decorative Arts

2597. Antiques. The Antiques treasury of furniture and other decorative arts at Winterthur, Williamsburg, Sturbridge, Ford Museum, Cooperstown, Deerfield [and] Shelburne. Edited by Alice Winchester and the staff of Antiques magazine. New York, Dutton, 1959. 320 p. illus. (part col.)
59–12514 NK806.A5

A revised and updated compilation of seven special issues of *Antiques* magazine which featured early American furnishings. Each of the seven museums is the subject of a separate chapter. A comparative chronology of crafts, compiled by Helen Comstock, is appended. *The Treasure House of Early American Rooms* (New York, Viking Press [1963] 179 p. A Winterthur book), by John A. H. Sweeney, and *100 Most Beautiful Rooms in America* (New York, Studio Publications [1958] 210 p.), by Helen Comstock, reveal the manner in which fine furniture has been used in rooms with notable decor.

2598. Comstock, Helen, *ed.* The concise encyclopedia of American antiques. New York, Hawthorn Books [1958] 2 v. (543 p.) illus., facsims. 58–5628 NK805.C65

A description of various kinds of American artifacts now regarded as "antiques." The chapters are written by specialists and are accompanied by glossaries and short bibliographies. Some chapters are limited to items made before 1830; others extend to the end of the 19th century. The first volume is devoted to such conventional antiques as furniture, silver, and glassware. The second deals with more unusual articles, including mechanical toys,

maps, ship models, stamps, dime novels, Valentines, and Christmas cards. *A Fortune in the Junk Pile* (New York, Crown [1963] 440 p.), by Dorothy H. Jenkins, is a handbook intended to help the average person identify antiques. In *American Antiques, 1800–1900, a Collector's History and Guide* (New York, Odyssey Press [1965] 203 p.), Joseph T. Butler surveys the ornate furnishings which characterized the 19th century.

2599. Hayward, Arthur H. Colonial lighting. 3d enl. ed. With a new introduction and supplement, "Colonial chandeliers," by James R. Marsh. New York, Dover Publications [1962] 198 p. illus. 62–6720 NK8360.H3 1962

An updated edition of no. 5786 in the 1960 *Guide*.

2600. Revi, Albert C. American pressed glass and figure bottles. New York, Nelson [1964] 446 p. 64–14510 NK5112.R4

Bibliography: p. 413.

An encyclopedic survey of manufacturers, listing 74 firms, summarizing their respective histories, and describing the patterns of their products. Numerous illustrations and an index to patterns supplement the text. *American Cut and Engraved Glass* (New York, Nelson [1965] 497 p.), by the same author, contains a roster of companies belonging to the National Association of Cut Glass Manufacturers and an illustrated list of trademarks and labels for cutglass wares. Robert Koch's *Louis C. Tiffany, Rebel in Glass* (New York, Crown [1964] 246 p.) is a biography of a world-famous designer of exotic colored glassware.

# J. Museums

2601. Hosmer, Charles B. Presence of the past; a history of the preservation movement in the United States before Williamsburg. New York, Putnam [1965] 386 p. illus.
65–13292 E159.H77

Bibliography: p. 349–372.

A selective survey of historic preservation in the United States from its beginnings in the mid-19th century to the 1920's, when professionalization began to overtake what had been primarily a field for amateurs. Preservation originated as a grassroots movement motivated by a wide variety of nonarchitectural considerations ranging from sentimentalism to commercialism. The establishment in 1910 of the Society for the Preservation of New England Antiquities, which made architectural beauty or originality its primary criterion, was a landmark in the history of preservation. The author includes a discussion of methods used in acquiring property and of the fundamentals of preservation—criteria for selection, techniques of restoration, and economics of maintenance. *History of the National Trust for Historic Preservation* ([Washington] National Trust for Historic Preservation [1965] 115 p.), by David E. Finley, one of the founders, covers the period 1947–63.

2602. Spaeth, Eloise. American art museums and galleries; an introduction to looking. New York, Harper [1960] 282 p. illus.

60–10429 N510.S6

Bibliography: [265]–266.

In this general guide, the author describes each institution, relating pertinent historical facts and indicating the scope of the collections and the most important works of art. Few college and university museums are included, and the large metropolitan museums are mentioned only briefly on the grounds that they have their own descriptive brochures. More intensive analyses of specific museum collections are offered in *A Guide to the Art Museums of New England* (New York, Harcourt, Brace [1958] 270 p.), by Samson L. Faison, and *Guide to Art Museums in the United States:* [v. 1] *East Coast: Washington to Miami* (New York, Duell, Sloan & Pearce [1958] 243 p.), by W. Aubrey Cartwright. *Museums, U.S.A.; a History and a Guide* (Garden City, N.Y., Doubleday, 1965. 395 p.), by Herbert and Marjorie Katz, is a survey of the development of all types of museums in the United States.

# XXVII

# Land and Agriculture

A GROWING concern about the deteriorating quality of the natural environment—the pollution of air, water, and soil, the depletion of nonrenewable resources, the extinction of numerous species of wildlife—suggested the possible desirability of modifying this chapter to accommodate an aggregation of works on conservation, which in the 1960 *Guide* have no designated place. In that publication, some works on conserving the environment are in various sections in Chapter XXVII; others are in Chapter VI, Geography, and Chapter XXVIII, Economic Life. In the *Supplement* such works have been placed together in two new sections in this chapter: Section G, Conservation: General, and Section H, Conservation: Special. Section E, which in the 1960 *Guide* is entitled Forests, National Parks, has been renamed Forests and Forestry, and the subject of national parks is regarded as being encompassed by Section H.

The new sections do not entirely solve the problem of placing each entry under a precisely suitable subject heading. Forests and Forestry could readily have been combined with Conservation: Special, but because of its relatively large size and its nearness in location to the conservation sections, it has been retained. Furthermore, a number of publications dealing with natural science but not stressing conservation are included in the *Supplement,* and these are entered by subject, as in the 1960 *Guide,* in such sections as D, Plants and Animals, Chapter VI.

## A. Land

2603. Bertrand, Alvin L., *and* Floyd L. Corty, *eds.*
Rural land tenure in the United States, a socio-economic approach to problems, programs, and trends. Baton Rouge, Louisiana State University Press [1962] 313 p. 62–16212 HD1156.A3B4

Combining the approaches of rural sociology and agricultural economics, this volume, which was sponsored by the Southwest Land Tenure Research Committee, presents a general synthesis of informa-
tion and an analysis of tenure problems in their total social aspect. The editors wrote two chapters each and teamed together as the coauthors of three more. Although the book is intended primarily for the specialist, basic terms are defined and fundamental concepts are explained. Aaron M. Sakolski's *Land Tenure and Land Taxation in America* (New York, R. Schalkenbach Foundation [1957] 316 p.) is a history of land settlement and the evolution of land tenure.

2604. Carstensen, Vernon R., *ed*. The public lands; studies in the history of the public domain. Madison, University of Wisconsin Press, 1963 [°1962] 522 p.

62–21554 HD216.C3 1963

Bibliographies at the ends of chapters.

2605. Homestead Centennial Symposium, *University of Nebraska, 1962*. Land use policy and problems in the United States. Edited by Howard W. Ottoson. Lincoln, University of Nebraska Press [1963] 470 p. 63–9096 HD205 1962.H6

Bibliographies at the ends of chapters.

These two collections of papers on the history of the public domain were published in recognition of separate anniversaries. As the name suggests, the Homestead Centennial Symposium celebrated the 100th anniversary of the Homestead Act. The participants were drawn from diverse disciplines, and their statements range over the social, economic, and political aspects of public land policy and administration. *The Public Lands* was prepared in observance of the 150th anniversary of the General Land Office, predecessor of the Bureau of Land Management. An advisory board selected representative articles on the history of public land from among those that its members regarded as the best published during the previous 50 years. Carstensen, a member of the advisory board, notes that the volume is intended to supplement, rather than supplant, the standard histories of the public domain.

2606. Dana, Samuel Trask. Forest and range policy, its development in the United States. New York, McGraw-Hill, 1956. 455 p. (The American forestry series) 55–11168 SD565.D3

Bibliography: p. 426–434.

"Fur, fish, farms, and forest" were the basis of the colonial economy, and forests on the east coast conditioned the first policies relating to forestry and range and resource management. Later influences were the westward expansion, the exploitation of gold and silver, the rise of commercial agriculture and forestry, the development of national parks and forests, and the conservation movement. The author focuses on broad subjects, chronologically presented, and concludes with a view of the future. He is coauthor of two pilot studies on land ownership and its influence on land management, initiated and published in Washington by the American Forestry Association: *California Lands* (1958. 308 p.), by Dana and Myron Krueger, and *Minnesota Lands* (1960. 463 p.), by Dana, John H. Allison, and Russell N. Cunningham. A third pilot study conducted under the same sponsorship is *North Carolina Lands* (1964. 372 p.), by Kenneth B. Pomeroy and James G. Yoho.

2607. Higbee, Edward C. The American oasis; the land and its uses. New York, Knopf, 1957. 262 p. 56–5788 S441.H6

Bibliography: p. 261–262.

2608. Resources for the Future. Land for the future, by Marion Clawson, R. Burnell Held [and] Charles H. Stoddard. Baltimore, Published for Resources for the Future by the Johns Hopkins Press [1960] xix, 570 p.

60–9917 HD205 1960.R4

Bibliographical footnotes.

According to *The American Oasis,* such factors as a large percentage of arable land and a high degree of mechanization cause the United States to be "an oasis of plenty in what is largely a hungry world." The author views the general agricultural picture, clarifies regional differences within the country, describes the methods of the best agriculturists, and stresses the magnitude of the task of feeding the world's population. *Land for the Future* examines the need for agricultural lands along with the demands for urbanization, recreation, forestry, grazing, and other purposes. Many graphs and tables and several appendixes illustrate and support the text. The authors offer a projection of expected land use to the year 2000. Marion Clawson's *Man and Land in the United States* (Lincoln, University of Nebraska Press, 1964. 178 p.) is a brief historical survey of land use, from conditions that prevailed before European settlers arrived to the modified landscape of today.

2609. Resources for the Future. The federal lands: their use and management, by Marion Clawson and Burnell Held. Baltimore, Published for Resources for the Future by the Johns Hopkins Press [1957] xxi, 501 p. illus.

57–12121 HD216.R4

Bibliographical footnotes.

Clawson, who draws upon his experience as Director of the Bureau of Land Management in the Department of the Interior, 1948–53, and Held, who studied pertinent agency records in detail, question whether the business of administering the Federal lands has kept pace with the social and economic growth of the country and urge a critical, imaginative reexamination of management policies. Two interpretive histories of public policy toward one type of land use are Phillip O. Foss' *Politics and Grass; the Administration of Grazing on the Public Domain* (Seattle, University of Washington Press, 1960. 236 p.) and Wesley C. Calef's *Private Grazing and Public Lands; Studies of the Local Management of the Taylor Grazing Act* ( [Chicago] University of Chicago Press [1960] 292 p.).

# B. Agriculture: History

2610. Bogue, Allan G. From prairie to corn belt; farming on the Illinois and Iowa prairies in the nineteenth century. Chicago, University of Chicago Press [1963] 310 p.

63–20913 HD1773.A3B6

Bibliography: p. 289–303.

In the upper watershed of the Mississippi River, "there lies a great farming region where farmers key their operations to the corn crop as they do nowhere else in the United States." The author analyzes the problems confronting the prairie farmer, 1830–1900, and portrays him breaking the land, harvesting the crops, tending livestock, and amassing capital. By 1900 the pioneer's work was done, and his successors "were moving forward into the golden age." Carefully detailed and more limited in scope is Margaret B. Bogue's *Patterns From the Sod; Land Use and Tenure in the Grand Prairie, 1850–1900* (Springfield, Illinois State Historical Library, 1959. 327 p. Collections of the Illinois State Historical Library, v. 34. Land series, v. 1). A brief, easily read history of "the most important plant in the United States" is *Corn and Its Early Fathers* ([East Lansing] Michigan State University Press, 1956. 134 p.), by Henry A. Wallace and William L. Brown.

2611. Case, Harold C. M., *and* Donald B. Williams. Fifty years of farm management. Urbana, University of Illinois Press, 1957. 386 p.

56–6707 S561.C317

Bibliographical footnotes.

The science of farm management is a product of the commercial and capitalistic aspects of 20th-century agriculture. Before that time the emphasis was on production techniques. The authors make special reference to research, extension, and teaching as developed by the land-grant colleges and the U. S. Department of Agriculture. Attention is directed to the emergence of research procedures and to the adoption of management practices rather than to the evolution of the practices themselves. A specialized study of farm financing is Alvin S. Tostlebe's *Capital in Agriculture: Its Formation and Financing Since 1870* (Princeton, Princeton University Press, 1957. 232 p. Studies in capital formation and financing, 2), sponsored by the National Bureau of Economic Research.

2612. Hargreaves, Mary Wilma M. Dry farming in the northern Great Plains, 1900–1925. Cambridge, Harvard University Press, 1957. 587 p. (Harvard economic studies, v. 101)

56–11281 S441.H29

Bibliographical footnotes.

In the 20th century, dry farming, or "agriculture without irrigation in regions of limited natural precipitation," was an experiment. Begun by settlers who were poorly suited to the venture, it was sustained by diligence, scientific research, and railroad expansion. Although the author confines her discussion to eastern Montana and the western Dakotas in the first quarter of the 20th century, her conclusions are broadly relevant to the problems common to all dry areas.

2613. Holt, Rackham. George Washington Carver, an American biography. Rev. ed. Garden City, N.Y., Doubleday [1963] 360 p.

62–11430 S417.C3H6 1963

An updated edition of no. 5825 in the 1960 *Guide*.

2614. Rasmussen, Wayne D., *ed.* Readings in the history of American agriculture. Urbana, University of Illinois Press, 1960. 340 p.

60–8342 S441.R34

Selected readings: p. 312–320.

When the Constitution was adopted, nine of every 10 working persons were employed on farms. By 1960, one farmer was growing food and fiber for himself and 22 other persons. The interim development was spectacular. The selections in this volume, many of which are from obscure sources, deal with such topics as the first planting of corn by the colonists, the modification of Old World practices by the environment of the New, the technological revolution at the time of the Civil War, the impact of increasing industrialization, the growing importance of domestic and foreign markets, the further technological changes associated with World War II, and current sales and distribution problems. *Harvest, an Anthology of Farm Writing* (New York, Appleton-Century [1964] 424 p.), edited by Wheeler McMillen, is a collection of personal reminiscences and literary selections stressing the idyllic aspects of farm life.

2615. Saloutos, Theodore. Farmer movements in the South 1865–1933. Berkeley, University of California Press, 1960. 354 p. (University of California publications in history, v. 64)

60–63657 E173.C15 vol. 64

Bibliography: p. 333–346.

This companion volume to *Agricultural Discontent in the Middle West, 1900–1939,* by Saloutos and John D. Hicks (no. 5831 in the 1960 *Guide*), is concentrated on the crusades to relieve numerous farmer grievances. Socioeconomically oriented, it is less a study of personalities than of the effective agencies—the Grange, Agricultural Wheel, Southern Alliance, Populist Party, Farmers Union, Southern Cotton Association, and other cotton and tobacco associations—which were able to express the southern farmer's discontent. Occasionally in harmony with the common needs of society as a whole, the aspirations of these groups were broadly influential and helped to determine trends throughout the Nation. A brief historical account, with supporting documents, is Fred A. Shannon's *American Farmers' Movements* (Princeton, N.J., Van Nostrand [1957] 192 p. An Anvil original, no. 28).

2616. Shideler, James H. Farm crisis, 1919–1923. Berkeley, University of California Press, 1957. 345 p. 57–10502 HD1761.S54

"Bibliographical notes": p. 297–301. Bibliographical references included in "Notes" (p. 303–331).

"The turning point in the great economic, political, and social trends of agriculture" was the period of economic dislocations in the years immediately following World War I. Emerging from the conflict as a creditor nation, the United States could no longer dispose of its surplus farm goods by sending them abroad for repayment of debts. Overproduction, high production costs, burdensome distribution charges, and the diminution of foreign markets—all contributed to the development of agriculture's long-lasting depression. The author examines changes in outlook and leadership as the farmers, encountering a "convergence of difficulties," attempted to improve their status through self-help.

# C. Agriculture: Practice

2617. Higbee, Edward C. American agriculture: geography, resources, conservation. New York, Wiley [1958] 399 p. 58–10803 S441.H59

Bibliographies at the ends of chapters.

The author, a geographer and an agricultural economist, blends his knowledge of both fields in a textbook for students of the agricultural sciences, vocational agriculture, conservation, and geography. He discusses agricultural regions of the United States, the underlying reasons for agricultural specialization within them, and selected farms which illustrate wise use and conservation of their resources. Two major topics are the West with its governing problem of aridity and the East with its humidity and resultant diverse focus. In *Farms and Farmers in an Urban Age* (New York, Twentieth Century Fund, 1963. 183 p.), the same author examines for the layman the transformation of agriculture from a way of life into a modern capitalistic enterprise. Lauren K. Soth, in *An Embarrassment of Plenty* (New York, Crowell [1965] 209 p.), analyzes the dual farm problem: increasing production and lagging income. *The Farmer and His Customers* (Norman, University of Oklahoma Press [1957] 99 p.), by Ladd Haystead, is a brief picture of "just where farming is today, its problems, its weaknesses, and its place in the United States of the future."

2618. Murray, William G., *and* Aaron G. Nelson. Agricultural finance. 4th ed. Ames, Iowa State University Press [1960] 486 p. 60–11129 HG2051.U5M88 1960

References at the ends of chapters.

An updated edition of no. 5848 in the 1960 *Guide*.

2619. Shotwell, Louisa R. The harvesters; the story of the migrant people. Garden City, N.Y., Doubleday, 1961. 242 p. 61–9552 HD1525.S48

Bibliography: p. [215]–237.

The author's purpose is "to portray the complex setting in which migrant families of different ethnic backgrounds live and work; to identify the thorny issues their migrancy raises for themselves, for the communities and the states that recruit their labor, and for the national economy; and to attempt a foreshadowing of what lies ahead for them." The people are fictitious, but their experiences are authentic. "Everything that happens to them has happened to real migrant people somewhere." Two other accounts are *The Slaves We Rent* (New York, Random House [1965] 171 p.), by Truman E. Moore, and *They Harvest Despair; the Migrant Farm Worker* (Boston, Beacon Press [1965] 158 p.), based on award-winning articles published in the *New York World-Telegram and Sun* in 1961, by Dale Wright.

2620. U.S. *Dept. of Agriculture.* Power to produce. Washington, U.S. Govt. Print. Off. [1960] 480 p. (*Its* Yearbook of agriculture, 1960)
Agr 60–362   S21.A35   1960

Agriculture's contribution to and benefits from the technological revolution in the United States are the subject of this collection of relatively short articles on the farmer's uses of power, which is defined by editor Alfred Stefferud as ranging from machines and oil to muscles and thought. The history, potentialities, and physical effects of power rather than its social, political, and humanitarian aspects are emphasized. Clear, nontechnical language traces power in the past and present — on the land, in the harvest, in the market, and in research. A section of illustrations juxtaposes old and new tools, machines, and methods.

2621. U. S. *Farmer Cooperative Service.* Farmer cooperatives in the United States. Washington, 1955 [i.e. 1956] 252 p. (*Its* FCS bulletin 1)
Agr 56–153   HD1484.A45

Bibliographical footnotes.

A revised edition of no. 5842 in the 1960 *Guide*. Two related works are *Agricultural Cooperation; Selected Readings* (Minneapolis, University of Minnesota Press [1957] 576 p.), edited by Martin A. Abrahamsen and Claud L. Scroggs, and *Farmers in Business, Studies in Cooperative Enterprise* (Washington, American Institute of Cooperation [1963] 450 p.), by Joseph G. Knapp, Administrator of the Farmer Cooperative Service in the Department of Agriculture.

2622. Wilcox, Walter W., *and* Willard W. Cochrane. Economics of American agriculture. 2d ed. Englewood Cliffs, N.J., Prentice-Hall, 1960. 538 p.   60–10780   HD1761.W435   1960

References at the ends of chapters.

An updated edition of no. 5850 in the 1960 *Guide*.

## D. Agriculture: Government Policies

2623. Campbell, Christiana McFadyen. The Farm Bureau and the New Deal; a study of the making of national farm policy, 1933-40. Urbana, University of Illinois Press, 1962. 215 p.
62–13210   HD1761.C3   1962

Bibliography: p. [196]–201.

The most influential of the farm organizations in the period of the New Deal was the American Farm Bureau Federation. Establishing and promoting a sectional alliance between the farmers of the Midwest and those of the South, the Farm Bureau concentrated on achieving compromises between agriculture and other interest groups, such as labor and business, in the making of national economic policy. Price policy was the organization's chief preoccupation. To raise the price of farm products became the predominant objective. The author of this monograph, winner of the Agricultural History Society award for 1961, sets forth an array of both facts and interpretations. William J. Block concentrates on a special controversy in *The Separation of the Farm Bureau and the Extension Service* (Urbana, University of Illinois Press, 1960. 304 p. Illinois studies in the social sciences, v. 47). *Roosevelt's Farmer: Claude R. Wickard in the New Deal* (New York, Columbia University Press, 1961 [°1955] 424 p.), by Dean Albertson, is a biography of the man who was Franklin D. Roosevelt's Secretary of Agriculture, 1940–45.

2624. Cochrane, Willard W. The city man's guide to the farm problem. Minneapolis, University of Minnesota Press [1965] 242 p.
65–20831   HD1761.C595   1965

Bibliographical footnotes.

A survey of farming populations and operations for the "interested layman who wants to make sense out of the farm problem." The author appeals to the urban dweller who has the financial and political means to be influential. Emphasis is on two aspects of the problem: overproduction and rural unemployment. In *The Great Farm Problem* (Chicago, Regnery, 1959. 235 p.), William H. Peterson advocates as a simple solution the discontinuance of support and subsidies and the restoration of a free market. Geoffrey S. Shepherd's *Farm Policy; New Directions* (Ames, Iowa State University Press [°1964] 292 p.) points to the oversupply of farmers as the root of the problem and urges a massive program to help those who want to choose a new vocation.

2625. Hathaway, Dale E. Government and agriculture: public policy in a democratic society. New York, Macmillan [1963] 412 p.
63–11797   HD1761.H383

Bibliographical footnotes.

2626. Paarlberg, Donald. American farm policy, a case study of centralized decision-making.

New York, J. Wiley [1964] xiv, 375 p.

64–14996 HD1761.P13

Two textbooks which analyze the costs and the benefits of agriculture's technological success. The authors review farm policies in terms of attitudes, goals, and ideals, describe their consequences, and speculate about their future. *Government and Agriculture,* a study of farm policy in its political setting, is focused specifically on price and income patterns since World War II. The author explains the industry's growth as well as its decline in relative economic importance. Assuming the inevitability of Government intervention, he suggests ways to raise farm income and to increase returns from the physical and human investments. The author of *American Farm Policy* traces the origins and consequences of Government intervention. Taking a pragmatic rather than a doctrinaire approach, he examines the present price support and production control programs. In an outline for the future, he urges, among other things, reduced price supports and more fully individualized decision-making. *Who's Behind Our Farm Policy?* ([New York] Praeger [1957, °1956] 374 p.), by Wesley McCune, is a journalistic description of "the people, organizations and pressures involved in the running national debate of farm policy."

2627. U. S. *Dept. of Agriculture. Agricultural History Branch.* Century of service: the first 100 years of the United States Department of Agriculture. [By Gladys L. Baker, and others. Washington] Centennial Committee, U. S. Dept. of Agriculture; [for sale by the Superintendent of Documents, U. S. Govt. Print. Off., 1963] xv, 560 p. Agr 63–175 S21.C8 1963

"Literature cited": p. 419–439.

Established in 1862, the Department of Agriculture began inauspiciously. The news of its appearance, and of the first Commissioner's appointment, attracted relatively slight public attention. For 50 years the Department's growth was slow. This official history is devoted largely to the period of rapid development beginning with World War I and emphasizes factual information rather than criticism or interpretation. The appendix contains brief biographies of Commissioners, Secretaries, Under Secretaries, and Assistant Secretaries; a historical list of heads of departmental agencies; a description of each agency's organization; and a chronology of major events. The Department's *Yearbook of Agriculture* for 1962, *After a Hundred Years* (Washington, U. S. Govt. Print. Off. [1962] 688 p.), is a "sampler of progress" since 1862.

## E. Forests and Forestry

2628. Allen, Shirley W., *and* Grant W. Sharpe. An introduction to American forestry. 3d ed. New York, McGraw-Hill, 1960. 466 p. (The American forestry series)

60–6956 SD371.A6 1960

References at the ends of chapters.

A revised edition of no. 5862 in the 1960 *Guide.* The Society of American Foresters' publication, *American Forestry: Six Decades of Growth* (Washington, 1960. 319 p.), edited by Henry Clepper and Arthur B. Meyer, is a history of forestry after 1900 and a summary of the society's influence in the field during that period. In *Timber and Men; the Weyerhaeuser Story* (New York, Macmillan [1963] 704 p.), Ralph W. Hidy, Frank E. Hill, and Allan Nevins have produced a scholarly history of the Weyerhaeuser enterprise from its beginning in 1860, when Frederick Weyerhaeuser and Frederick C. A. Denkmann started, with a defunct sawmill, a lumber business which grew into the largest wood products empire in the world. The Weyerhaeusers were pioneers in forest fire control and in planned forestry, demonstrating leadership in the practices of

selective logging and sustained yield through reforestation.

2629. Carhart, Arthur H. The national forests. New York, Knopf, 1959. 289 p.

59–5433 SD426.C2

Designed by the publisher as a companion to Freeman Tilden's book, *The National Parks; What They Mean to You and Me* (no. 5866 in the 1960 *Guide*) Carhart's volume surveys the national forests, emphasizing their multiple resources and uses. An introductory chapter identifies 150 forests — which together encompass 18 million acres — in terms of timber production, watershed protection, resources and recreation, history, and administration. The bulk of the text is devoted to nine forest regions — their geological history, weather, climate, soils, trees, management, preservation, economic uses, and folklore. Michael Frome's *Whose Woods These Are: The Story of the National Forests* (Garden City, N.Y., Doubleday, 1962. 360 p.) explores selected forests with sensitive attention to all their uses, from tree farming to wilderness. In *The Forest Ranger, a Study in Administrative Behavior* (Baltimore, Published for Resources for the Future by Johns Hopkins Press [1960] 259 p.), Herbert Kaufman describes the implementation of resource management programs in the U. S. Forest Service.

2630. McGeary, Martin Nelson. Gifford Pinchot, forester-politician. Princeton, N.J., Princeton University Press, 1960. 481 p.

60–12232   E664.P62M2

Bibliography: p. 467–471.

Heir to wealth, Pinchot perplexed his Yale classmates by choosing to become a forester. Forestry was an undeveloped field, and one so new that he had to go to Europe for professional education. Upon his return he traveled, loafed, and took odd jobs for a year. Finally a genuine opportunity opened. In 1892, he became forest manager on the "Biltmore Estate" of George W. Vanderbilt, near Asheville, N.C. From then on he was intensely active, ultimately becoming head of the Forest Service in the Department of Agriculture. He was chosen for the chairmanship of the National Conservation Commission in 1908 and for the presidency of the National Conservation Association in 1910. He also founded the school of forestry at Yale. From forestry he turned to politics, serving twice as Governor of Pennsylvania. Although this biography emphasizes Pinchot's political career, the author summarizes the contribution made by "America's first trained forester." George T. Morgan's *William B. Greeley, a Practical Forester, 1879–1955* (St. Paul, Forest History Society, 1961. 82 p.) is a brief biography of one of Pinchot's disciples.

2631. Platt, Rutherford H.   The great American forest. Illustrations by Stanley Wyatt. Englewood Cliffs, N.J., Prentice-Hall [1965] 271 p. ([Prentice-Hall series in nature and natural history])

65–25253   SD140.P55

The first volume in a new series on nature and natural history, illustrated with woodcuts and full-page photographs and combining technical description and esthetic appreciation. The author discusses the historical evolution of trees, their chemical and physical makeup, and their importance in relation to other natural resources. He also deals with the significance of leaf shedding, the regional characteristics of American forest types, and the variety of forest-related living things. He concludes with a plea for preservation of wilderness areas: "If only people would catch a vision of our fabulous forests, their ancient heritage, their beauty and beneficence, their meaning for our lives today . . . before it is too late."

2632. Shirley, Hardy L.   Forestry and its career opportunities. 2d ed. New York, McGraw-Hill [1964] 454 p. (The American forestry series)

63–16468   SD371.S5   1964

References at the ends of chapters.

An updated edition of no. 5865 in the 1960 *Guide.* The Society of American Foresters' *Forestry Education in America Today and Tomorrow* (Washington, 1963. 402 p.), by Samuel Trask Dana and Evert W. Johnson, is a progress report on professional education in forestry and related fields of natural resource management.

# F.  Animal Husbandry

2633. Dale, Edward E.   The range cattle industry; ranching on the Great Plains from 1865 to 1925. [New ed.] Norman, University of Oklahoma Press [1960]  xv, 207 p.

60–10552   SF196.U5D18   1960

Bibliography: p. 187–200.

A revised edition of no. 5868 in the 1960 *Guide.*

2634. Frink, Maurice.   When grass was king; contributions to the Western Range Cattle Industry Study. Boulder, University of Colorado Press, 1956. xv, 465 p. illus.

56–13159   HD9433.U4F7

Bibliography: p. 124–131, 322–330, 442–450.

CONTENTS.—When grass was king, by Maurice Frink.—British interests in the range cattle indus-

try, by W. Turrentine Jackson.—A "genius for handling cattle": John W. Iliff, by Agnes W. Spring.

2635. Schlebecker, John T.   Cattle raising on the Plains, 1900–1961. Lincoln, University of Nebraska Press, 1963. 323 p. illus.

63–14691   HD9433.U4S35

Bibliography: p. 291–310.

"Deeply rooted in the old world and ancient times," Frink observes, "cattle growing as a commercial enterprise on the western plains of the United States has helped for a hundred years and more to feed, clothe and otherwise nourish the people of our own and other lands." *When Grass Was King* covers the cattle industry in New Mexico, Colorado, Wyoming, and Montana during the period 1865–95. *Cattle Raising on the Plains* encompasses all 10 of the States which have a portion of the Great Plains within their boundaries and depicts the adjustments which cattlemen of the 20th century made to their environment. Paul C. Henlein's *Cattle Kingdom in the Ohio Valley, 1783–1860* (Lexington, University of Kentucky Press [1959] 198 p.) portrays a virtually forgotten period of importance for the beef-cattle industry in the East. In *The Hereford in America,* 2d ed. (Kansas City, Mo. [1960] 500 p.), Donald R. Ornduff traces the story of one breed of beef cattle from its origins in England.

2636. Lampard, Eric E. The rise of the dairy industry in Wisconsin; a study in agricultural change, 1820–1920. Madison, State Historical Society of Wisconsin, 1963. 466 p. illus.
63–64496 HD9275.U7W66
Bibliography: p. [429]–446.
By the early 20th century, Wisconsin had become the leading dairy State. Scientific research, education, regulation, improved breeding, and progress in marketing and transportation had helped to convert dairying as a domestic and seasonal activity into a year-round, factory-supplemented, production system providing a stable income. A characteristic

of the enterprise was that "it shared both the tribulations of agriculture and the triumphs of manufacture: it epitomized the industrial revolution." This economic analysis is highly detailed and copiously footnoted.

2637. Smithcors, J. F. The American veterinary profession, its background and development. Ames, Iowa State University Press [1963] 704 p.
63–16672 SF623.S65
A history of the veterinary profession from colonial times to the present. The author describes the slow development of American veterinary science up to the mid-19th century, then traces the growth of the organized profession, beginning with the founding in 1863 of the United States Veterinary Medical Association, now called the American Veterinary Medical Association. He suggests that the lack of a veterinary service in the early years of the country and the apparent immunity of animals to disease for a century or more led people to think that animals needed little attention. Consequently, the livestock industry was threatened with extinction before the value of veterinary science was apparent. The book is illustrated with many reproductions of paintings, photographs, and veterinary advertisements.

## G. Conservation: General

2638. Hays, Samuel P. Conservation and the gospel of efficiency; the progressive conservation movement, 1890–1920. Cambridge, Harvard University Press, 1959. 297 p. (Harvard historical monographs, 40) 59–9274 HC103.7.H3
"Bibliographical note": p. [277]–282. Bibliographical footnotes.
The conservation movement was born in an era characterized by Theodore Roosevelt's spirit of management and administration. The author of this history of Federal regulation defines conservation as "planned and efficient progress" in the development and use of all natural resources. The conservationists were concerned with resource use rather than ownership. They endeavored to apply scientific and technological means to limit the pattern of exploitation in the use of raw materials. Sharing the appreciation of big business for "large-scale capital organization, technology, and industry-wide cooperation and planning to abolish the uncertainties and waste of competitive resource use," Roosevelt, Gifford Pinchot, and Francis G. Newlands promoted the rationally planned development

and utilitarian use of water, forests, and rangelands. Two historical monographs on other aspects of the conservation movement are *The Politics of Conservation: Crusades and Controversies, 1897–1913* (Berkeley, University of California Press, 1962. 207 p. University of California publications in history, v. 70), by Elmo R. Richardson and *Federal Conservation Policy, 1921–1933* (Berkeley, University of California Press, 1963. 221 p. University of California publications in history, v. 76), by Donald C. Swain.

2639. Held, R. Burnell, *and* Marion Clawson. Soil conservation in perspective. Baltimore, Published for Resources for the Future by the Johns Hopkins Press [1965] 344 p. illus.
65–22946 S624.A1H4
Bibliographical footnotes.
For more than 30 years, soil conservation has been a major national program. The prime concerns of this volume are the economics of soil use and misuse and the social and political relationships involved. The authors conclude that, despite major

accomplishments, "a big job remains to be done, regardless of how that job is defined and measured." Future successes will necessitate the resolution of fundamental conflicts within current programs of the Department of Agriculture, as well as adaptation to the changing character of conservation problems. A companion volume resulting from the same general research project is Robert J. Morgan's *Governing Soil Conservation: Thirty Years of the New Decentralization* ([Baltimore] Published for Resources for the Future by the Johns Hopkins Press [1965] 399 p.), which deals with administrative problems rather than conservation practices.

2640. Parson, Ruben L. Conserving American resources. 2d ed. Englewood Cliffs, N.J., Prentice-Hall [1964] 521 p. illus.

64–10843 S930.P3 1964

Notes: p. 493–508.

Because it draws upon a number of disciplines for its subject matter, an introductory course in the conservation of natural resources can be approached from any of several directions. This textbook is by a resource geographer who offers a "development of concepts rather than a recitation of facts; an exhortation to think and participate rather than an exposition on statistics and techniques." Employing a style calculated to lighten the weight of a technical subject, he appeals for expanded citizen involvement in conservation activities. A compilation reflecting the wide variety of material to be found outside the standard text is *Readings in Resource Management and Conservation* (Chicago, University of Chicago Press [1965] 609 p.), edited by Ian Burton and Robert W. Kates. *Resources in America's Future; Patterns of Requirements and Availabilities, 1960–2000* ([Baltimore] Published for Resources for the Future by the Johns Hopkins Press [1963] 1017 p.), by Hans H. Landsberg, Leonard L. Fischman, and Joseph L. Fisher, is a study in depth supported by 500 pages of statistical appendixes and notes.

2641. Udall, Stewart L. The quiet crisis. Introduction by John F. Kennedy. New York, Holt, Rinehart & Winston [1963] 209 p. illus.

63–21463 S930.U3

Bibliographical notes in "Acknowledgements": p. 193–196.

"America today stands poised on a pinnacle of wealth and power, yet we live in a land of vanishing beauty, of increasing ugliness, of shrinking open space, and of an over-all environment that is diminished daily by pollution and noise and blight. This, in brief, is the quiet conservation crisis of the 1960's." Aided by an outline suggested by Wallace Stegner, Kennedy's Secretary of the Interior presents a vivid historical review of man's relationship to land in the United States. The story evolves largely through the exploits of key individuals — ranging from Daniel Boone to Frederick Law Olmsted — whose roles were influential in the development and implementation of conservation philosophies. The author concludes with a request for the development of a land ethic to serve as a guide to resource use. "A land ethic for tomorrow," he maintains, "should be as honest as Thoreau's *Walden,* and as comprehensive as the sensitive science of ecology. It should stress the oneness of our resources and the live-and-help-live logic of the great chain of life."

## H. Conservation: Special

2642. Carlson, Rachel L. Silent spring. Drawings by Lois and Louis Darling. Boston, Houghton Mifflin, 1962. 368 p.

60–5148 SB959.C3

List of principal sources: p. 301–355.

2643. U. S. *President's Science Advisory Committee. Environmental Pollution Panel.* Restoring the quality of our environment. Report. [Washington] The White House, 1965. 317 p.

66–60170 TD180.U55

Bibliography: p. 131–133.

The primary thesis of *Silent Spring* is that the synthetic pesticides pose a threat to man and to many species of plants and animals that are important to his welfare. Such chemicals, even when spread in diluted quantities, can be combined again by the cells of the lower forms of life until they reach densities far above the level of safety. As an alternative to the use of synthetics to control pests, the author advocates such biological solutions as sterilization by X-ray and the introduction of enemy species. One of the major papers in *Restoring the Quality of Our Environment* is a discussion of the biological methods of pest control and the need for developing them further. Another of the papers supports the Carson thesis that pesticides can accumulate in passing through the food chain. The panel's concern extends far beyond the subject of pesticides, however, to include the whole range of pollutants—in air, soil, and water. Smoke from chimneys, carbon dioxide from automobile exhausts, wastes from industries, and nitrates from fertilized fields are all within the range of the panel's interests. The general report, apart from appended papers on special subjects, summarizes the effects of pollution, the sources from which it comes, and the directions in which pollution control should now turn.

2644. Hart, Henry C. The dark Missouri. Madison, University of Wisconsin Press, 1957. 260 p.          57–7704   HD1695.M5H3
   Bibliographical notes: p. 230–253.
"In the heart of America civilized man has yet to make his peace with nature, even after a century of effort. For him the ways of the Missouri are dark still." Examining the Missouri River Basin from the anthropological, geological, and historical points of view, the author reviews drought and flood cycles, population changes, and the many plans to enable man to achieve harmony with the river and its power both to create and destroy. Despite all that has been accomplished, he maintains, the area is still improperly developed and "seems destined to pay the price of another Kansas City flood, another drought throughout the Northern Plains." In Reclamation in the United States (Caldwell, Idaho, Caxton Printers, 1961. 486 p.), Alfred R. Golzé discusses the problems of irrigating desert lands in order to render them productive.

2645. Ise, John. Our national park policy; a critical history. Baltimore, Published for Resources for the Future by Johns Hopkins Press [1961]   701 p.          60–15704   SB482.A1I75
   Bibliographical footnotes.
In 1960 the national park system comprised 180 areas covering nearly 23 million acres. It existed "not as a result of public demand but because a few farsighted, unselfish, and idealistic men and women foresaw the national need and got the areas established and protected in one way or another, fighting public inertia and selfish commercial interests at every step." The author follows the system's growth from the establishment of Yellowstone Park in 1872 to the present. Early parks receive individual treatment. After the creation of the National Park Service in 1916, the story unfolds chronologically through the administrations of the agency's directors. "Most of our national parks should have been much larger," Ise comments, "with far more in wilderness or primitive areas." The National Park Service publication, Parks for America; a Survey of Park and Related Resources in the Fifty States and a Preliminary Plan ([Washington, For sale by the Supt. of Docs., U. S. Govt. Print. Off.] 1964. 485 p.), describes existing facilities and projects future needs.

2646. Matthiessen, Peter. Wildlife in America. Drawings by Bob Hines. New York, Viking Press, 1959. 304 p.      59–11635   SK361.M36
   Bibliography: p. 289–294.
"The finality of extinction is awesome, and not unrelated to the finality of eternity." The author begins his story with a documented account of the death of the last two known specimens of the great auk. They died needlessly, and for the first time an animal species native to North America was rendered extinct by the hand of man. "This book is a history of North American wildlife, of the great auk and other creatures present and missing, of how they vanished, where, and why; and of what is presently being done that North America may not become a wasteland of man's creation, in which no wild thing can live." Three thoughtful and well-illustrated volumes on wildlife conservation are The Land and Wildlife of North America (New York, Time, Inc. [1964] 200 p. Life nature library), by Peter Farb; Exploring Our National Wildlife Refuges, 2d ed., rev. (Boston, Houghton Mifflin, 1963. 340 p.), by Devereux Butcher; and the U. S. Bureau of Sport Fisheries and Wildlife publication Waterfowl Tomorrow ([Washington, For sale by the Supt. of Docs., U.S. Govt. Print. Off., 1964] 770 p.), edited by Joseph P. Linduska.

2647. National Geographic Society, Washington, D.C. Book Service. America's wonderlands; the scenic national parks and monuments of the United States. Washington, National Geographic Society [1959] 510 p. (World in color library)          59–14338   E160.N24
In this volume, as in a number of the National Geographic Society's publications, articles by different authors are integrated into a coherent whole, with informal texts built around pictures of people and landscapes. National Parks of the West (Menlo Park, Calif., Lane Magazine & Book Co. [1965] 319 p.), by the editors of Sunset Books and Sunset Magazine, is a briefer work, artistically illustrated. Ansel Adams' These We Inherit; the Parklands of America (San Francisco, Sierra Club [1962] 103 p.) is an album by an acknowledged master of natural landscape photography. Devereux Butcher's Exploring Our National Parks and Monuments, 5th ed. (Boston, Houghton Mifflin, 1956. 288 p.) is an updated edition of a work mentioned in the annotation for no. 5866 in the 1960 Guide.

2648. Tilden, Freeman. The State parks, their meaning in American life. New York, Knopf, 1962. 496 p.     62–17547  E160.T53

A companion volume to one of the author's earlier works, *The National Parks, What They Mean to You and Me,* no. 5866 in the 1960 *Guide.* In 1921 the National Conference on State Parks first met to urge legislation for "recreation areas within states which would be comparable in purpose, in choice, in administration, and in resultant benefits" to the national parks. This warmly written book shows the growth and results of the State park movement. A discussion of the history, philosophy, and management policies of State parks is followed by descriptions of outstanding State recreation areas, monuments, beaches, parks, and parkways in four major geographical areas and by "thumbnail sketches" of individual parks.

2649. Wilderness Conference, *8th, San Francisco, 1963.* Tomorrow's wilderness. San Francisco, Sierra Club [1963] 262 p. (*Its* [Proceedings])     60–45889  QH75.W5 1963

The Sierra Club is a conservation organization founded in 1892 by John Muir to explore, enjoy, and protect the Nation's scenic resources of parks, wilderness, and wildlife. Since 1949 it has sponsored biennial wilderness conferences which have steadily broadened in concern, traversing the subject from the practical problems of trip organization to the theory, philosophy, and meaning of preservation. Like all the proceedings published since 1959, this volume is the work of a diverse group of wilderness enthusiasts and is illustrated with photographs by Ansel Adams and others. *This Is the American Earth* (San Francisco, Sierra Club [1960] 89 p.), by Adams and Nancy Newhall, is a poetic essay in word and picture and has been acclaimed a masterpiece in nature appreciation.

# XXVIII

# Economic Life

In the *Supplement* and in the 1960 *Guide*, Section I, Finance: General, and Section J, Finance: Special, considered together, form the largest unit devoted to a single topic in Chapter XXVIII. Although the two sections on labor and the two on business, when respectively combined, are equal in size in the 1960 *Guide*, in the *Supplement* labor has more entries than business. The change perhaps reflects an increased interest in the problems confronted by the workingman as well as in those created by him in his organized efforts to improve his status. The number of entries in Section A, General Works: Histories, in the *Supplement* represent the most conspicuous proportionate increase in an individual section. The most striking decrease is in Section E, Transportation: General, which is limited to one entry in the *Supplement*.

## A. General Works: Histories

2650. Arrington, Leonard J. Great Basin Kingdom; an economic history of the Latter-Day Saints, 1830–1900. Cambridge, Harvard University Press, 1958. xviii, 534 p. illus. (Studies in economic history)     58–12961  HC107.U8A8
  Bibliography: p. [415]–420.
  A study of Mormon concepts and the efforts of the church leadership to develop an economy in harmony with those concepts. The author points up the strengths and weaknesses of attempting a development program in an isolated, mountainous, semiarid region without outside capital. Founded for religious purposes and dominated by religious leaders, the community practiced economic innovations in establishing the pioneer settlements. Despite the external strains on their economy and the

conflict of their policies with those of the government, the Mormons worked out a financial system which resulted in successful cooperative living. Arrington concludes that the Mormon economic experience was, "to use the words of Thomas O'Dea, a heightening, a more explicit formulation, and a summation of American experience generally."

2651. Conference on Research in Income and Wealth. Trends in the American economy in the nineteenth century. A report of the National Bureau of Economic Research, New York. Princeton, Princeton University Press, 1960. 780 p. illus. (*Its* Studies in income and wealth, v. 24)

        60–6680  HC106.3.C714 vol. 24

"Contains most of the papers presented at the joint sessions of the Economic History Association and the Conference on Research in Income and Wealth held in Williamstown, Massachusetts, in September 1957."

Includes bibliographical references.

Statistical studies of such economic magnitudes as balance of payments, commodity output, and investment and income components. Each author attempts to use existing statistics as the basis for a comprehensive estimate of his particular subject. The overall effort is experimental, and the findings are tentative, but in his introduction to the volume, William N. Parker concludes that utilizing national income as the framework for the studies "appears to give a certain form to economic statistics and suggests a certain discipline and direction to further quantitative work."

2652. Dorfman, Joseph. The economic mind in American civilization. New York, Viking, 1946–59. 5 v.      45–11318  HB119.A2D6

"Bibliographic notes" at the end of each volume.

CONTENTS.—v. 1–2. 1606–1865.—v. 3. 1865–1918.—v. 4–5. 1918–1933.

Volumes 4 and 5 conclude this series, of which the first three volumes are no. 5876 in the 1960 *Guide.* In examining economic development as influenced by sociology, philosophy, psychology, industrial management, and public policy, the author emphasizes the works of professional economists but does not neglect others who made contributions to economic thought. He also includes brief references to the influence of foreign economists. One theorist whose views he discusses is John M. Clark, author of *Economic Institutions and Human Welfare* (New York, Knopf, 1957. 285 p.), a collection of essays dealing with community factors underlying freedom of choice and individual liberty. In *Founders of American Economic Thought and Policy* (New York, Bookman Associates [1958] 442 p.), Virgle Glenn Wilhite discusses the doc-

trines of such representative thinkers as William Douglass, Hugh Vance, Pelatiah Webster, Tench Coxe, Alexander Hamilton, Benjamin Franklin, John Taylor, and Albert Gallatin and shows how their ideas have shaped the course of American life. *The Rise of American Economic Thought* (Philadelphia, Chilton [1960] 202 p.), edited by Henry W. Spiegel, is a combined sourcebook and interpretive study that begins with the Puritans and ends with the late 19th-century economists.

2653. The Economic history of the United States. New York, Rinehart [1945–62] 8 v.

        45–7376  HC103.E25

In this cooperative series to be completed in 10 volumes, five of which are listed in no. 5877 in the 1960 *Guide,* three additional volumes have been published: *The Emergence of a National Economy, 1775–1815* (v. 2, 1962. 424 p.), by Curtis P. Nettels, *The Farmer's Age; Agriculture, 1815–1860* (v. 3, 1960. 460 p.), by Paul W. Gates, and *Industry Comes of Age; Business, Labor, and Public Policy, 1860–1897* (v. 6, 1961. 445 p.), by Edward C. Kirkland. Harold U. Faulkner's standard one-volume college text, *American Economic History,* 8th ed. (New York, Harper [1960] 816 p. Harper's historical series) is an updated version of a work mentioned in the annotation for no. 5877 in the 1960 *Guide.*

2654. Hickman, Bert G. Growth and stability of the postwar economy. Washington, Brookings Institution [1960] 426 p.

        60–53654  HC106.5.H48

Bibliographical footnotes.

Comparing the period from 1945 to 1958 with the 1920's, the author examines the business cycles of the postwar period, the importance of the abnormal disturbances caused by war and cold war, and the extent to which postwar developments were affected by structural changes in the economy. He also analyzes current conditions and offers predictions for the future. Simon S. Kuznets, in *Postwar Economic Growth* (Cambridge, Belknap Press of Harvard University Press, 1964. 148 p.), seeks to determine whether economic growth can be achieved without domestic and international conflicts and erosions of personal liberty. *Postwar Economic Trends in the United States* (New York, Harper [1960] 384 p. Massachusetts Institute of Technology. Center for International Studies. American project series), a collection of essays edited by Ralph E. Freeman, covers such subjects as the evolution of the economy, changes in specific industries, international economic relations, income distribution, and analyses of fiscal, monetary, financial, and labor policies. In *The U.S. Economy in the 1950's*

(New York, Norton [1963] 308 p.), Harold G. Vatter places the history of the decade in the context of longrun economic growth.

2655. Kelso, Louis O., *and* Mortimer J. Adler. The capitalist manifesto. New York, Random House [1958] 265 p. 58–5268 HB501.K43

Kelso worked for a decade to devise a new statement of capitalistic economics, while Adler searched for an economic formulation to sustain his concept of a sound political democracy. In this volume they collaborate in advocating a positive capitalistic program and rebutting partisans of the welfare state. They reexamine the nature of private property, production, distribution, economic freedom, and economic democracy. In *The Roots of Capitalism,* rev. ed. (Princeton, N.J., Van Nostrand [1965] 222 p.), John Chamberlain exhibits a deep faith in free enterprise and its attendant benefits as he surveys capitalistic systems from the 18th century to the present.

2656. Resources for the Future. Energy in the American economy, 1850–1975; an economic study of its history and prospects, by Sam H. Schurr and Bruce C. Netschert, with Vera F. Eliasberg, Joseph Lerner [and] Hans H. Landsberg. Baltimore, Johns Hopkins Press [1960] xxii, 774 p. illus. 60–14304 HD9545.R45

Bibliographical footnotes.

The annual per capita consumption of energy in the United States in the 1950's was about six times the world average. The authors believe that the high demands of the economy in 1975 can be met if appropriate actions are taken. Their purpose here, however, is neither to forecast nor to guide; rather, they seek to provide a large body of basic information which will be helpful to those responsible for reaching policy decisions.

2657. Robertson, Ross M. History of the American economy. 2d ed. New York, Harcourt, Brace & World [1964] 630 p. illus. 64–15591 HC103.R58 1964

Bibliography: p. 661–677.

An introductory textbook by a professor of economics at the University of Indiana. The author traces and explains changes in economic institutions, analyzes economic growth, and tests propositions of economic theory. He concludes that although in the past the American market system has performed the function of allocating basic resources with a high degree of efficiency, in the future increased government intervention will be necessary. *American Economic History* (New York, McGraw-Hill, 1961. 560 p.), edited by Seymour E. Harris, is an anthology of articles relating the past to the present. *The Economic Growth of the United States, 1790–1860* (Englewood Cliffs, N.J., Prentice-Hall, 1961. 304 p.), by Douglass C. North, reveals the relationship between growth and the evolution of a market economy in which the behavior of prices of goods, services, and productive factors was the major element in any explanation of economic change. In *The Roots of American Economic Growth, 1607–1861; an Essay in Social Causation* (New York, Harper & Row [1965] 234 p.), Stuart W. Bruchey finds the origins of American industrialism to be in "community will and acts of government, the structure of society and its values, knowledge and education, attitudes toward technological change, the actions of private investors, and the effects of widening markets."

# B. Other General Works

2658. Berle, Adolf A. The American economic republic. New York, Harcourt, Brace & World [1965] xxi, 247 p. (A Harvest book, HB83) 65–7509 HB119.A2B4 1965

Bibliographical references included in "Notes" (p. 219–238).

An outline of the theory and practice of the American economic system and the role of government in the economy. The author deals successively with theory, organization and structure, and underlying social values. He strongly discounts economic determinism. "Morals, culture, education, and their development and expansion," he maintains, "are not the product of an economic system. They are the motives, the drawing power, and the causes of its being." The same author's *Power Without Property* (New York, Harcourt, Brace [1959] 184 p.) explores a relatively new trend in American corporate organization—the separation of ownership from control. In *Challenge to Affluence,* rev. and expanded ed. (New York, Vintage Books [1965] 183 p.), Gunnar Myrdal proposes reforms for the American economic system.

2659. Edwards, Edgar O., *ed.* The Nation's economic objectives. [Chicago] Published for

William Marsh Rice University by University of Chicago Press [1964] 167 p. (Rice University semicentennial publications)

64–15816  HC106.5.E39

Bibliographical footnotes.

Eight previously unpublished essays by well-known economists appraising economic objectives, their origins and evolution, and the conditions necessary for their fulfillment. The authors deal with such national goals as full employment, stability, international cooperation, social and economic security, and economic freedom, and draw comparisons between the United States and other countries. Sumner H. Slichter's *Potentials of the American Economy; Selected Essays* (Cambridge, Harvard University Press, 1961. 467 p. Wertheim publications in industrial relations), edited by John T. Dunlop, reflects the major fields of interest and the persistently optimistic views of a leading American economist (1892–1959).

2660.  Fainsod, Merle, Lincoln Gordon, *and* Joseph C. Palamountain.  Government and the American economy. 3d ed. New York, Norton [1959] 996 p.  59–6084  HD3616.U47F3  1959
"Selected readings": p. 929–949.

An updated edition of no. 5885 in the 1960 *Guide*. A textbook with a slightly different emphasis is *Business, Government and Public Policy* (Princeton, N.J., Van Nostrand [°1964] 461 p. Van Nostrand series in business administration and economics), by Asher Isaacs and Reuben E. Slesinger.

2661.  Fishman, Betty G., *and* Leo Fishman.  The American economy.  Princeton, N.J., Van Nostrand [1962] 822 p. (Van Nostrand series in business administration and economics)

62–4085  HB171.5.F56

A textbook for introductory courses at the college level, in which the authors concentrate on topics viewed as likely to be most relevant to the everyday life of the student after he leaves college.

2662.  Tennessee Valley Authority.  TVA: the first twenty years; a staff report.  Edited by Roscoe C. Martin. [University, Ala.] University of Alabama Press, 1956. 282 p. illus.

56–13072  HN79.A135A54

Essays analyzing the Tennessee Valley Authority's legal foundations, general objectives, and worldwide influence. Together, they summarize what has been accomplished in flood control—the main reason for the agency's establishment—as well as in such areas as fertilizer research, reforestation, farm cooperatives, malaria and stream pollution control, and the development of recreational resources. Because of its achievements, the TVA project has been visited and studied by representatives of many underdeveloped countries interested in techniques of regional development.

## C. Industry: General

2663.  Adams, Walter, *ed.*  The structure of American industry; some case studies. 3d ed. New York, Macmillan [1961] 603 p.

61–5944  HC106.A34  1961

Suggested readings at the ends of chapters.

An updated edition of no. 5901 in the 1960 *Guide*. Alfred D. Chandler's *Strategy and Structure: Chapters in the History of the Industrial Enterprise* (Cambridge, M.I.T. Press, 1962. 463 p. M.I.T. Press research monographs) reveals the evolution of industrial organization citing four corporations —General Motors, Standard Oil of New Jersey, Du Pont, and Sears, Roebuck—which pioneered in adopting new structures to meet changing needs. In *The Great Organizers* (New York, McGraw-Hill, 1960. 277 p.), Ernest Dale reexamines some of the foundations of organization theory by analyz-ing the work of several men who played leading roles in organizing such companies as Du Pont, General Motors, and Westinghouse.

2664.  Glover, John G., *and* Rudolph L. Lagai, *eds.*  The development of American industries, their economic significance. 4th ed. New York, Simmons-Boardman [1959] 835 p.

59–7035  HC103.G5  1959

An updated edition of no. 5906 in the 1960 *Guide*. Wolfgang P. Strassmann's *Risk and Technological Innovation; American Manufacturing Methods During the Nineteenth Century* (Ithaca, N.Y., Cornell University Press [1959] 249 p.) is concerned with the interaction of two social forces—business enterprise and technological change—which produced the industrial revolution.

# D. Industry: Special

2665. Belden, Thomas G., *and* Marva R. Belden. The lengthening shadow; the life of Thomas J. Watson. Boston, Little, Brown [1962] 332 p.

61–8065    HD9999.B94I52

"A note on the sources": p. [319] "Selected bibliography": p. [321]–[327]

Watson (1874-1956), founder and president of IBM, started as a bookkeeper at $6 a week in Painted Post, N.Y., after a year at a business college. Following a stormy career with the National Cash Register Company, he joined a small firm in a shaky financial condition, the Computing-Tabulating-Recording Company, of which he became president. Changing the company name in 1924 to International Business Machines, he emphasized the importance of the individual, internationalism, faith in democracy and capitalism, and the family spirit in business. Successfully opposing labor unions, he advocated loyalty to the company. IBM prospered during the New Deal years and especially during World War II. Watson's personal assets reached nearly a hundred million dollars. "World Peace through World Trade" summarized his philosophy and became the slogan of IBM and the International Chamber of Commerce, of which he served as president.

2666. Kogan, Herman. The long white line; the story of Abbott Laboratories. New York, Random House [1963] 309 p. illus.

63–19530    RS68.A2K6

Bibliography: p. 293–295.

Wallace C. Abbott (1857–1921) was a Vermont farm boy who belatedly completed his education and obtained his M.D. degree from the University of Michigan at the age of 28. The next year he bought a firm consisting of a medical practice and a drugstore in Ravenswood, then a suburb of Chicago. Here he embarked on the manufacture of "dosimetric granules," each containing a precise quantity of an active drug within a sugar coating. By 1894 his business had grown into the Abbott Alkaloidal Company with its own publishing house and magazine. In 1914 the name was changed to Abbott Laboratories. After World War I the firm was in a position to build a new 26-acre plant in North Chicago and to absorb other drug manufacturers in Philadelphia, St. Louis, and Indianapolis. Recent products include Sucaryl for dieters and such antibiotics as Erythrocin and Spontin.

*The Chemical Industry: Viewpoints and Perspectives* (New York, Interscience [°1963] 426 p.), edited by Conrad Berenson, presents 47 selections dealing with the commercial activities of the chemical process industries.

2667. Leeston, Alfred M., John A. Crichton, *and* John C. Jacobs. The dynamic natural gas industry; the description of an American industry from the historical, technical, legal, financial, and economic standpoints. Norman, University of Oklahoma Press [1963] 464 p. illus.

62–16486    TP723.L37

Bibliography: p. 424–450.

The natural gas industry began in this country in the village of Fredonia, N.Y., where the first well was completed in 1821. Although natural gas had been discovered and employed for fuel in the Orient many centuries before, it first became a primary source of energy in the United States. The principal producers in the early stages were the Eastern States, with the Pittsburgh area of western Pennsylvania leading in the production and consumption of natural gas in 1885. Today the Southwest is the Nation's chief source of supply. The authors describe the gas industry "as it is, rather than as it ought to be." Their basic economic position is that "the most important factor in the growth of the natural gas industry is the freedom of the markets in which this industry operates." Another major fuel-supplying industry is the subject of Carroll L. Christenson's *Economic Redevelopment in Bituminous Coal; the Special Case of Technological Advance in United States Coal Mines, 1930–1960* (Cambridge, Harvard University Press, 1962. 312 p. Wertheim publications in industrial relations).

2668. McDonald, Forrest. Insull. [Chicago] University of Chicago Press [1962] 350 p.

62–18110    CT275.I6M3

Bibliographical footnotes.

Samuel Insull (1859–1938), beginning his career as Thomas A. Edison's private secretary, became "America's most powerful businessman of the twenties—and its most publicized businessman villain in the early thirties." Arriving in 1881 from London at the inception of the electrical industry, Insull assumed charge of Edison's business ventures. He initiated the centralized electric business, organized the Edison General Electric Company, and worked out a system of product distribution which much of American industry copied. David G. Loth's *Swope of G.E.* (New York, Simon & Schuster, 1958. 309 p.) is the biography of Gerard Swope (1872–1957), who, as president of General Electric, initiated the proposals of unemployment insurance and social security which influenced the New Deal. *The Economics of the Electrical Machinery Industry* ([New York] New York University Press, 1962. 374 p.), by Jules Backman, is a study of the fourth-largest industry in the United States.

2669. Riley, John J. A history of the American soft drink industry; bottled carbonated beverages, 1807–1957. Washington, American Bottlers of Carbonated Beverages, 1958. 302 p. illus.
        58–49342  HD9348.U52R49
Bibliographical references included in "Supplementary notes to the chapters" (p. [219]–240).
PARTIAL CONTENTS.—pt. 1. The evolution of the American flavored soft drink, and of the terminology.—pt. 2. The European development of simulated effervescent waters during the early 1800's.—pt. 3. The early development of the flavored carbonated beverage in America, 1807–1900.—pt. 4. The American industry in the twentieth century and its commercial development, 1900–1957.—pt. 5. The American industry in the twentieth century and its mechanical development, 1900–1957.—pt. 6. The literature, trade press, and industry associations.—pt. 7. Chronology of industry background and development: 1807–1957. *The Big Drink; the Story of Coca-Cola* (New York, Random House [1960] 174 p.), by Ely J. Kahn, is an account of an American soft drink which can be found almost anywhere in the world today. In *Cornflake Crusade* (New York, Rinehart [1957] 305 p.) Gerald Carson views the American cereal industry as a direct offspring of the 19th-century Seventh-day Adventist religious movement.

2670. Temin, Peter. Iron and steel in nineteenth-century America, an economic inquiry. Cambridge, M.I.T. Press, Massachusetts Institute of Technology [1964] 304 p. (M.I.T. monographs in economics)    64–22211  HD9515.T4
    Bibliography: p. 286–297.
From 1830 to 1900 the production of rails and the use of the Bessemer converter were the influences which determined the direction of the development of the iron and steel industry. The author's inquiry concerns the interaction of these two influences with gradual and cumulative processes that typify much of the industrialization of the 19th century and that demonstrate the increasing sophistication in the use of heat and the growing demand for iron and steel. In his analysis, Temin concentrates on three variables: quantity and composition of production, methods of production, and the nature of the firms in the industry.

2671. Williamson, Harold F., *and others*. The American petroleum industry. Evanston [Ill.] Northwestern University Press [1959–63] 2 v. illus.    59–12043  HD9565.W5
    Bibliographical references included in "Endnotes."
CONTENTS.—v. 1. The age of illumination, 1859–1899.—v. 2. The age of energy, 1899–1959.
The first volume "traces the story of American petroleum, from its inception as the medicinal by-product of salt well operations through the peak of its subsequent development as a source of illumination for a large portion of the world's population"; the second "is an account of the transformation of the industry from its primary role as a producer of illuminants to its current status as a major supplier of energy." *Enterprise in Oil; a History of Shell in the United States* (New York, Appleton-Century-Crofts, 1957. 815 p.), by Kendall Beaton; *History of Humble Oil & Refining Company; a Study in Industrial Growth* (New York, Harper [ᶜ1959] 769 p.), by Henrietta M. Larson and Kenneth W. Porter; and *Formative Years in the Far West; a History of Standard Oil Company of California and Predecessors Through 1919* (New York, Appleton-Century-Crofts [1962] 694 p.), by Gerald T. White, portray the development of individual oil companies.

# E. Transportation: General

2672. Pegrum, Dudley F. Transportation: economics and public policy. Homewood, Ill. R. D. Irwin, 1963. 625 p. illus. (The Irwin series in economics)    63–8442  HE206.P4

"Selected references for further reading": p. 601–610.
The author reviews the historical development of transportation systems, discusses transportation as

an economic activity, delineates its place in the American economy, explains the basic economic principles which bear on transportation, applies them to an analysis of the present structure, traces the development of regulation, describes national transportation policy, and suggests solutions to the basic problems of transportation in large metropolitan areas. *Issues in Transportation Economics* (Columbus, Ohio, C. E. Merrill Books [1965] 349 p.), edited by Karl M. Ruppenthal, is devoted entirely to current problems in the field.

# F. Transportation: Special

2673. Carr, Albert H. Z. John D. Rockefeller's secret weapon. New York, McGraw-Hill [1962] 383 p.          62–10598 CT275.R75C3
Bibliography: p. 361–368.

The first and crucial element of Rockefeller's ascendancy in the oil industry was his deft manipulation of his "secret weapon," the tank car. He utilized the Union Tank Car Company to give the Standard Oil Company a commanding lead over independent refiners, who had to ship oil in costly barrels. Although the Union Tank Car Company became less dominant in the industry after World War I, it experienced a renascence in the late 1950's. In *The Development of American Petroleum Pipelines; a Study in Private Enterprise and Public Policy, 1862–1906* (Ithaca, N.Y., Published for the American Historical Association [by] Cornell University Press [1956] 307 p.), Arthur M. Johnson indicates the importance of the role of pipelines in the formative period of the petroleum industry.

2674. Caves, Richard E. Air transport and its regulators; an industry study. Cambridge, Harvard University Press, 1962. 479 p. illus. (Harvard economic studies, v. 120)
          62–17216 TL521.C39
Bibliography: p. [453]–469.

An analysis of the operations of domestic passenger airlines in the United States and of their regulation by the Civil Aeronautics Board under the authority of the Civil Aeronautics Act of 1938. The author outlines the major economic elements of the air transport industry's market structure, examines the policies of the Civil Aeronautics Board, describes the airlines' patterns of market conduct, assesses the industry's efficiency, and suggests changes in the Civil Aeronautics Board's policies that might improve the airlines' performance.

2675. Cranmer, Horace Jerome. New Jersey in the automobile age; a history of transportation. Princeton, N.J., Van Nostrand, 1964. 139 p. illus. (The New Jersey historical series, v. 23)
          65–293 HE213.N5C7
"Bibliographical note": p. 129–131.

"The history of America in the nineteenth century may be told in terms of the impact of transportation innovations on a predominantly agricultural economy. The advent of turnpikes, canals, steamboats, and above all, railroads worked a tremendous transformation. The essence of this transformation lay in so drastically reducing transport costs as to create a single nation-wide market within which all producers could compete." The author stresses the importance of government planning and regulation in the development of ports and harbors; in the building of highways, tunnels, bridges, and airports; and in the operation of railroads and pipelines. He asserts that the solution to New Jersey's transportation problem lies in mass transit rather than in the expansion of highway, river crossing, and parking facilities. "Diversion of freight traffic from over-crowded roads to under-utilized rails would provide the least expensive solution to New Jersey's transportation problem in the automobile age."

2676. Cutler, Carl C. Queens of the western ocean; the story of America's mail and passenger sailing lines. With a foreword by Chester W. Nimitz. Annapolis, U.S. Naval Institute [1961] xxi, 672 p. illus. 61–11247 HE745.C8
Bibliographical references included in "Notes" (p. 360–367).

The establishment of the Black Ball Line's first regularly scheduled sailings in 1818 marked the beginning of an era of travel for culture and pleasure. In the following 40-year period, mail and passenger ships improved greatly in quality and comfort. This history spans the period from 1607 to 1860, after which steamboats largely displaced sailing ships. The author admires the sailing vessels and their crews and considers their disappearance a distinct loss. Six appendixes, totaling more than 200 pages, offer details about American sailing vessels, their tonnages, owners, captains, and eventual fates. In *Seaports South of Sahara; the Achievements of an American Steamship Service* (New York, Appleton-Century-Crofts [1959] 316 p.), Robert G. Albion focuses on the Farrell Lines in tracing the evolution of the United States-African trade and describing American maritime policy since 1914. In *United States Shipping Policy* (New York, Published for the Council on Foreign Relations by Harper, 1956. 230 p. Publications of the Council on Foreign Relations), Wytze Gorter argues that Government policies toward shipping need extensive revision.

2677. Goodrich, Carter. Government promotion of American canals and railroads, 1800–1890. New York, Columbia University Press, 1960. 382 p. map.                     60–6546  HE1051.G6
Bibliography: p. [353]–364.

Public promotion of internal improvements was a national phenomenon throughout the 19th century and played a role in the development of every part of the Union. The author concentrates on the controversial issues of competition and cooperation between government and business in the creation of canals and railroads. He is also the editor of a later work, *Canals and American Economic Development* (New York, Columbia University Press, 1961. 303 p.), which emphasizes the Erie Canal, the Pennsylvania Mainline, and the New Jersey Canals. *The Long Haul West; the Great Canal Era, 1817–1850* (New York, Putnam [1958] 320 p.), by Madeline S. Waggoner, is a colorful description of the canal era and especially of the planning, financing, building, and operation of the Erie Canal.

2678. Hilton, George W., *and* John F. Due. The electric interurban railways in America. Stanford, Calif., Stanford University Press, 1960. 463. p. illus.                     60–5383  HE4451.H55
Bibliographical references included in "Notes" (p. [427]–436) "Bibliographical note": p. [437]

"The electric interurban railway played a major but short-lived role in the development of intercity passenger transport. Basically, it provided a transitional step from almost sole reliance upon the steam railroad to an almost equally complete dependence on the automobile." The rapid growth of the interurbans took place between 1901 and 1918. By 1918 a decline set in, and the industry was virtually annihilated by the decade of the Great Depression. Since the interurbans never experienced a period of prolonged prosperity, their abandonment was finally brought about by the need for increased capital expenditures for repairs and replacements and for the payment of major damage claims. This study offers a general history of the industry and capsule histories of individual lines. *The Interurban Era* ([Milwaukee] Kalmbach [1961] 432 p.), by William D. Middleton, is a pictorial history of the industry.

2679. McCague, James. Moguls and iron men; the story of the first transcontinental railroad. New York, Harper & Row [1964] 392 p. illus.                     64–18061  HE2791.C455M3
Bibliography: p. 379–382.

As a financial and an engineering feat and as a symbol of national unity, the building of the transcontinental railroad was an event which stirred contemporaries deeply. The author describes this formidable enterprise, which culminated in the meeting of the Central Pacific, building eastward, and the Union Pacific, building westward. He questions the generally accepted story of the excess profits made by the Credit Mobilier, the Union Pacific's construction contractor. *A Work of Giants; Building the First Transcontinental Railroad* (New York, McGraw-Hill [1962] 367 p.), by Wesley S. Griswold, is extensively documented and contains numerous photographs. In *Burlington Route; a History of the Burlington Lines* (New York, Knopf, 1965. 623 p.), Richard C. Overton recounts the story of a 12-mile branch line that was built near Chicago in 1849 and that grew to a system of more than 8,500 miles. *Rebel of the Rockies; a History of the Denver and Rio Grande Western Railroad* (New Haven, Yale University Press, 1962. 395 p. Yale Western Americana series, [2]), by Robert G. Athearn, is a study of railroading in the Colorado Rockies.

2680. Nevins, Allan. Ford. By Allan Nevins with the collaboration of Frank Ernest Hill. New York, Scribner, 1954–[63] 3 v. illus.                     54–6305  CT275.F68N37
Bibliographical footnotes. Bibliography: v. 1, p. 653–664.
CONTENTS.—1. The times, the man, the company.—2. Expansion and challenge, 1915–1933.—[3] Decline and rebirth, 1933–1962.

The first two volumes are no. 5939 in the 1960 *Guide;* the third concludes the study. In *My Years With General Motors* (Garden City, N.Y., Doubleday, 1964 [ᶜ1963] 472 p.), Alfred P. Sloan tells of his long association with the organization as president and as chairman of the board.

2681. Rae, John B. American automobile manufacturers: the first forty years. Philadelphia, Chilton Co., Book Division [1959] 223 p.
                    59–5769  HD9710.U52R3
"Notes on sources": p. 209–212.

A study of management leadership and the way it met challenges and problems in the automobile industry. The author gives detailed information regarding the inventors of some of the early cars and the managers who formed the automobile companies which emerged as industrial giants. He considers the relationship between technological change and industrial advance in the light of the sources and availability of capital, the accessibility of materials and markets, the organization of business, and the supply of labor. Frank R. Donovan's *Wheels for a Nation* ([New York] Crowell [1965] 303 p.) reflects American enthusiasm for automobiles and reveals aspects of their influence on American life. Profusely illustrated, *Esquire's American Autos and Their Makers* ([New York, Esquire, Inc.; distributed by Harper & Row, 1963] 192 p.), by David J. Wilkie, begins with self-propelled road vehicles in 1769, brings the story to the present, and reveals designs for the future.

2682. Stover, John F. American railroads. [Chicago] University of Chicago Press [1961] 302 p. illus. (The Chicago history of American civilization)　　　　61–8081　HE2751.S7

"Suggested reading": p. 272–281.

A longtime student of railroad history, the author examines the industry's growth and development, its role in shaping the course of American history, and its decline after World War I. He concludes that a healthy railroad system is still needed and urges the public, the railroad workers and managers, and government at all levels to cooperate in re-creating and maintaining it. *Great Railroad Photographs, U.S.A.* (Berkeley, Calif., Howell-North Books, 1964. 243 p.), by Lucius M. Beebe and Charles Clegg, recalls the romance of the steam age. In *Transcontinental Railway Strategy, 1869–1893* (Philadelphia, University of Pennsylvania Press [1962] 443 p.), Julius Grodinsky describes the struggle for control of the limited natural facilities and capital funds for the risky business of providing pioneer railroad transportation.

2683. Taff, Charles A. Commercial motor transportation. 3d ed. Homewood, Ill., R. D. Irwin, 1961. 701 p. illus.
　　　　61–12901　HE5623.T3　1961
Bibliography: p. 677–688.
An updated edition of no. 5942 in the 1960 *Guide*.

## G. Commerce: General

2684. Converse, Paul D., Harvey W. Huegy, *and* Robert V. Mitchell. Elements of marketing. 7th ed. Englewood Cliffs, N.J., Prentice-Hall [1965] xv, 710 p. 65–10330 HF5415.C55 1965
Bibliographical foontotes.
An updated edition of no. 5945 in the 1960 *Guide*.

2685. Fortune. Marketing: change and exchange; readings from Fortune. Edited by H. C. Barksdale. New York, Holt, Rinehart & Winston [1964] 322 p. illus.　64–19809　HF5415.F567
These articles "describe and define the dramatic changes that are taking place in markets and products. They also report the adjustments being made in marketing institutions and distribution processes to adapt to new conditions. Together

they present a picture of marketing—change and exchange—in four dimensions: markets, products, institutions, and processes." In *The Distribution Revolution* (New York, I. Washburn [1960] 150 p.), Walter Hoving maintains that the field of distribution rather than that of production offers the most promising source of solutions to the economic problems of the world.

2686. Richert, Gottlieb Henry, Warren G. Meyer, *and* Peter G. Haines. Retailing; principles and practices. 4th ed. New York, Gregg Pub. Division, McGraw-Hill [1962] 504 p. illus.
　　　　61–10138　HF5429.R52　1962
An updated edition of no. 5949 in the 1960 *Guide*.

# H. Commerce: Special

2687. Britt, Steuart H. The spenders. New York, McGraw-Hill, 1960. 293 p. (McGraw-Hill series in marketing and advertising)

60–14994  HC110.C6B7

"Some suggested readings": p. 267–271.

A psychologist as well as a professor of marketing and advertising, the author views American business as the servant of the American consumer. He outlines the motives, wants, and needs of the typical consumer, his opportunities for spending his money and leisure, and the way in which he spends them. Brand images, packaging, advertising, and pricing are shown to affect the success or failure of products. Britt also investigates the present use and possible future applications of marketing and motivation research. In *The Waste Makers* (New York, D. McKay [1960] 340 p.), Vance O. Packard demonstrates how waste and consumption have become virtues in American society. He is especially critical of industry's shoddy construction of furniture; the planned obsolescence of cars, electrical appliances, and other products; and the consequent depletion of natural resources. *The Consumer in Our Economy* (Boston, Houghton Mifflin [1962] 473 p.), by David B. Hamilton, is a textbook that applies the tools of sociology and anthropology along with those of economics.

2688. Fuller, Alfred C. A foot in the door; the life appraisal of the original Fuller brush man [by] Alfred C. Fuller as told to Hartzell Spence. New York, McGraw-Hill [1960] 250 p. illus.

60–14996  HD9999.B865F84

The autobiography of a poor farm boy who founded the Fuller Brush Company, one of the largest enterprises of its kind in the world. A modest man and a devout Christion Scientist, the author attributes his success to the unfailing guidance of God. Imbued with an idealistic and dedicated spirit, he considers himself to have been "a benefactor to the housewives, a crusader against unsanitary kitchens and inadequately cleaned homes." He listened to suggestions for improvements from his customers and manufactured his wares accordingly. *The Charles Ilfeld Company; a Study of the Rise and Decline of Mercantile Capitalism in New Mexico* (Cambridge, Harvard University Press, 1961. 431 p. Harvard studies in business history, 20), by William J. Parish, is a history of a mercantile firm which operated in the Southwest for almost a century, exemplifying the contribution of businessmen in building and maintaining the economic life of a region. In *Bergdorf's on the Plaza; the Story of Bergdorf Goodman and a Half-Century of American Fashion* (New York, Knopf, 1956. 244 p.), Booton Herndon traces simultaneously the rise of Edwin Goodman from a modest tailor to an international fashion authority and the history of a store representing 50 years of good taste in women's fashions.

2689. Humphrey, Don D. The United States and the Common Market; a background study. New York, Praeger [1962] 176 p. (Books that matter)

62–18585  HF1455.H83

Bibliographical footnotes.

An examination of the United States tariff and trade program from the time of the Trade Agreements Act of 1934 to the trade expansion bill proposed by President Kennedy in 1962 and enacted into law. The author argues strongly in favor of tariff reduction and trade expansion as the chief devices for stimulating competition and economic growth in this country. *American Business and Public Policy; the Politics of Foreign Trade* (New York, Atherton Press, 1963. 499 p. The Atherton Press political science series), by Raymond A. Bauer, Ithiel de Sola Pool, and Lewis A. Dexter, covers the extensions of the Trade Agreements Act under Presidents Eisenhower and Kennedy. In *Raw Materials; a Study of American Policy* (New York, Published for the Council on Foreign Relations by Harper, 1958. 403 p.), Percy W. Bidwell recounts the postwar efforts of producers in the United States to protect themselves from foreign competition. In *The European Community and American Trade; a Study in Atlantic Economics and Policy* (New York, Published for the Council on Foreign Relations by Praeger [1965, °1964] 188 p.), Randall W. Hinshaw views the Common Market and related developments in Europe from the American standpoint.

2690. Lebhar, Godfrey M. Chain stores in America, 1859–1962. 3d ed. New York, Chain Store Pub. Corp. [1963] 430 p. illus.

63–2856  HF5468.L332  1963

Bibliographical footnotes.

An updated edition of no. 5961 in the 1960 *Guide*. In *A History of the Department Store* (New York, Macmillan, 1960. 387 p.), John W. Ferry states that the improved economic conditions of the last century, the entrance of women into the labor market, and the expansion of transportation facilities have provided impetus for the department store. The United States and the British Commonwealth are regarded as having set the world pattern. *And the Price is Right* (Cleveland, World Pub. Co. [1958] 318 p.), by Margaret C. Harriman, is a humorous account of the first hundred years of R. H. Macy and Company, one of the largest and best known department stores in the world.

2691. Pares, Richard. Yankees and Creoles; the trade between North America and the West Indies before the American Revolution. London, New York, Longmans, Green [1956] 168 p. illus.
56–1249    HF3074.P3
Bibliographical footnotes.

Without the trade which was carried on before the American Revolution between North America and the West Indies, "the sugar colonies could not have existed and the North American colonies could not have developed." The author's objective is "to throw some new light on the people who conducted this trade, the purposes for which they conducted it, and the methods by which they did so." In *The Maritime Commerce of Colonial Philadelphia* (Madison, State Historical Society of Wisconsin for the Dept. of History, University of Wisconsin, 1963. 312 p.), Arthur L. Jensen concludes that the pre-Revolutionary period "saw most Philadelphia merchants trying to walk gingerly on a thin line between abject submission to British policies which they considered unwise and unjust and support of measures of opposition which they feared could lead only to bloodshed, separation from the mother country, and eventual economic ruin." Robert A. Davison's *Isaac Hicks; New York Merchant and Quaker, 1767–1820* (Cambridge, Harvard University Press, 1964. 217 p. Harvard studies in business history, 22) is the story of a businessman whose loyalty to Quaker values was no handicap to financial success.

2692. Phillips, Paul C. The fur trade. With concluding chapters by J. W. Smurr. Norman, University of Oklahoma Press [1961] 2 v. illus.           61–6499   HD9944.A2P47
Bibliography: v. 2, p. 577–656.

A study of the vast economic and geographical extent of the fur trade from the 16th century onward, of its effect on business and politics in the Western Hemisphere, Europe, and Asia, and of the international problems arising from it. "Rivalries for the fur trade produced many diplomatic crises, and there were indications that furs were important in the economic and political imperialism that guided much of the colonization of North America." The author, who was working on the book's concluding chapters at the time of his death in 1956, interprets the roles of John Jacob Astor and other major figures and describes the operations of fur companies, trading organizations, and trappers. In *A Majority of Scoundrels; an Informal History of the Rocky Mountain Fur Company* (New York, Harper [1961] 432 p.) Don Berry describes a fur company which became a legend, although it was short lived and never produced large profits.

2693. Sandage, Charles H., *and* Vernon R. Fryburger. Advertising: theory and practice. 6th ed. Homewood, Ill., R. D. Irwin, 1963. 663 p. illus.           63–16893   HF5823.S25  1963
Bibliographical footnotes.

An updated edition of no. 5962 in the 1960 *Guide*. In *The Responsibilities of American Advertising; Private Control and Public Influence, 1920–1940* (New Haven, Yale University Press, 1958. 232 p. Yale publications in American studies, 2), Otis A. Pease analyzes the extent to which concepts of public responsibility existed in national advertising in newspapers and magazines for a 20-year period. In *The Story of Advertising* (New York, Ronald Press [1958] 512 p.), James P. Wood traces the long and varied history of advertising from its origins with the simple street criers of ancient Greece and Rome to the modern and complex business it is today. *The Golden Fleece; Selling the Good Life to Americans* (New York, Macmillan [1963] 305 p.) is a critical examination of the advertising business by Joseph J. Seldin, owner of an agency.

# I. Finance: General

2694. Chandler, Lester V. The economics of money and banking. 4th ed. New York, Harper & Row [1964] xiv, 606 p. illus.
64–12793 HG221.C448 1964
Selected readings at the ends of chapters.

An updated edition of no. 5975 in the 1960 *Guide.* In *Money, Banking, and Economic Welfare* (New York, McGraw-Hill, 1960. 578 p.), Paul B. Trescott offers an analysis intended in part to serve as a guide for future monetary and financial policies. *The Management of Money; a Survey of American Experience* (Chicago, Rand McNally [1964] 422 p. Rand McNally economics series), by Harold Barger, emphasizes the period from 1913, when the Federal Reserve System was established, to the present.

2695. Guthmann, Harry G., *and* Herbert E. Dougall. Corporate financial policy. 4th ed. Englewood Cliffs, N.J., Prentice-Hall, 1962. 776 p. illus. 62–18830 HG4011.G85 1962
"Selected reference list": p. 693–747.

An updated edition of no. 5967 in the 1960 *Guide.*

2696. Hansen, Alvin H. Business cycles and national income. Expanded ed. With a revised bibliography by Richard V. Clemence. New York, Norton [1964] xx, 721 p. illus.
63–21708 HB3711.H312 1964
Bibliography: p. 699–710.

The author, an advocate of Keynesian economics with its emphasis on investment as the strategic element in business, brings together from his previous writings his most important ideas on business cycles, national income, and proposed policies for avoiding cyclical fluctuations. In *Capital in the American Economy* (Princeton, N.J., Princeton University Press, 1961. 664 p. National Bureau of Economic Research. Studies in capital formation and financing, 9), Simon S. Kuznets examines long term trends in capital formation (since 1870) and in financing (since 1900). In *The National Wealth of the United States in the Postwar Period* (Princeton, [N.J.] Princeton University Press, 1962. 434 p. National Bureau of Economic Research. Studies in capital formation and financing, 10), Raymond W. Goldsmith estimates the national wealth in the period from 1945 through 1958 and offers his findings in annotated, summarized tables.

2697. Sharp, Ansel M., *and* Bernard F. Sliger. Public finance; an introduction to the study of the public economy. Homewood, Ill., Dorsey Press, 1964. 411 p. illus. (The Dorsey series in economics) 64–11715 HJ257.S47
Bibliographies at the ends of chapters.

"The study of economics is the study of man making decisions in a world where there is a scarcity of resources relative to human wants." This general textbook surveys governmental decision-making in regard to scarce resources. The author inquires into the "facts, techniques, principles, theories, rules, and policies" related to taxing, borrowing, and spending, which are viewed as "the operations of government pertaining to the use of scarce resources." In *Federal Lending and Economic Stability* (Washington, Brookings Institution [1965] 185 p.), George F. Break explores the economic consequences of direct lending by the Federal Government, especially the possibilities of its use to stabilize the economy.

2698. Studenski, Paul, *and* Herman E. Krooss. Financial history of the United States: fiscal, monetary, banking, and tariff, including financial administration and State and local finance. 2d ed. New York, McGraw-Hill [1963] 605 p.
62–21575 HG181.S83 1963
Bibliography: p. 489–503.

An updated edition of no. 5973 in the 1960 *Guide.* Milton Friedman and Anna J. Schwartz in *A Monetary History of the United States, 1867–1960* (Princeton, Princeton University Press, 1963. 860 p. National Bureau of Economic Research. Studies in business cycles, 12) support the quantity theory of money, which holds that the stock of money is the major determinant of economic history. The authors trace the changes in the stock of money in the United States for almost a century and analyze the reflex influences exerted on the course of events. *A History of the Dollar* (New York, Columbia University Press, 1957. 308 p.), by Arthur Nussbaum, is concerned with the political, economic, and psychological factors underlying the monetary history of the United States.

# J. Finance: Special

2699. Aubrey, Henry G. The dollar in world affairs: an essay in international financial policy. New York, Published for the Council on Foreign Relations by Harper & Row [1964] 295 p.
63–21750 HG3883.U7A85
Bibliographical references included in "Notes" (p. 264–277).

An interpretation of the relationship between the strength of the dollar in world finance and the role of the United States in world affairs. In the author's opinion, the dollar "cannot be stronger — and need not be weaker—than the purpose this country has set itself in the world, and while these tasks—toward the less developed countries, the Communist bloc, and within the Western community — are acknowledged as the West's common objectives, the dollar will serve as a common, not just a national, financial instrument." Thirteen collaborators offer their views in *The Dollar in Crisis* (New York, Harcourt, Brace & World [1961] 309 p.), edited by Seymour E. Harris.

2700. Burch, Philip H. Highway revenue and expenditure policy in the United States. New Brunswick, N.J., Rutgers University Press [1962] xiv, 315 p. illus. 62–13759 HE355.B8
Bibliography: p. 288–305.

A description and analysis of policies pursued by Federal, State, and local governments. Before 1934, highway planning in the United States was conducted on an intermittent basis. In that year Congress passed the Hayden-Cartwright Act, section 11 of which stipulated that up to 1½ percent of a State's Federal aid allotment could be used for highway planning and research. After World War II, in particular, highway planning surveys served as guides for remedying deficiences in State road networks. The author focuses primary attention on the problem of disbursement of funds, especially at the State level. He observes that each State's highway department is perhaps involved in more bitter disputes than any other State agency. Public emotion is readily aroused over questions of which roads should be built or improved first and how much money should be appropriated.

2701. De Bedts, Ralph F. The New Deal's SEC: the formative years. New York, Columbia University Press, 1964. 226 p.
64–14236 HG4556.U6D38
Bibliography: p. [207]–217.

The first Securities and Exchange Commission was appointed by President Franklin D. Roosevelt in 1934. Established to protect the investing public, the SEC became one of the most influential of the New Deal reform agencies. The author "attempts to consider not only the historical origins and antecedents of the SEC but also its growth and formative years in the light of the financial and political happenings of the times and in relationship to the many individuals involved." *A Study of Mutual Funds* (Washington, U.S. Govt. Print. Off., 1962. 595 p. 87th Congress, 2d session. House report no. 2274), prepared by the Wharton School of Finance and Commerce of the University of Pennsylvania, describes the structure of the industry, the growth of investment companies, the performance and market impact of the funds, and the relationship between the funds and their investment advisers.

2702. Edwards, James D. History of public accounting in the United States. East Lansing, Bureau of Business and Economic Research, Graduate School of Business Administration, Michigan State University [1960] 368 p. illus. (MSU business studies, 1960) 60–63369 HF5616.U5E3
Bibliography: p. 308–327.

Legal recognition was first given the profession of independent certified public accountant in 1896 in New York State, although the earliest activities of public accountants antedated the American Revolution. The American Association of Public Accountants, founded in 1886, ultimately became the American Institute of Certified Public Accountants. The author develops his narrative chronologically, beginning with the antecedents of American public accounting in England and Scotland and concluding with the recognition of the CPA as a professional who is often called upon in matters of business policy. The book is addressed especially to accountants, students entering the accounting field, and business historians.

2703. Kimmel, Lewis H. Federal budget and fiscal policy, 1789–1958. Washington, Brookings Institution [1959] 337 p.
59–9512 HJ2050.K
Bibliographical footnotes.

From 1789 to the 1930's the Federal budget was viewed chiefly in terms of money costs, and Government activities were considered a burden on the economy. The annually balanced budget was almost universally accepted as a prerequisite for financial stability and economic growth. As a consequence of the Depression of the thirties, however, a revolutionary change in theory and policy led to the concepts of pump-priming, compensatory fiscal policy, and the assumption by the Government of responsibility for economic growth and cyclical stability. Fiscal theorists today regard the budget as an instrument of economic policy. *A Primer on Government Spending* (New York, Random House [1963] 120 p.), by Robert L. Heilbroner and Peter L. Bernstein, attempts to clarify "the words that frighten us—government spending, deficit financing, the national debt, growth, inflation—in clear, vivid, and, above all, simple terms." *The American Way in Taxation: Internal Revenue, 1862–1963* (Englewood Cliffs, N.J., Prentice-Hall [1963] 301 p.), edited by Lillian Doris, is a historical survey of the Federal tax system and a recognition of the centennial of the Internal Revenue Service.

2704. Leffler, George L. The stock market. 3d ed., revised by Loring C. Farwell. New York, Ronald Press Co. [1963] 654 p. illus.
63–10640 HG4551.L35 1963
Includes bibliography.

A revised edition of no. 5982 in the 1960 *Guide*. *The Big Board: A History of the New York Stock Market* (New York, Free Press [1965] 395 p.), by Robert Sobel, concentrates on the New York Stock Exchange and the men who were central to American investment banking and brokerage. Leonard L. Levinson's *Wall Street; a Pictorial History* (New York, Ziff-Davis Pub. Co. [1961] 376 p.) is profusely illustrated with prints, photographs, and cartoons. In *Populists, Plungers, and Progressives; a Social History of Stock and Commodity Speculation, 1890–1936* (Princeton, N. J., Princeton University Press, 1965. 299 p.), Cedric B. Cowing traces the ideological opposition to stock market speculation from the efforts of the Populists to the regulatory legislation of the New Deal.

2705. Maxwell, James A. Financing State and local governments. Washington, Brookings Institution [1965] xvii, 276 p. (Brookings Institution. Studies of government finance)
65–26007 HJ275.M39
Bibliography: p. 263–265.

A nontechnical analysis to help the interested citizen understand the fiscal problems of his own State and community. The author discusses the various ways in which States and localities raise and spend their money, most of which is allotted to

education, public welfare, health, roads, hospitals, police, and sanitation; he also recommends courses of action for the future. Statistical tables are provided throughout the text and in the appendix.

2706. Mowbray, Albert H., *and* Ralph H. Blanchard. Insurance; its theory and practice in the United States. 5th ed. New York, McGraw-Hill, 1961. 617 p. (McGraw-Hill insurance series)
60–13767 HG8051.M75 1961
Bibliography: p. 591–597.

An updated edition of no. 5990 in the 1960 *Guide*. Frank J. Angell's *Insurance: Principles and Practices* (New York, Ronald Press [1959] 894 p.) is a textbook suitable for the layman as well as the college student. *The Life Insurance Enterprise, 1885–1910; a Study in the Limits of Corporate Power* (Cambridge, Belknap Press of Harvard University Press, 1963. 338 p.), by Morton Keller, is concerned with the quest for power to which the leaders of the great life insurance companies were dedicated and with the life insurance business as a social institution.

2707. Prochnow, Herbert V., *ed.* The Federal Reserve System. New York, Harper [1960] 393 p. illus.
60–6767 HG2563.P7
Suggested readings at the ends of chapters.

A collection of articles that together narrate the history of the Federal Reserve System, describe its operations, evaluate its place in the Nation's financial and business structure, analyze its impact on banks and other types of financial institutions, and explore its relationship to the economy generally. In *The Federal Reserve and the American Dollar: Problems and Policies, 1946–1964* (Chapel Hill, University of North Carolina Press [1965] 321 p.), James L. Knipe traces and evaluates American monetary management since 1946. In *Nicholas Biddle, Nationalist and Public Banker, 1786–1844* ([Chicago] University of Chicago Press [1959] 428 p.), Thomas P. Govan recounts the efforts of Biddle to influence Presidents Madison and Monroe to establish the Bank of the United States and his service as its director and president. Lester V. Chandler's *Benjamin Strong, Central Banker* (Washington, Brookings Institution [1958] 495 p.) is a biography of the Governor of the Federal Reserve Bank of New York, 1914–28, who played a strong role in shaping the Federal Reserve System in its formative years.

2708. Trescott, Paul B. Financing American enterprise; the story of commercial banking. New York, Harper & Row [1963] 304 p.
63–8006 HG2471.T7

Bibliographical references included in "Notes" (p. 283–292).

A publication commemorating the passage of the National Currency Act of 1863, which created national banking in its modern sense and encouraged the ultimate establishment of approximately 13,000 banks in the commercial banking system. The author devotes a large portion of his study to an exposition of the relation between bank credit and the evolution of the Nation's economy. He deals at length with the role of banks in the development of important firms, industries, and categories of business enterprise. Other aspects of the history of banks, such as their monetary functions and the evolution of government regulation, are also discussed.

2709. Unger, Irwin. The greenback era; a social and political history of American finance, 1865–1879. Princeton, N.J., Princeton University Press, 1964. 467 p. 63–18651 HG604.U5
Bibliography: p. 417–441.

The Civil War brought about sweeping financial changes and made problems of money and banking the subject of vital national concern. The author seeks to evaluate the neo-Populist economic theories of post bellum America. These views, notably propounded by Charles A. Beard, are essentially dualistic (capitalist versus farmer and worker, debtor versus creditor, East versus West, conservative versus radical, hard money versus soft money) and are grounded in economic determinism. Unger argues that both the dualism and the determinism are oversimplifications. He also concludes that despite the changes effected by the Civil War, much of the prewar structure of power and social prestige survived.

2710. Williamson, Jeffrey G. American growth and the balance of payments, 1820–1913; a study of the long swing. Chapel Hill, University of North Carolina Press [1964] xviii, 298 p. 64–13563 HG3883.U7W5 1964
Bibliography: p. [288]–294.

A study of the relationship between the Nation's internal growth and its balance of payments. The author examines the movements of goods, gold, and capital during a period in which "this country's domestic development was undergoing significant long waves in its pace of growth." He believes the accumulated evidence justifies the assumption of the existence of Kuznets cycles (each approximately 15 to 20 years in duration) in the Nation's domestic development, and he uses these cycles as a chronological framework in his analysis. He concludes that periods of rapid growth tended to generate dollar scarcity and that periods of sluggish growth resulted in dollar surplus. His analysis is supported by 69 tables and 37 charts.

# K. Business: General

2711. Chamberlain, John. The enterprising Americans; a business history of the United States. New York, Harper & Row [°1963] 282 p. 62–9886 HC106.C52
Bibliography: p. 265–272.

A popular narrative of the achievements of leading businessmen from the colonial period to the present. The author treats business as a primary creative force in this country's development. The genius of "busy-ness"—the innovations of inventors and technicians working with profit-seeking enterprisers—is viewed as a main factor in economic growth. Initiative combined with Old World mercantilist traditions and New World opportunities resulted in a propitious environment for the success of the American businessman. Much of this account appeared originally as a series in *Fortune* magazine. Thomas C. Cochran's *Basic History of American Business* (Princeton, N.J., Van Nostrand [1959] 191 p. An Anvil original, no. 39) is a brief survey coupled with documents relating to the many facets of business life. In *American Business Cycles, 1865–1897* (Chapel Hill, University of North Carolina Press [1959] 244 p.), Rendigs Fels, concludes that internal influences, as opposed to influences of an international character, were primarily responsible for cyclical fluctuations in the economy.

2712. Dimock, Marshall E. Business and government; issues of public policy. 4th ed. New York, Holt, Rinehart & Winston [1961] 505 p. illus. 61–7854 HD3616.U47D5 1961
Bibliographies at the ends of chapters.

An updated edition of no. 6006 in the 1960 *Guide*. Howard R. Smith's *Government and Business; a Study in Economic Evolution* (New York, Ronald Press [1958] 802 p.) chronicles "the step-by-step process through which government acquired the multitudinous responsibilities it now performs in connection with economic activities in the United States."

2713. Eells, Richard S. F. The meaning of modern business; an introduction to the philosophy of large corporate enterprise. New York, Columbia University Press, 1960. 427 p.

60–8393 HD2731.E36

Bibliographical references included in "Notes" (p. [341]–403).

A study of the corporation and its philosophy of business. The author used two models as the framework for his analysis of the nature and functions of the corporate form of enterprise: the "traditional" corporation which serves the profit motives of its stockholders and the "metrocorporation" which has broad social purposes and objectives. As the ideal form of business, he proposes the "well tempered" corporation, one "tempered to its times, and more specifically to the requirements of a pluralistic society grounded on the principles of democracy, individual liberty, and the rule of law as a safeguard to freedom."

2714. McGuire, Joseph W. Business and society. New York, McGraw-Hill [1963] 312 p.

63–13013 HF5343.M2

Includes bibliography.

Business operations play a dominant role in contemporary society and broadly affect its culture and values. The impact of business has produced an abundance that has altered the American character. The interdependence of business and government in the modern age has radically transformed the nature of the free enterprise system and tradi-tional consumer habits. Struggling with the problem of goals, values, and ethics in a business world, the author calls for a new ideology to guide businessmen in their decisionmaking. *Business Policy and Its Environment* (New York, Holt, Rinehart & Winston [1965] 368 p.), edited by Thomas Moranian, Donald Grunewald, and Richard C. Reidenbach, contains reprinted articles and lectures on the effects of social environment on the formation of business policy. *Business Enterprise in Its Social Setting* (Cambridge, Harvard University Press, 1959. 286 p.), by Arthur H. Cole, attempts "to extend a bridge between history and theory" and to bring together economic, business administration, sociology, and history as tools of analysis.

2715. Petersen, Elmore, Edward Grosvenor Plowman, *and* Joseph M. Trickett. Business organization and management. 5th ed. Homewood, Ill., R. D. Irwin, 1962. 341 p.

62–18175 HF5351.P48 1962

Bibliographies at the ends of chapters.

An updated edition of no. 6009 in the 1960 *Guide.* In *Business Management and Public Policy* (Homewood, Ill., R. D. Irwin, 1958. 402 p.), Richard N. Owens considers the problems faced by management in dealing with "stockholders, customers, management personnel, employees, labor unions, competitors, suppliers, and the general public." Hugh G. J. Aitken's *Taylorism at Watertown Arsenal; Scientific Management in Action, 1908–1915* (Cambridge, Harvard University Press, 1960. 269 p.) is a case study of the application of the Taylor system of management and its impact at the Watertown Arsenal.

# L. Business: Special

2716. Collins, Orvis F., *and* David G. Moore. The enterprising man. East Lansing, Bureau of Business and Economic Research, Graduate School of Business Administration, Michigan State University, 1964. xvii, 254 p. (MSU business studies, 1964) 64–63821 HB601.C5686

"Notes and References": p. 247–250.

A behavioral study of entrepreneurs. The authors define an entrepreneur as a man "who has developed an ongoing business activity where none existed before" and base their study on research into the origins, motivations, and patterns of behavior of successful entrepreneurs. After defining their terminology and outlining the scope of their study, they analyze the motivations of the typical entrepreneur, applying the results of interviews and Thematic Apperception Tests. They also compare the entrepreneur with the managerial executive. In *Little Business in the American Economy* (Urbana, University of Illinois Press, 1958. 135 p. Illinois studies in the social sciences, v. 42), Joseph D. Phillips discusses the place and the problems of small economic units in the American economy. In *The Politics of Small Business* (Washington, Public Affairs Press [1961] 150 p.), Harmon Zeigler describes the activities of organizations such as the National Small Business Men's Association, the National Federation of Independent Business, and the Small Business Administration.

2717. Gordon, Robert A., *and* James E. Howell. Higher education for business. New York, Columbia University Press, 1959. 491 p.

        59–16886  HF1131.G6

Bibliographical footnotes. "The literature on personal qualities contributing to business success": p. [453]–455.

A report sponsored by the Ford Foundation on the current state of business education at the college and university level. The authors studied the curricula, educational methods, faculties, students, and goals of schools of business administration. They point out areas in which changes are needed to effect a broader and more rigorous educational program. Among their recommendations are the following: the standards of admission and the performance of students should be raised, research should be emphasized, and the curricula should be reorganized to stress courses of an analytical nature. Another analysis of the same subject, financed by the Carnegie Corporation, is *The Education of American Businessmen; a Study of University-College Programs in Business Administration* (New York, McGraw-Hill, 1959. 740 p. The Carnegie series in American education), by Frank C. Pierson and others.

2718. Grodinsky, Julius. Jay Gould, his business career, 1867–1892. Philadelphia, University of Pennsylvania Press [1957] 627 p. maps.

        56–12389  CT275.G6G7

"Bibliographical Note": p. 11–14.

A detailed examination of the business policies and practices of a leading trader, businessman, and capitalist in an era of unregulated business competition. A master of corporate negotiation and security trading, Gould started as a speculator and at age 31 was on the Erie Railroad board of directors. He gained control of several major railroads, including the Union Pacific, the Wabash, and the Erie. He manipulated unscrupulously, using "every stock-rigging device then known." Despite his disregard of business ethics, however, he introduced new methods of corporate finance and "set precedents which were later followed by investment bankers and by state and federal legislators." Edward C. Kirkland's *Dream and Thought in the Business Community, 1860–1900* (Ithaca, N.Y., Cornell University Press [1956] 175 p.) is a series of essays on the attitudes of prominent businessmen toward the economic, social, and political issues of their day.

2719. Kaplan, Abraham D. H. Big enterprise in a competitive system. Rev. ed. Washington, Brookings Institution [1964] xv, 240 p.

        64–8754  HC106.5.K36 1964

Bibliographical footnotes.

A revised edition of no. 6020 in the 1960 *Guide*. *The Corporation Take-Over* (New York, Harper & Row [c1964] 280 p.), edited by Andrew Hacker, and *Big Business and Free Men* (New York, Harper [1959] 205 p.), by James C. Worthy, are discussions of the place of big businesses in society and the consequences of their use of power.

2720. Miller, William, *ed.* Men in business; essays on the historical role of the entrepreneur. With 2 additional essays on American business leaders, not included in the original edition. New York, Harper & Row [1962] 389 p. (Harper torchbooks, TB1081. The Academy library)

        62–52879  HF3023.A2M5  1962

Bibliographical notes: p. [339]–389.

An updated edition of no. 6023 in the 1960 *Guide*.

2721. Patterson, Robert T. The great boom and panic, 1921–1929. Chicago, H. Regnery [1965] xiv, 282 p. illus.

        65–15267  HB3717  1929.P3

Bibliography: p. 247–264.

In this informal history of the economic boom of the 1920's and the crash of 1929, the author hypothesizes that inflation, prosperity, and mounting speculation deluded people into believing that everyone could grow rich by investing in the stock market. The economy was shaped by the Federal Reserve Board's policy of "easy money" and the large quantity of stocks bought "on margin." In the early autumn of 1929, the great boom collapsed and was followed by an extended and painful deflation, of which the panic of October and November was only the beginning.

2722. Schriftgiesser, Karl. Business comes of age; the story of the Committee for Economic Development and its impact upon the economic policies of the United States, 1942–1960. New York, Harper [1960] 248 p.

        60–5709  HB1.C573S3

Organized in 1942 as a representative of the liberal and progressive elements of big business, the Committee for Economic Development has joined with scholars to perform research and propose policy. Its first program was to study the prospects for the postwar economy and to identify methods of preventing depression. The success of its publications has assured it a role in shaping public and private economic policy, and its influence is viewed by the author of this study as having been highly beneficial.

2723. Wiebe, Robert H. Businessmen and reform: a study of the Progressive movement.

Cambridge, Harvard University Press, 1962. 283 p.
62–18718   E743.W59

Bibliography: p. [225]–231. Bibliographical references included in "Notes" (p. [233]–271).

An analysis of the relationship between businessmen and Progressivism, based on research among manuscripts of leading businessmen, congressional reports, business publications, and trade journals.

The author points out the diverse interests within the business community at the beginning of the 20th century. Businessmen opposed many reforms, but in the development of economic regulations they supported major changes and laid "their claim as progressives." At least one segment of the business community supported such programs for Federal control as railroad regulations, labor laws, tariff revisions, and banking reforms.

## M.  Labor: General

2724.  Barbash, Jack.  Labor's grass roots; a study of the local union.  New York, Harper [1961]  250 p.          61–14839   HD6508.B352
Bibliographical footnotes.

A composite picture of the internal government of local unions.  After presenting the governmental structure as a whole, the author analyzes each of the major working parts and discusses the roles of the business agent, the steward, and the rank and file worker.  *The Worker Views His Union* ([Chicago] University of Chicago Press [1958] 299 p.), by Joel I. Seidman and others, includes many excerpts from interviews with workers.

2725.  Barbash, Jack, *ed.*  Unions and union leadership: their human meaning.  New York, Harper [1959]  xxii, 348 p.
59–9937   HD6508.B354
Bibliographical footnotes.

A collection of writings relating the union to contemporary industrial society and emphasizing the ordinary, "non-glamorous" aspects of the union experience.  To ensure a balanced presentation, the editor includes essays by such academic writers as Selig Perlman, Daniel Bell, and Irving Bernstein along with articles by labor reporters.  The volume encompasses a broad view of the American labor movement, biographies of labor leaders, discussions of styles of unionism, and analyses of problems encountered by labor in society today.  In *Intellectuals in the Labor Unions; Organizational Pressures on Professional Roles* (Glencoe, Ill., Free Press [1956] 336 p.), Harold L. Wilensky appraises the functions and influences of intellectuals in the unions and their role in the decisionmaking process.

2726.  Dulles, Foster Rhea.  Labor in America, a history.  2d rev. ed.  New York, Crowell, 1960.  435 p.          60–14543   HD8066.D8 1960
"Bibliographical Notes": p. 414–422.

An updated edition of no. 6034 in the 1960 *Guide*.

2727.  Kerr, Clark.  Labor and management in industrial society.  Garden City, N.Y., Anchor Books [1964]  xxvi, 372 p.
64–19279   HD6961.K43
"A401."
Bibliographical footnotes.

Four issues recur in the area of industrial relations: the maintenance of freedom in a machine-dominated society; the achievement of peace among labor, management, and the state; the possibilities for progress in a highly organized and bureaucratized nation; and the role of technology in the interaction of managers and workers.  The author discusses manifestations of these questions as they appeared on the American labor front from 1953 to 1961.  He aims as well at attaining an overall view of economic development and reverts often to such themes as the impact of industrialization on the course of world history and the wisdom of looking beyond the American system in the 20th century.  In *Automation and Industrial Relations* (New York, Holt, Rinehart, & Winston [1963] 360 p.  Modern management series) Edward B. Shils explores the effects of modern technology on jobs and on management and union policies.

2728.  Leiserson, William M.  American trade union democracy.  With a foreword by Sumner H. Slichter.  New York, Columbia University Press, 1959.  354 p.  59–8112  HD6508.L43
Bibliographical footnotes.

In his study of the normal operations of trade union governments, the author concentrates on national unions as the power centers of the union movement.  He considers the question of whether or not the great influence exerted by the unions in political and economic life is becoming a threat to freedom.  To enable the reader to form his own opinion, Leiserson describes in detail the work of the union convention, the division of the executive power, and the operation of the judicial process and draws analogies between union government and the governments of church and state.

2729. Peterson, Florence. American labor unions, what they are and how they work. 2d rev. ed. New York, Harper & Row [1963] 271 p.
63–10629  HD6508.P42  1963
An updated edition of no. 6035 in the 1960 *Guide*.

2730. Reynolds, Lloyd G. Labor economics and labor relations. 4th ed. Englewood Cliffs, N.J., Prentice-Hall [1964] 568 p. illus.
64–22311  HD4901.R47  1964
Selected readings at the ends of chapters.

An updated edition of no. 6037 in the 1960 *Guide*. In a similar work, *The Labor Sector* (New York, McGraw-Hill [ᶜ1965] 758 p.), Neil W. Chamberlain deals with comparable topics but also devotes a section to the household's position in the economy. Using labor as a source of income, the family unit regulates the labor supply by deciding the amount of time each member will exchange on the market for remunerated employment. With its wages, the family purchases goods and services; its buying power is thus another influence on the economy. Furthermore, in its strivings for financial security, the household is partly responsible for the rise of the labor unions with the problems and benefits they bring to society.

2731. Taylor, George W., *and* Frank C. Pierson, *eds*. New concepts in wage determination.

New York, McGraw-Hill, 1957. 336 p. (McGraw-Hill labor management series)
56–11057  HD4909.T3
Bibliographical footnotes.

Realizing the need for a systematic treatment of wage theory, the contributors to this volume wish to establish a common frame of reference. They depart from the traditional view in which wages form an integral part of general economic theory. The editors point out in the preface that "wage theory should be closely, but not exclusively, tied to general theory." Contrary to the usual narrow outlook, maximum gain is not the only goal of economic activity; the men who determine wages operate from several perspectives and seek diversified ends in their economic dealings. In addition, "institutional environment," government intervention in industrial relations, and community attitudes and social customs affect the wage-setting process. Consequently, the editors maintain, the traditional restrictive analysis, which does not take these variables into account, cannot provide a full understanding of wage economics.

2732. Updegraff, Clarence M., *and* Whitley P. McCoy. Arbitration of labor disputes. 2d ed., by Clarence M. Updegraff. Washington, B[ureau of] N[ational] A[ffairs, 1961] 321 p.
60–16683  KF3424.U5  1961
Bibliographical footnotes.
An updated edition of no. 6058 in the 1960 *Guide*.

## N. Labor: Special

2733. Baker, Elizabeth F. Technology and woman's work. New York, Columbia University Press, 1964. xvi, 460 p.  64–22559  HD6095.B3
Bibliography: p. [443]–450.

In the 18th century, American women first left their spinning wheels at home for the spinning jennies in the factories. Women have been finding employment outside the home in increasing numbers ever since. The author traces the historical and economic factors which have taken women out of household manufactures into offices, factories, and shops. Although primarily concerned with women in nonprofessional jobs, the author also discusses women in teaching, nursing, social work, and other professional fields. Finally, she considers the relationship between women and labor unions and the impact of protective labor legislation on the female work force.

2734. Bernstein, Irving. The lean years; a history of the American worker, 1920–1933. Boston, Houghton Mifflin, 1960. 577 p. illus.
60–9143  HD8072.B37
Bibliographical references included in "Notes" (p. 517–559).

The author's direct style and the photographs of riots, breadlines, and life in the "urban jungle" recreate the demoralization of workers during the twenties and early thirties. Characterizing the period as one of economic disparity between the great mass of poor workers and the wealthy few, he examines the laborer's place in this unbalanced society, the disorganized state of the labor movement, the power tactics used by employers to quash any potential union strength, and the position of labor in relation to the law. He then discusses several aspects of the country's ordeal following the stock market crash and describes the policies of the Hoover administration during the early years of the Depression. *Labor and the New Deal* (Madison, University of Wisconsin Press, 1957. 393 p.), a collection of essays edited by Milton Derber and Edwin Young, indicates what present-day labor institutions owe to developments in the New Deal period.

2735. Chamberlain, Neil W., *and* James W. Kuhn. Collective bargaining. 2d ed. New York, McGraw-Hill [1965] 451 p. illus.

   64–23640   HD6483.C48   1965
Bibliographical footnotes.

An updated edition of no. 6046 in the 1960 *Guide*. In *Strategy and Collective Bargaining Negotiation* (New York, McGraw-Hill [1963] 192 p. Publications of the Wertheim Committee), Carl M. Stevens develops a theoretical framework for labor-management bartering. In *The Impact of Collective Bargaining on Management* (Washington, Brookings Institution [1960] 982 p.), Sumner H. Slichter, James J. Healy, and Edward Robert Livernash draw upon their intensive field research in actual union-management confrontation. *The Impact of the Professional Engineering Union* (Boston, Division of Research, Graduate School of Business Administration, Harvard University, 1961. 419 p.), by Richard E. Walton, is a study of the significance of collective bargaining engaged in by scientists and engineers.

2736. Saposs, David J. Communism in American unions. New York, McGraw-Hill, 1959. 279 p. (McGraw-Hill labor management series)

   59–7318   HD6508.S24
After brief mention of the early radicalism preceding the Communist movement, the author traces Communist infiltration of the American Federation of Labor and the Congress of Industrial Organizations. He states that, because Communist organizers could penetrate the CIO at its formation, they managed to reach the national level of leadership. Although less successful in the well-established AFL, they did infiltrate some of its affiliates. Saposs concludes that in spite of exposures, expulsions, and defeats, Communism continues to undermine democracy in the unions.

2737. Taft, Philip. The A. F. of L. in the time of Gompers. New York, Harper [1957] xx, 508 p.   57–6741   HD8055.A5T3
Bibliographical footnotes.

2738. Taft, Philip. The A. F. of L. from the death of Gompers to the merger. New York, Harper [1959] 499 p. 59–7064 HD8055.A5T28
Includes bibliographical references.

Drawing on official and private records, minutes of conventions and executive council meetings, and letters of federation officials, the author presents a sympathetic history of the AFL. In the first of these two publications, he examines the problems inherent in the organizing activities of the federation and in the formation of policies concerning immigration and Negro labor. He also evaluates the quality of leadership provided by Samuel Gompers. In the second work, Taft analyzes the structure and jurisdiction of the AFL and delineates the steps leading to the merger with the CIO. In *American Labor Unions and Politics, 1900–1918* (Carbondale, Southern Illinois University Press, 1958. 358 p.), Marc Karson discusses such topics as the role of the Roman Catholic Church in the labor movement, the AFL's support of the Democratic Party, and the reasons for the absence of a national labor party in the United States.

# XXIX

# Constitution and Government

THE INTRODUCTION to Chapter XXIX in the 1960 *Guide* noted the growing literature on American political thought. That scholars have continued to probe this area is evident from the number of entries in the present Section A, treating such topics as conservatism, the democratic tradition, and patterns of antidemocratic thought. The history of the Constitution (Section B) has also held the attention of scholars, several of whom have placed particular emphasis on the document's origins. Works on government in general (Section E) are likewise numerous, especially in the category of textbooks, which are represented here by a conventional descriptive survey, an analysis of the dynamics of government, an examination of intergovernmental relations on the Federal, State, and local levels, and a compilation of readings. Two publications are devoted to general appraisals of the Presidency (Section F), and related works are focused on such special topics as assistants to the President, Presidential succession, and the transition that occurs when a President belonging to one political party is succeeded by one who belongs to another party. Three of the works on Congress (Section G) are by men who discuss their experiences as members. Proportionately fewer publications appear in the sections on administration and State and local government in the *Supplement* than in the 1960 *Guide*. Perhaps the major reason for the difference is that most scholarly monographs in these fields are too limited in scope to be appropriate for this bibliography; almost half of the works chosen for Sections H, I, J, and K are textbooks, which have the appropriate breadth of coverage.

## A. Political Thought

2739. Auerbach, M. Morton. The conservative illusion. New York, Columbia University Press, 1959. 359 p.      59–10698   JA84.U5A9
   Bibliography: p. [333]–337.

"Conservatism has no way of making the crucial transition from values to reality, from theory to practice; and in the limited periods of history when it *seemed* to make this transition, it was able to do so only for reasons which contradicted its premises." The author bases this statement on an examination of European conservative thought from Plato to Edmund Burke and of the "new conservatism" in the United States as represented by Russell Kirk, Peter Viereck, Clinton Rossiter, and Reinhold Niebuhr. Having thus dismissed the conservative formulation, Auerbach suggests a critical examination of three alternatives: liberalism, radicalism or equalitarianism, and authoritarianism.

2740. Ekirch, Arthur A. The American democratic tradition: a history. New York, Macmillan [1963] 338 p.    63–18793 JK31.E5
Bibliography: p. 317–321.
In an attempt "to survey and analyze both the idea and practice of democracy for the entire sweep of American history," the author traces the American democratic tradition from colonial times to the Cold War period. He notes an increasing popular emphasis on social and economic rather than merely political democracy and identifies two factors that help to explain the origin and growth of American democracy—the heritage of dissent and the hope that every grievance could be redressed in the American environment. Democracy has become part of almost every aspect of American life, "a new kind of secular religion." The emphasis in American democratic thought is shifting, however, "from individual freedom and liberty to the collective security of the group." Ekirch concludes that, with the threat of nuclear war, the future of the democratic tradition depends "as never before upon the achievement of world peace and international understanding."

2741. Grimes, Alan P. American political thought. Rev. ed. New York, Holt, Rinehart & Winston [1960] 556 p.    60–7493 JA84.U5G7 1960
Includes bibliography.
A revised edition of no. 6062 in the 1960 *Guide*. *The Essential Lippmann; a Political Philosophy for Liberal Democracy* (New York, Random House [1963] 552 p.), edited by Clinton Rossiter and James Lare, is a selection from the political writings of Walter Lippmann over the period 1913–63.

2742. Mason, Alpheus T. Free government in the making; readings in American political thought. 3d ed. New York, Oxford University Press, 1965. xix, 929 p.
65–10151 JK11 1965.M3
Includes bibliographies.
An updated edition of no. 6065 in the 1960 *Guide*.

2743. Mason, Alpheus T., *and* Richard H. Leach. In quest of freedom; American political thought and practice. Englewood Cliffs, N.J., Prentice-Hall, 1959. 568 p. 59–11129 JK31.M35
Includes bibliography.
An interpretation of American political thought from John Locke through the Supreme Court's decision on school segregation in 1954. Noting that American politics "esteems aggressive, self-reliant individuals" and that "the doers are also the thinkers," the authors highlight the writings of James Otis, John Adams, Thomas Jefferson, John Taylor, John C. Calhoun, Thorstein Veblen, Woodrow Wilson, and Franklin Roosevelt. They define various enduring political principles in the United States and note that American political thought is constantly making new adjustments so that individual freedom and initiative can be combined with the necessities of social cohesion.

2744. Nagel, Paul C. One nation indivisible; the Union in American thought, 1776–1861. New York, Oxford University Press, 1964. 328 p.
64–11235 JK311.N2
Bibliographical references included in "Notes" (p. 289–318).
A discussion of the significance of the concept and ideology of "Union" from the Revolution to the Civil War. The author quotes from a variety of sources indicating the widespread intellectual and emotional appeal of the Union cult and contends that Union served as a verbal icon until the Civil War dispelled the spiritual illusion of unity and advanced technology and communications demonstrated the impossibility of physical disunity.

2745. Rossiter, Clinton L. Conservatism in America; the thankless persuasion. 2d ed., rev. New York, Vintage Books [1962] 306 p.
62–2229 JK31.R58 1962
Includes bibliography.
An updated edition of no. 6067 in the 1960 *Guide*.

2746. Schattschneider, Elmer E. The semisovereign people; a realist's view of democracy in America. New York, Holt, Rinehart & Winston [1960] 147 p.    60–14798 JK271.S23
The author describes his book as "an attempt to work out a theory about the relation between organization and conflict, the relation between political organization and democracy, and the organizational alternatives open to the American people. The assumption made throughout is that the nature of political organization depends on the conflicts exploited in the political system." He discusses the "contagiousness of conflict" in a free society, the scope and bias of the pressures under which the system operates, and "the displacement of conflicts," which is a prime instrument of political party strat-

egy. The election of 1896 is interpreted as "the best example in American history of the successful substitution of one conflict for another." American democracy is considered to be "a competitive political system in which competing leaders and organizations define the alternatives of public policy in such a way that the public can participate in the decision-making process." The people profit by this system but, according to Schattschneider, they cannot do the work of the system—that is, govern. They are "powerless if the political enterprise is not competitive" and are thus semisovereign rather than sovereign.

2747. Spitz, David. Patterns of anti-democratic thought; an analysis and a criticism, with special reference to the American political mind in recent times. Rev. ed. New York, Free Press [1965] 347 p. (A Free Press paperback)
62–21616 JC481.S65 1965
Bibliographical references included in "Notes" (p. 297–334).
An updated edition of no. 6069 in the 1960 *Guide*.

# B. Constitutional History

2748. Brown, Robert E. Reinterpretation of the formation of the American Constitution. Boston, Boston University Press [1963] 63 p. (The Gaspar G. Bacon lectures on the Constitution of the United States) 63–13735 JK119.B7
Includes bibliography.

2749. McDonald, Forrest. We the people; the economic origins of the Constitution. Chicago, University of Chicago Press [1958] 436 p. (A Publication of the American History Research Center) 58–14905 JK146.M27
Bibliographical footnotes.

Two studies of *An Economic Interpretation of the Constitution of the United States* (1913), by Charles A. Beard. Using the same basic approach that Brown applied earlier to his *Charles Beard and the Constitution* (cited in the annotation for no. 3046 in the 1960 *Guide*), McDonald employs a highly detailed statistical analysis and presents a mass of evidence indicating that Beard's thesis is not valid. His method is that which Beard himself proposed for verification. McDonald concludes that Beard's "dynamic element," the holding of public securities, is without significance and outlines instead a method for the "pluralistic study of the Constitution" which he thinks will offer sounder possibilities. In his 1963 study, Brown supports his reinterpretation of the Constitution and its ratification by reexamining the nature of American colonial society and the American Revolution. He portrays American colonial society as "predominately middle-class, with much economic opportunity, a broad franchise, representation that favored the agricultural areas, educational facilities for the common man, and much religious freedom." Colonial America was "much more liberal than we have previously believed," and the Revolution was an attempt "to preserve an already democratic middle-class society."

2750. Dietze, Gottfried. The Federalist, a classic on federalism and free government. Baltimore, Johns Hopkins Press [1960] 378 p.
60–11204 JK155.D5
Bibliography: p. 355–358. Bibliographical footnotes.
An interpretive analysis of *The Federalist* as a classic of Western political thought and as the outstanding American contribution to the literature of constitutional democracy and federalism. The author's purpose is to demonstrate how *The Federalist* advances "beyond the orthodox conception of the purpose of federation, by advocating federalism not only as a means for maintaining the security of the federating states from foreign powers or peace among the members, but also—and especially—as a means for securing the individual's freedom from governmental control." The ideal implicit in the papers is that "the democratic principle of popular participation in government, as a mere means, is subordinate to the liberal principle of the protection of the individual, as the end." Two recent editions of the classic volume by Hamilton, Madison, and Jay are *The Federalist* (Middletown, Conn., Wesleyan University Press, 1961. 672 p.), edited by Jacob E. Cooke, and *The Federalist* (Cambridge, Mass., Belknap Press of Harvard University Press, 1961. 572 p. The John Harvard Library), edited by Benjamin F. Wright.

2751. Kelly, Alfred H., *and* Winfred A. Harbison. The American Constitution; its origins and development. 3d ed. New York, Norton [1963] 1125 p. 63–8030 JK31.K4 1963
Includes bibliography.

An updated edition of no. 6077 in the 1960 *Guide*. In *The Reins of Power; a Constitutional History of the United States* (New York, Hill & Wang [1963] 216 p.), Bernard Schwartz describes the impact of major Supreme Court decisions on the evolution of constitutional government.

2752. Lee, Charles R. The Confederate Constitutions. Chapel Hill, University of North Carolina Press [1963] 225 p.

63–4415 KFZ9000.L4

Bibliography: p. [201]–220.

A study of the framing and adoption of the two Confederate Constitutions, the provisional and the permanent. In the author's view, the South's conception of the Union as a compact between individually sovereign states culminated in secession and was embodied in these Confederate Constitutions, which included conspicuous provisions to protect minority rights and preserve State sovereignty. The "most significant constitutional guarantee of the position of the minority" is provided by Article V, which enables a minority of three States to initiate the process of amending the basic law. Lee notes that, besides representing the ultimate constitutional expression of the philosophy of States' rights, the Confederate Constitutions made "a valuable contribution through the legacy of government reform," inasmuch as they contained provisions aimed at correcting the spoils system, maintaining the Government's fiscal integrity, and providing for an executive budget and the appearance of Cabinet officers on the floor of Congress. The U.S. Constitution and the permanent Constitution of the Confederacy are compared in parallel columns in an appendix.

2753. Main, Jackson Turner. The antifederalists; critics of the Constitution, 1781–1788. Chapel Hill, Published for the Institute of Early American History and Culture at Williamsburg, Va., by the University of North Carolina Press [1961] 308 p. 61–17904 JK116.M2

"Historiographical and bibliographical essay": p. 293–297. Bibliographical footnotes.

A detailed study of the antifederalist critics of the Constitution. The author regards antifederalism as a mixture of two points of view: advocacy of a weak central government by wealthy, usually agrarian, interests, and preference for a government democratically controlled by the many, principally among small farmers. The origins and intensity of antifederalist sentiment are discussed, but primary attention is devoted to the months between the publication of the Constitution and its adoption. Two books containing selections from the writings and speeches against ratification of the Constitution are *The Antifederalist Papers* ([East Lansing, Mich.] Michigan State University Press, 1965. 258 p.), edited by Morton Borden, and *The States Rights Debate: Antifederalism and the Constitution* (Englewood Cliffs, N.J., Prentice-Hall [1964] 206 p. A Spectrum book), edited by Alpheus T. Mason.

2754. Rossiter, Clinton L. Alexander Hamilton and the Constitution. New York, Harcourt, Brace & World [1964] 372 p.

64–11540 KF363.H3R6

Bibliographical references included in "Notes" (p. 259–348).

An analysis of Hamilton's role in the struggle for ratification and implementation of the Constitution. On the basis of research in letters, diaries, and public statements of Hamilton and his contemporaries, Rossiter discusses Hamilton's contributions to the Constitution, his exposition of constitutional law and theory, and the political philosophy which crowned his efforts. In particular, the author analyzes the importance of Hamilton's efforts toward obtaining a broad construction for the Constitution, his advocacy of a strongly instituted Presidency, his insistence on Supreme Court primacy over the courts of the States, and his role in the establishment of the first Bank of the United States. The study includes a comparison of Hamilton's ideas and objectives with those of Thomas Jefferson.

2755. Smith, James M., *and* Paul L. Murphy, *eds.* Liberty and justice; a historical record of American constitutional development. New York, Knopf, 1958. 566 p.

59–5061 KF4541.A7S6 1958

A collection of 276 American historical documents dated from 1606 to 1956, selected to illustrate the integral role of constitutional evolution in the major transformations of the American social order. The material consists of statutes, reports, resolutions, petitions, Presidential messages, court decisions, and other official documents, as well as letters, pamphlets, newspaper commentaries, and sermons. Twelve chapters deal with developments up to the Civil War, eight are devoted to the period from the Civil War through the 1920's, and eight concentrate on recent changes in such areas as government-business relations and civil liberties. A short introductory essay begins each chapter.

## C. Constitutional Law

2756. Columbia University. *Legislative Drafting Research Fund*. Constitutions of the United States, national and State. Dobbs Ferry, N.Y., Oceana Publications [1962]  2 v.
61–18391  KF4530.C6
Prepared under the direction of John M. Kernochan as part of a broad program of State constitutional studies developed jointly by the Brookings Institution, the National Municipal League, and Columbia University, this compilation includes the texts of constitutions in force in the United States, with amendments through December 31, 1960. A historical note on the present and earlier constitutions precedes each text.

2757. Forkosch, Morris D.  Constitutional law. Brooklyn, Foundation Press, 1963.  xxi, 541 p.  63–1348  KF4550.F6
Bibliographical footnotes.
An introduction to Federal constitutional law, geared to the special requirements of students. Among the topics discussed are the Constitution and its background, judicial review, the Federal system, the amending process, Federal powers and limitations, State powers, Federal-State conflicts, and the rights of persons as against both Federal and State Governments. The author describes the commerce clause as "the greatest single peacetime source of federal power, especially as against the states," and the due process clause as the greatest single peacetime limitation on the States as regards individual rights. A comprehensive casebook aimed at providing a body of basic material for college upperclassmen or first-year law school students is *Cases in Constitutional Law,* 2d ed. (New York, Appleton-Century-Crofts [1963]  945 p.  ACC political science series), by Robert E. Cushman and Robert F. Cushman.

2758. Hirschfield, Robert S.  The Constitution and the Court; the development of the basic law through judicial interpretation. New York, Random House [1962]  257 p. (Studies in political science, PS40)  62–10672  KF4550.Z9H55
"Cases and selected bibliography": p. 240–252.
A demonstration of what the author believes is the "essential element in the dynamism of American government"—the process of constitutional development and change through judicial interpretation of basic law. The bulk of this paperback is devoted to the Supreme Court's activity in the fields of economic regulation, racial equality, civil liberty and national security, and wartime government.

2759. Schmidhauser, John R.  Constitutional law in the political process. Chicago, Rand McNally [1963]  544 p. illus. (Rand McNally political science series)  63–7578  KF8700.A7S3
A behavioral study of the role of the Supreme Court in the American political process. As background for his analysis of the political significance of the Court's role as an instrument of government, the author cites articles, essays, judicial decisions, legislative debates, and election campaign documents chosen primarily for the social and political issues involved. Among the topics covered are democratic theory and the administration of justice, the Constitution and the status of individuals and groups, Federal judicial authority, the hierarchy of American courts, the traditions and procedures of judicial institutions, the selection of Federal judges, the crucial role of the bar, the Supreme Court and social change, and the roots of judicial behavior. In *Constitutional Politics* (New York, Holt, Rinehart & Winston [1960]  735 p.), Glendon A. Schubert focuses on the decisionmaking behavior of Supreme Court Justices and their role in the development of national policy.

2760. Schwartz, Bernard.  A commentary on the Constitution of the United States.  New York, Macmillan [1963–65]  2 pts. in 3 v.
62–19994  KF4550.S3
Bibliographical references included in "Notes" (pt. 1, v. 2, p. 307–437). "Table of Cases": pt. 1, v. 2, p. 439–472.
CONTENTS.—pt. 1.  The powers of Government: v. 1.  Federal and State powers.  v. 2.  Powers of the President.—pt. 2.  The rights of property.
The initial volumes in a planned comprehensive study of the Constitution. The first part deals with the powers of the Federal Government which enable it to fulfill its designated purpose; part 2 discusses the rights of property; subsequent volumes will cover the rights of the individual. The author bases his analysis on two significant characteristics of the Constitution—its role as a source of governmental authority and its emphasis on the restrictions of governmental power.

2761. U.S. *Constitution*. The Constitution of the United States of America; analysis and interpretation. Annotations of cases decided by the Supreme Court of the United States to June 22, 1964. Prepared by the Legislative Reference Service, Library of Congress, Norman J. Small, editor, and Lester S. Jayson, supervising editor. [Rev. ed.] Washington, U.S. Govt. Print. Off., 1964. 1693 p. (88th Congress, 1st session. Senate. Document no. 39) 65–61050 Law

An updated edition of no. 6102 in the 1960 *Guide*.

# D. Civil Liberties and Rights

2762. Abernathy, Mabra Glenn. The right of assembly and association. Columbia, University of South Carolina Press, 1961. 263 p.
61–9384 K4778.A3 1961
Includes bibliography.

The purpose of this analysis is "to outline the scope of the right of assembly in the United States and to point out those areas in which it might be practicable to permit a freer exercise" of this right and its cognate right of association than is now the general rule. Governmental restrictions on these rights are considered "constitutionally permissible" in several areas. The most substantial restriction lies in the law of unlawful assembly. "Assemblies in the public streets" is another situation which has caused conflicts between constitutional rights and local legal restrictions. In the author's view, extraordinary efforts must be made to ensure that local authorities "be as well schooled as possible in the subject of individual rights." He emphasizes that the right of assembly is primarily designed to protect and encourage the interchange of opinions and ideas. Noting that there is a wide range of discriminatory practices concerning assemblies in public parks by local authorities, Abernathy calls for revision of municipal ordinances in line with Supreme Court decisions. Federal protection of the right of assembly derives from the Court's broad power of review under the 14th amendment and from existing Federal civil and criminal remedies, but the latter, the author indicates, are meager, insufficient, and in need of expansion.

2763. Brant, Irving. The Bill of Rights; its origin and meaning. Indianapolis, Bobbs-Merrill [1965] 567 p. 65–21401 KF4749.B7
"Bibliographical notes": p. 527–544.

The origins of constitutional liberties in the United States are approached through an examination of the English and American background to the rights identified in the first 10 amendments to the Constitution. Protections provided in the fifth and sixth amendments against self-incrimination, arbitrary arrest, and secret trial have roots in abuses perpetrated under the King's Star Chamber tribunal. The idea of freedom of the press, embodied in the first amendment, was strengthened in America by the successful defense in 1733 of Peter Zenger against Crown charges of libel. The author uses early court and legislative records of both England and the Colonies to support his lines of argument and, in the light of this evidence, reviews and evaluates historical arguments contained in major opinions of the U.S. Supreme Court.

2764. Caughey, John W. In clear and present danger; the crucial state of our freedoms. [Chicago] University of Chicago Press [1958] 207 p. 58–10815 JC599.U5C36

Traditional freedoms in the United States, the author believes, were put "in clear and present danger" by the national demand for security against communism. The "narrowing of our freedom" is identified in the laws enacted, cases decided, congressional and executive behavior, and the growth of demagoguery. The author traces the security measures taken in the years after World War II, the growth of McCarthyism, the "orgy of Communist baiting," the investigating committees, and "decline and fall of the Fifth Amendment," and the attacks upon academic freedom, noting that all of these contributed to a wholesale decline in individual freedoms. Supreme Court decisions subsequently did much to temper the excesses of the early 1950's, but many of the restrictions upon individual liberties had been institutionalized and continued to operate. The author advocates containment of the Communist minority "without violating or sacrificing the freedoms which are the American birthright."

2765. Cornell University. Cornell studies in civil liberties. Robert E. Cushman, advisory editor. Ithaca, Cornell University Press, 1946–65. 19 v.

Four new studies and one revised edition have been added to no. 6110 in the 1960 *Guide*. They are *Tenure in American Higher Education: Plans, Practices, and the Law* ([1959] 212 p. 59–10438.

LB2334.B95), by Clark Byse and Louis Joughin; Henry W. Edgerton's *Freedom in the Balance: Opinions Relating to Civil Liberties* ([1960] 278 p. 60–3038. KF4748.E3), edited by Eleanor Bontecou; *The Presidency and Individual Liberties* ([1961] 239 p. 61–8206. JK518.L6), by Richard P. Longaker; *First Amendment Freedoms: Selected Cases on Freedom of Religion, Speech, Press, Assembly* ([1963] 933 p. 63–18091. KF4770. A7K65), edited by Milton R. Konvitz; and *Bill of Rights Reader: Leading Constitutional Cases,* 3d ed., rev. and enl. ([1965] 941 p. 65–19199. KF4748.K6 1965), edited by Milton R. Konvitz, a revised edition of no. 6121 in the 1960 *Guide.*

2766. Dumbauld, Edward. The Bill of Rights and what it means today. Norman, University of Oklahoma Press [1957] xv, 242 p.

57–5954 KF4749.D8

Bibliography: p. 223–235.

Study of the adoption of the first 10 amendments to the Constitution and of their adaptation to current conditions. After presenting a detailed account of the contributions of the several States and of the successive congressional drafts of the Bill of Rights, the author discusses the function of current judicial interpretation in determining the implementation of the amendments. He concludes that the Bill of Rights has served as the conservator of the spirit of the Declaration of Independence in the Constitution and that its specific provisions continue to demonstrate their practical utility. *Sources of our Liberties* ([Chicago] American Bar Foundation [1959] 456 p.), edited by Richard L. Perry, is a collection of the major legal sources of individual freedoms in the United States. *The Supreme Court and Civil Liberties,* 2d ed. (Dobbs Ferry, N.Y., Published for the American Civil Liberties Union [by] Oceana Publishers, 1963. 189 p.), by Osmond K. Fraenkel, is a concise summary of Supreme Court decisions in cases involving civil liberties.

2767. Gellhorn, Walter. American rights; the Constitution in action. New York, Macmillan, 1960. 232 p.     60–5408 KF4750.G43 1960

An examination of the ways in which the Constitution has protected individual rights. The author considers the Constitution itself to be a vague bulwark against oppression. Its principles acquire solidity and significance "through the erratic, sometimes conflicting currents of judicial decision," but "in the end, the Constitution always becomes what the People of America will it to be." In *Individual Freedom and Governmental Restraints* (Baton Rouge, Louisiana State University Press [1956] 215 p. The Edward Douglass White lectures on citizenship), Gellhorn traces the increasing tendency for judicial responsibilities to be transferred to administrative agencies.

2768. Hudon, Edward G. Freedom of speech and press in America. Foreword by William O. Douglas. Washington, Public Affairs Press [1963] 224 p.     62–22380 KF4770.H8

"Table of Cases": p. 213–217.

The author believes that first amendment freedoms have been subject to severe strains because the history of this amendment "has been one of uncertainty although it was adopted to end uncertainty." By recourse to 18th-century thought and principle, as well as to the events which "provoked men to act as they did when the Amendment was adopted," he expects that a more stable interpretation can be found. The adoption of the amendment is discussed, its English and colonial background is outlined, and the history of cases and decisions relating to it is traced from the Alien and Sedition Laws to the present. Hudon concludes that the theory of natural law motivated the creation of the Bill of Rights but has never governed Court interpretations of its provisions. He advocates a return to natural law principles as the best approach to the meaning of the first amendment.

2769. Johnson, Donald O. The challenge to American freedoms; World War I and the rise of the American Civil Liberties Union. [Lexington] For the Mississippi Valley Historical Association, University of Kentucky Press, 1963. 243 p.

63–12388 JC599.U5J58

Essay on bibliography.

A study of the American Civil Liberties Union (ACLU) and its predecessor organizations and of their attempts to defend civil liberties in the years during and immediately after the First World War. Specific issues discussed include the treatment of conscientious objectors by the Army, prosecutions under the Espionage Acts, deportation of alien radicals by the Justice Department, and censorship of socialist and pacifist publications by the Post Office Department. The author considers that the civil liberties movement had its origin among pacifist and antimilitarist groups in 1914 and was formalized through the founding of the National Civil Liberties Bureau (NCLB) in 1917 and the ACLU in 1919. "Few Americans have ever been so intolerant of their fellow men as Americans in the First World War," according to Johnson, and it was not only acts of the Government that kept the NCLB occupied but also direct action by "gangs of angry patriots." Although led by men of moderate views who were able to unite fragments of the Progressive movement, the NCLB-ACLU gained a reputation for radicalism which the author regards as unwarranted; he notes that even in the 1920's the ACLU never publicly defended any doctrine other than its own of unlimited freedom of speech, press, and assembly.

2770. Kauper, Paul G. Civil liberties and the Constitution. Ann Arbor, University of Michigan Press [1962] 237 p. 62–7723 KF4749.K37

An analysis of recent major decisions of the Supreme Court in the area of civil liberties, based on the author's lectures at the Special Summer School for Lawyers held in June 1961 at the University of Michigan Law School. Among the topics covered are the church-state controversy, censorship and obscenity legislation, the right of association, civil rights for Negroes, and the Federal Government's role in restricting as well as protecting civil liberties. Supreme Court decisions in these areas are considered important not only for their intrinsic significance but also because they "reveal the fluidity and movement that characterize the whole process of constitutional interpretation." In *Frontiers of Constitutional Liberty* (Ann Arbor, University of Michigan Law School, 1956. 251 p. The Thomas M. Cooley lectures, 7th ser.), Kauper discusses law in relation to the flexibility of interpretation of the Constitution.

2771. Levy, Leonard W. Jefferson & civil liberties; the darker side. Cambridge, Belknap Press of Harvard University Press, 1963. 225 p. (A publication of the Center for the Study of the History of Liberty in America, Harvard University)
63–19140 JC599.U5L45

Bibliography: p. 179–186.

The author regards Jefferson as one of the greatest American politicians and the foremost spokesman of his generation but considers his libertarian standards "too shallow to prevail as more than rhetoric when pitted against the acid test of experience and crisis."

Finding "a strong pattern of unlibertarian, even anti-libertarian thought and behavior extending throughout Jefferson's long career," Levy notes that this unfamiliar Jefferson "at one time or another supported loyalty oaths; countenanced internment camps for political suspects; drafted a bill of attainder; urged prosecution for seditious libel; trampled on the Fourth Amendment; condoned military despotism; used the army to enforce laws in time of peace; censored reading; chose professors for their political opinions; and endorsed the doctrine that the means, however odious, were justified by the ends." These acts, according to the author, resulted not from hypocrisy but from the fact that Jefferson was simply not as libertarian as later Americans liked to think and was willing to sacrifice civil liberties for what he believed were more urgent political causes.

2772. Levy, Leonard W. Legacy of suppression; freedom of speech and press in early American history. Cambridge, Belknap Press of Harvard University Press, 1960. xiv, 353 p.
60–8449 JC591.L2

Bibliography: p. [321]–339.

An interpretation of the origins and early significance of the freedom of speech and press clause of the first amendment. The author examines early English legal theory and the experience of the American colonists between 1735 and the Revolution. He concludes "that the generation which adopted the Constitution and the Bill of Rights did not believe in a broad scope for freedom of expression, particularly in the realm of politics." Freedom of speech developed very late, as an offshoot of freedom of the press and had no legal recognition in England or America before the ratification of the first amendment in 1791. Only in 1798 did a modern and mature doctrine of these freedoms as championed by the followers of Jefferson appear in America. In *The Case for Liberty* (Chapel Hill, University of North Carolina Press [1965] 254 p.), Helen D. H. Miller summarizes colonial court cases utilized by the proponents of the Bill of Rights.

# E. Government: General

2773. Anderson, James E. The emergence of the modern regulatory state. Washington, Public Affairs Press [1962] 172 p.
62–18336 JK901.A75

An examination of the theories of regulation developed during the years from 1887 to 1917. The author notes that within this 30-year period a considerable body of legislation dealing with railroads, trusts and monopolies, impure foods and drugs, banking, labor conditions, and tariffs was proposed and much of it enacted into law. He discusses the shift from State to national control in many areas of regulation and interprets the entire regulatory movement as "an effort to extend democratic control over the economic system and to infuse it with a social conscience."

2774. Burns, James MacGregor, *and* Jack W. Peltason. Government by the people; the dynamics of American national, State, and local government. 5th ed. Englewood Cliffs, N.J., Prentice-Hall, 1963. 914 p. 63–11089 JK274.B855 1963

First edition published in 1952 as two separate works under titles: *Government by the People; the Dynamics of American National Government,* and *Government by the People; the Dynamics of American State and Local Government.*

An updated edition of no. 6134 in the 1960 *Guide.* The same authors have edited a book of supplementary readings, *Functions and Policies of American Government* (Englewood Cliffs, N.J., Prentice-Hall, 1962. 450 p.). In a succinct study, *Congress and the President* (Chicago, Scott, Foresman [1965] 197 p. Scott, Foresman American government series), Louis W. Koenig explores the pluralistic nature of policymaking.

2775. Graves, William Brooke. American intergovernmental relations: their origins, historical development, and current status. New York, Scribner [1964] xx, 984 p. illus.
64–11248 JK325.G75
Includes bibliographical references.

A textbook treatment of the evolution of American federalism. The author traces the origins and development of intergovernmental relations on the Federal, State, and local levels. *The Structure of American Federalism* ([London] Oxford University Press, 1961. 206 p.) is a study by an English political scientist, Maurice J. C. Vile. In *The American Partnership* ([Chicago] University of Chicago Press [1962] 358 p.), Daniel J. Elazar develops the thesis that the cooperative character of Federal-State programs has changed relatively little since the 19th century despite the increase in the "velocity of government." In *The Cities and the Federal System* (New York, Atherton Press [1965] 200 p.), Roscoe C. Martin comments favorably upon the increasing interaction between the Federal Government and the cities.

2776. McKay, Robert B. Reapportionment; the law and politics of equal representation. New York, Twentieth Century Fund, 1965. 498 p.
65–26764 KF4905.M3
Bibliography: p. [477]–485.

This appraisal of representative government in the United States seeks to clarify the implications of the constitutional principles announced by the Supreme Court in 1964 regarding legislative apportionment and congressional districting. The author discusses the political theory upon which the legislative aspects of representative government are based and reviews the series of cases in which the "one man, one vote" principle evolved, including *Baker* v. *Carr* (1962) and *Reynolds* v. *Sims* (1964). Against this background, McKay explores the prospects for the future, placing final emphasis on the possibilities for local diversity among State apportionment formulas. *Legislative Apportionment* (New York, Harper & Row [1964] 181 p.), edited by Howard D. Hamilton, is a collection of readings.

2777. Ogg, Frederic A. Ogg and Ray's Introduction to American Government [by] William H. Young. 12th ed. New York, Appleton-Century-Crofts [1962] 957 p. illus.
62–15133 JK421.05 1962
Includes bibliography.
An updated edition of no. 6137 in the 1960 *Guide.*

2778. Powell, Norman J., *and* Daniel P. Parker, *eds.* Major aspects of American Government. New York, McGraw-Hill [°1963] 369 p. (McGraw-Hill series in political science)
62–19250 JK31.P6
Includes bibliography.

Readings for college students, organized under such topics as "The American Value System," "Congress in Action and Interaction," "The Presidency as Power and Myth," "Politics, Parties, and Politicking," "Public Opinion, Pressure Groups, and Propaganda," "The United States in the World Context," and "Public Administration." Most of the selections are taken from public documents, congressional debates, legal opinions, and speeches and articles by political figures and scholars. Short editorial comments introduce the selections. *Politics and Government in the United States,* national, State, and local ed. (New York, Harcourt, Brace & World [1965] 1004 p.), edited by Alan F. Westin, is a compilation covering a wider range of problems and viewpoints.

2779. Rourke, Francis E. Secrecy and publicity; dilemmas of democracy. Baltimore, Johns Hopkins Press [1961] 236 p.
61–10736 JK468.S4R6
A study of the conflict inherent in a democracy between the Government's need to regulate the flow of information to the public and the public's need to know. Although Rourke acknowledges the necessity for secrecy to protect national security, he sees in government control of information the grave danger that public opinion "may become all too submissive

or inadequately critical of the follies and fallacies by which it is often led." Two unique characteristics of American society are cited as compounding this dilemma—the "passion for publicity" and the lack of a tradition to sustain governmental privacy such as is common in Western European democracies. The author describes the growth of secrecy in American bureaucracy; the dilemma of Congress, caught between its antagonism to executive secrecy and its desire to protect national security; the Presidential power to control information; and government manipulation of public opinion. The most reliable defense against the excesses of government propaganda and official secrecy is found in political pluralism and governmental balance of power, as well as in an independent and aggressive press. In the end, however, "there is no simple way of reconciling the conflicting claims of publicity, secrecy, and democracy."

2780. Schmeckebier, Laurence F., *and* Roy B. Eastin. Government publications and their use. Rev. ed. Washington, D.C., Brookings Institution [1961] 476 p. 61–7718 Z1223.Z7S3 1961
An updated edition of no. 6138 in the 1960 *Guide*.

# F. The Presidency

2781. Binkley, Wilfred E. President and Congress. 3d rev. ed. New York, Vintage Books [1962] 403 p. 62–2230 JK516.B5 1962
An updated edition of no. 6140 in the 1960 *Guide*.
In *Presidential Power; the Politics of Leadership* (New York, Wiley [1960] 224 p.), Richard E. Neustadt analyzes the President's personal power on the basis of an examination of the ways in which it was wielded by Franklin D. Roosevelt, Truman, and Eisenhower. Theodore C. Sorensen's *Decision-Making in the White House* (New York, Columbia University Press, 1963. 94 p.), two lectures first delivered at Columbia as the Gino Speranza lectures for 1963, illuminates the decisionmaking process during the years of the Kennedy administration.

2782. Corwin, Edward S. The President, office and powers, 1787–1957; history and analysis of practice and opinion. 4th rev. ed. New York, New York University Press, 1957. 519 p.
57–11573 KF5051.C6 1957
Bibliographical references included in "Notes" (p. 315–496).
An updated edition of no. 6143 in the 1960 *Guide*.
*The Ultimate Decision* (New York, G. Braziller, 1960. 290 p.), edited by Ernest R. May, is a collection of nine essays on the ways in which wartime Presidents have managed their immense responsibilities under the constitutional provision making the President the Commander in Chief of the Armed Forces.

2783. Feerick, John D. From failing hands; the story of Presidential succession. Foreword by Paul A. Freund. New York, Fordham University Press [1965] xiv, 368 p. 65–14917 JK609.F4
Bibliography: p. 349–361.

A history of the formulation and execution of the Presidential succession acts of 1792, 1886, and 1947. The author examines the critical moments surrounding the succession of Vice Presidents to the Presidency, discusses the increasing importance of the Vice Presidency, and suggests improvements in the succession mechanism. Donald Young's *American Roulette, the History and Dilemma of the Vice Presidency* (New York, Holt, Rinehart & Winston [1965] 367 p.) is an anecdotal account of the Vice Presidents of the United States from John Adams to Lyndon B. Johnson.

2784. Henry, Laurin L. Presidential transitions. Washington, Brookings Institution [1960] xviii, 755 p. 60–53252 E743.H4
Bibliographical footnotes.
A study of four occasions on which the Presidency has passed from one major party to the other in this century: the Taft-Wilson transition of 1912–13; the Wilson-Harding transition of 1920–21; the Hoover-Roosevelt transition of 1932–33; and the Truman-Eisenhower transition of 1952–53. In each case the author describes how the President and President-elect prepared for the transfer, how the new President organized his administration and fulfilled his commitments, and how the institutions of Government contributed to and were affected by what occurred. The author identifies two broad requirements for effective transitions: continuity of leadership and administrative performance and responsiveness of Government to the new leadership. *Changing Administrations* (Washington, Brookings Institution [1965] 147 p.), by David T. Stanley, concentrates on the transfer of responsibility in six Federal organizations in the early 1960's.

2785. Koenig, Louis W.  The invisible Presidency. New York, Rinehart [1960]  438 p.

60–5341  E176.K6

Includes bibliography.

An investigation of the personalities, activities, and accomplishments of important Presidential assistants and favorites.  Among the careers considered are those of Alexander Hamilton, Martin Van Buren, William Loeb, Edward M. House, Thomas C. Corcoran, Harry Hopkins, and Sherman Adams. In general, the relationship between a President and his aides has been deeply personal, with the latter performing a variety of important tasks for him. The author concludes with a criticism of the recent growth of committees and of the staffs of Presidential assistants.  In *The President's Cabinet* (Cambridge, Harvard University Press, 1959.  327 p. Harvard's political studies), Richard F. Fenno approaches the cabinet as an "advisory, decisionmaking and coordinating body," analyzing its close relationship with the President as well as its role within the larger political system.  In *The Cabinet and Congress* (New York, Columbia University Press, 1960.  310 p.), John S. Horn explores an area often neglected in political studies.

2786. Rossiter, Clinton L.  The American Presidency.  With a new introduction by D. W.

Brogan.  New York, Time, Inc. [ᶜ1963]  xxi, 319 p.

63–25745  JK516.R6  1963

Bibliography: [309]–311.

An examination of the sources and limits of power in the Presidency, which the author considers to be "one of the few truly successful institutions created by men in their endless quest for the blessings of free government."  Constitutional provisions, custom, the practice of other nations, and the logic of history have created a variety of Presidential functions, among which the author cites the following as major roles: chief of state, Chief Executive, Commander in Chief, chief diplomat, chief legislator, chief of party, protector of the peace, manager of prosperity, and world leader.  On the other hand, the uses of Presidential power are circumscribed by numerous constitutional provisions, institutional arrangements, political pressures, and nongovernmental sources of power.  Rossiter uses this structure in evaluating the performance of various Presidents.  In *The Man in the White House,* rev. ed.  (New York, Harper & Row [1964]  274 p.  Harper colophon books, CN/46), Wilfred E. Binkley traces transformations in the Presidential office from Washington to Eisenhower.  *The Chief Executive* (New York, Harcourt, Brace & World [1964]  435 p.), by Louis W. Koenig, emphasizes the limitations on Presidential power.

## G. Congress

2787. Beck, Carl.  Contempt of Congress; a study of the prosecutions initiated by the Committee on Un-American Activities, 1945–1957. New Orleans, Hauser Press [1959]  263 p.  [The Galleon series in economics, history, and political science]  59–15941  KF9405.B4  1959

"Selected bibliography": p. [253]–258.  Bibliographical footnotes.

The origin and development of the power of Congress to prosecute for contempt are reviewed and specific cases are traced through the House Committee on Un-American Activities, the Congress, and the courts.  Among the constitutional issues discussed are the questions of fourth-amendment restraints on the power to subpoena the documents of private organizations, first-amendment limitations on the power to compel disclosure of political opinions, and the degree of protection against self-incrimination available to witnesses under the fifth amendment.  A synopsis of contempt citations from 1787 to 1943, a list of contempt citations from 1944

to 1958, and a statistical analysis of the citations are appended.

2788. Berman, Daniel M.  In Congress assembled; the legislative process in the National Government. New York, Macmillan [1964]  xv, 432 p.

64–14974  JK1061.B44

Bibliography: p. 405–412.  Bibliographical footnotes.

A critical appraisal of the U.S. Congress in its dual aspects as a legislative body and an organization of politicians.  In support of his contention that Congress as now constituted bears little resemblance to the legislative body envisaged by the framers of the Constitution, the author examines various political influences on the legislative process, including campaign procedures, political organization in Congress, activities of pressure groups, and the relationships between the executive and legislative branches and between individual Congressmen and their constituents.  The same author offers a case study of the legislative process in *A Bill Becomes a Law: The Civil Rights Act of 1960* (New York, Macmillan [1962] 143 p.). The two branches of the national legislature are discussed in *Forge of Democracy: The House of Representatives* (New York, D. McKay [1963] 496 p.), by Neil MacNeil, and *Citadel, the Story of the U.S. Senate* (New York, Harper [ᶜ1957] 274 p.), by William S. White.

2789. Burnham, James. Congress and the American tradition. Chicago, H. Regnery Co., 1959. 363 p.      59–9849   JK1061.B78

A discussion of the distribution and limitations of power under the American system of government, with particular reference to the role of Congress. According to the author, expansion of the Government and its increasing intervention in social life have been at the expense of the lawmaking, fiscal, and investigatory powers of Congress and its control of warmaking and foreign affairs. He concludes with a discussion of the future position of Congress within the American political system. *Congressional Control of Administration* (Washington, Brookings Institution [1964] 306 p.), by Joseph P. Harris, examines congressional efforts to control governmental operations and the difficulties involved in exercising such control owing to the growth of executive functions. In *Congressional Control of Federal Spending* (Detroit, Wayne State University Press, 1960. 188 p.), Robert A. Wallace reviews the influence exerted by Congress through its control over appropriations.

2790. Clapp, Charles L. The Congressman; his work as he sees it. Washington, Brookings Institution [1963] 452 p.   63–23202   JK1021.C55

Bibliographical footnotes.

An examination of the Congressman's role within the framework of the established procedures of the House of Representatives, based on extensive interviews and a series of panel discussions. The study covers such topics as the choice of House Speaker and floor leaders, the traditions of seniority, party discipline, intraparty blocs, and interpersonal relationships within the House and between Congressmen and their constituents. In *U.S. Senators and Their World* (Chapel Hill, University of North Carolina Press [1960] 303 p.), Donald R. Matthews studies background, performance, and work patterns of the men who served in the Senate during the years 1947–57.

2791. Clark, Joseph S. Congress: the sapless branch. New York, Harper & Row [1964] xviii, 268 p.      64–12669   JK1061.C57

Bibliographical references included in "Notes" (p. 253–257).

An examination of formal and real party structure in the U. S. Congress. A serious discrepancy exists between these, according to the author, owing to outworn organization and procedures, which in turn serve to invalidate publicly approved party platforms. Senator Clark considers that the Congress is neither effective nor representative and calls for reforms in congressional procedures. His analysis includes characterizations of both the House and Senate and a discussion of relationships between Congress and the President and between Congressmen and their constituents. In *House Out of Order* (New York, Dutton, 1965. 253 p.), Representative Richard W. Bolling suggests ways of restructuring the House of Representatives. *New Perspectives on the House of Representatives* (Chicago, Rand McNally [ᶜ1963] 392 p. Rand McNally political science series), edited by Robert L. Peabody and Nelson W. Polsby, is a collection of recent studies of the House as a political institution. *The Congress and America's Future* (Englewood Cliffs, N.J., Prentice-Hall [1965] 185 p. A Spectrum book S-AA-13), edited by David B. Truman for the American Assembly, consists of essays on the functions of Congress in dealing with current and potential needs and problems.

2792. Congressional Quarterly Service, *Washington, D.C.* Congress and the Nation, 1945–1964; a review of government and politics in the postwar years. Washington [1965] xxii, 1784, 231a p. illus.     65–22351   KF49.C653

A summary of major legislation and the national political scene for the years after World War II, covering such areas as foreign relations, national security, economics, labor, agriculture, education, welfare, and natural resources. Included are a biographical index of the Members of the 79th through the 88th Congresses, a record of key votes, a report on national and State elections during the period, and a review of 216 major Supreme Court cases. Congressional politics during the immediate post-Civil War period are discussed by the English historian William R. Brock in *An American Crisis: Congress and Reconstruction, 1865–1867* ([New York] St. Martin's Press [1963] 312 p.). Information on Senatorial graft during the same period can be found in *Of Snuff, Sin, and the Senate* (Chicago, Follett Pub. Co., 1965. 360 p.), by Robert Rienow and Leona T. Rienow.

2793. Evins, Joe L. Understanding Congress. New York, C. N. Potter [1963] 304 p.     63–18878   JK1061.E85

Includes bibliography.

The author, for 16 years a Congressman from Tennessee, notes the "lack of true appreciation of the work of Congress" and attributes it not only to the fact that Congress is "a highly complicated institution with a unique character and little similarity to any other body, political, civil, or private" but also to the failure on the part of Congressmen themselves to fully explain their work to the country. A vivid and detailed description of the Congressman's life on Capitol Hill is included, as well as discussions of the functions, organization, and procedures of Congress, its place in domestic and world affairs, and its relationships with the political parties, the Presidency, and the Supreme Court. *Member of the House* (New York, Scribner [1962] 195 p.), a collection of constituent-oriented newsletters written by Representative Clem Miller of California over a three-year period and edited by John W. Baker, provides insights into the activities and problems of a U.S. Congressman.

2794. Galloway, George B. History of the United States House of Representatives. [Rev. ed] Washington, U.S. Govt. Print. Off., 1965. 218 p. (89th Congress, 1st session. House document no. 250)          65–65604  JK1316.G22

A study of administrative growth and procedural change in the House of Representatives, prepared for the House Committee on House Administration of the 89th Congress. The author traces the evolution of the structure and organization of Congress, with particular reference to the development of the committee system and the pattern of leadership. Other aspects considered include party government, the performance of legislative functions, relations with the Senate and the President, and the role of the individual Representative. *The United States Senate, 1787–1801; a Dissertation on the First Fourteen Years of the Upper Legislative Body* (Washington, U.S. Govt. Print. Off., 1962. 325 p. 87th Congress, 1st session. Senate Documents no. 64), by Roy Swanstrom is a detailed history of the early years of the upper house.

2795. Green, Harold P., *and* Alan Rosenthal. Government of the atom; the integration of powers. New York, Atherton Press, 1963. 281 p. (The Atherton Press political science series)
          63–8916  HD9698.U52G7  1963
Bibliographical footnotes.

The authors cite the Joint Committee on Atomic Energy as a notable exception to the pattern of increasing ascendency of the executive branch over Congress in the fields of foreign and defense affairs. Since its creation under the Atomic Energy Act of 1946, the committee has played an unprecedented role in the formulation of national policy. The study covers not only the evolution and functions of the committee but also such broad areas as executive-legislative relations and the performance of congressional committees as institutions. *The Truman Committee* (New Brunswick, N.J., Rutgers University Press [1964] 207 p.), by Donald H. Riddle, is a study of the history and performance of the Senate Special Committee Investigating the National Defense Program. In *The House Rules Committee* (Indianapolis, Bobbs-Merrill [1963] 142 p. The advanced studies in political science), James A. Robinson assesses the powers and procedures of that committee through an analysis of its documents.

2796. Kofmehl, Kenneth T. Professional staffs of Congress. [West Lafayette, Ind., 1962] 282 p. (Purdue University studies: humanities series)
          62–63211  JK1083.K6
Bibliographical references included in "Notes" (p. 231–268).

An analytical and descriptive study of the enlarged professional staff created to assist Congress during the first six years following enactment of the Legislative Reorganization Act of 1946, which provided for the enlargement. In the author's view, these years were the formative period for most of the professional staffing subsequently available to members of Congress. He concentrates on committee staffs, office staffs, and the Office of the Legislative Counsel. His conclusion is that the increased staffing was desirable but that Congress should resist tendencies to expand it still further. A postscript is devoted to major trends in congressional staffing from 1953 through 1961.

## H. Administration: General

2797. Kilpatrick, Franklin P., Milton C. Cummings, *and* M. Kent Jennings. The image of the Federal service. Washington, Brookings Institution [1964] xvii, 301 p.
          64–13789  JK691.K44

Bibliographical footnotes.

An analysis of the results of a cross-sectional poll of public attitudes toward the civil service and the Federal Government as an employer, prompted by growing competition between private and Federal organizations for talented manpower. The authors suggest a number of changes in Federal personnel organization, policies, and procedures. The data themselves are presented in a companion volume, *Source Book of a Study of Occupational Values and the Image of the Federal Service* (Washington, Brookings Institution [1964] 681 p.), by the same authors. In *The Job of the Federal Executive* (Washington, Brookings Institution [1958] 241 p.), Marver H. Bernstein analyzes various factors involved in effective Federal administration.

2798. Millett, John D. Government and public administration; the quest for responsible performance. New York, McGraw-Hill, 1959. 484 p. (McGraw-Hill series in political science)
58–13883   JK421.M5

A study of the ways in which American political institutions operate "to keep the great apparatus of public administration subject to some degree of political responsibility." The author notes the separate identity of government bureaucracy and its position of tactical superiority over the decisionmaking branches but considers that these branches, acting in concert, provide the instrumentalities for keeping bureaucracy responsible: the legislative by determining public policy through laws, the executive by its supervisory role and its part in determining national policy, and the judicial by its concern for constitutional limitations and its share in political power.

2799. Nigro, Felix A. Modern public administration. New York, Harper & Row [1965] 531 p.                        65–11140   JF1351.N5

Bibliographies at ends of chapters.

A textbook on the problems of administration at all governmental levels, with emphasis on adaptability to current developments and needs. Edward W. Weidner's *Technical Assistance in Public Administration Overseas* (Chicago, Public Administration Service [1964] 247 p.) is a review of programs sponsored by the United Nations, the Ford Foundation, consulting firms, and American universities.

## I. Administration: Special

2800. Karl, Barry Dean. Executive reorganization and reform in the New Deal, the genesis of administrative management, 1900–1939. Cambridge, Mass., Harvard University Press, 1963. 292 p.                        63–13813   JK691.K35

Includes bibliography.

In 1936 President Franklin Delano Roosevelt created the Committee on Administrative Management and appointed Louis Brownlow, Charles E. Merriam, and Luther H. Gulick as its members. The committee was instructed "to make a study of the relation of the existing regular organizations of the Executive Branch of the Government," including the many new agencies created to cope with the depression. The committee's report led to passage of the Administrative Reorganization Act of 1939, which set up the Executive Office of the President and a White House staff, enabled the President to appoint administrative assistants, and authorized him to effect additional reorganization. In this study, the author combines biographies of the committee members with historical narrative and theoretical analysis. In *Congress and the Challenge of Big Government* (New York, Bookman Associates [°1958] 129 p. Bookman monograph series), Oscar Kraines examines the "first comprehensive Congressional investigations into administration," begun in 1885.

2801. Powell, Norman J. Personnel administration in government. Englewood Cliffs, N.J., Prentice-Hall, 1956. 548 p.   56–9003   JK421.P6

Bibliography: p. 487–510.

A textbook study of the "principal ideas and data fundamental to thinking out and working out effective personnel programs and policies in the public service." In addition to discussing general principles and problems of government personnel administration, the author covers such specific matters as program guidelines, recruiting, selection, employee relations, position classification, pay schedules, career service, and in-service training. He notes that research is providing the administrator with new and objective means for dealing with his problems but that in practice these usually have limitations. Public personnel administration thus remains "a value-laden area of study with components both of science and art."

2802. Stahl, Oscar Glenn, William E. Mosher, *and* J. Donald Kingsley. Public personnel administration. 5th ed. New York, Harper & Row [1962] 531 p.        62–19728   JK765.S68   1962

Includes bibliography.

An updated edition of no. 6188 in the 1960 *Guide.*

2803. Warner, William Lloyd, *and others*. The American Federal executive; a study of the social and personal characteristics of the civilian and military leaders of the United States Federal Government. New Haven, Yale University Press, 1963. xvii, 405 p. illus.                63–7952  JK723.E9W3

A sociological study of Federal executive personnel, based on an anlysis of questionnaires sent to more than 12,000 military and civilian administrators. The authors devote particular attention to the executives' family and educational backgrounds, the career routes leading to their present positions, and their social and occupational mobility as compared to that of leaders in private industry. *The Assistant Secretaries* (Washington, D.C., The Brookings Institution [1965] 310 p.), by Dean E. Mann with Jameson W. Doig, is a study of recruitment and appointment on one executive level.

# J. State Government

2804. Adrian, Charles R. State and local governments, a study in the political process. New York, McGraw-Hill, 1960. 531 p. (McGraw-Hill series in political science)    59–15042  JK2408.A3
"For further reading": p. 517–521.

An examination of the general patterns of State and local parties and election campaigns, the characteristics of executives, legislatures, and judiciaries, and their performance in such fields as education, public welfare, and water supply. The author defines the political process as "a method by which individual wants, which become social wants, are met by government and social-political policies emerge as imperfect compromises among the conflicting interests of society," and his analysis draws heavily on the social sciences and humanities. *State and Local Governments: A Case Book* ([University] University of Alabama Press, 1963. 669 p.), prepared by a group of political scientists for the Inter-University Case Program and edited by Edwin A. Bock, is a collection of 25 case studies which portray situations, atmospheres, processes, and tactics in American government below the Federal level. *State and Local Government & Politics,* 2d ed., rev. & enl. (New York, Random House [1962] 425 p.), by Robert S. Babcock, is a textbook which focuses on specific political problems and the dynamics of the political process. In *The Office of Governor in the United States* (University, Ala., University of Alabama Press, 1956. 417 p.), Coleman B. Ransone concentrates on executive functions at the State level.

2805. Anderson, William, Clara Penniman, *and* Edward W. Weidner. Government in the fifty States. New York, Holt, Rinehart & Winston [1960] 509 p. illus.    60–9131  JK2408.A7  1960
Includes bibliography.

An updated edition of *State and Local Government in the United States,* no. 6196 in the 1960 *Guide.*

2806. Jewell, Malcolm E. The State legislature: politics and practice. New York, Random House [1962] 146 p. (Studies in political science, PS37)    62–10673  JK2488.J4

A paperback study of the State legislatures in the United States, with emphasis on the political character of these institutions. Since political patterns vary widely among the States, the author develops a theoretical model legislature, based on a vigorous two-party system as an analytical aid in clarifying the actual functions of the party system in legislatures and estimating the likelihood of achieving increased party responsibility in the legislative process. Specific topics discussed include the election of legislators, voting alignments in the legislature, its political organization, and the Governor as legislator. The author considers a lack of political responsibility to be the fundamental weakness of some legislatures and concludes that a strong two-party system within a State offers the greatest possibility of achieving responsible government. He notes a recent weakening of Republican strongholds in the North and inroads by the Republicans in the South and border areas, a situation which has resulted in there now being "probably more state legislatures where politics is based on the competition of closely balanced parties than at any other time in American history."

2807. Pennsylvania. University. *Fels Institute of Local and State Government.* Government studies, Fels Institute series. Philadelphia, University of Pennsylvania Press [1958–63] 5 v.

A series commemorating the 20th anniversary of the Fels Institute of Local and State Government and the 75th of the Wharton School of Finance and Commerce, both of the University of Pennsylvania. The Fels Institute was founded in 1937 under the direction of Stephen B. Sweeney, professor of governmental administration at the University of Pennsylvania, as an affiliate of the Wharton School. The series is made up of five scholarly monographs devoted to "problems of current and long-range significance which are of particular interest to students of local and state goverment." Case studies of Pennsylvania situations predominate, but the analyses have broad applications. The individual volumes are as follows: *Education for Administrative Careers in Government Service* ([1958] 366 p. 58–12719. JF1338.A259), edited by Stephen B. Sweeney; *Metropolitan Analysis* ([1958] 189 p. 58–8137.

HT109.S9), also edited by Sweeney; *Planning Municipal Investment, a Case Study of Philadelphia* ([1961] 293 p. 61–5540. HJ9307.P4B7 1961), by William H. Brown and Charles E. Gilbert; *State Government in Transition; Reforms of the Leader Administration, 1955–1959* ([1963] 309 p. 63–7864. JK3638 1959.S57), by Reed M. Smith; and *Four Cities; a Study in Comparative Policy Making* ([1963] 334 p. 63–7853. JS323.W53), by Oliver P. Williams and Charles R. Adrian.

## K. Local Government

2808. Banfield, Edward C., *and* James Q. Wilson. City politics. Cambridge, Harvard University Press, 1963. 362 p. illus. (Publications of the Joint Center for Urban Studies of the Massachusetts Institute of Technology and Harvard University)

63–19134 JS331.B28

Bibliographical footnotes.

An introductory study of urban government as a political rather than an administrative process. Among the topics considered are the effects of a greater or lesser concentration of authority within the city, ways in which power is accumulated, and "the fundamental cleavage between the public-regarding, Anglo-Saxon Protestant, middle-class ethos and the private-regarding, lower-class, immigrant ethos." *Urban Government* ([New York] Free Press of Glencoe [1961] 593 p.), a collection of readings on urban politics and administration edited by Banfield, is intended to serve as a supplementary text.

2809. Blair, George S. American local government. New York, Harper & Row [1964] 619 p. illus. 64–12787 JS331.B48

Includes bibliographies.

A textbook in which a comparative and functional approach is taken to various divisions of local government, including counties, cities, townships, towns, and schools. Another textbook, concentrating on rural governments, is *Local Government in Rural America* (New York, Appleton-Century-Crofts [1957] 584 p. ACC political science series), by Clyde F. Snider. A study of recently formed local government units is Robert G. Smith's *Public Authorities, Special Districts, and Local Government* (Washington, National Association of Counties Research Foundation [1964] 225 p.).

2810. Connery, Robert H., *and* Richard H. Leach. The Federal Government and metropolitan

areas. Cambridge, Harvard University Press, 1960. 275 p. (Government in metropolitan areas)

60–7990 JS323.C58

Includes bibliography.

This study, conducted by the Government in Metropolitan Areas Project, explores governmental problems "thrust to the fore by the revolutionary expansion of urban populations in the United States and the resulting new patterns of metropolitan settlement." Among the topics discussed are the effects of existing Federal programs on metropolitan areas, representation of metropolitan interests in Washington, and ways in which Congress and the executive branch have failed to meet metropolitan problems. Arguments for and against the creation of a Department of Urban Affairs are also reviewed. The authors note that although any approach must take into account the American federal system under which the primary responsibility for solving urban problems lies with local and State governments, interstate and international situations which neither the local community nor the States can handle alone are also involved. The Federal Government must therefore "take the initiative in meeting the challenge of the metropolis." Specific recommendations are presented concerning highways, water resources, water and air pollution, airports, military installations and defense industries, civil defense, and housing and urban renewal.

2811. Phillips, Jewell C. Municipal government and administration in America. New York, Macmillan [1960] 648 p. illus.

60–5247 JS331.P46

Bibliographies at the ends of chapters.

A textbook covering the functions and operation of municipal governments within the context of intergovernmental relations. Particular attention is devoted to the effectiveness of governmental structures in dealing with urban problems. The dynamic quality of urban populations and the consequent effects on the functions of city government are emphasized in another textbook, Benjamin Baker's *Urban Government* (Princeton, N.J., Van Nostrand [1957] 572 p. Van Nostrand political science series). In a report entitled *Governmental Manpower for Tomorrow's Cities* (New York, McGraw-Hill [1962] 201 p.), the Municipal Manpower Commission, organized under a Ford Foundation study grant, discusses the difficulties experienced by American urban governments in their attempts to attract and retain qualified administrative, professional, and technical personnel.

2812. Smith, Thelma E. Guide to the municipal government of the city of New York. 8th ed. New York, Record Press, 1960. 278 p.

60–9986 JS1228.S6 1960

An updated edition of Rebecca B. Rankin's *Guide to the Municipal Government of the City of New York*, no. 6214 in the 1960 *Guide*.

# XXX

# Law and Justice

THE WORKS classified under History (Sections A and B) in this chapter are for the most part scholarly monographs on relatively narrow topics. In Section A are publications devoted to such topics as British statutes in American law, 1776–1836, and law and authority in early Massachusetts. Section B, which is almost twice as large as any other section in the chapter, includes biographies of six Supreme Court Justices. Also in the same section, however, are a general history of the Court, an examination of its role in American life, and a discussion of its function as guardian of fundamental freedoms. With the exception of a five-volume work on jurisprudence, Section C, General Views, consists largely of essays and addresses. Monographic digests of American law of the type entered in Section D in the 1960 *Guide* appear to have been superseded in many instances by other kinds of publications; as a consequence, a text on civil procedure is the single entry in this section of the *Supplement*. Studies of what takes place in the courtroom are divided between Section E, Courts and Judges, and Section F, The Judicial Process. In the former are books emphasizing the role of the judges; in the latter are works dealing primarily with arrests, lawyers, and juries. The law as a profession falls within Section H, which includes the writings of three trial lawyers.

## A. History: General

2813.  Brown, Elizabeth G.  British statutes in American law, 1776–1836. In consultation with William Wirt Blume. Ann Arbor, University of Michigan Law School, 1964. 377 p. (Michigan legal studies)          64–64845  KF366.B7

The American Colonies were denied the right to incorporate the whole of Anglican law in their legal process, but once independence was declared and such restrictions were nullified, the adoption of suitable British statutes offered a solution to the need for a body of laws in the new Republic. This study, intended primarily for the scholar, explores the extent to which such statutes, without reenactment, were either declared or considered to be in force. *Law and Authority in Colonial America* (Barre, Mass., Barre Publishers [1965] 208 p.), edited by George A. Billias, is a collection of essays which take a more general approach to the same subject.

2814.  Haskins, George L.  Law and authority in early Massachusetts; a study in tradition and design. New York, Macmillan, 1960. 298 p.

    60–6416 KFM2478.H3 1960

Bibliographical notes: p. 232–287.

The introductory volume in a planned series, covering the first 20 years of the Massachusetts Bay settlement. Noting that "in early Massachusetts the law appears both as an anchor to tradition and a vehicle for change," the author traces the evolution of the Colony's institutions and instruments of government and describes in broad outline the development of substantive law in these first two decades. The study includes a discussion of the influence exerted by Puritan doctrines and aspirations and of the more general topic of state-church relations in society.

2815. Hurst, James W. Law and social process in United States history; five lectures delivered at the University of Michigan, November 9, 10, 11, 12, and 13, 1959. Ann Arbor, University of Michigan Law School, 1960. 361 p. (The Thomas M. Cooley lectures, 9th ser.) 61–62695 KF358.H8

The author discusses four features which, he maintains, have been greatly responsible for shaping the distinctive roles and character of law in the United States: force—the Government's "legitimated monopoly of violence"; constitutionalism—the belief in law based on a fundamental document; procedure—the formal steps through which the law is executed; and resource allocation—reliance upon law as a major means of determining how natural and human resources will be used. American experience has been characterized by change rather than stability, according to Hurst, a situation which places heavy demands on legal order, and inertia has tended to prevail over deliberated decision in producing this change. The same author analyzes the effect that law and court decisions may have on a particular type of activity in *Law and Economic Growth; the Legal History of the Lumber Industry in Wisconsin, 1836–1915* (Cambridge, Mass., Belknap Press of Harvard University Press, 1964. 946 p.). Samuel Mermin's *Jurisprudence and Statecraft; the Wisconsin Development Authority and Its Implications* (Madison, University of Wisconsin Press, 1963. 252 p.) demonstrates the interplay of the many factors that influence legal and social reform.

2816. Morris, Richard B. Studies in the history of American law, with special reference to the seventeenth and eighteenth centuries. 2d ed. Philadelphia, J. M. Mitchell Co., 1959 [°1958] 285 p.

    59–14510 KF361.M67 1959

Includes bibliography.

A revised edition of no. 6230 in the 1960 *Guide*.

2817. Paul, Arnold M. Conservative crisis and the rule of law; attitudes of bar and bench, 1887–1895. Ithaca, N.Y. Published for the American Historical Association [by] Cornell University Press [1960] 256 p. 61–88 KF5130.P3 1960

Bibliography: p. 238–247.

In the late 19th century, a "new judicialism" emerged as the principal bulwark of defense against demands for economic adjustment, according to the author. Judicial intervention in economic conflict was aimed at circumscribing reform movements and legislation which had been stimulated by the effects of intense industrialization. Court decisions were at times major factors in perpetuating the inequalities that accompanied this socioeconomic growth. In support of his position, the author discusses specific instances relating to income tax legislation, trusts and entrenched capital, injunctions against labor, and delimitation of police power in the name of due process of law and freedom of contract.

# B. History: The Supreme Court

2818. Frank, John P. Marble palace; the Supreme Court in American life. New York, Knopf, 1958. 301 p. 58–12628 KF8748.F65

A former law clerk to Associate Justice Hugo L. Black discusses the Supreme Court as a governmental institution which plays a vital balancing role between conflicting interests. After reviewing the Court's jurisdiction, enforcement of its decisions, selection of its members, and techniques used by lawyers and justices during litigation, the author examines special functions of the Court in such areas as civil liberties, the economy, international affairs, and maintenance of a balance between the National and State Governments. *The Judiciary* (Boston, Allyn & Bacon, 1965. 122 p. The Allyn & Bacon series in American Government), by Henry J. Abraham, is a concise survey of the Supreme Court's role in government. In *The Least Dangerous Branch* (Indianapolis, Bobbs-Merrill [°1962] 303 p.), Alexander M. Bickel considers the Court's impact on society, using the idea of judicial supremacy as a point of departure. The problems of judicial selection, the external forces operating upon the Court, and the evolution of its procedures and customs are discussed by John R. Schmidhauser in *The Supreme Court: Its Politics, Personalities, and Procedures* (New York, Holt, Rinehart & Winston [1960] 163 p.).

2819.  Harper, Fowler V.  Justice Rutledge and the bright constellation.  Indianapolis, Bobbs-Merrill [1965]  xxv, 406 p.
64–8430  KF8745.R87H37
Bibliographical references included in "Notes" (p. 379–398).

In his initial inaugural address, Thomas Jefferson referred to the first eight amendments to the Constitution as the "Bright Constellation." During his six-year service on the Supreme Court, 1943–49, Associate Justice Wiley B. Rutledge promoted recognition of the basic American liberties inherent in those amendments.  The author describes Justice Rutledge's origins, gives the background of his appointment to the bench, and discusses key judicial decisions involving fundamental freedoms and procedural rights.  Noting that Rutledge's views, often expressed in dissent, did not prevail until after his death in 1949, Harper traces the influence of the Justice's opinions to 1965.

2820.  Howe, Mark De Wolfe.  Justice Oliver Wendell Holmes.  Cambridge, Belknap Press of Harvard University Press, 1957–63.  2 v.
57–6348  KF8745.H6H65
CONTENTS.— 1. The shaping years, 1841–1870. 2. The proving years, 1870–1882.

Volume 1 of this projected multivolume biography is no. 6241 in the 1960 *Guide*. The second volume continues the "account of a young man's progress towards intellectual accomplishment," with primary emphasis on an analysis of Holmes' classic study, *The Common Law* (no. 6222 in the 1960 *Guide*).  This work occupied much of Holmes' time and energy for six years before its publication in 1881, although during the period covered by the second volume in this biography he also managed to serve as an editor of the *American Law Review* and to lecture at Harvard and at the Lowell Institute, in addition to practicing law.  In 1882 he was appointed a professor at Harvard Law School, and in December of that year he accepted a seat on the Massachusetts Supreme Judicial Court.  Howe has also prepared a special edition of *The Common Law* (Cambridge, Belknap Press of Harvard University Press, 1963.  338 p.  The John Harvard library).

2821.  Lewis, Anthony.  Gideon's trumpet.  New York, Random House [1964]  262 p.
64–11986  Law

Bibliographic references included in "Notes" (p. [239]–252).  "Suggested readings": p. [253]–256.

A study of two judicial issues, federalism and the right to counsel, as they apply in the case of Clarence Gideon, an indigent convicted of breaking and entering with the intent to commit petty larceny. Gideon appealed his case to the U.S. Supreme Court on the grounds that he had not been represented by counsel.  The case is traced from the *forma pauperis* petition and arguments by the court-appointed counsel to Justice Hugo L. Black's opinion that the sixth amendment's general guarantee of counsel in criminal prosecutions is extended to cases in State courts by the 14th amendment.  This decision broadened an earlier Supreme Court interpretation requiring counsel for indigents in capital cases. Gideon eventually won a verdict of not guilty in the same Florida court which had originally convicted him.  The account includes a discussion of the problems confronting the attorney for the State of Florida and of the questions of States' rights raised by the case.  Another fundamental decision is chronicled by Alan F. Westin in *The Anatomy of a Constitutional Law Case: Youngstown Sheet and Tube Co. v. Sawyer; the Steel Seizure Decision* (New York, Macmillan [1958]  183 p.).  The entire 1962–63 term of the Court is discussed by James E. Clayton in *The Making of Justice* (New York, Dutton, 1964.  319 p.).

2822.  Lewis, Walker.  Without fear or favor; a biography of Chief Justice Roger Brooke Taney.  Boston, Houghton Mifflin, 1965.  556 p.
65–18490  KF8745.T3L4
Bibliography: p. [539]–546.

Taney (1777–1864) succeeded John Marshall in 1836 to sit as the fifth Chief Justice of the U.S. Supreme Court, a post in which he served until his death.  The author reviews Taney's activities before the appointment, noting that a high point of his career was his support, as Secretary of the Treasury, of Andrew Jackson's "war" against the Bank of the United States.  Taney's judicial opinions on many key subjects, according to the author, "provided the creative hypothesis around which a whole branch of law developed," particularly in the field of commercial law.  The Dred Scott decision (1856), which held in effect that a Negro could not be a citizen of the United States, subjected Taney to severe criticism.  His opinion in *ex parte Merryman* (1861), on the other hand, which ruled against executive suspension of the writ of *habeas corpus* without legislative approval, is often praised as one of the greatest expositions of individual liberty in the Nation's history.

2823. Magrath, C. Peter. Morrison R. Waite; the triumph of character. New York, Macmillan [1963] 334 p. 63–14340 KF8745.W27M3

The author describes the pervasive corruption of the Grant era from which Chief Justice Waite emerged, briefly reviews Waite's early life and career, and discusses in detail the difficulties confronting the Supreme Court during his tenure (1874–88). Two categories of problems were of primary concern to the Court, according to the author, reintegrating the South with the rest of the Nation and coping with the advances in technology and finance. The 13th, 14th, and 15th amendments were designed to protect the newly freed Negro, but the Court interpreted them narrowly, believing the States could adequately handle the issue of race. Maintaining a suitable climate for the reconciliation was considered the paramount judicial obligation. Although later the Court denied the States the right to regulate business and strictly construed Congress' power as well, in *Munn* v. *Illinois* (1877) it declared a State regulatory statute valid. The author concludes that Chief Justice Waite's major achievement was "personal." By "quiet dignity and careful observance of the judicial proprieties he did much to add new luster to the Court's tarnished reputation."

2824. Mason, Alpheus T. The Supreme Court from Taft to Warren. Baton Rouge, Louisiana State University Press, 1958. 250 p.
58–10292 KF8748.M3 1958

James Madison envisioned that one function of the Supreme Court would be to protect individuals and minorities while permitting government by the majority. The author examines this role as reflected in the legal philosophies of the four Chief Justices preceding Earl W. Warren. He notes that for William Howard Taft, the concept of property was bedrock; the commerce clause of the Constitution was designed to accommodate change facilitating the growth of business. The primary value in Charles Evans Hughes' philosophy was stability, but he modified his views quickly to maintain judicial supremacy against Franklin D. Roosevelt's "court-packing" proposal. Harlan Fiske Stone, who had "an acute awareness of the role the Court must and should play in the American scheme of government," advocated judicial restraint. Relatively little attention is devoted to the seven-year term of Fred M. Vinson, upon whose death in 1953 Warren was appointed Chief Justice. In *Politics and the Warren Court* (New York, Harper & Row [1965] 299 p.), Alexander M. Bickel examines the interaction between Supreme Court decisions and public policies during the 12-year period beginning in 1954, with

emphasis on civil rights, legislative reapportionment, and public education.

2825. Mason, Alpheus T. William Howard Taft, Chief Justice. New York, Simon & Schuster [1965] 354 p. 65–11166 KF8745.T27M3

Although Taft's tenure as Chief Justice constituted only one phase in a long career, he left as a legacy for the people of the United States a judiciary better able to cope with society's needs. Among his proposals, only reorganization of the lower Federal courts and alteration of the Supreme Court's jurisdiction were accepted immediately, Mason notes, but he laid the groundwork for more extensive reform, especially in the rules of procedure which were finally adopted in 1938. Taft was a consummate lobbyist, according to the author, and campaigned hard for a seat on the high bench, for reform measures, and for candidates for vacant seats on the Supreme Court. Mason sees Taft as a dominant personality whose views were well founded, deep seated, and basically conservative. He finds it ironic that Taft should be best remembered for judicial reforms that facilitated a progressivism which he distrusted and that his broad construction of the commerce clause has permitted widespread experimentation of a kind that disconcerted him. In *A Supreme Court Justice Is Appointed* (New York, Random House [1964] 242 p. Random House studies in political science, PS46), David J. Danelski describes Taft's role in the nomination of Pierce Butler.

2826. Pfeffer, Leo. The liberties of an American; the Supreme Court speaks. 2d ed. enl. [Boston] Beacon Press [1963] 328 p. (Beacon paperback, 168) 63–14156 KF4749.P45 1963
Bibliography: p. [305]–307.

A discussion of the Supreme Court's function in defining and protecting constitutional privileges. The author compares decisions made before 1937 with those which have been handed down since and concludes that the Court has become the chief guardian of fundamental freedoms. This role is illustrated most clearly in its increasing willingness, particularly since midcentury, to handle issues involving civil rights. In general, Pfeffer maintains, the Court's vigor has resulted in a clearer, more precise definition of the freedoms basic to the American experiment in government.

2827. Pfeffer, Leo. This honorable Court; a history of the United States Supreme Court. Boston, Beacon Press [1965] 470 p.
65–13536 KF8742.P34
Bibliography: p. 429–434.

The author views the role of the Supreme Court as a threefold paradox: the Court uses customs and instruments of a judicial nature but performs important political and legislative functions; while so acting, it is beyond effective attack upon its status or powers; and its decisions impinging upon the political and legislative processes are accepted despite its inability to compel compliance. This history of the Court is intended as a starting point in the development of an understanding of the paradox and thus of the functioning of our governmental system. The author reviews the treatment accorded each of the three branches in the Constitution and discusses some of the Court's crucial decisions against their historical background. In *The American Supreme Court* ([Chicago] University of Chicago Press [1960] 260 p. The Chicago history of American civilization), Robert G. McCloskey also reviews the relationship between the Court and American society.

2828.  Schmidhauser, John R.  The Supreme Court as final arbiter in Federal-State relations, 1789–1957.  Chapel Hill, University of North Carolina Press [1958]  241 p.
              58–3675  KF8748.S275  1968
    Bibliography: p. [231]–235.

A study of the origins of the Supreme Court's power in Federal-State relations and of the manner in which that power has been exercised. The author defends the Court against recent States' rights charges of "judicial usurpation" of power, asserting that the records of the Convention of 1787 and of the State ratifying conventions, as well as the legislative history of the first Judiciary Act, indicate unmistakably that the Founding Fathers intended to give the Supreme Court the responsibility for monitoring the Federal system. The crises and difficulties subsequently faced by the Court are understandable, he finds, in part because it has frequently been either behind the times, as in the early period of the New Deal, or ahead of the times, as in recent years. In addition, personal preferences of the judges have led to the adoption of doctrines which violated or strained constitutional proprieties, according to Schmidhauser.

2829.  Schubert, Glendon A.  The Presidency in the courts.  Minneapolis, University of Minnesota Press [1957]  391 p.
              57–5803  KF5050.S35

2830.  Murphy, Walter F.  Congress and the Court; a case study in the American political process.  [Chicago] University of Chicago Press [1962]  307 p.     62–9739  KF8748.M84

Bibliographical references included in "Notes" (p. 269–296).

*The Presidency in the Courts* is an analysis of judicial behavior as it relates to the powers of the Presidency. Schubert concludes that the most significant aspect of judicial review of Presidential orders is its ineffectiveness and argues that "the elected representatives of the people—the President and the Congress—must decide the great questions of constitutional law." The author of *Congress and the Court* examines the Supreme Court's decisions under Chief Justice Earl W. Warren and the response of Congress to those decisions. He notes that the Court handed down a number of decisions which had significant effects in shaping public policy and that Congress then considered—but in only one instance adopted—proposals to reverse the Court's policies. In the end, however, the Court withdrew from policymaking activities. In *Congress Versus the Supreme Court, 1957–1960* (Minneapolis, University of Minnesota Press [1961] 168 p.), Charles Herman Pritchett concentrates on efforts of the 85th and 86th Congresses to curb the Court.

2831.  Shapiro, Martin.  Law and politics in the Supreme Court; new approaches to political jurisprudence.  [New York]  Free Press of Glencoe [1964]  364 p.    64–23078  KF8748.S5
    Bibliographical references included in "Notes" (p. 334–356).

As an aid to law students, the author provides background in political concepts which clarify the sources and implications of Supreme Court doctrines and decisions. The study is intended to bridge the gap between political and legal learning. On the basis of an approach which combines judicial realism and sociological jurisprudence, Shapiro defines the major roles of the Court and analyzes each of them in detail. In *The Supreme Court on Trial* (New York, Atherton Press, 1963. 308 p.), Charles S. Hyneman uses *Brown* v. *Board of Education* (1954) as a case study in examining the place of the Court in the political system.

2832.  Silver, David M.  Lincoln's Supreme Court.  Urbana, University of Illinois Press, 1956.  272 p.  (Illinois studies in the social sciences, v. 38)
           56–5688  H31.I4  v. 38
    Bibliography: p. 241–249.

Taking a basically historical rather than legalistic approach, the author describes and evaluates the Supreme Court's relationship to Lincoln and to the Union during the Civil War. The study covers radical attempts to "modify, pack, or destroy the Supreme Court," as well as "the attitudes of the various members of the Court as the war opens, the politics behind the appointment of four Associate Justices and a Chief Justice, decisions of vital, war-related cases, examination of the normal business of the wartime Court, proposals to lure aged Democratic Justices into retirement, the role of the Justices on circuit, the revamping of the Court under its new Republican Chief Justice, Salmon P. Chase, and the absolution of its former Democratic head, Roger B. Taney." In the Prize Cases, according to the author, the Court handed down its most significant decisions of the period: Lincoln's proclamation instituting a blockade of the entire coastline of the Confederacy, based solely on Presidential authority, was upheld as constitutional.

2833. Thomas, Helen S. Felix Frankfurter; scholar on the bench. Baltimore, Johns Hopkins Press [1960] 381 p. 60–11571 KF8745.F7T44
Bibliographical footnotes.

A biography which includes an examination of Justice Frankfurter's writings, speeches, and judicial opinions. Displaying great faith in the legislative branch, Frankfurter advocated a limited role for the judiciary in trying to solve the problems of an evolving society, according to the author, and legislative intent based on policy was thus accorded great weight in his findings. Although sudden breaks in the nature of the Court's decisions were not desirable, *stare decisis* was not to be blindly followed where new bodies of knowledge, not extant at the time of earlier decisions, had become available. The Constitution, although written, only set up bounds within which great flexibility could be exercised to accommodate new developments. Frankfurter believed that the court's function was to direct the Constitution, which he referred to as a stream of history.

2834. Westin, Alan F., ed. An autobiography of the Supreme Court; off-the-bench commentary by the Justices. New York, Macmillan [1963] 475 p. 63–10707 Law
Bibliography: p. 35–47.

An anthology of out-of-court commentary by U.S. Supreme Court Justices from 1790 to 1962. Asserting that the public "can profit from as much explanatory commentary in speeches and books as the Justices can produce without disrupting the sense of corporate privacy and the reputation for impartial judging," the author presents a variety of selections which include statements about the Court as an institution, about constitutional law issues, and about fellow Justices. Each item represents the thinking of the Justice after he joined the Court and secured a view from the inside. *The Constitution and the Supreme Court*, 2d ed. (New York, Dodd, Mead, 1965. 681 p.), edited by Wallace Mendelson, uses actual decisions to reveal the current status of constitutional law.

## C. General Views

2835. Association of American Law Schools. Selected essays on constitutional law, 1938–1962. Compiled and edited by a committee of the Association of American Law Schools: Edward L. Barrett, Jr. [and others] St. Paul, West Pub. Co., 1963 971 p. 63–4245 KF4550.A2A782
Bibliographical footnotes.

A supplement to No. 6090 in the 1960 *Guide*.

2836. Griswold, Erwin N. Law and lawyers in the United States; the common law under stress. Cambridge, Harvard University Press, 1965 [°1964] 152 p. 65–2274 KF298.G7 1965
Bibliographical footnotes.

A series of lectures delivered in London by the dean of the Harvard University Law School. Various aspects of the law of the United States are discussed, including the American legal profession, problems of federalism, and civil rights.

2837. Hand, Learned. The spirit of liberty; papers and addresses. Collected and with an introduction and notes by Irving Dilliard. 3d ed., enl. New York, Knopf, 1960. xxx, 310 p.
60–10956 KF213.H3 1960
A revised edition of no. 6264 in the 1960 *Guide*.

2838. Henson, Ray D., ed. Landmarks of law; highlights of legal opinion. New York, Harper [1960] 461 p. 60–7558 Law

A collection of essays which provide a variety of 20th-century views on the subject of jurisprudence, including those of Oliver Wendell Holmes, Roscoe Pound, and Felix Frankfurter. The substance of law is illustrated with comments on such topics as evidence, right to privacy, and proof, as well as on legal guidelines governing insurance, community property, and compensation. Of particular interest is the article in which Samuel D. Warren and Louis

D. Brandeis laid the foundations for modern recognition of the "right to privacy."

2839. Mendelson, Wallace. Justices Black and Frankfurter: conflict in the Court. [Chicago] University of Chicago Press [1961] 151 p.

61–5781  KF8748.M4 1961

"The main trouble with the Supreme Court is a general misunderstanding of its role in American government," according to the author, who seeks to dispel at least a part of that misunderstanding in this book. Emphasis is placed on Justices Hugo L. Black and Felix Frankfurter "not because they must be accepted as heroes" but because they "represent with uncommon ability two great, if differing, traditions in American jurisprudence." Mendelson notes that both consider it inevitable that the Court must make laws as well as interpret them. The difference between the two views lies in the extent to which each asserts the lawmaking should be carried. Frankfurter is pictured as an advocate of restraint, as one who would keep judicial legislation to a minimum. Black is portrayed as an activist, one to whom the making of law is the heart of the judicial process. The former position tends to produce dispersion of governmental power and the latter centralization, the author believes, and "eventually, perhaps, we will have to choose between them."

2840. Pound, Roscoe. Jurisprudence. St. Paul, West Pub. Co., 1959. 5 v.  59–3463 Law
CONTENTS.—v. 1. Jurisprudence. The end of law.—v. 2. The nature of law.—v. 3. The scope and subject matter of law. Sources, forms, modes of growth.—v. 4. Application and enforcement of law. Analysis of general juristic conceptions.—v. 5. The system of law. Index.

A preeminent legal scholar surveys the philosophy of law and the science of its administration. This monumental study represents a summation of and,

to some extent, supplement to the author's prolific writings. The discourses cover a wide variety of areas, including legal philosophy, analytical jurisprudence, legal history, comparative law, technical or professional elements in law, and sociological jurisprudence. The scope of the study, which Pound worked on intermittently for 47 years, extends from about 1750 B.C. through the late 1930's. Throughout the work runs the theme of "the difference between law and a law, that law is not a mere aggregate of rules of law nor the legal order a glorified system of policing." In *Roscoe Pound and Criminal Justice* (Dobbs Ferry, N.Y., Published for National Council on Crime and Delinquency by Oceana Publications, 1965. 261 p.), Sheldon Glueck has brought together a selection of the jurist's articles and addresses on criminal justice, probation, and court organization which have been long out of print or to which access is difficult.

2841. Swisher, Carl B. The Supreme Court in modern role. Rev. ed. [New York] New York University Press, 1965. 221 p. (James Stokes lectureship on politics)

65–19522  KF8748.S93 1965

Includes bibliographies.

As the Nation moves further from conditions existing in 1789, the Supreme Court must rely more on its estimates of current society than on history in its search for constitutional meaning. When situations with which it is faced are novel and lack effectively authoritative precedents, the author asserts, the Court must be particularly dynamic or creative. Modern problems "occur not so much in connection with the scope of property rights, as in earlier years, as with the rights of persons and groups of persons in relation to the law." Critical circumstances are discussed in which the Court has dealt with such problems as subversion, race, and the changing place of the military in our traditionally civilian culture.

# D. Digests of American Law

2842. James, Fleming. Civil procedure. Boston, Little, Brown, 1965. xx, 747 p.

65–17621  KF8840.J3

A textbook for basic courses in civil procedure, by a professor of law at Yale University. On the basis of his experience in teaching such a course for

more than 30 years, James summarizes subjects given extensive treatment in large works unsuitable for use as textbooks and includes new developments that have significantly changed the nature of procedure. Of particular interest to the layman is the author's step-by-step review of the progression of a civil action.

# E. Courts and Judges

2843. Goldfarb, Ronald L. The contempt power. New York, Columbia University Press, 1963. 366 p. 63–20342 KF9415.G6 1963
Bibliography: p. [351]–356.
The author explores the ramifications of the power to punish contempt, which he defines in a general sense as "an act of disobedience or disrespect toward a judicial or legislative body of government, or interference with its orderly process, for which a summary punishment is usually exacted." Various related topics are discussed, including the extralegal significance of the contempt power.

2844. Justice for the child; the juvenile court in transition. Edited by Margaret Keeney Rosenheim. New York, Free Press of Glencoe [1962] 240 p. 62–15349 KF9709.J86
Bibliographical notes and selected references at the ends of chapters.
A collection of articles which examine various aspects of the treatment accorded juvenile offenders and the functioning of the courts which administer this treatment. Among the topics considered are constitutional rights in the juvenile court, juvenile courts and due process, and the origin, purpose, and failings of the American juvenile court system.

2845. Llewellyn, Karl N. The common law tradition: deciding appeals. Boston, Little, Brown, 1960. 565 p. 60–14465 KF9050.L58
An examination and defense of the role of the appellate courts of the United States. According to Llewellyn, "The bar is so much bothered about these courts that we face a crisis in confidence which packs danger." Lawyers lament the "death of *stare decisis*" and complain that legal opinions are products of uncontrolled judicial will. The decisionmaking of the appellate courts, however, is "more reckonable and stable than is the deciding done in most other phases of American life on most other types of fighting issue." Many of the existing deficiencies in the appellate system, the author asserts, are effects rather than causes of an unfavorable image and obscure true characteristics. The numerous factors which have grown or been built into the system are reviewed, with specific attention to such special aspects as the meaning and use of precedent and the craftsmanship and style of judges. Everyday case situations rather than landmark decisions are cited in support of the author's argument.

Appendixes provide additional illustrative material and commentary.

2846. Mayers, Lewis. The American legal system; the administration of justice in the United States by judicial, administrative, military, and arbitral tribunals. Rev. ed. New York, Harper & Row [1964] 594 p. 63–17711 KF8700.M36 1964
Bibliography: p. 568–573. Bibliographical footnotes.
A revised edition of no. 6289 in the 1960 *Guide*.

2847. Murphy, Walter F., *and* Charles Herman Pritchett, *eds.* Courts, judges, and politics; an introduction to the judicial process. New York, Random House [1961] 707 p. 61–9678 KF8700.A7M8
A collection of cases and essays which analyze and illustrate the functioning of the judiciary in the context of the American political process," intended for students of government, law, and public affairs. Materials were selected with a view to developing "a clearer understanding of the role which American judges and courts, as they perform their historic function of settling disputes and dispensing justice, play in the process of democratic policy formation." In addition to cases and essays, the editors have included excerpts from personal letters, books, legal codes, and fiction. In *The Role of Domestic Courts in the International Legal Order* ([Syracuse, N.Y.] Syracuse University Press, 1964. 184 p. The Procedural aspects of international law series), Richard A. Falk argues that foreign policy considerations must not be allowed to control the outcome of judicial proceedings in international law cases litigated in domestic courts.

2848. Schubert, Glendon A., *ed.* Judicial behavior; a reader in theory and research. Chicago, Rand McNally [1964] 603 p. illus. (Rand McNally political science series) 64–17638 KF8775.A7S3
Bibliographical footnotes.
An anthology of materials illustrating the development of the behavioral approach to the study of the judicial process. In contrast to traditional empirical approaches, this type of investigation represents "a fusion of theories and methods developed in various social sciences in order to study

scientifically why judges make the decisions that they do." The studies are divided into three major categories: historical background; relationships between judicial behavior and the social sciences, specifically cultural anthropology, political sociology and social psychology; and prediction of judicial behavior. The relative newness of this analytical method is reflected in the fact that more than half of the 45 contributions were published after 1961. A pioneer work in the field is Schubert's *Quantitative Analysis of Judicial Behavior* (Glencoe, Ill., Free Press [1960, °1959] 392 p.). He also employs a behavioral approach in *The Judicial Mind; the Attitudes and Ideologies of Supreme Court Justices, 1946–1963* (Evanston, Ill., Northwestern University Press [1965] 295 p.).

2849. Schulman, Sidney. Toward judicial reform in Pennsylvania; a study in court reorganization. Philadelphia, University of Pennsylvania, the Law School, Institute of Legal Research, 1962. 281 p. (Studies in law and administration)

62–18050 KFP508.S3

A comprehensive survey of "courthouse government" in Pennsylvania in which the author discusses the system's deficiencies and offers a plan for court reorganization. Schulman's investigation covers a broad sphere, from traffic court operations to the selection of State supreme court judges, and his proposals range from a draft for constitutional reform to the organization of small citizen pressure groups as a means of stimulating change. State court procedure is also the subject of *Dispatch and Delay; a Field Study of Judicial Administration in Pennsylvania* (Philadelphia, Institute of Legal Research, Law School, University of Pennsylvania, 1961. 426 p. Studies in law and administration), by A. Leo Levin and Edward A. Woolley.

2850. Virtue, Maxine B. Survey of metropolitan courts; final report. Prepared for the University of Michigan Law School and the Section of Judicial Administration of the American Bar Association. Ann Arbor, University of Michigan Press [1962] xxv, 523 p. (Michigan legal studies)

62–9960 KF8737.V5

Bibliography: p. 475–491.

Tremendous growth in jurisdictional area and in population mobility and diversity have produced metropolitan judicial structures of confusing variety and characterized by overlapping and conflicting responsibilities, according to the author, and as a result the courts have become inefficient, overburdened, and chaotic. Initiated by the University of Michigan Law School, this survey investigates the composition, machinery, and functions of courts in communities that have outgrown city and county boundaries. On the basis of the results, general conclusions are offered and solutions for problems are suggested. The author recommends consolidation and streamlining of the "hodge-podge of scattered tribunals" existing within the metropolitan structure and notes that the "entrenched judiciary must guard against permitting their respect for traditional structures to offer a block to needed administrative change." She commends the trend toward the use of specialized judges within the framework of a flexible general court. In *Urban Justice; Municipal Courts in Tennessee* (Knoxville, Bureau of Public Administration, University of Tennessee, 1964. 101 p.), a study of administrative justice in city courts, Richard G. Sheridan criticizes municipal judiciaries for laxity in adhering to due process.

## F. The Judicial Process

2851. Busch, Francis X. Law and tactics in jury trials. Encyclopedic ed. Indianapolis, Bobbs-Merrill [1959–63] 5 v.

59–1175 KF8915.B8

A revised and greatly enlarged edition of no. 6296 in the 1960 *Guide,* accompanied by a *General Index* ([1964] 514 p.) and kept up to date by cumulative supplements.

2852. Cheatham, Elliott E. A lawyer when needed. New York, Columbia University Press, 1963. 128 p. (James S. Carpentier lectures, 1963)

63–19857 KF9646.A75C44

Bibliographical footnotes.

Six lectures delivered at Columbia University by the Charles Evans Hughes professor of law emeritus at that institution. Cheatham explores the practical and ethical factors which underlie the call for measures to make counsel more readily available, examines the special problem of providing counsel for defendants who are highly unpopular, and discusses the need for counsel in various kinds of civil cases. One aspect of the problem is examined by Lee Silverstein in *Defense of the Poor in Criminal Cases in American State Courts* (Chicago, 1965. 276 p.), an American Bar Foundation field study.

2853. Jacob, Herbert. Justice in America; courts, lawyers, and the judicial process. Boston, Little, Brown [1965] 215 p.

65–16550 KF8700.Z9J3

Bibliographical footnotes.

A political analysis of the administration of justice in the courts, with a description of overall court structure and operations. The author defines two broad functions of the courts — enforcing norms and making policy — and takes the position that the courts, although directed by different decision-making rules, act as political institutions performing functions similiar to those of legislative and executive bodies. The roles played by lawyers, judges, and juries are reviewed, recent suggestions for judicial reform are assessed, and the inadequacy of legal research upon which to base improvements is noted.

2854. LaFave, Wayne R. Arrest; the decision to take a suspect into custody. [Boston] Little, Brown, 1965. xxxiv, 540 p. (American Bar Foundation. Administration of criminal justice series) 65–16283 KF9625.L3

Bibliographical footnotes.

The first report of an American Bar Foundation survey of criminal justice. The decision to arrest, the first step in the administration of justice, was the subject of a pilot study, conducted in Michigan, Wisconsin, and Kansas, which covered the choices and subsequent forms of action at all stages of the arrest procedure. The report stresses "those issues which are important and difficult for the well-staffed, competent, and honest police department, prosecutor's office, trial court, or correctional agency." A more general study, written principally for the layman, is *From Arrest to Release* (Springfield, Ill., C. C. Thomas [1958] 235 p.), by Marshall Houts.

2855. McCart, Samuel W. Trial by jury; a complete guide to the jury system. [2d ed.] rev. Philadelphia, Chilton Books [1965] 204 p.

65–9292 KF8972.M3 1965

The author traces the jury system from its beginnings in English history, noting its gradual emergence as an instrument of justice superior to a system of trial by judge. He considers the right to trial by jury to be a cornerstone of individual freedom and encourages citizen awareness as a means of preventing its erosion. Charles W. Join-

er's *Civil Justice and the Jury* (Englewood Cliffs, N.J., Prentice-Hall, 1962. 238 p.) examines the history and structure of the American system of justice and appraises its success in upholding the Nation's ideals.

2856. Rosenberg, Maurice. The pretrial conference and effective justice; a controlled test in personal injury litigation. With a preface by Tom C. Clark. New York, Columbia University Press, 1964. xvi, 249 p. illus.

64–8492 KFN2337.R6

Bibliography: p. [230]–242.

Advocates of the pretrial conference consider it to be the answer to docket congestion; opponents argue that it bypasses, and thus weakens, the adversary system. At such a conference, the attorneys inform the judge of matters which might unfold in the forthcoming trial. A judicial order specifying further steps to be taken is then prepared. When this study began, the New Jersey Rules of Civil Practice required that a pretrial conference be held at a certain point in every personal injury case filed in the State's major courts. In response to criticism of the rule, the chief justice of the State supreme court asked the Columbia University Project for Effective Justice to plan a controlled experiment testing the effect of the pretrial conference. Rosenberg reports the results of that study, as a consequence of which the pretrial conference was made optional in negligence cases.

2857. Rubin, Sol. Psychiatry and criminal law: illusions, fictions, and myths. Dobbs Ferry, N.Y., Oceana Publications, 1965. xvi, 219 p.

64–19354 KF9242.Z9R8

Bibliographical footnotes.

In 1843 the House of Lords ruled in the case of Daniel M'Naghten that "to establish a defence on the ground of insanity, it must be clearly proved that at the time of committing of the act, the party accused was laboring under such a defect of reason, from disease of the mind, as not to know the nature and quality of the act he was doing; or if he did know it, that he did not know he was doing what was wrong." The author contrasts this ruling with *Durham* v. *United States* (1954), in which the U.S. Court of Appeals in the District of Columbia held that "an accused is not criminally responsible if his unlawful act was the product of mental disease or mental defect." Under the more widely applied M'Naghten rule an insane person who at the time of the act knew right from wrong is subject to punishment for his crime; under the Durham rule he is not. Rubin's view is that more leniency is desirable than is available under the M'Naghten rule but that the Durham rule achieves that leniency in the wrong way. He advocates a Model Sentencing Act under which the M'Naghten rule would be combined with expanded judicial discretion. In *Psychiatric Justice* (New York, Macmillan [1965] 282 p.), Thomas S. Szasz uses the case approach to show the distortions that have sometimes occurred when the psychiatrist has served as a gatherer of evidence.

2858. Russell, Francis. Tragedy in Dedham; the story of the Sacco-Vanzetti case. New York, McGraw-Hill [1962] 478 p.

62–13822   KF224.S2R85

Noting that the meaning of the Sacco-Vanzetti trial for law and society today lies not so much in the question of innocence or guilt as in its implications for legal process and justice, the author details the crime, the trial, the appeals, the executions, and the reaction, with emphasis on the political and social forces which influenced the case. On the basis of his analysis of pressures to which the judicial process and those responsible for its execution are contin-

ually subjected, Russell raises a number of questions regarding an individual's rights before the law. Another famous trial and the issues of legal process that arose in connection with it are discussed in Edward D. Radin's *Lizzie Borden: The Untold Story* (London, Gollancz, 1961. 269 p.).

2859. Younger, Richard D. The people's panel; the grand jury in the United States, 1634–1941. Providence, American History Research Center, Brown University Press, 1963. 263 p.

63–12993   KF9642.Y6

A history of the grand jury in the United States, the movements to abolish it, and its resurgence and renewed practice since a low point in the late 1920's. Demonstrating the important role the grand jury has played within the context of American social and political development, Younger stresses its effectiveness against imperial interference during the colonial period, against outside pressures in the Western territories, and in the South during Reconstruction. He advocates grand jury investigations in cases involving alleged fraud or corruption in private or public life.

## G. Administrative Law

2860. Nelson, Dalmas H. Administrative agencies of the USA, their decisions and authority. Detroit, Wayne State University Press, 1964. 341 p. (Wayne State University studies, no. 13)

63–13433   KF5407.N4

Bibliography: p. 326–334.

The author examines the growth of the quasi-judicial authority of Federal agencies and analyzes the argument that administrative adjudication is a violation of the constitutional separation of powers. Specific types of administrative law interpretation are reviewed and recommendations are made for the reform of agency procedures. In *The Lawyer and Administrative Agencies* (Englewood Cliffs, N.J., Prentice-Hall, 1957. 331 p.), Frank E. Cooper discusses the numerous problems attorneys face in representing clients before administrative tribunals.

2861. Woll, Peter. Administrative law, the informal process. Berkeley, University of California Press, 1963. 203 p.

63–10409   KF5402.Z9W6

Bibliographical notes.

2862. Forkosch, Morris D. A treatise on administrative law. Indianapolis, Bobbs-Merrill [1956] 856 p.   56–58483   KF5402.F65

Woll develops the hypothesis that administrative adjudication, because of the requirements of public policy and the demands for speed, has become primarily informal in its process. In analyzing the significance of this development, he discusses the growth of administrative law and the role of administrative agencies within our legal system. Forkosch, a professor of law at Brooklyn Law School, offers a broad survey of the entire field of administrative law, which he considers to encompass both the law administered by an agency and the law that binds it. His comprehensive monograph stresses the legal and constitutional principles involved in administrative law. In *The Language of Dissent* (Cleveland, World Pub. Co. [1959] 314 p.), Lowell B. Mason, a former member of the Federal Trade Commission, argues against the "vagaries and injustices of Federal administrative law."

# H. Lawyers and the Legal Profession

2863. Chroust, Anton Hermann. The rise of the
legal profession in America. Norman, University of Oklahoma Press [1965] 2 v.
65–11230  KF361.C47
Bibliographical footnotes.
CONTENTS.— v. 1. The colonial experience.— v. 2.
The Revolution and the post-Revolution era.
A history of the legal profession in the United
States from its colonial beginnings to the mid-19th
century. The author discusses the varying paths
along which American legal systems emerged in the
New England, Middle Atlantic, and Southern Colonies under the influence of English law. He finds
in his study that by 1776 wide differences existed
among the three areas. The period between the
Revolution and 1840 is referred to by the author as
the "Golden Age" for both the law and the lawyer
in the United States. In spite of the demanding
conditions created by this unsettled period, it was
distinguished by the breadth and quality of the formative law established and by the number of outstanding individual lawyers. Under such men as
John Marshall of Virginia, Daniel Webster of Massachusetts, and Thomas Ruffin of North Carolina,
the concept and range of law greatly expanded.

2864. Darrow, Clarence S. Attorney for the
damned, edited and with notes by Arthur
Weinberg. Foreword by William O. Douglas.
New York, Simon & Schuster, 1957. 552 p.
57–12408  KF213.D3W4
Bibliography: p. 547–548.
It was Lincoln Steffens who applied the title of
"attorney for the damned" to Clarence Darrow.
Among the "damned" for whom the lawyer pleads
in this selection of his addresses are Nathan F. Leopold and Richard A. Loeb (1924) and Lt. Thomas
H. Massie (1932). Darrow also defends himself
against a bribery charge before a Los Angeles jury
(1912) and attacks the Tennessee anti-evolution law
in the Scopes trial (1924). Each selection is accompanied by a foreword giving the setting, legal background, and human factors involved and an afterword disclosing the verdict and subsequent effects of
the trial.

2865. Gertz, Elmer. A handful of clients. Chicago, Follett Pub. Co., 1965. xv, 379 p.
65–16544  Law
A personal account of clients and causes represented by the author. Among the topics covered are
the stratagems and techniques employed in guiding
Nathan F. Leopold's unsuccessful appeal for executive clemency in 1956 and his successful plea for
parole in 1958. Gertz carries the Leopold story on
through his winning of a judgment of liability
against Meyer Levin's novel *Compulsion* (1958)
and the motion picture and play based upon it for
having appropriated Leopold's name, likeness, and
personality. Other causes discussed include the successful defense of Henry Miller's *Tropic of Cancer*
(1935) against bans based on charges of obscenity.
*Life Plus 99 Years* (Garden City, N.Y., Doubleday,
1958. 381 p.) is Nathan F. Leopold's autobiography.

2866. Grossman, Joel B. Lawyers and judges; the
ABA and the politics of judicial selection.
New York, J. Wiley [1965] 228 p.
65–16409  KF8776.G7
Bibliographical footnotes.
An examination of the American Bar Association's role in the selection of Federal judges. Because of the specialized professional background of
its members, the ABA believes that it deserves a
voice in the staffing of the Federal courts. Working
through its Standing Committee on Federal Judiciary, the ABA seeks to diminish political considerations in judicial appointments and to influence the
standards to be employed in the selection process.
To date, according to Grossman, these efforts have
had a diffuse impact: the most import achievements
have been in establishing a liaison with the Attorney
General's office and in advocating minimal standards of selection; the greatest disappointment has
stemmed from an inability to build a similarly close
relationship with the Senate. The author concludes
that the ABA's function as adviser and consultant
in the process of recruiting judges "certainly makes
sense" but warns that there is "reason for grave concern" when that organization's influence results in
the veto of a prospective judicial nomination.

2867. Hamilton, Alexander. The law practice of
Alexander Hamilton; documents and com-
mentary. Julius Goebel, Jr., editor. New York,
Published under the auspices of the William Nelson
Cromwell Foundation by Columbia University
Press, 1964. 898 p.    64–13900  KF363.H3G6
Bibliographical footnotes.
Volume one of a projected two-volume documen-
tary reconstruction of the law practice of the man
who became the Nation's first Secretary of the

Treasury. Each group of documents is prefaced by an introductory commentary and many individual documents are accompanied by summaries of relevant circumstances. In attempting to establish Hamilton's professional capacities and to chronicle his possible contributions to the growth of law, Goebel uses briefs wherever possible to uncover the lawyer's learning, acumen, resourcefulness, and discipline of mind. A further goal of the study is to illustrate the type of litigation which was pressing in the early years of the Nation's independence. One conspicuous category concerned the property rights of Loyalists. Goebel notes that, motivated by views of national honor, safety, and advantage, Hamilton strongly opposed statutes that were designed to penalize the Tories. By appealing to international law in several instances, he helped to set important precedents for its acceptance and use in the United States.

2868. Nizer, Louis. My life in court. Garden City, N.Y., Doubleday [1961] 542 p.
61–12563 KF220.N5

A prominent trial lawyer reviews seven of his major cases and, in so doing, paints a graphic picture of the courtroom attorney at work. "The lawyer's task is to reconstruct past events and adduce the persuasive facts for his client. He is like the archeologist who must find and exhume old evidence." Asserting that real trials are far more dramatic and far more challenging to the attorney's intellect than stereotyped presentations on the stage or in motion pictures and television indicate, Nizer introduces the reader to various critical problems encountered in the courtroom, such as those relating to opening statements, the admissibility of evidence, cross-examination, and the judge's charge to the jury. Of particular interest is a discussion of the libel suit brought by Quentin Reynolds against Westbrook Pegler. As Reynolds' attorney, Nizer won an unprecedented kind of settlement: in compensatory damages, $1, a sum which was subject to taxation; in punitive damages, $200,000, which was nontaxable.

2869. Smigel, Erwin O. The Wall Street lawyer: professional organization man? [New York] Free Press of Glencoe [1964] 369 p.
64–16968 KF297.S45 1964

A sociological study of the large law firms of Wall Street, the attorneys that work for them, and the effects of these organizations on the lawyers themselves, on their clients, and on the law. Smigel concludes that, despite the size of these firms, individual creativity not only survives but in some ways thrives, and that the firms in fact have a tendency to lead into the frontiers of new law. A useful complement to *The Wall Street Lawyer* is Jerome E. Carlin's *Lawyers on Their Own; a Study of Individual Practitioners in Chicago* (New Brunswick, N.J., Rutgers University Press [1962] 234 p.).

2870. Williams, Edward Bennett. One man's freedom. Introduction by Eugene V. Rostow. New York, Atheneum, 1962. 344 p.
62–11689 KF373.W466A32

Asserting that every man's right to counsel must be respected and that the work of a lawyer must transcend the identity of his client, the author devotes a large segment of this work to the undesirable effects which, he maintains, many congressional committee investigations have had on fundamental liberties, particularly the privilege of refraining from testifying against oneself and the right to trial by due process. He supports the view that the proper role of hearings is one of obtaining information necessary for intelligent legislation and not one of exposure for its own sake.

# XXXI

# Politics, Parties, Elections

SECTION B, Politics: Special, in the *Supplement* has more entries than its counterpart in the 1960 *Guide*. Books on State legislators, Jews in politics, Negroes in politics, the Ku Klux Klan in politics, and the reasons for which people in general become involved in politics are among the works chosen to represent the increased number of publications appropriate for inclusion as special studies of politics. As in the 1960 *Guide,* Section C, Political Parties, in the *Supplement* is more than twice as large as any other section in this chapter; the entries include four works on American communism, four on the Republican Party, two on the Jeffersonian Republicans, one on the Democratic Party, and one revealing a four-party structure in modern American politics. Although Section I, Reform, is limited to one entry—an analysis of the movement culminating in the Civil Service Act of 1883—works on other types of reform appear in Section D, Local Studies.

## A. Politics: General

2871. Adrian, Charles R., *and* Charles Press. The American political process. New York, McGraw-Hill [1965] 756 p. illus.
64–25164  JK274.A5294
Bibliographies at the ends of chapters.
A descriptive survey of politics in the United States, based on a behavioral approach to an analysis of the relationship of political events to the individual and to the society. The authors discuss the political process by which public policy is made, devoting special attention to the influence of public ideology or "folk philosophy." Projections of current demographic, social, economic, and political trends are reviewed from the standpoint of their possible implications for a democratic system of government. Lectures by eight scholars representing both the traditional and behavioral approaches to political science are presented in *Continuing Crisis in American Politics* (Englewood Cliffs, N.J., Prentice-Hall [1963] 174 p. A Spectrum book, S-54), edited by Marian D. Irish.

2872. Key, Valdimer O. Politics, parties, & pressure groups. 5th ed. New York, Crowell [1964] 738 p.    64–11799  JF2051.K4 1964
Bibliographical footnotes.
A revised edition of no. 6335 in the 1960 *Guide.*

2873. Plano, Jack C., *and* Milton Greenberg. The American political dictionary. New York, Holt, Rinehart & Winston [1962] 383 p.

62–18757 JK9.P55

More than 1,100 entries covering terms, agencies, court cases, and statutes considered "most relevant for a basic comprehension of American government, institutions, practices, and problems." For each entry, a basic definition and a statement of its significance are provided. The arrangement of chapters closely parallels that followed in most textbooks on American government; for example, there are chap-

ters dealing with the Constitution, political parties, and each of the three basic governmental branches. The historical origins and uses of approximately a thousand political terms, including some employed in Europe, are outlined in *American Political Terms* (Detroit, Wayne State University Press, 1962. 516 p.), by Hans Sperber and Travis Trittschuh. A shorter dictionary, emphasizing current terms and illustrated with reproductions of political cartoons, is *The Crescent Dictionary of American Politics* (New York, Macmillan, 1962. 182 p.), by Eugene J. McCarthy.

## B. Politics: Special

2874. Barber, James D. The lawmakers: recruitment and adaptation to legislative life. New Haven, Yale University Press, 1965. 314 p. (Yale studies in political science, 11)

65–11172 JK1976.B3

Bibliography: p. 262–263. Bibliographical references included in "Notes" (p. 285–310).

By examining politics "as a personal experience of the politician," Barber seeks to describe the types of persons attracted to political candidacy in the United States. His analysis is based on information obtained through 27 intensive interviews with State legislators, replies to questionnaires, direct observation of committee meetings, caucuses, and plenary sessions, and books, newspapers, and official documents. The two major variables measured in the appraisal are the level of activity and the degree of commitment to office by the individual politician. Barber identifies four types of legislators: the "Spectator," characterized by modest achievement, limited skills, and restricted ambition; the "Advertiser," high in activity, yet viewing the office as the basis for another career; the "Reluctant," low in activity and in willingness to return — serving, under protest, through his commitment to civic duty; and the "Lawmaker," who seeks the nomination, campaigns hard, and, if elected, finds important roles to play. The nature of leadership in general is examined in Barber's compilation of readings from the works of a number of prominent scholars, *Political Leadership in American Government* (Boston, Little, Brown [1964] 360 p.).

2875. Fuchs, Lawrence H. The political behavior of American Jews. Glencoe, Ill., Free Press [1956] 220 p. 56–6875 E184.J5F8
Bibliographical footnotes.

The author asserts that ethno-religious block voting is virtually a thing of the past and, although acknowledging an unusual cohesiveness and solidarity within the Jewish community, points out that individuals within that community belong to a variety of interest groups. He notes that American Jews have historically been identified with movements and parties stressing civil liberties and general equality. Their early political allegiance to the party of Jefferson and Jackson was lost in the controversy over slavery. The advent of Wilsonian idealism instigated a movement back to the Democratic Party. Fuchs also examines the independent behavior of Jews who have been attracted to minor parties, particularly those with socialist creeds. A clear illustration of the influence that group identification may exert is presented in *The Political World of American Zionism* (Detroit, Wayne State University Press, 1961. 431 p.), by Samuel Halperin.

2876. Lane, Robert E. Political life: why people get involved in politics. Glencoe, Ill., Free Press [1959] 374 p. 58–6485 JA74.L25
A comprehensive study of electoral participation in voting and officeholding in the United States. Among the specific topics discussed are acquisition and use of the franchise, changing voter patterns, the individual's political motives and attitudes, and the influences exerted by social institutions such as churches, professional organizations, and mass media. In conclusion, the social and individual consequences of popular participation in government are evaluated, ways to obtain a higher degree of political participation are suggested, and the social disadvantages which some of them might entail are noted.

2877. Lubell, Samuel. The future of American politics. 3d ed., rev. New York, Harper &

Row [1965] 270 p. (Harper colophon books, CN74K) 66–11177 E743.L85 1965
A revised edition of no. 6346 in the 1960 *Guide*.

2878. Mitchell, William C. The American polity; a social and cultural interpretation. New York, Free Press of Glencoe [1962] 434 p.
62–15346 JA84.U5M65
Bibliography: p. 421-426.

A sociological approach is taken in this attempt to synthesize institutional and behavioral data in an overall examination of the American political system. Among the questions considered are those pertaining to the polity's integration, its maintenance, societal goals, allocation of values and costs, and distribution of benefits.

2879. Rice, Arnold S. The Ku Klux Klan in American politics. Introduction by Harry Golden. Washington, Public Affairs Press [1962] 150 p. 61–8449 HS2330.K63R5
References: p. 130–139.

An introductory evaluation of the Klan in the 20th century. Concentrating on Klanism in the South, Rice describes the nature and sources of the movement in its various stages of success and failure. He notes that the year 1915 marked the new beginning of a Ku Klux Klan organization patterned after the original order which flourished during the Reconstruction era. Political involvement was a prominent part of Klan activity in the 1920's, but by 1942, according to the author, aroused public wrath, politically unskilled leaders, and dissipated energies had brought the order into disrepute and decline. The movement reappeared after World War II, however, and beginning in 1954 achieved new momentum through its opposition to civil rights.

2880. Ulmer, S. Sidney, *ed.* Introductory readings in political behavior. Chicago, Rand Mc-

Nally [1961] 465 p. (Rand McNally political science series) 61–10183 JA74.U5

A selection of essays in which behavioral data are applied to the study of government and politics. Among the topics considered are the psychological and social bases of political behavior, characteristics of groups, factors influencing decision, and problems of communication, power, and individual response to varying roles. A broader study, in which an attempt is made to define the origins of political behavior, is James C. Davies' *Human Nature in Politics* (New York, Wiley [1963] 403 p.).

2881. Wilson, James Q. Negro politics; the search for leadership. Glencoe, Ill., Free Press [1960] 342 p. 60–10906 JK1924.W5
Bibliographical notes: p. 319–333.

An analysis of political leadership in major Negro communities outside the South. Among the several large cities studied, Chicago is singled out for detailed analysis. Separate sections are devoted to a description of Negro community political organization, an analysis of civic life and Negro-white relations, and a discussion of the principal dimensions of leadership. The author believes that, within the Northern Negro community, the "omnicompetent" men—often ministers—who have dealt with a wide range of issues are being replaced by representatives of the middle class who specialize by area of interest and competence. A study of community leadership in a Southern city is *The Negro Leadership Class* (Englewood Cliffs, N.J., Prentice-Hall [1963] 171 p. A Spectrum book), by Daniel C. Thompson. In *The Negro Politician* (Chicago, Johnson Pub. Co., 1964. 213 p.), Edward T. Clayton assesses the role of leaders at various levels of political affairs throughout the United States.

## C. Political Parties

2882. Binkley, Wilfred E. American political parties, their natural history. 4th ed., enl. New York, Knopf, 1962. 486 p.
62–52807 JK2261.B5 1962
Bibliography: p. 469–486.
An updated edition of no. 6347 in the 1960 *Guide*.

2883. Bone, Hugh A. Party committees and national politics. Seattle, University of Wash-

ington Press, 1958. xv, 256 p.
58-10481 JK2276.B6
Bibliography: p. 245–249.
An examination of the structure and operations of eight committees of the two major political parties at the national level. Included in the discussion are the Republican and Democratic National Committees, the four House and Senate campaign committees, and two Senate policy committees. Noting

the amorphous, decentralized character of the party system, the author emphasizes that each committee is only a part of the greater structure of the national parties, sharing responsibilities in such vital areas as finance, patronage, publicity, and public relations. He concludes that committee powers are both unpredictable and questionable. Another study which delineates the important role played by national party committees is *Politics Without Power* (New York, Atherton Press, 1964. 246 p. The Atherton Press political science series), by Cornelius P. Cotter and Bernard C. Hennessy.

2884. Burns, James MacGregor. The deadlock of democracy; four-party politics in America. With revisions. Englewood Cliffs, N.J., Prentice-Hall [1963] 376 p. (A Spectrum book, S-95)

64–4219 E183.B96 1963

Bibliographical references included in "Sources" (p. 343–368).

According to the author, the political system of the United States has become entrapped by the Madisonian system, in which conflicting interests check each other and in turn check national power. In the first half of the book, Burns analyzes American political history in terms of this Madisonian model and its Jeffersonian opposite, based on moderate majority rule. The remainder of the text is devoted to a reassessment of American democracy in action. This country's polity is described as being characterized by a four-party system (two congressional parties, motivated by local interests, and two presidential parties, which emphasize matters of national and international concern) that necessitates government by "consensus and coalition," rather than a two-party arrangement that "allows the winning party to govern and the losers to oppose." The author proposes a restoration of the Jeffersonian system with two-party competition and improved, revitalized leadership.

2885. Chambers, William N. Political parties in a new Nation: the American experience, 1776–1809. New York, Oxford University Press, 1963. 231 p. 63–12551 E302.1.C45

Summary of sources: p. 209–218.

An interpretive essay tracing early American politics from nonparty beginnings to the emergence of the modern two-party system. After reviewing the factional politics which characterized the Nation from the time of the Revolution until adoption of the Constitution, the author concentrates on the Federalist-Republican conflict of the 1790's. The adoption of a federal government in lieu of the Confederation created a political arena on a national scale and led to the appearance of national parties,

Chambers observes. Although several issues made this situation all but inevitable, he notes that debate over international affairs—and over Jay's Treaty in particular—greatly stimulated the formation of issue-oriented parties. Joseph Charles deals with party politics during the same period in three essays published under the title *The Origins of the American Party System* (Williamsburg, Va., Institute of Early American History and Culture, 1956. 147 p.). The subject is further explored in *The Making of the American Party System, 1789–1809* (Englewood Cliffs, N.J., Prentice-Hall [1965] 177 p. A Spectrum book, S-115), edited by Noble E. Cunningham.

2886. Cunningham, Noble E. The Jeffersonian Republicans; the formation of party organization, 1789–1801. Chapel Hill, Published for the Institute of Early American History and Culture at Williamsburg by the University of North Carolina Press [°1957] 279 p. 58–1263 JK2316.C8

"Bibliographical note": p. [264]–266. Bibliographical footnotes.

2887. Cunningham, Noble E. The Jeffersonian Republicans in power; party operations, 1801–1809. Chapel Hill, Published for the Institute of Early American History and Culture at Williamsburg, Va., by the University of North Carolina Press [1963] 318 p. 63–21074 JK2316.C82

"Bibliographical note": p. [306]–310. Bibliographical footnotes.

The first volume reviews the events surrounding the germination of political parties in the evolving Nation and outlines the gradual progression of party growth. The second volume discusses the formative years in the development of the Nation's political system. The author notes that, even with Jefferson's election in 1800, the role of political parties had not yet become fully established. The second volume also covers State components in the national party structure and includes a State-by-State survey of party machinery. A general history of early party development is *The Democratic Party: Jefferson to Jackson* (New York, Fordham University Press [1962] 240 p.), by Herbert J. Clancy. Shaw Livermore relates the political history of the Federalist Party during the transitional period between Madison and Jackson in *The Twilight of Federalism; the Disintegration of the Federalist Party, 1815–1830* (Princeton, N.J., Princeton University Press, 1962. 292 p.).

2888. De Santis, Vincent P. Republicans face the Southern question: the new departure years, 1877–1897. Baltimore, Johns Hopkins Press, 1959. 275 p. (The Johns Hopkins University studies in historical and political science, ser. 77, no. 1)

        59–10767  H31.J6 ser. 77, no. 1
Bibliographical footnotes.

2889. Hirshson, Stanley P. Farewell to the bloody shirt; Northern Republicans & the Southern Negro, 1877–1893. Introduction by David Donald. Bloomington, Indiana University Press [1962] 334 p.        62–8975  E661.H58
    Bibliography: p. 259–273.
In an introduction to Hirshon's book, David Donald of Princeton University notes that the fundamental problem facing the Republican Party after 1877 was the apparently permanent Democratic national majority. In an effort to destroy this supremacy in the South, Republican leaders significantly modified the party position on the race question, according to Hirshson. He analyzes the shifting political position taken by Northern Republicans toward the Negro between 1877 and 1893 and recalls that some Republicans advocated a party in the South based on the Negro vote, whereas an opposing school urged the development of a white Republican organization in the South. De Santis covers much the same period, concentrating on Republican policy and strategy within the South. Witnessing the end of military reconstruction and the restoration of "home rule," the party leaders failed to conciliate the Southern whites and deemed it increasingly expedient to abandon the Negro altogether. The author points out that the "'lily-white' movements of the 1920's had their origins in the 1880's."

2890. Draper, Theodore. The roots of American communism. New York, Viking Press, 1957. 498 p. (Communism in American life)
        57–6433  HX83.D7
    Bibliographical notes: p. 399-458.

2891. Draper, Theodore. American communism and Soviet Russia, the formative period. New York, Viking Press, 1960. 558 p. (Communism in American life)    60–7672  HX83.D68
    Bibliographical notes: p. 445–531.
These two separate but sequential works cover the political history of communism in the United States through 1929. The first study analyzes the background and growth of the movement which led to formal organization of the American Communist Party in 1919. Draper observes that the impetus for polarization and formal organization of the pro-Communist left, originally absorbed within earlier leftwing movements, was supplied by American participation in World War I, combined with the success of the Bolshevik revolution in Russia. He uses Communist source materials to trace the emergence of a specific Russian influence on the American leftwing after 1917. In the later study, the author concentrates on the first decade of the party's existence as basic to an understanding of its fundamental nature. He re-creates the party personalities and the intraparty struggles which culminated in 1929 with complete Soviet domination over "nationalists" in the movement. A general account of the party's history is presented by Irving Howe and Lewis Coser in *The American Communist Party, a Critical History, 1919–1957* (Boston, Beacon Press [°1957] 593 p.).

2892. Eldersveld, Samuel J. Political parties; a behavioral analysis. Chicago, Rand McNally [1964] 613 p. (Rand McNally political science series)    64–17633  JK2265.E4
    Bibliographical footnotes.
"The disparity between our firm philosophical belief in party organization and our imperfect and uncertain knowledge about party organization can only be resolved by persistent behavioral research into the party structure," asserts the author. Using this approach, he systematically appraises the political party in the United States as a distinct social group operating within society. Data for the study were obtained from an investigation of the structure and activity of the Democratic and Republican Parties of Wayne County (Detroit), Mich., during the 1956 presidential campaign. Eldersveld characterizes the party as a miniature political system with distinctive patterns of power distribution. A succinct monograph on party politics and electoral behavior in the United States is *The American Party System and the American People* (Englewood Cliffs, N.J., Prentice-Hall [1963] 115 p. Foundations of modern political science series), by Fred I. Greenstein.

2893. Glazer, Nathan. The social basis of American communism. New York, Harcourt, Brace [1961] 244 p. (Communism in American life)    61–11911  JK2391.C5G55
    Bibliographical references included in "Notes" (p. 196–238).
A sociological study of the kinds of groups from which the American Communist Party has recruited its members. Membership, observes the author, has been the "treasure" of the party. Members were recruited in distinct ways, subjected to special training, and treated as a deployable resource. Party ideology and strategy determined that the major targets for recruiting were native-born industrial workers and Negroes. Social realities in America revealed over the years, however, that these groups did not fit the traditional Communist theoretical categories, and enormous efforts to capture them

ended largely in failure. Meanwhile, the greatest and most significant responses came first from the existing Socialist Party and later from immigrant workers whose backgrounds made membership neither eccentric nor exceptional. An unexpected response came from middle class and professional groups, which became prominent in the late 1930's. Wilson Record makes a more thorough appraisal of the lack of American Negro response to communism in *Race and Radicalism; the NAACP and the Communist Party in Conflict* (Ithaca, N.Y., Cornell University Press [1964] 237 p. Communism in American life). The actual process by which a Communist member is trained is examined by Frank S. Meyer in *The Moulding of Communists* (New York, Harcourt, Brace [1961] 214 p. Communism in American life).

2894. Hollingsworth, Joseph R. The whirligig of politics; the democracy of Cleveland and Bryan. Chicago, University of Chicago Press [1963] 263 p. illus.                    63–18846   E661.H72
"Bibliographical notes": p. 242–250. Bibliographical footnotes.

A history of the Democratic Party from the beginning of Cleveland's second administration through the elections of 1904. By 1893 the party had fully recovered from the "maladies" bred by the Civil War, Hollingsworth asserts, but the financial panic and severe economic depression which followed Cleveland's inauguration produced a wide divergence of opinion as to remedies and strengthened new divisive forces within the party. The insistent presence of the Populist Party heightened the turmoil and, reflecting the violent tensions between agrarian and industrial values, the Democratic Party entered the 20th century in disastrous disarray. In an era of new political leaders, such as William Jennings Bryan, John Peter Altgeld, and Theodore Roosevelt, both parties became increasingly aware of the Nation's growing international involvement, and world affairs became a primary issue. In *The Presidential Election of 1896* (Madison, University of Wisconsin Press, 1964. 436 p.), Stanley L. Jones discusses the importance to the Democratic Party of the urban vote and the futility of "free silver" as a winning issue, decisively demonstrated with McKinley's first victory over Bryan.

2895. Mayer, George H. The Republican Party, 1854–1964. New York, Oxford University Press, 1964. 563 p.         64–11232   JK2356.M3
Bibliographical references included in "Notes" (p. 521–548).

2896. Moos, Malcolm C. The Republicans; a history of their party. New York, Random House [1956]   564 p.         56–5195   JK2356.M6

Two studies of the development of the Republican Party, with emphasis on the national organization and only limited coverage of State and local politics. Mayer analyzes the operations of Republican administrations, assessing the Presidents, tracing the records of the party's Congressmen, and seeking to clarify the impact of social and economic forces on the party and its leaders. Among the major subjects discussed are secession, Reconstruction, tariffs, expansion, the League of Nations, and the depression. In his 1956 study, Moos seeks to ascertain and evaluate the ambitions and achievements of the Republican Party throughout its history, augmenting factual reporting with human interest sidelights. Donald B. Johnson examines a unique period in party history in *The Republican Party and Wendell Willkie* (Urbana, University of Illinois Press, 1960. 354 p.)

2897. Porter, Kirk H., *and* Donald B. Johnson, *comps.* National party platforms, 1840–1960. [2d ed.] Urbana, University of Illinois Press, 1961 [ᶜ1956] 640 p.
61–65727   JK2255.P6   1961
_____ _____ Supplement 1964. Urbana, University of Illinois Press, 1965. 58 p.
JK2255.P6   1961 Suppl.
A revised edition of no. 6367 in the 1960 *Guide*.

2898. Remini, Robert V. The election of Andrew Jackson. Philadelhpia, Lippincott [1963] 224 p.  (Critical periods of history)
63–17677   E380.R4
Bibliography: p. 221–224.

An essay on the "profound changes" which occurred in the politics of the United States during the 1828 presidential election. Particular attention is given to the transformations in the structuring of the party organizations as they sought to create mass support for their candidates. The victory which placed Andrew Jackson in the White House is largely attributed to the Democratic Party's revitalization, brought about by Martin Van Buren and other party leaders. The real significance of the 1828 election, the author concludes, lay not in the "rise of the common man" but in the return of active competition between two national parties. This development in turn offered the ordinary citizen an elaborate party machinery "through which he could more effectively control the operation of government and shape public policy." An earlier study by the same author, *Martin Van Buren and the Making of the Democratic Party* (New York, Columbia University Press, 1959. 271 p.), focuses on the New York leader as the man giving direction to new political forces in the shaping of the Democratic Party and as one of the first "professional politicians" in American history.

2899. Rossiter, Clinton L. Parties and politics in America. Ithaca, N.Y., Cornell University Press [1960] 205 p.        60–16163  E183.R7
Bibliographical references included in "Notes" (p. 189–198).
A series of lectures delivered at Cornell University in 1960. The existence of a persistent and "tyrannic" two-party system, Rossiter observes, is particularly obvious in the instinctive way in which one major party or the other moves to absorb the most challenging third party in a given period. Another marked feature of the system is the lack of ideological or programmatic commitment on the outer edges of each party. Thus organizational loyalty and service tend to blur, and programs and voters overlap. William Goodman analyzes party organization and the bases of bipartisanism in *The Two-Party System in the United States,* 3d ed. (Princeton, N.J., Van Nostrand [1964] 672 p. Van Nostrand political science series). A selection of supplementary readings on the subject is presented in *The American Party System* (New York, Macmillan [1965] 466 p.), edited by John R. Owens and P. J. Staudenraus.

2900. Shannon, David A. The decline of American Communism; a history of the Communist Party of the United States since 1945. New York, Harcourt, Brace [1959] 425 p. (Communism in American life)   59–11770  JK2391.C5S5
Bibliographical essay: p. 375–378. Bibliographical notes: p. 379–411.
The author discusses the postwar readjustments of the U. S. Communist Party, its dealings with the Progressive Party of 1948, and its problems during the anti-Communist drive of the late forties and early fifties. Particular stress is placed on the devastating effects on party morale occasioned by the Soviet denunciation of Stalin in 1956 and the crushing of the Hungarian Revolution. The account ends with the losing struggle for power in the American party by the unorthodox "nationalist" elements, highlighted in 1958 by the death of the *Daily Worker* and the simultaneous resignation of editor John Gates from the organization. These events, states the author, accompanied by an 85-percent drop in membership, signified the passing of an era in Communist history. In *The Story of an American Communist* (New York, Nelson [1958] 221 p.), John Gates tells of his long membership in the party and of his final disenchantment.

# D. Local Studies

2901. Garrett, Charles. The La Guardia years; machine and reform politics in New York City. New Brunswick, N.J., Rutgers University Press [1961] 423 p.        61–10262  F128.5.G25
Bibliographical note: p. 403–405.
A history of municipal reform in New York City, with emphasis on the three-term Fusion Party administration of Fiorello La Guardia. Set in an era of depression and urban expansion, this study covers the welfare, policies, administrative reorganization, and coalition politics which strengthened a counter movement to the growing chaos in New York and established hopeful precedents for action against modern city problems. In *Governing New York City* (New York, Russell Sage Foundation, 1960. 815 p.), Wallace S. Sayre and Herbert Kaufman examine current political processes in the city.

2902. Litt, Edgar. The political cultures of Massachusetts. Cambridge, Mass., M.I.T. Press [1965] xiv, 224 p.        65–26663  F64.L58
Bibliography: p. 213–217.

Massachusetts government is analyzed as a highly decentralized system serving innumerable interest groups. A transformed political order has emerged, according to the author, based on coalitions led by new managerial professional groups, with added academician influence. These groupings have cut across the old alignments based on social class and ethno-religious background. Four current cultural identifications, with their historical settings, are defined by the author: the Patrician and the Yeoman, urban and smalltown professionals of old-stock lineage; the Worker, of the new-stock, low-income groups; and the Manager, a member of the high-income, professional-technical class of increasingly new-stock heritage. Although the traditional groupings still wield influence, Litt observes a strong trend away from urban industrial centers and toward suburbia. The evolution of Massachusetts party politics in the early years of United States independence is traced by Paul Goodman in *The Democratic-Republicans of Massachusetts* (Cambridge, Harvard University Press, 1964. 281 p. A publication of the

Center for the Study of the History of Liberty in America).

2903. Lockard, Duane. New England State politics. Princeton, N.J., Princeton University Press, 1959. 347 p.  59–5600  JK2295.A11216
A political analysis of the States of New Hampshire, Vermont, Maine, Massachusetts, Rhode Island, and Connecticut. The author notes that, despite a common "Yankee" heritage and many regional similarities, the six States vary widely in their politics. Lockard examines the historical coalitions in New England, and evaluates the increasingly complex ethnic, social, and economic factors in the politics of the area, relating recent trends to current problems and to transitions taking place in State political systems throughout the Nation.

2904. Lockard, Duane. The politics of State and local government. New York, Macmillan [1963] 566 p.  63–13569  JK2408.L6
Bibliography: p. 544–558.
A general descriptive textbook. Noting the new demands placed on democratic government by changes in society, as well as the increasing concern over the proper distribution of power among governmental units, Lockard first reviews the adjustments taking place in Federal-State-local government relations and then devotes the major portion of his text to the structure, functions, and political dynamics of State and municipal governments. He identifies four basic challenges to be faced in the next few decades: population expansion, social instability, economic transition, and subsequent political pressures. A collection of essays undertaking a comparative analysis of State institutions is *Politics in the American States* (Boston, Little, Brown [1965] 493 p.), edited by Herbert Jacob and Kenneth N. Vines. An insight into intermittent movements toward municipal reform in major American cities is provided by Lorin W. Peterson in *The Day of the Mugwump* (New York, Random House [1961] 366 p.).

2905. Sindler, Allan P. Huey Long's Louisiana: State politics, 1920-1952. Baltimore, Johns Hopkins Press, 1956. xv, 316 p.
56–11664  F375.L846
"Bibliographical essays": p. 287–302. Bibliographical footnotes.
A study of Huey Long's career as Governor, Senator, and political boss, with an analysis of the major political events in Louisiana over a period of three critical decades. Sindler discusses the movement for reform in the 1920's, which paved the way for Long and his "Share-Our-Wealth" program, describes the rise of the "Long faction," and notes its dominance even after Long's assassination at the State Capitol in 1935. In *The Louisiana Elections of 1960* (Baton Rouge, Louisiana State University Press, 1963. 126 p. Louisiana State University studies. Social science series, no. 9), William C. Havard, Rudolf Heberle, and Perry H. Howard describe what they consider to be the almost complete breakdown of the Long and anti-Long bifactional system, identifying the gubernatorial campaign of 1960 as a possible major turning point in Louisiana politics.

2906. Sorauf, Francis J. Party and representation, legislative politics in Pennsylvania. New York, Atherton Press [1963] 173 p. (The American Political Science Association series)
63–13840  JK2295.P43S6
A study of the interaction of legislator, party, and constituency in State government, based on an analysis of Pennsylvania politics. The author considers that the degree to which discipline is fostered in party-backed candidates depends upon the party's success in controlling the issues and character of an election, and he therefore concentrates on the party function, beginning with the finding and recruiting of a candidate. The extent of party domination over the direct primary and the general election is discussed, and an attempt is made to judge the responses of the successful candidate to the competing demands of party, constituency, and personal philosophy.

## E. Machines and Bosses

2907. Curley, James M. I'd do it again, a record of all my uproarious years. Englewood Cliffs, N.J., Prentice-Hall [1957] 372 p.
57–8558  F70.C83
Beginning in 1896, James M. Curley engaged in Boston-Irish politics for half a century. In addition to holding many minor municipal posts, he was four times mayor of Boston, once Governor of Massachusetts, and twice a U.S. Congressman. With language and humor suggesting the skilled stump rouser, Curley recalls episodes from his long and colorful career. From an ethical point of view, many of the

maneuvers he recounts are marginal at best, but they are considered by some to have been necessary in view of the intolerable and unyielding conditions that faced Boston's immigrant groups. A novel which is thought by many critics to be based on Curley's life and which focuses on the circumstances surrounding contentious boss manipulations is Edwin O'Connor's *The Last Hurrah* (Boston, Little, Brown [ᶜ1956] 427 p.).

2908. Martin, Ralph G. The bosses. New York, Putnam [1964] 349 p.

64–18010 E183.M25

"Notes and references": p. 331–336.

A discussion of the techniques of "bossism" as developed and utilized by six major 20th-century politicians in the United States. Mark Hanna is depicted as the first and, to date, the last, national boss, one who largely created the framework of national political campaign tactics used today. Edward H. Crump of Memphis gained State as well as city power on a program of civic improvement. Jersey City under Frank Hague, according to the author, "was among the most ruthlessly ruled, among the most corrupt, cities in the country." Boston's James M. Curley is shown as unique for the power of his personality above that of his machine. The career of Jordan Chambers in St. Louis exemplifies the independent Negro leadership emerging in the 1940's. Quietly persuasive John M. Bailey of Connecticut is used to illustrate today's new breed of political boss. Crump and Anton J. Cermak are the respective subjects of William D. Miller's *Mr. Crump of Memphis* (Baton Rouge, Louisiana State Univer-sity Press, 1964. 373 p. Southern biography series) and Alex Gottfried's *Boss Cermak of Chicago* (Seattle, University of Washington Press, 1962. 459 p.).

2909. Steele, Robert V. P. A debonair scoundrel; an episode in the moral history of San Francisco by Lately Thomas [pseud.] New York, Holt, Rinehart & Winston [1962] 422 p.

62–12137 JS1449.S75

Bibliography: p. 407–411.

Bossism is seen in its most unprincipled aspects in this presentation of an "unforgotten, avoided chapter"—an "uneasy memory, primly swept under the carpet of civic consciousness"—in the "flamboyant" history of San Francisco. The author traces the bizarre career of Abraham Ruef, who purportedly ruled the city through Mayor Eugene F. Schmitz, elected in 1901. Ruef built an empire of graft based firmly on his control of the Union Labor Party, the account recalls. Aided and abetted by railroad magnates and other "robber barons," he paralyzed San Francisco's political echelons through systematic corruption and threat. These maneuvers touched every part of the city government and extended into picaresque private enterprises, such as elegant restaurant-brothels, which for an extorted fee received Ruef's "protection." The story is seasoned further with murder, attempted assassination, and suicide. In a protracted series of prosecutions, 1906-10, which the author emphasizes heavily and from which he extracts much of his information, a few dedicated reformers finally caused Ruef's downfall. He was convicted of bribery and imprisoned.

## F. Pressures

2910. Key, Valdimer O. Public opinion and American democracy. New York, Knopf, 1961. 566 p. 61–14321 HM261.K4

Noting that "governments must concern themselves with the opinions of their citizens, if only to provide a basis for repression of disaffection," the author undertakes to explain the character and force of public opinion in a democratic political system. He discusses the various influences which affect opinion at all levels of society and examines the beliefs, outlooks, faiths, and conditions conducive to the maintenance of government. Most important in understanding "the puzzle of how democratic regimes manage to function," Key concludes, are the hazily articulated motives, values, rules, and expectations prevailing at the highest political levels.

2911. Milbrath, Lester W. The Washington lobbyists. Chicago, Rand McNally [1963] xiv, 431 p. (Rand McNally political science series) 63–8243 JK1118.M5

Bibliography: p. 399–421.

"Lobbyist" is used in American politics to designate an individual—other than a citizen acting on his own behalf—who seeks to influence the actions of a government decisionmaker. The present study is based on personal interviews with Washington lobbyists and some of the persons toward whom they direct their efforts. It seeks to establish lobbyists as a special political skill group, denote their purposes and characteristics, and analyze their impact on governmental decisions at a national level. In an effort to dispel a general public uneasiness regarding professional lobbyists, the author underscores their activity as an important link between organized interests and government—the means through which the desires of special groups are channeled into the decisionmaking process.

2912. Monsen, R. Joseph., *and* Mark W. Cannon. The makers of public policy: American power groups and their ideologies. New York, McGraw-Hill [1965] 355 p.

64–7938    HN58.M6

Bibliographical footnotes.

In their analysis of political participation in a democracy, the authors point out that unless an individual is associated with some organized group he is unlikely to influence the course of government. They note that major power groups play a predominant role in making public policy at the national

level and the diversity of interests among various segments of the population must be reconciled with such groups. Negotiation and compromise among competing groups are meaningful and expected functions of government. In the present study, the authors concentrate chiefly on occupational groups and their broad ideologies, dividing them into two categories based on degree of organization and characteristic programs. In the category of formally organized power groups fall the representatives of business, the professions, labor, agriculture, and public school teachers; informally organized groups are the intellectuals, the civil bureaucracy, and the military bureaucracy (allied with veterans' organizations); they "compose, with Negroes, the major makers of public policy." The effects of these groups on domestic policies are given priority over their influence on foreign issues in this study.

## G. Elections: Machinery

913. David, Paul T., Ralph M. Goldman, *and* Richard C. Bain. The politics of national party conventions. [Washington] Brookings Institution [1960] xv, 592 p.    60–7422 JK2255.D39

Bibliographical footnotes.

After reviewing the origins of the national party convention during the Jacksonian era, the authors analyze this institution as a means of selecting presidential nominees. An updated and condensed version for the general reader, edited by Kathleen Sproul, was also published under the title *The Politics of National Party Conventions* (New York, Vintage Books [1964] 368 p.). Both versions include detailed information on the delegates, their organization, their decisionmaking processes, and their voting patterns. Richard C. Bain's *Convention Decisions and Voting Records* (Washington, Brookings Institution [1960] 327, [127] p.) provides a running account of convention proceedings of the two major parties since 1832 and a record of important convention votes.

2914. Eaton, Herbert. Presidential timber; a history of nominating conventions, 1868–1960. [New York] Free Press of Glencoe [1964] 528 p.

64–16971 E661.E2

Bibliography: p. 511–518.

A study of 32 presidential nominees from 1868 to 1960, in which the author attempts to determine how and why they were selected by their parties. Emphasizing the specific steps leading to nominations in the national conventions, Eaton examines

political issues and events largely for their effects on these choices. He notes that some of the conventions raised little conflict, renominating incumbent Presidents by acclamation, but that others involved controversy, surprise, and compromise. In 1924, for example, the Democrats required 103 ballots to nominate John W. Davis. Drama and irony also appear in the account, for example, in James G. Blaine's oratory in Congress to clear his reputation before the Republican convention of 1876 and in the classic political misplay in 1900, when Thomas C. Platt, hoping to elevate Theodore Roosevelt into political oblivion, helped him to win the Republican vice-presidential nomination.

2915. Heard, Alexander. The costs of democracy. Chapel Hill, University of North Carolina Press [1960] xxv, 493 p.    60–10532 JK1991.H39

Bibliographical footnotes.

One way to study the complex relationships existing in politics, asserts the author, is to analyze the financial linkages by which people and groups are connected. Exploring the highly controversial realm of campaign financing, he illuminates both the nature of the American political system and the attitudes of many citizens toward it. Among the areas examined are the sources of political funds, their effects on elections, past efforts to control campaign financing, and proposals for future action. Heard concludes that in national politics today money is indispensable to nomination of a candidate but in itself is insufficient to guarantee his election. A final chapter suggests measures which might be adopted to ensure greater equality among the parties and their candidates, including direct public subsidies to party activities, State support to political publicity, and Federal-State tax incentives for political donations.

2916. Kelley, Stanley. Political campaigning; problems in creating an informed electorate. Washington, Brookings Institution [1960] 163 p.
60–14637   JF2051.K38

In an attempt to define standards for evaluating campaigning in contemporary politics, the author examines current campaign practices, identifies deviations from the customary guidelines, and advances

suggestions for reform. Campaign discussion serves primarily an informative function, according to the author, helping voters to make rational decisions at the polls. Earlier practices which curtailed this dialog, he maintains, have largely disappeared: political machines, for instance, have declined in strength, and fraud is restricted. Two areas of current concern are the problems surrounding unfair personal attacks and those involving the often unidentifiable authorship of campaign statements. A portrait of the 1964 presidential election from primary to final vote is offered by the National Broadcasting Company's news staff in *Somehow It Works* (Garden City, N.Y., Doubleday [1965] 233 p.), edited by Gene Shalit and Lawrence K. Grossman.

# H. Elections: Results

2917. Michigan. University. *Survey Research Center.* The American voter [by] Angus Campbell [and others] New York, Wiley [1960] 573 p.
60–11615   JK1976.M5

Bibliographical footnotes.

An effort to identify the major factors which bring a voted to his decision at the polls. The study is based on nationwide surveys of large samples accumulated as early as 1948 but with major emphasis given to the 1952 and 1956 elections. Smaller samples recorded in midterm elections are also considered. The range of the study extends from the immediate determinants of voter attitudes to broader, more remote factors such as party identification, group membership, population movement, and personality. A chronological and analytical survey of behavior in national campaigns after World War II is *Presidential Elections, 1948–1960* (Salt Lake City, Institute of Government, University of Utah, 1961. 58 p. Research monograph no. 4), by Robert Blanchard, Richard Meyer, and Blaine Morley.

2918. Roseboom, Eugene H. A history of presidential elections. [2d ed.] New York, Macmillan [1964] 600 p.
64–17369   E183.R69   1964

Bibliography: p. 573–586.

An analysis of 44 contests for the position of Chief Executive, through the 1960 campaign. The conventions and events subsequent to them are reviewed, with particular attention to the actions and interactions of the candidates, party leaders, bosses, and others immediately involved in the political contests. The author sees special significance in the course of presidential campaigns in the decades im-

mediately preceding and following the Civil War, the period of the sectionalist breakdown of the Democratic Party and the rise of the Republican Party. Statistics on presidential elections are available in *A Statistical History of the American Presidential Elections* (New York, Ungar [1963] 247 p.), compiled by Svend Petersen.

2919. Schmidt, Karl M. Henry A. Wallace, quixotic crusade, 1948. [Syracuse] Syracuse University Press, 1960. 362 p. (Men and movements series)
60–16440   E815.S35

Bibliography: p. 336–347.

A chronicle of the Progressive Party and its activities from Wallace's 1946 break with President Truman over foreign policy to the party's organizational disintegration in 1950. Primary attention is devoted to the 1948 campaign and to Wallace's personal philosophy and characteristics as a presidential candidate. Schmidt identifies a number of factors which he considers essential for a successful third party movement and notes the extent to which they appeared in the cycle of the Progressive drive. He also discusses special handicaps faced by the party, particularly its underlying doctrine stressing peaceful coexistence and its attempt "to introduce tolerant politics into a period of intolerance."

2920. Thomson, Charles A. H., *and* Frances M. Shattuck. The 1956 presidential campaign. Washington, Brookings Institution [1960] xv, 382 p.
60–12085   E839.T48

Bibliographical footnotes.

One of the first attempts to prepare a single-volume study of the presidential election process in its entirety, with emphasis on the major interests, values, and activities combined in a campaign. The authors review the years of preparation preceding the nominating convention in 1956, including the important midterm elections of 1954 and the immediate preconvention activities, and then analyze the various convention maneuvers carried out in committee meetings, corridors, and "smoked-filled rooms." The post-convention electioneering is viewed as having had three distinct phases, which are treated separately. The first phase consisted of each candidate's initial "swing" around the country; the second phase drew the major issues closer around foreign policy; and the last seven days of campaigning were filled with the candidates' reactions to the crisis over the Suez-Sinai invasion by England, France, and Israel. Morris Janowitz and Dwaine Marvick anticipated the combined use of theory and empirical research in their interpretation of the 1952 presidential election, *Competitive Pressure and Democratic Consent*, 2d ed. (Chicago, Quadrangle Books, 1964 [°1956] 123 p.). A brief comparative study, which tests possible Republican inroads into sectional Democratic solidarity, largely in 1952 and 1956, is Donald S. Strong's *Urban Republicanism in the South* (University, Ala., Bureau of Public Administration, University of Alabama, 1960. 69 p.).

2921. White, Theodore H. The making of the President, 1960. New York, Atheneum Publishers, 1961. 400 p.     61–9259 E840.W5
An account which conveys much of the drama and significance of the 1960 presidential contest from the planning stages in 1959 through John F. Kennedy's election in November 1960. The author examines the issues of race, religion, leadership, national growth, and national defense and evaluates the unprecedented television debates in which Kennedy and Republican candidate Richard M. Nixon confronted each other. An appraisal of the political developments resulting from the campaign is offered in *The Presidential Election and Transition, 1960–1961* (Washington, Brookings Institution [1961] 353 p.), a collection of 12 essays edited by Paul T. David. The background and effects of the television confrontations of the candidates are examined in *The Great Debates* ([Bloomington] Indiana University Press [1962] 439 p.), a series of readings edited by Sidney Kraus.

2922. White, Theodore H. The making of the President, 1964. New York, Atheneum Publishers, 1965. 431 p.     65–18328 E850.W5
In a companion volume to the preceding entry, White chronicles the 1964 presidential campaign and the election in which Lyndon B. Johnson overwhelmingly defeated Barry Goldwater. Although lacking much of the drama of 1960, the 1964 election was nonetheless significant in many respects. The split which developed in the Republican Party, for example, is characterized by the author as reflecting "a bitterness which reached a point of morbid intensity." This mood was manifest in the primaries, in which the party's liberal and moderate elements failed to stop the conservative drive. The subsequent nomination went to Goldwater at the San Francisco convention in what the author terms a political coup d'état, but the intraparty conflict continued. For the Democrats, on the other hand, there was no nomination issue, although a brief drama was enacted over the choice of a vice-presidential candidate. The author describes the campaigns waged by each party, outlining the various strategies and their subsequent successes or failures, and devotes a special section to the development and meaning of the civil rights question.

# I. Reform

2923. Hoogenboom, Ari A. Outlawing the spoils; a history of the civil service reform movement, 1865–1883. Urbana, University of Illinois Press, 1961. 306 p.     61–6537 JK686.H7 1961
Bibliography: p. 269–278.
The conflict over civil service reform in the United States is traced from the Presidency of Andrew Johnson to the passage of the Pendleton Act under Chester A. Arthur. The author suggests that "the civil service reform movement fits into an 'out' versus 'in' pattern." The "outs," he maintains, found that the period following the Civil War failed to measure up to their expectations, and, frustrated, turned to reform. Specific attention is devoted to Representative Thomas Allen Jenckes, who was the recognized congressional leader of the movement until 1871, and to the move by Rutherford B. Hayes to displace Roscoe Conkling as the controller of patronage in the New York customhouse. Hoogenboom notes that the triumph of the reformers was short lived but that after 1900 the movement was revived in the broad spectrum of Progressive ideology.

# XXXII

# Books and Libraries

IRONICALLY, the book trade, which produces and distributes an ever increasing number of publications on a wide variety of topics, is itself the subject of relatively few volumes. Because of the dearth of scholarly studies of the field as a whole, most entries on book production deal with individual publishers, printers, or bibliophiles.

The lack of scholarly research in book form extends into the area of library literature. For example, librarians' views on such current issues as intellectual freedom, censorship, and the social responsibility of libraries are more likely to be found in professional journals than in books. Two of the most significant directions of development, in the library field, however, are represented in Section F, Librarianship and Library Use. That librarians are increasingly aware of the importance of both community involvement and computer technology is reflected respectively in a collection of reports on library service and community relations and in the proceedings of a conference on libraries and automation.

## A. Printing and Publishing: General

2924. Gross, Gerald, *ed*. Publishers on publishing. New York, R. R. Bowker Co. [1961] 491 p.
61–19878 Z278.G778
An anthology of 36 self-portraits of great American and British publishers, past and present, selected "to reveal the publisher as a man—and as a man of business." The nature of the portraits varies considerably: some are solely personal reminiscences; some offer discussions of the philosophical, moral, and commercial aspects of publishing; and some comment on such diverse topics as censorship, book reviewing, and author-publisher relationships. A briefer and more cohesive collection of essays on publishing is *Now, Barabbas* (New York, Harper & Row [1964] 228 p.), by William Jovanovich, the president of Harcourt, Brace & Company.

2925. Smith, Roger H., *ed*. The American reading public: what it reads, why it reads; from inside education and publishing, view of present status, future trends; the Daedalus symposium, with rebuttals and other new material. New York, R. R. Bowker [1964, °1963] 268 p.
63–22265 Z1003.S646
A collection of 20 articles, 13 of which originally appeared in the winter 1963 issue of *Daedalus*. Written chiefly by publishing executives, the essays attempt to define the character of contemporary book publishing, selling, and reviewing as well as the services they render to the "*engaged* segment of the American Reading Public." Each chapter is preceded by brief summaries of the essays included in it, and a detailed index is appended.

2926. Sutton, Walter. The western book trade: Cincinnati as a nineteenth-century publishing and book-trade center; containing a directory of Cincinnati publishers, booksellers, and members of allied trades, 1796–1880, and a bibliography. Columbus, Ohio State University Press for the Ohio Historical Society, 1961. 360 p. illus.

60–16600 Z473.S93

A history of publishing in the "Literary Emporium of the West" from the early 19th century until the beginning of the Civil War. Cincinnati flourished as the American book trade center west of the Allegheny Mountains during this period, largely owing to its advantageous geographical position in the steam age—at the center of the Ohio River Valley. With the development of the railroad, however, a few Eastern publishing centers were able to supply books to the entire Nation, river trade declined, and Chicago surpassed Cincinnati as chief distributor of books west of the mountains. Among the publishing houses discussed are the firms of J. A. and U. P. James, H. W. Derby, and Robert Clarke.

## B. Individual Publishers

2927. Exman, Eugene. The brothers Harper; a unique publishing partnership and its impact upon the cultural life of America from 1817 to 1853. New York, Harper & Row [1965] xvi, 415 p. illus. 65–14651 Z473.H29E9
"Bibliographical notes": p. 363–377.
A review of the first 36 years of the publishing house created by the four Harper brothers. The author traces the development of the Harper enterprise from its beginnings as a job printing operation with two handpresses to its eventual status as the largest book-printing establishment in the United States. Exman notes that the firm not only developed a strong list of original American books (including *Moby Dick* and *Two Years Before the Mast*) but also became the Nation's leader in publishing reprints of English books. The history is divided topically rather than chronologically. Appendixes include a complete list of the books in the *Harper's Family Library* and the *Harper's School District Library,* two series which helped to establish the company's reputation and prosperity.

2928. Kogan, Herman. The great EB; the story of the Encyclopaedia Britannica. [Chicago] University of Chicago Press [1958] 338 p. illus.
58–8379 AE5.E44K6
An anecdotal history covering the 14 numbered editions of the encyclopedia published between 1768 and 1929, when a policy of continuous revision was adopted. The author devotes particular attention to the business maneuvers responsible for perpetuating the *Encyclopaedia Britannica* and its image as the ultimate in reference works, noting that before becoming an autonomous corporation in 1957, the encyclopedia had been associated with such diverse organizations as *The Times* (London), the Cambridge University Press, and Sears, Roebuck and Company. A different view is presented in *The Myth of the Britannica* (New York, Grove Press [1964] 390 p.), by Harvey Einbinder, who concentrates on the encyclopedia's weaknesses and argues that it is not the paragon of authoritativeness it purports to be.

2929. Portrait of a publisher, 1915–1965. With an introduction by Paul A. Bennett. New York, The Typophiles, 1965. 2 v. (Typophile chap books, 42–43) 65–28266 Z473.K72P6
CONTENTS.—1. Reminiscences and reflections, by A. A. Knopf.—2. Alfred A. Knopf and the Borzoi imprint: recollections and appreciations.
Selections from Alfred A. Knopf's own writings and addresses, essays written to commemorate earlier anniversaries of Knopf and his company, and new pieces by librarians, book designers, other publishers, and authors currently published under the Borzoi imprint. The collection, which marks the 50th anniversary of the publishing house established by Knopf when he was 23 years old, provides many insights not only into the career of a publisher who has contributed significantly to the improvement of the design and content of American books but also into many facets of contemporary book publishing.

2930. Tryon, Warren S. Parnassus Corner; a life of James T. Fields, publisher to the Victorians. Boston, Houghton Mifflin, 1963. xiv, 445 p. illus. 62–14207 Z473.F5T7
Bibliography: p. [413]–431.
The biographer characterizes James Thomas Fields as a man with a keen business sense coupled with amiability and intense literary interests which enabled him to guide the evolution of Boston's obscure Old Corner Bookstore into one of the Nation's greatest publishers of fine literature. Fields' company was the first to publish such American classics as *Evangeline* (1847) and *The Scarlet Letter*

(1850); he was himself a published poet; and when Ticknor & Fields purchased the *Atlantic Monthly,* he proved an able successor to James Russell Lowell as editor. When Fields retired, he sold his interest in the company to a partnership headed by James Ripley Osgood. Only two years later, a new partnership was formed with Henry O. Houghton's Riverside Press and its publishing subsidiary, Hurd & Houghton. In 1880, Osgood retired, and Houghton, Mifflin & Company was established. Osgood's career in publishing is traced by Carl J. Weber in *The Rise and Fall of James Ripley Osgood* (Waterville, Me., Colby College Press, 1959. 283 p. Colby College monograph no. 22).

## C. Book Production: Technology and Art

2931. Bennett, Paul A., *ed.* Postscripts on Dwiggins, essays & recollectons, by Dorothy Abbe [and others] With a selective check list compiled by Dorothy Abbe and Rollo G. Silver. New York, The Typophiles, 1960. 2 v. (271 p.) illus. (Typophile chap books, no. 35, 36)

60–4471 Z232.D975B4

Bibliography: v. 2, p. 255–268.

William Addison Dwiggins (1880–1956) was one of this country's most distinguished artists in the areas of calligraphy, lettering, typography, book illustration, and book design, and this "biography by recollection and reminiscence" reflects his varied interests. He worked with a number of trade publishers—notably Alfred A. Knopf—as well as with such publishers of deluxe editions as the Limited Editions Club. Among the better known of his typeface designs are Electra, in which *Postscripts on Dwiggins* is set, and Caledonia. Specimens of his graphic work are presented in the final pages of volume 1. *Elmer Adler in the World of Books* (New York, The Typophiles, 1964. 114 p. Typophile chap books, 39), also edited by Bennett, is a study of another prominent figure in 20th-century book design.

2932. Eckman, James R. The heritage of the printer. v. 1. Philadelphia, North American Pub. Co., 1965. 209 p. illus.

65–22399 Z208.E23

These articles, which originally appeared in various numbers of the periodical *Printing Impressions,* describe both original and imported tools of the printer in America—composing machines, printing presses, and typefaces—and provide an informal account of major figures in the printing world. Primary attention is given to the last half of the 19th and the first third of the 20th centuries. A related work which traces the beginnings of the typefounding industry in the United States is Rollo G. Silver's *Typefounding in America, 1787–1825* (Charlottesville, Published for the Bibliographical Society of the University of Virginia [by the] University Press of Virginia [1965] 139 p.).

## D. Book Selling and Collecting

2933. Powell, Lawrence C. Books in my baggage; adventures in reading and collecting. Cleveland, World Pub. Co. [1960] 255 p.

59–11538 Z992.P64

As university librarian on the Los Angeles campus of the University of California and director of the William Andrews Clark Memorial Library, the author has been an avid collector of books both for his university and for his personal library. These 23 essays about books, book collecting, and reading have been drawn in part from three earlier volumes published in limited editions by the Ward Ritchie Press of Los Angeles—*Islands of Books, The Alchemy of Books,* and *Books West Southwest*—and were written to describe the satisfactions "derived from a life in which reading and living have become inseparably blended."

2934. Rogers, William G. Wise men fish here; the story of Frances Steloff and the Gotham Book Mart. New York, Harcourt, Brace & World [ᶜ1965] 246 p. illus. 64–18293 Z473.G63R6

Founded in 1920 by Frances Steloff, the Gotham Book Mart in New York City's theater district early became a haven for litterateurs. Readers and writers alike met at GBM, where the conversation, books, and little magazines they wanted were available. In addition to selling to such frequent visitors as Christopher Morley, Theodore Dreiser, H. L. Mencken, and Marianne Moore, Miss Steloff organized a fund from which needy writers (of whom Henry Miller was one of the more prominent) could draw. Rogers' history concentrates on the first 25 years of the Gotham Book Mart and its exceptionally colorful clientele, but the final pages reveal that its proprietress, at the age of 78, still demonstrates, according to Marianne Moore, that "the way to handle books best is to have parties and get the writers and readers together."

2935. Wolf, Edwin. Rosenbach; a biography, by Edwin Wolf, 2nd, with John F. Fleming. Cleveland, World Pub. Co. [1960] 616 p. illus.

60–15992  Z473.R7W6

Abraham Simon Wolf Rosenbach grew from a "baby bibliomaniac" to one of the world's best-known antiquarian booksellers, according to his biographers. Among his early patrons were J. Pierpont Morgan and the Widener family, who established the Widener Library at Harvard. Rosen-bach's sound critical perception enabled him to stand above the fashionable literary preferences and prompted him to buy for a low price the original manuscript of James Joyce's *Ulysses* when the work was less than two years old and had a limited audience. Among his more spectacular purchases were the certified copy of the Declaration of Independence, various copies of the Gutenberg Bible, and the original manuscript of *Alice in Wonderland*. *Henry Stevens of Vermont, American Rare Book Dealer in London, 1845–1886* (Amsterdam, N. Israel, 1963. 348 p.), by Wyman W. Parker, is the biography of a 19th-century antiquarian dealer whose "greatest services to scholarship were the transfer of rare books from Europe to America and the supplying of English libraries with large numbers of American books." The Grolier Club publication, *Grolier 75* ([New York, 1959] 240 p.), a collection of biographies of past members, was prepared to mark the 75th anniversary of "the oldest American club devoted exclusively to the arts of the book."

## E. Libraries

2936. Eaton, Thelma, *ed*. Contributions to American library history. Champaign, Ill., Distributed by Illini Union Bookstore [1961] xvii, 277 p. illus.

61–3095  Z731.E25

This collection of articles, written by historians and librarians during the last quarter of the 19th century and the first few years of the 20th century, deals with various kinds of libraries in a number of cities and States from the colonial period onward. The book is intended to provide students of librarianship with a historical background for understanding the library movement. *An American Library History Reader* (Hamden, Conn., Shoe String Press, 1961 [°1960] 464 p. Contributions to library literature), compiled by John D. Marshall, is a source collection of recent historical and biographical essays.

2937. Woodford, Frank B. Parnassus on Main Street; a history of the Detroit Public Library. With a foreword by Ralph R. Shaw. Illustrated by Donald G. Blaney. Detroit, Wayne State University Press, 1965. 487 p.  65–11820  Z733.D49W6

Bibliographical references included in "Notes" (p. 442–465).

The Detroit Public Library, described as one of the first free public libraries in the United States, opened in 1865 and developed as an integral part of the Detroit educational system. The author traces the expansion of the functions and facilities of the library from 1865 to 1965 against the broad background of local and national social and political events. He emphasizes two aspects of the library's development which were in occasional conflict: the library's increasing importance as a central cultural and intellectual institution and its position as a public institution subject to local political influence.

# F. Librarianship and Library Use

2938. Conference on Libraries and Automation, *Airlie Foundation, 1963.* Libraries and automation; proceedings, edited by Barbara Evans Markuson. Washington, Library of Congress, 1964. 268 p. illus.   64–62653   Z699.C6   1963

The report of a conference sponsored by the Library of Congress, the National Science Foundation, and the Council on Library Resources, Inc.  Among the objectives of the meeting were the establishment of a dialog between computer experts and professional librarians engaged in automation research, identification of areas in which there was overlapping or duplication of effort in library automation programs, and familiarization of librarians with the most recent technical advances in the field.  The proceedings are divided into seven sections covering the library of the future, file organization and conversion, file storage and access, graphic storage, output printing, library communications networks, and the automation of library systems.  *Automation and the Library of Congress* (Washington, Library of Congress, 1963 [i.e. 1964]  88 p.) is the report, by Gilbert W. King and other technical experts, of a two-year survey undertaken for the Library of Congress to determine the desirability and feasibility of automating bibliographic operations in large research libraries, with particular emphasis on the Library of Congress.

2939. Coplan, Kate, *and* Edwin Castagna, *eds.* The library reaches out; reports on library service and community relations by some leading American librarians.  Dobbs Ferry, N.Y., Oceana Publications, 1965.  xiv, 403 p. illus.
65–22164   Z665.C755
Includes bibliographical references.

A survey of library service and communication, written by librarians who, according to the editors, were selected to contribute because of their distinguished professional stature and their outstanding record of accomplishment in their respective fields.  Although emphasis is placed on the public library, one article each is devoted to school, university, State, and regional libraries.  One aspect of public library service is treated comprehensively in *Library Adult Education, the Biography of an Idea* (New York, Scarecrow Press, 1963.  550 p.), in which Margaret E. Monroe discusses the evolution of the library's role in community adult education in the United States between the early 1920's and the early 1960's.  Out of the Symposium on Library Functions in the Changing Metropolis, held in Dedham, Mass., in 1963, came *The Public Library and the City* (Cambridge, M.I.T. Press [1965]  216 p.  A Publication of the Joint Center for Urban Studies of the Massachusetts Institute of Technology and Harvard University), edited by Ralph W. Conant; it provides a new look at the urban library by urban social scientists, economists, historians, sociologists, political scientists, planners, communications experts, library scholars, and library administrators.

2940. Holley, Edward G.  Charles Evans: American bibliographer.  Urbana, University of Illinois Press, 1963.  343 p.  (Illinois contributions to librarianship, no. 7)   63-10315   Z1004.E85H6
Bibliography: p. 323–330.

2941. Williamson, William L.  William Frederick Poole and the modern library movement. New York, Columbia University Press, 1963.  203 p. illus.  (Columbia University studies in library service, no. 13)   63–14110   Z720.P6W5
Bibliography: p. [193]–196.

Charles Evans held a variety of positions in American libraries of the late 19th century, but his most significant contribution to scholarship was his *American Bibliography; a Chronological Dictionary of All Books, Pamphlets, and Periodical Publications Printed in the United States of America From the Genesis of Printing in 1639 Down to and Including the Year 1820* (1903–34.  12 v.).  Evans did not reach the goal announced in the title of his work, but he did carry through the letter "M" of 1799.  "Almost singlehandedly," Holley observes, "he accomplished what one of his colleagues has hailed as 'one of the greatest bibliographical compilations of all time.'"  *William Frederick Poole and the Modern Library Movement* is the biography of a mentor of Charles Evans.  Poole headed the Boston Athenaeum, the Cincinnati Public Library, the Chicago Public Library, and the Newberry Library.  He prepared *Poole's Index to Periodical Literature,* the pioneer index to American and English periodicals, served as president of both the American Library Association and the American Historical Association, and wrote numerous articles, reviews, and books.

2942. Schick, Frank L., *ed.* The future of library service: demographic aspects and implications. Urbana, University of Illinois, Graduate School of Library Science, 1962 [ᶜ1961]  286 p. illus. (Illinois contributions to librarianship, no. 6)
62–62687  Z731.S3

Includes bibliographies.

Demographic projections are cited which indicate that, in addition to being 37 percent larger than in 1960, the population of the United States in 1980 will be more urbanized and better educated. The average age will be younger, but the proportion of people 65 years of age and over will have increased. The library's function in the light of these and other demographic projections is the central topic of this group of articles reprinted from the July and October 1961 issues of *Library Trends.* The contributors discuss characteristic services to be expected in various kinds of libraries and also give consideration to documentation and to books, serial publications, and audiovisual materials as library resources. The concluding article reflects the point of view of the American Library Association concerning appropriate governmental action for adequate library development. Verner W. Clapp, in *The Future of the Research Library* (Urbana, University of Illinois Press, 1964.  114 p.  Phineas L. Windsor series [i.e. lectures] in librarianship [no. 8]  1963), discusses possible means by which the general research library of the future can meet the increasing need for it to make available to users the persistently multiplying "informational records of mankind."

2943. Shores, Louis.  Mark Hopkins' log, and other essays.  Selected by John David Marshall.  Hamden, Conn., Shoe String Press, 1965.  383 p.  65–12144  Z665.S48

Includes bibliographical references.

Articles, essays, addresses, and lectures by the dean of the Florida State University Library School. Selected from Shores' publications in journals and anthologies during the years from 1928 to 1964, these writings stress the role of the librarian in fostering a "continuous communicability" between books and people.  *Of, by, and for Librarians* (Hamden, Conn., Shoe String Press, 1960.  335 p. Contributions to library literature), compiled by John D. Marshall, is an anthology of miscellaneous articles and essays on books, libraries, and the library profession.  Essays on reference librarianship exclusively have been brought together by Arthur R. Rowland in *Reference Services* (Hamden, Conn., Shoe String Press, 1964.  259 p.  Contributions to library literature, no. 5).

# Index

☆ U.S. GOVERNMENT PRINTING OFFICE: 1976 O—428-227